THE DAVID
FOSTER
WALLACE
READER

ALSO BY DAVID FOSTER WALLACE

The Broom of the System

Girl with Curious Hair

Signifying Rappers (with Mark Costello)

Infinite Jest

A Supposedly Fun Thing I'll Never Do Again

Brief Interviews with Hideous Men

Everything and More

Oblivion

Consider the Lobster

McCain's Promise

This Is Water

The Pale King

Both Flesh and Not

THE DAVID
FOSTER
WALLACE
READER

LITTLE, BROWN AND COMPANY

New York   Boston   London

Copyright © 2014 by The David Foster Wallace Literary Trust

Little, Brown and Company
Hachette Book Group
1290 Avenue of the Americas, New York, NY 10104
littlebrown.com

First Edition: November 2014

Little, Brown and Company is a division of Hachette Book Group, Inc.
The Little, Brown name and logo are trademarks of Hachette Book Group, Inc.

The publisher is not responsible for websites (or their content) that are not owned by the publisher.

Copyright acknowledgments appear on pages 961–963.

Library of Congress Cataloging-in-Publication Data

Wallace, David Foster.
  [Works. Selections]
  The David Foster Wallace Reader / David Foster Wallace. — First edition.
    pages cm
  ISBN 978-0-316-18239-3 (hardback) / 978-0-316-34120-2 (Limited Edition)
  I. Title.
  PS3573.A425635A6 2014
  813'.54—dc22   2014032157

10 9 8 7 6 5 4 3 2 1

RRD-C

Printed in the United States of America

Contents

TEACHING MATERIALS

NONFICTION

Introduction

The purpose of this *David Foster Wallace Reader* is simple: to gather in one volume a selection of the most celebrated, most enjoyable, funniest, and most remarkable work by this always-remarkable writer. It is a Greatest Hits collection of novel excerpts, short fiction, and essays that we hope will delight readers who know Wallace's work already and show those new to him the amazing breadth of subjects, characters, ideas, interiors, landscapes, emotions, and human interaction in his writing. We also believe that teachers will find here an ideal introduction for students.

Assembling this book was a collaboration between the executors of the David Foster Wallace Literary Trust and Wallace's editor at Little, Brown and Company. We agreed on a core group of excerpts, stories, and essays that were essential to any collection of Wallace's work, argued over others, and sought broader suggestions from writers, critics, and colleagues. Those who kindly aided in the process are listed below. A few took the further step of writing an afterword to a piece they recommended. Brief biographies of these contributors appear at the book's end.

Nearly everything in this *Reader* has been published previously in Wallace's novels, story collections, and essay collections, and the versions here are the original, full texts, rather than the shortened versions that were sometimes created for magazine publication. There are two new works. One is the first story in the book, "The Planet Trillaphon as It Stands in Relation to the Bad Thing," which was published in the *Amherst Review* when Wallace was an undergraduate there. It is an astonishing exploration of psychological pain and self-consciousness. The other is a selection of teaching materials. Wallace taught undergraduate creative writing classes at Emerson College, Illinois State University, and Pomona College, and poured enormous care into creating syllabi, reading lists, and pop quizzes to help his students learn to write well. This section is introduced by his mother, Sally Foster Wallace, with whom he shared a boundless love of grammar and linguistic rigor.

We hope we have gathered here a representation of the range, depth, and layers of Wallace's creations—the complexity of thought and emotion, and the desire to disturb and tickle and demolish and annoy, even to break hearts, that lived alongside his intent to astonish and entertain. This collection could easily have been two or three times as long as it is, and we forced ourselves to leave out many excellent works in an effort to keep to a manageable length. There is writing in all of Wallace's books that is every bit as powerful as what's included here, and we hope you will be moved to read those books in full.

We would like to take this opportunity to thank Sam Freilich, Victoria Matsui, and Mario J. Pulice for their work and care in creating this book, and Marlena Bittner for her kindness and support in everything connected with David and his books.

— *Bonnie Nadell*
— *Karen Green*
— *Michael Pietsch*

Advisers

Matthew Baldwin
Jo Ann Beard
Sven Birkerts
Tom Bissell
Stephen Burn
Blake Butler
Mark Costello
Kevin J. H. Dettmar
Anne Fadiman
Jonathan Franzen
Rivka Galchen
Gerald Howard

Malcolm Knox
Hari Kunzru
Nam Le
Nick Maniatis
Lorrie Moore
Simon Prosser
James Ryerson
George Saunders
Mike Schur
Deborah Treisman
David L. Ulin
Sally Foster Wallace

THE DAVID
FOSTER
WALLACE
READER

FICTION

The Planet Trillaphon as
It Stands in Relation to the Bad Thing

I'VE BEEN ON antidepressants for, what, about a year now, and I suppose I feel as if I'm pretty qualified to tell what they're like. They're fine, really, but they're fine in the same way that, say, living on another planet that was warm and comfortable and had food and fresh water would be fine: it would be fine, but it wouldn't be good old Earth, obviously. I haven't been on Earth now for almost a year, because I wasn't doing very well on Earth. I've been doing somewhat better here where I am now, on the planet Trillaphon, which I suppose is good news for everyone involved.

Antidepressants were prescribed for me by a very nice doctor named Dr. Kablumbus at a hospital to which I was sent ever so briefly following a really highly ridiculous incident involving electrical appliances in the bathtub about which I really don't wish to say a whole lot. I had to go to the hospital for physical care and treatment after this very silly incident, and then two days later I was moved to another floor of the hospital, a higher, whiter floor, where Dr. Kablumbus and his colleagues were. There was a certain amount of consideration given to the possibility of my undergoing E.C.T., which is short for "Electro-Convulsive Therapy," but E.C.T. wipes out bits of your memory sometimes — little details like your name and where you live, etc. — and it's also in other respects just a thoroughly scary thing, and we — my parents and I — decided against it. New Hampshire, which is the state where I live, has a law that says E.C.T. cannot be administered without the patient's knowledge and consent. I regard this as an extremely good law. So antidepressants were prescribed for me instead by Dr. Kablumbus, who can be said really to have had only my best interests at heart.

If someone tells about a trip he's taken, you expect at least some explanation of why he left on the trip in the first place. With this in mind perhaps I'll tell some things about why things weren't too good for me on

Earth for quite a while. It was extremely weird, but, three years ago, when I was a senior in high school, I began to suffer from what I guess now was a hallucination. I thought that a huge wound, a really huge and deep wound, had opened on my face, on my cheek near my nose...that the skin had just split open like old fruit, that blood was seeping out, all dark and shiny, that veins and bits of yellow cheek-fat and red-gray muscle were plainly visible, even bright flashes of bone, in there. Whenever I'd look in the mirror, there it would be, that wound, and I could feel the twitch of the exposed muscle and the heat of the blood on my cheek, all the time. But when I'd say to a doctor or to Mom or to other people, "Hey, look at this open wound on my face, I'd better go to the hospital," they'd say, "Well, hey, there's no wound on your face, are your eyes OK?" And yet whenever I'd look in the mirror, there it would be, and I could always feel the heat of the blood on my cheek, and when I'd feel with my hand my fingers would sink in there really deep into what felt like hot gelatin with bones and ropes and stuff in it. And it seemed like everyone was always looking at it. They'd seem to stare at me really funny, and I'd think "Oh God, I'm really making them sick, they see it, I've got to hide, get me out of here." But they were probably only staring because I looked all scared and in pain and kept my hand to my face and was staggering like I was drunk all over the place all the time. But at the time, it seemed so real. Weird, weird, weird. Right before graduation—or maybe a month before, maybe—it got really bad, such that when I'd pull my hand away from my face I'd see blood on my fingers, and bits of tissue and stuff, and I'd be able to smell the blood, too, like hot rusty metal and copper. So one night when my parents were out somewhere I took a needle and some thread and tried to sew up the wound myself. It hurt a lot to do this, because I didn't have any anesthetic, of course. It was also bad because, obviously, as I know now, there was really no wound to be sewn up at all, there. Mom and Dad were less than pleased when they came home and found me all bloody for real and with a whole lot of jagged unprofessional stitches of lovely bright orange carpet-thread in my face. They were really upset. Also, I made the stitches too deep—I apparently pushed the needle incredibly deep—and some of the thread got stuck way down in there when they tried to pull the stitches out at the hospital and it got infected later and then they had to make a *real* wound back at the hospital to get it all out and drain it and clean it out. That was highly ironic. Also, when I was making the stitches too deep I guess I ran the needle into a few nerves in my cheek and destroyed them, so now sometimes bits of my face will get numb for no reason, and my mouth will sag on the left side a bit. I know it sags for sure and that I've got this cute scar, here, because it's not just a matter of looking in the mirror and seeing it and feeling it; other people tell me they see it too, though they do this very tactfully.

Anyway, I think that year everyone began to see that I was a troubled little soldier, including me. Everybody talked and conferred and we all decided that it would probably be in my best interests if I deferred admission to Brown University in Rhode Island, where I was supposedly all set to go, and instead did a year of "Post-Graduate" schoolwork at a very good and prestigious and expensive prep school called Phillips Exeter Academy conveniently located right there in my home town. So that's what I did. And it was by all appearances a pretty successful period, except it was still on Earth, and things were increasingly non-good for me on Earth during this period, although my face had healed and I had more or less stopped having the hallucination about the gory wound, except for really short flashes when I saw mirrors out of the corners of my eyes and stuff.

But, yes, all in all things were going increasingly badly for me at that time, even though I was doing quite well in school in my little "Post-Grad" program and people were saying, "Holy cow, you're really a very good student, you should just go on to college right now, why don't you?" It was just pretty clear to me that I *shouldn't* go right on to college then, but I couldn't say that to the people at Exeter, because my reasons for saying I shouldn't had nothing to do with balancing equations in Chemistry or interpreting Keats poems in English. They had to do with the fact that I was a troubled little soldier. I'm not at this point really dying to give a long gory account of all the cute neuroses that more or less around that time began to pop up all over the inside of my brain, sort of like wrinkly gray boils, but I'll tell a few things. For one thing, I was throwing up a lot, feeling really nauseated all the time, especially when I'd wake up in the morning. But it could switch on anytime, the second I began to think about it: if I felt OK, all of a sudden I'd think, "Hey, I don't feel nauseated at all, here." And it would just switch on, like I had a big white plastic switch somewhere along the tube from my brain to my hot and weak stomach and intestines, and I would just throw up all over my plate at dinner or my desk at school or the seat of the car, or my bed, or wherever. It was really highly grotesque for everyone else, and intensely unpleasant for me, as anyone who has ever felt really sick to his stomach can appreciate. This went on for quite a while, and I lost a lot of weight, which was bad because I was quite thin and non-strong to begin with. Also, I had to have a lot of medical tests on my stomach, involving delicious barium-drinks and being hung upside down for X-rays, and so on, and once I even had to have a spinal tap, which hurt more than anything has ever hurt me in my life. I am never ever going to have another spinal tap.

Also, there was this business of crying for no reason, which wasn't painful but was very embarrassing and also quite scary because I couldn't control it. What would happen is that I'd cry for no reason, and then I'd get sort of scared that I'd cry or that once I started to cry I wouldn't be able to stop, and this state of being scared would very kindly activate this other white switch on the tube between my brain with its boils and my hot eyes, and off I'd go even worse, like a skateboard that you keep pushing along. It was very embarrassing at school, and incredibly embarrassing with my family, because they would think it was their fault, that they had done something bad. It would have been incredibly embarrassing with my friends, too, but by that time I really didn't have very many friends. So that was kind of an advantage, almost. But there was still everyone else. I had little tricks I employed with regard to the "crying problem." When I was around other people and my eyes got all hot and full of burning salt-water I would pretend to sneeze, or even more often to yawn, because both these things can explain someone's having tears in his eyes. People at school must have thought I was just about the sleepiest person in the world. But, really, yawning doesn't exactly explain the fact that tears are just running down your cheeks and raining down on your lap or your desk or making little wet star-puckers on your exam papers and stuff, and not too many people get super-red eyes just from yawning. So the tricks probably weren't too effective. It's weird but even now, here on the planet Trillaphon, when I think about it at all, I can hear the snap of the switch and my eyes more or less start to fill up, and my throat aches. That is bad. There was also the fact that back then I got so I couldn't stand silence, really couldn't stand it at all. This was because when there was no noise from outside the little hairs on my eardrums or wherever would manufacture a noise all by themselves, to keep in practice or something. This noise was sort of a high, glittery, metallic, spangly hum that really for some reason scared the living daylights out of me and just about drove me crazy when I heard it, the way a mosquito in your ear in bed at night in summer will just about drive you crazy when you hear it. I began to look for noise sort of the way a moth looks for light. I'd sleep with the radio on in my room, watch an incredible amount of loud television, keep my trusty Sony Walkman on at all times at school and walking around and on my bike (that Sony Walkman was far and away the best Christmas present I have ever received). I would even maybe sometimes talk to myself when I had just no other recourse to noise, which must have seemed very crazy to people who heard me, and I suppose *was* very crazy, but not in the way they supposed. It wasn't as if I thought I was two people who could have a dialogue, or as if I heard voices from Venus or anything. I knew I was just one person, but this one person, here, was a troubled little soldier who could withstand neither the substance nor the implications of the noise produced by the inside of his own head.

Anyway, all this extremely delightful stuff was going on while I was doing well and making my otherwise quite worried and less-than-pleased parents happy school-wise during the year, and then while I was working for Exeter Building and Grounds Department during the following summer, pruning bushes and crying and throwing up discreetly into them, and while I was packing and having billions of dollars of clothes and electrical appliances bought for me by my grandparents, getting all ready to go to Brown University in Rhode Island in September. Mr. Film, who was more or less my boss at "B and G," had a riddle that he thought was unbelievably funny, and he told it to me a lot. He'd say, "What's the color of a bowel movement?" And when I didn't say anything he'd say. "Brown! har har har!" He'd laugh, and I'd smile, even after about the four-trillionth time, because Mr. Film was on the whole a fairly nice man, and he didn't even get mad when I threw up in his truck once. I told him my scar was from getting cut up with a knife in high school, which was essentially the truth.

So I went off to Brown University in the fall, and it turned out to be very much like "P.G." at Exeter: it was supposed to be all hard but it really wasn't, so I had plenty of time to do well in classes and have people say "Outstanding" and still be neurotic and weird as hell, so that my roommate, who was a very nice, squeakingly healthy guy from Illinois, understandably asked for a single instead and moved out in a few weeks and left me with a very big single all my very own. So it was just little old me and about nine billion dollars worth of electronic noise-making equipment, there in my room, after that. It was quite soon after my roommate moved out that the Bad Thing started. The Bad Thing is more or less the reason why I'm not on Earth anymore. Dr. Kablumbus told me after I told him as best I could about the Bad Thing that the Bad Thing was "severe clinical depression." I am sure that a doctor at Brown would have told me pretty much the same thing, but I didn't ever go to see anyone at Brown, mainly because I was afraid that if I ever opened my mouth in that context stuff would come out that would ensure that I'd be put in a place like the place I was put after the hilariously stupid business in the bathroom.

I really don't know if the Bad Thing is really depression. I had previously sort of always thought that depression was just sort of really intense sadness, like what you feel when your very good dog dies, or when Bambi's mother gets killed in *Bambi*. I thought that it was that you frowned or maybe even cried a little bit if you were a girl and said "Holy cow, I'm really depressed, here," and then your friends if you have any come and cheer you up or take you out and get you ploughed and in the morning it's like a faded color and in a couple days it's gone altogether. The Bad Thing—which I guess is what is really depression—is very different, and indescribably worse. I guess I should say rather *sort of* indescribably, because I've heard different people try to describe "real" depression over the last couple years. A very glib guy on the television said some people liken it to being underwater, under a body of water that has no surface, at least for you, so that no matter what direction you go, there will only be more water, no fresh air and freedom of movement, just restriction and suffocation, and no light. (I don't know how apt it is to say it's like being underwater, but maybe imagine the moment in which you realize, at which it hits you that there is *no surface for you,* that you're just going to drown in there no matter which way you swim; imagine how you'd feel at that exact moment, like Descartes at the start of his second thing, then imagine that feeling in all its really delightful choking intensity spread out over hours, days, months…that would maybe be more apt.) A really lovely poet named Sylvia Plath, who unfortunately isn't living anymore, said that it's like having a jar covering you and having all the air pumped out of the jar, so you can't breathe any good air (and imagine the moment when your movement is invisibly stopped by the glass and you realize you're *under glass…*). Some people say it's like having always before you and under you a huge black hole without a bottom, a black, black hole, maybe with vague teeth in it, and then your being part of the hole, so that you fall even when you stay where you are (…maybe when you realize *you're* the hole, nothing else…).

I'm not incredibly glib, but I'll tell what I think the Bad Thing is like. To me it's like being completely, totally, utterly sick. I will try to explain what I mean. Imagine feeling really sick to your stomach. Almost everyone has felt really sick to his or her stomach, so everyone knows what it's like: it's less than fun. OK. OK. But that feeling is localized: it's more or less just your stomach. Imagine your whole body being sick like that: your feet, the big muscles in your legs, your collarbone, your head, your hair, everything, all just as sick as a fluey stomach. Then, if you can imagine that, please imagine it even more spread out and total. Imagine that every cell in your body, every single cell in your body is as sick as that nauseated stomach. Not just your own cells, even, but the e. coli and lactobacilli in you, too, the mitochondria, basal bodies, all sick and boiling and hot like maggots in your neck, your brain, all over, everywhere, in everything. All just *sick* as hell. Now imagine that every single *atom* in every single cell in your body is sick like that, sick, intolerably sick. And every proton and neutron in every atom . . . swollen and throbbing, off-color, sick, with just no chance of throwing up to relieve the feeling. Every electron is sick, here, twirling off balance and all erratic in these funhouse orbitals that are just thick and swirling with mottled yellow and purple poison gases, everything off balance and woozy. Quarks and neutrinos out of their minds and bouncing sick all over the place, bouncing like crazy. Just imagine that, a sickness spread utterly through every bit of you, even the bits of the bits. So that your very . . . very *essence* is characterized by nothing other than the feature of sickness; you and the sickness are, as they say, "one."

That's kind of what the Bad Thing is like at its roots. Everything in you is sick and grotesque. And since your only acquaintance with the whole world is through parts of you — like your sense-organs and your mind, etc. — and since these parts are sick as hell, the whole world as you perceive it and know it and are in it comes at you through this filter of bad sickness and becomes bad. As everything becomes bad in you, all the good goes out of the world like air out of a big broken balloon. There's nothing in this world you know but horrible rotten smells, sad and grotesque and lurid pastel sights, raucous or deadly-sad sounds, intolerable open-ended situations lined on a continuum with just no end at all . . . Incredibly stupid, hopeless ideas. And just the way when you're sick to your stomach you're kind of scared way down deep that it might maybe never go away, the Bad Thing scares you the same way, only worse, because the fear is itself filtered through the bad disease and becomes bigger and worse and hungrier than it started out. It tears you open and gets in there and squirms around.

Because the Bad Thing not only attacks you and makes you feel bad and puts you out of commission, it especially attacks and makes you feel bad and puts out of commission precisely those things that are necessary in order for you to fight the Bad Thing, to maybe get better, to stay alive. This is hard to understand, but it's really true. Imagine a really painful disease that, say, attacked your legs and your throat and resulted in a really bad pain and paralysis and all-around agony in these areas. The disease would be bad enough, obviously, but the disease would also be open-ended; you wouldn't be able to do anything about it. Your legs would be all paralyzed and would hurt like hell . . . but you wouldn't be able to run for help for those poor legs, just exactly because your legs would be too sick for you to run anywhere at all. Your throat would burn like crazy and you'd think it was just going to explode...but you wouldn't be able to call out to any doctors or anyone for help, precisely because your throat would be too sick for you to do so. This is the way the Bad Thing works: it's especially good at attacking your defense mechanisms. The way to fight against or get away from the Bad Thing is clearly just to think differently, to reason and argue with yourself, just to change the way you're perceiving and sensing and processing stuff. But you need your mind to do this, your brain cells with their atoms and your mental powers and all that, your *self*, and that's exactly what the Bad Thing has made too sick to work right. That's exactly what it has made sick. It's made you sick in just such a way that you can't get better. And you start thinking about this pretty vicious situation, and you say to yourself, "Boy oh boy, how the heck is the Bad Thing able to do this?" You think about it—really hard, since it's in your best interests to do so—and then all of a sudden it sort of dawns on you...that the Bad Thing is able to do this to you because *you're* the Bad Thing yourself! The Bad Thing is you. Nothing else: no bacteriological infection or having gotten conked on the head with a board or a mallet when you were a little kid, or any other excuse; you are the sickness yourself. It is what "defines" you, especially after a little while has gone by. You realize all this, here. And that, I guess, is when if you're all glib you realize that there is no surface to the water, or when you bonk your nose on the jar's glass and realize you're trapped, or when you look at the black hole and it's wearing your face. That's when the Bad Thing just absolutely eats you up, or rather when you just eat yourself up. When you kill yourself. All this business about people committing suicide when they're "severely depressed"; we say, "Holy cow, we must do something to stop them from killing themselves!" That's wrong. Because all these people have, you see, by this time *already* killed themselves, where it really counts. By the time these people swallow entire medicine cabinets or take naps in the garage or whatever, they've already been killing themselves for ever so long. When they "commit suicide," they're just being orderly. They're just giving external form to an event the substance of which already exists and has existed in them over time. Once you realize what's going on, the event of self-destruction for all practical purposes exists. There's not much a person is apt to do in this situation, except "formalize" it, or, if you don't quite want to do that, maybe "E.C.T." or a trip away from the Earth to some other planet, or something.

Anyway, this is more than I intended to say about the Bad Thing. Even now, thinking about it a little bit and being introspective and all that, I can feel it reaching out for me, trying to mess with my electrons. But I'm not on Earth anymore.

I made it through my first little semester at Brown University and even got a prize for being a very good introductory Economics student, two hundred dollars, which I promptly spent on marijuana, because smoking marijuana keeps you from getting sick to your stomach and throwing up. It really does: they give it to people undergoing chemotherapy for cancer, sometimes. I had smoked a lot of marijuana ever since my year of "P.G." schoolwork to keep from throwing up, and it worked a lot of the time. It just bounced right off the sickness in my atoms, though. The Bad Thing just laughed at it. I was a very troubled little soldier by the end of the semester. I longed for the golden good old days when my face just bled.

In December the Bad Thing and I boarded a bus to go from Rhode Island to New Hampshire for the holiday season. Everything was extremely jolly. Except just coming out of Providence, Rhode Island, the bus driver didn't look carefully enough before he tried to make a left turn and a pickup truck hit our bus from the left side and smunched the left front part of the bus and knocked the driver out of his seat and down into the well where the stairs onto and off of the bus are, where he broke his arm and I think his leg and cut his head fairly badly. So we had to stop and wait for an ambulance for the driver and a new bus for us. The driver was incredibly upset. He was sure he was going to lose his job, because he'd messed up the left turn and had had an accident, and also because he hadn't been wearing his seat belt—clear evidence of which was the fact that he had been knocked way out of his seat into the stairwell, which everybody saw and would say they saw—which is against the law if you're a bus driver in just about any state of the Union. He was almost crying, and me too, because he said he had about seventy kids and he really needed that job, and now he would be fired. A couple of passengers tried to soothe him and calm him down, but understandably no one came near me. Just me and the Bad Thing, there. Finally the bus driver just kind of passed out from his broken bones and that cut, and an ambulance came and they put him under a rust-colored blanket. A new bus came out of the sunset and a bus executive or something came too, and he was really mad when some of the incredibly helpful passengers told him what had happened. I knew that the bus driver was probably going to lose his job, just as he had feared would happen. I felt unbelievably sorry for him, and of course the Bad Thing very kindly filtered this sadness for me and made it a lot worse. It was weird and irrational but all of a sudden I felt really strongly as though the bus driver were really *me*. I really felt that way. So I felt just like he must have felt, and it was awful. I wasn't just sorry for him, I was sorry *as* him, or something like that. All courtesy of the Bad Thing. Suddenly I had to go somewhere, really fast, so I went to where the driver's stretcher was in the open ambulance and went in to look at him, there. He had a bus company ID badge with his picture, but I couldn't really see anything because it was covered by a streak of blood from his head. I took my roughly a hundred dollars and a bag of "sinsemilla" marijuana and slipped it under his rusty blanket to help him feed all his kids and not get sick and throw up, then I left really fast again and got my stuff and got on the new bus. It wasn't until, what, about thirty minutes later on the nighttime highway that I realized that when they found that marijuana with the driver they'd think it was maybe his all along and he really *would* get fired, or maybe even sent to jail. It was kind of like I'd framed him, killed him, except he was also me, I thought, so it was really confusing. It was like I'd symbolically killed myself or something, because I felt he was me in some deep sense. I think at that moment I felt worse than I'd ever felt before, except for that spinal tap, and that was totally different. Dr. Kablumbus says that's when the Bad Thing really got me by the balls. Those were really his words. I'm really sorry for what I did and what the Bad Thing did to the bus driver. I really sincerely only meant to help him, as if he were me. But I sort of killed him, instead.

I got home and my parents said "Hey, hello, we love you, congratulations," and I said "Hello, hello, thank you, thank you." I didn't exactly have the "holiday spirit," I must confess, because of the Bad Thing, and because of the bus driver, and because of the fact that we were all three of us the same thing in the respects that mattered at all.

The highly ridiculous thing happened on Christmas Eve. It was very stupid, but I guess almost sort of inevitable given what had gone on up to then. You could just say that I'd already more or less killed myself internally during the fall semester, and symbolically with respect to that bus driver, and now like a tidy little soldier I had to "formalize" the whole thing, make it neat and right-angled and external; I had to fold down the corners and make hospital corners. While Mom and Dad and my sisters and Nanny and Pop-Pop and Uncle Michael and Aunt Sally were downstairs drinking cocktails and listening to a beautiful and deadly-sad record about a crippled boy and the three kings on Christmas night, I got undressed and got into a tub full of warm water and pulled about three thousand electrical appliances into that tub after me. However, the consummate silliness of the whole incident was made complete by the fact that most of the appliances were cleverly left unplugged by me in my irrational state. Only a couple were actually "live," but they were enough to blow out the power in the house and make a big noise and give me a nice little shock indeed, so that I had to be taken to the hospital for physical care. I don't know if I should say this, but what got shocked really the worst were my reproductive organs. I guess they were sort of out of the water part-way and formed a sort of bridge for the electricity between the water and my body and the air. Anyway, their getting shocked hurt a lot and also I am told had consequences that will become more significant if I ever want to have a family or anything. I am not overly concerned about this. My family was concerned about the whole incident, though; they were less than pleased, to say the least. I had sort of half passed out or gone to sleep, but I remember hearing the water sort of fizzing, and their coming in and saying "Oh my God, hey!" I remember they had a hard time because it was just pitch-black in that bathroom, and they more or less only had me to see by. They had to be extremely careful getting me out of the tub, because they didn't want to get shocked themselves. I find this perfectly understandable.

Once a couple days went by in the hospital and it became clear that boy and reproductive organs were pretty much going to survive, I made my little vertical move up to the White Floor. About the White Floor—the Troubled Little Soldier Floor—I really don't wish to go into a gigantic amount of detail. But I will tell some things. The White Floor was white, obviously, but it wasn't a bright, hurty white, like the burn ward. It was more of a soft, almost grayish white, very bland and soothing. Now that I come to think back on it, just about everything about the White Floor was soft and unimposing and . . . *demure,* as if they tried really hard there not to make any big or strong impressions on any of their guests—sense-wise or mind-wise—because they knew that just about any real impression on the people who needed to go to the White Floor was probably going to be a bad impression, after being filtered through the Bad Thing.

The White Floor had soft white walls and soft light-brown carpeting, and the windows were sort of frosty and very thick. All the sharp corners on things like dressers and bedside tables and doors had been beveled-off and sanded round and smooth, so it all looked a little strange. I have never heard of anyone trying to kill himself on the sharp corner of a door, but I suppose it is wise to be prepared for all possibilities. With this in mind, I'm sure, they made certain that everything they gave you to eat was something you could eat without a knife or a fork. Pudding was a very big item on the White Floor. I had to wear a bit of a thing while I was a guest there, but I certainly wasn't strapped down in my bed, which some of my colleagues

were. The thing I had to wear wasn't a straitjacket or anything, but it was
certainly tighter than your average bathrobe, and I got the feeling they
could make it even tighter if they felt it was in my best interests to do so.
When someone wanted to smoke a tobacco cigarette, a psychiatric nurse
had to light it, because no guest on the White Floor was allowed to have
matches. I also remember that the White Floor smelled a lot nicer than the
rest of the hospital, all feminine and kind of dreamy, like ether.

Dr. Kablumbus wanted to know what was up, and I more or less told
him in about six minutes. I was a little too tired and torn up for the Bad
Thing to be super bad right then, but I was pretty glib. I rather liked Dr.
Kablumbus, although he sucked on very nasty-smelling candies all the
time — to help him stop smoking, apparently — and he was a bit irritating
in that he tried to talk like a kid — using a lot of curse words, etc. — when
it was just quite clear that he wasn't a kid. He was very understanding,
though, and it was awfully nice to see a doctor who didn't want to do stuff
to my reproductive organs all the time. After he knew the general scoop,
Dr. Kablumbus laid out the options to me, and then to my parents and me.
After we all decided not to therapeutically convulse me with electricity.
Dr. Kablumbus got ready to let me leave the Earth via antidepressants.

Before I say anything else about Dr. Kablumbus or my little trip, I want
to tell very briefly about my meeting a colleague of mine on the White
Floor who is unfortunately not living anymore, but not through any fault
of her own whatsoever, rather through the fault of her boyfriend, who
killed her in a car crash by driving drunk. My meeting and making the
acquaintance of this girl, whose name is May, even now stands out in my
memory as more or less the last good thing that happened to me on Earth.
I happened to meet May one day in the TV room because of the fact that
her turtleneck shirt was on inside out. I remember *The Little Rascals* was
on and I saw the back of a blond head belonging to who knows what sex,
there, because the hair was really short and ragged. And below that head
there was the size and fabric-composition tag and the white stitching that
indicates the fact that one's turtleneck shirt is on inside out. So I said,
"Excuse me, did you know your shirt was on inside out?" And the person,
who was May, turned around and said, "Yes I know that." When she
turned I could not help noticing that she was unfortunately very pretty. I
hadn't seen that this was a pretty girl, here, or else I almost certainly
wouldn't have said anything whatsoever. I have always tried to avoid
talking to pretty girls, because pretty girls have a vicious effect on me in
which every part of my brain is shut down except for the part that says
unbelievably stupid things and the part that is aware that I am saying

unbelievably stupid things. But at this point I was still too tired and torn up to care much, and I was just getting ready to leave Earth, so I just said what I thought, even though May was disturbingly pretty. I said, "Why do you have it on inside out?" referring to the shirt. And May said, "Because the tag scratches my neck and I don't like that." Understandably, I said, "Well, hey, why don't you just cut the tag out?" To which I remember May replied, "Because then I couldn't tell the front of the shirt." "What?" I said, wittily. May said, "It doesn't have any pockets or writing on it or any-thing. The front is just exactly like the back. Except the back has the tag on it. So I wouldn't be able to tell." So I said, "Well, hey, if the front's just like the back, what difference does it make which way you wear it?" At which point May looked at me all seriously, for about eleven years, and then said, "It makes a difference to me." Then she broke into a big deadly-pretty smile and asked me tactfully where I got my scar. I told her I had had this annoying tag sticking out of my cheek....

So just more or less by accident May and I became friends, and we talked some. She wanted to write made-up stories for a living. I said I didn't know that could be done. She was killed by her boyfriend in his drunken car only ten days ago. I tried to call May's parents just to say that I was incredibly sorry yesterday, but their answering service informed me that Mr. and Mrs. Aculpa had gone out of town for an indefinite period. I can sympathize, because I am "out of town," too.

Dr. Kablumbus knew a lot about psychopharmaceuticals. He told my parents and me that there were two general kinds of antidepressants: tri-cyclics and M.A.O. inhibitors (I can't remember what "M.A.O." stands for exactly, but I have my own thoughts with respect to the matter). Apparently both kinds worked well, but Mr. Kablumbus said that there were certain things you couldn't eat and drink with M.A.O. inhibitors, like beer, and certain kinds of sausage. My Mom was afraid I would forget and maybe eat and drink some of these things, so we all conferred and decided to go with a tricyclic. Dr. Kablumbus thought this was a very good choice.

Just as with a long trip you don't reach your destination right away, so with antidepressants you have to "go up" on them; i.e., you start with a very tiny little dose and work your way up to a full-size dose in order to get your blood level accustomed and all that. So in one way my trip to the planet Trillaphon took over a week. But in another way, it was like being off Earth and on the planet Trillaphon right from the very first morning after I started. The big difference between the Earth and the planet Trillaphon, of course, is distance: the planet Trillaphon is very very far away. But there are other differences that are sort of more immediate and intrinsic. I think the air on the planet Trillaphon must not be as rich in oxygen or nutrition or something, because you get a lot tireder a lot faster there. Just shoveling snow off a sidewalk or running to catch a bus or shooting a couple baskets or walking up a hill to sled down gets you very, very tired. Another annoying thing is that the planet Trillaphon is tilted ever so slightly on its axis or something, so that the ground when you look at it isn't quite level; it lists a little to starboard. You get used to this fairly quickly, though, like getting your "sea legs" when you're on a ship.

Another thing is that the planet Trillaphon is a very sleepy planet. You have to take your antidepressants at night, and you better make sure there is a bed nearby, because it will be bedtime incredibly soon after you take them. Even during the day, the resident of the planet Trillaphon is a sleepy little soldier. Sleepy and tired, but too far away to be super-troubled.

This has nothing to do with the very ridiculous incident in the bathtub on Christmas Eve, but there is something electrical about the planet Trillaphon. On Trillaphon for me there isn't the old problem of my head making silence into a spangly glitter, because my tricyclic antidepressant — "Tofranil" — makes a sort of electrical noise of its own that drowns the spangle out completely. The new noise isn't incredibly pleasant, but it's better than the old noises, which I really couldn't stand at all. The new noise on my planet is kind of a high-tension electric trill. That's why for almost a year now I've somehow always gotten the name of my antidepressant wrong when I'm not looking right at the bottle: I've called it "Trillaphon" instead of "Tofranil," because "Trillaphon" is more trilly and electrical, and it just sounds more like what it's like to be there. But the electricalness of the planet Trillaphon is not just a noise. I guess if I were all glib like May is I'd say that "the planet Trillaphon is simply characterized by a more electrical way of life." It is, sort of. Sometimes on the planet Trillaphon the hairs on your arms will stand up and a chill will go through the big muscles in your legs and your teeth will vibrate when you close your mouth, as if you're under a high-tension line, or by a transformer. Sometimes you'll crackle for no reason and see blue things. And even the sound of your brain-voice when you think thoughts to yourself on the planet Trillaphon is different than it was on Earth; now it sounds like it's coming from a sort of speaker connected to you only by miles and miles and miles of wire, like you're back listening to the "Golden Days of Radio."

It is very hard to read on the planet Trillaphon, but that is not too inconvenient, because I hardly ever read anymore, except for "Newsweek" magazine, a subscription which I got for my birthday. I am twenty-one years old.

May was seventeen years old. Now sometimes I'll sort of joke with myself and say that I need to switch to an M.A.O. inhibitor. May's initials are M.A., and when I think about her now I get so sad I go "O!" In a way, I would understandably like to inhibit the "M.A.:O." I'm sure Dr. Kablumbus would agree that it is in my own best interests to do so. If the bus driver I more or less killed had the initials M.A., that would be incredibly ironic.

Communications between Earth and the planet Trillaphon are hard, but they are very inexpensive, so I am definitely probably going to call the Aculpas to say just how sorry I am about their daughter, and maybe even that I more or less loved her.

The big question is whether the Bad Thing is on the planet Trillaphon. I don't know if it is or not. Maybe it has a harder time in a thinner and less nutritious atmosphere. I certainly do, in some respects. Sometimes, when I don't think about it, I think I have just totally escaped the Bad Thing, and that I am going to be able to lead a Normal and Productive Life as a lawyer or something here on the planet Trillaphon, once I get so I can read again.

Being far away sort of helps with respect to the Bad Thing.

Except that is just highly silly when you think about what I said before concerning the fact that the Bad Thing is really

Afterword

For me—knowing who David Foster Wallace would become, even having known him, albeit slightly, and sitting as I write this across the hall from the office that was his—rereading "The Planet Trillaphon as It Stands in Relation to the Bad Thing" today is an absolutely brutal experience. Apart from some "lite" pieces published in the Amherst humor magazine he coedited, this is his first published piece of fiction. And it's a body blow.

"The Planet Trillaphon" is neither a memoir nor a technical piece about clinical depression and suicide. It's a short story, by one of the late twentieth century's most distinctive voices. And I love the voice here. Take that opening sentence, which our narrator manages to qualify in six different ways: "I've been on antidepressants for, *what, about* a year now, and *I suppose I feel as if* I'm *pretty* qualified to tell what they're like." Listen to the faux-yokel Midwestern interjections that pepper the characters' speech: "Boy oh boy," "holy cow," "well, hey," "how the heck." Midwestern, too, the narrator's reticence: "I really don't wish to go into a gigantic amount of detail" (following which, he goes into a gigantic amount of detail). The tone, while not perfectly managed, is wonderfully varied: long, urgent paragraphs swelling under the pressure of speech alternate with comic under- and overstatement. (Billions of dollars of clothes and electrical appliances? Really?)

While some near and dear to me have suffered with clinical depression, I've known only transient, situational depression, what the narrator describes as "just sort of really intense sadness." Reading "The Planet Trillaphon" I felt, for the first time, like I understood the vicious logic of real depression: how it feeds on and amplifies itself, establishes a closed loop between what D. T. Max terms "anxiety" and "the fear of anxiety." There's a bruised, frightened human heart at the center of "Trillaphon." A troubled little soldier. It creates a powerful irony—that this story, given over to a narrator who laments his inability to make others understand what he's going through, so effectively communicates his pain to us.

And there are two beating hearts here: our narrator's and that of the woman he "more or less loved," May. More precisely, May Aculpa—a cringe-inducing pun on *mea culpa*, "through my fault," from the Confiteor. In the course of *The Crying of Lot 49*, Thomas Pynchon's protagonist Oedipa Maas comes to realize that there is a "high magic to low puns"; so, too, here. May "wanted to write made-up stories for a living," a thing the narrator had thought impossible. Haunted by "Trillaphon"'s porous boundary between fact and fiction, I wonder whether it isn't the notion of "making up" stories, imaginatively inventing new stories, rather than rehashing and rehearsing his own, that strikes the narrator as fantastic.

—*Kevin J. H. Dettmar*

THE BROOM OF THE SYSTEM

1

1981

MOST REALLY PRETTY girls have pretty ugly feet, and so does Mindy Metalman, Lenore notices, all of a sudden. They're long and thin and splay-toed, with buttons of yellow callus on the little toes and a thick stair-step of it on the back of the heel, and a few long black hairs are curling out of the skin at the tops of the feet, and the red nail polish is cracking and peeling in curls and candy-striped with decay. Lenore only notices because Mindy's bent over in the chair by the fridge picking at some of the polish on her toes; her bathrobe's opening a little, so there's some cleavage visible and everything, a lot more than Lenore's got, and the thick white towel wrapped around Mindy's wet washed shampooed head is coming undone and a wisp of dark shiny hair has slithered out of a crack in the folds and curled down all demurely past the side of Mindy's face and under her chin. It smells like Flex shampoo in the room, and also pot, since Clarice and Sue Shaw are smoking a big thick j-bird Lenore got from Ed Creamer back at Shaker School and brought up with some other stuff for Clarice, here at school.

What's going on is that Lenore Beadsman, who's fifteen, has just come all the way from home in Shaker Heights, Ohio, right near Cleveland, to visit her big sister, Clarice Beadsman, who's a freshman at this women's college, called Mount Holyoke; and Lenore's staying with her sleeping bag in this room on the second floor of Rumpus Hall that Clarice shares with her roommates, Mindy Metalman and Sue Shaw. Lenore's also come to sort of check out this college, a little bit. This is because even though she's just fifteen she's supposedly quite intelligent and thus accelerated and already a junior at Shaker School and thus thinking about college, application-wise, for next year. So she's visiting. Right now it's a Friday night in March.

Sue Shaw, who's not nearly as pretty as Mindy or Clarice, is bringing the joint over here to Mindy and Lenore, and Mindy takes it and lets her toe alone for a second and sucks the bird really hard, so it glows bright and a seed snaps loudly and bits of paper ash go flying and floating, which Clarice and Sue find super funny and start laughing at really hard, whooping and clutching at each other, and Mindy breathes it in really deep and holds it in and passes the bird to Lenore, but Lenore says no thank you.

"No thank you," says Lenore.

"Go ahead, you brought it, why not...," croaks Mindy Metalman, talking the way people talk without breathing, holding on to the smoke.

"I know, but it's track season at school and I'm on the team and I don't smoke during the season, I can't, it kills me," Lenore says.

So Mindy shrugs and finally lets out a big breath of pale used-up smoke and coughs a deep little cough and gets up with the bird and takes it over across the room to Clarice and Sue Shaw, who are by a big wooden stereo speaker listening to this song, again, by Cat Stevens, for like the tenth time tonight. Mindy's robe's more or less open, now, and Lenore can see some pretty amazing stuff, but Mindy just walks across the room. Lenore can at this point divide all the girls she's known neatly into girls who think deep down they're pretty and girls who deep down think they're really not. Girls who think they're pretty don't care much about their bathrobes being undone and are good at makeup and like to walk when people are watching, and they act different when there are boys around; and girls like Lenore, who don't think they're too pretty, tend not to wear makeup, and run track, and wear black Converse sneakers, and keep their bathrobes pretty well fastened at all times. Mindy sure is pretty, though, except for her feet.

The Cat Stevens song is over again, and the needle goes up by itself, and obviously none of these three feel like moving all the way to start it again, so they're just sitting back in their hard wood desk chairs, Mindy in her faded pink terry robe with one shiny smooth leg all bare and sticking out; Clarice in her Desert boots and her dark blue jeans that Lenore calls her shoe-horn jeans, and that white western shirt she'd worn at the state fair the time she'd had her purse stolen, and her blond hair flooding all over the shirt, and her eyes very blue right now; Sue Shaw with her red hair and a green sweater and green tartan skirt and fat white legs with a bright red pimple just over one knee, legs crossed with one foot jiggling one of those boat shoes, with the sick white soles — Lenore dislikes that kind of shoe a lot.

Clarice after a quiet bit lets out a long sigh and says, in whispers, "Cat . . . is . . . *God*," giggling a little at the end. The other two giggle too.

"God? How can Cat be God? Cat exists." Mindy's eyes are all red.

"That's offensive and completely blaphemous," says Sue Shaw, eyes wide and puffed and indignant.

"*Blaphe*mous?" Clarice dies, looks at Lenore. "*Blas*phemous," she says. Her eyes aren't all that bad, really, just unusually cheerful, as if she's got a joke she's not telling.

"Blissphemous," says Mindy.

"Blossphemous."

"Blousephemous."

"Bluesphemous."

"Boisterous."

"Boisteronahalfshell."

"Bucephalus."

"Barney Rubble."

"Baba Yaga."

"Bolshevik."

"*Blaphe*mous!"

They're dying, doubled over, and Lenore's laughing that weird sympathetic laugh you laugh when everybody else is laughing so hard they make you laugh too. The noise of the big party downstairs is coming through the floor and vibrating in Lenore's black sneakers and the arms of the chair. Now Mindy slides out of her desk chair all limp and shlomps down on Lenore's sleeping bag on the floor next to Clarice's pretend-Persian ruglet from Mooradian's in Cleveland, and Mindy modestly covers her crotch with a corner of her robe, but Lenore still can't help but see the way her breasts swell up into the worn pink towel cloth of the robe, all full and stuff, even lying down on her back, there, on the floor. Lenore unconsciously looks down a little at her own chest, under her flannel shirt.

"Hunger," Sue Shaw says after a minute. "Massive, immense, uncontrollable, consuming, uncontrollable, *hunger*."

"This is so," says Mindy.

"We will wait" — Clarice looks at her watch on the underside of her wrist — "one, that is *one* hour, before eating anything what-soentirelyever."

"No we can't possibly *possibly* do that."

"But do it we shall. As per room discussions of not one week ago, when we explicitly agreed that we shall not gorge when utterly flapped, lest we get fat and repulsive, like Mindy, over there, you poor midge."

"Fart-blossom," Mindy says absently, she's not fat and she knows it, Lenore knows it, they all know it.

"A lady at all times, that Metalman," Clarice says. Then, after a minute, "Speaking of which, you might just maybe either fix your robe or get dressed or get up off your back in Lenore's stuff, I'm not really all up for giving you a gynecological exam, which is sort of what you're making us do, here, O Lesbia of Thebes."

"Stuff and bother," says Mindy, or rather, "Stuth and bozzcr"; and she gets up swaying and reaching for solid things, goes over to the door that goes into her little single bedroom off the bathroom. She got there first in September and took it, Clarice had said in a letter, this Playboy-Playmatish JAP from Scarsdale, and she's shedding what's left of her bathrobe, battered into submission, leaving it all wet in Lenore's lap in the chair by the door, and going through the door with her long legs, deliberate steps. Shuts the door.

Clarice looks after her when she's gone and shakes her head a tiny bit and looks over at Lenore and smiles. There are sounds of laughter downstairs, and cattle-herd sounds of lots of people dancing. Lenore just loves to dance.

Sue Shaw takes a big noisy drink of water out of a big plastic Jetsons glass on her desk up by the front door. "Speaking of which, you didn't by any chance happen to see Splittstoesser this morning?" she says.

"Nuh-uh," says Clarice.

"She was with Proctor."

"So?"

"At seven o'clock? Both in nighties, all sleepy and googly, coming out of her room, together? Holding *hands*?"

"Hmmm."

"Now if anybody ever told me that *Splittstoesser...*"

"I thought she was engaged to some guy."

"She is."

They both laugh like hell.

"Awww."

"Who's Splittstoesser?" Lenore asks.

"Nancy Splittstoesser, at dinner? The girl in the red V-neck, with the earrings that were really little fists?"

"Oh. But what about her?"

Clarice and Sue look at each other and start to laugh again. Mindy

Metalman comes back in, in gym shorts and an inside-out sweatshirt with the arms cut off. Lenore looks at her and smiles at the floor.

"What?" Mindy knows something's up right away.

"Splittstoesser and Proctor," Sue gets out.

"I meant to *ask* you." Mindy's eyes get all wide. "They're in the bathroom this morning? In the same *shower?*"

"Ahh, no!" Sue's going to die, Mindy starts to laugh too, that weird sympathetic laugh, looking around at them.

"They're, uh, together now? I thought Nancy was engaged."

"She...is," Clarice making Lenore laugh, too.

"Godfrey Jaysus."

It settles down after a while. Sue does the "Twilight Zone" theme in a low voice. "Who...will be struck next...?"

"Not entirely sure I even understand what you guys are, uh..." Lenore is asking, looking around.

So Clarice tells Lenore all this business about how Pat Proctor's a bull and what bulls are and how quite a few of the girls get pretty friendly and all, here at this women's college.

"You're kidding."

"No."

"That's just incredibly gross." And this sets Mindy and Sue off again. Lenore looks at them. "Well doesn't that kind of thing sort of give you guys the creeps a little bit? I mean I—"

"Well it's just part of life and everything, what people want to do is more or less their own..." Clarice is putting the needle on that song again.

There's a silence for about half the song. Mindy's at her toes, again, over at the bunkbeds. "The thing is, I don't know if we should say," says Sue Shaw, looking over at Clarice, "but Nancy Splittstoesser sort of got assaulted right before Thanksgiving, on the path out by the Widget House, and I think she—"

"Assaulted?" Lenore says.

"Well, raped, I guess, really."

"I see." Lenore looks up behind Sue at a poster over Clarice's desk, which is of a really muscular guy, without a shirt on, making all his muscles from the back, his back all shiny and bulging every which way. The poster's old and ripped at the edges from tape; it had been in Clarice's room at home and their father had not been pleased, the light from the high ceiling makes a bright reflection at the back of the man's head and hides it in white.

"I think it kind of messed her up," says Sue.

"How hard to understand," Lenore says softly. "Raped. So she just doesn't like males now, because of that, or—?"

"Well I think it's hard to say, Lenore," Clarice with her eyes closed, playing with a button on her shirt pocket. She's in front of their air vent, with her chair leaning back, and her hair's all over, a yellow breeze around her cheeks. "Probably just safe to say she's pretty confused and messed up temporarily, 'ntcha think?"

"Sure, I guess."

"You a virgin Lenore?" Mindy's on the lower bunk, Sue's bed, with her picked and flakey feet up and toes hooked into the springs on the underside of Clarice's mattress.

"You bitch," Clarice says to Mindy.

"I'm just *asking*," says Mindy. "I doubt Lenore's too hung up about what—"

"Yes I'm a virgin, I mean I've never had, you know, sexual intercourse with anybody," Lenore says, smiling at Clarice that it's OK, really. "Are you a virgin Mindy?"

Mindy laughs. "Oh very much so."

Sue Shaw snorts into her water. "Mindy's saving herself for the right marine battalion." Clarice and Lenore laugh.

"Fuck you in the ear," Mindy Metalman says mildly, she's all relaxed, almost asleep. Her legs are all curved and faintly muscular and the skin's so smooth it almost glows because she'd recently gotten "waxed" at home, she'd told Lenore, whatever that meant.

"This happen a lot?"

"What happen?"

"Rapes and assaults and stuff?"

Clarice and Sue look away, all calm. "Sometimes, probably, who knows, it's hard to say, because it gets covered up or not reported or something a lot of the time, the College isn't exactly nuts about—"

"Well how many times that you know of?"

"I dle know. About maybe, I guess I know of about ten women—"

"*Ten?*"

"...."

"How many women do you even know total, here?"

"Lenore, *I* don't know," Clarice says. "It's just not...it's just common sense, is what it is, really. If you're careful, you know, and stay off the paths at night..."

"Security's really good here, really," says Sue Shaw. "They'll give you rides just about anywhere on campus at night if it's far, and there's a shuttle bus that goes from the library and the labs back here to the rear dorms every hour, with an armed guard, and they'll take you right up to the—"

"*Armed guard?*"

"Some of them are pretty cute, too." Clarice winks at Lenore.

"You never told me about any of this stuff at Christmas, Clarice. Armed guards and stuff. Doesn't it bother you? I mean back at home—"

"I don't think it's too different anywhere else, Lenore," says Clarice. "I don't think it is. You get used to it. It's really just common sense."

"Still, though."

"There is of course the issue of the party," says Mindy Metalman from the bunk, pretty obviously changing the subject. The noise is still loud from underneath their room.

What's going on is that the dorm is giving a really big party, here, tonight, downstairs, with a bitching band called Spiro Agnew and the Armpits and dancing and men and beer with ID's. It's all really cute and clever, and at dinner downstairs Lenore saw them putting up plastic palm trees and strings of flowers, and some of the girls had plastic grass skirts, because tonight's was a theme party, with the theme being Hawaiian: the name of the party on a big lipstick banner on a sheet out in front of Rumpus said it was the "Comonawannaleiya" party, which Lenore thought was really funny and clever, and they were going to give out leis, ha, to all the men who came from other schools and could get in with ID's. They had a whole room full of leis, Lenore had seen after dinner.

"There is that," says Clarice.

"Thus."

"So."

"Not me," says Sue Shaw. "Nawmeboy, never again, I said it and I meant it. *Pas moi.*"

Clarice laughs and reaches over for the Jetsons glass.

"The issue, however," says Mindy from the bed, her sweatshirt slipped all down at the shoulder and about ready to fall off, it looks like, "the issue is the fact that there is...food, *food* down in the dining room, spread under the laughing fingers of the plastic palms, that we all helped buy."

"This is true," Clarice sighs, hitting the repeat on the stereo. Her eyes are so blue they look hot, to Lenore.

"And all we've got is just those far too scrumptious mashed potatoes in the fridge," Mindy says, which is true, just a clear Tuperware dish full of salty Play-Doh Rumpus mashed potatoes, which was all they could steal at dinner, seeing as how the kitchen ran out of cookies, then the bread...

"But you guys said no way you'd go down," says Lenore. " 'Member you guys kept telling me how gross it was, these parties, mixers, and like a meat market, and how you could get sucked in, 'as it were,' you said, and how you just had to avoid going down at all costs, and how I shouldn't, you know..." She looks around, she wants to go down, she loves to dance, she has a killer new dress she got at Tempo in East Corinth for just such a—

"She wants to go, Clarice," Mindy says, throwing her legs over the side of the bunk and sitting up with a bounce, "and she *is* our guest, and there is the Dorito factor, and if we stayed for like six quick minutes..."

"So I see." Clarice looks all droopy-lidded at Lenore and sees her eagerness and has to smile. Sue Shaw is at her desk with her back turned, her butt is really pretty fat and wide in the chair, pooching over the sides, Lenore sees.

Clarice sighs. "The thing is Lenore you just don't know. These things are so unbelievably tiresome, unpleasant, we went all first semester and you just really literally get nauseated, physically ill after a while, ninety-nine point nine percent of the men who come are just lizards, reptiles, and it's clear awfully fast that the whole thing is really just nothing more than a depressing ritual, a rite that we're expected by God knows who to act out, over and over. You can't even have conversations. It's really repulsive." And she drinks water out of the Jetsons glass. Sue Shaw is nodding her head at her desk.

"I say what we do," Mindy Metalman hits the floor and claps her hands, "is Lenore goes and puts on that *fabulous* violet dress I saw you hang up, and we three stay and attend to the rest of this joint, for a second, and then we all just scamper down really quick, and Lenore gets a condensed liberal arts education and one or two dances while we steal about seven *tons* of food, then we come right back up, David Letterman's on in less than an hour."

"No," says Sue Shaw.

"Well then you can stay here, nipplehead, we'll get over it, if one semi-bad experience is going to make you hide away like a—"

"Fine, look, let's just do that." Clarice looks less than thrilled. They all look at each other. Lenore gets a nod from Clarice and jumps up and goes to Mindy's little annex bedroom to put on her dress as Clarice starts glaring in earnest at Mindy and Mindy gives little stuff-it signals to Sue Shaw, over in the corner.

Lenore brushes her teeth in a tiny bathroom redolent of Metalman and Shaw, washes her face, dries it with a towel off the floor, puts Visine in, finds some of that bright wet-looking lipstick Mindy owns in an old Tampax box on the toilet, gets the lipstick out, knocks the Tampax box over, a compact falls in the toilet and she has to fish it out, her shirt's wet, the arm's soaked, she takes the shirt off and goes into Mindy's bedroom. She has to get her bra, since the dress fabric is really thin, violet cotton, pretty as hell with her brown hair, which is luckily clean, and a bit of lipstick, she looks eighteen, very nearly, and her bra's in the bottom of her bag on Mindy's bed. Lenore rummages in her bag. Mindy's room is really a sty, clothes all over, an Exercycle, big James Dean poster on the inside of the door, Richard Gere too oh of course, pictures of some nonfamous guy on a sailboat, *Rolling Stone* magazine covers, Journey concert poster, super-high ceiling like the other rooms, here with a bright blanket tacked one side on the ceiling and one on the wall and sagging, a becalmed candy sail. There's a plastic thing on the dresser, and Lenore knows it's a Pill-holder, for the Pill, because Clarice has got one and so does Karen Daughenbaugh, who's more or less Lenore's best friend at Shaker School. There's the bra, Lenore puts it on. The dress. Combs her hair with a long red comb that has black hair in it and smells like Flex.

A scritch. The Cat Stevens goes off all of a sudden, in the main room. There's loud knocking on the front door, Lenore can hear. She comes back in with the others with her white dress pumps in her hand as Sue Shaw opens the door and Mindy tries to disperse smoke with an album cover. There's two guys outside, filling the doorway, grinning, in matching blue blazers and tartan ties and chinos and those shoes. There's nobody with them.

"Hey and howdy, ma'am," says one of them, a big, tall, tan-in-the-spring-type guy with thick blond hair and a sculptured part and a cleft chin and bright green eyes. "Does Melinda Sue Metalman live here, by any chance at all?"

"How did you get up here," says Sue Shaw. "No one gets upstairs here without an escort, see."

The one guy beams. "Please to meet you. Andy 'Wang-Dang' Lang; my colleague, Biff Diggerence." And he not very subtly pushes the door open with one big hand, and Sue goes back a little on her heels, and the two just walk right in, all of a sudden, Wang-Dang and Biff. Biff's shorter than Lang, and broader, a rectangular person. They've both got Comonawannaleiya cups, with beer, in their hands. They're a bit tight, apparently. Biff especially: his jaw is slack and eyes are dull and his cheeks are all red in hot patches.

Wang-Dang Lang finally says to Sue, while he's looking at Clarice, "Well I'm just afraid your security personnel here are pretty trusting, 'cause when I told them I was Father Mustafa Metalman, Miss Metalman's second cousin and spiritchul advisor, and then gave them some spiritchul advice of their own, they just..." He stops and looks around and whistles. "Unbelievably nice room here. Biff you ever see ceilings so *hah* in a dorm?"

Lenore sits back down in her chair by the door to Mindy's room, barefoot, watching. Mindy pulls up her sweatshirt. Clarice and Sue face the two men, their arms crossed.

"I'm Mindy Metalman," says Mindy Metalman. The guys don't even look over at her for a second, they're still looking the room over, then the tall one looks at Mindy, and he starts nudging Biff, staring at her.

"Hi Mindy, I'm Wang-Dang Lang, Biff Diggerence on my right, here," gesturing, looking at Mindy all wide-eyed still. Comes over and shakes her hand, Mindy sort of shakes it back, looking around at the others.

"Do I know you?"

Wang-Dang smiles. "Well now quite regrettably I must say no, but you do, if I'm not entirely mistaken, know Doug Dangler, over at Amherst College? He's my roommate, or rather me and Biff's roommate? And when we said how we were comin' over here to the Comonolay party, the Dangle-man just said 'Wanger,' he said, he said 'Wanger, Melinda Metalman lives in Rumpus Hall, and I'd really be just ever so much more than obliged if you'd pay your respects, to her, for me,' and so I—"

"Doug Dangler?" Mindy's eyes are mad eyes, Lenore sees, sort of. "Listen I do *not* know any Doug Dangler at Amherst, I think you're mixed up, so maybe you just better go back downst—"

"Sure you know Doug, Doug's a kick-ass guy," the aforementioned Biff is heard from, short and broad with watery denim eyes dull and beady with party, and a little blond beardish thing sprouting from his chin, making it look a little like an armpit, Lenore thinks. His voice is low and rather engagingly grunty. Lang's is soft and smooth and nice, although he does seem to fall in and out of some sort of accent, at times. He says:

"Ma'am now I know for a fact you met Doug Dangler because he told me all about it, at length." His bottle-green eyes fall on Lenore. "It was at a party at Femur Hall, right after Christmas break and Winterterm and all? You were standing talking to this guy, and y'all were more than a little taken with each other, when the guy very unfortunately got taken slightly under the weather and vomited a tiny bit in your purse? *That* was Doug Dangler." Lang smiles triumphantly. Biff Diggerence laughs ogg-ogg, his shoulders go up and down together. Lang continues, "And he said how he was real sorry and could he pay to have your purse cleaned? And but you said no and were all…mind-bogglingly nice about it, and when you were rescuing items from your purse you on purpose dropped that piece of paper that had your name and box number and phone and all on it, that phone bill? Doug picked that sucker up, and that's how you met him," smiling, nodding.

"*That* was that guy?" Mindy says. "He said I gave him my name on purpose? That's just a lie. That was utterly disgusting. I had to throw that purse away. He, I remember he came up to me" (to Clarice and Sue) "and put his hand on the hem of my sweater, and said how he had this hangnail that had got caught on my sweater, and how he couldn't get away, it was stuck, ha ha, but he did it for like *two hours*, until finally he threw up on me." To Wang-Dang Lang she says, "He was bombed out of his mind. He was so drunk he was actually drooling. I remember drool was coming out of his mouth."

"Well now Melinda surely you know how we can all tend to get that way at certain times." Lang nudges Biff Diggerence, who almost falls on Sue Shaw, who squeals and backs toward the door with her arms crossed.

"Look, I think you better leave," Clarice says from now over by Lenore. "We're all really tired and you're really not supposed to be up here without—"

"But, now, we just got here, really," Wang-Dang Lang smiles. He looks around again. "I couldn't impose on you ladies for a small can of beer, could I, by any chance, if you maht possibly…?" gesturing over at Sue's little fridgelette by the bunks. And then he sits down in Sue's wooden desk chair by the door, by a speaker. Biff still stands by Sue, facing Clarice and Lenore. Sue looks at Clarice, Mindy at Biff, who grins yellowly, Wang-Dang Lang over at Lenore in her chair at the back by Mindy's door, sitting watching. Lenore feels like a clot in her pretty violet dress and bit of lipstick and bare feet, wondering what to do with her shoes, if she should throw a shoe at Lang, it's got a sharp heel, are the police on their way?

"Look, we don't have any beer, and if we did it's just rude for you guys to come in here uninvited and ask us for beer, and I *don't* know Doug Dangler, and I think we'd really just appreciate it if you'd leave."

"I'm sure there's all the beer you could possibly want downstairs," Clarice says.

Biff Diggerence now belches a huge belch, one of almost unbelievable duration, clearly a specialty, then he has another swallow out of his Comonawannaleiya cup. Lenore involuntarily mutters something about how disgusting this burp was; all eyes go to her. Lang smiles broadly:

"Well hi there. What's *your* name?"

"Lenore Beadsman," says Lenore.

"Whey you from, Lenore?"

"Lenore's my sister," Clarice says, moving toward the door and looking at Biff Diggerence. "She's fifteen and she's visiting and she's invited, which I'm afraid you're really not, so if you'll just let me out for a quick second, here..."

Biff Diggerence steps over like a dancer, with a flourish, to block the door with his body.

"Hmmm," says Clarice. She looks at Mindy Metalman. Mindy goes over to Lenore, gets her damp robe off the back of the chair, puts it on over her armless sweatshirt. Lang smiles warmly. Biff watches Mindy for a second, then turns around abruptly at the door, starts banging his head on the door, over and over, really hard. Wang-Dang Lang laughs. The banging isn't all that loud compared with the noise of the party and all, though, suddenly, because the music's now a lot louder, they must have opened the dining room doors at eleven.

"Thing about Biff," Wang-Dang Lang shouts over the pounding to Clarice and Mindy Metalman, "beer does not entirely agree with him because he is, we've found, for some reason physically incapable of... um...emptying his stomach in crisis. As they say. Just can't do it, 'matter how much he drinks, which is often more than can be explained by known physical laws. It's dangerous, right Digger?" Wang-Dang shouts over to the pounding Biff. "So instead of booting, the big fella here finds himself having recourse to..."

"...Pounding his head against the wall," Clarice finishes for him with a little mouth-smile, she obviously remembers Creamer and Geralamo and company, Lenore can tell. Lang nods at Clarice with an engaging grin. Biff finally stops and turns back around, resting his back against the door, beaming, with a red forehead, a little cross-eyed. The muscles in his big neck are corded. He closes his eyes and leans back and breathes heavily.

"Well if we could just stay and rest up and catch our breaths for just a couple of seconds for the second half of the big luau, down there, we'll be more than obliged to you," says Lang. "And I'll be giving old Doug the bad and from what I can see most unfortchinit news about your not remembering him, Melinda-Sue. He'll be hurt, I'll just tell you right now, in advance. He is a shy and sinsitive person."

"Seems like a common problem over there at Amherst," says Clarice. Lenore smiles at her.

Meanwhile Mindy has gone over to the ashtray to see about the corpse of the joint. Lenore can tell Mindy's decided not to be intimidated, all of a sudden. Mindy's shiny legs through the robe are now right by Wang-Dang Lang's face, he's still sitting in the chair, his nose about even with her waist. Lang looks down at his shoes, with the white soles, he's shy, almost, Mindy makes even him shy, Lenore sees. Mindy resuscitates the joint with a big plastic lighter that says "When God Made Man She Was Only Joking." She pauses, watches it. It glows, she takes it back with her to the edge of Sue Shaw's bed, sits down, faces Lang off the end of the bunk. The room's all quiet, except for party noise, underneath. Mindy concentrates on the j-bird, then pauses again, then looks at Lang and holds the joint out to him.

"Well now aren't you kind," Lang says softly. He takes a bit of a polite puff, smiles at Mindy.

"Who *are* you guys, anyway?" Mindy asks. Clarice and Sue are glaring at her.

Lang stops and smiles broadly, taken aback. Holds out his hand. "I personally am Andrew Sealander 'Wang-Dang' Lang, class of '83, from Nugget Bluff, Texas, residing now at 666 Psi Phi fraternity, Amherst College, Massachusetts, U.S.A."

"A sophomore."

"Affirmative. As is Bernard Werner 'Biff' Diggerence, of Shillington, Pennsylvania." A pause, all pregnant. Lang looks up at Biff, who seems still to be sleeping at the door.

"We've actually, I'll tell you ladies in confidence, been sent out," Wang-Dang leans all conspiratorially toward Mindy and Lenore. "We've actually been sent out for what could be termed our 'nitiation."

"Oh, shit," Clarice says, her arms crossed, leaning against the wall. Biff Diggerence is now showing signs of life; he's to be seen stroking Sue Shaw's hair with a hot-dog finger, and winking down at her, making clicking noises with the corner of his mouth, as Sue whimpers and gets set to cry.

"Initiation?" Mindy says.

"Affirmative. The High Demiurge and Poobah of the Psi Phi fraternal order of brothers himself has sent us out on a...," a burp, here, "...a sort of quest, you might say. We find ourselves in search of personal decoration."

"Decoration."

"Auto...graphs," Biff laughs ogg and gives a little pound on the wall with the back of his head, for emphasis.

"Autographs?"

"We need you girls to sign our asses," says Biff, coming to the point, smiling down at Sue Shaw.

"Sign your asses?" says Mindy Metalman.

"That is unfortunately affirmative," Lang says, flashing a smile full of bright teeth over at Lenore. "We are required...," fishing for a piece of paper in the pocket of his blazer, perusing, "...we are requahred to secure the signatures of no fewer than *fahv* of Mount Holyoke's loveliest before sunrise tomorrow. We figger of course we can sign each other, being friends and all, but that's just one each." He looks around significantly at each of the girls, gives Lenore a bit of a wink. "Means we need, according to my figures, four more."

Lenore notices Sue Shaw sitting there all quiet, looking at her leather shoes with the white soles. Biff's hands are in Sue's bright red hair.

"So wait," says Clarice. "You mean you want us to sign your bottoms?"

"Please."

"*Bare?*"

"Well, clearly yes, that's the whole—"

"Sweet shrieking mother of Christ what nerve." Clarice says in amazement, staring at Lang. "And it just never occurred to you geniuses that we might say no? I'm saying no."

"Your prerogative entirely," says Wang-Dang Lang. " 'Course we very regrettably will find ourselves unable to leave until you do." He now has his hand lightly on Mindy's bare leg, Lenore notices. Lenore shivers a bit. Clarice makes a sudden move for the door, Biff moves in front of the knob, Clarice stops, Biff pounds the door with the back of his head again, a few times, emphasizing the general state of affairs.

Clarice stops, clearly now for a second just so mad she can't really say or do anything at all. "You shiny bastards," she finally gets out. "You Amherst guys, U-Mass too, all of you. Just because you're bigger, physically just take up more space, you think—*do* you think?—think you can rule everything, make women do whatever stupid rotten disgusting stuff you say you want just because you're drunk? Well up yours, sideways." She looks from Lang to Biff. "You come over to our parties, grinning like apes on the bus no doubt, you get smeared in about two minutes, trash us, act like we're meat, or furniture, think you can just...," looking around, "*invade* us, our *room*, for no other reason than that you're just stronger, that you can block the door and pound your big greasy stupid heads on it? Screw you. Screw you."

Lang laughs. "Regrettably an invitation extended in anger, I'm afraid." He laughs again. Mindy smiles a bit, too. Lang's hand is still on her leg.

But Biff is miffed, here, suddenly. "Well screw you right back Miss Rodeo Shirt," he says to Clarice, obviously now in one of those alcoholically articulate periods. "Just come off it. This place is just the biggest...," looking around, "the biggest giant joke!" He looks to Lang for support; Lang is whispering something to Mindy Metalman.

But Biff is pissed. "You have these parties that you advertise out our ears, all this cute teasing bullshit, 'Come to the Comonawannaleiya party, get lei'd at the door,' ha. 'Win a trip to the hot tubs for two,' blah-blah-blah. You're just teases of the cockular sort, is what you are. So we come, like you ask and advertise for, and we put on ties, and we come over, and then we find you got security guards at the doors, with freaking *guns*, and we gotta have our hands stamped like fifth-graders for beer, and all the girls look at us like we're rapists, and plus, besides, all the girls down there look like Richard Nixon, while all the real babes lock themselves up up here—"

"Like you lovely ladies, you must admit," Wang-Dang Lang says with a smile.

Biff Diggerence whirls and whomps the door with his forehead a few times, really hard. He stays facing the door, his sails apparently windless, for a moment.

"I'm afraid he's quite inebriated," says Lang.

Lenore stands up, in her dress. "Please let me out."

Lang and Mindy stand. Sue stands. Everyone's standing with Lenore. Lang smiles and nods his head. "So if you'd just be kind enough to put your...Jocelyn Hancock on...my...," struggling with the belt of his chinos. Mindy looks away. Biff, still breathing at the door, does his belt too. He even brought a pen; Lenore can see it sticking out of his pocket.

"No, I'm not going to touch you, much less sign you," says Lenore.

Wang-Dang Lang looks at her, vaguely puzzled. "Well then we're real unfortunately not going to be able to leave."

"That's fortunately of very little concern to me because I'm not going to be here because I'm leaving," Lenore says.

"I'll sign," Sue Shaw says quietly.

Clarice stares at Sue. "What?"

"I want them out. I'll sign." She doesn't look up. She looks at her shoes. Biff's pants drop with a heavy sound, he's still facing the door. His bottom is big, broad, white, largely hairless. A vulnerable bottom, really. Lenore evaluates it calmly.

"Whuboutchoo, Melinda-Sue?" Lang asks Mindy. Lang's in his underpants.

Mindy really looks at Lang, looks him in the eye. There's no expression on her. After a moment she says, "Sure, why not."

"*You* can sign the front if you want," laughs Wang-Dang.

"This is disgusting. I'm leaving, let me leave, please," says Lenore. She turns. "You're a coward," she says to Sue Shaw. "You have ugly feet," she says to Mindy Metalman. "Look at her feet, Andy, before you do anything rash." She turns to the door. "Get out of the way, Boof, or whatever your name is."

Biff turns, the first time Lenore's ever seen a man naked. "No."

Lenore throws one of her spiky white high-heeled dress shoes, the kind with the metal straps, at Biff Diggerence's head. It misses his head and hits the door above him and makes a loud sound and the heel sticks in the wood of the door. The white shoe hangs there. As if the noise of the shoe's hitting the door were just the last straw, Sue Shaw gives a yelp and begins to cry a little, although she's still a bit dry from being recently stoned. She has Biff's pen in her hand.

"Let me leave or I'll put out your eye with my shoe," Lenore says to Biff, hefting her other shoe. Wang-Dang Lang is holding Mindy Metalman's hand.

"Let her out, she doesn't even go here," says Clarice. "I'll sign too, you drips."

"Let me out," says Lenore.

Biff finally gets away from the door, still holding his empty Comonawannaleiya cup. He has to go over anyway, obviously, to present his bottom to Sue Shaw, there in the corner. He takes little comic steps because his pants are down around his ankles, and Lenore sees his genitals bob and waggle as he takes his tiny shuffles over to Sue. Lenore runs past in bare feet, gets her shoe out of the door. Pulls it out, the heel, looks back. Lang is kissing Mindy's creamy cheek, with a faraway, laughing expression, in his underwear. Sue is kneeling, signing Biff. Clarice has her arms crossed. Tapping her fingers on her arms.

Lenore runs out into the tiled hall, away. Outside there will be air, Lenore wants out of Rumpus Hall very much, and gets out, finally she does, but only after negotiating a hall door, a stair door, a hall door, and a front door, all locked tight from the inside. Out in the crusty March lawn, by the wash of the well-lit street, amid crowds of boys in blue blazers going up the walk, putting Certs in their mouths, she enjoys a brief nosebleed.

5

1990

/a/

Suppose someone had said to me, ten years ago, in Scarsdale, or on the commuter train, suppose the person had been my next-door neighbor, Rex Metalman, the corporate accountant with the unbelievable undulating daughter, suppose this was back in the days before his lawn mania took truly serious hold and his nightly paramilitary sentry-duty with the illuminated riding mower and the weekly planeloads of DDT dropping from the sky in search of perhaps one sod webworm nest and his complete intransigence in the face of the reasonable and in the beginning polite requests of one or even all of the neighbors that hostilities against the range of potential lawn enemies that obsessed him be toned down, at least in scale, before all this drove a wedge the size of a bag of Scott's into our tennis friendship, suppose Rex Metalman had speculated in my presence, then, that ten years later, which is to say now, I, Rick Vigorous, would be living in Cleveland, Ohio, between a biologically dead and completely offensive-smelling lake and a billion-dollar man-made desert, that I would be divorced from my wife and physically distanced from the growth of my son, that I would be operating a firm in partnership with an invisible person, little more, it seems clear now, than a corporate entity interested in failure for tax purposes, the firm publishing things perhaps even slightly more laughable than nothing at all, and that perched high atop this mountain of the unthinkable would be the fact that I was in love, grossly and pathetically and fiercely and completely in love with a person eighteen count them eighteen years younger than I, a woman from one of Cleveland's first families, who lives in a city owned by her father but who works answering telephones for something like four dollars an hour, a woman whose uniform of white cotton dress and black Converse hightop sneakers is an unanalyzable and troubling constant, who takes somewhere, I suspect, between five and eight showers a day, who works in neurosis like a whaler in scrim-shaw, who lives with a schizophrenically narcissistic bird and an almost certainly nymphomaniacal bitch of a roommate, and who finds in me, somewhere, who knows where, the complete lover . . . suppose all this were said to me by Rex Metalman, leaning conversationally with his flamethrower over the fence between our properties as I stood with a rake in my hand, suppose Rex had said all this to me, then I almost certainly would have replied that the likelihood of all *that* was roughly equal to the probability of young Vance Vigorous, then eight and at eight in certain respects already more of a man than I, that young Vance, even as we stood there to be seen kicking a football up into the cold autumn sky and down through a window, his laughter echoing forever off the closed colored suburban trees, of strapping Vance's eventually turning out to be a . . . a *homosexual*, or something equally unlikely or preposterous or totally out of the question.

Now the heavens resound with unkind giggles. Now that it's become undeniably apparent even to me that I have a son who lends to the expression "fruit of my loins" whole new vistas of meaning, that I am here and do do what I do when there is anything to do, when I feel an empty draft and look down and find a hole in my chest and spy, in the open polyurethane purse of Lenore Beadsman, among the aspirins and bars of hotel soap and lottery tickets and the ridiculous books that mean nothing at all, the clenched purple fist of my own particular heart, what am I to say to Rex Metalman and Scarsdale and the sod webworms and the past, except that it does not exist, that it has been obliterated, that footballs never climbed into crisp skies, that my support checks disappear into a black void, that a man can be and is and must be reborn, at some point, perhaps points? Rex would be confused and would, as whenever confused, hide his discomfort by dynamiting an area of his lawn. I would stand, cold rake in white hand, knowing what I know, in a rain of dirt and grass and worms, and shake my head at all around me.

Then who is this girl who owns me, whom I love? I refuse to ask or answer who she is. *What* is she? This is a thin-shouldered, thin-armed, big-breasted girl, a long-legged girl with feet larger than average, feet that tend to point out a bit when she walks . . . in her black basketball sneakers. Did I say troubling? These are shoes that I love. I will confess that I once in a moment of admittedly irresponsible degeneracy tried to make love to one of the shoes, a 1989 All-Star hightop, when Lenore was in the shower, but failed to be able to bring the thing off, for familiar reasons.

But what of Lenore, of Lenore's hair? Here is hair that is clearly within and of itself every color—blond and red and jet-black-blue and honeynut—but which effects an outward optical compromise with possibility that consists of appearing simply dull brown, save for brief teasing glimpses out of the corner of one's eye. The hair hangs in bangs, and the sides curve down past Lenore's cheeks and nearly meet in points below her chin, like the brittle jaws of an insect of prey. Oh, the hair can bite. I've been bitten by the hair.

And her eyes. I cannot say what color Lenore Beadsman's eyes are; I cannot look at them; they are the sun to me.

They are blue. Her lips are full and red and tend to wetness and do not ask but rather demand, in a pout of liquid silk, to be kissed. I kiss them often, I admit it, it is what I do, I am a kisser, and a kiss with Lenore is, if I may indulge a bit for a moment here, not so much a kiss as it is a dislocation, a removal and rude transportation of essence from self to lip, so that it is not so much two human bodies coming together and doing the usual things with their lips as it is two sets of lips spawned together and joined in kind from the beginning of post-Scarsdale time, achieving full ontological status only in subsequent union and trailing behind and below them, as they join and become whole, two now utterly superfluous fleshly bodies, drooping outward and downward from the kiss like the tired stems of overblossomed flora, trailing shoes on the ground, husks. A kiss with Lenore is a scenario in which I skate with buttered soles over the moist rink of lower lip, sheltered from weathers by the wet warm overhang of upper, finally to crawl between lip and gum and pull the lip to me like a child's blanket and stare over it with beady, unfriendly eyes out at the world external to Lenore, of which I no longer wish to be part.

That I must in the final analysis remain part of the world that is external to and other from Lenore Beadsman is to me a source of profound grief. That others may dwell deep, deep within the ones they love, drink from the soft cup at the creamy lake at the center of the Object of Passion, while I am fated forever only to intuit the presence of deep recesses while I poke my nose, as it were, merely into the foyer of the Great House of Love, agitate briefly, and make a small mess on the doormat, pisses me off to no small degree. But that Lenore finds such tiny frenzies, such conversations just inside the Screen Door of Union, to be not only pleasant and briefly diverting but somehow apparently right, fulfilling, significant, in some sense wonderful, quite simply and not at all surprisingly makes me feel the same way, enlarges my sense of it and me, sends me hurrying up the walk to that Screen Door in my best sportjacket and flower in lapel as excited as any schoolboy, time after time, brings me charging to the cave entrance in leopardskin shirt, *avec* club, bellowing for admittance and promising general kickings of ass if I am impeded in any way.

We met, oddly enough, not at the Bombardini Building, but at the office of the counselor whose ear it turned out we shared, Dr. Curtis Jay, a good man but a strange and in general I'm coming to believe thoroughly poor psychologist, about whom I don't wish to speak at the moment because I am more than a little incensed at his latest and completely preposterous interpretation of a certain dream that has recently been recurring and troubling me not a little, a dream having to do with Queen Victoria, manipulative prowess, and mice — obviously to any reasonable sensitivity a profoundly sexual dream, which Dr. Jay tiresomely insists is not sexually fixated but has rather to do with what he terms "hygiene anxiety," which I simply and flatly reject, along with Jay's whole Blentnerian hygiene-bent, which I believe he has at some level both pirated from and added to Lenore's own private well of neurotic cathex; rather I know that that's the case, because one of Dr. Jay's redeeming qualities, and certainly the chief reason why I continue to see him in the face of mounting evidence of major incompetence, is the fact that he is also completely unethical and an incorrigible gossip who tells me all of what Lenore tells him. All of it.

Lenore and I met in Dr. Jay's reception room, I clankily leaving his office, she waiting in the other fabric track-chair in flowing white gown and worn black Converses, reading, her legs crossed ankle on knee. I knew I had seen her at the firm's switchboard, had in fact gotten my paper from her that very day, and what with the setting I was a little embarrassed, but Lenore, oh so very Lenorishly I know now, was not. She said hello, and called me Mr. Vigorous, and said she hoped we would have things to publish soon, she felt in her marrow we would. She said "marrow." She said she was seeing Dr. Jay chiefly for help with feelings of disorientation and identity-confusion and lack of control, which I could to an extent understand, because I knew her to be the daughter of the proprietor of Stonecipheco Baby Food Products, one of Cleveland's very leading and if I may say so in my perception evil industries, at any rate certain to be an oppressive and unignorable influence in the life of anyone in any way connected with its helm. I recall that at this point her mechanical chair on its track was caused to move toward the door of the inner office of Dr. Jay — whose fondness for useless gadgets would, I'm convinced, be of significant interest to his colleagues — and we called goodbye. I looked at the back of her neck as she disappeared into Jay's lair, undid the seat belt of my own ridiculous carnival appliance, and went out into the brown lake breezes with a lighter heart, somehow.

How did things progress, after that? I see for the most part not isolated events, not history, but a montage, to some sort of music, not any sort of brisk or invigorating The Fighter Gets Ready For The Big Fight montage, but rather a gauzy, tinkly thing, Rick Vigorous Fashions An Infatuation With Someone About The Same Age As His Own Child And Prepares To Make A Complete Ass Of Himself Over And Over, moving in water-color, over which is imposed in even more liquid hues the ghostly scene of Lenore and me running toward each other in slow motion through the pale gelatin of our respective inhibitions and various troubles.

I see me getting my *Plain Dealer* every morning from Lenore over the switchboard counter, blushing and enduring the snorts of Candy Mandible or of Ms. Prietht, both of whom I loathe. I see me looking for Lenore in Dr. Jay's waiting room, her time never again coinciding with mine, me slumped in my chair as it moves slowly, noisily, toward Jay's inner office. I see me, at night, in my bed, in my apartment, performing my two-fingered Ritual of Solace, while over my head swim filmy visions in which a certain flowing, predatory-haired, black-shoed figure begins to predominate. I see me squirming in my chair in Dr. Jay's office, wanting to ask him about Lenore Beadsman, to spill the emotional beans, but too embarrassed to do so yet, feeling like an idiot while Jay strokes his walrus mustache with his perfumed hankie and sagely interprets my discomfort and distraction as signs of an impending "breakthrough," and urges me to double the number of my weekly visits.

Finally I see me, fed up with the whole business, unable to concentrate on my lack of work at the firm, unable to do any useful work on the *Review*, which really did, thank God, require real work. So I see me lurking one day like a ridiculous furtive spying child behind a marble pillar, within snapping reach of the jaws of the Erieview shadow, in the lobby of the Bombardini Building, waiting for Judith Prietht to hearken to one of the many daily calls of her impossibly small bladder. I see me accosting Lenore Beadsman in the claustrophobic cubicle after Prietht leaves. I see Lenore looking up to smile at my approach. I see me exhausting the subject of the weather, then asking Lenore if she might perhaps care to have a drink, with me, after work. I see one of the rare occasions I've encountered in which the word "nonplussed" might profitably be used in description. I see Lenore momentarily nonplussed.

"I don't really drink," she said, after a moment, looking back down at her book.

I felt a sinking. "You don't drink liquid of any sort?" I asked her.

Lenore looked back up at me and gave a slow smile. Her moist lips curved up softly. They really did. I resisted the urge to lunge into disaster right there in the lobby. "I drink liquid," she admitted, after a moment.

"Splendid. What sort of liquid do you prefer to drink?"

"Ginger ale's an especially good liquid, I've always thought," she said, laughing. We were both laughing. I had a fierce and painful erection, one which, thanks to one of the few advantages of my physical character, was not even a potential source of embarrassment.

"I know a wonderful place where they serve ginger ale in thin glasses, with tiny straws," I said. I was referring to a bar.

"Sounds super."

"Good."

I see us in a bar, I hear a piano I did not hear, I feel me getting thinly intoxicated on perhaps half a weak Canadian Club and distilled water, having to urinate almost at once and coming back and having to urinate again right away. I see Lenore's lips close around the tiny short straw of her ginger ale with a natural delicate ease that sent shivers through the large muscles of my legs. We were made for each other. I see me learning all about Lenore, Lenore in one of her pricelessly rare unself-conscious moments telling me of a life she would, I can say now, come to believe was in some sense not hers.

Lenore had a sister and two brothers. Her sister was married to a rising executive at Stonecipheco and was in some vague way connected with the tanning-parlor industry. One brother was an academic in Chicago who was not well. One brother was on the last leg of his first year at Amherst College, in Amherst, Massachusetts. [I, Rick Vigorous, I insert here, had gone to Amherst.] What a coincidence, I said, I went to Amherst too. Gosh, said Lenore. I remember how the jaws of her hair caressed the straw as she drew the ginger ale out of the tall frosted glass. Yes, she said, her brother was at Amherst, her father had gone to Amherst, her sister had gone to Mount Holyoke, a few miles away [how well I knew], her grandfather had gone to Amherst, her great-grandfather had gone to Amherst, her grandmother and great-grandmother to Mount Holyoke, her great-grandmother on to Cambridge in the twenties, where she had been a student of Wittgenstein, she still had notes from his classes.

Which brother was at Amherst now?

Her brother LaVache.

Where had her other brother gone to school? What was her other brother's name? Would she like another ginger ale, with a tiny straw?

Yes that would be fine, his name was John, her other brother's name was really Stonecipher but he used LaVache which was his middle name and had been their mother's maiden name. John, the oldest, hadn't gone to college as such, he had a Ph.D. from U. Chicago, he had in junior high school proved certainly hitherto unprovable things, with a crayon from Lenore's own crayon box, on a Batman writing tablet, and had shocked hell out of everyone, and had gotten a Ph.D. a few years later without really going to any classes.

This was the one who was now not well.

Yes.

It was hoped that it was nothing serious.

It was unfortunately very serious. He was in his room, in Chicago, unable to receive any but a very few visitors, having problems eating food. Lenore did not wish to talk about it, at that point, obviously.

So then, where had Lenore gone to school, had Lenore gone to Mount Holyoke?

No, Lenore had not liked Mount Holyoke very much, she had gone to Oberlin, a small coed college south of Cleveland. Her sister's husband had gone there, too. Lenore had graduated two years ago next month. And I had gone to Amherst?

Yes, I had gone to Amherst, class of '69, had taken a quick Masters in English at Columbia, had gone to work at the publishing firm of Hunt and Peck, on Madison Avenue, in New York City.

That was a huge firm.

Yes. And for reasons that remain unclear, I was very successful there. I made obscene amounts of money for the House, rose to such dizzying editorial heights that my salary became almost enough to live on. I married Veronica Peck. I moved to Scarsdale, New York, a short distance from the City. I had a son. He was now eighteen.

Eighteen?

Yes. I was forty-two, after all. I was divorced, too, by the way.

I sure didn't look forty-two.

How sweet. I was squirming like this in my seat because I remembered a phone call I just had to make, for the firm.

I am back. I sure made a lot of really quick calls. Who was the Frequent in Frequent and Vigorous, anyway, could she ask.

This was to an extent unclear. Monroe Frequent, I knew, was a fabulously wealthy clothier and inventor. He had invented the beige leisure suit. He had invented the thing that buzzes when a car is started without the seat belts being fastened. He was now, understandably, a recluse. I had been approached by a representative in wrap-around sunglasses. Interest in publishing. Outside New York and environs. Bold, new. Huge amounts of capital to invest. Full partnership for me. A salary out of all proportion to industry norm. If it's assumed, as is reasonable, that our Frequent is

Monroe Frequent, then it's becoming clear that Frequent and Vigorous is really just a crude tax dodge.

Golly.

Yes. The only real benefit for me was having the opportunity to start my own quarterly. A literary thing. Enthusiastic agreement to the condition. An air of legitimacy lent to the whole enterprise right off the bat, on Frequent's view.

The *Frequent Review?*

Yes. Last year's issues sold well.

It was a good quarterly.

How kind.

There was also the Norslan account, of course.

Yes, if publishing monosyllabic propaganda praising the virtues of a clearly ineffective and carcinogenic pesticide to be disseminated among the graft-softened bureaucracies of Third World countries could be considered an account, there was the Norslan account. Why on earth did she work as a telephone operator?

Well, she obviously needed money to buy food. Her best friend, Mandible, who had gone to Oberlin too for a while, worked as an operator. Et cetera.

Why didn't she work at Stonecipheco for undoubtedly more money and thus more food?

Food was not the issue. She felt little enough control over her life as it was. A job at Stonecipheco, or a home with her father and her old governess in Shaker Heights, would only localize and intensify feelings of helplessness, loss of individual efficacy of will. I hear me hearing the voice of Dr. Jay. I see me pounding the drum of my courage with a swizzle stick and trying to press my knee against Lenore's under the tiny plastic-wood table, and finding that her legs were not there. Me sweeping the area under the table with my leg, her not being there at all. Me being insanely curious about where her legs were.

I articulated my inability to understand this feeling of lack of control. Surely we all dealt with and reconciled ourselves to a life many of whose features were out of our control. It was part of living in a world full of other people with other interests. I was close to wetting my pants again.

No, that wasn't it. Such a general feeling of dislocation would not be a problem. The problem was a localized feeling. An intuition that her own personal perceptions and actions and volitions were not under her control.

What did "control" mean?

Who knew.

Was this a religious thing? A deterministic crisis? I had had a friend...

No. Determinism would be fine if she were able to feel that what determined her was something objective, impersonal, that she were just a tiny part of a large mechanism. If she didn't feel as though she were being used.

Used.

Yes. As if what she did and said and perceived and thought were having some sort of...function beyond herself.

Function. Alarm bells. Dr. Jay, after all. A plot thing?

No, not a plot thing, definitely not a plot thing, she wasn't making herself understood. The points of her hair swung like pendula below her chin as she shook her head. My napkin had unfortunately fallen under the table. How clumsy of me. Her legs were there, but curled back, underneath her chair, ankles crossed. Alarm bells or no, I wanted first to reach for an ankle, then to pee.

No, she simply felt—at times, mind you, not all the time, but at sharp and distinct intuitive moments—as if she had no real existence, except for what she said and did and perceived and et cetera, and that these were, it seemed at such times, not really under her control. There was nothing pure.

Hmmm.

Could we talk about something else? Why for instance did *I* see Dr. Jay?

Oh, just some dream-orientation, general rapping. I had a sort of detached interest in the whole analysis scene, really. My problems were without exception very tiny. Hardly worth discussing at that point. I saw Jay in particular because I liked him least of any of the [very many] Cleveland clinicians with whom I'd rapped. I found an atmosphere of antagonism vital to the whole process, somehow. Lenore too? No, Lenore had been referred to Jay by a physician, friend of the family, old old crony of her great-grandmother, a physician to whom Lenore had gone with a persistent nosebleed problem. She'd stayed ever since. She found Jay irritating but fascinating. Did I find him fascinating? Actually, I went simply to ride the chairs; I found the chairs fun things. A release.

The chairs. She loved the heavy clanking pull as the chain drew her down the track to the Sanctum. She had gone to a fair once with her brother and her governess, and had ridden a rollercoaster that at the start had pulled and clanked like that. Sometimes she really almost expected a drastic rollercoaster plunge when she entered Jay's inner office. [Give it time.] She had gone to the state fair in Columbus once with her sister Clarice and they had gotten lost in the House of Mirrors and Clarice's purse had been stolen by a man who had pretended to be a reflection until the very last moment. It had been scary as hell.

What did her mother do?

She was hanging out, more or less, in Wisconsin.

Were her parents divorced?

Not exactly. Could we go. She had to be at work to give me my paper in the morning, after all. Very late all of a sudden. Had she eaten, would she like something to eat? Ginger ale was surprisingly filling. Her car was in the shop, choke trouble. She had taken the bus to work that day. Well then. She had one of those new cars made by Mattel, also the maker of Hot Wheels. Only slightly larger than same. Really more toy than car. And so on.

I see us driving down the insanely shaped Inner Belt of 1-271 South, toward lower East Corinth. I see Lenore in the car keeping her knees together and swinging both legs over to the side, toward me, so that I touch her knee with the back of my hand as I shift.

With my stomach I see disaster. I see me dropping Lenore off at her place, us on the porch of a huge gray house that looked black in the soft darkness of the April night, the house Lenore in a small voice said belonged to an oral surgeon who lent out two rooms to her and Mandible and one to a girl who worked for her sister at CabanaTan. Lenore lived with Mandible. I see her thanking me for the ginger ale and the ride. I see me leaning, lunging over the rustle of the white collar of her dress and kissing her before she has finished saying thank you. I see her kicking me, in the knee, where the knee nerve is, with a sneaker that is revealed to be surprisingly heavy and hard. I see me squealing and holding my knee and sitting down heavily on a step of the porch bristling with nails. I see me howling and holding my knee with one hand and my ass with the other and pitching headlong into an empty flowerbed of soft spring earth. I see Lenore kneeling beside me — how sorry, she didn't know what made her do that, I had surprised her, she had been taken by surprise, oh shit what had she done. I see me with dirt in my nose, I see lights going on in the gray house, in other houses. I am horribly sensitive to pain and almost begin to cry. I see Lenore run through the door of the oral surgeon's house. I see my car tilting ever closer as I hop madly toward it on one leg. I am convinced that I heard the voice of Candy Mandible high overhead.

I knew that I loved Lenore Beadsman when she failed to appear for work the next day. Mandible informed me with wide eyes that Lenore had assumed she was fired. I called Lenore's landlady, the surgeon's wife, a two-hundred-pound Bible-thumping born-again fanatic. I asked her to inform Lenore that she was in fact not fired. I apologized to Lenore. She was incredibly embarrassed. I was embarrassed. Her supervisor, the switchboard supervisor, Walinda Peahen, really did want to fire Lenore, ostensibly for not showing up for work. Walinda dislikes Lenore for her privileged background. I am Walinda's supervisor. I soothed her. Lenore began to hand me my paper as before.

Where are you now?

For there was the magic night later, a magic night, untalkaboutable, when my heart was full of heat and my bottom had healed and I left the office in a trance before six, descended, on wire, saw across the dark empty stone lobby Lenore in her cubicle, alone, for the moment Priethtless, reading, the switchboard mute as usual. I slipped across the blackly shadowed floor and melted into the white desk-lamp light of the tiny office, behind Lenore at her console. She looked up at me and smiled and looked back down at her book. She was not reading. Through the giant window high over the cubicle a thin spear of the orange-brown light of a Cleveland sunset, saved and bent for a moment by some kindly chemical cloud around the Erieview blackness, fell like a beacon on the soft patch of cream just below Lenore's right ear, on her throat. I bent in my trance and pressed my lips gently to the spot. The sudden beeping of the switchboard mechanism was the beating of my heart, transported into Lenore's purse.

And Lenore Beadsman slowly took her right hand and slid it back up my own neck, cradling with soft hesitant warmth the right side of my jaw and cheek, her long fingers with their dull bitten nails holding me in position against her throat, comforting, her head now tilted left so I could feel the tiny thunder of an artery against my lips. I lived, truly and completely and for the first time in a very long time, in that moment. Lenore said, "Frequent and Vigorous" into the phone she held with her left hand, looking out into the approaching black. The magic of the night was that the magic has lasted. Come to work.

11

/c/

"THERE IS AN ominous rumbling in my ears."

"That's the engine, right outside the window."

"No, the engine is a piercing, nerve-jangling, screaming whine. I'm talking about an ominous rumbling."

"...."

"My ears are going to hurt horribly on this flight, I know. The change in pressure is going to make my ears hurt like hell."

"Rick, in my purse are like fifty packs of gum. I'll keep shoving gum in your mouth, and you'll chew, and swallow your saliva, and your ears will be OK. We've discussed this already."

"Maybe I'd better have a piece now, all unwrapped and ready to go in my hand."

"Here, then."

"Bless you, Lenore."

"A story, please."

"A story? Here?"

"I'm really in the mood for a story. Maybe a story will take your mind off your ears."

"My ears, God. I'd almost begun to have hopes of forgetting, what with the gum in my hand, and you go and mention my ears."

"Let's just have a minimum of spasms, here in public, on the plane, with a pilot and stewardess who're probably going to tell my father everything we do and say."

"How comforting."

"Just no spasms, please."

"But a story."

"Please."

"...."

"I know you've got some. I saw manila envelopes in your suitcase when I put stuff in."

"Lord, they're getting ready to take off. We're moving. My ears are rumbling like mad."

" . . . "

"Ironically enough, a man, in whom the instinct to love is as strong and natural and instinctive as can possibly be, is unable to find someone really to love."

"We're starting the story? Or is this just a Vigorous pithy?"

"The story is underway. The aforementioned pre-sarcastic-interruption fact is because this man, in whom the instincts and inclinations are so strong and pure, is completely unable to control these strong and pure instincts and inclinations. What invariably happens is that the man meets a halfway or even quarterway desirable woman, and he immediately falls head over heels in love with her, right there, first thing, on the spot, and blurts out 'I love you' as practically the first thing he says, because he can't control the intensely warm feelings of love, and not just lust, now, it's made clear, but deep, emotionally intricate, passionate love, the feelings that wash over him, and so immediately at the first opportunity he says 'I love you,' and his pupils dilate until they fill practically his whole eyes, and he moves unself-consciously toward the woman in question as if to touch her in a sexual way, and the women he does this to, which is more or less every woman he meets, quite understandably don't react positively to this, a man who says 'I love you' right away, and makes a bid for closeness right away, and so the women as an invariable rule reject him verbally on the spot, or hit him with their purse, or worst of all run away, screaming screams only he and they can hear."

"Look down a second, Rick. Out the window."

"Where?"

"Right down there."

"Heavens, I know her! That's . . ."

"Jayne Mansfield."

"Jayne Mansfield, right. What's she doing as a town? Is that East Corinth?"

"I'll explain later."

"My God, will you look at that west border. That 271. That's the Inner Belt. I've driven over that."

"Meanwhile, back with the lover whose love drives the lovee away with silent screams."

"Right. So the man is understandably not too happy. Not only is he denied the opportunity to love, but it's the very strength and intensity of his own love-urge that denies him the opportunity, which denial thus understandably causes him exponentially more sadness and depression and frustration than it would you or me, in whom the instincts are semi-under-control, and so semi-satisfiable."

"More gum?"

"And so the man is in a bad way, and he loses his job at the New York State Department of Weights and Measures, at which he'd been incredibly successful before the love-intensity problem got really bad, and now he wanders the streets of New York City, living off the bank account he'd built up during his days as a brilliant weights-and-measures man, wandering the streets, stopping only when he falls in love, getting slapped or laughed at or hearing silent screams. And this goes on, for months, until one day in Times Square he sees a discreet little Xeroxed ad on a notice board, an ad for a doctor who claims to be a love therapist, one who can treat disorders stemming from and connected to the emotion of love."

"What, like a sex therapist?"

"No, as a matter of fact it says *'Not A Sex Therapist'* in italics at the bottom of the ad, and it gives an address, and so the man, who is neither overjoyed with his life nor overwhelmed with alternatives for working out his problems, hops the subway and starts heading across town to the love therapist's office. And in his car on the subway there are four women, three of them reasonably desirable, and he falls in love in about two seconds with each of the three in turn, and gets hit, laughed at, and subjected to a silent scream, respectively, and then eventually he looks over at the fourth woman, who's conspicuously fat, and has stringy hair, and Coke-bottle glasses, and an incredibly weak chin, weaker even than mine, and so the fourth woman is prohibitively undesirable, even for the man, and besides she's very hard to see because she's pressed back into the shadow of the rear of the car, with her coat collar pulled up around her neck, which neck is also encased in a thick scarf. Did I mention it was March in New York City?"

"No."

"Well it is, and she's in a scarf, pressed back into the shadow, with her cheek pressed against the grimy graffiti-spattered wall of the subway car, clutching an old Thermos bottle that's jutting half-way out of her coat pocket, and she just basically looks like one of those troubled cases you don't want to mess with, which cases New York City does not exactly have a scarcity of."

"You're telling me."

"And then on top of everything else the fat stringy-haired woman with the Thermos has been watching the man telling the other three women that he loves them, and making bids for closeness, out of the corner of her eye, as she hugs the wall of the car in shadow, and then so when she sees the man even look at her, at all, she obviously flips out, it really bothers her, and she bolts for the door of the subway car, as fast as she can bolt, which isn't too fast, because now it becomes clear that one of her legs is roughly one half the length of the other, but still she bolts, and the car is just pulling into a station, and the door opens, and out she flies, and in her excessive haste she drops the old Thermos she'd been clutching, and it rolls down the floor of the subway, and it finally clunks against the man's shoe, and he picks it up, and it's just an old black metal Thermos, but on the bottom is a piece of masking tape on which is written in a tiny faint hand a name and an address, which he and we assume to be the woman's, in Brooklyn, and so the man resolves to give the woman back her Thermos, since it was probably he and his inappropriate emotional behavior that had caused her to drop it in the first place. Besides, the love therapist's office is in Brooklyn, too.

"And so the man arrives at the love therapist's office, and actually wouldn't ordinarily have gotten in to see the love therapist at all, because she's apparently a truly great and respected love therapist, and incredibly busy, and her appointment calendar is booked up months in advance, but, as it happens, the love therapist's receptionist is a ravingly desirable woman, and the man immediately and involuntarily falls head over heels in love with her, and actually begins involuntarily reciting love poems to her, then eventually sort of passes out, swoons from the intensity of his love, and falls to the carpeted floor, and so the receptionist runs in and tells the love therapist what's happened, that this is obviously a guy who really needs to be seen right away, out here, on the rug, and so the love therapist skips her lunch hour, which she was just about to take, and they pick the man up off the reception-area rug and carry him into the office and revive him with cold water, and he gets an appointment right away.

"And it turns out that one of the reasons why this love therapist is so great is that she can usually hew to the bone of someone's love-problem in one appointment, and doesn't keep the patient stringing along month after expensive month with vague predictions of breakthrough, which we are both in a position to appreciate the desirability of, I think, and so the love therapist hews to the bone of the man's problem, and tells the man that surprisingly enough it's not that his emotional love-mechanism is too strong, but rather that some of its important features are actually too *weak*, because one of the big things about real love is the power to discriminate and decide whom and on the basis of what criteria to love, which the man is very obviously unable to do—witness the fact that the man fell deeply and intricately for the receptionist without even knowing her, and has already said 'I love you' to the love therapist, herself, about ten times, involuntarily. What the man needs to do, the love therapist says, is to strengthen his love-discrimination mechanism by being around women and trying not to fall in love with them. Since this obviously will be hard for the man to do at the start, the love therapist suggests that he begin by finding some woman so completely and entirely undesirable, looks-wise and personality-wise, that it won't be all that hard to keep from falling in love with her right away, and then proceeding to hang around her as much as he can, to begin to strengthen the mechanism that lets men hang around with women without necessarily falling in love with them. And the man is dazed from the one-two punch of the ravingly desirable receptionist and the wise and kind and obviously exceedingly competent and also not unerotic love therapist, but the back part of his brain, the part that deals with basic self-preservation, knows that things cannot keep going as they have been, and he resolves to give the love therapist's advice a try, and then he happens to look down at the Thermos he's still holding, and he sees the piece of masking tape with the name and address of the Thermos woman on it, and he has an epiphany-ish flashback to the subway, and sees that the Thermos woman is just a prime candidate for non-love, stringyhair-and-uneven-leg-wise, and clearly-troubled-personality-wise, and as the scene ends we see him looking speculatively at the Thermos and then at the love therapist."

"How's the gum doing?"

"New piece, please."

"Here."

" . . . . "

"Is the gum working?"

"Do you hear me complaining yet?"

"Good point."

"And so as the next scene opens it's a few days later, and the man and the Thermos woman are walking in Central Park, or rather walking and limping, respectively, and they're holding hands, although for the man it's just a friendly platonic hand-holding, although we're not sure what it is for the Thermos woman, and it's made clear that the man had gone to the Thermos address and had talked to the woman and had, after a reasonably long time and many visits, broken down some of her really pathological shyness and introversion, though only some. And they're walking hand in

hand, although it's inconvenient, because the woman clearly has a pathological need always to be in shadow, and so they keep having to veer all
over Central Park to find shadow that she'll be able to walk in, and she
also has a pathological need to keep her neck covered, and keeps fingering
at one of the seemingly uncountable number of scarves she owns, and she
also strangely always seems to want to have only her right side facing the
man, she keeps her left side turned away at all times, so all the man ever
sees of her is her right profile, and as he turns from time to time and moves
relative to her she keeps moving and positioning herself like mad to keep
only her right side facing him."

"...."

"And she also seems really aloof and not emotionally connected with
anyone outside herself at all, except her family, who live in Yonkers, but as
the man works to exercise his love-discrimination mechanism and starts
hanging around the woman and beginning to get to know her better, it
seems clear to him that she actually *wants* to be connected with people
outside herself, very much, but can't, for some strange reason that he can't
figure out, but knows has something to do with the shadows, the scarves,
and the profiles."

"...."

"And a funny thing happens. The man begins to like the Thermos
woman. Not love, but *like*, which is something the man has never experienced before, and finds different, because it involves directing a lot more
emotional attention to the actual other person than the old uncontrollable
passionate love had involved, involves caring about the whole other person, including the facets and features that have nothing whatsoever to do
with the man. And now it's implied that what has happened is that the
man has for the first time become really *connected* to a person other than
himself, that he had not really ever been connected before, that his intense-
love tendency, which might at first glance have seemed like the ultimate
way to connect, has really been a way *not* to connect, at all, both in its
results and, really, as a little psychological analysis is by implication
indulged in, in its subconscious intent. The inability to bring the discriminating faculty of love to bear on the world outside him has been what has
kept the man from connecting with that world outside him, the same way
the Thermos woman has been kept from connecting by the mysterious
shadow-scarf-and-profile thing.

"Which thing, by the way, really begins to bother the man, and makes
him intensely curious, especially as he begins to feel more and more connected to the woman, though not exactly in a passionate-love way, and

thinks he feels her yearning to connect, too. And so he gradually wins her trust and affection, and she responds by starting to wash her hair, and dieting, and buying an extra thick shoe for her obscenely short leg, and things progress, although the Thermos woman is still clearly pathologically hung up about something. And then one night in very early April, after a walk all around the quainter parts of Brooklyn, the man takes the Thermos woman back to her apartment and has sex with her, seduces her, gets her all undressed — except, compassionately, for her scarf — and he makes love to her, and it's at first surprisingly, but then when we think about it not all that surprisingly, revealed that this is the first time this incredibly passionate, love-oriented man, who's about thirty, has ever had sex with anybody, at all."

"...."

"Um, first time for the Thermos woman, too."

"...."

"...."

"What's the matter?"

"My ear! Shit! God!"

"Try to swallow."

"...."

"Try to yawn."

"...."

"...."

"Good God. I so hate airplanes, Lenore. I can think of no more convincing demonstration of my devotion to you than my coming on this trip. I am flying for you."

"You're going to get to see Amherst in the very early fall. You said early fall in Amherst used to make you weep with joy."

"...."

"You're less pale. Can we assume the ear is better?"

"Jesus."

"...."

"So they have sex, and the man is able to be gentle and caring, which we can safely intuit he couldn't have been, passion-wise, if he'd really been hopelessly in love in his old way with the Thermos woman, and the Thermos woman weeps tears of joy, at all the gentleness and caring, and we can practically hear the thud as she falls in love with the man, and she really begins to think it's possible to connect with someone in the world outside her. And they're lying in bed, and their limbs are unevenly intertwined, and the man is resting his head on the little shelf of the Thermos woman's weak chin, and he's playing idly with the scarf around her neck, which playing pathologically bothers the woman, which the man notices, and curiosity and concern wash over him, and he tries tentatively and experimentally slowly to undo the scarf and take it off, and the Thermos woman tenses all her muscles but through what is obviously great strength of will doesn't stop him, although she's weeping for real, now, and the man gently, and with kisses and reassurances, removes the scarf, throws it aside, and in the dimness of the bedroom sees something more than a little weird on the woman's neck, and he goes and turns on the light, and in the light of the bedroom it's revealed that the woman has a pale-green tree toad living in a pit at the base of her neck, on the left side."

"Pardon me?"

"In a perfectly formed and non-woundish pit on the left side of the Thermos woman's neck is a tiny tree toad, pale green, with a white throat that puffs rhythmically out and in. The toad stares up at the man from the woman's neck with sad wise clear reptilian eyes, the clear and delicate lower lids of which blink upward, in reverse. And the woman is weeping, her secret is out, she has a tree toad living in her neck."

"Is it my imagination, or did this story just get really weird all of a sudden?"

"Well, the context is supposed to explain and so minimize the weirdness. The tree toad in the pit in her neck is the thing that has kept the Thermos woman from connecting emotionally with the world outside her: it has been what has kept her in sadness and confusion, see also darkness and shadow, what has bound and constrained her, see also being wrapped in a scarf, what has kept her from facing the external world, see also staying in profile all the time. The tree toad is the mechanism of nonconnection and alienation, the symbol and cause of the Thermos woman's isolation; yet it also becomes clear after a while that she is emotionally attached to the tree toad in a very big way, and cares more for it and gives it more attention than she gives herself, there in the privacy of her apartment. And the man also discovers that all the scarves the woman wears to cover up and hide the tree toad are full of tiny holes, air holes for the toad, holes that are practically invisible and that the woman herself makes via millions of tiny punctures of the cloth with a pin, late at night."

"*My* ear even hurts a little. We must be really high."

"So that the very thing that has made the woman unconnected when she wants to be connected and so has made her extremely unhappy is also the center of her life, a thing she cares a lot about, and is even, in certain ways the man can't quite comprehend, proud of, and proud of the fact that she can feed the pale-green tree toad bits of food off her finger, and that it will let her scratch its white throat with a letter opener. So now things are understandably ambiguous, and it's not clear whether deep down at the core of her being the Thermos woman really wants to connect, after all, at all. Except as time goes by and the man continues to hang around, exercising his non-love love-mechanism, being gentle and caring, the woman falls more and more for him, and clearly wants to connect, and her relation with the tree toad in the pit in her neck gets ambiguous, and at times she's hostile toward it and flicks at it cruelly with her fingernail, except at other times she falls back into not wanting to connect, and so dotes on the tree toad, and scratches it with the letter opener, and is aloof toward the man. And this goes on and on, and she falls for the man on the whole more and more. And the man begins to be unsure about his formerly definitely non-love feelings for this strange and not too pretty but still quite complex and in many ways brave and in all ways certainly very interesting Thermos woman, and so his whole love-situation gets vastly more complicated than it's ever been before."

"Listen, would you like a Canadian Club? I can get Jennifer to bring you a Canadian Club."

"Not too tasty with gum, I'm afraid, of which I would however like another piece."

"Coming right up."

"And so things are complicated, and the man earns the Thermos woman's trust more and more, and finally one night she brings him to her family's home in Yonkers, for a family get-together and dinner, and the man meets her whole family, and he knows right away something's up, because they all have scarves around their necks, and they're clearly extremely on edge about there being an outsider in their midst, but anyway they all sit around the living room for a while, in uncomfortable silence, with cocktails, and Cokes for the little kids, and then they sit down to dinner, and right before they all sit down, the Thermos woman looks significantly at the man, and then at her father, and then in a gesture of letting the family know she's clued the man into her secret condition and initiated some kind of nascent emotional connection, she undoes her scarf and throws it aside, and her tree toad gives a little chirrup, and there's a moment of incredibly tense silence, and then the father slowly undoes and discards his scarf, too, and in the pit in the left side of his neck there's a mottle-throated fan-wing moth, and then the whole rest of the family undo their scarves, too, and they all have little animals living in pits in their necks: the mother has a narrow-tailed salamander, one brother has a driver ant, one sister has a wolf spider, another brother has an axolotl, one of the little children has a sod webworm. Et cetera et cetera."

"I think I feel the need for context again."

"Well, the father explains to the man, as the family is sitting around the table, eating, and also feeding their respective neck-tenants little morsels off the tips of their fingers, that their family is from an ancient and narratively unspecified area in Eastern Europe, in which area the people have always stood in really ambiguous relations to the world outside them, and that the area's families were internally fiercely loyal, and their members were intimately and thoroughly connected with one another, but that the family units themselves were fiercely independent, and tended to view just about all non-family-members as outsiders, and didn't connect with them, and that the tiny animals in their necks, which specific animal-types used to be unique to each family and the same for each member of a particular family, in the old days, were symbols of this difference from and non-connection with the rest of the outside world. But then the father goes on to say that these days inbreeding and the passage of time were making the animal-types in the necks of the family-members different, and that also, regrettably, some younger members of the fiercely loyal families were now inclined to resent the secrecy and non-connection with the world that having animals in their necks required and entitled them to, and that some members of his own family had unfortunately given him to understand that they weren't entirely happy about the situation. And here he and all the other members of the family stop eating and glare at the Thermos woman, there in her glasses, who is silently trying to feed her tree toad a bit of pot roast off the tip of her finger. And the man's heart just about breaks with pity for the Thermos woman, who so clearly now stands in such an ambiguous relation to everything and everyone around her, and his heart almost breaks, and he also realizes in an epiphany-ish flash that he has sort of fallen in love with the Thermos woman, in a way, though not in the way he'd fallen for any of the uncountable number of women he'd fallen in love with before."

"Look down a second, if it doesn't hurt your ear. I think we're over Pennsylvania. I thought I saw a hex sign on a barn roof. We're past Lake Erie, at least."

"Thank God. Drowning in sludge is one of my special horrors."

". . . ."

"And so things are complicated, enormously complicated, and the man feels he's now experiencing the kind of strong discriminating love the love therapist had been recommending, so he's pleased, and also maybe I neglected to mention he's long since toned down his head-over-heels-in-love-in-public inclinations, things are now much more under control, and with all his professional weight-measure experience, plus his new-found amorous restraint, he manages to land a fairly good job with a company that makes scales, and he's doing pretty well, although he does miss that exciting head-busting rush of hot feeling he used to get from being madly, passionately, non-discriminatingly in love. But the Thermos woman is clearly undergoing even more complicated changes and feelings than the man; she's obviously fallen in love with him, and her nascent connection with him is obviously arousing in her a desire to begin to connect emotionally with the entire outside world, and she gets more concerned with and attentive to her own appearance; she loses more weight, and buys contact lenses to replace the Coke-bottle glasses, and gets a perm, and there's still of course the problem of chinlessness and leg-length, but still. But most of all she now noticeably begins to perceive the green tree toad in the pit in her neck as a definite problem, and ceases to identify herelf with it and non-connection, and begins instead to identify herself with herself and connection. But now her perception of the tiny toad as a definite problem, which is, remember, a function of her new world view and desire to connect, now paradoxically causes her enormous grief and distress, because, now that she feels a bit connected to the world, she no longer feels that she *wants* to stay in shadow and present only profiles — so far so good — but that now even though she doesn't want to hide away she feels more than ever as though she *ought* to, because she's got a reptile living in a pit in her neck, after all, and is to that extent alienated and different and comparatively disgusting, with respect to the world she now wants to connect with."

"Aren't tree toads amphibians, really?"

"Wise-ass. Amphibian in a pit in her neck. But she suddenly and ominously gets even more fanatical about being in shadow and wearing the scarves, even though these are obviously alienating things: the more she wants to be accepted by the world, the more she's beaten back by her heightened perception of her own difference, amphibian-tenant-wise. She becomes absolutely obsessed with the green tree toad, and gives it a really hard time with her fingernail, and cries, and tells the man she hates the toad, and the man tries to cheer her up by taking her out dancing at a nightclub that has lots of shadows. Gum, please."

" . . . . "

"And things get worse, and the Thermos woman is now drinking a lot, sitting in her apartment, and as she's drinking, the man will look at her sadly, as he sits nearby working on the design for a scale; and the tree toad, when it's not busy getting flicked by a fingernail, will look at the man and blink sadly, from the lower lid up, there in the pit in the Thermos woman's neck."

"...."

"And now, disastrously, it's late April. It's the height of spring, almost. Have you ever been around someplace that has tree toads, in the spring, Lenore?"

"Oh, no."

"They sing. It's involuntary. It's instinctive. They sing and chirrup like mad. And this, I rather like to think, is why the tree toad looked sadly at the man as the man was looking sadly at the drinking Thermos woman: the tree toad has its own nature to be true to, too. The toad's maybe aware that its singing will have a disastrous effect on the Thermos woman, right now, because whereas in the past she always just used to keep herself hidden away, in the spring, in the singing season, now she's clearly torn by strong desires to connect, to be a part of the world. And so maybe the tree toad knows it's hurting the Thermos woman, maybe irreparably, by chirruping like mad, but what can it do? And the singing clearly drives the Thermos woman absolutely insane with frustration and horror, and her urges both to connect and to hide away in shadow are tearing at her like hell, and it's all pathetic, and also, as should by now be apparent, more than a little ominous."

"Oh, God."

"And one day, not long after the toad began singing in the apartment, as the air is described as getting soft and sweet and tinged with gentle promises of warmth, with a flowery smell all around, even in New York City, the man gets a call at work from the Thermos woman's father, in Yonkers: it seems that the Thermos woman had thrown herself in front of the subway and killed herself that morning in a truly horrible way."

"Sweet Jesus."

"And the man is obviously incredibly upset, and doesn't even thank the father for calling him, even though it was quite a thing for the Eastern European father to do, what with the man being an outsider, et cetera, and so but the man is incredibly upset, and doesn't even go to the funeral, he's so frantic, and he discovers now—the hard way—that he really was connected to the Thermos woman, really and truly, deeply and significantly, and that the severing of an established connection is exponentially more painful than the rejection of an attempted connection, and he wallows in grief, and also disastrously his old love problem immediately comes roaring back stronger than ever, and the man is falling passionately in love with anything with a pulse, practically, and now, disastrously, men as well as women, and he's perceived as a homosexual, and starts getting regularly beaten up at work, and then he loses his job when he tells his supervisor he's in love with him, and he's back out wandering the streets, and now he starts falling in love with children, too, which is obviously frowned upon by society, and he commits some gross though of course involuntary indiscretions, and gets arrested, and thrown in jail overnight, and he's in a truly horrible way, and he curses the love therapist for even suggesting that he try to love with his discriminating love-faculty."

"May I please ask a question?"

"Yes."

"Why didn't the Thermos woman just take the tree toad out of her neck and put it in a coffee can or something?"

"*A*, the implication is that the only way the animal-in-neck people can rid themselves of the animals in their necks is to die, see for instance the subway, and *b*, you're totally, completely missing what I at any rate perceive to be the point of the story."

"...."

"And the man is in a horrible way, and his old love problem is raging, together with and compounded by his continued grief at the severed Thermos-woman-connection, and his desire never ever to connect again, which desire itself stands in a troublingly ambiguous and bad-way-producing relation to the original love problem. And so things are just horrible. And they go on this way for about a week, and then one night in May the man is lying totally overcome by grief and by his roughly twenty-five fallings in love and run-ins with the police that day, and he's almost out of his mind, lying in a very bad way there on the rug of his apartment, and suddenly there's an impossibly tiny knock at the apartment door."

"Oh, no."

"What do you mean, 'Oh, no'?"

"...."

"Well he opens the door, and there on the floor of the hall outside his apartment is the Thermos woman's tiny delicate pale-green tree toad, blinking up at him, from the lower eyelid up, with its left rear foot flattened and trailing way behind it and obviously hurt, no doubt we're to assume from the subway episode, which episode however the toad at least seemed to have survived."

"Wow."

"And the story ends with the man, bleary-eyed and punchy from grief and love and connection-ambiguity, at the door, staring down at the tiny pale-green tree toad, which is still simply looking up at him, blinking sadly in reverse, and giving a few tentative little chirrups. And they're just there in the hall looking at each other as the story ends."

"Wow."

"I think I'd like to try two pieces of gum at once, please."

". . . ."

"It's clearly not right for the *Frequent Review*, but I'm going to write a personal rejection note in which I say that I personally liked it, and thought it had possibilities, though it was not as yet a finished piece."

"Another troubled-collegiate-mind submission?"

"That's the very strong sense I get, although the kid tried to pass himself off as much older in his cover letter, and included what I have now determined to be a phony bibliography of published material."

"Lordy."

"I'm suddenly monstrously hungry, Lenore."

"I know for a fact there are sandwiches. Let me buzz Jennifer."

". . . ."

Afterword

That was fun, wasn't it?

I had the pleasure of acquiring and editing—or trying to edit—David Foster Wallace's brilliant first novel, *The Broom of the System*. This basically fulfilled every idealistic and naive dream I ever had of being the editor who discovered the best writer of his generation, and I was only thirty-six at the time. Imagine the thrill of turning the pages of a manuscript from a completely unknown young author and encountering such instances of bravura storytelling as you have just read. John Keats wrote one of his greatest poems about that feeling, "On First Looking into Chapman's Homer." Like him, "Then felt I like some watcher of the skies / When a new planet swims into his ken." Planet DFW had swum into view.

The Broom of the System is a novel of ideas, most of them deriving from the gnomic philosopher Ludwig Wittgenstein. I was a little thin, to put it mildly, on my Wittgenstein, so before setting down to edit—or try to edit—the novel, I read a compact Modern Masters volume to bone up on his work. That didn't help much, frankly, as David overwhelmed most of my queries and reservations with an unstoppable volley of high-IQ verbiage. Still, to this day I can quote Wittgenstein's solemn admonition "Whereof one cannot speak, thereof one must be silent," which is a guaranteed conversation stopper.

So I left the brainy big-picture stuff to David's big brain and concentrated on the intense local pleasures to be experienced in his virtuoso deployment of linguistic facility and narrative velocity, of which this tree toad episode is such an outstanding example. The parallel John Irving send-up in the novel involving a headlong attempt to save a dying baby may be even better; certainly David wiped the floor with the competition when he read that section at his first-ever public reading, in 1987 at New York's McBurney Y. I was there, and that evening a star was born.

One final note. In reading this piece, I connected two dots I never had before. David once told me that one of his favorite movies was the 1989 cult film *How to Get Ahead in Advertising*, starring Richard Grant as an advertising copywriter blocked on an ad for pimple cream. He discovers that a boil on his neck is actually growing into a replica of his head, one that gives voice to all his darkest impulses about hucksterism and success, and eventually replaces him. A similar literalization of a psychic state of alienation of course informs the passage you've just read, and it was a technique David would continue to use and refine.

—*Gerald Howard*

GIRL WITH CURIOUS HAIR

Little Expressionless Animals

Iᴛ's 1976. The sky is low and full of clouds. The gray clouds are bulbous and wrinkled and shiny. The sky looks cerebral. Under the sky is a field, in the wind. A pale highway runs beside the field. Lots of cars go by. One of the cars stops by the side of the highway. Two small children are brought out of the car by a young woman with a loose face. A man at the wheel of the car stares straight ahead. The children are silent and have very white skin. The woman carries a grocery bag full of something heavy. Her face hangs loose over the bag. She brings the bag and the white children to a wooden fencepost, by the field, by the highway. The children's hands, which are small, are placed on the wooden post. The woman tells the children to touch the post until the car returns. She gets in the car and the car leaves. There is a cow in the field near the fence. The children touch the post. The wind blows. Lots of cars go by. They stay that way all day.

It's 1970. A woman with hair like fire sits several rows from a movie theater's screen. A child in a dress sits beside her. A cartoon has begun. The child's eyes enter the cartoon. Behind the woman is darkness. A man sits behind the woman. He leans forward. His hands enter the woman's hair. He plays with the woman's hair, in the darkness. The cartoon's reflected light makes faces in the audience flicker: the woman's eyes are bright with fear. She sits absolutely still. The man plays with her red hair. The child does not look over at the woman. The theater's cartoons, previews of coming attractions, and feature presentation last almost three hours.

Alex Trebek goes around the "JEOPARDY!" studio wearing a button that says PAT SAJAK LOOKS LIKE A BADGER. He and Sajak play racquetball every Thursday.

It's 1986. California's night sky hangs bright and silent as an empty palace. Little white sequins make slow lines on streets far away under Faye's warm apartment.

Faye Goddard and Julie Smith lie in Faye's bed. They take turns lying on each other. They have sex. Faye's cries ring out like money against her penthouse apartment's walls of glass.

Faye and Julie cool each other down with wet towels. They stand naked at a glass wall and look at Los Angeles. Little bits of Los Angeles wink on and off, as light gets in the way of other light.

Julie and Faye lie in bed, as lovers. They compliment each other's bodies. They complain against the brevity of the night. They examine and reexamine, with a sort of unhappy enthusiasm, the little ignorances that necessarily, Julie says, line the path to any real connection between persons. Faye says she had liked Julie long before she knew that Julie liked her.

They go together to the *O.E.D.* to examine the entry for the word "like."

They hold each other. Julie is very white, her hair prickly short. The room's darkness is pocked with little bits of Los Angeles, at night, through glass. The dark drifts down around them and fits like a gardener's glove. It is incredibly romantic.

On 12 March 1988 it rains. Faye Goddard watches the freeway outside her mother's office window first darken and then shine with rain. Dee Goddard sits on the edge of her desk in stocking feet and looks out the window, too. "JEOPARDY!"'s director stands with the show's public relations coordinator. The key grip and cue-card lady huddle over some notes. Alex Trebek sits alone near the door in a canvas director's chair, drinking a can of soda. The room is reflected in the dark window.

"We need to know what you told her so we can know whether she'll come," Dee says.

"What we have here, Faye, is a twenty-minutes-tops type of thing," says the director, looking at the watch on the underside of her wrist. "Then we're going to be in for at least another hour's setup and studio time. Or we're short a slot, meaning satellite and mailing overruns."

"Not to mention a boy who's half catatonic with terror and general neurosis right this very minute," Muffy deMott, the P.R. coordinator, says softly. "Last I saw, he was fetal on the floor outside Makeup."

Faye closes her eyes.

"My husband is watching him," says the director.

"Thank you ever so much, Janet," Dee Goddard says to the director. She looks down at her clipboard. "All the others for the four slots are here?"

"Everybody who's signed up. Most we've ever had. Plus a rather scary retired WAC who's not even tentatively slotted till late April. Says she can't wait any longer to get at Julie."

"But no Julie," says Muffy deMott.

Dee squints at her clipboard. "So how many is that all together, then?"

"Nine," Faye says softly. She feels at the sides of her hair.

"We got nine," says the director; "enough for at least the full four slots with a turnaround of two per slot." The rain on the aluminum roof of the Merv Griffin Enterprises building makes a sound in this room, like the frying of distant meat.

"And I'm sure they're primed," Faye says. She looks at the backs of her hands, in her lap. "What with Janet assuming the poor kid will bump her. Your new mystery data guru."

"Don't confuse the difference between me, on one hand, and what I'm told to do," says the director.

"He won't bump her," the key grip says, shaking her head. She's chewing gum, stimulating a little worm of muscle at her temple.

Alex Trebek, looking at his digital watch, begins his pre-slot throat-clearing, a ritual. Everyone in the room looks at him.

Dee says, "Alex, perhaps you'd put the new contestants in the booth for now, tell them we may or may not be experiencing a slight delay. Thank them for their patience."

Alex rises, straightens his tie. His soda can rings out against the metal bottom of a wastebasket. He clears his throat.

"A good host and all that." Dee smiles kindly.

"Gotcha."

Alex leaves the door open. The sun breaks through the clouds outside. Palm trees drip and concrete glistens. Cars sheen by, their wipers on Sporadic. Janet Goddard, the director, looks down, pretends to study whatever she's holding. Faye knows that sudden sunlight makes her feel unattractive.

In the window, Faye sees Dee's outline check its own watch with a tiny motion. "Questions all lined up?" the outline asks.

"Easily four slots' worth," says the key grip; "categories set, all monitors on the board check. Joan's nailing down the sequence now."

"That's my job," Faye says.

"Your job," the director hisses, "is to tell Mommy here where your spooky little girlfriend could possibly be."

"Alex'll need all the cards at the podium very soon," Dee tells the grip.

"Is what your job is today." Janet stares at Faye's back.

Faye Goddard gives her ex-stepfather's wife, Janet Goddard, the finger, in the window. "One of those for every animal question," she says.

The director rises, calls Faye a bitch who looks like a praying mantis, and leaves through the open door, closing it.

"Bitch," Faye says.

Dee complains with a weak smile that she seems simply to be surrounded by bitches. Muffy deMott laughs, takes a seat in Alex's chair. Dee eases off the desk. A splinter snags and snaps on a pantyho. She assumes a sort of crouch next to her daughter, who is in the desk chair, at the window, her bare feet resting on the sill. Dee's knees crackle.

"If she's not coming," Dee says softly, "just tell me. Just so I can get a jump on fixing it with Merv. Baby."

It is true that Faye can see her mother's bright-faint image in the window. Here is her mother's middle-aged face, the immaculately colored and styled red hair, the sore-looking wrinkles that triangulate around her mouth and nose, trap and accumulate base and makeup as the face moves through the day. Dee's eyes are smoke-red, supported by deep circles, pouches of dark blood. Dee is pretty, except for the circles. This year Faye has been able to see the dark bags just starting to budge out from beneath her own eyes, which are her father's, dark brown and slightly thyroidic. Faye can smell Dee's breath. She cannot tell whether her mother has had anything to drink.

Faye Goddard is twenty-six; her mother is fifty.

Julie Smith is twenty.

Dee squeezes Faye's arm with a thin hand that's cold from the office.

Faye rubs at her nose. "She's not going to come, she told me. You'll have to bag it."

The key grip leaps for a ringing phone.

"I lied," says Faye.

"My girl." Dee pats the arm she's squeezed.

"I sure didn't hear anything," says Muffy deMott.

"Good," the grip is saying. "Get her into Makeup." She looks over at Dee. "You want her in Makeup?"

"You did good," Dee tells Faye, indicating the closed door.

"I don't think Mr. Griffin is well," says the cue-card lady.

"He and the boy deserve each other. We can throw in the WAC. We can call *her* General Neurosis."

Dee uses a thin hand to bring Faye's face close to her own. She kisses her gently. Their lips fit perfectly, Faye thinks suddenly. She shivers, in the air-conditioning.

"JEOPARDY!" QUEEN DETHRONED AFTER THREE-YEAR REIGN
—Headline, *Variety*, 13 March 1988.

"Let's all be there," says the television.

"Where else would I be?" asks Dee Goddard, in her chair, in her office, at night, in 1987.

"We bring good things to life," says the television.

"So did I," says Dee. "I did that. Just once."

Dee sits in her office at Merv Griffin Enterprises every weeknight and kills a tinkling pitcher of wet weak martinis. Her office walls are covered with store-bought aphorisms. Humpty Dumpty was pushed. When the going gets tough the tough go shopping. Also autographed photos. Dee and Bob Barker, when she wrote for "Truth or Consequences." Merv Griffin, giving her a plaque. Dee and Faye between Wink Martindale and Chuck Barris at a banquet.

Dee uses her remote matte-panel to switch from NBC to MTV, on cable. Consumptive-looking boys in makeup play guitars that look more like jets or weapons than guitars.

"Does your husband still look at you the way he used to?" asks the television.

"Safe to say not," Dee says drily, drinking.

"She drinks too much," Julie Smith says to Faye.

"It's for the pain," Faye says, watching.

Julie looks through the remote viewer in Faye's office. "For killing the pain, or feeding it?"

Faye smiles.

Julie shakes her head. "It's mean to watch her like this."

"You deserve a break today," says the television. "Milk likes you. The more you hear, the better we sound. Aren't you hungry for a flame-broiled Whopper?"

"No I am not hungry for a flame-broiled Whopper," says Dee, sitting up straight in her chair. "No I am not hungry for it." Her glass falls out of her hand.

"It was nice what she said about you, though." Julie is looking at the side of Faye's face. "About bringing one good thing to life."

Faye smiles as she watches the viewer. "Did you hear about what Alex did today? Sajak says he and Alex are now at war. Alex got in the engineer's booth and played with the Applause sign all through "The Wheel" 's third slot. The audience was like applauding when people lost turns and stuff. Sajak says he's going to get him."

"So you don't forget," says the television. "Look at all you get."

"Wow," says Dee. She sleeps in her chair.

Faye and Julie sit on thin towels, in 1987, at the edge of the surf, nude, on a nude beach, south of Los Angeles, just past dawn. The sun is behind them. The early Pacific is lilac. The women's feet are washed and abandoned by a weak surf. The sky's color is kind of grotesque.

Julie has told Faye that she believes lovers go through three different stages in getting really to know one another. First they exchange anecdotes and inclinations. Then each tells the other what she believes. Then each observes the relation between what the other says she believes and what she in fact *does*.

Julie and Faye are exchanging anecdotes and inclinations for the twentieth straight month. Julie tells Faye that she, Julie, best likes: contemporary poetry, unkind women, words with univocal definitions, faces whose expressions change by the second, an obscure and limited-edition Canadian encyclopedia called *LaPlace's Guide to Total Data*, the gentle smell of powder that issues from the makeup compacts of older ladies, and the *O.E.D.*

"The encyclopedia turned out to be lucrative, I guess you'd have to say."

Julie sniffs air that smells yeasty. "It got to be just what the teachers tell you. The encyclopedia was my friend."

"As a child, you mean?" Faye touches Julie's arm.

"Men would just appear, one after the other. I felt so sorry for my mother. These blank, silent men, and she'd hook up with one after the other, and they'd move in. And not one single one could love my brother."

"Come here."

"Sometimes things would be ugly. I remember her leading a really ugly life. But she'd lock us in rooms when things got bad, to get us out of the way of it." Julie smiles to herself. "At first sometimes I remember she'd give me a straightedge and a pencil. To amuse myself. I could amuse myself with a straightedge for hours."

"I always liked straightedges, too."

"It makes worlds. I could make worlds out of lines. A sort of jagged magic. I'd spend all day. My brother watched."

There are no gulls on this beach at dawn. It's quiet. The tide is going out.

"But we had a set of these *LaPlace's Data Guides.* Her fourth husband sold them to salesmen who went door-to-door. I kept a few in every room she locked us in. They did, really and truly, become my friends. I got to be able to feel lines of consistency and inconsistency in them. I got to know them really well." Julie looks at Faye. "I won't apologize if that sounds stupid or dramatic."

"It doesn't sound stupid. It's no fun to be a kid with a damaged brother and a mother with an ugly life, and to be lonely. Not to mention locked up."

"See, though, it was *him* they were locking up. I was just there to watch him."

"An autistic brother simply cannot be decent company for somebody, no matter how much you loved him, is all I mean," Faye says, making an angle in the wet sand with her toe.

"Taking care of him took incredible amounts of time. He wasn't company, though; you're right. But I got so I wanted him with me. He got to be my job. I got so I associated him with my identity or something. My right to take up space. I wasn't even eight."

"I can't believe you don't hate her," Faye says.

"None of the men with her could stand to have him around. Even the ones who tried couldn't stand it after a while. He'd just stare and flap his arms. And they'd say sometimes when they looked in my mother's eyes they'd see him looking out." Julie shakes some sand out of her short hair. "Except he was bright. He was totally inside himself, but he was bright. He could stare at the same thing for hours and not be bored. And it turned out he could read. He read very slowly and never out loud. I don't know what the words seemed like to him." Julie looks at Faye. "I pretty much taught us both to read, with the encyclopedia. Early. The illustrations really helped."

"I can't believe you don't hate her."

Julie throws a pebble. "Except I don't, Faye."

"She abandoned you by a road because some guy told her to."

Julie looks at the divot where the pebble was. The divot melts. "She really loved this man who was with her." She shakes her head. "He made her leave *him*. I think she left me to look out for him. I'm thankful for that. If I'd been without him right then, I don't think there would have been any me left."

"Babe."

"*I'd* have been in hospitals all this time, instead of him."

"What, like he'd have been instantly unautistic if you weren't there to take care of him?"

Among things Julie Smith dislikes most are: greeting cards, adoptive parents who adopt without first looking inside themselves and evaluating their capacity for love, the smell of sulphur, John Updike, insects with antennae, and animals in general.

"What about kind women?"

"But insects are maybe the worst. Even if the insect stops moving, the antennae still wave around. The antennae never stop waving around. I can't stand that."

"I love you, Julie."

"I love you too, Faye."

"I couldn't believe I could ever love a woman like this."

Julie shakes her head at the Pacific. "Don't make me sad."

Faye watches a small antennaeless bug skate on legs thin as hairs across the glassy surface of a tidal pool. She clears her throat.

"OK," she says. "This is the only line on an American football field of which there is only one."

Julie laughs. "What is the fifty."

"This, the only month of the year without a national holiday, is named for the Roman emperor who..."

"What is August."

The sun gets higher; the blood goes out of the blue water.

The women move down to stay in the waves' reach.

"The ocean looks like a big blue dog to me, sometimes," Faye says, looking. Julie puts an arm around Faye's bare shoulders.

'We loved her like a daughter,' said "JEOPARDY!" public relations coordinator Muffy deMott. 'We'll be sorry to see her go. Nobody's ever influenced a game show like Ms. Smith influenced "JEOPARDY!"'

—Article, *Variety*, 13 March 1988.

Weak waves hang, snap, slide. White fingers spill onto the beach and melt into the sand. Faye can see dark sand lighten beneath them as the water inside gets tugged back out with the retreating tide.

The beach settles and hisses as it pales. Faye is looking at the side of Julie Smith's face. Julie has the best skin Faye's ever seen on anyone anywhere. It's not just that it's so clear it's flawed, or that here in low sun off water it's the color of a good blush wine; it has the texture of something truly alive, an elastic softness, like a ripe sheath, a pod. It is vulnerable and has depth. It's stretched shiny and tight only over Julie's high curved cheekbones; the bones make her cheeks hollow, her eyes deep-set. The outlines of her face are like clefs, almost Slavic. Everything about her is sort of permeable: even the slim dark gap between her two front teeth seems a kind of slot, some recessive invitation. Julie has used the teeth and their gap to stimulate Faye with a gentle deftness Faye would not have believed.

Julie has looked up. "Why, though?"

Faye looks blankly, shakes her head.

"Poetry, you were talking about." Julie smiles, touching Faye's cheek.

Faye lights a cigarette in the wind. "I've just never liked it. It beats around bushes. Even when I like it, it's nothing more than a really oblique way of saying the obvious, it seems like."

Julie grins. Her front teeth have a gap. "Olé," she says. "But consider how very, very few of us have the equipment to deal with the obvious."

Faye laughs. She wets a finger and makes a scoreboard mark in the air. They both laugh. An anomalous wave breaks big in the surf. Faye's finger tastes like smoke and salt.

Pat Sajak and Alex Trebek and Bert Convy sit around, in slacks and loosened neckties, in the Merv Griffin Entertainment executive lounge, in the morning, watching a tape of last year's World Series. On the lounge's giant screen a batter flails at a low pitch.

"That was low," Trebek says.

Bert Convy, who is soaking his contact lenses, squints at the replay.

Trebek sits up straight. "Name the best low-ball hitter of all time."

"Joe Pepitone," Sajak says without hesitation.

Trebek looks incredulous. "Joe Pepitone?"

"Willie Stargell was a great low-ball hitter," says Convy. The other two men ignore him.

"Reggie Jackson was great," Sajak muses.

"Still is," Trebek says, looking absently at his nails.

A game show host has a fairly easy professional life. All five of a week's slots can be shot in one long day. Usually one hard week a month is spent on performance work at the studio. The rest of the host's time is his own. Bert Convy makes the rounds of car shows and mall openings and "Love Boat" episodes and is a millionaire several times over. Pat Sajak plays phenomenal racquetball, and gardens, and is learning his third language by mail. Alex, known in the industry as the most dedicated host since Bill Cullen, is to be seen lurking almost daily in some area of the MGE facility, reading, throat-clearing, grooming, worrying.

There's a hit. Sajak throws a can of soda at the screen. Trebek and Convy laugh.

Sajak looks over at Bert Convy. "How's that tooth, Bert?"

Convy's hand strays to his mouth. "Still discolored," he says grimly.

Trebek looks up. "You've got a discolored tooth?"

Convy feels at a bared canine. "A temporary thing. Already clearing up." He narrows his eyes at Alex Trebek. "Just don't tell Merv about it."

Trebek looks around, as if to see who Convy is talking to. "Me? This guy right here? Do I look like that sort of person?"

"You look like a game show host."

Trebek smiles broadly. "Probably because of my perfect and beautiful and flawless teeth."

"Bastard," mutters Convy.

Sajak tells them both to pipe down.

———

The dynamics of the connection between Faye Goddard and Julie Smith tend, those around them find, to resist clear articulation. Faye is twenty-six and has worked Research on the "JEOPARDY!" staff for the past forty months. Julie is twenty, has foster parents in La Jolla, and has retained her "JEOPARDY!" championship through over seven hundred market-dominating slots.

Forty months ago, game-show production mogul Merv Griffin decided to bring the popular game "JEOPARDY!" back from syndicated oblivion, to retire Art Flemming in favor of the waxily handsome, fairly distinguished, and prenominately dedicated Alex Trebek, the former model who'd made his bones in the game show industry hosting the short-lived "High Rollers" for Barris/NBC. Dee Goddard, who'd written for shows as old as "Truth or Consequences" and "Name That Tune," had worked Promotion/Distribution on "The Joker's Wild," and had finally produced the commercially shaky but critically acclaimed "Gambit," was hired by MGE as the new "JEOPARDY!" 's production executive. A period of disordered tension followed Griffin's decision to name Janet Lerner Goddard—forty-eight, winner of two Clios, but also the wife of Dee's former husband—as director of the revised show; and in fact Dee is persuaded to stay only when Merv Griffin's executive assistant puts in a personal call to New York, where Faye Goddard, having left Bryn Mawr in 1982 with a degree in library science, is doing an editorial stint at *Puzzle* magazine. Merv's right-hand man offers to put Faye on staff at "JEOPARDY!" as Category-/Question-researcher.

Faye works for her mother.

Summer, 1985, Faye has been on the "JEOPARDY!" team maybe four months when a soft-spoken and weirdly pretty young woman comes in off the freeway with a dirty jeans jacket, a backpack, and a *Times* classified ad detailing an MGE contestant search. The girl says she wants "JEOPARDY!"; she's been told she has a head for data. Faye interviews her and is mildly intrigued. The girl gets a solid but by no means spectacular score on a CBE general knowledge quiz, this particular version of which turns out to feature an important zoology section. Julie Smith barely makes it into an audition round.

In a taped audition round, flanked by a swarthy Shriner from Encino and a twig-thin Redding librarian with a towering blond wig, Julie takes the game by a wide margin, but has trouble speaking clearly into her microphone, as well as difficulty with the quirky and distinctive "JEOPARDY!" inversion by which the host "asks" the answer and a contestant supplies the appropriate question. Faye gives Julie an audition score of three out of five. Usually only fives and fours are to be called back. But Alex Trebek, who spends at least part of his free time haunting audition rounds, likes the girl, even after she turns down his invitation for a cola at the MGE commissary; and Dee Goddard and Muffy deMott pick Julie out for special mention from among eighteen other prospectives on the audition tape; and no one on the staff of a program still in its stressful initial struggle to break back into a respectable market share has anything against hauntingly attractive young female contestants. Etc. Julie Smith is called back for insertion into the contestant rotation sometime in early September 1985.

"JEOPARDY!" slots forty-six through forty-nine are shot on 17 September. Ms. Julie Smith of Los Angeles first appears in the forty-sixth slot. No one can quite remember who the reigning champion was at that time.

Palindromes, Musical Astrology, The Eighteenth Century, Famous

Edwards, The Bible, Fashion History, States of Mind, Sports Without Balls.

Julie runs the board in both rounds. Every question. Never been done before, even under Flemming. The other two contestants, slack and gray, have to be helped off-stage. Julie wins $22,500, every buck on the board, in half an hour. She earns no more in this first match only because a flustered Alex Trebek declares the Final Jeopardy wagering round moot, Julie Smith having no incentive to bet any of her winnings against opponents' scores of $0 and –$400, respectively. A wide-eyed and grinning Trebek doffs a pretend cap to a blank-faced Julie as electric bongos rattle to the running of the closing credits.

Ten minutes later Faye Goddard locates a missing Julie Smith in a remote section of the contestants' dressing area. (Returning contestants are required to change clothes between each slot, conducing to the illusion that they've "come back again tomorrow.") It's time for "JEOPARDY!" slot forty-seven. A crown to defend and all that. Julie sits staring at herself in a harsh makeup mirror framed with glowing bulbs, her face loose and expressionless. She has trouble reacting to stimuli. Faye has to get her a wet cloth and talk her through dressing and practically carry her upstairs to the set.

Faye is in the engineer's booth, trying to communicate to her mother her doubts about whether the strange new champion can make it through another televised round, when Janet Goddard calmly directs her attention to the monitor. Julie is eating slot forty-seven and spitting it out in little pieces. Lady Bird Johnson's real first name turns out to be Claudia. The Florida city that produces more Havana cigars than all of Cuba is revealed to be Tampa. Julie's finger abuses the buzzer. She is on Alex's answers with the appropriate questions before he can even end-punctuate his clues. The first-round board is taken. Janet cuts to commercial. Julie sits at her little desk, staring out at a hushed studio audience.

Faye and Dee watch Julie as the red lights light and Trebek's face falls into the worn creases of a professional smile. Something happens to Julie Smith when the red lights light. Just a something. The girl who gets a three-score and who stares with no expression is gone. Every concavity in that person now looks to have come convex. The camera lingers on her. It seems to ogle. Often Julie appears on-screen while Trebek is still reading a clue. Her face, on-screen, gives off an odd lambent UHF flicker; her expression, brightly serene, radiates a sort of oneness with the board's data.

Trebek manipulates the knot of his tie. Faye knows he feels the something, the odd, focused flux in the game's flow. The studio audience gasps and whispers as Julie supplies the Latin name for the common radish.

"No one knows the Latin word for radish," Faye says to Dee. "That's one of those deadly ones I put in on purpose in every game."

The other two contestants' postures deteriorate. Someone in the audience loudly calls Julie's name.

Trebek, who has never before had an audience get away from him, gets more and more flustered. He uses forty expensive seconds relating a tired anecdote involving a Dodgers game he saw with Tom Brokaw. The audience hoots impatiently for the game to continue.

"Bad feeling, here," Faye whispers. Dee ignores her, bends to the monitor.

Janet signals Alex for a break. Moist and upstaged, Alex promises America that he'll be right back, that he's eager to inquire on-air about the tremendous Ms. Smith and the even more tremendous personal sacrifices she must have made to have absorbed so much data at such a tender age.

"JEOPARDY!" breaks for a Triscuit advertisement. Faye and Dee stare at the monitor in horror. The studio audience is transfixed as Julie Smith's face crumples like a Kleenex in a pocket. She begins silently to weep. Tears move down the clefs of her cheeks and drip into her mike, where for some reason they hiss faintly. Janet, in the booth, is at a loss. Faye is sent for a cold compress but can't make the set in time. The lights light. America watches Julie Smith murder every question on the Double Jeopardy board, her face and vinyl jacket slickered with tears. Trebek, suddenly and cucumbrously cool, pretends he notices nothing, though he never asks (and never in hundreds of slots does he ask) Julie Smith any of the promised personal questions.

The game unfolds. Faye watched a new, third Julie respond to answer after answer. Julie's face dries, hardens. She is looking at Trebek with eyes narrowed to the width of paper cuts.

In Final Jeopardy, her opponents again cashless, Julie coolly overrides Trebek's moot-motion and bets her entire twenty-two-five on the fact that the first part of Peking Man discovered was a parenthesis-shaped fragment of mandible. She ends with $45,000. Alex pretends to genuflect. The audience applauds. There are bongos. And in a closing moment that Faye Goddard owns, captured in a bright glossy that hangs over her iron desk, Julie Smith, on television, calmly and deliberately gives Alex Trebek the finger.

A nation goes wild. The switchboards at MGE and NBC begin jangled two-day symphonies. Pat Sajak sends three-dozen long-stemmed reds to

Julie's dressing table. The market share for the last segment of "JEOP-ARDY!" slot forty-seven is a fifty—on a par with Super Bowls and assas-sinations. This is 17 September 1985.

"My favorite word," says Alex Trebek, "is *moist*. It is my favorite word, especially when used in combination with my second-favorite word, which is *induce*." He looks at the doctor. "I'm just associating. Is it OK if I just associate?"

Alex Trebek's psychiatrist says nothing.

"A dream," says Trebek. "I have this recurring dream where I'm stand-ing outside the window of a restaurant, watching a chef flip pancakes. Except it turns out they're not pancakes—they're faces. I'm watching a guy in a chef's hat flip faces with a spatula."

The psychiatrist makes a church steeple with his fingers and contem-plates the steeple.

"I think I'm just tired," says Trebek. "I think I'm just bone weary. I con-tinue to worry about my smile. That it's starting to maybe be a tired smile. Which is *not* an inviting smile, which is professionally worrying." He clears his throat. "And it's the *worry* I think that's making me tired in the first place. It's like a vicious smiling-circle."

"This girl you work with," says the doctor.

"And Convy reveals today that he's getting a discolored tooth," Trebek says. "Tell me *that* augurs well, why don't you."

"This contestant you talk about all the time."

"She lost," Trebek says, rubbing the bridge of his nose. "She lost yester-day. Don't you read papers, ever? She lost to her own brother, after Janet and Merv's exec snuck the damaged little bastard in with a rigged five audition and a board just crawling with animal questions."

The psychiatrist hikes his eyebrows a little. They are black and angled, almost hinged.

"Queer story behind that," Trebek says, manipulating a broad bright cufflink to produce lines of reflected window-light on the ceiling's tile. "I got it about fourth-hand, but still. Parents abandoned the children, as kids. There was the girl and her brother, Lunt. Can you imagine a cham-pion named Lunt? Lunt was autistic. Autistic to where this was like a mannequin of a kid instead of a kid. Muffy said Faye said the girl used to carry him around like a suitcase. Then finally he and the girl got aban-doned out in the middle of nowhere somewhere. By the parents. Grisly. She got adopted and the brother was institutionalized. In a state institu-tion. This hopelessly autistic kid, who it turns out he's got the whole

LaPlace's Data Guide memorized. They were both forced to somehow memorize this thing, as kids. And I thought *I* had a rotten childhood, boy." Trebek shakes his head. "But he got put away, and the girl got adopted by some people in La Jolla who were not, from the sense I get, princes among men. She ran away. She got on the show. She kicked ass. She was fair and a good sport and took no crapola. She used her prize money to pay these staggering bills for Lunt's autism. Moved him to a private hospital in the desert that was supposed to specialize in sort of... *yanking* people outside themselves. Into the world." Trebek clears his throat.

"And I guess they yanked him OK," he says, "at least to where he could talk. Though he still hides his head under his arm whenever things get tense. Plus he's weird-looking. And but he comes and bumps her off with this torrent of zoology data." Trebek plays with the cufflink. "And she's gone."

"You said in our last hour together that you thought you loved her."

"She's a lesbian," Trebek says wearily. "She's a lesbian through and through. I think she's one of those political lesbians. You know the kind? The kind with the anger? She looks at men like they're unsightly stains on the air. Plus she's involved with our ditz of a head researcher, which if you don't think the F.C.C. took a dim view of *that* little liaison you've got another...."

"Free-associate," orders the doctor.

"Image association?"

"I have no problem with that."

"I invited the girl for coffee, or a Tab, years ago, right at the start, in the commissary, and she gave me this haunting, moisture-inducing look. Then tells me she could never imbibe caffeine with a man who wore a digital watch. The hell she says. She gave me the finger on national television. She's practically got a crewcut. Sometimes she looks like a vampire. Once, in the contestant booth—the contestant booth is where we keep all the contestants for all the slots—once one of the lights in the booth was flickering, they're fluorescent lights—and she said to get her the hell out of that booth, that flickering fluorescence made her feel like she was in a nightmare. And there *was* a sort of nightmary quality to that light, I remember. It was like there was a pulse in the neon. Like blood. Everybody in the booth got nervous." Trebek strokes his mustache. "Odd girl. Something odd about her. When she smiled things got bright, too focused. It took the fun out of it, somehow.

"I love her, I think," Trebek says. "She has a way with a piece of data. To see her with an answer...Is there such a thing as an intellectual caress? I think of us together: seas part, stars shine spotlights...."

"And this researcher she's involved with?"

"Nice enough girl. A thick, friendly girl. Not fantastically bright. A little emotional. Has this adoration-versus-loathing thing with her mother." Trebek ponders. "My opinion: Faye is the sort of girl who's constantly surfing on her emotions. You know? Not really in control of where they take her, but not quite ever wiping out, yet, either. A psychic surfer. But scary-looking, for so young. These black, bulging, buggy eyes. Perfectly round and black. Impressive breasts, though."

"Mother-conflicts?"

"Faye's mother is one very tense production exec. Spends far too much time obsessing about not obsessing about the fact that our director is her ex-husband's wife."

"A woman?"

"Janet Lerner Goddard. Worst director I've ever worked with. Dee hates her. Janet likes to play with Dee's head; it's a head that admittedly tends to be full of gin. Janet likes to put little trinkety reminders of Dee's ex in Dee's mailbox at the office. Old bills, tie clips. She plays with Dee's mind. Dee's obsessing herself into stasis. She's barely able to even function at work anymore."

"Image associated with this person?"

"You know those ultra-modern rifles, where the mechanisms of aiming far outnumber those of firing? Dee's like that. God am I worried about potentially ever being like that."

The psychiatrist thinks they have done all they can for today. He shows Trebek the door.

"I also really like the word *bedizen*," Trebek says.

In those first fall weeks of 1985, a public that grows with each Nielsen sweep discerns only two areas of even potential competitive vulnerability in Ms. Julie Smith of Los Angeles. One has to do with animals. Julie is simply unable to respond to clues about animals. In her fourth slot, categories in Double Jeopardy include Marsupials and Zoological Songs, and an eidetic pharmacist from Westwood pushes Julie all the way to Final Jeopardy before she crushes him with a bold bet on Eva Braun's shoe size.

In her fifth slot (and what is, according to the game's publicized rules, to be her last—if a winner, she'll be retired as a five-time champion), Julie goes up against a spectacularly fat Berkeley mailman who claims to be a co-founder of the California chapter of MENSA. The third contestant is a neurasthenic (but gorgeous — Alex keeps straightening his tie) Fullerton stenographer who wipes her lips compulsively on the sleeve of her blouse. The stenographer quickly accumulates a negative score, and becomes hysterically anxious during the second commercial break, convinced by the skunked, vengeful, and whispering mailman that she will have to pay "JEOPARDY!" the nine hundred dollars she's down before they will let her leave the set. Faye dashes out during Off-Air; the woman cannot seem to be reassured. She keeps looking wildly at the exits as Faye runs offstage and the red lights light.

A bell initiates Double Jeopardy. Julie, refusing to meet the audience's eye, begins pausing a bit before she reponds to Alex. She leaves openings. Only the mailman capitalizes. Julie stays ahead of him. Faye watches the stenographer, who is clearly keeping it together only through enormous exercise of will. The mailman closes on Julie. Julie assumes a look of distaste and runs the board for several minutes, down to the very last answer, Ancient Rome For A Thousand: author of *De Oratore* who was executed by Octavian in 43 b.c. Julie's finger hovers over the buzzer; she looks to the stenographer. The mailman's eyes are closed in data-search. The stenographer's head snaps up. She looks wildly at Julie and buzzes in with Who is Tully. There is a silence. Trebek looks at his index card. He shakes his head. The stenographer goes to –$1,900 and seems to suffer something resembling a petit mal seizure.

Faye watches Julie Smith buzz in now and whisper into her mike that, though Alex was doubtless looking for the question Who is Cicero, in point of fact one Marcus Tullius Cicero, 106–43 b.c., was known variously as both Cicero *and* Tully. Just as Augustus's less-common appellation is Octavian, she points out, indicating the card in the host's hand. Trebek looks at the card. Faye flies to the Resource Room. The verdict takes only seconds. The stenographer gets the credit and the cash. Out of the emotional red, she hugs Julie on-camera. The mailman fingers his lapels. Julie smiles a really magnificent smile. Alex, generally moved, declaims briefly on the spirit of good clean competition he's proud to have witnessed here today. Final Jeopardy sees Julie effect the utter annihilation of the mailman, who is under the impression that the first literature in India was written by Kipling. The slot pulls down a sixty-five share. Hardly anyone notices Julie's and the stenographer's exchange of phone numbers as the bongos play. Faye gets a tongue-lashing from Muffy deMott on the inestimable importance of researching all possible questions to a given answer. The shot of Julie buzzing in with the correction makes the "Newsmakers" column of *Newsweek*.

That night Merv Griffin's executive assistant calls an emergency policy meeting of the whole staff. MGE's best minds take counsel. Alex and Faye are invited to sit in. Faye calls downstairs for coffee and Cokes and Merv's special seltzer.

Griffin murmurs to his right-hand man. His man has a shiny face and a black toupee. The man nods, rises:

"Can't let her go. Too good. Too hot. She's become the whole show. Look at these figures." He brandishes figures.

"Rules, though," says the director. "Five slots, retire undefeated, come back for Champion's Tourney in April. Annual event. Tradition. Art Flemming. Fairness to whole contestant pool. An ethics type of thing."

Griffin whispers into his shiny man's ear. Again the man rises.

"Balls," the shiny man says to the director. "The girl's magic. Figures do not lie. The Triscuit people have offered to double the price on thirty-second spots, long as she stays." He smiles with his mouth but not his eyes, Faye sees. "Shoot, Janet, we could just call this the Julia Smith Show and still make mints."

"Julie," says Faye.

"Absolutely."

Griffin whispers up at his man.

"Need Merv mention we should all see substantial salary and benefit incentives at work here?" says the shiny man, flipping a watch fob. "A chance here to be industry heroes. Heroines. MGE a Camelot. You, all of you, knights." Looks around. "Scratch that. Queens. Entertainment Amazons."

"You don't get rid of a sixty share without a fight," says Dee, who's seated next to Faye, sipping at what looks to Faye a little too much like water. The director whispers something in Muffy deMott's ear.

There's a silence. Griffin rises to stand with his man. "I've seen the tapes, and I'm impressed as I've never been impressed before. She's like some lens, a filter for that great unorganized force that some in the industry have spent their whole lives trying to locate and focus." This is Merv Griffin saying this. Eyes around the table are lowered. "What is that force?" Merv asks quietly. Looks around. He and his man sit back down.

Alex goes to the door to relieve a winded gofer of refreshments.

Griffin whispers and the shiny man rises. "Merv posits that this force, ladies, gentleman, is the capacity of facts to transcend their internal factual limitations and become, in and of themselves, meaning, feeling. This girl not only kicks facts in the ass. This girl informs trivia with import. She makes it human, something with the power to emote, evoke, induce, cathart. She gives the game the simultaneous transparency and mystery all of us in the industry have groped for, for decades. A sort of union of contestantorial head, heart, gut, buzzer finger. She is, or can become, the game show incarnate. She is mystery."

"What, like a cult thing?" Alex Trebek asks, opening a can of soda at arm's length.

Merv Griffin gives Trebek a cold stare.

Merv's man's face gleams. "See that window?" he says. "That's where the rules go. Out the window." Feels at his nose. "Does your conscientious entertainer retain—and here I say think about all the implications of 'retention,' here"—looking at Janet—"I mean does he cling blindly to rules for their own sake when the very goal and purpose and *idea* of those rules walks right in off the street and into the hearts of every Triscuit consumer in the free world?"

"Safe to say not," Dee says drily.

The man: "So here's the scoop. She stays till she's bumped. We cannot and will not give her any help on-air. Off-air she gets anything within what Merv defines as reason. We get her to play a little ball, go easy on the board when strategy allows, give the other players a bit of a shot. We tell her we want to play ball. DeMott here is one of our carrots."

Muffy deMott wipes her mouth on a commissary napkin. "I'm a carrot?"

"If the girl plays ball, then you, deMott, you start in on helping the kid shelter her income. Tell her we'll give her shelter under MGE. Take her from the seventy bracket to something more like a twenty. Kapisch? She's got to play ball, with a carrot like that."

"She sends all her money to a hospital her brother's in," Faye says softly, next to her mother.

"Hospital?" Merv Griffin asks. "What hospital?"

Faye looks at Griffin. "All she told me was her brother was in Arizona in a hospital because he has trouble living in the world."

"The world?" Griffin asks. He looks at his man.

Griffin's man touches his wig carefully, looks at Muffy. "Get on that, deMott," he says. "This hospitalized brother thing. If it's good P.R., see that it's P.'d. Take the girl aside. Fill her in. Tell her about the rules and the window. Tell her she's here as long as she can hang." A significant pause. "Tell her Merv might want to do lunch, at some point."

Muffy looks at Faye. "All right."

Merv Griffin glances at his watch. Everyone is instantly up. Papers are shuffled.

"Dee," Merv says from his chair, absently fingering a canine tooth. "You and your daughter stay for a moment, please."

Idaho, Coins, Truffaut, Patron Saints, Historical Cocktails, Animals, Winter Sports, 1879, The French Revolution, Botanical Songs, The Talmud, 'Nuts to You.'

One contestant, slot two-eighty-seven, 4 December 1986, is a bespectacled teenage boy with a smear of acne and a shallow chest in a faded Mozart T-shirt; he claims on-air to have revised the Western solar calendar into complete isomorphism with the atomic clocks at the U.S. Bureau of Time Measurement in Washington. He eyes Julie beadily. Any and all of his winnings, he says, will go toward realizing his father's fantasy. His father's fantasy turns out to be a spa, in the back yard of the family's Orange County home, with an elephant on permanent duty at either side of the spa, spouting.

"God am I tired," Alex intones to Faye over a soda and handkerchief at the third commercial break. Past Alex, Faye sees Julie, at her little desk, looking out at the studio audience. People in the audience vie for her attention.

The boy's hopes for elephants are dashed in Final Jeopardy. He claims shrilly that the Islamic week specifies no particular sabbath.

"Friday," Julie whispers.

Alex cues bongos, asks the audience to consider the fact that Californians never ("*never*," he emphasizes) seem to face east.

"Just the facts on the brother who can't live in the world is all I want," Merv Griffin says, pushing at his cuticles with a paper clip. Dee makes soft sounds of assent.

"The kid's autistic," Faye says. "I can't really see why you'd want data on a damaged person."

Merv continues to address himself to Dee. "What's wrong with him exactly. Are there different degrees of autisticness. Can he talk. What's his prognosis. Would he excite pathos. Does he look too much like the girl. And et cetera."

"We want total data on Smith's brother," iterates the gleaming face of Merv's man.

"Why?"

Dee looks at the empty glass in her hand.

"The potential point," Merv murmurs, "is can the brother do with a datum what she can do with a datum." He switches the paper clip to his left hand. "Does the fact that he has, as Faye here put it, trouble being in the world, together with what have to be impressive genetics, by association," he smiles, "add up to mystery status? Game-show incarnation?" He works a cuticle. "Can he do what she can do?"

"Imagine the possibilities," says the shiny man. "We're looking way down the road on this thing. A climax type of deal, right? Antigone-thing. If she's going to get bumped sometime, we obviously want a bumper with the same kind of draw. The brother's expensive hospitalization at the sister's selfless expense is already great P.R."

"Is he mystery, I want to know," says Merv.

"He's *austistic*," Faye says, staring bug-eyed. "Meaning they're like trying to teach him just to talk coherently. How not to go into convulsions whenever somebody looks at him. You're thinking about maybe trying to put him on the air?"

Merv's man stands at the dark office window. "Imagine sustaining the mystery beyond the individual girl herself, is what Merv means. The mystery of total data, that mystery made a sort of antic, ontic self-perpetuation. We're talking fact sustaining feeling, right through the change that inevitably attends all feeling, Faye."

"We're thinking perpetuation, is what we're thinking," says Merv. "Every thumb over at Triscuit is up, on this one."

Dee's posture keeps deteriorating as they stand there.

"Remember, ladies," Merv's man says from the window. "You're either part of the solution, or you're part of the precipitate." He guffaws. Griffin slaps his knee.

Nine months later Faye is back in the office of Griffin's man. The man has different hair. He says:

"I say two words to you, Faye. I say F.C.C., and I say separate apartments. We do not I repeat not need even a whiff of scandal. We do not need a "Sixty-Four-Thousand-Dollar-Question"–type-scandal kind of deal. Am I right? So I say to you F.C.C., and separate pads.

"You do good research, Faye. We treasure you here. I've personally heard Merv use the word *treasure* in connection with your name."

"I don't give her any answers," Faye says. The man nods vigorously.

Faye looks at the man. "She doesn't need them."

"All I'm saying to you is let's make our dirty linen a private matter," says the shiny man. "Treasure or no. So I say keep your lovely glass apartment, that I hear so much about."

That first year, ratings slip a bit, as they always do. They level out at incredible. MGE stock splits three times in nine months. Alex buys a car so expensive he's worried about driving it. He takes the bus to work. Dee and the cue-card lady acquire property in the canyons. Faye explores IRAs with the help of Muffy deMott. Julie moves to a bungalow in Burbank, continues to live on fruit and seeds, and sends everything after her minimal, post-shelter taxes to the Palo Verde Psychiatric Hospital in Tucson. She turns down a *People* cover. Faye explains to the *People* people that Julie is basically a private person.

It quickly gets to the point where Julie can't go out anywhere without some sort of disguise. Faye helps her select a mustache and explains to her about not too much glue.

Extrapolation from LAX Airport flight-plan data yields a scenario in which Merv Griffin's shiny man, "JEOPARDY!" director Janet Goddard, and a Mr. Mel Goddard, who works subsidiary rights at Screen Gems, board the shiny man's new Piper Cub on the afternoon of 17 September 1987, fly nonstop to Tucson, Arizona, and enjoy a three-day stay among flying ants and black spiders and unimaginable traffic and several sizzling, carbonated summer monsoons.

> Dethroning Ms. Smith after 700-plus victories last night was one 'Mr. Lunt' of Arizona, a young man whose habit of hiding his head under his arm at crucial moments detracted not at all from the virtuosity with which he worked a buzzer and board that had, for years, been the champion's own.
>
> —Article, *Variety*, 13 March 1988.

WHAT NEXT FOR SMITH?
> —Headline, *Variety*, 14 March 1988.

Los Angeles at noon today in 1987 is really hot. A mailman in mailman shorts and wool knee socks sits eating his lunch in the black guts of an open mailbox. Air shimmers over the concrete like fuel. Sunglasses ride every face in sight.

Faye and Julie are walking around west L.A. Faye wears a bathing suit and rubber thongs. Her thongs squeak and slap.

"You did *what?*" Faye says. "You did *what* for a living before you saw our ad?"

"A psychology professor at UCLA was doing tests on the output of human saliva in response to different stimuli. I was a professional subject."

"You were a professional salivator?"

"It paid me, Faye. I was seventeen. I'd had to hitch from La Jolla. I had no money, no place to stay. I ate seeds."

"What, he'd like ring bells or wave chocolate at you and see if you'd drool?"

Julie laughs, gap-toothed, in mustache and sunglasses, her short spiked hair hidden under a safari hat. "Not exactly."

"So what, then?"

Faye's thongs squeak and slap.

"Your shoes sound like sex," Julie says.

"Don't think even one day doesn't go by," says veteran reference-book sales representative P. Craig Lunt in the office of the game-show production mogul who's looking studiously down, manipulating a plastic disk, trying to get a BB in the mouth of a clown.

Dee Goddard and Muffy deMott sit in Dee's office, overlooking the freeway, today, at noon, in the air-conditioning, with a pitcher of martinis, watching the "All New Newlywed Game."

"It's the 'All New Newlywed Game'!" says the television.

"Weak show," says Dee. "All they do on this show is humiliate newlyweds. A series of low gags."

"I like this show," Muffy says, reaching for the pitcher that's refrigerating in front of the air-conditioner. "It's people's own fault if they're going to let Bob Eubanks embarrass them on national daytime just for a drier or a skimobile."

"Cheap show. Mel got a look at their books once. A really...a really chintzy operation." Dee jiggles a lemon twist.

Bob Eubanks' head fills the screen.

"Jesus will you look at the size of the head on that guy."

"Youthful-looking, though," Muffy muses. "He never seems to age. I wonder how he does it."

"He's traded his soul for his face. He worships bright knives. He makes sacrifices to dark masters on behalf of his face."

Muffy looks at Dee.

"A special grand prize chosen just for you," says the television.

Dee leans forward. "Will you just look at that head. His forehead simply *dominates* the whole shot. They must need a special lens."

"I sort of like him. He's sort of funny."

"I'm just glad he's on the inside of the set, and I'm on the outside, and I can turn him off whenever I want."

Muffy holds her drink up to the window's light and looks at it. "And of course you never lie there awake in the dark considering the possibility that it's the other way around."

Dee crosses her ankles under her chair. "Dear child, we are in this business precisely to make sure that that is *not* a possibility."

They both laugh.

"You hear stories, though," Muffy says. "About these lonely or somehow disturbed people who've had only the TV all their lives, their parents or whomever started them right off by plunking them down in front of the set, and as they get older the TV comes to be their whole emotional world, it's all they have, and it becomes in a way their whole way of defining themselves as existents, with a distinct identity, that they're outside the set, and everything else is inside the set." She sips.

"Stay right where you are," says the television.

"And then you hear about how every once in a while one of them gets on TV somehow. By accident," says Muffy. "There's a shot of them in the crowd at a ball game, or they're interviewed on the street about a referendum or something, and they go home and plunk right down in front of the set, and all of a sudden they look and they're *inside* the set." Muffy pushes her glasses up. "And sometimes you hear about how it drives them mad, sometimes."

"There ought to be special insurance for that or something," Dee says, tinkling the ice in the pitcher.

"Maybe that's an idea."

Dee looks around. "You seen the vermouth around here anyplace?"

Julie and Faye walk past a stucco house the color of Pepto-Bismol. A VW bus is backing out of the driveway. It sings the high sad song of the Volkswagen-in-reverse. Faye wipes her forehead with her arm. She feels moist and sticky, something hot in a Baggie.

"But so I don't know what to tell them," she says.

"Being involved with a woman doesn't automatically make you a lesbian," says Julie.

"It doesn't make me Marie Osmond, either, though."

Julie laughs. "A cross you'll have to bear." She takes Faye's hand.

Julie and Faye take walks a lot. Faye drives over to Julie's place and helps her into her disguise. Julie wears a mustache and hat, Bermuda shorts, a Hawaiian shirt, and a Nikon.

"Except what if I am a lesbian?" Faye asks. She looks at a small child methodically punching a mild-faced father in the back of the thigh while the father buys Häagen-Dazs from a vendor. "I mean, what if I am a lesbian, and people ask me why I'm a lesbian?" Faye releases Julie's hand to pinch sweat off her upper lip. "What do I say if they ask me why?"

"You anticipate a whole lot of people questioning you about your sexuality?" Julie asks. "Or are there particular people you're worried about?"

Faye doesn't say anything.

Julie looks at her. "I can't believe you really even care."

"Maybe I do. What questions I care about aren't really your business. You're why I might be a lesbian; I'm just asking you to tell me what I can say."

Julie shrugs. "Say whatever you want." She has to keep straightening her mustache, from the heat. "Say lesbianism is simply one kind of response to Otherness. Say the whole point of love is to try to get your fingers through the holes in the lover's mask. To get some kind of hold on the mask, and who cares how you do it."

"I don't want to hear mask theories, Julie," Faye says. "I want to hear what I should really tell people."

"Why don't you just tell me which people you're so worried about."

Faye doesn't say anything. A very large man walks by, his face red as steak, his cowboy boots new, a huge tin star pinned to the lapel of his business suit.

Julie starts to smile.

"Don't smile," says Faye.

They walk in silence. The sky is clear and spread way out. It shines in its own sun, glassy as aftershave.

Julie smiles to herself, under her hat. The smile's cold. "You know what's fun, if you want to have fun," she says, "is to make up explanations. Give people reasons, if they want reasons. Anything you want. Make reasons up. It'll surprise you—the more improbable the reason, the more satisfied people will be."

"That's fun?"

"I guarantee you it's more fun than twirling with worry over the whole thing."

"Julie?" Faye says suddenly. "What about if you lose, sometime? Do we stay together? Or does our being together depend on the show?"

A woman in terry-cloth shorts is giving Julie a pretty brazen look.

Julie looks away, in her hat.

"Here's one," she says. "If people ask, you can give them this one. You fall totally in love with a man who tells you he's totally in love with you, too. He's older. He's important in terms of business. You give him all of yourself. He goes to France, on important business. He won't let you come. You wait for days and don't hear from him. You call him in France, and a woman's voice says a French hello on the phone, and you hear the man's electric shaver in the background. A couple days later you get a hasty French postcard he'd mailed on his first day there. It says: 'Scenery is here. Wish you were beautiful.' You reel into lesbianism, from the pain."

Faye looks at the curved side of Julie's face, deep skin of a perfect white grape.

Julie says: "Tell them this man who broke your heart quickly assumed in your memory the aspects of a political cartoon: enormous head, tiny body, all unflattering features exaggerated."

"I can tell them all men everywhere look that way to me now."

"Give them this one. You meet a boy, at your East Coast college. A popular and beautiful and above all—and this is what attracts you most—a terribly *serious* boy. A boy who goes to the library and gets out a copy of *Gray's Anatomy*, researches the precise location and neurology of the female clitoris—simply, you're convinced, to allow him to give you pleasure. He plays your clitoris, your whole body, like a fine instrument. You fall for the boy completely. The intensity of your love creates what you could call an organic situation: a body can't walk without legs; legs can't walk without a body. He becomes your body."

"But pretty soon he gets tired of my body."

"No, he gets obsessed with your body. He establishes control over your own perception of your body. He makes you diet, or gain weight. He makes you exercise. He supervises your haircuts, your make-overs. Your body can't make a move without him. You get muscular, from the exercise. Your clothes get tighter and tighter. He traces your changing outline on huge sheets of butcher's paper and hangs them in his room in a sort of evolutionary progression. Your friends think you're nuts. You lose all your friends. He's introduced you to all his friends. He made you turn slowly around while he introduced you, so they could see you from every conceivable angle."

"I'm miserable with him."

"No, you're deliriously happy. But there's not much you, at the precise moment you're feeling most complete."

"He makes me lift weights while he watches. He has barbells in his room."

"Your love," says Julie, "springs from your incompleteness, but also reduces you to another's prosthetic attachment, calcified by the Medusa's gaze of his need."

"I told you I didn't want abstractions about this stuff," Faye says impatiently.

Julie walks, silent, with a distant frown of concentration. Faye sees a big butterfly beat incongruously at the smoke-black window of a long limousine. The limousine is at a red light. Now the butterfly falls away from the window. It drifts aimlessly to the pavement and lies there, bright.

"He makes you lift weights, in his room, at night, while he sits and watches," Julie says quietly. "Pretty soon you're lifting weights nude while he watches from his chair. You begin to be uneasy. For the first time you taste something like degradation in your mouth. The degradation tastes like tea. Night after night it goes. Your mouth tastes like tea when he eventually starts going outside, to the window, to the outside of the window at night, to watch you lift weights nude."

"I feel horrible when he watches through the window."

"Plus, eventually, his friends. It turns out he starts inviting all his friends over at night to watch through the window with him as you lift weights. You're able to make out the outlines of all the faces of his friends. You can see them through your own reflection in the black glass. The faces are rigid with fascination. The faces remind you of the carved faces of pumpkins. As you look you see a tongue come out of one of the faces and touch the window. You can't tell whether it's the beautiful serious boy's tongue or not."

"I reel into lesbianism, from the pain."

"You still love him, though."

Faye's thongs slap. She wipes her forehead and considers.

"I'm in love with a guy and we get engaged and I start going over to his parents' house with him for dinner. One night I'm setting the table and I hear his father in the living room laughingly tell the guy that the penalty for bigamy is two wives. And the guy laughs too."

An electronics shop pulls up alongside them. Faye sees a commercial behind the big window, reflected in the fly's-eye prism of about thirty televisions. Alan Alda holds up a product between his thumb and forefinger. Smiles at it.

"You're in love with a man," says Julie, "who insists that he can love you only when you're standing in the exact center of whatever room you're in."

Pat Sajak plants lettuce in the garden of his Bel Air home. Bert Convy boards his Lear, bound for an Indianapolis Motor Home Expo.

"A dream," says Alex Trebek to the doctor with circumflex brows. "I have this dream where I'm standing smiling over a lectern on a little hill in the middle of a field. The field, which is verdant and clovered, is covered with rabbits. They sit and look at me. There must be several million rabbits in that field. They all sit and look at me. Some of them lower their little heads to eat clover. But their eyes never leave me. They sit there and look at me, a million bunny rabbits, and I look back."

"Uncle," says Patricia ("Patty-Jo") Smith-Tilley-Lunt, stout and loose-faced behind the cash register of the Holiday Inn Restaurant at the Holiday Inn, Interstate 70, Ashtabula, Ohio:
    "Uncle uncle uncle uncle."

"No," says Faye. "I meet a man in the park. We're both walking. The man's got a tiny puppy, the cutest and most beautiful puppy I've ever seen. The puppy's on a little leash. When I meet the man, the puppy wags its tail so hard that it loses its little balance. The man lets me play with the puppy. I scratch its stomach and it licks my hand. The man has a picnic lunch in a hamper. We spend all day in the park, with the puppy. By sundown I'm totally in love with the man with the puppy. I stay the night with him. I let him inside me. I'm in love. I start to see the man and the puppy whenever I close my eyes.
    "I have a date with the man in the park a couple days later. This time he's got a different puppy with him, another beautiful puppy that wags its tail and licks my hand, and the man's hand. The man says it's the first puppy's brother."
    "Oh Faye."
    "And but this goes on, me meeting with the man in the park, him having a different puppy every time, and the man is so warm and loving and attentive toward both me and the puppies that soon I'm totally in love. I'm totally in love on the morning I follow the man to work, just to surprise him, like with a juice and Danish, and I follow him and discover that he's actually a professional cosmetics researcher, who performs product experiments on puppies, and kills them, and dissects them, and that before he

experiments on each puppy he takes it to the park, and walks it, and uses the beautiful puppies to attract women, who he seduces."

"You're so crushed and revolted you become a lesbian," says Julie.

Pat Sajak comes close to skunking Alex Trebek in three straight games of racquetball. In the health club's locker room Trebek experiments with a half-Windsor and congratulates Sajak on the contract renewal and iterates hopes for no hard feeling re that Applause-sign gag, still. Sajak says he's forgotten all about it, and calls Trebek big fella; and there's some towel-snapping and general camaraderie.

"I need you to articulate for me the dynamics of this connection between Faye Goddard and Julie Smith," Merv Griffin tells his shiny executive. His man stands at the office window, watching cars move by on the Hollywood Freeway, in the sun. The cars glitter.

"You and your mother happen to go to the movies," Faye says. She and Julie stand wiping themselves in the shade of a leather shop's awning. "You're a child. The movie is *Son of Flubber,* from Disney. It lasts pretty much the whole afternoon." She gathers her hair at the back of her neck and lifts it. "After the movie's over and you and your mother are outside, on the sidewalk, in the light, your mother breaks down. She has to be restrained by the ticket man, she's so hysterical. She tears at her beautiful hair that you've always admired and wished you could have had too. She's totally hysterical. It turns out a man in the theater behind you was playing with your mother's hair all through the movie. He was touching her hair in a sexual way. She was horrified and repulsed, but didn't make a sound, the whole time, I guess for fear that you, the child, would discover that a strange man in the dark was touching your mother in a sexual way. She breaks down on the sidewalk. Her husband has to come. She spends a year on antidepressants. Then she drinks.

"Years later her husband, your stepfather, leaves her for a woman. The woman has the same background, career interests, and general sort of appearance as your mother. Your mother gets obsessed with whatever slight differences between herself and the woman caused your stepfather to leave her for the woman. She drinks. The woman plays off her emotions, like the insecure and basically shitty human being she is, by dressing as much like your mother as possible, putting little mementos of your stepfather in your mother's In-box, coloring her hair the same shade of red as your mother does. You all work together in the same tiny but terrifyingly

powerful industry. It's a tiny and sordid and claustrophobic little community, where no one can get away from the nests they've fouled. You reel
into confusion. You meet this very unique and funny and sad and one-of-
a-kind person."

"The rain in Spain," director Janet Goddard says to a huge adolescent boy
so plump and pale and vacant he looks like a snowman. "I need you to say
'The rain in Spain' without having your head under your arm.

"Pretend it's a game," she says.

It's true that, the evening before Julie Smith's brother will beat Julie Smith
on her seven-hundred-and-forty-first "JEOPARDY!" slot, Faye tells Julie
about what Merv Griffin's man and the director have done. The two
women stand clothed at Faye's glass wall and watch distant mountains
become Hershey kisses in an expanding system of shadow.

Faye tells Julie that it's because the folks over at MGE have such respect
and admiration for Julie that they want to exercise careful control over the
choice of who replaces her. That to MGE Julie is the mystery of the game
show incarnate, and that the staff is understandably willing to do pretty
much anything at all in the hopes of hanging on to that power of mystery
and incarnation through the inevitability of change, loss. Then she says
that that was all just the shiny executive's bullshit, what she just said.

Julie asks Faye why Faye has not told her before now what is going to
happen.

Faye asks Julie why Julie sends all her sheltered winnings to her brother's doctors, but will not talk to her brother.

Julie isn't the one who cries.

Julie asks whether there will be animal questions tomorrow.

There will be lots and lots of animal questions tomorrow. The director
has personally compiled tomorrow's categories and answers. Faye's been
temporarily assigned to help the key grip try to repair a defectively lit *E* in
the set's giant "JEOPARDY!" logo.

Faye asks why Julie likes to make up pretend reasons for being a lesbian.
She thinks Julie is really a lesbian because she hates animals, somehow.
Faye says she does not understand this. She cries, at the glass wall.

Julie lays her hands flat on the clean glass.

Faye asks Julie whether Julie's brother can beat her.

Julie says that there is no way her brother can beat her, and that deep
down in the silence of himself her brother knows it. Julie says that she will
always know every fact her brother knows, plus one.

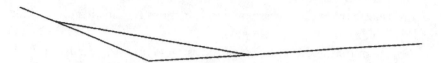

Through the window of the Makeup Room Faye can see a gray paste of clouds moving back over the sun. There are tiny flecks of rain on the little window.

Faye tells the makeup lady she'll take over. Julie's in the makeup chair, in a spring blouse and faded cotton skirt, and sandals. Her legs are crossed, her hair spiked with mousse. Her eyes, calm and bright and not at all bored, are fixed on a point just below her own chin in the lit mirror. A very small kind smile for Faye.

"You're late I love you," Faye whispers.

She applies base.

"Here's one," Julie says.

Faye blends the border of the base into the soft hollows under Julie's jaw.

"Here's one," says Julie. "To hold in reserve. For when you're really on the spot. They'll eat it up."

"You're not going to get bumped. He's too terrified to stand up, even. I had to step over him on the way down here."

Julie shakes her head. "Tell them you were eight. Your brother was silent and five. Tell them your mother's face hung tired from her head, that first men and then she herself made her ugly. That her face just hung there with love for a blank silent man who left you touching wood forever by the side of the road. Tell them how you were left by your mother by a field of dry grass. Tell them the field and the sky and the highway were the color of old laundry. Tell them you touched a post all day, your hand and a broken baby's bright-white hand, waiting for what had always come back, every single time, before."

Faye applies powder.

"Tell them there was a cow." Julie swallows. "It was in the field, near where you held the fence. Tell them the cow stood there all day, chewing at something it had swallowed long ago, and looking at you. Tell them how the cow's face had no expression on it. How it stood there all day, looking at you with a big face that had no expression." Julie breathes. "How it almost made you need to scream. The wind sounds like screams. Stand there touching wood all day with a baby who is silence embodied. Who can, you know, stand there forever, waiting for the only car it knows, and not once have to understand. A cow watches you, standing, the same way it watches anything."

A towelette takes the excess powder. Julie blots her lipstick on the blotter Faye holds out.

"Tell them that, even now, you cannot stand animals, because animals' faces have no expression. Not even the possibility of it. Tell them to look, really to look, into the face of an animal, sometime."

Faye runs a gentle pick through Julie's moist spiked hair.

Julie looks at Faye in a mirror bordered with bulbs. "Then tell them to look closely at men's faces. Tell them to stand perfectly still, for time, and to look into the face of a man. A man's face has nothing on it. Look closely. Tell them to look. And not at what the faces do—men's faces never stop moving—they're like antennae. But all the faces do is move through different configurations of blankness."

Faye looks for Julie's eyes in the mirror.

Julie says, "Tell them there are no holes for your fingers in the masks of men. Tell them how could you ever even hope to love what you can't grab onto."

Julie turns her makeup chair and looks up at Faye. "That's when I love you, if I love you," she whispers, running a finger down her white powdered cheek, reaching to trace an angled line of white onto Faye's own face. "Is when your face moves into expression. Try to look out from yourself, different, all the time. Tell people that you know your face is least pretty at rest."

She keeps her fingers on Faye's face. Faye closes her eyes against tears. When she opens them Julie is still looking at her. She's smiling a wonderful smile. Way past twenty. She takes Faye's hands.

"You asked me once how poems informed me," she says. Almost a whisper—her microphone voice. "And you asked whether we, us, depended on the game, to even be. Baby?"—lifting Faye's face with one finger under the chin—"Remember? Remember the ocean? Our dawn ocean, that we loved? We loved it because it was like us, Faye. That ocean was *obvious*. We were looking at something obvious, the whole time." She pinches a nipple, too softly for Faye even to feel. "Oceans are only oceans when they move," Julie whispers. "Waves are what keep oceans from just being very big puddles. Oceans are just their waves. And every wave in the ocean is finally going to meet what it moves toward, and break. The whole thing we looked at, the whole time you asked, was obvious. It was obvious and a poem because it was us. See things like that, Faye. Your own face, moving into expression. A wave, breaking on a rock, giving up its shape in a gesture that *expresses* that shape. See?"

It wasn't at the beach that Faye had asked about the future. It was in

Los Angeles. And what about the anomalous wave that came out of nowhere and broke on itself?

Julie is looking at Faye. "See?"

Faye's eyes are open. They get wide. "You don't like my face at rest?"

The set is powder-blue. The giant "JEOPARDY!" logo is lowered. Its *E* flickers a palsied fluorescent flicker. Julie turns her head from the sick letter. Alex has a flower in his lapel. The three contestants' names appear in projected cursive before their desks. Alex blows Julie the traditional kiss. Pat Sajak gives Faye a thumbs-up from stage-opposite. He gestures. Faye looks around the curtain and sees a banana peel on the pale blue carpet, carefully placed in the tape-marked path Alex takes every day from his lectern to the board full of answers. Dee Goddard and Muffy deMott and Merv Griffin's shiny man hunch over monitors in the director's booth. Janet Goddard arranges a shot of a pale round boy who dwarfs his little desk. The third contestant, in the middle, feels at his makeup a little. Faye smells powder. She watches Sajak rub his hands together. The red lights light. Alex raises his arms in greeting. There is no digital watch on his wrist.

The director, in her booth, with her headset, says something to camera two.

Julie and the audience look at each other.

Afterword

The word *expression* is dulled from overuse. This is the story in which twenty-five-year-old Wallace sharpens it up and cuts into a topic to which he'll always return: the difficulty, the near impossibility—as he sees it—of interpersonal connection. What does it mean to be expressionless? To wear a mask. What would it take to worm that mask off its wearer—your lover, your parent, your sibling, your friend?

If being expressionless is the result of trauma, as it is in this story, then self-expression must be healthy. But somehow, in the cities of the developed world, expressing yourself has started to feel like work. We're constantly exhorted toward ever-greater feats of affect; to be that little bit more creative; to commit to our goals; to give service with a smile, feigning excitement like contestants on a game show. When life takes on this game-show quality—fake, regimented, spiritually exhausted—expressivity pulls in two directions, both toward and away from truthfulness. It can be another kind of mask, the kind that eats away at the face until you're no longer sure what your off-camera reaction would be. Few writers would turn to *Jeopardy!* for clues to the human condition, but Wallace is always interested in Waste Lands of one kind or another. He looks in the most debased places, those apparently most empty of redemptive possibility. He is, after all, a writer who set a novel in a tax office.

The conference room banter of his television hosts and executives is pitch-perfect. Wallace brings his usual fierce intellectual attack and an ear that sometimes seems almost supernatural in such a young writer. Yes, we think. This is how Alex Trebek and Pat Sajak and Bert Convy really talk when they're watching the World Series in the "Merv Griffin Entertainment executive lounge." It doesn't matter if it's true. It doesn't matter if no such lounge exists, though one suspects (probably wrongly) that Wallace sourced floor plans and wallpaper samples, and knew the exact contents of the liquor cabinet. The vast cynicism of corporate decision-making serves as a backdrop for star-crossed lovers cautiously exploring the possibility of a sincere relationship, trying to be real in a world that doesn't value reality. And of course it features a central character whose childhood best friend was the encyclopedia, perhaps an avatar of Wallace himself: the postmodernist yearning for sincerity, daring his reader to unmask.

—Hari Kunzru

My Appearance

I AM A WOMAN who appeared in public on "Late Night with David Letterman" on March 22, 1989.

In the words of my husband Rudy, I am a woman whose face and attitudes are known to something over half of the measurable population of the United States, whose name is on lips and covers and screens. And whose heart's heart is invisible, and unapproachably hidden. Which is what Rudy thought could save me from all this appearance implied.

The week that surrounded March 22, 1989 was also the week David Letterman's variety-and-talk show featured a series of videotaped skits on the private activities and pastimes of executives at NBC. My husband, whose name is better known inside the entertainment industry than out of it, was anxious: he knew and feared Letterman; he claimed to know for a fact that Letterman loved to savage female guests, that he was a misogynist. It was on Sunday that he told me he felt he and Ron and Ron's wife Charmian ought to prepare me to handle and be handled by Letterman. March 22 was to be Wednesday.

On Monday, viewers accompanied David Letterman as he went deep-sea fishing with the president of NBC's News Division. The executive, whom my husband had met and who had a pappus of hair sprouting from each red ear, owned a state-of-the-art boat and rod and reel, and apparently deep-sea fished without hooks. He and Letterman fastened bait to their lines with rubber bands.

"He's waiting for the poor old bastard to even think about saying holy mackerel," Rudy grimaced, smoking.

On Tuesday, Letterman perused NBC's chief of Creative Development's huge collection of refrigerator magnets. He said:

"Is this entertainment ladies and gentlemen? Or what?"

I had the bitterness of a Xanax on my tongue.

We had Ramon haul out some videotapes of old "Late Night" editions, and watched them.

"How do you feel?" my husband asked me.

In slow motion, Letterman let drop from a rooftop twenty floors above a cement lot several bottles of champagne, some plump fruit, a plate-glass window, and what looked, for only a moment, like a live piglet.

"The hokeyness of the whole thing is vital," Rudy said as Letterman dropped a squealing piglet off what was obviously only a pretend rooftop in the studio; we saw something fall a long way from the original roof to hit cement and reveal itself to be a stuffed piglet. "But that doesn't make him benign." My husband got a glimpse of his image in our screening room's black window and rearranged himself. "I don't want you to think the hokeyness is real."

"I thought hokeyness was pretty much understood not to be real," I said.

He directed me to the screen, where Paul Shaffer, David Letterman's musical sidekick and friend, was doing a go-figure with his shoulders and his hands.

We had both taken Xanaxes before having Ramon set up the video-tapes. I also had a glass of chablis. I was very tired by the time the refriger-ator magnets were perused and discussed. My husband was also tired, but he was becoming increasingly concerned that this particular appearance could present problems. That it could be serious.

The call had come from New York the Friday before. The caller had con-gratulated me on my police drama being picked up for its fifth season, and asked whether I'd like to be a guest on the next week's "Late Night with David Letterman," saying Mr. Letterman would be terribly pleased to have me on. I tentatively agreed. I have few illusions left, but I'm darn proud of our show's success. I have a good character, work hard, play her well, and practically adore the other actors and people associated with the series. I called my agent, my unit director, and my husband. I agreed to accept an appearance on Wednesday, March 22. That was the only inter-val Rudy and I had free in a weekly schedule that denied me even two days to rub together: my own series tapes Fridays, with required read-throughs and a Full Dress the day before. Even the 22nd, my husband pointed out over drinks, would mean leaving L.A.X. very early Wednesday morning, since I was contracted to appear in a wiener commercial through Tuesday. My agent had thought he could reschedule the wiener shoot—the people at Oscar Mayer had been very accommodating throughout the whole campaign—but my husband had a rule for himself about honoring contracted obligations, and as his partner I chose also to try to live according to this rule. It meant staying up terribly late Tuesday to watch David Letterman and the piglet and refrigerator magnets and an unending succession of eccentrically talented pets, then catching a predawn flight the next morning: though "Late Night"'s taping didn't begin until 5:30 E.S.T., Rudy had gone to great trouble to arrange a lengthy strategy session with Ron beforehand.

Before I fell asleep Tuesday night, David Letterman had Teri Garr put on a Velcro suit and fling herself at a Velcro wall. That night his NBC Bookmobile featured a *1989 Buyer's Guide to New York City Officials;* Letterman held the book up to view while Teri hung behind him, stuck to the wall several feet off the ground.

"That could be you," my husband said, ringing the kitchen for a glass of milk.

The show seemed to have a fetish about arranging things in lists of ten. We saw what the "Late Night" research staff considered the ten worst television commercials ever. I can remember number five or four: a German automobile manufacturer tried to link purchase of its box-shaped car to sexual satisfaction by showing, against a background of woodwinds and pines, a languid Nordic woman succumbing to the charms of the car's stickshift.

"Well I'm certainly swayed," Letterman said when the clip had ended. "Aren't you, ladies and gentlemen?"

He offered up a false promo for a cultural program PBS had supposedly decided against inserting into next fall's lineup. The promo was an understated clip of four turbaned Kurdistani rebels, draped in small-arms gear, taking time out from revolution to perform a Handel quartet in a meadow full of purple flowers. The bud of culture flourishing even in the craggiest soil, was the come-on. Letterman cleared his throat and claimed that PBS had finally submitted to conservative PTA pressure against the promo. Paul Shaffer, to a drum roll, asked why this was so. Letterman grinned with an embarrassment Rudy and I both found attractive. There were, again, ten answers. Two I remember were Gratuitous Sikhs and Violets, and Gratuitous Sects and Violins. Everyone hissed with joy. Even Rudy laughed, though he knew no such program had ever been commissioned by PBS. I laughed sleepily and shifted against his arm, which was out along the back of the couch.

David Letterman also said, at various intervals, "Some fun now, boy." Everyone laughed. I can remember not thinking there was anything especially threatening about Letterman, though the idea of having to be peeled off a wall upset me.

Nor did I care one bit for the way the airplane's ready, slanted shadow rushed up the runway to join us as we touched down. By this time I was quite upset. I even jumped and said *Oh* as the plane's front settled into its shadow on the landing. I broke into tears, though not terribly. I am a woman who simply cries when she's upset; it does not embarrass me. I was exhausted and tense. My husband touched my hair. He argued that I shouldn't have a Xanax, though, and I agreed.

"You'll need to be sharp," was the reason. He took my arm.

The NBC driver had put our bags far behind us; I heard the trunk's solid sound.

"You'll need to be both sharp and prepared," my husband said. He judged that I was tense enough to want simply to agree; Rudy did know human nature.

But I was irritable by now. Part of my tension about appearing knew where it came from. "Just how much preparation am I supposed to need?" I said. Charmian and I had already conferred long-distance about my appearance. She'd advised solidity and simplicity. I would be seen in a plain blue outfit, no jewelry. My hair would be down.

Rudy's concerns were very different. He claimed to fear for me.

"I don't see this dark fearful thing you seem to see in David Letterman," I told him. "The man has freckles. He used to be a local weatherman. He's witty. But so am *I*, Rudy." I did want a Xanax. "We both know me. I'm an actress who's now forty and has four kids, you're my second husband, you've made a successful career change, I've had three dramatic series, the last two have been successful, I have an Emmy nomination, I'm probably never going to have a feature-film career or be recognized seriously for my work as an actress." I turned in the back seat to look at him. "So so *what?* All of this is known. It's all way out in the open already. I honestly don't see what about me or us is savageable."

My husband ran his arm, which was well-built, out along the back seat's top behind us. The limousine smelled like a fine purse; its interior was red leather and buttery soft. It felt almost wet. "He'll give you a huge amount of grief about the wiener thing."

"Let him," I said.

As we were driven up through a borough and extreme southeast Manhattan, my husband became anxious that the NBC driver, who was young and darkly Hispanic, might be able to hear what we were saying to one another, even though there was a thick glass panel between us in back and the driver up front, and an intercom in the panel had to be activated to communicate with him. My husband felt at the glass and at the intercom's grille. The driver's head was motionless except to check traffic in mirrors. The radio was on for our enjoyment; classical music drifted through the intercom.

"He can't hear us," I said.

"...if this were somehow taped and played back on the air while you looked on in horror?" my husband muttered as he satisfied himself about the intercom. "Letterman would eat it up. We'd look like absolute idiots."

"Why do you insist that he's mean? He doesn't seem mean."

Rudy tried to settle back as serious Manhattan began to go by. "This is the man, Edilyn, who publicly asked Christie Brinkley what state the Kentucky Derby is run in."

I remembered what Charmian had said on the phone and smiled.

"But was she or wasn't she unable to answer correctly?"

My husband smiled, too. "Well she was *flustered*," he said. He touched my cheek, and I his hand. I began to feel less jittery.

He used his hand and my cheek to open my face toward his. "Edilyn," he said, "meanness is not the issue. The issue is *ridiculousness*. The bastard feeds off ridiculousness like some enormous Howdy-Doodyesque parasite. The whole show feeds on it; it swells and grows when things get absurd. Letterman starts to look gorged, dark, shiny. Ask Teri about the Velcro. Ask Lindsay about that doctored clip of him and the Pope. Ask Nigel or Charmian or Ron. You've heard them. Ron could tell you stories that'd curl your toes."

I had a compact in my purse. My skin was sore and hot from on-air makeup for two straight days. "He's likeable, though," I said. "Letterman. When we watched, it looked to me as though he likes to make himself look ridiculous as much as he does the guests. So he's not a hypocrite."

We were in a small gridlock. A disheveled person was trying to clean the limousine's windshield with his sleeve. Rudy tapped on the glass panel until the driver activated the intercom. He said we wished to be driven directly to Rockefeller Center, where "Late Night" taped, instead of going first to our hotel. The driver neither nodded nor turned.

"That's part of what makes him so dangerous," my husband said, lifting his glasses to massage the bridge of his nose. "The whole thing feeds off *everybody's* ridiculousness. It's the way the audience can tell he *chooses* to ridicule himself that exempts the clever bastard from real ridicule." The young driver blew his horn; the vagrant fell away.

We were driven west and slightly uptown; from this distance I could see the building where Letterman taped and where Ron worked in an office on the sixtieth floor. Ron used to be professionally associated with my husband before Rudy made the decision to go over to Public Television. We were all still friends.

"It will be on how your ridiculousness is *seen* that whether you stand or fall depends," Rudy said, leaning into my compact's view to square the knot of his tie.

Less and less of Rockefeller's skyscraper was visible as we approached. I asked for half a Xanax. I am a woman who dislikes being confused; it upsets me. I wanted after all, to be both sharp and relaxed.

"Appear," my husband corrected, "both sharp and relaxed."

"You will be made to look ridiculous," Ron said. He and my husband sat together on a couch in an office so high in the building my ears felt as they'd felt at take-off. I faced Ron from a mutely expensive chair of canvas stretched over steel. "That's not in your control," Ron said. "How you respond, though, is."

"Is what?"

"In your control," Ron said, raising his glass to his little mouth.

"If he wants to make me look silly I guess he's welcome to try," I said. "I guess."

Rudy swirled the contents of his own glass. His ice tinkled. "That's just the attitude I've been trying to cultivate in her," he said to Ron. "She thinks he's really like what she sees."

The two of them smiled, shaking their heads.

"Well he isn't really like that, of course," Ron told me. Ron has maybe the smallest mouth I have ever seen on a human face, though my husband and I have known him for years, and Charmian, and they've been dear friends. His mouth is utterly lipless and its corners are sharp; the mouth seems less a mouth than a kind of gash in his head. "Because no one's like that," he said. "That's what he sees as his great insight. That's why everything on the show is just there to be ridiculed." He smiled. "But that's our edge, that we know that, Edilyn. If you know in advance that you're going to be made to look ridiculous, then you're one step ahead of the game, because then you can make *yourself* look ridiculous, instead of letting *him* do it to you."

Ron I thought I could at least understand. "I'm supposed to make myself look ridiculous?"

My husband lit a cigarette. He crossed his legs and looked at Ron's white cat. "The big thing here is whether we let Letterman make fun of you on national television or whether you beat him to the punch and join in the fun and do it yourself." He looked at Ron as Ron stood. "By *choice*,"

Rudy said. "It's on that issue that we'll stand or fall." He exhaled. The couch was in a patch of sunlight. The light, this high, seemed bright and cold. His cigarette hissed, gushing smoke into the lit air.

Ron was known even then for his tendency to fidget. He would stand and sit and stand. "That's good advice, Rudolph. There are definite do's and don't's. Don't look like you're trying to be witty or clever. That works with Carson. It doesn't work with Letterman."

I smiled tiredly at Rudy. The long cigarette seemed almost to be *bleeding* smoke, the sunlight on the couch was so bright.

"Carson would play along with you," Rudy nodded. "Carson's *sincere*."

"Sincerity is out," Ron said. "The joke is now *on* people who're sincere."

"Or who are sincere-seeming, who think they're sincere, Letterman would say," my husband said.

"That's well put," Ron said, looking me closely up and down. His mouth was small and his head large and round, his knee up, elbow on his knee, his foot on the arm of another thin steel chair, his cat swirling a lazy figure-eight around the foot on the floor. "That's the cardinal sin on 'Late Night.' That's the Adidas heel of every guest that he mangles." He drank. "Just be aware of it."

"I think that's it: I think being seen as being *aware* is the big thing, here," my husband said, spitting a sliver of drink-ice into his hand. Ron's cat approached and sniffed at the bit of ice. The heat of my husband's proffering fingers was turning the sliver to water as I looked at my husband blankly. The cat sneezed.

I smoothed the blue dress I'd slipped on in Letterman's putty-colored green room. "What I want to know is is he going to make fun of me over the wiener spots," I told Ron. I had become truly worried about at least this. The Mayer people had been a class act throughout the whole negotiations and campaign, and I thought we had made some good honest attractive commercials for a product that didn't claim to be anything more than occasional and fun. I didn't want Oscar Mayer wieners to be made to look ridiculous because of me; I didn't want to be made to look as though I'd prostituted my name and face and talents to a meat company. "I mean, will he go beyond making fun? Will he get savage about it?"

"Not if you do it first!" Rudy and Ron said together, looking at each other. They laughed. It was an in-joke. I laughed. Ron turned and made himself another small drink. I sipped my own. My cola's ice kept hitting my teeth. "That's how to defuse the whole thing," Ron said.

My husband ground out his cigarette. "Savage yourself before he can savage you." He held out his glass to Ron.

"Make sure you're seen as making fun of yourself, but in a self-aware and ironic way." The big bottle gurgled as Ron freshened Rudy's drink.

I asked whether it might be all right if I had just a third of a Xanax.

"In other words, appear the way Letterman appears, on Letterman," Ron gestured as if to sum up, sitting back down. "Laugh in a way that's somehow deadpan. Act as if you knew from birth that everything is clichéd and hyped and empty and absurd, and that that's *just* where the fun is."

"But that's not the way I am at all."

The cat yawned.

"That's not even the way I act when I'm acting," I said.

"Yes," Ron said, leaning toward me and pouring a very small splash of liquor on my glass's ice cubes, furred with frozen cola.

"Of *course* that's not you," my husband said, lifting his glasses. When tense, he always rubbed at the red dents his frames imposed on his nose. It was a habit. "That's why this is serious. If a you shows its sweet little bottom anywhere near the set of 'Late Night,' it'll get the hell savaged out of it." He tamped down another cigarette, looking at Ron.

"At least she's looking terrific," Ron said, smiling. He felt at his sharp little mouth, his expression betraying what looked to me like tenderness. Toward me? We weren't particularly close. Not like Ron's wife and I. The liquor tasted smoky. I closed my eyes. I was tired, confused and nervous; I was also a bit angry. I looked at the watch I'd gotten for my birthday.

I am a woman who lets her feelings show rather than hide them; it's just healthier that way. I told Ron that when Charmian had called she'd said that David Letterman was a little shy but basically a nice man. I said I felt now as though maybe the *extreme* nervousness I was feeling was my husband's fault, and now maybe Ron's; and that I very much wanted either a Xanax or some constructive, supportive advice that wouldn't demand that I be artificial or empty or on my guard to such an extent that I vacuumed the fun out of what was, when you got right down to it, supposed to be nothing more than a fun interview.

Ron smiled very patiently as he listened. Rudy was dialing a talent coordinator. Ron instructed Rudy to say that I wasn't really needed downstairs for makeup until after 5:30: tonight's monologue was long and involved, and a skit on the pastime of another NBC executive would precede me.

My husband began to discuss the issue of trust, as it related to awareness.

It turned out that an area of one wall of Ron's office could be made to slide automatically back, opening to view several rows of monitors, all of which received NBC feeds. Beneath a local weatherman's set-up and the March

22 broadcast of "Live at Five," the videotaping of "Late Night"'s opening sequence had begun. The announcer, who wore a crewneck sweater, read into an old-fashioned microphone that looked like an electric razor with a halo:

"Ladies and gentlemen!" he said. "A man who is, even as we speak, *checking his fly: DAVID LETTERMAN!*"

There was wild applause; the camera zoomed in on a tight shot of the studio's APPLAUSE sign. On all the monitors appeared the words LATE NIGHT APPLAUSE — SIGN — CAM. The words flashed on and off as the audience cheered. David Letterman appeared out of nowhere in a hideous yachting jacket and wrestling sneakers.

"What a *fine* crowd," he said.

I felt at the fuzz of Pepsi and fine rum on my ice. My finger left a clear stripe in the fuzz. "I *really* don't think this is necessary."

"Trust us, Edi."

"Ron, talk to him," I said.

"Testing," said Ron.

Ron stood near the couch's broad window, which was no longer admitting direct sunlight. The window faced south; I could see rooftops bristling with antennae below, hear the tiny sounds of distant car horns. Ron held a kind of transmitting device, compact enough to fit in his soft palm. My husband had his head cocked and his thumb up as Ron tested the signal. The little earplug in Rudy's ear was originally developed to allow sportscasters to take direction and receive up-to-the-minute information without having to stop talking. My husband had sometimes found it useful in the technical direction of live comedy before he made the decision to leave commercial television. He removed the earplug and cleaned it with his handkerchief.

The earplug, which was supposed to be flesh-colored, was really prosthesis-colored. I told them I emphatically did *not* want to wear a pork-colored earplug and take direction from my husband on not being sincere.

"No," my husband corrected, "being *not-sincere*."

"There's a difference," Ron said, trying to make sense of the transmitter's instructions, which were mostly in Korean.

But I wanted to be both sharp and relaxed, and to get downstairs and have this over with. I did want a Xanax.

And so my husband and I entered into negotiations.

"Thank you," Paul Shaffer told the studio audience. "Thank you so much." I laughed, in the wings, in the long jagged shadows produced by lights at many angles. There was applause for Shaffer. The APPLAUSE sign was again featured on camera.

From this distance Letterman's hair looked something like a helmet, I thought. It seemed thick and very solid. He kept putting index cards in the big gap between his front teeth and fiddling with them. He and the staff quickly presented a list of ten medications, both over-the-counter and 'scrip, that resembled well-known candies in a way Letterman claimed was insidious. He showed slides side by side, for comparison. It was true that Advils looked just like brown M&M's. Motrin, in the right light, were SweetTarts. A brand of MAO inhibitor called Nardil looked just like the tiny round Red Hots we'd all eaten as children.

"Eerie or what?" Letterman asked Paul Shaffer.

And the faddish anti-anxiety medication Xanax was supposed to resemble miniatures of those horrible soft pink-orange candy peanuts that everyone sees everywhere but no one will admit ever to having tasted.

I had gotten a Xanax from my husband, finally. It had been Ron's idea. I touched my ear and tried to drive the earplug deeper, out of sight. I arranged my hair over my ear. I was seriously considering taking the earplug out.

My husband did know human nature. "A deal's a deal" kept coming into my ear.

The florid young aide with me had told me I was to be the second guest on the March 22 edition of "Late Night with David Letterman." Appearing first was to be the executive coordinator of NBC Sports, who was going to be seen sitting in the center of a circle of exploding dynamite, for fun. Also on the bill with me was the self-proclaimed king of kitchen-gadget home sales.

We saw a short veterinary film on dyspepsia in swine.

"Your work has gone largely unnoticed by the critics, then," the video-tape showed Letterman saying to the film's director, a veterinarian from Arkansas who was panicked throughout the interview because, the electric voice in my ear maintained, he didn't know whether to be serious about his life's work with Letterman, or not.

The executive coordinator of NBC Sports apparently fashioned perfect rings of high explosive in his basement workshop, took them into his backyard, and sat inside explosions; it was a hobby. David Letterman asked the NBC executive to please let him get this straight: that somebody who sat in the exact center of a perfect circle of dynamite would be completely safe, encased in a vacuum, a sort of storm's eye — but that if so much as one stick of dynamite in the ring was defective, the explosion could, in theory, kill the executive?

"Kill?" Letterman kept repeating, looking over at Paul Shaffer, laughing.

The Bolsheviks had used the circle ceremoniously to "execute" Russian noblemen they really wanted to spare, the executive said; it was an ancient and time-honored illusion. I thought he looked quite distinguished, and decided that sense played no part in the hobbies of men.

As I waited for my appearance, I imagined the coordinator in his Westchester backyard's perfect center, unhurt but encased as waves of concussed dynamite whirled around him. I imagined something tornadic, colored pink—since the dynamite piled on-stage was pink.

But the real live explosion was gray. It was disappointingly quick, and sounded flat, though I laughed when Letterman pretended that they hadn't gotten the explosion properly taped and that the executive coordinator of NBC Sports, who looked as though he'd been given a kind of cosmic slap, was going to have to do the whole thing over again. For a moment the coordinator thought Letterman was serious.

"See," Ron had said as it became time for me to be made up, "there's no way he *can* be serious, Edilyn. He's a millionaire who wears wrestling sneakers."

"One watches him," my husband said, bent to check the fit of the cold pink plug in my ear, "and one envisions a whole nation, watching, nudging each other in the ribs."

"Just get in there and nudge," Ron said encouragingly. I looked at his mouth and head and cat. "Forget all the rules you've ever learned about appearing on talk shows. This kid's turned it inside out. Those rules of television humor are what he makes the most fun of." His eyes went a bit cold. "He's making money ridiculing the exact things that have put him in a position to make money ridiculing things."

"Well, there's been a kind of parricidal mood toward rules in the industry for quite some time," my husband said as we waited for the elevator's ascent. "He sure as hell didn't invent it." Ron lit his cigarette for him, smiling sympathetically. We both knew what Rudy was talking about. The Xanax was beginning to take effect, and I felt good. I felt psyched up to appear.

"You could say it's like what happened over at 'Saturday Night Live,' " Ron said. "It's the exact same phenomena. The cheap sets that are supposed to look even cheaper than they are. The home-movie mugging for the cameras, the backyard props like Monkey-Cam or Thrill-Cam or coneheads of low-grade mâché. 'Late Night,' 'SNL'—they're *anti*-shows."

We were at the back of the large silent elevator. It seemed not to be moving. It seemed like a room unto itself. Rudy had pressed 6. Both my ears were crackling. Ron was speaking slowly, as if I couldn't possibly understand.

"But even if something's an anti-show, if it's a hit, it's a *show*," Ron said. He got his cat to lift its head, and scratched its throat.

"So just imagine the strain the son of a bitch is under," my husband muttered.

Ron smiled coolly, not looking at Rudy.

My husband's brand of cigarette is a foreign sort that lets everyone know that something is on fire. The thing hissed and popped and gushed as he inhaled, looking steadily at his old superior. Ron looked at me.

"Remember how 'SNL' had those great parodies of commercials right after the show's opening, Edilyn? Such great parodies that it always took you a while to even realize they were parodies and not commercials? And how the anti-commercials were a hit? So *then* what happened?" Ron asked me. I said nothing. Ron liked to ask questions and then answer them. We arrived on Letterman's floor. Rudy and I got out behind him.

"What happened," he said over his shoulder, "is that the sponsors started putting commercials on 'SNL' that were almost like the *parodies* of the commercials, so that it took you a while to realize that these were even real commercials in the first place. So the sponsors were suddenly guaranteed huge audiences that watched their commercials very, very closely—hoping, of course, that they'd be parodies." Secretaries and interns rose to attention as Ron passed with us; his cat yawned and stretched in his arms.

"*But*," Ron laughed, still not looking at my husband, "But instead, the sponsors had turned the anti-commercials' joke around on 'SNL' and were *using* it, using the joke to manipulate the very same audience the parodies had made fun of them for manipulating in the first place."

Studio 6-A's stage doors were at the end of a carpeted hall, next to a huge poster that showed David Letterman taking a picture of whoever was taking his picture for the poster.

"So really being a certain way or not isn't a question that can come up, on shows like this," Rudy said, tapping an ash, not looking at Ron.

"Were those great days or what?" Ron whispered into the ear of the cat he nuzzled.

The locked studio doors muffled the sounds of much merriment. Ron entered a code on a lit panel by the Letterman poster. He and Rudy were going back upstairs to watch from Ron's office, where the wall of monitors would afford them several views of me at once.

"You'll just have to act, is all," my husband said, brushing the hair back from my ear. He touched my cheek. "You're a talented and multifaceted actress."

And Ron, manipulating the cat's white paw in a pretend goodbye, said, "And she *is* an actress, Rudolph. With you helping her we'll help you turn this thing just the right way."

"And she appreciates it, sir. More than she knows right now."

"So I'm to be a sort of anti-guest?" I said.

"*Terribly* nice to see you," is what David Letterman said to me. I had followed my introduction on-stage; the sweatered attendant conducted me by the elbow and peeled neatly away as I hit the lights.

"Terribly, nay, *grotesquely* nice to see you," Letterman said.

"He's scanning for pretensions," crackled my ear. "Pockets of naïve self-importance. Something to stick a pin in. Anything."

"Yas," I drawled to David Letterman. I yawned, touching my ear absently.

Close up, he looked depressingly young. At most thirty-five. He congratulated me on the series' renewal, the Emmy nomination, and said my network had handled my unexpected pregnancy well on the show's third year, arranging to have me seen only behind waist-high visual impediments for thirteen straight episodes.

"That was fun," I said sarcastically. I laughed drily.

"Big, *big* fun," Letterman said, and the audience laughed.

"Oh Jesus God let him see you're being sarcastic and dry," my husband said.

Paul Shaffer did a go-figure with his hands in response to something Letterman asked him.

David Letterman had a tiny label affixed to his cheek (he did have freckles); the label said MAKEUP. This was left over from an earlier joke, during his long monologue, when Letterman had returned from a commercial air-break with absolutely everything about him labeled. The sputtering fountain between us and the footlights was overhung with a crudely lettered arrow: DANCING WATERS.

"So then Edilyn any truth to the rumors linking that crazy thing over at your husband's network and the sort of secondary rumors...." He looked from his index card to Paul Shaffer. "Gee you know Paul it says 'secondary rumors' here; is it OK to go ahead and call them secondary rumors? What does that mean, anyway, Paul: 'secondary rumors'?"

"We in the band believe it could mean any of... really any of hundreds of things, Dave," Shaffer said, smiling. I smiled. People laughed.

The voice of Ron came over the air in my ear: "Say *no*." I imagined a wall of angles of me, the wound in Ron's head and the transmitting thing at the wound, my husband seated with his legs crossed and his arm out along the back of wherever he was.

"... secondary or not, about you and Tito's fine, fine program perhaps, ah, leaving commercial television altogether at the end of next season and maybe moving over to that other, unnamed, uncommercial network?"

I cleared my throat. "Absolutely every rumor about my husband is true." The audience laughed.

Letterman said, "Ha *ha*." The audience laughed even harder.

"As for me," I smoothed my skirt in that way prim women do, "I know next to nothing, David, about the production or business sides of the show. I am a woman who *acts*."

"And, you know, wouldn't that look terrific emblazoned on the T-shirts of women everywhere?" Letterman asked, fingering his tiepin's label.

"And was it ever a crazy thing over at his network, Dave, from what I heard," said Reese, the NBC Sports coordinator, on my other side, in another of these chairs that seemed somehow disemboweled. Around Reese's distinguished eyes were two little raccoon-rings of soot, from his hobby's explosion. He looked to Letterman. "A power struggle in public TV?"

"Kind of like a... a bloody *coup* taking place in the League of Women Voters, wouldn't you say, Edilyn?"

I laughed.

"Riot squads and water-cannon moving in on a faculty tea."

Letterman and Reese and Shaffer and I were falling about the place. The audience was laughing.

"Polysyllables must just be *flying*," I said.

"Really... really *grammatically correct* back-stabbing going on all over...."

We all tried to pull ourselves together as my husband gave me some direction.

"The point is I'm afraid I just don't know," I said, as Letterman and Shaffer were still laughing and exchanging looks. "In fact," I said, "I'm not even all that aware or talented or multifaceted an actress."

David Letterman was inviting the audience, whom he again called ladies and gentlemen (which I liked) to imagine I AM A WOMAN WHO *ACTS* emblazoned on a shirt.

"That's why I'm doing those commercials you're seeing all the time now," I said lightly, yawning.

"Well, and now hey, I wanted to ask you about that, Edilyn," Letterman said. "The problem, ah, is that"—he rubbed his chin—"I'll need to ask you what they're commercials *for* without anyone of course mentioning the fine...fine and may I say delicious?"

"Please do."

"Delicious product by name." He smiled. "Since that would be a commercial itself right there."

I nodded, smiled. My earplug was silent. I looked around the stage innocently, pretending to stretch, whistling a very famous jingle's first twelve-note bar.

Letterman and the audience laughed. Paul Shaffer laughed. My husband's electric voice crackled approvingly. I could also hear Ron laughing in the background; his laugh did sound deadpan.

"I think that probably gives us a good clear picture, yes," Letterman grinned. He threw his index card at a pretend window behind us. There was an obviously false sound of breaking glass.

The man seemed utterly friendly.

My husband transmitted something I couldn't make out because Letterman had put his hands behind his head with its helmet of hair and was saying "So then I guess *why,* is the thing, Edilyn. I mean we *know* about the dollars, the big, *big* dollars over there in, ah, prime time. They scribble vague hints, *allusions,* really, is all, they're such big dollars, about prime-time salaries in the washrooms here at NBC. They're amounts that get discussed only in low tones. Here you are," he said, "you've had, what, three quality television series? *Countless* guest-appearances on other programs...?"

"A hundred and eight," I said.

He looked aggrieved at the camera a moment as the audience laughed. "...Virtually *countless* guest-credits," he said. "You've got a critically acclaimed police drama that's been on now, what, three years? four years? You've got this..." he looked at an index card "...talented daughter who's done several fine films and who's currently in a series, you've got a husband who's a mover and a shaker, basically a legend in comedy development...."

"Remember 'Laugh-In'?" said the NBC Sports coordinator. "'Flip Wilson'? 'The Smothers'? Remember 'Saturday Night Live' back when it was good, for a few years there?" He was shaking his head in admiration.

Letterman released his own head. "So series, daughter's series, Emmy nomination, husband's virtually countless movings and shakings and former series, one of the best marriages in the industry if not the Northern, ah, Hemisphere..." He counted these assets off on his hands. His hands were utterly average. "You're *loaded*, sweetie," he said. "If I may." He smiled and played with his coffee mug. I smiled back.

"So then Edilyn a nation is wondering what's the deal with going off and doing these... *wiener* commercials," he asked in a kind of near-whine that he immediately exaggerated into a whine.

Rudy's small voice came: "See how he exaggerated the whine the minute he saw how—?"

"Because I'm not a great actress, David," I said.

Letterman looked stricken. For a moment in the angled white lights I looked at him and he looked stricken for me. I was positive I was dealing with a basically sincere man.

"Those things you listed," I said, "are assets, is all they are." I looked at him. "They're my assets, David, they're not me. I'm an actress in commercial television. Why not act in television commercials?"

"Be honest," Rudy hissed, his voice slight and metallic as a low-quality phone. Letterman was pretending to sip coffee from an empty mug.

"Let's be honest," I said. The audience was quiet. "I just had a very traumatic birthday, and I've been shedding illusions right and left. You're now looking at a woman with no illusions, David."

Letterman seemed to perk up at this. He cleared his throat. My earplug hissed a direction *never* to use the word "illusions."

"That's sort of a funny coincidental thing," Letterman was saying speculatively. "I'm an illusion with no *women*; say do you... detect a sort of parallel, there, Paul?"

I laughed with the audience as Paul Shaffer did a go-figure from the bandstand.

"Doom," my husband transmitted from the office of a man whose subordinates fished without hooks and sat in exploding circles. I patted at the hair over my ear.

I said, "I'm *forty*, David. I turned forty just last week. I'm at the point now where I think I have to know what I am." I looked at him. "I have four kids. Do you know of many working commercial-television actresses with four kids?"

"There are actresses who have four kids," Letterman said. "Didn't we have a lovely and talented young lady with four kids on, recently, Paul?"

"Name ten actresses with four kids," Shaffer challenged.

Letterman did a pretend double-take at him. *"Ten?"*

"Meredith Baxter Birney?" Reese said.

"Meredith Baxter Birney," Letterman nodded. "And Loretta Swit has four kids, doesn't she, Paul?"

"Marion Ross?"

"I think Meredith Baxter Birney actually has *five* kids, in fact, Dave," said Paul Shaffer, leaning over his little organ's microphone. His large bald spot had a label on it that said BALD SPOT.

"I guess the point, gentlemen"—I interrupted them, smiling—"is that I've got kids who're already bigger stars than I. I've appeared in two feature films, total, in my whole career. Now that I'm forty, I'm realizing that with two films, but three pretty long series, my mark on this planet is probably not going to be made in features. David, I'm a television actress."

"You're a *woman who acts* in television," Letterman corrected, smiling.

"And now a woman in television commercials, too." I shrugged as if I just couldn't see what the big deal was.

Paul Shaffer, still leaning over his organ, played a small but very sweet happy-birthday tune for me.

Letterman had put another card between his teeth. "So what I think we're hearing you saying, then, is that you didn't think the wiener-commercial thing would hurt your career, is the explanation."

"Oh no, God, no, not at all," I laughed. "I didn't mean that at *all*. I mean this *is* my career, right? Isn't that what we were just talking about?"

Letterman rubbed his chin. He looked at the Sports coordinator. "So then fears such as...say maybe something like compromising your integrity, some, ah, art factor: not a factor in this decision, is what you're saying."

Ron was asking Rudy to let him have the remote transmitter a moment.

"But there *were* art factors," I said. "Ever try to emote with meat, David?" I looked around. "Any of you? To dispense mustard like you *mean* it?"

Letterman looked uncomfortable. The audience made odd occasional sounds: they couldn't tell whether to laugh. Ron was beginning to transmit to me in a very calm tone.

"To still look famished on the fifteenth frank?" I said as Letterman smiled and sipped at his mug. I shrugged. "Art all over the place in those commercials, David."

I barely heard Ron's little voice warning me to be aware of the danger of appearing at all defensive. For Letterman appeared suddenly diffident, reluctant about something. He looked stage-left, then at his index card, then at me. "It's just Edilyn I guess a cynic, such as maybe Paul over there"—Shaffer laughed—"might be tempted to ask you...I mean," he said, "with all those assets we just listed together, with you being quote unquote, ah, loaded...and now this is just something someone like Paul gets curious about, certainly not our business," he felt uncomfortably at his collar; "this question then with all due respect of how *any* amount of money, even vast amounts, could get a talented, if not great then certainly we'd both agree acclaimed, and above all *loaded* actress...to emote with meat."

Either Ron or Rudy whispered Oh my God.

"To be *famished* for that umpteenth frank she's putting all that...*mustard* on," Letterman said, his head tilted, looking me in what I distinctly remember as the right eye. "And this is something we'll certainly understand if you don't want to go into, I mean...am I right Paul?"

He did look uncomfortable. As if he'd been put up to this last-minute. I was looking at him as if he were completely mad. Now that he'd gotten his silly question out I felt as if he and I had been having almost separate conversations since my appearance's start. I genuinely yawned.

"Just be honest," Ron was saying.

"Go ahead and tell him about the back taxes," Rudy whispered.

"Look," I said, smiling, "I think one of us hasn't been making themselves clear, here. So may I just be honest?"

Letterman was looking stage-left as if appealing to someone. I was sure he felt he'd gone too far, and his discomfort had quieted the audience like a death.

I smiled until my silence got his attention. I leaned toward him conspiratorially. After an uncertain pause he leaned over his desk toward me. I looked slowly from side to side. In a stage whisper I said *"I did the wiener commercials for nothing."*

I worked my eyebrows up and down.

Letterman's jaw dropped.

"For nothing," I said, "but art, fun, a few cases of hot dogs, and the feeling of a craft well plied."

"Oh, now, come now, really," Letterman said, leaning back and grabbing his head. He pretended to appeal to the studio audience: "Ladies and gentlemen..."

"A feeling I'm sure we all know well here." I smiled with my eyes closed. "In fact, I called *them*. I volun*teered*. Almost *begged*. You should have seen it. You should have been there. Not a pretty sight."

"What a kid," Paul Shaffer tossed in, pretending to wipe at an eye under his glasses. Letterman threw his index card at him, and the Sound man in his red sweater hit another pane of glass with his hammer. I heard Ron telling Rudy this was inspired. Letterman seemed now suddenly to be having the time of his life. He smiled; he said ha *ha*; his eyes came utterly alive; he looked like a very large toy. Everyone seemed to be having a ball. I touched my ear and heard my husband thanking Ron.

We talked and laughed for one or two minutes more about art and self-acceptance being inestimably more important than assets. The interview ended in a sort of explosion of good will. David Letterman made confetti out of a few of his body's labels. I was frankly sorry it was over. Letterman smiled warmly at me as we went to commercial.

It was then that I felt sure in my heart all the angst and conference, Rudy's own fear, had been without point. Because, when we cut to that commercial message, David Letterman was still the *same way*. The director, in his cardigan, sawed at his throat with a finger, a cleverly photographed bumper filled all 6-A's monitors, the band got funky under Shaffer's direction, and the cameras' lights went dark. Letterman's shoulders sagged; he leaned tiredly across his obviously cheap desk and mopped at his forehead with a ratty-looking tissue from his yachting jacket's pocket. He smiled from the depths of himself and said it *was* really grotesquely nice having me on, that the audience was certainly getting the very most for its entertainment dollar tonight, that he hoped for her sake my daughter Lynnette had even one half the stage presence I had, and that if he'd known what a thoroughly engaging guest I'd be, he himself would have moved molehills to have me on long before this.

"He really said that," I told my husband later in the NBC car. "He said 'grotesquely nice,' 'entertainment dollar,' and that I was an engaging guest. And no one was listening."

Ron had gotten a driver and gone ahead to pick up Charmian and would meet us at the River Café, where the four of us try to go whenever Rudy and I are able to get into town. I looked at our own driver, up ahead, through the panel; his hat was off, his hair close-clipped, his whole head as still as a photo.

My husband in the back seat with me held my hand in his hands. His necktie and handkerchief were square and flush. I could almost smell his relief. He was terribly relieved when I saw him after the taping. Letterman had explained to the audience that I needed to be on my way, and I'd been escorted off as he introduced the self-proclaimed king of kitchen-gadget home sales, who wore an Elks pin.

"Of course he really said that," my husband said. "It's just the sort of thing he'd say."

"Exactly," I maintained, looking at what his hands held.

We were driven south.

"But that doesn't mean he's really that way," he said, looking at me very directly. Then he too looked at our hands. Our three rings were next to each other. I felt a love for him, and moved closer on the soft leather seat, my face hot and sore. My empty ear did feel a bit violated.

"Any more than you're really the way you were when we were handling him better than I've ever seen him handled," he said. He looked at me admiringly. "You're a talented and multifaceted actress," he said. "You took direction. You kept your head and did us both credit and survived an appearance on an anti-show." He smiled. "You did good work."

I moved away from my husband just enough to look at his very clean face. "I wasn't acting, with David Letterman," I told him. And I was sincere. "It was more you and Ron that I had to...handle." Rudy's smile remained. "I would've taken Ron's earplug out altogether, agreement or not, if Charmian hadn't had me wear my hair down. It would have hurt the man's feelings. And I knew the minute I sat across that silly desk from him I wasn't going to need any direction. He wasn't savage." I said. "He was *fun*, Rudy. I had fun."

He lit a long Gauloise, smiling. "Did it just for fun?" he asked wryly. He pretended almost to nudge my ribs. A high-rent district that I had remembered as a low-rent district went by on both sides of us.

And I'll say that I felt something dark in my heart when my husband almost nudged me there. I felt that it was a sorry business indeed when my own spouse couldn't tell I was being serious. And I told him so.

"I was just the way I am," I maintained.

And I saw in Rudy's face what my face must have betrayed when I hadn't a clue about what he and Ron or even David had been talking about. And I felt the same queer near-panic I imagine now he must have felt all week. We both listened as something sweetly baroque filtered through the limousine intercom's grille.

"It's like my birthday," I said, holding my second husband's hand in mine. "We agreed, on my birthday. I'm forty, and have both grown and tiny children, and a husband who is dear to me, and I'm a television actress who's agreed to represent a brand of wiener. We drank *wine* to that, Rudy. We held the facts out and looked, together. We agreed just last week about the way I am. What other way is there for me to be, now?"

My husband disengaged his hand and felt at the panel's grille. The

Spanish driver's hatless head was cocked. A part of his neck was without pigment, I saw. The lighter area was circular; it spiraled into his dark hair and was lost to me.

"He leaned across right up to me, Rudy. I could see every little part of his face. He was freckled. I could see little pinheads of sweat, from the lights. A tiny mole, near that label. His eyes were the same denim color Jamie and Lynnette's eyes get in the summer. I looked at him. I *saw* him."

"But we told you, Edilyn," my husband said, reaching into his jacket pocket. "What put him there, here and now, for you to see, is that he *can't* be seen. That's what the whole thing's about, now. That no one is really the way they have to be seen."

I looked at him. "You really think that's true."

His cigarette crackled. "Doesn't matter what I think. That's what the show is about. They make it true. By watching him."

"You believe that," I said.

"I believe what I see," he said, putting his cigarette down to manipulate the bottle's cap. The thing's typed label read TAKE SEVERAL, OFTEN. "If it wasn't true, could he use it the way he does...?"

"That strikes me as really naïve."

"...The way we used to?" he said.

Certain pills are literally bitter. When I'd finished my drink from the back seat's bar, I still tasted the Xanax on the back of my tongue. The adrenaline's ebb had left me very tired. We broke out of the tall buildings near the water. I watched the Manhattan Bridge pass. The late sun came into view. It hung to our right, red. We both looked at the water as we were driven past. The sheet of its surface was wound-colored under the March sunset.

I swallowed. "So you believe no one's really the way we see them?"

I got no response. Rudy's eyes were on the window.

"Ron doesn't really have a mouth, I noticed today. It's more like a gash in his head." I paused. "You needn't defer to him in our personal lives just because of your decisions in business, Rudy." I smiled. "We're loaded, sweetie."

My husband laughed without smiling. He looked at the last of the sun-colored water as we approached the Brooklyn Bridge's system of angled shadow.

"Because if no one is really the way we see them," I said, "that would include me. And you."

Rudy admired the sunset out loud. He said it looked explosive, hanging, all round, just slightly over the water. Reflected and doubled in that bit of river. But he'd been looking only at the water. I'd watched him.

*   *   *

"Oh, *my*," is what David Letterman said when Reese the coordinator's distinguished but raccoon-ringed face had resolved out of a perfect ring of exploded explosives. Months later, after I'd come through something by being in its center, survived in the stillness created by great disturbance from which I, as cause, perfectly circled, was exempt, I'd be struck all over again by what a real and simply *right* thing it was for a person in such a place to say.

And I have remembered and worked hard to show that, if nothing else at all, I am a woman who speaks her mind. It is the way I have to see myself, to live.

And so I did ask my husband, as we were driven in our complimentary limousine to join Ron and Charmian and maybe Lindsay for drinks and dinner across the river at NBC's expense, just what way he thought he and I really were, then, did he think.

Which turned out to be the mistake.

INFINITE JEST

O

Year of Glad

I AM SEATED IN an office, surrounded by heads and bodies. My posture is consciously congruent to the shape of my hard chair. This is a cold room in University Administration, wood-walled, Remington-hung, double-windowed against the November heat, insulated from Administrative sounds by the reception area outside, at which Uncle Charles, Mr. deLint and I were lately received.

I am in here.

Three faces have resolved into place above summer-weight sportcoats and half-Windsors across a polished pine conference table shiny with the spidered light of an Arizona noon. These are three Deans — of Admissions, Academic Affairs, Athletic Affairs. I do not know which face belongs to whom.

I believe I appear neutral, maybe even pleasant, though I've been coached to err on the side of neutrality and not attempt what would feel to me like a pleasant expression or smile.

I have committed to crossing my legs I hope carefully, ankle on knee, hands together in the lap of my slacks. My fingers are mated into a mirrored series of what manifests, to me, as the letter X. The interview room's other personnel include: the University's Director of Composition, its varsity tennis coach, and Academy prorector Mr. A. deLint. C.T. is beside me; the others sit, stand and stand, respectively, at the periphery of my focus. The tennis coach jingles pocket-change. There is something vaguely digestive about the room's odor. The high-traction sole of my complimentary Nike sneaker runs parallel to the wobbling loafer of my mother's half-brother, here in his capacity as Headmaster, sitting in the chair to what I hope is my immediate right, also facing Deans.

The Dean at left, a lean yellowish man whose fixed smile nevertheless has the impermanent quality of something stamped into uncooperative material, is a personality-type I've come lately to appreciate, the type who delays need of any response from me by relating my side of the story for me, to me. Passed a packet of computer-sheets by the shaggy lion of a Dean at center, he is speaking more or less to these pages, smiling down.

'You are Harold Incandenza, eighteen, date of secondary-school graduation approximately one month from now, attending the Enfield Tennis Academy, Enfield, Massachusetts, a boarding school, where you reside.' His reading glasses are rectangular, court shaped, the sidelines at top and bottom. 'You are, according to Coach White and Dean [unintelligible], a regionally, nationally, and continentally ranked junior tennis player, a potential O.N.A.N.C.A.A. athlete of substantial promise, recruited by Coach White via correspondence with Dr. Tavis here commencing... February of this year.' The top page is removed and brought around neatly to the bottom of the sheaf, at intervals. 'You have been in residence at the Enfield Tennis Academy since age seven.'

I am debating whether to risk scratching the right side of my jaw, where there is a wen.

'Coach White informs our offices that he holds the Enfield Tennis Academy's program and achievements in high regard, that the University of Arizona tennis squad has profited from the prior matriculation of several former E.T.A. alumni, one of whom was one Mr. Aubrey F. deLint, who appears also to be with you here today. Coach White and his staff have given us —'

The yellow administrator's usage is on the whole undistinguished, though I have to admit he's made himself understood. The Director of Composition seems to have more than the normal number of eyebrows. The Dean at right is looking at my face a bit strangely.

Uncle Charles is saying that though he can anticipate that the Deans might be predisposed to weigh what he avers as coming from his possible appearance as a kind of cheerleader for E.T.A., he can assure the assembled Deans that all this is true, and that the Academy has presently in residence no fewer than a third of the continent's top thirty juniors, in age brackets all across the board, and that I here, who go by 'Hal,' usually, am 'right up there among the very cream.' Right and center Deans smile professionally; the heads of deLint and the coach incline as the Dean at left clears his throat:

'—belief that you could well make, even as a freshman, a real contribution to this University's varsity tennis program. We are pleased,' he either says or reads, removing a page, 'that a competition of some major sort here has brought you down and given us the chance to sit down and chat together about your application and potential recruitment and matriculation and scholarship.'

'I've been asked to add that Hal here is seeded third, Boys' 18-and-Under Singles, in the prestigious WhataBurger Southwest Junior Invitational out at the Randolph Tennis Center—' says what I infer is Athletic Affairs, his cocked head showing a freckled scalp.

'Out at Randolph Park, near the outstanding El Con Marriott,' C.T. inserts, 'a venue the whole contingent's been vocal about finding absolutely top-hole thus far, which—'

'Just so, Chuck, and that according to Chuck here Hal has already justified his seed, he's reached the semifinals as of this morning's apparently impressive win, and that he'll be playing out at the Center again tomorrow, against the winner of a quarterfinal game tonight, and so will be playing tomorrow at I believe scheduled for 0830—'

'Try to get under way before the godawful heat out there. Though of course a dry heat.'

'—and has apparently already qualified for this winter's Continental Indoors, up in Edmonton, Kirk tells me—' cocking further to look up and left at the varsity coach, whose smile's teeth are radiant against a violent sunburn—'Which is something indeed.' He smiles, looking at me. 'Did we get all that right Hal.'

C.T. has crossed his arms casually; their triceps' flesh is webbed with mottle in the air-conditioned sunlight. 'You sure did. Bill.' He smiles. The two halves of his mustache never quite match. 'And let me say if I may that Hal's excited, excited to be invited for the third year running to the Invitational again, to be back here in a community he has real affection for, to visit with your alumni and coaching staff, to have already justified his high seed in this week's not unstiff competition, to as they say still be in it without the fat woman in the Viking hat having sung, so to speak, but of course most of all to have a chance to meet you gentlemen and have a look at the facilities here. Everything here is absolutely top-slot, from what he's seen.'

There is a silence. DeLint shifts his back against the room's panelling and recenters his weight. My uncle beams and straightens a straight watchband. 62.5% of the room's faces are directed my way, pleasantly expectant. My chest bumps like a dryer with shoes in it. I compose what I project will be seen as a smile. I turn this way and that, slightly, sort of directing the expression to everyone in the room.

There is a new silence. The yellow Dean's eyebrows go circumflex. The two other Deans look to the Director of Composition. The tennis coach has moved to stand at the broad window, feeling at the back of his crew-cut. Uncle Charles strokes the forearm above his watch. Sharp curved palm-shadows move slightly over the pine table's shine, the one head's shadow a black moon.

'Is Hal all right, Chuck?' Athletic Affairs asks. 'Hal just seemed to... well, grimace. Is he in pain? Are you in pain, son?'

'Hal's right as rain,' smiles my uncle, soothing the air with a casual hand. 'Just a bit of a let's call it maybe a facial tic, slightly, at all the adren-aline of being here on your impressive campus, justifying his sccd so far without dropping a set, receiving that official written offer of not only waivers but a living allowance from Coach White here, on Pac 10 letter-head, being ready in all probability to sign a National Letter of Intent right here and now this very day, he's indicated to me.' C.T. looks to me, his look horribly mild. I do the safe thing, relaxing every muscle in my face, emptying out all expression. I stare carefully into the Kekuléan knot of the middle Dean's necktie.

My silent response to the expectant silence begins to affect the air of the room, the bits of dust and sportcoat-lint stirred around by the AC's vents dancing jaggedly in the slanted plane of windowlight, the air over the table like the sparkling space just above a fresh-poured seltzer. The coach, in a slight accent neither British nor Australian, is telling C.T. that the whole application-interface process, while usually just a pleasant formality, is probably best accentuated by letting the applicant speak up for himself. Right and center Deans have inclined together in soft conference, forming a kind of tepee of skin and hair. I presume it's probably *facilitate* that the tennis coach mistook for *accentuate*, though *accelerate*, while clunkier than *facilitate*, is from a phonetic perspective more sensible, as a mistake. The Dean with the flat yellow face has leaned forward, his lips drawn back from his teeth in what I see as concern. His hands come together on the confer-ence table's surface. His own fingers look like they mate as my own four-X series dissolves and I hold tight to the sides of my chair.

We need candidly to chat re potential problems with my application, they and I, he is beginning to say. He makes a reference to candor and its value.

'The issues my office faces with the application materials on file from you, Hal, involve some test scores.' He glances down at a colorful sheet of standardized scores in the trench his arms have made. 'The Admissions staff is looking at standardized test scores from you that are, as I'm sure you know and can explain, are, shall we say... subnormal.' I'm to explain.

It's clear that this really pretty sincere yellow Dean at left is Admissions. And surely the little aviarian figure at right is Athletics, then, because the facial creases of the shaggy middle Dean are now pursed in a kind of distanced affront, an I'm-eating-something-that-makes-me-really-appreciate-the-presence-of-whatever-I'm-drinking-along-with-it look that spells professionally Academic reservations. An uncomplicated loyalty to standards, then, at center. My uncle looks to Athletics as if puzzled. He shifts slightly in his chair.

The incongruity between Admissions's hand- and face-color is almost wild. '—verbal scores that are just quite a bit closer to zero than we're comfortable with, as against a secondary-school transcript from the institution where both your mother and her brother are administrators—' reading directly out of the sheaf inside his arms' ellipse—'that this past year, yes, has fallen off a bit, but by the word I mean "fallen off" to outstanding from three previous years of frankly incredible.'

'Off the charts.'

'Most institutions do not even *have* grades of A with multiple pluses after it,' says the Director of Composition, his expression impossible to interpret.

'This kind of…how shall I put it…incongruity,' Admissions says, his expression frank and concerned, 'I've got to tell you sends up a red flag of potential concern during the admissions process.'

'We thus invite you to explain the appearance of incongruity if not outright shenanigans.' Students has a tiny piping voice that's absurd coming out of a face this big.

'Surely by *incredible* you meant very very very impressive, as opposed to literally quote "incredible," surely,' says C.T., seeming to watch the coach at the window massaging the back of his neck. The huge window gives out on nothing more than dazzling sunlight and cracked earth with heat-shimmers over it.

'Then there is before us the matter of not the required two but *nine* separate application essays, some of which of nearly monograph-length, each without exception being—' different sheet—'the adjective various evaluators used was quote "stellar"—'

Dir. of Comp.: 'I made in my assessment deliberate use of *lapidary* and *effete.*'

'—but in areas and with titles, I'm sure you recall quite well, Hal: "Neoclassical Assumptions in Contemporary Prescriptive Grammar," "The Implications of Post-Fourier Transformations for a Holographically Mimetic Cinema," "The Emergence of Heroic Stasis in Broadcast Entertainment"—'

' "Montague Grammar and the Semantics of Physical Modality"?'

' "A Man Who Began to Suspect He Was Made of Glass"?'

' "Tertiary Symbolism in Justinian Erotica"?'

Now showing broad expanses of recessed gum. 'Suffice to say that there's some frank and candid concern about the recipient of these unfortunate test scores, though perhaps explainable test scores, being these essays' sole individual author.'

'I'm not sure Hal's sure just what's being implied here,' my uncle says. The Dean at center is fingering his lapels as he interprets distasteful computed data.

'What the University is saying here is that from a strictly academic point of view there are admission problems that Hal needs to try to help us iron out. A matriculant's first role at the University is and must be as a student. We couldn't admit a student we have reason to suspect can't cut the mustard, no matter how much of an asset he might be on the field.'

'Dean Sawyer means the court, of course, Chuck,' Athletic Affairs says, head severely cocked so he's including the White person behind him in the address somehow. 'Not to mention O.N.A.N.C.A.A. regulations and investigators always snuffling around for some sort of whiff of the smell of impropriety.'

The varsity tennis coach looks at his own watch.

'Assuming these board scores are accurate reflectors of true capacity in this case,' Academic Affairs says, his high voice serious and sotto, still looking at the file before him as if it were a plate of something bad, 'I'll tell you right now my opinion is it wouldn't be fair. It wouldn't be fair to the other applicants. Wouldn't be fair to the University community.' He looks at me. 'And it'd be especially unfair to Hal himself. Admitting a boy we see as simply an athletic asset would amount to just using that boy. We're under myriad scrutiny to make sure we're not using anybody. Your board results, son, indicate that we could be accused of using you.'

Uncle Charles is asking Coach White to ask the Dean of Athletic Affairs whether the weather over scores would be as heavy if I were, say, a revenue-raising football prodigy. The familiar panic at feeling misperceived is rising, and my chest bumps and thuds. I expend energy on remaining utterly silent in my chair, empty, my eyes two great pale zeros. People have promised to get me through this.

Uncle C.T., though, has the pinched look of the cornered. His voice takes on an odd timbre when he's cornered, as if he were shouting as he receded. 'Hal's grades at E.T.A., which is I should stress an *Acad*emy, not simply a camp or factory, accredited by both the Commonwealth of Massachusetts and the North American Sports Academy Association, it's focused on the total needs of the player and student, founded by a towering intellectual figure whom I hardly need name, here, and based by him on the rigorous Oxbridge Quadrivium-Trivium curricular model, a school fully staffed and equipped, by a fully certified staff, should show that my nephew here can cut just about any Pac 10 mustard that needs cutting, and that—'

DeLint is moving toward the tennis coach, who is shaking his head.

'—would be able to see a distinct flavor of minor-sport prejudice about this whole thing,' C.T. says, crossing and recrossing his legs as I listen, composed and staring.

The room's carbonated silence is now hostile. 'I think it's time to let the actual applicant himself speak out on his own behalf,' Academic Affairs says very quietly. 'This seems somehow impossible with you here, sir.'

Athletics smiles tiredly under a hand that massages the bridge of his nose. 'Maybe you'd excuse us for a moment and wait outside, Chuck.'

'Coach White could accompany Mr. Tavis and his associate out to reception,' the yellow Dean says, smiling into my unfocused eyes.

'—led to believe this had all been ironed out in advance, from the—' C.T. is saying as he and deLint are shown to the door. The tennis coach extends a hypertrophied arm. Athletics says 'We're all friends and colleagues here.'

This is not working out. It strikes me that EXIT signs would look to a native speaker of Latin like red-lit signs that say HE LEAVES. I would yield to the urge to bolt for the door ahead of them if I could know that bolting for the door is what the men in this room would see. DeLint is murmuring something to the tennis coach. Sounds of keyboards, phone consoles as the door is briefly opened, then firmly shut. I am alone among administrative heads.

'—offense intended to anyone,' Athletic Affairs is saying, his sportcoat tan and his necktie insigniated in tiny print—'beyond just physical abilities out there in play, which believe me we respect, *want*, believe me.'

'—question about it we wouldn't be so anxious to chat with you directly, see?'

'—that we've known in processing several prior applications through Coach White's office that the Enfield School is operated, however impressively, by close relations of first your brother, who I can still remember the way White's predecessor Maury Klamkin wooed that kid, so that grades' objectivity can be all too easily called into question—'

'By whomsoever's calling—N.A.A.U.P., ill-willed Pac 10 programs, O.N.A.N.C.A.A.—'

The essays are old ones, yes, but they are mine; *de moi*. But they are, yes, old, not quite on the application's instructed subject of Most Meaningful Educational Experience Ever. If I'd done you one from the last year, it would look to you like some sort of infant's random stabs on a keyboard, and to you, who use *whomsoever* as a subject. And in this new smaller company, the Director of Composition seems abruptly to have actuated, emerged as both the Alpha of the pack here and way more effeminate than he'd seemed at first, standing hip-shot with a hand on his waist, walking with a roll to his shoulders, jingling change as he pulls up his pants as he slides into the chair still warm from C.T.'s bottom, crossing his legs in a way that inclines him well into my personal space, so that I can see multiple eyebrow-tics and capillary webs in the oysters below his eyes and smell fabric-softener and the remains of a breath-mint turned sour.

'...a bright, solid, but very shy boy, we know about your being very shy, Kirk White's told us what your athletically built if rather stand-offish younger instructor told him,' the Director says softly, cupping what I feel to be a hand over my sportcoat's biceps (surely not), 'who simply needs to swallow hard and trust and tell his side of the story to these gentlemen who bear no maliciousness none at all but are doing our jobs and trying to look out for everyone's interests at the same time.'

I can picture deLint and White sitting with their elbows on their knees in the defecatory posture of all athletes at rest, deLint staring at his huge thumbs, while C.T. in the reception area paces in a tight ellipse, speaking into his portable phone. I have been coached for this like a Don before a RICO hearing. A neutral and affectless silence. The sort of all-defensive game Schtitt used to have me play: the best defense: let everything bounce off you; do nothing. I'd tell you all you want and more, if the sounds I made could be what you hear.

Athletics with his head out from under his wing: '—to avoid admission procedures that could be seen as primarily athletics-oriented. It could be a mess, son.'

'Bill means the appearance, not necessarily the real true facts of the matter, which you alone can fill in,' says the Director of Composition.

'—the appearance of the high athletic ranking, the subnormal scores, the over-academic essays, the incredible grades vortexing out of what could be seen as a nepotistic situation.'

The yellow Dean has leaned so far forward that his tie is going to have a horizontal dent from the table-edge, his face sallow and kindly and no-shit-whatever:

'Look here, Mr. Incandenza, Hal, please just explain to me why we couldn't be accused of using you, son. Why nobody could come and say to us, why, look here, University of Arizona, here you are using a boy for just his body, a boy so shy and withdrawn he won't speak up for himself, a jock with doctored marks and a store-bought application.'

The Brewster's-Angle light of the tabletop appears as a rose flush behind my closed lids. I cannot make myself understood. 'I am not just a jock,' I say slowly. Distinctly. 'My transcript for the last year might have been dickied a bit, maybe, but that was to get me over a rough spot. The grades prior to that are *de moi*.' My eyes are closed; the room is silent. 'I cannot make myself understood, now.' I am speaking slowly and distinctly. 'Call it something I ate.'

It's funny what you don't recall. Our first home, in the suburb of Weston, which I barely remember — my eldest brother Orin says he can remember being in the home's backyard with our mother in the early spring, helping the Moms till some sort of garden out of the cold yard. March or early April. The garden's area was a rough rectangle laid out with Popsicle sticks and twine. Orin was removing rocks and hard clods from the Moms's path as she worked the rented Rototiller, a wheelbarrow-shaped, gas-driven thing that roared and snorted and bucked and he remembers seemed to propel the Moms rather than vice versa, the Moms very tall and having to stoop painfully to hold on, her feet leaving drunken prints in the tilled earth. He remembers that in the middle of the tilling I came tear-assing out the door and into the backyard wearing some sort of fuzzy red Pooh-wear, crying, holding out something he said was really unpleasant-looking in my upturned palm. He says I was around five and crying and was vividly red in the cold spring air. I was saying something over and over; he couldn't make it out until our mother saw me and shut down the tiller, ears ringing, and came over to see what I was holding out. This turned out to have been a large patch of mold — Orin posits from some dark corner of the Weston home's basement, which was warm from the furnace and flooded every spring. The patch itself he describes as horrific: darkly green, glossy, vaguely hirsute, speckled with parasitic fungal points of yellow, orange, red. Worse, they could see that the patch looked oddly incomplete, gnawed-on; and some of the nauseous stuff was smeared around my open mouth. 'I ate this,' was what I was saying. I held the patch out to the Moms, who had her contacts out for the dirty work, and at first, bending way down, saw only her crying child, hand out, proffering; and in that most maternal of reflexes she, who feared and loathed more than anything spoilage and filth, reached to take whatever her baby held out—as in how many used heavy Kleenex, spit-back candies, wads of chewed-out gum in how many theaters, airports, backseats, tournament lounges? O. stood there, he says, hefting a cold clod, playing with the Velcro on his puffy coat, watching as the Moms, bent way down to me, hand reaching, her lowering face with its presbyopic squint, suddenly stopped, froze, beginning to I.D. what it was I held out, countenancing evidence of oral contact with same. He remembers her face as past describing. Her outstretched hand, still Rototrembling, hung in the air before mine.

'I ate this,' I said.

'Pardon me?'

O. says he can only remember (sic) saying something caustic as he limboed a crick out of his back. He says he must have felt a terrible impending anxiety. The Moms refused ever even to go into the damp basement. I had stopped crying, he remembers, and simply stood there, the size and shape of a hydrant, in red PJ's with attached feet, holding out the mold, seriously, like the report of some kind of audit.

O. says his memory diverges at this point, probably as a result of anxiety. In his first memory, the Moms's path around the yard is a broad circle of hysteria:

'*God!*' she calls out.

'Help! My son ate this!' she yells in Orin's second and more fleshed-out recollection, yelling it over and over, holding the speckled patch aloft in a pincer of fingers, running around and around the garden's rectangle while O. gaped at his first real sight of adult hysteria. Suburban neighbors' heads appeared in windows and over the fences, looking. O. remembers me tripping over the garden's laid-out twine, getting up dirty, crying, trying to follow.

'God! Help! My son ate this! Help!' she kept yelling, running a tight pattern just inside the square of string; and my brother Orin remembers noting how even in hysterical trauma her flight-lines were plumb, her footprints Native-American-straight, her turns, inside the ideogram of string, crisp and martial, crying 'My son ate this! Help!' and lapping me twice before the memory recedes.

'My application's not bought,' I am telling them, calling into the darkness of the red cave that opens out before closed eyes. 'I am not just a boy who plays tennis. I have an intricate history. Experiences and feelings. I'm complex.

'I *read*,' I say. 'I study and read. I bet I've read everything you've read. Don't think I haven't. I consume libraries. I wear out spines and ROM-drives. I do things like get in a taxi and say, "The library, and step on it." My instincts concerning syntax and mechanics are better than your own, I can tell, with due respect.

'But it transcends the mechanics. I'm not a machine. I feel and believe. I have opinions. Some of them are interesting. I could, if you'd let me, talk and talk. Let's talk about anything. I believe the influence of Kierkegaard on Camus is underestimated. I believe Dennis Gabor may very well have been the Antichrist. I believe Hobbes is just Rousseau in a dark mirror. I believe, with Hegel, that transcendence is absorption. I could interface you guys right under the table,' I say. 'I'm not just a creātus, manufactured, conditioned, bred for a function.'

I open my eyes. 'Please don't think I don't care.'

I look out. Directed my way is horror. I rise from the chair. I see jowls sagging, eyebrows high on trembling foreheads, cheeks bright-white. The chair recedes below me.

'Sweet mother of Christ,' the Director says.

'I'm fine,' I tell them, standing. From the yellow Dean's expression, there's a brutal wind blowing from my direction. Academics' face has gone instantly old. Eight eyes have become blank discs that stare at whatever they see.

'Good God,' whispers Athletics.

'Please don't worry,' I say. 'I can explain.' I soothe the air with a casual hand.

Both my arms are pinioned from behind by the Director of Comp., who wrestles me roughly down, on me with all his weight. I taste floor.

'What's *wrong?*'

I say '*Nothing* is wrong.'

'It's all *right!* I'm *here!*' the Director is calling into my ear.

'Get help!' cries a Dean.

My forehead is pressed into parquet I never knew could be so cold. I am arrested. I try to be perceived as limp and pliable. My face is mashed flat; Comp.'s weight makes it hard to breathe.

'Try to listen,' I say very slowly, muffled by the floor.

'What in God's name are those…,' one Dean cries shrilly, '…those *sounds?*'

There are clicks of a phone console's buttons, shoes' heels moving, pivoting, a sheaf of flimsy pages falling.

'*God!*'

'*Help!*'

The door's base opens at the left periphery: a wedge of halogen hall-light, white sneakers and a scuffed Nunn Bush. 'Let him *up!*' That's deLint.

'There is nothing wrong,' I say slowly to the floor. 'I'm in here.'

I'm raised by the crutches of my underarms, shaken toward what he must see as calm by a purple-faced Director: 'Get a *grip,* son!'

DeLint at the big man's arm: '*Stop* it!'

'I am not what you see and hear.'

Distant sirens. A crude half nelson. Forms at the door. A young Hispanic woman holds her palm against her mouth, looking.

'I'm not,' I say.

You have to love old-fashioned men's rooms: the citrus scent of deodorant disks in the long porcelain trough; the stalls with wooden doors in frames of cool marble; these thin sinks in rows, basins supported by rickety alphabets of exposed plumbing; mirrors over metal shelves; behind all the voices the slight sound of a ceaseless trickle, inflated by echo against wet porcelain and a cold tile floor whose mosaic pattern looks almost Islamic at this close range.

The disorder I've caused revolves all around. I've been half-dragged, still pinioned, through a loose mob of Administrative people by the Comp. Director—who appears to have thought variously that I am having a seizure (prying open my mouth to check for a throat clear of tongue), that I am somehow choking (a textbook Heimlich that left me whooping), that I am psychotically out of control (various postures and grips designed to transfer that control to him)—while about us roil deLint, trying to restrain the Director's restraint of me, the varsity tennis coach restraining deLint, my mother's half-brother speaking in rapid combinations of polysyllables to the trio of Deans, who variously gasp, wring hands, loosen neckties, waggle digits in C.T.'s face, and make *pases* with sheafs of now-pretty-clearly-superfluous application forms.

I am rolled over supine on the geometric tile. I am concentrating docilely on the question why U.S. restrooms always appear to us as infirmaries for public distress, the place to regain control. My head is cradled in a knelt Director's lap, which is soft, my face being swabbed with dusty-brown institutional paper towels he received from some hand out of the crowd overhead, staring with all the blankness I can summon into his jowls' small pocks, worst at the blurred jaw-line, of scarring from long-ago acne. Uncle Charles, a truly unparalleled slinger of shit, is laying down an enfilade of same, trying to mollify men who seem way more in need of a good brow-mopping than I.

'He's fine,' he keeps saying. 'Look at him, calm as can be, lying there.'

'You didn't see what *happened* in there,' a hunched Dean responds through a face webbed with fingers.

'Excited, is all he gets, sometimes, an excitable kid, impressed with —'

'But the *sounds* he made.'

'Undescribable.'

'Like an animal.'

'*Sub*animalistic noises and sounds.'

'Nor let's not forget the *gestures*.'

'Have you ever gotten *help* for this boy Dr. Tavis?'

'Like some sort of animal with something in its mouth.'

'This boy is damaged.'

'Like a stick of butter being hit with a mallet.'

'A writhing animal with a knife in its eye.'

'What were you possibly *about*, trying to enroll this —'

'And his *arms*.'

'You didn't see it, Tavis. His arms were —'

'Flailing. This sort of awful reaching drumming wriggle. *Waggling*,' the group looking briefly at someone outside my sight trying to demonstrate something.

'Like a time-lapse, a flutter of some sort of awful...growth.'

'Sounded most of all like a drowning goat. A goat, drowning in something viscous.'

'This strangled series of bleats and —'

'Yes they *waggled*.'

'So suddenly a bit of excited waggling's a crime, now?'

'You, sir, are in trouble. You are *in trouble*.'

'His face. As if he was strangling. Burning. I believe I've seen a vision of hell.'

'He has some trouble communicating, he's communicatively challenged, no one's denying that.'

'The boy needs *care*.'

'Instead of caring for the boy you send him here to *enroll, compete?*'

'Hal?'

'You have not in your most dreadful fantasies dreamt of the amount of *trouble* you have bought yourself, Dr. so-called Headmaster, *educator*.'

'...were given to understand this was all just a formality. You took him aback, is all. Shy—'

'And you, White. You sought to *recruit* him!'

'—and terribly impressed and excited, in there, without us, his support system, whom you asked to leave, which if you'd—'

'I'd only seen him play. On court he's gorgeous. Possibly a genius. We had no idea. The brother's in the bloody NFL for God's sake. Here's a top player, we thought, with Southwest roots. His stats were off the chart. We watched him through the whole WhataBurger last fall. Not a waggle or a noise. We were watching ballet out there, a mate remarked, after.'

'Damn right you were watching ballet out there, White. This boy is a balletic athlete, a player.'

'Some kind of athletic savant then. Balletic compensation for deep problems which *you* sir choose to disguise by muzzling the boy in there.' An expensive pair of Brazilian espadrilles goes by on the left and enters a stall, and the espadrilles come around and face me. The urinal trickles behind the voices' small echoes.

'—haps we'll just be on our way,' C.T. is saying.

'The integrity of my sleep has been forever compromised, sir.'

'—think you could pass off a damaged applicant, fabricate credentials and shunt him through a kangaroo-interview and inject him into all the rigors of college life?'

'Hal here *functions,* you ass. Given a supportive situation. He's fine when he's by himself. Yes he has some trouble with excitability in conversation. Did you once hear him try to deny that?'

'We witnessed something only marginally *mammalian* in there, sir.'

'Like hell. Have a look. How's the excitable little guy doing down there, Aubrey, does it look to you?'

'You, sir, are quite possibly ill. This affair is not concluded.'

'What *ambulance?* Don't you guys *listen?* I'm telling you there's—'

'Hal? Hal?'

'Dope him up, seek to act as his mouthpiece, muzzling, and now he lies there catatonic, staring.'

The crackle of deLint's knees. 'Hal?'

'—inflate this publicly in any distorted way. The Academy has distinguished alumni, litigators at counsel. Hal here is provably competent. Credentials out the bazoo, Bill. The boy reads like a vacuum. *Digests* things.'

I simply lie there, listening, smelling the paper towel, watching an espadrille pivot.

'There's more to life than sitting there interfacing, it might be a news-flash to you.'

And who could not love that special and leonine roar of a public toilet?

Not for nothing did Orin say that people outdoors down here just scuttle in vectors from air conditioning to air conditioning. The sun is a hammer. I can feel one side of my face start to cook. The blue sky is glossy and fat with heat, a few thin cirri sheared to blown strands like hair at the rims. The traffic is nothing like Boston. The stretcher is the special type, with restraining straps at the extremities. The same Aubrey deLint I'd dismissed for years as a 2-D martinet knelt gurneyside to squeeze my restrained hand and say 'Just hang in there, Buckaroo,' before moving back into the administrative fray at the ambulance's doors. It is a special ambulance, dispatched from I'd rather not dwell on where, with not only paramedics but some kind of psychiatric M.D. on board. The medics lift gently and are handy with straps. The M.D., his back up against the ambulance's side, has both hands up in dispassionate mediation between the Deans and C.T., who keeps stabbing skyward with his cellular's antenna as if it were a sabre, outraged that I'm being needlessly ambulanced off to some Emergency Room against my will and interests. The issue whether the damaged even have interested wills is shallowly hashed out as some sort of ultra-mach fighter too high overhead to hear slices the sky from south to north. The M.D. has both hands up and is pat-ting the air to signify dispassion. He has a big blue jaw. At the only other emergency room I have ever been in, almost exactly one year back, the psy-chiatric stretcher was wheeled in and then parked beside the waiting-room chairs. These chairs were molded orange plastic; three of them down the row were occupied by different people all of whom were holding empty pre-scription bottles and perspiring freely. This would have been bad enough, but in the end chair, right up next to the strap-secured head of my stretcher, was a T-shirted woman with barnwood skin and a trucker's cap and a bad starboard list who began to tell me, lying there restrained and immobile, about how she had seemingly overnight suffered a sudden and anomalous gigantism in her right breast, which she referred to as a titty; she had an almost parodic Québecois accent and described the 'titty's' presenting his-tory and possible diagnoses for almost twenty minutes before I was rolled away. The jet's movement and trail seem incisionish, as if white meat behind the blue were exposed and widening in the wake of the blade. I once saw the word *KNIFE* finger-written on the steamed mirror of a nonpublic bath-room. I have become an infantophile. I am forced to roll my closed eyes either up or to the side to keep the red cave from bursting into flames from the sunlight. The street's passing traffic is constant and seems to go 'Hush, hush, hush.' The sun, if your fluttering eye catches it even slightly, gives you the blue and red floaters a flashbulb gives you. 'Why *not?* Why *not?* Why not *not,* then, if the best reasoning you can contrive is why not?' C.T.'s voice, receding with outrage. Only the gallant stabs of his antenna are now visible, just inside my sight's right frame. I will be conveyed to an Emergency Room of some kind, where I will be detained as long as I do not respond to questions, and then, when I do respond to questions, I will be sedated; so it will be inversion of standard travel, the ambulance and ER: I'll make the journey first, then depart. I think very briefly of the late Cosgrove Watt. I think of the hypophalangial Grief-Therapist. I think of the Moms, alphabetizing cans of soup in the cabinet over the microwave. Of Himself's umbrella hung by its handle from the edge of the mail table just inside the Headmaster's House's foyer. The bad ankle hasn't ached once this whole year. I think of John N. R. Wayne, who would have won this year's WhataBurger, standing watch in a mask as Donald Gately and I dig up my father's head. There's very little doubt that Wayne would have won. And Venus Williams owns a ranch outside Green Valley; she may well attend the 18's Boys' and Girls' finals. I will be out in plenty of time for tomorrow's semi; I trust Uncle Charles. Tonight's winner is almost sure to be Dymphna, sixteen but with a birthday two weeks under the 15 April deadline; and Dymphna will still be tired tomorrow at 0830, while I, sedated, will have slept like a graven image. I have never before faced Dymphna in tournament play, nor played with the sonic balls the blind require, but I watched him barely dispatch Petropolis Kahn in the Round of 16, and I know he is mine.

It will start in the E.R., at the intake desk if C.T.'s late in following the ambulance, or in the green-tiled room after the room with the invasive-digital machines; or, given this special M.D.-supplied ambulance, maybe on the ride itself: some blue-jawed M.D. scrubbed to an antiseptic glow with his name sewn in cursive on his white coat's breast pocket and a quality desk-set pen, wanting gurneyside Q&A, etiology and diagnosis by Socratic method, ordered and point-by-point. There are, by the *O.E.D. VI's* count, nineteen nonarchaic synonyms for *unresponsive,* of which nine are Latinate and four Saxonic. I will play either Stice or Polep in Sunday's final. Maybe in front of Venus Williams. It will be someone blue-collar and unlicensed, though, inevitably—a nurse's aide with quick-bit nails, a hospital security guy, a tired Cuban orderly who addresses me as *jou*—who will, looking down in the middle of some kind of bustled task, catch what he sees as my eye and ask So yo then man what's *your* story?

—pages 3-17

Year of the Depend Adult Undergarment

WHERE WAS THE woman who said she'd come. She said she would come. Erdedy thought she'd have come by now. He sat and thought. He was in the living room. When he started waiting one window was full of yellow light and cast a shadow of light across the floor and he was still sitting waiting as that shadow began to fade and was intersected by a brightening shadow from a different wall's window. There was an insect on one of the steel shelves that held his audio equipment. The insect kept going in and out of one of the holes on the girders that the shelves fit into. The insect was dark and had a shiny case. He kept looking over at it. Once or twice he started to get up to go over closer to look at it, but he was afraid that if he came closer and saw it closer he would kill it, and he was afraid to kill it. He did not use the phone to call the woman who'd promised to come because if he tied up the line and if it happened to be the time when maybe she was trying to call him he was afraid she would hear the busy signal and think him disinterested and get angry and maybe take what she'd promised him somewhere else.

She had promised to get him a fifth of a kilogram of marijuana, 200 grams of unusually good marijuana, for $1250 U.S. He had tried to stop smoking marijuana maybe 70 or 80 times before. Before this woman knew him. She did not know he had tried to stop. He always lasted a week, or two weeks, or maybe two days, and then he'd think and decide to have some in his home one more last time. One last final time he'd search out someone new, someone he hadn't already told that he had to stop smoking dope and please under no circumstances should they procure him any dope. It had to be a third party, because he'd told every dealer he knew to cut him off. And the third party had to be someone all-new, because each time he got some he knew this time had to be the last time, and so told them, asked them, as a favor, never to get him any more, ever. And he never asked a person again once he'd told them this, because he was proud, and also kind, and wouldn't put anyone in that kind of contradictory position. Also he considered himself creepy when it came to dope, and he was afraid that others would see that he was creepy about it as well. He sat and thought and waited in an uneven X of light through two different windows. Once or twice he looked at the phone. The insect had disappeared back into the hole in the steel girder a shelf fit into.

She'd promised to come at one certain time, and it was past that time. Finally he gave in and called her number, using just audio, and it rang several times, and he was afraid of how much time he was taking tying up the line and he got her audio answering device, the message had a snatch of ironic pop music and her voice and a male voice together saying we'll call you back, and the 'we' made them sound like a couple, the man was a handsome black man who was in law school, she designed sets, and he didn't leave a message because he didn't want her to know how much now he felt like he needed it. He had been very casual about the whole thing. She said she knew a guy just over the river in Allston who sold high-resin dope in moderate bulk, and he'd yawned and said well, maybe, well, hey, why not, sure, special occasion, I haven't bought any in I don't know how long. She said he lived in a trailer and had a harelip and kept snakes and had no phone, and was basically just not what you'd call a pleasant or attractive person at all, but the guy in Allston frequently sold dope to theater people in Cambridge, and had a devoted following. He said he was trying to even remember when was the last time he'd bought any, it had been so long. He said he guessed he'd have her get a decent amount, he said he'd had some friends call him in the recent past and ask if he could get them some. He had this thing where he'd frequently say he was getting dope mostly for friends. Then if the woman didn't have it when she said she'd have it for him and he became anxious about it he could tell the woman that it was his friends who were becoming anxious, and he was sorry to bother the woman about something so casual but his friends were anxious and bothering him about it and he just wanted to know what he could maybe tell them. He was caught in the middle, is how he would represent it. He could say his friends had given him their money and were now anxious and exerting pressure, calling and bothering him. This tactic was not possible with this woman who'd said she'd come with it because he hadn't yet given her the $1250. She would not let him. She was well off. Her family was well off, she'd said to explain how her condominium was as nice as it was when she worked designing sets for a Cambridge theater company that seemed to do only German plays, dark smeary sets. She didn't care much about the money, she said she'd cover the cost herself when she got out to the Allston Spur to see whether the guy was at home in the trailer as she was certain he would be this particular afternoon, and he could just reimburse her when she brought it to him. This arrangement, very casual, made him anxious, so he'd been even more casual and said sure, fine, whatever. Thinking back, he was sure he'd said *whatever,* which in retrospect worried him because it might have sounded as if he didn't care at all, not at all, so little that it wouldn't matter if she forgot to get it or call, and once he'd made the decision to have marijuana in his home one more time it mattered a lot. It mattered a lot. He'd been too casual with the woman, he should have made her take $1250 from him up front, claiming politeness, claiming he didn't want to inconvenience her financially over something so trivial and casual. Money created a sense of obligation, and he should have wanted the woman to feel obliged to do what she'd said, once what she'd said she'd do had set him off inside. Once he'd been set off inside, it mattered so much that he was somehow afraid to show how much it mattered. Once he had asked her to get it, he was committed to several courses of action. The insect on the shelf was back. It didn't seem to do anything. It just came out of the hole in the girder onto the edge of the steel shelf and sat there. After a while it would disappear back into the hole in the girder, and he was pretty sure it didn't do anything in there either. He felt similar to the insect inside the girder his shelf was connected to, but was not sure just how he was similar. Once he'd decided to own marijuana one more last time, he was committed to several courses of action. He had to modem in to the agency and say that there was an emergency and that he was posting an e-note on a colleague's TP asking her to cover his calls for the rest of the week because he'd be out of contact for several days due to this emergency. He had to put an audio message on his answering device saying that starting that afternoon he was going to be unreachable for several days. He had to clean his bedroom, because once he had dope he would not leave his bedroom except to go to the refrigerator and the bathroom, and even then the trips would be very quick. He had to throw out all his beer and liquor, because if he drank alcohol and smoked dope at the same time he would get dizzy and ill, and if he had alcohol in the house he could not be relied on not to drink it once he started smoking dope. He'd had to do some shopping. He'd had to lay in supplies. Now just one of the insect's antennae was protruding from the hole in the girder. It protruded, but it did not move. He had had to buy soda, Oreos, bread, sandwich meat, mayonnaise, tomatoes, M&M's, Almost Home cookies, ice cream, a Pepperidge Farm frozen chocolate cake, and four cans of canned chocolate frosting to be eaten with a large spoon. He'd had to log an order to rent film cartridges from the InterLace entertainment outlet. He'd had to buy antacids for the discomfort that eating all he would eat would cause him late at night. He'd had to buy a new bong, because each time he finished what simply had to be his last bulk-quantity of marijuana he decided that that was it, he was through, he didn't even like it anymore, this was it, no more hiding, no more imposing on his colleagues and putting different messages on his answering device and moving his car away from his condominium and closing his windows and curtains and blinds and living in quick vectors between his bedroom's InterLace teleputer's films and his refrigerator and his toilet, and he would take the bong he'd used and throw it away wrapped in several plastic shopping bags. His refrigerator made its own ice in little cloudy crescent blocks and he loved it, when he had dope in his home he always drank a great deal of cold soda and ice water. His tongue almost swelled at just the thought. He looked at the phone and the clock. He looked at the windows but not at the foliage and blacktop driveway beyond the windows. He had already vacuumed his venetian blinds and curtains, everything was ready to be shut down. Once the woman who said she'd come had come, he would shut the whole system down. It occurred to him that he would disappear into a hole in a girder inside him that supported something else inside him. He was unsure what the thing inside him was and was unprepared to commit himself to the course of action that would be required to explore the question. It was now almost three hours past the time when the woman had said she would come. A counselor, Randi, with an *i*, with a mustache like a Mountie, had told him in the outpatient treatment program he'd gone through two years ago that he seemed insufficiently committed to the course of action that would be required to remove substances from his lifestyle. He'd had to buy a new bong at Bogart's in Porter Square, Cambridge because whenever he finished the last of the substances on hand he always threw out all his bongs and pipes, screens and tubes and rolling papers and roach clips, lighters and Visine and Pepto-Bismol and cookies and frosting, to eliminate all future temptation. He always felt a sense of optimism and firm resolve after he'd discarded the materials. He'd bought the new bong and laid in fresh supplies this morning, getting back home with everything well before the woman had said she would come. He thought of the new bong and new little packet of round brass screens in the Bogart's bag on his kitchen table in the sunlit kitchen and could not remember what color this new bong was. The last one had been orange, the one before that a dusky rose color that had turned muddy at the bottom from resin in just four days. He could not remember the color of this new last and final bong. He considered getting up to check the color of the bong he'd be using but decided that obsessive checking and convulsive movements could compromise the atmosphere of casual calm he needed to maintain while he waited, protruding but not moving, for the woman he'd met at a design session for his agency's small campaign for her small theater company's new Wedekind festival, while he waited for this woman, with whom he'd had intercourse twice, to honor her casual promise. He tried to decide whether the woman was pretty. Another thing he laid in when he'd committed himself to one last marijuana vacation was petroleum jelly. When he smoked marijuana he tended to masturbate a great deal, whether or not there were opportunities for intercourse, opting when he smoked for masturbation over intercourse, and the petroleum jelly kept him from returning to normal function all tender and sore. He was also hesitant to get up and check the color of his bong because he would have to pass right by the telephone console to get to the kitchen, and he didn't want to be tempted to call the woman who'd said she would come again because he felt creepy about bothering her about something he'd represented as so casual, and was afraid that several audio hang-ups on her answering device would look even creepier, and also he felt anxious about maybe tying up the line at just the moment when she called, as she certainly would. He decided to get Call Waiting added to his audio phone service for a nominal extra charge, then remembered that since this was positively the last time he would or even could indulge what Randi, with an *i*, had called an addiction every bit as rapacious as pure alcoholism, there would be no real need for Call Waiting, since a situation like the present one could never arise again. This line of thinking almost caused him to become angry. To ensure the composure with which he sat waiting in light in his chair he focused his senses on his surroundings. No part of the insect he'd seen was now visible. The clicks of his portable clock were really composed of three smaller clicks, signifying he supposed preparation, movement, and readjustment. He began to grow disgusted with himself for waiting so anxiously for the promised arrival of something that had stopped being fun anyway. He didn't even know why he liked it anymore. It made his mouth dry and his eyes dry and red and his face sag, and he hated it when his face sagged, it was as if all the integrity of all the muscles in his face was eroded by marijuana, and he got terribly self-conscious about the fact that his face was sagging, and had long ago forbidden himself to smoke dope around anyone else. He didn't even know what its draw was anymore. He couldn't even be around anyone else if he'd smoked marijuana that same day, it made him so self-conscious. And the dope often gave him a painful case of pleurisy if he smoked it for more than two straight days of heavy continuous smoking in front of the InterLace viewer in his bedroom. It made his thoughts jut out crazily in jagged directions and made him stare raptly like an unbright child at entertainment cartridges—when he laid in film cartridges for a vacation with marijuana, he favored cartridges in which a lot of things blew up and crashed into each other, which he was sure an unpleasant-fact specialist like Randi would point out had implications that were not good. He pulled his necktie down smooth while he gathered his intellect, will, self-knowledge, and conviction and determined that when this latest woman came as she surely would this would simply be his very last mari- juana debauch. He'd simply smoke so much so fast that it would be so unpleasant and the memory of it so repulsive that once he'd consumed it and gotten it out of his home and his life as quickly as possible he would never want to do it again. He would make it his business to create a really bad set of debauched associations with the stuff in his memory. The dope scared him. It made him afraid. It wasn't that he was afraid of the dope, it was that smoking it made him afraid of everything else. It had long since stopped being a release or relief or fun. This last time, he would smoke the whole 200 grams—120 grams cleaned, destemmed—in four days, over an ounce a day, all in tight heavy economical one-hitters off a quality vir- gin bong, an incredible, insane amount per day, he'd make it a mission, treating it like a penance and behavior-modification regimen all at once, he'd smoke his way through thirty high-grade grams a day, starting the moment he woke up and used ice water to detach his tongue from the roof of his mouth and took an antacid—averaging out to 200 or 300 heavy bong-hits per day, an insane and deliberately unpleasant amount, and he'd make it a mission to smoke it continuously, even though if the marijuana was as good as the woman claimed he'd do five hits and then not want to take the trouble to load and one-hit any more for at least an hour. But he would force himself to do it anyway. He would smoke it all even if he didn't want it. Even if it started to make him dizzy and ill. He would use discipline and persistence and will and make the whole experience so unpleasant, so debased and debauched and unpleasant, that his behavior would be henceforward modified, he'd never even want to do it again because the memory of the insane four days to come would be so firmly, terribly emblazoned in his memory. He'd cure himself by excess. He pre- dicted that the woman, when she came, might want to smoke some of the 200 grams with him, hang out, hole up, listen to some of his impressive collection of Tito Puente recordings, and probably have intercourse. He had never once had actual intercourse on marijuana. Frankly, the idea repelled him. Two dry mouths bumping at each other, trying to kiss, his self-conscious thoughts twisting around on themselves like a snake on a stick while he bucked and snorted dryly above her, his swollen eyes red and his face sagging so that its slack folds maybe touched, limply, the folds of her own loose sagging face as it sloshed back and forth on his pillow, its mouth working dryly. The thought was repellent. He decided he'd have her toss him what she'd promised to bring, and then would from a distance toss back to her the $1250 U.S. in large bills and tell her not to let the door hit her on the butt on the way out. He'd say *ass* instead of *butt*. He'd be so rude and unpleasant to her that the memory of his lack of basic decency and of her tight offended face would be a further disincentive ever, in the future, to risk calling her and repeating the course of action he had now committed himself to.

He had never been so anxious for the arrival of a woman he did not want to see. He remembered clearly the last woman he'd involved in his trying just one more vacation with dope and drawn blinds. The last woman had been something called an appropriation artist, which seemed to mean that she copied and embellished other art and then sold it through a prestigious Marlborough Street gallery. She had an artistic manifesto that involved radical feminist themes. He'd let her give him one of her smaller paintings, which covered half the wall over his bed and was of a famous film actress whose name he always had a hard time recalling and a less famous film actor, the two of them entwined in a scene from a well-known old film, a romantic scene, an embrace, copied from a film history textbook and much enlarged and made stilted, and with obscenities scrawled all over it in bright red letters. The last woman had been sexy but not pretty, as the woman he now didn't want to see but was waiting anxiously for was pretty in a faded withered Cambridge way that made her seem pretty but not sexy. The appropriation artist had been led to believe that he was a former speed addict, intravenous addiction to methamphetamine hydrochloride[1] is what he remembered telling that one, he had even described the awful taste of hydrochloride in the addict's mouth immediately after injection, he had researched the subject carefully. She had been further led to believe that marijuana kept him from using the drug with which he really had a problem, and so that if he seemed anxious to get some once she'd offered to get him some it was only because he was heroically holding out against much darker deeper more addictive urges and he needed her to help him. He couldn't quite remember when or how she'd been given all these impressions. He had not sat down and outright bold-faced lied to her, it had been more of an impression he'd conveyed and nurtured and allowed to gather its own life and force. The insect was now entirely visible. It was on the shelf that held his digital equalizer. The insect might never actually have retreated all the way back into the hole in the shelf's girder. What looked like its reemergence might just have been a change in his attention or the two windows' light or the visual context of his surroundings. The girder protruded from the wall and was a triangle of dull steel with holes for shelves to fit into. The metal shelves that held his audio equipment were painted a dark industrial green and were originally made for holding canned goods. They were designed to be extra kitchen shelves. The insect sat inside its dark shiny case with an immobility that seemed like the gathering of a force, it sat like the hull of a vehicle from which the engine had been for the moment removed. It was dark and had a shiny case and antennae that protruded but did not move. He had to use the bathroom. His last piece of contact from the appropriation artist, with whom he had had intercourse, and who during intercourse had sprayed some sort of perfume up into the air from a mister she held in her left hand as she lay beneath him making a wide variety of sounds and spraying perfume up into the air, so that he felt the cold mist of it settling on his back and shoulders and was chilled and repelled, his last piece of contact after he'd gone into hiding with the marijuana she'd gotten for him had been a card she'd mailed that was a pastiche photo of a doormat of coarse green plastic grass with *WELCOME* on it and next to it a flattering publicity photo of the appropriation artist from her Back Bay gallery, and between them an unequal sign, which was an equal sign with a diagonal slash across it, and also an obscenity he had assumed was directed at him magisculed in red grease pencil along the bottom, with multiple exclamation points. She had been offended because he had seen her every day for ten days, then when she'd finally obtained 50 grams of genetically enhanced hydroponic marijuana for him he had said that she'd saved his life and he was grateful and the friends for whom he'd promised to get some were grateful and she had to go right now because he had an appointment and had to take off, but that he would doubtless be calling her later that day, and they had shared a moist kiss, and she had said she could feel his heart pounding right through his suit coat, and she had driven away in her rusty unmuffled car, and he had gone and moved his own car to an underground garage several blocks away, and had run back and drawn the clean blinds and curtains, and changed the audio message on his answering device to one that described an emergency departure from town, and had drawn and locked his bedroom blinds, and had taken the new rose-colored bong out of its Bogart's bag, and was not seen for three days, and ignored over two dozen audio messages and protocols and e-notes expressing concern over his message's emergency, and had never contacted her again. He had hoped she would assume he had succumbed again to methamphetamine hydrochloride and was sparing her the agony of his descent back into the hell of chemical dependence. What it really was was that he had again decided those 50 grams of resin-soaked dope, which had been so potent that on the second day it had given him an anxiety attack so paralyzing that he had gone to the bathroom in a Tufts University commemorative ceramic stein to avoid leaving his bedroom, represented his very last debauch ever with dope, and that he had to cut himself off from all possible future sources of temptation and supply, and this surely included the appropriation artist, who had come with the stuff at precisely the time she'd promised, he recalled. From the street outside came the sound of a dumpster being emptied into an E.W.D. land barge. His shame at what she might on the other hand perceive as his slimy phallocentric conduct toward her made it easier for him to avoid her, as well. Though not shame, really. More like being uncomfortable at the thought of it. He had had to launder his bedding twice to get the smell of the perfume out. He went into the bathroom to use the bathroom, making it a point to look neither at the insect visible on the shelf to his left nor at the telephone console on its lacquer workstation to the right. He was committed to touching neither. Where was the woman who had said she'd come. The new bong in the Bogart's bag was orange, meaning he might have misremembered the bong before it as orange. It was a rich autumnal orange that lightened to more of a citrus orange when its plastic cylinder was held up to the late-afternoon light of the window over the kitchen sink. The metal of its stem and bowl was rough stainless steel, the kind with a grain, unpretty and all business. The bong was half a meter tall and had a weighted base covered in soft false suede. Its orange plastic was thick and the carb on the side opposite the stem had been raggedly cut so that rough shards of plastic protruded from the little hole and might well hurt his thumb when he smoked, which he decided to consider just part of the penance he would undertake after the woman had come and gone. He left the door to the bathroom open so that he would be sure to hear the telephone when it sounded or the buzzer to the front doors of his condominium complex when it sounded. In the bathroom his throat suddenly closed and he wept hard for two or three seconds before the weeping stopped abruptly and he could not get it to start again. It was now over four hours since the time the woman had casually committed to come. Was he in the bathroom or in his chair near the window and near his telephone console and the insect and the window that had admitted a straight rectangular bar of light when he began to wait. The light through this window was coming at an angle more and more oblique. Its shadow had become a parallelogram. The light through the southwest window was straight and reddening. He had thought he needed to use the bathroom but was unable to. He tried putting a whole stack of film cartridges into the dock of the disc-drive and then turning on the huge teleputer in his bedroom. He could see the piece of appropriation art in the mirror above the TP. He lowered the volume all the way and pointed the remote device at the TP like some sort of weapon. He sat on the edge of his bed with his elbows on his knees and scanned the stack of cartridges. Each cartridge in the dock dropped on command and began to engage the drive with an insectile click and whir, and he scanned it. But he was unable to distract himself with the TP because he was unable to stay with any one entertainment cartridge for more than a few seconds. The moment he recognized what exactly was on one cartridge he had a strong anxious feeling that there was something more entertaining on another cartridge and that he was potentially missing it. He realized that he would have plenty of time to enjoy all the cartridges, and realized intellectually that the feeling of deprived panic over missing something made no sense. The viewer hung on the wall, half again as large as the piece of feminist art. He scanned cartridges for some time. The telephone console sounded during this interval of anxious scanning. He was up and moving back out toward it before the first ring was completed, flooded with either excitement or relief, the TP's remote device still in his hand, but it was only a friend and colleague calling, and when he heard the voice that was not the woman who had promised to bring what he'd committed the next several days to banishing from his life forever he was almost sick with disappointment, with a great deal of mistaken adrenaline now shining and ringing in his system, and he got off the line with the colleague to clear the line and keep it available for the woman so fast that he was sure his colleague perceived him as either angry with him or just plain rude. He was further upset at the thought that his answering the telephone this late in the day did not jibe with the emergency message about being unreachable that would be on his answering device if the colleague called back after the woman had come and gone and he'd shut the whole system of his life down, and he was standing over the telephone console trying to decide whether the risk of the colleague or someone else from the agency calling back was sufficient to justify changing the audio message on the answering device to describe an emergency departure this evening instead of this afternoon, but he decided he felt that since the woman had definitely committed to coming, his leaving the message unchanged would be a gesture of fidelity to her commitment, and might somehow in some oblique way strengthen that commitment. The E.W.D. land barge was emptying dumpsters all up and down the street. He returned to his chair near the window. The disk drive and TP viewer were still on in his bedroom and he could see through the angle of the bedroom's doorway the lights from the high-definition screen blink and shift from one primary color to another in the dim room, and for a while he killed time casually by trying to imagine what entertaining scenes on the unwatched viewer the changing colors and intensities might signify. The chair faced the room instead of the window. Reading while waiting for marijuana was out of the question. He considered masturbating but did not. He didn't reject the idea so much as not react to it and watch as it floated away. He thought very broadly of desires and ideas being watched but not acted upon, he thought of impulses being starved of expression and drying out and floating dryly away, and felt on some level that this had something to do with him and his circumstances and what, if this grueling final debauch he'd committed himself to didn't somehow resolve the problem, would surely have to be called his problem, but he could not even begin to try to see how the image of desiccated impulses floating dryly related to either him or the insect, which had retreated back into its hole in the angled girder, because at this precise time his telephone and his intercom to the front door's buzzer both sounded at the same time, both loud and tortured and so abrupt they sounded yanked through a very small hole into the great balloon of colored silence he sat in, waiting, and he moved first toward the telephone console, then over toward his intercom module, then convulsively back toward the sounding phone, and then tried somehow to move toward both at once, finally, so that he stood splay-legged, arms wildly out as if something's been flung, splayed, entombed between the two sounds, without a thought in his head.

—pages 17–27

O

IN THE EIGHTH American-educational grade, Bruce Green fell dreadfully in love with a classmate who had the unlikely name of Mildred Bonk. The name was unlikely because if ever an eighth-grader looked like a Daphne Christianson or a Kimberly St.-Simone or something like that, it was Mildred Bonk. She was the kind of fatally pretty and nubile wraithlike figure who glides through the sweaty junior-high corridors of every nocturnal emitter's dreamscape. Hair that Green had heard described by an overwrought teacher as 'flaxen'; a body which the fickle angel of puberty—the same angel who didn't even seem to know Bruce Green's zip code—had visited, kissed, and already left, back in sixth; legs which not even orange Keds with purple-glitter-encrusted laces could make unserious. Shy, iridescent, coltish, pelvically anfractuous, amply busted, given to diffident movements of hand brushing flaxen hair from front of dear creamy forehead, movements which drove Bruce Green up a private tree. A vision in a sundress and silly shoes. Mildred L. Bonk.

And then but by tenth grade, in one of those queer when-did-that-happen metamorphoses, Mildred Bonk had become an imposing member of the frightening Winchester High School set that smoked full-strength Marlboros in the alley between Senior and Junior halls and that left school altogether at lunchtime, driving away in loud low-slung cars to drink beer and smoke dope, driving around with sound-systems of illegal wattage, using Visine and Clorets, etc. She was one of them. She chewed gum (or worse) in the cafeteria, her dear diffident face now a bored mask of Attitude, her flaxen locks now teased and gelled into what looked for all the world like the consequence of a finger stuck into an electric socket. Bruce Green saved up for a low-slung old car and practiced Attitude on the aunt who'd taken him in. He developed a will.

And, by the year of what would have been graduation, Bruce Green was way more bored, imposing, and frightening than even Mildred Bonk, and he and Mildred Bonk and tiny incontinent Harriet Bonk-Green lived just off the Allston Spur in a shiny housetrailer with another frightening couple and with Tommy Doocey, the infamous harelipped pot-and-sundries dealer who kept several large snakes in unclean uncovered aquaria, which smelled, which Tommy Doocey didn't notice because his upper lip completely covered his nostrils and all he could smell was lip. Mildred Bonk got high in the afternoon and watched serial-cartridges, and Bruce Green had a steady job at Leisure Time Ice, and for a while life was more or less one big party.

—pages 38–39

Year of the Depend Adult Undergarment

HERE'S HAL INCANDENZA, age seventeen, with his little brass one-hitter, getting covertly high in the Enfield Tennis Academy's underground Pump Room and exhaling palely into an industrial exhaust fan. It's the sad little interval after afternoon matches and conditioning but before the Academy's communal supper. Hal is by himself down here and nobody knows where he is or what he's doing.

Hal likes to get high in secret, but a bigger secret is that he's as attached to the secrecy as he is to getting high.

A one-hitter, sort of like a long FDR-type cigarette holder whose end is packed with a pinch of good dope, gets hot and is hard on the mouth — the brass ones especially — but one-hitters have the advantage of efficiency: every particle of ignited pot gets inhaled; there's none of the incidental secondhand-type smoke from a party bowl's big load, and Hal can take every iota way down deep and hold his breath forever, so that even his exhalations are no more than slightly pale and sick-sweet-smelling.

Total utilization of available resources = lack of publicly detectable waste.

The Academy's tennis courts' Lung's Pump Room is underground and accessible only by tunnel. E.T.A. is abundantly, embranchingly tunnelled. This is by design.

Plus one-hitters are small, which is good, because let's face it, anything you use to smoke high-resin dope with is going to stink. A bong is big, and its stink is going to be like commensurately big, plus you have the foul bong-water to deal with. Pipes are smaller and at least portable, but they always come with only a multi-hit party bowl that disperses nonutilized smoke over a wide area. A one-hitter can be wastelessly employed, then allowed to cool, wrapped in two baggies and then further wrapped and sealed in a Ziploc and then enclosed in two sport-socks in a gear bag along with the lighter and eyedrops and mint-pellets and the little film-case of dope itself, and it's highly portable and odor-free and basically totally covert.

As far as Hal knows, colleagues Michael Pemulis, Jim Struck, Bridget C. Boone, Jim Troeltsch, Ted Schacht, Trevor Axford, and possibly Kyle D. Coyle and Tall Paul Shaw, and remotely possibly Frannie Unwin, all know Hal gets regularly covertly high. It's also not impossible that Bernadette Longley knows, actually; and of course the unpleasant K. Freer always has suspicions of all kinds. And Hal's brother Mario knows a thing or two. But that's it, in terms of public knowledge. And but even though Pemulis and Struck and Boone and Troeltsch and Axford and occasionally (in a sort of medicinal or touristic way) Stice and Schacht all are known to get high also, Hal has actually gotten actively high only with Pemulis, on the rare occasions he's gotten high with anybody else, as in in person, which he avoids. He'd forgot: Ortho ('The Darkness') Stice, of Partridge KS, knows; and Hal's oldest brother, Orin, mysteriously, even long-distance, seems to know more than he's coming right out and saying, unless Hal's reading more into some of the phone-comments than are there.

Hal's mother, Mrs. Avril Incandenza, and her adoptive brother Dr. Charles Tavis, the current E.T.A. Headmaster, both know Hal drinks alcohol sometimes, like on weekend nights with Troeltsch or maybe Axford down the hill at clubs on Commonwealth Ave.; The Unexamined Life has its notorious Blind Bouncer night every Friday where they card you on the Honor System. Mrs. Avril Incandenza isn't crazy about the idea of Hal drinking, mostly because of the way his father had drunk, when alive, and reportedly his father's own father before him, in AZ and CA; but Hal's academic precocity, and especially his late competitive success on the junior circuit, make it clear that he's able to handle whatever modest amounts she's pretty sure he consumes — there's no way someone can seriously abuse a substance and perform at top scholarly and athletic levels, the E.T.A. psych-counselor Dr. Rusk assures her, especially the high-level-athletic part — and Avril feels it's important that a concerned but unsmothering single parent know when to let go somewhat and let the two high-functioning of her three sons make their own possible mistakes and learn from their own valid experience, no matter how much the secret worry about mistakes tears her gizzard out, the mother's. And Charles supports whatever personal decisions she makes in conscience about her children. And God knows she'd rather have Hal having a few glasses of beer every so often than absorbing God alone knows what sort of esoteric designer compounds with reptilian Michael Pemulis and trail-of-slime-leaving James Struck, both of whom give Avril a howling case of the maternal fantods. And ultimately, she's told Drs. Rusk and Tavis, she'd rather have Hal abide in the security of the knowledge that his mother trusts him, that she's trusting and supportive and doesn't judge or gizzard-tear or wring her fine hands over his having for instance a glass of Canadian ale with friends every now and again, and so works tremendously hard to hide her maternal dread of his possibly ever drinking like James himself or James's father, all so that Hal might enjoy the security of feeling that he can be up-front with her about issues like drinking and not feel he has to hide anything from her under any circumstances.

Dr. Tavis and Dolores Rusk have privately discussed the fact that not least among the phobic stressors Avril suffers so uncomplainingly with is a black phobic dread of hiding or secrecy in all possible forms with respect to her sons.

Avril and C.T. know nothing about Hal's penchants for high-resin Bob Hope and underground absorption, which fact Hal obviously likes a lot, on some level, though he's never given much thought to why. To why he likes it so much.

E.T.A.'s hilltop grounds are traversable by tunnel. Avril I., for example, who never leaves the grounds anymore, rarely travels above ground, willing to hunch to take the off-tunnels between Headmaster's House and her office next to Charles Tavis's in the Community and Administration Bldg., a pink-bricked white-pillared neo-Georgian thing that Hal's brother Mario says looks like a cube that has swallowed a ball too big for its stomach.[3] Two sets of elevators and one of stairs run between the lobby, reception area, and administrative offices on Comm.-Ad.'s first floor and the weight room, sauna, and locker/shower areas on the sublevel below it. One large tunnel of elephant-colored cement leads from just off the boys' showers to the mammoth laundry room below the West Courts, and two smaller tunnels radiate from the sauna area south and east to the subbasements of the smaller, spherocubular, proto-Georgian buildings (housing classrooms and subdormitories B and D); these two basements and smaller tunnels often serve as student storage space and hallways between various prorectors[4] private rooms. Then two even smaller tunnels, navigable by any adult willing to assume a kind of knuckle-dragging simian posture, in turn connect each of the subbasements to the former optical and film-development facilities of Leith and Ogilvie and the late Dr. James O. Incandenza (now deceased) below and just west of the Headmaster's House (from which facilities there's also a fair-diametered tunnel that goes straight to the lowest level of the Community and Administration Bldg., but its functions have gradually changed over four years, and it's now too full of exposed wiring and hot-water pipes and heating ducts to be really passable) and to the offices of the Physical Plant, almost directly beneath the center row of E.T.A. outdoor tennis courts, which offices and custodial lounge are in turn connected to E.T.A.'s Lung-Storage and -Pump Rooms via a pargeted tunnel hastily constructed by the TesTar All-Weather Inflatable Structures Corp., which together with the folks over at ATHSCME Industrial Air Displacement Devices erects and services the inflatable dendriurethane dome, known as the Lung, that covers the middle row of courts for the winter indoor season. The crude little rough-sided tunnel between Plant and Pump is traversable only via all-fours-type crawling and is essentially unknown to staff and Administration, popular only with the Academy's smaller kids' Tunnel Club, as well as with certain adolescents with strong secret incentive to crawl on all fours.

The Lung-Storage Room is basically impassable from March through November because it's full of intricately folded dendriurethane Lung-material and dismantled sections of flexible ducting and fan-blades, etc. The Pump Room is right next to it, though you have to crawl back out into the tunnel to get to it. On the engineering diagrams the Pump Room's maybe about twenty meters directly beneath the centermost courts in the middle row of courts, and looks like a kind of spider hanging upside-down—an unfenestrated oval chamber with six man-sized curved ducts radiating up and out to exit points on the grounds above. And the Pump Room has six radial openings, one for each upcurving duct: three two-meter vents with huge turbine-bladed exhaust fans bolted into their grilles and three more 2M's with reversed ATHSCME intake fans that allow air from the ground above to be sucked down and around the room and up into the three exhaust vents. The Pump Room is essentially like a pulmonary organ, or the epicenter of a massive six-vectored wind tunnel, and when activated roars like a banshee that's slammed its hand in a door, though the P.R.'s in full legit operation only when the Lung is up, usually November-March. The intake fans pull ground-level winter air down into and around the room and through the three exhaust fans and up the out-take ducts into networks of pneumatic tubing in the Lung's sides and dome: it's the pressure of the moving air that keeps the fragile Lung inflated.

When the courts' Lung is down and stored, Hal will descend and walk and then hunch his way in to make sure nobody's in the Physical Plant quarters, then he'll hunch and crawl to the P.R., gear bag in his teeth, and activate just one of the big exhaust fans and get secretly high and exhale palely through its blades into the vent, so that any possible odor is blown through an outtake duct and expelled through a grille'd hole on the west side of the West Courts, a threaded hole, with a flange, where brisk white-suited ATHSCME guys will attach some of the Lung's arterial pneumatic tubing at some point soon when Schtitt et al. on Staff decide the real weather has moved past enduring for outdoor tennis.

During winter months, when any expelled odor would get ducted up into the Lung and hang there conspicuous, Hal mostly goes into a remote subdormitory lavatory and climbs onto a toilet in a stall and exhales into the grille of one of the little exhaust fans in the ceiling; but this routine lacks a certain intricate subterranean covert drama. It's another reason why Hal dreads Interdependence Day and the approach of the Whata-Burger classic and Thanksgiving and unendurable weather, and the erection of the Lung.

Recreational drugs are more or less traditional at any U.S. secondary school, maybe because of the unprecedented tensions: post-latency and puberty and angst and impending adulthood, etc. To help manage the intrapsychic storms, etc. Since the place's inception, there's always been a certain percentage of the high-caliber adolescent players at E.T.A. who manage their internal weathers chemically. Much of this is good clean temporary fun; but a traditionally smaller and harder-core set tends to rely on personal chemistry to manage E.T.A.'s special demands—dexedrine or low-volt methedrine[5] before matches and benzodiazapenes[6] to come back down after matches, with Mudslides or Blue Flames at some understanding Comm. Ave. nightspot[7] or beers and bongs in some discreet Academy corner at night to short-circuit the up-and-down cycle, mushrooms or X or something from the Mild Designer class[8]—or maybe occasionally a little Black Star,[9] whenever there's a match- and demand-free weekend, to basically short out the whole motherboard and blow out all the circuits and slowly recover and be almost neurologically reborn and start the gradual cycle all over again...this circular routine, if your basic wiring's OK to begin with, can work surprisingly well throughout adolescence and sometimes into one's like early twenties, before it starts to creep up on you.

But so some E.T.A.s—not just Hal Incandenza by any means—are involved with recreational substances, is the point. Like who isn't, at some life-stage, in the U.S.A. and Interdependent regions, in these troubled times, for the most part. Though a decent percentage of E.T.A. students aren't at all. I.e. involved. Some persons can give themselves away to an ambitious pursuit and have that be all the giving-themselves-away-to-something they need to do. Though sometimes this changes as the players get older and the pursuit more stress-fraught. American experience seems to suggest that people are virtually unlimited in their need to give themselves away, on various levels. Some just prefer to do it in secret.

An enrolled student-athlete's use of alcohol or illicit chemicals is cause for immediate expulsion, according to E.T.A.'s admissions catalogue. But the E.T.A. staff tends to have a lot more important stuff on its plate than policing kids who've already given themselves away to an ambitious competitive pursuit. The administrative attitude under first James Incandenza and then Charles Tavis is, like, why would anybody who wanted to compromise his faculties chemically even come here, to E.T.A., where the whole point is to stress and stretch your faculties along multiple vectors.[10] And since it's the alumni prorectors who have the most direct supervisory contact with the kids, and since most of the prorectors themselves are depressed or traumatized about not making it into the Show and having to come back to E.T.A. and live in decent but subterranean rooms off the tunnels and work as assistant coaches and teach laughable elective classes—which is what the eight E.T.A. prorectors do, when they're not off playing Satellite tournaments or trying to make it through the qualifying rounds of some serious-money event—and so they're morose and low on morale, and feel bad about themselves, often, as a rule, and so also not all that surprisingly tend to get high now and then themselves, though in a less covert or exuberant fashion than the hard-core students' chemical cadre, but so given all this it's not hard to see why internal drug-enforcement at E.T.A. tends to be flaccid.

The other nice thing about the Pump Room is the way it's connected by tunnel to the prorectors' rows of housing units, which means men's rooms, which means Hal can crawl, hunch, and tiptoe into an unoccupied men's room and brush his teeth with his portable Oral-B and wash his face and apply eyedrops and Old Spice and a plug of wintergreen Kodiak and then saunter back to the sauna area and ascend to ground level looking and smelling right as rain, because when he gets high he develops a powerful obsession with having nobody—not even the neurochemical cadre—know he's high. This obsession is almost irresistible in its force. The amount of organization and toiletry-lugging he has to do to get secretly high in front of a subterranean outtake vent in the pre-supper gap would make a lesser man quail. Hal has no idea why this is, or whence, this obsession with the secrecy of it. He broods on it abstractly sometimes, when high: this No-One-Must-Know thing. It's not fear per se, fear of discovery. Beyond that it all gets too abstract and twined up to lead to anything, Hal's brooding. Like most North Americans of his generation, Hal tends to know way less about why he feels certain ways about the objects and pursuits he's devoted to than he does about the objects and pursuits themselves. It's hard to say for sure whether this is even exceptionally bad, this tendency.

At 0015h., 2 April, the medical attaché's wife is just leaving the Mount Auburn Total Fitness Center, having played five six-game pro-sets in her little Mideast-diplomatic-wife-tennis-circle's weekly round-robin, then hung around the special Silver-Key-Members' Lounge with the other ladies, unwrapping her face and hair and playing Narjees[11] and all smoking kif and making extremely delicate and oblique fun of their husbands' sexual idiosyncrasies, laughing softly with their hands over their mouths. The medical attaché, at their apartment, is still viewing the unlabelled cartridge, which he has rewound to the beginning several times and then configured for a recursive loop. He sits there, attached to a congealed supper, watching, at 0020h., having now wet both his pants and the special recliner.

—pages 49–54

Autumn — Year of Dairy Products from the American Heartland

DRUG ADDICTS DRIVEN to crime to finance their drug addiction are not often inclined toward violent crime. Violence requires all different kinds of energy, and most drug addicts like to expend their energy not on their professional crime but on what their professional crime lets them afford. Drug addicts are often burglars, therefore. One reason why the home of someone whose home has been burglarized feels violated and unclean is that there have probably been drug addicts in there. Don Gately was a twenty-seven-year-old oral narcotics addict (favoring Demerol and Talwin[12]), and a more or less professional burglar; and he was, himself, unclean and violated. But he was a gifted burglar, when he burgled — though the size of a young dinosaur, with a massive and almost perfectly square head he used to amuse his friends when drunk by letting them open and close elevator doors on, he was, at his professional zenith, smart, sneaky, quiet, quick, possessed of good taste and reliable transportation — with a kind of ferocious jolliness in his attitude toward his livelihood.

As an active drug addict, Gately was distinguished by his ferocious and jolly élan. He kept his big square chin up and his smile wide, but he bowed neither toward nor away from any man. He took zero in the way of shit and was a cheery but implacable exponent of the Don't-Get-Mad-Get-Even school. Like for instance once, after he'd done a really unpleasant three-month bit in Revere Holding on nothing more than a remorseless North Shore Assistant District Attorney's circumstantial suspicion, finally getting out after 92 days when his P.D. got the charges dismissed on a right-to-speedy brief, Gately and a trusted associate[13] paid a semiprofessional visit to the private home of this Assistant D.A. whose zeal and warrant had cost Gately a nasty impromptu detox on the floor of his little holding-cell. Also a believer in the Revenge-Is-Tastier-Chilled dictum, Gately had waited patiently until the 'Eye On People' section of the *Globe* mentioned the A.D.A. and his wife's presence at some celebrity charity sailing thing out in Marblehead. Gately and the associate went that night to the A.D.A.'s private home in the upscale Wonderland Valley section of Revere, killed the power to the home with a straight shunt in the meter's inflow, then clipped just the ground wire on the home's pricey HBT alarm, so that the alarm'd sound after ten or so minutes and create the impression that the perps had somehow bungled the alarm and been scared off in the middle of the act. Later that night, when Revere's and Marblehead's Finest summoned them home, the A.D.A. and his wife found themselves minus a coin collection and two antique shotguns and nothing more. Quite a few other valuables were stacked on the floor of the living room off the foyer like the perps hadn't had time to get them out of the house. Everything else in the burglarized home looked undisturbed. The A.D.A. was a jaded pro: he walked around touching the brim of his hat[14] and reconstructed probable events: the perps looked like they'd bungled disabling the alarm all the way and had got scared off by the thing's siren when the alarm's pricey HBT alternate ground kicked in at 300 v. The A.D.A. soothed his wife's sense of violation and uncleanliness. He calmly insisted on sleeping there in their home that very night; no hotel: it was like crucial to get right back on the emotional horse, in cases like this, he insisted. And then the next day the A.D.A. worked out the insurance and reported the shotguns to a buddy at A.T.F.[15] and his wife calmed down and life went on.

About a month later, an envelope arrived in the A.D.A.'s home's exquisite wrought-iron mailbox. In the envelope were a standard American Dental Association glossy brochure on the importance of daily oral hygiene—available at like any dentist's office anywhere—and two high-pixel Polaroid snapshots, one of big Don Gately and one of his associate, each in a Halloween mask denoting a clown's great good professional cheer, each with his pants down and bent over and each with the enhanced-focus handle of one of the couple's toothbrushes protruding from his bottom.

Don Gately had sense enough never to work the North Shore again after that. But he ended up in hideous trouble anyway, A.D.A.-wise. It was either bad luck or kismet or so forth. It was because of a cold, a plain old human rhinovirus. And not even Don Gately's cold, is what made him finally stop and question his kismet.

The thing started out looking like tit on a tray, burglary-wise. A beautiful neo-Georgian home in a wildly upscale part of Brookline was set nicely back from an unlit pseudo-rural road, had a chintzy SentryCo alarm system that fed, idiotically enough, on a whole separate 330 v AC 90 Hz cable with its own meter, didn't seem to be on anything like a regular P.M.-patrol route, and had, at its rear, flimsily tasteful French doors surrounded by dense and thorn-free deciduous shrubbery and blocked off from the garage's halogen floods by a private E.W.D.-issue upscale dumpster. It was in short a real cock-tease of a home, burglary-wise, for a drug addict. And Don Gately straight-shunted the alarm's meter and, with an associate,[16] broke and entered and crept around on huge cat feet.

Except unfortunately the owner of the house turned out to be still home, even though both of his cars and the rest of his family were gone. The little guy was asleep sick in bed upstairs in acetate pajamas with a hot water bottle on his chest and half a glass of OJ and a bottle of NyQuil[17] and a foreign book and copies of *International Affairs* and *Interdependent Affairs* and a pair of thick specs and an industrial-size box of Kleenex on the bedside table and an empty vaporizer barely humming at the foot of the bed, and the guy was to say the least nonplussed to wake up and see high-filter flashlights crisscrossing over the unlit bedroom walls and bureau and teak chiffonnier as Gately and associate scanned for a wall-safe, which surprisingly like 90% of people with wall-safes conceal in their master bedroom behind some sort of land- or seascape painting. People turned out so identical in certain root domestic particulars it made Gately feel strange sometimes, like he was in possession of certain overlarge private facts to which no man should be entitled. Gately had a way stickier conscience about the possession of some of these large particular facts than he did about making off with other people's personal merchandise. But then all of a sudden in mid-silent-search for a safe here's this upscale homeowner turning out to be home with a nasty head-cold while his family's out on a two-car foliage-tour in what's left of the Berkshires, writhing groggily and NyQuilized around on the bed and making honking adenoidal sounds and asking what in bloody *hell* is the meaning of this, except he's saying it in Québecois French, which means to these thuggish U.S. drug addicts in Halloween-clowns' masks exactly nothing, he's sitting up in bed, a little and older-type homeowner with a football-shaped head and gray van Dyke and eyes you can tell are used to corrective lenses as he switches on the bright bedside lamp. Gately could easily have screwed out of there and never looked back; but here indeed, in the lamplight, is a seascape over next to the chiffonnier, and the associate has a quick peek and reports that the safe behind it is to laugh at, it can be opened with harsh language, almost; and oral narcotics addicts tend to operate on an extremely rigid physical schedule of need and satisfaction, and Gately is at this moment firmly in the need part of the schedule; and so D. W. Gately disastrously decides to go ahead and allow a nonviolent burglary to become in effect a robbery—which the operative legal difference involves either violence or the coercive threat of same—and Gately draws himself up to his full menacing height and shines his flashlight in the little homeowner's rheumy eyes and addresses him the way menacing criminals speak in popular entertainment—*d*'s for *th*'s, various apocopes, and so on—and takes hold of the guy's ear and conducts him down to a kitchen chair and binds his arms and legs to the chair with electrical cords neatly clipped from refrigerator and can-opener and M. Café-brand Automatic Café-au-Lait-Maker, binds him just short of gangrenously tight, because he's hoping the Berkshire foliage is prime and the guy's going to be soloing in this chair for a good stretch of time, and Gately starts looking through the kitchen's drawers for the silverware—not the good-silver-for-company silverware; that was in a calfskin case underneath some neatly folded old spare Christmas wrapping in a stunning hardwood-with-ivory-inlay chest of drawers in the living room, where over 90% of upscale people's good silver is always hidden, and has already been promoted and is piled[18] just off the foyer—but just the regular old everyday flatware silverware, because the vast bulk of homeowners keep their dish towels two drawers below their everyday-silverware drawer, and God's made no better call-for-help-stifling gag in the world than a good old oily-smelling fake-linen dish towel; and the bound guy in the cords on the chair suddenly snaps to the implications of what Gately's looking for and is struggling and saying: Do not gag me, I have a terrible cold, my nose she is a brick of the snot, I have not the power to breathe through the nose, for the love of God please do not gag my mouth; and as a gesture of goodwill the homeowner tells Gately, who's rummaging, the combination of the bedroom's seascape safe, except in French numbers, which together with the honking adenoidal inflection the guy's grippe gives his speech doesn't even sound like human speech to Gately, and but also the guy tells Gately there are some antique pre-British-takeover Québecois gold coins in a calfskin purse taped to the back of an undistinguished Impressionist landscape in the living room. But everything the Canadian homeowner says means no more to poor old Don Gately, whistling a jolly tune and trying to look menacing in his clown's mask, than the cries of, say, North Shore gulls or inland grackles; and sure enough the towels are two drawers under the spoons, and here comes Gately across the kitchen looking like a sort of Bozo from hell, and the Québecer guy's mouth goes oval with horror, and into that mouth goes a balled-up, faintly greasy-smelling kitchen towel, and across the guy's cheeks and over the dome of protruding linen goes some fine-quality fibrous strapping tape from the drawer under the decommissioned phone—why does everybody keep the serious mailing supplies in the drawer nearest the kitchen phone?—and Don Gately and associate finish their swift and with-the-best-of-intentions nonviolent business of stripping the Brookline home as bare as a post-feral-hamster meadow, and they relock the front door and hit the unlit road in Gately's reliable and double-mufflered 4 x 4. And the bound, wheezing, acetate-clad Canadian—the right-hand man to probably the most infamous anti-O.N.A.N. organizer north of the Great Concavity, the lieutenant and trouble-shooting trusted adviser who selflessly volunteered to move with his family to the savagely American area of metro Boston to act as liaison between and general leash-holder for the half-dozen or so malevolent and mutually antagonistic groups of Québecer Separatists and Albertan ultra-rightists united only in their fanatical conviction that the U.S.A.'s Experialistic 'gift' or 'return' of the so-calledly 'Reconfigured' Great Convexity to its northern neighbor and O.N.A.N. ally constituted an intolerable blow to Canadian sovereignty, honor, and hygiene—this homeowner, unquestionably a V.I.P., although admittedly rather a covert V.I.P., or probably more accurately a 'P.I.T.,'[19] in French, this meek-looking Canadian-terrorism-coordinator—bound to his chair, thoroughly gagged, sitting there, alone, under cold fluorescent kitchen lights,[20] the rhinovirally afflicted man, gagged with skill and quality materials—the guy, having worked so hard to partially clear one clotted nasal passage that he tore intercostal ligaments in his ribs, soon found even that pinprick of air blocked off by mucus's implacable lava-like flow once again, and so has to tear more ligaments trying to breach the other nostril, and so on; and after an hour of struggle and flames in his chest and blood on his lips and the white kitchen towel from trying frantically to tongue the towel out past the tape, which is quality tape, and after hopes skyrocketing when the doorbell rings and then hopes blackly dashed when the person at the door, a young woman with a clipboard and chewing gum who's offering promotional coupons good for Happy Holidays discounts on member-ships of six months or more at a string of Boston non-UV tanning salons, shrugs in her parka and makes a mark on the clipboard and blithely retreats down the long driveway to the pseudo-rural road, an hour of this or more, finally the Québecois P.I.T., after unspeakable agony—slow suf-focation, mucoidal or no, being no day at the Montreal Tulip-Fest—at the height of which agony, hearing his head's pulse as receding thunder and watching his vision's circle shrink as a red aperture around his sight rotates steadily in from the edges, at the height of which he could think only, despite the pain and panic, of what a truly dumb and silly way this was, after all this time, to die, a thought which the towel and tape denied expression via the rueful grin with which the best men meet the dumbest ends—this Guillaume DuPlessis passed bluely from this life, and sat there, in the kitchen chair, 250 clicks due east of some really spectacular autumn foliage, for almost two nights and days, his posture getting more and more military as rigor mortis set in, with his bare feet looking like purple loaves of bread, from the lividity; and when Brookline's Finest were finally summoned and got him unbound from the coldly lit chair, they had to carry him out as if he were still seated, so militarily comme-il-faut had his limbs and spine hardened. And poor old Don Gately, whose professional habit of killing power with straight shunts to a meter's inflow was pretty much a signature M.O., and who had, of course, a special place in the heart of a remorseless Revere A.D.A. with judicial clout throughout Boston's three counties and beyond, an of course particularly remorseless A.D.A., as of late, whose wife now needed Valium even just to floss, and was patiently awaiting his chance, the A.D.A. was, coldly biding his time, being a patient Get-Even and Cold-Dish man just like Don Gately, who was, through no will to energy-consuming violence on his part, in the sort of a hell of a deep-shit mess that can turn a man's life right around.

Year of the Depend Adult Undergarment: InterLace Telentertainment, 932/1864 R.I.S.C. power-TPs w/ or w/o console, Pink$_2$, post-Primestar D.S.S. dissemination, menus and icons, pixel-free Internet Fax, tri- and quad-modems w/ adjustable baud, Dissemination-Grids, screens so high-def you might as well be there, cost-effective videophonic conferencing, internal Froxx CD-ROM, electronic *couture*, all-in-one consoles, Yushi-tyu nanoprocessors, laser chromotography, Virtual-capable media-cards, fiberoptic pulse, digital encoding, killer apps; carpal neuralgia, phosphenic migraine, gluteal hyperadiposity, lumbar stressae.

—*pages 55–60*

As of Year of the Depend Adult Undergarment

THE ENFIELD TENNIS Academy has been in accredited operation for three pre-Subsidized years and then eight Subsidized years, first under the direction of Dr. James Incandenza and then under the administration of his half-brother-in-law Charles Tavis, Ed.D. James Orin Incandenza—the only child of a former top U.S. jr. tennis player and then promising young pre-Method actor who, during the interval of J. O. Incandenza's early formative years, had become a disrespected and largely unemployable actor, driven back to his native Tucson AZ and dividing his remaining energies between stints as a tennis pro at ranch-type resorts and then short-run productions at something called the Desert Beat Theater Project, the father, a dipsomaniacal tragedian progressively crippled by obsessions with death by spider-bite and by stage fright and with a bitterness of ambiguous origin but consuming intensity toward the Method school of professional acting and its more promising exponents, a father who somewhere around the nadir of his professional fortunes apparently decided to go down to his Raid-sprayed basement workshop and build a promising junior athlete the way other fathers might restore vintage autos or build ships inside bottles, or like refinish chairs, etc.—James Incandenza proved a withdrawn but compliant student of the game and soon a gifted jr. player—tall, bespectacled, domineering at net—who used tennis scholarships to finance, on his own, private secondary and then higher education at places just about as far away from the U.S. Southwest as one could get without drowning. The United States government's prestigious O.N.R.[23] financed his doctorate in optical physics, fulfilling something of a childhood dream. His strategic value, during the Federal interval G. Ford-early G. Bush, as more or less the top applied-geometrical-optics man in the O.N.R. and S.A.C., designing neutron-scattering reflectors for thermo-strategic weapons systems, then in the Atomic Energy Commission—where his development of gamma-refractive indices for lithium-anodized lenses and panels is commonly regarded as one of the big half-dozen discoveries that made possible cold annular fusion and approximate energy-independence for the U.S. and its various allies and protectorates—his optical acumen translated, after an early retirement from the public sector, into a patented fortune in rearview mirrors, light-sensitive eyewear, holographic birthday and Xmas greeting cartridges, videophonic Tableaux, homolosine-cartography software, nonfluorescent public-lighting systems and film-equipment; then, in the optative retirement from hard science that building and opening a U.S.T.A.-accredited and peda-gogically experimental tennis academy apparently represented for him, into 'après-garde' experimental- and conceptual-film work too far either ahead of or behind its time, possibly, to be much appreciated at the time of his death in the Year of the Trial-Size Dove Bar—although a lot of it (the experimental- and conceptual-film work) was admittedly just plain pretentious and unengaging and bad, and probably not helped at all by the man's very gradual spiral into the crippling dipsomania of his late father.[24]

The tall, ungainly, socially challenged and hard-drinking Dr. Incandenza's May-December[25] marriage to one of the few bona fide bombshell-type females in North American academia, the extremely tall and high-strung but also extremely pretty and gainly and teetotalling and classy Dr. Avril Mondragon, the only female academic ever to hold the Macdonald Chair in Prescriptive Usage at the Royal Victoria College of McGill University, whom Incandenza'd met at a U. Toronto conference on Reflective vs. Reflexive Systems, was rendered even more romantic by the bureaucratic tribulations involved in obtaining an Exit- and then an Entrance-Visa, to say nothing of a Green Card, for even a U.S.-spoused Professor Mon-dragon whose involvement, however demonstrably nonviolent, with cer-tain members of the Québecois-Separatist Left while in graduate school had placed her name on the R.C.M.P.'s notorious 'Personnes à Qui On Doit Surveiller Attentivement' List. The birth of the Incandenzas' first child, Orin, had been at least partly a legal maneuver.

It is known that, during the last five years of his life, Dr. James O. Incandenza liquidated his assets and patent-licenses, ceded control over most of the Enfield Tennis Academy's operations to his wife's half-brother—a former engineer most recently employed in Amateur Sports Administration at Throppinghamshire Provincial College, New Bruns-wick, Canada—and devoted his unimpaired hours almost exclusively to the production of documentaries, technically recondite art films, and mordantly obscure and obsessive dramatic cartridges, leaving behind a substantial (given the late age at which he bloomed, creatively) number of completed films and cartridges, some of which have earned a small aca-demic following for their technical feck and for a pathos that was somehow both surreally abstract and CNS-rendingly melodramatic at the same time.

Professor James O. Incandenza, Jr.'s untimely suicide at fifty-four was held a great loss in at least three worlds. President J. Gentle (F.C.), acting on behalf of the U.S.D.D.'s O.N.R. and O.N.A.N.'s post-annular A.E.C., conferred a posthumous citation and conveyed his condolences by classified ARPA-NET Electronic Mail. Incandenza's burial in Québec's L'Islet County was twice delayed by annular hyperfloration cycles. Cornell University Press announced plans for a festschrift. Certain leading young quote 'après-garde' and 'anticonfluential' filmmakers employed, in their output for the Year of the Trial-Size Dove Bar, certain oblique visual gestures — most involving the chiaroscuro lamping and custom-lens effects for which Incandenza's distinctive deep focus was known — that paid the sort of deep-insider's elegaic tribute no audience could be expected to notice. An interview with Incandenza was posthumously included in a book on the genesis of annulation. And those of E.T.A.'s junior players whose hypertrophied arms could fit inside them wore black bands on court for almost a year.

—pages 63–65

Winter B.S. 1960 — Tucson Az

JIM NOT THAT way Jim. That's no way to treat a garage door, bending stiffly down at the waist and yanking at the handle so the door jerks up and out jerky and hard and you crack your shins and my ruined knees, son. Let's see you bend at the healthy knees. Let's see you hook a soft hand lightly over the handle feeling its subtle grain and pull just as exactly gently as will make it come to you. Experiment, Jim. See just how much force you need to start the door easy, let it roll up out open on its hidden greasy rollers and pulleys in the ceiling's set of spiderwebbed beams. Think of all garage doors as the well-oiled open-out door of a broiler with hot meat in, heat roiling out, hot. Needless and dangerous ever to yank, pull, shove, thrust. Your mother is a shover and a thruster, son. She treats bodies outside herself without respect or due care. She's never learned that treating things in the gentlest most relaxed way is also treating them and your own body in the most efficient way. It's Marlon Brando's fault, Jim. Your mother back in California before you were born, before she became a devoted mother and long-suffering wife and breadwinner, son, your mother had a bit part in a Marlon Brando movie. Her big moment. Had to stand there in saddle shoes and bobby sox and ponytail and put her hands over her ears as really loud motorbikes roared by. A major thespian moment, believe you me. She was in love from afar with this fellow Marlon Brando, son. Who? Who. Jim, Marlon Brando was the archetypal new-type actor who ruined it looks like two whole generations' relations with their own bodies and the everyday objects and bodies around them. No? Well it was because of Brando you were opening that garage door like that, Jimbo. The disrespect gets learned and passed on. Passed down. You'll know Brando when you watch him, and you'll have learned to fear him. *Brando,* Jim, Jesus, B-r-a-n-d-o. Brando the new archetypal tough-guy rebel and slob type, leaning back on his chair's rear legs, coming crooked through doorways, slouching against everything in sight, trying to *dominate* objects, showing no artful respect or care, yanking things toward him like a moody child and using them up and tossing them crudely aside so they miss the wastebasket and just lie there, ill-used. With the over-clumsy impetuous movements and postures of a moody infant. Your mother is of that new generation that moves against life's grain, across its warp and baffles. She may have loved Marlon Brando, Jim, but she didn't understand him, is what's ruined her for everyday arts like broilers and garage doors and even low-level public-park knock-around tennis. Ever see your mother with a broiler door? It's carnage, Jim, it's to cringe to see it, and the poor dumb thing thinks it's tribute to this slouching slob-type she loved as he roared by. Jim, she never intuited the gentle and cunning economy behind this man's quote harsh sloppy unstudied approach to objects. The way he'd oh so clearly practiced a chair's back-leg tilt over and over. The way he studied objects with a welder's eye for those strongest centered seams which when pressured by the swinishest slouch still support. She never...never sees that Marlon Brando felt himself as body so keenly he'd *no need* for manner. She never sees that in his quote careless way he actually really touched whatever he touched as if it were part of him. Of his own body. The world he only seemed to manhandle was for him sentient, feeling. And no one...and she never understood that. Sour sodding grapes indeed. You can't envy someone who can be that way. Respect, maybe. Maybe *wistful* respect, at the very outside. She never saw that Brando was playing the equivalent of high-level quality tennis across sound stages all over both coasts, Jim, is what he was really doing. Jim, he moved like a careless fingerling, one big muscle, muscularly naïve, but always, notice, a fingerling at the center of a clear current. That kind of animal grace. The bastard wasted *no* motion, is what made it art, this brutish no-care. His was a tennis player's dictum: touch things with consideration and they will be yours; you will own them; they will move or stay still or move for you; they will lie back and part their legs and yield up their innermost seams to you. Teach you all their tricks. He knew what the Beats know and what the great tennis player knows, son: learn to do nothing, with your whole head and body, and everything will be done by what's around you. I know you don't understand. Yet. I know that goggle-eyed stare. I know what it means all too well, son. It's no matter. You will. Jim, I know what I know.

I'm predicting it right here, young sir Jim. You are going to be a great tennis player. I was near-great. You will be truly great. You will be the real thing. I know I haven't taught you to play yet, I know this is your first time, Jim, Jesus, relax, I know. It doesn't affect my predictive sense. You will overshadow and obliterate me. Today you are starting, and within a very few years I know all too well you will be able to beat me out there, and on the day you first beat me I may well weep. It'll be out of a sort of selfless pride, an obliterated father's terrible joy. I feel it, Jim, even here, standing on hot gravel and looking: in your eyes I see the appreciation of angle, a prescience re spin, the way you already adjust your overlarge and apparently clumsy child's body in the chair so it's at the line of best force against dish, spoon, lens-grinding appliance, a big book's stiff bend. You do it unconsciously. You have no idea. But I watch, very closely. Don't ever think I don't, son.

You will be poetry in motion, Jim, size and posture and all. Don't let the posture-problem fool you about your true potential out there. Take it from me, for a change. The trick will be transcending that overlarge head, son. Learning to move just the way you already sit still. Living in your body.

This is the communal garage, son. And this is our door in the garage. I know you know. I know you've looked at it before, many times. Now... now *see* it, Jim. See it as body. The dull-colored handle, the clockwise latch, the bits of bug trapped when the paint was wet and now still protruding. The cracks from this merciless sunlight out here. Original color anyone's guess, boyo. The concave inlaid squares, how many, bevelled at how many levels at the borders, that pass for decoration. Count the squares, maybe... let's see you treat this door like a lady, son. Twisting the latch clockwise with one hand that's right and.... I guess you'll have to pull harder, Jim. Maybe even harder than that. Let me... *that's* the way she wants doing, Jim. Have a look. Jim, this is where we keep this 1956 Mercury Montclair you know so well. This Montclair weighs 3,900 pounds, give or take. It has eight cylinders and a canted windshield and aerodynamic fins, Jim, and has a maximum flat-out road-speed of 95 m.p.h. per. I described the shade of the paint job of this Montclair to the dealer when I first saw it as bit-lip red. Jim, it's a machine. It will do what it's made for and do it perfectly, but only when stimulated by someone who's made it his business to know its tricks and seams, as a body. The stimulator of this car must know the car, Jim, feel it, be inside much more than just the... the compartment. It's an object, Jim, a body, but don't let it fool you, sitting here, mute. It will *respond*. If given its due. With artful care. It's a body and will respond with a well-oiled purr once I get some decent oil in her and all Mercuryish at up to 95 big ones per for just that driver who treats its body like his own, who *feels* the big steel body he's inside, who quietly and unnoticed feels the nubbly plastic of the grip of the shift up next to the wheel when he shifts just as he feels the skin and flesh, the muscle and sinew and bone wrapped in gray spiderwebs of nerves in the blood-fed hand just as he feels the plastic and metal and flange and teeth, the pistons and rubber and rods of the amber-fueled Montclair, when he shifts. The bodily red of a well-bit lip, parping along at a silky 80-plus per. Jim, a toast to our knowledge of bodies. To high-level tennis on the road of life. Ah. Oh.

Son, you're ten, and this is hard news for somebody ten, even if you're almost five-eleven, a possible pituitary freak. Son, you're a body, son. That quick little scientific-prodigy's mind she's so proud of and won't quit twittering about: son, it's just neural spasms, those thoughts in your mind are just the sound of your head revving, and head is still just body, Jim. Commit this to memory. Head is body. Jim, brace yourself against my shoulders here for this hard news, at ten: you're a machine a body an object, Jim, no less than this rutilant Montclair, this coil of hose here or that rake there for the front yard's gravel or sweet Jesus this nasty fat spider flexing in its web over there up next to the rake-handle, see it? See it? *Latrodectus mactans*, Jim. Widow. Grab this racquet and move gracefully and feelingly over there and kill that widow for me, young sir Jim. Go on. Make it say 'K.' Take no names. There's a lad. Here's to a spiderless section of communal garage. Ah. Bodies bodies everywhere. A tennis ball is the ultimate body, kid. We're coming to the crux of what I have to try to impart to you before we get out there and start actuating this fearsome potential of yours. Jim, a tennis ball is the ultimate body. Perfectly round. Even distribution of mass. But empty inside, utterly, a vacuum. Susceptible to whim, spin, to force—used well or poorly. It will reflect your own character. Characterless itself. Pure potential. Have a look at a ball. Get a ball from the cheap green plastic laundry basket of old used balls I keep there by the propane torches and use to practice the occasional serve, Jimbo. Attaboy. Now look at the ball. Heft it. Feel the weight. Here, I'll...tear the ball... open. Whew. See? Nothing in there but evacuated air that smells like a kind of rubber hell. Empty. Pure potential. Notice I tore it open along the seam. It's a body. You'll learn to treat it with consideration, son, some might say a kind of love, and it will open for you, do your bidding, be at your beck and soft lover's call. The thing truly great players with hale bodies who overshadow all others have is a way with the ball that's called, and keep in mind the garage door and broiler, *touch*. Touch the ball. Now that's...that's the touch of a player right there. And as with the ball so with that big thin slumped overall body, sir Jimbo. I'm predicting it right now. I see the way you'll apply the lessons of today to yourself as a physical body. No more carrying your head at the level of your chest under round slumped shoulders. No more tripping up. No more overshot reaches, shattered plates, tilted lampshades, slumped shoulders and caved-in chest, the simplest objects twisting and resistant in your big thin hands, boy. Imagine what it feels like to be this ball, Jim. Total physicality. No revving head. Complete presence. Absolute potential, sitting there potentially absolute in your big pale slender girlish hand so young its thumb's unwrinkled at the joint. My thumb's wrinkled at the joint, Jim, some might say gnarled. Have a look at this thumb right here. But I still treat it as my own. I give it its due. You want a drink of this, son? I think you're ready for a drink of this. No? Nein? Today, Lesson One out there, you become, for better or worse, Jim, a man. A player. A body in commerce with bodies. A helmsman at your own vessel's tiller. A machine in the ghost, to quote a phrase. Ah. A ten-year-old freakishly tall bow-tied and thick-spectacled citizen of the.... I drink this, sometimes, when I'm not actively working, to help me accept the same painful things it's now time for me to tell you, son. Jim. Are you ready? I'm telling you this now because you have to know what I'm about to tell you if you're going to be the more than near-great top-level tennis player I know you're going to be eventually very soon. Brace yourself. Son, get ready. It's glo...gloriously painful. Have just maybe a taste, here. This flask is silver. Treat it with due care. Feel its shape. The near-soft feel of the warm silver and the calfskin sheath that covers only half its flat rounded silver length. An object that rewards a considered touch. Feel the slippery heat? That's the oil from my fingers. My oil, Jim, from my body. Not my hand, son, feel the flask. Heft it. Get to know it. It's an object. A vessel. It's a two-pint flask full of amber liquid. Actually more like half full, it seems. So it seems. This flask has been treated with due care. It's never been dropped or jostled or crammed. It's never had an errant drop, not drop *one,* spilled out of it. I treat it as if it can feel. I give it its due, as a body. Unscrew the cap. Hold the calfskin sheath in your right hand and use your good left hand to feel the cap's shape and ease it around on the threads. Son...son, you'll have to put that what is that that *Columbia Guide to Refractive Indices Second Edition* down, son. Looks heavy anyway. A tendon-strainer. Fuck up your pronator teres and surrounding tendons before you even start. You're going to have to put down the book, for once, young Sir Jimbo, you never try to handle two objects at the same time without just aeons of diligent practice and care, a

Brando-like dis... and well *no* you don't just drop the book, son, you don't just just don't *drop* the big old *Guide to Indices* on the dusty garage floor so it raises a square bloom of dust and gets our nice white athletic socks all gray before we even hit the court, boy, *Jesus* I just took five minutes explaining how the key to being even a potential player is to treat the things with just exactly the... here lemme have this... that books aren't just *dropped* with a crash like bottles in the trashcan they're *placed*, guided, with senses on Full, feeling the edges, the pressure on the little floor of both hands' fingers as you bend at the knees with the book, the slight gassy shove as the air on the dusty floor... as the floor's air gets displaced in a soft square that raises no dust. Like soooo. Not like *so*. Got me? Got it? Well now don't be that way. Son, don't be that way, now. Don't get all oversensitive on me, son, when all I'm trying to do is help you. Son, Jim, I *hate* this when you do this. Your chin just disappears into that bow-tie when your big old overhung lower lip quivers like that. You look chinless, son, and big-lipped. And that cape of mucus that's coming down on your upper lip, the way it shines, don't, just don't, it's revolting, son, you don't want to revolt people, you have to learn to control this sort of oversensitivity to hard truths, this sort of thing, take and exert some goddamn *control* is the whole point of what I'm taking this whole entire morning off rehearsal with not one but two vitally urgent auditions looming down my neck so I can show you, planning to let you move the seat back and touch the shift and maybe even... maybe even drive the Montclair, God knows your feet'll reach, right Jimbo? Jim, hey, why not drive the Montclair? Why not you drive us over, starting today, pull up by the courts where today you'll—here, look, see how I unscrew it? the cap? with the soft very outermost tips of my gnarled fingers which I wish they were steadier but I'm exerting control to control my anger at that chin and lip and the cape of snot and the way your eyes slant and goggle like some sort of mongoloid child's when you're threatening to cry but just the very tips of the fingers, here, the most sensitive parts, the parts bathed in warm oil, the whorled pads, I feel them singing with nerves and blood I let them extend... further than the warm silver hip-flask's cap's very top down its broadening cone where to where the threads around the upraised little circular mouth lie hidden while with the other warm singing hand I gently grip the leather holster so I can feel the way the whole flask feels as I guide... guide the cap around on its silver threads, hear that? stop that and listen, hear that? the sound of threads moving through well-machined grooves, with great care, a smooth barbershop spiral, my whole hand right through the pads of my fingertips less... less unscrewing, here, than guiding, per-

suading, reminding the silver cap's body what it's built to do, machined to
do, the silver cap knows, Jim, I know, you know, we've been through this
before, leave the book *alone,* boy, it's not going anywhere, so the silver cap
leaves the flask's mouth's warm grooved lips with just a snick, hear that?
that faintest snick? not a rasp or a grinding sound or harsh, not a harsh
brutal Brando-esque rasp of attempted domination but a snick a . . .
nuance, there, ah, oh, like the once you've heard it never mistakable *ponk*
of a true-hit ball, Jim, well pick it *up* then if you're afraid of a little dust,
Jim, pick the book *up* if it's going to make you all goggle-eyed and chinless
honestly Jesus why do I try I try and try just wanted to introduce you to
the broiler's garage and let you drive, maybe, feeling the Montclair's body,
taking my time to let you pull up to the courts with the Montclair's shift
in a neutral glide and the eight cylinders thrumming and snicking like a
healthy heart and the wheels all perfectly flush with the curb and bring
out my good old trusty laundry . . . laundry basket of balls and racquets and
towels and flask and my *son,* my flesh of my flesh, white slumped flesh of
my flesh who wanted to embark on what I predict right now will be a tennis career that'll put his busted-up used-up old Dad back square in his little place, who wanted to maybe for once be a real boy and learn how to
play and have fun and frolic and play around in the unrelieved sunshine
this city's so fuck-all famous for, to enjoy it while he can because did your
mother tell you we're moving? That we're moving back to California finally
this spring? We're moving, son, I'm harking one last attempted time to
that celluloid siren's call, I'm giving it the one last total shot a man's obligation to his last waning talent deserves, Jim, we're headed for the big
time again at last for the first time since she announced she was having
you, Jim, hitting the road, celluloid-bound, so say adios to that school and
that fluttery little moth of a physics teacher and those slumped chinless
slide-rule-wielding friends of no now wait I didn't mean it I meant I
wanted to tell you *now,* ahead of time, your mother and I, to give you
plenty of notice so you could *adjust* this time because oh you made it so
unmisinterpretably *clear* how this last move to this trailer park upset you
so, didn't you, to a mobile home with chemical toilet and bolts to hold it in
place and widow-webs everyplace you look and grit settling on everything
like dust out here instead of the Club's staff quarters I got us removed
from or the house it was clearly my fault we couldn't afford anymore. It
was my fault. I mean who else's fault would it be? Am I right? That we
moved your big soft body with allegedly not enough notice and that east-
side school you cried over and that Negro research resource librarian there
with the hair out to here that . . . that lady with the upturned nose on tiptoe

all the time I have to tell you she seemed so consummate east-side Tucsonian all self-consciously not of this earth's grit urging us to quote nurture your optical knack with physics with her nose upturned so you could see up in there and on her toes like something skilled overhead had sunk a hook between her big splayed fingerling's nostrils and were reeling skyward up toward the aether little by little I'll bet those heelless pumps are off the floor altogether by now son what do you say son what do you think...no, go on, cry, don't inhibit yourself, I won't say a word, except it's getting to me less all the time when you do it, I'll just warn you, I think you're overworking the tears and the...it's getting less effec...effective with me each time you use it though we know we both know don't we just between you and me we know it'll always work on your mother, won't it, never fail, she'll every time take and bend your big head down to her shoulder so it looks obscene, if you could see it, pat-patting on your back like she's burping some sort of slumping oversized obscene bow-tied infant with a book straining his pronator teres, crying, will you do this when you're grown? Will there be episodes like this when you're a man at your own tiller? A citizen of a world that won't go pat-pat-there-there? Will your face crumple and bulge like this when you're six-and-a-half grotesque feet tall, six-six-plus like your grandfather may he rot in hell's rubber vacuum when he finally kicks on the tenth tee and with your flat face and no chin just like him on that poor dumb patient woman's fragile wet snotty long-suffering shoulder did I tell you what he did? Did I tell you what he did? I was your age Jim here take the flask no give it here, oh. Oh. I was thirteen, and I'd started to play well, seriously, I was twelve or thirteen and playing for years already and he'd never been to watch, he'd never come once to where I was playing, to watch, or even changed his big flat expression even once when I brought home a trophy I won trophies or a notice in the paper TUCSON NATIVE QUALIFIES FOR NATIONAL JR CH'SHIPS he never acknowledged I even existed as I was, not as I do you, Jim, not as I take care to bend over backwards way, *way* out of my way to let you know I *see* you recognize you am aware of you as a body care about what might go on behind that big flat face bent over a homemade prism. He plays golf. Your grandfather. Your grandpappy. Golf. A golf man. Is my tone communicating the contempt? Billiards on a big table, Jim. A bodiless game of spasmodic flailing and flying sod. A quote unquote sport. Anal rage and checkered berets. This is almost empty. This is just about it, son. What say we rain-check this. What say I put the last of this out of its amber misery and we go in and tell her you're not feeling up to snuff enough again and we're rain-checking your first introduction to the Game till this weekend and we'll head over this weekend and do two straight days both days and give you a really extensive intensive intro to a by all appearances limitless future. Intensive gentleness and bodily care equals great tennis, Jim. We'll go both days and let you plunge right in and get wet all over. It's only five dollars. The court fee. For one lousy hour. Each day. Five dollars each day. Don't give it a thought. Ten total dollars for an intensive weekend when we live in a glorified trailer and have to share a garage with two DeSotos and what looks like a Model A on blocks and my Montclair can't afford the kind of oil she deserves. Don't look like that. What's money or my rehearsals for the celluloid auditions we're moving 700 miles for, auditions that may well comprise your old man's last shot at a life with any meaning at all, compared to my *son?* Right? Am I right? Come here, kid. C'mere c'mere c'mere c'mere. That's a boy. That's my J.O.I. of a guy of a joy of boy. That's my kid, in his body. He never came once, Jim. Not once. To watch. Mother never missed a competitive match, of course. Mother came to so many it ceased to mean anything that she came. She became part of the environment. Mothers are like that, as I'm sure you're aware all too well, am I right? Right? Never came once, kiddo. Never lumbered over all slumped and soft and cast his big grotesque long-even-at-midday shadow at any court I performed on. Till one day he came, once. Suddenly, once, without precedent or warning, he...came. Ah. Oh. I heard him coming long before he hove into view. He cast a long shadow, Jim. It was some minor local event. It was some early-round local thing of very little consequence in the larger scheme. I was playing some local dandy, the kind with fine equipment and creased white clothing and country-club lessons that still can't truly play, even, regardless of all the support. You'll find you often have to endure this type of opponent in the first couple rounds. This gleaming hapless lox of a kid was some client of my father's son...son of one of his clients. So he came for the client, to put on some sham show of fatherly concern. He wore a hat and coat and tie at 95° plus. The client. Can't recall the name. There was something canine about his face, I remember, that his kid across the net had inherited. My father wasn't even sweating. I grew up with the man in this town and never once saw him sweat, Jim. I remember he wore a boater and the sort of gregariously plaid uniform professional men had to wear on the weekends then. They sat in the indecisive shade of a scraggly palm, the sort of palm that's just crawling with black widows, in the fronds, that come down without warning, that hide lying in wait in the heat of midday. They sat on the blanket my mother always brought—my mother, who's dead, and the client. My father stood apart, sometimes in the waving shade, sometimes not, smoking a long filter. Long filters had come into fashion. He never sat on the ground. Not in the American Southwest he didn't. There was a man with a healthy respect for spiders. And *never* on the ground under a palm. He knew he was too grotesquely tall and ungainly to stand up in a hurry or roll screaming out of the way in a hurry in case of falling spiders. They've been known to be willing to drop right out of the trees they hide in, in the daytime, you know. Drop right on you if you're sitting on the ground in the shade. He was no fool, the bastard. A golfer. They all watched. I was right there on the first court. This park no longer exists, Jim. Cars are now parked on what used to be these rough green asphalt courts, shimmering in the heat. They were right there, watching, their heads going back and forth in that windshield-wiper way of people watching quality tennis. And was I nervous, young sir J.O.I.? With the one and only Himself there in all his wooden glory there, watching, half in and out of the light, expressionless? I was not. I was in my body. My body and I were one. My wood Wilson from my stack of wood Wilsons in their trapezoid presses was a sentient expression of my arm, and I felt it singing, and my hand, and they were alive, my well-armed hand was the secretary of my mind, lithe and responsive and *senza errori*, because I knew myself as a body and was fully inside my little child's body out there, Jim, I was in my big right arm and scarless legs, safely ensconced, running here and there, my head pounding like a heart, sweat purled on every limb, running like a veldt-creature, leaping, frolicking, striking with maximum economy and minimum effort, my eyes on the ball and the corners both, I was two, three, a couple shots ahead of both me and the hapless canine client's kid, handing the dandy his pampered ass. It was carnage. It was a scene out of nature in its rawest state, Jim. You should have been there. The kid kept bending over to get his breath. The smoothly economical frolicking I was doing contrasted starkly compared to the heavily jerky way he was being forced to stomp around and lunge. His white knit shirt and name-brand shorts were soaked through so you could see the straps of his jock biting into the soft ass I was handing him. He wore a flitty little white visor such as fifty-two-year-old women at country clubs and posh Southwestern resorts wear. I was, in a word, deft, considered, prescient. I made him stomp and stagger and lunge. I wanted to humiliate him. The client's long sharp face was sagging. My father had no face, it was sharply shadowed and then illuminated in the wagging fronds' shadow he half stood in but was wreathed in smoke from the long filters he fancied, long plastic filtered holders, yellowed at the stem, in imitation of the President, as courtiers once spluttered with the King...veiled in shade and then lit smoke. The client didn't know enough to keep quiet. He thought he was at a ball game or something. The client's voice carried. Our first court was right near the tree they sat under. The client's legs were out in front of them and protruded from the sharp star of frond-shade. His slacks were lattice-shadowed from the pattern of the fence his son and I played just behind. He was drinking the lemonade my mother had brought for me. She made it fresh. He said I was good. My father's client did. In that emphasized way that made his voice carry. You know, son? Good godfrey Incandenza old trout but that lad of yours is *good*. Unquote. I heard him say it as I ran and whacked and frolicked. And I heard the tall son of a bitch's reply, after a long pause during which the world's whole air hung there as if lifted and left to swing. Standing at the baseline, or walking back to the baseline, to either serve or receive, one of the two, I heard the client. His voice carried. And then later I heard my father's reply, may he rot in a green and empty hell. I heard what...what he said in reply, sonbo. But not until after I'd fallen. I insist on this point, Jim. Not until after I'd started to fall. Jim, I'd been in the middle of trying to run down a ball way out of mortal reach, a rare blind lucky dribbler of a drop-shot from the overgroomed lox across the net. A point I could have more than afforded to concede. But that's not the way I...that's not the way a real player plays. With respect and due effort and care for every point. You want to be great, near-great, you give every ball everything. And then some. You concede nothing. Even against loxes. You play right up to your limit and then pass your limit and look back at your former limit and wave a hankie at it, embarking. You enter a trance. You feel the seams and edges of everything. The court becomes a...an extremely unique place to be. It will do everything for you. It will let nothing escape your body. Objects move as they're made to, at the lightest easiest touch. You slip into the clear current of back and forth, making delicate X's and L's across the harsh rough bright green asphalt surface, your sweat the same temperature as your skin, playing with such ease and total mindless effortless effort and and and entranced concentration you don't even stop to consider whether to run down every ball. You're barely aware you're doing it. Your body's doing it for you and the court and Game's doing it for your body. You're barely involved. It's magic, boy. Nothing touches it, when it's right. I predict it. Facts and figures and curved glass and those elbow-straining books of yours' lightless pages are going to seem flat by comparison. Static. Dead and white and flat. They don't begin to....It's like a dance, Jim. The point is I was too bodily respectful to slip up and fall on my own, out there. And the other point is I started to fall forward even *before* I started to hear him reply, standing there: Yes, But He'll *Never Be Great*. What he said in no way made me fall forward. The unlovely opponent had dribbled one just barely over the too-low public-park net, a freak accident, a mishit drop-shot, and another man on another court in another early-round laugher would have let it dribble, conceded the affordable, not tried to wave a hankie from the vessel of his limit. Not race on all eight healthy scarless cylinders desperately forward toward the net to try to catch the goddamn thing on the first bounce. Jim, but any man can slip. I don't know what I slipped on, son. There were spiders well-known to infest the palms' fronds all along the courts' fences. They come down at night on threads, bulbous, flexing. I'm thinking it could have been a bulbous goo-filled widow I stepped and slipped on, Jim, a spider, a mad rogue spider come down on its thread into the shade, flabby and crawling, or that leapt suicidally right from an overhanging frond onto the court, probably making a slight flabby hideous sound when it landed, crawling around on its claws, blinking grotesquely in the hot light it hated, that I stepped on rushing forward and killed and slipped on the mess the big loathsome spider made. See these scars? All knotted and ragged, like something had torn at my own body's knees the way a slouching Brando would just rip a letter open with his teeth and let the envelope fall on the floor all wet and rent and torn? All the palms along the fence were sick, they had palm-rot, it was the A.D. year 1933, of the Great Bisbee Palm-Rot epidemic, all through the state, and they were losing their fronds and the fronds were blighted and the color of really old olives in those old slim jars at the very back of the refrigerator and exuded a sick sort of pus-like slippery discharge and sometimes abruptly fell from trees curving back and forth through the air like celluloid pirates' paper swords. God I hate fronds, Jim. I'm thinking it could have been either a daytime *latrodectus* or some pus from a frond. The wind blew cruddy pus from the webbed fronds onto the court, maybe, up near the net. Either way. Something poisonous or infected, at any rate, unexpected and slick. All it takes is a second, you're thinking, Jim: the body betrays you and down you go, on your knees, sliding on sandpaper court. Not so, son. I used to have another flask like this, smaller, a rather more cunning silver flask, in the glove compartment of my Montclair. Your devoted mother did something to it. The subject has never been mentioned between us. Not so. It was a *foreign* body, or a substance, not my body, and if anybody did any betraying that day I'm telling

you sonny kid boy it was something *I* did, Jimmer, I may well have
betrayed that fine young lithe tan unslumped body, I may very well have
gotten rigid, overconscious, careless of it, listening for what my father,
who I respected, I *respected* that man, Jim, is what's sick, I knew he was
there, I was conscious of his flat face and filter's long shadow, I knew him,
Jim. Things were different when I was growing up, Jim. I hate...Jesus I
hate saying something like this, this things-were-different-when-I-was-a-
lad-type cliché shit, the sort of cliché fathers back then spouted, assuming
he said anything at all. But it was. Different. Our kids, my generation's
kids, they...now you, this post-Brando crowd, you new kids can't like us
or dislike us or respect us or not as human beings, Jim. Your parents. No,
wait, you don't have to pretend you disagree, don't, you don't have to say it,
Jim. Because I know it. I could have predicted it, watching Brando and
Dean and the rest, and I know it, so don't splutter. I blame no one your
age, boyo. You see parents as kind or unkind or happy or miserable or
drunk or sober or great or near-great or failed the way you see a table
square or a Montclair lip-red. Kids today...you kids today somehow don't
know how to *feel*, much less love, to say nothing of respect. We're just bodies to you. We're just bodies and shoulders and scarred knees and big bel-
lies and empty wallets and flasks to you. I'm not saying something cliché
like you take us for granted so much as I'm saying you cannot...imagine
our absence. We're so present it's ceased to mean. We're environmental.
Furniture of the world. Jim, I could imagine that man's absence. Jim, I'm
telling you you cannot imagine my absence. It's my fault, Jim, home so
much, limping around, ruined knees, overweight, under the Influence,
burping, nonslim, sweat-soaked in that broiler of a trailer, burping, farting, frustrated, miserable, knocking lamps over, overshooting my reach.
Afraid to give my last talent the one shot it demanded. Talent is its own
expectation, Jim: you either live up to it or it waves a hankie, receding forever. Use it or lose it, he'd say over the newspaper. I'm...I'm just afraid of
having a tombstone that says HERE LIES A PROMISING OLD
MAN. It's...potential may be worse than none, Jim. Than no talent to
fritter in the first place, lying around guzzling because I haven't the balls
to...God I'm I'm so *sorry*. Jim. You don't deserve to see me like this. I'm
so scared, Jim. I'm so scared of dying without ever being really *seen*. Can
you understand? Are you enough of a big thin prematurely stooped young
bespectacled man, even with your whole life still ahead of you, to understand? Can you see I was giving it all I had? That I was *in* there, out there
in the heat, listening, webbed with nerves? A self that touches all edges,

I remember she said. I felt it in a way I fear you and your generation never could, son. It was less like falling than being shot out of something, is the way I recall it. It did not did *not* happen in slow motion. One minute I was at a dead and beautiful forward run for the ball, the next minute there were hands at my back and nothing underfoot like a push down a stairway. A rude whip-lashing shove square in the back and my promising body with all its webs of nerves pulsing and firing was in full airborne flight and came down on my knees this flask is empty right down on my knees with all my weight and inertia on that scabrous hot sandpaper surface forced into what was an exact parody of an imitation of contemplative prayer, sliding forward. The flesh and then tissue and bone left twin tracks of brown red gray white like tire tracks of bodily gore extending from the service line to the net. I slid on my flaming knees, rushed past the dribbling ball and toward the net that ended my slide. Our slide. My racquet had gone pinwheeling off Jim and my racquetless arms out before me sliding Jim in the attitude of a mortified monk in total prayer. It was given me to hear my father pronounce my bodily existence as not even potentially great at the moment I ruined my knees forever, Jim, so that even years later at USC I never got to wave my hankie at anything beyond the near- and almost-great and would-have-been-great-*if,* and later could never even hope to audition for those swim-trunk and Brylcreem beach movies that snake Avalon is making his mint on. I do not insist that the judgment and punishing fall are . . . were connected, Jim. Any man can slip out there. All it takes is a second of misplaced respect. Son, it was more than a father's voice, carrying. My mother cried out. It was a religious moment. I learned what it means to be a body, Jim, just meat wrapped in a sort of flimsy nylon stocking, son, as I fell kneeling and slid toward the stretched net, myself seen by me, frame by frame, torn open. I may have to burp, belch, son, son, telling you what I learned, son, my . . . my love, too late, as I left my knees' meat behind me, slid, ended in a posture of supplication on my knees' disclosed bones with my fingers racquetless hooked through the mesh of the net, across which, the net, the sopped dandy had dropped his pricey gut-strung Davis racquet and was running toward me with his visor askew and his hands to his cheeks. My father and the client he was there to perform for dragged me upright to the palm's infected shade where she knelt on the plaid beach-blanket with her knuckles between her teeth, Jim, and I felt the religion of the physical that day, at not much more than your age, Jim, shoes filling with blood, held under the arms by two bodies big as yours and dragged off a public court with two extra lines. It's a pivotal, it's a seminal, religious day when you get to both hear and feel your destiny at the same moment, Jim. I got to notice what I'm sure you've noticed long ago, I know, I know you've seen me brought home on occasions, dragged in the door, under what's called the Influence, son, helped in by cabbies at night, I've seen your long shadow grotesquely backlit at the top of the house's stairs I helped pay for, boy: how the drunk and the maimed both are dragged forward out of the arena like a boneless Christ, one man under each arm, feet dragging, eyes on the aether.

—pages 157–169

○

TENNIS AND THE FERAL PRODIGY, NARRATED BY HAL
INCANDENZA, AN 11.5-MINUTE DIGITAL ENTERTAINMENT
CARTRIDGE DIRECTED, RECORDED, EDITED,
AND — ACCORDING TO THE ENTRY FORM — WRITTEN
BY MARIO INCANDENZA, IN RECEIPT OF NEW-NEW-
ENGLAND REGIONAL HONORABLE MENTION IN INTERLACE
TELENTERTAINMENT'S ANNUAL 'NEW EYES, NEW VOICES'
YOUNG FILMMAKERS' CONTEST, APRIL IN THE YEAR OF
THE YUSHITYU 2007 MIMETIC-RESOLUTION-CARTRIDGE-
VIEW-MOTHERBOARD-EASY-TO-INSTALL UPGRADE FOR
INFERNATRON/INTERLACE TP SYSTEMS FOR HOME, OFFICE
OR MOBILE (SIC), ALMOST EXACTLY THREE YEARS AFTER
DR. JAMES O. INCANDENZA PASSED FROM THIS LIFE

HERE IS HOW to put on a big red tent of a shirt that has *ETA* across the chest in gray.

Please ease carefully into your supporter and adjust the elastic straps so the straps do not bite into your butt and make bulged ridges in your butt that everyone can see once you've sweated through your shorts.

Here is how to wrap your torn ankle so tightly in its flesh-tone Ace bandages your left leg feels like a log.

Here is how to win, later.

This is a yellow iron-mesh Ball-Hopper full of dirty green dead old balls. Take them to the East Courts while the dawn is still chalky and no one's around except the mourning doves that infest the pines at sunrise, and the air is so sopped you can see your summer breath. Hit serves to no one. Make a mess of balls along the base of the opposite fence as the sun hauls itself up over the Harbor and a thin sweat breaks and the serves start to boom. Stop thinking and let it flow and go boom, boom. The shiver of the ball against the opposite fence. Hit about a thousand serves to no one while Himself sits and advises with his flask. Older men's legs are white and hairless from decades in pants. Here is the set of keys a stride's length before you in the court as you serve dead balls to no one. After each serve you must almost fall forward into the court and in one smooth motion bend and scoop up the keys with your left hand. This is how to train yourself to follow through into the court after the serve. You still, years after the man's death, cannot keep your keys anywhere but on the floor.

This is how to hold the stick.

Learn to call the racquet a stick. Everyone does, here. It's a tradition: The Stick. Something so much an extension of you deserves a sobriquet.

Please look. You'll be shown exactly once how to hold it. This is how to hold it. Just like this. Forget all the near-Eastern-slice-backhand-grip bafflegab. Just say Hello is all. Just shake hands with the calfskin grip of the stick. This is how to hold it. The stick is your friend. You will become very close.

Grasp your friend firmly at all times. A firm grip is essential for both control and power. Here is how to carry a tennis ball around in your stick-hand, squeezing it over and over for long stretches of time — in class, on the phone, in lab, in front of the TP, a wet ball for the shower, ideally squeezing it at all times except during meals. See the Academy dining hall, where tennis balls sit beside every plate. Squeeze the tennis ball rhythmically month after year until you feel it no more than your heart squeezing blood and your right forearm is three times the size of your left and your arm looks from across a court like a gorilla's arm or a stevedore's arm pasted on the body of a child.

Here is how to do extra individual drills before the Academy's A.M. drills, before breakfast, so that after the thousandth ball hit just out of reach by Himself, with his mammoth wingspan and ghastly calves, urging you with nothing but smiles on to great and greater demonstrations of effort, so that after you've gotten your third and final wind and must vomit, there is little inside to vomit and the spasms pass quickly and an east breeze blows cooler past you and you feel clean and can breathe.

Here is how to don red and gray E.T.A. sweats and squad-jog a weekly 40 km. up and down urban Commonwealth Avenue even though you would rather set your hair on fire than jog in a pack. Jogging is painful and pointless, but you are not in charge. Your brother gets to ride shotgun while a senile German blows BBs at your legs both of them laughing and screaming *Schnell*. Enfield is due east of the Marathon's Hills of Heartbreak, which are just up Commonwealth past the Reservoir in Newton. Urban jogging in a sweaty pack is tedious. Have Himself hunch down to put a long pale arm around your shoulders and tell you that his own father had told him that talent is sort of a dark gift, that talent is its own expectation: it is there from the start and either lived up to or lost.

Have a father whose own father lost what was there. Have a father who lived up to his own promise and then found thing after thing to meet and surpass the expectations of his promise in, and didn't seem just a whole hell of a lot happier or tighter wrapped than his own failed father, leaving you yourself in a kind of feral and flux-ridden state with respect to talent.

Here is how to avoid thinking about any of this by practicing and playing until everything runs on autopilot and talent's unconscious exercise becomes a way to escape yourself, a long waking dream of pure play.

The irony is that this makes you very good, and you start to become regarded as having a prodigious talent to live up to.

Here is how to handle being a feral prodigy. Here is how to handle being seeded at tournaments, signifying that seeding committees composed of old big-armed men publicly expect you to reach a certain round. Reaching at least the round you're supposed to is known at tournaments as 'justifying your seed.' By repeating this term over and over, perhaps in the same rhythm at which you squeeze a ball, you can reduce it to an empty series of phonemes, just formants and fricatives, trochaically stressed, signifying zip.

Here is how to beat unseeded, wide-eyed opponents from Iowa or Rhode Island in the early rounds of tournaments without expending much energy but also without seeming contemptuous.

This is how to play with personal integrity in a tournament's early rounds, when there is no umpire. Any ball that lands on your side and is too close to call: call it fair. Here is how to be invulnerable to gamesmanship. To keep your attention's aperture tight. Here is how to teach yourself, when an opponent maybe cheats on the line-calls, to remind yourself that what goes around comes around. That a poor sport's punishment is always self-inflicted.

Try to learn to let what is unfair teach you.

Here is how to spray yourself down exactly once with Lemon Pledge, the ultimate sunscreen, then discover that when you go out and sweat into it it smells like close-order skunk.

Here is how to take nonnarcotic muscle relaxants for the back spasms that come from thousands of serves to no one.

Here is how to weep in bed trying to remember when your torn blue ankle didn't hurt every minute.

This is the whirlpool, a friend.

Here is how to set up the electric ball machine at dawn on the days Himself is away living up to what will be his final talent.

Here is how to tie a bow tie. Here is how to sit through small openings of your father's first art films, surrounded by surly foreign cigarette smoke and conversations so pretentious you literally cannot believe them, you're sure you have misheard them. Pretend you're engaged by the jagged angles and multiple exposures without pretending you have the slightest idea what's going on. Assume your brother's expression.

Here is how to sweat.

Here is how to hand a trophy to Lateral Alice Moore to put in the E.T.A. lobby's glass case under its system of spotlights and small signs.

What is unfair can be a stern but invaluable teacher.

Here is how to pack carbohydrates into your tissues for a four-singles two-doubles match day in a Florida June.

Please learn to sleep with perpetual sunburn.

Expect some rough dreams. They come with the territory. Try to accept them. Let them teach you.

Keep a flashlight by your bed. It helps with the dreams.

Please make no extramural friends. Discourage advances from outside the circuit. Turn down dates.

If you do exactly the rehabilitative exercises They assign you, no matter how silly and tedious, the ankle will mend more quickly.

This type of stretch helps prevent the groin-pull.

Treat your knees and elbow with all reasonable care: you will have them with you for a long time.

Here is how to turn down an extramural date so you won't be asked again. Say something like I'm terribly sorry I can't come out to see *8½* revived on a wall-size Cambridge Celluloid Festival viewer on Friday, Kimberly, or Daphne, but you see if I jump rope for two hours then jog backwards through Newton till I puke They'll let me watch match-cartridges and then my mother will read aloud to me from the *O.E.D.* until 2200 lights-out, and c.; so you can be sure that henceforth Daphne/Kimberly/Jennifer will take her adolescent-mating-dance-type-ritual-socialization business somewhere else. Be on guard. The road widens, and many of the detours are seductive. Be constantly focused and on alert: feral talent is its own set of expectations and can abandon you at any one of the detours of so-called normal American life at any time, so be *on guard*.

Here is how to *schnell.*

Here is how to go through your normal adolescent growth spurt and have every limb in your body ache like a migraine because selected groups of muscles have been worked until thick and intensile and they resist as the sudden growth of bone tries to stretch them, and they ache all the time. There is medication for this condition.

If you are an adolescent, here is the trick to being neither quite a nerd nor quite a jock: be no one.

It is easier than you think.

Here is how to read the monthly E.T.A. and U.S.T.A. and O.N.A.N.T.A. rankings the way Himself read scholars' reviews of his multiple-exposure melodramas. Learn to care and not to care. They mean the rankings to help you determine where you are, not who you are. Memorize your monthly rankings, and forget them. Here is how: never tell anyone where you are.

This is also how not to fear sleep or dreams. Never tell anyone where you are. Please learn the pragmatics of expressing fear: sometimes words that seem to express really *invoke.*

This can be tricky.

Here is how to get free sticks and strings and clothes and gear from Dunlop, Inc. as long as you let them spraypaint the distinctive Dunlop logo on your sticks' strings and sew logos on your shoulder and the left pocket of your shorts and use a Dunlop gear-bag, and you become a walk-ing lunging sweating advertisement for Dunlop, Inc.; this is all as long as you keep justifying your seed and preserving your rank; the Dunlop, Inc. New New England Regional Athletic Rep will address you as 'Our gray swan'; he wears designer slacks and choking cologne and about twice a year wants to help you dress and has to be slapped like a gnat.

Be a Student of the Game. Like most clichés of sport, this is profound. You can be shaped, or you can be broken. There is not much in between. Try to learn. Be coachable. Try to learn from everybody, especially those who fail. This is hard. Peers who fizzle or blow up or fall down, run away, disappear from the monthly rankings, drop off the circuit. E.T.A. peers waiting for deLint to knock quietly at their door and ask to chat. Oppo-nents. It's all educational. How promising you are as a Student of the Game is a function of what you can pay attention to without run-ning away. Nets and fences can be mirrors. And between the nets and fences, opponents are also mirrors. This is why the whole thing is scary. This is why all opponents are scary and weaker opponents are especially scary.

See yourself in your opponents. They will bring you to understand the

Game. To accept the fact that the Game is about managed fear. That its object is to send from yourself what you hope will not return.

This is your body. They want you to know. You will have it with you always.

On this issue there is no counsel; you must make your best guess. For myself, I do not expect ever really to know.

But in the interval, if it is an interval: here is Motrin for your joints, Noxzema for your burn, Lemon Pledge if you prefer nausea to burn, Contracol for your back, benzoin for your hands, Epsom salts and anti-inflammatories for your ankle, and extracurriculars for your folks, who just wanted to make sure you didn't miss anything they got.

—pages 172–176

○

SELECTED TRANSCRIPTS OF THE RESIDENT–INTERFACE–
DROP-IN-HOURS OF MS. PATRICIA MONTESIAN, M.A.,
C.S.A.C.,[58] EXECUTIVE DIRECTOR, ENNET HOUSE
DRUG AND ALCOHOL RECOVERY HOUSE (SIC), ENFIELD
MA, 1300–1500H., WEDNESDAY, 4 NOVEMBER — YEAR OF
THE DEPEND ADULT UNDERGARMENT

'BUT THERE'S THIS *way* he drums his fingers on the table. Not even like really drumming. More like in-way between drumming and like this *scratching, picking,* the way you see somebody picking at dead skin. And without any kind of rhythm, see, constant and never-stopping but with no kind of rhythm you could grab onto and follow and stand. Totally like *whacked, insane.* Like the kind of sounds you can imagine a girl hears in her head right before she kills her whole family because somebody took the last bit of peanut butter or something. You know what I'm saying? The sound of a fucking mind coming apart. You know what I'm saying? So yeah, yes, OK, the short answer is when he wouldn't quit with the drumming at supper I sort of poked him with my fork. Sort of. I could see how maybe somebody could have thought I sort of stabbed him. I offered to get the fork out, though. Let me just say I'm ready to make amends at like anytime. For my part in it. I'm *owning* my part in it is what I'm saying. Can I ask am I going to get Restricted for this? Cause I have this Overnight tomorrow that Gene he approved already in the Overnight Log. If you want to look. But I'm not trying to get out of owning my part of the, like, occurrence. If my Higher Power who I choose to call God works through you saying I've got some kind of a punishment due, I won't try to get out of a punishment. If I've got one due. I just wanted to ask. Did I mention I'm grateful to be here?'

'I'm not *denying* anything. I'm simply asking you to define "alcoholic." How can you ask me to attribute to myself a given term if you refuse to define the term's meaning? I've been a reasonably successful personal-injury attorney for sixteen years, and except for that one ridiculous so-called seizure at the Bar Association dinner this spring and that clot of a judge banning me from his courtroom — and let me just say that I can support my contention that the man masturbates under his robe behind the bench with *detailed* corroboration from both colleagues and Circuit Court laundry personnel — with the exception of less than a handful of incidents I've held my liquor and my head as high as many a taller advocate. Believe you me. How old are you, young lady? I am not *in denial* so to speak about anything empirical and objective. Am I having pancreas problems? Yes. Do I have trouble recalling certain intervals in the Kemp and Limbaugh administrations? No contest. Is there a spot of domestic turbulence surrounding my intake? Why yes there is. Did I experience yes some formication in detox? I did. I have no problem forthrightly admitting things I can grasp. For*m*icate, with an *m*, yes. But what is this you demand I admit? Is it *denial* to delay signature until the vocabulary of the contract is clear to all parties so bound? Yes, yes, you don't follow what I mean here, good! And you're reluctant to proceed without clarification. I rest. I cannot deny what I don't understand. This is my position.'

'So I'm sitting there waiting for my meatloaf to cool and suddenly there's a simply *sphincter*-loosening shriek and here's Nell in the air with a steak-fork, positively *aloft*, *leaping* across the table, in *flight*, horizontal, I mean Pat the girl's body is literally *parallel* to the surface of the table, *hurling* herself at me, with this upraised fork, shrieking something about the sound of *peanut* butter. I mean my God. Gately and Diehl had to pull the fork out of my hand and the tabletop both. To give you an idea. Of the *savagery*. Don't even ask me about the pain. Let's don't even get into that, I assure you. They *offered* me Percocet[59] at the emergency room, is all I'll say about the levels of pain involved. I told them I was in recovery and powerless over narcotics of any sort. Please don't even ask me how moved they were at my courage if you don't want me to get weepy. This whole experience has me right on the edge of a complete hysterical *fit*. So but yes, guilty, I may very well have been tapping on the table. Excuse me for occupying space. And then she ever so *magnaminously* says she'll apologize if I will. Well come again I said? Come *again?* I mean my God. I'm sitting there attached to the table by tines. I know bashing, Pat, and this was unabashed bashing at its most fascist. I respectfully ask that she be kicked out of here on her enormous rear-end. Let her go back to whatever fork-wielding district she came from, with her Hefty bag full of gauche clothes. Honestly. I know part of this process is learning to live in a community. The give and take, to let go of personality issues, turn them over. Et cetera. But is it not also supposed to be and here I quote the handbook a *safe* and *nurturing* environment? I have seldom felt less nurtured than I did impaled on that table I have to say. The pathetic harassments of Minty and McDade are bad enough. I can get bashed back at the Fenway. I did not come here to get bashed on some pretense of table-tapping. I'm dangerously close to saying either that... that *specimen* goes or I do.'

'I'm awful sorry to bother. I can come back. I was wondering if maybe there was any special Program prayer for when you want to hang yourself.'

'I want understanding I have no denial I am drug addict. Me, I know that I am addicted since the period of before Miami. I am no trouble to stand up in the meetings and say I am Alfonso, I am drug addict, powerless. I am knowing powerlessness since the period of Castro. But I cannot stop even since I know. This I have fear. I fear I do not stop when I admit I am Alfonso, powerless. How does to admit I am powerless make me stop what the thing is I am powerless to stop? My head it is crazy from this fearing of no power. I am now hope for *power*, Mrs. Pat. I want to advice. Is hope of power the bad way for Alfonso as drug addict?'

'Sorry to barge, there, P.M. Division called again about the thing with the vermin. The word was *ultimatum* that they said.'

'Sorry if I'm bothering you about something that isn't a straightforward treatment interface thing. I'm up there trying to do my Chore. I've got the men's upstairs bathroom. There's something... Pat there's something in the toilet up there. That won't flush. The thing. It won't go away. It keeps reappearing. Flush after flush. I'm only here for instructions. Possibly also protective equipment. I couldn't even describe the thing in the toilet. All I can say is if it was produced by anything human then I have to say I'm really worried. Don't even ask me to describe it. If you want to go up and have a look, I'm a 100% confident it's still there. It's made it real clear it's not going anywhere.'

'Alls I know is I put a Hunt's Pudding Cup in the resident fridge like I'm supposed to at 1300 and da-da-da and at 1430 I come down all primed for pudding that I paid for myself and it's not there and McDade comes on all concerned and offers to help me look for it and da-da, except if you look I look and here's the son of a whore got this big thing of pudding on his chin.'

'Yeah but except so how can I answer just yes or no to do I want to stop the coke? Do I think I want to absolutely I think I want to. I don't have a septum no more. My septum's been like fucking dissolved by coke. See? You see anything like a septum when I lift up like that? I've absolutely with my whole heart thought I wanted to stop and so forth. Ever since with the septum. So but so since I've been wanting to stop this whole time, why couldn't I stop? See what I'm saying? Isn't it all about wanting to and so on? And so forth? How can living here and going to meetings and all do anything except make me want to stop? But I think I already want to stop. How come I'd even be here if I didn't want to stop? Isn't being here proof I want to stop? But then so how come I can't stop, if I want to stop, is the thing.'

'This kid had a harelip. Where it goes like, you know, *thith*. But his went way up. Further up. He sold bad speed but good pot. He said he'd cover our part of the rent if we kept his snakes supplied with mice. We were smoking up all our cash so what's to do. They ate mice. We had to go into pet stores and pretend to be real heavily into mice. Snakes. He kept snakes. Doocy. They smelled bad. He never cleaned the tanks. His lip covered his nose. The harelip. My guess he couldn't smell what they smelled like. Or something would have got done. He had a thing for Mildred. My girlfriend. I don't know. She probably has a problem too. I don't know. He had a thing for her. He'd keep saying shit like, with all these *t-h*'s, he'd go Tho you want to fuck me, Mildred, or what? We don't hath t'eat each other or nothin. He'd say shit like this with me right there, dropping mice into these tanks, holding my breath. The mice had to be alive. All in this godawful voice like somebody's holding their nose and can't say *s*. He didn't wash his hair for two years. We had like an in-joke on how long he wouldn't wash his hair and we'd make X's on the calendar every week. We had a lot of these in-type jokes, to help us stand it. We were wasted I'd say

90% of the time. Nine-O. But he never did the whole time we were there. Wash. When she said we had to leave or she was taking off and taking Harriet was when she said when I was at work he started telling her how to have sex with a chicken. He said he had sex with the chickens. It was a trailer out past the dumpster-dock in the Spur, and he kept a couple chickens under it. No wonder they ran like hell when anybody came. He'd been like sexually abusing fowls. He kept talking to her about it, with all *t-h*'s, like You hath to like *thcrew* them on, but when you come they jutht thort of *fly* off of you. She said she drew the line. We left and went to Pine Street shelter and she stayed for a while till this guy with a hat said he had a ranch in New Jersey and off she goes, and with Harriet. Harriet's our daughter. She's going to be three. She says it *free*, though. I doubt now the kid'll ever say a single *t-h* her whole life. And I don't even know where in New Jersey. Does New Jersey even have ranches? I'd been in school with her since grade school. Mildred. We were like childhood sweethearts. And then this guy who got her old cot at the shelter I got lice from. He moves into her cot and then I start to get lice. I was still trying to deliver ice to machines at gas stations. Who wouldn't have to get high just to stand it?'

'So this purports to be a disease, alcoholism? A disease like a cold? Or like cancer? I have to tell you, I have never heard of anyone being told to pray for relief from cancer. Outside maybe certain very rural parts of the American South, that is. So what is this? You're *ordering* me to pray? Because I allegedly have a disease? I dismantle my life and career and enter nine months of low-income treatment for a *disease,* and I'm prescribed prayer? Does the word *retrograde* signify? Am I in a sociohistorical era I don't know about? What exactly is the story here?'

'Fine, fine. Fine. Just completely fine. No problem at all. Happy to be here. Feeling better. Sleeping better. Love the chow. In a word, couldn't be finer. The grinding? The tooth-grinding? A tic. A jaw-strengthener. Expression of all-around fineness. Likewise the thing with the eyelid.'

'But I did *too* try. I been trying all *month*. I been on four interviews. They didn't none of them start till 11, and I'm like what's the point get up early sit around here I don't have to be down there till 11? I filled out applications *ever*day. Where'm I suppose to go? You can't kick me out just for the moth — they don't call me back if I'm *trying*. Snot my *fault*. Go on and ask

Clenette. Ask that Thrale girl and them if I ain't been trying. You *can't*. This is just so *fucked up*.

'I *said* where'm I suppose to *go* to?'

'I'm on a month's Full-House Restriction for using freaking mouthwash? Newsflash: news bulletin: mouthwash is for spitting out! It's like 2% proof!'

'It's about somebody *else*'s farting, why I'm here.'

'I'll gladly identify myself if you'll first simply explain what it is I'm identifying myself *as*. This is my position. You're requiring me to attest to facts I do not possess. The term for this is "duress." '

'So my offense is what, misdemeanor gargling?'

'I'll come back when you're free.'

'It's back. For a second there I hoped. I had hope. Then there it was again.'

'First just let me say one thing.'

—*pages 176–181*

○

IF, BY THE virtue of charity or the circumstance of desperation, you ever chance to spend a little time around a Substance-recovery halfway facility like Enfield MA's state-funded Ennet House, you will acquire many exotic new facts. You will find out that once MA's Department of Social Services has taken a mother's children away for any period of time, they can always take them away again, D.S.S., like at will, empowered by nothing more than a certain signature-stamped form. I.e. once deemed Unfit—no matter why or when, or what's transpired in the meantime—there's nothing a mother can do.

Or for instance that people addicted to a Substance who abruptly stop ingesting the Substance often suffer wicked papular acne, often for months afterward, as the accumulations of Substance slowly leave the body. The Staff will inform you that this is because the skin is actually the body's biggest excretory organ. Or that chronic alcoholics' hearts are—for reasons no M.D. has been able to explain—swollen to nearly twice the size of civilians' human hearts, and they never again return to normal size. That there's a certain type of person who carries a picture of their therapist in their wallet. That (both a relief and kind of an odd let-down) black penises tend to be the same general size as white penises, on the whole. That not all U.S. males are circumcised.

That you can cop a sort of thin jittery amphetaminic buzz if you rapidly consume three Millennial Fizzies and a whole package of Oreo cookies on an empty stomach. (Keeping it down is required, however, for the buzz, which senior residents often neglect to tell newer residents.)

That the chilling Hispanic term for whatever interior disorder drives the addict back again and again to the enslaving Substance is *tecato gusano*, which apparently connotes some kind of interior psychic worm that cannot be sated or killed.

That black and Hispanic people can be as big or bigger racists than white people, and then can get even more hostile and unpleasant when this realization seems to surprise you.

That it is possible, in sleep, for some roommates to secure a cigarette from their bedside pack, light it, smoke it down to the quick, and then extinguish it in their bedside ashtray—without once waking up, and without setting anything on fire. You will be informed that this skill is usually acquired in penal institutions, which will lower your inclination to complain about the practice. Or that even Flents industrial-strength expandable-foam earplugs do not solve the problem of a snoring roommate if the roommate in question is so huge and so adenoidal that the snores in question also produce subsonic vibrations that arpeggio up and down your body and make your bunk jiggle like a motel bed you've put a quarter in.

That females are capable of being just as vulgar about sexual and elimi-natory functions as males. That over 60% of all persons arrested for drug- and alcohol-related offenses report being sexually abused as children, with two-thirds of the remaining 40% reporting that they cannot remember their childhoods in sufficient detail to report one way or the other on abuse. That you can weave hypnotic Madame Psychosis–like harmonies around the minor-D scream of a cheap vacuum cleaner, humming to yourself as you vacuum, if that's your Chore. That some people really do look like rodents. That some drug-addicted prostitutes have a harder time giving up prostitution than they have giving up drugs, with their explana-tion involving the two habits' very different directions of currency-flow. That there are just as many idioms for the female sex-organ as there are for the male sex-organ.

That a little-mentioned paradox of Substance addiction is: that once you are sufficiently enslaved by a Substance to need to quit the Substance in order to save your life, the enslaving Substance has become so deeply important to you that you will all but lose your mind when it is taken away from you. Or that sometime after your Substance of choice has just been taken away from you in order to save your life, as you hunker down for required A.M. and P.M. prayers, you will find yourself beginning to pray to be allowed literally to lose your mind, to be able to wrap your mind in an old newspaper or something and leave it in an alley to shift for itself, without you.

That in metro Boston the idiom of choice for the male sex-organ is: *Unit*, which is why Ennet House residents are wryly amused by E.M.P.H. Hospital's designations of its campus's buildings.

That certain persons simply will not like you no matter what you do. Then that most nonaddicted adult civilians have already absorbed and accepted this fact, often rather early on.

That no matter how smart you thought you were, you are actually way less smart than that.

That AA and NA and CA's 'God' does not apparently require that you believe in Him/Her/It before He/She/It will help you.[69] That, *pace* macho bullshit, public male weeping is not only plenty masculine but can actually feel *good* (reportedly). That *sharing* means talking, and *taking somebody's inventory* means criticizing that person, plus many additional pieces of Recoveryspeak. That an important part of halfway-house Human Immuno-Virus prevention is not leaving your razor or toothbrush in communal bathrooms. That apparently a seasoned prostitute can (reportedly) apply a condom to a customer's Unit so deftly he doesn't even know it's on until he's history, so to speak.

That a double-layered steel portable strongbox w/ tri-tumblered lock for your razor and toothbrush can be had for under $35.00 U.S./$38.50 O.N.A.N. via Home-Net Hardware, and that Pat M. or the House Manager will let you use the back office's old TP to order one if you put up a sustained enough squawk.

That over 50% of persons with a Substance addiction suffer from some other recognized form of psychiatric disorder, too. That some male prostitutes become so accustomed to enemas that they cannot have valid bowel movements without them. That a majority of Ennet House residents have at least one tattoo. That the significance of this datum is unanalyzable. That the metro Boston street term for not having any money is: *sporting lint*. That what elsewhere's known as Informing or Squealing or Narcing or Ratting or Ratting Out is on the streets of metro Boston known as 'Eating Cheese,' presumably spun off from the associative nexus of *rat*.

That nose-, tongue-, lip-, and eyelid-rings rarely require actual penetrative piercing. This is because of the wide variety of clip-on rings available. That nipple-rings do require piercing, and that clitoris- and glans-rings are not things anyone thinks you really want to know the facts about. That sleeping can be a form of emotional escape and can with sustained effort be abused. That female chicanos are not called chicanas. That it costs $225 U.S. to get a MA driver's license with your picture but not your name. That purposeful sleep-deprivation can also be an abusable escape. That gambling can be an abusable escape, too, and work, shopping, and shoplifting, and sex, and abstention, and masturbation, and food, and exercise, and meditation/prayer, and sitting so close to Ennet House's old D.E.C. TP cartridge-viewer that the screen fills your whole vision and the screen's static charge tickles your nose like a linty mitten.[70]

That you do not have to like a person in order to learn from him/her/it.

That loneliness is not a function of solitude. That it is possible to get so angry you really do see everything red. What a 'Texas Catheter' is. That some people really do steal — will steal things that are *yours*. That a lot of U.S. adults truly cannot read, not even a ROM hypertext phonics thing with HELP functions for every word. That cliquey alliance and exclusion and gossip can be forms of escape. That logical validity is not a guarantee of truth. That evil people never believe they are evil, but rather that *everyone else* is evil. That it is possible to learn valuable things from a stupid person. That it takes effort to pay attention to any one stimulus for more than a few seconds. That you can all of a sudden out of nowhere want to get high with your Substance so bad that you think you will surely die if you don't, and but can just sit there with your hands writhing in your lap and face wet with craving, can want to get high but instead just sit there, wanting to but not, if that makes sense, and if you can gut it out and not hit the Substance during the craving the craving will eventually *pass*, it will go away — at least for a while. That it is statistically easier for low-IQ people to kick an addiction than it is for high-IQ people. That the metro Boston street term for panhandling is: *stemming*, and that it is regarded by some as a craft or art; and that professional stem-artists actually have like little professional colloquia sometimes, little conventions, in parks or public-transport hubs, at night, where they get together and network and exchange feedback on trends and techniques and public relations, etc. That it is possible to abuse OTC cold- and allergy remedies in an addictive manner. That Nyquil is over 50 proof. That boring activities become, perversely, much less boring if you concentrate intently on them. That if enough people in a silent room are drinking coffee it is possible to make out the sound of steam coming off the coffee. That sometimes human beings have to just sit in one place and, like, *hurt*. That you will become way less concerned with what other people think of you when you realize how seldom they do. That there is such a thing as raw, unalloyed, agendaless kindness. That it is possible to fall asleep during an anxiety attack.

That concentrating intently on anything is very hard work.

That addiction is either a disease or a mental illness or a spiritual condition (as in 'poor of spirit') or an O.C.D.-like disorder or an affective or character disorder, and that over 75% of the veteran Boston AAs who want to convince you that it is a disease will make you sit down and watch them write *DISEASE* on a piece of paper and then divide and hyphenate the word so that it becomes *DIS–EASE*, then will stare at you as if expecting you to undergo some kind of blinding epiphanic realization, when really (as G. Day points tirelessly out to his counselors) changing

DISEASE to *DIS–EASE* reduces a definition and explanation down to a simple description of a feeling, and rather a whiny insipid one at that.

That most Substance-addicted people are also addicted to thinking, meaning they have a compulsive and unhealthy relationship with their own thinking. That the cute Boston AA term for addictive-type thinking is: *Analysis-Paralysis.* That cats will in fact get violent diarrhea if you feed them milk, contrary to the popular image of cats and milk. That it is simply more pleasant to be happy than to be pissed off. That 99% of compulsive thinkers' thinking is about themselves; that 99% of this self-directed thinking consists of imagining and then getting ready for things that are going to happen to them; and then, weirdly, that if they stop to think about it, that 100% of the things they spend 99% of their time and energy imagining and trying to prepare for all the contingencies and consequences of are *never good.* Then that this connects interestingly with the early-sobriety urge to pray for the literal loss of one's mind. In short that 99% of the head's thinking activity consists of trying to scare the everliving shit out of itself. That it is possible to make rather tasty poached eggs in a microwave oven. That the metro-street term for really quite wonderful is: *pisser.* That everybody's sneeze sounds different. That some people's moms never taught them to cover up or turn away when they sneeze. That no one who has been to prison is ever the same again. That you do not have to have sex with a person to get crabs from them. That a clean room feels better to be in than a dirty room. That the people to be most frightened of are the people who are the most frightened. That it takes great personal courage to let yourself appear weak. That you don't have to hit somebody even if you really really want to. That no single, individual moment is in and of itself unendurable.

That nobody who's ever gotten sufficiently addictively enslaved by a Substance to need to quit the Substance and has successfully quit it for a while and been straight and but then has for whatever reason gone back and picked up the Substance again has *ever* reported being glad that they did it, used the Substance again and gotten re-enslaved; not ever. That *bit* is a metro Boston street term for a jail sentence, as in 'Don G. was up in Billerica on a six-month bit.' That it's impossible to kill fleas by hand. That it's possible to smoke so many cigarettes that you get little white ulcerations on your tongue. That the effects of too many cups of coffee are in no way pleasant or intoxicating.

That pretty much everybody masturbates.

Rather a lot, it turns out.

That the cliché 'I don't know who I am' unfortunately turns out to be more than a cliché. That it costs $330 U.S. to get a passport in a phony name. That other people can often see things about you that you yourself cannot see, even if those people are stupid. That you can obtain a major credit card with a phony name for $1500 U.S., but that no one will give you a straight answer about whether this price includes a verifiable credit history and line of credit for when the cashier slides the phony card through the register's little verification-modem with all sorts of burly security guards standing around. That having a lot of money does not immunize people from suffering or fear. That trying to dance sober is a whole different kettle of fish. That the term *vig* is street argot for the bookmaker's commission on an illegal bet, usually 10%, that's either subtracted from your winnings or added to your debt. That certain sincerely devout and spiritually advanced people believe that the God of their understanding helps them find parking places and gives them advice on Mass. Lottery numbers.

That cockroaches can, up to a certain point, be lived with.

That 'acceptance' is usually more a matter of fatigue than anything else.

That different people have radically different ideas of basic personal hygiene.

That, perversely, it is often more fun to want something than to have it.

That if you do something nice for somebody in secret, anonymously, without letting the person you did it for know it was you or anybody else know what it was you did or in any way or form trying to get credit for it, it's almost its own form of intoxicating buzz.

That anonymous generosity, too, can be abused.

That having sex with someone you do not care for feels lonelier than not having sex in the first place, afterward.

That it is permissible to *want*.

That everybody is identical in their secret unspoken belief that way deep down they are different from everyone else. That this isn't necessarily perverse.

That there might not be angels, but there are people who might as well be angels.

That God—unless you're Charlton Heston, or unhinged, or both—speaks and acts entirely through the vehicle of human beings, if there is a God.

That God might regard the issue of whether you believe there's a God or not as fairly low on his/her/its list of things s/he/it's interested in re you.

That the smell of Athlete's Foot is sick-sweet v. the smell of podiatric Dry Rot is sick-sour.

That a person—one with the Disease/-Ease—will do things under the influence of Substances that he simply would not ever do sober, and that some consequences of these things cannot ever be erased or amended.[71] Felonies are an example of this.

As are tattoos. Almost always gotten on impulse, tattoos are vividly, chillingly permanent. The shopworn 'Act in Haste, Repent at Leisure' would seem to have been almost custom-designed for the case of tattoos. For a while, the new resident Tiny Ewell got first keenly interested and then weirdly obsessed with people's tattoos, and he started going around to all the residents and outside people who hung around Ennet House to help keep straight, asking to check out their tattoos and wanting to hear about the circumstances surrounding each tattoo. These little spasms of obsession—like first with the exact definition of *alcoholic,* and then with Morris H.'s special tollhouse cookies until the pancreatitis-flare, then with the exact kinds of corners everybody made their bed up with—these were part of the way Tiny E. temporarily lost his mind when his enslaving Substance was taken away. The tattoo thing started out with Tiny's white-collar amazement at just how many of the folks around Ennet House seemed to have tattoos. And the tattoos seemed like potent symbols of not only whatever they were pictures of but also of the chilling irrevocability of intoxicated impulses.

Because the whole thing about tattoos is that they're permanent, of course, irrevocable once gotten—which of course the irrevocability of a tattoo is what jacks up the adrenaline of the intoxicated decision to sit down in the chair and actually get it (the tattoo)—but the chilling thing about the intoxication is that it seems to make you consider only the adrenaline of the moment itself, not (in any depth) the irrevocability that produces the adrenaline. It's like the intoxication keeps your tattoo-type-class person from being able to project his imagination past the adrenaline of the impulse and even consider the permanent consequences that are producing the buzz of excitement.

Tiny Ewell'll put this same abstract but not very profound idea in a whole number of varied ways, over and over, obsessively almost, and still fail to get any of the tattooed residents interested, although Bruce Green will listen politely, and the clinically depressed Kate Gompert usually won't have the juice to get up and walk away when Tiny starts in, which makes Ewell seek her out vis-à-vis tattoos, though she hasn't got a tattoo.

But they don't have any problem with showing Tiny their tatts, the residents with tatts don't, unless they're female and the thing is in some sort of area where there's a Boundary Issue.

As Tiny Ewell comes to see it, people with tattoos fall under two broad headings. First there are the younger scrofulous boneheaded black-T-shirt-and-spiked-bracelet types who do not have the sense to regret the impulsive permanency of their tatts, and will show them off to you with the same fake-quiet pride with which someone more of Ewell's own social stratum would show off their collection of Dynastic crockery or fine Sauvignon. Then there are the more numerous (and older) second types, who'll show you their tattoos with the sort of stoic regret (albeit tinged with a bit of self-conscious pride about the stoicism) that a Purple-Hearted veteran displays toward his old wounds' scars. Resident Wade McDade has complex nests of blue and red serpents running down the insides of both his arms, and is required to wear long-sleeved shirts every day to his menial job at Store 24, even though the store's heat always loses its mind in the early A.M. and it's always wicked motherfucking hot in there, because the store's Pakistani manager believes his customers will not wish to purchase Marlboro Lights and Mass. Giga-bucks lottery tickets from someone with vascular-colored snakes writhing all over his arms.[72] McDade also has a flaming skull on his left shoulderblade. Doony Glynn has the faint remains of a black dotted line tattooed all the way around his neck at about Adam's-apple height, with instruction-manual-like directions for the removal of his head and maintenance of the disengaged head tattooed on his scalp, from the days of his Skinhead youth, which now the tattooed directions take patience and a comb and three of April Cortelyu's barrettes for Tiny even to see.

Actually, a couple weeks into the obsession Ewell broadens his dermo-taxonomy to include a third category, Bikers, of whom there are presently none in Ennet House but plenty around the area's AA meetings, in beards and leather vests and apparently having to meet some kind of weight-requirement of at least 200 kilos. *Bikers* is the metro Boston street term for them, though they seem to refer to themselves usually as Scooter-Puppies, a term which (Ewell finds out the hard way) non-Bikers are not invited to use. These guys are veritable one-man tattoo festivals, but when they show them to you they're disconcerting because they'll bare their tatts with the complete absence of affect of somebody just showing you like a limb or a thumb, not quite sure why you want to see or even what it is you're looking at.

A like *N.B.* that Ewell ends up inserting under the heading *Biker* is that every professional tattooist everybody who can remember getting their tattoos remembers getting them from was, from the sound of everybody's general descriptions, a Biker.

W/r/t the Stoic-Regret group within Ennet House, it emerges that the male tattoos with women's names on them tend, in their irrevocability, to be especially disastrous and regretful, given the extremely provisional nature of most addicts' relationships. Bruce Green will have *MILDRED BONK* on his jilted right triceps forever. Likewise the *DORIS* in red-dripping Gothic script just below the left breast of Emil Minty, who yes apparently did love once. Minty also has a palsied and amateur swastika with the caption *FUCK NIGERS* on a left biceps he is heartily encouraged to keep covered, as a resident. Chandler Foss has an undulating banner with a redly inscribed *MARY* on one forearm, said banner now mangled and necrotic because Foss, dumped and badly coked out one night, tried to nullify the romantic connotations of the tatt by inscribing *BLESSED VIRGIN* above the *MARY* with a razor blade and a red Bic, with predictably ghastly results. Real tattoo artists (Ewell gets this on authority after a White Flag Group meeting from a Biker whose triceps' tattoo of a huge disembodied female breast being painfully squeezed by a disembodied hand which is *itself* tattooed with a disembodied breast and hand communicates real tattoo-credibility, as far as Tiny's concerned) real tatt-artists are always highly trained professionals.

What's sad about the gorgeous violet arrow-pierced heart with *PAMELA* incised in a circle around it on Randy Lenz's right hip is that Lenz has no memory either of the tattoo-impulse and -procedure or of anybody named Pamela. Charlotte Treat has a small green dragon on her calf and another tattoo on a breast she's set a Boundary about letting Tiny see. Hester Thrale has an amazingly detailed blue and green tattoo of the planet Earth on her stomach, its poles abutting pubis and breasts, an equatorial view of which cost Tiny Ewell two weeks of doing Hester's weekly Chore. Overall searing-regret honors probably go to Jennifer Belbin, who has four uncoverable black teardrops descending from the corner of one eye, from one night of mescaline and adrenalized grief, so that from more than two meters away she always looks like she has flies on her, Randy Lenz points out. The new black girl Didi N. has on the plane of her upper abdomen a tattered screaming skull (off the same stencil as McDade's, but w/o the flames) that's creepy because it's just a tattered white outline: Black people's tattoos are rare, and for reasons Ewell regards as fairly obvious they tend to be just white outlines.

Ennet House alumnus and volunteer counselor Calvin Thrust is quietly rumored to have on the shaft of his formerly professional porn-cartridge-performer's Unit a tattoo that displays the magiscule initials *CT* when the Unit is flaccid and the full name *CALVIN THRUST* when hyperemic. Tiny Ewell has soberly elected to let this go unsubstantiated. Alumna and v.c. Danielle Steenbok once got the bright idea of having eyeliner-colored tattoos put around both eyes so she'd never again have to apply eyeliner, not banking on the inevitable fade that over time's turned the tattoos a kind of nauseous dark-green she now has to constantly apply eyeliner to cover up.

Current female live-in Staffer Johnette Foltz has undergone two of the six painful procedures required to have the snarling orange-and-blue tiger removed from her left forearm and so now has a snarling tiger minus a head and one front leg, with the ablated parts looking like someone determined has been at her forearm with steel wool. Ewell decides this is what gives profundity to the tattoo-impulse's profound irrevocability: Having a tatt removed means just exchanging one kind of disfigurement for another. There are Tingly and Diehl's identical palmate-cannabis-leaf-on-inner-wrist tattoos, though Tingly and Diehl are from opposite shores and never crossed paths before entering the House.

Nell Gunther refuses to discuss tattoos with Tiny Ewell in any way or form.

For a while, Tiny Ewell considers live-in Staffer Don Gately's home-made jailhouse tattoos too primitive to even bother asking about.

He'd made a true pest of himself, though, Ewell did, when at the height of the obsession this one synthetic-narc-addicted kid came in who refused to be called anything but his street name, Skull, and lasted only like four days, but who'd been a walking exhibition of high-regret ink—both arms tattooed with spiderwebs at the elbows, on his fishy-white chest a naked lady with the same kind of overlush measurements Ewell remembered from the pinball machines of his Watertown childhood. On Skull's back a half-m.-long skeleton in a black robe and cowl playing the violin in the wind on a crag with *THE DEAD* in maroon on a vertical gonfalonish banner unfurling below; on one biceps either an icepick or a mucronate dagger, and down both forearms a kind of St. Vitus's dance of leather-winged dragons with the words—on both forearms—*HOW DO YOU LIK YOUR BLUEYED BOY NOW MR DETH!?*, the typos of which, Tiny felt, only served to heighten Skull's whole general tatt-gestalt's intended effect, which Tiny presumed was primarily to repel.

In fact Tiny E.'s whole displacement of obsession from bunks' hospital corners to people's tattoos was probably courtesy of this kid Skull, who on his second night in the newer male residents' Five-Man Room had shed his electrified muscle-shirt and was showing off his tattoos in a bone-headed regretless first-category fashion to Ken Erdedy while R. Lenz did headstands against the closet door in his jockstrap and Ewell and Geoffrey D. had their wallets' credit cards spread out on Ewell's drum-tight bunk and were trying to settle a kind of admittedly childish argument about who had the more prestigious credit cards—Skull flexing his pectorals to make the overdeveloped woman on his chest writhe, reading his forearms to Erdedy, etc.—and Geoffrey Day had looked up from his

AmEx (Gold, to Ewell's Platinum) and shaken his moist pale head at Ewell and asked rhetorically what had ever happened to good old traditional U.S. tattoos like *MOM* or an anchor, which for some reason touched off a small obsessive explosion in Ewell's detox-frazzled psyche.

Probably the most poignant items in Ewell's survey are the much-faded tattoos of old Boston AA guys who've been sober in the Fellowship for decades, the crocodilic elder statesmen of the White Flag and Allston Groups and the St. Columbkill Sunday Night Group and Ewell's chosen Home Group, Wednesday night's Better Late Than Never Group (Nonsmoking) at St. Elizabeth's Hospital just two blocks down from the House. There is something queerly poignant about a deeply faded tattoo, a poignancy something along the lines of coming upon the tiny and poignantly unfashionable clothes of a child long-since grown up in an attic trunk somewhere (the clothes, not the grown child, Ewell confirmed for G. Day). See, e.g., White Flag's cantankerous old Francis ('Ferocious Francis') Gehaney's right forearm's tatt of a martini glass with a naked lady sitting in the glass with her legs kicking up over the broad flaring rim, with an old-style Rita Hayworth–era bangs-intensive hairstyle. Faded to a kind of underwater blue, its incidental black lines gone soot-green and the red of the lips/nails/*SUBIKBAY'62USN4-07* not lightened to pink but more like decayed to the dusty red of fire through much smoke. All these old sober Boston blue-collar men's irrevocable tattoos fading almost observably under the low-budget fluorescence of church basements and hospital auditoria—Ewell watched and charted and cross-referenced them, moved. Any number of good old U.S.N. anchors, and in Irish Boston sooty green shamrocks, and several little frozen tableaux of little khaki figures in G.I. helmets plunging bayonets into the stomachs of hideous urine-yellow bucktoothed Oriental caricatures, and screaming eagles with their claws faded blunt, and *SEMPER FI,* all autolyzed to the point where the tattoos look like they're just under the surface of a murky-type pond.

A tall silent hard-looking old black-haired BLTN-Group veteran has the terse and hateful single word *PUSSY* in what's faded to pond-scum green down one liver-spotted forearm; but yet the fellow transcends even stoic regret by dressing and carrying himself as if the word simply wasn't there, or was so irrevocably there there was no point even thinking about it: there's a deep and tremendously compelling dignity about the old man's demeanor w/r/t the *PUSSY* on his arm, and Ewell actually considers approaching this fellow re the issue of sponsorship, if and when he feels it's appropriate to get an AA sponsor, if he decides it's germane in his case.

Near the conclusion of this two-month obsession, Tiny Ewell

approaches Don Gately on the subject of whether the jailhouse tattoo should maybe comprise a whole separate phylum of tattoo. Ewell's personal feeling is that jailhouse tattoos aren't poignant so much as grotesque, that they seem like they weren't a matter of impulsive decoration or self-presentation so much as simple self-mutilation arising out of boredom and general disregard for one's own body and the aesthetics of decoration. Don Gately's developed the habit of staring coolly at Ewell until the little attorney shuts up, though this is partly to disguise the fact that Gately usually can't follow what Ewell's saying and is unsure whether this is because he's not smart or educated enough to understand Ewell or because Ewell is simply out of his fucking mind.

Don Gately tells Ewell how your basic-type jailhouse tatt is homemade with sewing needles from the jailhouse canteen and some blue ink from the cartridge of a fountain pen promoted from the breast pocket of an unalert Public Defender, is why the jailhouse genre is always the same night-sky blue. The needle is dipped in the ink and jabbed as deep into the tattooee as it can be jabbed without making him recoil and fucking up your aim. Just a plain ultraminimal blue square like Gately's got on his right wrist takes half a day and hundreds of individual jabs. How come the lines are never quite straight and the color's never quite all the way solid is it's impossible to get all the individualized punctures down to the same uniform deepness in the, like, twitching flesh. This is why jailhouse tatts always look like they were done by sadistic children on rainy afternoons. Gately has a blue square on his right wrist and a sloppy cross on the inside of his mammoth left forearm. He'd done the square himself, and a cellmate had done the cross in return for Gately doing a cross on the cellmate. Oral narcotics render the process both less painful and less tedious. The sewing needle is sterilized in grain alcohol, which Gately explains that the alcohol is got by taking mess-hall fruit and mashing it up and adding water and secreting the whole mess in a Ziploc just inside the flush-hole thing of the cell's toilet, to, like, foment. The sterilizing results of this can be consumed, as well. Bonded liquor and cocaine are the only things hard to get inside of M.D.C. penal institutions, because the expense of them gets everybody all excited and it's only a matter of time before somebody goes and eats cheese. The inexpensive C-IV oral narcotic Talwin can be traded for cigarettes, however, which can in turn be got at the canteen or won at cribbage and dominoes (M.D.C. regs prohibit straight-out cards) or got in mass quantities off smaller inmates in return for protection from the romantic advances of larger inmates. Gately is right-handed and his arms are roughly the size of Tiny Ewell's legs. His wrist's jailhouse square is canted and has sloppy extra blobs at three of the corners. Your average jailhouse tatt can't be removed even with laser surgery because it's incised so deep in. Gately is polite about Tiny Ewell's inquiries but not expansive, i.e. Tiny has to ask very specific questions about whatever he wishes to know and then gets a short specific answer from Gately to just that question. Then Gately stares at him, a habit Ewell tends to complain about at some length up in the Five-Man Room. His interest in tattoos seems to be regarded by Gately not as invasive but as the temporary obsession of a still-quivering Substanceless psyche that in a couple weeks will have forgot all about tattoos, an attitude Ewell finds condescending in the extremus. Gately's attitude toward his own primitive tattoos is a second-category attitude, with most of the stoicism and acceptance of his tatt-regret sincere, if only because these irrevocable emblems of jail are minor Rung Bells compared to some of the fucked-up and *really* irrevocable impulsive mistakes Gately'd made as an active drug addict and burglar, not to mention their consequences, the mistakes', which Gately's trying to accept he'll be paying off for a real long time.

—*pages 200–211*

○

THE BATHROOM HAS a hook and a mirrored medicine cabinet over the sink and is off the bedroom. Molly Notkin's bedroom looks like the bedroom of someone who stays in bed for serious lengths of time. A pair of pantyhose has been tossed onto a lamp. There are not crumbs but whole portions of crackers protruding from the gray surf of wopsed-up bedding. A photo of the phalloneurotic New Yorker with the same fold-out triangular support as the blank cartridge's anti-ad. A Ziploc of pot and EZ-Widers and seeds in the ashtray. Books with German and Cyrillic titles lie open in spine-cracking attitudes on the colorless rug. Joelle's never liked the fact that Notkin's father's photograph is nailed at iconic height to the wall above the headboard, a systems planner out of Knoxville TN, his smile the smile of a man who wears white loafers and a squirting carnation. And why are bathrooms always way brighter lit than whatever room they're off? On the private side of the bathroom door she's had to take two damp towels off the top of to close all the way, the same rotten old hook for a lock never quite ever seeming to want to fit its receptacle in the jamb, the party's music now some horrible collection of mollified rock classics with all soft rock's grim dental associations, the business side of the door is hung with a Selective Automation of Knoxville calendar from before Subsidized Time and cut-out photos of Kinski as Paganini and Léaud as Doinel and a borderless still of the crowd scene in what looks like Peterson's *The Lead Shoes* and rather curiously the offprinted page of J. van Dyne, M.A.'s one and only published film-theory monograph.[81] Joelle can smell, through her veil and own stale exhalations, the little room's complicated spice of sandalwood rubble in a little violet-ribboned pomander and deodorant soap and the sharp decayed-lemon odor of stress-diarrhea. Low-budget celluloid horror films created ambiguity and possible elision by putting *?* after *THE END*, is what pops into her head: *THE END?* amid the odors of mildew and dicky academic digestion?

Joelle's mother's family had no indoor plumbing. It is all right. She represses all bathetic this-will-be-the-last-thing-I-smell thought-patterns. Joelle is going to have Too Much Fun in here. It was beyond all else so much *fun,* at the start. Orin had neither disapproved nor partaken; his urine was an open book because of football. Jim hadn't disapproved so much as been vacant with disinterest. His Too Much was neat bourbon, and he had lived life to the fullest, and then gone in for detoxification, again and again. This had been simply too much fun, at the start. So much better even than nasaling the Material up through rolled currency and waiting for the cold bitter drip at the back of your throat and cleaning the newly spacious apartment to within an inch of its life while your mouth twitches and writhes unbidden beneath the veil. The 'base frees and con-denses, compresses the whole experience to the implosion of one terrible shattering spike in the graph, an afflated orgasm of the heart that makes her feel, truly, *attractive,* sheltered by limits, deveiled and loved, observed and alone and sufficient and female, full, as if watched for an instant by God. She always sees, after inhaling, right at the apex, at the graph's spike's tip, Bernini's 'Ecstasy of St. Teresa,' behind glass, at the Vittoria, for some reason, the saint recumbent, half-supine, her flowing stone robe lifted by the angel in whose other hand a bare arrow is raised for that best descent, the saint's legs frozen in opening, the angel's expression not char-ity but the perfect vice of barb-headed love. The stuff had been not just her encaging god but her lover, too, fiendish, angelic, of rock. The toilet seat is up. She can hear a helicopter's chop somewhere overhead east, a traffic helicopter over Storrow, and Molly Notkin's shriek as an enormous glass crash sounds off in the living room, imagines her beard hanging aslant and her mouth ellipsed with champagne's foam as she waves off the break-age that signals good Party, can hear through the door the ecstatic Melinda's apologies and Molly's laugh, which sounds like a shriek:

'Oh everything falls off the wall sooner or later.'

Joelle has lifted her veil back to cover her skull like a bride. Since she threw away her pipes and bowls and screens again this A.M. she is going to have to be resourceful. On the counter of an old sink the same not-quite white as the floor and ceiling (the wallpaper is a maddening uncountable pattern of roses twined in garlands on sticks) on the counter are an old splay-bristled toothbrush, tube of Gleem rolled neatly up from the bot-tom, unsavory old NoCoat scraper, rubber cement, NeGram, depilatory ointment, tube of Monostat not squeezed from the bottom, phony-beard whiskerbits and curled green threads of used mint floss and Parapectolin and a wholly unsqueezed tube of diaphragm-foam and no makeup but serious styling gel in a big jar with no lid and hairs around the rim and an empty tampon box half-filled with nickels and pennies and rubber bands, and Joelle sweeps an arm across the counter and squunches everything over to the side under the small rod with a washcloth wrung viciously out and dried in the tight spiral of a twisted cord, and if some items do totter and fall to the floor it is all right because everything eventually has to fall. On the cleared counter goes Joelle's misshapen purse. The absence of veil dulls the bathroom's smells, somehow.

She's been resourceful before, but this is the most deliberate Joelle has been able to be about it in something like a year. From the purse she removes the plastic Pepsi container, a box of wooden matches kept dry in a resealable baggie, two little thick glycine bags each holding four grams of pharmaceutical-grade cocaine, a single-edge razor blade (increasingly tough to find), a little black Kodachrome canister whose gray lid she pops and discards to reveal baking soda sifted fine as talc, the empty glass cigar tube, a folded square of Reynolds Wrap foil the size of a playing card, and an amputated length of the bottom of a quality wire coat hanger. The overhead light casts shadows of her hands over what she needs, so she turns on the light over the medicine cabinet's mirror as well. The light stutters and hums and bathes the counter with cold lithium-free fluorescence. She undoes the four pins and removes the veil from her head and places it on the counter with the rest of the Material. Lady Delphina's little glycine baglets have clever seals that are green when sealed and blue and yellow when not. She taps half a glycine's worth into the cigar tube and adds half again as much baking soda, spilling some of the soda in a parenthesis of bright white on the counter. This is the most deliberate she's been able to be in at least a year. She turns the sink's C knob and lets the water get really cold, then cranks the volume back to a trickle and fills the rest of the tube to the top with water. She holds the tube up straight and gently taps on its side with a blunt unpainted nail, watching the water slowly darken the powders beneath it. She produces a double rose of flame in the mirror that illuminates the right side of her face as she holds the tube over the matches' flame and waits for the stuff to begin to bubble. She uses two matches, twice. When the tube gets too hot to hold she takes and folds her veil and uses it as a kind of oven-mitt over the fingers of her left hand, careful (from habit and experience) not to let the bottom corners get close enough to the flame to brown. After it's bubbled for just a second Joelle shakes out the matches with a flourish and tosses them in the toilet to hear that briefest of hisses. She takes up the black wire prod from the hanger and begins to stir and mash the just-bubbled stuff in the tube, feeling it thicken quickly and its resistance to the wire's tiny circles increase. It was when her hands started to tremble during this part of the cooking procedure that she'd first known she liked this more than anyone can like anything and still live. She is not stupid. The Charles rolling away far below the windowless bathroom is vividly blue, more mildly blue on top from the fresh rainwater that had made purple rings appear and widen, a deeper Magic Marker–type blue below the dilute layer, gulls stamped to the cleared sky, motionless as kites. A bulky thump sounds from behind the large flat-top Enfield hill on the river's south shore, a large but relatively shapeless projectile of drums wrapped in brown postal paper and belted with twine hurtling in a broad upward arc that bothers the gulls into dips and wheels, the brown package quickly a pinpoint in the yet-hazy sky to the north, where a yellow-brown cloud hangs just above the line between sky and terrain, its top slowly dispersing and opening out so that the cloud looks like a not very pretty sort of wastebasket, waiting. Inside, Joelle hears only a bit of the bulky thump, which could be anything. The only other thing besides what she's about to do too much of here right now she'd ever come close to feeling this way about: In Joelle's childhood, Paducah, not too bad a drive from Shiny Prize, still had a few public movie theaters, six and eight separate auditoria clustered in single honeycombs at the edges of interstate malls. The theaters always ended in -*plex*, she reflected. The Thisoplex and Thatoplex. It had never struck her as odd. And she never saw even one film there, as a girl, that she didn't just about die with love for. It didn't matter what they were. She and her own personal Daddy up in the front row, they sat in the front rows of the narrow little overinsulated -plexes up in neck-crick territory and let the screen fill their whole visual field, her hand in his lap and their big box of Crackerjacks in her hand and sodapops secure in little rings cut out of the plastic of their seats' arms; and he, always with a wooden match in the corner of his mouth, pointing up into the rectangular world at this one or that one, performers, giant flawless 2D beauties iridescent on the screen, telling Joelle over and over again how she was prettier than this one or that one right there. Standing in the placid line as he bought the -plex's paper tickets that looked like grocery receipts, knowing that she was going to love the celluloid entertainment no matter what it was, wonderfully innocent, still thinking *quality* referred to the living teddy bears in Qantas commercials, standing hand-held, eyes even with his wallet's back-pocket bulge, she'd never so much again as in that line felt so *taken care of*, destined for big-screen entertainment's unalloyed good fun, never once again until starting in with this lover, cooking and smoking it, five years back, before Incandenza's death, at the start. The punter never made her feel quite so *taken care of*, never made her feel about to be entered by something that didn't know she was there and yet was all about making her feel good anyway, coming in. Entertainment is blind.

The improbable thing of the whole thing is that, when the soda and water and cocaine are mixed right and heated right and stirred just right as the mix cools down, then when the stuff's too stiff to stir and is finally ready to come on out it comes out slick as shit from a goat, just an inverted-ketchup-bottle thump and out the son of a fucking whore slides, one molded cylinder hardened onto the black wire, its snout round from the glass tube's bottom. The average pre-chopped freebase rock looks like a .38 round. What Joelle now slides with three fillips from the cigar tube is a monstrous white wiener, a county-fair corn dog, its sides a bit rough, like mâché, a couple clots left on the inside of the tube that are what you forage and smoke before the Chore Boys and panties.

She is now a little under two deliberate minutes from Too Much Fun for anyone mortal to hope to endure. Her unveiled face in the dirty lit mirror is shocking in the intensity of its absorption. Out in the bedroom doorway she can hear Reeves Mainwaring telling some helium-voiced girl that life is essentially one long search for an ashtray. Too Much Fun. She uses the razor blade to cross-section chunks out of the freebase wiener. You can't whittle thin deli-shaved flakes off because they'll crumble back to powder right away and they anyway don't smoke as well as you'd think. Blunt chunks are S.O.P. Joelle chops out enough chunks for maybe twenty good-sized hits. They form a little quarry on the soft cloth of her folded veil on the counter. Her Brazilian skirt is no longer damp. Reeves Mainwaring's blond imperial often had little bits of food residue in it. 'The Ecstasy of St. Teresa' is on perpetual display at the Vittoria in Rome and she never got to see it. She will never again say *And Lo* and invite people to watch darkness dance on the face of the deep. 'The Face of the Deep' had been the title she'd suggested for Jim's unseen last cartridge, which he'd said would be too pretentious and then used that skull-fragment out of the *Hamlet* graveyard scene instead, which talk about pretentious she'd laughed. His frightened look when she'd laughed is for the life of her the last facial-expression memory she can remember of the man. Orin had referred to his father sometimes as Himself and sometimes as The Mad

Stork and once in a slip as The Sad Stork. She lights one wooden match and blows it right out and touches the hot black head to the side of the plastic pop bottle. It melts right through and makes a little hole. The helicopter was probably a traffic helicopter. Somebody at their Academy had had some connection to some traffic helicopter that had had an accident. She can't for the life of her. No one out there knows she is in here getting ready to have Too Much. She can hear Molly Notkin calling through rooms about has anyone seen Keck. In her first theory seminar Reeves Mainwaring had called one film 'wretchedly ill-conceived' and another 'desperately acquiescent' and Molly Notkin had pretended to have a coughing fit and had had a Tennessee accent and that was how they met. The Reynolds Wrap is to make a screen that will rest in the bottle's open top. A regular dope screen is the size of a thimble, its sides spread like an opening bud. Joelle uses the point of some curved nail scissors on the back of the toilet to poke tiny holes in the rectangle of aluminum foil and shapes it into a shallow funnel large enough to siphon gasoline, narrowing its tip to fit in the bottle's mouth. She now owns a pipe with a monster-sized bowl and screen, now, and puts in enough chunklets to make five or six hits at once. The little rocks lie there piled and yellow-white. She puts her lips experimentally to the melted hole in the side of the bottle and draws, then, very deliberately, lights another match and extinguishes it and makes the hole bigger. The idea that she'll never see Molly Notkin or the cerebral Union or her U.H.I.D. support-brothers and -sisters or the YYY engineer or Uncle Bud on a roof or her stepmother in the Locked Ward or her poor personal Daddy again is sentimental and banal. The idea of what she's about in here contains all other ideas and makes them banal. Her glass of juice is on the back of the toilet, half-empty. The back of the toilet is lightly sheened with condensation of unknown origin. These are facts. This room in this apartment is the sum of very many specific facts and ideas. There is nothing more to it than that. Deliberately setting about to make her heart explode has assumed the status of just one of these facts. It was an idea but now is about to become a fact. The closer it comes to becoming concrete the more abstract it seems. Things get very abstract. The concrete room was the sum of abstract facts. Are facts abstract, or are they just abstract representations of concrete things? Molly Notkin's middle name is Cantrell. Joelle puts two more matches together and prepares to strike them, breathing rapidly in and out like a diver preparing for a long descent.

'I say is someone in there?' The voice is the young post-New Formalist from Pittsburgh who affects Continental and wears an ascot that won't stay

tight, with that hesitant knocking of when you know perfectly well someone's in there, the bathroom door composed of thirty-six that's three times a
lengthwise twelve recessed two-bevelled squares in a warped rectangle of
steam-softened wood, not quite white, the bottom outside corner right here
raw wood and mangled from hitting the cabinets' bottom drawer's wicked
metal knob, through the door and offset 'Red' and glowering actors and
calendar and very crowded scene and pubic spiral of pale blue smoke from
the elephant-colored rubble of ash and little blackened chunks in the foil
funnel's cone, the smoke's baby-blanket blue that's sent her sliding down
along the wall past knotted washcloth, towel rack, blood-flower wallpaper
and intricately grimed electrical outlet, the light sharp bitter tint of a heated
sky's blue that's left her uprightly fetal with chin on knees in yet another
North American bathroom, deveiled, too pretty for words, maybe the
Prettiest Girl Of All Time (Prettiest G.O.A.T.), knees to chest, slew-footed
by the radiant chill of the claw-footed tub's porcelain, Molly's had somebody lacquer the tub in blue, lacquer, she's holding the bottle, recalling
vividly its slogan for the last generation was The Choice of a Nude Generation, when she was of back-pocket height and prettier by far than any of the
peach-colored titans they'd gazed up at, his hand in her lap her hand in the
box and rooting down past candy for the Prize, more fun way too much fun
inside her veil on the counter above her, the stuff in the funnel exhausted
though it's still smoking thinly, its graph reaching its highest spiked prick,
peak, the arrow's best descent, so good she can't stand it and reaches out for
the cold tub's rim's cold edge to pull herself up as the white- party-noise
reaches, for her, the sort of stereophonic precipice of volume to teeter on just
before the speakers blow, people barely twitching and conversations stretto-
ing against a ghastly old pre-Carter thing saying 'We've Only Just Begun,'
Joelle's limbs have been removed to a distance where their acknowledgment
of her commands seems like magic, both clogs simply gone, nowhere in
sight, and socks oddly wet, pulls her face up to face the unclean medicine-
cabinet mirror, twin roses of flame still hanging in the glass's corner, hair of
the flame she's eaten now trailing like the legs of wasps through the air of
the glass she uses to locate the de-faced veil and what's inside it, loading up
the cone again, the ashes from the last load make the world's best filter: this
is a fact. Breathes in and out like a savvy diver—

'Look here then who's that in there? Is someone in there? Do open up.
I'm on one foot then the other out here. I say Notkin someone's been in
here locked in and, well, sounding unwell, amid rather a queer scent.'

—and is knelt vomiting over the lip of the cool blue tub, gouges on the tub's lip revealing sandy white gritty stuff below the lacquer and porcelain, vomiting muddy juice and blue smoke and dots of mercuric red into the claw-footed trough, and can hear again and seems to see, against the fire of her closed lids' blood, bladed vessels aloft in the night to monitor flow, searchlit helicopters, fat fingers of blue light from one sky, searching.

—pages 234–240

14 November
Year of the Depend Adult Undergarment

POOR TONY KRAUSE had a seizure on the T. It happened on a Gray Line train from Watertown to Inman Square, Cambridge. He'd been drinking codeine cough syrup in the men's room of the Armenian Foundation Library in horrid central Watertown MA for over a week, darting out from cover only to beg a scrip from hideous Equus Reese and then dash in at Brooks Pharmacy, wearing a simply vile ensemble of synthetic-fiber slacks and suspenders and tweed Donegal cap he'd had to cadge from a longshoremen's union hall. Poor Tony couldn't dare wear anything comely, not even the Antitoi brothers' red leather coat, not since that poor woman's bag had turned out to have a heart inside. He had simply never felt so beset and overcome on all sides as the black July day when it fell to his lot to boost a heart. Who wouldn't wonder Why Me? He didn't dare dress expressive or ever go back to the Square. And Emil still had him marked for de-mapping as a consequence of that horrid thing with Wo and Bobby C last winter. Poor Tony hadn't dared show one feather east of Tremont St. or at the Brighton Projects or even Delphina's in backwater Enfield since last Xmas, even after Emil simply dematerialized from the street-scene; and now since 29 July he was *non grata* at Harvard Square and environs; and even the sight of an Oriental now gave him palpitations—say nothing of an Aigner accessory.

Thus Poor Tony had no way to cop for himself. He could trust no one enough to inject their wares. S. T. Cheese and Lolasister were no more trustworthy than he himself; he didn't even want them to know where he slept. He began drinking cough syrup. He managed to get Bridget Tender-hole and the strictly rough-trade Stokely Dark Star to cop for him on the wink for a few weeks, until Stokely died in a Fenway hospice and then Bridget Tenderhole was shipped by her pimp to Brockton under maddeningly vague circumstances. Then Poor Tony had read the dark portents and swallowed the first of his pride and hid himself even more deeply in a dumpster-complex behind the I.B.P.W.D.W.[102] Local #4 Hall in Fort Point downtown and resolved to stay hidden there for as long as he could swallow the pride to send Lolasister out to acquire heroin, accepting w/o pride or complaint the shameless rip-offs the miserable bitch perpetrated upon him, until a period in October when Lolasister went down with hepatitis-G and the supply of heroin dried horribly up and the only people even copping enough to chip were people in a position to dash here and there to great beastly lengths under an open public-access sky and no friend, no matter how dear or indebted, could afford to cop for another. Then, wholly friend- and connectionless, Poor Tony, in hiding, began to Withdraw From Her- oin. Not just get strung out or sick. Withdraw. The words echoed in his neuralgiac and wigless head with the simply most awful sinister-footsteps- echoing-in-deserted-corridor quality. Withdrawal. The Wingless Fowl. Turkeyfication. Kicking. The Old Cold Bird. Poor Tony had never once had to Withdraw, not all the way down the deserted corridor of With- drawal, not since he first got strung at seventeen. At the very worst, some- one kind had always found him charming, if things got dire enough to have to rent out his charms. Alas thus about the fact that his charms were now at low ebb. He weighed fifty kilos and his skin was the color of summer squash. He had terrible shivering-attacks and also perspired. He had a sty that had scraped one eyeball as pink as a bunny's. His nose ran like twin spigots and the output had a yellow-green tinge he didn't think looked promising at *all*. There was an uncomely dry-rot smell about him that even he could smell. In Watertown he tried to pawn his fine auburn wig w/ removable chignon and was cursed at in Armenian because the wig had infestations from his own hair below. Let's not even mention the Armenian pawnbroker's critique of his red leather coat.

Poor Tony got more and more ill as he further Withdrew. His symptoms themselves developed symptoms, troughs and nodes he charted with morbid attention in the dumpster, in his suspenders and horrid tweed cap, clutching a shopping bag with his wig and coat and comely habiliments he could nei- ther wear nor pawn. The empty Empire Displacement Co. dumpster he was hiding in was new and apple-green and the inside was bare dimpled iron, and it remained new and unutilized because persons declined to come near enough to utilize it. It took some time for Poor Tony to realize why this was so; for a brief interval it had seemed like a break, fortune's one wan smile. An E.W.D. land-barge crew set him straight in language that left quite a bit of tact to be wished for, he felt. The dumpster's green iron cover also leaked when it rained, and it contained already a colony of ants along one wall, which insects Poor Tony had ever since a neurasthenic childhood feared and detested in particular, ants; and in direct sunlight the quarters became a hellish living environment from which even the ants seemed to vanish.

With each step further into the black corridor of actual Withdrawal, Poor Tony Krause stamped his foot and simply refused to believe things could feel any worse. Then he stopped being able to anticipate when he needed to as it were visit the powder room. A fastidious gender-dysphoric's horror of incontinence cannot properly be described. Fluids of varying consistency began to pour w/o advance notice from several openings. Then of course they stayed there, the fluids, on the summer dumpster's iron floor. There they were, not going anywhere. He had no way to clean up and no way to cop. His entire set of interpersonal associations consisted of persons who did not care about him plus persons who wished him harm. His own late obstetrician father had rended his own clothing in symbolic shiva in the Year of the Whopper in the kitchen of the Krause home, 412 Mount Auburn Street, horrid central Watertown. It was the incontinence plus the prospect of 11/4's monthly Social Assistance checks that drove Poor Tony out for a mad scampering relocation to an obscure Armenian Foundation Library men's room in Watertown Center, wherein he tried to arrange a stall as comfortingly as he could with shiny magazine photos and cherished knickknacks and toilet paper laid down around the seat, and flushed repeatedly, and tried to keep true Withdrawal at some sort of bay with bottles of Codinex Plus. A tiny percentage of codeine gets metabolized into good old C_{17}-morphine, affording an agonizing hint of what real relief from The Bird might feel like. I.e. the cough syrup did little more than draw the process out, extend the corridor—it slowed up time.

Poor Tony Krause sat on the insulated toilet in the domesticated stall all day and night, alternately swilling and gushing. He held his high heels up at 1900h. when the library staff checked the stalls and turned off all the lights and left Poor Tony in a darkness within darkness so utter he had no idea where his own limbs were or went. He left that stall maybe once every two days, scampering madly to Brooks in cast-off shades and a kind of hood or shawl made pathetically of brown men's-room paper towels.

Time began to take on new aspects for him, now, as Withdrawal progressed. Time began to pass with sharp edges. Its passage in the dark or dim-lit stall was like time was being carried by a procession of ants, a gleaming red martial column of those militaristic red Southern-U.S. ants that build hideous tall boiling hills; and each vile gleaming ant wanted a minuscule little portion of Poor Tony's flesh in compensation as it helped bear time slowly forward down the corridor of true Withdrawal. By the second week in the stall time itself seemed the corridor, lightless at either end. After more time time then ceased to move or be moved or be move-throughable and assumed a shape above and apart, a huge, musty-feathered, orange-eyed wingless fowl hunched incontinent atop the stall, with a kind of watchful but deeply uncaring personality that didn't seem keen on Poor Tony Krause as a person at all, or to wish him well. Not one little bit. It spoke to him from atop the stall, the same things, over and over. They were unrepeatable. Nothing in even Poor Tony's grim life-experience prepared him for the experience of time with a shape and an odor, squatting; and the worsening physical symptoms were a spree at Bonwit's compared to time's black assurances that the symptoms were merely hints, signposts pointing up at a larger, far more dire set of Withdrawal phenomena that hung just overhead by a string that unravelled steadily with the passage of time. It would not keep still and would not end; it changed shape and smell. It moved in and out of him like the very most feared prison-shower assailant. Poor Tony had once had the hubris to fancy he'd had occasion really to shiver, ever, before. But he had never truly really shivered until time's cadences—jagged and cold and smelling oddly of deodorant—entered his body via several openings—cold the way only damp cold is cold—the phrase he'd had the gall to have imagined he understood was the phrase *chilled to the bone*—shard-studded columns of chill entering to fill his bones with ground glass, and he could hear his joints' glassy crunch with every slightest shift of hunched position, time ambient and in the air and entering and exiting at will, coldly; and the pain of his breath against his teeth. Time came to him in the falcon-black of the library night in an orange mohawk and Merry Widow w/ tacky Amalfo pumps and nothing else. Time spread him and entered him roughly and had its way and left him again in the form of endless gushing liquid shit that he could not flush enough to keep up with. He spent the longest morbid time trying to fathom whence all the shit came from when he was ingesting nothing at all but Codinex Plus. Then at some point he realized: time had become the shit itself: Poor Tony had become an hourglass: time moved through him now; he ceased to exist apart from its jagged-edged flow. He now weighed more like 45 kg. His legs were the size his comely arms had been, before Withdrawal. He was haunted by the word *Zuckung*, a foreign and possibly Yiddish word he did not recall ever before hearing. The word kept echoing in quick-step cadence through his head without meaning anything. He'd naïvely assumed that going mad meant you were not aware of going mad; he'd naïvely pictured madmen as forever laughing. He kept seeing his sonless father again — removing the training wheels, looking at his pager, wearing a green gown and mask, pouring iced tea in a pebbled glass, tearing his sportshirt in filial woe, grabbing his shoulder, sinking to his knees. Stiffening in a bronze casket. Being lowered under the snow at Mount Auburn Cemetery, through dark glasses from a distance. 'Chilled to the *Zuckung*.' When, then, even the funds for the codeine syrup were exhausted, he still sat on the toilet of the rear stall of the A.F.L. loo, surrounded by previously comforting hung habilements and fashion-magazine photographs he'd fastened to the wall with tape cadged on the way in from the Reference desk, sat for almost a whole nother night and day, because he had no faith that he could stem the flow of diarrhea long enough to make it anywhere — if anywhere to go presented itself — in his only pair of gender-appropriate slacks. During hours of lit operation, the men's room was full of old men who wore identical brown loafers and spoke Slavic and whose rapid-fire flatulence smelled of cabbage.

Toward the end of the day of the second syrupless afternoon (the day of the seizure) Poor Tony Krause began to Withdraw from the cough syrup's alcohol and codeine and demethylated morphine, now, as well as from the original heroin, yielding a set of sensations for which not even his recent experience had prepared him (the alcohol-Withdrawal especially); and when the true D.T.-type big-budget visuals commenced, when the first glossy and minutely hirsute army-ant crawled up his arm and refused ghost-like to be brushed away or hammered dead, Poor Tony threw his hygienic pride into time's porcelain maw and pulled up his slacks — mortifyingly wrinkled from 10+ days puddled around his ankles — made what slight cosmetic repairs he could, donned his tacky hat with Scotch-taped scarf of paper towels, and lit out in last-ditch desperation for Cambridge's Inman Square, for the sinister and duplicitous Antitoi brothers, their Glass-Entertainment-'N-Notions-fronted operations center he'd long ago vowed never again to darken the door of and but now figured to be his place of very last resort, the Antitois, Canadians of the Québec subgenus, sinister and duplicitous but when it came down to it rather hapless political insurgents he'd twice availed of services through the offices of Lolasister, now the only persons anywhere he could claim somehow owed him a kindness, since the affair of the heart.

In his coat and skallycap-over-scarf on Watertown Center's underground Gray Line platform, when the first hot loose load fell out into the baggy slacks and down his leg and out around his high heel — he still had only his red high heels with the crossing straps, which the slacks were long enough to mostly hide — Poor Tony closed his eyes against the ants formicating up and down his arms' skinny length and screamed a soundless interior scream of utter and soul-scalded woe. His beloved boa fit almost entirely in one breast pocket, where it stayed in the name of discretion. On the crowded train itself, then, he discovered that he'd gone in three weeks from being a colorful and comely albeit freakishly comely person to being one of those loathsome urban specimens that respectable persons on T-trains slide and drift quietly away from without even seeming to notice they're even there. His scarf of paper towels had come partly untaped. He smelled of bilirubin and yellow sweat and wore week-old eyeliner that simply did not fly if one needed a shave. There had been some negative urine-incidents as well, in the slacks, to round matters out. He had simply never in his life felt so unattractive or been so sick. He wept silently in shame and pain at the passage of each brightly lit public second's edge, and the driver ants that boiled in his lap opened needle-teethed little insectile mouths to catch the tears. He could feel his erratic pulse in his sty. The Gray Line was of the Green- and Orange-Line trundling-behemoth-type train, and he sat all alone at one end of the car, feeling each slow second take its cut.

When it descended, the seizure felt less like a separate distinct health-crisis than simply the next exhibit in the corridor of horrors that was the Old Cold Bird. In actual fact the seizure—a kind of synaptic firefight in Poor Tony's desiccated temporal lobes—was caused entirely by Withdrawal not From Heroin but from plain old grain alcohol, which was Codinex Plus cough syrup's primary ingredient and balm. He'd consumed upwards of sixteen little Eighty-Proof bottles of Codinex per day for eight days, and so was cruising for a real neurochemical bruising when he just up and stopped. The first thing that didn't augur very well was a shower of spark-sized phosphenes from the ceiling of the swaying train, this plus the fiery violet aura around the heads of the respectables who'd quietly retreated as far as possible from the various puddles in which he sat. Their clean pink faces looked somehow stricken, each inside a hood of violet flame. Poor Tony didn't know that his silent whimpers had ceased to be silent, was why everyone in the car had gotten so terribly interested in the floor-tiles between their feet. He knew only that the sudden and incongruous smell of Old Spice Stick Deodorant, Classic Original Scent—unbidden and unexplainable, his late obstetric Poppa's brand, not smelled for years—and the tiny panicked twitters with which Withdrawal's ants skittered glossily up into his mouth and nose and disappeared (each of course taking its tiny pincered farewell bite as it went) augured some new and vivider exhibit on the corridor's horizon. He'd become, at puberty, violently allergic to the smell of Old Spice. As he soiled himself and the plastic seat and floor once again the Classic Scent of times past intensified. Then Poor Tony's body began to swell. He watched his limbs become airy white dirigibles and felt them deny his authority and detach from him and float sluggishly up snout-first into the steel-mill sparks the ceiling rained. He suddenly felt nothing, or rather Nothing, a pre-tornadic stillness of zero sensation, as if he were the very space he occupied.

Then he had a seizure.[103] The floor of the subway car became the ceiling of the subway car and he was on his arched back in a waterfall of light, gagging on Old Spice and watching his tumid limbs tear-ass around the car's interior like undone balloons. The booming *Zuckung Zuckung Zuckung* was his high heels' heels drumming on the soiled floor's tile. He heard a rushing train-roar that was no train on earth and felt a vascular roaring rushing that until the pain hit seemed like the gathering of a kind of orgasm of the head. His head inflated hugely and creaked as it stretched, inflating. Then the pain (seizures *hurt*, is what few civilians have occasion to know) was the sharp end of a hammer. There was a squeak and rush of release inside his skull and something shot from him into the air. He saw Bobby ('C') C's blood misting upward in the hot wind of the Copley blower. His father knelt beside him on the ceiling in a well-rended sleeveless tee-, extolling the Red Sox of Rice and Lynn. Tony wore summer taffeta. His body flopped around without OK from HQ. He didn't feel one bit like a puppet. He thought of gaffed fish. The gown had 'a thousand flounces and a saucy bodice of lace crochet.' Then he saw his father, green-gowned and rubber-gloved, leaning to read the headlines off the skin of a fish a newspaper had wrapped. That had never happened. The largest-print headline said PUSH. Poor Tony flopped and gasped and pushed down inside and the utter red of the blood that feeds sight bloomed behind his fluttering lids. Time wasn't passing so much as kneeling beside him in a torn tee-shirt disclosing the rodent-nosed tits of a man who disdains the care of his once-comely bod. Poor Tony convulsed and drummed and gasped and fluttered, a fountain of light all around him. He felt a piece of nourishing and possibly even intoxicating meat in the back of his throat but elected not to swallow it but swallowed it anyway, and was immediately sorry he did; and when his father's bloody-rubbered fingers folded his teeth back to retrieve the tongue he'd swallowed he refused absolutely to bite down ungratefully on the hand that was taking his food, then without authorization he pushed and bit down and took the gloved fingers clean off, so there was rubber-wrapped meat in his mouth again and his father's head exploded into needled antennae of color like an exploding star between his gown's raised green arms and a call for *Zuckung* while Tony's heels drummed and struggled against the widening stirrups of light they were hoisted into while a curtain of red was drawn wetly up over the floor he stared down at, Tony, and he heard someone yelling for someone to Give In, Err, with a hand on his lace belly as he bore down to PUSH and he saw the legs in the stirrups they held would keep spreading until they cracked him open and all the way inside-out on the ceiling and his last worry was that red-handed Poppa could see up his dress, what was hidden.

—*pages 299–306*

8 November
Year of the Depend Adult Undergarment
Interdependence Day
Gaudeamus Igitur

BOSTON AA IS like AA nowhere else on this planet. Just like AA everyplace else, Boston AA is divided into numerous individual AA Groups,
and each Group has its particular Group name like the Reality Group or
the Allston Group or the Clean and Sober Group, and each Group holds
its regular meeting once a week. But almost all Boston Groups' meetings
are speaker meetings. That means that at the meetings there are recovering alcoholic speakers who stand up in front of everybody at an amplified
podium and 'share their experience, strength, and hope.'[131] And the singular thing is that these speakers are not ever members of the Group that's
holding the meeting, in Boston. The speakers at one certain Group's
weekly speaker meeting are always from some other certain Boston AA
Group. The people from the other Group who are here at like your Group
speaking are here on something called a Commitment. Commitments are
where some members of one Group commit to hit the road and travel to
another Group's meeting to speak publicly from the podium. Then a bunch
of people from the host Group hit the opposite lane of the same road on
some other night and go to the visiting Group's meeting, to speak. Groups
always trade Commitments: you come speak to us and we'll come speak to
you. It can seem bizarre. You always go elsewhere to speak. At your own
Group's meeting you're a host; you just sit there and listen as hard as you
can, and you make coffee in 60-cup urns and stack polystyrene cups in big
ziggurats and sell raffle tickets and make sandwiches, and you empty ashtrays and scrub out urns and sweep floors when the other Group's speakers
are through. You never share your experience, strength, and hope on-stage
behind a fiberboard podium with its cheap nondigital PA system's mike
except in front of some *other* metro Boston Group.[132] Every night in

Boston, bumper-stickered cars full of totally sober people, wall-eyed from caffeine and trying to read illegibly scrawled directions by the dashboard lights, crisscross the city, heading for the church basements or bingo halls or nursing-home cafeterias of other AA Groups, to put on Commitments. Being an active member of a Boston AA Group is probably a little bit like being a serious musician or like athlete, in terms of constant travel.

The White Flag Group of Enfield MA, in metropolitan Boston, meets Sundays in the cafeteria of the Provident Nursing Home on Hanneman Street, off Commonwealth Avenue a couple blocks west of Enfield Tennis Academy's flat-topped hill. Tonight the White Flag Group is hosting a Commitment from the Advanced Basics Group of Concord, a suburb of Boston. The Advanced Basics people have driven almost an hour to get here, plus there's always the problem of signless urban streets and directions given over the phone. On this coming Friday night, a small horde of White Flaggers will drive out to Concord to put on a reciprocal Commitment for the Advanced Basics Group. Travelling long distances on signless streets trying to parse directions like 'Take the second left off the rotary by the driveway to the chiropractor's' and getting lost and shooting your whole evening after a long day just to speak for like six minutes at a plywood podium is called 'Getting Active With Your Group'; the speaking itself is known as '12th-Step Work' or 'Giving It Away.' Giving It Away is a cardinal Boston AA principle. The term's derived from an epigrammatic description of recovery in Boston AA: 'You give it up to get it back to give it away.' Sobriety in Boston is regarded as less a gift than a sort of cosmic loan. You can't pay the loan back, but you can pay it *forward*, by spreading the message that despite all appearances AA works, spreading this message to the next new guy who's tottered in to a meeting and is sitting in the back row unable to hold his cup of coffee. The only way to hang onto sobriety is to give it away, and even just 24 hours of sobriety is worth doing anything for, a sober day being nothing short of a daily miracle if you've got the Disease like he's got the Disease, says the Advanced Basics member who's chairing this evening's Commitment, saying just a couple public words to the hall before he opens the meeting and retires to a stool next to the podium and calls his Group's speakers by random lot. The chairperson says he didn't used to be able to go 24 lousy *minutes* without a nip, before he Came In. 'Coming In' means admitting that your personal ass is kicked and tottering into Boston AA, ready to go to any lengths to stop the shitstorm. The Advanced Basics chairperson looks like a perfect cross between pictures of Dick Cavett and Truman Capote[133] except this guy's also like totally, almost flamboyantly bald, and to top it off he's wearing a bright-black country-western shirt with baroque curlicues of white Nodie-piping across the chest and shoulders, and a string tie, plus sharp-toed boots of some sort of weirdly imbricate reptile skin, and overall he's riveting to look at, grotesque in that riveting way that flaunts its grotesquerie. There are more cheap metal ashtrays and Styrofoam cups in this broad hall than you'll see anywhere else ever on earth. Gately's sitting right up front in the first row, so close to the podium he can see the tailor's notch in the chair-person's outsized incisors, but he enjoys twisting around and watching everybody come in and mill around shaking water off their outerwear, try-ing to find empty seats. Even on the night of the I.-Day holiday, the Provi-dent's cafeteria is packed by 2000h. AA does not take holidays any more than the Disease does. This is the big established Sunday P.M. meeting for AAs in Enfield and Allston and Brighton. Regulars come every week from Watertown and East Newton, too, often, unless they're out on Commitments with their own Groups. The Provident cafeteria walls, painted an indeci-sive green, are tonight bedecked with portable felt banners emblazoned with AA slogans in Cub-Scoutish blue and gold. The slogans on them appear way too insipid even to mention what they are. E.g. 'ONE DAY AT A TIME,' for one. The effete western-dressed guy concludes his opening exhortation, leads the opening Moment of Silence, reads the AA Pre-amble, pulls a random name out of the Crested Beaut cowboy hat he's holding, makes a squinty show of reading it, says he'd like to call Advanced Basics' first random speaker of the evening, and asks if his fellow Group-member John L. is in the house, here, tonight.

John L. gets up to the podium and says, 'That is a question I did not used to be able to answer.' This gets a laugh, and everybody's posture gets subtly more relaxed, because it's clear that John L. has some sober time in and isn't going to be one of those AA speakers who's so wracked with self-conscious nerves he makes the empathetic audience nervous too. Everybody in the audience is aiming for total empathy with the speaker; that way they'll be able to receive the AA message he's here to carry. Empathy, in Boston AA, is called Identification.

Then John L. says his first name and what he is, and everybody calls Hello.

White Flag is one of the area AA meetings Ennet House requires its residents to attend. You have to be seen at a designated AA or NA meeting every single night of the week or out you go, discharged. A House Staff member has to accompany the residents when they go to the designated meetings, so they can be officially seen there.[134] The residents' House counselors suggest that they sit right up at the front of the hall where they can see the pores in the speaker's nose and try to Identify instead of Compare. Again, *Identify* means empathize. Identifying, unless you've got a stake in Comparing, isn't very hard to do, here. Because if you sit up front and listen hard, all the speakers' stories of decline and fall and surrender are basically alike, and like your own: fun with the Substance, then very gradually less fun, then significantly less fun because of like blackouts you suddenly come out of on the highway going 145 kph with companions you do not know, nights you awake from in unfamiliar bedding next to somebody who doesn't even resemble any known sort of mammal, three-day blackouts you come out of and have to buy a newspaper to even know what town you're in; yes gradually less and less actual fun but with some physical need for the Substance, now, instead of the former voluntary fun; then at some point suddenly just very little fun at all, combined with terrible daily hand-trembling need, then dread, anxiety, irrational phobias, dim siren-like memories of fun, trouble with assorted authorities, knee-buckling headaches, mild seizures, and the litany of what Boston AA calls Losses—

'Then come the day I lost my job to drinking.' Concord's John L. has a huge hanging gut and just no ass at all, the way some big older guys' asses seem to get sucked into their body and reappear out front as gut. Gately, in sobriety, does nightly sit-ups out of fear this'll all of a sudden happen to him, as age thirty approaches. Gately is so huge no one sits behind him for several rows. John L. has the biggest bunch of keys Gately's ever seen. They're on one of those pull-outable-wire janitor's keychains that clips to a belt loop, and the speaker jangles them absently, unaware, his one tip of the hat to public nerves. He's also wearing gray janitor's pants. 'Lost my damn job,' he says. 'I mean to say I still knew where it was and whatnot. I just went in as usual one day and there was some other fellow doing it,' which gets another laugh.

—then more Losses, with the Substance seeming like the only consolation against the pain of the mounting Losses, and of course you're in Denial about it being the Substance that's causing the very Losses it's consoling you about—

'Alcohol destroys *slowly* but *thoroughly* is what a fellow said to me the first night I Come In, up in Concord, and that fellow ended up becoming my sponsor.'

—then less mild seizures, D.T.s during attempts to taper off too fast, introduction to subjective bugs and rodents, then one more binge and more formicative bugs; then eventually a terrible acknowledgment that some line has been undeniably crossed, and fist-at-the-sky, as-God-is-my-witness vows to buckle down and lick this thing for good, to quit for all time, then maybe a few white-knuckled days of initial success, then a slip, then more pledges, clock-watching, baroque self-regulations, repeated slips back into the Substance's relief after like two days' abstinence, ghastly hangovers, head-flattening guilt and self-disgust, superstructures of additional self-regulations (e.g. not before 0900h. not on a worknight, only when the moon is waxing, only in the company of Swedes) which also fail—

'When I was drunk I wanted to get sober and when I was sober I wanted to get drunk,' John L. says; 'I lived that way for years, and I submit to you that's not livin, that's a fuckin death-in-life.'

—then unbelievable psychic pain, a kind of peritonitis of the soul, psychic agony, fear of impending insanity (why can't I quit if I so want to quit, unless I'm insane?), appearances at hospital detoxes and rehabs, domestic strife, financial free-fall, eventual domestic Losses—

'And then I lost my wife to drinking. I mean I still knew where she was and whatnot. I just went in one day and there was some other fellow doing it,' at which there's not all that much laughter, lots of pained nods: it's often the same all over, in terms of domestic Losses.

—then vocational ultimatums, unemployability, financial ruin, pancreatitis, overwhelming guilt, bloody vomiting, cirrhotic neuralgia, incontinence, neuropathy, nephritis, black depressions, searing pain, with the Substance affording increasingly brief periods of relief; then, finally, no relief available anywhere at all; finally it's impossible to get high enough to freeze what you feel like, being this way; and now you hate the Substance, *hate* it, but you still find yourself unable to stop doing it, the Substance, you find you finally want to stop more than anything on earth and it's no fun doing it anymore and you can't believe you ever liked doing it and but you *still* can't stop, it's like you're totally fucking bats, it's like there's two yous; and when you'd sell your own dear Mum to stop and still, you find, can't stop, then the last layer of jolly friendly mask comes off your old friend the Substance, it's midnight now and all masks come off, and you all of a sudden see the Substance as it really is, for the first time you see the Disease as it really is, really has been all this time, you look in the mirror at midnight and see what owns you, what's become what you are—

'A fuckin livin death, I tell you it's not being near alive, by the end I was undead, not alive, and I tell you the idea of dyin was nothing compared to the idea of livin like that for another five or ten years and only *then* dyin,' with audience heads nodding in rows like a wind-swept meadow; *boy* can they ever Identify.

—and then you're in serious trouble, very serious trouble, and you know it, finally, deadly serious trouble, because this Substance you thought was your one true friend, that you gave up all for, gladly, that for so long gave you relief from the pain of the Losses your love of that relief caused, your mother and lover and god and compadre, has finally removed its smily-face mask to reveal centerless eyes and a ravening maw, and canines down to here, it's the Face In The Floor, the grinning root-white face of your worst nightmares, and the face is your own face in the mirror, now, it's *you*, the Substance has devoured or replaced and become *you*, and the puke-, drool- and Substance-crusted T-shirt you've both worn for weeks now gets torn off and you stand there looking and in the root-white chest where your heart (given away to It) should be beating, in its exposed chest's center and centerless eyes is just a lightless hole, more teeth, and a beckoning taloned hand dangling something irresistible, and now you see you've been had, screwed royal, stripped and fucked and tossed to the side like some stuffed toy to lie for all time in the posture you land in. You see now that It's your enemy and your worst personal nightmare and the trouble It's gotten you into is undeniable and you *still* can't stop. Doing the Substance now is like attending Black Mass but you still can't stop, even though the Substance no longer gets you high. You are, as they say, Finished. You cannot get drunk and you cannot get sober; you cannot get high and you cannot get straight. You are behind bars; you are in a cage and can see only bars in every direction. You are in the kind of a hell of a mess that either ends lives or turns them around. You are at a fork in the road that Boston AA calls your *Bottom*, though the term is misleading, because everybody here agrees it's more like someplace very high and unsupported: you're on the edge of something tall and leaning way out forward....

If you listen for the similarities, all these speakers' Substance-careers seem to terminate at the same cliff's edge. You are now Finished, as a Substance-user. It's the jumping-off place. You now have two choices. You can either eliminate your own map for keeps—blades are the best, or else pills, or there's always quietly sucking off the exhaust pipe of your repossessable car in the bank-owned garage of your familyless home. Something whimpery instead of banging. Better clean and quiet and (since your whole career's been one long futile flight from pain) painless. Though of the alcoholics and drug addicts who compose over 70% of a given year's suicides, some try to go out with a last great garish Balaclavan gesture: one longtime member of the White Flag Group is a prognathous lady named Louise B. who tried to take a map-eliminating dive off the old Hancock Building downtown in B.S. '81 but got caught in the gust of a rising thermal only six flights off the roof and got blown cartwheeling back up and in through the smoked-glass window of an arbitrage firm's suite on the thirty-fourth floor, ending up sprawled prone on a high-gloss conference table with only lacerations and a compound of the collarbone and an experience of willed self-annihilation and external intervention that has left her rabidly Christian—rabidly, as in foam—so that she's comparatively ignored and avoided, though her AA story, being just like everybody else's but more spectacular, has become metro Boston AA myth. But so when you get to this jumping-off place at the Finish of your Substance-career you can either take up the Luger or blade and eliminate your own personal map—this can be at age sixty, or twenty-seven, or seventeen—or you can get out the very beginning of the Yellow Pages or InterNet Psych-Svce File and make a blubbering 0200h. phone call and admit to a gentle grandparentish voice that you're in trouble, deadly serious trouble, and the voice will try to soothe you into hanging on until a couple hours go by and two pleasantly earnest, weirdly calm guys in conservative attire appear smiling at your door sometime before dawn and speak quietly to you for hours and leave you not remembering anything from what they said except the sense that they used to be eerily like you, just where you are, utterly fucked, and but now somehow aren't anymore, fucked like you, at least they didn't seem like they were, unless the whole thing's some incredibly involved scam, this AA thing, and so but anyway you sit there on what's left of your furniture in the lavender dawnlight and realize that by now you literally have no other choices besides trying this AA thing or else eliminating your map, so you spend the day killing every last bit of every Substance you've got in one last joyless bitter farewell binge and resolve, the next day, to go ahead and swallow your pride and maybe your common sense too and try these meetings of this 'Program' that at best is probably just Unitarian happy horseshit and at worst is a cover for some glazed and canny cult-type thing where they'll keep you sober by making you spend twenty hours a day selling cellophane cones of artificial flowers on the median strips of heavy-flow roads. And what defines this cliffish nexus of exactly two total choices, this miserable road-fork Boston AA calls your Bottom, is that at this point you feel like maybe selling flowers on median strips might not be so bad, not compared to what you've got going, personally, at this juncture. And this, at root, is what unites Boston AA: it turns out this same resigned, miserable, brainwash-and-exploit-me-if-that's-what-it-takes-type desperation has been the jumping-off place for just about every AA you meet, it emerges, once you've actually gotten it up to stop darting in and out of the big meetings and start walking up with your wet hand out and trying to actually personally meet some Boston A As. As the one particular tough old guy or lady you're always particularly scared of and drawn to says, nobody ever Comes In because things were going really well and they just wanted to round out their P.M. social calendar. Everybody, but *everybody* Comes In dead-eyed and puke-white and with their face hanging down around their knees and with a well-thumbed firearm-and-ordnance mail-order catalogue kept safe and available at home, map-wise, for when this last desperate resort of hugs and clichés turns out to be just happy horseshit, for you. You are not unique, they'll say: this initial hopelessness unites every soul in this broad cold salad-bar'd hall. They are like Hindenburg-survivors. Every meeting is a reunion, once you've been in for a while.

And then the palsied newcomers who totter in desperate and miserable enough to Hang In and keep coming and start feebly to scratch beneath the unlikely insipid surface of the thing, Don Gately's found, then get united by a second common experience. The shocking discovery that the thing actually does seem to work. Does keep you Substance-free. It's improbable and shocking. When Gately finally snapped to the fact, one day about four months into his Ennet House residency, that quite a few days seemed to have gone by without his playing with the usual idea of slipping over to Unit #7 and getting loaded in some nonuremic way the courts couldn't prove, that several days had gone without his even *thinking* of oral narcotics or a tightly rolled duBois or a cold foamer on a hot day…when he realized that the various Substances he didn't used to be able to go a day without absorbing hadn't even like *occurred* to him in almost a week, Gately hadn't felt so much grateful or joyful as just plain shocked. The idea that AA might actually somehow *work* unnerved him. He suspected some sort of trap. Some new sort of trap. At this stage he and the other Ennet residents who were still there and starting to snap to the fact that AA might work began to sit around together late at night going batshit together because it seemed to be impossible to figure out just *how* AA worked. It did, yes, tentatively seem maybe actually to be working, but Gately couldn't for the life of him figure out how just sitting on hemorrhoid-hostile folding chairs every night looking at nose-pores and listening to clichés could work. Nobody's ever been able to figure AA out, is another binding commonality. And the folks with serious time in AA are infuriating about questions starting with *How.* You ask the scary old guys How AA Works and they smile their chilly smiles and say Just Fine. It just works, is all; end of story. The newcomers who abandon common sense and resolve to Hang In and keep coming and then find their cages all of a sudden open, mysteriously, after a while, share this sense of deep shock and possible trap; about newer Boston AAs with like six months clean you can see this look of glazed suspicion instead of beatific glee, an expression like that of bug-eyed natives confronted suddenly with a Zippo lighter. And so this unites them, nervously, this tentative assemblage of possible glimmers of something like hope, this grudging move toward maybe acknowledging that this unromantic, unhip, clichéd AA thing—so unlikely and unpromising, so much the inverse of what they'd come too much to love—might really be able to keep the lover's toothy maw at bay. The process is the neat reverse of what brought you down and In here: Substances start out being so magically great, so much the interior jigsaw's missing piece, that at the start you just know, deep in your gut, that they'll never let you down; you just know it. But they do. And then this goofy slapdash anarchic system of low-rent gatherings and corny slogans and saccharin grins and hideous coffee is so lame you just *know* there's no way it could ever possibly work except for the utterest morons...and then Gately seems to find out AA turns out to be the very loyal friend he thought he'd had and then lost, when you Came In. And so you Hang In and stay sober and straight, and out of sheer hand-burned-on-hot-stove terror you heed the improbable-sounding warnings not to stop pounding out the nightly meetings even after the Substance-cravings have left and you feel like you've got a grip on the thing at last and can now go it alone, you still don't try to go it alone, you heed the improbable warnings because by now you have no faith in your own sense of what's really improbable and what isn't, since AA seems, improbably enough, to be working, and with no faith in your own senses you're confused, flummoxed, and when people with AA time strongly advise you to keep coming you nod robotically and keep coming, and you sweep floors and scrub out ashtrays and fill stained steel urns with hideous coffee, and you keep getting ritually down on your big knees every morning and night asking for help from a sky that still seems a burnished shield against all who would ask aid of it—how can you pray to a 'God' you believe only morons believe in, still?—but the old guys say it doesn't yet matter what you believe or don't believe, Just Do It they say, and like a shock-trained organism without any kind of independent human will you do exactly like you're told, you keep coming and coming, nightly, and now you take pains not to get booted out of the squalid halfway house you'd at first tried so hard to get discharged from, you Hang In and Hang In, meeting after meeting, warm day after cold day...; and not only does the urge to get high stay more or less away, but more general life-quality-type things—just as improbably promised, at first, when you'd Come In—things seem to get progressively somehow better, inside, for a while, then worse, then even better, then for a while worse in a way that's still somehow better, realer, you feel weirdly unblinded, which is good, even though a lot of the things you now see about yourself and how you've lived are horrible to have to see—and by this time the whole thing is so improbable and unparsable that you're so flummoxed you're convinced you're maybe brain-damaged, still, at this point, from all the years of Substances, and you figure you'd better Hang In in this Boston AA where older guys who seem to be less damaged—or at least less flummoxed by their damage—will tell you in terse simple imperative clauses exactly what to do, and where and when to do it (though never How or Why); and at this point you've started to have an almost classic sort of Blind Faith in the older guys, a Blind Faith in them born not of zealotry or even belief but just of a chilled conviction that you have no faith whatsoever left in yourself;[135] and now if the older guys say Jump you ask them to hold their hand at the desired height, and now they've got you, and you're free.

Another Advanced Basics Group speaker, whose first name Gately loses in the crowd's big Hello but whose last initial is E., an even bigger guy than John L., a green-card Irishman in a skallycap and Sinn Fein sweatshirt, with a belly like a swinging sack of meal and a thoroughly visible ass to back it up, is sharing his hope's experience by listing the gifts that have followed his decision to Come In and put the plug in the jug and the cap on the phentermine-hydrochloride bottle[136] and stop driving long-haul truck routes in unbroken 96-hour metal-pedalled states of chemical psychosis. The rewards of his abstinence, he stresses, have been more than just spiritual. Only in Boston AA can you hear a fifty-year-old immigrant wax lyrical about his first solid bowel movement in adult life.

''d been a confarmed bowl-splatterer for yars b'yond contin'. 'd been barred from t'facilities at o't' troock stops twixt hair'n Nork for yars. T'wallpaper in de loo a t'ome hoong in t'ese carled sheets froom t'wall, ay till yo. But now woon dey…ay'll remaember't'always. T'were a wake to t'day ofter ay stewed oop for me ninety-dey chip. Ay were tray moents sobber. Ay were thar on t'throne a't'ome, yo new. No't'put too fain a point' on it, ay prodooced as er uzhal and…and ay war soo amazed as to no't'be-laven' me yairs. 'Twas a sone so wonefamiliar at t'first ay tought ay'd droped me wallet in t'loo, do yo new. Ay tought ay'd droped me wallet in t'loo as Good is me wetness. So doan ay bend twixt m'knays and'ad a luke in t'dim o't'loo, and codn't belave me'yize. So gud paple ay do then ay drope to m'knays by t'loo an't'ad a *rail* luke. A loaver's luke, d'yo new. And friends t'were loavely past me pur poewers t'say. T'were a *tard* in t'loo. A *rail tard*. T'were farm an' teppered an' aiver so jaintly aitched. T'luked… *conestroocted* instaid've sprayed. T'luked as ay fel't'in me 'eart Good 'imsailf maint a tard t'luke. Me friends, this tard'o'mine practically had a poolse. Ay sted doan own m'knays an tanked me Har Par, which ay choose t'call me Har Par Good, an' ay been tankin me Har Par own m'knays aiver sin, marnin and natetime an in t'loo's'well, aiver sin.' The man's red-leather face radiant throughout. Gately and the other White Flaggers fall about, laugh from the gut, a turd that practically had a pulse, an ode to a solid dump; but the lightless eyes of certain palsied back-row newcomers widen with a very private Identification and possible hope, hardly daring to imagine.... A certain Message has been Carried.

Gately's biggest asset as an Ennet House live-in Staffer—besides the size thing, which is not to be discounted when order has to be maintained in a place where guys come in fresh from detox still in Withdrawal with their eyes rolling like palsied cattle and an earring in their eyelid and a tattoo that says BORN TO BE UNPLEASANT—besides the fact that his upper arms are the size of cuts of beef you rarely see off hooks, his big plus is he has this ability to convey his own experience about at first hating AA to new House residents who hate AA and resent being forced to go and sit up in nose-pore-range and listen to such limply improbable clichéd drivel night after night. Limp AA looks, at first, and actually limp it sometimes really is, Gately tells the new residents, and he says no way he'd expect them to believe on just his say-so that the thing'll work if they're miserable and desperate enough to Hang In against common sense for a while. But he says he'll clue them in on a truly great thing about AA: *they can't kick you out.* You're In if you say you're In. Nobody can get kicked out, not for any reason. Which means you can say *anything* in here. Talk about solid turds all you want. The molecular integrity of shit is small potatoes. Gately says he defies the new Ennet House residents to try and shock the smiles off these Boston AAs' faces. Can't be done, he says. These folks have literally heard it all. Enuresis. Impotence. Priapism. Onanism. Projectile-incontinence. Autocastration. Elaborate paranoid delusions, the grandiosest megalomania, Communism, fringe-Birchism, National-Socialist-Bundism, psychotic breaks, sodomy, bestiality, daughter-diddling, exposures at every conceivable level of indecency. Coprophilia and -phagia. Four-year White Flagger Glenn K.'s personally chosen Higher Power is *Satan*, for fuck's sake. Granted, nobody in White Flag much likes Glenn K., and the thing with the hooded cape and makeup and the candelabrum he carries around draw some mutters, but Glenn K. is a member for exactly as long as he cares to Hang In.

So say anything you want, Gately invites them. Go to the Beginner Meeting at 1930h. and raise your shaky mitt and tell the unlacquered truth. Free-associate. Run with it. Gately this morning, just after required

A.M. meditation, Gately was telling the tatt-obsessed little new lawyer guy Ewell, with the hypertensive flush and little white beard, telling him how he, Gately, had perked up considerably at 30 days clean when he found he could raise his big mitt in Beginner Meetings and say publicly just how much he hates this limp AA drivel about gratitude and humility and miracles and how he hates it and thinks it's horseshit and hates the AAs and how they all seem like limp smug moronic self-satisfied shit-eating pricks with their lobotomized smiles and goopy sentiment and how he wishes them all violent technicolor harm in the worst way, new Gately sitting there spraying vitriol, wet-lipped and red-eared, *trying* to get kicked out, purposely *trying* to outrage the AAs into giving him the boot so he could quick-march back to Ennet House and tell crippled Pat Montesian and his counselor Gene M. how he'd been given the boot at AA, how they'd pleaded for honest sharing of innermost feelings and OK he'd honestly shared his deepest feelings on the matter of *them* and the grinning hypocrites had shaken their fists and told him to screw...and but so in the meetings the poison would leap and spurt from him, and how but he found out all that these veteran White Flaggers would do as a Group when he like vocally wished them harm was nod furiously in empathetic Identification and shout with maddening cheer 'Keep Coming!' and one or two Flaggers with medium amounts of sober time would come up to him after the meeting and say how it was so good to hear him share and holy *mackerel* could they ever Identify with the deeply honest feelings he'd shared and how he'd done them the service of giving them the gift of a real 'Remember-When'-type experience because they could now remember feeling just exactly the same way as Gately, when they first Came In, only they confess not then having the spine to honestly share it with the Group, and so in a bizarre improbable twist they'd have Gately ending up standing there feeling like some sort of AA hero, a prodigy of vitriolic spine, both frustrated and elated, and before they bid him orevwar and told him to come back they'd make sure to give him their phone numbers on the back of their little raffle tickets, phone numbers Gately wouldn't dream of actually calling up (to say *what*, for chrissakes?) but which he found he rather liked having in his wallet, to just carry around, just in case of who knew what; and then plus maybe one of these old Enfield-native White Flag guys with geologic amounts of sober time in AA and a twisted ruined old body and clear bright-white eyes would hobble sideways like a crab slowly up to Gately after a meeting in which he'd spewed vitriol and reach way up to clap him on his big sweaty shoulder and say in their fremitic smoker's croak that Well you at least seem like a ballsy little bastard, all full of piss and vinegar and whatnot, and that just maybe you'll be OK, Don G., just maybe, just Keep Coming, and, if you'd care for a spot of advice from somebody who likely spilled more booze in his day than you've even consumed in yours, you might try to just simply sit down at meetings and relax and take the cotton out of your ears and put it in your mouth and shut the fuck up and just listen, for the first time perhaps in your life really *listen*, and maybe you'll end up OK; and they don't offer their phone numbers, not the really old guys, Gately knows he'd have to eat his pride raw and actually *request* the numbers of the old ruined grim calm longtimers in White Flag, 'The Crocodiles' the less senior White Flaggers call them, because the old twisted guys all tend to sit clustered together with hideous turd-like cigars in one corner of the Provident cafeteria under a 16 X 20 framed glossy of crocodiles or alligators sunning themselves on some verdant riverbank somewhere, with the maybe-joke legend OLD-TIMERS CORNER somebody had magisculed across the bottom of the photo, and these old guys cluster together under it, rotating their green cigars in their misshapen fingers and discussing completely mysterious long-sober matters out of the sides of their mouths. Gately sort of fears these old AA guys with their varicose noses and flannel shirts and white crew cuts and brown teeth and coolly amused looks of appraisal, feels like a kind of low-rank tribal knucklehead in the presence of stone-faced chieftains who rule by some unspoken shamanistic fiat,[137] and so of course he hates them, the Crocodiles, for making him feel like he fears them, but oddly he also ends up looking forward a little to sitting in the same big nursing-home cafeteria with them and facing the same direction they face, every Sunday, and a little later finds he even enjoys riding at 30 kph tops in their perfectly maintained 25-year-old sedans when he starts going along on White Flag Commitments to other Boston AA Groups. He eventually heeds a terse suggestion and starts going out and telling his grisly personal story publicly from the podium with other members of White Flag, the Group he gave in and finally officially joined. This is what you do if you're new and have what's called The Gift of Desperation and are willing to go to any excruciating lengths to stay straight, you officially join a Group and put your name and sobriety-date down on the Group secretary's official roster, and you make it your business to start to get to know other members of the Group on a personal basis, and you carry their numbers talismanically in your wallet; and, most important, you get Active With Your Group, which here in Gately's Boston AA *Active* means not just sweeping the footprinty floor after the Lord's Prayer and making coffee and emptying ashtrays of gasper-butts and ghastly spit-wet cigar

ends but also showing up regularly at specified P.M. times at the White
Flag Group's regular haunt, the Elit (the final *e*'s neon's ballast's out) Diner
next to Steve's Donuts in Enfield Center, showing up and pounding down
tooth-loosening amounts of coffee and then getting in well-maintained
Crocodilian sedans whose suspensions' springs Gately's mass makes sag
and getting driven, wall-eyed with caffeine and cigar fumes and general
public-speaking angst, to like Lowell's Joy of Living Group or Charles-
town's Plug In The Jug Group or Bridgewater State Detox or Concord
Honor Farm with these guys, and except for one or two other pale wall-
eyed newcomers with The Gift of utter Desperation it's mostly Crocodiles
with geologic sober time in these cars, it's mostly the guys that've stayed
sober in White Flag for decades who still go on every single booked Commitment, they go every time, dependable as death, even when the Celtics
are on Spontaneous-Dis they hit the old Commitment trail, they remain
rabidly Active With Their Group; and the Crocodiles in the car invite
Gately to see the coincidence of long-term contented sobriety and rabidly
tireless AA Activity as not a coincidence at all. The backs of their necks
are complexly creased. The Crocodiles up front look into the rearview
mirror and narrow their baggy bright-white eyes at Gately in the sagging
backseat with the other new guys, and the Crocodiles say they can't even
begin to say how many new guys they've seen Come In and then get
sucked back Out There, Come In to AA for a while and Hang In and put
together a little sober time and have things start to get better, head-wise
and life-quality-wise, and after a while the new guys get cocky, they
decide they've gotten '*Well*,' and they get really busy at the new job sobriety's allowed them to get, or maybe they buy season Celtics tickets, or they
rediscover pussy and start chasing pussy (these withered gnarled toothless
totally postsexual old fuckers actually say *pussy*), but one way or another
these poor cocky clueless new bastards start gradually drifting away from
rabid Activity In The Group, and then away from their Group itself, and
then little by little gradually drift away from any AA meetings at all, and
then, without the protection of meetings or a Group, in time — oh there's
always plenty of time, the Disease is fiendishly patient — how in time they
forget what it was like, the ones that've cockily drifted, they forget who
and what they are, they forget about the Disease, until like one day they're
at like maybe a Celtics-Sixers game, and the good old Fleet/First Interstate Center's hot, and they think what could just one cold foamer hurt,
after all this sober time, now that they've gotten '*Well*.' Just one cold one.
What could it hurt. And after that one it's like they'd never stopped, if
they've got the Disease. And how in a month or six months or a year they

have to Come *Back* In, back to the Boston AA halls and their old Group, tottering, D.T.ing, with their faces hanging down around their knees all over again, or maybe it's five or ten years before they can get it up to get back In, beaten to shit again, or else their system isn't ready for the recurred abuse again after some sober time and they die Out There—the Crocodiles are always talking in hushed, 'Nam-like tones about *Out There*—or else, worse, maybe they kill somebody in a blackout and spend the rest of their lives in MCI-Walpole drinking raisin jack fermented in the seatless toilet and trying to recall what they did to get in there, Out There; or else, worst of all, these cocky new guys drift back Out There and have nothing sufficiently horrible to Finish them happen at all, just go back to drinking 24/7/365, to not-living, behind bars, undead, back in the Disease's cage all over again. The Crocodiles talk about how they can't count the number of guys that've Come In for a while and drifted away and gone back Out There and died, or not gotten to die. They even point some of these guys out—gaunt gray spectral men reeling on sidewalks with all that they own in a trashbag—as the White Flaggers drive slowly by in their well-maintained cars. Old emphysemic Francis G. in particular likes to slow his LeSabre down at a corner in front of some jack-legged loose-faced homeless fuck who'd once been in AA and drifted cockily out and roll down his window and yell 'Live it up!'

Of course—the Crocodiles dig at each other with their knobby elbows and guffaw and wheeze—they say when they tell Gately to either Hang In AA and get rabidly Active or else die in slime of course it's only a *suggestion*. They howl and choke and slap their knees at this. It's your classic in-type joke. There are, by ratified tradition, no 'musts' in Boston AA. No doctrine or dogma or rules. They can't kick you out. You don't have to do what they say. Do exactly as you please—if you still trust what seems to please you. The Crocodiles roar and wheeze and pound on the dash and bob in the front seat in abject AA mirth.

Boston AA's take on itself is that it's a benign anarchy, that any order to the thing is a function of Miracle. No regs, no musts, only love and support and the occasional humble suggestion born of shared experience. A non-authoritarian, dogma-free movement. Normally a gifted cynic, with a keen bullshit-antenna, Gately needed over a year to pinpoint the ways in which he feels like Boston AA really is actually sub-rosa dogmatic. You're not supposed to pick up any sort of altering Substance, of course; that goes without saying; but the Fellowship's official line is that if you do slip or drift or fuck up or forget and go Out There for a night and absorb a Substance and get all your Disease's triggers pulled again they want you to know they not only invite but urge you to come on back to meetings as quickly as possible. They're pretty sincere about this, since a lot of new people slip and slide a bit, total-abstinence-wise, in the beginning. Nobody's supposed to judge you or snub you for slipping. Everybody's here to help. Everybody knows that the returning slippee has punished himself enough just being Out There, and that it takes incredible desperation and humility to eat your pride and wobble back In and put the Substance down again after you've fucked up the first time and the Substance is calling to you all over again. There's the sort of sincere compassion about fucking up that empathy makes possible, although some of the AAs will nod smugly when they find out the slippee didn't take some of the basic suggestions. Even newcomers who can't even start to quit yet and show up with suspicious flask-sized bulges in their coat pockets and list progressively to starboard as the meeting progresses are urged to keep coming, Hang In, stay, as long as they're not too disruptive. Inebriates are discouraged from driving themselves home after the Lord's Prayer, but nobody's going to wrestle your keys away. Boston AA stresses the utter autonomy of the individual member. Please say and do whatever you wish. Of course there are about a dozen basic suggestions,[138] and of course people who cockily decide they don't wish to abide by the basic suggestions are constantly going back Out There and then wobbling back in with their faces around their knees and confessing from the podium that they didn't take the suggestions and have paid full price for their willful arrogance and have learned the hard way and but now they're back, by God, and this time they're going to follow the suggestions to the bloody *letter* just see if they don't. Gately's sponsor Francis ('Ferocious Francis') G., the Crocodile that Gately finally got up the juice to ask to be his sponsor, compares the totally optional basic suggestions in Boston AA to, say for instance if you're going to jump out of an airplane, they 'suggest' you wear a parachute. But of course you do what you want. Then he starts laughing until he's coughing so bad he has to sit down.

The bitch of the thing is you have to *want* to. If you don't *want* to do as you're told—I mean as it's suggested you do—it means that your own personal will is still in control, and Eugenio Martinez over at Ennet House never tires of pointing out that your personal will is the web your Disease sits and spins in, still. The will you call your own ceased to be yours as of who knows how many Substance-drenched years ago. It's now shot through with the spidered fibrosis of your Disease. His own experience's term for the Disease is: *The Spider*.[139] You have to Starve The Spider: you have to surrender your will. This is why most people will Come In and Hang In only after their own entangled will has just about killed them. You have to want to surrender your will to people who know how to Starve The Spider. You have to want to take the suggestions, want to abide by the traditions of anonymity, humility, surrender to the Group conscience. If you don't obey, nobody will kick you out. They won't have to. You'll end up kicking *yourself* out, if you steer by your own sick will. This is maybe why just about everybody in the White Flag Group tries so hard to be so disgustingly humble, kind, helpful, tactful, cheerful, nonjudgmental, tidy, energetic, sanguine, modest, generous, fair, orderly, patient, tolerant, attentive, truthful. It isn't like the Group makes them do it. It's more like that the only people who end up able to hang for serious time in AA are the ones who willingly try to be these things. This is why, to the cynical newcomer or fresh Ennet House resident, serious AAs look like these weird combinations of Gandhi and Mr. Rogers with tattoos and enlarged livers and no teeth who used to beat wives and diddle daughters and now rhapsodize about their bowel movements. It's all optional; do it or die.

So but like e.g. Gately puzzled for quite some time about why these AA meetings where nobody kept order seemed so orderly. No interrupting, fisticuffery, no heckled invectives, no poisonous gossip or beefs over the tray's last Oreo. Where was the hard-ass Sergeant at Arms who enforced these principles they guaranteed would save your ass? Pat Montesian and Eugenio Martinez and Ferocious Francis the Crocodile wouldn't answer Gately's questions about where's the enforcement. They just all smiled coy smiles and said to Keep Coming, an apothegm Gately found just as trite as 'Easy Does It!' 'Live and Let Live!'

How do trite things get to be trite? Why is the truth usually not just un-but *anti*-interesting? Because every one of the seminal little mini-epiphanies you have in early AA is always polyesterishly banal, Gately admits to residents. He'll tell how, as a resident, right after that one Harvard Square industrial-grunge post-punk, this guy whose name was Bernard but insisted on being called Plasmatron-7, right after old Plasmatron-7 drank nine bottles of NyQuil in the men's upstairs head and pitched forward face-first into his instant spuds at supper and got discharged on the spot, and got fireman-carried by Calvin Thrust right out to Comm. Ave.'s Green Line T-stop, and Gately got moved up from the newest guys' 5-Man room to take Plasmatron-7's old bunk in the less-new guys' 3-Man room, Gately had an epiphanic AA-related nocturnal dream he'll be the first to admit was banally trite.[140] In the dream Gately and row after row of totally average and non-unique U.S. citizens were kneeling on their knees on polyester cushions in a crummy low-rent church basement. The basement was your average low-rent church basement except for this dream-church's basement walls were of like this weird thin clean clear glass. Everybody was kneeling on these cheap but comfortable cushions, and it was weird because nobody seemed to have any clear idea why they were all on their knees, and there was like no tier-boss or sergeant-at-arms-type figure around coercing them into kneeling, and yet there was this sense of some compelling unspoken reason why they were all kneeling. It was one of those dream things where it didn't make sense but did. And but then some lady over to Gately's left got off her knees and all of a sudden stood up, just like to stretch, and the minute she stood up she was all of a sudden yanked backward with terrible force and sucked out through one of the clear glass walls of the basement, and Gately had winced to get ready for the sound of serious glass, but the glass wall didn't shatter so much as just let the cartwheeling lady sort of melt right through, and healed back over where she'd melted through, and she was gone. Her cushion and then Gately notices a couple other polyester cushions in some of the rows here and there were empty. And it was then, as he was looking around, that Gately in his dream looked slowly up overhead at the ceiling's exposed pipes and could now all of a sudden see, rotating slow and silent through the basement a meter above the different-shaped and -colored heads of the kneeling assembly, he could see a long plain hooked stick, like the crook of a giant shepherd, like the hook that appears from stage-left and drags bad acts out of tomato-range, moving slowly above them in French-curled circles, almost demurely, as if quietly scanning; and when a mild-faced guy in a cardigan happened to stand up and was hooked by the hooked stick and pulled ass-over-teakettle out through the soundless glass membrane Gately turned his big head as far as he could without leaving the cushion and could see, now, just outside the wall's clean pane, trolling with the big stick, an extraordinarily snappily dressed and authoritative figure manipulating the giant shepherd's crook with one hand and coolly examining the nails of his other hand from behind a mask that was simply the plain yellow smily-face circle that accompanied invitations to have a nice day. The figure was so impressive and trustworthy and casually self-assured as to be both soothing and compelling. The authoritative figure radiated good cheer and abundant charm and limitless patience. It manipulated the big stick in the coolly purposeful way of the sort of angler who you know isn't going to throw back anything he catches. The slow silent stick with the hook he held was what kept them all kneeling below the baroque little circumferences of its movement overhead.

One of Ennet House's live-in Staffers' rotating P.M. jobs is to be awake and on-call in the front office all night for Dream Duty—people in early recovery from Substances often get hit with real horror-show dreams, or else traumatically seductive Substance-dreams, and sometimes trite but important epiphanic dreams, and the Staffer on Dream Duty is required to be up doing paperwork or sit-ups or staring out the broad bay window in the front office downstairs, ready to make coffee and listen to the residents' dreams and offer the odd practical upbeat Boston-AA-type insight into possible implications for the dreamer's progress in recovery—but Gately had no need to clomp downstairs for a Staffer's feedback on this one, since it was so powerfully, tritely obvious. It had come clear to Gately that Boston AA had the planet's most remorselessly hard-ass and efficient sergeant at arms. Gately lay there, overhanging all four sides of his bunk, his broad square forehead beaded with revelation: Boston AA's Sergeant at Arms stood *outside* the orderly meeting halls, in that much-invoked Out There where exciting clubs full of good cheer throbbed gaily below lit signs with neon bottles endlessly pouring. AA's patient enforcer was always and everywhere Out There: it stood casually checking its cuticles in the astringent fluorescence of pharmacies that took forged Talwin scrips for a hefty surcharge, in the onionlight through paper shades in the furnished rooms of strung-out nurses who financed their own cages' maintenance with stolen pharmaceutical samples, in the isopropyl reek of the storefront offices of stooped old chain-smoking MD's whose scrip-pads were always out and who needed only to hear 'pain' and see cash. In the home of a snot-strangled Canadian VIP and the office of an implacable Revere A.D.A. whose wife has opted for dentures at thirty-five. AA's disciplinarian looked damn good and smelled even better and dressed to impress and his blank black-on-yellow smile never faltered as he sincerely urged you to have a nice day. Just one more last nice day. Just one.

And that was the first night that cynical Gately willingly took the basic suggestion to get down on his big knees by his undersized spring-shot Ennet House bunk and Ask For Help from something he still didn't believe in, ask for his own sick Spider-bit will to be taken from him and fumigated and squished.

But and plus in Boston AA there is, unfortunately, dogma, too, it turns out; and some of it is both dated and smug. And there's an off-putting jargon in the Fellowship, a psychobabbly dialect that's damn near impossible to follow at first, says Ken Erdedy, the college-boy ad exec semi-new at Ennet House, complaining to Gately at the White Flag meeting's raffle-break. Boston AA meetings are unusually long, an hour and a half instead of the national hour, but here they also have this formal break at about 45 minutes where everybody can grab a sandwich or Oreo and a sixth cup of coffee and stand around and chat, and bond, where people can pull their sponsors aside and confide some trite insight or emotional snafu that the sponsor can swiftly, privately validate but also place in the larger imperative context of the primary need not to absorb a Substance today, just today, no matter what happens. While everybody's bonding and interfacing in a bizarre system of catchphrases, there's also the raffle, another Boston idiosyncrasy: the newest of the White Flag newcomers trying to Get Active In Group Service wobble around with rattan baskets and packs of tickets, one for a buck and three for a fin, and the winner eventually gets announced from the podium and everyone hisses and shouts 'Fix!' and laughs, and the winner wins a Big Book or an *As Bill Sees It* or a *Came To Believe*, which if he's got some sober time in and already owns all the AA literature from winning previous raffles he'll stand up and publicly offer it to any newcomer who wants it, which means any newcomer with enough humble desperation to come up to him and ask for it and risk being given a phone number to carry around in his wallet.

At the White Flag raffle-break Gately usually stands around chainsmoking with the Ennet House residents, so that he's casually available to answer questions and empathize with complaints. He usually waits til after the meeting to do his own complaining to Ferocious Francis, with whom Gately now shares the important duty of 'breaking down the hall,' sweeping floors and emptying ashtrays and wiping down the long cafeteria tables, which F.F.G.'s function is limited because he's on oxygen and his function consists mostly of standing there sucking oxygen and holding an unlit cigar while Gately breaks down the hall. Gately rather likes Ken Erdedy, who came into the House about a month ago from some cushy Belmont rehab. Erdedy's an upscale guy, what Gately's mother would have called a yuppie, an account executive at Viney and Veals Advertising downtown his Intake form said, and though he's about Gately's age he's so softly good-looking in that soft mannequinish way Harvard and Tufts schoolboys have, and looks so smooth and groomed all the time even in jeans and a plain cotton sweater, that Gately thinks of him as much younger, totally ungrizzled, and refers to him mentally as 'kid.' Erdedy's in the House mainly for 'marijuana addiction,' which Gately has a hard time Identifying with anybody getting in enough trouble with weed to leave his job and condo to bunk in a room full of tattooed guys who smoke in their sleep, and to work like pumping gas (Erdedy just started his nine-month humility job at the Merit station down by North Harvard St. in Allston) for 32 minimum-wage hours a week. Or to have his leg be joggling like that all the time from tensions of Withdrawal: from fucking grass? But it's not Gately's place to say what's bad enough to make somebody Come In and what isn't, not for anybody else but himself, and the shapely but big-time-troubled new girl Kate Gompert—who mostly just stays in her bed in the new women's 5-Woman room when she isn't at meetings, and is on a Suicidality Contract with Pat, and isn't getting the usual pressure to get a humility job, and gets to get some sort of scrip-meds out of the meds locker every morning—Kate Gompert's counselor Danielle S. reported at the last Staff Meeting that Kate had finally opened up and told her she'd mostly Come In for weed, too, and not the light-weight prescription tranqs she'd listed on her Intake form. Gately used to treat weed like tobacco. He wasn't like some other narcotics addicts who smoked weed when they couldn't get anything else; he always smoked weed and could always get something else and simply smoked weed while he did whatever else he could get. Gately doesn't miss weed much. The shocker-type AA Miracle is he doesn't much miss the Demerol, either, today.

A hard November wind is spattering goopy sleet against the broad windows all around the hall. The Provident Nursing Home cafeteria is lit by a checkerboard array of oversized institutional bulbs overhead, a few of which are always low and give off fluttery strobes. The fluttering bulbs are why Pat Montesian and all the other photic-seizure-prone area AAs never go to White Flag, opting for the Freeway Group over in Brookline or the candyass Lake Street meeting up in West Newton on Sunday nights, which Pat M. bizarrely drives all the way up from her home down on the South Shore in Milton to get to, to hear people talk about their analysts and Saabs. There is no way to account for people's taste in AA. The White Flag hall is so brightly lit up all Gately can see out any of the windows is a kind of shiny drooling black against everybody's pale reflection.

Miracle's one of the Boston AA terms Erdedy and the brand-new and very shaky veiled girl resident standing over him complain they find hard to stomach, as in 'We're All Miracles Here' and 'Don't Leave Five Minutes Before The Miracle Happens' and 'To Stay Sober For 24 Hours Is A Miracle.'

Except the brand-new girl, either Joelle V. or Joelle D., who said she'd hit the occasional meeting in the past before her Bottom and had been roundly repelled, and is still pretty much cynical and repelled, she said on the way down to Provident under Gately's direct new-resident supervision, says she finds even the word *Miracle* preferable to the constant AA talk about 'the Grace of God,' which reminds her of wherever she grew up, where she's indicated places of worship were often aluminum trailers or fiberboard shacks and church-goers played with copperheads in the services to honor something about serpents and tongues.

Gately's also observed how Erdedy's also got that Tufts-Harvard way of speaking without seeming to move his lower jaw.

'It's as if it's its own country or something,' Erdedy complains, legs crossed in maybe a bit of a faggy schoolboy way, looking around at the raffle-break, sitting in Gately's generous shadow. 'The first time I ever talked, over at the St. E's meeting on Wednesday, somebody comes up after the Lord's Prayer and says "Good to hear you, I could really I.D. with that bottom you were sharing about, the isolating, the can't-and-can't, it's the greenest I've felt in months, hearing you." And then gives me this raffle ticket with his phone number that I didn't ask for and says I'm right where I'm supposed to be, which I have to say I found a bit patronizing.'

The best noise Gately produces is his laugh, which booms and reassures, and a certain haunted hardness goes out of his face when he laughs. Like most huge men, Gately has kind of a high hoarse speaking voice; his larynx sounds compressed. 'I still hate that right-where-you're-supposed-to-be thing,' he says, laughing. He likes that Erdedy, sitting, looks right up at him and cocks his head slightly to let Gately know he's got his full attention. Gately doesn't know that this is a requisite for a white-collar job where you have to show you're attending fully to clients who are paying major sums and get to expect an overt display of full attention. Gately is still not yet a good judge of anything about upscale people except where they tend to hide their valuables.

Boston AA, with its emphasis on the Group, is intensely social. The raffle-break goes on and on. An intoxicated street-guy with a venulated nose and missing incisors and electrician's tape wrapped around his shoes is trying to sing 'Volare' up at the empty podium microphone. He is gently, cheerfully induced offstage by a Crocodile with a sandwich and an arm around the shoulders. There's a certain pathos to the Crocodile's kindness, his clean flannel arm around the weatherstained shoulders, which pathos Gately feels and likes being able to feel it, while he says 'But at least the "Good to hear you" I quit minding. It's just what they say when somebody's got done speaking. They can't say like "Good job" or "You spoke well," cause it can't be anybody's place here to judge if anybody else did good or bad or whatnot. You know what I'm saying, Tiny, there?'

Tiny Ewell, in a blue suit and laser chronometer and tiny shoes whose shine you could read by, is sharing a dirty aluminum ashtray with Nell Gunther, who has a glass eye which she amuses herself by usually wearing so the pupil and iris face in and the dead white and tiny manufacturer's specifications on the back of the eye face out. Both of them are pretending to study the blond false wood of the tabletop, and Ewell makes a bit of a hostile show of not looking up or responding to Gately or entering into the conversation in any way, which is his choice and on him alone, so Gately lets it go. Wade McDade has a Walkman going, which is technically OK at the raffle-break although it's not a real good idea. Chandler Foss is flossing his teeth and pretending to throw the used floss at Jennifer Belbin. Most of the Ennet House residents are mingling satisfactorily. The couple of residents that are black are mingling with other blacks.[141] The Diehl kid and Doony Glynn are amusing themselves telling homosexuality jokes to Morris Hanley, who sits smoothing his hair with his fingertips, pretending to not even acknowledge, his left hand still bandaged. Alfonso Parias-Carbo is standing with three Allston Group guys, smiling broadly and nodding, not understanding a word anybody says. Bruce Green has gone downstairs to the men's head and amused Gately by asking his permission first. Gately told him to go knock himself out. Green has good big arms and no gut, even after all the Substances, and Gately suspects he might have played some ball at some point. Kate Gompert is totally by herself at a nonsmoking table over by a window, ignoring her pale reflection and making little cardboard tents out of her raffle tickets and moving them around. Clenette Henderson clutches another black girl and laughs and says 'Girl!' several times. Emil Minty is clutching his head. Geoff Day in his black turtleneck and blazer keeps lurking on the fringes of various groups of people pretending he's part of the conversations. No immediate sign of Burt F. Smith or Charlotte Treat. Randy Lenz, in his cognito white mustache and sideburns, is doubtless at the pay phone in the northeast corner of the Provident lobby downstairs: Lenz spends nearly unacceptable amounts of time either on a phone or trying to get in position to use a phone. 'Cause what I like,' Gately says to Erdedy (Erdedy really is listening, even though there's a compellingly cheap young woman in a brief white skirt and absurd black mesh stockings sitting with her legs nicely crossed — one-strap low-spike black Ferragamos, too — at the periphery of his vision, and the woman is with a large man, which makes her even more compelling; and also the veiled new girl's breasts and her hips' clefs are compelling and distracting, next to him, even in a long baggy loose blue sweater that matches the embroidered selvage around her veil), 'What I think I like is how "It was good to hear you" ends up, like, saying two separate things together.' Gately's also saying this to Joelle, who it's weird but you can tell she's looking at you, even through the linen veil. There's maybe half a dozen or so other veiled people in the White Flag hall tonight; a decent percentage of people in the

11-Step Union of the Hideously and Improbably Deformed are also in 12-Step fellowships for other issues besides hideous deformity. Most of the room's veiled AAs are women, though there is this one male veiled U.H.I.D. guy that's an active White Flagger, Tommy S. or F., who years ago nodded out on a stuffed acrylic couch with a bottle of Rémy and a lit Tiparillo—the guy now wears U.H.I.D. veils and a whole spectrum of silk turtlenecks and assorted hats and classy lambskin driving gloves. Gately's had the U.H.I.D.-and-veil philosophy explained to him in passing a couple times but still doesn't much get it, it seems like a gesture of shame and concealment, still, to him, the veil. Pat Montesian had said there's been a few other U.H.I.D.s who'd gone through Ennet House prior to the Year of Dairy Products From the American Heartland, which is when new resident Gately came wobbling in, but this Joelle van Dyne, who Gately feels he has zero handle on yet as a person or how serious she is about putting down Substances and Coming In to really get straight, this Joelle is the first veiled resident Gately's had under him, as a Staffer. This Joelle girl, that wasn't even on the two-month waiting list for Intake, got in overnight under some private arrangement with somebody on the House's Board of Directors, upscale Enfield guys into charity and directing. There'd been no Intake interview with Pat at the House; the girl just showed up two days ago right after supper. She'd been up at Brigham and Women's for five days after some sort of horrific O.D.-type situation said to have included both defib paddles and priests. She'd had real luggage and this like Chinese portable dressing-screen thing with clouds and pop-eyed dragons that even folded lengthwise took both Green and Parias-Carbo to lug upstairs. There's been no talk of a humility job for her, and Pat's counseling the girl personally. Pat's got some sort of privately directed arrangement with the girl; Gately's already seen enough private-type arrangements between certain Staffers and residents to feel like it's maybe kind of a character defect of Ennet House. A girl from the Brookline Young People's Group over in a cheerleader skirt and slut-stockings is ignoring all the ashtrays and putting her extra-long gasper out on the bare tabletop two rows over as she laughs like a seal at something an acne'd guy in a long camelhair car coat he hasn't taken off and sockless leather dance-shoes Gately's never seen at a meeting before says. And he's got his hand on hers as she grinds the gasper out. Something like putting a cigarette out against the wood-grain plastic tabletop, which Gately can already see the ragged black burn-divot that's formed, it's something the rankness of which would never have struck him one way or the other, before, until Gately took on half the break-down-the-hall-and-wipe-down-the-tables

job at Ferocious Francis G.'s suggestion, and now he feels sort of propri-
etary about the Provident's tabletops. But it's not like he can go over and
take anybody else's inventory and tell them how to behave. He settles for
imagining the girl pinwheeling through the air toward a glass wall.

'When they say it it sort of means like what you said was good for them,
it helped them out somehow,' he says, 'but plus now also I like saying it
myself because if you think about it it also means it was good to be *able* to
hear you. To really hear.' He's trying subtly to alternate and look at Erdedy
and Joelle both, like he's addressing them both. It's not something he's
good at. His head's too big to be subtle with. 'Because I remember for like
the first sixty days or so I couldn't hear shit. I didn't hear nothing. I'd just
sit there and Compare, I'd go to myself, like, "I never rolled a car," "I never
lost a wife," "I never bled from the rectum." Gene would tell me to just
keep coming for a while and sooner or later I'd start to be able to both
listen and hear. He said it's hard to really hear. But he wouldn't say what
was the difference between hearing and listening, which pissed me off.
But after a while I started to really *hear*. It turns out—and this is just for
me, maybe—but it turned out *hearing* the speaker means like all of a sudden hearing how fucking similar the way he felt and the way I felt were,
Out There, at the Bottom, before we each Came In. Instead of just sitting
here resenting being here and thinking how he bled from the ass and I
didn't and how that means I'm not as bad as him yet and I can still be Out
There.'

One of the tricks to being of real service to newcomers is not to lecture or
give advice but only talk about your own personal experience and what you
were told and what you found out personally, and to do it in a casual but positive and encouraging way. Plus you're supposed to try and Identify with the
newcomer's feelings as much as possible. Ferocious Francis G. says this is one
of the ways guys with just a year or two sober can be most helpful: being able
to sincerely ID with the newly Sick and Suffering. Ferocious Francis told
Gately as they were wiping down tables that if a Crocodile with decades of
sober AA time can still sincerely empathize and Identify with a whacked-out
bug-eyed Disease-ridden newcomer then there's something deeply fucked up
about that Crocodile's recovery. The Crocodiles, decades sober, live in a
totally different spiritual galaxy, inside. One long-timer describes it as he has
a whole new unique interior spiritual castle, now, to live in.

Part of this new Joelle girl's pull for Ken Erdedy isn't just the sexual
thing of her body, which he finds made way sexier by the way the overlarge blue coffee-stained sweater tries to downplay the body thing without
being so hubristic as to try to hide it—sloppy sexiness pulls Erdedy in like

a well-groomed moth to a lit window—but it's also the veil, wondering what horrific contrast to the body's allure lies swollen or askew under that veil; it gives the pull a perverse sideways slant that makes it even more distracting, and so Erdedy cocks his head a little more up at Gately and narrows his eyes to make his listening-look terribly intense. He doesn't know that there's an abstract distance in the look that makes it seem like he's studying a real bitch of a 7-iron on the tenth rough or something; the look doesn't communicate what he thinks his audience wants it to.

The raffle-break is winding down as everybody starts to want their own ashtray. Two more big urns of coffee emerge from the kitchen door over by the literature table. Erdedy is probably the second-biggest leg-and-foot-joggler in present residence, after Geoffrey D. Joelle v. D. now says something very strange. It's a very strange little moment, right at the end of the raffle-break, and Gately later finds it impossible to describe it in his Log entry for the P.M. shift. It is the first time he realizes that Joelle's voice—crisp and rich and oddly empty, her accent just barely Southern and with a strange and it turns out Kentuckian lapse in the pronunciation of all apicals except *s*—is familiar in a faraway way that both makes it familiar and yet lets Gately be sure he's never once met her before, Out There. She inclines the plane of her blue-bordered veil briefly toward the floor's tile (very bad tile, scab-colored, nauseous, worst thing about the big room by far), brings it back up level (unlike Erdedy she's standing, and in flats is nearly Gately's height), and says that she's finding it especially hard to take when these earnest ravaged folks at the lectern say they're 'Here But For the Grace of God,' except that's not the strange thing she says, because when Gately nods hard and starts to interject about 'It was the same for—' and wants to launch into a fairly standard Boston AA agnostic-soothing riff about the 'God' in the slogan being just shorthand for a totally subjective and up-to-you 'Higher Power' and AA being merely spiritual instead of dogmatically religious, a sort of benign anarchy of subjective spirit, Joelle cuts off his interjection and says that but that *her* trouble with it is that 'But For the Grace of God' is a subjunctive, a counterfactual, she says, and can make sense only when introducing a conditional clause, like e.g. 'But For the Grace of God I *would* have died on Molly Notkin's bathroom floor,' so that an indicative transposition like 'I'm here But For the Grace of God' is, she says, literally senseless, and regardless of whether she *hears* it or not it's meaningless, and that the foamy enthusiasm with which these folks can say what in fact means nothing at all makes her want to put her head in a Radarange at the thought that Substances have brought her to the sort of pass where this is the sort of language she has to have Blind Faith in. Gately looks at a rectangular blue-selvaged expanse of clean linen whose gentle rises barely allude to any features below, he looks at her and has no idea whether she's serious or not, or whacked, or trying like Dr. Geoff Day to erect Denial-type fortifications with some kind of intellectualish showing-off, and he doesn't know what to say in reply, he has absolutely nothing in his huge square head to Identify with her with or latch onto or say in encouraging reply, and for an instant the Provident cafeteria seems pin-drop silent, and his own heart grips him like an infant rattling the bars of its playpen, and he feels a greasy wave of an old and almost unfamiliar panic, and for a second it seems inevitable that at some point in his life he's going to get high again and be back in the cage all over again, because for a second the blank white veil levelled at him seems a screen on which might well be projected a casual and impressive black and yellow smily-face, grinning, and he feels all the muscles in his own face loosen and descend kneeward; and the moment hangs there, distended, until the White Flag raffle coordinator for November, Glenn K., glides up to the podium mike in his scarlet velour caparison and makeup and candelabrum with candles the same color as the floor tile and uses the plastic gavel to formally end the break and bring things back to whatever passes here for order, for the raffle drawing. The Watertown guy with middle-level sober time who wins the Big Book publicly offers it to any newcomer that wants it, and Gately is pleased to see Bruce Green raise a big hand, and decides he'll just turn it over and ask Ferocious Francis G. for feedback on subjunctives and countersexuals, and the infant leaves its playpen alone inside him, and the rivets of the long table his seat's attached to make a brief distressed noise as he sits and settles in for the second half of the meeting, asking silently for help to be determined to try to really hear or die trying.

—*pages 343–367*

Winter, B.S. 1963, Sepulveda CA

I REMEMBER[208] I was eating lunch and reading something dull by Bazin when my father came into the kitchen and made himself a tomato juice beverage and said that as soon as I was finished he and my mother needed my help in their bedroom. My father had spent the morning at the commercial studio and was still all in white, with his wig with its rigid white parted hair, and hadn't yet removed the television makeup that gave his real face an orange cast in daylight. I hurried up and finished and rinsed my dishes in the sink and proceeded down the hall to the master bedroom. My mother and father were both in there. The master bedroom's valance curtains and the heavy lightproof curtain behind them were all slid back and the venetian blinds up, and the daylight was very bright in the room, the decor of which was white and blue and powder-blue.

My father was bent over my parents' large bed, which was stripped of bedding all the way down to the mattress protector. He was bent over, pushing down on the bed's mattress with the heels of his hands. The bed's sheets and pillows and powder-blue coverlet were all in a pile on the carpet next to the bed. Then my father handed me his tumbler of tomato juice to hold for him and got all the way on top of the bed and knelt on it, pressing down vigorously on the mattress with his hands, putting all his weight into it. He bore down hard on one area of the mattress, then let up and pivoted slightly on his knees and bore down with equal vigor on a different area of the mattress. He did this all over the bed, sometimes actually walking around on the mattress on his knees to get at different areas of the mattress, then bearing down on them. I remember thinking the bearing-down action looked very much like emergency compression of a heart patient's chest. I remember my father's tomato juice had grains of pepperish material floating on the surface. My mother was standing at the bedroom window, smoking a long cigarette and looking at the lawn, which I had watered before I ate lunch. The uncovered window faced south. The room blazed with sunlight.

'Eureka,' my father said, pressing down several times on one particular spot.

I asked whether I could ask what was going on.

'Goddamn bed squeaks,' he said. He stayed on his knees over the one particular spot, bearing down on it repeatedly. There was now a squeaking sound from the mattress when he bore down on the spot. My father looked up and over at my mother next to the bedroom window. 'Do you or do you not hear that?' he said, bearing down and letting up. My mother tapped her long cigarette into a shallow ashtray she held in her other hand. She watched my father press down on the squeaking spot.

Sweat was running in dark orange lines down my father's face from under his rigid white professional wig. My father served for two years as the Man from Glad, representing what was then the Glad Flaccid Plastic Receptacle Co. of Zanesville, Ohio, via a California-based advertising agency. The tunic, tight trousers, and boots the agency made him wear were also white.

My father pivoted on his knees and swung his body around and got off the mattress and put his hand at the small of his back and straightened up, continuing to look at the mattress.

'This miserable cock-sucking bed your mother felt she needed to hang on to and bring with us out here for quote sentimental value has started squeaking,' my father said. His saying 'your mother' indicated that he was addressing himself to me. He held his hand out for his tumbler of tomato juice without having to look at me. He stared darkly down at the bed. 'It's driving us fucking nuts.'

My mother balanced her cigarette in her shallow ashtray and laid the ashtray on the windowsill and bent over from the foot of the bed and bore down on the spot my father had isolated, and it squeaked again.

'And at night this one spot here we've isolated and identified seems to spread and metastisate until the whole Goddamn bed's replete with squeaks.' He drank some of his tomato juice. 'Areas that gibber and squeak,' my father said, 'until we both feel as if we're being eaten by rats.' He felt along the line of his jaw. 'Boiling hordes of gibbering squeaking ravenous rapacious rats,' he said, almost trembling with irritation.

I looked down at the mattress, at my mother's hands, which tended to flake in dry climates. She carried a small bottle of moisturizing lotion at all times.

My father said, 'And I have personally had it with the aggravation.' He blotted his forehead on his white sleeve.

I reminded my father that he'd mentioned needing my help with something. At that age I was already taller than both my parents. My mother was taller than my father, even in his boots, but much of her height was in her legs. My father's body was denser and more substantial.

My mother came around to my father's side of the bed and picked the bedding up off the floor. She started folding the sheets very precisely, using both arms and her chin. She stacked the folded bedding neatly on top of her dresser, which I remember was white lacquer.

My father looked at me. 'What we need to do here, Jim, is take the mattress and box spring off the bed frame under here,' my father said, 'and expose the frame.' He took time out to explain that the bed's bottom mattress was hard-framed and known uniformly as a box spring. I was looking at my sneakers and making my feet alternately pigeon-toed and then penguin-toed on the bedroom's blue carpet. My father drank some of his tomato juice and looked down at the edge of the bed's metal frame and felt along the outline of his jaw, where his commercial studio makeup ended abruptly at the turtleneck collar of his white commercial tunic.

'The frame on this bed is old,' he told me. 'It's probably older than you are. Right now I'm thinking the thing's bolts have maybe started coming loose, and that's what's gibbering and squeaking at night.' He finished his tomato juice and held the glass out for me to take and put somewhere. 'So we want to move all this top crap out of the way, entirely'—he gestured with one arm—'entirely out of the way, get it out of the room, and expose the frame, and see if we don't maybe just need to tighten up the bolts.'

I wasn't sure where to put my father's empty glass, which had juice residue and grains of pepper along the inside's sides. I poked at the mattress and box spring a little bit with my foot. 'Are you sure it isn't just the mattress?' I said. The bed's frame's bolts struck me as a rather exotic first-order explanation for the squeaking.

My father gestured broadly. 'Synchronicity surrounds me. Concord,' he said. 'Because that's what your mother thinks it is, also.' My mother was using both hands to take the blue pillowcases off all five of their pillows, again using her chin as a clamp. The pillows were all the overplump polyester fiberfill kind, because of my father's allergies.

'Great minds think alike,' my father said.

Neither of my parents had any interest in hard science, though a great uncle had accidentally electrocuted himself with a field series generator he was seeking to patent.

My mother stacked the pillows on top of the neatly folded bedding on her dresser. She had to get up on her tiptoes to put the folded pillowcases on top of the pillows. I had started to move to help her, but I couldn't decide where to put the empty tomato juice glass.

'But you just want to hope it isn't the mattress,' my father said. 'Or the box spring.'

My mother sat down on the foot of the bed and got out another long cigarette and lit it. She carried a little leatherette snap-case for both her cigarettes and her lighter.

My father said, 'Because a new frame, even if we can't get the bolts squared away on this one and I have to go get a new one. A new frame. It wouldn't be too bad, see. Even top-shelf bed frames aren't that expensive. But new mattresses are outrageously expensive.' He looked at my mother. 'And I mean fucking *outrageous*.' He looked down at the back of my mother's head. 'And we bought a new box spring for this sad excuse for a bed not five years ago.' He was looking down at the back of my mother's head as if he wanted to confirm that she was listening. My mother had crossed her legs and was looking with a certain concentration either at or out the master bedroom window. Our home's whole subdivision was spread along a severe hillside, which meant that the view from my parents' bedroom on the first floor was of just sky and sun and a foreshortened declivity of lawn. The lawn sloped at an average angle of 55° and had to be mowed horizontally. None of the subdivision's lawns had trees yet. 'Of course that was during a seldom-discussed point in time when your mother had to assume the burden of assuming responsibility for finances in the household,' my father said. He was now perspiring very heavily, but still had his white professional toupee on, and still looked at my mother.

My father acted, throughout our time in California, as both symbol and spokesman for the Glad F.P.R. Co.'s Individual Sandwich Bag Division. He was the first of two actors to portray the Man from Glad. He was inserted several times a month in a mock-up of a car interior, where he would be filmed in a tight trans-windshield shot receiving an emergency radio summons to some household that was having a portable-food-storage problem. He was then inserted opposite an actress in a generic kitchen-interior set, where he would explain how a particular species of Glad Sandwich Bag was precisely what the doctor ordered for the particular portable-food-storage problem at issue. In his vaguely medical uniform of all white, he carried an air of authority and great evident conviction, and earned what I always gathered was an impressive salary, for those times, and received, for the first time in his career, fan mail, some of which bordered on the disturbing, and which he sometimes liked to read out loud at night in the living room, loudly and dramatically, sitting up with a nightcap and fan mail long after my mother and I had gone to bed.

I asked whether I could excuse myself for a moment to take my father's empty tomato juice glass out to the kitchen sink. I was worried that the residue along the inside sides of the tumbler would harden into the kind of precipitate that would be hard to wash off.

'For Christ's sake Jim just put the thing down,' my father said.

I put the tumbler down on the bedroom carpet over next to the base of my mother's dresser, pressing down to create a kind of circular receptacle for it in the carpet. My mother stood up and went back over by the bedroom window with her ashtray. We could tell she was getting out of our way.

My father cracked his knuckles and studied the path between the bed and the bedroom door.

I said I understood my part here to be to help my father move the mattress and box spring off the suspect bed frame and well out of the way. My father cracked his knuckles and replied that I was becoming almost frighteningly quick and perceptive. He went around between the foot of the bed and my mother at the window. He said, 'I want to let's just stack it all out in the hall, to get it the hell out of here and give us some room to maneuver.'

'Right,' I said.

My father and I were now on opposite sides of my parents' bed. My father rubbed his hands together and bent and worked his hands between the mattress and box spring and began to lift the mattress up from his side of the bed. When his side of the mattress had risen to the height of his shoulders, he somehow inverted his hands and began pushing his side up rather than lifting it. The top of his wig disappeared behind the rising mattress, and his side rose in an arc to almost the height of the white ceiling, exceeded 90°, toppled over, and began to fall over down toward me. The mattress's overall movement was like the crest of a breaking wave, I remember. I spread my arms and took the impact of the mattress with my chest and face, supporting the angled mattress with my chest, outspread arms, and face. All I could see was an extreme close-up of the woodland floral pattern of the mattress protector.

The mattress, a Simmons Beauty Rest whose tag said that it could not by law be removed, now formed the hypotenuse of a right dihedral triangle whose legs were myself and the bed's box spring. I remember visualizing and considering this triangle. My legs were trembling under the mattress's canted weight. My father exhorted me to hold and support the mattress. The respectively sharp plastic and meaty human smells of the mattress and protector were very distinct because my nose was mashed up against them.

My father came around to my side of the bed, and together we pushed the mattress back up until it stood up at 90° again. We edged carefully apart and each took one end of the upright mattress and began jockeying it off the bed and out the bedroom door into the uncarpeted hallway.

This was a King-Size Simmons Beauty Rest mattress. It was massive but had very little structural integrity. It kept curving and curling and wobbling. My father exhorted both me and the mattress. It was flaccid and floppy as we tried to jockey it. My father had an especially hard time with his half of the mattress's upright weight because of an old competitive-tennis injury.

While we were jockeying it on its side off the bed, part of the mattress on my father's end slipped and flopped over and down onto a pair of steel reading lamps, adjustable cubes of brushed steel attached by toggle bolts to the white wall over the head of the bed. The lamps took a solid hit from the mattress, and one cube was rotated all the way around on its toggle so that its open side and bulb now pointed at the ceiling. The joint and toggle made a painful squeaking sound as the cube was wrenched around upward. This was also when I became aware that even the reading lamps were on in the daylit room, because a faint square of direct lamplight, its four sides rendered slightly concave by the distortion of projection, appeared on the white ceiling above the skewed cube. But the lamps didn't fall off. They remained attached to the wall.

'God damn it to hell,' my father said as he regained control of his end of the mattress.

My father also said, 'Fucking son of a...' when the mattress's thickness made it difficult for him to squeeze through the doorway still holding his end.

In time we were able to get my parents' giant mattress out in the narrow hallway that ran between the master bedroom and the kitchen. I could hear another terrible squeak from the bedroom as my mother tried to realign the reading lamp whose cube had been inverted. Drops of sweat were falling from my father's face onto his side of the mattress, darkening part of the protector's fabric. My father and I tried to lean the mattress at a slight supporting angle against one wall of the hallway, but because the floor of the hallway was uncarpeted and didn't provide sufficient resistance, the mattress wouldn't stay upright. Its bottom edge slid out from the wall all the way across the width of the hallway until it met the baseboard of the opposite wall, and the upright mattress's top edge slid down the wall until the whole mattress sagged at an extremely concave slumped angle, a dry section of the woodland floral mattress protector stretched drum-tight over the slumped crease and the springs possibly damaged by the deforming concavity.

My father looked at the canted concave mattress sagging across the width of the hall and moved one end of it a little with the toe of his boot and looked at me and said, 'Fuck it.'

My bow tie was rumpled and at an angle.

My father had to walk unsteadily across the mattress in his white boots to get back to my side of the mattress and the bedroom behind me. On his way across he stopped and felt speculatively at his jaw, his boots sunk deep in woodland floral cotton. He said 'Fuck it' again, and I remember not being clear about what he was referring to. Then my father turned and started unsteadily back the way he had come across the mattress, one hand against the wall for support. He instructed me to wait right there in the hallway for one moment while he darted into the kitchen at the other end of the hall on a very brief errand. His steadying hand left four faint smeared prints on the wall's white paint.

My parents' bed's box spring, though also King-Size and heavy, had just below its synthetic covering a wooden frame that gave the box spring structural integrity, and it didn't flop or alter its shape, and after another bit of difficulty for my father—who was too thick through the middle, even with the professional girdle beneath his Glad costume—after another bit of difficulty for my father squeezing with his end of the box spring through the bedroom doorway, we were able to get it into the hall and lean it vertically at something just over 70° against the wall, where it stayed upright with no problem.

'That's the way she wants doing, Jim,' my father said, clapping me on the back in exactly the ebullient way that had prompted me to have my mother buy an elastic athletic cranial strap for my glasses. I had told my mother I needed the strap for tennis purposes, and she had not asked any questions.

My father's hand was still on my back as we returned to the master bedroom. 'Right, then!' my father said. His mood was now elevated. There was a brief second of confusion at the doorway as each of us tried to step back to let the other through first.

There was now nothing but the suspect frame left where the bed had been. There was something exoskeletal and frail-looking about the bed frame, a plain low-ratio rectangle of black steel. At each corner of the rectangle was a caster. The casters' wheels had sunk into the pile carpet under the weight of the bed and my parents and were almost completely submerged in the carpet's fibers. Each of the frame's sides had a narrow steel shelf welded at 90° to its interior's base, so that a single rectangular narrow shelf perpendicular to the frame's rectangle ran all around the frame's interior. This shelf was obviously there to support the bed's occupants and King-Size box spring and mattress.

My father seemed frozen in place. I cannot remember what my mother was doing. There seemed to be a long silent interval of my father looking closely at the exposed frame. The interval had the silence and stillness of dusty rooms immersed in sunlight. I briefly imagined every piece of furniture in the bedroom covered with sheets and the room unoccupied for years as the sun rose and crossed and fell outside the window, the room's daylight becoming staler and staler. I could hear two power lawnmowers of slightly different pitch from somewhere down our subdivision's street. The direct light through the master bedroom's window swam with rotating columns of raised dust. I remember it seemed the ideal moment for a sneeze.

Dust lay thick on the frame and even hung from the frame's interior support-shelf in little gray beards. It was impossible to see any bolts anywhere on the frame.

My father blotted sweat and wet makeup from his forehead with the back of his sleeve, which was now dark orange with makeup. 'Jesus will you look at that mess,' he said. He looked at my mother. 'Jesus.'

The carpeting in my parents' bedroom was deep-pile and a darker blue than the pale blue of the rest of the bedroom's color scheme. I remember the carpet as more a royal blue, with a saturation level somewhere between moderate and strong. The rectangular expanse of royal blue carpet that had been hidden under the bed was itself carpeted with a thick layer of clotted dust. The rectangle of dust was gray-white and thick and unevenly layered, and the only evidence of the room's carpet below was a faint sick bluish cast to the dust-layer. It looked as if dust had not drifted under the bed and settled on the carpet inside the frame but rather had somehow taken root and grown on it, upon it, the way a mold will take root and gradually cover an expanse of spoiled food. The layer of dust itself looked a little like spoiled food, bad cottage cheese. It was nauseous. Some of the dust-layer's uneven topography was caused by certain lost- and litter-type objects that had found their way under the bed—a flyswatter, a roughly *Variety*-sized magazine, some bottletops, three wadded Kleenex, and what was probably a sock—and gotten covered and textured in dust.

There was also a faint odor, sour and fungal, like the smell of an over-used bathmat.

'Jesus, there's even a smell,' my father said. He made a show of inhaling through his nose and screwing up his face. 'There's even a fucking *smell*.' He blotted his forehead and felt his jaw and looked hard at my mother. His mood was no longer elevated. My father's mood surrounded him like a field and affected any room he occupied, like an odor or a certain cast to the light.

'When was the last time this got cleaned under here?' my father asked my mother.

My mother didn't say anything. She looked at my father as he moved the steel frame around a little with his boot, which raised even more dust into the window's sunlight. The bed frame seemed very lightweight, moving back and forth noiselessly on its casters' submerged wheels. My father often moved lightweight objects absently around with his foot, rather the way other men doodle or examine their cuticles. Rugs, magazines, telephone and electrical cords, his own removed shoe. It was one of my father's ways of musing or gathering his thoughts or trying to control his mood.

'Under what presidential administration was this room last deep-cleaned, I'm standing here prompted to fucking muse out loud,' my father said.

I looked at my mother to see whether she was going to say anything in reply.

I said to my father, 'You know, since we're discussing squeaking beds, my bed squeaks, too.'

My father was trying to squat down to see whether he could locate any bolts on the frame, saying something to himself under his breath. He put his hands on the frame for balance and almost fell forward when the frame rolled under his weight.

'But I don't think I even really noticed it until we began to discuss it,' I said. I looked at my mother. 'I don't think it bothers me,' I said. 'Actually, I think I kind of like it. I think I've gradually gotten so used to it that it's become almost comforting. At this juncture,' I said.

My mother looked at me.

'I'm not complaining about it,' I said. 'The discussion just made me think of it.'

'Oh, we hear your bed, don't you worry,' my father said. He was still trying to squat, which drew his corset and the hem of his tunic up and allowed the top of his bottom's crack to appear above the waist of his white pants. He shifted slightly to point up at the master bedroom's ceiling. 'You so much as turn over in bed up there? We hear it down here.' He took one steel side of the rectangle and shook the frame vigorously, sending up a shroud of dust. The bed frame seemed to weigh next to nothing under his hands. My mother made a mustache of her finger to hold back a sneeze.

He shook the frame again. 'But it doesn't aggravate us the way this rodential son of a whore right here does.'

I remarked that I didn't think I'd ever once heard their bed squeak before, from upstairs. My father twisted his head around to try to look up at me as I stood there behind him. But I said I'd definitely heard and could confirm the presence of a squeak when he'd pressed on the mattress, and could verify that the squeak was no one's imagination.

My father held a hand up to signal me to please stop talking. He remained in a squat, rocking slightly on the balls of his feet, using the rolling frame to keep his balance. The flesh of the top of his bottom and crack-area protruded over the waist of his pants. There were also deep red folds in the back of his neck, below the blunt cut of the wig, because he was looking up and over at my mother, who was resting her tailbone on the sill of the window, still holding her shallow ashtray.

'Maybe you'd like to go get the vacuum,' he said. My mother put the ashtray down on the sill and exited the master bedroom, passing between me and the dresser piled with bedding. 'If you can... if you can remember where it is!' my father called after her.

I could hear my mother trying to get past the King-Size mattress sagging diagonally across the hall.

My father was rocking more violently on the balls of his feet, and now the rocking had the sort of rolling, side-to-side quality of a ship in high seas. He came very close to losing his balance as he leaned to his right to get a handkerchief from his hip pocket and began using it to reach out and flick dust off something at one corner of the bed frame. After a moment he pointed down next to a caster.

'Bolt,' he said, pointing at the side of a caster. 'Right there's a bolt.' I leaned in over him. Drops of my father's perspiration made small dark coins in the dust of the frame. There was nothing but smooth lightweight black steel surface where he was pointing, but just to the left of where he was pointing I could see what might have been a bolt, a little stalactite of clotted dust hanging from some slight protrusion. My father's hands were broad and his fingers blunt. Another possible bolt lay several inches to the right of where he pointed. His finger trembled badly, and I believe the trembling might have been from the muscular strain on his bad knees, trying to hold so much new weight in a squat for an extended period. I heard the telephone ring twice. There had been an extended silence, with my father pointing at neither protrusion and me trying to lean in over him.

Then, still squatting on the balls of his feet, my father placed both hands on the side of the frame and leaned out over the side into the rectangle of dust inside the frame and had what at first sounded like a bad coughing fit. His hunched back and rising bottom kept me from watching him. I remember deciding that the reason the frame was not rolling under his hands' pressure was that my father had so much of his weight on it, and that maybe my father's nervous system's response to heavy dust was a cough-signal instead of a sneeze-signal. It was the wet sound of material hitting the dust inside the rectangle, plus the rising odor, that signified to me that, rather than coughing, my father had been taken ill. The spasms involved made his back rise and fall and his bottom tremble under his white commercial slacks. It was not too uncommon for my father to be taken ill shortly after coming home from work to relax, but now he seemed to have been taken really ill. To give him some privacy, I went around the frame to the side of the frame closest to the window where there was direct light and less odor and examined another of the frame's casters. My father was whispering to himself in brief expletive phrases between the spasms of his illness. I squatted easily and rubbed dust from a small area of the frame and wiped the dust on the carpet by my feet. There was a small carriage-head bolt on either side of the plating that attached the caster to the bed frame. I knelt and felt one of the bolts. Its round smooth head made it impossible either to tighten or loosen. Putting my cheek to the carpet and examining the bottom of the little horizontal shelf welded to the frame's side, I observed that the bolt seemed threaded tightly and completely through its hole, and I decided it was doubtful that any of the casters' platings' bolts were producing the sounds that reminded my father of rodents.

Just at this time, I remember, there was a loud cracking sound and my area of the frame jumped violently as my father's illness caused him to faint and he lost his balance and pitched forward and lay prone and asleep over his side of the bed frame, which as I rolled away from the frame and rose to my knees I saw was either broken or very badly bent. My father lay face-down in the mixture of the rectangle's thick dust and the material he'd brought up from his upset stomach. The dust his collapse raised was very thick, and as the new dust rose and spread it attenuated the master bedroom's daylight as decisively as if a cloud had moved over the sun in the window. My father's professional wig had detached and lay scalp-up in the mixture of dust and stomach material. The stomach material appeared to be mostly gastric blood until I recalled the tomato juice my father had been drinking. He lay face-down, with his bottom high in the air, over the side of the bed frame, which his weight had broken in half. This was how I accounted for the loud cracking sound.

I stood out of the way of the dust and the window's dusty light, feeling along the line of my jaw and examining my prone father from a distance. I remember that his breathing was regular and wet, and that the dust mixture bubbled somewhat. It was then that it occurred to me that when I'd been supporting the bed's raised mattress with my chest and face preparatory to its removal from the room, the dihedral triangle I'd imagined the mattress forming with the box spring and my body had not in fact even been a closed figure: the box spring and the floor I had stood on did not constitute a continuous plane.

Then I could hear my mother trying to get the heavy canister vacuum cleaner past the angled Simmons Beauty Rest in the hall, and I went to help her. My father's legs were stretched out across the clean blue carpet between his side of the frame and my mother's white dresser. His feet's boots were at a pigeon-toed angle, and his bottom's crack all the way down to the anus itself was now visible because the force of his fall had pulled his white slacks down even farther. I stepped carefully between his legs.

'Excuse me,' I said.

I was able to help my mother by telling her to detach the vacuum cleaner's attachments and hand them one at a time to me over the width of the slumped mattress, where I held them. The vacuum cleaner was manufactured by Regina, and its canister, which contained the engine, bag, and evacuating fan, was very heavy. I reassembled the vacuum and held it while my mother made her way back across the mattress, then handed the vacuum cleaner back to her, flattening myself against the wall to let her pass by on her way into the master bedroom.

'Thanks,' my mother said as she passed.

I stood there by the slumped mattress for several moments of a silence so complete that I could hear the street's lawnmowers all the way out in the hall, then heard the sound of my mother pulling out the vacuum cleaner's retractable cord and plugging it into the same bedside outlet the steel reading lamps were attached to.

I made my way over the angled mattress and quickly down the hall, made a sharp right at the entrance to the kitchen, crossed the foyer to the staircase, and ran up to my room, taking several stairs at a time, hurrying to get some distance between myself and the vacuum cleaner, because the sound of vacuuming has always frightened me in the same irrational way it seemed a bed's squeak frightened my father.

I ran upstairs and pivoted left at the upstairs landing and went into my room. In my room was my bed. It was narrow, a twin bed, with a headboard of wood and frame and slats of wood. I didn't know where it had come from, originally. The frame held the narrow box spring and mattress much higher off the floor than my parents' bed. It was an old-fashioned bed, so high off the floor that you had to put one knee up on the mattress and clamber up into it, or else jump.

That is what I did. For the first time since I had become taller than my parents, I took several running strides in from the doorway, past my shelves' collection of prisms and lenses and tennis trophies and my scale-model magneto, past my bookcase, the wall's still-posters from Powell's *Peeping Tom* and the closet door and my bedside's high-intensity standing lamp, and jumped, doing a full swan dive up onto my bed. I landed with my weight on my chest with my arms and legs out from my body on the indigo comforter on my bed, squashing my tie and bending my glasses' temples slightly. I was trying to make my bed produce a loud squeak, which in the case of my bed I knew was caused by any lateral friction between the wooden slats and the frame's interior's shelf-like slat-support.

But in the course of the leap and the dive, my overlong arm hit the heavy iron pole of the high-intensity standing lamp that stood next to the bed. The lamp teetered violently and began to fall over sideways, away from the bed. It fell with a kind of majestic slowness, resembling a felled tree. As the lamp fell, its heavy iron pole struck the brass knob on the door to my closet, shearing the knob off completely. The round knob and half its interior hex bolt fell off and hit my room's wooden floor with a loud noise and began then to roll around in a remarkable way, the sheared end of the hex bolt stationary and the round knob, rolling on its circumference, circling it in a spherical orbit, describing two perfectly circular motions on two distinct axes, a non-Euclidian figure on a planar surface, i.e., a cycloid on a sphere:

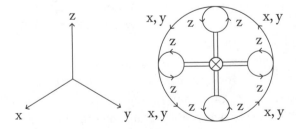

The closest conventional analogue I could derive for this figure was a cycloid, L'Hôpital's solution to Bernoulli's famous Brachistochrone Problem, the curve traced by a fixed point on the circumference of a circle rolling along a continuous plane. But since here, on the bedroom's floor, a circle was rolling around what was itself the circumference of a circle, the cycloid's standard parametric equations were no longer apposite, those equations' trigonometric expressions here becoming themselves first-order differential equations.

Because of the lack of resistance or friction against the bare floor, the knob rolled this way for a long time as I watched over the edge of the comforter and mattress, holding my glasses in place, completely distracted from the minor-D shriek of the vacuum below. It occurred to me that the movement of the amputated knob perfectly schematized what it would look like for someone to try to turn somersaults with one hand nailed to the floor. This was how I first became interested in the possibilities of annulation.

—pages 491–503

○

IT IS STARTING to get quietly around Ennet House that Randy Lenz has found his own dark way to deal with the well-known Rage and Powerlessness issues that beset the drug addict in his first few months of abstinence.

The nightly AA or NA meetings get out at 2130h. or 2200h., and curfew isn't until 2330, and every Ennet resident mostly carpools back to the House with whatever residents have cars, or some of them go out in cars for massive doses of ice cream and coffee.

Lenz is one of the ones with a car, a heavily modified old Duster, white with what look like 12-gauge blasts of rust over the wheelwells, with oversized rear tires and an engine so bored-out for heavy-breathing speed it's a small miracle he still has a license.

Lenz sets loafer one outside Ennet House only after sunset, and then only in his white toupee and mustache and billowing tall-collared topcoat, and goes only to the required nightly meetings; and the thing is that he'll never drive his own car to the meetings. He always thumbs along with somebody else and adds to the crowd in their car. And then he always has to sit in the northernmost seat in the car, for some reason, using a compass and napkin to plot out what the night's major direction of travel'll be and then figuring out what seat he'll have to be in to stay maximally north. Both Gately and Johnette Foltz have had to make a nightly routine of telling the other residents that Lenz is teaching them valuable patience and tolerance.

But then after the meeting lets out, Lenz never thumbs back with anybody. He always walks back to the House after meetings. He says it's that he needs the air, what with being shut up in the crowded House all day and avoiding doors and windows, hiding from both sides of the Justice System.

And then one Wednesday after the Brookline Young People's AA up

Beacon by Chestnut Hill it takes him right up to 2329 to get home, almost two hours, even though it's like a half-hour walk and even Burt Smith did it in September in under an hour; and Lenz gets back just at curfew and without saying a word to anybody books right up to his and Glynn's and Day's room, Polo topcoat flapping and powdered wig shedding powder, and sweating, and making an unacceptable classy-shoed racket running up the men's side's carpetless stairs, which Gately didn't have time to go up and address because of having to deal with Bruce Green and Amy J. separately both missing curfew.

Lenz abroad in the urban night, solo, on almost a nightly basis, sometimes carrying a book.

Residents who seem to make it a point to go off alone a lot are red-flagged at Thursday's All-Staff Meeting in Pat's office as clear relapse-risks. But they've pulled spot-urines on Lenz five times, and the three times the lab didn't fuck up the E.M.I.T. test Lenz's urine's come back clean. Gately's basically decided to just let Lenz be. Some newcomers' Higher Power is like Nature, the sky, the stars, the cold-penny tang of the autumn air, who knows.

So Lenz abroad in the night, unaccompanied and disguised, apparently strolling. He's mastered the streets' cockeyed grid around Enfield-Brighton-Allston. South Cambridge and East Newton and North Brookline and the hideous Spur. He takes side-streets home from meetings, mostly. Low-rent dumpster-strewn residential streets and Projects' driveways that become alleys, gritty passages behind stores and dumpsters and warehouses and loading docks and Empire Waste Displacement's mongo hangars, etc. His loafers have a wicked shine and make an elegant dancerly click as he walks along with his hands in his pockets and open coat flared wide, scanning. He scans for several nights before he even becomes aware of why or what he might be scanning for.[224] He moves nightly through urban-animal territory. Liberated housecats and hard-core strays ooze in and out of shadows, rustle in dumpsters, fuck and fight with hellish noises all around him as he walks, senses very sharp in the downscale night. You got your rats, your mice, your stray dogs with tongues hanging and countable ribs. Maybe the odd feral hamster and/or raccoon. Everything slinky and furtive after sunset. Also non-stray dogs that clank their chains or bay or lunge, when he goes by yards with dogs. He prefers to move north but will move east or west on the streets' good sides. His shoes' fine click precedes him by several hundred meters on cement of varying texture.

Sometimes near drainage pipes he sees serious rats, or sometimes near cat-free dumpsters. The first conscious thing he did was a rat that this one time he came on some rats in a wide W-E alley by the loading dock out behind the Svelte Nail Co. just east of Watertown on N. Harvard St. What night was that. It'd been coming back from East Watertown, which meant More Will Be Revealed NA with Glynn and Diehl instead of St. E.'s Better Late Than Never AA with the rest of the House's herd, so a Monday. So on a Monday he'd been strolling through this one alley, his steps echoing trebled back off the cement sides of the docks and the north left wall he hugged, scanning without knowing what he was scanning for. Up ahead there was the Stegosaurus-shape of a Svelte Co. dumpster as versus your lower slimmer E.W.D.-type dumpster. There were dry skulky sounds issuing from the dumpster's shadow. He hadn't consciously picked anything up. The alley's surface was coming apart and Lenz barely broke his dancerly stride picking a kilo-sized chunk of tar-shot concrete. It was rats. Two big rats were going at a half-eaten wiener in a mustardy paper tray from a Lunchwagon in a recess between the north wall and the dumpster's barge-hitch. Their hideous pink tails were poking out into the alley's dim light. They didn't move as Randy Lenz came up behind them on the toes of his loafers. Their tails were meaty and bald and like twitched back and forth, twitching in and out of the dim yellow light. The big flat-top chunk came down on most of one rat and a bit of the other rat. There'd been godawful twittering squeaks, but the major hit on the one rat also made a very solid and significant noise, some aural combination of a tomato thrown at a wall and a pocketwatch getting clocked with a hammer. Material came out of the rat's anus. The rat lay on its side in a very bad medical way, its tail twitching and anus material and there were little beads of blood on its whiskers that looked black, the beads, in the sodium security-lights along the Svelte Nail Co. roof. Its side heaved; its back legs were moving like it was running, but this rat wasn't going anywhere. The other rat had vanished under the dumpster, dragging its rear region. There were more chunks of dismantled street lying all over. When Lenz brought another down on the head of the rat he consciously discovered what he liked to say at the moment of issue-resolution was: 'There.'

Demapping rats became Lenz's way of resolving internal-type issues for the first couple weeks of it, walking home in the verminal dark.

Don Gately, House chef and shopper, buys these huge econo-size boxes of Hefty[225] bags that get stored under the kitchen sink for whoever's got Trash for their weekly chore. Ennet House generates serious waste.

So after vermin started to get a little ho-hum and insignificant, Lenz starts cabbaging a Hefty bag out from under the sink and taking it with him to meetings and walking back home with it. He keeps a trashbag neatly folded in an inside pocket of his topcoat, a billowing top-collared Lauren-Polo model he loves and uses a daily lint-roller on. He also takes along a little of the House's Food-Bank tunafish in a Zip-loc baggie in another pocket, which your average drug addict has expertise in rolling baggies into a cylinder so they're secure and odor-free.

The Ennet House residents call Hefty bags 'Irish Luggage'—even McDade—it's a street-term.

Randy Lenz found that if he could get an urban cat up close enough with some outstretched tuna he could pop the Hefty bag over it and scoop up from the bottom so the cat was in the air in the bottom of the bag, and then he could tie the bag shut with the complimentary wire twist-tie that comes with each bag. He could put the closed bag down next to the vicinity's northernmost wall or fence or dumpster and light a gasper and hunker down up next to the wall to watch the wide variety of changing shapes the bag would assume as the agitated cat got lower on air. The shapes got more and more violent and twisted and mid-air with the passage of a minute. After it stopped assuming shapes Lenz would dab his butt with a spitty finger to save the rest for later and get up and untie the twist-tie and look inside the bag and go: 'There.' The 'There' turned out to be crucial for the sense of brisance and closure and resolving issues of impotent rage and powerless fear that like accrued in Lenz all day being trapped in the northeastern portions of a squalid halfway house all day fearing for his life, Lenz felt.

There evolved for Lenz a certain sportsman's hierarchy of types of cats and neighborhoods of types of your abroad cats; and he becomes a connoisseur of cats the same way a deep-sea sportsman knows the fish-species that fight most fiercely and excitatingly for their marine lives. The best and most fiercely alive cats could usually claw their way out of a Hefty bag, though, which created this conundrum where the ones most worth watching assuming bagged shapes were the ones Lenz risked maybe not getting his issues resolved on. Watching a spike-furred hissing cat run twisting away still half wrapped in a plastic bag made Lenz admire the cat's fighting spirit but still feel unresolved.

So the next stage is Lenz gives Ms. Charlotte Treat or Ms. Hester Thrale some of his own $ when they go down to the Palace Spa or Father/Son to buy smokes or LifeSavers and has them start to get him special Hefty SteelSak[226] trashbags, fiber-reinforced for your especially sharp or uncooperative waste needs, described by Ken E. as 'Irish Guccis,' extra resilient and a businesslike gunmetal-gray in tone. Lenz has such a panoply of strange compulsive habits that a request for SteelSaks barely raises a brow on anybody.

And then he doubles them, the special reinforced bags, and employs industrial-growth pipe-cleaners as twist-ties, and then now the grittiest most salutary cats make the doubled bags assume all manners of wickedly abstract twisting shapes, even sometimes moving the closed bags a couple dozen m. down the alley in a haphazard hopping-like fashion, until finally the cat runs out of gas and resolves itself and Lenz's issues into one nightly shape.

Lenz's interval of choice for this is the interval 2216h. to 2226h. He doesn't consciously know why this interval. Anchovies turn out to be even more effective than tuna. A Program of Attraction, he recalls coolly, strolling along. His northern routes back to the House are restricted by the priority to keep Brighton Best Savings Bank's rooftop digital Time and Temperature display in view as much as possible. B.B.S.B. displays both EST and Greenwich Mean, which Lenz approves of. The liquid-crystal data sort of melts upward into view on the screen and then disappears from the bottom up and is replaced by new data. Mr. Doony R. Glynn said at the House's Community Meeting Monday once that one time in B.S. 1989 A.D. after he'd done a reckless amount of a hallucinogen he'd refer to only as 'The Madame' he'd gone around for several subsequent weeks under a Boston sky that instead of a kindly curved blue dome with your clouds and your stars and sun was a flat square coldly Euclidian grid with black axes and a thread-fine reseau of lines creating grid-type coordinates, the whole grid the same color as a D.E.C. HD viewer-screen when the viewer's off, that sort of dead deepwater gray-green, with the DOW Ticker running up one side of the grid and the NIKEI Index running down the other, and the Time and Celsius Temp to like serious decimal points flashing along the bottom axis of the sky's screen, and whenever he'd go to a real clock or get a *Herald* and check the like DOW the skygrid would turn out to have been totally accurate; and that several unbroken weeks of this sky overhead had sent Glynn off first to his mother's Stoneham apartment's fold-out couch and then into Waltham's Metropolitan State Hospital for a month of Haldol[227] and tapioca, to get out from under the empty-grid accurate sky, and says it makes his ass wet to this day to even think about the grid-interval; but Lenz had thought it sounded wicked nice, the sky as digital timepiece. And also between 2216 and 2226 the ATHSCME giant fans off up at the Sunstrand Plaza within earshot were typically shut off for daily de-linting, and it was quiet except for the big Ssshhh of a whole urban city's vehicular traffic, and maybe the odd E.W.D. airborne deliverer catapulted up off Concavityward, its little string of lights arcing northeast; and of course also sirens, both the Eurotrochaic sirens of ambulances and the regular U.S.-sounding sirens of the city's very Finest, Protecting and Serving, keeping the citizenry at bay; and the winsome thing about sirens in the urban night is that unless they're right up close where the lights bathe you in red-blue-red they always sound like they're terribly achingly far away, and receding, calling to you across an expanding gap. Either that or they're on your ass. No middle distance with sirens, Lenz reflects, walking along and scanning.

Glynn hadn't come right out and said *Euclidian*, but Lenz had gotten the picture all right. Glynn had thin hair and an invariant three-day growth of gray stubble and diverticulitis that made him stoop somewhat over, and remaining physique-type issues from a load of bricks falling on his head from a Workers Comp scam gone rye that included crossed eyes that Lenz overheard the veiled girl Joe L. tell Clenette Henderson and Didi Neaves the man was so cross-eyed he could stand in the middle of the week and see both Sundays.

Lenz has gotten high on organic cocaine two or three, maybe half a dozen times tops, secretly, since he came into Ennet House in the summer, just enough times to keep him from going totally out of his fucking mind, utilizing lines from the private emergency stash he kept in a kind of rectangular bunker razor-bladed out of three hundred or so pages of Bill James's gargantuan Large-Print *Principles of Psychology and The Gifford Lectures on Natural Religion*. Such totally occasional Substance-ingestions in a run-down sloppy-clocked House where he's cooped up and under terrible stress all day every day, hiding from threats from two different legal directions, with, upstairs at all times, calling to him, a 20-gram stash from the underreported South End two-way attempted scam whose very bad luck had forced him into hiding in squalor and rooming with the likes of fucking Geoffrey D. — cocaine-ingestion this occasional and last-resort is such a marked reduction of Use & Abuse for Lenz that it's a bonerfied miracle and clearly constitutes as much miraculous sobriety as total abstinence would be for another person without Lenz's unique sensitivities and psychological makeup and fucking intolerable daily stresses and difficulty unwinding, and he accepts his monthly chips with a clear conscience and a head unmuddled by doubting: he knows he's sober. He's smart about it: he's never ingested cocaine on his solo walks home from meetings, which is where the Staff'd expect him to ingest if he was going to ingest. And never in Ennet House itself, and only once in the forbidden #7 across the roadlet. And anybody with half a clue can beat an E.M.I.T. urine-screen: a cup of lemon juice or vinegar down the hatch'll turn the lab's reading into gibberish; a trace of powdered bleach on the fingertips and let the stream play warmly over the fingertips on its way into the cup while you banter with Don G. A Texas catheter's a pain to get piss for and put on, plus the obscene size of the thing's receptacle for his Unit gives Lenz inadequacy-issues, and he's only used it twice, both times when Johnette F. took the urine and he could embarrass her into turning away. Lenz owns a Texas Cathy from his last halfway house in Quincy, in what Lenz recalls as the Year of the Maytag Quietmaster.

And then it turned out, when a cat aggrieved Lenz by scratching his wrist in a particularly hostile fashion on the way into the receptacle, that doubled Hefty SteelSaks were such quality-reinforced products they could hold something razor-clawed and frantically in-motion and still survive a direct swung hit against a NO PARKING sign or a telephone pole without splitting open, even when what was inside split nicely open; and so that technique got substituted around United Nations Day, because even though it was too quick and less meditative it allowed Randy Lenz to take a more active role in the process, and the feeling of (temporary, nightly) issues-resolution was more definitive when Lenz could swing a twisting ten-kilo burden hard against a pole and go: 'There,' and hear a sound. On banner nights the doubled bag would continue for a brief period of time to undergo a subtle flux of smaller, more subtle and connoisseur-oriented shapes, even after the melony sound of hard impact, along with further smaller sounds.

Then it was discovered that resolving them directly inside the yards and porches of the people that owned them provided more adrenal excitation and thus more sense of what Bill James one time called a *Catharsis* of resolving, which Lenz felt he could agree. A small can of oil in its own little baggie, for squeaky gates. But because SteelSak trashbags—and then also tunafish mixed with anchovies and Raid ant poison from behind the Ennet residents' fridge—caused too much resultant noise to allow for lighting a gasper and hunkering down to meditatively watch, Lenz developed the habit of setting the resolution in motion and then booking on out of the yard into the urban night, his Polo topcoat billowing, hurdling fences and running over the hoods of cars and etc. For a period during the two-week interval of give-them-poison-tuna-and-run Lenz had brief recourse to a small Caldor-brand squeeze-bottle of kerosene, plus of course his lighter; but a Wednesday night on which the alight cat ran (as alight cats will, like hell) but ran after *Lenz,* seemingly, leaping the same fences Lenz hurdled and staying on his tail and not only making an unacceptable attention-calling racket but also illuminating Lenz to the scopophobic view of passing homes until it finally decided to drop to the ground and expire and smolder thereupon—Lenz considered this his only really close call, and took an enormous and partly non-north route home, with every siren sounding up-close and on his personal ass, and barely got in by 2330h., and ran right up to the 3-Man room. This was the night Lenz had to have another recourse to the hollowed-out cavity in his *Principles of Psychology and The Gifford Lectures on Natural Religion* after just beating curfew home, which who wouldn't need a bit of an unwinder after a stressful close-call-type situation with a flaming cat chasing you and screaming in a way that made porch lights go on all up and down Sumner Blake Rd.; except but instead of an unwinder the couple or few lines of uncut Bing proved to be on this occasion an *un*-unwinder—which happens, sometimes, depending on one's like spiritual condition when ingesting it through a rolled dollar bill off the back of the john in the men's can—and Lenz barely made it through switching his car's parking spot at 2350h. before the verbal torrent started, and after lights-out had only gotten up to age eight in the oral autobiography that followed in the 3-Man when Geoff D. threatened to go get Don G. and have Lenz forcibly stifled, and Lenz was scared to go downstairs to find somebody to listen and so for the rest of the night he had to lie there in the dark, mute, with his mouth twisting and writhing—it always twisted and writhed on the times the Bing proved to be a rev-upper instead of a rough-edge-smoother—and pretending to be asleep, with phosphenes like leaping flaming shapes dancing behind his quivering lids, listening to Day's moist gurgles and Glynn's apnea and thinking that each siren abroad out there in the urban city was meant for him and coming closer, with Day's illuminated watch-face in his fucking tableside drawer instead of out where anybody with some stress and anxiety could check the time from time to time.

So after the incident with the flaming cat from hell and before Halloween Lenz had moved on and up to the Browning X444 Serrated he even had a shoulder-holster for, from his previous life Out There. The Browning X444 has a 25-cm. overall length, with a burl-walnut handle with a brass butt-cap and a point Lenz'd sharpened the clip out of when he got it and a single-edge Bowie-style blade with .1-mm. serrations that Lenz owns a hone for and tests by dry-shaving a little patch of his tan forearm, which he loves.

The Browning X444, combined with blocks of Don Gately's highly portable cornflake-garnish meatloaf, were for canines, which your urban canines tended to be nonferal and could be found within the confinement of their pet-owners' fenced yards on a regularer basis than the urban-cat species, and who are less suspicious of food and, though more of a personal-injury risk to approach, do not scratch the hand that feeds them.

For when the dense square of meatloaf is taken out and unwrapped from the Zip-loc and proffered from the edgelet of yard out past the fence by the sidewalk, the dog at issue invariably stops with the barking and/or lunging and its nose flares and it becomes totally uncynical and friendly and comes to the end of its chain or the fence Lenz stands behind and makes interested noises and if Lenz holds the meat-item just up out of reach the dog if its rope or chain will permit it it'll go up on the hind legs and sort of play the fence with its front paws, jumping eagerly, as Lenz dangles the meat.

Day had had some Recovery-Issue paperback he was reading that Lenz had a look at one P.M. in their room when Day was downstairs with Ewell and Erdedy telling each other their windbagathon stories, lying on Day's mattress with his shoes on and trying to fart into the mattress as much as possible: some line in the book had arrested Lenz's attention: something about the more basically Powerless an individual feels, the more the likelihood for the propensity for violent acting-out—and Lenz found the observation to be sound.

The only serious challenge to using the Browning X444 is that Lenz has to make sure to get around behind the dog before he cuts the dog's throat, because the bleeding is far-reaching in its intensity, and Lenz is now on his second R. Lauren topcoat and third pair of dark wool slacks.

Then once near Halloween in an alley behind Blanchard's Liquors off Allston's Union Square Lenz comes across a street drunk in a chewed-looking old topcoat in the deserted alley taking a public leak against the side of a dumpster, and Lenz envisualizes the old guy both cut and on fire and dancing jaggedly around hitting at himself while Lenz goes 'There,' but that's as close as Lenz comes to that kind of level of resolution; and it's maybe to his credit that he's a little off his psychic feed for a few days after that close call, and inactive with pets circa 2216h.

Lenz has nothing much against his newer fellow resident Bruce Green, and when one Sunday night after the White Flag Green asks can he walk along with Lenz on the walk back after the Our Father Lenz says Whatever and lets Green walk with him, and is inactive during this night's 2216 interval as well. Except after a couple nights of Green strolling home along with him, first from the White Flag and then from St. Columbkill's on Tuesday and a double 1900–2200 shot of St. E.'s Sharing and Caring NA and then BYP on Wed., Green following him around like a terrier from mtg. to mtg. and then home, it begins to like emerge on Lenz that Bruce G. is starting to treat this walking-through-the-urban-P.M.-with-Randy-Lenz thing as like a regular fucking thing, and Lenz starts to jones about it, the unresolved Powerless Rage issues that the thing is now he's gotten so he's used to resolving them on a more or less nightly basis, so that being unable to be freely alone to be active with the Browning X444 or even a SteelSak during the 2216–2226h. interval causes this pressure to build up like almost a Withdrawal-grade pressure. But on the other side of the hand, walking with Green has its positive aspects as well. Like that Green doesn't complain about lengthy detours to keep a mainly north/northeastern orientation to the walks when possible. And Lenz enjoys a sympathetic and listening ear to have around; he has numerous aspects and experiences to mull over and issues to organize and mull, and (like many people hardwired for organic stimulants) talking is sort of Lenz's way of thinking. And but most of the ears of the other residents at Ennet House are not only unsympathetic but are attached to great gaping flapping oral mouths which keep horning into the conversation with the mouths' own opinions and issues and aspects — most of the residents are the worst listeners Lenz has ever seen. Bruce Green, on the hand's positive side, hardly says anything. Bruce Green is quiet the way certain stand-up type guys you want to have there with you beside you if a beef starts going down are quiet, like self-contained. Yet Green is not so quiet and unresponding that it's like with some silent people where you start to wonder if he's listening with a sympathizing ear or if he's really drifting around in his own self-oriented thoughts and not even listening to Lenz, etc., treating Lenz like a radio you can tune in or out. Lenz has a keen antenna for people like this and their stock is low on his personal exchange. Bruce Green inserts low affirmatives and 'No shit's and 'Fucking-A's, etc., at just the right places to communicate his attentions to Lenz. Which Lenz admires.

So it's not like Lenz just wants to blow Green off and tell him to go peddle his papers and let him the fuck alone after Meetings so he can solo. It would have to be handled in a more diplomatic fashion. Plus Lenz finds himself nervous at the prospect of offending Green. It's not like he's scared of Green in terms of physically. And it's not like he's concerned Green would be the Ewell- or Day-type you have to stressfully worry about maybe going and ratting out on Lenz's place of whereabouts to the Finest and everything like that. Green has a strong air of non-rat about him which Lenz admires. So it's not like he's frightened to blow Green off; it's more like very tense and tightly wound.

Plus it agitates Lenz that he has the feeling that it really wouldn't be any big deal to Green that much one way or the other, and that Lenz feels like he's spending all this stress tensely worrying about his side of something that Green would barely think about for more than a couple seconds, and it enrages Lenz that he can know in his head that the tense worry about how to diplomatize Green into leaving him alone is unnecessary and a waste of time and tension and yet still not be able to stop worrying about it, which all only increases the sense of Powerlessness that Lenz is impotent to resolve with his Browning and meatloaf as long as Green continues to walk home with him.

And the schizoid cats with clotted fur that lurk around Ennet House cringing and neurotic and afraid of their own shadow are too risky, for the female residents are always formulating attachments to them. And Pat M.'s Golden Retrievers would be tattlemount to legal suicide. On a Saturday c. 2221h., Lenz found a miniature bird that had fallen out of some nest and was sitting bald and pencil-necked on the lawn of Unit #3 flapping ineffectually, and went in with Green and ducked Green and went back outside to #3's lawn and put the thing in a pocket and went in and put it down the garbage disposal in the kitchen sink of the kitchen, but still felt largely impotent and unresolved.

—pages 538–547

○

As at all D.S.A.S.-certified halfway facilities, Ennet House's resident curfew is 2330h. From 2300 to 2330, the Staffer on night-duty has to do head-counts and sit around like somebody's mom waiting for different residents to come in. There's always ones that always like to cut it close and play with the idea of getting Discharged for something picayune so it won't be their fault. Tonight Clenette H. and the deeply whacked-out Yolanda W. come back in from Footprints[246] around 2315 in purple skirts and purple lipstick and ironed hair, tottering on heels and telling each other what a wicked time they just had. Hester Thrale undulates in in a false fox jacket at 2320 as usual even though she has to be up at like 0430 for the breakfast-shift at the Provident Nursing Home and sometimes eats breakfast with Gately, both of their faces nodding down perilously close to their Frosted Flakes. Chandler Foss and the spectrally thin April Cortelyu come in from someplace with postures and expressions that arouse comments and force Gately to Log a possible issue about an in-House relationship. Gately has to bid goodnight to two craggy-faced brunette ex-residents who've been planted on the couch all night talking cults. Emil Minty and Nell Gunther and sometimes Gavin Diehl (who Gately did three weeks of a municipal bit with, once, at Concord Farm) make a nightly point of going to smoke outside on the front porch and coming in only after Gately says twice he's got to lock the door, just as some limp rebellious gesture. Tonight they're closely followed by a mustacheless Lenz, who sort of oozes through the door just as Gately's going through his keys to get the key to lock it, and kind of brushes by and goes up to the 3-Man without a word, which he's been doing a lot lately, which Gately has to Log, plus the fact that it's now after 2330 and he can't account for either the semi-new girl Amy J. or—more upsetting—Bruce Green. Then Green knocks at the front door at 2336—Gately has to Log the exact time and then it's his call whether to unlock the door. After curfew Staff doesn't have to unlock the door. Many a bad-news resident gets effectively bounced this way. Gately lets him in. Green's never come close to missing curfew before and looks godawful, skin potato-white and eyes vacant. And a big quiet kid is one thing, but Green looks at the floor of Pat's office like it's a loved one while Gately gives him the required ass-chewing; and Green takes the standard dreaded week's Full House Restriction[247] in such a vacantly hangdog way, and is so lamely vague when Gately asks does he want to tell him where he's been at and why he couldn't make 2330 and whether there's anything that's an issue that he might want to share with Staff, so unresponsive that Gately feels like he has no choice but to pull an immediate spot-urine on Green, which Gately hates doing not only because he plays cribbage with Green and feels like he's taken Green under the old Gately wing and is probably the closest thing to a sponsor the kid's got but also because urine samples taken after Unit #2's clinic's closed[248] have to be stored overnight in the little Staff miniature fridgelette in Don Gately's basement room—the only fridge in the House that no resident could conceivably dicky into—and Gately hates to have a warm blue-lidded cup of somebody's goddamn urine in his fridgelette with his pears and Polar seltzer, etc. Green submits to Gately's cross-armed presence in the men's head as Green produces a urine so efficiently and with so little bullshit that Gately is able to take the lidded cup between gloved thumb and finger and get it downstairs and tagged and Logged and down in the fridgelette in time to not be late for getting the residents' cars moved, the night-shift's biggest pain in the ass; but then his final head-count at 2345 reminds Gately that Amy J. isn't back, and she hasn't called, and Pat has told him the decision to Discharge after a missed curfew is his call, and at 2350 Gately makes the decision, and has to get Treat and Belbin to go up into the 5-Woman room and pack the girl's stuff up in the same Irish Luggage she'd brought it in Monday, and Gately has to put the trashbags on the front porch with a quick note explaining the Discharge and wishing the girl good luck, and has to call Pat's answering device down in Milton and leave word of a mandatory Curfew-Discharge at 2350h., so Pat can hear about it first thing in the A.M. and schedule interviews to fill the available bed ASAP, and then with a hissed curse Gately remembers the anti-big-hanging-gut situps he's sworn to himself to do every night before 0000, and it's 2356, and he has time to do only 20 with his huge discolored sneakers wedged under the frame of the office's black vinyl couch before it's unavoidably time to supervise moving the residents' cars around.

Gately's predecessor as male live-in Staff, a designer-narcotics man who's now (via Mass Rehab) learning to repair jet engines at East Coast AeroTech, once described residents' vehicles to Gately as a continuing boil on the ass of night Staff. Ennet House lets any resident with a legally registered vehicle and insurance keep their car at the House, if they want, during residency, to use for work and nightly meetings, etc., and the Enfield Marine Public Health Hospital goes along, except they put authorized parking for all the Units' clients out in the little street right outside the House. And since metro Boston's serious fiscal troubles in the third year of Subsidized Time there's been this hellish municipal deal where only one side of any street is legal for parking, and the legal side switches abruptly at 0000h., and cruisers and municipal tow trucks prowl the streets from 0001h. on, writing $95.00 tickets and/or towing suddenly-illegally-parked vehicles to a region of the South End so blasted and dangerous no cabbie with anything to live for will even go there. So the interval 2355h.–0005h. in Boston is a time of total but not very spiritual community, with guys in skivvies and ladies in mud-masks staggering out yawning into the crowded midnight streets and disabling their alarms and revving and all trying to pull out and do a U and find a parallel-parking place facing the other way. There's nothing very mysterious about the fact that metro Boston's battery- and homicide-rates during this ten-minute interval are the highest per diem, so that ambulances and paddy wagons are especially aprowl at this hour, too, adding to the general clot and snarl.

Since the E.M.P.H.H. Units' catatonics and enfeebled people rarely own registered vehicles, it's generally pretty easy to find places along the little road to switch to, but it's a constant sore point between Pat Montesian and the E.M.P.H.H. Board of Regents that Ennet House residents don't get to park overnight in the big off-street lot by the condemned hospital building—the lot's spaces are reserved for all the different Units' professional staff starting at 0600h., and E.M. Security got sick of staffs' complaints about drug addicts' poorly maintained autos still sitting there taking up their spots in the A.M.—and that Security won't consider changing the little E.M. streetlet's nightly side-switch to 2300h., before Ennet Houses' D.S.A.S.-required curfew; E.M.'s Board claims it's a municipal ordinance that they can't be expected to mess with just to accommodate one tenant, while Pat's memos keep pointing out that the Enfield Marine Hospital complex is state- not city-owned, and that Ennet House residents are the only tenants who face the nightly car-moving problem, since just about everyone else is catatonic or enfeebled. And so on.

But so every P.M. at like 2359 Gately has to lock up the lockers and Pat's cabinets and desk drawers and the door to the front office and put the phone console's answering machine on and personally escort all residents who own cars out post-curfew outside into the little nameless streetlet, and for somebody with Gately's real limited managerial skills the head-aches involved are daunting: he has to herd the vehicular residents together just inside the locked front door; he has to threaten the residents he's herded together into staying together by the door while he clomps upstairs to get the one or two drivers who always forget and fall asleep before 0000—and this straggler-collecting is a particular pain in the ass if the straggler's a female, because he has to unlock and press the Male Coming Up button by the kitchen, and the 'buzzer' sounds more like a klaxon, and wakes the edgiest female residents up with an ugly surge of adrenaline, and Gately as he clomps up the stairs gets roundly bitched out by all the mud-masked heads sticking out into the female hall, and he by regulation can't go into the sleeper's bedroom but has to pound on the door and keep shouting out his gender and get one of the straggler's roommates to wake her up and get her dressed and to the bedroom door; so he has to retrieve the stragglers and chew them out and threaten them with both a Restriction and a possible tow while herding them quick-walking down the stair-case to join the main car-owner herd as quickly as possible before the main herd can like disperse. They'll always disperse if he takes too long getting stragglers; they'll get distracted or hungry or need an ashtray or just get impatient and start looking at the whole car-moving-after-curfew thing as an imposition on their time. Their early-recovery Denial makes it impossi-ble for them to imagine their own car getting towed instead of, say, some-body else's car. It's the same Denial Gately can see at work in the younger B.U. or -C. students when he's driving Pat's Aventura to the Food Bank or Purity Supreme when they'll fucking walk right out in the street against the light in front of the car, whose brakes are fortunately in top shape. Gately's snapped to the fact that people of a certain age and level of like life-experience believe they're immortal: college students and alcoholics/ addicts are the worst: they deep-down believe they're exempt from the laws of physics and statistics that ironly govern everybody else. They'll piss and moan your ear off if somebody else fucks with the rules, but they don't deep down see themselves subject to them, the same rules. And they're constitutionally unable to learn from anybody else's experience: if some jaywalking B.U. student does get splattered on Comm. or some House resident does get his car towed at 0005, your other student's or addict's response to this will be to ponder just what imponderable difference makes it possible for that other guy to get splattered or towed and not him, the ponderer. They never doubt the difference—they just ponder it. It's like a kind of idolatry of uniqueness. It's unvarying and kind of spirit-killing for a Staffer to watch, that the only way your addict ever learns anything is the hard way. It has to happen to *them* to like upset the idolatry. Eugenio M. and Annie Parrot always recommend letting everybody get towed at least once, early on in their residency, to help make believers out of them in terms of laws and rules; but Gately for some reason on his night-shifts can't do it, cannot fucking *stand* to have one of his people get towed as long as there's something he can do to prevent it, and then plus if they do get towed there's the nail-chewing hassle of arranging their transport to the South End's municipal lot the next day, fielding calls from bosses and supplying verification of residents' carlessness in terms of getting to work without letting the boss know that the carless employee is a resident of a halfway house, which is totally sacred private residents' private information to give out or not—Gately breaks a full-body sweat just thinking about the managerial headaches involved in a fucking tow, so he'll spend time herding and regathering and chewing the absentminded asses of residents who Gene M. says have such calloused asses still it's a waste of Gately's time and spirit: you have to let them learn for themselves.[249]

Gately alerts Thrale and Foss and Erdedy and Henderson,[250] and Morris Hanley, and drags the new kid Tingley out of the linen closet, and Nell Gunther—who's fucking sacked out slack-mouthed on the couch, in violation—and lets them all get coats and herds them together by the locked front door. Yolanda W. says she left personal items in Clenette's car and can she come. Lenz owns a car but doesn't answer Gately's yell up the stairs. Gately tells the herd to stay put and that if anybody leaves the herd he's going to take a personal interest in their discomfort. Gately clomps up the stairs and into the 3-Man room, plotting different fun ways to wake Lenz up without bruises that'd show. Lenz is not asleep but is wearing personal-stereo headphones, plus a jock strap, doing handstand-pushups up against the wall by Geoffrey Day's rack, his bottom only inches from Day's pillow and farting in rhythm to the pushups' downstrokes, as Day lies there in pajamas and Lone Ranger sleep mask, hands folded over his heaving chest, lips moving soundlessly. Gately's maybe a little rough about grabbing Lenz's calf and lifting him off his hands and using his other big hand on Lenz's hip to twirl him around upright like a drill-team's rifle, but Lenz's cry is of over-ebullient greeting, not pain, but it sends both Day and Gavin Diehl bolt-upright in their racks, and then they curse as Lenz hits the floor. Lenz starts saying he'd let time completely get away from him and didn't know what time it was. Gately can hear the herd down by the front door at the bottom of the stairs stamping and chuffing and getting ready to maybe disperse.

Up this close, Gately doesn't even need his Staffer's eerie seventh sense to sense that Lenz is clearly wired on either 'drines or Bing. That Lenz has been visited by the Sergeant at Arms. Lenz's right eyeball is wobbling around in its socket and his mouth writhing in that way and he has that Nietzschean supercharged aura of a wired individual, and all the time he's throwing on slacks and topcoat and incognitoizing wig and getting almost pitched headfirst down the stairs by Gately he's telling this insane breathless whopper about his finger once getting cut off and then spontaneously regentrifying itself back on, and his mouth is writhing in that fish-on-a-gaff way distinctive of a sustained L-Dopa surge, and Gately wants to pull an immediate urine, *immediate,* but meanwhile the cars' herd's edges are just starting to widen in that way that precedes distraction and dispersal, and they're angry not at Lenz for straggling but at Gately for even bothering with him, and Lenz pantomimes the akido Serene But Deadly Crane stance at Ken Erdedy, and it's 0004h. and Gately can see tow trucks aprowl way down on Comm. Ave., coming this way, and he jangles his keys and unlocks all three curfew-locks on the front door and gets everybody out in the scrotum-tightening November cold and out down the walk to the line of their cars in the little street and stands there on the porch watching in just orange shirtsleeves, making sure Lenz doesn't bolt before he can pull a spot-urine and extract an admission and Discharge him officially, feeling a twinge of conscience at so looking forward to giving Lenz the administrative shoe, and Lenz jabbers nonstop to whoever's closest all the way to his Duster, and everybody goes to their car, and the backwash around Gately from the open House door is hot and people in the living room provide loud feedback on the draft from the open door, the sky overhead immense and dimensional and the night so clear you can see stars hanging in a kind of lacteal goo, and out on the streetlet a couple car doors are squeaking and slamming and some people are conversing and delaying just to make Staff have to stand there in shirtsleeves on the cold porch, a small nightly sideways ball-busting rebellious gesture, when Gately's eye falls on Doony R. Glynn's specialty-disembowelled old dusty-black VW Bug parked with the other cars on the now-illicit street-side, its rear-mount engine's guts on full glittered display under the little street's lights, and Glynn's upstairs in bed tonight legitimately prostrate with diverticulitis, which for insurance reasons means Gately has to go back in and ask some resident with a driver's license to come move Glynn's VW across the street, which is humiliating because it means admitting publicly to these specimens that he, Gately, doesn't have a valid license, and the sudden heat of the living room confuses his goose-pimples, and nobody in the living room will admit to have a driver's license, and it turns out the only licensed resident who's still vertical and downstairs is Bruce Green, who's in the kitchen expressionlessly stirring a huge amount of sugar into a cup of coffee with his bare blunt finger, and Gately finds himself having to ask for managerial assistance from a kid he likes and has just bitched out and extracted urine from, which Green minimizes the humiliation of the whole thing by volunteering to help the second he hears the words *Glynn* and *fucking car,* and goes to the living room closet to get out his cheap leather jacket and fingerless gloves, and but Gately now has to leave the residents outside still unsupervised for a second to go clomping upstairs and verify that it's kosher with Glynn for Bruce Green to move his car.[251] The 2-Man seniorest males' bedroom has a bunch of old AA bumper-stickers on it and a calligraphic poster saying EVERYTHING I'VE EVER LET GO OF HAS CLAW MARKS ON IT, and the answer to Gately's knock is a moan, and Glynn's little naked-lady bedside lamp he brought in with him is on, he's in his rack curled on his side clutching his abdomen like a kicked man. McDade is illicitly sitting on Foss's rack reading one of Foss's motorcycle magazines and drinking Glynn's Millennial Fizzy with stereo headphones on, and he hurriedly puts out his cigarette when Gately enters and closes the little drawer in the bedside table where Foss keeps his ashtray just like everybody else.[252] The street outside sounds like Daytona—a drug addict is like physically unable to start a car without gunning the engine. Gately looks quickly out the west window over Glynn's rack to verify that all the unsupervised headlights going down the little street are Uing and coming back the right way to repark. Gately's forehead is wet and he feels the start of a greasy headache, from managerial stress. Glynn's crossed eyes are glassy and feverish and he's softly singing the lyrics to a Choosy Mothers song to a tune that isn't the song's tune.

'Doon,' Gately whispers.

One of the cars is coming back down the street a little fast for Gately's taste. Anything involving residents that happens on the grounds after curfew is his responsibility, the House Manager's made clear.

'Doon.'

It's the bottom eye, grotesquely, that rolls up at Gately. 'Don.'

'*Doon.*'

'Don Doon the witch is dead.'

'Doon, I need to let Green move your car.'

'Vehicle's black, Don.'

'*Brucie Green* needs your keys so's we can switch your car over, brother, it's midnight.'

'My Black Bug. My baby. The Roachmobile. The Doonulater's wheels. His mobility. His exposed baby. His slice of the American Pie. Simonize my baby when I'm gone, Don Doon.'

'Keys, Doony.'

'Take them. Take it. Want you to have it. One true friend. Brought me Ritz crackers and a Fizz. Treat it like a roachlady. Shiny, black, hard, mobile. Needs Premium and a weekly wax.'

'Doon. You got to show me where's the keys, brother.'

'And the bowel. Gotta weekly shine the pipes in the bowel. Exposed to view. With a soft cloth. The mobile roach. The bowelmobile.'

The heat coming off Glynn is face-tightening.

'You feel like you got a fever, Doon?' At one point elements of Staff thought Glynn might be playing sick to get out of looking for a job after losing his menial job at Brighton Fence & Wire. All Gately knows about diverticulitis is that Pat said it's intestinal and alcoholics can get it in recovery from impurities in bottom-shelf blends that the body's trying to expel. Glynn's had physical complaints all through his residency, but nothing like this here. His face is gray and waxy with pain and there's a yellowish crust on his lips. Glynn's got a real severe adtorsion, and the bottom eye is rolled up at Gately with a terrible delirious glitter, the top eye rolling around like a cow's eye. Gately still cannot bring himself to feel another man's forehead. He settles for punching Glynn very lightly on the shoulder.

'You think we need to take you over to St. E.'s to get your intestine looked at, Doon, do you think?'

'Hoits, Don.'

'You think you—?'

Because he's worrying about what if a resident comas or dies on his shift, and then feeling shame that this is his worry, the squeal of brakes and raised voices' noises down out front hasn't registered on Gately right away, but Hester Thrale's unmistakable high-B# scream does—i.e. register—and now serious feet running up the stairs:

Green's face in the doorway, red in round patches high on his cheeks: 'Come out.'

'The fuck's the problem out—'

Green: 'Come *now* Gately.'

Glynn sotto: 'Mother.'

Gately doesn't get to even ask Green what the fuck again on the stairs because Green is down ahead out the door so fast; the damn front door's been open all this time. A watercolor of a retrieverish dog cants and then falls from the wall on the staircase from the vibrations of Gately taking two stairs down at a time. He doesn't take time to grab his coat off Pat's couch. All he's got on is a donated orange bowling shirt with the name *Moose* cursive-stitched on the breast and SHUCO-MIST M.P.S. in ghastly aqua blocks across the back,[253] and he feels every follicle on his body hump up again as the cold encases him on the front porch and the wheelchair-ramp down to the little walkway. The night is cold and glycerine-clear and quite still. Very distant sounds of car horns and raised voices down on Comm. Green's receding at a run off up the little streetlet into a glare of highbeams that diffracts in the clouds of Gately's breath, so even as Gately walks briskly[254] in Green's leather-smelling backwash toward a rising hubbub of curses and Lenz's high-speed voice and Thrale's glass-shattering cries and Henderson and Willis talking shit angrily to somebody and the sound of Joelle v.D.'s veiled head in an upstairs window that isn't the 5-Women room's shouting something down to Gately as he appears in the street, even as he closes in it takes a while for the scene to decoct out of the fog of his breath and its shifting spears of color against the headlights. He passes Glynn's disembowelled and illegally parked Bug. Several of the residents' cars are idling at haphazard angles of mid-U-turn in the middle of the street, and in front of them is a modified dark Montego with highbeams and jacked rear wheels and a turbo's carnivorous idle. Two almost Gately-sized bearded guys in loose like bowling-wear shirts with flowers or suns on them and what look like big faggy necklaces of flowers around what would be their necks if they had necks turn out to be chasing Randy Lenz around this Montego car. Yet another guy with a necklace and a plaid Donegal is holding the rest of the residents at bay on the lawn of #4 with a nasty-looking Item[255] expertly held. Everything now slightly slows down; at the sight of an Item held on his residents there's almost a kind of mechanistic click as Gately's mind shifts into a different kind of drive. He gets very cool and clear and his headache recedes and his breathing slows. It's not so much that things slow as break into frames.

The ruckus has aroused the old nurse in #4 who Asks For Help, and her spectral figure is splayed in a nightie against an upstairs #4 window yelling '*Eeeeeeyelp!*' Hester Thrale now has her pink-nailed hands over her eyes and is screaming over and over for nobody to hurt nobody especially her. It's the Bulldog Item that holds the attention. The two guys chasing Lenz around the Montego are unarmed but look coldly determined in a way Gately recognizes. They're not wearing coats either but they don't look cold. All this appraisal's taking only seconds; it only takes time to list it. They have vaguely non-U.S. beards and are each about ⅔ Gately's size. They take turns coming around the car and running past the headlights' glare and Gately can see they have similar froggy lippy pale foreign faces. Lenz is talking at the guys nonstop, mostly imprecating. They're all three going around and around the car like a cartoon. Gately's still walking up as he sees all this. It's obvious to appraisal the foreignish guys aren't real bright because of they're chasing Lenz in tandem instead of heading around the car in opposite directions to trap him in like a pincer. They all three stop and start, Lenz across the car from them. Some of the at-bay residents are yelling to Lenz. Like most coke-dealers Lenz is quick on his feet, his topcoat billowing and then settling whenever he stops. Lenz's voice is nonstop—he's alternately inviting the guy to perform impossible acts and advancing baroque arguments for how whatever they think he did there's no way he was even in the same area code as whatever happened that they think he did. The guys keep speeding up like they want to catch Lenz just to shut him up. Ken Erdedy has his hands up and his car keys in his hand; his legs look like he's about to wet himself. Clenette and the new black girl, clearly veterans at gunpoint-etiquette, are prone on the lawn with their fingers laced behind their heads. Nell Gunther's assumed Lenz's old martial-arts Crane stance, hands twisted into flat claws, eyeing the guy's .44, which pans coolly back and forth over the residents. This smaller guy gets the most frames the slowest. He's got on a plaid hunting cap that keeps Gately from seeing if he's foreign also. But the guy's holding the weapon in the classic Weaver stance of somebody that can really shoot—left foot slightly forward, slightly hunched, a two-handed grip with the right arm cocked elbow-out so the Item's held high up in front of the guy's face, up to his sighting eye. This is how policemen and Made Guys from the North End shoot. Gately knows weapons way better than sobriety, still. And the Item—if the guy trig-pulls on some resident that resident's going down—the Item's some customized version of a U.S. .44 Bulldog Special, or maybe a Nuck or Brazilian clone, blunt and ugly and with a bore like the mouth of a cave. The stout alcoholic kid Tingley has both hands to his cheeks and is 100% at bay. The piece's been modified, Gately can appraise. The barrel's been vented out near the muzzle to cut your Bulldog's infamous recoil, the hammer's bobbed, and the thing's got a fat Mag Na Port or -clone grip like the metro Finest favor. This is not a weekend-warrior or liquor-store-holdup type Item; it's one that's made real specifically for putting projectiles into people. It's not a semiauto but is throated for a fucking speed-loader, which Gately can't see if the guy's got a speed-loader under the loose floral shirt but needs to assume the guy's got near-unlimited shots with a speed-loader. The North Shore Finest on the other hand wrap their grips in this like colored gauze that wicks sweat. Gately tries to recall a past associate's insufferable ammo-lectures when under the influence—your Bulldog and clones can take anything from light target loads and wadcutter to Colt SofTip dum-dums and worse. He's pretty sure this thing could put him down with one round; he's not sure. Gately's never been shot but he's seen guys shot. He feels something that is neither fear nor excitement. Joelle van D. is shouting stuff you can't make out, and Erdedy at bay on the lawn's calling out to her to get her head out of the whole picture. Gately's been bearing down this whole brief time, both seeing his breath and hearing it, beating his arms across his chest to keep some feeling in his hands. You could almost call what he feels a kind of jolly calm. The unAmerican guys chase Lenz and then stop across the car facing him for a second and then get furious again and chase him. Gately guesses he ought to be grateful the third guy doesn't come over and just shoot him. Lenz puts both hands on whatever part of the car he stops at and sends language out across the car at the two guys. Lenz's white wig is askew and he's got no mustache, you can see. E.M. Security, normally so scrupulous with their fucking trucks at 0005h., is nowhere around, lending weight to yet another cliché. If you asked Gately what he was feeling right this second he'd have no idea. He's got a hand up shading his eyes and closes on the Montego as things further clarify. One of the guys now you can see has Lenz's disguise's mustache in two fingers and keeps holding it up and brandishing it at Lenz. The other guy issues stilted but colorful threats in a Canadian accent, so it emerges on Gately it's Nucks, the trio Lenz has managed to somehow enrage is Nucks. Gately cops a black surge of Remember-Whenning, the babbling little football-head Québecer he'd killed by gagging a man with a bad cold. This line of thinking is intolerable. Joelle's overhead shout to for Christ's sake somebody call Pat mixes in and out of the Help lady's cries. It occurs to Gately that the Help lady has cried Wolf for so many years that real shouts for real help are all going to be ignored. The residents all look to Gately as he crosses the street directly into the Montego's wash of light. Hester Thrale screams out Look out there's a Item. The plaid-hat Nuck pans stiffly to sight at Gately, his elbow up around his ear. It occurs to Gately if you fire with an Item right up to your sighting-eye like that won't you get a face full of cordite. There's a break in the circular action around the throbbing car as Lenz shouts *Don* with great gusto just as the Help lady shouts for

Help. The Nuck with the Item has backed up several steps to keep the residents in his peripheral vision while he sights square on Gately as the massive Nuck holding the mustache across the car tells Gately if he was him he'd return to whence he came, him, to avoid the trouble. Gately nods and beams. Nucks really do pronounce *the* with a *z*. Both the car and Lenz are between Gately and the large Nucks, Lenz's back to Gately. Gately stands quietly, wishing he felt different about potential trouble, less almost jolly. Late in Gately's Substance and burglary careers, when he'd felt so low about himself, he'd had sick little fantasies of saving somebody from harm, some innocent party, and getting killed in the process and getting eulogized at great length in bold-faced *Globe* print. Now Lenz breaks away from the hood of the car and dashes Gately's way and around behind him to stand behind him, spreading his arms wide to put a hand on each of Gately's shoulders, using Don Gately like a shield. Gately's stance has the kind of weary resolution of like You'll Have to Go Through Me. The only anxious part of him can see the Log entry he'll have to make if residents come to physical grief on his shift. For a moment he can almost smell the smells of the penitentiary, armpits and Pomade and sour food and cribbage-board-wood and reefer and mopwater, the rich piss stink of a zoo's lion house, the smell of the bars you lace your hands through and stand there, looking out. This line of thinking is intolerable. He's neither goosepimpled nor sweating. His senses haven't been this keen in over a year. The stars in their jelly and dirty sodium lamplight and stark white steer-horns of headlights splayed at residents' different angles. Star-chocked sky, his breath, faraway horns, low trill of ATHSCMEs way to the north. Thin keen cold air in his wide-open nose. Motionless heads at #5's windows.

The Nuck duo with flowers chasing Lenz come around this side and now break away from the car toward them. Now Hester Thrale at Gately's right periphery breaks away from the cluster and runs for it off into the night across the lawn and behind #4, waving her arms and screaming, and Minty and McDade and Parias-Carbo and Charlotte Treat appear out of Ennet House's back door across the hedge and mill and jostle amid the mops and old furniture on Ennet's back porch, watching, and a couple of the more mobile catatonics appear on the porch of the Shed across the little street, staring at the spect-op, all this flummoxing the smaller one so he keeps swinging the Item stiffly this way and that way, trying to keep way more people at potential bay. The two alien foreigners that want Lenz's map bear down slowly across the Montego's headlights toward where Lenz is holding Gately like a shield. The larger one that's so large his luauish shirt won't even button all the way holding out the mustache adopts the overly reasonable tone that always precedes a serious-type beef. He reads Gately's bowling shirt in the headlight and says reasonably that Moose still has a chance to keep out of what they've got no beef with him, them. Lenz is pouring a diarrheatic spatter of disclaimers and exhortations into Gately's right ear. Gately shrugs at the Nucks like he's got no choice but to be here. Green's just looking at them. It occurs to Gately by White Flag suggestion that who gives a fuck how it'd look, he ought to hit his knees right here on the headlit blacktop and ask for guidance on this from a Higher Power. But he stands there, Lenz chattering in his shadow. The fingernails of Lenz's hand on Gately's shoulder have horseshoes of dried blood in the creases between nail and finger, and there's a coppery smell off Lenz that isn't just fear. It occurs to Gately that if he'd pulled the instant spot-urine he'd wanted on Lenz this whole snafu wouldn't maybe be happening. The one Nuck is holding Lenz's disguise's mustache out at them like a blade. Lenz hasn't asked the time once, notice. Then the other Nuck's got his hand down at his side and a real blade's gleam appears in that hand with the familiar *snick*. At the blade's sound the situation becomes even more automatic and Gately feels adrenaline's warmth spread through him as his subdural hardware clicks deeper into a worn familiar long-past track. Having no choice now not to fight and things simplify radically, divisions collapse. Gately's just one part of something bigger he can't control. His face in the left headlight has dropped into its fight-expression of ferocious good cheer. He says he's responsible for these people on these private grounds tonight and is part of this whether he wants to be or not, and can they talk this out because he doesn't want to have to fight them. He says twice very distinctly that he does not want to fight them. He's no longer divided enough to think about whether this is true. His eyes are on the two men's maple-leaf belt buckles, the part of the body where you can't get suckered by a feint. The guys shake their manes and say they're going to unembowel this craven *bâtard* here like this *sans-Christe bâtard* killed somebody they call either Pépé or Bébé, and if Moose has any self-interest he'll backpedal away from there's no way it is his duty to get frapped or fropped for this sick gutless U.S.A. *bâtard* in his womanly wig. Lenz, apparently thinking they're Brazilian, pops his head around Gately's flank and calls them *maricones* and tells them they can suck his *bâtard* is what they can do. Gately has just division enough to almost wish he didn't feel such a glow of familiar warmth, a surge of almost sexual competence, as the two shriek at Lenz's taunts and split and curve in at them an arm's length apart, walking gradually faster, like unstoppable inertia, but stupidly too close together. At two meters off they charge, shedding petals and unisonly bellowing something in Canadian.

It's always that everything always speeds up and slows down both. Gately's smile broadens as he's shoved slightly forward by Lenz as Lenz recoils backward off him to run from the guys' shrieking charge. Gately takes the shove's momentum and bodychecks the enormous Nuck holding the mustache into the Nuck holding the blade, who goes down with an *euf* of expelled air. The first Nuck has hold of Gately's bowling shirt and rips it and punches Gately in the forehead and audibly breaks his hand, letting go of Gately to grab his hand. The punch makes Gately stop thinking in any sort of spiritual terms at all. Gately takes the man's broken hand's arm he's holding out and with his eyes on the ground's other Nuck breaks the arm over his knee, and as the guy goes down on one knee Gately takes the arm and pirouettes around twisting the broken arm behind the guy's back and plants his sneaker on the guy's floral back and forces him forward so there's a sick crack and he feels the arm come out of the socket, and there's a high foreign scream. The Nuck with the blade who was down slashes Gately's calf through his jeans as the guy rolls gracefully left and starts to rise, up on one knee, knife out front, a guy that knows his knives and can't be closed with while he's got the blade up. Gately feints and takes one giant step and gets all his weight into a Rockette kick that lands high up under the Nuck's beard's chin and audibly breaks Gately's big toe in the sneaker and sends the man curving out back into the dazzle of the high-beams, and there's a metallic boom of him landing on the Montego's hood and the click and skitter of the blade landing somewhere on the street beyond the car. Gately on one foot, holding his toe, and his slashed calf feels hot. His smile is broad but impersonal. It's impossible, outside choreographed entertainment, to fight two guys together at once; they'll kill you; the trick to fighting two is to make sure and put one down for long enough that he's out of the picture long enough to put the other guy down. And this first larger one with the extreme arm-trouble is clutching himself as he rolls, trying to rise, still perversely holding the white mustache. You can tell this is a real beef because nobody's saying anything and the sounds from everybody else have receded to the sounds stands' crowds make and Gately hops over and uses the good foot to kick the Nuck twice in the side of the big head and then without a thought in his head moves down the guy and lines it up and drops to one knee with all his weight on the guy's groin, resulting in an indescribable sound from the guy and a shout from J.v.D. overhead and a flat crack from the lawn and Gately's punched so hard in the shoulder he's spun around on one knee and almost goes over backwards and the shoulder goes hotly numb, which tells Gately he's gotten shot instead of punched in the shoulder. He never got shot before. **SHOT IN SOBRIETY** in bold headline caps goes across his mind's eye like a slow train as he sees the third Nuck with his cap pushed back and Nuck face contorted with cordite in his good stance with elbow back up drawing a second bead on Don's big head from #4's lawn with the bore's lightless eye and a little pubic curl of smoke coming up from the vented muzzle, and Gately can't move and forgets to pray, and then the bore zagging up and away as it blooms orange as good old Bruce Green's got the Nuck from behind in a half-nelson with his hand in the necklace of flowers and with the other hand is forcing the cocked elbow down and the Item skyward away from Gately's head as it blooms with that flat crack of a vented muzzle. The first thing somebody's who's shot wants to do is throw up, which by the way the larger Nuck with the breezeblocked crotch under Gately's doing all over his beard and flower necklace and Gately's leg's thigh as Gately weaves on one knee on the guy's groin still. The lady yells for Help. Now a meaty thwack as Nell Gunther on the lawn leaps several twirling meters and kicks the Nuck Green's half-nelsoning in the face with her paratrooper-boot's heel, and the guy's hat flies off and his head snaps back and hits Green's face, and there's the pop of Green's nose breaking but he doesn't let go, and the guy's slumped forward in the Parkinsonian half-bow of a guy in a quality half-nelson, with the guy's Item-hand's arm still up in the air with Green's arm like they're dancing, and good old Green doesn't even let go to hold his spurting nose, and now that the Nuck's restrained, notice, here comes Lenz barrelling in howling from the hedge's shadows and leaping and he tackles the Nuck and Green both, and they're a roil of clothes and legs on the lawn, the Item not in sight. Ken Erdedy still has his hands up. Gately, still kneeling shot on the Nuck's sickeningly softened groin, Gately hears the second Nuck trying to slide himself off the hood of the Montego and hops and wobbles over. Joelle v.D. keeps yelling something monosyllabic from what can't be her window. Don goes to the Montego's front bumper and punches the large man carefully in the kidneys with his good arm and takes him by the thick foreign hair and slides him back up the hood and begins banging his head off the Montego's windshield. He remembers how he'd stay in luxury furnished North Shore apts. with G. Fackelmann and T. Kite and they'd gradually strip the place and sell the appointments off until they were sleeping in a totally bare apartment. Green has risen bloody-faced, and Lenz is on the lawn with his heaving topcoat covering him and the third Nuck, and Clenette H. and Yolanda W. are now up and not at bay and circling them and getting solid high-heel kicks into the Nuck's and some-times hopefully Lenz's ribs, reciting 'Motha*fucka*' and landing a kick each time they get to *fu*. Gately, canted way over to the side, methodically beats his Nuck's shaggy head against the windshield so hard that spidered stars are appearing in the shatterproof glass until something in the head gives with a sort of liquid crunch. Petals from the guy's necklace are all over the hood and Gately's torn shirt. Joelle v.D. in her terry robe and gauze veil and still clutching a toothbrush has climbed out onto the little balcony outside the 5-Woman's window and into a skinny ailanthus beside it and is coming down, showing about two meters of spectacularly undeformed thigh, shouting Gately's name by the first name, which he likes. Gately leaves the largest Nuck prone on the idling hood, his head resting in a shatter-frosted head-shaped recession in the windshield. It occurs to Ken Erdedy, looking up into the oak past his upraised hands, that this deformed veiled girl likes Don Gately in an extracurricular way, it would seem. Gately, toe and shoulder or no, has looked strictly all-business this whole time. He's projected a sort of white-collar attitude of cheery competence and sangfroid. Erdedy's found he rather likes standing there with his hands up in a gesture of noncombatant status while the Afro-American girls curse and kick and Lenz continues to roll around with the uncon-scious man hitting him and going 'There, *there*,' and Gately moves back-ward between the second fellow in the windshield and the first fellow he'd originally disarmed, his smile now as empty as a pumpkin's grin. Chan-dler Foss is trying on the third fellow's plaid hunting cap. There's a sound in #4 of somebody trying to force a warped window. An Empire W.D.V. is launched with a kind of spronging thud and whistles overhead, climbing, its warning-light wrap of like Xmas lights winking red and green as Don Gately starts to come over in the direction of the lawn and the fellow who appears to have winged him and then veers drunkenly and changes direc-tion and in three one-foot hops is over to the vomit-covered first Nuck, the one who'd called Gately Moose and punched him in the forehead. There's the slow trundle of the Green T and exhortations from Minty as Gately begins stomping on the supine face of the Nuck with the heel of his good foot as if he were killing cockroaches. The guy's movable arm is wag-gling pathetically in the air around Gately's shoe as it rises and falls. Gate-ly's hideous torn orange shirt's whole right side is dark and his right arm drips blackly and seems weirdly set in its socket. Lenz is up and adjusting his wig and brushing off. The veiled girl has hit a rough part some three meters up and is hanging from a limb and kicking, Erdedy staring Coper-nically up her flapping robe. The new Tingley kid sits cross-legged in the grass and rocks as the black ladies continue stomping the inert Nuck. You can hear Emil Minty and Wade McDade exhorting Yolanda W. to use the spike heel. Charlotte Treat is reciting the Serenity Prayer over and over. Bruce Green has his head back and his finger held like a mustache under his nostrils. Hester Thrale can still be heard way off down Warren Street, receding, as Gately wobbles back from the Nuck's map and sits heavily down in the little street, in shadow except for his huge head in the Nucks' car's lights, sitting there with his head on his knees. Lenz and Green move in toward him the cautious way you approach a big animal that's hurt. Joelle van Dyne lands on her feet. The lady at the high warped window shouts for Helphelphelphelp*help*. Minty and McDade come down off the back porch, finally, McDade for some reason wielding a mop. Everybody except Lenz and Minty looks unwell.

Joelle runs just like a girl, Erdedy notes.[256] She gets out through the many-angled cars into the street just as Gately decides to lie down.

It's not like passing out. It's just a decision Gately makes to like lie back with his knees bent and pointing up into the sky's depth, which seems to bulge and recede with the pulse in his right shoulder, which has now gone dead cold, which means there will very soon be pain, he predicts.

He waves off concern with the left hand and goes 'Flesh-wound' the second Joelle's bare feet and robe's hem are in view.

'Son of a fucking *bitch*.'

'Flesh-wound.'

'Are you ever *bleeding*.'

'Thanks for the feedback.'

You can hear Henderson and Willis off in the background still going '*fu*.'

'I think you can tell them he's probably subdued,' Gately pointing off in what he thinks is #4's lawn's direction. His lying flat gives him a double-chin, he can feel, and pulls his big face into a smile. His big present fear is throwing up in front of and maybe partly on Joelle v.D., whose calves he's noted.

Now Lenz's lizard-skin loafers with grass stains at the toes. 'Don what can I say.'

Gately struggles to sit back up. 'You got fucking armed *Nucks* wanting your ass too?'

Revealing a kind of blackly kimonoish thing under, Joelle has taken off the terry robe and folds the robe into a kind of trapezoidal pad and is kneeling over Gately's shoulder, straddling his arm, pressing down on the pad with the heels of her hands.

'Owie.'

'Lenz he's really bleeding bad here.'

'I'm groping to even know what to begin to say, Don.'

'You owe me urine, Lenz.'

'I think there's two of them, like, desisted.' Wade McD.'s unlaced high-tops, his voice breathy with awe.

'He's bleeding really bad I said.'

'You mean deceased.'

'There's one of their shoes in one of them's fucking eye.'

'Tell Ken to put his hands down for Christ's sake.'

'Oh fucking *God.*'

Gately can feel his eyes crossing and uncrossing by themselves.

'He soaking right through it man look at that shit.'

'This man needs an ambulance.'

Somebody else female says God again and Gately's hearing warbles a bit as Joelle snaps at her to shut up. She leans down and in, so Gately can see up at what looks like a regular human female chin and makeupless lower lip under the veil's billowing hem. 'Whom should we call?' she asks him.

'Call Pat's machine and Calvin. You have to dial 9. Tell them to come down.'

'I'm going to be sick.'

'Airdaddy!' Minty is shouting at Ken E.

'Tell her to call Annie and the E.M. office down there and do some like strategic thing.'

'Where the fuck is Security when it isn't just innocent recovering cars to get towed?'

'And call Pat,' Gately says.

A forest of footwear and bare feet and shins all around him, and heads too high to see. Lenz screaming back to somebody in the House: 'Call a fucking *am*bulance already.'

'Regulate the voice, man.'

'Fucking call about *five* ambulances is more like it.'

'Motha*fucka.*'

'Ssshh.'

'I just never saw anything *like* that.'

'Nuh-uh,' Gately gasps, trying to rise and deciding he just likes it better lying down. 'Don't call one for me.'

'This is the straight and narrow?'

'By doze is fide.'

'He doesn't *want* one he said.'

Green's and Minty's boots, Treat's purple plastic shower-thongs. Somebody has on Clearasil, he can smell.

'Seen some righteous ass-kickings in my past, brother, but—'

Somebody male screams back off to the right.

'Just don't try and walk me around,' Gately grins up.

'Dipshit.'

'He can't go in no E.R. with a gunshot,' Minty says to Lenz, whose shoes keep moving to get himself north of everybody.

'Somebody turn off the car will you?'

'I wouldn't touch nothing.'

Gately focuses at where the Joelle girl's eyes would be. Her thighs are forked way wide to straddle his arm, which is numb and doesn't feel like his. She's bearing down on him. She smells strange but good. She's got all her weight on her bathrobe's pad. She weighs roughly nothing. The first threads of pain are starting to radiate out of the shoulder and down the side and into the neck. Gately hasn't looked down at the shoulder, on purpose, and he tries to wedge his left hand's finger under the shoulder to see if anything went through. The night's so clear the stars shine right through people's heads.

'Green.'

'I'b dot touchig dothig, dud worry.'

'Look at his *head*.'

Her kimono's shoulders are humped and glassy black in the Montego's light. Gately's brain keeps wanting to go away inside himself. When you start to feel deeply cold that's shock and blood-loss. Gately sort of wills himself to stay right here, looks over past Joelle's hand at Lenz's fine shoes. 'Lenz. You and Green. Get me inside.'

'Green!'

The circle of stars' heads' faces above are all faceless from the headlights' shadows. Some car engines have shut off and some haven't. One of the cars has a twittering fan-belt. Somebody's suggesting to call the genuine Finest—Erdedy—which everybody greets with scorn at his naïveté. Gately's figuring Staff from the Shed or #4 has called them or at least dialed down to Security. By the time he was ten only his pinkie-finger would fit in the dialer's holes of his mother's old princess phone; he exerts will to uncross his eyes and stay right here; he in the worst way does not want to be lying here with a gunshot in shock trying to deal with the Finest.

'I think one of these guys is, like, expired.'

'No shit Shylock.'

'*Nobody call.*' Gately yells it up and out. He's afraid he's going to vomit when they stand him up. 'Nobody call nobody til you get me in.' He can smell Green's leather jacket overhead. Bits of grass and whatnot drifting down onto him from where Lenz is still brushing off his clothes, and coins of blood on the street from Green's nose. Joelle tells Lenz if he doesn't cut something out she's going to hand him his ass. Gately's whole right side had gone deadly cold. To Joelle he says, 'I'm Supervised. I'll go to jail sure.'

'You got fucking eyewitnesses out the ass behind you Don man,' either McDade or Glynn says, but it can't be Glynn, for some reason he tries to bring up inside him. And it seems like Charlotte T.'s voice saying Ewell's trying to get in Pat's office to call but Gately locked Pat's door.

'Nobody call *anyone!*' Joelle shouts up and out. She smells good.

'They're calling!'

'Get him off the phone! Say prank for Christ's sake! You hear me?' Her kimono smells good. Her voice has a Staff-like authority. The scene out here has changed: Gately's down, Madame Psychosis is in charge.

'We're going to get him up and we're going to get him inside,' she says to the circle. 'Lenz.'

There's impending static-crackle and the sound of a serious set of keys.

Her voice is that one Madame lady's voice on no-subscription radio, from out of nowhere he's all of a sudden sure, is where he heard that odd empty half-accented voice before.

'Secyotty! Hold it *right* thaah.' It's at least luckily one of the ex-football E.M. Security guys, that spends half his shift down at the Life and then goes up and down the streetlet all night playing with his service baton and singing sea chanties off-key, that's just impressively qualified to Come In to AA with them.

Joelle: 'Erdedy—deal with him.'

'Pardon me?'

'It's the drunk,' Gately gets out.

Joelle's looking up at presumably Ken E. 'Go over and look high-income and respectable at him. Verbalize at him. Distract him while we get him inside before the real ones come.'

'How am I supposed to explain all these prone figures draped over cars?'

'For Christ's sake Ken he's not a mental titan—distract him with something shiny or something. Get your thumb out of your ass and move.'

Gately's smile has reached his eyes. 'You're Madame on the FM, is how I knew you.'

Erdedy's squeaky shoe and the obese guy's radio and keys. 'Who hold it? As in desist?'

'Se*cyotty* I said *halt!*'

Green and Lenz bending in, white breath all over and Green's dripping nose the same copper smell as Lenz.

'I knew I knew you,' Gately says to Joelle, whose veil remains inscrutable.

'If I could ask you to specify halt from what.'

'Get his back up here first,' Green tells Lenz.

'Not crazy about all this blood,' Lenz is saying.

Many hands slide under his back; the shoulder blooms with colorless fire. The sky looks so 3-D you could like dive in. The stars distend and sprout spikes. Joelle's warm legs shift with her weight to keep pressure on the pad. The squishing sound Gately knows means the robe's soaked through. He wants somebody to congratulate him for not having thrown up. You can tell some of the stars are nearer and some far, down there. What Gately's always thought of as the Big Question Mark is really the Big Dipper.

'I'm *oddering* desist until who's in chahge that I can repot the si*chation.*' The Security guy's hammered, his name's Sidney or Stanley and he wears his Security-hat and baton shopping in the Purity Supreme and always asks Gately how it's hanging. His shoes' uppers are blasted along the feet's insides the way fat men that have to walk a lot's are; his ex-ballplayer's collops and big hanging gut are one of Gately's great motivators for nightly situps. Gately turns his head to throw up a little on both Green and Joelle, who both ignore it.

'Oh sorry. Oh shit I hate that.'

Joelle v.D. runs a hand down Gately's wet arm that leaves a warm wake, the hand, and then gently squeezes as much of the wrist as she can get her hand around. 'And Lo,' she says softly.

'Jesus his leg's all bloody too.'

'Boy do I know guys loved that show you did.' A tiny bit more throwing up.

'Now we're going to lift him very gently and get the feet under.'

'Here Green man get over here on the south why don't you.'

'I'm oddering the whole sitchation halt it *right* thaah whe*yaah.*'

Lenz and Green's shoes coming together and moving apart at either side of Gately, faces coming down in a fish-eye lens, lifting:

'Ready?'

—*pages 601–619*

O

AND RE ENNET House resident Kate Gompert and this depression issue:

Some psychiatric patients—plus a certain percentage of people who've gotten so dependent on chemicals for feelings of well-being that when the chemicals have to be abandoned they undergo a loss-trauma that reaches way down deep into the soul's core systems—these persons know first-hand that there's more than one kind of so-called 'depression.' One kind is low-grade and sometimes gets called *anhedonia*[280] or *simple melancholy*. It's a kind of spiritual torpor in which one loses the ability to feel pleasure or attachment to things formerly important. The avid bowler drops out of his league and stays home at night staring dully at kick-boxing cartridges. The gourmand is off his feed. The sensualist finds his beloved Unit all of a sudden to be so much feelingless gristle, just hanging there. The devoted wife and mother finds the thought of her family about as moving, all of a sudden, as a theorem of Euclid. It's a kind of emotional novocaine, this form of depression, and while it's not overtly painful its deadness is disconcerting and...well, depressing. Kate Gompert's always thought of this anhedonic state as a kind of radical abstracting of everything, a hollowing out of stuff that used to have affective content. Terms the undepressed toss around and take for granted as full and fleshy—*happiness, joie de vivre, preference, love*—are stripped to their skeletons and reduced to abstract ideas. They have, as it were, denotation but not connotation. The anhedonic can still speak about happiness and meaning et al., but she has become incapable of feeling anything in them, of understanding anything about them, of hoping anything about them, or of believing them to exist as anything more than concepts. Everything becomes an outline of the thing. Objects become schemata. The world becomes a map of the world. An anhedonic can navigate, but has no location. I.e. the anhedonic becomes, in the lingo of Boston AA, Unable To Identify.

It's worth noting that, among younger E.T.A.s, the standard take on Dr.

J. O. Incandenza's suicide attributes his putting his head in the microwave to this kind of anhedonia. This is maybe because anhedonia's often associated with the crises that afflict extremely goal-oriented people who reach a certain age having achieved all or more than all than they'd hoped for. The what-does-it-all-mean-type crisis of middle-aged Americans. In fact this is in fact not what killed Incandenza at all. In fact the presumption that he'd achieved all his goals and found that the achievement didn't confer meaning or joy on his existence says more about the students at E.T.A. than it says about Orin's and Hal's father: still under the influence of the deLint-like carrot-and-stick philosophies of their hometown coaches rather than the more paradoxical Schtitt/Incandenza/Lyle school, younger athletes who can't help gauging their whole worth by their place in an ordinal ranking use the idea that achieving their goals and finding the gnawing sense of worthlessness still there in their own gut as a kind of psychic bogey, something that they can use to justify stopping on their way down to dawn drills to smell flowers along the E.T.A. paths. The idea that achievement doesn't automatically confer interior worth is, to them, still, at this age, an abstraction, rather like the prospect of their own death — 'Caius Is Mortal' and so on. Deep down, they all still view the competitive carrot as the grail. They're mostly going through the motions when they invoke anhedonia. They're mostly small children, keep in mind. Listen to any sort of sub-16 exchange you hear in the bathroom or food line: 'Hey there, how are you?' 'Number eight this week, is how I am.' They all still worship the carrot. With the possible exception of the tormented LaMont Chu, they all still subscribe to the delusive idea that the continent's second-ranked fourteen-year-old feels exactly twice as worthwhile as the continent's #4.

Deluded or not, it's still a lucky way to live. Even though it's temporary. It may well be that the lower-ranked little kids at E.T.A. are proportionally happier than the higher-ranked kids, since we (who are mostly not small children) know it's more invigorating to *want* than to *have*, it seems. Though maybe this is just the inverse of the same delusion.

Hal Incandenza, though he has no idea yet of why his father really put his head in a specially-dickied microwave in the Year of the Trial-Size Dove Bar, is pretty sure that it wasn't because of standard U.S. anhedonia. Hal himself hasn't had a bona fide intensity-of-interior-life-type emotion since he was tiny; he finds terms like *joie* and *value* to be like so many variables in rarified equations, and he can manipulate them well enough to satisfy everyone but himself that he's in there, inside his own hull, as a human being — but in fact he's far more robotic than John Wayne. One of his troubles with his Moms is the fact that Avril Incandenza believes she knows him inside and out as a human being, and an internally worthy one at that, when in fact inside Hal there's pretty much nothing at all, he knows. His Moms Avril hears her own echoes inside him and thinks what she hears is him, and this makes Hal feel the one thing he feels to the limit, lately: he is lonely.

It's of some interest that the lively arts of the millennial U.S.A. treat anhedonia and internal emptiness as hip and cool. It's maybe the vestiges of the Romantic glorification of *Weltschmerz,* which means world-weariness or hip ennui. Maybe it's the fact that most of the arts here are produced by world-weary and sophisticated older people and then consumed by younger people who not only consume art but study it for clues on how to be cool, hip—and keep in mind that, for kids and younger people, to be hip and cool is the same as to be admired and accepted and included and so Unalone. Forget so-called peer-pressure. It's more like peer-*hunger.* No? We enter a spiritual puberty where we snap to the fact that the great transcendent horror is loneliness, excluded encagement in the self. Once we've hit this age, we will now give or take anything, wear any mask, to fit, be part-of, not be Alone, we young. The U.S. arts are our guide to inclusion. A how-to. We are shown how to fashion masks of ennui and jaded irony at a young age where the face is fictile enough to assume the shape of whatever it wears. And then it's stuck there, the weary cynicism that saves us from gooey sentiment and unsophisticated naïveté. Sentiment equals naïveté on this continent (at least since the Reconfiguration). One of the things sophisticated viewers have always liked about J. O. Incandenza's *The American Century as Seen Through a Brick* is its unsubtle thesis that naïveté is the last true terrible sin in the theology of millennial America. And since sin is the sort of thing that can be talked about only figuratively, it's natural that Himself's dark little cartridge was mostly about a myth, viz. that queerly persistent U.S. myth that cynicism and naïveté are mutually exclusive. Hal, who's empty but not dumb, theorizes privately that what passes for hip cynical transcendence of sentiment is really some kind of fear of being really human, since to be really human (at least as he conceptualizes it) is probably to be unavoidably sentimental and naïve and goo-prone and generally pathetic, is to be in some basic interior way forever infantile, some sort of not-quite-right-looking infant dragging itself anaclitically around the map, with big wet eyes and froggy-soft skin, huge skull, gooey drool. One of the really American things about Hal, probably, is the way he despises what it is he's really lonely for: this hideous internal self, incontinent of sentiment and need, that pules and writhes just under the hip empty mask, anhedonia.[281]

The American Century as Seen Through a Brick's main and famous key-image is of a piano-string vibrating—a high D, it looks like—vibrating, and making a very sweet unadorned solo sound indeed, and then a little thumb comes into the frame, a blunt moist pale and yet dingy thumb, with disreputable stuff crusted in one of the nail-corners, small and unlined, clearly an infantile thumb, and as it touches the piano string the high sweet sound immediately dies. And the silence that follows is excruciating. Later in the film, after much mordant and didactic panoramic brick-following, we're back at the piano-string, and the thumb is removed, and the high sweet sound recommences, extremely pure and solo, and yet now somehow, as the volume increases, now with something rotten about it underneath, there's something sick-sweet and overripe and potentially putrid about the one clear high D as its volume increases and increases, the sound getting purer and louder and more dysphoric until after a surprisingly few seconds we find ourselves right in the middle of the pure undampered sound longing and even maybe praying for the return of the natal thumb, to shut it up.

Hal isn't old enough yet to know that this is because numb emptiness isn't the worst kind of depression. That dead-eyed anhedonia is but a remora on the ventral flank of the true predator, the Great White Shark of pain. Authorities term this condition *clinical depression* or *involutional depression* or *unipolar dysphoria*. Instead of just an incapacity for feeling, a deadening of soul, the predator-grade depression Kate Gompert always feels as she Withdraws from secret marijuana is *itself* a feeling. It goes by many names—*anguish, despair, torment,* or q.v. Burton's *melancholia* or Yevtuschenko's more authoritative *psychotic depression*—but Kate Gompert, down in the trenches with the thing itself, knows it simply as *It*.

It is a level of psychic pain wholly incompatible with human life as we know it. *It* is a sense of radical and thoroughgoing evil not just as a feature but as the essence of conscious existence. *It* is a sense of poisoning that pervades the self at the self's most elementary levels. *It* is a nausea of the cells and soul. *It* is an unnumb intuition in which the world is fully rich and animate and un-map-like and also thoroughly painful and malignant and antagonistic to the self, which depressed self *It* billows on and coagulates around and wraps in *Its* black folds and absorbs into *Itself,* so that an almost mystical unity is achieved with a world every constituent of which means painful harm to the self. *Its* emotional character, the feeling Gompert describes *It* as, is probably mostly indescribable except as a sort of double bind in which any/all of the alternatives we associate with human agency—sitting or standing, doing or resting, speaking or keeping silent, living or dying—are not just unpleasant but literally horrible.

It is also lonely on a level that cannot be conveyed. There is no way Kate

Gompert could ever even begin to make someone else understand what clinical depression feels like, not even another person who is herself clinically depressed, because a person in such a state is incapable of empathy with any other living thing. This anhedonic Inability To Identify is also an integral part of *It*. If a person in physical pain has a hard time attending to anything except that pain,[282] a clinically depressed person cannot even perceive any other person or thing as independent of the universal pain that is digesting her cell by cell. Everything is part of the problem, and there is no solution. It is a hell for one.

The authoritative term *psychotic depression* makes Kate Gompert feel especially lonely. Specifically the *psychotic* part. Think of it this way. Two people are screaming in pain. One of them is being tortured with electric current. The other is not. The screamer who's being tortured with electric current is not psychotic: her screams are circumstantially appropriate. The screaming person who's not being tortured, however, is psychotic, since the outside parties making the diagnoses can see no electrodes or measurable amperage. One of the least pleasant things about being psychotically depressed on a ward full of psychotically depressed patients is coming to see that none of them is really psychotic, that their screams are entirely appropriate to certain circumstances part of whose special charm is that they are undetectable by any outside party. Thus the loneliness: it's a closed circuit: the current is both applied and received from within.

The so-called 'psychotically depressed' person who tries to kill herself doesn't do so out of quote 'hopelessness' or any abstract conviction that life's assets and debits do not square. And surely not because death seems suddenly appealing. The person in whom *Its* invisible agony reaches a certain unendurable level will kill herself the same way a trapped person will eventually jump from the window of a burning high-rise. Make no mistake about people who leap from burning windows. Their terror of falling from a great height is still just as great as it would be for you or me standing speculatively at the same window just checking out the view; i.e. the fear of falling remains a constant. The variable here is the other terror, the fire's flames: when the flames get close enough, falling to death becomes the slightly less terrible of two terrors. It's not desiring the fall; it's terror of the flames. And yet nobody down on the sidewalk, looking up and yelling 'Don't!' and 'Hang on!', can understand the jump. Not really. You'd have to have personally been trapped and felt flames to really understand a terror way beyond falling.

But and so the idea of a person in the grip of *It* being bound by a

'Suicide Contract' some well-meaning Substance-abuse halfway house makes her sign is simply absurd. Because such a contract will constrain such a person only until the exact psychic circumstances that made the contract necessary in the first place assert themselves, invisibly and indescribably. That the well-meaning halfway-house Staff does not understand *Its* overriding terror will only make the depressed resident feel more alone.

One fellow psychotically depressed patient Kate Gompert came to know at Newton-Wellesley Hospital in Newton two years ago was a man in his fifties. He was a civil engineer whose hobby was model trains—like from Lionel Trains Inc., etc.—for which he erected incredibly intricate systems of switching and track that filled his basement recreation room. His wife brought photographs of the trains and networks of trellis and track into the locked ward, to help remind him. The man said he had been suffering from psychotic depression for seventeen straight years, and Kate Gompert had had no reason to disbelieve him. He was stocky and swart with thinning hair and hands that he held very still in his lap as he sat. Twenty years ago he had slipped on a patch of 3-In-1-brand oil from his model-train tracks and bonked his head on the cement floor of his basement rec room in Wellesley Hills, and when he woke up in the E.R. he was depressed beyond all human endurance, and stayed that way. He'd never once tried suicide, though he confessed that he yearned for unconsciousness without end. His wife was very devoted and loving. She went to Catholic Mass every day. She was very devout. The psychotically depressed man, too, went to daily Mass when he was not institutionalized. He prayed for relief. He still had his job and his hobby. He went to work regularly, taking medical leaves only when the invisible torment got too bad for him to trust himself, or when there was some radical new treatment the psychiatrists wanted him to try. They'd tried Tricyclics, M.A.O.I.s, insulin-comas, Selective-Serotonin-Reuptake Inhibitors,[283] the new and side-effect-laden Quadracyclics. They'd scanned his lobes and affective matrices for lesions and scars. Nothing worked. Not even high-amperage E.C.T. relieved *It*. This happens sometimes. Some cases of depression are beyond human aid. The man's case gave Kate Gompert the howling fantods. The idea of this man going to work and to Mass and building miniaturized railroad networks day after day after day while feeling anything like what Kate Gompert felt in that ward was simply beyond her ability to imagine. The rationo-spiritual part of her knew this man and his wife must be possessed of a courage way off any sort of known courage-chart. But in her toxified soul Kate Gompert felt only a paralyzing horror at the idea of the squat dead-eyed man laying toy track slowly and carefully in the silence of his wood-panelled rec room, the silence total except for the sounds of the track being oiled and snapped together and laid into place, the man's head full of poison and worms and every cell in his body screaming for relief from flames no one else could help with or even feel.

The permanently psychotically depressed man was finally transferred to a place on Long Island to be evaluated for a radical new type of psychosurgery where they supposedly went in and yanked out your whole limbic system, which is the part of the brain that causes all sentiment and feeling. The man's fondest dream was anhedonia, complete psychic numbing. I.e. death in life. The prospect of radical psychosurgery was the dangled carrot that Kate guessed still gave the man's life enough meaning for him to hang onto the windowsill by his fingernails, which were probably black and gnarled from the flames. That and his wife: he seemed genuinely to love his wife, and she him. He went to bed every night at home holding her, weeping for it to be over, while she prayed or did that devout thing with beads.

The couple had gotten Kate Gompert's mother's address and had sent Kate an Xmas card the last two years, Mr. and Mrs. Ernest Feaster of Wellesley Hills MA, stating that she was in their prayers and wishing her all available joy. Kate Gompert doesn't know whether Mr. Ernest Feaster's limbic system got yanked out or not. Whether he achieved anhedonia. The Xmas cards had had excruciating little watercolor pictures of locomotives on them. She could barely stand to think about them, even at the best of times, which the present was not.

—Pages 692–698

O

JOELLE USED TO like to get really high and then clean. Now she was finding she just liked to clean. She dusted the top of the fiberboard dresser she
and Nell Gunther shared. She dusted the oval top of the dresser's mirror's
frame and cleaned off the mirror as best she could. She was using Kleenex
and stale water from a glass by Kate Gompert's bed. She felt oddly averse
to putting on socks and clogs and going down to the kitchen for real
cleaning supplies. She could hear the noise of all the post-meeting
nighttime residents and visitors and applicants down there. She could feel
their voices in the floor. When the dental nightmare tore her upright
awake her mouth was open to scream out, but the scream was Nell G.
down in the living room, whose laugh always sounds like she's being
eviscerated. Nell preempted Joelle's own scream. Then Joelle cleaned.
Cleaning is maybe a form of meditation for addicts too new in recovery to
sit still. The 5-Woman's scarred wood floor had so much grit all over she
could sweep a pile of grit together with just an unappliquéd bumper
sticker she'd won at B.Y.P. Then she could use damp Kleenex to get up
most of the pile. She had only Kate G.'s little bedside lamp on, and she
wasn't listening to any YYY tapes, out of consideration for Charlotte
Treat, who was unwell and missed her Saturday Night Lively Mtng. on
Pat's OK and was now asleep, wearing a sleep mask but not her foam earplugs. Expandable foam earplugs were issued to every new Ennet resident,
for reasons the Staff said would clarify for them real quick, but Joelle hated
to wear them — they shut out exterior noise, but they made your head's
pulse audible, and your breath sounded like someone in a space suit — and
Charlotte Treat, Kate Gompert, April Cortelyu, and the former Amy
Johnson had all felt the same way. April said the foam plugs made her
brain itch.

It had started with Orin Incandenza, the cleaning. When relations
were strained, or she was seized with anxiety at the seriousness and

possible impermanence of the thing in the Back Bay's co-op, the getting high and cleaning became an important exercise, like creative visualization, a preview of the discipline and order with which she could survive alone if it came to that. She would get high and visualize herself solo in a dazzlingly clean space, every surface twinkling, every possession in place. She saw herself being able to pick, say, dropped popcorn up off the rug and ingest it with total confidence. An aura of steely independence surrounded her when she cleaned the co-op, even with the little whimpers and anxious moans that exited her writhing mouth when she cleaned high. The place had been provided nearly gratis by Jim, who said so little to Joelle on their first several meetings that Orin kept having to reassure her that it wasn't disapproval—Himself was missing the part of the human brain that allowed for being aware enough of other people to disapprove of them, Orin had said—or dislike. It was just how The Mad Stork was. Orin had referred to Jim as 'Himself' or 'The Mad Stork'—family nicknames, both of which gave Joelle the creeps even then.

It'd been Orin who introduced her to his father's films. The Work was then so obscure not even local students of serious film knew the name. The reason Jim kept forming his own distribution companies was to ensure distribution. He didn't become notorious until after Joelle'd met him. By then she was closer to Jim than Orin had ever been, part of which caused part of the strains that kept the brownstone co-op so terribly clean.

She'd barely thought consciously of any Incandenzas for four years before Don Gately, who for some reason kept bringing them bubbling up to mind. They were the second-saddest family Joelle'd ever seen. Orin felt Jim disliked him to the precise extent that Jim was even aware of him. Orin had spoken about his family at length, usually at night. On how no amount of punting success could erase the psychic stain of basic fatherly dislike, failure to be seen or acknowledged. Orin'd had no idea how banal and average his same-sex-parent-issues were; he'd felt they were some hideous exceptional thing. Joelle'd known her mother didn't much like her from the first time her own personal Daddy'd told her he'd rather take Pokie to the pictures alone. Much of the stuff Orin said about his family was dull, gone stale from years of never daring to say it. He credited Joelle with some strange generosity for not screaming and fleeing the room when he revealed the banal stuff. *Pokie* had been Joelle's family nickname, though her mother'd never called her anything but Joelle. The Orin she knew first felt his mother was the family's pulse and center, a ray of light incarnate, with enough depth of love and open maternal concern to almost make up for a father who barely existed, parentally. Jim's internal life was to Orin a black hole, Orin said, his father's face any room's fifth wall. Joelle had struggled to stay awake and attentive, listening, letting Orin get the stale stuff out. Orin had no idea what his father thought or felt about anything. He thought Jim wore the opaque blank facial expression his mother in French sometimes jokingly called *Le Masque*. The man was so blankly and irretrievably hidden that Orin said he'd come to see him as like autistic, almost catatonic. Jim opened himself only to the mother. They all did, he said. She was there for them all, psychically. She was the family's light and pulse and the center that held tight. Joelle could yawn in bed without looking like she was yawning. The children's name for their mother was 'the Moms.' As if there were more than one of her. His younger brother was a hopeless retard, Orin had said. Orin recalled the Moms used to tell him she loved him about a hundred times a day. It nearly made up for Himself's blank stare. Orin's basic childhood memory of Jim had been of an expressionless stare from a great height. His mother had been really tall, too, for a girl. He'd said he'd found it secretly odd that none of the brothers were taller. His retarded brother was stunted to about the size of a fire hydrant, Orin reported. Joelle cleaned behind the filthy room's radiator as far as she could reach, being careful not to touch the radiator. Orin described his childhood's mother as his emotional sun. Joelle remembered her own personal Daddy's Uncle T.S. talking about how her own personal Daddy'd thought his own Momma 'Hung the God Damn Moon,' he'd said. The radiators on Ennet House's female side stayed on at all times, 24/7/365. At first Joelle had thought Mrs. Avril Incandenza's high-watt maternal love had maybe damaged Orin by bringing into sharper relief Jim's remote self-absorption, which would have looked, by comparison, like neglect or dislike. That it had maybe made Orin too emotionally dependent on his mother—why else would he have been so traumatized when a younger brother had suddenly appeared, specially challenged from birth and in need of even more maternal attention than Orin? Orin, late one night on the co-op's futon, recalled to Joelle his skulking in and dragging a wastebasket over and inverting it next to his infant brother's special crib, holding a heavy box of Quaker Oats high above his head, preparing to brain the needy infant. Joelle had gotten an A- in Developmental Psych. the semester before. And also dependent psychologically, Orin, it seemed, or even metaphysically—Orin said he'd grown up, first in a regular house in Weston and then at the Academy in Enfield, grown up dividing the human world into those who were open, readable, trustworthy, v. those so closed and hidden that you had no clue what they thought of you but could pretty damn well imagine it couldn't be anything all that marvelous or else why hide it? Orin had recounted that he'd started to see himself getting closed and blank and hidden like that, as a tennis player, toward the end of his junior career, despite all the Moms's frantic attempts to keep him from hiddenness. Joelle had thought of B.U.'s Nickerson Field's 30,000 voices' openly roared endorsement, the sound rising with the punt to a kind of amniotic pulse of pure positive noise. Versus tennis's staid and reserved applause. It had all been so easy to figure and see, then, listening, loving Orin and feeling for him, poor little rich and prodigious boy—all this was before she came to know Jim and the Work.

Joelle scrubbed at the discolored square of fingerprints around the light-switch until the wet Kleenex disintegrated into greebles.

Never trust a man on the subject of his own parents. As tall and basso as a man might be on the outside, he nevertheless sees his parents from the perspective of a tiny child, still, and will always. And the unhappier his childhood was, the more arrested will be his perspective on it. She's learned this through sheer experience.

Greebles had been her own mother's word for the little bits of sleepy goo you got in your eyes' corners. Her own personal Daddy called them 'eye-boogers' and used to get them out for her with the twisted corner of his hankie.

Though it's not as if you could trust parents on the subject of their memory of their children either.

The cheap glass shade over the ceiling's light was black with interior grime and dead bugs. Some of the bugs looked like they might have been from long-extinct species. The loose grime alone filled half an empty Carefree box. The more stubborn crud would take a scouring pad and ammonia. Joelle put the shade aside for until she'd shot down to the kitchen to toss out different boxes of crud and wet Kleenex and grab some serious Chore-type supplies from under the sink.

Orin had said she was the third-neatnikest person he knew after his Moms and a former player he'd played with with Obsessive Compulsive Disorder, a dual diagnosis with which the U.H.I.D. membership was rife. But at the time the import had missed her. At that time it had never occurred to her that Orin's pull toward her could have had anything either pro or con to do with his mother. Her biggest worry was that Orin was pulled only by what she looked like, which her personal Daddy'd warned her the sweetest syrup draws the nastiest flies, so to watch out.

Orin hadn't been anything like her own personal Daddy. When Orin was out of the room it had never seemed like a relief. When she was home, her own Daddy never seemed to be out of the room for more than a few seconds. Her mother said she hardly even tried to talk to him when his Pokie was home. He kind of trailed her around from room to room, kind of pathetically, talking batons and low-pH chemistry. It was like when she exhaled he inhaled and vice versa. He was all through the house. He was real present at all times. His presence penetrated a room and outlasted him there. Orin's absence, whether for class or practice, emptied the co-op out. The place seemed vacuumed and buffed sterile before the cleaning even started, when he went. She didn't feel lonely in the place without him, but she did feel alone, what alone was going to feel like, and she, no one's fool,[305] was erecting fortifications real early into it.

It was Orin, of course, who'd introduced them. He'd had this stubborn idea that Himself would want to use her. In the Work. She was too pretty for somebody not to want to arrange, capture. Better Himself than some weak-chinned academic. Joelle'd protested the whole idea. She had a brainy girl's discomfort about her own beauty and its effect on folks, a caution intensified by the repeated warnings of her personal Daddy. Even more to the immediate point, her filmic interests lay behind the lens. She'd do the capturing thank you very much. She wanted to make things, not appear in them. She had a student filmmaker's vague disdain for actors. Worst, Orin's idea's real project was developmentally obvious: he thought he could somehow get to his father through her. That he pictured himself having weighty, steeple-fingered conversations with the man, Joelle's appearance and performance the subjects. A three-way bond. It made her real uneasy. She theorized that Orin unconsciously wished her to mediate between himself and 'Himself,' just as it sounded like his mother had. She was uneasy about the excited way Orin predicted that his father wouldn't be able to '*resist using*' her. She was extra uneasy about how Orin referred to his father as 'Himself.' It seemed painfully blatant, developmental-arrest-wise. Plus she felt—only a little less than she made it sound, on the futon at night, protesting—she'd felt uneasy at the prospect of any sort of connection with the man who had hurt Orin so, a man so monstrously tall and cold and remotely hidden. Joelle heard a howl and a crash from the kitchen, followed by McDade's tubercular laugh. Twice Charlotte Treat sat up in sleep, glistening with fever, and said in a flat dead voice something that sounded for all the world like 'Trances in which she did not breathe,' and then fell back, out. Joelle was trying to pin down a queer rancid-cinnamon smell that came from the back of a closet stuffed with luggage. It was especially hard to clean when you weren't supposed to be allowed to touch any other resident's stuff.

She might have known from the Work. The man's Work was amateur-ish, she'd seen, when Orin had had his brother—the unretarded one—lend them some of The Mad Stork's Read-Only copies. Was *ama-teurish* the right word? More like the work of a brilliant optician and tech-nician who was an amateur at any kind of real communication. Technically gorgeous, the Work, with lighting and angles planned out to the frame. But oddly hollow, empty, no sense of dramatic *towardness*—no narrative movement toward a real story; no emotional movement toward an audi-ence. Like conversing with a prisoner through that plastic screen using phones, the upperclassman Molly Notkin had said of Incandenza's early oeuvre. Joelle thought them more like a very smart person conversing with himself. She thought of the significance of the moniker 'Himself.' Cold. *Pre-Nuptial Agreement of Heaven and Hell*—mordant, sophisticated, campy, hip, cynical, technically mind-bending; but cold, amateurish, hid-den: no risk of empathy with the Job-like protagonist, whom she felt like the audience was induced to regard like somebody sitting atop a dunk-tank. The lampoons of 'inverted' genres: archly funny and sometimes insightful but with something provisional about them, like the finger-exercises of someone promising who refused to really sit down and play something to test that promise. Even as an under-grad Joelle'd been con-vinced that parodists were no better than camp-followers in ironic masks, satires usually the work of people with nothing new themselves to say.[306] '*The Medusa v. the Odalisque*'—cold, allusive, inbent, hostile: the only feel-ing for the audience one of contempt, the meta-audience in the film's the-ater presented as objects long before they turn to blind stone.

But there had been flashes of something else. Even in the early oeuvre, before Himself made the leap to narratively anticonfluential but unironic melodrama she helped prolong the arc of, where he dropped the technical fireworks and tried to make characters move, however inconclusively, and showed courage, abandoned everything he did well and willingly took the risk of appearing amateurish (which he had). But even in the early Work—flashes of something. Very hidden and quick. Almost furtive. She noticed them only when alone, watching, without Orin and his rheostat's dimmer, the living room's lights up high like she liked them, liked to see herself and everything else in the room with the viewer—Orin liked to sit in the dark and enter what he watched, his jaw slackening, a child raised on multichannel cable TV. But Joelle began—on repeated view-ing whose original purpose was to study how the man had blocked out scenes, for an Advanced Storyboard course she went the extra click in—she began to see little flashes of something. The *M v. O.*'s three quick cuts to the sides of the gorgeous combatants' faces, twisted past recognition with some kind of torment. Each cut to a flash of pained face had followed the crash of a petrified spectator toppling over in her chair. Three split-seconds, no more, of glimpses of facial pain. And not pain at wounds—they never touched each other, whirling with mirrors and blades; the defenses of both were impenetrable. More like as if what their beauty was doing to those drawn to watch it ate them alive, up there on stage, the flashes seemed to suggest. But just three flashes, each almost subliminally quick. Accidents? But not one shot or cut in the whole queer cold film was accidental—the thing was clearly s-boarded frame by frame. Must have taken hundreds of hours. Astounding technical anality. Joelle kept trying to Pause the cartridge on the flashes of facial torment, but these were the early days of InterLace cartridges, and the Pause still distorted the screen just enough to keep her from seeing what she wanted to study. Plus she got the creepy feeling the man had upped the film-speed in these few-frame human flashes, to thwart just such study. It was like he couldn't help putting human flashes in, but he wanted to get them in as quickly and unstudyably as possible, as if they compromised him somehow.

Orin Incandenza had been only the second boy ever to approach her in a male-female way.[307] The first had been shiny-chinned and half blind on Everclear punch, an All-Kentucky lineman for the Shiny Prize Biting Shoats team back in Shiny Prize KY, at a cookout to which the Boosters had invited the Pep and Baton girls; and the lineman had looked like a little shy boy as he confessed, by way of apologizing for almost splashing her when he threw up, that she was just too Goddamn-all petrifyingly pretty to approach any other way but liquored up past all horror. The lineman'd confessed the whole team's paralyzing horror of the prettiness of varsity Pep's top twirler, Joelle. Orin confessed to his private name for her. The memory of that H.S. afternoon remained real strong. She could smell the mesquite smoke and the blue pines and the YardGuard spray, hear the squeals of the stock they butchered and cleaned in symbolic prep for the opener against the N. Paducah Technical H.S. Rivermen. She could still see the swooning lineman, wet-lipped and confessing, keeping himself upright against an immature blue pine until the blue pine's trunk finally gave with a snap and crash.

Until that cookout and confession she'd somehow thought it was her own personal Daddy, somehow, discouraging dates and male-female approaches. The whole thing had been queer, and lonely, until she'd been approached by Orin, who made no secret of the fact that he had balls of unrejectable steel where horrifyingly pretty girls were concerned.

But it wasn't even the subjective identification she felt, watching, she felt, somehow, for the flashes and seeming non-seqs that betrayed something more than cold hip technical abstraction. Like e.g. the 240-second motionless low-angle shot of Gianlorenzo Bernini's 'Ecstasy of St. Teresa,' which—yes—ground *Pre-Nuptial...*'s dramatic movement to an annoying halt and added nothing that a 15- or 30-second still shot wouldn't have added just as well; but on the fifth or sixth reviewing Joelle started to see the four-minute motionless shot as important for what was absent: the whole film was from the alcoholic sandwich-bag salesman's POV,[308] and the alcoholic sandwich-bag salesman—or rather his head—was on-screen every moment, even when split-screened against the titanic celestial marathon seven-card-stud-with-Tarot-cards game—his rolling eyes and temples' dents and rosary of upper-lip sweat was imposed nonstop on the screen and viewer... except for the four narrative minutes the alcoholic sandwich-bag salesman stood in the Vittorio's Bernini room, and the climactic statue filled the screen and pressed against all four edges. The statue, the sensuous presence of the thing, let the alcoholic sandwich-bag salesman escape himself, his tiresome ubiquitous involuted head, she saw, was the thing. The four-minute still shot maybe wasn't just a heavy-art gesture or audience-hostile herring. Freedom from one's own head, one's inescapable P.O.V.—Joelle started to see here, oblique to the point of being hidden, an emotional thrust, since the mediated transcendence of self was just what the apparently decadent statue of the orgasmic nun claimed for itself as subject. Here then, after studious (and admittedly kind of boring) review, was an unironic, almost *moral* thesis to the campy abstract mordant cartridge: the film's climactic statue's stasis presented the theoretical subject as the emotional effect—self-forgetting as the Grail—and—in a covert gesture almost moralistic, Joelle thought as she glanced at the room-lit screen, very high, mouth writhing as she cleaned—presented the self-forgetting of alcohol as inferior to that of religion/art (since the consumption of bourbon made the salesman's head progressively swell, horrendously, until by the film's end its dimensions exceeded the frame, and he had a nasty and humiliating time squeezing it through the front door of the Vittorio).

It didn't much matter once she'd met the whole family anyhow, though. The Work and reviewings were just an inkling—usually felt on the small manageable bits of coke that helped her see deeper, harder, and so maybe not even objectively accessible in the Work itself—a lower-belly intuition that the punter's hurt take on his father was limited and arrested and maybe unreal.

With Joelle makeupless and stone-sober and hair up in a sloppy knot, the introductory supper with Orin and Himself at Legal Seafood up in Brookline[309] betrayed nothing much at all, save that the director seemed more than able to resist 'using' Joelle in any capacity—she saw the tall man slump and cringe when Orin told him the P.G.O.A.T. majored in F&C[310]—Jim'd told her later she'd seemed too conventionally, commercially pretty to consider using in any of that period's Work, part of whose theoretical project was to militate against received U.S. commercial-prettiness-conventions—and that Orin was so tense in 'Himself' 's presence that there wasn't room for any other real emotion at the table, Orin gradually beginning to fill up silences with more and faster nonstop blather until both Joelle and Jim were embarrassed at the fact that the punter hadn't touched his steamed grouper or given anyone else space for a word of reply.

Jim later told Joelle that he simply didn't know how to speak with either of his undamaged sons without their mother's presence and mediation. Orin could not be made to shut up, and Hal was so completely shut down in Jim's presence that the silences were excruciating. Jim said he suspected he and Mario were so easy with each other only because the boy had been too damaged and arrested even to speak to until he was six, so that both he and Jim had got a chance to become comfortable in mutual silence, though Mario did have an interest in lenses and film that had nothing to do with fathers or needs to please, so that the interest was something truly to share, the two of them; and even when Mario was allowed to work crew on some of Jim's later Work it was without any of the sort of pressures to interact or bond via film that there'd been with Orin and Hal and tennis, at which Jim (Orin informed her) had been a late-blooming junior but a top collegian.

Jim referred to the Work's various films as 'entertainments.' He did this ironically about half the time.

In the cab (that Jim had hailed for them), on the way back home from Legal Seafood, Orin had beaten his fine forehead against the plastic partition and wept that he couldn't seem to communicate with Himself without his mother's presence and mediation. It wasn't clear how the Moms mediated or facilitated communication between different family-members, he said. But she did. He didn't have one fucking clue how Himself felt about his abandoning a decade's tennis for punting, Orin wept. Or about Orin's being truly great at it, at something, finally. Was he proud, or jealously threatened, or judgmental that Orin had quit tennis, or what?

The 5-Woman's room's mattresses were too skinny for their frames, and the rims of the frames between the slats were appallingly clotted with dust, with female hair entwined and involved in the dust, so that it took one Kleenex just to wet the stuff down, several dry ones to wipe the muck out. Charlotte Treat had been too sick to shower for days, and her frame and slats were hard to be near.

At Joelle's first interface with the whole sad family unit—Thanksgiving, Headmaster's House, E.T.A., straight up Comm. Ave. in Enfield—Orin's Moms Mrs. Incandenza ('Please do call me Avril, Joelle') had been gracious and warm and attentive without obtruding, and worked unobtrusively hard to put everyone at ease and to facilitate communication, and to make Joelle feel like a welcomed and esteemed part of the family gathering—and something about the woman made every follicle on Joelle's body pucker and distend. It wasn't that Avril Incandenza was one of the tallest women Joelle had ever seen, and definitely the tallest pretty older woman with immaculate posture (Dr. Incandenza slumped something awful) she'd ever met. It wasn't that her syntax was so artless and fluid and imposing. Nor the near-sterile cleanliness of the home's downstairs (the bathroom's toilet seemed not only scrubbed but waxed to a high shine). And it wasn't that Avril's graciousness was in any conventional way fake. It took a long time for Joelle even to start to put a finger on what gave her the howling fantods about Orin's mother. The dinner itself—no turkey; some politico-familial in-joke about no turkey on Thanksgiving—was delicious without being grandiose. They didn't even sit down to eat until 2300h. Avril drank champagne out of a little fluted glass whose level somehow never went down. Dr. Incandenza (no invitation to call him Jim, she noticed) drank at a tri-faceted tumbler of something that made the air above it shimmer slightly. Avril put everyone at ease. Orin did credible impressions of famous figures. He and little Hal made dry fun of Avril's Canadian pronunciation of certain diphthongs. Avril and Dr. Incandenza took turns cutting up Mario's salmon. Joelle had a weird half-vision of Avril hiking her knife up hilt-first and plunging it into Joelle's breast. Hal Incandenza and two other lopsidedly muscular boys from the tennis school ate like refugees and were regarded with gentle amusement. Avril dabbed her mouth in a patrician way after every bite. Joelle wore girl-clothes, her dress's neckline very high. Hal and Orin looked vaguely alike. Avril directed every fourth comment to Joelle, to include her. Orin's brother Mario was stunted and complexly deformed. There was a spotless doggie-dish under the table, but no dog, and no mention was ever made of a dog. Joelle noticed Avril also directed every fourth comment to Orin, Hal, and Mario, like a cycle of even inclusion. There was New York white

and Albertan champagne. Dr. Incandenza drank his drink instead of
wine, and got up several times to freshen his drink in the kitchen. A massive hanging garden behind Avril's and Hal's captains' chairs cut complex
shadows into the UV light that made the table's candles' glow a weird
bright blue. The director was so tall he seemed to rise forever, when he rose
with his tumbler. Joelle had the queerest indefensible feeling that Avril
wished her ill; she kept feeling different areas of hair stand up. Everybody
Please-and-Thank-You'd in a way that was sheer Yankee WASP. After his
second trip to the kitchen, Dr. Incandenza molded his twice-baked potatoes into an intricate futuristic cityscape and suddenly started to discourse
animatedly on the 1946 breakup of Hollywood's monolithic Studio system and the subsequent rise of the Method actors Brando, Dean, Clift
et al., arguing for a causal connection. His voice was mid-range and mild
and devoid of accent. Orin's Moms had to be over two meters tall, way
taller than Joelle's own personal Daddy. Joelle could somehow tell Avril
was the sort of female who'd been ungainly as a girl and then blossomed
and but who'd only become really beautiful later in life, like thirty-five.
She'd decided Dr. Incandenza looked like an ecologically poisoned crane,
she told him later. Mrs. Incandenza put everyone at ease. Joelle imagined
her with a conductor's baton. She never did tell Jim that Orin called him
The Mad or Sad Stork. The whole Thanksgiving table inclined very subtly
toward Avril, very slightly and subtly, like heliotropes. Joelle found herself
doing it too, the inclining. Dr. Incandenza kept shading his eyes from the
UV plant-light in a gesture that resembled a salute. Avril referred to her
plants as her Green Babies. At some point out of nowhere, little Hal
Incandenza, maybe ten, announced that the basic unit of luminous intensity is the Candela, which he defined for no one in particular as the
luminous intensity of 1/600,000 of a square meter of a cavity at the
freezing-temperature of platinum. All the table's males wore coats and
ties. The larger of Hal's two tennis partners passed out dental stimulators,
and no one made fun of him. Mario's grin seemed both obscene and sincere. Hal, whom Joelle wasn't crazy about, kept asking wasn't anybody
going to ask him the freezing-temperature of platinum. Joelle and Dr.
Incandenza found themselves in a small conversation about Bazin, a
film-theorist Himself detested, making a tormented face at the name.
Joelle intrigued the optical scientist and director by explaining Bazin's
disparagement of self-conscious directorial expression as historically connected to the neo-Thomist Realism of the 'Personalistes,' an aesthetic
school of great influence over French Catholic intellectuals circa 1930–
1940—many of Bazin's teachers had been eminent Personalistes. Avril

encouraged Joelle to describe rural Kentucky. Orin did a long impression of late pop-astronomer Carl Sagan expressing televisual awe at the cosmos' scale. 'Billions and billions,' he said. One of the tennis friends burped just awfully, and no one reacted to the sound in any way. Orin said '*Billions* and *billions* and *billions*' in the voice of Sagan. Avril and Hal had a brief good-natured argument about whether the term *circa* could modify an interval or only a specific year. Then Hal asked for several examples of something called Haplology. Joelle kept fighting urges to slap the sleek little show-offy kid upside the head so hard his bow-tie would spin. 'The universe:'—Orin continued long after the wit had worn thin—'cold, immense, incredibly universal.' The subjects of tennis, baton-twirling, and punting never came up: organized sports were never once mentioned. Joelle noticed that nobody seemed to look directly at Dr. Incandenza except her. A curious flabby white mammarial dome covered part of the Academy's grounds outside the dining room's window. Mario plunged his special fork into Dr. Incandenza's potato-cityscape, to general applause and certain grating puns on the term *deconstruction* from the insufferable Hal kid. Everyone's teeth were dazzling in the candlelight and UV. Hal wiped Mario's snout, which seemed to run continuously. Avril invited Joelle by all means to make a Thanksgiving call home to her family in rural Kentucky if she wished. Orin said the Moms was herself originally from rural Québec. Joelle was on her seventh glass of wine. Orin's fingering his half-Windsor kept looking more and more like a signal to somebody. Avril urged Dr. Incandenza to find a way to include Joelle in a production, since she was both a film student and a now a heartily welcome honorary addition to the family. Mario, reaching for the salad, fell out of his chair, and was helped up by one of the tennis players amid much hilarity. Mario's deformities seemed wide-ranging and hard to name. Joelle decided he looked like a cross between a puppet and one of the big-headed carnivores from Spielberg's old special-effects orgies about reptiles. Hal and Avril hashed out whether *misspoke* was a bona fide word. Dr. Incandenza's tall narrow head kept inclining toward his plate and then slowly rising back up in a way that was either meditative or tipsy. Deformed Mario's broad smile was so constant you could have hung things from the corners of it. In a fake Southern-belle accent that was clearly no jab at Joelle, more like a Scarlett O'Hara accent, Avril said she did declare that Albertan champagne always gave her 'the vapors.' Joelle noticed that pretty much everybody at the table was smiling, broadly and constantly, eyes shiny in the plants' odd light. She was doing it herself, too, she noticed; her cheek muscles were starting to ache. Hal's larger friend kept pausing to use his dental stimulator. Nobody else was using their dental stimulator, but everyone held one politely, as if getting ready to use it. Hal and the two friends made odd spasmic one-handed squeezing motions, periodically. No one seemed to notice. Not once in Orin's presence did anyone mention the word *tennis*. He had been up half the previous night vomiting with anxiety. Now he challenged Hal to name the freezing-point of platinum. Joelle couldn't for the life of her remember either of the names of poor old Spielberg's old computer-enhanced celluloid dinosaur things, though her own Daddy'd personally taken her to each one. At some point Orin's father got up to go freshen his drink and never returned.

Just before dessert—which was on fire—Orin's Moms had asked whether they could perhaps all join hands secularly for a moment and simply be grateful for all being together. She made a special point of asking Joelle to include her hands in the hand-holding. Joelle held Orin's hand and Hal's smaller friend's hand, which was so callused up it felt like some sort of rind. Dessert was Cherries Jubilee with gourmet New Brunswick ice cream. Dr. Incandenza's absence from the table went unmentioned, almost unnoticed, it seemed. Both Hal and his nonstimulating friend pleaded for Kahlua, and Mario flapped pathetically at the tabletop in imitation. Avril made a show of gazing at Orin in mock-horror as he produced a cigar and clipper. There was also a blancmange. The coffee was decaf with chickory. When Joelle looked over again, Orin had put his cigar away without lighting it.

The dinner ended in a kind of explosion of goodwill.

Joelle'd felt half-crazed. She could detect nothing fake about the lady's grace and cheer toward her, the goodwill. And at the same time felt sure in her guts' pit that the woman could have sat there and cut out Joelle's pancreas and thymus and minced them and prepared sweetbreads and eaten them chilled and patted her mouth without batting an eye. And unremarked by all who leaned her way.

On the way back home, in a cab whose company's phone-number Hal had summoned from memory, Orin hung his leg over Joelle's crossed legs and said that if anybody could have been counted on to see that the Stork needed to use Joelle somehow, it was the Moms. He asked Joelle twice how she'd liked her. Joelle's cheek muscles ached something awful. When they got back to the brownstone co-op on that last pre-Subsidized Thanksgiving was the first historical time Joelle intentionally did lines of cocaine to keep from sleeping. Orin couldn't ingest anything during the season even if he wanted to: B.U.'s major-sport teams Tested randomly. So Joelle was awake at 0400, cleaning back behind the refrigerator for the second time, when Orin cried out in the nightmare she'd somehow felt should have been hers.

—pages 736–747

11 November
Year of the Depend Adult Undergarment

PART OF MARIO's footage for the documentary they're letting him do on this fall's E.T.A. consists of Mario just walking around different parts of the Academy with the Bolex H64 camera strapped to his head and joined by coax cable to the foot-treadle, which he holds against his sweatered chest with one hand and operates with the other. At 2100 at night it's cold out. The Center Courts are brightly lit, but only one court is being used, Gretchen Holt and Jolene Criess still winding up some sort of marathon challenge from the P.M. session, the hands around their grips bluish and sweaty hair frozen into electrified spikes, pausing between points to blow noses on sleeves, wearing so many layers of sweats they look barrel-bodied out there, and Mario doesn't bother with the change in film-speed he'd need to record them through the steamed window of Schtitt's room, where he is. The room's noise is deafening.

Coach Schtitt's room is 106, next to his office on the first floor of Comm.-Ad., past Dr. Rusk's office and down a two-corner hall from the lobby.

It's a big empty room, built for its stereo. Hardwood floor in need of sanding, a wooden chair and a cane chair, an army cot. A little low table just big enough for Schtitt's pipe rack. A folding card table folded up and leaning against the wall. Acoustic damping-tile on all the walls and nothing decorative hanging or mounted on the walls. Acoustic tiling on the ceiling also, with a bare overhead light with a long chain mounted in a dirty ceiling fan with a short chain. The fan never rotates but sometimes emits a sound of faulty wiring. There's a faint odor of Magic Marker in the room. There is nothing upholstered, no pillow on the cot, nothing soft to absorb or deflect the sound of the equipment stacked on the floor, the black Germanness of a top-shelf sound system, a Mario-sized speaker in each corner of the room with the cloth cover removed so each woofer's cone is exposed and mightily throbbing. Schtitt's room is soundproofed.

The window faces the Center Courts, the transom and observatory directly overhead and mangling the shadows of the courts' lights. The window is right over the radiator, which when the stereo is off makes odd hollow ringing clanky clunks as if someone deep underground were having at the pipes with a hammer. The cold window over the radiator is steamed and trembles slightly with Wagnerian bass.

Gerhardt Schtitt is asleep in the cane chair in the middle of the empty room, his head thrown back and arms hanging, hands treed with arteries you can see his slow pulse in. His feet are stolidly on the floor, his knees spread way out wide, the way Schtitt always has to sit, on account of his varicoceles. His mouth is partly open and a dead pipe hangs at an alarming angle from its corner. Mario records him sleeping for a little while, looking very old and white and frail, yet also obscenely fit. What's on and making the window shiver and condensed droplets gather and run in little bullet-headed lines down the glass is a duet that keeps climbing in pitch and emotion: a German second tenor and a German soprano are either very happy or very unhappy or both. Mario's ears are extremely sensitive. Schtitt sleeps only amid excruciatingly loud European opera. He's shared with Mario several different tales of grim childhood experiences at a BMW-sponsored 'Quality-Control-Orientated' Austrian Akademie to account for his REM-peculiarities. The soprano leaves the baritone and goes up to a high D and just hangs there, either shattered or ecstatic. Schtitt doesn't stir, not even when Mario falls twice, loudly, trying to get to the door with his hands over his ears.

The Community-Administration stairwells are narrow and no-nonsense. Red railings of cold iron whose red is one coat of primer. Steps and walls of raw-colored rough cement. The sort of sandy echo in there that makes you take stairs as fast as possible. The salve makes a sucking sound. The upper halls are empty. Low voices and lights from under the doors on the second floor. 2100 is still mandatory Study Period. There won't be serious movement till 2200, when the girls will drift from room to room, congregating, doing whatever packs of girls in robes and furry slippers do late at night, until deLint kills all the dormitory lights at the dorms' main breaker around 2300. Isolated movement: a door down the hall opens and shuts, the Vaught twins are heading down the hall to the bathroom at the far end, wearing only an enormous towel, one of their heads in curlers. One of the falls in Mr. Schtitt's room had been on the burnt hip, and squunched salve from the bandage is starting to darken the corduroys at that side of the pelvis, though there is zero pain. Three tense voices behind Carol Spodek and Shoshana Abram's door, lists of degrees and focal lengths, a study group for Mr. Ogilvie's 'Reflections on Refraction' exam tomorrow. A girl's voice from he can't tell which room says 'Steep hot beach sea' twice very distinctly and then is still. Mario is leaning back against a wall in the hallway, panning idly. Felicity Zweig emerges from her door by the stairwell carrying a soap-dish and wearing a towel tied at that breast-level, as if there were breasts, moving toward Mario on her way to the head. She puts her hand out straight at his head's camera, a kind of distant stiff-arm as she passes:

'I'm wearing a towel.'

'I understand,' Mario says, using his arms to turn himself around and pointing the lens at the bare wall.

'I'm wearing a *towel.*'

Brisk controlled sounds of retching from behind Diane Prins's door. Mario gets a couple seconds of Zweig hurrying away in the towel, tiny little bird steps, looking terribly fragile.

The stairwells smell like the cement they're made of.

Behind 310, Ingersoll and Penn's door, is the faint rubbery squeak of somebody moving around on crutches. Someone in 311 is yelling 'Boner check! Boner check!' A lot of the third floor is for boys under fourteen. The hall carpet up here is ectoplasmically stained, the expanses of wall between doors hung with posters of professional players endorsing gear. Someone has drawn a goatee and fangs on an old Donnay poster of Mats Wilander, and the poster of Gilbert Treffert is defaced with anti-Canadian slurs. Otis Lord's door has *Infirmary* next to his name on the door's name-card. Penn's room's door's card's name also had *Infirmary.* Sounds of someone talking low to someone who's sobbing from Beak, Whale, and Virgilio's room, and Mario resists an impulse to knock. LaMont Chu's door next door is completely covered with magazines' action-shots of matches. Mario is leaning back to get footage of the door when LaMont Chu exits the bathroom at this end in a terry robe and thongs and wet hair, literally whistling 'Dixie.'

'Mario!'

Mario gets him bearing down, his calves hairless and muscular, hair-water dripping onto his robe's shoulders with each step. 'LaMont Chu!'

'What's happening?'

'Nothing's happening!'

Chu stands there just within conversation-range. He's only slightly taller than Mario. A door down the hall opens and a head sticks out and scans and then withdraws.

'Well.' Chu squares his shoulders and looks into the camera atop Mario's head. 'You want me to say something for posterity?'

'Sure!'

'What should I say?'

'You can say anything you want!'

Chu draws himself way up and looks penetrating. Mario checks the meter on his belt and uses the treadle to shorten the focal length and adjust the angle of the camera's lens slightly downward, right at Chu, and there are tiny grinding adjustment-sounds from the Bolex.

Chu's still just standing there. 'I can't think what to say.'

'That happens to me all the time.'

'The minute your invitation became official my mind went blank.'

'That can happen.'

'There's just this staticky blank field in there now.'

'I know just what you mean.'

They stand there silent, the camera's mechanism emitting a tiny whir.

Mario says 'You just got out of the shower, I can tell.'

'I was talking with good old Lyle downstairs.'

'Lyle's terrific!'

'I was going to just whip right over into the showers, but the locker room's got this, like, odor.'

'It's always great to talk with good old Lyle.'

'So I came up here.'

'Everything you're saying is very good.'

LaMont Chu stands there a moment looking at Mario, who's smiling and Chu can tell wants to nod furiously, but can't, because he needs to keep the Bolex steady. 'What I was doing, I was filling Lyle in on the Eschaton debacle, telling him about the lack of hard info, the conflicted rumors that are going around, about how Kittenplan and some of the Big Buds are going to get blamed. About disciplinary action for the Buds.'

'Lyle's just an outstanding person to go to with concerns,' Mario says, fighting not to nod furiously.

'Lord's head and Penn's leg, the Postman's broken nose. What's going to happen to the Incster?'

'You're acting perfectly natural. This is very good.'

'I'm asking if you've heard from Hal what they're going to do, if he's in on the blame from Tavis. Pemulis and Kittenplan I can see, but I'm having trouble with the idea of Struck or your brother taking discipline for what happened out there. They were strictly from spectation for the whole thing. Kittenplan's Bud is Spodek, and she wasn't even out there.'

'I'm getting all this, you'll be glad to know.'

Chu is now looking at Mario, which for Mario is weird because he's looking through the viewfinder, a lens-eye view, which means when Chu looks down from the lens to look at Mario it looks to Mario like he's looking down south somewhere along Mario's thorax.

'Mario, I'm asking if Hal's told you what they're going to do to anybody.'

'Is this what you're saying, or are you asking me?'

'Asking.'

Chu's face looks slightly oval and convex through the lens's fish-eye, a jutting aspect. 'So what if I want to use this that you're saying for the documentary I've been asked to make?'

'Jesus, Mario, use whatever you want. I'm just saying I have conscience-trouble with the idea of Hal and Troeltsch. And Struck didn't even seem like he was conscious for the debacle itself.'

'I should tell you I feel like we're getting the totally real LaMont Chu here.'

'Mario, camera to one side, I'm standing here dripping asking you for Hal's impressions of when Tavis called them in, as in did he give you impressions. Van Vleck at lunch said he yesterday saw Pemulis and Hal coming out of Tavis's office with the Association urine-guy holding them both by the ear. Van Vleck said Hal's face was the color of Kaopectate.'

Mario directs the lens at Chu's shower-thongs so he can look over the viewfinder at Chu. 'Are you saying this, or is this what happened?'

'That's what I'm asking *you*, Mario, if Hal told you what happened.'

'I follow what you're saying.'

'So you asked whether I was asking, and I'm asking you about it.'

Mario zooms in very tight: Chu's complexion is a kind of creamy green, with not one follicle in view. 'LaMont, I'm going to find you and tell you whatever Hal tells me, this is so good.'

'So then you haven't talked to Hal?'

'When?'

'Jesus, Mario, it's like trying to talk to a rock with you sometimes.'

'This is going very well!'

Someone gargling. Guglielmo Redondo's voice going through the rosary, it sounds like, just inside his and Esteban Reynes's door. The Clipperton Suite in East House had had a bright-yellow strip of B.P.D. plastic for over a month, he remembers. The Boys Room door a different kind of wood than the room doors. The Clipperton Suite had a glued picture of Ross Reat pretending to kiss Clipperton's ring at the net. The roar of a toilet and a stall door's squeak. The Academy's plumbing is high-pressure. It takes Mario longer to walk down a set of stairs than to walk up. Red primer stains his hand, he has to hold the railing so tight.

The special hush of lobby carpet, and smells of Benson & Hedges brand cigarettes in the reception area off the lobby. The little hall doors that are always closed and never locked. The rubber sheaths on the knobs. Benson & Hedges cost $5.60 O.N.A.N. a pack at Father & Son grocery down the hill. Lateral Alice Moore's desk's plaque's DANGER: THIRD RAIL light is unilluminated, and her word-processing setup wears its cover of frosted plastic. The blue chairs have the faint imprints of people's bottoms. The waiting room is empty and dim. Some light from the lit courts outside. From under double doors is lamplight, much attenuated by double doors, from the Headmaster's office, which Mario doesn't explore; Tavis is unnerved into such gregarity around Mario it's awkward for all parties.[316] If you asked Mario whether he got on with his Uncle C.T. he'd say: Sure. The Bolex's light-meter is in the No Way range. Most of the waiting area's available light comes from the doorless Dean of Females's office. Meaning the Moms is: In.

Heavy shag carpet is especially treacherous for Mario when he's top-heavy with equipment. Avril Incandenza, a fiend for light, has the whole bank of overheads going, two torchères and some desk lamps, and a B&H cigarette on fire in the big clay ashtray Mario'd made her at Rindge and Latin School. She is swivelled around in her swivel-chair, facing out the big window behind her desk, listening to someone on the phone, holding the transmitter violin-style under her chin and holding up a stapler, checking its load. Her desk has what looks like a skyline of stacks of file folders and books in neat cross-hatched stacks; nothing teeters. The open book on top facing Mario is Dowty, Wall and Peters's seminal *Introduction to Montague Semantics,*[317] which has very fascinating illustrations that Mario doesn't look at this time, trying to film the cock of the Moms's head and the phone's extended antenna against the cumulus of her hair from behind, capturing her back unawares.

But the sound of Mario entering even a shag-carpeted room is unmistakable, plus she can see his reflection in the window.

'Mario!' Her arms go up in a V, stapler open in one hand, facing the window.

'The Moms!' It's a good ten meters past the seminar table and viewer and portable blackboard to the far part of the office where the desk is, and each step on the deep shag is precarious, Mario resembling a very old brittle-boned man or someone carrying a load of breakables down a slick hill.

'Hel*lo!*' She's addressing his reflection in the quartered window, watching him put the treadle down carefully on the desk and struggle with the pack on his back. 'Not you,' she tells the phone. She points the stapler at the image of the Bolex on the image of his head. 'Are we On-Air?'

Mario laughs. 'Would you like to be?'

She tells the phone she's still here, that Mario's come in.

'I don't want to intercept your call.'

'Don't be absurd.' She talks past the phone at the window. She rotates her swivel-chair to face Mario, the receiver's antenna describing a half moon and now pointing up at the window behind her. There are two blue chairs like the reception-area chairs in front of her desk; she doesn't indicate to Mario to sit. Mario's most comfortable standing and leaning into the support of the police lock he's trying to detach from his canvas plastron and lower, shucking the pack off his back at the same time. Avril looks at him like the sort of stellar mother where just looking at her kid gives her joy. She doesn't offer to help him get the lock's lead brace out of the pack because she knows he'd feel completely comfortable asking for her help if he needed it. It's like she feels these two sons are the people in her life with whom so little important needs to be said that she loves it. The Bolex and support-yoke and viewfinder over his forehead and eyes give Mario an underwater look. His movements, setting and bracing his police lock, are at once graceless and deft. The lit Center Courts, now empty, are visible out the left side of Avril's window, if you lean far forward and look. Someone has forgotten a gear bag and pile of sticks out by the net-post of Court 17.

Silences between them are totally comfortable. Mario can't tell if the person on the phone is still talking or if Avril just hasn't put the dead phone down. She still holds the black stapler. Its jaws are open and it looks alligatorish in her hand.

'Is this you passing through the neighborhood poking a head in to say hello? Or am I a subject, tonight?'

'You can be a subject, Moms.' He moves the big head around in a weary circle. 'I get tired from wearing this.'

'It gets heavy. I've held it.'

'It's good.'

'I remember his making that. He took such care making that. It's the last time I believe he enjoyed himself on something, thoroughly.'

'It's terrific!'

'He took weeks putting everything together.'

He likes to look at her, too, leaning in and letting her know he likes looking. They are the two least embarrassable people either of them knows. She's rarely here this late; she has a big study at the HmH. The only thing that ever shows she's tired is that her hair gets a sort of huge white cowlick, like a rolling ocean comber of hair, and just on one side, the side with the phone, sticking up and touching the antenna. Her hair has been pure white since Mario can first remember seeing her looking down at him through the incubator's glass. Pictures of her own father's hair were like that. It goes down the middle of her back against the chair and down both arms, hanging off the arms near the elbow. Its part shows her pink scalp. She keeps the hair very clean and well-combed. She has one of Mr. deLint's big whistles around her neck. The big cowlick casts a bent shadow on the sill of the window. There's a maple-leaf flag and a 50-star U.S.A. flag hanging limp off brass poles on either side of the window; in an extreme corner are fleur-de-lis pennons on tall sharp polished sticks. C.T.'s office has an O.N.A.N. flag and a 49-star U.S.A. flag.[318]

'I had quality interface dialogue with LaMont Chu upstairs. But I made the girl Felicity, the really thin one—she got upset. She said only a towel.'

'Felicity will be just fine. So you're just strolling. Peripatetic footage.' She refuses to adjust syntax, to speak in any way down to him, it'd be beneath him, though he seems not to mind when most people do it, speak down.

Nor will she ask about the burn on his pelvis unless he brings it up. She's careful to keep her oar out of Mario's health stuff unless he brings things up, out of concern that it might be taken as intrusive or smothering.

'I saw your lights. Why is the Moms here, still, I thought to myself.'

She made as if to clutch her head. 'Don't ask. I'll starting whingeing. Tomorrow's going to be hellishly busy.' Mario didn't hear her say good-bye to the man as she put down the phone so the antenna now points at Mario's chest. She's putting out the nub of the Benson & Hedge against the rooster-comb holder he'd squeezed and karate-chopped and put down the bowl's center, when he made it, after she'd said she wanted it to be an ashtray. 'You give me such pleasure standing there, all outfitted for work,' she said. 'Aprowl.' She ground individual sparks out in the bowl. She had the idea that her smoking around Mario made him worry, though he'd never said anything about it one way or the other. 'I have a breakfast engagement at 07, which means I have to do final swotting and whacking for morning classes now, so I just lurched back over here to do it instead of carrying everything back and forth.'

'Are you tired?'

She just smiled at him.

'This is off.' Pointing at his head. 'I turned it off.'

To look at them, you'd never guess these two persons were related, one sitting and one standing canted forward.

'Will you eat with us? I hadn't even thought of dinner until I saw you. I don't even know what there might be for dinner. Many Wonders.[319] Turkey cartilage. Your bag is by the radio. Will you stay again? Charles is still in conference, I believe, he said.'

'About the debracle with the Eschaton and the Postman's nose?'

'A person from a magazine has come to do a piece of reportage on your brother. Charles is speaking to her in lieu of any of the students. You may speak to her about Orin if you like.'

'She's been *aprowl* for Hal, Ortho said.'

Avril has a certain way of cocking her fine head at him.

'Your poor Uncle Charles has been with Thierry and this magazine person since this afternoon.'

'Have you talked to him?'

'I've been trying to buttonhole your brother. He's not in your room. The Pemulis person was seen by Mary Esther taking their truck before Study Period. Is Hal with him, Mario?'

'I haven't seen Hal since lunchtime. He said he'd had a tooth thing.'

'I didn't even find out he'd been to see Zeggarelli until today.'

'He asked about how the burn on my pelvis is.'

'Which I won't ask about unless you'd care to discuss how it's coming along.'

'It's fine. Plus Hal said he wishes I'd come back and sleep there.'

'I left two messages asking him to let me know how the tooth was. Love-o, I feel bad I wasn't there for him. Hal and his teeth.'

'Did C.T. tell what happened? Was he upset? Was that C.T. on the phone you were with?' Mario can't see why the Moms would call C.T. on the phone when he was in there right across the hall behind his doors. When she didn't smoke a lot of the time she held a pen in her mouth; Mario didn't know why. Her college mug has about a hundred blue pens in it, on the desk. She likes to square herself in her chair, sitting up extra straight and grasping the chair's arms in a commanding posture. She looks like something Mario can't place when she does this. He keeps thinking the word *typhoon*. He knows she's not trying to consciously be commanding with him.

'How was your own day, I want to hear.'

'Hey Moms?'

'I determined years ago that my position needs to be that I trust my children, and I'd never traffic in third-party hearsay when the lines of communication with my children are as open and judgment-free as I'm fortunate they are.'

'That seems like a really good position. Hey Moms?'

'So I have no problem waiting to hear about Eschaton, teeth, and urine from your brother, who'll come to me the moment it's appropriate for him to come to me.'

'Hey Moms?'

'I'm right here, Love-o.'

Tycoon is the term her commanding way of sitting suggests, grasping her chair, a pen clamped in her teeth like a businessman's cigar. There were other carpet-prints in the heavy shag.

'Moms?'

'Yes.'

'Can I ask you a thing?'

'Please do.'

'This is off,' again indicating the silent apparatus on his head.

'Is this a confidential thing, then?'

'There isn't any secret. My day was I was wondering about something. In my mind.'

'I'm right here for you anytime day or night, Mario, as you are for me, as I am for Hal and we all are for each other.' She gestures in a hard-to-describe way. 'Right here.'

'Moms?'

'I am right here with my attention completely focused on you.'

'How can you tell if somebody's sad?'

A quick smile. 'You mean whether someone's sad.'

A smile back, but still earnest: 'That improves it a lot. *Whether* someone's sad, how can you tell so you're sure?'

Her teeth are not discolored; she gets them cleaned at the dentist all the time for the smoking, a habit she despises. Hal inherited the dental problems from Himself; Himself had horrible dental problems; half his teeth were bridges.

'You're not exactly insensitive when it comes to people, Love-o,' she says.

'What if you, like, only *suspect* somebody's sad. How do you reinforce the suspicion?'

'Confirm the suspicion?'

'In your mind.' Some of the prints in the deep shag he can see are shoes, and some are different, almost like knuckles. His lordotic posture makes him acute and observant about things like carpet-prints.

'How would I, for my part, confirm a suspicion of sadness in someone, you mean?'

'Yes. Good. All right.'

'Well, the person in question may cry, sob, weep, or, in certain cultures, wail, keen, or rend his or her garments.'

Mario nods encouragingly, so the headgear clanks a little. 'But say in a case where they don't weep or rend. But you still have a suspicion which they're sad.'

She uses a hand to rotate the pen in her mouth like a fine cigar. 'He or she might alternatively sigh, mope, frown, smile halfheartedly, appear downcast, slump, look at the floor more than is appropriate.'

'But what if they don't?'

'Well, he or she may act out by seeming distracted, losing enthusiasm for previous interests. The person may present with what appears to be laziness, lethargy, fatigue, sluggishness, a certain passive reluctance to engage you. Torpor.'

'What else?'

'They may seem unusually subdued, quiet, literally "low." '

Mario leans all his weight into his police lock, which makes his head jut, his expression the sort of mangled one that expresses puzzlement, an attempt to reason out something hard. Pemulis called it Mario's Data-Search Face, which Mario liked.

'What if sometime they might act even less low than normal. But still these suspicions are in your mind.'

She's about the same height sitting as Mario upright and leaning forward. Now neither of them is quite looking at the other, both just a couple degrees off. Avril taps the pen against her front teeth. Her phone light is blinking, but there's no ringing. The thing's handset's antenna still points at Mario. Her hands are not her age. She hoists the executive chair back slightly to cross her legs.

'Would you feel comfortable telling me whether we're discussing a particular person?'

'Hey Moms?'

'Is there someone specific in whom you're intuiting sadness?'

'Moms?'

'Is this about Hal? Is Hal sad and for some reason not yet able to speak about it?'

'I'm just saying how to be generally sure.'

'And you have no idea where he is or whether he left the grounds this evening sad?'

Lunch today was the exact same as lunch yesterday: pasta with tuna and garlic, and thick wheaty bread, and required salad, and milk or juice, and pears in juice in a dish. Mrs. Clark had taken a Sick Morning off because when she came in this morning Pemulis at lunch said one of the breakfast girls had said there'd been brooms on the wall in an X of brooms, out of nowhere, on the wall, when she'd come in very early to fire up the Wheatina-cauldron, and nobody knowing how the brooms were there or why or who glued them on had upset Mrs. Clarke's nerves, who'd been with the Incandenzas since long before E.T.A., and had nerves.

'I didn't see Hal since lunchtime. He had an apple he cut into chunks and put peanut butter on, instead of pears in juice.'

Avril nods with vigor.

'LaMont didn't know either. Mr. Schtitt is asleep in his chair in his room. Hey Moms?'

Avril Incandenza can switch a Bic from one side of her mouth to the other without using her hand; she never knows she's doing it when she's doing it. 'Whether or not we're discussing anyone in particular, then.'

Mario smiles at her.

'Hypothetically, then, you may be picking up in someone a certain very strange type of sadness that appears as a kind of disassociation from itself, maybe, Love-o.'

'I don't know *disassociation*.'

'Well, love, but you know the idiom "not yourself" — "He's not himself today," for example,' crooking and uncrooking fingers to form quotes on either side of what she says, which Mario adores. 'There are, apparently, persons who are deeply afraid of their own emotions, particularly the painful ones. Grief, regret, sadness. Sadness especially, perhaps. Dolores describes these persons as afraid of obliteration, emotional engulfment. As if something truly and thoroughly felt would have no end or bottom. Would become infinite and engulf them.'

'*Engulf* means *obliterate*.'

'I am saying that such persons usually have a very fragile sense of themselves as persons. As existing at all. This interpretation is "existential," Mario, which means vague and slightly flaky. But I think it may hold true in certain cases. My own father told stories of his own father, whose potato farm had been in St. Pamphile and very much larger than my father's. My grandfather had had a marvelous harvest one season, and he wanted to invest money. This was in the early 1920s, when there was a great deal of money to be made on upstart companies and new American products. He apparently narrowed the field to two choices—Delaware-brand Punch, or an obscure sweet fizzy coffee substitute that sold out of pharmacy soda fountains and was rumored to contain smidgeons of cocaine, which was the subject of much controversy in those days. My father's father chose Delaware Punch, which apparently tasted like rancid cranberry juice, and the manufacturer of which folded. And then his next two potato harvests were decimated by blight, resulting in the forced sale of his farm. Coca-Cola is now Coca-Cola. My father said his father showed very little emotion or anger or sadness about this, though. That he somehow couldn't. My father said his father was frozen, and could feel emotion only when he was drunk. He would apparently get drunk four times a year, weep about his life, throw my father through the living room window, and disappear for several days, roaming the countryside of L'Islet Province, drunk and enraged.'

She's not been looking at Mario this whole time, though Mario's been looking at her.

She smiled. 'My father, of course, could himself tell this story only when *he* was drunk. He never threw anyone through any windows. He simply sat in his chair, drinking ale and reading the newspaper, for hours, until he fell out of the chair. And then one day he fell out of the chair and didn't get up again, and that was how your maternal grandfather passed away. I'd never have gotten to go to University had he not died when I was a girl. He believed education was a waste for girls. It was a function of his era; it wasn't his fault. His inheritance to Charles and me paid for university.'

She's been smiling pleasantly this whole time, emptying the butt from the ashtray into the wastebasket, wiping the bowl's inside with a Kleenex, straightening straight piles of folders on her desk. A couple odd long crinkly paper strips of bright red hung over the side of the wastebasket, which was normally totally empty and clean.

Avril Incandenza is the sort of tall beautiful woman who wasn't ever quite world-class, shiny-magazine-class beautiful, but who early on hit a certain pretty high point on the beauty scale and has stayed right at that point as she ages and lots of other beautiful women age too and get less beautiful. She's 56 years old, and Mario gets pleasure out of just getting to look at her face, still. She doesn't think she's pretty, he knows. Orin and Hal both have parts of her prettiness in different ways. Mario likes to look at Hal and at their mother and try to see just what slendering and spacing of different features makes a woman's face different from a man's, in attractive people. A male face versus a face you can just tell is female. Avril thinks she's much too tall to be pretty. She'd seemed much less tall when compared to Himself, who was seriously tall. Mario wears small special shoes, almost perfectly square, with weights at the heel and Velcro straps instead of laces, and a pair of the corduroys Orin Incandenza had worn in elementary school, which Mario still favors and wears instead of brand-new pants he's given, and a warm crewneck sweater that's striped like a flea.

'My point here is that certain types of persons are terrified even to poke a big toe into genuinely felt regret or sadness, or to get angry. This means they are afraid to live. They are imprisoned in something, I think. Frozen inside, emotionally. Why is this. No one knows, Love-o. It's sometimes called "suppression,"' with the fingers out to the sides again. 'Dolores believes it derives from childhood trauma, but I suspect not always. There may be some persons who are born imprisoned. The irony, of course, being that the very imprisonment that prohibits sadness's expression must itself feel intensely sad and painful. For the hypothetical person in question. There may be sad people right here at the Academy who are like this, Mario, and perhaps you're sensitive to it. You are not exactly insensitive when it comes to people.'

Mario scratches his lip again.

She says 'What I'll do'—leaning forward to write something on a Post-It note with a different pen than the one she has in her mouth—'is to write down for you the terms *disassociation, engulfment,* and *suppression,* which I'll put next to another word, *repression,* with an underlined unequal sign between them, because they denote entirely different things and should not be regarded as synonyms.'

Mario shifts slightly forward. 'Sometimes I get afraid when you forget you have to talk more simply to me.'

'Well then I'm both sorry for that and grateful that you can tell me about it. I do forget things. Particularly when I'm tired. I forget and just get going.' Lining the edges up and folding the little sticky note in half and then half again and dropping it into the wastebasket without having to look for where the wastebasket is. Her chair is a fine executive leather swivelling chair but it shrieks a little when she leans back or forward. Mario can tell she's making herself not look at her watch, which is all right.

'Hey Moms?'

'People, then, who are sad, but who can't let themselves feel sad, or express it, the sadness, I'm trying rather clunkily to say, these persons may strike someone who's sensitive as somehow just not quite right. Not quite there. Blank. Distant. Muted. Distant. *Spacey* was an American term we grew up with. Wooden. Deadened. Disconnected. Distant. Or they may drink alcohol or take other drugs. The drugs both blunt the real sadness and allow some skewed version of the sadness some sort of expression, like throwing someone through a living room window out into the flowerbeds she'd so very carefully repaired after the last incident.'

'Moms, I think I get it.'

'Is that better, then, instead of my maundering on and on?'

She's risen to pour herself coffee from the last black bit in the glass pot. So her back is almost to him as she stands there at the little sideboard. An old folded pair of U.S.A. football pants and a helmet are on top of one of the file cabinets by the flag. Her one memento of Orin, who won't talk to them or contact them in any way. She has an old mug with a cartoon of someone in a dress small and perspectively distant in a knee-high field of wheat or rye, that says *TO A WOMAN OUTSTANDING IN HER FIELD*. A blue blazer with an O.N.A.N.T.A. insignia is hung very neatly and straight on a wooden hanger from the metal tree of the coatrack in the corner. She's always had her coffee out of the *OUTSTANDING FIELD* mug, even in Weston. The Moms hangs up stuff like shirts and blazers neater and more wrinkle-free than anyone alive. The mug has a hair-thin brown crack down one side, but it's not dirty or stained, and she never gets lipstick on the rim the way other ladies over fifty years old pinken cups' rims.

Mario was involuntarily incontinent up to his early teens. His father and later Hal had changed him for years, never once judging or wrinkling their face or acting upset or sad.

'But except hey Moms?'

'I'm still right here.'

Avril couldn't change diapers. She'd come to him in tears, he'd been seven, and explained, and apologized. She just couldn't handle diapers. She just couldn't deal with them. She'd sobbed and asked him to forgive her and to assure her that he understood it didn't mean she didn't love him to death or find him repellent.

'Can you be sensitive to something sad even though the person isn't not himself?'

She especially likes to hold the coffee's mug in both hands. 'Pardon me?'

'You explained it very well. It helped a lot. Except what if it's that they're almost like even *more* themselves than normal? Than they were before? If it's not that he's blank or dead. If he's himself even more than before a sad thing happened. What if that happens and you still think he's sad, inside, somewhere?'

One thing that's happened as she got over fifty is she gets a little red sideways line in the skin between her eyes when she doesn't follow you. Ms. Poutrincourt gets the same little line, and she's twenty-eight. 'I don't follow you. How can someone be too much himself?'

'I think I wanted to ask you that.'

'Are we discussing your Uncle Charles?'

'Hey Moms?'

She pretends to knock her forehead at being obtuse. 'Mario Love-o, are *you* sad? Are you trying to determine whether I've been sensing that you *yourself* are sad?'

Mario's gaze keeps going from Avril to the window behind her. He can activate the Bolex's foot-treadle with his hands, if necessary. The Center Courts' towering lights cast an odd pall up and out into the night. The sky has a wind in it, and dark thin high clouds whose movement's pattern has a kind of writhing weave. All this is visible out past the faint reflections of the lit room, and up, the tennis lights' odd small lumes like criss-crossing spots.

'Though of course the sun would leave my sky if I couldn't assume you'd simply come and tell me you were sad. There would be no need for intuition about it.'

And plus then to the east, past all the courts, you can see some lights in houses in the Enfield Marine Complex below, and beyond that Commonwealth's cars' headers and store lights and the robed lit lady's downcast-looking statue atop St. Elizabeth's Hospital. Out the right to the north over lots of different lights is the red rotating tip of the WYYY transmitter, its spin's ring of red reflected in the visible Charles River, the Charles tumid with rain and snowmelt, illumined in patches by headlights on Memorial and the Storrow 500, the river unwinding, swollen and humped, its top a mosaic of oil rainbows and dead branches, gulls asleep or brooding, bobbing, head under wing.

The dark had a distanceless shape. The room's ceiling might as well have been clouds.

'Skkkkk.'

'Booboo?'

'Skk-kkk.'

'Mario.'

'Hal!'

'Were you asleep there, Boo?'

'I don't think I was.'

'Cause I don't want to wake you up if you were.'

'Is it dark or is it me?'

'The sun won't be up for a while, I don't think.'

'So it's dark then.'

'Booboo, I just had a wicked awful dream.'

'You were saying "Thank you Sir may I have another" several times.'

'Sorry Boo.'

'Numerous times.'

'Sorry.'

'I think I slept right through it.'

'Jesus, you can hear Schacht snoring all the way across. You can feel the snores' vibrations in your midsection.'

'I slept right through it. I didn't hear you even come in.'

'Quite a nice surprise to come in and see the good old many-pillowed Mario-shape in his rack again.'

'...'

'I hope you didn't move the bag back here just because it sounded like I might have been asking you. To.'

'I found somebody with tapes of old Psychosis, for until the return. I need you to show me how to ask somebody I don't know to borrow tapes, if we're both devoted.'

'...'

'Hey Hal?'

'Booboo, I dreamed I was losing my teeth. I dreamed that my teeth dry-rotted somehow into shale and splintered when I ate or spoke, and I was jettisoning fragments all over the place, and there was a long scene where I was pricing dentures.'

'All night last night people were coming up going where is Hal, have you seen Hal, what happened with CT and the urine doctor and Hal's urine. Moms asked me where's Hal, and I was surprised at that because of how she makes it a big point never to check up.'

'Then, without any sort of dream-segue, I'm sitting in a cold room, naked as a jaybird, in a flame-retardant chair, and I keep receiving bills in the mail for teeth. A mail carrier keeps knocking on the door and coming in without being invited and presenting me with various bills for teeth.'

'She wants you to know she trusts you at all times and you're too trustworthy to worry about or check up on.'

'Only not for any teeth of mine, Boo. The bills are for somebody *else's* teeth, not my teeth, and I can't seem to get the mail carrier to acknowledge this, that they're not for my teeth.'

'I promised LaMont Chu I'd tell him whatever information you told me, he was so concerned.'

'The bills are in little envelopes with plasticized windows that show the addressee part of the bills. I put them in my lap until the stack gets so big they start to slip off the top and fall to the floor.'

'LaMont and me had a whole dialogue about his concerns. I like LaMont a lot.'

'Booboo, do you happen to remember S. Johnson?'

'S. Johnson used to be the Moms's dog. That passed away.'

'And you remember how he died, then.'

'Hey Hal, you remember a period in time back in Weston when we were little that the Moms wouldn't go anywhere without S. Johnson? She took him with her to work, and had that unique car seat for him when she had the Volvo, before Himself had the accident in the Volvo. The seat was from the Fisher-Price Company. We went to Himself's opening of *Kinds of Light* at the Hayden[320] that wouldn't let in cigarettes or dogs and the Moms brought S. Johnson in a blind dog's harness-collar that went all the way around his chest with the square bar on the leash thing and the Moms wore those sunglasses and looked up and to the right the whole time so it looked like she was legally blind so they'd let S.J. into the Hayden with us, because he had to be there. And how Himself just thought it was a good one on the Hayden, he said.'

'I keep thinking about Orin and how he stood there and lied to her about S. Johnson's map getting eliminated.'

'She was sad.'

'I've been thinking compulsively about Orin ever since C.T. called us all in. When you think about Orin what do you think, Boo?'

'The best was remember when she had to fly and wouldn't put him in a cagey box and they wouldn't even let a blind dog on the plane, so she'd leave S. Johnson and leave him out tied to the Volvo and she'd make Orin put a phone out there with its antenna up during the day out by where S. Johnson was tied to the Volvo and she'd call on the phone and let it ring next to S. Johnson because she said how S. Johnson knew her unique personal ring on the phone and would hear the ring and know that he was thought about and cared about from afar, she said?'

'She was unbent where that dog was concerned, I remember. She bought some kind of esoteric food for it. Remember how often she bathed it?

'. . .'

'What was it with her and that dog, Boo?'

'And the day we were out rolling balls in the driveway and Orin and Marlon were there and S. Johnson was there lying there on the driveway tied to the bumper with the phone right there and it rang and rang and Orin picked it up and barked into it like a dog and hung it up and turned it off?'

'. . .'

'So she'd think it was S. Johnson? The joke that Orin thought was such a good one?'

'Jesus, Boo, I don't remember any of that.'

'And he said we'd get Indian Rub-Burns down both arms if we didn't pretend how we didn't know what she was talking about if and when she asked us about the bark on the phone when she got home?'

'The Indian Rub-Burns I remember far too well.'

'We were supposed to shrug and look at her like she was minus cards from her deck, or else?'

'Orin lied with a really pathological intensity, growing up, is what I've been remembering.'

'He made us laugh really hard a lot of times, though. I miss him.'

'I don't know whether I miss him or not.'

'I miss Family Trivia. Do you remember four times he let us sit in on when they played Family Trivia?'

'You've got a phenomenal memory for this stuff, Boo.'

'. . .'

'You probably think I'm wondering why you don't ask me about the thing with C.T. and Pemulis and the impromptu urine, after the Eschaton debacle, where the urologist took us right down to the administrative loo and was going to watch personally while we filled his cups, like watch it go in, the urine, to make sure it came from us personally.'

'I think I especially have a phenomenal memory for things I remember that I liked.'

'You can ask, if you like.'

'Hey Hal?'

'The key datum is that the O.N.A.N.T.A. guy didn't actually extract urine samples from us. We got to hold on to our urine, as the Moms no doubt knows quite well, don't kid yourself, from C.T.'

'I have a phenomenal memory for things that make me *laugh* is what I think it is.'

'That Pemulis, without self-abasement or concession of anything compromising, got the guy to give us thirty days—the Fundraiser, the WhataBurger, Thanksgiving Break, then Pemulis, Axford and I pee like racehorses into whatever-sized receptacles he wants, is the arrangement we made.'

'I can hear Schacht, you're right. Also the fans.'

'Boo?'

'I like the fans' sound at night. Do you? It's like somebody big far away goes like: it'sOKit'sOKit'sOKit'sOK, over and over. From very far away.'

'Pemulis—the alleged weak-stomached clutch-artist—Pemulis showed some serious brass under pressure, standing there over that urinal. He played the O.N.A.N.T.A. man like a fine instrument. I found myself feeling almost proud for him.'

'. . .'

'You might think I'm wondering why you aren't asking me why thirty days, why it was so important to extract thirty days from the blue-blazered guy before a G.C./M.S. scan. As in what is there to be afraid of, you might ask.'

'Hal, pretty much all I do is love you and be glad I have an excellent brother in every way, Hal.'

'Jesus, it's just like talking to the Moms with you sometimes, Boo.'

'Hey Hal?'

'Except with you I can feel you mean it.'

'You're up on your elbow. You're on your side, facing my way. I can see your shadow.'

'How does somebody with your kind of Panglossian constitution determine whether you're ever being lied to, I sometimes wonder, Booboo. Like what criteria brought to bear. Intuition, induction, reductio, what?'

'You always get hard to understand when you're up on your side on your elbow like this.'

'Maybe it just doesn't occur to you. Even the possibility. Maybe it's never once struck you that something's being fabricated, misrepresented, skewed. Hidden.'

'Hey Hal?'

'And maybe that's the key. Maybe then whatever's said to you is so completely believed by you that, what, it becomes sort of true in transit. Flies through the air toward you and reverses its spin and hits you true, however mendaciously it comes off the other person's stick.'

'. . .'

'You know, for me, Boo, people seem to lie in different but definite ways, I've found. Maybe I can't change the spin the way you can, and this is all I've been able to do, is assemble a kind of field guide to the different kinds of ways.'

'. . .'

'Some people, from what I've seen, Boo, when they lie, they become very still and centered and their gaze very concentrated and intense. They try to dominate the person they lie to. The person to whom they're lying. Another type becomes fluttery and insubstantial and punctuates his lie with little self-deprecating motions and sounds, as if credulity were the same as pity. Some bury the lie in so many digressions and asides that they like try to slip the lie in there through all the extraneous data like a tiny bug through a windowscreen.'

'Except Orin used to end up telling the truth even when he didn't think he was.'

'Would that that were a trait family-wide, Boo.'

'Maybe if we call him he'll come to the WhataBurger. You can see him if you want to if you ask, maybe.'

'Then there are what I might call your Kamikaze-style liars. These'll tell you a surreal and fundamentally incredible lie, and then pretend a crisis of conscience and retract the original lie, and then offer you the lie they really want you to buy instead, so the real lie'll appear as some kind of concession, a settlement with truth. That type's mercifully easy to see through.'

'The merciful type of lie.'

'Or then the type who sort of overelaborates on the lie, buttresses it with rococo formations of detail and amendment, and that's how you can always tell. Pemulis was like that, I always thought, til his performance over the urinal.'

'*Rococo*'s a pretty word.'

'So now I've established a subtype of the over-elaborator type. This is the liar who used to be an over-elaborator and but has somehow snapped to the fact that rococo elaborations give him away every time, so he changes and now lies tersely, sparely, seeming somehow bored, like what he's saying is too obviously true to waste time on.'

'. . .'

'I've established that as a sort of subtype.'

'You sound like you can always tell.'

'Pemulis could have sold that urologist land in there, Boo. It was an incredibly high-pressure moment. I never thought he had it in him. He was nerveless and stomachless. He projected a kind of weary pragmatism the urologist found impossible to discount. His face was a brass mask. It was almost frightening. I told him I never would have believed he had that kind of performance in him.'

'Psychosis live on the radio used to read an Eve Arden beauty brochure all the time where Eve Arden says: "The importance of a mask is to increase your circulation," quote.'

'The truth is nobody can *always* tell, Boo. Some types are just too good, too complex and idiosyncratic; their lies are too close to the truth's heart for you to tell.'

'I can't ever tell. You wanted to know. You're right. It never crosses my mind.'

'...'

'I'm the type that'd buy land, I think.'

'You remember my hideous phobic thing about monsters, as a kid?'

'Boy do I ever.'

'Boo, I think I no longer believe in monsters as faces in the floor or feral infants or vampires or whatever. I think at seventeen now I believe the only real monsters might be the type of liar where there's simply no way to tell. The ones who give nothing away.'

'But then how do you know they're monsters, then?'

'That's the monstrosity right there, Boo, I'm starting to think.'

'Golly Ned.'

'That they walk among us. Teach our children. Inscrutable. Brass-faced.'

—pages 755–774

Afterword

Here is Mario, severely deformed, burdened by backpack of lead and steel, Bolex camera mounted to his oversized head and co-axialed operating treadle to his square feet, walking-and-recording through the cold night. He's making a documentary for the Academy, searching for the real. He's good at his job—people forget he's there, drop their guard; when they talk they find that he listens, intently, nonjudgmentally. It's hard not to see Mario as a tragic incarnation of Wallace's *ars poetica,* hard not to despair at the corollary that the world, people, the *real,* may avail itself only to an artist who is apart, somehow stunted, somehow removed from feeling. The artist, given to recognizing life as material for art, becomes pinned beneath his own lens, becomes himself twisted by the process of twisting real into simulacrum.

(Mario interviewing LaMont Chu: "I should tell you I feel like we're getting the totally real LaMont Chu here.")

But Mario—epistemically bent, familial-dysautonomic—nevertheless feels. He may be insensate in the way of those invulnerable to others' opinions of them, but he loves. He loves Hal "so much it makes his heart beat hard." And he can't tell if Hal is sad. Is it in spite of or because of his specific love that he can't tell? "Mario, you and I are mysterious to each other," Hal says. (See too: "Jim's internal life was to Orin a black hole"; "Avril Incandenza believes she knows him inside and out as a human being…when in fact inside Hal there's pretty much nothing at all, he knows.") It's hard not to see Mario as a tragic totem of Wallace's metaphysics of love, hard not to despair at the implication that even a love as true and pure as Mario's for Hal can never apprehend, let alone dissolve, the gap between them.

What's left, then? Without true connection, communication. In Wallace's work—and this is what makes his work so singular, so necessary—art and ethics are conflated. The problem of art is a moral one: how are we to treat each other? Mario is sought out, trusted, and loved (by all but Orin) because he is good; he is open, empathetic, whole in his beliefs. His laugh is unfractioned, clutch-your-stomach happy. He likes Madame Psychosis because she talks about "heartbreak and people you loved dying and U.S. woe, stuff that was real"; similarly, he likes Ennet House because "it's very real: people are crying and making noise and getting less unhappy, and once he heard somebody say *God* with a straight face and nobody looked at them or looked down or smiled in any sort of way where you could tell they were worried inside."

Here's the thing: Mario exists without irony or self-consciousness; his notion of *realness* reflects this. What you see is what you get. But here's the thing: some of us — the rest of us? — *are* self-conscious, selfish, secretive, insecure. Vain and agitable. We cannot always tell the truth, cannot always laugh without social-gauging or self-looking, cannot stop ourselves acting from fear of being judged, being seen as naive. Through our self-consciousness, we are capable of twisting openness into something inbent, completely other-excluding (C.T.); twisting empathy into a tool of contempt, making people "Subjects" to be seduced to their own ruin (Orin); twisting graciousness into something creepy, not *right*, a form of emotional ransom — consummate mind-fuckery (Avril).

Unlike Mario, who "never changes," we are works in progress. Unlike Mario, whose face is fixed and one-layer deep, we are multiple and mask-wearing. And this is okay. Here is where Mario, as moral agent as well as artistic avatar, bangs up against his limitation: he does not, *cannot*, understand that self-consciousness — which, yes, ushers in ulteriority and irony, hypocrisy and every stripe of fakery — is also real, deeply real. For many of us, who cannot steer by single, simple stars (God, AA dogma, goo-prone sentimentality…) self-consciousness is our primary reality. There must be a way for us, too, to love, and be loved, to treat people right. It must be possible.

Here is Mario, fatigued from a night's work, braced against his police lock, asking his mother how you can tell if someone is sad. This is the book's saddest passage. Because every member of the Incandenza family is so sad — Mario could be talking about any of them — and because their sadnesses are so hidden, so remote from one another. Because Avril confesses herself when she tells Mario that "there are, apparently, persons who are deeply afraid of their own emotions…afraid to live." Because she loves her son (—her sons—Orin's presence in her life now reduced to a pair of football pants and helmet on the sideboard), but she can never know him, no matter how "open and judgment-free" her lines of communication with him. Because all she can do with Mario — and it is all Wallace can do, with each and every character in this book — is try her best to really see him, listen to him, hoping that just because two people are not connected doesn't mean they can't be a little less alone. Her best is not enough, and it must be enough. His best is more than we deserve.

—*Nam Le*

O

THE CEILING WAS breathing. It bulged and receded. It swelled and settled. The room was in St. Elizabeth's Hospital's Trauma Wing. Whenever he looked at it, the ceiling bulged and then deflated, shiny as a lung. When Don was a massive toddler his mother had put them in a little beach house just back of the dunes off a public beach in Beverly. The place was affordable because it had a big ragged hole in the roof. Origin of hole unknown. Gately's outsized crib had been in the beach house's little living room, right under the hole. The guy that owned the little cottages off the dunes had stapled thick clear polyurethane sheeting across the room's ceiling. It was an attempt to deal with the hole. The polyurethane bulged and settled in the North Shore wind and seemed like some monstrous vacuole inhaling and exhaling directly over little Gately, lying there, wide-eyed. The breathing polyurethane vacuole had seemed like it developed a character and personality as winter deepened and the winds grew worse. Gately, age like four, had regarded the vacuole as a living thing, and had named it Herman, and had been afraid of it. He couldn't feel the right side of his upper body. He couldn't move in any real sense of the word. The hospital room had that misty quality rooms in fevers have. Gately lay on his back. Ghostish figures materialized at the peripheries of his vision and hung around and then dematerialized. The ceiling bulged and receded. Gately's own breath hurt his throat. His throat felt somehow raped. The blurred figure in the next bed sat up very still in bed in a sitting position and seemed to have a box on its head. Gately kept having a terrible repetitious ethnocentric dream that he was robbing the house of an Oriental and had the guy tied to a chair and was trying to blindfold him with quality mailing twine from the drawer under the Oriental's kitchen phone. The Oriental kept being able to see around the twine and kept looking steadily at Gately and blinking inscrutably. Plus the Oriental had no nose or mouth, just a smooth expanse of lower-facial skin, and wore a silk robe and scary sandals, and had no hair on its legs.

What Gately perceived as light-cycles and events all out of normal sequence was really Gately going in and out of consciousness. Gately did not perceive this. It seemed to him more like he kept coming up for air and then being pushed below the surface of something. Once when Gately came up for air he found that resident Tiny Ewell was seated in a chair right up next to the bed. Tiny's little slim hand was on the bed's crib-type railing, and his chin rested on the hand, so his face was right up close. The ceiling bulged and receded. The room's only light was what spilled in from the nighttime hall. Nurses glided down the hall and past the door in sub-sonic footwear. A tall and slumped ghostish figure appeared to Gately's left, off past the blurred seated square-head boy's bed, slumped and flut-tering, appearing to rest its tailbone on the sill of the dark window. The ceiling rounded on down and then settled back flat. Gately rolled his eyes up at Ewell. Ewell had shaved off his blunt white goatee. His hair was so completely clean and white it took a faint pink cast from the pink of his scalp below. Ewell had been discoursing to him for an unknown length of time. It was Gately's first full night in St. Elizabeth's Hospital's Trauma Wing. He didn't know what night of the week it was. His circadian rhythm was the least of the personal rhythms that had been scrambled. His right side felt encased in a kind of hot cement. Also a sick throb in what he assumed was a toe. He wondered dimly about going to the bath-room, if and when. Ewell was right in the middle of speaking. Gately couldn't tell if Ewell was whispering. Nurses glided across the doorway's light. Their sneakers were so noiseless the nurses seemed to be on wheels. A stolid shadow of somebody in a hat was cast obliquely across the hall's tile floor just outside the room, as if a stolid figure were seated just outside the door, against the wall, in a hat.

'My wife's personal term for soul is *personality*. As in "There's some-thing incorrigibly dark in your personality, Eldred Ewell, and Dewars brings it out." '

The hall floor was pretty definitely white tile, with a cloudy overwaxed shine in the bright fluorescence out there. Some kind of red or pink stripe ran down the center of the hall. Gately couldn't tell if Tiny Ewell thought he was awake or unconscious or what.

'It was in the fall term of third grade as a child that I found myself fallen in with the bad element. They were a group of tough blue-collar Irish lads bussed in from the East Watertown projects. Runny noses, home-cut hair, frayed cuffs, quick with their fists, sports-mad, fond of sneaker-hockey on asphalt,' Ewell said, 'and yet, strangely, I, unable to do even one pull-up in the President's Physical Fitness Test, quickly became the leader of the pack we all fell into. The blue-collar lads all seemed to admire me for attributes that were not clear. We formed a sort of club. Our uniform was a gray skallycap. Our clubhouse was the dugout of a Little League diamond that had fallen into disuse. Our club was called the Money-Stealers' Club. At my suggestion we went with a descriptive name as opposed to euphemistic. The name was mine. The Irish lads acquiesced. They viewed me as the brains of the operation. I held them in a kind of thrall. This was due in large part to my capacity for rhetoric. Even the toughest and most brutish Irish lad respects a gilded tongue. Our club was formed for the express purpose of undertaking a bunko operation. We went around to people's homes after school, ringing the doorbell and soliciting donations for Project Hope Youth Hockey. There was no such organization. Our donation-receptacle was a Chock Full O' Nuts can with PROJECT HOPE YOUTH HOCKEY written on a strip of masking tape wrapped around the can. The lad who made the receptacle had spelled *PROJECT* with a *G* in the first draft. I ridiculed him for the error, and the whole club pointed at him and laughed. Brutally.' Ewell kept staring at the crude blue jailhouse square and canted cross on Gately's forearms. 'Our only visible credentials were kneepads and sticks we'd purloined from the P.E. stockroom. By my order, all were held carefully to conceal the *PPTY W. WTTN ELEM SCH* emblazoned down the side of every stick. One lad had a goalie mask on under his skallycap, the rest kneepads and carefully held sticks. The kneepads were turned inside-out for the same reason. I couldn't even skate, and my mother absolutely forbade rough play on asphalt. I wore a necktie and combed my hair carefully after each solicitation. I was the spokesperson. The mouthpiece, the bad lads called me. They were Irish Catholics all. Watertown from east to west is Catholic, Armenian, and Mixed. The Eastside boys all but genuflected to my gift for bullshit. I was exceptionally smooth with adults. I rang doorbells and the lads arrayed themselves behind me on the porch. I spoke of disadvantaged youth and team spirit and fresh air and the meaning of competition and alternatives to the after-school streets' bad element. I spoke of mothers in support-hose and war-injured older brothers with elaborate prostheses cheering disadvantaged lads on to victory against far better-equipped teams. I discovered that I had a gift for it, the emotional appeal of adult rhetoric. It was the first time I felt personal power. I was unrehearsed and creative and moving. Hard-case homeowners who came to the door in sleeveless Ts holding tallboys of beer with stubble and expressions of minimal charity were often weeping openly by the time we left their porch. I was called a fine lad and a good kid and a credit to me Mum and Da. My hair was tousled so often I had to carry a mirror and comb. The coffee can became hard to carry back to the dugout, where we hid it behind a cinderblock bench-support. We'd netted over a hundred dollars by Halloween. This was a serious amount in those days.'

Tiny Ewell and the ceiling kept receding and then looming in, bulging roundly. Figures Gately didn't know from Adam kept popping in and out of fluttery view in different corners of the room. The space between his bed and the other bed seemed to distend and then contract with a slow sort of boinging motion. Gately's eyes kept rolling up in his head, his upper lip mustached with sweat. 'And I was revelling in the fraud of it, the discovery of the gift,' Ewell was saying. 'I was flushed with adrenaline. I had tasted power, the verbal manipulation of human hearts. The lads called me the gilded blarneyman. Soon the first-order fraud wasn't enough. I began secretly filching receipts from the club's Chock Full O' Nuts can. Embezzling. I persuaded the lads it was too risky to keep the can in the open-air dugout and took personal charge of the can. I kept the can in my bedroom and persuaded my mother that it contained Christmas-connected gifts and must under no circumstances be inspected. To my underlings in the club I claimed to be rolling the coins and depositing them in a high-interest savings account I'd opened for us in the name Franklin W. Dixon. In fact I was buying myself Pez and Milky Ways and *Mad* magazines and a Creeple Peeple–brand Deluxe Oven-and-Mold Set with six different colors of goo. This was in the early 1970s. At first I was discreet. Grandiose but discreet. At first the embezzlement was controlled. But the power had roused something dark in my personality, and the adrenaline drove it forward. Self-will run riot. Soon the club's coffee can was empty by each weekend's end. Each week's haul went toward some uncontrolled Saturday binge of puerile consumption. I doctored up flamboyant bank statements to show the club, in the dugout. I got more loquacious and imperious with them. None of the lads thought to question me, or the purple Magic Marker the bank statements were done in. I was not dealing with intellectual titans here, I knew. They were nothing but malice and muscle, the worst of the school's bad element. And I ruled them. Thrall. They trusted me completely, and the rhetorical gift. In retrospect they probably could not conceive of any sane third-grader with glasses and a necktie trying to defraud them, given the inevitably brutal consequences. Any *sane* third-grader. But I was no longer a sane third-grader. I lived only to feed the dark thing in my personality, which told me any consequences could be forestalled by my gift and grand personal aura.

'But then of course eventually Christmas hove into view.' Gately tries to stop Ewell and say 'hove?' and finds to his horror that he can't make any sounds come out. 'The meaty Catholic Eastside bad-element lads now wanted to tap their nonexistent Franklin W. Dixon account to buy support-hose and sleeveless Ts for their swarthy blue-collar families. I held them off as long as I could with pedantic blather on interest penalties and fiscal years. Irish Catholic Christmas is no laughing matter, though, and for the first time their swarthy eyes began to narrow at me. Things at school grew increasingly tense. One afternoon, the largest and swarthiest of them assumed control of the can in an ugly dugout coup. It was a blow from which my authority never recovered. I began to feel a gnawing fear: my denial broke: I realized I'd gradually embezzled far more than I could ever make good. At home, I began talking up the merits of private-school curricula at the dinner table. The can's weekly take fell off sharply as holiday expenses drained homeowners of change and patience. This bear-market in giving was attributed by some of the club's swarthier lads to my deficiencies. The whole club began muttering in the dugout. I began to learn that one could perspire heavily even in a bitterly cold open-air dugout. Then, on the first day of Advent, the lad now in charge of the can produced childish-looking figures and announced the whole club wanted their share of the accrued booty in the Dixon account. I bought time with vague allusions to co-signatures and a misplaced passbook. I arrived home with chattering teeth and bloodless lips and was forced by my mother to swallow fish-oil. I was consumed with puerile fear. I felt small and weak and evil and consumed by dread of my embezzlement's exposure. Not to mention the brutal consequences. I claimed intestinal distress and stayed home from school. The telephone began ringing in the middle of the night. I could hear my father saying "Hello? *Hello?*" I did not sleep. My personality's dark part had grown leathery wings and a beak and turned on me. There were still several days until Christmas vacation. I'd lie in bed panicked during school hours amid piles of ill-gotten *Mad* magazines and Creeple Peeple figures and listen to the lonely handheld bells of the Salvation Army Santas on the street below and think of synonyms for *dread* and *doom*. I began to know shame, and to know it as grandiosity's aide-de-camp. My unspecific digestive illness wore on, and teachers sent cards and concerned notes. On some days the door-buzzer would buzz after school hours and my mother would come upstairs and say "How *sweet*, Eldred," that there were swarthy and cuff-frayed but clearly good-hearted boys in gray skallycaps on the stoop asking after me and declaring that they were *keenly* awaiting my return to school. I began to gnaw on the bathroom's soap in the morning to make a convincing case for staying home. My mother was alarmed at the masses of bubbles I vomited and threatened to consult a specialist. I felt myself moving closer and closer to some cliff-edge at which everything would come out. I longed to be able to lean into my mother's arms and weep and confess all. I could not. For the shame. Three or four of the Money-Stealers' Club's harder cases took up afternoon positions by the nativity scene in the churchyard across from our house and stared stonily up at my bedroom window, pounding their fists in their palms. I began to understand what a Belfast Protestant must feel. But even more prospectively dreadful than pummellings from Irish Catholics was the prospect of my parents' finding out my personality had a dark thing that had driven me to grandiose wickedness and left me there.'

Gately has no idea how Ewell feels about him making no responses, whether Ewell doesn't like it or even notices it or what. He can breathe OK, but something in his raped throat won't let whatever's supposed to vibrate to speak vibrate.

'Finally, on the day before my gastroenterologist appointment, when my mother was down the street at a speculum party, I crept downstairs from my sick bed and stole over a hundred dollars from a shoebox marked I.B.E.W. LOCAL 517 PETTY SLUSH in the back of my father's den's closet. I'd never dreamed of resorting to the shoebox before. Stealing from my own parents. To remit funds I'd stolen from dull-witted boys with whom I'd stolen them from adults I'd lied to. My feelings of fear and despicability only increased. I now felt ill for real. I lived and moved in the shadow of something dark that hovered just overhead. I vomited without aid of emetic, now, but secretly, so I could return to school; I couldn't face the prospect of a whole Christmas vacation of swarthy sentries pounding their palms outside the house. I converted my father's union's bills to small change and paid off the Money-Stealers' Club and got pummelled anyway. Apparently on general bad-element principles. I discovered the latent rage in followers, the fate of the leader who falls from the mob's esteem. I was pummelled and given a savage wedgie and hung from a hook in my school locker, where I remained for several hours, swollen and mortified. And going home was worse; home was no refuge. For home was the scene of the third-order crime. Of theft cubed. I couldn't sleep. I tossed and turned. There were night terrors. I was unable to eat, no matter how long after supper I had to stay at the table. The more worried about me my par-

ents became, the greater my shame. I felt a shame and personal despicability no third-grader should have to feel. The holidays were not jolly. I
looked back over the autumn and failed to recognize anyone named
Eldred K. Ewell Jr. It no longer seemed a question of insanity or dark
parts of me. I had stolen from neighbors, slum-children, and family, and
bought myself sweets and toys. Under any tenable definition of *bad,* I was
bad. I resolved to toe the virtuous line from then on. The shame and horror was too awful: I had to remake myself. I resolved to do whatever was
required to see myself as good, remade. I never knowingly committed
another felony. The whole shameful interval of the Money-Stealers' Club
was moved to mental storage and buried there. Don, I'd forgotten it ever
happened. Until the other night. Don, the other night, after the fracas and
your display of reluctant *se offendendo,*[337] after your injury and the whole
aftermath…Don, I dreamed the whole mad repressed third-grade interval of grandiose perfidy all over again. Vividly and completely. When I
awoke, I was somehow minus my goatee and my hair was center-parted in
a fashion I haven't favored for forty years. The bed was soaked, and there
was a gnawed-looking cake of McDade's special anti-acne soap in my
hand.'

Gately starts to short-term recall that he was offered I.V.-Demerol for
the pain of his gunshot wound immediately on admission to the E.R. and
has been offered Demerol twice by shift-Drs. who haven't bothered to
read the HISTORY OF NARCOTICS DEPENDENCY NO SCHED-
ULE C-IV + MEDIC. that Gately'd made Pat Montesian swear she'd
make them put in italics on his file or chart or whatever, first thing. Last
night's emergency surgery was remedial, not extractive, because the big
pistol's ordnance had apparently fragmented on impacting and passed
through the meters of muscle that surrounded Gately's Humorous ball
and Scalpula socket, passing through and missing bone but doing great
and various damage to soft tissues. The E.R.'s Trauma Specialist had prescribed Toradol-IM[338] but had warned that the pain after the surgery's
general anesthetic wore off was going to be unlike anything Gately had
ever imagined. The next thing Gately knew he was upstairs in a Trauma
Wing room that trembled with sunlight and a different Dr. was speculat-
ing to either Pat M. or Calvin T. that the invasive foreign body had been
treated with something unclean, beforehand, possibly, because Gately's
developed a massive infection, and they're monitoring him for something
he heard as *Noxzema* but is really toxemia. Gately also wanted to protest
that his body was 100% American, but he seemed temporarily unable to
vocalize aloud. Later it was nighttime and Ewell was there, intoning. It

was totally unclear what Ewell wanted from Gately or why he was choosing this particular time to share. Gately's right shoulder was almost the same size as his head, and he had to roll his eyes up and over like a cow to see Ewell's hand on the railing and his face floating above it.

'And how will I administer the Ninth Step when it comes time to make amends? How can I start to make reparations? Even if I could remember the homes of the citizens we defrauded, how many could still be there, living? The club lads have doubtless scattered into various low-rent districts and dead-end careers. My father lost the I.B.E.W.[339] account under the Weld administration and has been dead since 1993. And the revelations would kill my mother. My mother is very frail. She uses a walker, and arthritis has twisted her head nearly all the way around on her neck. My wife jealously protects my mother from all unpleasant facts regarding me. She says someone has to do it. My mother believes right this minute I'm at a nine-month Banque-de-Genève-sponsored tax-law symposium in the Alsace. She keeps sending me knitted skiwear that doesn't fit, from the rest home.

'Don, this buried interval and the impost I've carried ever since may have informed my whole life. Why I was drawn to tax law, helping wealthy suburbanites two-step around their fair share. My marriage to a woman who looks at me as if I were a dark stain at the back of her child's trousers. My whole descent into somewhat-heavier-than-normal drinking may have been some instinctive attempt to bury third-grade feelings of despicability, submerge them in an amber sea.

'I don't know what to do,' Ewell said.

Gately was on enough Toradol-IM to make his ears ring, plus a saline drip with Doryx.[340]

'I don't want to remember despicabilities I can do nothing about. If this is a sample of the "More Will Be Revealed," I hereby lodge a complaint. Some things seem better left submerged. No?'

And everything on his right side was on fire. The pain was getting to be emergency-type pain, like scream-and-yank-your-charred-hand-off-the-stove-type pain. Parts of him kept sending up emergency flares to other parts of him, and he could neither move nor call out.

'I'm scared,' from what seemed somewhere overhead and rising, was the last thing Gately heard Ewell whisper as the ceiling bulged down toward them. Gately wanted to tell Tiny Ewell that he could totally fucking I.D. with Ewell's feelings, and that if he, Tiny, could just hang in and tote that bale and put one little well-shined shoe in front of the other everything would end up all right, that the God of Ewell's Understanding would find some way for Ewell to make things right, and then he could let the despicable feelings go instead of keeping them down with Dewars, but Gately couldn't connect the impulse to speak with actual speech, still. He settled for trying to reach his left hand across and pat Ewell's hand on the railing. But his own breadth was too far to reach across. And then the white ceiling came all the way down and made everything white.

He seemed to sort of sleep. He fever-dreamed of dark writhing storm clouds writhing darkly and screaming on down the beach at Beverly MA, the winds increasing over his head until Herman the polyurethane vacuole burst from the force, leaving a ragged inhaling maw that tugged at Gately's XXL Dr. Dentons. A blue stuffed brontosaurus was sucked upward out of the crib and disappeared into the maw, spinning. His mother was getting the shit beaten out of her by a man with a shepherd's crook in the kitchen and couldn't hear Gately's frantic cries for help. He broke through the crib's bars with his head and went to the front door and ran outside. The black clouds up the beach lowered and roiled, funnelling sand, and as Gately watched he saw a tornado's snout emerge from the clouds and slowly lower. It looked as if the clouds were either giving birth or taking a shit. Gately ran across the beach to the water to escape the tornado. He ran through the crazed breakers to deep warm water and submerged himself and stayed under until he ran out of breath. It was now no longer clear if he was little Bimmy or the grown man Don. He kept coming up briefly for a great sucking breath and then going back under where it was warm and still. The tornado stayed in one place on the beach, bulging and receding, screaming like a jet, its opening a breathing maw, lightning coming off the funnel-cloud like hair. He could hear the tiny tattered sounds of his mother calling his name. The tornado was right by the beach house and the whole house trembled. His mother came out the front door, wild-haired and holding a bloody Ginsu knife, calling his name. Gately tried to call for her to come into the deep water with him, but even he couldn't hear his calls against the scream of the storm. She dropped the knife and held her head as the funnel pointed its pointy maw her way. The beach house exploded and his mother flew through the air toward the funnel's intake, arms and legs threshing, as if swimming in wind. She vanished into the maw and was pulled spinning up into the tornado's vortex. Shingles and boards followed her. No sign of the shepherd's crook of the man who'd hurt her. Gately's right lung burned horribly. He saw his mother for the last time when lightning lit up the funnel's cone. She was whirling around and around like something in a drain, rising, seeming to swim, bluely backlit. The burst of lightning was the white of the sunlit room when he came up for air and opened his eyes. His mother's tiny rotating imago faded against the ceiling. What seemed like heavy breathing was him trying to scream. The skinny bed's sheets were soaked and he needed a piss something bad. It was daytime and his right side was in no way numb, and he was immediately nostalgic for the warm-cement feeling of when it was numb. Tiny Ewell was gone. His every pulse was an assault on his right side. He didn't think he could stand it for even another second. He didn't know what would happen, but he didn't think he could stand it.

Later somebody who was either Joelle van D. or a St. E's nurse in a U.H.I.D. veil was running a cold washcloth over his face. His face was so big it took some time to cover it all. It seemed too tender a touch on the cloth for a nurse, but then Gately heard the clink of I.V. bottles being changed or R.N.ishly messed with somewhere overhead behind him. He was unable to ask about changing the sheets or going to the bathroom. Some time after the veiled lady left, he just gave up and let the piss go, and instead of feeling wet heat he heard the rising metallic sound of something filling up somewhere near the bed. He couldn't move to lift the covers and see what he was hooked up to. The blinds were up, and the room was so bright-white in the sunlight everything looked bleached and boiled. The guy with either the square head or the box on his head had been taken off someplace, his bed unmade and one crib-railing down. There were no ghostish figures or figures in mist. The hallway was no brighter than the room, and Gately couldn't see any shadows of anybody in a hat. He didn't even know if last night had been real. The pain kept making his lids flutter. He hadn't cried over pain since he was four. His last thought before letting his lids stay shut against the brutal white of the room was that he'd maybe been castrated, which was how he'd always heard the term *catheterized*. He could smell rubbing alcohol and a kind of vitamin stink, and himself.

At some point a probably real Pat Montesian came in and got her hair in his eye when she kissed his cheek and told him if he could just hang in and concentrate on getting well everything would be fine, that everything at the House was back to normal, more or less, and essentially fine, that she was so sorry he'd had to handle a situation like that alone, without support or counsel, and that she realized full well Lenz and the Canadian thugs hadn't given him enough time to call anybody, that he'd done the very best he could with what he'd had to work with and had nothing to feel horrid about, to let it go, that the violence hadn't been relapse-type thrill-seeking violence but simply doing the best he could at that moment and trying to stand up for himself and for a resident of the House. Pat Montesian was dressed as usual entirely in black, but formally, as in for taking somebody to court, and her formalwear looked like a Mexican widow's. She really had said the words *thug* and *horrid*. She said not to worry, the House was a community and it took care of its own. She kept asking if he was sleepy. Her hair's red was a different and less radiant red than the red of Joelle van D.'s hair. The left side of her face was very kind. Gately had very little understanding of what she was talking about. He was kind of surprised the Finest hadn't come calling already. Pat didn't know about the remorseless A.D.A. or the suffocated Nuck: Gately'd tried hard to share openly about the wreckage of his past, but some issues still seemed suicidal to share about. Pat said that Gately was showing tremendous humility and willingness sticking to his resolution about nothing stronger than non-narcotic painkillers, but that she hoped he'd remember that he wasn't in charge of anything except putting himself in his Higher Power's hands and following the dictates of his heart. That codeine or maybe Percoset[341] or maybe even Demerol wouldn't be a relapse unless his heart of hearts that knew his motives thought it would be. Her red hair was down and looked uncombed and mashed in on the side; she looked frazzled. Gately wanted very much to ask Pat about the legal fallout of the other night's thug-fracas. He realized she kept asking if he was sleepy because his attempts to speak looked like yawns. His inability to still speak was like speechlessness in bad dreams, airless and hellish, horrid.

What made the whole interface with Pat M. possibly unreal was that right at the end for no reason Pat M. burst into tears, and for no reason Gately got so embarrassed he pretended to pass out, and slept again, and probably dreamed.

Almost certainly dreamed and unreal was the interval when Gately came up with a start and saw Mrs. Lopate, the objay dart from the Shed that they come and install next to the Ennet House viewer some days, sitting there in a gunmetal wheelchair, face contorted, head cocked, hair stringy, looking not at him but more like seemingly at whatever array of I.V. bottles and signifying monitors hung above and behind his big crib, so not speaking or even looking at him but still in some sense being there *with* him, somehow. Even though there was no way she could have really been there, it was the first time Gately realized that the catatonic Mrs. L. had been the same lady he'd seen touching the tree in #5's front lawn late at night, some nights, when he'd first come on Staff. That they were the same person. And that this realization was real even though the lady's presence in the room was not, the complexities of which made his eyes roll up in his head again as he passed back out again.

Then at some later point Joelle van Dyne was sitting in a chair just outside the railing of the bed, veiled, wearing sweatpants and a sweater that was starting to unravel, in a pink-bordered veil, not saying anything, probably looking at him, probably thinking he was unconscious with his eyes open, or delirious with Noxzema. The whole right side of himself hurt so bad each breath was like a hard decision. He wanted to cry like a small child. The girl's silence and the blankness of her veil frightened him after a while, and he wished he could ask her to come back later.

Nobody'd offered him anything to eat, but he wasn't hungry. There were I.V. tubes going into the backs of both hands and the crook of his left elbow. Other tubing exited him lower down. He didn't want to know. He kept trying to ask his heart if just codeine would be a relapse, according to the heart, but his heart was declining to comment.

Then at some point Ennet House alum and senior counselor Calvin Thrust came roaring in and pulled up a chair and straddled it backwards like a slow-tease stripper, slumping and draping his arms over the back of the chair, gesturing with an unlit rodney as he spoke. He told Gately that man he looked like shit something heavy had fell on. But he told Gately he should get a gander of the other guys, the Nucks in Polynesian-wear. Thrust and the House Manager had got there before E.M.P.H.H. Security could drag the Finest away from issuing midnight street-side citations down on Comm. Ave., he told Gately. Lenz and Green and Alfonso Parias-Carbo had dragged/carried the passed-out Gately inside and laid him on the black vinyl couch in Pat's office, where Gately had come to and told them ixnay on the ambulanceay and to please wake him up in five more minutes, and then passed out for serious real. Parias-Carbo seemed like he'd suffered a mild intestinal hernia from dragging/carrying Gately, but he was being a man about it and had refused codeine downstairs at the E.R. and was expressing gratitude for the growth experience, and the thoraxic lump was receding nicely. Calvin Thrust's breath smelled of smoke and old scrambled eggs. Gately had once seen a cheap bootleg cartridge of a young Calvin Thrust having sex with a lady with only one arm on what looked like a crude homemade trapeze. The cartridge's lighting and production values had been real low-quality, and Gately had been in and out of a Demerol-nod, but he was 98% sure it had been the young Calvin Thrust. Calvin Thrust said how right there over Gately's unconscious form in the office Randy Lenz had begun womaning right off how of course he, Randy Lenz, was going to somehow get blamed for Gately and the Nucks getting fucked up and why didn't they just get it over with and give him the administrative Shoe right now without going through the sham motions of deliberating. Bruce Green had rammed Lenz up against Pat's cabinets and shaken him like a margarita, but refused to rat out Lenz or say why irate Canadians might think a specimen as dickless as Lenz might have demapped their friend. The matter was under investigation, but Thrust confessed to a certain admiration for Green's refusal to eat cheese. Brucie G. had suffered a broken nose in the beef and now had a terrific set of twin shiners. Calvin Thrust said both he, Calvin Thrust, and the House Manager had immediately on arrival pegged Lenz as either coked up or 'drined to the gills on some 'drine, and Thrust said he summoned every Oreida of self-control sobriety'd blessed him with and had quietly taken Lenz out of the office into the special Disabled Bedroom next door and over the sound of Burt F. Smith coughing up little pieces of lung in his sleep he said he'd real controlledly given Lenz the choice of voluntarily resigning his Ennet residency on the spot or submitting to a spot-urine and a room-search and everything like that, plus to questioning by the Finest, who were pretty doubtless even now on route with the fleet of ambulances for the Nucks. Meanwhile, Thrust said—gesturing with the gasper and occasionally leaning forward to see whether Gately was still conscious and to tell him he looked like shit, meanwhile—Gately had been lying there passed out, wedged with two full filing cabinets to keep him from rolling off the couch he was wider than, and was bleeding in a very big way, and nobody knew how to, like, *affix* a turnipcut to a shoulder, and the good-bodied new girl with the cloth mask was bending over the arm of the couch applying pressure to towels on Gately's bleeding, and her partly-open robe was yielding a view that even brought Alfonso P.-C. around from his herniated fetal posture on the floor, and Thrust and the House Manager were taking turns Asking for Help to intuitively know what they ought to do with Gately, because it was well known that he was on Probie against a real serious bit, and with all due trust and respect to Don it wasn't clear at that point from the scattered damaged Canadian forms still in different prone positions out in the street who'd done what to who in defense of whatever or not, and the Finest tend to take a keen interest in huge guys who come into E.R.'s with spectacular gunshot wounds, and but then when Pat M. pulled up in the Aventura laying rubber a couple minutes later she'd screamed rather unserenely at Thrust for not having already rikky-ticked Don Gately over to St. E.'s on his own already. Thrust said he'd let go of Pat's screaming like water off a duck, revealing that Pat M. had been under felony-weight domestic stress at

home, he knew. He said and but so Gately was too heavy to carry unconscious for more than a few meters, even with the masked girl filling in for
Parias-Carbo, and they'd just barely got Gately outside still in his wet
bowling shirt and laid him briefly on the sidewalk and covered him with
Pat's black suede car-coat while Thrust maneuvered his beloved Corvette
up as close to Gately as possible. The sounds of sirens on the way up
Comm. Ave. mixed with the sounds of severely fucked-up Canadians
returning to whatever passed with Nucks for consciousness and calling for
what they called *medecins,* and with the crazed-squirrel sound of Lenz
trying to start his rusted-out brown Duster, which had a bad solenoid.
They'd heaved Gately's dead weight in the 'Vette and Pat M. drove interference like a madwoman in her turbocharged Aventura. Pat let the
masked girl ride shotgun with her because the masked girl wouldn't quit
asking her to let her come too. The House Manager stayed behind to represent Ennet House to E.M.P.H.H. Security and the somewhat less bull-
shittable BPD-Finest. The sirens got steadily closer, which added to the
confusion because senile and mobile-vegetable residents of both Unit #4
and the Shed had been drawn out on the frozen lawns by the freakas, and
the mix of several kinds of sirens didn't do them a bit of good, and they
started flapping and shrieking and running around and adding to the
medical confusion of the whole scene, which by the time him and Pat
pulled out of there was a fucking millhouse and everything like that.
Thrust asks rhetorically how much does Don fucking *weigh,* anyway,
because moving the front buckets way up to where like dwarfs put them
and putting Gately's carcass across the back seat of the 'Vette had required
all available hands and even Burt F.S.'s stumps, had been like trying to get
something humongous through a door that's way smaller than the humongous thing was and everything like that. Thrust occasionally tapped his
gasper like he thought it was lit. The first squad cars had come fishtailing
around the Warren-Comm. corner just as they all came out of the E.M.
driveway onto Warren. Pat in her car up ahead had made an arm-motion
that could have been either waving coolly at the passing Finest or uncoolly
clutching her head. Thrust said had he mentioned Gately's blood? Gately'd bled all over Pat M.'s vinyl couch and filing cabinets and carpet, the
little E.M. streetlet, the sidewalk, Pat M.'s black suede car-coat, pretty
much everybody's winter coats, and the beloved upholstery of Thrust's
beloved Corvette, which upholstery Thrust might add had been new, and
dear. But he said not to worry about it, Thrust said: the fucking blood was
the least of the problems. Gately didn't like the sound of that at all, and
started trying to blink at him in a kind of crude code, to get his attention,

but Thrust either didn't notice it or thought it was like a post-operative tic. Thrust's hair was always combed straight back like a mobster. Thrust said at the St. E.'s E.R. how the E.R. crew had been quick and ingenious about getting Gately out of the 'Vette and onto a double-width gurney, though they did have some trouble lifting the gurney so they could get the legs with wheels set up under it so the guys in white could roll him in with more guys in white walking briskly alongside of him and leaning over him and applying pressure and barking little orders in terse code like they always do in E.R.s and everything like that, in emergencies. Thrust says he couldn't tell if they could tell right away it was a spectacular gunshot wound, nobody used the G-word or anything like that. Thrust had babbled something about a chain-saw while Pat nodded furiously. The chief two things Gately kept blinking rhythmically to try to find out were: did anybody end up getting killed, meaning the Nucks; and has this one certain A.D.A.-type figure that always wore a hat come in from Essex County or given any sign of getting wind of Gately's whereabouts or involvement; and—so really three things—and will any of the Ennet House residents that were right there on the scene from start to finish look respectable enough on paper to have creditibility as like legal witnesses. Plus he wouldn't mind knowing what the fuck Thrust was thinking of, scaring Lenz off and letting him screw off into the urban night leaving Gately maybe holding the statutory bag. Most of Calvin Thrust's legality-experience was filmic and petty-vice. Thrust eventually describes that one of the House Manager's key coups of quick thinking was doing a quick TP-scan and finding out which of the residents out there milling around with the catatonics on the street had up-in-the-air legal issues such that they needed to be secloistered in the protected area of the House out of legal sight by the time the BPD's Finest hit the scene. He says in his view it was lucky for Gately that he (Gately) was such a massive son of a bitch and had so much blood, because even so Gately'd lost huge volumes of blood all over people's upholstery and was in shock and everything like that by the time they got him on the double-width gurney, his face cheese-colored and his lips blue and muttering all this shock-type stuff, but even so here he (Gately) was, not exactly ready for a *GQ* cover but still sucking air. Thrust said in the waiting room at the E.R., where they wouldn't let a working man smoke down there either, he said then the arrogant new girl resident in the white veil had up and tried to take Thrust's inventory for letting Randy L. resign and decamp before his part in Gately's legal embryoglio could be nailed down, and Pat M. had been pretty unconditionally loving about it but it was obvious she wasn't thrilled with Thrust's tactics either and everything like that. Gately blinked furiously to signify his agreement with Joelle's position. Calvin Thrust gestured stoically with his cigarette and said he'd told Pat M. the truth: he always told the truth, no matter how unpleasant for himself, today: he said he'd said he'd encouraged Lenz to rikky-tick out of there because otherwise he was afraid that he (Thrust) was going to eliminate Lenz's map on the spot, out of rage. Lenz's solenoid appeared to have been on the permanent dicky, because the rusty Duster was seen by new resident Amy J. real early the next A.M. getting towed from its wrong-side-of-the-street spot in front of #3 when Amy J. slunk back to the House all jonesy and hungover to get her Hefty bag full of evicted personal shit, Lenz apparently having abandoned his wheels and fleen off by foot during all the Finest's confusion and static with the ambulance drivers that who could blame them didn't want to take Canadians because of horrible paperwork for Health Card reimbursement for Nucks. The House Manager had gone so far as planting herself out in front of the House's locked front door with her not-all-that-small arms and legs spread out, blocking the door, assertively stating at whatever Finest tried to enter that Ennet House was court-mandated Protected by the Commonwealth of MA and could only be entered with a Court Order and three working days' mandated time for the House to file an injunction and wait for a ruling, and the Finest and even the booger-eating morons from E.M.P.H.H. Security were successfully held in bay and kept out, therefore, by her, alone, and Pat M. was considering rewarding the House Manager's coolness under fire by promoting her to Assistant Director next month when the present Assistant Director left to go get certified in jet-engine maintenance at East Coast Aerotech on a Mass Rehab grant.

Gately's eyes keep rolling up in his head, only partly from pain.

Unless he actually had a lit gasper going, Calvin Thrust always has this way of being only technically wherever he was. There was always this air of imminent departure about him, like a man whose beeper was about to sound. It's like a lit gasper was psychic ballast for him or something. Everything he said to Gately seemed like it was going to be the last thing he said right before he looked at his watch and slapped his forehead and left.

Thrust said whatever that Nuck that the residents allege shot him shot him with was serious ordnance, because there'd been bits of Gately's shoulder and bowling shirt all over the complex's little street. Thrust pointed at the huge bandage and asked whether they'd talked to Gately yet about was he going to get to keep what was left of the mutilated shoulder and arm. Gately found that the only audible sound he could make sounded like a run-over kitten. Thrust mentioned that Danielle S.'d been over to Mass Rehab with Burt F.S. and had reported how they were doing miraculous things with prosfeces these days. Gately's eyes were rolling around in his head and he was making pathetic little scared aspirated sounds as he pictured himself with a hook and parrot and patch making piratical 'Arr Matey' sounds from the AA podium. He felt a terrible certainty that the whole nerve-assembly network that connected the human voice-box to the human mind and let somebody ask for crucial legal and medical feedback must run through the right human shoulder. All kinds of fucking shunts and crazy interconnections with nerves, he knew. He imagined himself with one of those solar-cell electric shaver voice-box prosfeces he has to hold up to his throat (maybe with his hook), trying to Carry the Message with it from the podium, sounding like an automatic teller or ROM-audio interface. Gately wanted to know what day the next day was and whether any of Lenz's Nucks had been demapped, and what the official capacity of the guy was in the hat who'd been sitting just outside the door to the room either last night or the night before, his hat's shadow cast in a kind of parallelogram across the open doorway, and if the guy was still there, assuming the sight of the guy's hatted shadow had been valid and not phantasmic, and he wondered how they went about cuffing you if one of your arms' shoulders was mutilated and the size of your head. If Gately took anything deeper than a half-breath, a mind-bending sheet of pain goes down his right side. He even breathed like a sick kitten, more like throbbing than breathing. Thrust said Hester Thrale had apparently disappeared sometime during the freakas and never came back. Gately could remember her running screaming off into the urban night. Thrust said her Alfa Romeo got towed the next A.M. right along with Lenz's bum Duster, and her stuff's been duly bagged and is on the porch and everything familiar like that. Thrust said they found this mysteriously huge stash of high-quality Irish Luggage during the Staff's search of Lenz's room, and the House looks to be fixed for trash- and eviction-bags for the next fiscal year. Discharged residents' bagged possessions stay on the porch for three days, and Gately's trying to calculate the present date from this fact. Thrust says Emil Minty got a Full House Restriction for getting observed removing one of Hester Thrale's undergarments from her bag on the porch, for reasons nobody much wants to speculate about. Kate Gompert and Ruth van Cleve supposedly went to hit an NA meeting in Inman Square and got supposedly mugged and separated, and then only Ruth van Cleve showed up back at the House, and Pat's sworn out a P.C. warrant for Gompert because of the girl's other psych and suicide issues. Gately discovers he doesn't even all that much care whether anybody thought to call Stavros L. at the Shattuck about Gately's day job. Thrust smoothed his hair back and said what else let's see. Johnette Foltz is so far covering Gately's shifts and said to say he's in her prayers. Chandler Foss finished out his nine months and graduated but came back the next morning and hung around for Morning Meditation, which has to be a good sign sobriety-wise for the old Chandulator. Jennifer Belbin did get indicted on the bad-check issue up in Wellfleet Circuit Court, but they're going to let her finish out her residency at the House before anything goes to trial, which her P.D. said graduating the House is guaranteed to get her bit cut in at least half. The Asst. Director had gone up to court with Belbin on her own time. Doony Glynn's still laid up with the diveritis thing, and can be neither coaxed nor threatened out of his fetal position in bed, and the House Manager's trying to breast-work through the red tape at Health to get them to OK him admission to St. E.'s even though he's got insurance fraud on his yellow sheet, part of his own past-wreckage. A guy that had gone through the House back when Thrust did and had stayed sober in AA for four solid years had suddenly out of nowhere slipped up and took The First Drink the same day as the Lenz freakas, and predictably ended getting totally shitfaced, and went and fell off the end of the Fort Point pier—like literally took a long walk on a short pier, apparently—and sank like a rock, and the memorial service is today, which is why Thrust is going to have to take off in a second here, he says. The new kid Tingley's coming out of the linen closet for up to an hour at a time and is taking solid food and Johnette's quit lobbying to have the kid sent over to Met State. The even newer new guy now that's come in to take Chandler Foss's spot's name is Dave K. and is one grim story to behold, Thrust assures him, a junior executive guy at ATHSCME Air Displacement, an upscale guy with a picket house and kids and a worried wife with tall hair, who this Dave K.'s bottom was he drank half a liter of Cuerva at some ATHSCME Interdependence Day office party and everything like that and got in some insane drunken limbo-dance challenge with a rival executive and tried to like limbo under a desk or a chair or something insanely low, and got his spine all fucked up in a limbo-lock, maybe permanently: so the newest new guy scuttles around the Ennet House living room like a crab, his scalp brushing the floor and his knees trembling with effort. Danielle S. thinks Burt F.S. might have batorial ammonia or some kind of chronic lung thing, and Geoff D.'s trying to get the other residents to sign a petition to get Burt barred from the kitchen and dining room because Burt can't cover his mouth when he coughs, understandably. Thrust says Clenette H. and Yolanda W. are taking meals in their room and are under orders not to come down or go near any windows, because of what happened to the map of the Nuck they allegedly stomped and everything like that. Gately mews and blinks like mad. Thrust says everybody's being real supportive of Jenny B. and encouraging her to turn the Wellfleet indictment over to her Higher Power. The Shed staff are still rolling the catatonic lady's wheelchair over from the Shed to the House on scheduled A.M.'s, and Thrust says Johnette had to write up Minty and Diehl for putting one of those gag-arrows that are curved in the middle and look like there's an arrow through your head over the catatonic lady's paralyzed head yesterday and leaving her slumped by the TP like that all day. Plus Thrale's panties; so suddenly in twelve hours Minty's just one more offense away from getting the Shoe, which Thrust is already personally shining the tip of his very sharpest shoe, in hopes. The biggest issue at the House Bitch and Complaint meeting was that earlier this week it turns out Clenette H. had brung in this whole humongous shitload of cartridges she said they were getting ready to throw in the dumpster up at the swank tennis school up the hill she works at, and she promoted them and hauled them down to the House, and the residents all have a wild hair because Pat says Staff has to preview the cartridges for suitability and sex before they can be put out for the residents, and the residents are all bitching that this'll take forever and it's just the fucking Staff hoarding the new entertainment when the House's TP's just about on its hands and knees in the entertainment desert starving for new entertainment. McDade bitched at the meeting that if he had to watch *Nightmare on Elm Street XXII: The Senescence* one more time he was going to take a brody off the House's roof.

Plus Thrust says Bruce Green hasn't shared word one to Staff about his feelings about anything to do with Lenz or Gately's embryoglio; that he just sits around waiting for somebody to read his mind; that his roommates have complained that he thrashes and shouts about nuts and cigars in his sleep.

Calvin Thrust, four years sober, straddling the backwards chair, keeps inclining himself ever more forward in the posture of a man who's at any moment going to push up off out of the chair and leave. He reports how something deep in the previously hopelessly arrogant-seeming 'Tiny' Ewell seems like it's broken and melted, spiritually speaking: the guy shaved off his Kentucky Chicken beard, was heard weeping in the 5-Man head, and was observed by Johnette taking out the kitchen trash in secret even though his Chore this week was Office Windows. Thrust had discovered fine dining in sobriety, and has the beginning of chins. His hair is slicked back with odorless stuff at all times, and he has a more or less permanent sore on his upper lip. Gately for some reason keeps imagining Joelle van Dyne dressed as Madame Psychosis sitting in a plain chair in the 3-Woman room eating a peach and looking out the open window at the crucifix atop St. Elizabeth's Hospital's prolix roof. The crucifix isn't big, but it's up so high it's visible from most anywhere in Enfield-Brighton. Sees Joelle delicately pulling the veil out to get the peach up under it. Thrust says Charlotte Treat's T-cell count is down. She's needlepointing Gately some kind of *GET BETTER A DAY AT A TIME ASSUMING THAT'S GOD'S WILL* doily, but it's been slow going, because Treat's developed some kind of goopy Virus-related eye infection that's got her bumping into walls, and her counselor Maureen N. at the Staff Meeting wanted Pat to consider having her transferred to an HIV halfway house up in Everett that's got some recovering addicts in there. Morris Hanley, speaking of T-cells, has baked some cream-cheese brownies for Gately as a nurturing gesture, but then the twats at the Trauma Wing's nurses' station, like, *impounded* them from Thrust when he came up, but he'd had a couple on the way over in the bloodstained 'Vette and he could assure Don that Hanley's brownies were worth killing a loved one for and everything like that. Gately feels a sudden rush of anxiety over the issue of who's cooking the House supper in his absence, like will they know to put corn flakes in the meat loaf, for texture. He finds Thrust insufferable and wishes he'd just fucking go already, but has to admit he's less conscious of the horrific pain when somebody's there, but that that's mostly because the drowned panic of not being able to ask questions or have any input into what somebody's saying is so awful it sort of dwarfs the pain. Thrust puts his unlit gasper behind his ear where Gately predicts hair-tonic will render it unsmokable, looks conspiratorially around back over each shoulder, leans in so his face is visible between two bars of the bed's side-railing, and bathes Gately's face in old eggs and smoke as he leans in and quietly says that Gately'll be psyched to hear that all the residents that were at the embryoglio—except Lenz and Thrale and the ones that aren't in a legal position to step forward and like that, he says—he says they've most of them all come forward and filed depositions, that the BPD's Finest, plus some rather weirder Federal guys with goofy-looking archaic crew cuts, probably involved because of the like inter-O.N.A.N. element of the Nucks—here Gately's big heart skips and sinks—have come around and been voluntarily admitted inside, on Pat's written OK, and they took depositions, which is like testifying on paper, and the depositions look to be basically 110% behind Don Gately and support a justifiable señorio of either self-defense or Lenz-defense. Several testimonies indicate the Nucks gave the impression of being under the influence of aggressive-type Substances. The single biggest problem right now, Thrust says Pat says, is the missing alleged Item. As in the .44 Item Gately was plugged with's whereabouts are missing, Thrust says. The last resident to depose to seeing it was Green, who says he took it away from the Nuck the nigger girls stomped, whereupon he, Green, says he dropped it on the lawn. Whereupon it liked vanished from legal view. Thrust says that in his legal view the Item's the thing that makes the difference between a señorio of ironshod self-defense and one of just maybe a huge fucking beef in which Gately got mysteriously plugged at some indefinite point while rearranging a couple Canadian maps with his huge bare hands. Gately's heart is now somewhere around his bare hairy shins, at the mention of Federal crewcuts. His attempted plea for Thrust to come out and say did he actually kill anybody *did he* sounds like that crushed kitten again. The pain of the terror is past standing, and it helps him surrender and quit trying, and he relaxes his legs and decides Thrust gets to not say whatever he wants, that the reality right this second is that he's mute and powerless over Thrust. Thrust leans in and hugs the back of the chair and says Clenette Henderson and Yolanda Willis are on Full House Restriction in their room to keep them from coming down and maybe fucking themselves over legally in a deposition. Because the Nuck with the plaid hat with the ear-flaps and the missing alleged Item had expired on the spot from a spike heel through the right eye, as he was getting the shit stomped out of him as only female niggers can stomp, and everything like that, and Yolanda Willis had very shrewdly left the shoe and spike heel right there protruding from the guy's map with her toe-prints all over its insides — meaning presumably the shoe's — so producing the Item was going to be in her strong legal interests too, as well, as Thrust analyzes the legal landscape. Thrust says Pat's limped around and appealed to every single resident personally, and everybody's submitted more or less voluntarily to a room- and property-search and everything like that, and still no large-caliber Item has turned up, though Nell Gunther's hidden Oriental-knife collection sure made an impression. Thrust predicts it'll be strongly in Gately's lego-judicial interest and everything like that to ransack his brain and mind for where and with who he last saw the alleged gun. The sun was starting to go down over the West Newton hills through the double-sealed windows, now, trembling slightly, and the windowlight against the far wall was ruddled and bloody. The heater vents kept making a sound like a distant parent gently shushing. When it starts to get dark out is when the ceiling breathes. And everything like that.

—pages 809–827

Notes and Errata

1. Methamphetamine hydrochloride, a.k.a. crystal meth.

3. E.T.A. is laid out as a cardioid, with the four main inward-facing bldgs. convexly rounded at the back and sides to yield a cardioid's curve, with the tennis courts and pavilions at the center and the staff and students' parking lots in back of Comm.-Ad. forming the little bashed-in dent that from the air gives the whole facility the Valentine-heart aspect that still wouldn't have been truly cardioid if the buildings themselves didn't have their convex bulges all derived from arcs of the same r, a staggering feat given the uneven ground and wildly different electrical-and-plumbing-conduit wallspace required by dormitories, administrative offices, and polyresinous Lung, pull-offable probably by on the whole East Coast one guy, E.T.A.'s original architect, Avril's old and very dear friend, the topology world's closed-curve-mapping-Übermensch A.Y. ('Vector-Field') Rickey of Brandeis U., now deceased, who used to wow Hal and Mario in Weston by taking off his vest without removing his suit jacket, which M. Pemulis years later exposed as a cheap parlor-trick-exploitation of certain basic features of continuous functions, which revelation Hal mourned in a Santa's-not-real type of secret way, and which Mario simply ignored, preferring to see the vest thing as plain magic.

4. Those younger staffers who double as academic and athletic instructors are, by convention at North American tennis academies, known as 'prorectors.'

5. Known usually as 'drines—i.e. lightweight speed: Cylert, Tenuate,[a] Fastin, Preludin, even sometimes Ritalin. It's worth an N.B. that, unlike Jim Troeltsch or the Preludin-happy Bridget Boone, Michael Pemulis (out of maybe some queer sort of blue-collar street-type honor) rarely ingests any 'drines before a match, reserving them for recreation—some people are wired to find heart-pounding eye-wobbling 'drine-stimulation recreational.

> a. Tenuate's the trade name of diethylpropion hydrochloride, Marion Merrell Dow Pharmaceuticals, technically a prescription antiobesity agent, favored by some athletes for its mildly euphoric and resources-rallying properties w/o the tooth-grinding and hideous post-blood-spike crash that the hairier-chested 'drines like Fastin and Cylert inflict, though with a discomfitting tendency to cause post-spike ocular nystagmus. Nystagmus or no nystagmus, Tenuate's a particular favorite of Michael Pemulis, who hoards for personal ingestion every 75-mg. white Tenuate capsule he can lay hands on, and does not sell or trade them, except sometimes to roommate Jim Troeltsch, who nags Pemulis for them and also goes into Pemulis's special entrepôt-yachting-cap and promotes still more of them on the sly, a couple at a time, feeling that they help his sports-color-commentary loquacity, which secret promotions Pemulis knows about all too well, and is biding his time to retaliate, never you fear.

6. Lightweight tranqs: Valium-III and Valrelease, good old dependable Xanax, Dalmane, Buspar, Serax, even Halcion (legally available in Canada, unbelievably, still); with those kids inclined toward a heavier slide—reds, Meprospan, 'Happy Patch' transdermals, Miltown, Stelazine, the odd injury-'scrip Darvon) never lasting for more than a couple seasons for the obvious reason that serious tranqs can make even breathing seem like

too much trouble to go to, the cause of a meaty percentage of tranq-related deaths being attributed off the record by Emergency Room personnel to 'P.S.' or 'Pulmonary Sloth.'

7. Top jr. players are for the most part pretty cautious with alcohol, mostly because the physical consequences of heavy intake—like nausea and dehydration and poor hand-eye interface—make high-level performance almost impossible. Very few other standard substances have prohibitive short-term hangovers, actually, though an evening of even synthetic cocaine will make the next day's Dawn Drills very unpleasant indeed, which is why so few of E.T.A.'s hard core do cocaine, though there's also the issue of expense: though many E.T.A.s are the children of upscale parents, the children themselves are rarely flush with $ from home, since the gratification of pretty much every physical need is either taken care of or prohibited by E.T.A. itself. It's maybe worth noting that the same people hardwired to enjoy recreational 'drines also tend to gravitate toward cocaine and methedrine and other engine-revvers, while another broad class of more naturally higher-strung types tend more toward the edge-bevelling substances: tranqs, cannabis, barbiturates, and—yes—alcohol.

8. I.e.: psylocibin; Happy Patches[a]; MDMA/Xstasy (bad news, though, X); various low-tech manipulations of the benzene-ring in methoxy-class psychedelics, usually homemakable; synthetic dickies like MMDA, DMA, DMMM, 2CB, para-DOT I-VI, etc.—though note this class doesn't and shouldn't include CNS-rattlers like STP, DOM, the long-infamous West-U.S.-Coast 'Grievous Bodily Harm' (gamma hydroxybutyric acid), LSD-25 or -32, or DMZ/M.P. Enthusiasm for this stuff seems independent of neurologic type.

    a. Homemade transdermals, usually MDMA or Muscimole, with DDMS or the over-counter-available DMSO as the transdermal carrier.

9. A.k.a. LSD-25, often with a slight 'drine kicker added, called 'Black Star' because in metro Boston the available acid usually comes on chip-sized squares of thin cardboard with a black stencilled star on them, all from a certain shadowy node of supply down in New Bedford. All acid and Grievous Bodily Harm, like cocaine and heroin, come into Boston mostly from New Bedford MA, which in turn gets most of its supply from Bridgeport CT, which is the true lower intestine of North America, Bridgeport, be advised, if you've never been through there.

10. Like most sports academies, E.T.A. maintains the gentle fiction that 100% of its students are enrolled at their own ambitious volition and not that of, say for instance, their parents, some of whom (tennis-parents, like the stage-mothers of Hollywood legend) are bad news indeed.

11. An involved Arab women's game involving little shells and a quilted gameboard—rather like mah jongg without rules, by the diplomatic and medical husbands' estimate.

12. Meperedine hydrochloride and pentazocine hydrochloride, Schedule C-II and C-IV[a] narcotic analgesics, respectively, both from the good folks over at Sanofi Winthrop Pharm-Labs, Inc.

    a. Following the Continental Controlled Substance Act of Y.T.M.P., O.N.A.N.D.E.A.'s hierarchy of analgesics/antipyretics/anxiolytics establishes drug-classes of Category-II through Category-VI, with C-II's (e.g. Dilaudid,

Demerol) being judged the heaviest w/r/t dependence and possible abuse, down to C-VI's that are about as potent as a kiss on the forehead from Mom.

13. Though masked in the evidentiary photo and never once given up or named by Gately to anyone, this can be presumed to have been one Trent ('Quo Vadis') Kite, Gately's old and once-gifted friend from his Beverly MA childhood.

14. This A.D.A.'s little personal trademark was that he always wore an anachronistic but quality Stetson-brand businessman's hat with a decorative feather in the band, and frequently touched or played with the hat in tense situations.

15. The Bureau of Alcohol/Tobacco/Firearms, at that time under the temporary aegis of the United States Office of Unspecified Services.

16. Extremely unpleasant Québecois-insurgents-and-cartridge-related subsequent developments make it clear that this was (again) Trent ('Quo Vadis') Kite.

17. The codeineless kind, though—almost the first physical datum Gately took in in the nasty flashbulb-flash shock of the occupied bedroom's light coming on, to give you an idea of an oral-narcotics man's depth of psychic investment.

18. On top of the seascape safe's more negotiable contents, themselves on top of an unplugged and head-parked and absolutely top-hole genuine InterLace state-of-the-art TP/viewer ensemble in a multishelved hardwood rollable like entertainment-system-console thing, with a cartridge-dock and double-head drive in a compartment underneath with doors with classy little brass maple-leaf knob things and several shelves crammed tight with upscale arty-looking film cartridges, which latter Don Gately's colleague just about drooled all over the parquet flooring at the potential discriminating-type-fence-value of, potentially, if they were rare or celluloid-transferred or not available on the InterLace Dissemination Grid.

19. *'Une Personne de l'Importance Terrible,'* presumably.

20. Fluorescence has been banned in Québec, as have computerized telephone solicitations, the little ad-cards that fall out of magazines and have to be looked at to be picked up and thrown in the trash, and the mention of any religious holiday whatsoever to sell any sort of product or service, is just one reason why his volunteering to come live down here was selfless.

23. Office of Naval Research, U.S.D.D.

24.

JAMES O. INCANDENZA: A FILMOGRAPHY[a]

The following listing is as complete as we are able to make it. Because the twelve years of Incandenza's directorial activity also coincided with large shifts in film venue—from public art cinemas, to VCR-capable magnetic recordings, to InterLace TelEntertainment laser dissemination and reviewable storage disk laser cartridges—and because Incandenza's output itself comprises industrial, documentary, conceptual, advertorial,

---

a. From Comstock, Posner, and Duquette, 'The Laughing Pathologists: Exemplary Works of the Anticonfluential *Après Garde:* Some Analyses of the Movement Toward Stasis in North American Conceptual Film (w/ Beth B., Vivienne Dick, James O. Incandenza, Vigdis Simpson, E. and K. Snow).' *ONANite Film and Cartridge Studies Annual,* vol. 8, nos. 1-3 (Year of D.P. from the A.H.), pp. 44–117.

technical, parodic, dramatic noncommercial, nondramatic ('anticonfluential') noncommercial, nondramatic commercial, and dramatic commercial works, this filmmaker's career presents substantive archival challenges. These challenges are also compounded by the facts that, first, for conceptual reasons, Incandenza eschewed both L. of C. registration and formal dating until the advent of Subsidized Time, secondly, that his output increased steadily until during the last years of his life Incandenza often had several works in production at the same time, thirdly, that his production company was privately owned and underwent at least four different changes of corporate name, and lastly that certain of his high-conceptual projects' agendas required that they be titled and subjected to critique but never filmed, making their status as film subject to controversy.

Accordingly, though the works are here listed in what is considered by archivists to be their probable order of completion, we wish to say that the list's order and completeness are, at this point in time, not definitive.

Each work's title is followed: by either its year of completion, or by 'B.S.,' designating undated completion before Subsidization; by the production company; by the major players, if credited; by the storage medium's ('film' 's) gauge or gauges; by the length of the work to the nearest minute; by an indication of whether the work is in black and white or color or both; by an indication of whether the film is silent or in sound or both; by (if possible) a brief synopsis or critical overview; and by an indication of whether the work is mediated by celluloid film, magnetic video, InterLace Spontaneous Dissemination, TP-compatible InterLace cartridge, or privately distributed by Incandenza's own company(ies). The designation UNRELEASED is used for those works which never saw distribution and are now publicly unavailable or lost.

Cage.[b] Dated only 'Before Subsidization.' Meniscus Films, Ltd. Uncredited cast; 16 mm.; .5 minutes; black and white; sound. Soliloquized parody of a broadcast-television advertisement for shampoo, utilizing four convex mirrors, two planar mirrors, and one actress. UNRELEASED

Kinds of Light. B.S. Meniscus Films, Ltd. No cast; 16 mm.; 3 minutes; color; silent. 4,444 individual frames, each of which photo depicts lights of different source, wavelength, and candle power, each reflected off the same unpolished tin plate and rendered disorienting at normal projection speeds by the hyperretinal speed at which they pass. CELLULOID, LIMITED METROPOLITAN BOSTON RELEASE, REQUIRES PROJECTION AT .25 NORMAL SPROCKET DRIVE

Dark Logics. B.S. Meniscus Films, Ltd. Players uncredited; 35 mm.; 21 minutes; color; silent w/ deafening Wagner/Sousa soundtrack. Griffith tribute, Iimura parody. Child-sized but severely palsied hand turns pages of incunabular manuscripts in mathematics, alchemy, religion, and bogus political autobiography, each page

---

b. With the possible exception of *Cage III—Free Show,* Incandenza's *Cage* series bears no discernible relation to Sidney Peterson's 1947 classic, *The Cage.*

comprising some articulation or defense of intolerance and hatred. Film's dedication to D. W. Griffith and Taka Iimura. UNRELEASED

Tennis, Everyone? B.S. Heliotrope Films, Ltd./U.S.T.A. Films. Documentary cast w/ narrator Judith Fukuoka-Hearn; 35 mm.; 26 minutes; color; sound. Public relations/advertorial production for United States Tennis Association in conjunction with Wilson Sporting Goods, Inc. MAGNETIC VIDEO

'*There Are No Losers Here.*' B.S. Heliotrope Films, Ltd./U.S.T.A. Films. Documentary cast w/ narrator P. A. Heaven; 35 mm.; color; sound. Documentary on B.S. 1997 U.S.T.A. National Junior Tennis Championships, Kalamazoo MI and Miami FL, in conjunction with United States Tennis Association and Wilson Sporting Goods. MAGNETIC VIDEO

Flux in a Box. B.S. Heliotrope Films, Ltd./Wilson Inc. Documentary cast w/ narrator Judith Fukuoka-Hearn; 35 mm.; 52 minutes; black and white/color; sound. Documentary history of box, platform, lawn, and court tennis from the 17th-century Court of the Dauphin to the present. MAGNETIC VIDEO

Infinite Jest (I). B.S. Meniscus Films, Ltd. Judith Fukuoka-Hearn; 16/35 mm.; 90(?) minutes; black and white; silent. Incandenza's unfinished and unseen first attempt at commercial entertainment. UNRELEASED

Annular Fusion Is Our Friend. B.S. Heliotrope Films, Ltd./Sunstrand Power & Light Co. Documentary cast w/ narrator C. N. Reilly; Sign-Interpreted for the Deaf; 78 mm.; 45 minutes; color; sound. Public relations/advertorial production for New England's Sunstrand Power and Light utility, a nontechnical explanation of the processes of DT-cycle lithiumized annular fusion and its applications in domestic energy production. CELLULOID, MAGNETIC VIDEO

Annular Amplified Light: Some Reflections. B.S. Heliotrope Films/Sunstrand Power & Light

Co. Documentary cast w/ narrator C. N. Reilly; Sign-Interpreted for the Deaf; 78 mm.; 45 minutes; color; sound. Second infomercial for Sunstrand Co., a nontechnical explanation of the applications of cooled-photon lasers in DT-cycle lithiumized annular fusion. CELLULOID, MAGNETIC VIDEO

Union of Nurses in Berkeley. B.S. Meniscus Films, Ltd. Documentary cast; 35 mm.; 26 minutes; color; silent. Documentary and closed-caption interviews with hearing-impaired RNs and LPNs during Bay Area health care reform riots of 1996. MAGNETIC VIDEO, PRIVATELY RELEASED BY MENISCUS FILMS, LTD.

Union of Theoretical Grammarians in Cambridge. B.S. Meniscus Films, Ltd. Documentary cast; 35 mm.; 26 minutes; color; silent w/ heavy use of computerized distortion in facial close-ups. Documentary and closed-caption interviews with participants in the public Steven Pinker–Avril M. Incandenza debate on the political implications of prescriptive grammar during the infamous Militant Grammarians of Massachusetts convention credited with helping incite the M.I.T. language riots of B.S. 1997. UNRELEASED DUE TO LITIGATION

Widower. B.S. Latrodectus Mactans Productions. Cosgrove Watt, Ross Reat; 35 mm.; 34 minutes; black and white; sound. Shot on location in Tucson AZ, parody of broadcast television domestic comedies, a cocaine-addicted father (Watt) leads his son (Reat) around their desert property immolating poisonous spiders. CELLULOID; INTERLACE TELENT CARTRIDGE RERELEASE #357–75–00 (Y.P.W.)

Cage II. B.S. Latrodectus Mactans Productions. Cosgrove Watt, Disney Leith; 35 mm.; 120 minutes; black and white; sound. Sadistic penal authorities place a blind convict (Watt) and a deaf-mute convict (Leith) together in 'solitary confinement,' and the two men attempt to devise ways of communicating with each other. LIMITED CELLULOID RUN; RERELEASED ON MAGNETIC VIDEO

Death in Scarsdale. B.S. Latrodectus Mactans Productions. Cosgrove Watt, Marlon R. Bain; 78 mm.; 39 minutes; color; silent w/ closed-caption subtitles. Mann/Allen parody, a world-famous dermatological endocrinologist (Watt) becomes platonically obsessed with a boy (Bain) he is treating for excessive perspiration, and begins himself to suffer from excessive perspiration. UNRELEASED

Fun with Teeth. B.S. Latrodectus Mactans Productions. Herbert G. Birch, Billy Tolan, Pam Heath; 35 mm.; 73 minutes; black and white; silent w/ non-human screams and howls. Kosinski/Updike/Peckinpah parody, a dentist (Birch) performs sixteen unanesthetized root-canal procedures on an academic (Tolan) he suspects of involvement with his wife (Heath). MAGNETIC VIDEO, PRIVATELY RELEASED BY LATRODECTUS MACTANS PROD.

Infinite Jest (II). B.S. Latrodectus Mactans Productions. Pam Heath; 35/78 mm.; 90(?) minutes; black and white; silent. Unfinished, unseen attempt at remake of *Infinite Jest (I).* UNRELEASED

Immanent Domain. B.S. Latrodectus Mactans Productions. Cosgrove Watt, Judith Fukuoka-Hearn, Pam Heath, Pamela-Sue Voorheis, Herbert G. Birch; 35 mm.; 88 minutes; black and white w/ microphotography; sound. Three memory-neurons (Fukuoka-Hearn, Heath, Voorheis (w/ polyurethane costumes)) in the Inferior frontal gyrus of a man's (Watt's) brain fight heroically to prevent their displacement by new memory-neurons as the man undergoes intensive psychoanalysis. CELLULOID; INTERLACE TELENT CARTRIDGE RERELEASE #340–03–70 (Y.P.W.)

Kinds of Pain. B.S. Latrodectus Mactans Productions. Anonymous cast; 35/78 mm.; 6 minutes; color; silent. 2,222 still-frame close-ups of middle-aged white males suffering from almost every conceivable type of pain, from an ingrown toenail to cranio-facial neuralgia to inoperable colo-rectal neoplastis. CELLULOID, LIM-ITED METRO BOSTON RELEASE, REQUIRES PROJECTION AT .25 NORMAL SPROCKET-DRIVE

Various Small Flames. B.S. Latrodectus Mactans Productions. Cosgrove Watt, Pam Heath, Ken N. Johnson; 16 mm.; 25 minutes w/ recursive loop for automatic replay; color; silent w/ sounds of human coitus appropriated from and credited to Caballero Control Corp. adult videos. Parody of neoconceptual structuralist films of Godbout and Vodriard, n-frame images of myriad varieties of small household flames, from lighters and birthday candles to stovetop gas rings and grass clippings ignited by sunlight through a magnifying glass, alternated with antinarrative sequences of a man (Watt) sitting in a dark bedroom drinking bourbon while his wife (Heath) and an Amway representative (Johnson) have acrobatic coitus in the background's lit hallway. UNRELEASED DUE TO LITIGATION BY 1960s US CONCEPTUAL DIRECTOR OF *VARIOUS SMALL FIRES* ED RUSCHA—INTERLACE TELENT CARTRIDGE RERELEASE #330–54–94 (Y.T.-S.D.B.)

Cage III—Free Show. B.S. Latrodectus Mactans Productions/Infernatron Animation Concepts, Canada. Cosgrove Watt, P. A. Heaven, Everard Maynell, Pam Heath; partial animation; 35 mm.; 65 minutes; black and white; sound. The figure of Death (Heath) presides over the front entrance of a carnival sideshow whose spectators watch performers undergo unspeakable degradations so grotesquely compelling that the spectators' eyes become larger and larger until the spectators themselves are transformed into gigantic eyeballs in chairs, while on the other side of the sideshow tent the figure of Life (Heaven) uses a megaphone to invite fairgoers to an exhibition in which, if the fairgoers consent to undergo unspeakable degradations, they can witness ordinary persons gradually turn into gigantic eyeballs. INTERLACE TELENT FEATURE CARTRIDGE #357–65–65

'*The Medusa v. the Odalisque.*' B.S. Latrodectus Mactans Productions. Uncredited cast; zone-plating laser holography by James O. Incandenza and Urquhart Ogilvie, Jr.; holographic fight-choreography by Kenjiru Hirota courtesy of Sony Entertainment-Asia; 78 mm.; 29 minutes; black and white; silent w/ audience-noises appropriated from network broadcast television. Mobile holograms of two visually lethal mythologic females duel with reflective surfaces onstage while a live crowd of spectators turns to stone. LIMITED CELLULOID RUN; PRIVATELY RE-RELEASED ON MAGNETIC VIDEO BY LATRODECTUS MACTANS PRODUCTIONS

The Machine in the Ghost: Annular Holography for Fun and Prophet. B.S. Heliotrope Films, Ltd./National Film Board of Canada. Narrator P. A. Heaven; 78 mm.; 35 minutes; color; sound. Nontechnical introduction to theories of annular enhancement and zone-plating and their applications in high-resolution laser holography. UNRELEASED DUE TO US/CANADIAN DIPLOMATIC TENSIONS

Homo Duplex. B.S. Latrodectus Mactans Productions. Narrator P. A. Heaven; Super-8 mm.; 70 minutes; black and white; sound. Parody of Woititz and Shulgin's 'poststructural antidocumentaries,' interviews with fourteen Americans who are named John Wayne but are not the legendary 20th-century film actor John Wayne. MAGNETIC VIDEO (LIMITED RELEASE)

Zero-Gravity Tea Ceremony. B.S. Latrodectus Mactans Productions. Ken N. Johnson, Judith Fukuoka-Hearn, Otto Brandt, E. J. Kenkle; 35 mm.; 82 minutes; black and white/color; silent. The intricate *Ocha-Kai* is conducted 2.5 m. off the ground in the Johnson Space Center's zero-gravity-simulation chamber. CELLULOID; INTERLACE TELENT RERELEASE #357-40-01 (Y.P.W.)

Pre-Nuptial Agreement of Heaven and Hell. B.S. Latrodectus Mactans Productions/ Infernatron Animation Concepts, Canada. Animated w/ uncredited voices; 35 mm.; 59 minutes; color; sound. God and Satan play poker with Tarot cards for the soul of an alcoholic sandwich-bag salesman obsessed with Bernini's 'The Ecstasy of St. Teresa.' PRIVATELY RELEASED ON CELLULOID AND MAGNETIC VIDEO BY LATRODECTUS MACTANS PRODUCTIONS

The Joke. B.S. Latrodectus Mactans Productions. Audience as reflexive cast; 35 mm. × 2 cameras; variable length; black and white; silent. Parody of Hollis Frampton's 'audience-specific events,' two Ikegami EC-35 video cameras in theater record the 'film' 's audience and project the resultant raster onto screen—the theater audience watching itself watch itself get the obvious 'joke' and become increasingly self-conscious and uncomfortable and hostile supposedly comprises the film's involuted 'antinarrative' flow. Incandenza's first truly controversial project, *Film & Kartridge Kultcher's* Sperber credited it with 'unwittingly sounding the death-knell of post-poststructural film in terms of sheer annoyance.' NONRECORDED MAGNETIC VIDEO SCREEN-ABLE IN THEATER VENUE ONLY, NOW UNRELEASED

Various Lachrymose U.S. Corporate Middle-Management Figures. Unfinished. UNRELEASED

Every Inch of Disney Leith. B.S. Latrodectus Mactans Productions/Medical Imagery of Alberta, Ltd. Disney Leith; computer-enlarged 35 mm./x 2 m.; 253 minutes; color; silent. Miniaturized, endoscopic, and microinvasive cameras traverse entire exterior and interior of one of Incandenza's technical crew as he sits on a folded serape in the Boston Common listening to a public forum on uniform North American metricization. PRIVATE RELEASE ON MAGNETIC VIDEO BY LATRO-DECTUS MACTANS PRODUCTIONS; INTERLACE TELENT RERE-LEASE #357-56-34 (Y.P.W.)

Infinite Jest (III). B.S. Latrodectus Mactans Productions. Uncredited cast; 16/35 mm.; color; sound. Unfinished, unseen remake of *Infinite Jest (I), (II).* UNRELEASED

Found Drama I.
Found Drama II.
Found Drama III. . . . conceptual, conceptually unfilmable. UNRELEASED

The Man Who Began to Suspect He Was Made of Glass. Year of the Whopper. Latrodectus Mactans Productions. Cosgrove Watt, Gerhardt Schtitt; 35 mm.; 21 minutes; black and white; sound. A man undergoing intensive psychotherapy discovers that he is brittle, hollow, and transparent to others, and becomes either transcendentally enlightened or schizophrenic. INTERLACE TELENT FEATURE CARTRIDGE #357–59–00

Found Drama V.
Found Drama VI. . . . conceptual, conceptually unfilmable. UNRELEASED

The American Century as Seen Through a Brick. Year of the Whopper. Latrodectus Mactans Productions. Documentary cast w/ narration by P. A. Heaven; 35 mm.; 52 minutes; color w/ red filter and oscillophotography; silent w/ narration. As U.S. Boston's historical Back Bay streets are stripped of brick and repaved with polymerized cement, the resultant career of one stripped brick is followed, from found-art temporary installation to displacement by E.W.D. catapult to a waste-quarry in southern Québec to its use in the F.L.Q.-incited anti-O.N.A.N. riots of January/Whopper, all intercut with ambiguous shots of a human thumb's alterations in the interference pattern of a plucked string. PRIVATELY RELEASED ON MAGNETIC VIDEO BY LATRODECTUS MACTANS PRODUCTIONS

The ONANtiad. Year of the Whopper. Latrodectus Mactans Productions/Claymation action sequences © Infernatron Animation Concepts, Canada. Cosgrove Watt, P. A. Heaven, Pam Heath, Ken N. Johnson, Ibn-Said Chawaf, Squyre Frydell, Marla-Dean Chumm, Herbert G. Birch, Everard Meynell; 35 mm.; 76 minutes; black and white/color; sound/silent. Oblique, obsessive, and not very funny claymation love triangle played out against live-acted backdrop of the inception of North American Interdependence and Continental Reconfiguration. PRIVATELY RELEASED ON MAGNETIC VIDEO BY LATRODECTUS MACTANS PRODUCTIONS

The Universe Lashes Out. Year of the Whopper. Latrodectus Mactans Productions. Documentary cast w/ narrator Herbert G. Birch; 16 mm.; 28 minutes; color; silent w/ narration. Documentary on the evacuation of Atkinson NH/New Québec at the inception of Continental Reconfiguration. MAGNETIC VIDEO (LIMITED RELEASE)

Poultry in Motion. Year of the Whopper. Latrodectus Mactans Productions. Documentary cast w/ narrator P. A. Heaven; 16 mm.; 56 minutes; color; silent w/ narration. Documentary on renegade North Syracuse NNY turkey farmers' bid to prevent toxification of Thanksgiving crop by commandeering long, shiny O.N.A.N. trucks to transplant over 200,000 pertussive fowl south to Ithaca. MAGNETIC VIDEO (LIMITED RELEASE)

Found Drama IX.
Found Drama X.
Found Drama XI. . . . conceptual, conceptually unfilmable. UNRELEASED

Möbius Strips. Year of the Whopper. Lactrodectus Mactans Productions. 'Hugh G. Rection,' Pam Heath, 'Bunny Day,' 'Taffy Appel'; 35 mm.; 109 minutes; black and white; sound. Pornography-parody, possible parodic homage to Fosse's *All That Jazz*, in which a theoretical physicist ('Rection'), who can only achieve creative mathematical insight during coitus, conceives of Death as a lethally beautiful woman (Heath). INTERLACE TELENT FEATURE CARTRIDGE #357–65–32 (Y.W.)

Wave Bye-Bye to the Bureaucrat. Year of the Whopper. Latrodectus Mactans Productions. Everard Maynell, Phillip T. Smothergill, Paul Anthony Heaven, Pamela-Sue Voorheis; 16 mm.; 19 minutes; black and white; sound. Possible parody/homage to B.S. public-service-announcement cycle of Church of Jesus Christ of Latter-Day Saints,[c] a harried commuter is mistaken for Christ by a child he knocks over.

Blood Sister: One Tough Nun. Year of the Tucks Medicated Pad. Latrodectus Mactans Productions. Telma Hurley, Pam Heath, Marla-Dean Chumm, Diane Saltoone, Soma Richardson-Levy, Cosgrove Watt; 35 mm.; 90 minutes; color; sound. Parody of revenge/recidivism action genre, a formerly delinquent nun's (Hurley's) failure to reform a juvenile delinquent (Chumm) leads to a rampage of recidivist revenge. INTERLACE TELENT PULSE-DISSEMINATION 21 JULY Y.T.M.P., CARTRIDGE #357–87–04

Infinite Jest (IV). Year of the Tucks Medicated Pad. Latrodectus Mactans Productions. Pam Heath (?), 'Madame Psychosis'(?); 78 mm.; 90 minutes(?); color; sound. Unfinished, unseen attempt at completion of *Infinite Jest (III)*. UNRELEASED

Let There Be Lite. Year of the Tucks Medicated Pad. Poor Yorick Entertainment Unlimited. Documentary cast w/ narrator Ken N. Johnson; 16mm.; 50 minutes(?); black and white; silent w/ narration. Unfinished documentary on genesis of reduced-calorie bourbon industry. UNRELEASED

Untitled. Unfinished. UNRELEASED

No Troy. Year of the Whopper. Latrodectus Mactans Productions. No cast; liquid-surface holography by Urquhart Ogilvie, Jr.; 35 mm.; 7 minutes; enhanced color; silent.

---

c. See Romney and Sperber, 'Has James O. Incandenza Ever Even Once Produced One Genuinely Original or Unappropriated or Nonderivative Thing?' *Post-Millennium Film Cartridge Journal*, nos. 7–9 (Fall/Winter, Y.P.W.), pp. 4–26.

Scale-model holographic recreation of Troy NY's bombardment by miscalibrated Waste Displacement Vehicles, and its subsequent elimination by O.N.A.N. cartographers. MAGNETIC VIDEO (PRIVATE RELEASE LIMITED TO NEW BRUNSWICK, ALBERTA, QUÉBEC) Note: Archivists in Canada and the U.S. West Coast do not list *No Troy* but do list titles *The Violet City* and *The Violet Ex-City*, respectively, leading scholars to conclude that the same film was released under several different appellations.

Untitled. Unfinished. UNRELEASED

Valuable Coupon Has Been Removed. Year of the Tucks Medicated Pad. Poor Yorick Entertainment Unlimited. Cosgrove Watt, Phillip T. Smothergill, Diane Saltoone; 16 mm.; 52 minutes; color; silent. Possible Scandinavian-psychodrama parody, a boy helps his alcoholic-delusional father and disassociated mother dismantle their bed to search for rodents, and later he intuits the future feasibility of D.T.-cycle lithiumized annular fusion. CELLULOID (UNRELEASED)

Baby Pictures of Famous Dictators. Year of the Tucks Medicated Pad. Poor Yorick Entertainment Unlimited. Documentary or uncredited cast w/ narrator P. A. Heaven; 16 mm.; 45 minutes; black and white; sound. Children and adolescents play a nearly incomprehensible nuclear strategy game with tennis equipment against the real or holographic(?) backdrop of sabotaged ATHSCME 1900 atmospheric displacement towers exploding and toppling during the New New England Chemical Emergency of Y.W. CELLULOID (UNRELEASED)

Stand Behind the Men Behind the Wire. Year of the Tucks Medicated Pad. Poor Yorick Entertainment Unlimited. Documentary cast w/ narrator Soma Richardson-Levy; Super-8 mm.; 52 minutes; black and white/color; sound. Shot on location north of Lowell MA, documentary on Essex County Sheriff's Dept. and Massachusetts Department of Social Services' expedition to track, verify, capture, or propitiate the outsized feral infant alleged to have crushed, gummed, or picked up and dropped over a dozen residents of Lowell in January, Y.T.M.P. INTERLACE TELENT CARTRIDGE #357–12–56

As of Yore. Year of the Tucks Medicated Pad. Poor Yorick Entertainment Unlimited. Cosgrove Watt, Marlon Bain; 16/78 mm.; 181 minutes; black and white/color; sound. A middle-aged tennis instructor, preparing to instruct his son in tennis, becomes intoxicated in the family's garage and subjects his son to a rambling monologue while the son weeps and perspires. INTERLACE TELENT CARTRIDGE #357–16–09

The Clever Little Bastard. Unfinished, unseen. UNRELEASED

The Cold Majesty of the Numb. Unfinished, unseen. UNRELEASED

Good-Looking Men in Small Clever Rooms That Utilize Every Centimeter of Available Space With Mind-Boggling Efficiency. Unfinished due to hospitalization. UNRELEASED

Low-Temperature Civics. Year of the Tucks Medicated Pad. Poor Yorick Entertainment Unlimited. Cosgrove Watt, Herbert G. Birch, Ken N. Johnson, Soma Richardson-Levy, Everard Maynell, 'Madame Psychosis,' Phillip T. Smothergill, Paul Anthony Heaven; 35 mm.; 80 minutes; black and white; sound. Wyler parody in which four sons (Birch, Johnson, Maynell, Smothergill) intrigue for control of a sandwich-bag conglomerate after their CEO father (Watt) has an ecstatic encounter with Death ('Psychosis') and becomes irreversibly catatonic. NATIONAL DISSEMINATION IN INTERLACE TELENT'S 'CAVALCADE OF EVIL' SERIES—JANUARY/YEAR OF TRIAL-SIZE DOVE BAR—AND INTERLACE TELENT CARTRIDGE #357-89-05

(At Least) Three Cheers for Cause and Effect. Year of the Tucks Medicated Pad. Poor Yorick Entertainment Unlimited. Cosgrove Watt, Pam Heath, 'Hugh G. Rection'; 78 mm.; 26 minutes; black and white; sound. The headmaster of a newly constructed high-altitude sports academy (Watt) becomes neurotically obsessed with litigation over the construction's ancillary damage to a V.A. hospital far below, as a way of diverting himself from his wife's (Heath's) poorly hidden affair with the academically renowned mathematical topologist who is acting as the project's architect ('Rection'). CELLULOID (UNRELEASED)

(The) Desire to Desire. Year of the Tucks Medicated Pad. Poor Yorick Entertainment Unlimited. Robert Lingley, 'Madame Psychosis,' Marla-Dean Chumm; 35 mm.; 99 minutes(?); black and white; silent. A pathology resident (Lingley) falls in love with a beautiful cadaver ('Psychosis') and the paralyzed sister (Chumm) she died rescuing from the attack of an oversized feral infant. Listed by some archivists as unfinished. UNRELEASED

Safe Boating Is No Accident. Year of the Tucks Medicated Pad(?). Poor Yorick Entertainment Unlimited/X-Ray and Infrared Photography by Shuco-Mist Medical Pressure Systems, Enfield MA. Ken N. Johnson, 'Madame Psychosis,' P. A. Heaven. Kierkegaard/Lynch (?) parody, a claustrophobic water-ski instructor ('Johnson), struggling with his romantic conscience after his fiancée's ('Psychosis's) face is grotesquely mangled by an outboard propeller, becomes trapped in an overcrowded hospital elevator with a defrocked Trappist monk, two overcombed missionaries for the Church of Jesus Christ of Latter-Day Saints, an enigmatic fitness guru, the Massachusetts State Commissioner for Beach and Water Safety, and seven severely intoxicated opticians with silly hats and exploding cigars. Listed by some archivists as completed the following year, Y.T.-S.D.B. UNRELEASED

Very Low Impact. Year of the Tucks Medicated Pad. Poor Yorick Entertainment Unlimited. Marla-Dean Chumm, Pam Heath, Soma Richardson-Levy-O'Byrne; 35 mm.; 30 minutes; color; sound. A narcoleptic aerobics instructor (Chumm) struggles to hide her condition from students and employers. POSTHUMOUS RELEASE Y.W.-Q.M.D.; INTERLACE TELENT CARTRIDGE #357-97-29

The Night Wears a Sombrero. Year of the Tucks Medicated Pad (?): Ken N. Johnson, Phillip T. Smothergill, Dianne Saltoone, 'Madame Psychosis'; 78 mm.; 105 minutes; color; silent/sound. Parody/homage to Lang's *Rancho Notorious,* a nearsighted apprentice cowpoke (Smothergill), swearing vengeance for a gunslinger's (Johnson's) rape of what he (the cowpoke) mistakenly believes is the motherly brothel-owner (Saltoone) he (the cowpoke) is secretly in love with, loses the trail of the gunslinger after misreading a road sign and is drawn to a sinister Mexican ranch where Oedipally aggrieved gunslingers are ritually blinded by a mysterious veiled nun ('Psychosis'). Listed by some archivists as completed the preceding year, Y.W. INTERLACE TELENT CARTRIDGE #357–56–51

Accomplice! Year of the Tucks Medicated Pad. Poor Yorick Entertainment Unlimited. Cosgrove Watt, Stokely 'Dark Star' McNair; 16 mm.; 26 minutes; color; sound. An aging pederast mutilates himself out of love for a strangely tattooed street hustler. INTERLACE TELENT CARTRIDGE #357-10-10 withdrawn from dissemination after *Cartridge Scene* reviewers called *Accomplice!* '…the stupidest, nastiest, least subtle and worst-edited product of a pretentious and wretchedly uneven career.' NOW UNRELEASED

Untitled. Unfinished. UNRELEASED

Untitled. Unfinished. UNRELEASED

Untitled. Unfinished. UNRELEASED

Dial C for Concupiscence. Year of the Trial-Size Dove Bar. Poor Yorick Entertainment Unlimited. Soma Richardson-Levy-O'Byrne, Marla-Dean Chumm, Ibn-Said Chawaf, Yves Francoeur; 35 mm.; 122 minutes; black and white; silent w/ subtitles. Parodic *noir*-style tribute to Bresson's *Les Anges du Peché,* a cellular phone operator (Richardson-Levy-O'Byrne), mistaken by a Québecois terrorist (Francoeur) for another cellular phone operator (Chumm) the FLQ had mistakenly tried to assassinate, mistakes his mistaken attempts to apologize as attempts to assassinate her (Richardson-Levy-O'Byrne) and flees to a bizarre Islamic religious community whose members communicate with each other by means of semaphore flags, where she falls in love with an armless Near Eastern medical attaché (Chawaf). RELEASED IN INTERLACE TELENT'S 'HOWLS FROM THE MARGIN' UNDERGROUND FILM SERIES—MARCH/Y.T.-S.D.B.—AND INTERLACE TELENT CARTRIDGE #357–75–43

Insubstantial Country. Year of the Trial-Size Dove Bar. Poor Yorick Entertainment Unlimited. Cosgrove Watt; 16 mm.; 30 minutes; black and white; silent/sound. An unpopular après-garde filmmaker (Watt) either suffers a temporal lobe seizure and becomes mute or else is the victim of everyone else's delusion that his (Watt's) temporal lobe seizure has left him mute. PRIVATE CARTRIDGE RELEASE BY POOR YORICK ENTERTAINMENT UNLIMITED

It Was a Great Marvel That He Was in the Father Without Knowing Him. Year of the Trial-Size Dove Bar. Poor Yorick Entertainment Unlimited. Cosgrove Watt, Phillip T. Smothergill; 16 mm.; 5 minutes; black and white; silent/sound. A father (Watt), suffering from the delusion that his etymologically precocious son (Smothergill) is pretending to be mute, poses as a 'professional conversationalist' in order to draw the boy out. RELEASED IN INTERLACE TELENT'S 'HOWLS FROM THE MARGIN' UNDERGROUND FILM SERIES—MARCH/ Y.T.-S.D.B.—AND INTERLACE TELENT CARTRIDGE #357-75-50

Cage IV—Web. Unfinished. UNRELEASED

Cage V—Infinite Jim. Unfinished. UNRELEASED

Death and the Single Girl. Unfinished. UNRELEASED.

The Film Adaptation of Peter Weiss's 'The Persecution and Assassination of Marat as Performed by the Inmates of the Asylum at Charenton Under the Direction of the Marquis de Sade.' Year of the Trial-Size Dove Bar. Poor Yorick Entertainment Unlimited. James O. Incandenza, Disney Leith, Urquhart Ogilvie, Jr., Jane Ann Prickett, Herbert G. Birch, 'Madame Psychosis,' Marla-Dean Chumm, Marlon Bain, Pam Heath, Soma Richardson-Levy-O'Byrne-Chawaf, Ken N. Johnson, Dianne Saltoone; Super-8 mm.; 88 minutes; black and white; silent/sound. Fictional 'interactive documentary' on Boston stage production of Weiss's 20th-century play within play, in which the documentary's chemically impaired director (Incandenza) repeatedly interrupts the inmates' dumbshow-capering and Marat and Sade's dialogues to discourse incoherently on the implications of Brando's Method Acting and Artaud's Theatre of Cruelty for North American filmed entertainment, irritating the actor who plays Marat (Leith) to such an extent that he has a cerebral hemorrhage and collapses onstage well before Marat's scripted death, whereupon the play's nearsighted director (Ogilvie), mistaking the actor who plays Sade (Johnson) for Incandenza, throws Sade into Marat's medicinal bath and throttles him to death, whereupon the extra-dramatic figure of Death ('Psychosis') descends *deus ex machina* to bear Marat (Leith) and Sade (Johnson) away, while Incandenza becomes ill all over the theater audience's first row. 8 MM. SYNC-PROJECTION CELLULOID. UNRELEASED DUE TO LITIGATION, HOSPITALIZATION

Too Much Fun. Unfinished. UNRELEASED

The Unfortunate Case of Me. Unfinished. UNRELEASED

Sorry All Over the Place. Unfinished. UNRELEASED

Infinite Jest (V?). Year of the Trial-Size Dove Bar. Poor Yorick Entertainment Unlimited. 'Madame Psychosis'; no other definitive data. Thorny problem for archivists. Incandenza's last film, Incandenza's death occurring during its post-production. Most archival authorities list as unfinished, unseen. Some list as completion of *Infinite Jest (IV)*, for which Incandenza also used 'Psychosis,' thus list the film under Incandenza's output for Y.T.M.P. Though no scholarly synopsis or report of viewing exists, two short essays in different issues of *Cartridge Quarterly East* refer to the film as 'extraordinary'[d] and 'far and away [James O. Incandenza's] most entertaining and compelling work.'[e] West Coast archivists list the film's gauge as '16…78…n mm.,' basing the gauge on critical allusions[f] to 'radical experiments in viewers' optical perspective and context' as *IJ(V?)*'s distinctive feature. Though Canadian archivist Tête-Bêche lists the film as completed and privately distributed by P.Y.E.U. through posthumous provisions in the filmmaker's will, all other comprehensive filmographies have the film either unfinished or UNRELEASED, its Master cartridge either destroyed or vaulted *sui testator*.

25. More like July-October, actually.

58. Certified (by the Commonwealth of Massachusetts) Substance Abuse Counselor.

59. Oxycodone hydrochloride w/ acetaminophen, C-II Class, Du Pont Pharmaceuticals.

69. NA = Narcotics Anonymous; CA = Cocaine Anonymous. In some cities there are also Psychedelics Anonymous, Nicotine Anonymous (also, confusingly, called NA), Designer Drugs Anonymous, Steroids Anonymous, even (especially in and around Manhattan) something called Prozac Anonymous. In none of these Anonymous fellowships anywhere is it possible to avoid confronting the God stuff, eventually.

70. Not to mention, according to some hard-line schools of 12-Step thought, yoga, reading, politics, gum-chewing, crossword puzzles, solitaire, romantic intrigue, charity work, political activism, N.R.A. membership, music, art, cleaning, plastic surgery, cartridge-viewing even at normal distances, the loyalty of a fine dog, religious zeal, relentless helpfulness, relentless other-folks'-moral-inventory-taking, the development of hard-line schools of 12-Step thought, ad darn near infinitum, including 12-Step fellowships themselves, such that quiet tales sometimes go around the Boston AA community of certain incredibly advanced and hard-line recovering persons who have pared away potential escape after potential escape until finally, as the stories go, they end up sitting in a bare chair, nude, in an unfurnished room, not moving but also not sleeping or meditating or abstracting, too advanced to stomach the thought of the potential emotional escape of doing anything whatsoever, and just end up sitting there completely motion- and escapeless until a long

---

d. E. Duquette, 'Beholden to Vision: Optics and Desire in Four Après Garde Films,' *Cartridge Quarterly East*, vol. 4 no. 2, Y.W.-Q.M.D., pp. 35-39.

e. Anonymous, 'Seeing v. Believing,' *Cartridge Quarterly East*, vol. 4 no. 4, Y.W.-Q.M.D., pp. 93–95.

f. Ibid.

time later all that's found in the empty chair is a very fine dusting of off-white ashy stuff that you can wipe away completely with like one damp paper towel.

71. The Boston AA slogan w/r/t this phenomenon is 'You Can't Unring a Bell.'

72. About which Pakistani manager and his ancestry and ratty little mustache and officious management style McDade has a colorful thing or two to say, boy.

81. 'Theory and Praxis in Peckinpah's Use of Red,' *Classic Cartridge Studies* vol. IX, nos. 2 & 3, YY2007MRCVMETIUFI/ITPSFH,O,OM(s).

102. International Brotherhood of Pier, Wharf, and Dock Workers.

103. A quote 'episode of excessive neuronal discharge manifested by motor, sensory and/or [psychic] dysfunction, with or without unconsciousness and/or convulsive [movements],' plus eye-rolling and tongue-swallowing.

131. Before Boston Groups' regular speaker meetings there are often closed, half-hour Beginners' Discussion Meetings, where newcomers can share their cluelessness, weakness, and despair in a warm supportive private atmosphere.

132. The word *Group* in *AA Group* is always capitalized because Boston AA places enormous emphasis on joining a Group and identifying yourself as a member of this larger thing, the Group. Likewise caps in like *Commitment, Giving It Away,* and c.

133. Gately's little bedroom in the damp Ennet House basement is plastered all over every part of every wall that's dry enough to take tape with cutout Scotch-taped photos of all sorts of variegated and esoteric celebrities past and present, which are varied as residents throw magazines into the E.M.P.H.H. dumpsters and are frequently selected because the celebrities are somehow grotesque; it's a kind of compulsive habit held over from Gately's fairly dysfunctional North Shore childhood, when he'd been a clipping and taping fiend.

134. And if you're brand-new, as in like your first three days, and so on mandatory nonpunitive House Restriction—like veiled Joelle van Dyne, who entered the House just today, 11/8, Interdependence Day, after the E.R. physician at Brigham and Women's Hospital who last night had pumped her full of Inderal[a] and nitro had looked upon her unveiled face and been deeply affected, and had taken a special interest, a consequence of which after Joelle regained consciousness and speech had involved placing a call to Pat Montesian, whose paralyzing alcoholic stroke the physician had treated in this very same E.R. almost seven years before, and in whose case he'd also taken a special interest and had followed, such that he was now a personal friend of the sober Pat M.'s and sat honorarily on Ennet House's Board of Directors, so that his call to Pat's home on Saturday night had gotten Joelle into the House on the spot, as of Interdependence Day A.M.'s discharge from B&W, leap-frogging literally dozens of waiting-list people and putting Joelle into Ennet House's intensive program of residential treatment literally before she even knew what was happening, which in retrospect might have been lucky—if you're this new you're actually not supposed ever to leave the Staffer's sight, though in practice this rule gets suspended when you have to go to the ladies' room and the Staffer's male, or vice versa.

    a. Propranolol hydrochloride, Wyeth-Ayerst, a beta-blocking antihypertensive.

135. A conviction common to all who Hang In with AA, after a while, and abstracted in the slogan 'My Best Thinking Got Me Here.'

136. Trade-name Fastin, ®SmithKline Beecham Inc., a low-level 'drine not unlike Tenuate, though w/ more associated tooth-grinding.

137. None of these are Don Gately's terms.

138. In e.g. Boston: join Group, get Active, get phone #s, get sponsor, audio-call sponsor daily, hit meetings daily, pray like fiend for release from Disease, don't kid self that you can still buy rodneys in liquor stores or date your dealer's niece or think for a second you can still hang out in bars playing darts and just drinking Millennial Fizzies or vanilla Yoo-Hoos, etc.

139. Volunteer Counselor Eugenio ('Gene') M. favors entomologic tropes and analogies, which is especially effective with brand-new residents fresh from subjective safaris through the Kingdom of Bugs.

140. Don G.'s North Shore's vulgate signifier for trite/banal is: *limp.*

141. Likewise that his private term for blacks is *niggers,* which is unfortunately still all he knows.

208. From Ch. 16, 'The Awakening of My Interest in Annular Systems,' in *The Chill of Inspiration: Spontaneous Reminiscences by Seventeen Pioneers of DT-Cycle Lithiumized Annular Fusion,* ed. Prof. Dr. Günther Sperber, Institut für Neutronenphysik und Reaktortechnik, Kernforschungszentrum Karlsruhe, U.R.G., available in English in ferociously expensive hardcover only, © Y.T.M.P. from Springer-Verlag Wien NNY.

224. Q.v. William James on '…that latent process of unconscious preparation often preceding a sudden awakening to the fact that the mischief is irretrievably done,' the line that actually snapped Lenz to what he was up to when he chanced to read it in a huge large-print edition he'd found behind a bookshelf along the north wall of the Ennet living room of something called *The Principles of Psychology with The Gifford Lectures on Natural Religion,* by William James (obviously), available in EZC large-font print from Microsoft/NAL–Random House–Ticknor, Fields, Little, Brown and Co., © Y.T.M.P., a volume that's come to mean a great deal to Lenz.

225. ® The Mobil Chemical Co.'s Consumer Products Branch's Plastics Division, Pittsford NNY.

226. ® Ibid.

227. A.k.a. Haloperidol, McNeil Pharmaceutical, 5 mg./ml. pre-filled syringes: picture several cups of Celestial Seasonings' Cinnamon Soother tea followed by a lead-filled sap across the back of the skull.

246. A depressing new Sober Club in Somerville's Davis Square where AAs and NAs—mostly new and young—get heartbreakingly dolled up and dance stiffly and tremble with sober sexual anxiety and they stand around with Cokes and M.F.s telling each other how great it is to be in an intensely social venue with all your self-conscious inhibitions unmedicated and screaming in your head. The smiles alone in these places are excruciating to see.

247. A Restriction means just no Overnight that week and an extra Chore; a House Restriction means you have to be back an hour after work and nightly meetings; Full House is no leaving the House except for work and meetings, and 15 minutes to get back, and no even leaving to buy smokes or a paper, or even to go out in the lawn for oxygen, and one violation means a Discharge: F.H.R. is Ennet's version of the Hole, and it's dreaded.

248. Ennet House takes its urines over to the methadone clinic, which has all manner of clients who have to submit weekly urines to courts and programs, and the clinic lets Ennet put its urines gratis in the weekly batch the clinic sends out to an E.M.I.T.-

mill clinic all the way out in Natick, and in return every once in a while Pat gets a call from the trollish little social worker who runs #2 about some client down there who's decided he wants off the methadone, as well, and Pat will shoot the client way up on the Interview list and give him an interview and usually let the client in—Calvin T. and Danielle S. had both originally gotten into Ennet House this way, i.e. via #2.

249. It's maybe significant that Don Gately never once failed to clean up any vomit or incontinence his mother'd just drunkenly left there or passed out in, no matter how pissed off or disgusted he was or how sick he himself was: not once.

250. (who owns a Lincoln, Henderson does, origins unknown and suspicious)

251. This is all for Insurance Reasons, the Staff sheet on which Gately doesn't understand all the language of, and fears.

252. It's against House rules to smoke upstairs in the bedrooms—more Insurance Reasons—and a week's Restriction is supposed to be mandatory, and Pat's personally a fanatic about the rule, but Gately, much as he fears the grim boilerplate on the Insurance Sheet, always pretends he doesn't see anything when he sees somebody smoking up here, since when he was a resident he actually used to sometimes smoke *in his sleep* he was so tense, and every once in a while will wake up and find that he has again, i.e. lit a gasper and apparently smoked it and put it out all in his sleep, down in bed in his Staff oubliette in the basement.

253. (the items from the House's donated-clothes baskets that fit Gately being few and far)

254. Gately's made it an iron point never again ever to run, once he got straight.

255. NNE street argot for any kind of handgun.

256. (Erdedy's hands still up, w/ keys)

280. *Anhedonia* was apparently coined by Ribot, a Continental Frenchman, who in his 19th-century *Psychologie des Sentiments* says he means it to denote the psycho-equivalent of *analgesia*, which is the neurologic suppression of pain.

281. This had been one of Hal's deepest and most pregnant abstractions, one he'd come up with once while getting secretly high in the Pump Room. That we're all lonely for something we don't know we're lonely for. How else to explain the curious feeling that he goes around feeling like he misses somebody he's never even met? Without the universalizing abstraction, the feeling would make no sense.

282. (the big reason why people in pain are so self-absorbed and unpleasant to be around)

283. S.S.R.I.s, of which Zoloft and the ill-fated Prozac were the ancestors.

305. (she thought then)

306. Some of her and Jim's best arguments had been over the connotations of 'Everybody's a critic,' which Jim had liked to repeat with all different shades and pitches of ironic double-edge.

307. Joelle van Dyne and Orin Incandenza each remember themselves as the original approachee. It's unclear which if either's memory is accurate, though it's noteworthy that this is one of only two total times Orin has perceived himself as the approachee, the other being the 'Swiss hand-model' on whose nude flank he's been furiously tracing infinity signs all during the *Moment* Subject's absence.

308. = point of view.

316. Like e.g. the times C.T. and the Moms would come out to Logan to pick

Mario and Himself up from a filming trip, Mario lugging gear, Himself damp and pasty from the cabin pressure and not enough leg-room and his sportcoat pockets always clicking with little plastic bottles with unopenable caps, and in the car up to Enfield Mario's uncle would keep up an Opheliac mad monologue of chatter that would get Himself's poor teeth grinding so bad that when they pulled over to the breakdown lane and Mario came around to open the door and let Himself lean out and be ill there'd be grit in the throw-up that came out, white dental visible grit, from all the grinding.

317. © B.S. 1981, Routledge & Kegan Paul Plc, London UK, wildly expensive hdcover; not on disk.

318. Maine having been lost altogether, recall.

319. Incandenza family idiom for leftovers.

320. Main library, M.I.T., East Cambridge.

337. Latin blunder for self-defense's *se defendendo* is *sic,* either a befogged muddling of a professional legal term, or a post-Freudian slip, or (least likely) a very oblique and subtle jab at Gately from a Ewell intimate with the graveyard scene from *Hamlet*—namely V.i. 9.

338. Ketorolac tromethamine, a non-narcotic analgesic, little more than Motrin with ambition—®Syntex Labs.

339. International Brotherhood of Electrical Workers.

340. Doxycycline hyclate, an I.V.-antibiotic—®Parke-Davis Pharmaceuticals.

341. Oxycodone hydrochloride + acetaminophen, a Schedule C-III narcotic oral analgesic—®Du Pont Pharmaceuticals.

BRIEF INTERVIEWS WITH HIDEOUS MEN

A Radically Condensed History of Postindustrial Life

WHEN THEY WERE introduced, he made a witticism, hoping to be liked. She laughed extremely hard, hoping to be liked. Then each drove home alone, staring straight ahead, with the very same twist to their faces.

The man who'd introduced them didn't much like either of them, though he acted as if he did, anxious as he was to preserve good relations at all times. One never knew, after all, now did one now did one now did one.

Brief Interviews with Hideous Men

B.I. #14 08-96

St. Davids PA

'It's cost me every sexual relationship I ever had. I don't know why I do it. I'm not a political person, I don't consider myself. I'm not one of these America First, read the newspaper, will Buchanan get the nod people. I'll be doing it with some girl, it doesn't matter who. It's when I start to come. That it happens. I'm not a Democrat. I don't even vote. I freaked out about it one time and called a radio show about it, a doctor on the radio, anonymously, and he diagnosed it as the uncontrolled yelling of involuntary words or phrases, frequently insulting or scatological, which is coprolalia is the official term. Except when I start to come and always start yelling it it's not insulting, it's not obscene, it's always the same thing, and it's always so weird but I don't think insulting. I think it's just weird. And uncontrolled. It's like it comes out the same way the spooge comes out, it feels like that. I don't know what it's about and I can't help it.'

Q.

' "Victory for the Forces of Democratic Freedom!" Only way louder. As in really shouting it. Uncontrollably. I'm not even thinking it until it comes out and I hear it. "Victory for the Forces of Democratic Freedom!" Only louder than that: "*VICTORY—*" '

Q.

'Well it totally freaks them out, what do you think? And I just about die of the embarrassment. I don't ever know what to say. What do you say if you just shouted "Victory for the Forces of Democratic Freedom!" right when you came?'

Q.

'It wouldn't be so embarrassing if it wasn't so totally fucking weird. If I had any clue about what it was about. You know?'

Q....

'God, now I'm embarrassed as hell.'

Q.

'But all there *is* is the once. That's what I mean about it costing. I can tell how bad it freaks them out, and I get embarrassed and never call them again. Even if I try to explain. And it's the ones that'll act all understanding like they don't care and it's OK and they understand and it doesn't matter that embarrass me the worst, because it's so fucking weird to yell "Victory for the Forces of Democratic Freedom!" when you're shooting off that I can always tell they're totally freaked out and just condescending down to me and pretending they understand, and those are the ones where actually I actually end up almost getting pissed off and don't even feel embarrassed not calling them or totally avoiding them, the ones that say "I think I could love you anyway." '

B.I. #40 06-97

BENTON RIDGE OH

'It's the arm. You wouldn't think of it as a asset like that would you. But it's the arm. You want to see it? You won't get disgusted? Well here it is. Here's the arm. This is why I go by the name Johnny One-Arm. I made it up, not anybody being, like, hardhearted—me. I see how you're trying to be polite and not look at it. Go ahead and look though. It don't bother me. Inside my head I don't call it the arm I call it the Asset. How all would you describe it? Go on. You think it'll hurt my feelings? You want to hear me describe it? It looks like a arm that changed its mind early on in the game when it was in Mama's stomach with the rest of me. It's more like a itty tiny little flipper, it's little and wet-looking and darker than the rest of me is. It looks wet even when it's dry. It's not a pretty sight at all. I usually keep it in the sleeve until it's time to haul it out and use it for the Asset. Notice the shoulder's normal, it's just like the other shoulder. It's just the arm. It'll only go down to like the titty-nipple of my chest here, see? It's a little sucker. It ain't pretty. It moves fine, I can move it around fine. If you look close here at the end there's these little majiggers you can tell started out wanting to be fingers but didn't form. When I was in her stomach. The other arm—see? It's a normal arm, a little muscley on account of using it all the time. It's normal and long and the right color, that's the arm I show all the time, most times I keep the other sleeve pinned up so it don't look to be even anything like a arm in there at all. It's strong though. The arm is. It's hard on the eyes but it's strong, sometimes I'll try and get them to armwrestle it to see how strong it is. It's a strong little flippery sucker. If they think they can stand to

touch it. I always say if they don't think they can stand touching it why that's
OK, it don't hurt my feelings. You want to touch it?'

Q.

'That's all right. That is all right.'

Q.

'What it is is—well first there's always some girls around. You know
what I mean? At the foundry there, at the Lanes. There's a tavern right
down by the bus stop there. Jackpot—that's my best friend—Jackpot and
Kenny Kirk—Kenny Kirk's his cousin, Jackpot's, that are both over me at
the foundry cause I finished school and didn't get in the union till
after—they're real good-looking and normal-looking and Good With
The Ladies if you know what I mean, and there's always girls hanging
back around. Like in a group, a bunch or group of all of us, we'll all just
hang back, drink some beers. Jackpot and Kenny're always going with one
of them or the other and then the ones they're going with got friends. You
know. A whole, say, group of us there. You follow the picture here? And
I'll start hanging back with this one or that one, and after a while the first
stage is I'll start in to telling them how I got the name Johnny One-Arm
and about the arm. That's a stage of the thing. Of getting some pussy
using the Asset. I'll describe the arm while it's still up in the sleeve and
make it sound like just about the ugliest thing you ever did see. They'll get
this look on their face like Oh You Poor Little Fella You're Being Too
Hard On Yourself You Shouldn't Be Shameful Of The Arm. So on. How
I'm such a nice young fella and it breaks their heart to see me talk about
my own part of me that way especially since it weren't any fault of mine to
get born with the arm. At which time when they start with that stage of it
the next stage is I ask them do they want to see it. I say how I'm shameful
of the arm but somehow I trust them and they seem real nice and if they
want I'll unpin the sleeve and let the arm out and let them look at the arm
if they think they could stand it. I'll go on about the arm until they can't
hardly stand to hear no more about it. Sometimes it's a ex of Jackpot's
that's the one that starts hanging back with me down at Frame Eleven
over to the Lanes and saying how I'm such a good listener and sensitive
not like Jackpot or Kenny and she can't believe there's any way the arm's as
bad as I'm making out and like that. Or we'll be hanging back at her place
in the kitchenette or some such and I'll go It's So Hot I Feel Like Taking
My Shirt Off But I Don't Want To On Account Of I'm Shameful Of The
Arm. Like that. There's numerous, like, stages. I never out loud call it the
Asset believe you me. Go on and touch it whenever you get a mind to.
One of the stages is I know after some time I really am starting to come

off creepy to the girl, I can tell, cause all I can talk about is the arm and how wet and flippery it is but how it's strong but how I'd just about up and die if a girl as nice and pretty and perfect as I think she is saw it and got disgusted, and I can tell all the talk starts creeping them up inside and they start to secretly think I'm kind of a loser but they can't back out on me cause after all here they been all this time saying all this nice shit about what a sensitive young fella I am and how I shouldn't be shameful and there's no way the arm can be that bad. In this stage it's like they're committed into a corner and if they quit hanging back with me now why they know I can go It Was Because Of The Arm.'

Q.

'Usually long about two weeks, like that. The next is your critical-type stage where I show them the arm. I wait till it's just her and me alone someplace and I haul the sucker out. I make it seem like they talked me into it and now I trust them and they're who I finally feel like I can let it out of the sleeve and show it. And I show it to her just like I just did you. There's some additional things too I can do with it that look even worse, make it look—see that? See this right here? It's cause there ain't even really a elbow bone, it's just a—'

Q.

'Or some of your ointments or Vaseline-type jelly on it to make it look even wetter and shinier. The arm's not a pretty sight at all when I up and haul it out on them I'm telling you right now. It just about makes them puke, the sight of it the way I get it. Oh and a couple run out, some skedoodle right out the door. But your majority? Your majority of them'll swallow hard a time or two and go Oh It's It's It's Not Too Bad At All but they're looking over all away and try and not look at my face which I've got this totally shy and scared and trusting face on at the time like this one thing I can do where I can make my lip even tremble a little. Ee? Ee anh? And ever time sooner or later within inside, like, five minutes of it they'll up and start crying. They're in way over their head, see. They're, like, committed into a corner of saying how it can't be that ugly and I shouldn't be shameful and then they see it and I see to it it is ugly, ugly ugly ugly and now what do they do? Pretend? Shit girl most of these girls around here think Elvis is alive someplace. These are not girl wonders of the brain. It breaks them down ever time. They get even worse if I ask them Oh Golly What's Wrong, how come they're crying, Is It The Arm and they have to say It Ain't The Arm, they have to, they have to try and pretend it ain't the arm that it's how they feel so sad for me being so shameful of something that ain't a big deal at all they have to say. Oftentimes with their face in their hands and crying. Your climactic stage then is then I up and come over to where she's at and sit down and now I'm the one that's comforting them. A, like, factor here I found out the hard way is when I go in to hold them and comfort them I hold them with the good side. I don't give them no more of the Asset. The Asset's wrapped back up safe out of sight in the sleeve now. They're broke down crying and I'm the one holding them with the good arm and go It's OK Don't Cry Don't Be Sad Being Able To Trust You Not To Get Disgusted By The Arm Means So Very Very Much To Me Don't You See You Have Set Me Free Of Being Shameful Of The Arm Thank You Thank You and so on while they put their face in my neck and just cry and cry. Sometimes they get me crying too. You following all this?'

Q. . . .

'More pussy than a toilet seat, man. I shit you not. Go on and ask Jackpot and Kenny if you want about it. Kenny Kirk's the one named it the Asset. You go on.'

Forever Overhead

HAPPY BIRTHDAY. Your thirteenth is important. Maybe your first really public day. Your thirteenth is the chance for people to recognize that important things are happening to you.

Things have been happening to you for the past half year. You have seven hairs in your left armpit now. Twelve in your right. Hard dangerous spirals of brittle black hair. Crunchy, animal hair. There are now more of the hard curled hairs around your privates than you can count without losing track. Other things. Your voice is rich and scratchy and moves between octaves without any warning. Your face has begun to get shiny when you don't wash it. And two weeks of a deep and frightening ache this past spring left you with something dropped down from inside: your sack is now full and vulnerable, a commodity to be protected. Hefted and strapped in tight supporters that stripe your buttocks red. You have grown into a new fragility.

And dreams. For months there have been dreams like nothing before: moist and busy and distant, full of yielding curves, frantic pistons, warmth and a great falling; and you have awakened through fluttering lids to a rush and a gush and a toe-curling scalp-snapping jolt of feeling from an inside deeper than you knew you had, spasms of a deep sweet hurt, the streetlights through your window blinds cracking into sharp stars against the black bedroom ceiling, and on you a dense white jam that lisps between legs, trickles and sticks, cools on you, hardens and clears until there is nothing but gnarled knots of pale solid animal hair in the morning shower, and in the wet tangle a clean sweet smell you can't believe comes from anything you made inside you.

The smell is, more than anything, like this swimming pool: a bleached sweet salt, a flower with chemical petals. The pool has a strong clear blue smell, though you know the smell is never as strong when you are actually in the blue water, as you are now, all swum out, resting back along the shallow end, the hip-high water lapping at where it's all changed.

Around the deck of this old public pool on the western edge of Tucson is a Cyclone fence the color of pewter, decorated with a bright tangle of locked bicycles. Beyond this a hot black parking lot full of white lines and glittering cars. A dull field of dry grass and hard weeds, old dandelions' downy heads exploding and snowing up in a rising wind. And past all this, reddened by a round slow September sun, are mountains, jagged, their tops' sharp angles darkening into definition against a deep red tired light. Against the red their sharp connected tops form a spiked line, an EKG of the dying day.

The clouds are taking on color by the rim of the sky. The water is spangles off soft blue, five-o'clock warm, and the pool's smell, like the other smell, connects with a chemical haze inside you, an interior dimness that bends light to its own ends, softens the difference between what leaves off and what begins.

Your party is tonight. This afternoon, on your birthday, you have asked to come to the pool. You wanted to come alone, but a birthday is a family day, your family wants to be with you. This is nice, and you can't talk about why you wanted to come alone, and really truly maybe you didn't want to come alone, so they are here. Sunning. Both your parents sun. Their deck chairs have been marking time all afternoon, rotating, tracking the sun's curve across a desert sky heated to an eggy film. Your sister plays Marco Polo near you in the shallows with a group of thin girls from her grade. She is being blind now, her Marco's being Polo'd. She is shut-eyed and twirling to different cries, spinning at the hub of a wheel of shrill girls in bathing caps. Her cap has raised rubber flowers. There are limp old pink petals that shake as she lunges at blind sound.

There at the other end of the pool is the diving tank and the high board's tower. Back on the deck behind is the SN CK BAR, and on either side, bolted above the cement entrances to dark wet showers and lockers, are gray metal bullhorn speakers that send out the pool's radio music, the jangle flat and tinny thin.

Your family likes you. You are bright and quiet, respectful to elders—though you are not without spine. You are largely good. You look out for your little sister. You are her ally. You were six when she was zero and you had the mumps when they brought her home in a very soft yellow blanket; you kissed her hello on her feet out of concern that she not catch your mumps. Your parents say that this augured well. That it set the tone. They now feel they were right. In all things they are proud of you, satisfied, and they have retreated to the warm distance from which pride and satisfaction travel. You all get along well.

Happy Birthday. It is a big day, big as the roof of the whole southwest sky. You have thought it over. There is the high board. They will want to leave soon. Climb out and do the thing.

Shake off the blue clean. You're half-bleached, loose and soft, tenderized, pads of fingers wrinkled. The mist of the pool's too-clean smell is in your eyes; it breaks light into gentle color. Knock your head with the heel of your hand. One side has a flabby echo. Cock your head to the side and hop—sudden heat in your ear, delicious, and brain-warmed water turns cold on the nautilus of your ear's outside. You can hear harder tinnier music, closer shouts, much movement in much water.

The pool is crowded for this late. Here are thin children, hairy animal men. Disproportionate boys, all necks and legs and knobby joints, shallow-chested, vaguely birdlike. Like you. Here are old people moving tentatively through shallows on stick legs, feeling at the water with their hands, out of every element at once.

And girl-women, women, curved like instruments or fruit, skin burnished brown-bright, suit tops held by delicate knots of fragile colored string against the pull of mysterious weights, suit bottoms riding low over the gentle juts of hips totally unlike your own, immoderate swells and swivels that melt in light into a surrounding space that cups and accommodates the soft curves as things precious. You almost understand.

The pool is a system of movement. Here now there are: laps, splash fights, dives, corner tag, cannonballs, Sharks and Minnows, high fallings, Marco Polo (your sister still It, halfway to tears, too long to be It, the game teetering on the edge of cruelty, not your business to save or embarrass). Two clean little bright-white boys caped in cotton towels run along the poolside until the guard stops them dead with a shout through his bullhorn. The guard is brown as a tree, blond hair in a vertical line on his stomach, his head in a jungle explorer hat, his nose a white triangle of cream. A girl has an arm around a leg of his little tower. He's bored.

Get out now and go past your parents, who are sunning and reading, not looking up. Forget your towel. Stopping for the towel means talking and talking means thinking. You have decided being scared is caused mostly by thinking. Go right by, toward the tank at the deep end. Over the tank is a great iron tower of dirty white. A board protrudes from the top of the tower like a tongue. The pool's concrete deck is rough and hot against your bleached feet. Each of your footprints is thinner and fainter. Each shrinks behind you on the hot stone and disappears.

Lines of plastic wieners bob around the tank, which is entirely its own thing, empty of the rest of the pool's convulsive ballet of heads and arms. The tank is blue as energy, small and deep and perfectly square, flanked by lap lanes and SN CK BAR and rough hot deck and the bent late shadow of the tower and board. The tank is quiet and still and healed smooth between fallings.

There is a rhythm to it. Like breathing. Like a machine. The line for the board curves back from the tower's ladder. The line moves in its curve, straightens as it nears the ladder. One by one, people reach the ladder and climb. One by one, spaced by the beat of hearts, they reach the tongue of the board at the top. And once on the board, they pause, each exactly the same tiny heartbeat pause. And their legs take them to the end, where they all give the same sort of stomping hop, arms curving out as if to describe something circular, total; they come down heavy on the edge of the board and make it throw them up and out.

It's a swooping machine, lines of stuttered movement in a sweet late bleach mist. You can watch from the deck as they hit the cold blue sheet of the tank. Each fall makes a white that plumes and falls into itself and spreads and fizzes. Then blue clean comes up in the middle of the white and spreads like pudding, making it all new. The tank heals itself. Three times as you go by.

You are in line. Look around. Look bored. Few talk in the line. Everyone seems by himself. Most look at the ladder, look bored. You almost all have crossed arms, chilled by a late dry rising wind on the constellations of blue-clean chlorine beads that cover your backs and shoulders. It seems impossible that everybody could really be this bored. Beside you is the edge of the tower's shadow, the tilted black tongue of the board's image. The system of shadow is huge, long, off to the side, joined to the tower's base at a sharp late angle.

Almost everyone in line for the board watches the ladder. Older boys watch older girls' bottoms as they go up. The bottoms are in soft thin cloth, tight nylon stretch. The good bottoms move up the ladder like pendulums in liquid, a gentle uncrackable code. The girls' legs make you think of deer. Look bored.

Look out past it. Look across. You can see so well. Your mother is in her deck chair, reading, squinting, her face tilted up to get light on her cheeks. She hasn't looked to see where you are. She sips something sweet out of a bright can. Your father is on his big stomach, back like the hint of a hump of a whale, shoulders curling with animal spirals, skin oiled and soaked red-brown with too much sun. Your towel is hanging off your chair and a corner of the cloth now moves—your mother hit it as she waved away a sweat bee that likes what she has in the can. The bee is back right away, seeming to hang motionless over the can in a sweet blur. Your towel is one big face of Yogi Bear.

At some point there has gotten to be more line behind you than in front of you. Now no one in front except three on the slender ladder. The woman right before you is on the low rungs, looking up, wearing a tight black nylon suit that is all one piece. She climbs. From above there is a rumble, then a great falling, then a plume and the tank reheals. Now two on the ladder. The pool rules say one on the ladder at a time, but the guard never shouts about it. The guard makes the real rules by shouting or not shouting.

This woman above you should not wear a suit as tight as the suit she is wearing. She is as old as your mother, and as big. She is too big and too white. Her suit is full of her. The backs of her thighs are squeezed by the suit and look like cheese. Her legs have abrupt little squiggles of cold blue shattered vein under the white skin, as if something were broken, hurt, in her legs. Her legs look like they hurt to be squeezed, full of curled Arabic lines of cold broken blue. Her legs make you feel like your own legs hurt.

The rungs are very thin. It's unexpected. Thin round iron rungs laced in slick wet Safe-T felt. You taste metal from the smell of wet iron in shadow. Each rung presses into the bottoms of your feet and dents them. The dents feel deep and they hurt. You feel heavy. How the big woman over you must feel. The handrails along the ladder's sides are also very thin. It's like you might not hold on. You've got to hope the woman holds on, too. And of course it looked like fewer rungs from far away. You are not stupid.

Get halfway up, up in the open, big woman placed above you, a solid bald muscular man on the ladder underneath your feet. The board is still high overhead, invisible from here. But it rumbles and makes a heavy flapping sound, and a boy you can see for a few contained feet through the thin rungs falls in a flash of a line, a knee held to his chest, doing a splasher. There is a huge exclamation point of foam up into your field of sight, then scattered claps into a great fizzing. Then the silent sound of the tank healing to new blue all over again.

More thin rungs. Hold on tight. The radio is loudest here, one speaker at ear-level over a concrete locker room entrance. A cool dank whiff of the locker room inside. Grab the iron bars tight and twist and look down behind you and you can see people buying snacks and refreshments below. You can see down into it: the clean white top of the vendor's cap, tubs of ice cream, steaming brass freezers, scuba tanks of soft drink syrup, snakes of soda hose, bulging boxes of salty popcorn kept hot in the sun. Now that you're overhead you can see the whole thing.

There's wind. It's windier the higher you get. The wind is thin; through the shadow it's cold on your wet skin. On the ladder in the shadow your skin looks very white. The wind makes a thin whistle in your ears. Four more rungs to the top of the tower. The rungs hurt your feet. They are thin and let you know just how much you weigh. You have real weight on the ladder. The ground wants you back.

Now you can see just over the top of the ladder. You can see the board. The woman is there. There are two ridges of red, hurt-looking callus on the backs of her ankles. She stands at the start of the board, your eyes on her ankles. Now you're up above the tower's shadow. The solid man under you is looking through the rungs into the contained space the woman's fall will pass through.

She pauses for just that beat of a pause. There's nothing slow about it at all. It makes you cold. In no time she's at the end of the board, up, down on it, it bends low like it doesn't want her. Then it nods and flaps and throws her violently up and out, her arms opening out to inscribe that circle, and gone. She disappears in a dark blink. And there's time before you hear the hit below.

Listen. It does not seem good, the way she disappears into a time that passes before she sounds. Like a stone down a well. But you think she did not think so. She was part of a rhythm that excludes thinking. And now you have made yourself part of it, too. The rhythm seems blind. Like ants. Like a machine.

You decide this needs to be thought about. It may, after all, be all right to do something scary without thinking, but not when the scariness is the not thinking itself. Not when not thinking turns out to be wrong. At some point the wrongnesses have piled up blind: pretend-boredom, weight, thin rungs, hurt feet, space cut into laddered parts that melt together only in a disappearance that takes time. The wind on the ladder not what anyone would have expected. The way the board protrudes from shadow into light and you can't see past the end. When it all turns out to be different you should get to think. It should be required.

The ladder is full beneath you. Stacked up, everyone a few rungs apart. The ladder is fed by a solid line that stretches back and curves into the dark of the tower's canted shadow. People's arms are crossed in the line. Those on the ladder's feet hurt and they are all looking up. It is a machine that moves only forward.

Climb up onto the tower's tongue. The board turns out to be long. As long as the time you stand there. Time slows. It thickens around you as your heart gets more and more beats out of every second, every movement in the system of the pool below.

The board is long. From where you stand it seems to stretch off into nothing. It's going to send you someplace which its own length keeps you from seeing, which seems wrong to submit to without even thinking.

Looked at another way, the same board is just a long thin flat thing covered with a rough white plastic stuff. The white surface is very rough and is freckled and lined with a pale watered red that is nevertheless still red and not yet pink—drops of old pool water that are catching the light of the late sun over sharp mountains. The rough white stuff of the board is wet. And cold. Your feet are hurt from the thin rungs and have a great ability to feel. They feel your weight. There are handrails running above the beginning of the board. They are not like the ladder's handrails just were. They are thick and set very low, so you almost have to bend over to hold on to them. They are just for show, no one holds them. Holding on takes time and alters the rhythm of the machine.

It is a long cold rough white plastic or fiberglass board, veined with the sad near-pink color of bad candy.

But at the end of the white board, the edge, where you'll come down with your weight to make it send you off, there are two areas of darkness. Two flat shadows in the broad light. Two vague black ovals. The end of the board has two dirty spots.

They are from all the people who've gone before you. Your feet as you stand here are tender and dented, hurt by the rough wet surface, and you see that the two dark spots are from people's skin. They are skin abraded from feet by the violence of the disappearance of people with real weight. More people than you could count without losing track. The weight and abrasion of their disappearance leaves little bits of soft tender feet behind, bits and shards and curls of skin that dirty and darken and tan as they lie tiny and smeared in the sun at the end of the board. They pile up and get smeared and mixed together. They darken in two circles.

No time is passing outside you at all. It is amazing. The late ballet below is slow motion, the overbroad movements of mimes in blue jelly. If you wanted you could really stay here forever, vibrating inside so fast you float motionless in time, like a bee over something sweet.

But they should clean the board. Anybody who thought about it for even a second would see that they should clean the end of the board of people's skin, of two black collections of what's left of before, spots that from back here look like eyes, like blind and cross-eyed eyes.

Where you are now is still and quiet. Wind radio shouting splashing not here. No time and no real sound but your blood squeaking in your head.

Overhead here means sight and smell. The smells are intimate, newly clear. The smell of bleach's special flower, but out of it other things rise to you like a weed's seeded snow. You smell deep yellow popcorn. Sweet tan oil like hot coconut. Either hot dogs or corn dogs. A thin cruel hint of very dark Pepsi in paper cups. And the special smell of tons of water coming off tons of skin, rising like steam off a new bath. Animal heat. From overhead it is more real than anything.

Look at it. You can see the whole complicated thing, blue and white and brown and white, soaked in a watery spangle of deepening red. Everybody. This is what people call a view. And you knew that from below you wouldn't look nearly so high overhead. You see now how high overhead you are. You knew from down there no one could tell.

He says it behind you, his eyes on your ankles, the solid bald man, Hey kid. They want to know. Do your plans up here involve the whole day or what exactly is the story. Hey kid are you okay.

There's been time this whole time. You can't kill time with your heart. Everything takes time. Bees have to move very fast to stay still.

Hey kid he says Hey kid are you okay.

Metal flowers bloom on your tongue. No more time for thinking. Now that there is time you don't have time.

Hey.

Slowly now, out across everything, there's a watching that spreads like hit water's rings. Watch it spread out from the ladder. Your sighted sister and her thin white pack, pointing. Your mother looks to the shallows where you used to be, then makes a visor of her hand. The whale stirs and jiggles. The guard looks up, the girl around his leg looks up, he reaches for his horn.

Forever below is rough deck, snacks, thin metal music, down where you once used to be; the line is solid and has no reverse gear; and the water, of course, is only soft when you're inside it. Look down. Now it moves in the sun, full of hard coins of light that shimmer red as they stretch away into a mist that is your own sweet salt. The coins crack into new moons, long shards of light from the hearts of sad stars. The square tank is a cold blue sheet. Cold is just a kind of hard. A kind of blind. You have been taken off guard. Happy Birthday. Did you think it over. Yes and no. Hey kid.

Two black spots, violence, and disappear into a well of time. Height is not the problem. It all changes when you get back down. When you hit, with your weight.

So which is the lie? Hard or soft? Silence or time?

The lie is that it's one or the other. A still, floating bee is moving faster than it can think. From overhead the sweetness drives it crazy.

The board will nod and you will go, and eyes of skin can cross blind into a cloud-blotched sky, punctured light emptying behind sharp stone that is forever. That is forever. Step into the skin and disappear.

Hello.

The Depressed Person

THE DEPRESSED PERSON was in terrible and unceasing emotional pain, and the impossibility of sharing or articulating this pain was itself a component of the pain and a contributing factor in its essential horror.

Despairing, then, of describing the emotional pain or expressing its utterness to those around her, the depressed person instead described circumstances, both past and ongoing, which were somehow related to the pain, to its etiology and cause, hoping at least to be able to express to others something of the pain's context, its—as it were—shape and texture. The depressed person's parents, for example, who had divorced when she was a child, had used her as a pawn in the sick games they played. The depressed person had, as a child, required orthodonture, and each parent had claimed—not without some cause, given the Medicean legal ambiguities of the divorce settlement, the depressed person always inserted when she described the painful struggle between her parents over the expense of her orthodonture—that the other should be required to pay for it. And the venomous rage of each parent over the other's petty, selfish refusal to pay was vented on their daughter, who had to hear over and over again from each parent how the other was unloving and selfish. Both parents were well off, and each had privately expressed to the depressed person that s/he was, of course, if push came to shove, willing to pay for all the orthodonture the depressed person needed and then some, that it was, at its heart, a matter not of money or dentition but of "principle." And the depressed person always took care, when as an adult she attempted to describe to a trusted friend the circumstances of the struggle over the cost of her orthodonture and that struggle's legacy of emotional pain for her, to concede that it may very well truly have appeared to each parent to have been, in fact, just that (i.e., a matter of "principle"), though unfortunately not a "principle" that took into account their daughter's needs or her feelings at receiving the emotional message that scoring petty points off each other was more important to her parents than her own maxillofacial health and thus constituted, if considered from a certain perspective, a form of parental neglect or abandonment or even outright abuse, an abuse clearly connected—here the depressed person nearly always inserted that her therapist concurred with this assessment—to the bottomless, chronic adult despair she suffered every day and felt hopelessly trapped in. This was just one example. The depressed person averaged four interpolated apologies each time she recounted for supportive friends this type of painful and damaging past circumstance on the telephone, as well as a sort of preamble in which she attempted to describe how painful and frightening it was not to feel able to articulate the chronic depression's excruciating pain itself but to have to resort to recounting examples that probably sounded, she always took care to acknowledge, dreary or self-pitying or like one of those people who are narcissistically obsessed with their "painful childhoods" and "painful lives" and wallow in their burdens and insist on recounting them at tiresome length to friends who are trying to be supportive and nurturing, and bore them and repel them.

The friends whom the depressed person reached out to for support and tried to open up to and share at least the contextual shape of her unceasing psychic agony and feelings of isolation with numbered around half a dozen and underwent a certain amount of rotation. The depressed person's therapist—who had earned both a terminal graduate degree and a medical degree, and who was the self-professed exponent of a school of therapy which stressed the cultivation and regular use of a supportive peer-community in any endogenously depressed adult's journey toward healing—referred to these female friends as the depressed person's Support System. The approximately half-dozen rotating members of this Support System tended to be either former acquaintances from the depressed person's childhood or else girls she had roomed with at various stages of her school career, nurturing and comparatively undamaged women who now lived in all manner of different cities and whom the depressed person often had not seen in person for years and years, and whom she often called late in the evening, long-distance, for sharing and support and just a few well-chosen words to help her get some realistic perspective on the day's despair and get centered and gather together the strength to fight through the emotional agony of the next day, and to whom, when she telephoned, the depressed person always began by saying that she apologized if she was dragging them down or coming off as boring or self-pitying or repellent or taking them away from their active, vibrant, largely pain-free long-distance lives.

The depressed person also made it a point, when reaching out to members of her Support System, never to cite circumstances like her parents' endless battle over her orthodonture as the *cause* of her unceasing adult depression. The "Blame Game" was too easy, she said; it was pathetic and contemptible; and besides, she'd had quite enough of the "Blame Game" just listening to her fucking parents all those years, the endless blame and recrimination the two had exchanged over her, through her, using the depressed person's (i.e., the depressed person as a child's) own feelings and needs as ammunition, as if her valid feelings and needs were nothing more than a battlefield or theater of conflict, weapons which the parents felt they could deploy against each other. They had displayed far more interest and passion and emotional availability in their hatred of each other than either had shown toward the depressed person herself, as a child, the depressed person confessed to feeling, sometimes, still.

The depressed person's therapist, whose school of therapy rejected the transference relation as a therapeutic resource and thus deliberately eschewed confrontation and "should"-statements and all normative, judging, "authority"-based theory in favor of a more value-neutral bioexperiential model and the creative use of analogy and narrative (including, but not necessarily mandating, the use of hand puppets, polystyrene props and toys, role-playing, human sculpture, mirroring, drama therapy, and, in appropriate cases, whole meticulously scripted and storyboarded Childhood Reconstructions), had deployed the following medications in an attempt to help the depressed person find some relief from her acute affective discomfort and progress in her (i.e., the depressed person's) journey toward enjoying some semblance of a normal adult life: Paxil, Zoloft, Prozac, Tofranil, Wellbutrin, Elavil, Metrazol in combination with unilateral ECT (during a two-week voluntary in-patient course of treatment at a regional Mood Disorders clinic), Parnate both with and without lithium salts, Nardil both with and without Xanax. None had delivered any significant relief from the pain and feelings of emotional isolation that rendered the depressed person's every waking hour an indescribable hell on earth, and many of the medications themselves had had side effects which the depressed person had found intolerable. The depressed person was currently taking only very tiny daily doses of Prozac, for her A.D.D. symptoms, and of Ativan, a mild nonaddictive tranquilizer, for the panic attacks which made the hours at her toxically dysfunctional and unsupportive workplace such a living hell. Her therapist gently but repeatedly shared with the depressed person her (i.e., the therapist's) belief that the very best medicine for her (i.e., the depressed person's) endogenous depression was the cultivation and regular use of a Support System the depressed person felt she could reach out to share with and lean on for unconditional caring and support. The exact composition of this Support System and its one or two most special, most trusted "core" members underwent a certain amount of change and rotation as time passed, which the therapist had encouraged the depressed person to see as perfectly normal and OK, since it was only by taking the risks and exposing the vulnerabilities required to deepen supportive relationships that an individual could discover which friendships could meet her needs and to what degree.

The depressed person felt that she trusted the therapist and made a concerted effort to be as completely open and honest with her as she possibly could. She admitted to the therapist that she was always extremely careful to share with whomever she called long-distance at night her (i.e., the depressed person's) belief that it would be whiny and pathetic to blame her constant, indescribable adult pain on her parents' traumatic divorce or their cynical use of her while they hypocritically pretended that each cared for her more than the other did. Her parents had, after all—as her therapist had helped the depressed person to see—done the very best they could with the emotional resources they'd had at the time. And she had, after all, the depressed person always inserted, laughing weakly, eventually gotten the orthodonture she'd needed. The former acquaintances and roommates who composed her Support System often told the depressed person that they wished she could be a little less hard on herself, to which the depressed person often responded by bursting involuntarily into tears and telling them that she knew all too well that she was one of those dreaded types of people of everyone's grim acquaintance who call at inconvenient times and just go on and on about themselves and whom it often takes several increasingly awkward attempts to get off the telephone with. The depressed person said that she was all too horribly aware of what a joyless burden she was to her friends, and during the long-distance calls she always made it a point to express the enormous gratitude she felt at having a friend she could call and share with and get nurturing and support from, however briefly, before the demands of that friend's full, joyful, active life took understandable precedence and required her (i.e., the friend) to get off the telephone.

The excruciating feelings of shame and inadequacy which the depressed person experienced about calling supportive members of her Support System long-distance late at night and burdening them with her clumsy attempts to articulate at least the overall context of her emotional agony were an issue on which the depressed person and her therapist were currently doing a great deal of work in their time together. The depressed person confessed that when whatever empathetic friend she was sharing with finally confessed that she (i.e., the friend) was dreadfully sorry but there was no helping it she absolutely *had* to get off the telephone, and had finally detached the depressed person's needy fingers from her pantcuff and gotten off the telephone and back to her full, vibrant long-distance life, the depressed person almost always sat there listening to the empty apian drone of the dial tone and feeling even more isolated and inadequate and contemptible than she had before she'd called. These feelings of toxic shame at reaching out to others for community and support were issues which the therapist encouraged the depressed person to try to get in touch with and explore so that they could be processed in detail. The depressed person admitted to the therapist that whenever she (i.e., the depressed person) reached out long-distance to a member of her Support System she almost always visualized the friend's face, on the telephone, assuming a combined expression of boredom and pity and repulsion and abstract guilt, and almost always imagined she (i.e., the depressed person) could detect, in the friend's increasingly long silences and/or tedious repetitions of encouraging clichés, the boredom and frustration people always feel when someone is clinging to them and being a burden. She confessed that she could all too well imagine each friend now wincing when the telephone rang late at night, or during the conversation looking impatiently at the clock or directing silent gestures and facial expressions of helpless entrapment to all the other people in the room with her (i.e., the other people in the room with the "friend"), these inaudible gestures and expressions becoming more and more extreme and desperate as the depressed person just went on and on and on. The depressed person's therapist's most noticeable unconscious personal habit or tic consisted of placing the tips of all her fingers together in her lap as she listened attentively to the depressed person and manipulating the fingers idly so that her mated hands formed various enclosing shapes — e.g., cube, sphere, pyramid, right cylinder — and then appearing to study or contemplate them. The depressed person disliked this habit, though she would be the first to admit that this was chiefly because it drew her attention to the therapist's fingers and fingernails and caused her to compare them with her own.

The depressed person had shared with both the therapist and her Support System that she could recall, all too clearly, at her third boarding school, once watching her roommate talk to some unknown boy on their room's telephone as she (i.e., the roommate) made faces and gestures of repulsion and boredom with the call, this self-assured, popular and attractive roommate finally directing at the depressed person an exaggerated pantomime of someone knocking on a door, continuing the pantomime with a desperate expression until the depressed person understood that she was to open the room's door and step outside and knock loudly on the open door so as to give the roommate an excuse to get off the telephone. As a schoolgirl, the depressed person had never spoken of the incident of the boy's telephone call and the mendacious pantomime with that particular roommate—a roommate with whom the depressed person hadn't clicked or connected at all, and whom she had resented in a bitter, cringing way that had made the depressed person despise herself, and had not made any attempt to stay in touch with after that endless sophomore second semester was finished—but she (i.e., the depressed person) had shared her agonizing memory of the incident with many of the friends in her Support System, and had also shared how bottomlessly horrible and pathetic she had felt it would have been to have been that nameless, unknown boy at the other end of that telephone, a boy trying in good faith to take an emotional risk and to reach out and try to connect with the confident roommate, unaware that he was an unwelcome burden, pathetically unaware of the silent pantomimed boredom and contempt at the telephone's other end, and how the depressed person dreaded more than almost anything ever being in the position of being someone you had to appeal silently to someone else in the room to help you contrive an excuse to get off the telephone with. The depressed person would therefore always implore any friend she was on the telephone with to tell her the very *second* she (i.e., the friend) was getting bored or frustrated or repelled or felt she had other more urgent or interesting things to do, to please for God's sake be utterly up-front and frank and not spend one second longer on the phone with the depressed person than she (i.e., the friend) was absolutely glad to spend. The depressed person knew perfectly well, of course, she assured the therapist, how pathetic such a need for reassurance might come off to someone, how it could all too possibly be heard not as an open invitation to get off the telephone but actually as a needy, self-pitying, contemptibly manipulative plea for the friend *not* to get off the telephone, *never* to get off the telephone. The therapist[1] was diligent, whenever the depressed person shared her concern about how some statement or action might

---

[1] The multiform shapes the therapist's mated fingers assumed nearly always resembled, for the depressed person, various forms of geometrically diverse cages, an association which the depressed person had not shared with the therapist because its symbolic significance seemed too overt and simple-minded to waste their time together on. The therapist's fingernails were long and shapely and well maintained, whereas the depressed person's fingernails were compulsively bitten so short and ragged that the quick sometimes protruded and began spontaneously to bleed.

"seem" or "appear," in supporting the depressed person in exploring how these beliefs about how she "seemed" or "came off" to others made her feel.

It felt demeaning; the depressed person felt demeaned. She said it felt demeaning to call childhood friends long-distance late at night when they clearly had other things to do and lives to lead and vibrant, healthy, nurturing, intimate, caring partner-relationships to be in; it felt demeaning and pathetic to constantly apologize for boring someone or to feel that you had to thank them effusively just for being your friend. The depressed person's parents had eventually split the cost of her orthodonture; a professional arbitrator had finally been hired by their lawyers to structure the compromise. Arbitration had also been required to negotiate shared payment schedules for the depressed person's boarding schools and Healthy Eating Lifestyles summer camps and oboe lessons and car and collision insurance, as well as for the cosmetic surgery needed to correct a malformation of the anterior spine and alar cartilage of the depressed person's nose which had given her what felt like an excruciatingly pronounced and snoutish pug nose and had, coupled with the external orthodontic retainer she had to wear twenty-two hours a day, made looking at herself in the mirrors of her rooms at her boarding schools feel like more than any person could possibly stand. And yet also, in the year that the depressed person's father had remarried, he—in either a gesture of rare uncompromised caring or a *coup de grâce* which the depressed person's mother had said was designed to make her own feelings of humiliation and superfluousness complete—had paid in toto for the riding lessons, jodhpurs, and outrageously expensive boots the depressed person had needed in order to gain admission to her second-to-last boarding school's Riding Club, a few of whose members were the only girls at this particular boarding school whom the depressed person felt, she had confessed to her father on the telephone in tears late one truly horrible night, even remotely accepted her and had even minimal empathy or compassion in them at all and around whom the depressed person hadn't felt so totally snout-nosed and brace-faced and inadequate and rejected that it had felt like a daily act of enormous personal courage even to leave her room to go eat dinner in the dining hall.

The professional arbitrator her parents' lawyers had finally agreed on for help in structuring compromises on the costs of meeting the depressed person's childhood needs had been a highly respected Conflict-Resolution Specialist named Walter D. ("Walt") DeLasandro Jr. As a child, the depressed person had never met or even laid eyes on Walter D. ("Walt") DeLasandro Jr., though she had been shown his business card—complete with its parenthesized invitation to informality—and his name had been invoked in her hearing on countless childhood occasions, along with the fact that he billed for his services at a staggering $130 an hour plus expenses. Despite overwhelming feelings of reluctance on the part of the depressed person—who knew very well how much like the "Blame Game" it might sound—her therapist had strongly supported her in taking the risk of sharing with members of her Support System an important emotional breakthrough she (i.e., the depressed person) had achieved during an Inner-Child-Focused Experiential Therapy Retreat Weekend which the therapist had supported her in taking the risk of enrolling in and giving herself open-mindedly over to the experience of. In the I.-C.-F.E.T. Retreat Weekend's Small-Group Drama-Therapy Room, other members of her Small Group had role-played the depressed person's parents and the parents' significant others and attorneys and myriad other emotionally toxic figures from the depressed person's childhood and, at the crucial phase of the drama-therapy exercise, had slowly encircled the depressed person, moving in and pressing steadily in together on her so that she could not escape or avoid or minimize, and had (i.e., the small group had) dramatically recited specially pre-scripted lines designed to evoke and awaken blocked trauma, which had almost immediately provoked the depressed person into a surge of agonizing emotional memories and long-buried trauma and had resulted in the emergence of the depressed person's Inner Child and a cathartic tantrum in which the depressed person had struck repeatedly at a stack of velour cushions with a bat made of polystyrene foam and had shrieked obscenities and had reexperienced long-pent-up and festering emotional wounds, one of which[2] being a deep vestigial rage over the fact that Walter D. ("Walt") DeLasandro Jr. had been able to bill her parents $130 an hour plus expenses for being put in the middle and playing the role of mediator and absorber of shit from both sides while she (i.e., the depressed person, as a child) had had to perform essentially the same coprophagous services on a more or less daily basis for *free*, for *nothing*, services which were not only grossly unfair and inappropriate for an emotionally sensitive child to be made to feel required to perform but about which her parents had then turned around and tried to make *her*, the depressed person *herself*, as a *child*, feel *guilty* about the staggering cost of Walter D. DeLasandro Jr. the Conflict-Resolution Specialist's services, as if the repeated hassle and expense of Walter D. DeLasandro Jr. were *her* fault and only undertaken on *her* spoiled little snout-nosed snaggletoothed behalf instead of simply because of her fucking parents' utterly fucking *sick* inability to communicate and share

---

2 (i.e., one of which purulent wounds)

honestly and work through their own sick, dysfunctional issues with each other. This exercise and cathartic rage had enabled the depressed person to get in touch with some really core resentment-issues, the Small-Group Facilitator at the Inner-Child-Focused Experiential Therapy Retreat Weekend had said, and could have represented a real turning point in the depressed person's journey toward healing, had the rage and velour-cushion-pummeling not left the depressed person so emotionally shattered and drained and traumatized and embarrassed that she had felt she had no choice but to fly back home that night and miss the rest of the I.-C.-F.E.T.R. Weekend and the Small-Group Processing of all the exhumed feelings and issues.

The eventual compromise which the depressed person and her therapist worked out together as they processed the unburied resentments and the consequent guilt and shame at what could all too easily appear to be just more of the self-pitying "Blame Game" that attended the depressed person's experience at the Retreat Weekend was that the depressed person would take the emotional risk of reaching out and sharing the experience's feelings and realizations with her Support System, but only with the two or three elite, "core" members whom the depressed person currently felt were there for her in the very most empathetic and unjudgingly supportive way. The most important provision of the compromise was that the depressed person would be permitted to reveal to them her reluctance about sharing these resentments and realizations and to inform them that she was aware of how pathetic and blaming they (i.e., the resentments and realizations) might sound, and to reveal that she was sharing this potentially pathetic "breakthrough" with them only at her therapist's firm and explicit suggestion. In validating this provision, the therapist had objected only to the depressed person's proposed use of the word "pathetic" in her sharing with the Support System. The therapist said that she felt she could support the depressed person's use of the word "vulnerable" far more wholeheartedly than she could support the use of "pathetic," since her gut (i.e., the therapist's gut) was telling her that the depressed person's proposed use of "pathetic" felt not only self-hating but also needy and even somewhat manipulative. The word "pathetic," the therapist candidly shared, often felt to her like a defense-mechanism the depressed person used to protect herself against a listener's possible negative judgments by making it clear that the depressed person was already judging herself far more severely than any listener could possibly have the heart to. The therapist was careful to point out that she was not judging or critiquing or rejecting the depressed person's use of "pathetic" but was merely trying to openly and honestly share the feelings which its use brought up for her in the context of their relationship. The therapist, who by this time had less than a year to live, took a brief time-out at this point to share once again with the depressed person her (i.e., the therapist's) conviction that self-hatred, toxic guilt, narcissism, self-pity, neediness, manipulation, and many of the other shame-based behaviors with which endogenously depressed adults typically presented were best understood as psychological defenses erected by a vestigial wounded Inner Child against the possibility of trauma and abandonment. The behaviors, in other words, were primitive emotional prophylaxes whose real function was to preclude intimacy; they were psychic armor designed to keep others at a distance so that they (i.e., others) could not get emotionally close enough to the depressed person to inflict any wounds that might echo and mirror the deep vestigial wounds of the depressed person's childhood, wounds which the depressed person was unconsciously determined to keep repressed at all costs. The therapist—who during the year's cold months, when the abundant fenestration of her home office kept the room chilly, wore a pelisse of hand-tanned Native American buckskin that formed a somewhat ghastlily moist-looking flesh-colored background for the enclosing shapes her joined hands formed in her lap as she spoke—assured the depressed person that she was not trying to lecture her or impose on her (i.e., on the depressed person) the therapist's own particular model of depressive etiology. Rather, it simply felt appropriate on an intuitive "gut" level at this particular point in time for the therapist to share some of her own feelings. Indeed, as the therapist said that she felt comfortable about positing at this point in the therapeutic relationship between them, the depressed person's acute chronic mood disorder could actually itself be seen as constituting an emotional defense-mechanism: i.e., as long as the depressed person had the depression's acute affective discomfort to preoccupy her and take up her emotional attention, she could avoid feeling or getting in touch with the deep vestigial childhood wounds which she (i.e., the depressed person) was apparently still determined to keep repressed.[3]

---

3 The depressed person's therapist was always extremely careful to avoid appearing to judge or blame the depressed person for clinging to her defenses, or to suggest that the depressed person had in any way consciously *chosen* or *chosen to cling to* a chronic depression whose agony made her (i.e., the depressed person's) every waking hour feel like more than any person could possibly endure. This renunciation of judgment or imposed value was held by the therapeutic school in which the therapist's philosophy of healing had evolved over almost fifteen years of clinical experience to be integral to the combination of unconditional support and complete honesty about feelings which composed the nurturing professionalism required for a productive therapeutic journey toward authenticity and intrapersonal wholeness. Defenses against intimacy, the depressed person's therapist's experiential theory held, were nearly always arrested or vestigial survival-mechanisms; i.e., they had, at one time, been environmentally appropriate and necessary and had very prob-

Several months later, when the depressed person's therapist suddenly and unexpectedly died—as the result of what was determined by authorities to be an "accidentally" toxic combination of caffeine and homeopathic appetite suppressant but which, given the therapist's extensive medical background and knowledge of chemical interactions, only a person in very deep denial indeed could fail to see must have been, on some level, intentional—without leaving any sort of note or cassette or encouraging final words for any of the persons and/or clients in her life who had, despite all their debilitating fear and isolation and defense-mechanisms and vestigial wounds from past traumas, come to connect intimately with her and let her in emotionally even though it meant making themselves vulnerable to the possibility of loss- and abandonment-traumas, the depressed person found the trauma of this fresh loss and abandonment so shattering, its resultant agony and despair and hopelessness so unbearable, that she was, ironically, now forced to reach frantically and repeatedly out on a nightly basis to her Support System, sometimes calling three or even four long-distance friends in an evening, sometimes calling the same friends twice in one night, sometimes at a very late hour, sometimes even—the depressed person felt sickeningly sure—waking them up or interrupting them in the midst of healthy, joyful sexual intimacy with their partner. In other words, sheer survival, in the turbulent wake of her feelings of shock and grief and loss and abandonment and bitter betrayal following the therapist's sudden death, now compelled the depressed person to put aside her innate feelings of shame and inadequacy and embarrassment at being a pathetic burden and to lean with all her might on the empathy and emotional nurture of her Support System, despite the fact that this, ironically, had been one of the two areas in which the depressed person had most vigorously resisted the therapist's counsel.

Even on top of the shattering abandonment-issues it brought up, the therapist's unexpected death also could not have occurred at a worse time from the perspective of the depressed person's journey toward inner healing, coming as it (i.e., the suspicious death) did just as the depressed person

---

ably served to shield a defenseless childhood psyche against potentially unbearable trauma, but in nearly all cases they (i.e., the defense-mechanisms) had become inappropriately imprinted and arrested and were now, in adulthood, no longer environmentally appropriate and in fact now, paradoxically, actually caused a great deal more trauma and pain than they prevented. Nevertheless, the therapist had made it clear from the outset that she was in no way going to pressure, hector, cajole, argue, persuade, flummox, trick, harangue, shame, or manipulate the depressed person into letting go of her arrested or vestigial defenses before she (i.e., the depressed person) felt ready and able to risk taking the leap of faith in her own internal resources and self-esteem and personal growth and healing to do so (i.e., to leave the nest of her defenses and freely and joyfully fly).

was beginning to work through and process some of her core shame- and resentment-issues concerning the therapeutic process itself and the intimate therapist-patient relationship's impact on her (i.e., on the depressed person's) unbearable isolation and pain. As part of her grieving process, the depressed person shared with supportive members of her Support System the fact that she felt she had, she had realized, experienced significant trauma and anguish and isolation-feelings even in the therapeutic relationship itself, a realization which she said she and the therapist had been working intensively together to explore and process. For just one example, the depressed person shared long-distance, she had discovered and struggled in therapy to work through her feeling that it was ironic and demeaning, given her parents' dysfunctional preoccupation with money and all that that preoccupation had cost her as a child, that she was now, as an adult, in the position of having to pay a therapist $90 an hour to listen patiently to her and respond honestly and empathetically; i.e., it felt demeaning and pathetic to feel forced to *buy* patience and empathy, the depressed person had confessed to her therapist, and was an agonizing echo of the exact same childhood pain which she (i.e., the depressed person) was so very anxious to put behind her. The therapist — after attending closely and unjudgingly to what the depressed person later admitted to her Support System could all too easily have been interpreted as mere niggardly whining about the expense of therapy, and after a long and considered pause during which both the therapist and the depressed person had gazed at the ovoid cage which the therapist's mated hands in her lap at that moment composed[4] — had responded that, while on a purely intellec-

---

4 The therapist—who was substantially older than the depressed person but still younger than the depressed person's mother, and who, other than in the condition of her fingernails, resembled that mother in almost no physical or stylistic respects—sometimes annoyed the depressed person with her habit of making a digiform cage in her lap and changing the shapes of the cage and gazing down at the geometrically diverse cages during their work together. Over time, however, as the therapeutic relationship deepened in terms of intimacy and sharing and trust, the sight of the digiform cages irked the depressed person less and less, eventually becoming little more than a distraction. Far more problematic in terms of the depressed person's trust- and self-esteem-issues was the therapist's habit of from time to time glancing up very quickly at the large sunburst-design clock on the wall behind the suede easy chair in which the depressed person customarily sat during their time together, glancing (i.e., the therapist glancing) very quickly and almost furtively at the clock, such that what came to bother the depressed person more and more over time was not that the therapist was looking at the clock but that the therapist was apparently trying to *hide* or *disguise* the fact that she was looking at the clock. The depressed person—who was agonizingly sensitive, she admitted, to the possibility that anyone she was trying to reach out and share with was secretly bored or repelled or desperate to get away from her as quickly as possible, and was commensurately hyper-

tual or "head" level she might respectfully disagree with the substance or "propositional content" of what the depressed person was saying, she (i.e., the therapist) nevertheless wholeheartedly supported the depressed person

---

vigilant about any slight movements or gestures which might imply that a listener was conscious of the time or eager for time to pass, and never once failed to notice when the therapist glanced ever so quickly either up at the clock or down at the slender, elegant wristwatch whose timepiece rested hidden from the depressed person's view against the underside of the therapist's slim wrist — had finally, late in the first year of the therapeutic relationship, broken into sobs and shared that it made her feel totally demeaned and invalidated whenever the therapist appeared to try to hide the fact that she wished to know the exact time. Much of the depressed person's work with the therapist in the first year of her (i.e., the depressed person's) journey toward healing and intrapersonal wholeness had concerned her feelings of being uniquely and repulsively boring or convoluted or pathetically self-involved, and of not being able to trust that there was genuine interest and compassion and caring on the part of a person to whom she was reaching out for support; and in fact the therapeutic relationship's first significant breakthrough, the depressed person told members of her Support System in the agonizing period following the therapist's death, had come when the depressed person, late in the therapeutic relationship's second year, had gotten sufficiently in touch with her own inner worth and resources to be able to share assertively with the therapist that she (i.e., the respectful but assertive depressed person) would prefer it if the therapist would simply look openly up at the helioform clock or openly turn her wrist over to look at the underside's wristwatch instead of apparently believing — or at least engaging in behavior which made it appear, from the depressed person's admittedly hypersensitive perspective, as if the therapist believed — that the depressed person could be fooled by her dishonestly sneaking an observation of the time into some gesture that tried to look like a meaningless glance at the wall or an absent manipulation of the cagelike digiform shape in her lap.

Another important piece of therapeutic work the depressed person and her therapist had accomplished together — a piece of work which the therapist had said she personally felt constituted a seminal leap of growth and deepening of the trust and level of honest sharing between them — occurred in the therapeutic relationship's third year, when the depressed person had finally confessed that she also felt it was demeaning to be spoken to as the therapist sometimes spoke to her, i.e., that the depressed person felt patronized, condescended to, and/or treated like a child at those times during their work together when the therapist would start tiresomely lallating over and over and over again what her therapeutic philosophies and goals and wishes for the depressed person were; plus not to mention, while they were on the whole subject, that she (i.e., the depressed person) also sometimes felt demeaned and resentful whenever the therapist would look up from her lap's hands' cage at the depressed person and her (i.e., the therapist's) face would once again assume its customary expression of calm and boundless patience, an expression which the depressed person admitted she knew (i.e., the depressed person knew) was intended to communicate unjudging attention and interest and support but which nevertheless sometimes from the depressed person's perspective looked to her more like emotional detachment, like clinical distance, like mere professional interest the depressed person was purchasing instead of the intensely *personal* interest and empathy and compassion she often felt she had spent her whole life starved for. It made her angry, the depressed person confessed; she often felt angry and resentful at being nothing but the object of the therapist's professional compassion or of the putative "friends" in her pathetic "Support System" 's charity and abstract guilt.

in sharing whatever feelings the therapeutic relationship itself brought up in her (i.e., in the depressed person[5]) so that they could work together on processing them and exploring safe and appropriate environments and contexts for their expression.

---

5 Though the depressed person had, she later acknowledged to her Support System, been anxiously watching the therapist's face for evidence of a negative reaction as she (i.e., the depressed person) opened up and vomited out all these potentially repulsive feelings about the therapeutic relationship, she nevertheless was by this point in the session benefiting enough from a kind of momentum of emotional honesty to be able to open up even further and tearfully share with the therapist that it also felt demeaning and even somehow abusive to know that, for example, today (i.e., the day of the depressed person and her therapist's seminally honest and important piece of relationship-work together), at the moment the depressed person's time with the therapist was up and they had risen from their respective recliners and hugged stiffly goodbye until their next appointment together, that at that very moment all of the therapist's seemingly intensely personally focused attention and support and interest in the depressed person would be withdrawn and then effortlessly transferred onto the next pathetic contemptible whiny self-involved snaggletoothed pig-nosed fat-thighed *shiteater* who was waiting out there right outside reading a used magazine and waiting to lurch in and cling pathetically to the hem of the therapist's pelisse for an hour, so desperate for a personally interested friend that they would pay almost as much per month for the pathetic temporary illusion of a friend as they paid in fucking *rent*. The depressed person knew all too perfectly well, she conceded—holding up a pica-gnawed hand to prevent the therapist from interrupting—that the therapist's professional detachment was in fact not at all incompatible with true caring, and that the therapist's careful maintenance of a professional, rather than a personal, level of caring and support and commitment meant that this support and caring could be counted on to always Be There for the depressed person and not fall prey to the normal vicissitudes of less professional and more personal interpersonal relationships' inevitable conflicts and misunderstandings or natural fluctuations in the therapist's own personal mood and emotional availability and capacity for empathy on any particular day; not to mention that her (i.e., the therapist's) professional detachment meant that at least within the confines of the therapist's chilly but attractive home office and of their appointed three hours together each week the depressed person could be totally honest and open about her own feelings without ever having to be afraid that the therapist would take those feelings personally and become angry or cold or judgmental or derisive or rejecting or would ever shame or deride or abandon the depressed person; in fact that, ironically, in many ways, as the depressed person said she was all too aware, the therapist was actually the depressed person's—or at any rate the isolated, agonized, needy, pathetic, selfish, spoiled, wounded-Inner-Child part of the depressed person's—absolutely *ideal* personal friend: i.e. here, after all, was a person (viz., the therapist) who would always Be There to listen and really care and empathize and be emotionally available and giving and to nurture and support the depressed person and yet would demand absolutely nothing back from the depressed person in terms of empathy or emotional support or in terms of the depressed person ever really caring about or even considering the therapist's own valid feelings and needs as a human being. The depressed person also knew perfectly well, she had acknowledged, that it was in fact the $90 an hour which made the therapeutic relationship's simulacrum of friendship so ideally one-sided: i.e. the only expectation or demand the therapist placed on the depressed person was for the contracted hourly $90;

The depressed person's recollections of the therapist's patient, attentive, and unjudging responses to even her (i.e., the depressed person's) most spiteful and childishly arrested complaints felt as if they brought on further, even more unbearable feelings of loss and abandonment, as well as

---

after that one demand was satisfied, everything in the relationship got to be for and about the depressed person. On a rational, intellectual, "head" level, the depressed person was completely aware of all these realities and compensations, she told the therapist, and so of course felt that she (i.e., the depressed person) had no rational reason or excuse for feeling the vain, needy, childish feelings she had just taken the unprecedented emotional risk of sharing that she felt; and yet the depressed person confessed to the therapist that she nevertheless still felt, on a more basic, emotionally intuitive or "gut" level, that it truly was demeaning and insulting and pathetic that her chronic emotional pain and isolation and inability to reach out forced her to spend $1,080 a month to purchase what was in many respects a kind of fantasy-friend who could fulfill her childishly narcissistic fantasies of getting her own emotional needs met by another without having to reciprocally meet or empathize with or even consider the other's own emotional needs, an other-directed empathy and consideration which the depressed person tearfully confessed she sometimes despaired of ever having it in her to give. The depressed person here inserted that she often worried, despite the numerous traumas she had suffered at the hands of attempted relationships with men, that it was in fact her own inability to get outside her own toxic neediness and to Be There for another and truly emotionally *give* which had made those attempts at intimate, mutually nurturing partner-relationships with men such an agonizingly demeaning across-the-board failure.

The depressed person had further inserted in her seminal sharing with the therapist, she later told the select elite "core" members of her Support System after the therapist's death, that her (i.e., the depressed person's) resentments about the $1,080/month cost of the therapeutic relationship were in truth less about the actual expense—which she freely admitted she could afford—than about the demeaning *idea* of paying for artificially one-sided friendship and narcissistic-fantasy-fulfillment, then had laughed hollowly (i.e., the depressed person had laughed hollowly during the original insertion in her sharing with the therapist) to indicate that she heard and acknowledged the unwitting echo of her cold, niggardly, emotionally unavailable parents in the stipulation that what was objectionable was not the actual expense but the idea or "*principle*" of the expense. What it really felt like, the depressed person later admitted to supportive friends that she had confessed to the compassionate therapist, was as if the $90 hourly therapeutic fee were almost a kind of ransom or "protection money," purchasing the depressed person an exemption from the scalding internal shame and mortification of telephoning distant former friends she hadn't even laid fucking *eyes* on in years and had no legitimate claim on the friendship of anymore and telephoning them uninvited at night and intruding on their functional and blissfully ignorantly joyful if perhaps somewhat shallow lives and leaning shamelessly on them and constantly reaching out and trying to articulate the essence of the depression's terrible and unceasing pain even when it was this very pain and despair and loneliness that rendered her, she knew, far too emotionally starved and needy and self-involved to be able ever to truly Be There in return for her long-distance friends to reach out to and share with and lean on in return, i.e. that hers (i.e., the depressed person's) was a contemptibly greedy and narcissistic omnineediness that only a complete idiot would not fully expect the members of her so-called "Support System" to detect all too easily in her, and to be totally repelled by, and to stay on the telephone with only out

fresh waves of resentment and self-pity which the depressed person knew all too well were repellent in the extreme, she assured the friends who composed her Support System, trusted friends whom the depressed person was by this time calling almost constantly, sometimes now even during

---

of the barest and most abstract human charity, all the while rolling their eyes and making faces and looking at the clock and wishing that the telephone call were over or that she (i.e., the pathetically needy depressed person on the phone) would call anyone else but her (i.e., the bored, repelled, eye-rolling putative "friend") or that she'd never historically been assigned to room with the depressed person or had never even gone to that particular boarding school or even that the depressed person had never been born and didn't even exist, such that the whole thing felt totally, unendurably pathetic and demeaning "*if the truth be told*," if the therapist really wanted the "*totally honest and uncensored sharing*" she always kept "alleging [she] want[ed]," the depressed person later confessed to her Support System she had hissed derisively at the therapist, her face (i.e., the depressed person's face during the seminal but increasingly ugly and humiliating third-year therapy session) working in what she imagined must have been a grotesque admixture of rage and self-pity and complete humiliation. It had been the imaginative visualization of what her own enraged face must have looked like which had caused the depressed person to begin at this late juncture in the session to weep, pule, snuffle, and sob in real earnest, she shared later with trusted friends. For no, if the therapist really wanted the truth, the actual "gut"-level truth underneath all her childishly defensive anger and shame, the depressed person had shared from a hunched and near-fetal position beneath the sunburst clock, sobbing but making a conscious choice not to bother wiping her eyes or even her nose, the depressed person *really* felt that what was *really* unfair was that she felt able—even here in therapy with the trusted and compassionate therapist—that she felt able to share only painful circumstances and historical insights about her depression and its etiology and texture and numerous symptoms instead of feeling truly able to communicate and articulate and express the depression's terrible unceasing agony *itself*, an agony that was the overriding and unendurable reality of her every black minute on earth—i.e., not being able to share the way it truly *felt*, what the depression made her *feel like* inside on a daily basis, she had wailed hysterically, striking repeatedly at her recliner's suede armrests—or to reach out and communicate and express it to someone who could not only listen and understand and care but could or would actually *feel it* with her (i.e., feel what the depressed person felt). The depressed person confessed to the therapist that what she felt *truly* starved for and really *truly* fantasized about was having the ability to somehow really truly literally "*share*" it (i.e., the chronic depression's ceaseless torment). She said that the depression felt as if it was so central and inescapable to her identity and who she was as a person that not being able to share the depression's inner feeling or even really describe what it felt like felt to her for example like feeling a desperate, life-or-death need to describe the sun in the sky and yet being able or permitted only to point to shadows on the ground. She was so very tired of pointing at shadows, she had sobbed. She (i.e., the depressed person) had then immediately broken off and laughed hollowly at herself and apologized to the therapist for employing such a floridly melodramatic and self-pitying analogy. The depressed person shared all this later with her Support System, in great detail and sometimes more than once a night, as part of her grieving process following the therapist's death from homeopathic caffeinism, including her (i.e., the depressed person's) reminiscence that the therapist's display of compassionate and unjudging attention to everything the depressed person had finally opened up and vented and hissed and

the day, from her workplace, dialing her closest friends' long-distance work numbers and asking them to take time away from their own challenging, stimulating careers to listen supportively and share and dialogue and help the depressed person find some way to process this grief and loss and find some way to survive. Her apologies for burdening these friends during daylight hours at their workplaces were elaborate, involved, vociferous, baroque, mercilessly self-critical, and very nearly constant, as were her expressions of gratitude to the Support System just for Being There for her, just for allowing her to begin again to be able to trust and take the risk of reaching out, even just a little, because the depressed person shared that she felt as if she had been discovering all over again, and with a shattering new clarity now in the wake of the therapist's abrupt and wordless abandonment, she shared over her workstation's headset telephone, just how agonizingly few and far between were the people whom she could ever hope to really communicate and share with and forge healthy, open, trusting, mutually nurturing relationships to lean on. For example, her work environment—as the depressed person readily acknowledged she'd whined about at tiresome length many times before—was totally dysfunctional and toxic, and the totally unsupportive emotional atmosphere there made the idea of trying to bond in any mutually nurturing way with coworkers a grotesque joke. And the depressed person's attempts to reach out in her emotional isolation and try to cultivate and develop caring friends and relationships in the community through church groups or nutrition and holistic stretching classes or community woodwind ensembles and the like had proved so excruciating, she shared, that she had all but begged the therapist to withdraw her gentle suggestion that the depressed person try her best to do so. And then as for the idea of girding herself once again and venturing out there into the emotionally Hobbesian meat market of the "dating scene" and trying once again to find and

---

spewed and whined and puled about during the traumatically seminal breakthrough session had been so formidable and uncompromising that she (i.e., the therapist) had blinked far less often than any nonprofessional listener the depressed person had ever shared with face-to-face had ever blinked. The two currently most trusted and supportive "core" members of the depressed person's Support System had responded, almost verbatim, that it sounded as though the depressed person's therapist had been very special, and that the depressed person clearly missed her very much; and the one particularly valuable and empathetic and elite, physically ill "core" friend whom the depressed person leaned on more heavily than on any other support during the grieving process suggested that the single most loving and appropriate way to honor both the therapist's memory and the depressed person's own grief over her loss might be for the depressed person to try to become as special and caring and unflaggingly nurturing a friend to herself as the late therapist had been.

establish any healthy, caring, functional connections with men, whether in a physically intimate partner-relationship or even just as close and supportive friends—at this juncture in her sharing the depressed person laughed hollowly into the headset telephone she wore at the terminal inside her cubicle at her workplace and asked whether it was really even necessary, with a friend who knew her as well as whatever member of her Support System she was presently sharing with did, to go into why the depressed person's intractable depression and highly charged self-esteem- and trust-issues rendered that idea a pie-in-the-sky flight of Icarusian fancy and denial. To take just one example, the depressed person shared from her workstation, in the second semester of her junior year at college there had been a traumatic incident in which the depressed person had been sitting alone on the grass near a group of popular, self-assured male students at an intercollegiate lacrosse game and had distinctly overheard one of the men laughingly say, of a female student the depressed person knew slightly, that the only substantive difference between this woman and a restroom toilet was that the toilet did not keep pathetically following you around after you'd used it. Sharing with supportive friends, the depressed person was now suddenly and unexpectedly flooded with emotional memories of the early session during which she had first told the therapist of this incident: they had been doing basic feelings-work together during this awkward opening stage of the therapeutic process, and the therapist had challenged the depressed person to identify whether the overheard slur had made her (i.e., the depressed person) feel primarily more angry, lonely, frightened, or sad.[6, 6(A)]

---

6 The depressed person, trying desperately to open up and allow her Support System to help her honor and process her feelings about the therapist's death, took the risk of sharing her realization that she herself had rarely if ever used the word "sad" in the therapeutic process's dialogues. She had usually used the words "despair" and "agony," and the therapist had, for the most part, acquiesced to this admittedly melodramatic choice of words, though the depressed person had long suspected that the therapist probably felt that her (i.e., the depressed person's) choice of "agony," "despair," "torment," and the like was at once melodramatic—hence needy and manipulative—on the one hand, and minimizing— hence shame-based and toxic—on the other. The depressed person also shared with long-distance friends during the shattering grieving process the painful realization that she had never once actually come right out and asked the therapist what she (i.e., the therapist) was thinking or feeling at any given moment during their time together, nor had asked, even once, what she (i.e., the therapist) actually thought of her (i.e., of the depressed person) as a human being, i.e. whether the therapist personally liked her, didn't like her, thought she was a basically decent v. repellent person, etc. These were merely two examples.

6(A) As a natural part of the grieving process, sensuous details and emotional memories flooded the depressed person's agonized psyche at random moments and in ways impossible to predict, pressing in on her and clamoring for expression and processing. The

By this stage in the grieving process following the therapist's possible death by her own (i.e., by the therapist's own) hand, the depressed person's feelings of loss and abandonment had become so intense and overwhelming and had so completely overridden her vestigial defense-mechanisms that, for example, when whatever long-distance friend the depressed person had reached out to finally confessed that she (i.e., the "friend") was dreadfully sorry but there was no helping it she absolutely *had* to get off the telephone and back to the demands of her own full, vibrant, undepressed life, a primal instinct for what felt like nothing more than basic emotional survival now drove the depressed person to swallow every last pulverized remnant of pride and to beg shamelessly for two or even just one more minute of the friend's time and attention; and, if the "empathetic friend," after expressing her hope that the depressed person would find a way to be more gentle and compassionate with herself, held firm and gracefully terminated the conversation, the depressed person now spent hardly any time at all listening dully to the dial tone or gnawing the cuticle of her index finger or grinding the heel of her hand savagely into her forehead or feeling anything much at all beyond sheer primal desperation as she hurriedly dialed the next ten-digit number on her Support System Telephone List, a list which by this point in the grieving process had been photocopied several times and placed in the depressed person's address book, workstation terminal's PHONE.VIP file, billfold, zippered interior security compartment of her purse, minilocker at the Holistic Stretching and Nutrition Center, and in a special homemade pocket inside the back cover of the leatherbound Feelings Journal which the depressed person—at her late therapist's suggestion—carried with her at all times.

---

therapist's buckskin pelisse, for example, though the therapist had seemed almost fetishistically attached to the Native American garment and had worn it, seemingly, on a near-daily basis, was always immaculately clean and always presented an immaculately raw and moist-looking flesh-tone backdrop to the varioform cagelike shapes the therapist's unconscious hands composed—and the depressed person shared with members of her Support System, after the therapist's death, that it had never been clear to her how or by what process the pelisse's buckskin was able to stay so clean. The depressed person confessed to sometimes imagining narcissistically that the therapist wore the immaculate flesh-colored garment only for their particular appointments together. The therapist's chilly home office also contained, on the wall opposite the bronze clock and behind the therapist's recliner, a stunning molybdenum desk-and-personal-computer-hutch ensemble, one shelf of which was lined, on either side of the deluxe Braun coffeemaker, with small framed photographs of the late therapist's husband and sisters and son; and the depressed person often broke into fresh sobs of loss and despair and self-excoriation on her cubicle's headset telephone as she confessed to her Support System that she had never once even asked the therapist's loved ones' names.

The depressed person shared, with each available member of her Support System in turn, some portion of the flood of emotionally sensuous memories of the session during which she had first opened up and told the late therapist of the incident in which the laughing men had compared the female college student to a toilet, and shared that she had never been able to forget the incident, and that, even though she had not had much of a personal relationship or connection to the female student whom the men had compared to a toilet or even known her very well at all, the depressed person had, at the intercollegiate lacrosse game, been filled with horror and empathic despair at the pathos of the idea of that female student being the object of such derision and laughing intergender contempt without her (i.e., the female student, to whom the depressed person again admitted she had had very little connection) ever even knowing it. It seemed to the depressed person very likely that her (i.e., the depressed person's) whole later emotional development and ability to trust and reach out and connect had been deeply scarred by this incident; she chose to make herself open and vulnerable by sharing—albeit only with the one single most trusted and elite and special "core" member of her current Support System—that she had admitted to the therapist that she was, even today, as a putative adult, often preoccupied with the idea that laughing groups of people were often derisive and demeaning of her (i.e., of the depressed person) without her knowledge. The late therapist, the depressed person shared with her very closest long-distance confidante, had pointed to the memory of the traumatic incident in college and the depressed person's reactive presumption of derision and ridicule as a classic example of the way an adult's arrested vestigial emotional defense-mechanisms could become toxic and dysfunctional and could keep the adult emotionally isolated and deprived of community and nurturing, even from herself, and could (i.e., the toxic vestigial defenses could) deny the depressed adult access to her own precious inner resources and tools for both reaching out for support and for being gentle and compassionate and affirming with herself, and that thus, paradoxically, arrested defense-mechanisms helped contribute to the very pain and sadness they had originally been erected to forestall.

It was while sharing this candid, vulnerable four-year-old reminiscence with the one particular "core" Support System–member whom the grieving depressed person felt she now most deeply trusted and leaned on and could really communicate over the headset telephone with that she (i.e., the depressed person) suddenly experienced what she would later describe as an emotional realization nearly as traumatic and valuable as the realization she had experienced nine months prior at the Inner-Child-Focused

Experiential Therapy Retreat Weekend before she had felt simply too cathartically drained and enervated to be able to continue and had had to fly home. I.e., the depressed person told her very most trusted and supportive long-distance friend that, paradoxically, she (i.e., the depressed person) appeared to have somehow found, in the extremity of her feelings of loss and abandonment in the wake of the therapist's overdose of natural stimulants, the resources and inner respect for her own emotional survival required for her finally to feel able to risk trying to follow the second of the late therapist's two most challenging and difficult suggestions and to begin openly asking certain demonstrably honest and supportive others to tell her straight out whether they ever secretly felt contempt, derision, judgment, or repulsion for her. And the depressed person shared that she now, finally, after four years of whiny and truculent resistance, proposed at last really to begin actually asking trusted others this seminally honest and possibly shattering question, and that because she was all too aware of her own essential weakness and defensive capacities for denial and avoidance, she (i.e., the depressed person) was choosing to commence this unprecedentedly vulnerable interrogative process now, i.e., with the elite, incomparably honest and compassionate "core" Support System–member with whom she was sharing via her workstation's headset right this moment.[7] The depressed person here paused momentarily to insert the additional fact that she had firmly resolved to herself to ask this potentially deeply traumatizing question without the usual pathetic and irritating defense-mechanisms of preamble or apology or interpolated self-criticism. She wished to hear, with no holds barred, the depressed person averred, the one very most valuable and intimate friend in her current Support System's brutally honest opinion of her as a person, the potentially negative and judging and hurtful parts as well as the positive and affirming and supportive and nurturing parts. The depressed person stressed that she was serious about this: whether it sounded melodramatic or not, the brutally honest assessment of her by an objective but deeply

---

7 The singularly valuable and supportive long-distance friend to whom the depressed person had decided she was least mortified about posing a question this fraught with openness and vulnerability and emotional risk was an alumna of one of the depressed person's very first childhood boarding schools, a surpassingly generous and nurturing divorced mother of two in Bloomfield Hills, Michigan, who had recently undergone her second course of chemotherapy for a virulent neuroblastoma which had greatly reduced the number of responsibilities and activities in her full, functional, vibrantly other-directed adult life, and who thus was now not only almost always at home but also enjoyed nearly unlimited conflict-free availability and time to share on the telephone, for which the depressed person was always careful to enter a daily prayer of gratitude in her Feelings Journal.

caring other felt to her, at this point in time, like an almost literal matter of life and death.

For she was frightened, the depressed person confessed to the trusted and convalescing friend, profoundly, unprecedentedly frightened by what she was beginning to feel she was seeing and learning and getting in touch with about herself in the grieving process following the sudden death of a therapist who for nearly four years had been the depressed person's closest and most trusted confidante and source of support and affirmation and—with no offense in any way intended to any members of her Support System—her very best friend in the world. Because what she had discovered, the depressed person confided long-distance, when she took her important daily Quiet Time[8] now, during the grieving process, and got quiet and centered and looked deep within, was that she could neither feel nor identify any real feelings within herself for the therapist, i.e. for the therapist as a person, a person who had died, a person who only somebody in truly stupefying denial could fail to see had probably taken her own life, and thus a person who, the depressed person posited, had possibly herself suffered levels of emotional agony and isolation and despair which were comparable to or perhaps—though it was only on a "head" or purely abstract intellectual level that she seemed to be able even to entertain this possibility, the depressed person confessed over the headset telephone—even exceeded the depressed person's own. The depressed person shared that the most frightening implication of this (i.e., of the fact that, even when she centered and looked deep within herself, she felt she could locate no real feelings for the therapist as an autonomously valid human being) appeared to be that all her agonized pain and despair since the therapist's suicide had in fact been all and only for *herself*, i.e. for *her* loss, *her* abandonment, *her* grief, *her* trauma and pain and primal affective survival. And, the depressed person shared that she was taking the additional risk of revealing, even more frightening, that this shatteringly terrifying set of realizations, instead now of awakening in her any feelings of compassion, empathy, and other-directed grief for the therapist as a person, had—and here the depressed person waited patiently for an episode of retching in the especially available trusted friend to pass so that she could take the risk of sharing this with her—that these shatteringly frightening realizations had seemed, terrifyingly, merely to have brought up and cre-

---

8 (i.e., carefully arranging her morning schedule to permit the twenty minutes the therapist had long suggested for quiet centering and getting in touch with feelings and owning them and journaling about them, looking inside herself with a compassionate, unjudging, almost clinical detachment)

ated still more and further feelings in the depressed person about *herself*. At this point in the sharing, the depressed person took a time-out to solemnly swear to her long-distance, gravely ill, frequently retching but still caring and intimate friend that there was no toxic or pathetically manipulative self-excoriation here in what she (i.e., the depressed person) was reaching out and opening up and confessing, only profound and unprecedented fear: the depressed person was frightened for herself, for as it were "[her]*self*"—i.e. for her own so-called "character" or "spirit" or as it were "soul" i.e. for her own capacity for basic human empathy and compassion and caring—she told the supportive friend with the neuroblastoma. She was asking sincerely, the depressed person said, honestly, desperately: what kind of person could seem to feel nothing—"*nothing*," she emphasized—for anyone but herself? Maybe not *ever?* The depressed person wept into the headset telephone and said that right here and now she was shamelessly begging her currently very best friend and confidante in the world to share her (i.e., the friend with the virulent malignancy in her adrenal medulla's) brutally candid assessment, to pull no punches, to say nothing reassuring or exculpatory or supportive which she did not honestly believe to be true. She trusted her, she assured her. For she had decided, she said, that her very life itself, however fraught with agony and despair and indescribable loneliness, depended, at this point in her journey toward true healing, on inviting—even if necessary laying aside all possible pride and defense and *begging for*, she interpolated—the judgment of certain trusted and very carefully selected members of her supportive community. So, the depressed person said, her voice breaking, she was begging her now single most trusted friend to share her very most private judgment of the depressed person's "character" 's or "spirit" 's capacity for human caring. She needed her feedback, the depressed person wept, even if that feedback was partly negative or hurtful or traumatic or had the potential to push her right over the emotional edge once and for all—even, she pleaded, if that feedback lay on nothing more than the coldly intellectual or "head" level of objective verbal description; she would settle even for that, she promised, hunched and trembling in a near-fetal position atop her workstation cubicle's ergonomic chair—and therefore now urged her terminally ill friend to go on, to not hold back, to let her have it: what words and terms might be applied to describe and assess such a solipsistic, self-consumed, endless emotional vacuum and sponge as she now appeared to herself to be? How was she to decide and describe—even to herself, looking inward and facing herself—what all she'd so painfully learned said about her?

OBLIVION

Good Old Neon

MY WHOLE LIFE I've been a fraud. I'm not exaggerating. Pretty much all
I've ever done all the time is try to create a certain impression of me in
other people. Mostly to be liked or admired. It's a little more complicated
than that, maybe. But when you come right down to it it's to be liked,
loved. Admired, approved of, applauded, whatever. You get the idea. I did
well in school, but deep down the whole thing's motive wasn't to learn or
improve myself but just to do well, to get good grades and make sports
teams and perform well. To have a good transcript or varsity letters to
show people. I didn't enjoy it much because I was always scared I wouldn't
do well enough. The fear made me work really hard, so I'd always do well
and end up getting what I wanted. But then, once I got the best grade or
made All City or got Angela Mead to let me put my hand on her breast, I
wouldn't feel much of anything except maybe fear that I wouldn't be able
to get it again. The next time or next thing I wanted. I remember being
down in the rec room in Angela Mead's basement on the couch and having her let me get my hand up under her blouse and not even really feeling
the soft aliveness or whatever of her breast because all I was doing was
thinking, 'Now I'm the guy that Mead let get to second with her.' Later
that seemed so sad. This was in middle school. She was a very big-hearted,
quiet, self-contained, thoughtful girl—she's a veterinarian now, with her
own practice—and I never even really saw her, I couldn't see anything
except who I might be in her eyes, this cheerleader and probably number
two or three among the most desirable girls in middle school that year.
She was much more than that, she was beyond all that adolescent ranking
and popularity crap, but I never really let her be or saw her as more,
although I put up a very good front as somebody who could have deep

conversations and really wanted to know and understand who she was inside.

Later I was in analysis, I tried analysis like almost everybody else then in their late twenties who'd made some money or had a family or whatever they thought they wanted and still didn't feel that they were happy. A lot of people I knew tried it. It didn't really work, although it did make everyone sound more aware of their own problems and added some useful vocabulary and concepts to the way we all had to talk to each other to fit in and sound a certain way. You know what I mean. I was in regional advertising at the time in Chicago, having made the jump from media buyer for a large consulting firm, and at only twenty-nine I'd made creative associate, and verily as they say I was a fair-haired boy and on the fast track but wasn't happy at all, whatever *happy* means, but of course I didn't say this to anybody because it was such a cliché — 'Tears of a Clown,' 'Richard Cory,' etc. — and the circle of people who seemed important to me seemed much more dry, oblique and contemptuous of clichés than that, and so of course I spent all my time trying to get them to think I was dry and jaded as well, doing things like yawning and looking at my nails and saying things like, '*Am I happy?* is one of those questions that, if it has got to be asked, more or less dictates its own answer,' etc. Putting in all this time and energy to create a certain impression and get approval or acceptance that then I felt nothing about because it didn't have anything to do with who I really was inside, and I was disgusted with myself for always being such a fraud, but I couldn't seem to help it. Here are some of the various things I tried: EST, riding a ten-speed to Nova Scotia and back, hypnosis, cocaine, sacrocervical chiropractic, joining a charismatic church, jogging, pro bono work for the Ad Council, meditation classes, the Masons, analysis, the Landmark Forum, the Course in Miracles, a right-brain drawing workshop, celibacy, collecting and restoring vintage Corvettes, and trying to sleep with a different girl every night for two straight months (I racked up a total of thirty-six for sixty-one and also got chlamydia, which I told friends about, acting like I was embarrassed but secretly expecting most of them to be impressed — which, under the cover of making a lot of jokes at my expense, I think they were — but for the most part the two months just made me feel shallow and predatory, plus I missed a great deal of sleep and was a wreck at work — that was also the period I tried cocaine). I know this part is boring and probably boring you, by the way, but it gets a lot more interesting when I get to the part where I kill myself and discover what happens immediately after a person dies. In terms of the list, psychoanalysis was pretty much the last thing I tried.

The analyst I saw was OK, a big soft older guy with a big ginger mustache and a pleasant, sort of informal manner. I'm not sure I remember him alive too well. He was a fairly good listener, and seemed interested and sympathetic in a slightly distant way. At first I suspected he didn't like me or was uneasy around me. I don't think he was used to patients who were already aware of what their real problem was. He was also a bit of a pill-pusher. I balked at trying antidepressants, I just couldn't see myself taking pills to try to be less of a fraud. I said that even if they worked, how would I know if it was me or the pills? By that time I already knew I was a fraud. I knew what my problem was. I just couldn't seem to stop. I remember I spent maybe the first twenty times or so in analysis acting all open and candid but in reality sort of fencing with him or leading him around by the nose, basically showing him that I wasn't just another one of those patients who stumbled in with no clue what their real problem was or who were totally out of touch with the truth about themselves. When you come right down to it, I was trying to show him that I was at least as smart as he was and that there wasn't much of anything he was going to see about me that I hadn't already seen and figured out. And yet I wanted help and really was there to try to get help. I didn't even tell him how unhappy I was until five or six months into the analysis, mostly because I didn't want to seem like just another whining, self-absorbed yuppie, even though I think even then I was on some level conscious that that's all I really was, deep down.

Right from the start, what I liked best about the analyst was that his office was a mess. There were books and papers everyplace, and usually he had to clear things off the chair so I could sit down. There was no couch, I sat in an easy chair and he sat facing me in his beat-up old desk chair whose back part had one of those big rectangles or capes of back-massage beads attached to it the same way cabbies often put them on their seat in the cab. This was another thing I liked, the desk chair and the fact that it was a little too small for him (he was not a small guy) so that he had to sit sort of almost hunched with his feet flat on the floor, or else sometimes he'd put his hands behind his head and lean way back in the chair in a way that made the back portion squeak terribly when it leaned back. There always seems to be something patronizing or a little condescending about somebody crossing their legs when they talk to you, and the desk chair didn't allow him to do this—if he ever crossed his legs his knee would have been up around his chin. And yet he had apparently never gone out and gotten himself a bigger or nicer desk chair, or even bothered to oil the medial joint's springs to keep the back from squeaking, a noise that I know would have driven me up the wall if it had been my chair and I had to spend all day in it. I noticed all this almost right away. The little office also reeked of pipe tobacco, which is a pleasant smell, plus Dr. Gustafson never took notes or answered everything with a question or any of the cliché analyst things that would have made the whole thing too horrible to keep going back whether it even helped or not. The whole effect was of a sort of likable, disorganized, laid-back guy, and things in there actually did get better after I realized that he probably wasn't going to do anything to make me quit fencing with him and trying to anticipate all his questions so I could show that I already knew the answer—he was going to get his $65 either way—and finally came out and told him about being a fraud and feeling alienated (I had to use the uptown word of course, but it was still the truth) and starting to see myself ending up living this way for the rest of my life and being completely unhappy. I told him I wasn't blaming anybody for my being a fraud. I had been adopted, but it was as a baby, and the stepparents who adopted me were better and nicer than most of the biological parents I knew anything about, and I was never yelled at or abused or pressured to hit .400 in Legion ball or anything, and they took out a second mortgage to send me to an elite college when I could have gone scholarship to U.W.–Eau Claire, etc. Nobody'd ever done anything bad to me, every problem I ever had I'd been the cause of. I was a fraud, and the fact that I was lonely was my own fault (of course his ears pricked up at *fault*, which is a loaded term) because I seemed to be so totally self-centered and fraudulent that I experienced everything in terms of how it affected people's view of me and what I needed to do to create the impression of me I wanted them to have. I said I knew what my problem was, what I couldn't do was stop it. I also admitted to Dr. Gustafson some of the ways I'd been jerking him around early on and trying to make sure he saw me as smart and self-aware, and said I'd known early on that playing around and showing off in analysis were a waste of time and money but that I couldn't seem to help myself, it just happened automatically. He smiled at all this, which was the first time I remember seeing him smile. I don't mean he was sour or humorless, he had a big red friendly face and a pleasant enough manner, but this was the first time he'd smiled like a human being having an actual conversation. And yet at the same time I already saw what I'd left myself open for—and sure enough he says it. 'If I understand you right,' he says, 'you're saying that you're basically a calculating, manipulative person who always says what you think will get somebody to approve of you or form some impression of you you think you want.' I told him that was maybe a little simplistic but basically accurate, and he said further that as he understood it I was saying that I felt as if I was trapped in this false way of being and unable ever to be totally open and tell the truth irregardless of whether it'd make me look good in others' eyes or not. And I somewhat resignedly said yes, and that I seemed always to have had this fraudulent, calculating part of my brain firing away all the time, as if I were constantly playing chess with everybody and figuring out that if I wanted them to move a certain way I had to move in such a way as to induce them to move that way. He asked if I ever played chess, and I told him I used to in middle school but quit because I couldn't be as good as I eventually wanted to be, how frustrating it was to get just good enough to know what getting really good at it would be like but not being able to get that good, etc. I was laying it on sort of thick in hopes of distracting him from the big insight and question I realized I'd set myself up for. But it didn't work. He leaned back in his loud chair and paused as if he were thinking hard, for effect—he was thinking that he was going to get to feel like he'd really earned his $65 today. Part of the pause always involved stroking his mustache in an unconscious way. I was reasonably sure that he was going to say something like, 'So then how were you able to do what you just did a moment ago?,' in other words meaning how was I able to be honest about the fraudulence if I was really a fraud, meaning he thought he'd caught me in some kind of logical contradiction or paradox. And I went ahead and played a little dumb, probably, to get him to go ahead and say it, partly because I still held out some hope that what he'd say might be more discerning or incisive than I had predicted. But it was also partly because I liked him, and liked the way he seemed genuinely pleased and excited at the idea of being helpful but was trying to exercise professional control over his facial expression in order to make the excitement look more like simple pleasantness and clinical interest in my case or whatever. He was hard not to like, he had what is known as an engaging manner. By way of decor, the office wall behind his chair had two framed prints, one being that Wyeth one of the little girl in the wheat field crawling uphill toward the farmhouse, the other a still life of two apples in a bowl on a table by Cézanne. (To be honest, I only knew it was Cézanne because it was an Art Institute poster and had a banner with info on a Cézanne show underneath the painting, which was a still life, and which was weirdly discomfiting because there was something slightly off about the perspective or style that made the table look crooked and the apples look almost square.) The prints were obviously there to give the analyst's patients something to look at, since many people like to look around or look at things on the wall while they talk. I didn't have any trouble looking right at him most of the time I was in there, though. He did have a talent for putting you at ease, there was no question about it. But I had no illusions that this was the same as having enough insight or firepower to find some way to really help me, though.

There was a basic logical paradox that I called the 'fraudulence paradox' that I had discovered more or less on my own while taking a mathematical logic course in school. I remember this as being a huge undergrad lecture course that met twice a week in an auditorium with the professor up on stage and on Fridays in smaller discussion sections led by a graduate assistant whose whole life seemed to be mathematical logic. (Plus all you had to do to ace the class was sit down with the assigned textbook that the prof was the editor of and memorize the different modes of argument and normal forms and axioms of first-order quantification, meaning the course was as clean and mechanical as logic itself in that if you put in the time and effort, out popped the good grade at the other end. We only got to paradoxes like the Berry and Russell Paradoxes and the incompleteness theorem at the very end of the term, they weren't on the final.) The fraudulence paradox was that the more time and effort you put into trying to appear impressive or attractive to other people, the less impressive or attractive you felt inside—you were a fraud. And the more of a fraud you felt like, the harder you tried to convey an impressive or likable image of yourself so that other people wouldn't find out what a hollow, fraudulent person you really were. Logically, you would think that the moment a supposedly intelligent nineteen-year-old became aware of this paradox, he'd stop being a fraud and just settle for being himself (whatever that was) because he'd figured out that being a fraud was a vicious infinite regress that ultimately resulted in being frightened, lonely, alienated, etc. But here was the other, higher-order paradox, which didn't even have a form or name—I didn't, I couldn't. Discovering the first paradox at age nineteen just brought home to me in spades what an empty, fraudulent person I'd basically been ever since at least the time I was four and lied to my stepdad because I'd realized somehow right in the middle of his asking me if I'd broken the bowl that if I said I did it but 'confessed' it in a sort of clumsy, implausible way, then he wouldn't believe me and would instead believe that my sister Fern, who's my stepparents' biological daughter, was the one who'd actually broken the antique Moser glass bowl that my stepmom had inherited from her biological grandmother and totally loved, plus it would lead or induce him to see me as a kind, good stepbrother who was so anxious to keep Fern (whom I really did like) from getting in trouble that I'd be willing to lie and take the punishment for it for her. I'm not explaining this very well. I was only four, for one thing, and the realization didn't hit me in words the way I just now put it, but rather more in terms of feelings and associations and certain mental flashes of my stepparents' faces with various expressions on them. But it happened that fast, at only four, that I figured out how to create a certain impression by knowing what effect I'd produce in my stepdad by implausibly 'confessing' that I'd punched Fern in the arm and stolen her Hula Hoop and had run all the way downstairs with it and started Hula-Hooping in the dining room right by the sideboard with all my stepmom's antique glassware and figurines on it, while Fern, forgetting all about her arm and hoop because of her concern over the bowl and other glassware, came running downstairs shouting after me, reminding me about how important the rule was that we weren't supposed to play in the dining room....Meaning that by lying in such a deliberately unconvincing way I could actually get everything that a direct lie would supposedly get me, plus look noble and self-sacrificing, plus also make my stepparents feel good because they always tended to feel good when one of their kids did something that showed character, because it's the sort of thing they couldn't really help but see as reflecting favorably on them as shapers of their kids' character. I'm putting all this in such a long, rushing, clumsy way to try to convey the way I remember it suddenly hit me, looking up at my stepfather's big kindly face as he held two of the larger pieces of the Moser bowl and tried to look angrier than he really felt. (He had always thought the more expensive pieces ought to be kept secure in storage somewhere, whereas my stepmom's view was more like what was the point of having nice things if you didn't have them out where people could enjoy them.) How to appear a certain way and get him to think a certain thing hit me just that fast. Keep in mind I was only around four. And I can't pretend it felt bad, realizing it—the truth is it felt great. I felt powerful, smart. It felt a little like looking at part of a puzzle you're doing and you've got a piece in your hand and you can't see where in the larger puzzle it's supposed to go or how to make it fit, looking at all the holes, and then all of a sudden in a flash you see, for no reason right then you could point to or explain to anyone, that if you turn the piece this one certain way it will fit, and it does, and maybe the best way to put it is that in that one tiny instant you feel suddenly connected to something larger and much more of the complete picture the same way the piece is. The only part I'd neglected to anticipate was Fern's reaction to getting blamed for the bowl, and punished, and then punished even worse when she continued to deny that she'd been the one playing around in the dining room, and my stepparents' position was that they were even more upset and disappointed about her lying than they were about the bowl, which they said was just a material object and not ultimately important in the larger scheme of things. (My stepparents spoke this way, they were people of high ideals and values, humanists. Their big ideal was total honesty in all the family's relationships, and lying was the worst, most disappointing infraction you could commit, in their view as parents. They tended to discipline Fern a little more firmly than they did me, by the way, but this too was an extension of their values. They were concerned about being fair and having me be able to feel that I was just as much their real child as Fern was, so that I'd feel maximally secure and loved, and sometimes this concern with fairness caused them to bend a little too far over backward when it came to discipline.) So that Fern, then, got regarded as being a liar when she was not, and that must have hurt her way more than the actual punishment did. She was only five at the time. It's horrible to be regarded as a fraud or to believe that people think you're a fraud or liar. It's possibly one of the worst feelings in the world. And even though I haven't really had any direct experience with it, I'm sure it must be doubly horrible when you were actually telling the truth and they didn't believe you. I don't think Fern ever quite got over that episode, although the two of us never talked about it afterward except for one sort of cryptic remark she made over her shoulder once when we were both in high school and having an argument about something and Fern was storming out of the house. She was sort of a classically troubled adolescent — smoking, makeup, mediocre grades, dating older guys, etc. — whereas I was the family's fair-haired boy and had a killer G.P.A. and played varsity ball, etc. One way to put it is that I looked and acted much better on the surface then than Fern did, although she eventually settled down and ended up going on to college and is now doing OK. She's also one of the funniest people on earth, with a very dry, subtle sense of humor — I like her a lot. The point being that that was the start of my being a fraud, although it's not as if the broken-bowl episode was somehow the origin or cause of my fraudulence or some kind of childhood trauma that I'd never gotten over and had to go into analysis to work out. The fraud part of me was always there, just as the puzzle piece, objectively speaking, is a true piece of the puzzle even before you see how it fits. For a while I thought that possibly one or the other of my biological parents had been frauds or had carried some type of fraud gene or something and that I had inherited it, but that was a dead end, there was no way to know. And even if I did, what difference would it make? I was still a fraud, it was still my own unhappiness that I had to deal with.

Once again, I'm aware that it's clumsy to put it all this way, but the point is that all of this and more was flashing through my head just in the interval of the small, dramatic pause Dr. Gustafson allowed himself before delivering his big reductio ad absurdum argument that I couldn't be a total fraud if I had just come out and admitted my fraudulence to him just now. I know that you know as well as I do how fast thoughts and associations can fly through your head. You can be in the middle of a creative meeting at your job or something, and enough material can rush through your head just in the little silences when people are looking over their notes and waiting for the next presentation that it would take exponentially longer than the whole meeting just to try to put a few seconds' silence's flood of thoughts into words. This is another paradox, that many of the most important impressions and thoughts in a person's life are ones that flash through your head so fast that *fast* isn't even the right word, they seem totally different from or outside of the regular sequential clock time we all live by, and they have so little relation to the sort of linear, one-word-after-another-word English we all communicate with each other with that it could easily take a whole lifetime just to spell out the contents of one split-second's flash of thoughts and connections, etc.—and yet we all seem to go around trying to use English (or whatever language our native country happens to use, it goes without saying) to try to convey to other people what we're thinking and to find out what they're thinking, when in fact deep down everybody knows it's a charade and they're just going through the motions. What goes on inside is just too fast and huge and all interconnected for words to do more than barely sketch the outlines of at most one tiny little part of it at any given instant. The internal head-speed or whatever of these ideas, memories, realizations, emotions and so on is even faster, by the way—exponentially faster, unimaginably faster—when you're dying, meaning during that vanishingly tiny nanosecond between when you technically die and when the next thing happens, so that in reality the cliché about people's whole life flashing before their eyes as they're dying isn't all that far off—although the *whole life* here isn't really a sequential thing where first you're born and then you're in the crib and then you're up at the plate in Legion ball, etc., which it turns out that that's what people usually mean when they say 'my whole life,' meaning a discrete, chronological series of moments that they add up and call their lifetime. It's not really like that. The best way I can think of to try to say it is that it all happens at once, but that *at once* doesn't really mean a finite moment of sequential time the way we think of time while we're alive, plus that what turns out to be the meaning of the term *my life* isn't even close to what we think we're talking about when we say 'my life.' Words and chronological time create all these total misunderstandings of what's really going on at the most basic level. And yet at the same time English is all we have to try to understand it and try to form anything larger or more meaningful and true with anybody else, which is yet another paradox. Dr. Gustafson—whom I would meet again later and find out that he had almost nothing to do with the big doughy repressed guy sitting back against his chair's beads in his River Forest office with colon cancer in him already at that time and him knowing nothing yet except that he didn't feel quite right down there in the bathroom lately and if it kept on he'd make an appointment to go in and ask his internist about it—Dr. G. would later say that the whole *my whole life flashed before me* phenomenon at the end is more like being a whitecap on the surface of the ocean, meaning that it's only at the moment you subside and start sliding back in that you're really even aware there's an ocean at all. When you're up and out there as a whitecap you might talk and act as if you know you're just a whitecap on the ocean, but deep down you don't think there's really an ocean at all. It's almost impossible to. Or like a leaf that doesn't believe in the tree it's part of, etc. There are all sorts of ways to try to express it.

And of course all this time you've probably been noticing what seems like the really central, overarching paradox, which is that this whole thing where I'm saying words can't really do it and time doesn't really go in a straight line is something that you're hearing as words that you have to start listening to the first word and then each successive word after that in chronological time to understand, so if I'm saying that words and sequential time have nothing to do with it you're wondering why we're sitting here in this car using words and taking up your increasingly precious time, meaning aren't I sort of logically contradicting myself right at the start. Not to mention am I maybe full of B.S. about knowing what happens—if I really did kill myself, how can you even be hearing this? Meaning am I a fraud. That's OK, it doesn't really matter what you think. I mean it probably matters to you, or you think it does—that isn't what I meant by *doesn't matter*. What I mean is that it doesn't really matter what you think about me, because despite appearances this isn't even really about me. All I'm trying to do is sketch out one little part of what it was like before I died and why I at least thought I did it, so that you'll have at least some idea of why what happened afterward happened and why it had the impact it did on who this is really about. Meaning it's like an abstract or sort of intro, meant to be very brief and sketchy...and yet of course look how much time and English it's seeming to take even to say it. It's interesting if you really think about it, how clumsy and laborious it seems to be to convey even the smallest thing. How much time would you even say has passed, so far?

One reason why Dr. Gustafson would have made a terrible poker player or fraud is that whenever he thought it was a big moment in the analysis he would always make a production of leaning back in his desk chair, which made that loud sound as the back tilted back and his feet went back on their heels so the soles showed, although he was good at making the position look comfortable and very familiar to his body, like it felt good doing that when he had to think. The whole thing was both slightly over-dramatic and yet still likable for some reason. Fern, by the way, has red-dish hair and slightly asymmetrical green eyes — the kind of green people buy tinted contact lenses to get — and is attractive in a sort of witchy way. I think she's attractive, anyway. She's grown up to be a very poised, witty, self-sufficient person, with maybe just the slightest whiff of the perfume of loneliness that hangs around unmarried women around age thirty. The fact is that we're all lonely, of course. Everyone knows this, it's almost a cliché. So yet another layer of my essential fraudulence is that I pretended to myself that my loneliness was special, that it was uniquely my fault because I was somehow especially fraudulent and hollow. It's not special at all, we've all got it. In spades. Dead or not, Dr. Gustafson knew more about all this than I, so that he spoke with what came off as genuine authority and pleasure when he said (maybe a little superciliously, given how obvious it was), 'But if you're constitutionally false and manipulative and unable to be honest about who you really are, Neal' (Neal being my given name, it was on my birth certificate when I got adopted), 'how is it that you were able to drop the sparring and manipulation and be honest with me a moment ago' (for that's all it had been, in spite of all the English that's been expended on just my head's partial contents in the tiny interval between then and now) 'about who you really are?' So it turned out I'd been right in predicting what his big logical insight was going to be. And although I played along with him for a while so as not to prick his bubble, inside I felt pretty bleak indeed, because now I knew that he was going to be just as pliable and credulous as everyone else, he didn't appear to have anything close to the firepower I'd need to give me any hope of getting helped out of the trap of fraudulence and unhappiness I'd constructed for myself. Because the real truth was that my confession of being a fraud and of having wasted time sparring with him over the previous weeks in order to manipulate him into seeing me as exceptional and insightful had itself been kind of manipulative. It was pretty clear that Dr. Gustafson, in order to survive in private practice, could not be totally stupid or obtuse about people, so it seemed reasonable to assume that he'd noticed the massive amount of fencing and general showing off I'd been doing during the first weeks of the analysis, and thus had come to some conclusions about my apparently desperate need to make a certain kind of impression on him, and though it wasn't totally certain it was thus at least a decent possibility that he'd sized me up as a basically empty, insecure person whose whole life involved trying to impress people and manipulate their view of me in order to compensate for the inner emptiness. It's not as if this is an incredibly rare or obscure type of personality, after all. So the fact that I had chosen to be supposedly 'honest' and to diagnose myself aloud was in fact just one more move in my campaign to make sure Dr. Gustafson understood that as a patient I was uniquely acute and self-aware, and that there was very little chance he was going to see or diagnose anything about me that I wasn't already aware of and able to turn to my own tactical advantage in terms of creating whatever image or impression of myself I wanted him to see at that moment. His big supposed insight, then—which had as its ostensible, first-order point that my fraudulence could not possibly be as thoroughgoing and hopeless as I claimed it was, since my ability to be honest with him about it logically contradicted my claim of being incapable of honesty—actually had as its larger, unspoken point the claim that he could discern things about my basic character that I myself could not see or interpret correctly, and thus that he could help me out of the trap by pointing out inconsistencies in my view of myself as totally fraudulent. The fact that this insight that he appeared so coyly pleased and excited about was not only obvious and superficial but also wrong—this was depressing, much the way discovering that somebody is easy to manipulate is always a little depressing. A corollary to the fraudulence paradox is that you simultaneously want to fool everyone you meet and yet also somehow always hope that you'll come across someone who is your match or equal and can't be fooled. But this was sort of the last straw, I mentioned I'd tried a whole number of different things that hadn't worked already. So *depressing* is a gross understatement, actually. Plus of course the obvious fact that I was paying this guy for help in getting out of the trap and he'd now showed that he didn't have the mental firepower to do it. So I was now thinking about the prospect of spending time and money driving in to River Forest twice a week just to yank the analyst around in ways he couldn't see so that he'd think that I was actually less fraudulent than I thought I was and that analysis with him was gradually helping me see this. Meaning that he'd probably be getting more out of it than I would, for me it would just be fraudulence as usual.

However tedious and sketchy all this is, you're at least getting an idea, I think, of what it was like inside my head. If nothing else, you're seeing how exhausting and solipsistic it is to be like this. And I had been this way my whole life, at least from age four onward, as far as I could recall. Of course, it's also a really stupid and egotistical way to be, of course you can see that. This is why the ultimate and most deeply unspoken point of the analyst's insight—namely, that who and what I believed I was was not what I really was at all—which I thought was false, was in fact true, although not for the reasons that Dr. Gustafson, who was leaning back in his chair and smoothing his big mustache with his thumb and forefinger while I played dumb and let him feel like he was explaining to me a contradiction I couldn't understand without his help, believed.

One of my other ways of playing dumb for the next several sessions after that was to protest his upbeat diagnosis (irrelevantly, since by this time I'd pretty much given up on Dr. Gustafson and was starting to think of various ways to kill myself without causing pain or making a mess that would disgust whoever found me) by means of listing the various ways I'd been fraudulent even in my pursuit of ways to achieve genuine and uncalculating integrity. I'll spare giving you the whole list again. I basically went all the way back to childhood (which analysts always like you to do) and laid it on. Partly I was curious to see how much he'd put up with. For example, I told him about going from genuinely loving ball, loving the smell of the grass and distant sprinklers, or the feel of pounding my fist into the glove over and over and yelling 'Hey, batterbatter,' and the big low red tumid sun at the game's start versus the arc lights coming on with a clank in the glowing twilight of the late innings, and of the steam and clean burned smell of ironing my Legion uniform, or the feel of sliding and watching all the dust it raised settle around me, or all the parents in shorts and rubber flip-flops setting up lawn chairs with Styrofoam coolers, little kids hooking their fingers around the backstop fence or running off after fouls. The smell of the ump's aftershave and sweat, the little whisk-broom he'd bend down and tidy the plate with. Mostly the feel of stepping up to the plate knowing anything was possible, a feeling like a sun flaring somewhere high up in my chest. And about how by only maybe fourteen all that had disappeared and turned into worrying about averages and if I could make All City again, or being so worried I'd screw up that I didn't even like ironing the uniform anymore before games because it gave me too much time to think, standing there so nerved up about doing well that night that I couldn't even notice the little chuckling sighs the iron made anymore or the singular smell of the steam when I hit the little button for steam. How I'd basically ruined all the best parts of everything like that. How sometimes it felt like I was actually asleep and none of this was even real and someday out of nowhere I was maybe going to suddenly wake up in midstride. That was part of the idea behind things like joining the charismatic church up in Naperville, to try to wake up spiritually instead of living in this fog of fraudulence. 'The truth shall set you free'—the Bible. This was what Beverly-Elizabeth Slane liked to call my holy roller phase. And the charismatic church really did seem to help a lot of the parishioners and congregants I met. They were humble and devoted and charitable, and gave tirelessly without thought of personal reward in active service to the church and in donating resources and time to the church's campaign to build a new altar with an enormous cross of thick glass whose crossbeam was lit up and filled with aerated water and was to have various kinds of beautiful fish swimming in it. (Fish being a prominent Christ-symbol for charismatics. In fact, most of us who were the most devoted and active in the church had bumper stickers on our cars with no words or anything except a plain line drawing of the outline of a fish—this lack of ostentation impressed me as classy and genuine.) But with the real truth here being how quickly I went from being someone who was there because he wanted to wake up and stop being a fraud to being somebody who was so anxious to impress the congregation with how devoted and active I was that I volunteered to help take the collection, and never missed one study group the whole time, and was on two different committees for coordinating fund-raising for the new aquarial altar and deciding exactly what kind of equipment and fish would be used for the crossbeam. Plus often being the one in the front row whose voice in the responses was loudest and who waved both hands in the air the most enthusiastically to show that the Spirit had entered me, and speaking in tongues—mostly consisting of d's and g's—except not really, of course, because in fact I was really just pretending to speak in tongues because all the parishioners around me were speaking in tongues and had the Spirit, and so in a kind of fever of excitement I was able to hoodwink even myself into thinking that I really had the Spirit moving through me and was speaking in tongues when in reality I was just shouting 'Dugga muggle ergle dergle' over and over. (In other words, so anxious to see myself as truly born-again that I actually convinced myself that the tongues' babble was real language and somehow less false than plain English at expressing the feeling of the Holy Spirit rolling like a juggernaut right through me.) This went on for about four months. Not to mention falling over backward whenever Pastor Steve came down the row popping people and popped me in the forehead with the heel of his hand, but falling over backward on purpose, not genuinely being struck down by the Spirit like the other people on either side of me (one of whom actually fainted and had to be brought around with salts). It was only when I was walking out to the parking lot one night after Wednesday Night Praise that I suddenly experienced a flash of self-awareness or clarity or whatever in which I suddenly stopped conning myself and realized that I'd been a fraud all these months in the church, too, and was really only saying and doing these things because all the real parishioners were doing them and I wanted everyone to think I was sincere. It just about knocked me over, that was how vividly I saw how I'd deceived myself. The revealed truth was that I was an even bigger fraud in church about being a newly reborn authentic person than I'd been before Deacon and Mrs. Halberstadt first rang my doorbell out of nowhere as part of their missionary service and talked me into giving it a shot. Because at least before the church thing I wasn't conning myself—I'd known that I was a fraud since at least age nineteen, but at least I'd been able to admit and face the fraudulence directly instead of B.S.ing myself that I was something I wasn't.

All this was presented in the context of a very long pseudo-argument about fraudulence with Dr. Gustafson that would take way too much time to relate to you in detail, so I'm just telling you about some of the more garish examples. With Dr. G. it was more in the form of a prolonged, multi-session back-and-forth on whether or not I was a total fraud, during which I got more and more disgusted with myself for even playing along. By this point in the analysis I'd pretty much decided he was an idiot, or at least very limited in his insights into what was really going on with people. (There was also the blatant issue of the mustache and of him always playing with it.) Essentially he saw what he wanted to see, which was just the sort of person I could practically eat for lunch in terms of creating whatever ideas or impressions of me I wanted. For instance, I told him about the period of trying jogging, during which I seemed never to fail to have to increase my pace and pump my arms more vigorously whenever someone drove by or looked up from his yard, so that I ended up with bone spurs and eventually had to quit altogether. Or spending at least two or three sessions recounting the example of the introductory meditation class at the Downers Grove Community Center that Melissa Betts of Settleman, Dorn got me to take, at which through sheer force of will I'd always force myself to remain totally still with my legs crossed and back perfectly straight long after the other students had all given up and fallen back on their mats shuddering and holding their heads. Right from the first class meeting, even though the small, brown instructor had told us to shoot for only ten minutes of stillness at the outset because most Westerners' minds could not maintain more than a few minutes of stillness and mindful concentration without feeling so restless and ill at ease that they couldn't stand it, I always remained absolutely still and focused on breathing my prana with the lower diaphragm longer than any of them, sometimes for up to thirty minutes, even though my knees and lower back were on fire and I had what felt like swarms of insects crawling all over my arms and shooting out of the top of my head—and Master Gurpreet, although he kept his facial expression inscrutable, gave me a deep and seemingly respectful bow and said that I sat almost like a living statue of mindful repose, and that he was impressed. The problem was that we were also all supposed to continue practicing our meditation on our own at home between classes, and when I tried to do it alone I couldn't seem to sit still and follow my breath for more than even a few minutes before I felt like crawling out of my skin and had to stop. I could only sit and appear quiet and mindful and withstand the unbelievably restless and horrible feelings when all of us were doing it together in the class—meaning only when there were other people to make an impression on. And even in class, the truth was that I was often concentrating not so much on following my prana as on keeping totally still and in the correct posture and having a deeply peaceful and meditative expression on my face in case anyone was cheating and had their eyes open and was looking around, plus also to ensure that Master Gurpreet would continue to see me as exceptional and keep addressing me by what became sort of his class nickname for me, which was 'the statue.'

Finally, in the final few class meetings, when Master Gurpreet told us to sit still and focused for only as long as we comfortably could and then waited almost an hour before finally hitting his small bell with the little silver thing to signal the period of meditation's end, only I and an extremely thin, pale girl who had her own meditation bench that she brought to class with her were able to sit still and focused for the whole hour, although at several different points I'd get so cramped and restless, with what felt like bright blue fire going up my spine and shooting invisibly out of the top of my head as blobs of color exploded over and over again behind my eyelids, that I thought I was going to jump up screaming and take a header right out the window. And at the end of the course, when there was also an opportunity to sign up for the next session, which was called Deepening the Practice, Master Gurpreet presented several of us with different honorary certificates, and mine had my name and the date and was inscribed in black calligraphy, CHAMPION MEDITATOR, MOST IMPRESSIVE WESTERN STUDENT, THE STATUE. It was only after I fell asleep that night (I'd finally sort of compromised and told myself I was practicing the meditative discipline at home at night by lying down and focusing on following my breathing very closely as I fell asleep, and it did turn out to be a phenomenal sleep aid) that while I was asleep I had the dream about the statue in the commons and realized that Master Gurpreet had actually in all likelihood seen right through me the whole time, and that the certificate was in reality a subtle rebuke or joke at my expense. Meaning he was letting me know that he knew I was a fraud and not even coming close to actually quieting my mind's ceaseless conniving about how to impress people in order to achieve mindfulness and honor my true inner self. (Of course, what he seemed not to have divined was that in reality I actually seemed to have no true inner self, and that the more I tried to be genuine the more empty and fraudulent I ended up feeling inside, which I told nobody about until my stab at analysis with Dr. Gustafson.) In the dream, I was in the town commons in Aurora, over near the Pershing tank memorial by the clock tower, and what I'm doing in the dream is sculpting an enormous marble or granite statue of myself, using a huge iron chisel and a hammer the size of those ones they give you to try to hit the bell at the top of the big thermometer-like thing at carnivals, and when the statue's finally done I put it up on a big bandstand or platform and spend all my time polishing it and keeping birds from sitting on it or doing their business on it, and cleaning up litter and keeping the grass neat all around the bandstand. And in the dream my whole life flashes by like that, the sun and moon go back and forth across the sky like windshield wipers over and over, and I never seem to sleep or eat or take a shower (the dream takes place in dream time as opposed to waking, chronological time), meaning I'm condemned to a whole life of being nothing but a sort of custodian to the statue. I'm not saying it was subtle or hard to figure out. Everybody from Fern, Master Gurpreet, the anorexic girl with her own bench, and Ginger Manley, to people from the firm and some of the media reps we bought time from (I was still a media buyer at this time) all walk by, some several times—at one point Melissa Betts and her new fiancé even spread out a blanket and have a sort of little picnic in the shade of the statue—but none of them ever look over or say anything. It's obviously another dream about fraudulence, like the dream where I'm supposedly a big pop star on-stage but all I really do is lip-synch to one of my stepparents' old Mamas and Papas records that's on a record player just off-stage, and somebody whose face I can't ever look over long enough to make out keeps putting his hand in the area of the record as if he's going to make it skip or scratch, and the whole dream makes my skin crawl. These dreams were obvious, they were warnings from my subconscious that I was hollow and a fraud and it was only a matter of time before the whole charade fell apart. Another of my stepmother's treasured antiques was a silver pocket-watch of her maternal grandfather's with the Latin RESPICE FINEM inscribed on the inside of the case. It wasn't until after she passed away and my stepfather said she'd wanted me to have it that I bothered to look up the term, after which I'd gotten the same sort of crawly feeling as with Master Gurpreet's certificate. Much of the nightmarish quality of the dream about the statue was due to the way the sun raced back and forth across the sky and the speed with which my whole life blew by like that, in the commons. It was obviously also my subconscious enlightening me as to the meditation instructor's having seen through me the whole time, after which I was too embarrassed even to go try to get a refund for the Deepening the Practice class, which there was now no way I felt like I could show up for, even though at the same time I also still had fantasies about Master Gurpreet becoming my mentor or guru and using all kinds of inscrutable Eastern techniques to show me the way to meditate myself into having a true self...

...Etc., etc. I'll spare you any more examples, for instance I'll spare you the literally countless examples of my fraudulence with girls—with the ladies as they say—in just about every dating relationship I ever had, or the almost unbelievable amount of fraudulence and calculation involved in my career—not just in terms of manipulating the consumer and manipulating the client into trusting that your agency's ideas are the best way to manipulate the consumer, but in the interoffice politics of the agency itself, like for example in sizing up what sorts of things your superiors want to believe (including the belief that they're smarter than you and that that's why they're your superior) and then giving them what they want but doing it just subtly enough that they never get a chance to view you as a sycophant or yes-man (which they want to believe they do not really want) but instead see you as a tough-minded independent thinker who from time to time bows to the weight of their superior intelligence and creative firepower, etc. The whole agency was one big ballet of fraudulence and of manipulating people's images of your ability to manipulate images, a virtual hall of mirrors. And I was good at it, remember, I thrived there.

It was the sheer amount of time Dr. Gustafson spent touching and smoothing his mustache that indicated he wasn't aware of doing it and in fact was subconsciously reassuring himself that it was still there. Which is not an especially subtle habit, in terms of insecurity, since after all facial hair is known as a secondary sex characteristic, meaning what he was really doing was subconsciously reassuring himself that something *else* was still there, if you know what I mean. This was some of why it was no real surprise when it turned out that the overall direction he wanted the analysis to proceed in involved issues of masculinity and how I understood my masculinity (my 'manhood' in other words). This also helped explain everything from the lost-female-crawling and two-testicle-shaped-objects-that-looked-deformed prints on the wall to the little African or Indian drum things and little figurines with (sometimes) exaggerated sex characteristics on the shelf over his desk, plus the pipe, the unnecessary size of his wedding band, even the somewhat overdone little-boy clutter of the office itself. It was pretty clear that there were some major sexual insecurities and maybe even homosexual-type ambiguities that Dr. Gustafson was subconsciously trying to hide from himself and reassure himself about, and one obvious way he did this was to sort of project his insecurities onto his patients and get them to believe that America's culture had a uniquely brutal and alienating way of brainwashing its males from an early age into all kinds of damaging beliefs and superstitions about what being a so-called 'real man' was, such as competitiveness instead of concert, winning at all costs, dominating others through intelligence or will, being strong, not showing your true emotions, depending on others seeing you as a real man in order to reassure yourself of your manhood, seeing your own value solely in terms of accomplishments, being obsessed with your career or income, feeling as if you were constantly being judged or on display, etc. This was later in the analysis, after the seemingly endless period where after every example of fraudulence I gave him he'd make a show of congratulating me on being able to reveal what I felt were shameful fraudulent examples, and said that this was proof that I had much more of an ability to be genuine than I (apparently because of my insecurities or male fears) seemed able to give myself credit for. Plus it didn't exactly seem like a coincidence that the cancer he was even then harboring was in his colon—that shameful, dirty, secret place right near the rectum—with the idea being that using your rectum or colon to secretly *harbor an alien growth* was a blatant symbol both of homosexuality and of the repressive belief that its open acknowledgment would equal disease and death. Dr. Gustafson and I both had a good laugh over this one after we'd both died and were outside linear time and in the process of dramatic change, you can bet on that. (*Outside time* is not just an expression or manner of speaking, by the way.) By this time in the analysis I was playing with him the way a cat does with a hurt bird. If I'd had an ounce of real self-respect I would have stopped and gone back to the Downers Grove Community Center and thrown myself on Master Gurpreet's mercy, since except for maybe one or two girls I'd dated he was the only one who'd appeared to see all the way through to the core of my fraudulence, plus his oblique, very dry way of indicating this to me betrayed a sort of serene indifference to whether I even understood that he saw right through me that I found incredibly impressive and genuine—here in Master Gurpreet was a man with, as they say, nothing to prove. But I didn't, instead I more or less conned myself into sticking with going in to see Dr. G. twice a week for almost nine months (toward the end it was only once a week because by then the cancer had been diagnosed and he was getting radiation treatments every Tuesday and Thursday), telling myself that at least I was trying to find some venue in which I could get help finding a way to be genuine and stop manipulating everybody around me to see 'the statue' as erect and impressive, etc.

Nor however is it strictly true that the analyst had nothing interesting to say or that he didn't sometimes provide helpful models or angles for looking at the basic problem. For instance, it turned out that one of his basic operating premises was the claim that there were really only two basic, fundamental orientations a person could have toward the world, (1) love and (2) fear, and that they couldn't coexist (or, in logical terms, that their domains were exhaustive and mutually exclusive, or that their two sets had no intersection but their union comprised all possible elements, or that:
'$(\forall x) ((Fx \rightarrow \sim (Lx)) \mathrel{\&} (Lx \rightarrow \sim (Fx))) \mathrel{\&} \sim ((\exists x) (\sim (Fx) \mathrel{\&} \sim (Lx)))$'),
meaning in other words that each day of your life was spent in service to one of these masters or the other, and 'One cannot serve two masters'—the Bible again—and that one of the worst things about the conception of competitive, achievement-oriented masculinity that America supposedly hardwired into its males was that it caused a more or less constant state of fear that made genuine love next to impossible. That is, that what passed for love in American men was usually just the need to be regarded in a certain way, meaning that today's males were so constantly afraid of 'not measuring up' (Dr. G.'s phrase, with evidently no pun intended) that they had to spend all their time convincing others of their masculine 'validity' (which happens to also be a term from formal logic) in order to ease their own insecurity, making genuine love next to impossible. Although it seemed a little bit simplistic to see this fear as just a male problem (try watching a girl stand on a scale sometime), it turns out that

Dr. Gustafson was very nearly right in this concept of the two masters—though not in the way that he, when alive and confused about his own real identity, believed—and even while I played along by pretending to argue or not quite understand what he was driving at, the idea struck me that maybe the real root of my problem was not fraudulence but a basic inability to really love, even to genuinely love my stepparents, or Fern, or Melissa Betts, or Ginger Manley of Aurora West High in 1979, whom I'd often thought of as the only girl I'd ever truly loved, though Dr. G.'s bromide about men being brainwashed to equate love with accomplishment or conquest also applied here. The plain truth was that Ginger Manley was just the first girl I ever went all the way with, and most of my tender feelings about her were really just nostalgia for the feeling of immense cosmic validation I'd felt when she finally let me take her jeans all the way off and put my so-called 'manhood' inside her, etc. There's really no bigger cliché than losing your virginity and later having all kinds of retrospective tenderness for the girl involved. Or what Beverly-Elizabeth Slane, a research technician I used to see outside of work when I was a media buyer, and had a lot of conflict with toward the end, said, which I don't think I ever told Dr. G. about, fraudulence-wise, probably because it cut a little too close to the bone. Toward the end she had compared me to some piece of ultra-expensive new medical or diagnostic equipment that can discern more about you in one quick scan than you could ever know about yourself—but the equipment doesn't care about you, you're just a sequence of processes and codes. What the machine understands about you doesn't actually *mean* anything to it. Even though it's really good at what it does. Beverly had a bad temper combined with some serious firepower, she was not someone you wanted to have pissed off at you. She said she'd never felt the gaze of someone so penetrating, discerning, and yet totally empty of care, like she was a puzzle or problem I was figuring out. She said it was thanks to me that she'd discovered the difference between being penetrated and really known versus penetrated and just violated—needless to say, these thanks were sarcastic. Some of this was just her emotional makeup—she found it impossible to really end a relationship unless all bridges were burned and things got said that were so devastating that there could be no possibility of a rapprochement to haunt her or prevent her moving on. Nevertheless it penetrated, I never did forget what she said in that letter.

Even if being fraudulent and being unable to love were in fact ultimately the same thing (a possibility that Dr. Gustafson never seemed to consider no matter how many times I set him up to see it), being unable to really love was at least a different model or lens through which to see the problem, plus initially it seemed like a promising way of attacking the fraudulence paradox in terms of reducing the self-hatred part that reinforced the fear and the consequent drive to try to manipulate people into providing the very approval I'd denied myself. (Dr. G.'s term for approval was *validation*.) This period was pretty much the zenith of my career in analysis, and for a few weeks (during a couple of which I actually didn't see Dr. Gustafson at all, because some sort of complication in his illness required him to go into the hospital, and when he came back he appeared to have lost not only weight but some kind of essential part of his total mass, and no longer seemed too large for his old desk chair, which still squeaked but now not as loudly, plus a lot of the clutter and papers had been straightened up and put in several brown cardboard banker's boxes against the wall under the two sad prints, and when I came back in to see him the absence of mess was especially disturbing and sad, for some reason) it was true that I felt some of the first genuine hope I'd had since the early, self-deluded part of the experiment with Naperville's Church of the Flaming Sword of the Redeemer. And yet at the same time these weeks also led more or less directly to my decision to kill myself, although I'm going to have to simplify and linearize a great deal of interior stuff in order to convey to you what actually happened. Otherwise it would take an almost literal eternity to recount it, we already agreed about that. It's not that words or human language stop having any meaning or relevance after you die, by the way. It's more the specific, one-after-the-other temporal ordering of them that does. Or doesn't. It's hard to explain. In logical terms, something expressed in words will still have the same 'cardinality' but no longer the same 'ordinality.' All the different words are still there, in other words, but it's no longer a question of which one comes first. Or you could say it's no longer the series of words but now more like some limit toward which the series converges. It's hard not to want to put it in logical terms, since they're the most abstract and universal. Meaning they have no connotation, you don't feel anything about them. Or maybe imagine everything anybody on earth ever said or even thought to themselves all getting collapsed and exploding into one large, combined, instantaneous sound—although *instantaneous* is a little misleading, since it implies other instants before and after, and it isn't really like that. It's more like the sudden internal flash when you see or realize something—a sudden flash or whatever of epiphany or insight. It's not just that it happens way faster than you could break the process down and arrange it into English, but that it happens on a scale in which there isn't even time to be aware of any sort of time at all in which it's happening, the flash—all you know is that there's a before and an after, and afterward you're different. I don't know if that makes sense. I'm just trying to give it to you from several different angles, it's all the same thing. Or you could think of it as being more a certain configuration of light than a word-sum or series of sounds, too, afterward. Which is in fact true. Or as a theorem's proof—because if a proof is true then it's true everywhere and all the time, not just when you happen to say it. The thing is that it turns out that logical symbolism really would be the best way to express it, because logic is totally abstract and outside what we think of as time. It's the closest thing to what it's really like. That's why it's the logical paradoxes that really drive people nuts. A lot of history's great logicians have ended up killing themselves, that is a fact.

And keep in mind this flash can happen anywhere, at any time.

Here's the basic Berry paradox, by the way, if you might want an example of why logicians with incredible firepower can devote their whole lives to solving these things and still end up beating their heads against the wall. This one has to do with big numbers—meaning really big, past a trillion, past ten to the trillion to the trillion, way up there. When you get way up there, it takes a while even to describe numbers this big in words. 'The quantity one trillion, four hundred and three billion to the trillionth power' takes twenty syllables to describe, for example. You get the idea. Now, even higher up there in these huge, cosmic-scale numbers, imagine now the very smallest number that can't be described in under twenty-two syllables. The paradox is that *the very smallest number that can't be described in under twenty-two syllables,* which of course is itself a description of this number, only has twenty-one syllables in it, which of course is under twenty-two syllables. So now what are you supposed to do?

At the same time, what actually led to it in causal terms, though, occurred during maybe the third or fourth week that Dr. G. was back seeing patients after his hospitalization. Although I'm not going to pretend that the specific incident wouldn't strike most people as absurd or even sort of insipid, as causes go. The truth is just that late at night one night in August after Dr. G.'s return, when I couldn't sleep (which happened a lot ever since the cocaine period) and was sitting up drinking a glass of milk or something and watching television, flipping the remote almost at random between different cable stations the way you do when it's late, I happened on part of an old *Cheers* episode from late in the series' run where the analyst character, Frasier (who went on to have his own show), and Lilith, his fiancée and also an analyst, are just entering the stage set of the underground tavern, and Frasier is asking her how her workday at her office went, and Lilith says, 'If I have one more yuppie come in and start whining to me about how he can't love, I'm going to throw up.' This line got a huge laugh from the show's studio audience, which indicated that they—and so by demographic extension the whole national audience at home as well—recognized what a cliché and melodramatic type of complaint the inability-to-love concept was. And, sitting there, when I suddenly realized that once again I'd managed to con myself, this time into thinking that this was a truer or more promising way to conceive of the problem of fraudulence—and, by extension, that I'd also somehow deluded myself into almost believing that poor old Dr. Gustafson had anything in his mental arsenal that could actually help me, and that the real truth was probably more that I was continuing to see him partly out of pity and partly so that I could pretend to myself that I was taking steps to becoming more authentic when in fact all I was doing was jerking a gravely ill shell of a guy around and feeling superior to him because I was able to analyze his own psychological makeup so much more accurately than he could analyze mine—the flash of realizing all this at the very same time that the huge audience-laugh showed that nearly everybody in the United States had probably already seen through the complaint's inauthenticity as long ago as whenever the episode had originally run—all this flashed through my head in the tiny interval it took to realize what I was watching and to remember who the characters of Frasier and Lilith even were, meaning maybe half a second at most, and it more or less destroyed me, that's the only way I can describe it, as if whatever hope of any way out of the trap I'd made for myself had been blasted out of midair or laughed off the stage, as if I were one of those stock comic characters who is always both the butt of the joke and the only person not to get the joke—and in sum I went to bed feeling as fraudulent, befogged, hopeless and full of self-contempt as I'd ever felt, and it was the next morning after that that I woke up having decided I was going to kill myself and end the whole farce. (As you probably recall, *Cheers* was an incredibly popular series, and even in syndication its metro numbers were so high that if a local advertiser wanted to buy time on it the slots cost so much that you pretty much had to build his whole local strategy around those slots.) I'm compressing a huge amount of what took place in my psyche that next-to-last night, all the different realizations and conclusions I reached as I lay there in bed unable to sleep or even move (no single series' line or audience-laugh is in and of itself going to constitute a reason for suicide, of course)—although to you I imagine it probably doesn't seem all that compressed at all, you're thinking here's this guy going on and on and why doesn't he get to the part where he kills himself and explain or account for the fact that he's sitting here next to me in a piece of high-powered machinery telling me all this if he died in 1991. Which in fact I knew I would from the moment I first woke up. It was over, I'd decided to end the charade.

After breakfast I called in sick to work and stayed home the whole day by myself. I knew that if I was around anyone I'd automatically lapse into fraudulence. I had decided to take a whole lot of Benadryl and then just as I got really sleepy and relaxed I'd get the car up to top speed on a rural road way out in the extreme west suburbs and drive it head-on into a concrete bridge abutment. Benadryl makes me extremely foggy and sleepy, it always has. I spent most of the morning on letters to my lawyer and C.P.A., and brief notes to the creative head and managing partner who had originally brought me aboard at Samieti and Cheyne. Our creative group was in the middle of some very ticklish campaign preparations, and I wanted to apologize for in any way leaving them in the lurch. Of course I didn't really feel all that sorry—Samieti and Cheyne was a ballet of fraudulence, and I was well out of it. The note was probably ultimately just so that the people who really mattered at S. & C. would be more apt to remember me as a decent, conscientious guy who it turned out was maybe just a little too sensitive and tormented by his personal demons—'Almost too good for this world' is what I seemed to be unable to keep from fantasizing a lot of them saying after news of it came through. I did not write Dr. Gustafson a note. He had his own share of problems, and I knew that in the note I'd spend a lot of time trying to seem as if I was being honest but really just dancing around the truth, which was that he was a deeply repressed homosexual or androgyne and had no real business charging patients to let him project his own maladjustments onto them, and that the truth was that he'd be doing himself and everybody else a favor if he'd just go over to Garfield Park and blow somebody in the bushes and try honestly to decide if he liked it or not, and that I was a total fraud for continuing to drive all the way in to River Forest to see him and bat him around like a catnip toy while telling myself there was some possible non-fraudulent point to it. (All of which, of course, even if they weren't dying of colon cancer right in front of you you still could never actually come out and say to somebody, since certain truths might well destroy them—and who has that right?)

I did spend almost two hours before taking the first of the Benadryl composing a handwritten note to my sister Fern. In the note I apologized for whatever pain my suicide and the fraudulence and/or inability to love that had precipitated it might cause her and my stepdad (who was still alive and well and now lived in Marin County, California, where he taught part-time and did community outreach with Marin County's homeless). I also used the occasion of the letter and all the sort of last-testament urgency associated with it to license apologizing to Fern about manipulating my stepparents into believing that she'd lied about the antique glass bowl in 1967, as well as for half a dozen other incidents and spiteful or fraudulent actions that I knew had caused her pain and that I had felt bad about ever since, but had never really seen any way to broach with her or express my honest regret for. (It turns out there are things that you can discuss in a suicide note that would just be too bizarre if expressed in any other kind of venue.) Just one example of such an incident was during a period in the mid-'70s, when Fern, as part of puberty, underwent some physical changes that made her look chunky for a year or two — not fat, but wide-hipped and bosomy and sort of much more broad than she'd been as a pre-teen — and of course she was very, very sensitive about it (puberty also being a time of terrible self-consciousness and sensitivity about one's body image, obviously), so much so that my stepparents took great pains never to say anything about Fern's new breadth or even ever to bring up any topics related to eating habits, diet and exercise, etc. And I for my own part never said anything about it either, not directly, but I had worked out all kinds of very subtle and indirect ways to torment Fern about her size in such a way that my stepparents never saw anything and I could never really be accused of anything that I couldn't then look all around myself with a shocked, incredulous facial expression as if I had no idea what she was talking about, such as just a quick raise of my eyebrow when her eyes met mine as she was having a second helping at dinner, or a quick little quiet, 'You sure you can fit into that?' when she came home from the store with a new skirt. The one I still remembered the most vividly involved the second-floor hall of our house, which was in Aurora and was a three-story home (including the basement) but not all that spacious or large, meaning a skinny three-decker like so many you always see all crammed together along residential streets in Naperville and Aurora. The second-floor hallway, which ran between Fern's room and the top of the stairway on one end and my room and the second-floor bathroom on the other, was cramped and somewhat narrow, but not anywhere close to as narrow as I would pretend that it was whenever Fern and I passed each other in it, with me squashing my back against the hallway wall and splaying my arms out and wincing as if there would barely be enough room for somebody of her unbelievable breadth to squeeze past me, and she would never say anything or even look at me when I did it but would just go on past me into the bathroom and close the door. But I knew it must have hurt her. A little while later, she entered an adolescent period where she hardly ate anything at all, and smoked cigarettes and chewed several packs of gum a day, and used a lot of makeup, and for a while she got so thin that she looked angular and a bit like an insect (although of course I never said that), and I once, through their bedroom's keyhole, overheard a brief conversation in which my stepmother said she was worried because she didn't think Fern was having her normal time of the month anymore because she had gotten so underweight, and she and my stepfather discussed the possibility of taking her to see some kind of specialist. That period passed on its own, but in the letter I told Fern that I'd always remembered this and certain other periods when I'd been cruel or tried to make her feel bad, and that I regretted them very much, although I said I wouldn't want to seem so egotistical as to think that a simple apology could erase any of the hurt I'd caused her when we were growing up. On the other hand, I also assured her that it wasn't as if I had gone around for years carrying excessive guilt or blowing these incidents out of all proportion. They were not life-altering traumas or anything like that, and in many ways they were probably all too typical of the sorts of cruelties that kids tend to inflict on each other growing up. I also assured her that neither these incidents nor my remorse about them had anything to do with my killing myself. I simply said, without going into anything like the level of detail I've given you (because my purpose in the letter was of course very different), that I was killing myself because I was an essentially fraudulent person who seemed to lack either the character or the firepower to find a way to stop even after I'd realized my fraudulence and the terrible toll it exacted (I told her nothing about the various different realizations or paradoxes, what would be the point?). I also inserted that there was also a good possibility that, when all was said and done, I was nothing but just another fast-track yuppie who couldn't love, and that I found the banality of this unendurable, largely because I was evidently so hollow and insecure that I had a pathological need to see myself as somehow exceptional or outstanding at all times. Without going into much explanation or argument, I also told Fern that if her initial reaction to these reasons for my killing myself was to think that I was being much, much too hard on myself, then she should know that I was already aware that that was the most likely reaction my note would produce in her, and had probably deliberately constructed the note to at least in part prompt just that reaction, just the way my whole life I'd often said and done things designed to prompt certain people to believe that I was a genuinely outstanding person whose personal standards were so high that he was far too hard on himself, which in turn made me appear attractively modest and unsmug, and was a big reason for my popularity with so many people in all different avenues of my life—what Beverly-Elizabeth Slane had termed my 'talent for ingratiation'—but was nevertheless basically calculated and fraudulent. I also told Fern that I loved her very much, and asked her to relay these same sentiments to Marin County for me.

Now we're getting to the part where I actually kill myself. This occurred at 9:17 PM on August 19, 1991, if you want the time fixed precisely. Plus I'll spare you most of the last couple hours' preparations and back-and-forth conflict and dithering, which there was a lot of. Suicide runs so counter to so many hardwired instincts and drives that nobody in his right mind goes through with it without going through a great deal of internal back-and-forth, intervals of almost changing your mind, etc. The German logician Kant was right in this respect, human beings are all pretty much identical in terms of our hardwiring. Although we are seldom conscious of it, we are all basically just instruments or expressions of our evolutionary drives, which are themselves the expressions of forces that are infinitely larger and more important than we are. (Although actually being conscious of this is a whole different matter.) So I won't really even try to describe the several different times that day when I sat in my living room and had a furious mental back-and-forth about whether to actually go through with it. For one thing, it was intensely mental and would take an enormous amount of time to put into words, plus it would come off as somewhat cliché or banal in the sense that many of the thoughts and associations were basically the same sorts of generic things that almost anyone who's confronting imminent death will end up thinking. As in, 'This is the last time I will ever tie my shoe,' 'This is the last time I will look at this rubber tree on top of the stereo cabinet,' 'How delicious this lungful of air right here tastes,' 'This is the last glass of milk I'll ever drink,' 'What a totally priceless gift this totally ordinary sight of the wind picking trees' branches up and moving them around is.' Or, 'I will never again hear the plaintive sound of the fridge going on in the kitchen' (the kitchen and breakfast nook are right off my living room), etc. Or, 'I won't see the sun come up tomorrow or watch the bedroom gradually undim and resolve, etc.,' and at the same time trying to summon the memory of the exact way the sun comes up over the humid fields and the wet-looking I-55 ramp that lay due east of my bedroom's sliding glass door in the morning. It had been a hot, wet August, and if I went through with killing myself I wouldn't ever get to feel the incremental cooling and drying that starts here around mid-September, or to see the leaves turn or hear them rustle along the edge of the courtyard outside S. & C.'s floor of the building on S. Dearborn, or see snow or put a shovel and bag of sand in the trunk, or bite into a perfectly ripe, ungrainy pear, or put a piece of toilet paper on a shaving cut. Etc. If I went in and went to the bathroom and brushed my teeth it would be the last time I did those things. I sat there and thought about that, looking at the rubber tree. Everything seemed to tremble a little, the way things reflected in water will tremble. I watched the sun begin to drop down over the townhouse developments going up south of Darien's corporation limit on Lily Cache Rd. and realized that I would never see the newest homes' construction and landscaping completed, or that the homes' white insulation wrap with the trade name TYVEK all over it flapping in all the wind out here would one day have vinyl siding or plate brick and color-coordinated shutters over it and I wouldn't see this happen or be able to drive by and know what was actually written there under all the nice exteriors. Or the breakfast nook window's view of the big farms' fields next to my development, with the plowed furrows all parallel so that if I lean and line their lines up just right they seem to all rush together toward the horizon as if shot out of something huge. You get the idea. Basically I was in that state in which a man realizes that everything he sees will outlast him. As a verbal construction I know that's a cliché. As a state in which to actually be, though, it's something else, believe me. Where now every movement takes on a kind of ceremonial aspect. The very sacredness of the world as seen (the same kind of state Dr. G. will try to describe with analogies to oceans and whitecaps and trees, you might recall I mentioned this already). This is literally about one one-trillionth of the various thoughts and internal experiences I underwent in those last few hours, and I'll spare both of us recounting any more, since I'm aware it ends up seeming somewhat lame. Which in fact it wasn't, but I won't pretend it was fully authentic or genuine, either. A part of me was still calculating, performing—and this was part of the ceremonial quality of that last afternoon. Even as I wrote my note to Fern, for instance, expressing sentiments and regrets that were real, a part of me was noticing what a fine and sincere note it was, and anticipating the effect on Fern of this or that heartfelt phrase, while yet another part was observing the whole scene of a man in a dress shirt and no tie sitting at his breakfast nook writing a heartfelt note on his last afternoon alive, the blondwood table's surface trembling with sunlight and the man's hand steady and face both haunted by regret and ennobled by resolve, this part of me sort of hovering above and just to the left of myself, evaluating the scene, and thinking what a fine and genuine-seeming performance in a drama it would make if only we all had not already been subject to countless scenes just like it in dramas ever since we first saw a movie or read a book, which somehow entailed that real scenes like the one of my suicide note were now compelling and genuine only to their participants, and to anyone else would come off as banal and even somewhat cheesy or maudlin, which is somewhat paradoxical when you consider—as I did, sitting there at the breakfast nook—that the reason scenes like this will seem stale or manipulative to an audience is that we've already seen so many of them in dramas, and yet the reason we've seen so many of them in dramas is that the scenes really are dramatic and compelling and let people communicate very deep, complicated emotional realities that are almost impossible to articulate in any other way, and at the same time still another facet or part of me realizing that from this perspective my own basic problem was that at an early age I'd somehow chosen to cast my lot with my life's drama's supposed audience instead of with the drama itself, and that I even now was watching and gauging my supposed performance's quality and probable effects, and thus was in the final analysis the very same manipulative fraud writing the note to Fern that I had been throughout the life that had brought me to this climactic scene of writing and signing it and addressing the envelope and affixing postage and putting the envelope in my shirt pocket (totally conscious of the resonance of its resting there, next to my heart, in the scene), planning to drop it in a mailbox on the way out to Lily Cache Rd. and the bridge abutment into which I planned to drive my car at speeds sufficient to displace the whole front end and impale me on the steering wheel and instantly kill me. Self-loathing is not the same thing as being into pain or a lingering death, if I was going to do it I wanted it instant.

On Lily Cache, the bridge abutments and sides' steep banks support State Route 4 (also known as the Braidwood Highway) as it crosses overhead on a cement overpass so covered with graffiti that most of it you can't even read. (Which sort of defeats the purpose of graffiti, in my opinion.) The abutments themselves are just off the road and about as wide as this car. Plus the intersection is isolated way out in the countryside around Romeoville, ten or so miles south of the southwest suburbs' limits. It is the true boonies. The only homes are farms set way back from the road and embellished with silos and barns, etc. At night in the summer the dewpoint is high and there's always fog. It's farm country. I've never once passed under 4 here without seeming to be the only thing on either road. The corn high and the fields like a green ocean all around, insects the only real noise.

Driving alone under creamy stars and a little cocked scythe of moon, etc. The idea was to have the accident and whatever explosion and fire was involved occur someplace isolated enough that no one else would see it, so that there would be as little an aspect of performance to the thing as I could manage and no temptation to spend my last few seconds trying to imagine what impression the sight and sound of the impact might make on someone watching. I was partly concerned that it might be spectacular and dramatic and might look as if the driver was trying to go out in as dramatic a way as possible. This is the sort of shit we waste our lives thinking about.

The ground fog tends to get more intense by the second until it seems that the whole world is just what's in your headlights' reach. High beams don't work in fog, they only make things worse. You can go ahead and try them but you'll see what happens, all they do is light up the fog so it seems even denser. That's kind of a minor paradox, that sometimes you can actually see farther with low beams than high. All right—and there's the construction and all the flapping TYVEK wrap on houses that if you really do do it you'll never see anyone live in. Although it won't hurt, it really will be instant, I can tell you that much. The fields' insects are almost deafening. If the corn's high like this and you watch as the sun sets you can practically watch them rise up out of the fields like some great figure's shadow rising. Mostly mosquitoes, I don't know what all they are. It's a whole insect universe in there that none of us will ever see or know anything about. Plus you'll notice the Benadryl doesn't help all that much once you're under way. That whole idea was probably ill-conceived.

All right, now we're coming to what I promised and led you through the whole dull synopsis of what led up to this in hopes of. Meaning what it's like to die, what happens. Right? This is what everyone wants to know. And you do, trust me. Whether you decide to go through with it or not, whether I somehow talk you out of it the way you think I'm going to try to do or not. It's not what anyone thinks, for one thing. The truth is you already know what it's like. You already know the difference between the size and speed of everything that flashes through you and the tiny inadequate bit of it all you can ever let anyone know. As though inside you is this enormous room full of what seems like everything in the whole universe at one time or another and yet the only parts that get out have to somehow squeeze out through one of those tiny keyholes you see under the knob in older doors. As if we are all trying to see each other through these tiny keyholes.

But it does have a knob, the door can open. But not in the way you think. But what if you could? Think for a second—what if all the infinitely dense and shifting worlds of stuff inside you every moment of your life turned out now to be somehow fully open and expressible afterward, after what you think of as *you* has died, because what if afterward now each moment itself is an infinite sea or span or passage of time in which to express it or convey it, and you don't even need any organized English, you can as they say open the door and be in anyone else's room in all your own multiform forms and ideas and facets? Because listen—we don't have much time, here's where Lily Cache slopes slightly down and the banks start getting steep, and you can just make out the outlines of the unlit sign for the farmstand that's never open anymore, the last sign before the bridge—so listen: What exactly do you think you are? The millions and trillions of thoughts, memories, juxtapositions—even crazy ones like this, you're thinking—that flash through your head and disappear? Some sum or remainder of these? Your *history?* Do you know how long it's been since I told you I was a fraud? Do you remember you were looking at the RESPICEM watch hanging from the rearview and seeing the time, 9:17? What are you looking at right now? Coincidence? What if no time has passed at all?* The truth is you've already heard this. That this is what it's like. That it's what makes room for the universes inside you, all the endless inbent fractals of connection and symphonies of different voices, the infinities you can never show another soul. And you think it makes you a fraud,

---

*One clue that there's something not quite real about sequential time the way you experience it is the various paradoxes of time supposedly passing and of a so-called 'present' that's always unrolling into the future and creating more and more past behind it. As if the present were this car—nice car by the way—and the past is the road we've just gone over, and the future is the headlit road up ahead we haven't yet gotten to, and time is the car's forward movement, and the precise present is the car's front bumper as it cuts through the fog of the future, so that it's *now* and then a tiny bit later a whole different *now,* etc. Except if time is really passing, how fast does it go? At what rate does the present change? See? Meaning if we use time to measure motion or rate—which we do, it's the only way you can—95 miles per hour, 70 heartbeats a minute, etc.—how are you supposed to measure the rate at which time moves? One second per second? It makes no sense. You can't even talk about time flowing or moving without hitting up against paradox right away. So think for a second: What if there's really no movement at all? What if this is all unfolding in the one flash you call the present, this first, infinitely tiny split-second of impact when the speeding car's front bumper's just starting to touch the abutment, just before the bumper crumples and displaces the front end and you go violently forward and the steering column comes back at your chest as if shot out of something enormous? Meaning that what if in fact this *now* is infinite and never really passes in the way your mind is supposedly wired to understand *pass,* so that not only your whole life but every single humanly conceivable way to describe and account for that life has time to flash like neon shaped into those connected cursive letters that businesses' signs and windows love so much to use through your mind all at once in the literally immeasurable instant between impact and death, just as you start forward to meet the wheel at a rate no belt ever made could restrain—THE END.

the tiny fraction anyone else ever sees? Of course you're a fraud, of course what people see is never you. And of course you know this, and of course you try to manage what part they see if you know it's only a part. Who wouldn't? It's called free will, Sherlock. But at the same time it's why it feels so good to break down and cry in front of others, or to laugh, or speak in tongues, or chant in Bengali—it's not English anymore, it's not getting squeezed through any hole.

So cry all you want, I won't tell anybody.

But it wouldn't have made you a fraud to change your mind. It would be sad to do it because you think you somehow have to.

It won't hurt, though. It will be loud, and you'll feel things, but they'll go through you so fast that you won't even realize you're feeling them (which is sort of like the paradox I used to bounce off Gustafson—is it possible to be a fraud if you aren't aware you're a fraud?). And the very brief moment of fire you'll feel will be almost good, like when your hands are cold and there's a fire and you hold your hands out toward it.

The reality is that dying isn't bad, but it takes forever. And that forever is no time at all. I know that sounds like a contradiction, or maybe just wordplay. What it really is, it turns out, is a matter of perspective. The big picture, as they say, in which the fact is that this whole seemingly endless back-and-forth between us has come and gone and come again in the very same instant that Fern stirs a boiling pot for dinner, and your stepfather packs some pipe tobacco down with his thumb, and Angela Mead uses an ingenious little catalogue tool to roll cat hair off her blouse, and Melissa Betts inhales to respond to something she thinks her husband just said, and David Wallace blinks in the midst of idly scanning class photos from his 1980 Aurora West H.S. yearbook and seeing my photo and trying, through the tiny little keyhole of himself, to imagine what all must have happened to lead up to my death in the fiery single-car accident he'd read about in 1991, like what sorts of pain or problems might have driven the guy to get in his electric-blue Corvette and try to drive with all that O.T.C. medication in his bloodstream—David Wallace happening to have a huge and totally unorganizable set of inner thoughts, feelings, memories and impressions of this little photo's guy a year ahead of him in school with the seemingly almost neon aura around him all the time of scholastic and athletic excellence and popularity and success with the ladies, as well as of every last cutting remark or even tiny disgusted gesture or expression on this guy's part whenever David Wallace struck out look-ing in Legion ball or said something dumb at a party, and of how impres-sive and authentically at ease in the world the guy always seemed, like an actual living person instead of the dithering, pathetically self-conscious outline or ghost of a person David Wallace knew himself back then to be. Verily a fair-haired, fast-track guy, whom in the very best human tradition David Wallace had back then imagined as happy and unreflective and wholly unhaunted by voices telling him that there was something deeply wrong with him that wasn't wrong with anybody else and that he had to spend all of his time and energy trying to figure out what to do and say in order to impersonate an even marginally normal or acceptable U.S. male, all this stuff clanging around in David Wallace '81's head every second and moving so fast that he never got a chance to catch hold and try to fight or argue against it or even really even feel it except as a knot in his stomach as he stood in his real parents' kitchen ironing his uniform and thinking of all the ways he could screw up and strike out looking or drop balls out in right and reveal his true pathetic essence in front of this .418 hitter and his witchily pretty sister and everyone else in the audience in lawn chairs in the grass along the sides of the Legion field (all of whom already probably saw through the sham from the outset anyway, he was pretty sure)—in other words David Wallace trying, if only in the second his lids are down, to somehow reconcile what this luminous guy had seemed like from the outside with whatever on the interior must have driven him to kill himself in such a dramatic and doubtlessly painful way—with David Wallace also fully aware that the cliché that you can't ever truly know what's going on inside somebody else is hoary and insipid and yet at the same time trying very consciously to prohibit that awareness from mocking the attempt or sending the whole line of thought into the sort of inbent spiral that keeps you from ever getting anywhere (considerable time having passed since 1981, of course, and David Wallace having emerged from years of literally indescribable war against himself with quite a bit more firepower than he'd had at Aurora West), the realer, more enduring and sentimental part of him commanding that other part to be silent as if looking it levelly in the eye and saying, almost aloud, 'Not another word.'

[→NMN.80.418]

Incarnations of Burned Children

THE DADDY WAS around the side of the house hanging a door for the tenant when he heard the child's screams and the Mommy's voice gone high between them. He could move fast, and the back porch gave onto the kitchen, and before the screen door had banged shut behind him the Daddy had taken the scene in whole, the overturned pot on the floortile before the stove and the burner's blue jet and the floor's pool of water still steaming as its many arms extended, the toddler in his baggy diaper standing rigid with steam coming off his hair and his chest and shoulders scarlet and his eyes rolled up and mouth open very wide and seeming somehow separate from the sounds that issued, the Mommy down on one knee with the dishrag dabbing pointlessly at him and matching the screams with cries of her own, hysterical so she was almost frozen. Her one knee and the bare little soft feet were still in the steaming pool, and the Daddy's first act was to take the child under the arms and lift him away from it and take him to the sink, where he threw out plates and struck the tap to let cold wellwater run over the boy's feet while with his cupped hand he gathered and poured or flung more cold water over the head and shoulders and chest, wanting first to see the steam stop coming off him, the Mommy over his shoulder invoking God until he sent her for towels and gauze if they had it, the Daddy moving quickly and well and his man's mind empty of everything but purpose, not yet aware of how smoothly he moved or that he'd ceased to hear the high screams because to hear them would freeze him and make impossible what had to be done to help his own child, whose screams were regular as breath and went on so long they'd become already a thing in the kitchen, something else to move quickly around. The tenant side's door outside hung half off its top hinge and moved slightly in the wind, and a bird in the oak across the driveway appeared to observe the door with a cocked head as the cries still came from inside. The worst scalds seemed to be the right arm and shoulder, the chest and stomach's red was fading to pink under the cold water and his feet's soft soles weren't blistered that the Daddy could see, but the toddler still made little fists and screamed except maybe now merely on reflex from fear, the Daddy would know he thought it possible later, small face distended and thready veins standing out at the temples and the Daddy kept saying he was here he was here, adrenaline ebbing and an anger at the Mommy for allowing this thing to happen just starting to gather in wisps at his mind's extreme rear and still hours from expression. When the Mommy returned he wasn't sure whether to wrap the child in a towel or not but he wet the towel down and did, swaddled him tight and lifted his baby out of the sink and set him on the kitchen table's edge to soothe him while the Mommy tried to check the feet's soles with one hand waving around in the area of her mouth and uttering objectless words while the Daddy bent in and was face to face with the child on the table's checked edge repeating the fact that he was here and trying to calm the toddler's cries but still the child breathlessly screamed, a high pure shining sound that could stop his heart and his bitty lips and gums now tinged with the light blue of a low flame the Daddy thought, screaming as if almost still under the tilted pot in pain. A minute, two like this that seemed much longer, with the Mommy at the Daddy's side talking sing-song at the child's face and the lark on the limb with its head to the side and the hinge going white in a line from the weight of the canted door until the first seen wisp of steam came lazy from under the wrapped tow-el's hem and the parents' eyes met and widened — the diaper, which when they opened the towel and leaned their little boy back on the checkered cloth and unfastened the softened tabs and tried to remove it resisted slightly with new high cries and was hot, their baby's diaper burned their hand and they saw where the real water'd fallen and pooled and been burning their baby boy all this time while he screamed for them to help him and they hadn't, hadn't thought and when they got it off and saw the state of what was there the Mommy said their God's first name and grabbed the table to keep her feet while the father turned away and threw a haymaker at the air of the kitchen and cursed both himself and the world for not the last time while his child might now have been sleeping if not for the rate of his breathing and the tiny stricken motions of his hands in the air above where he lay, hands the size of a grown man's thumb that had clutched the Daddy's thumb in the crib while he'd watched the Dad-dy's mouth move in song, his head cocked and seeming to see way past him into something his eyes made the Daddy lonesome for in a sideways way. If you've never wept and want to, have a child. Break your heart inside

454 • The David Foster Wallace Reader

and something will a child is the twangy song the Daddy hears again as if the radio's lady was almost there with him looking down at what they've done, though hours later what the Daddy most won't forgive is how badly he wanted a cigarette right then as they diapered the child as best they could in gauze and two crossed handtowels and the Daddy lifted him like a newborn with his skull in one palm and ran him out to the hot truck and burned custom rubber all the way to town and the clinic's ER with the tenant's door hanging open like that all day until the hinge gave but by then it was too late, when it wouldn't stop and they couldn't make it the child had learned to leave himself and watch the whole rest unfold from a point overhead, and whatever was lost never thenceforth mattered, and the child's body expanded and walked about and drew pay and lived its life untenanted, a thing among things, its self's soul so much vapor aloft, falling as rain and then rising, the sun up and down like a yoyo.

Afterword

I first read this story in December 2000, a time when the name David Foster Wallace was synonymous with *maximalist* and *encyclopedic* texts. After *Infinite Jest* and everything of his I'd read subsequently, "Incarnations of Burned Children" made me reevaluate the Wallace I thought I knew.

This is now one of a handful of Wallace pieces I regularly give to people when I'm asked who my favorite author is. I use it to introduce friends to his fiction, and I use it to teach short narrative to my high school English students. I've found that it always inspires intensely interesting conversations, whether the reader enjoys the story or not.

Why is "Incarnations of Burned Children" essential Wallace fiction? It is Wallace at his minimalist best, a single, hyper-compressed paragraph. As each sentence increases in length and tension, Wallace's amazing control of syntax feeds the narrative's pacing perfectly. It is an adept exploration of empathy, trauma, and taboo, and uses symbolism and narrative distance to powerful ends. Wallace succeeds in delivering to the reader what it is like to be the incarnation of a burned child, viewing the world at a distance, without judgment, conscious of everything yet far from the excruciating pain of it all. It is the most tense and horrific piece of writing I have read. It is also one of the finest.

(Fun fact: an early version of this story was part of some of the earliest work on *The Pale King*. Numerous characters in that novel experience some sort of childhood trauma that gives them unique abilities as adults. I'll leave it to you to figure out which character this burned child may have grown up to be...)

—*Nick Maniatis*

The Suffering Channel

1.

'BUT THEY'RE SHIT.'

'And yet at the same time they're art. Exquisite pieces of art. They're literally incredible.'

'No, they're literally shit is literally what they are.'

Atwater was speaking to his associate editor at *Style*. He was at the little twin set of payphones in the hallway off the Holiday Inn restaurant where he'd taken the Moltkes out to eat and expand their side of the whole pitch. The hallway led to the first floor's elevators and restrooms and to the restaurant's kitchen and rear area.

At *Style*, editor was more of an executive title. Those who did actual editing were usually called associate editors. This was a convention throughout the BSG subindustry.

'If you could just see them.'

'I don't want to see them,' the associate editor responded. 'I don't want to look at shit. Nobody wants to look at shit. Skip, this is the point: people do not want to look at shit.'

'And yet if you—'

'Even shit shaped into various likenesses or miniatures or whatever it is they're alleging they are.'

Skip Atwater's intern, Laurel Manderley, was listening in on the whole two way conversation. It was she whom Atwater'd originally dialed, since there was simply no way he was going to call the associate editor's head intern's extension on a Sunday and ask her to accept a collect call. *Style*'s whole editorial staff was in over the weekend because the magazine's Summer Entertainment double issue was booked to close on 2 July. It was a busy and extremely high stress time, as Laurel Manderley would point out to Skip more than once in the subsequent debriefing.

'No, no, but *not* shaped into, is the thing. You aren't—they come out that way. Already fully formed. Hence the term incredible.' Atwater was a plump diminutive boy faced man who sometimes unconsciously made a waist level fist and moved it up and down in time to his stressed syllables. A small and bell shaped *Style* salaryman, energetic and competent, a team player, unfailingly polite. Sometimes a bit overfastidious in presentation—for example, it was extremely warm and close in the little Holiday Inn hallway, and yet Atwater had not removed his blazer or even loosened his tie. The word among some of *Style*'s snarkier interns was that Skip Atwater resembled a jockey who had retired young and broken training in a big way. There was doubt in some quarters about whether he even shaved. Sensitive about the whole baby face issue, as well as about the size and floridity of his ears, Atwater was unaware of his reputation for wearing nearly identical navy blazer and catalogue slacks ensembles all the time, which happened to be the number one thing that betrayed his Midwest origins to those interns who knew anything about cultural geography.

The associate editor wore a headset telephone and was engaged in certain other editorial tasks at the same time he was talking to Atwater. He was a large bluff bearish man, extremely cynical and fun to be around, as magazine editors often tend to be, and known particularly for being able to type two totally different things at the same time, a keyboard under each hand, and to have them both come out more or less error free. *Style*'s editorial interns found this bimanual talent fascinating, and they often pressed the associate editor's head intern to get him to do it during the short but very intense celebrations that took place after certain issues had closed and everyone had had some drinks and the normal constraints of rank and deportment were relaxed a bit. The associate editor had a daughter at Rye Country Day School, where a number of *Style*'s editorial interns had also gone, as adolescents. The typing talent thing was also interesting because the associate editor had never actually written for *Style* or anyone else—he had come up through Factchecking, which was technically a division of Legal and answered to a whole different section of *Style*'s parent company. In any event, the doubletime typing explained the surfeit of clicking sounds in the background as the associate editor responded to a pitch he found irksome and out of character for Atwater, who was normally a consummate pro, and knew quite well the shape of the terrain that *Style*'s WHAT IN THE WORLD feature covered, and had no history of instability or substance issues, and rarely even needed much rewriting.

The editorial exchange between the two men was actually very rapid and clipped and terse. The associate editor was saying: 'Which think about it, you're going to represent how? You're going to propose we get photos of the man on the throne, producing? You're going to describe it?'

'Everything you're saying is valid and understandable and yet all I'm saying is if you could see the results. The pieces themselves.' The two pay-phones had a woodgrain frame with a kind of stiff steel umbilicus for the phone book. Atwater had claimed that he could not use his own phone because once you got far enough south of Indianapolis and Richmond there were not enough cellular relays to produce a reliable signal. Due to the glass doors and no direct AC, it was probably close to 100 degrees in the little passage, and also loud—the kitchen was clearly on the other side of the wall, because there was a great deal of audible clatter and shout-ing. Atwater had worked in a 24 hour restaurant attached to a Union 76 Truck 'n Travel Plaza while majoring in journalism at Ball State, and he knew the sounds of a short order kitchen. The name of the restaurant in Muncie had been simply: *EAT.* Atwater was facing away from everything and more or less concave, hunched into himself and the space of the phone, as people on payphones in public spaces so often are. His fist moved just below the little shelf where the slim GTE directory for Whitcomb–Mount Carmel–Scipio and surrounding communities rested. The technical name of the Holiday Inn's restaurant, according to the sign and menus, was Ye Olde Country Buffet. Hard to his left, an older couple was trying to get a great deal of luggage through the hallway's glass doors. It was only a matter of time before they figured out that one should just go through and hold the doors open for the other. It was early in the after-noon of 1 July 2001. You could also hear the associate editor sometimes talking to someone else in his office, which wasn't necessarily his fault or a way to marginalize Atwater, because other people were always coming in and asking him things.

A short time later, after splashing some cold water on his ears and face in the men's room, Atwater reemerged through the hallway's smeared doors and made his way through the crowds around the restaurant's buffet table. He had also used the sink's mirror to pump himself up a lit-tle—periods of self exhortation at mirrors were usually the only time he was fully conscious of the thing that he did with his fist. There were red heat lamps over many of the buffet's entrees, and a man in a partly crum-pled chef's hat was slicing prime rib to people's individual specs. The large room smelled powerfully of bodies and hot food. Everyone's face shone in the humidity. Atwater had a short man's emphatic, shoulder inflected walk. Many of the Sunday diners were elderly and wore special sunglasses with side flaps, the inventor of whom was possibly ripe for a WITW profile.

Nor does one hardly ever see actual flypaper anymore. Their table was almost all the way in front. Even across the crowded dining room it was not hard to spot them seated there, due to the artist's wife, Mrs. Moltke, whose great blond head's crown was nearly even with the hostess's lectern. Atwater used the head as a salient to navigate the room, his own ears and forehead flushed with high speed thought. Back at *Style*'s editorial offices on the sixteenth floor of 1 World Trade Center in New York, meanwhile, the associate editor was speaking with his head intern on the intercom while he typed internal emails. Mr. Brint Moltke, the proposed piece's subject, was smiling fixedly at his spouse, possibly in response to some remark. His entree was virtually untouched. Mrs. Moltke was removing mayo or dressing from the corner of her mouth with a pinkie and met Atwater's eye as he raised both arms:

'They're very excited.'

←

Part of the reason Atwater had had to splash and self exhort in the airless little men's room off the Holiday Inn restaurant was that the toll call had actually continued for several more minutes after the journalist had said '…pieces themselves,' and had become almost heated at the same time that it didn't really go anywhere or modify either side of the argument, except that the associate editor subsequently observed to his head intern that Skip seemed to be taking the whole strange thing more to heart than was normal in such a consummate pro.

'I do good work. I find it and I do it.'

'This is not about you or whether you could bring it in well,' the associate editor had said. 'This is simply me delivering news to you about what can happen and what can't.'

'I seem to recollect somebody once saying no way the parrot could ever happen.' Here Atwater was referring to a prior piece he'd done for *Style*.

'You're construing this as an argument about me and you. What this is really about is shit. Excrement. Human shit. It's very simple: *Style* does not run items about human shit.'

'But it's also art.'

'But it's also shit. And you're already tasked to Chicago for something else we're letting you look at because you pitched me, that's already dubious in terms of the sorts of things we can do. Correct me if I'm mistaken here.'

'I'm on that already. It's Sunday. Laurel's got me in for tomorrow all day. It's a two hour toot up the interstate. The two are a hundred and ten percent compatible.' Atwater sniffed and swallowed hard. 'You know I know this area.'

The other *Style* piece the associate editor had referred to concerned The Suffering Channel, a wide grid cable venture that Atwater had gotten Laurel Manderley to do an end run and pitch directly to the editor's head intern for WHAT IN THE WORLD. Atwater was one of three full time salarymen tasked to the WITW feature, which received .75 editorial pages per week, and was the closest any of the BSG weeklies got to freakshow or tabloid, and was a bone of contention at the very highest levels of *Style*. The staff size and large font specs meant that Skip Atwater was officially contracted for one 400 word piece every three weeks, except the juniormost of the WITW salarymen had been on half time ever since Eckleschafft-Böd had forced Mrs. Anger to cut the editorial budget for everything except celebrity news, so in reality it was more like three finished pieces every eight weeks.

'I'll overnight photos.'

'You will not.'

As mentioned, Atwater was rarely aware of the up and down fist thing, which as far as he could recall had first started in the pressure cooker environs of the Indianapolis *Star*. When he became aware he was doing it, he sometimes looked down at the moving fist without recognition, as if it were somebody else's. It was one of several lacunae or blind spots in Atwater's self concept, which in turn were part of why he inspired both affection and mild contempt around the offices of *Style*. Those he worked closely with, such as Laurel Manderley, saw him as without much protective edge or shell, and there were clearly some maternal elements in Laurel's regard for him. His interns' tendency to fierce devotion, in further turn, caused some at *Style* to see him as a manipulator, someone who complicitly leaned on people instead of developing his own inner resources. The former associate editor in charge of the magazine's SOCIETY PAGES feature had once referred to Skip Atwater as an emotional tampon, though there were plenty of people who could verify that she had been a person with all kinds of personal baggage of her own. As with institutional politics everywhere, the whole thing got very involved.

Also as mentioned, the editorial exchange on the telephone was in fact very rapid and compressed, with the exception of one sustained pause while the associate editor conferred with someone from Design about the shape of a pull quote, which Atwater could overhear clearly. The several beats of silence after that, however, could have meant almost anything.

'See if you get this,' the associate editor said finally. 'How about if I say to you what Mrs. Anger would say to me were I hypothetically as enthused as you are, and gave you the OK, and went up to the ed meeting and pitched it for let's say 10 September. Are you out of your mind. People are not interested in shit. People are disgusted and repelled by shit. That's why they call it shit. Not even to mention the high percentage of fall ad pages that are food or beauty based. Are you insane. Unquote.' Mrs. Anger was the Executive Editor of *Style* and the magazine's point man with respect to its parent company, which was the US division of Eckleschafft-Böd Medien.

'Although the inverse of that reasoning is that it's also wholly common and universal,' Atwater had said. 'Everyone has personal experience with shit.'

'But personal *private* experience.' Though technically included in the same toll call, this last rejoinder was part of a separate, subsequent conversation with Laurel Manderley, the intern who currently manned Atwater's phone and fax when he was on the road, and winnowed and vetted research items forwarded by the shades in Research for WHAT IN THE WORLD, and interfaced for him with the editorial interns. 'It's done in private, in a special private place, and flushed. People flush so it will go away. It's one of the things people don't want to be reminded of. That's why nobody talks about it.'

Laurel Manderley, who like most of the magazine's high level interns wore exquisitely chosen and coordinated professional attire, permitted herself a small diamond stud in one nostril that Atwater found slightly distracting in face to face exchanges, but she was extremely shrewd and pragmatic — she had actually been voted Most Rational by the Class of '96 at Miss Porter's School. She was also all but incapable of writing a simple declarative sentence and thus could not, by any dark stretch of the imagination, ever be any kind of rival for Atwater's salaryman position at *Style*. As he had with perhaps only one or two previous interns, Atwater relied on Laurel Manderley, and sounded her out, and welcomed her input so long as it was requested, and often spent large blocks of time on the phone with her, and had shared with her certain elements of his personal history, including pictures of the four year old schipperke mixes who were his pride and joy. Laurel Manderley, whose father controlled a large number of Blockbuster Video franchises throughout western Connecticut, and whose mother was in the final push toward certification as a Master Gardener, was herself destined to survive, through either coincidence or premonition, the tragedy by which *Style* would enter history two months hence.

Atwater rubbed his nose vertically with two fingers. 'Well, some people talk about it. You should hear little boys. Or men, in a locker room setting: "Boy, you wouldn't believe the dump I took last night." That sort of thing.'

'I don't want to hear that. I don't want to imagine that's what men talk to each other about.'

'It's not as if it comes up all that often,' Atwater conceded. He did feel a little uneasy talking about this with a female. 'My point is that the whole embarrassment and distaste of the issue is the point, if it's done right. The transfiguration of disgust. This is the UBA.' UBA was their industry's shorthand for upbeat angle, what hard news organs would call a story's hook. 'The let's say unexpected reversal of embarrassment and distaste. The triumph of creative achievement in even the unlikeliest places.'

Laurel Manderley sat with her feet up on an open file drawer of Atwater's desk, holding her phone's headset instead of wearing it. Slender almost to the point of clinical intervention, she had a prominent forehead and surprised eyebrows and a tortoiseshell barrette and was, like Atwater, extremely earnest and serious at all times. She had interned at *Style* for almost a year, and knew that Skip's only real weakness as a BSG journalist was a tendency to grand abstraction that was usually not hard to bring him back to earth on and get him to tone down. She knew further that this tendency was a form of compensation for what Skip himself believed was his chief flaw, an insufficient sense of the tragic which an editor at the *Indiana Star* had accused him of at an age when that sort of thing sank deep out of sight in the psyche and became part of your core understanding of who you are. One of Laurel Manderley's profs at Wellesley had once criticized her freshman essays for what he'd called their tin ear and cozening tone of unearned confidence, which had immediately become dark parts of her own self concept.

'So go write a Ph.D. thesis on the guy,' she had responded. 'But do not ask me to go to Miss Flick and make a case for making *Style* readers hear about somebody pooping little pieces of sculpture out of their butt. Because it's not going to happen.' Laurel Manderley now nearly always spoke her mind; her cozening days were behind her. 'I'd be spending credibility and asking Ellen to spend hers on something that's a lost cause.'

'You have to be careful what you ask people to do,' she had said. Sometimes privately a.k.a. Miss Flick, Ellen Bactrian was the WHAT IN THE WORLD section's head intern, a personage who was not only the associate editor's right hand but who was known to have the ear of someone high on Mrs. Anger's own staff on the 82nd floor, because Ellen Bactrian and this executive intern often biked down to work together from the Flatiron district on the extraordinary bicycle paths that ran all the way along the Hudson to almost Battery Park. It was said that they even had matching helmets.

For complicated personal and political reasons, Skip Atwater was uncomfortable around Ellen Bactrian and tried to avoid her whenever possible.

There were a couple moments of nothing but background clatter on his end of the phone.

'Who is this guy, anyhow?' Laurel Manderley had asked. 'What sort of person goes around displaying his own poo?'

2.

Indiana storms surprise no one. You can see them coming from half a state away, like a train on a very straight track, even as you stand in the sun and try to breathe. Atwater had what his mother'd always called a weather eye.

Seated together in the standard Midwest attitude of besotted amiability, the three of them had passed the midday hours in the Moltkes' sitting room with the curtains drawn and two rotating fans that picked Atwater's hair up and laid it down and made the little racks' magazines riffle. Laurel Manderley, who was something of a whiz at the cold call, had set this initial meeting up by phone the previous evening. The home was half a rented duplex, and you could hear its aluminum siding tick and pop in the assembling heat. A window AC chugged gamely in one of the interior rooms. The off white Roto Rooter van in the driveway had signified the Moltkes' side of the ranch style twin; Laurel's Internet directions to the address had been flawless as usual. The cul de sac was a newer development with abrasive cement and engineering specs still spraypainted on the curbs. Only the very western horizon showed piling clouds when Atwater pulled up in the rented Cavalier. Some of the homes' yards had not yet been fully sodded. There were almost no porches as such. The Moltkes' side's front door had had a US flag in an angled holder and an anodized cameo of perhaps a huge black ladybug or some kind of beetle attached to the storm door's frame, which one had to back slightly off the concrete slab in order to open. The slab's mat bid literal welcome.

The sitting room was narrow and airless and done mostly in green and a tawny type of maple syrup brown. It was thickly carpeted throughout. The davenport, chairs, and end tables had plainly been acquired as a set. A bird emerged at intervals from a catalogue clock; a knit sampler over the mantel expressed conventional wishes for the home and its occupants. The iced tea was kneebucklingly sweet. An odd stain or watermark marred the room's east wall, which Atwater educed was the load bearing wall that the Moltkes shared with the duplex's other side.

'I think I speak for a lot of folks when I want to know how it works. Just how you do it.' Atwater was in a padded rocker next to the television console and thus faced the artist and his wife, who were seated together on the davenport. The reporter had his legs crossed comfortably but was not actually rocking. He had spent a great deal of preliminary time chatting about the area and his memories of regional features and establishing a rapport and putting the Moltkes at ease. The recorder was out and on, but he was also going with a stenographer's notebook because it made him look a little more like the popular stereotype of someone from the press.

You could tell almost immediately that something was off about the artist and/or the marriage's dynamics. Brint Moltke sat hunched or slumped with his toes in and his hands in his lap, a posture reminiscent of a scolded child, but at the same time smiling at Atwater. As in smiling the entire time. It was not an empty professional corporate smile, but the soul effects were similar. Moltke was a thickset man with sideburns and graying hair combed back in what appeared to be a lopsided ducktail. He wore Sansabelt slacks and a dark blue knit shirt with his employer's name on the breast. You could tell from the dents in his nose that he sometimes wore glasses. A further idiosyncrasy that Atwater noted in Gregg shorthand was the arrangement of the artist's hands: their thumbs and forefingers formed a perfect lap level circle, which Moltke held or rather somehow directed before him like an aperture or target. He appeared to be unaware of this habit. It was a gesture both unsubtle and somewhat obscure in terms of what it signified. Combined with the rigid smile, it was almost the stuff of nightmares. Atwater's own hands were controlled and well behaved—his tic with the fist was entirely a private thing. The journalist's childhood hay fever was back with a vengeance, but even so he could not help detecting the Old Spice scent which Mr. Moltke emitted in great shimmering waves. Old Spice had been Skip's own father's scent and, reportedly, his father's father's before him.

The pattern of the davenport's upholstery, Skip Atwater also knew firsthand, was called Forest Floral.

↓

The WITW associate editor's typing feats were just one example of the various leveling traditions and shticks and reversals of protocol that made *Style*'s parties and corporate celebrations the envy of publishing interns throughout Manhattan. These fetes took place on the sixteenth floor and were usually open bar; some were even catered. The normally dry and insufferable head of Copyediting did impressions of various US presidents smoking dope that had to be seen to be believed. Given the right kinds of vodka and flame source, a senior receptionist from Haiti could be prevailed upon to breathe fire. A very odd senior paralegal in Permissions, who showed up to the office in foul weather gear nearly every day no matter what the forecast, turned out to have been in the original Broadway cast of *Jesus Christ Superstar*, and organized revues that could get kind of risqué. Some of the interns got bizarrely dressed up; nails were occasionally done in White Out. Mrs. Anger's executive intern had once worn a white leather suit with outrageous fringe and a set of cap pistols in a hiphugger belt and holster accessory. A longtime supervisor of shades used Crystal Light, Everclear, skinned fruit, and an ordinary office paper shredder to produce a libation she called Last Mango in Paris. The interns' annual ersatz awards show at the climax of Oscars Week often had people on the floor—one year they'd gotten Gene Shalit to appear. And so on and so forth.

Of arresting and demotic party traditions, however, none was so prized as Mrs. Anger's annual essay at self parody for the combination New Year's and closing of the Year's Most Stylish People double issue bash. Bedecked in costume jewelry, mincing and fluttering, affecting a falsetto and lorgnette, holding her head in such a way as to produce a double chin, tottering about with a champagne cocktail like one of those anserine dowagers in Marx Brothers films. It would be difficult to convey this routine's effect on morale and esprit. The rest of the publishing year, Mrs. Anger was a figure of near testamental awe and dread, serious as a heart attack. A veteran of Fleet Street and two separate R. Murdoch startups, wooed over from *Us* in 1994 under terms that were industry myth, Mrs. Anger had managed to put *Style* in the black for the first time in its history, and was said to enjoy influence at the very highest levels of Eckleschafft-Böd, and had worn one of the first Versace pantsuits ever seen in New York, and was nobody's fool whatsoever.

↓

Mrs. Amber Moltke, the artist's young spouse, wore a great billowing pastel housedress and flattened espadrilles and was, for better or worse, the sexiest morbidly obese woman Atwater had ever seen. Eastern Indiana was not short on big pretty girls, but this was less a person than a vista, a quarter ton of sheer Midwest pulchritude, and Atwater had already filled several narrow pages of his notebook with descriptions and analogies and abstract encomia to Mrs. Moltke, none of which could be used in the compressed piece he was even then conceiving how to pitch and submit. Some of the allure was atavistic, he acknowledged. Some was simply contrast, a relief from the sucking cheeks and starved eyes of Manhattan's women. He had personally seen *Style* interns weighing their food on small pharmaceutical scales before they consumed it. In one of the more abstract notebook entries, Atwater had theorized that Mrs. Moltke's was perhaps a sort of negative beauty that consisted mainly in her failure to be repellent. In another, he had compared her face and throat to whatever canids see in the full moon that makes them howl. The associate editor would never see one jot of material like this, obviously. Some BSG salarymen built their pieces gradually from the ground up. Atwater, trained originally as a background man for news dailies, constructed his own WITW pieces by pouring into his notebooks and word processor an enormous waterfall of prose which was then filtered more and more closely down to 400 words of commercial sediment. It was labor intensive, but it was his way. Atwater had colleagues who were unable even to start without a Roman numeral outline. *Style*'s daytime television specialist could compose his pieces only on public transport. So long as salarymen's personal quotas were filled and deadlines met, the BSG weeklies tended to be respectful of people's processes.

When as a child he had misbehaved or sassed her, Mrs. Atwater had made little Virgil go and cut from the fields' edge's copse the very switch with which she'd whip him. For most of the 1970s she had belonged to a splinter denomination that met in an Airstream trailer on the outskirts of Anderson, and she did spareth not the rod. His father had been a barber, the real kind, w/ smock and pole and rat tail combs in huge jars of Barbicide. Save the odd payroll data processor at Eckleschafft-Böd US, no one east of Muncie had access to Skip's true given name.

Mrs. Moltke sat with her spine straight and ankles crossed, her huge smooth calves cream white and unmarred by veins and the overall size and hue of what Atwater wrote were museum grade vases and funereal urns of the same antiquity in which the dead wore bronze masks and whole households were interred together. Her platter sized face was expressive and her eyes, though rendered small by the encasing folds of fat, were intelligent and alive. An Anne Rice paperback lay face down on the end table beside her fauxfrosted beverage tumbler and a stack of Butterick clothing patterns in their distinctive bilingual sleeves. Atwater, who held his pen rather high on the shaft, had already noted that her husband's eyes were flat and immured despite his constant smile. The lone time that Atwater had believed he was seeing his own father smile, it turned out to have been a grimace which presaged the massive infarction that had sent the man forward to lie prone in the sand of the horseshoe pit as the shoe itself sailed over the stake, the half finished apiary, a section of the simulation combat target range, a tire swing's supporting limb, and the backyard's pineboard fence, never to be recovered or even ever seen again, while Virgil and his twin brother had stood there wide eyed and red eared, looking back and forth from the sprawled form to the kitchen window's screen, their inability to move or cry out feeling, in later recall, much like the paralysis of bad dreams.

The Moltkes had already shown him the storm cellar and its literally incredible display, but Atwater decided to wait until he truly needed to visit the bathroom to see where the actual creative transfigurations took place. He felt that asking to be shown the bathroom as such, and then examining it while they watched him do so, would be awkward and unseemly. In her lap, the artist's wife had some kind of garment or bolt of orange cloth in which she was placing pins in a complicated way. A large red felt apple on the end table held the supply of pins for this purpose. She filled her whole side of the davenport and then some. One could feel the walls and curtains warming as the viscous heat outside beset the home. After one of the lengthy and uncomfortable attacks of what felt like aphasia that sometimes afflicted him with incidentals, Atwater was able to remember that the correct term for the apple was simply: pin cushion. One reason it was so discomfiting was that the detail was irrelevant. Likewise the twinge of abandonment he noticed that he felt whenever the near fan rotated back away from him. On the whole, though, the journalist's spirits were good. Part of it was actual art. But there was also something that felt solid and kind of invulnerable about returning to one's native area for legitimate professional reasons. He was unaware that the cadences of his speech had already changed.

After one or two awkward recrossings of his leg, Atwater had found a way to sit, with his weight on his left hip and the padded rocker held still against that weight, so that his right thigh formed a stable surface for taking notes. His iced tea, pebbled with condensation, was on a plastic coaster beside the cable converter box atop the television console. Atwater was particularly drawn to two framed prints on the wall above the davenport, matched renderings of retrievers, human eyed and much ennobled by the artist, each with some kind of dead bird in its mouth.

'I think I speak for a lot of folks when I say how curious I am to know how you do it,' Atwater said. 'Just how the whole thing works.'

There was a three beat pause in which no one moved or spoke and the fans' whines harmonized briefly and then diverged once more.

'I realize it's a delicate subject,' Atwater said.

Another stilted pause, only slightly longer, and then Mrs. Moltke signaled the artist to answer the man by swinging her great dimpled arm out and around and striking him someplace about the left breast or shoulder, producing a meaty sound. It was a gesture both practiced and without heat, and Moltke's only visible reaction, after angling hard to starboard and then righting himself, was to search within and answer as honestly as he could.

The artist said, 'I'm not sure.'

↓

The fliptop stenographer's notebook was partly for effect, but it was also what Skip Atwater had gotten in the habit of using out in the field for background at the start of his career, and its personal semiotics and mojo were profound; he was comfortable with it. He was, as a matter of professional persona, old school and low tech. Today's was a very different journalistic era, however, and in the Moltkes' sitting room his tiny professional tape recorder was also out and activated and resting atop a stack of recent magazines on the coffee table before the davenport. Its technology was foreign and featured a very sensitive built in microphone, though the unit also gobbled AAA cells, and the miniature cassettes for it had to be special ordered. BSG magazines as a whole being litigation conscious in the extreme, a *Style* salaryman had to submit all relevant notes and tapes to Legal before his piece could even be typeset, which was one more reason why the day of an issue's closing was so fraught and stressful, and why editorial staff and interns rarely got a whole weekend off.

Moltke's fingers' and thumbs' unconscious ring had naturally come apart when Amber had smacked him and he'd gone over hard against the davenport's right armrest, but now it was back as they all sat in the dim green curtainlight and smiled at one another. What might have sounded at first like isolated gunshots or firecrackers were actually new homes' carapaces expanding in the heat all up and down the Willkie development. No analogy for the digital waist level circle or aperture or lens or target or orifice or void seemed quite right, but it struck Atwater as definitely the sort of tic or gesture that meant something—the way in dreams and certain kinds of art things were never merely things but always seemed to stand for something else that you couldn't quite put a finger on—and the journalist had already shorthanded several reminders to himself to consider whether the gesture was some kind of unconscious visible code or might be a key to the question of how to represent the artist's conflicted response to his extraordinary but also undeniably controversial and perhaps even repulsive talent.

The recorder's battery indicator showed a strong clear red. Amber occasionally leaned forward over her sewing materials to check the amount of audiotape remaining. Once more, Atwater thanked the artist and his wife for opening their home to him on a Sunday, explaining that he had to head on up to Chicago for a day or two but then would be back to start in on deep background if the Moltkes decided to give their consent. He had explained that the type of personality driven article that *Style* was interested in running would be impossible without the artist's cooperation, and that there would be no point in his taking up any more of their time after today if Mr. and Mrs. Moltke weren't totally on board and as excited about the piece as everyone over at *Style* was. He had addressed this statement to the artist, but it had been Amber Moltke's reaction he noted.

On the same coffee table between them, beside the magazines and tape recorder and a small vase of synthetic marigolds, were three artworks allegedly produced through ordinary elimination by Mr. Brint F. Moltke. The pieces varied slightly in size, but all were arresting in their extraordinary realism and the detail of their craftsmanship—although one of Atwater's notes was a reminder to himself to consider whether a word like craftsmanship really applied in such a case. The sample pieces were the very earliest examples that Mrs. Moltke said she'd been able to lay hands on; they had been out on the table when Atwater arrived. There were literally scores more of the artworks arranged in vaguely familiar looking glass cases in the unattached storm cellar out back, an environment that seemed strangely perfect, though Atwater had seen immediately how difficult the storm cellar would be for any of *Style*'s photographers to light and shoot properly. By 11:00 AM, he was mouthbreathing due to hay fever.

Mrs. Moltke periodically fanned at herself in a delicate way and said she did believe it might rain.

When Atwater and his brother had been in the eighth grade, the father of a family just up the road in Anderson had run a length of garden hose from his vehicle's exhaust pipe to the interior and killed himself in the home's garage, after which the son in their class and everyone else in the family had gone around with a strange fixed smile that had seemed both creepy and courageous; and something in the hydraulics of Brint Moltke's smile on the davenport reminded Skip Atwater of the Haas family's smile.

↓

Omitted through oversight above: Nearly every Indiana community has some street, lane, drive, or easement named for Wendell L. Willkie, b. 1892, GOP, favorite son.

↓

The recorder's tiny tape's first side had been almost entirely filled by Skip Atwater answering Mrs. Moltke's initial questions. It had become evident pretty quickly whose show this was, in terms of any sort of piece, on their end. Chewing a piece of gum with tiny motions of her front teeth in the distinctive Indiana style, Mrs. Moltke had requested information on how any potential article would be positioned and when it was likely to run. She had asked about word counts, column inches, boxes, leader quotes, and shared templates. Hers was the type of infantly milky skin on which even the lightest contact would leave some type of blotch. She had used terms like conferral, serial rights, and *sic vos non vobis,* which latter Skip did not even know. She had high quality photographs of some of the more spectacular artworks in a leatherette portfolio with the Moltkes' name and address embossed on the cover, and Atwater was asked to provide a receipt for the portfolio's loan.

The tape's second side, however, contained Mr. Brint Moltke's own first person account of how his strange and ambivalent gift had first come to light, which emerged—the account did—after Atwater had phrased his query several different ways and Amber Moltke had finally asked the journalist to excuse them and removed her husband into one of the home's rear rooms, where they took inaudible counsel together while Atwater circumspectly chewed the remainder of his ice. The result was what Atwater later, in his second floor room at the Holiday Inn, after showering, applying crude first aid to his left knee, and struggling unsuccessfully to move or reverse the room's excruciating painting, had copied into his steno as certainly usable in some part or form for deep background/UBA, particularly if Mr. Moltke, who had appeared to warm to the task or at least to come somewhat alive, could be induced to repeat its substance on record in a sanitized way:

'It was on a field exercise in basic [training in the US Army, in which Moltke later saw action in Kuwait as part of a maintenance crew in Operation Desert Storm], and the fellows on shitter [latrine, hygienic] detail—[latrine] detail is they soak the [military unit's solid wastes] in gas and burn it with a [flamethrower]—and up the [material] goes and in the fire one of the fellows saw something peculiar there in amongst the [waste material] and calls the sergeant over and they kick up a [fuss] because at first they're thinking somebody tossed something in the [latrine] for a joke, which is against regs, and the sergeant said when he found out who it was he was going to crawl up inside the [responsible party's] skull and look out his eyeholes, and they made the [latrine] detail [douse] the fire and get it [the artwork] out and come to find it weren't a[n illicit or unpatriotic object], and they didn't know whose [solid waste] it was, but I was pretty sure it was mine [because subj. then reports having had prior experiences of roughly same kind, which renders entire anecdote more or less pointless, but could foreseeably be edited out or massaged].'

3.

The Mount Carmel Holiday Inn regretfully had neither scanner nor fax for guests' outgoing use, Atwater had been informed at the desk by a man whose blazer was nearly identical to his own.

Temperatures had fallen and the sodium streetlights come on by themselves as Skip Atwater drove the artist and his spouse home from Ye Olde Country Buffet with a styrofoam box of leavings for a dog he'd seen no sign of; and the great elms and locusts were beginning to yaw and two thirds of the sky to be stacked with enormous muttering masses of clouds that moved in and out of themselves as if stirred by a great unseen hand. Mrs. Moltke was in the back seat, and there was a terrible noise as the car hit the driveway's grade. Blinds that had been open on the duplex's other side were now closed, though there was still no vehicle in that side's drive. The other side's door had a US flag as well. As was also typical of severe weather conditions in the area, a gray luminescence to the light made everything appear greasy and unreal. The rear of the artist's company van listed a toll free number to dial if one had any concerns about the employee's driving.

It had emerged that the nearest Kinko's was in the nearby community of Scipio, which was only a dozen miles east on SR 252 but could be somewhat confusing to get around in because of indifferent signage. Scipio evidently also had a Wal Mart. It was Amber Moltke who suggested that they leave the artist to watch his Sunday Reds game in peace the way he liked to and proceed together in Atwater's rented Chevrolet to that Kinko's, and decide together which photos to scan in and forward, and to also go on and talk turkey in more depth respecting Skip's article on the Moltkes for *Style*. Atwater, whose fear of the region's weather was amply justified by childhood experience, was unsure about either driving or using the Moltke's land line to call Laurel Manderley during an impending storm that he was pretty sure would show up at least yellow on Doppler radar — though on the other hand he was not all that keen about returning to his room at the Holiday Inn, whose wall had an immovable painting of a clown that he found almost impossible to look at — and the journalist ended up watching half an inning of the first Cincinnati Reds game he had seen in a decade while sitting paralyzed with indecision on the Moltkes' davenport.

↓

Besides the facts that she walked without moving her arms and in general reminded him unpleasantly of the girl in *Election,* the core reason why Atwater feared and avoided Ellen Bactrian was that Laurel Manderley had once confided to Atwater that Ellen Bactrian — who had been in madrigals with Laurel Manderley for a year of their overlap at Wellesley, and at the outset of Laurel's internship more or less took the younger woman under her wing — had told her that in her opinion Skip Atwater was not really quite as spontaneous a person as he liked to seem. Nor was Atwater stupid, and he was aware that his being so disturbed over what Ellen Bactrian apparently thought of him was possible evidence that she might actually have him pegged, that he might be not only shallow but at root a kind of poseur. It was not exactly the nicest thing Laurel Manderley had ever done, and part of the fallout was that she was now in a position where she had to act as a sort of human shield between Atwater and Ellen Bactrian, who was responsible for a lot of the day to day administration of WHAT IN THE WORLD; and to be honest, it was a situation that Atwater sometimes exploited, and used Laurel's guilt over her indiscretion to get her to do things or to use her personal connections with Ellen Bactrian in ways that weren't altogether right or appropriate. The whole thing could sometimes get extremely complicated and awkward, but Laurel Manderley for the most part simply bowed to the reality of a situation she had helped create, and accepted it as a painful lesson in respecting certain personal lines and boundaries that turned out to be there for a reason and couldn't be crossed without inevitable consequences. Her father, who was the sort of person who had favorite little apothegms that could sometimes get under one's skin with constant repetition, liked to say, 'Education is expensive,' and Laurel Manderley felt she was now starting to understand how little this saying had really to do with tuition or petty complaint.

Because of some sort of hassle between *Style* and its imaging tech vendor over the terms of the service agreement, the fax machine that Skip Atwater shared with one other full time salaryman had had both a defunct ringer and a missing tray for over a month. Laurel Manderley was in stocking feet at Atwater's console formatting additional background on The Suffering Channel when the fax machine's red incoming light began blinking behind her. The Kinko's franchise in Scipio IN had no scanner, but it did have a digital faxing option that was vastly better than an ordinary low pixel fax. The images Atwater was forwarding to Laurel Manderley began to emerge from the unit's feeder, coiled slightly, detached, and floated in a back and forth fashion to the antistatic carpet. It would be almost 6:00 before she broke for a raisin and even saw them.

The first great grape sized drops were striking the windshield as the severely canted car left Scipio's commercial district, made two left turns in rapid succession, and proceeded out of town on a numbered county road whose gravel was so fresh it fairly gleamed in the gathering stormlight. Mrs. Moltke was navigating. Atwater now wore a mushroom colored Robert Talbott raincoat over his blazer. As was SOP for Indiana storms, there were several minutes of high winds and tentative spatters, followed by a brief eerie stillness that had the quality of an immense inhalation as gravel clattered beneath their chassis. Then fields and trees and cornrows' furrows all vanished in a sheet of sideways rain that sent vague tumbling things across the road ahead and behind. It was like nothing anyone east of Cleveland has ever seen. Atwater, whose father had been a Civil Defense volunteer during the F4 tornado that struck parts of Anderson in 1977, enjoined Amber to try to find something on the AM band that wasn't just concussive static. With the car's front seat unit moved all the way back to accommodate her, Atwater had to strain way out to reach the pedals, which made it difficult to lean forward anxiously and scan upward for assembling funnels. The odd hailstone made a musical sound against the rental's hood. The great myth is that the bad ones don't last long.

Amber Moltke directed Atwater through a murine succession of rural roads and even smaller roads off those roads until they were on little more than the ghost of a two track lane that cut through great whipping tracts of Rorschach shrubbery. Her instructions came primarily in the form of slight motions of her head and left hand, which were all she could move within the confines of her safety belt and harness, against which latter her body strained in several different places with resultant depressions and folds. Atwater's face was the same color as his raincoat by the time they reached their destination, some gap or terminus in the foliage which Amber explained was actually a kind of crude mesa whose vantage overlooked a large nitrogen fixative factory, whose complex and emberous lights at night were an attraction countywide. All that was visible at present was the storm working against the Cavalier's windshield like some sort of berserk car wash, but Atwater told Mrs. Moltke that he certainly appreciated her taking time out to let him absorb some of the local flavor. He watched her begin trying to disengage her seat's restraint system. The ambient noise was roughly equivalent to midcabin on a jetliner. There was, he could detect, a slight ammonial tang to the area's air.

Atwater had, by this point, helped Amber Moltke into the vehicle three separate times and out of it twice. Though technically fat, she presented more as simply huge, extrudent in all three dimensions. At least a half foot taller than the journalist, she managed to seem both towering and squat. Her release of the seat belt produced an effect not unlike an impact's airbag. Atwater's notebook already contained a description of Mrs. Moltke's fatness as being the smooth solid kind as opposed to the soft plumpness or billowing aspect or loose flapping fat of some obese people. There was no cellulite, no quivery or pendent or freehanging parts—she was enormous and firm, and fair the same way babies are. A head the size of a motorcycle tire was topped by a massive blond pageboy whose bangs were thick and not wholly even, receding into a complexly textured bale of curls in the rear areas. In the light of the storm she seemed to glow; the umbrella she carried was not for rain. 'I so much as get downwind of the sun and I burn,' had been Amber's explanation to Skip as the artist/husband held the great flowered thing out at arms' length to spread it in the driveway and then angle it up over the car's rear door just so.

→

Many of *Style*'s upper echelon interns convened for a working lunch at Chambers Street's Tutti Mangia restaurant twice a week, to discuss issues of concern and transact any editorial or other business that was pending, after which each returned to her respective mentor and relayed whatever was germane. It was an efficient practice that saved the magazine's paid staffers a great deal of time and emotional energy. Many of the interns at Monday's lunches traditionally had the Niçoise salad, which was outrageously good here.

They often liked to get two large tables squunched up together near the door, so that those who smoked could take turns darting out front to do so in the striped awning's shade. Which management was happy to do—conjoin the tables. It was an interesting station to serve or sit near. The *Style* interns all still possessed the lilting inflections and vaguely outraged facial expressions of adolescence, which were in sharp contrast to their extraordinary table manners and to the brisk clipped manner of their gestures and speech, as well as to the fact that their outfits' elements were nearly always members of the same color family, a very adult type of coordination that worked to convey a formal and businesslike tone to each ensemble. For reasons with origins much farther back in history than anyone at the table could have speculated about, a majority of the editorial interns at *Style* traditionally come from Seven Sisters colleges. Also at the table was one very plain but self possessed intern who worked with the design director up in *Style*'s executive offices on the 82nd floor. The two least conservatively dressed interns were senior shades from Research and also always wore, unless the day was really overcast, dark glasses to cover the red rings their jobs' goggles left around their eyes, which were slow to fade. It was also true that no fewer than five of the interns at the working lunch on 2 July were named either Laurel or Tara, although it's not as if people can help what their names are.

Laurel Manderley, who tended to favor very soft simple lines in business attire, wore a black Armani skirt and jacket ensemble with sheer hose and an objectively stunning pair of Miu Miu pumps that she'd picked up for next to nothing at a flea market in Milan the previous summer. Her hair was up and had a lacquer chopstick through the chignon. Ellen Bactrian often took a noon dance class on Mondays and was not at today's working lunch, though four of the other associate editors' head interns were there, one sporting a square cut engagement ring so large and garish that she made an ironic display of having to support her wrist with the other hand in order to show it around the table, which occasioned some snarky little internal emails back at *Style* over the course of the rest of the day.

Skip Atwater's bizarre and quixotic pitch for a WITW piece on some sort of handyman who purportedly excreted pieces of fine art out of his bottom in Indiana, while not the most pressing issue on this closing day for what was known as SE2, was certainly the most arresting and controversial. The interns ended up hashing out what came to be called the miraculous poo story in some detail, and the discussion was lively and far ranging, with passions aroused and a good deal of personal background information laid on the table, some of which would alter various power constellations in subtle ways that would not even emerge until preliminary work on the 10 September issue commenced later in the month.

At one point during the lunch, an editorial intern in a charcoal gray Yamamoto pantsuit related an anecdote of her fiancé's, with whom she had apparently exchanged every detail of their sexual histories as a condition for maximal openness and trust in their upcoming marriage. The anecdote, which the intern amused everyone by trying at first to phrase very delicately, involved her fiancé, as an undergraduate, performing cunnilingus on what was at that time one of Swarthmore's most beautiful and widely desired girls, with zero percent body fat and those great pillowy lips that were just then coming into vogue, when evidently she had, suddenly and without any warning...well, farted—the girl being gone down on had—and not at all in the sort of way you could minimize or blow off, according to the fiancé later, but rather 'one of those strange horrible hot ones that are so totally awful and rank.' The anecdote appeared to strike some kind of common chord or nerve: most of the interns at the table were laughing so hard they had to put their forks down, and some held their napkins to their mouths as if to bite them or hold down digestive matter. After the laughter tailed off, there was a brief inbent communal silence while the interns—most of whom were quite intelligent and had had exceptionally high board scores, particularly on the analytical component—tried to suss out just why they had all laughed and what was so funny about the conjunction of oral sex and flatus. There was also something just perfect about the editorial intern's jacket's asymmetrical cut, both incongruous and yet somehow inevitable, which was why Yamamoto was generally felt to be worth every penny. At the same time, it was common knowledge that there was something in the process or chemicals used in commercial dry cleaning that was unfriendly to Yamamotos' particular fabrics, and that they never lay or hung or felt quite so perfect after they'd been dry cleaned a couple times; so there was always a kernel of tragedy to the pleasure of wearing Yamamoto, which may have been a deeper part of its value. A more recent tradition was that the more senior of the interns usually enjoyed a glass of pinot grigio. The intern said that her fiancé tended to date his sexual adulthood as commencing with that incident, and liked to say that he had 'lost literally about twenty pounds of illusions in that one second,' and was now exceptionally, almost unnaturally comfortable with his body and bodies in general and their private functions, rarely even closing the bathroom door now when he went in there for what the intern referred to as big potty.

A fellow WITW staff intern, who also roomed with Laurel Manderley and three other Wellesleyites in a basement sublet near the Williamsburg Bridge, related a vignette that her therapist had once shared with her about dating his wife, whom the therapist had originally met when both of them were going through horrible divorces, and of their going out to dinner on one of their early dates and coming back and sitting with glasses of wine on her sofa, and of she all of a sudden saying, 'You have to leave,' and he not understanding, not knowing whether she was kicking him out or whether he'd said something inappropriate or what, and she finally explaining, 'I have to take a dump and I can't do it with you here, it's too stressful,' using the actual word dump, and of so how the therapist had gone down and stood on the corner smoking a cigarette and looking up at her apartment, watching the light in the bathroom's frosted window go on, and simultaneously, one, feeling like a bit of an idiot for standing out there waiting for her to finish so he could go back up, and, two, realizing that he loved and respected this woman for baring to him so nakedly the insecurity she had been feeling. He had told the intern that standing on that corner was the first time in quite a long time he had not felt deeply and painfully alone, he had realized.

Laurel Manderley's caloric regimen included very precise rules on what parts of her Niçoise salad she was allowed to eat and what she had to do to earn them. At today's lunch she was somewhat preoccupied. She had as yet told no one about any photos, to say nothing of any unannounced overnight package; and Atwater, who had spent the morning commuting to Chicago, made it a principle never to take cellular calls while he drove.

The longtime girl Friday for the associate editor of SURFACES, which was the section of *Style* that focused on health and beauty, had also been among the first of the magazine's interns not to bother changing into pumps on arrival but instead to wear, normally with a high end Chanel or DKBL suit, the same crosstrainers she had commuted in, which somehow for some strange reason worked, and had for a time split the editorial interns into two opposed camps regarding office footwear. She had also at some point spent a trimester at Cambridge, and still spoke with a slight British accent, and asked generally now whether anyone else who traveled abroad much had noticed that in German toilets the hole into which the poop is supposed to disappear when you flush is positioned way in front, so that the poop just sort of *lies* there in full view and there's almost no way you can avoid looking at it when you get up and turn around to flush. Which she observed was so almost stereotypically German, almost as if you were supposed to study and analyze your poop and make sure it passed muster before you flushed it down. Here a senior shade who seemed always to make it a point to wear something garishly retro on Mondays inserted a reminiscence about first seeing the word FAHRT in great block letters on signs all over Swiss and German rail stations, on childhood trips, and how she and her stepsisters had spent whole long Eurail rides cracking one another up by making childish jokes about travelers' various FAHRTS. Whereas, the SURFACES head intern continued with a slight cold smile at the shade's interruption, whereas in French toilets, though, the hole tended to be way in the back so that the poop vanished ASAP, meaning the whole thing was set up to be as elegant and tasteful as possible... although in France there was also the whole bidet issue, which many of the interns agreed always struck them as weird and kind of unhygienic. There was then a quick anecdote about someone's once having asked a French concierge about the really low drinking fountain in the salle de bains, which also struck a nerve of risibility at the table.

At different intervals, two or three of the interns who smoked would excuse themselves briefly and step out to smoke and then return—Tutti Mangia's management had made it clear that they didn't really want like eight people at a time out there under the awning.

'So then what about the US toilets here, with the hole in the middle and all this water so it all floats and goes around and around in a little dance before it goes down—what's up with that?'

The design director's intern wore a very simple severe Prada jacket over a black silk tee. 'They don't always go around and around. Some toilets are really fast and powerful and it's gone right away.'

'Maybe up on eighty-two it is!' Two of the newer staff interns leaned slightly toward each other as they laughed.

Laurel Manderley's roommate, who at Wellesley had played both field hockey and basketball and was a national finalist for a Marshall, asked how many of those at the table had had to read those ghastly pieces of Swift's in Post Liz Lit where he went on and on about women taking a crap and how supposedly traumatic it was for the swain when he found out that his beloved went to the bathroom like a normal human being instead of whatever sick mommy figure Swift liked to make women into, quoting the actual lines, ' "Send up an excremental Smell/To taint the Parts from whence they fell/the Pettycoats and Gown perfume/And waft a Stink round every Room,"' which a few people hazarded to say that it was maybe a little bit *disturbing* that Siobhan had seemingly memorized this... and thereupon the latter part of the discussion turned more toward intergender bathroom habits and the various small traumas of cohabitation with a male partner, or even just when you reached the stage where one or the other of you were staying over a lot, and the table conversation broke up into a certain number of overlapping smaller exchanges while some people ordered different kinds of coffee and Laurel Manderley sucked abstractedly on an olive pit.

'If you ask me, there's something sketchy about a guy whose bathroom is all full of those little deodorizers and scented candles. I always tend to think, here's somebody who kind of denies his own humanity.'

'It's bad news if it's a big deal either way. It's never a good sign.'

'But you don't want him totally uninhibited, don't get me wrong.'

'Because if he's going around farting in front of you or something, it means on some level he's thinking you're just one of the guys, and that's always bad news.'

'Because then how long before he's sitting there on the couch all day farting and telling you to go get him a beer?'

'If I'm out in the kitchen and Pankaj wants a beer or something, he *knows* he better say please.'

The shade who wore Pucci and two other research interns were evidently going with three guys from *Forbes* to some kind of infamous annual *Forbes* house party on Fire Island over the holiday weekend, which, since the Fourth was on Wednesday this year, meant the following weekend.

'I don't know,' THE THUMB's head intern said. 'My parents pass gas in front of each other. There's something sweet about it, like it's just another part of life together. They'll keep right on talking or whatever as if nothing happened.' THE THUMB was the name of the section of *Style* that contained mini reviews of film and television, as well as certain types of commercial music and books, each review accompanied by a special thumb icon whose angle conveyed visually how positive the assessment was.

'Although that in itself shows there's something different about it. If you sneeze or yawn, there's something said. A fart, though, is always ignored, even though everybody knows what's just happened.'

Some interns were laughing; some were not.

'The silence communicates some kind of unease about it.'

'A conspiracy of silence.'

'Shannon was on some friend of a friend thing at the Hat with some awful guy in she said an XMI Platinum sweater, with that awful Haverford type of jaunty misogyny, that was going on and on about why do girls always go to the bathroom together, like what's up with that, and Shannon looks at the guy like what planet did you just land from, and says well it should be obvious we're doing *cocaine* in there, is why.'

'One of those guys where you're like, hello, my eyes are *up here*.'

'Carlos says in some cultures the etiquette actually calls for passing gas in some situations.'

'The well known Korean thing about you burp to say thank you.'

'My parents had this running joke—they called a fart an intruder. They'd look at each other over the paper and be, like, "I do believe there's an intruder present." '

Laurel Manderley, who had had an idea, was rooting through her Fendi for her personal cell.

'My mom would just about drop over dead if anybody ever cut one in front of her. It's just not even imaginable.'

A circulation intern named Laurel Rodde, who as a rule favored DKNY, and who wasn't exactly unpopular but no one felt like they knew her very well despite all the time they all spent with one another, and who usually barely said a word at the working lunches, suddenly said: 'You know, did anybody when they were little ever have this thing where you think of your shit as sort of like your baby and sometimes want to hold it and talk to it and almost cry or feel guilty about flushing it and dream sometimes of your shit in a little sort of little stroller with a bonnet and bottle and still sometimes in the bathroom look at it and give a little wave like, bye bye, as it goes down, and then feel a void?' There was an uncomfortable silence. Some of the interns looked at one another out of the corner of their eye. They were at a stage where they were now too adult and socially refined to respond with a drawn out semicruel 'Oooo-kaaaay,' but you could tell that a few of them were thinking it. The circulation intern, who'd gone a bit pink, was bent to her salad once more.

←

Citing bridgework, Atwater again declined the half piece of gum that Mrs. Moltke offered. All the parked car's windows ran in a way that would have been pretty had there been more overall light. The rain had steadied to the point where he could just barely discern the outline of a large sign in the distance below, which Amber had told him marked the nitrogen fixative factory's entrance.

'The man's conflicted, is all,' Mrs. Moltke said. 'He's about the most private man you'd ever like to see. In the privy I mean.' She chewed her gum well, without extraneous noises. She had to be at least 6'1". 'It surely weren't like that at my house growing up, I can tell you. It's a matter of how folks grow up, wouldn't you say?'

'This is fascinating,' Atwater said. They had been parked at the little road's terminus for perhaps ten minutes. The tape recorder was placed on his knee, and the subject's wife now reached over across herself and turned it off. Her hand was large enough to cover the recorder and also make liberal contact with his knee on either side. Atwater still had the same pants size he'd had in college, though these slacks were obviously a great deal newer. In the low barometric pressure of the storm, he was now entirely stuffed up, and was mouth breathing, which caused his lower lip to hang outward and made him look even more childlike. He was breathing rather more rapidly than he was aware of.

It was not clear whether Amber's small smile was for him or herself or just what. 'I'm going to tell you some background facts that you can't write about, but it'll help you understand our situation here. Skip—can I call you Skip?'

'Please do.'

Rain beat musically on the Cavalier's roof and hood. 'Skip, between just us two now, what we've got here is a boy whose folks beat him witless all through growing up. That whipped on him with electric cords and burnt on him with cigarettes and made him eat out in the shed when his mother thought his manners weren't up to snuff for her high and mighty table. His daddy was all right, it was more his mother. One of this churchy kind that's so upright and proper in church but back at home she's crazy evil, whipped her own children with cords and I don't know what all.' At the mention of church, Atwater's facial expression had become momentarily inward and difficult to read. Amber Moltke's voice was low in register but still wholly feminine, with a quality that cut through the rain's sound even at low volume. It reminded Atwater somewhat of Lauren Bacall at the end of her career, when the aged actress had begun to look more and more like a scalded cat but still possessed of a voice that affected one's nervous system in profound ways, as a child.

The artist's wife said: 'I know that one time when he was a boy that she came in and I think caught Brint playing with himself maybe, and made him come down in the sitting room and do it in front of them, the family, that she made them all sit there and watch him. Do you follow what I'm saying, Skip?'

The most significant sign of an approaching tornado would be a greenish cast to the ambient light and a sudden drop in pressure that made one's ears pop.

'His daddy didn't outright abuse him, but he was half crazy,' Amber said, 'a deacon. A man under great pressure from his own demons that he wrestled with. And I know one time Brint saw her take and beat a little baby kittycat to death with a skillet for messing on the kitchen floor. When he was in his high chair, watching. A little kittycat. Well,' she said. 'What do you suppose a little boy's toilet training is going to be like with folks like that?'

Nodding vigorously being one of his tactics for drawing people out in interviews, Atwater was nodding at almost everything the subject's wife was saying. This, together with the fact that his arms were still out straight before him, lent him a somnambulist aspect. Wind gusts caused the car to shimmy slightly in the clearing's mud.

By this time, Amber Moltke had shifted her mass onto her left haunch and brought her great right leg up and was curled kittenishly in such a way as to incline herself toward Atwater, gazing at the side of his face. She smelled of talcum powder and Big Red. Her leg was like something you could slide down into some kind of unimaginable chasm. The chief outward sign that Atwater was affected one way or the other by the immense sexual force field around Mrs. Moltke was that he continued to grip the Cavalier's steering wheel tightly with both hands and to face directly ahead as though still driving. There was very little air in the car. He had an odd subtle sense of ascent, as if the car were slightly rising. There was no real sign of any type of overhead view, or even of the tiny road's dropoff to SR 252 and the nitrogen works that commenced just ahead—he was going almost entirely on Mrs. Moltke's report of where they were.

'This is a man, now, that will leave the premises to break wind. That closes the privy door and locks it and turns on the exhaust fan and this little radio he's got, and runs water, and sometimes puts a rolled up towel in the crack of the door when he's in there doing his business. Brint I mean.'

'I think I understand what you're saying.'

'Most times he can't do his business if there's somebody even there. In the house. The man thinks I believe him when he says he's going to just go driving around.' She sighed. 'So Skip, this is a very very shy individual in this department. He's wounded inside. He wouldn't hardly say boo when I first met him.'

Following college, Skip Atwater had done a year at IU-Indianapolis's prestigious grad journalism program, then landed a cub spot at the Indianapolis *Star,* and there had made no secret of his dream of someday writing a syndication grade human interest column for a major urban daily, until the assistant city editor who'd hired him told Skip in his first annual performance review, among other things, that as a journalist Atwater struck him as being polished but about two inches deep. After which performance review Atwater had literally run for the privacy of the men's room and there had struck his own chest with his fist several times because he knew that at heart it was true: his fatal flaw was an ineluctably light, airy prose sensibility. He had no innate sense of tragedy or preterition or complex binds or any of the things that made human beings' misfortunes significant to one another. He was all upbeat angle. The editor's blunt but kindly manner had made it worse. Atwater could write a sweet commercial line, he'd acknowledged. He had compassion, of a certain frothy sort, and drive. The editor, who always wore a white dress shirt and tie but never a jacket, had actually put his arm around Atwater's shoulders. He said he liked Skip enough to tell him the truth, because he was a good kid and just needed to find his niche. There were all different kinds of reporting. The editor said he had acquaintances at *USA Today* and offered to make a call.

Atwater, who also possessed an outstanding verbal memory, retained almost verbatim the questions Laurel Manderley had left him with on the phone at Ye Olde Country Buffet after he'd summarized the morning's confab and characterized the artist as catatonically inhibited, terribly shy, scared of his shadow, and so forth. What Laurel had said didn't yet add up for her in the story was how the stuff got seen in the first place: 'What, he gives it to somebody? This catatonically shy guy calls somebody into the bathroom and says, Hey, look at this extraordinary thing I just pooped out of me? I can't see anybody over age six doing that, much less somebody that shy. Whether it's a hoax or not, the guy's got to be some kind of closet exhibitionist,' she'd opined. Every instinct Atwater possessed had since been crying out that this was the piece's fulcrum and UBA, the universalizing element that made great soft news go: the conflict between Moltke's extreme personal shyness and need for privacy on the one hand versus his involuntary need to express what lay inside him through some type of personal expression or art. Everyone experienced this conflict on some level. Though lurid and potentially disgusting, the mode of production in this case simply heightened the conflict's voltage, underlined the stakes in bold, made it at once deep and accessible for *Style* readers, many of whom scanned the magazine in the bathroom anyway, all the salarymen knew.

Atwater, however, was, since the end of a serious involvement some years prior, also all but celibate, and tended to be extremely keyed up and ambivalent in any type of sexually charged situation, which unless he was off base this increasingly was—which in retrospect was partly why, in the stormy enclosure of the rental car with the pulverizingly attractive Amber Moltke, he had committed one of the fundamental errors in soft news journalism: asking a centrally important question before he was certain just what answer would advance the interests of the piece.

↓

Only the third shift attendant knew that R. Vaughn Corliss slept so terribly, twining in and out of the sheets with bleatings of the purest woe, foodlessly chewing, sitting up and looking wildly about, feeling at himself and moaning, crying out that no he wouldn't go there, not there not again no please. The high concept mogul was always up with the sun, and his first act after stripping the bed and placing his breakfast order was to erase the disk of the bedroom's monitor. A selected few nights' worth of these disks the attendant had slipped in during deep sleep and copied, however, as a de facto form of unemployment insurance, since Corliss's temper and caprice were well known; and the existence of these pirate disks was also known to certain representatives of Eckleschafft-Böd whose business it was to know such things.

It was only if, after sheep, controlled breathing, visualizing IV pentothal drips, and mentally reviewing in close detail a special collector's series of photographs of people on fire entitled *People on Fire,* Corliss still could not fall or fall back asleep that he'd resort to the failsafe: imagining the faces of everyone he had loved, hated, feared, known, or even ever seen all assembling and accreting as pixels into a pointillist image of a single great all devouring eye whose pupil was Corliss's own.

In the morning, the reinvented high concept cable entrepreneur's routine was invariant and always featured a half hour of pretend rowing on a machine that could simulate both resistance and crosscurrent, a scrupulously Fletcherized breakfast, and a session of the 28 lead facial biofeedback in which microelectric sensors were affixed to individual muscle groups and exhaustive daily practice yielded the ability to form, at will, any of the 216 facial expressions common to all known cultures. Corliss was in constant contact via headset cellular throughout this regimen.

Unlike most driven business visionaries he was not, when all was said and done, an unhappy man. He felt sometimes an odd complex emotion that, when broken down and examined in quiet reflection, revealed itself to be self envy, which appears near the top of certain Maslovian fulfillment pyramids as a rare and culturally specific form of joy. The sense Skip Atwater had gotten, after a brief and highly structured interface with

Corliss for a WITW piece on the All Ads cable channel in 1999, was that the producer's reclusive, eccentric persona was a conscious performance or imitation, and that Corliss (whom Atwater had personally liked and not found all that intimidating) was in reality a gregarious, backslapping, people type person who affected an hermetic torment for reasons which Atwater's notebooks contained several multipage theories on, none of which appeared in the article published in *Style*.

↓

Atwater and Mrs. Moltke were now unquestionably breathing each other's air; the Cavalier's glass surfaces were almost entirely steamed over. At the same time, an imperfection in its gasket's seal was allowing rain droplets to enter and move in a complex system of paths down his window. These branching paths and tributaries were in the left periphery of the journalist's vision; Amber Moltke's face loomed vividly in the right. Unlike Mrs. Atwater, the artist's wife had a good firm chin with no wattles, though her throat's girth was extraordinary—Atwater could not have gotten around it with both hands.

'The shyness and woundedness must be complex, though,' the journalist said. 'Given that the pieces are public. Publicly displayed.' He had already amassed a certain amount of technical detail about the preparation of the displays, back at the Moltkes' duplex. The pieces were not varnished or in any way chemically treated. They were, however, sprayed lightly with a fixative when fresh or new, to help preserve their shape and intricate detail—evidently some of the man's early work had become cracked or distorted when allowed to dry completely. Atwater knew that freshly produced pieces of art were placed on a special silver finish tray, an heirloom of some sort from Mrs. Moltke's own family, then covered in common kitchen plastic wrap and allowed to cool to room temperature before the fixative was applied. Skip could imagine the steam from a fresh new piece fogging the Saran's interior and making it difficult to see the thing itself until the wrap was removed and discarded. Only later, in the midst of all the editorial wrangling over his piece's typeset version, would Atwater learn that the fixative in question was a common brand of aerosol styling spray whose manufacturer advertised in *Style*.

Amber gave a brief laugh. 'We're not exactly talking the big time. Two bean festivals and the DAR craft show.'

'Well, and of course the fair.' Atwater was referring to the Franklin County Fair, which like most county fairs in eastern Indiana was held in

June, quite a bit earlier than the national average. The reasons for this were complicated, agricultural, and historically bound up with Indiana's refusal to participate in Daylight Savings Time, which caused no end of hassles for certain commodities markets at the Chicago Board of Trade. Atwater's own childhood experiences had been of the Madison County Fair, held during the third week of each June on the outskirts of Mounds State Park, but he assumed that all county fairs were roughly similar. He had unconsciously begun to do the thing with his fist again.

'Well, although the fair ain't exactly your big time either.'

Also from childhood experience, Skip Atwater knew that the slight squeaks and pops one could hear when Amber laughed were from different parts of her complex foundation garment as they strained and moved against one another. Her kneesized left elbow now rested on the seat back between them, leaving her left hand free to play and make tiny languid motions in the space between her head and his. A head nearly twice the size of Atwater's own. Her hair was wiglike in overall configuration, but it had a high protein luster no real wig could ever duplicate.

His right arm still rigidly out against the Cavalier's wheel, Atwater turned his head a few more degrees toward her. 'This, though, will be very public. *Style* is about as public as you can get.'

'Well, except for TV.'

Atwater inclined his head slightly to signify concession. 'Except for TV.'

Mrs. Moltke's hand, with its multiple different rings, was now within just inches of the journalist's large red right ear. She said: 'Well, I look at *Style*. I've been looking at *Style* for years. I don't bet there's a body in town that hasn't looked at *Style* or *People* or one of you all.' The hand moved as if it were under water. 'Sometimes it's hard keeping you all straight. After your girl there called, I said to Brint it was a man coming over from *People* when I was telling him to go on and get cleaned up for company.'

Atwater cleared his throat. 'So you see my point, then, which in no way forms any sort of argument against the piece or Mr. Moltke's—'

'Brint.'

'Against Brint's consenting to the piece.' Atwater would also every so often give a small but vigorous all body shiver, involuntary, rather like a wet dog shaking itself, which neither party commented on. Bits of wind-blown foliage hit the front and rear windshields and remained for a moment or two before they were washed away. The sky could really have been any color at all and there would be no way to know. Atwater now tried to rotate his entire upper body toward Mrs. Moltke: 'But he will need to know what he's in for. If my editors give the go ahead, which I should again stress I have every confidence they ultimately will, one condition is likely to be the presence of some sort of medical authority to authenticate the...circumstances of creation.'

'You're saying in there with him?' The gusts of her breath seemed to strike every little cilium on Atwater's cheek and temple. Her right hand still covered the recorder and several inches of Atwater's knee on either side. Her largo pulse was visible in the trembling of her bust, which was understandably prodigious and also now pointed Atwater's way. Probably no more than four inches separated the bust from his right arm, which was still held out stiffly and attached to the steering wheel. Atwater's other fist was pumping like mad down beside the driver's door.

'No, no, not necessarily, but probably right outside, and ready to perform various tests and procedures on the...on it the minute Mr. Moltke, Brint, is finished. Comes out with it.' Another intense little shiver.

Amber gave another small mirthless laugh.

'I'm sure you know what I mean,' Atwater said. 'Temperature and constitution and the lack of any sort of sign of any human hand or tool or anything employed in the...process of the...'

'And then it'll come out.'

'The piece, you mean,' Atwater said. She nodded. In a way that made no physical sense given their respective sizes, Atwater's eyes seemed now to be exactly level with hers, and without being aware of it he blinked whenever she did, though her hand's small circles often supervened.

Atwater said: 'As I've said, I have every confidence that yes, it will.'

At the same time, the journalist was also trying not to indulge himself by imagining Laurel Manderley's reaction to the faxed reproductions of the artist's pieces as they slowly emerged from the machine. He felt that he knew almost all the different permutations her face would go through.

Nor was it clear whether Mrs. Moltke was looking at his ear or at the underwater movements of her own hand up next to the ear. 'And what you're saying is then, why, to get ready, because once it comes out nothing will be the same. Because there'll be attention.'

'I would think so, yes.' He tried to turn a little further. 'Of various different kinds.'

'You're saying other magazines. Or TV, the Internet.'

'It's often difficult to predict the forms of public attention or to know in advance what—'

'But after this kind of amount of attention you're saying there might be art galleries wanting to handle it. For sale. Do art galleries do auctions, or they just put it out with a price sticker on it and folks come and shop, or what all?'

Atwater was aware that this was a very different type and level of exchange than the morning's confab in the Moltkes' home. It was hard for him not to feel that Amber might be patronizing him a bit, playing up to a certain stereotype of provincial naiveté—he did this himself in certain situations at *Style*. At the same time, he felt that to some extent she was sincere in deferring to him because he lived and worked in New York City, the cultural heart of the nation—Atwater was absurdly gratified by this kind of thing. The whole geographical deference issue could get very complicated and abstract. At the right periphery, he could see that a certain delicate pattern Amber was tracing in the air near his ear was actually the cartography of that ear, its spirals and intending whorls. Sensitive from childhood about his ears' size and hue, Atwater had worn either baseball caps or knit caps all the way through college.

Ultimately, the journalist's failure to think the whole thing through and decide just how to respond was itself a form of decision. 'I think they do both,' he told her. 'Sometimes there are auctions. Sometimes a special exhibit, and potential buyers will come for a large party on the first day, to meet the artist. Often called an art opening.' He was facing the windshield again. The rain came no less hard but the sky looked perhaps to be lightening—although, on the other hand, the steam of their exhalations against the window was itself whitish and might act as some type of optical filter. At any rate, Atwater knew that it was often at the trailing end of a storm front that funnels developed. 'The initial key,' he said, 'will be arranging for the right photographer.'

'Some professional type shots, you mean.'

'The magazine has both staff photographers and freelancers the photo people like to use for various situations. The politics of influencing them as to which particular photographer they might send all gets pretty involved, I'm afraid.' Atwater could taste his own carbon dioxide in the car's air. 'The key will be producing some images that are carefully lit and indirect and tasteful and yet at the same time emphatic in being able to show what he's able to . . . just what he's achieved.'

'Already. You mean the doodads he's come out with already.'

'There will be no way to even pitch it at the executive level without real photos, I don't think,' Atwater said.

For a moment there was only the wind and rain and a whisking sound of microfiber, due to Atwater's fist.

'You know what's peculiar? Is sometimes I can hear it and then other times not,' Amber said quietly. 'That you said up to home you were from back here, and sometimes I can hear it and then other times you sound more . . . all business, and I can't hear it in you at all.'

'I'm originally from Anderson.'

'Up by Muncie you mean. Where all the big mounds are.'

'Anderson's got the mounds, technically. Though I went to school in Muncie, at Ball State.'

'There's some more right here, up to Mixerville off the lake. They still say they don't know who all made those mounds. They just know they're old.'

'The sense I get is there are still competing theories.'

'Dave Letterman on the TV talks about Ball State all the time, that he was at. He's from here someplace.'

'He graduated long before I got there, though.'

She did touch his ear now, though her finger was too large to fit inside or trace the auricle's whorls and succeeded only in occluding Atwater's hearing on that side, so that he could hear his own heartbeat and his voice seemed newly loud to him over the rain:

'But with the operative question being whether he'll do it.'

'Brint,' she said.

'Respecting the subject of the piece.'

'If he'll sit still for it you mean.'

The finger kept Atwater from turning his head, so that he could not see whether Mrs. Moltke was smiling or had made a deliberate sally or just what. 'Since he's so agonizingly shy, as you've explained. You must—he's got to be able to see already that it will be, to some extent, a bit invasive.' Atwater was in no way acknowledging the finger in his ear, which did not move or turn but simply stayed there. The feeling of queer levitation persisted, however. 'Invasive of his privacy, of your privacy. And I don't exactly get the sense, which I respect, that Mr. Moltke burns to share his art with the world, or necessarily to get a lot of personal exposure.'

'He'll do it,' Amber said. The finger withdrew slightly but was still in contact with his ear. The very oldest she could possibly be was 28.

The journalist said: 'Because I'll be honest with you, I think it's an extraordinary thing and an extraordinary story, but Laurel and I are going to have to go right to the mat with the Executive Editor to secure a commitment to this piece, and it would make things really awkward if Mr. Moltke suddenly demurred or deferred or got cold feet or decided it was all just too private and invasive a process.'

She did not ask who Laurel was. She was wholly on her left flank now, her luminous knee up next to her hand on the Daewoo unit, and only the bunched hem of his raincoat separating her knee and his, her great bosom crushed and jutting and its heartbeat's quiver bringing one breast within inches of the Talbott's shawl collar. He kept envisioning her having to strike or swat the artist before he'd respond to the simplest query. And the strange fixed grin, which probably would not photograph well at all.

Again the artist's wife said: 'He'll do it.'

Unbeknownst to Atwater, the Cavalier's right hand tires were now sunk in mud almost to the valves. What he felt as an occult force rotating him up and over toward Mrs. Moltke in clear contravention of the most basic journalistic ethics was in fact simple gravity: the compartment was now at a 20 degree angle. Wind gusts shook the car like a maraca, and the journalist could hear the sounds of thrashing foliage and windblown debris doing God knew what to the rental's paint.

'I have no doubt,' the journalist said. 'I think I'm just trying to determine for myself why you're so sure, although obviously I'm going to defer to your judgment because he is your husband and if anyone knows another's heart it's obviously—'

What he felt in the first instant to be Mrs. Moltke's hand over his mouth turned out to be her forefinger held to his lips, chin, and lower jaw in an intimate shush. Atwater could not help wondering whether it was the same finger that had just been in his ear. Its tip was almost the width of both of his nostrils together.

'He will because he'll do it for me, Skip. Because I say.'

'Mn srtny gld t—'

'But go on and ask it.' Mrs. Moltke backed the finger off a bit. 'We should get it out here up front between us. Why I'd want my husband known for his shit.'

'Though of course the pieces are so much more than that,' Atwater said, his eyes appearing to cross slightly as he gazed at the finger. Another compact shiver, a whisking sound of fabric and his forehead running with sweat. The cinnamon heat and force of her exhalations like one of the heating grates along Columbus Circle where coteries of homeless sat in the winter in fingerless gloves and balaklava hoods, their eyes flat and pitiless as Atwater hurried past. He had to engage the car's battery in order to crack his window, and a burst of noise from the radio made him jump.

Amber Moltke appeared very still and intent. 'Still and all, though,' she said. 'To have your TV reporters or Dave Letterman or that skinny one real late at night making their jokes about it, and folks reading in *Style* and thinking about Brint's bowel, about him sitting there in the privy moving his bowel in some kind of special way to make something like that come out. Because that's his whole hook, Skip, isn't it. Why you're here in the first place. That it's his shit.'

→

It turned out that a certain Richmond IN firm did a type of specialty shipping where they poured liquid styrene around fragile items, producing a very light form fitting insulation. The Federal Express outlet named on the box's receipt, however, was in Scipio IN, which was also featured in the address on the Kinko's cover sheet that had accompanied Sunday's faxed photos, which faxes the next morning's Fed Ex rendered more or less moot or superfluous, so that Laurel Manderley couldn't quite see why Atwater'd gone to the trouble.

At Monday's working lunch, Laurel Manderley's deceptively simple idea with respect to the package's contents had been to hurry back and place them out on Ellen Bactrian's desk before she returned from her dance class, so that they would be sitting there waiting for her, and not to say a word or try to prevail on Ellen in any way, but simply to let the pieces speak for themselves. This was, after all, what her own salaryman appeared to have done, giving Laurel no warning whatsoever that art was on the way.

→

The following was actually part of a lengthy telephone conversation on the afternoon of 3 July between Laurel Manderley and Skip Atwater, the latter having literally limped back to the Mount Carmel Holiday Inn after negotiating an exhaustive and nerve wracking series of in situ authenticity tests at the artist's home.

'And what's with that address, by the way?'

'Willkie's an Indiana politician. The name is ubiquitous here. I think he may have run against Truman. Remember the photo of Truman holding up the headline?'

'No, I mean the half. What, fourteen and a half Willkie?'

'It's a duplex,' Atwater said.

'Oh.'

There had been a brief silence, one whose strangeness might have been only in retrospect.

'Who lives on the other side?'

There had been another pause. It was true that both salaryman and intern were extremely tired and discombobulated by this point.

The journalist said: 'I don't know yet. Why?'

To which Laurel Manderley had no good answer.

←

In the listing Cavalier, at or about the height of the thunderstorm, Atwater shook his head. 'It's more than that,' he said. He was, to all appearances, sincere. He appeared genuinely concerned that the artist's wife not think his motives exploitative or sleazy. Amber's finger was still right near his mouth. He told her it was not yet entirely clear to him how she viewed her husband's pieces or understood the extraordinary power they exerted. Rain and debris notwithstanding, the windshield was too steamed over for Atwater to see that the view of SR 252 and the fixative works was now tilted 30 or more degrees, like a faulty altimeter. Still facing forward with his eyes rotated way over to the right, Atwater told the artist's wife that his journalistic motives had been mixed at first, maybe, but that verily he did now believe. When they'd taken him through Mrs. Moltke's sewing room and out back and pulled open the angled green door and led him down the raw pine steps into the storm cellar and he'd seen the pieces all lined up in graduated tiers that way, something had happened. The truth was he'd been moved, and he said he'd understood then for the first time, despite some prior exposure to the world of art through a course or two in college, how people of discernment could say they felt moved and redeemed by serious art. And he believed this was serious, real, bona fide art, he told her. At the same time, it was also true that Skip Atwater had not been in a sexually charged situation since the previous New Year's annual YMSP2 party's bout of drunken fanny photocopying, when he'd gotten a glimpse of one of the circulation interns' pudenda as she settled on the Canon's plexiglass sheet, which afterward was unnaturally warm.

↓

Registered motto of Chicago IL's O Verily Productions, which for complicated business reasons appeared on its colophon in Portuguese:

CONSCIOUSNESS IS NATURE'S NIGHTMARE

↓

Amber Moltke, however, pointed out that if conventionally produced, the pieces would really be just small reproductions that showed a great deal of expression and technical detail, that what made them special in the first place was what they were and how they came out fully formed from her husband's behind, and she again asked rhetorically why on earth she would want these essential facts highlighted and talked about, that they were his shit—pronouncing the word shit in a very flat and matter of fact way—and Atwater admitted that he did wonder about this, and that the whole question of the pieces' production and how this rendered them somehow simultaneously both more and less natural than conventional artworks seemed dizzyingly abstract and complex, and that but in any event there would almost inevitably be some elements that some *Style* readers would find distasteful or invasive in an ad hominem way, and confessed that he did wonder, both personally and professionally, whether it wasn't possible that Mr. or at least Mrs. Moltke wasn't perhaps more ambivalent about the terms of public exposure than she was allowing herself to realize.

And Amber inclined even closer to Skip Atwater and said to him that she was not. That she'd thought on the whole business long and hard at the first soybean festival, long before *Style* even knew that Mr. and Mrs. B. F. Moltke of Mount Carmel even existed. She turned slightly to push at her mass of occipital curls, which had tightened shinily in the storm's moist air. Her voice was a dulcet alto with something almost hypnotic in the timbre. There were tiny random fragments of spindrift rain through the window's opened crack, and a planar flow of air that felt blessed, and the front seat's starboard list became more severe, which as he rose so very slowly gave Atwater the sensation that either he was physically enlarging or Mrs. Moltke was diminishing somewhat in relative size, or at any rate that the physical disparity between them was becoming less marked. It occurred to Atwater that he could not recall when he had eaten last. He could not feel his right leg anymore, and his ear's outer flange felt nearly aflame.

Mrs. Moltke said how she'd thought about it and realized that most people didn't even get such a chance, and that this here was hers, and Brint's. To somehow stand out. To distinguish themselves from the great huge faceless mass of folks that watched the folks that did stand out. On the TV and in venues like *Style*. In retrospect, none of this turned out to be true. To be known, to matter, she said. To have church or Ye Olde Buffet or the new Bennigan's at the Whitcomb Outlet Mall get quiet when her and Brint came in, and to feel people's eyes, the weight of their gaze. That it made a difference someplace when they came in. To pick up a copy of *People* or *Style* at the beautician's and see herself and Brint looking back out at her. To be on TV. That this was it. That surely Skip could understand. That yes, despite the overall dimness of Brint Moltke's bulb and a lack of personal verve that almost approached death in life, when she'd met the drain technician at a church dance in 1997 she'd somehow known that he was her chance. His hair had been slicked down with aftershave and he'd worn white socks with his good suit, and had missed a belt loop, and yet she'd known. Call it a gift, this power—she was different and marked to someday stand out and she'd known it. Atwater himself had worn white socks with dress slacks until college, when his fraternity brothers had finally addressed the issue in Mock Court. His right hand still gripping the steering wheel, Atwater's head was now rotated just as far as it would go in order to look more or less directly into Amber's great right eye, whose lashes ruffled his hair when she fluttered them. No more than a quarter moon of tire now showed above the mud on each of the right side's wheels.

What Amber appeared now to be confiding to him in the rented Cavalier struck Atwater as extremely open and ingenuous and naked. The sheer preterite ugliness of it made its admission almost beautiful, Atwater felt. Bizarrely, it did not occur to him that Amber might be speaking to him as a reporter instead of a fellow person. He knew that there was an artlessness about him that helped people open up, and that he possessed a measure of true empathy. It's why he considered himself fortunate to be tasked to WHAT IN THE WORLD rather than entertainment or beauty/fashion, budgets and prestige notwithstanding. The truth is that what Amber Moltke was confiding seemed to Atwater very close to the core of the American experience he wanted to capture in his journalism. It was also the tragic conflict at the heart of *Style* and all soft organs like it. The paradoxical intercourse of audience and celebrity. The suppressed awareness that the whole reason ordinary people found celebrity fascinating was that they were not, themselves, celebrities. That wasn't quite it. An odd thing was that his fist often stopped altogether when he thought abstractly. It was more the deeper, more tragic and universal conflict of which the celebrity paradox was a part. The conflict between the subjective centrality of our own lives versus our awareness of its objective insignificance. Atwater knew—as did everyone at *Style*, though by some strange unspoken consensus it was never said aloud—that this was the single great informing conflict of the American psyche. The management of insignificance. It was the great syncretic bond of US monoculture. It was everywhere, at the root of everything—of impatience in long lines, of cheating on taxes, of movements in fashion and music and art, of marketing. In particular, he thought it was alive in the paradoxes of audience. It was the feeling that celebrities were your intimate friends, coupled with the inchoate awareness that untold millions of people felt the same way—and that the celebrities themselves did not. Atwater had had contact with a certain number of celebrities (there was no way to avoid it at a BSG), and they were not, in his experience, very friendly or considerate people. Which made sense when one considered that celebrities were not actually functioning as real people at all, but as something more like symbols of themselves.

There had been eye contact between the journalist and Amber Moltke this whole time, and by now Atwater could also look down, as it were, to see the complex whorls and parts in the young wife's hair and the numerous clips and plastic clamps that were buried in its lustrous mass. There was still the occasional ping of hail. And it was also the world altering pain of accepting one's individual flaws and limitations and the tautological unattainability of our dreams and the dim indifference in the eyes of the circulation intern one tries, at the stroke of the true millennium, to share one's ambivalence and pain with. Most of these latter considerations occurred during a brief diversion from the exchange's main thread into something having to do with professional sewing and tatting and customized alterations, which evidently was what Amber did out of her home to help supplement her husband's income from TriCounty Roto Rooter: 'There's not a fiber swatch or pattern in this world I cannot work with, that's another gift it pleased God to bestow and I'm thankful, it's restful and creative and keeps me out of trouble, these hands are not ever idle'—she holding up for one moment an actual hand, which could likely have gone all the way around Atwater's head and still been able to touch finger to thumb.

Skip Atwater's one and only serious involvement ever had been with a medical illustrator for the Anatomical Monograph Company, which was located off the Pendleton Pike just outside Indianapolis proper, specializing in intricate exploded views of the human brain and upper spine, as well as in lower order ganglia for neurological comparison. She had been only 5'0", and toward the relationship's end Atwater hadn't cared one bit for the way she had looked at him when he undressed or got out of the shower. One evening he'd taken her to a Ruth's Chris and had almost a hallucination or out of body experience in which he'd viewed himself écorché style from her imagined perspective as he ate, his jaw muscles working redly and esophagus contracting to move bits of bolus down. Only days later had come the shattering performance review from the *Star*'s assistant city editor, and Skip's life had changed forever.

→

Early Tuesday morning was the second time ever that Laurel Manderley had ascended to the executive offices of *Style* magazine, which required getting out and transferring to a whole different elevator at the 70th floor. By prior arrangement, Ellen Bactrian had gone up first and verified that the coast was clear. The sun was barely up yet. Laurel Manderley was alone in the elevator, wearing dark wool slacks, very plain Chinese slippers, and a matte black Issey Miyake shirt that was actually made of paper but looked more like some type of very fine opaque tulle. She looked pale and a little unwell; she was not wearing her facial stud. Through some principle of physics she didn't understand, the box in her arms felt slightly heavier when the elevator was in motion. Its total weight was only a few pounds at most. Apparently Ellen Bactrian's commuting routine with the executive intern was a purely informal one whereby they always met up at some certain spot just north of the Holland Tunnel to bike down together, but if either one wasn't at the spot at the designated time, the other just rode on ahead. The whole thing was very laid back. The interior of the first elevator was brushed steel; the one up from 70 had inlaid paneling and a console with tiny directories next to each floor's button. The entire trip took over five minutes, although the elevators themselves were so fast that some of the executive staff wore special earplugs for the rapid ascent.

Her only other time up had been with two other new interns and the WITW associate editor, as part of general orientation, and in the elevator the associate editor had put his arms up over his head and made his hands sharp like a diver's and said: 'Up, up, and away.'

←

Ever since he was a little boy, a deep perfusive flush to Atwater's ears and surrounding tissues was the chief outward sign that his mind was working to process disparate thoughts and impressions much faster than its normal rate. At these times one could actually feel heat coming off the ear itself, which may have accounted for the rapid self fanning motions that the immense, creamily etiolated seamstress made as she came back on topic and shared the following personal experience. The daytime television celebrity Phillip Spaulding of *Guiding Light* had, at some past point that Amber didn't specify, made a live promotional appearance at the opening of a Famous Barr store at Richmond's Galleria Mall, and she and a girl-friend had gone to see him, and Amber said she had realized then that her deepest and most life informing wish, she realized, was to someday have strangers feel about her mere appearance someplace the way she had felt, inside, about getting to stand near enough to Phillip Spaulding (who was evidently a serious hottie indeed, despite something strange or strangely formed about the cartilage of his nose so that it looked like the tip almost had a little dimple or cleft like you'd more normally see on a human chin, which Amber and her girlfriend had decided they ultimately found cute, and made Phillip Spaulding even more of a hottie because it made him look more like a real human being instead of the almost too perfect mannequins these serials sometimes thought folks wanted to see all the time) to reach out between all the other people there and actually touch him if she'd wanted to.

Skip Atwater, in the course of an involved argument with himself later about whether he had more accurately *engaged in* or *been subject to* an act of fraternization with a journalistic subject, would identify this moment as the crucial fulcrum or tipping point of the whole exchange. Already tremendously keyed up and abstracted by Mrs. Moltke's confidences, he found himself nearly overcome by the ingenuous populism of the Phillip Spaulding anecdote, and wished to activate his tiny tape recorder and, if Amber wouldn't repeat the vignette, to at least get her to allow him to repeat and record its gist on tape, along with the date and approximate time — not that he would ever use it for this or any other piece, but just for his own record of a completely perfect representative statement of what it was like to be one of the people to and for whom he wished his work in *Style* to try to speak, as something to help provide objective dignification of his work and to so to speak hold up shieldlike against the voices in his head that mocked him and said all he really did was write fluff pieces for a magazine most people read in the bathroom. What happened was that Atwater's attempts to subtly work his fingers under Amber's right hand and pry the hand up off the tape recorder on his knee were, in retrospect, evidently interpreted as an attempt at handholding or some other kind of physical affection, and apparently had a profound effect on Mrs. Moltke, for it was then that she brought her great head all the way around between Atwater's face and the steering wheel, and they were kissing — or rather Atwater was kissing at the left corner of Amber Moltke's lip, while her mouth covered nearly the entire right side of the journalist's face all the way to the earlobe. The fluttering motions of his hands as they beat ineffectually at her left shoulder were no doubt similarly misperceived as passion. The movements of Amber's rapid disrobing then began to cause the rented sedan to heave this way and that, and drove its starboard side even more deeply into the overlook's mud, and a very muffled set of what could have been either screams or cries of excitement began to issue from the tilted vehicle; and anyone trying to look in either side's window would have been unable to see any part of Skip Atwater at all.

4.

In New York it starts out as a puzzling marginal entry, 411 on Dish, 105 on Metro Cable. Viewers find it difficult to tell whether it's supposed to be commercial or Community Access or what. At first it's just montages of well known photos involving anguish or pain: a caved in Jackie next to LBJ as he's sworn in on the plane, that agonized Vietcong with the pistol to his head, the naked kids running from napalm. There's something about seeing them one right after another. A woman trying to bathe her thalidomide baby, faces through the wire at Belsen, Oswald crumpled around Ruby's fist, a noosed man as the mob begins to hoist, Brazilians on the ledge of a burning highrise. A loop of 1,200 of these, four seconds per, running 5:00 PM–1:00 AM EST; no sound; no evident ads.

A venture capital subsidiary of Televisio Brasilia underwrites The Suffering Channel's startup, but you cannot tell that, watching, at first. The only credits are photo ©s and a complicated glyph for O Verily Productions. After a few weeks, stage one TSC also streams on the Web at OVP.com\ suff.~vide. The legalities of the video are more tortuous, and it takes almost twice as long as projected for TSC stage two, in which the still photo series is gradually replaced by video clips in a complex loop that expands by four to five new segments per day, depending. Still in the planning phase, TSC stage three is tentatively scheduled for experimental insertion during autumn '01 Sweeps, although, as is SOP with creative enterprises everywhere, there's always flexibility and room to maneuver built in.

Like nearly all members of the paid press, Skip Atwater watched a good deal of satellite TV, much of it marginal or late night, and knew the O Verily glyph quite well. He still had contacts among R. Vaughn Corliss's support staff because of the All Ads All The Time Channel piece, which O Verily had ended up regarding as a fortuitous part of its second wave marketing. The AAATC was still up and pulling in a solid cable share, although response to the insertion of real paid ads within the stream of artifact ads had not had the dynamic impact on revenues that O Verily's prospectus had promised it very well might. Like many viewers, Atwater had been able to tell almost immediately which ads in the loops were paid spots and which were aesthetic objects, and regarded them accordingly, sometimes zapping out the paid ads altogether. And while the differences between an ad as entertainment and an ad that really tried to sell something were fascinating to academics, and had helped to galvanize the whole field of Media Studies in the late 1990s, they did little for the All

Ads Channel's profitability. This was one reason why O Verily had had to outsource capitalization for The Suffering Channel, which was in turn why TSC had almost immediately begun positioning itself for acquisition by a major corporation—the Brazilian VCs had required a 24 percent return on a two year window, meaning that O Verily Productions would retain only nominal creative control if its revenues did not reach a certain floor, which R. Vaughn Corliss had never, from the very start, had any intention of allowing to occur.

In Chicago, O Verily Productions operated out of north side facilities just a few blocks down Addison from WGN's great uplink tower, past which landmark Skip Atwater's rented Cavalier yawed and squeaked—pulling severely to the right from a bent transaxle that had worn one tire nearly bald on the trip up Interstate 65, and with the driver's side door bowed dramatically out from inside as if from some horrific series of impacts, about which neither Hertz Inc. nor *Style*'s Accounting staff would be pleased at all—on 2 July at 10:10 AM, nearly two hours late, because it had turned out that any highway speed over 45 mph produced a sound like a great deal of loose change rattling around inside the vehicle's engine.

As of June '01, The Suffering Channel was in the late stages of acquisition by AOL Time Warner, which was itself in Wall Street freefall and involved in talks with Eckleschafft-Böd over a putative merger that would in reality constitute E-Böd white knighting AOL TW against hostile takeover from a consortium of interests led by MCI Premium. The Suffering Channel's specs were thus already in the Eckleschafft-Böd pipeline, and it had required less than an hour of email finagling for Laurel Manderley to acquire certain variably relevant portions of them on behalf of her salaryman.

↓

Subj: **Re: Condidential**
Date: 6/24/01 10:31:37 AM Eastern Daylight Time
Content-Type: text/html; charset = us-ascii
From: k_böttger@ecklbdus.com
To: l_manderle@stylebsgmag.com
<!DOCTYPE html PRIV "-//W2C//DTD HTML 3.01 Transitional//EN">
Totalp CT: 6
Content-Transfer-Encoding: 7bit
Descramble-Content Reference: 122-XXX-idvM32XX
<head>
<title><title>
<head>

Condidential

Product: The Suffering Channel

Type: Reality/Gaper

Desc. of Product: Real life still and moving images of most intense available moments of human anguish

Production Lic.: O Verily Productions, Chicago and Waukegan, Ill

FCC Lic. Var. Status: [see Attachments, below]

Current Distribution: Regional/test through Dish (Chic., NYC), Dillard Cable (NE, SE grid), Video Sodalvo (Braz), Webstream at OVP.com\suff.~vd

Proposed Distribution: National via TWC Premium Options package (est. 2002), TWC and AOL key = SUFFERCH

Proposed Carryable Rate: Subsc. = $0.95 monthly stack on TWC Premium Options (= 1.2% increase) w/ prorate 22.5% per subscr. mo. 1-12. Variable projected prorate from Arbitron/Hale subsc Sweeps thereafter (standard) (Note: tracks MCI Premium's Adult Film Channel rate variance per prorate—see attached AFC spreadsheet from MCI source SS2-B4, below)

Bkg on O Verily Prod: CEO & Creative Executive, V. Corliss, 41, b. Gurnee, Ill, BA, Emerson College, MBA & JD, Pepperdine Univ. 3 yrs assoc producer, Dick Clark Prod./NBC, TV's Bloopers & Practical Jokes. 3 yrs line producer, Television Program Enterprises, Lifestyles of the Rich and Famous, Runaway with the Rich and Famous. 3 yrs exec prod., O.V.P., Surprise Wedding! I-III, Shocking Moments in Couples Counseling! I-II, 2.5 years exec producer, All Ads All The Time Channel [see Attachments, below]

Current O.V.P. Assets, Including Capital Equipment and Receivables: [See Attached LLC filing and spreadsheets, below] (Note: At counsel re photo and video permissions, releases [see USCC/F §212, vi-xlii in Attachments]: Reudenthal and Voss, P.C., Chicago and NY [see Attachments]

Precis of Sample Tape, 2-21-01 [Enclosure, acquisition specs Attached], Contents:

(1) Low light security video, mothers of two children, aged 7 and 9, with late stage cancer, Blue Springs Memorial Hospital Palliative Care Unit, Independence, Mo.

(2) High light security video, 10 year old male owner (dog), elderly male owner (dog), adult female owner (cats) on Free Euthanasia Day, Maddox Co. Humane Society, Maddox, Ga.

(3) High light instructional video, 50 year old male coming abruptly awake on table during abdominal surgery, requires physical restraint. Audio quality very high. Brigham and Women's Hospital, Boston, Mass.

(4a) Handheld video, electroshock interrogation of adolescent male subject, *Chambre d'Interrogation,* Cloutier Prison, Cameroon (subtitles).

(4b) Appended low light video (quality poor), video clip (4a) is shown to subject's relatives (pres. parents?), one of whom is revealed as real subject of the interrogation (subtitles, facial closeups digitally enhanced).

(5) Covert (?) low light video, Catholic Outreach Services support group for families of victims of murder/violent crime, San Luis Obispo, Cal [rights pending, see Attachments].

(6) High light legal liability video, stage 4 root canal and crown procedure for 46 year old female allergic to all anesthetics, Off. Dahood Chaterjee DDS, East Stroudsburg, Penn.

(7) Unused BBC2 shoulder mount video clip of *Necklace Party,* Transvaal Civil Province C7, Pretoria, South Afr (audio excellent).

(8) Handheld video, middle aged Rwandan (?) couple murdered by group w/ agric. implements (no audio, facial closeups digitally enhanced).

(9) Handheld video, shark attack and attempts at resuscitation on 18(?) year old surfer, Stinson Beach, Cal [rights pending, see Attachments].

(10) High light videotaped suicide note and handgun suicide of 60 year old patent attorney, Rutherford, NJ.

(11) High light legal liability video, intake and assessment interview of 28 year old suicidal female, Newton Wellesley Hospital, Newton, Mass.

(12) Low light security video, parents identify remains of 13 year old raped/dec. child, Emerson County Coroner's Office, Brentley, Tx.

(13) Webcam digital video, gang rape in dormitory room of 22 year old female designing real time *My Life* Web Site for college course, Lambuth University, Jackson, Tenn (video quality/FPS poor, high gain audio excellent, some faces digitally obscured [see Attachments]).

(14) High light security video, change of dressing for 3rd degree female (?) burn patient, Josephthal Memorial Hospital Burns Unit, Lawrence, Kan.

(15) Unused Deutsch 2DF shoulder mount video clip of Cholera Dispensary, Chang Hua Earthquake Zone, PRC.

2-01 Arbitron Rate for 1st Loop Serial Broadcast: 6.2 ± .6

2-01 Arbitron Rate for 2nd Loop Serial Broadcast: 21.0 ± .6

...and so forth.

↓

Ellen Bactrian had them out and arranged on Mrs. Anger's desk when the executive intern came in carrying her bicycle at 7:10. Three of the pieces were upright, one more base intensive and kind of spread out. Each sat on its own blank sheet of typing paper; it was the 20 pound rag bond used for executive letters and memos at *Style*. The pieces were in no particular order. The two editorial interns were in matching chairs in the room's two far corners. Ellen Bactrian had short dark blond hair and an arc of studs along the rim of one ear that every so often caught the light just right and flashed. On the wall near the office door, a large photorealist portrait depicted Mrs. Anger in a glove tight Saint Laurent suit and what almost looked like the kind of Capezio pumps professional dancers wore.

The executive intern, who had been student body president at both Choate and Vassar, always wore form fitting bike shorts for the commute and then changed in the executive lounge. It was another sign of her over-all favor and influence that Mrs. Anger let her store the bicycle in her office, which locked. The executive intern's arrival that morning was ever so slightly late, because the SE2 issue had finally closed the previous day. Mrs. Anger herself rarely rolled in much before 9:30.

The executive intern stood there still holding her bike, which weighed only eight and a half pounds, and staring at the pieces while the smile she'd come in with emptied out. She was acknowledged as more or less defining the standard of excellence for interns at *Style*. At least 5'10" in flats, with long auburn tresses that shone in even the meanest fluorescence, she managed to seem at once worldly and ethereal, and moved through the corridors and semiattached cubicles of the magazine like a living refutation of everything Marx ever stood for.

'We decided you needed to see them,' Ellen Bactrian said, 'before anybody said anything to anybody one way or the other.'

'Great glittering God.' The executive intern's front teeth emerged and pressed lightly on her lower lip. She had unconsciously assumed the same position that Skip Atwater and Ellen Bactrian and many of the patrons of the soybean festivals and fair had—standing several feet away, her posture somewhat S shaped because of the twin impulses to approach and recoil. She had on a brain shaped helmet and a Vassar sweatshirt with the collar and cuffs removed and the white flocking of the interior allowed to show. Her athletic shoes had special attachments that evidently clipped to the racing bike's pedals. The shadow she cast back against the wall was complex and distended.

'Are they something?' Laurel Manderley said quietly. She and Ellen Bactrian had brought in some additional lamps from the conference room next door because something about the overhead lights hit the fixative wrong and produced glare. Each of the pieces was fully and evenly lit. The executive office area was much quieter and more dignified than the sixteenth floor, but also a bit cool and stiff, Laurel thought.

The executive intern still held the bicycle. 'You didn't actually...?'

'They're sort of laminated. Don't worry.' Laurel Manderley had applied the additional fixative herself per instructions relayed through Skip Atwater, who was even then boarding a commuter flight to Muncie out of Midway. Laurel Manderley, who had also handled the whole rental car exchange unpleasantness, knew his timetable to the minute. She had declined the optional thing with the Saran, though. She felt like she might literally faint at any time.

'So was I jerking you off, or what?' Ellen Bactrian asked the executive intern.

Laurel Manderley made a little ta da gesture: 'It's the miraculous poo.'

One of her bicycle's wheels still idly turned, but the executive intern's eyes had not once moved. She said: 'Something isn't even the word.'

↓

Established fact: Almost no adult remembers the details or psychic fallout of her own toilet training. By the time one might have cause to want to know, it has been so long that you have to try asking your parents—which rarely works, because most parents will deny not only recollection but even original involvement in anything having to do with your toilet training. Such denials are basic psychological protection, since parenting can sometimes be a nasty business. All these phenomena have been exhaustively researched and documented.

R. Vaughn Corliss's most tightly held secret vision or dream, dating from when he was just beginning to detach from Leach and TPE and to conceive of reinventing himself as a force in high concept cable: a channel devoted wholly to images of celebrities shitting. Reese Witherspoon shitting. Juliette Lewis shitting. Michael Jordan shitting. Longtime House Minority Whip Dick Gephardt shitting. Pamela Anderson shitting. George F. Will, with his bow tie and pruny mouth, shitting. Former PGA legend Hale Irwin shitting. Stones bassist Ron Wood shitting. Pope John Paul shitting as special attendants hold his robes' hems up off the floor. Leonard Maltin, Annette Bening, Michael Flatley, either or both of the

Olsen twins, shitting. And so on. Helen Hunt. *The Price Is Right*'s Bob Barker. Tom Cruise. Jane Pauley. Talia Shire. Yasser Arafat, Timothy McVeigh, Michael J. Fox. Former HUD Secretary Henry Cisneros. The idea of real time footage of Martha Stewart perched shitting amid the soaps and sachets and color coordinated linens of her Connecticut estate's master bathroom was so powerful that Corliss rarely allowed himself to imagine it. It was not a soporific conceit. It was also, obviously, private. Tom Clancy, Margaret Atwood, bell hooks. Dr. James Dobson. Beleaguered IL Governor George Ryan. Peter Jennings. Oprah. He told no one of this dream. Nor of his corollary vision of the images beamed into space, digitally sequenced for maximum range and coherence, and of advanced alien species studying this footage in order to learn almost everything necessary about planet earth circa 2001.

He wasn't a madman; it could never fly. Still, though. There was Reality TV, which Corliss himself had helped lay the ground floor of, and the nascent trend toward absorbing celebrities into the matrix of violation and exposure that was Reality: celebrity bloopers, celebrities showing you around their homes, celebrity boxing, celebrity political colloquy, celebrity blind dating, celebrity couples counseling. Even serving time at Leach's TPE, Corliss could see that the logic of such programming was airtight and led inexorably to the ultimate exposures: celebrity major surgical procedures, celebrity death, celebrity autopsy. It only seemed absurd from outside the logic. How far along the final arc would Slo Mo High Def Full Sound Celebrity Defecation be? How soon before the idea ceased being too loony to mention aloud, to float as a balloon before the laughing heads of Development and Legal? Not yet, but not never. They'd laughed at Murdoch in Perth, once, Corliss knew.

Laurel Manderley was the youngest of four children, and her toilet training, which commenced around 30 months, had been casual and ad hoc and basically no big deal. The Atwater brothers' own had been early, brutal, and immensely effective—it was actually during toilet training that the elder twin had first learned to pump his left fist in self exhortation.

Little Roland Corliss, whose nanny was an exponent of a small and unapologetically radical splinter of the Waldorf educational movement, had experienced no formal toilet training at all, but rather just the abrupt unexplained withdrawal of all diapers at age four. This was the same age at which he had entered Holy Calvary Lutheran Preschool, where unambiguous social consequences motivated him to learn almost immediately what toilets were for and how to use them, rather like the child who is rowed way out and then taught to swim the old fashioned way.

↓

BSG is magazine industry shorthand for the niche comprising *People, Us, In Style, In Touch, Style,* and *Entertainment Weekly.* (For demographic reasons, *Teen People* is not usually included among the BSGs.) The abbreviation stands for big soft glossy, with soft in turn meaning the very most demotic kind of human interest.

As of July 2001, three of the six major BSGs are owned by Eckleschafft-Böd Medien A.G., a German conglomerate that controls nearly 40 percent of all US trade publishing.

Like the rest of the mainstream magazine industry, each of the BSG weeklies subscribes to an online service that compiles and organizes all contracted stringers' submissions to both national wires and Gannett, of which submissions roughly 8 percent ever actually run in the major news dailies. A select company of editorial interns, known sometimes as shades because of the special anodized goggles required by OSHA for intensive screen time, is tasked to peruse this service.

Skip Atwater, who was one of the rare and old school BSG journalists who actually pitched pieces as well as receiving assignments, was also one of the few paid staffers at *Style* who bothered to review the online service for himself. As a practical matter, he did so only when he was not in the field, and then usually at night, after his dogs had again gone to sleep, sitting up in his Ball State Cardinals cap with a glass of ale and operating his home desktop according to instructions which Laurel Manderley's predecessor had configured as a special template that fit along the top of the unit's keyboard. An AP stringer out of Indianapolis, filing from the Franklin County Fair on what was alleged to be the second largest Monte Cristo sandwich ever assembled, had included a curio about displays of extremely intricate and high class figurines made out of what the stringer had spelled fasces. The objets d'art themselves were not described — they had been arrayed in glass cases that were difficult to get near because of the crowds around them, and people's hands and exhalations had apparently smeared the glass so badly that even when you did finally shoulder your way up close the interiors were half obscured. Later, Skip Atwater would learn that these slanted glass cabinets were acquired from the tax sale of a failed delicatessen in Greensburg IN, which for decades had had a small and anomalous Hasidic community.

It was a word padding aside in a throwaway item unflagged by any of *Style*'s shades, and from his own native experience Atwater was disposed to assume that the things were probably crude little Elvises or Earnhardts made of livestock waste…except the display banner's allegedly quoted *Hands Free Art Crafts* caught his eye. The phrase appeared to make no sense unless automation were involved, which, as applied to livestock waste, would be curious indeed. Curiosity, of course, being more or less Skip Atwater's oeuvre with regard to WHAT IN THE WORLD. Not curiosity as in tabloid or freakshow, or rather all right sometimes borderline freakshow but with an upbeat thrust. The content and tone of all BSGs were dictated by market research and codified down to the smallest detail: celebrity profiles, entertainment news, hot trends, and human interest, with human interest representing a gamut in which the occasional freakshow item had a niche — but the rhetoric was tricky. BSGs were at pains to distinguish themselves from the tabloids, whose target market was wholly different. *Style*'s WITW items were people centered and always had to be both credible and uplifting, or latterly there at least had to be ancillary elements that were uplifting and got thumped hard.

Atwater could thump with the best. And he was old school and energetic: he ran down two or three possible WITW stories for every one that got written, and pitched things, and could rewrite other men's copy if asked to. The politics of rewrites could get sticky, and interns often had to mediate between the salarymen involved, but Atwater was known around *Style*'s editorial offices as someone who could both rewrite and get rewritten without being an asshole about it. At root, his reputation with staffers and interns alike was based in this: his consistent failure to be an asshole. Which could, of course, be a double edged sword. He was seen as having roughly the self esteem of a prawn. Some at *Style* found him fussy or pretentious. Others questioned his spontaneity. Sometimes the phrase queer duck was used. There was the whole awkward issue of his monotone wardrobe. The fact that he actually carried pictures of his dogs in his wallet was either endearing or creepy, depending whom you asked. A few of the sharper interns intuited that he'd had to overcome a great deal in himself in order to get this far.

He knew just what he was: a professional soft news journalist. We all make our adjustments, hence the term well adjusted. A babyfaced bantam with ears about which he'd been savagely teased as a boy — Jughead, Spock, Little Pitcher. A polished, shallow, earnest, productive, consummate corporate pro. Over the past three years, Skip Atwater had turned in some

70 separate pieces to *Style,* of which almost 50 saw print and a handful of others ran under rewriters' names. A volunteer fire company in suburban Tulsa where you had to be a grandmother to join. When Baby Won't Wait—Moms who never made it to the hospital tell their amazing stories. Drinking and boating: The other DUI. Just who really *was* Slim Whitman. This Grass Ain't Blue—Kentucky's other cash crop. He Delivers—81 year old obstetrician welcomes the grandchild of his own first patient. Former Condit intern speaks out. Today's forest ranger: He doesn't just sit in a tower. Holy Rollers—Inline skateathon saves church from default. Eczema: The silent epidemic. Rock 'n' Roll High School—Which future pop stars made the grade? Nevada bikers rev up the fight against myasthenia gravis. Head of the Parade—From Macy's to the Tournament of Roses, this float designer has done them all. The All Ads All The Time cable channel. Rock of Ages—These geologists celebrate the millennium in a whole new way. Sometimes he felt that if not for his schipperkes' love he would simply blow away and dissipate like milkweed. The women who didn't get picked for *Who Wants to Marry a Millionaire:* Where did they come from, to what do they return. Leapin' Lizards—The Gulf Coast's new alligator plague. One Lucky Bunch of Cats—A terminally ill Lotto winner's astounding bequest. Those new home cottage cheese makers: Marvel or ripoff? Be(-Happy-)Atitudes—This Orange County pastor claims Christ was no sourpuss. Dramamine and NASA: The untold story. Secret documents reveal Wallis Simpson cheated on Edward VIII. A Whole Lotta Dough—Delaware teen sells $40,000 worth of Girl Scout cookies…and isn't finished yet! For these former agoraphobics, home is not where the heart is. Contra: The thinking person's square dance.

At the same time, it was acknowledged that Atwater's best had sometimes been those pieces he ran down himself and pitched, items that often pushed the BSG envelope. For 7 March '99, Atwater had submitted the longest WITW piece ever done for *Style,* on the case of a U. Maryland professor murdered in his apartment where the only witness was the man's African gray parrot, and all the parrot would repeat was 'Oh God, no, please no' and then gruesome noises, and on the veterinary hypnotist that the authorities had had working with the parrot to see what more they could get out of it. The UBA here had been the hypnotist and her bio and beliefs about animal consciousness, the central tensions being was she just a New Age loon along the lines of Beverly Hills pet therapists or was there really something to it, and if the parrot was hypnotizable as advertised and sang then what would be its evidentiary status in court.

Very early every morning of childhood, Mrs. Atwater's way of waking her two boys up was to stand between their beds and clap her hands loudly together, not stopping until their feet actually touched the bedroom floor, which now floated in the depths of Virgil Atwater's memory as a kind of sardonic ovation. Hopping Mad—This triple amputee isn't taking health care costs lying down. The meth lab next door! Mrs. Gladys Hine, the voice behind over 1,500 automated phone menus. The Dish—This Washington D.C. caterer has seen it all. Computer solitaire: The last addiction? No Sweet Talkin'—Blue M&Ms have these consumers up in arms. Dallas commuter's airbag nightmare. Menopause and herbs: Exciting new findings. Fat Chance— Lottery cheaters and the heavyweight squad that busts them. Seance secrets of online medium Duwayne Evans. Ice sculpture: How do they *do* that?

Atwater's best regarded piece ever so far, 3 July '00: A little girl in Upland CA had been born with an unpronounceable neurological condition whereby she could not form facial expressions, normal and healthy in every way with blond pigtails and a corgi named Skipper except her face was a flat staring granite mask, and the parents were starting a foundation for the incredibly over 5,000 other people worldwide who couldn't form normal facial expressions, and Atwater had run down, pitched, and landed 2,500 words for a piece only half of which was back matter, plus another two columns' worth of multiple photos of the girl reclined expressionless in her mother's lap, stony and staring under raised arms on a roller coaster, and so forth. Atwater had finally gotten the go ahead from the bimanual associate editor on the Suffering Channel piece because he'd done the '99 WITW fluffer on the All Ads All The Time Channel, which was also O Verily, and could truthfully posit a rapport with R. Vaughn Corliss, whose eccentric recluse persona formed a neat human hook—although the associate editor had said that where Atwater was ever going to find the UBA in the TSC story was anyone's guess and would stretch Atwater's skill set to the limit.

5.

The first of the dreams Laurel Manderley found so disturbing had occurred the same night that the digital photos of Brint Moltke's work had appeared on the floor below the fax and she had felt the queer twin impulses both to bend and get them and to run as fast as she could from the cubicle complex. An ominous vatic feeling had persisted throughout the rest of the evening, which was doubly unsettling to Laurel Manderley, because she normally believed about as much in intuition and the uncanny as US Vice President Dick Cheney did.

She lay late at night in the loft, her bunkmate encased in Kiehl's cream beneath her. The dream involved a small house that she somehow knew was the one with the fractional address that belonged to the lady and her husband in Skip Atwater's miraculous poo story. They were all in there, in the like living room or den, sitting there and either not doing anything or not doing anything Laurel Manderley could identify. The creepiness of the dream was akin to the fear she'd sometimes felt in her maternal grandparents' summer home in Lyford Cay, which had certain closet doors that opened by themselves whenever Laurel was in the room. It wasn't clear what Mr. and Mrs. Moltke looked like, or wore, or what they were saying, and at one point there was a dog standing in the middle of the room but its breed and even color were unclear. There was nothing overtly surreal or menacing in the scene. It seemed more like something generic or vague or tentative, like an abstract or outline. The only specifically strange thing was that the house had two front doors, even though one of them wasn't in the front but it was still a front door. But this fact could not begin to account for the overwhelming sense of dread Laurel Manderley felt, sitting there. There was a premonition of not just danger but evil. There was a creeping, ambient evil present, except even though present it was not in the room. Like the second front door, it was somehow both there and not. She couldn't wait to get out, she had to get out. But when she stood up with the excuse of asking to use the bathroom, even in the midst of asking she couldn't stand the feeling of evil and began running for the door in stocking feet in order to get out, but it was not the front door she ran for, it was the other door, even though she didn't know where it was, except she must know because there it was, with a decorative and terribly detailed metal scarab over the knob, and whatever the overwhelming evil was was right behind it, the door, but for some reason even as she's overcome with fear she's also reaching for the doorknob, she's going to open it, she can see herself starting to open it—and that's when she wakes. And then almost the totally exact same thing happens the next night, and she's afraid now that if she has it again then the next time she'll actually open the front door that isn't in front…and her fear of this possibility is the only thing she can put her finger on in trying to describe the dream to Siobhan and Tara on the train ride home Tuesday night, but there's no way to convey just why the two front door thing is so terrifying, since she herself can't even rationally explain it.

↓

The Moltkes were childless, but their home's bathroom lay off a narrow hallway whose east wall was hung with framed photos of Brint and Amber's friends' and relatives' children, as well as certain shots of the Moltkes themselves as youngsters. The presence in this hallway of Atwater, a freelance photographer who wore a Hawaiian shirt and smelled strongly of hair cream, and a Richmond IN internist whom Ellen Bactrian had personally found and engaged had already disarranged some of the photos, which now hung at haphazard angles and revealed partial cracks and an odd set of bulges in the wall's surface. There was one quite extraordinary shot of Amber at what had to have been her wedding's reception, radiant in white brocade and holding the cake's tiered platform in one hand while with the other she brought the cutter to bear. And what at first glance had looked like someone else was a Little League photo of Moltke himself, in uniform and holding an aluminum bat, the artist perhaps nine or ten and his batting helmet far too large. And so on.

Atwater's new rental car, a pointedly budget Kia that even he felt cramped in, sat in the Moltke's driveway with the MD's Lincoln Brougham just behind it. Moltke's company van was parked in the duplex's other driveway, which bespoke some kind of possible arrangement with the other side's occupant that Atwater, who felt more than a little battered and conflicted and ill at ease in Mrs. Moltke's presence, had not yet thought to inquire about. The artist's wife had objected strenuously to a procedure that she said both she and her husband found distasteful and degrading, and was now in her sewing room off the kitchen, whence the occasional impact of her foot on an old machine's treadle shook the hallway and caused the freelance photographer to have to readjust his light stands several different times.

The internist appeared to stand frozen in the gesture of a man looking at his watch. The photographer, for whom Atwater had had to wait over three hours in the Delaware County Airport, sat Indian style in a litter of equipment, picking at the carpet's nap like a doleful child. A large and very precise French curl of hair was plastered to the man's forehead with Brylcreem, whose scent was another of Skip Atwater's childhood associations, and he knew it was the heat of the arc lights that made the hair cream smell so strong. The journalist's left knee now ached no matter which way he distributed his weight. Every so often he pumped his fist at his side, but it was in a tentative and uninspired way.

In the wake of a slow moving front, the area's air was clear and dry and the sky a great cobalt expanse and Tuesday's overall weather both hot and almost autumnally crisp.

The Moltkes' home's bathroom door, a fiberboard model with interior hinges, was shut and locked. From its other side issued the sound of the sink and tub's faucets intermixed with snatches of conservative talk radio. Her husband was an intensely private and skittish bathroom individual, Mrs. Moltke had explained to the MD and photographer, due without doubt to certain abuses he'd suffered as a tiny child. Negotiations over the terms of authentication had taken place in the home's kitchen, and she had laid all this out with Mr. Moltke sitting right there beside her—Atwater had watched the man's hands instead of his face while Amber declaimed about her husband's bathroom habits and childhood trauma. Today she wore a great faded denim smock thing and seemed to loom in the periphery of Atwater's sight no matter where he looked, rather like the sky when one's outside.

At one point in the negotiations, Atwater had needed to use the bathroom and had gone in there and seen it. He really had had to go; it had not been a pretense. The Moltkes' toilet was in a small de facto alcove formed by the sink's counter and the wall that comprised the door jamb. The room smelled exquisitely of mildew. He could see that the wall behind the sink and toilet was part of the same east load bearer that ran along the hallway and sitting room and conjoined the duplex's other side. Atwater preferred a bathroom whose facilities were a bit farther from the door, for privacy's sake, but he could see that the only way to accomplish this here would have been to place the shower unit where the toilet now was, which given this shower's unusual size would be impossible. It was difficult to imagine Amber Moltke backing herself into this slender recess and settling carefully on the white oval seat to eliminate. Since the east wall also held the interior plumbing for all three of the room's fixtures, it stood to reason that the bathroom on the other side of the duplex abutted this one, and that its own plumbing also lay within the wall. For a moment, nothing but an ingrained sense of propriety kept Atwater from trying to press his ear to the wall next to the medicine cabinet to see whether he could hear anything. Nor would he ever have allowed himself to open the Moltkes' medicine cabinet, or to root in any serious way through the woodgrain shelves above the towel rack.

The toilet itself was a generic American Standard, its white slightly brighter than the room's walls and tile. The only noteworthy details were a large crack of some sort on the unpadded seat's left side and a rather sluggish flushing action. The toilet and area of floor around it appeared very clean. Atwater was also the sort of person who always made sure to put the seat back down when he was finished.

Evidently, Ellen Bactrian's brain trust had decided against presenting a short list of specific works or types of pieces they wanted the artist to choose from. The initial pitch that Laurel Manderley had been directed to instruct Atwater to make was that both the MD and photographer would be set up in there with Brint Moltke while he produced whatever piece he felt moved on this day to create. As predicted, Amber declared this totally unacceptable. The proffered compromise, then, was the presence of just the MD (which in fact was all they'd wanted in the first place, *Style* having no possible use for in medias photos). Mrs. Moltke, however, had nixed this as well—Brint had never produced an artwork with anyone else in the room. He was, she iterated once more, an incorrigibly private bathroom person.

During the parts of her presentation he'd already heard, the journalist noted in Gregg shorthand that the home's kitchen was carpeted and deployed a green and burgundy color scheme in its walls, counters, and cabinets, that Mrs. Amber Moltke must almost certainly have had some type of school or community theater experience, and that the broad plastic cup from which the artist had occasionally sipped coffee was from the top of a Thermos unit that was not itself in evidence. Of these observations, only the second had any bearing on the piece that would eventually run in *Style* magazine's final issue.

What had especially impressed Ellen Bactrian was Laurel Manderley's original suggestion that Skip pick up a portable fax machine at some Circuit City or Wal Mart on the way down from Muncie with the photographer—whose equipment had required the subcompact's seats to be moved forward as far as they would go, and who not only smoked in the nonsmoking rental but had this thing where he then fieldstripped each cigarette butt and put the remains carefully in the pocket of his Hawaiian shirt—and that the unit be hooked up to the Moltkes' kitchen phone, which had a clip outlet and could be switched back and forth from phone to fax with no problem. This allowed the MD, whose negotiated station was finally fixed at just outside the bathroom door, to receive the piece fresh ('hot off the griddle' had been the photographer's phrase, which had caused the circle of Moltke's digital mudra to quiver and distend for just a moment), to perform his immediate field tests, and to fax the findings directly to Laurel Manderley, signed and affixed with the same medical authorization number required by certain prescriptions.

'You understand that *Style* is going to have to have some corroboration,'

Atwater had said. This was at the height of the ersatz negotiations in the Moltkes' kitchen. He chose not to remind Amber that this entire issue had already been hashed out in the enmired Cavalier two days prior. 'It's not a matter of whether the magazine trusts you or not. It's that some readers are obviously going to be skeptical. *Style* cannot afford to look overcredulous or like a dupe to even a fraction of its readers.' He did not, in the kitchen, refer to the BSGs' concern with distinguishing themselves from tabloids, though he did say: 'They can't afford to let this look like a tabloid story.'

Both Amber Moltke and the photographer had been eating pieces of a national brand coffee cake that could evidently be heated in the microwave without becoming runny or damp. Her forkwork was deft and delicate and her face as broad across as two of Skip's own placed somehow side by side.

'Maybe we should just go on and let some tabloid do it, then,' she had replied coolly.

Atwater said: 'Well, should you decide to do that, then yes, credibility ceases to be an issue. The story gets inserted between Delta Burke's all fruit diet and reports of Elvis's profile in a photo of Neptune. But no other outlet picks up the story or follows it up. Tabloid pieces don't enter the mainstream.' He said: 'It's a delicate balance of privacy and exposure for you and Brint, I'm aware. You'll obviously have to make your own decision.'

Later, waiting in the narrow and redolent hallway, Atwater noted in Gregg that at some point he and Amber had ceased even pretending to include the artist in the kitchen's whole back and forth charade. And that the way his damaged knee really felt was this: ignominious.

↓

'Or here's one,' Laurel Manderley said. She was standing next to the tray-less fax machine, and the editorial intern who had regaled the previous day's working lunch with the intracunnilingual flatus vignette was seated at the other WITW salaryman's console a few feet away. Today the editorial intern — whose first name also happened to be Laurel, and who was a particularly close friend and protégé of Ellen Bactrian — wore a Gaultier skirt and a sleeveless turtleneck of very soft looking ash gray cashmere.

'Your own saliva,' said Laurel Manderley. 'You're swallowing it all the time. Is it disgusting to you? No. But now imagine gradually filling up a juice glass or something with your own saliva, and then drinking it all down.'

'That really is disgusting,' the editorial intern admitted.

'But why? When it's in your mouth it's not gross, but the minute it's outside of your mouth and you consider putting it back in, it becomes gross.'

'Are you suggesting it's somehow the same thing with poo?'

'I don't know. I don't think so. I think with poo, it's more like as long as it's inside us we don't think about it. In a way, poo only becomes poo when it's excreted. Until then, it's more like a part of you, like your inner organs.'

'It's maybe the same way we don't think about our organs, our livers and intestines. They're inside all of us—'

'They *are* us. Who can live without intestines?'

'But we still don't want to see them. If we see them, they're automatically disgusting.'

Laurel Manderley kept touching at the side of her nose, which felt naked and somewhat creepily smooth. She also had the kind of sick headache where it hurt to move her eyes, and whenever she moved her eyes she could not help but seem to feel all the complex musculature connecting her eyeballs to her brain, which made her feel even woozier. She said: 'But partly we don't like seeing them because if they're visible, that means there's something wrong, there's a hole or some kind of damage.'

'But we also don't even want to think about them,' the other Laurel said. 'Who sits there and goes, Now the salad I ate an hour ago is entering my intestines, now my intestines are pulsing and squeezing and moving the material along?'

'Our hearts pulse and squeeze, and we don't mind thinking about our heart.'

'But we don't want to see it. We don't even want to see our blood. We faint dead away.'

'Not menstrual blood, though.'

'True. I was thinking more of like a blood test, seeing the blood in the tube. Or getting a cut and seeing the blood come out.'

'Menstrual blood is disgusting, but it doesn't make you lightheaded,' Laurel Manderley said almost to herself, her large forehead crinkled with thought. Her hands felt as though they were shaking even though she knew no one else could see it.

'Maybe menstrual blood is ultimately more like poo. It's a waste thing, and disgusting, but it's not wrong that it's all of a sudden outside of you and visible, because the whole point is that it's supposed to get out, it's something you want to get rid of.'

'Or here's one,' Laurel Manderley said. 'Your skin isn't disgusting to you, right?'

'Sometimes my skin's pretty disgusting.'

'That's not what I mean.'

The other editorial intern laughed. 'I know. I was just kidding.'

'Skin's outside of us,' Laurel Manderley continued. 'We see it all the time and there's no problem. It's even aesthetic sometimes, as in so and so's got beautiful skin. But now imagine, say, a foot square section of human skin, just sitting there on a table.'

'Eww.'

'Suddenly it becomes disgusting. What's *that* about?'

The editorial intern recrossed her legs. The ankles above her slingback Jimmy Choos were maybe ever so slightly on the thick side, but she had on the sort of incredibly fine and lovely silk hose that you're lucky to be able to wear even once without totally ruining them. She said: 'Maybe again because it implies some kind of injury or violence.'

The fax's incoming light still had not lit. 'It seems more like the skin is decontextualized.' Laurel Manderley felt along the side of her nostril again. 'You decontextualize it and take it off the human body and suddenly it's disgusting.'

'I don't even like thinking about it, to be honest.'

↓

'I'm just telling you I don't like it.'

'Between you and I, I'd say I'm starting to agree. But it's out of our hands now, as they say.'

'You're saying you'd maybe prefer it if I hadn't gone to Miss Flick with them,' Laurel Manderley said on the telephone. It was late Tuesday afternoon. At certain times, she and Atwater used the name Miss Flick as a private code term for Ellen Bactrian.

'There was no other way to pitch it, I know. I know that,' Skip Atwater responded. 'Whatever's to blame is not that. You did what I think I would have asked you to do myself if I'd had my wits about me.' Laurel Manderley could hear the whispery whisk of his waist level fist. He said: 'Whatever culpability is mine,' which did not make that much sense to her. 'Somewhere some core part of it got past me on this one, I think.'

The *Style* journalist had been seated on the bed's edge on a spread out towel, checking the status of his injured knee. In the privacy of his motel room, Atwater was sans blazer and the knot of his necktie was loosened. The room's television was on, but it was tuned to the Spectravision base channel where the same fragment of song played over and over and the recorded voice of someone who was not Mrs. Gladys Hine welcomed you to the Mount Carmel Holiday Inn and invited you to press Menu in order to see options for movies, games, and a wide variety of in room entertainment, over and over; and Atwater had evidently misplaced the remote control (which in Holiday Inns tends to be very small) required for changing the channel or at the very least muting it. The left leg of his slacks was rolled neatly up to a point above the knee, every second fold reversed to prevent creasing. The television was a nineteen inch Symphonic on a swiveling base that was attached to the blondwood dresser unit facing the bed. It was the same second floor room he had checked into on Sunday—Laurel Manderley had somehow gotten Accounting to book the room straight through even though Atwater had spent the previous night in a Courtyard by Marriott on Chicago's near north side, for which motel the freelance photographer was even now bound, at double his normal daily rate, in preparation for tomorrow's combined coverage spectacle.

On the wall above the room's television was a large framed print of someone's idea of a circus clown's face and head constructed wholly out of vegetables. The eyes were olives and the lips peppers and the cheeks' spots of color small tomatoes, for example. Repeatedly, on both Sunday and today, Atwater had imagined some occupant of the room suffering a stroke or incapacitating fall and having to lie on the floor looking up at the painting and listening to the base channel's nine second message over and over, unable to move or cry out or look away. In some respects, Atwater's various tics and habitual gestures were designed to physicalize his consciousness and to keep him from morbid abstractions like this—he wasn't going to have a stroke, he wouldn't have to look at the painting or listen to the idiot tune over and over until a maid came in the next morning and found him.

'Because that's the only reason. I thought you knew she'd sent them.'

'And if I'd called in on time as I should have, we'd both have known and there would have been no chance of misunderstanding.'

'That's nice, but it's not really my point,' Laurel Manderley said. She was seated at Atwater's console, absently snapping and unsnapping a calfskin barrette. As was SOP with Skip and his interns, this telephone conversation was neither rapid nor clipped. It was shortly before 3:30 and 4:30 respectively, since Indiana does not adhere to the DST convention. Laurel Manderley would later tell Skip that she had been so tired and unwell on Tuesday that she'd felt almost translucent, and plus was upset that she would have to come in on the Fourth, tomorrow, in order to mediate between Atwater and Ellen Bactrian re the so called artist's appearance on

The Suffering Channel's inaugural tableau vivant thing, all of which had been literally thrown together in hours. It was not the way either of them normally worked.

Nor had *Style* ever before sought to conjoin two different pieces in process. It was this that signified to Skip Atwater that either Mrs. Anger or one of her apparatchiks had taken a direct hand. That he felt no discernible trace of either vindication or resentment about this was perhaps to his credit. What he did feel, suddenly and emphatically in the midst of the call, was that he might well be working for Laurel Manderley someday, that it would be she to whom he pitched pieces and pleaded for additional column inches.

For Laurel Manderley's own part, what she later realized she had been trying to do in the Tuesday afternoon telephone confab was to communicate her unease about the miraculous poo story without referring to her dream of spatial distortion and creeping evil in the Moltke couple's home. In the professional world, one does not invoke dreams in order to express reservations about an ongoing project. It just doesn't happen.

Skip Atwater said: 'Well, she did have my card. I gave her my card, of course. But not our Fed Ex number. You know I'd never do that.'

'But think—they got here Monday morning. Yesterday was Monday.'

'She spared no expense.'

'Skip,' Laurel Manderley said. 'Fed Ex isn't open on Sunday.'

The whisking sound stopped. 'Shit,' Atwater said.

'And I didn't even call them for the initial interview until almost Saturday night.'

'And Fed Ex isn't apt to be open Saturday night, either.'

'So the whole thing is just very creepy. So maybe you need to ask Mrs. Moltke what's going on.'

'You're saying she must have sent the pieces before you'd even called.' Atwater was not processing verbal information at his usual rate. One thing he was sure of was that he now had absolutely zero intention of telling Laurel Manderley about the potentially unethical fraternization in the Cavalier, which was also why he could say nothing to her of the whole knee issue.

A person who tended to have very little conscious recall of his own dreams, Atwater today could remember only the previous two nights' sensation of being somehow immersed in another human being, of having that person surround him like water or air. It did not exactly take an advanced clinical degree to interpret this dream. At most, Skip Atwater's mother had been only three fifths to two thirds the size of Amber Moltke, although if you considered Mrs. Atwater's size as it would appear to a small child, much of the disparity then vanished.

After the telephone conversation, seated there on the bed's protective towel, one of the other things that kept popping unbidden into Atwater's mind was the peculiar little unconscious signifier that Brint Moltke made when he sat, the strange abdominal circle or hole that he formed with his hands. He'd made the sign again today, in the home's kitchen, and Atwater could tell it was something Mr. Brint Moltke did a lot—it was in the way he sat, the way all of us have certain little trademark styles of gesturing when we speak or arranging various parts of our bodies when seated. In what he felt was his current state, Atwater's mind seemed able only to return to the image of the gesture again and again; he could get no further with it. In a similar vein, every time he had made a shorthand note to himself to inquire about the other side of the Moltkes' duplex, he would then promptly forget it. His stenographer's notebook later turned out to include a half dozen such notations. The clown's teeth were multicolored kernels of what Atwater's folks had called Indian corn, its hair a spherical nimbus of corn chaff, which happened to be the single most allergenic substance known to man. And yet at the same time the hands' circle seemed also a kind of signal, something that the artist perhaps wished to communicate to Atwater but didn't know how or was not even fully aware he wished to. The strange blank fixed smile was a different matter—it too was unsettling, but the journalist never felt that it might be trying to signify anything beyond itself.

Atwater had never before received any kind of sexual injury. The discoloration was chiefly along the leg's outside, but the swelling involved the kneecap, and this was clearly what was causing the real pain. The area of bruising extended from just below the knee to the lower thigh; certain features of the car door's armrest and window's controls were directly imprinted in the bruise's center and already yellowing. The knee had felt constricted in his slacks' left leg all day. It gave off a radioactive ache and was sensitive to even the lightest contact. Atwater examined it, breathing through his teeth. He felt the distinctive blend of repulsion and fascination nearly all people feel when examining a diseased or injured part of themselves. He also had the feeling that the knee now somehow existed in a more solid and emphatic way than the rest of him around it. It was something like the way he used to feel at the mirror in the bathroom as a boy, examining his protuberant ears from all different angles. The room was on the Holiday Inn's second level and opened onto an exterior balcony that overlooked the pool; the cement stairs up had also hurt the knee. He couldn't straighten his leg out all the way. In the afternoon light, his calf and foot appeared pale and extremely hairy, perhaps abnormally hairy. There were also spatial issues. He had allowed it to occur to him that the bruising was actually trapped blood leaking from injured blood vessels under the skin, and that the changes in color were signs of the trapped blood decomposing under the skin and of the human body's attempts to deal with the decaying blood, and as a natural result he felt lightheaded and insubstantial and ill.

He was not so much injured as sore and more or less pummeled feeling elsewhere, as well.

Another childhood legacy: When anything painful or unpleasant happened to his body, Skip Atwater often got the queer sense that he was in fact not a body that occupied space but rather just a bodyshaped area of space itself, impenetrable but empty, with a certain vacuous roaring sensation we tend to associate with empty space. The whole thing was very private and difficult to describe, although Atwater had had a long and interesting off the record conversation about it with the Oregon multiple amputee who'd organized a series of high profile anti HMO events in 1999. It also now occurred to him for the first time that 'gone in the stomach,' which was a regional term for nausea he'd grown up with and then jettisoned after college, turned out to be a much more acute, concise descriptor than all the polysyllables he and the one legged activist had hurled at one another over the whole interior spatial displacement epiphenomenon.

There was something essentially soul killing about the print of the vegetable head clown that had made Atwater want to turn it to the wall, but it was bolted or glued and could not be moved. It was really on there, and Atwater now was trying to consider whether hanging a bath towel or something over it would or would not perhaps serve to draw emotional attention to the print and make it an even more oppressive part of the room for anyone who already knew what was under the towel. Whether the painting was worse actually seen or merely, so to speak, alluded to. Standing angled at the bathroom's exterior sink and mirror unit, it occurred to him that these were just the sorts of overabstract thoughts that occupied his mind in motels, instead of the arguably much more urgent and concrete problem of finding the television's remote control. For some reason, the controls on the TV itself were inactive, meaning that the remote was the only way to change channels or mute the volume or even turn the machine off, since the relevant plug and outlet were too far behind the dresser to reach and the dresser unit, like the excruciating print, was bolted to the wall and could not be budged. There was a low knocking at the door, which Atwater did not hear over the repetitive tune and message because he was at the sink with the water running. Nor could he remember for certain whether it was heat or cold that was effective for swelling after almost 48 hours, though it was common knowledge that ice was what was indicated directly after. What he eventually decided was to prepare both a hot and a cold compress, and to alternate them, his left fist moving in self exhortation as he tried to recall his childhood scouting manual's protocol for contusions.

The second level's ice machine roared without cease in a large utility closet next to Atwater's room. His tie reknotted but the left leg of his slacks still rolled way up, the journalist had the Holiday Inn's distinctive lightweight ice bucket in his hand when he opened the door and stepped out into the ambient noise and chlorine smell of the balcony. His shoe nearly came down in the message before he saw it and stopped, one foot suspended in air, aware at the same time that chlorine was not the only scent in the balcony's wind. The "*HELP ME*" was ornate and calligraphic, quotation marks sic. In overall design, it was not unlike the cursive *HAPPY BIRTHDAY VIRGIL AND ROB, YMSP2 '00,* and other phrases of decorative icing on certain parties' cakes of his experience. But it was not made of icing. That much was immediately, emphatically clear.

Holding the bucket, his ears crimson and partly denuded leg still raised, the journalist was paralyzed by the twin urges to examine the message's workmanship more closely and to get far away as quickly as possible, perhaps even to check out altogether. He knew that great force of will would be required to try to imagine the various postures and contractions involved in producing the phrase, its detached and plumb straight underscoring, the tiny and perfectly formed quotation marks. Part of him was aware that it had not yet occurred to him to consider what the phrase might actually mean or imply in this context. In a sense, the content of the message was obliterated by the overwhelming fact of its medium and implied mode of production. The phrase terminated neatly at the second E's serif; there was no tailing off or spotting.

A faint human sound made Atwater look hard right—an older couple in golfing visors stood some yards off outside their door, looking at him and the balcony's brown cri de coeur. The wife's expression pretty much said it all.

←

All salarymen, staff, and upper level interns at *Style* had free corporate memberships to the large fitness center located on the second underground level of the WTC's South Tower. The only expense was a monthly locker fee, which was well worth it if you didn't want to schlep a separate set of exercise clothing along with you to the offices every day. Two of the facility's walls were lined with mirrored plate. There were no windows, but the center's cardio fitness area was replete with raised banks of television monitors whose high gain audios could be accessed with ordinary Walkman headphones, and the channels could be changed via touchpad controls that were right there on the consoles of all the machines except the stationary bicycles, which themselves were somewhat crude and used mainly for spinning classes, which were also offered gratis.

At midday on Tuesday 3 July, Ellen Bactrian and Mrs. Anger's executive intern were on two of the elliptical training machines along the fitness center's north wall. Ellen Bactrian wore a dark gray Fila unitard with Reebok crosstrainers. There was a neoprene brace on her right knee, but it was mostly prophylactic, the legacy of a soccer injury at Wellesley three seasons past. Multicolored fairy lights on the machines' sides spelled out the brand name of the elliptical trainers. The executive intern, in the same ensemble she'd worn for biking in to the *Style* offices that morning, had programmed her machine to the same medium level of difficulty as Ellen Bactrian's, as a kind of courtesy.

It being the lunch hour, the center's cardio fitness area was almost fully occupied. Every elliptical trainer was in use, though only a few of the interns were using headsets. The nearby StairMasters were used almost exclusively by midlevel financial analysts, all of whom had bristly cybernetic haircuts. Not for over 40 years had the crewcut and variations upon it been so popular; a SURFACES item on the phenom was not long in the offing.

Certain parts of a four way internal email exchange Tuesday morning had concerned what specified type(s) of piece the magazine should require the Indianan to produce under tightly controlled circumstances in order to verify that his abilities were not a hoax or some tasteless case of idiot savantism. The fourth member of this exchange had been the photo intern whose mammoth engagement ring at Tutti Mangia had occasioned so much cattiness during yesterday's SE2 closing. Some of the specs proposed for the authenticity test were: A 0.5 reproduction of the Academy Awards' well known Oscar statuette, G. W. F. Hegel's image of Napoleon as the world spirit on horseback, a WWII Pershing tank with rotating turret, any coherently identifiable detail from Rodin's *The Gates of Hell*, a buck with a twelve point rack, either the upper or lower portion of the ancient Etruscan *Mars of Todi*, and the well known tableau of several US Marines planting the flag on an Iwo Jiman atoll. The idea of any sort of Crucifixion or *Pietà* type piece was flamed the moment it was proposed. Although Skip Atwater had not yet been given his specific marching orders, Mrs. Anger's executive intern and Ellen Bactrian were both currently leaning toward a representation of the famous photograph in which Marilyn Monroe's skirts are blown upward by some type of vent in the sidewalk and the expression on her face is, to say the least, intimately familiar to readers of *Style*.

Some of the internal email exchange's topics and arguments had carried over into various different lunchtime colloquies and brainstorming sessions, including the present one in the World Trade Center's corporate fitness facility, which proceeded more or less naturally because an axiom of elliptical cardio conditioning is that your target heartrate and respiration are to stay just at the upper limit of what allows for normal conversation.

'But is the physical, so to speak handmade character of a piece of art part of the artwork's overall quality?'

That is, in elliptical training you want your breathing to be deep and rapid but not labored—Ellen Bactrian's rhetorical question took only a tiny bit longer to get out than a normal, at rest rhetorical question.

The executive intern responded: 'Do we all really value a painting more than a photograph anymore?'

'Let's say we do.'

The executive intern laughed. 'That's almost a textbook petitio principii.' She actually pronounced principii correctly, which almost no one can do.

'A great painting certainly sells for more than a great photograph, doesn't it?'

The executive intern was silent for several broad quadular movements of the elliptical trainer. Then she said: 'Why not just say rather that *Style*'s readership would not have a problem with the assumption that a good painting or sculpture is intrinsically better, more human and meaningful, than a good photo.'

Often, editorial brainstorming sounds like an argument, but it isn't—it's two or more people thinking aloud in a directed way. Mrs. Anger herself sometimes referred to the brainstorming process as dilation, but this was a vestige of her Fleet Street background, and no one on her staff aped the phrase.

A woman about their mothers' age was exhibiting near perfect technique on a rowing machine in the mirror, mouthing the words to what Ellen Bactrian thought she recognized as a Venetian bacarole. The other rowing machine was vacant. Ellen Bactrian said: 'But now, if we agree the human element's key, then does the physical process or processes by which the painting is produced, or any artwork, have anything to do with the artwork's quality?'

'By quality you're still referring to how good it is.'

It is difficult to shrug on an elliptical trainer. 'Good quote unquote.'

'Then the answer again is that what we're interested in is human interest, not some abstract aesthetic value.'

'And yet isn't the point that they're not mutually exclusive? How about all Picasso's affairs, or the thing with van Gogh's ear?'

'Yes, but van Gogh didn't paint with his ear.'

By habit, Ellen Bactrian avoided looking directly at their side by side reflections in the mirrored wall. The executive intern was at least three inches taller than she. The sounds of all the young men's legs working the StairMasters were at certain points syncopated, then not, then gradually syncopated again. The two editorial interns' movements on the elliptical trainers, on the other hand, appeared synchronized down to the smallest detail. Each of them had a bottle of water with a sports cap in her elliptical trainer's special receptacle, although they were not the same brands of bottled water. The fitness center's sonic environment was basically one large, complex, and rhythmic pneumatic clank.

Between breaths, an ever so slightly peevish or impatient tone entered Ellen Bactrian's voice: 'Then, say, the *My Left Foot* guy who painted with his left foot.'

'Or the idiot savant who can reproduce Chopin after one hearing,' the executive intern said. This was an indirect bit of massaging on her part, since there had been a WITW profile of just such an idiot savant in an issue the previous summer—the piece's UBA was that the retarded man's mother had battled heroically to keep him out of an institution.

Under the diffused high lumen lights of the cardio fitness area, the executive intern's quads and delts seemed like something out of an advertisement. Ellen Bactrian was fit and attractive, with a perfectly respectable body fat percentage, but around the executive intern she often felt squat and dumpy. An unhealthy part of her sometimes suspected that the executive intern liked exercising with her because it made her, the executive intern, feel comparatively even more willowy and scintillant and buff. What neither Ellen Bactrian nor anyone else at *Style* knew was that the executive intern had had a dark period in preparatory school during which she'd made scores of tiny cuts in the tender skin of her upper arms' insides and then squeezed reconstituted lemon juice into the cuts as penance for a long list of personal shortcomings, a list she had tracked daily in her journal in a special numerical key code that was totally unbreakable unless you knew exactly which page of *The Bell Jar* the code's numbers were keyed to. Those days were now behind her, but they were still part of who the executive intern was.

'Yes,' Ellen Bactrian said, 'although, although I'm no art critic, Skip's guy's pieces are also artworks of surpassing quality and value in their own right.'

'Although of course all the readers will get to see is photos —'

'*Maybe.*' Both interns laughed briefly. The issue of publishable photos had been one they'd all agreed that morning to table — there were, as the WITW associate editor sometimes liked to quip, bigger fish on the front burner.

Ellen Bactrian said: 'Although remember that even photos, if Amine's to be believed, if absolutely properly lit and detailed so that —'

'Except hold on, answer this — does this person have to actually be *familiar* with something to represent it the way he does?'

Both women were at a node of their computerized workout and were breathing almost heavily now. Amine Tadić was *Style* magazine's associate photo editor; her head intern had served as her proxy in the morning's email confab.

Ellen Bactrian said: 'What do you mean?'

'According to Laurel, this is a person with maybe like a year or two of community college. How on earth would he know Boccioni's *Unique Forms of Continuity in Space,* or what Anubis's head looks like?'

'Or for that matter which side the Liberty Bell's crack's on.'

'I sure didn't know it.'

Ellen Bactrian laughed. 'Laurel did. Or she said she did — obviously she could have looked it up.' Ellen Bactrian was also, on her own time, trying to learn how to type completely different things with each hand, à la the WHAT IN THE WORLD section's associate editor, for whom she had certain feelings that she knew perfectly well were SOP transference for an intelligent, ambitious woman her age, since the associate editor was both seductive and a textbook authority figure. Ellen Bactrian liked the associate editor's wife quite a lot, actually, and so took great pains to keep the whole bimanual thing in perspective.

The executive intern was able to reach down and hydrate without breaking rhythm, which on an elliptical trainer takes a great deal of practice. 'I'm saying: Does the man have to see or know something in order to represent it? Produce it? Let's say that if he does and it's all totally conscious and intentional, then he's a real artist.'

'But if he doesn't—'

'Which is why the unlikeliness of a Roto Rooter guy from Nowhere Indiana knowing futurism or the *Unique Forms* is relevant,' the executive intern said, wiping her forehead with a terry wristband.

'If he doesn't, it's some kind of, what, a miracle? Idiot savantry? Divine intervention?'

'Or else some kind of extremely sick fraud.'

Fraud was a frightening word to them both, for obvious reasons. One consequence of getting Mrs. Anger's executive intern in on the miraculous poo story was that Eckleschafft-Böd US's Legal people were now involved and devoting resources to the piece in a way that Laurel Manderley and Ellen Bactrian could never have caused, even given the WITW associate editor's own background in Legal. BSG weeklies rarely broke stories or covered anything that other media hadn't already premasticated. The prospect was both exciting and frightful.

The executive intern said: 'Or else maybe it's subconscious. Maybe his colon somehow knows things his conscious mind doesn't.'

'Is it the colon that determines the whole shape and configuration and everything of the... you know?'

The executive intern made a face. 'I don't know. I don't really want to think about it.'

'What is the colon, anyhow? Is it part of the intestines or is it technically its own organ?'

Ellen Bactrian's and the executive intern's fathers were both MDs in Westchester County NY, though the two men practiced different medical specialties and had never met. The executive intern periodically reversed the direction of her elliptical trainer's pedals, working her quadriceps and calves instead of the hamstrings and lower gluteals. Her facial expression throughout these periods of reversal was both intent and abstracted.

'Either way,' Ellen Bactrian said, 'it's obviously human interest right out the wazoo.' She then related the anecdote that Laurel Manderley had shared with her in the elevators on the way back down from the 82nd floor early that morning, about the DKNY clad circulation intern at lunch telling everybody that she sometimes pretended her waste was a baby and then expecting them to relate or to think her candor was somehow hip or brave.

For a moment there was nothing but the sound of two syncopated elliptical trainers. Then the executive intern said: 'There's a way to do this.' She blotted momentarily at her upper lip with the inside of her wristband. 'Joan would say we've been thinking about this all wrong. We've been thinking about the subject *of* the piece instead of the angle *for* the piece.' Joan referred to Mrs. Anger, the Executive Editor of *Style*.

'The UBA's been a problem from the start,' Ellen Bactrian said. 'What I told—'

The executive intern interrupted: 'There doesn't have to be a strict UBA, though, because we can take the piece out of WHAT IN THE WORLD and do it in SOCIETY PAGES. Is the miraculous poo phenomenon art, or miracle, or just disgusting.' She seemed not to be aware that her limbs' forward speed had increased; she was now forcing her workout's program instead of following it. SOCIETY PAGES was the section of *Style* devoted to soft coverage of social issues such as postnatal depression and the rain forest. According to the magazine's editorial template, SP items ran up to 600 words as opposed to WITW's 400.

Ellen Bactrian said: 'Meaning we include some bites from credible sources who think it *is* disgusting. We have Skip create controversy in the piece itself.' It was true that her use of Atwater's name in the remark was somewhat strategic—there were complex turf issues involved in altering a piece's venue within the magazine, and Ellen Bactrian could well imagine the WITW associate editor's facial expression and some of the cynical jokes he might make in order to mask his hurt at being shut out of the story altogether.

'No,' the executive intern responded. 'Not quite. We don't create the controversy, we cover it.' She was checking her sports watch even though there were digital clocks right there on the machines' consoles. Both women had met or exceeded their target heartrate for over half an hour.

A short time later, they were in the little tiled area where people toweled off after a shower. At this time of day, the locker room was steamy and extremely crowded. The executive intern looked like something out of Norse mythology. The hundreds of tiny parallel scars on the insides of her upper arms were all but invisible. It is a fact of life that certain people are corrosive to others' self esteem simply as a function of who and what they are. The executive intern was saying: 'The real angle is about coverage. *Style* is not foisting a gross or potentially offensive story on its readers. Rather, *Style* is doing soft coverage on a controversial story that already exists.'

Ellen Bactrian had two towels, one of which she had wrapped around her head in an immense lavender turban. 'So Atwater will just rotate over and do it for SOCIETY PAGES, you're saying? Or will Genevieve want to send in her own salaryman?' Genevieve was the given name of the new associate editor in charge of SOCIETY PAGES, with whom Ellen Bactrian's overman had already locked horns several times in editorial meetings.

The executive intern had inclined her head over to the side and was combing out a shower related tangle with her fingers. As was something of an unconscious habit, she bit gently at her lower lip in concentration. 'I'm like ninety percent sure this is the way to go,' she said. '*Style* is covering the human element of a controversy that's already raging.' At this point, they were at their rented lockers, which, in contradistinction to those on the men's side, were full length in order to facilitate hanging. Painstakingly modified with portable inset shelving and adhesive hooks, both the women's locker units were small marvels of organization.

Ellen Bactrian said: 'Meaning it will need to be done somewhere else first. SOCIETY PAGES covers the coverage and the controversy.' She favored Gaultier pinstripe slacks and sleeveless cashmere tops that could be worn either solo or under a jacket. So long as the slacks and top were in the same color family, sleeveless could still be all business — Mrs. Anger had taught them all that.

In what appeared to be another unconscious habit, the executive intern sometimes actually pressed the heel of her hand into her forehead when she was thinking especially hard. In a way, it was her version of Skip Atwater's capital flush. The opinion of nearly all the magazine's other interns was that the executive intern was operating on a level where she didn't have to be concerned about things like color families or maintaining a cool professional demeanor.

'But it can't be too big,' she said.

'The piece, or the venue?' Ellen Bactrian always had to pat the ear with all the studs in it dry with a disposable little antibiotic cloth.

'We don't want *Style* readers to already know the story. This is the tricky part. We want them to feel as if *Style* is their first exposure to a story whose existence still precedes their seeing it.'

'In a media sense, you mean.'

The executive intern's skirt was made of several dozen men's neckties all stitched together lengthwise in a complicated way. She and a Mauritanian exchange student in THE THUMB who wore hallucinatorily colored tribal garb were the only two interns at *Style* who could get away with this sort of thing. It was actually the executive intern, at a working lunch two summers past, who had originally compared Skip Atwater to a jockey who'd broken training, though she had said it in a light and almost affectionate way—coming from her, it had not sounded cruel. Over Memorial Day weekend, she had actually been a guest of Mrs. Anger at her summer home in Quogue, where she had reportedly played mahjongg with none other than Mrs. Hans G. Böd. Her future seemed literally without limit.

'Yes, though again, it's delicate,' the executive intern said. 'Think of it as not unlike the Bush daughters, or that thing last Christmas on Dodi's driver.' These were rough analogies, but they did convey to Ellen Bactrian the executive intern's basic thrust. In a broad sense, the cover the extant story angle was one of the standard ways BSGs distinguished themselves from both hard news glossies and the tabloids. On another level, Ellen Bactrian was also being informed that the overall piece was still her and the WHAT IN THE WORLD associate editor's baby; and the executive intern's repeated use of terms like tricky and delicate was designed both to flatter Ellen Bactrian and to apprise her that her editorial skill set would be amply tested by the challenges ahead.

Gaultier slacks held their crease a great deal better if your hanger had clips and they could hang from the cuffs. The voluptuous humidity of the locker room was actually good for the tiny wrinkles that always accumulated through the morning. Unbeknownst to Ellen Bactrian, lower level interns often referred to her and the executive intern in the same hushed and venerative tones. A constant sense that she was insufficient and ever at risk of exposing her incompetence was one of the ways Ellen Bactrian kept her edge. Were she to learn that she, too, was virtually assured of a salaried offer from *Style* at her internship's end, she would literally be unable to process the information—it might well send her over the edge, the executive intern knew. The way the girl now pressed at her forehead in unconscious imitation of the executive intern was a sign of just the kind of core insecurity the executive intern was trying to mitigate by bringing her along slowly and structuring their conversations as brainstorming rather than, for instance, her simply outright telling Ellen Bactrian how the miraculous poo story should be structured so that everyone made out. The executive intern was one of the greatest, most intuitive nurturers of talent

Mrs. Anger had ever seen — and she herself had interned under Katharine Graham, back in the day.

'So it can't be too big,' Ellen Bactrian was saying, first one hand against the locker and then the other as she adjusted her Blahniks' straps. She now spoke in the half dreamy way of classic brainstorming. 'Meaning we don't totally sacrifice the scoop element. We need just enough of a prior venue so the story already exists. We're covering a controversy instead of profiling some freakoid whose b.m. comes out in the shape of Anubis's head.' Her hair had almost completely air dried already.

The executive intern's belt for the skirt was two feet of good double hemp nautical rope. Her sandals were Laurent, open toe heels that went with nearly anything. She tied the ankles' straps with half hitches and began to apply just the tiniest bit of clear gloss. Ellen Bactrian had now turned and was looking at her:

'Are you thinking what I'm thinking?'

Their eyes met in the compact's little mirror, and the executive intern smiled coolly. 'Your salaryman's already out there. You said he's shuttling between the two pieces already, no?'

Ellen Bactrian said: 'But is there actual suffering involved?' She was already constructing a mental flow chart of calls to be made and arrangements undertaken and then dividing the overall list between herself and Laurel Manderley, whom she now considered a bit of a pistol.

'Well, listen — can he take orders?'

'Skip? Skip's a consummate pro.'

The executive intern was adjusting the balloon sleeves of her blouse. 'And according to him, the miraculous poo man is skittish on the story?'

'The word Laurel says Skip used was excruciated.'

'Is that even a word?'

'It's apparently totally the wife's show, in terms of publicity. The artist guy is scared of his own shadow — according to Laurel, he's sitting there flashing Skip secret signs like No, please God, no.'

'So how hard could it be to represent this to Atwater's All Ads person as comprising bona fide suffering?'

Ellen Bactrian's mental flow charts often contained actual boxes, Roman numerals, and multiarrow graphics — that's how gifted an administrator she was. 'You're talking about something live, then.'

'With the proviso that of course it's all academic until this afternoon's tests check out.'

'But do we know for sure he'll even go for it?'

The executive intern never brushed her hair after a shower. She just gave her head two or three shakes and let it fall gloriously where it might and turned, slightly, to give Ellen Bactrian the full effect:

'Who?' She had ten weeks to live.

6.

In what everyone at the next day's working lunch would agree was a masterstroke, the special limousine that arrived at 5:00 AM Wednesday to convey the artist and his wife to Chicago was like something out of a *Style* reader's dream. Half a city block long, white the way cruise ships and bridal gowns are white, it had a television and wet bar, opposing seats of cordovan leather, noiseless AC, and a thick glass shield between passenger compartment and driver that could be raised and lowered at the touch of a button on the woodgrain panel, for privacy. To Skip Atwater, it looked like the hearse of the kind of star for whom the whole world stops dead in its tracks to mourn. Inside, the Moltkes faced each other, their knees almost touching, the artist's hands obscured from view by the panels of his new beige sportcoat.

The salaryman's Kia trailing at a respectful distance, the limousine proceeded at dawn through the stolid caucasian poverty of Mount Carmel. There were only faint suggestions of faces behind its windows' darkened glass, but whoever was awake to see the limousine glide by could tell that whoever was in there looking out saw everything afresh, like coming out of a long coma.

↓

O Verily was, understandably, a madhouse. The time from initial pitch to live broadcast was 31 hours. The Suffering Channel would enter stage three at 8:00 PM CDT on 4 July, ten weeks ahead of schedule, with three tableaux vivant. There were five different line producers, and all of them were very busy indeed.

It was not Sweeps Week; but as the saying goes in cable, every week is Sweeps Week.

A 52 year old grandmother from Round Lake Beach IL had a growth in her pancreas. The needle biopsy w/ CAT assist at Rush Presbyterian would be captured live by a remote crew; so would the activities of the radiology MD and pathologist whose job was to stain the sample and determine whether the growth was malignant. The segment entailed two separate freelance crews, all of whom were IA union and on holiday double time. The second part of the feed would be split screen. In something of a permissions coup, they'd have the woman's face for the whole ten minutes it took for the stain to set and the pathologist to scope it. She and her husband would be looking at a monitor on which the pathology crew's real time feed would be displayed—viewers would get to see the verdict and her reaction to it at the same time.

Finding just the right host for the segments' intros and voiceovers was an immense headache, given that nearly every plausible candidate's agent was off for the Fourth, and that whomever The Suffering Channel cast they were then all but bound to stick with for at least one stage three cycle. Finalists were still being auditioned as late as 3:00 PM—and *Style* magazine's Skip Atwater, in a move whose judgment was later questioned all up and down the editorial line, ended up devoting a good part of his time, attention, and shorthand notes to these auditions, as well as to a lengthy and somewhat meandering Q&A with an assistant to the Reudenthal and Voss associate tasked to the day's multiform permissions and releases.

In 1996, an unemployed arc welder was convicted of abducting and torturing to death a Penn State coed named Carole Ann Deutsch. Over four hours of high quality audiotape had been recovered from the suspect's apartment and entered into evidence at trial. Voiceprint analysis confirmed that the screams and pleadings on the tapes—which were played for the jury, though not in open court—belonged to the victim. This tableau's venue was a hastily converted OVP conference room. For the first time, Carole Ann Deutsch's widowed father, of Glassport PA, would listen to selections from those tapes. There with him for support are the associate pastor from Mr. Deutsch's church and an APA certified trauma counselor whose sunburn, only hours old, presents some ticklish problems for the segment's makeup coordinator.

Longtime *People's Court* moderator Doug Llewellyn hosts. After lengthy and sometimes heated negotiations—during which at one point Mrs. Anger herself had to be contacted at home and enjoined to speak directly by cell to R. Vaughn Corliss, which Ellen Bactrian later said made her just about want to curl up and die—representatives of both the ACLU and the League of Decency are on hand for brief interviews by Skip Atwater of *Style*.

It is a clear Lucite commode unit atop a ten foot platform of tempered glass beneath which a video crew will record the real time emergence of either an iconically billowing and ecstatic Monroe or a five to seven inch *Winged Victory of Samothrace*, depending on dramatic last minute instructions. Suspended from the studio's lighting grid to a position directly before the commode unit, a special monitor taking feed from below will give the artist visual access to his own production for the first time ever in his career. He believes what he sees will be public.

In point of fact, the piece's physical emergence will not really be broadcast. The combined arguments of *Style*'s Ellen Bactrian and the Development heads of O Verily Productions finally persuaded Mr. Corliss it would be beyond the pale. Instead, the artist's wife has been interviewed on tape respecting Brint Moltke's abusive childhood and the terrific shame, ambivalence, and sheer human suffering involved in his unchosen art. Edited portions of this interview will compose the voiceover as TSC viewers watch the artist's face in the act of creation, its every wince and grimace captured by the special camera hidden within the chassis of the commode's monitor.

A consciência é o pesadelo da natureza.

It is, of course, malignant. Subsequently, though, Carole Ann Deutsch's father discomfits everyone by seeming less interested in the tapes than in justifying his appearance on the broadcast itself. His purpose for being here is to inform the public of what victims' loved ones go through, to humanize the process and raise awareness. He repeats this several times, but at no point does he share how he feels or what he feels he's gone through just now, listening. In the context of what he and the viewers have just heard, Mr. Deutsch's reaction comes off as almost obscenely abstract and disengaged. On the other hand, Doug Llewellyn's own evident humanity and ad lib skill in getting everyone through the segment testify to the soundness of his casting.

A slow chain pulls the commode assembly up an angled plane until the unit locks into place atop its Lucite pipe. Mrs. Moltke's been allowed in the control room. Virgil 'Skip' Atwater and the Reudenthal and Voss paralegal are back against one wall, out of the arc lights' wash, the journalist's whole face flushed with ibuprofen and hands folded monkishly over his abdomen. At the base of the plane, *Style*'s freelance photographer is down on one knee, going handheld, still in the same Hawaiian shirt. The famously reclusive R. Vaughn Corliss is nowhere in view. Doug Llewellyn's wardrobe furnished by Hugo Boss. The Malina blanket for the artist's lap and thighs, however, is the last minute fix of a production oversight, retrieved from the car of an apprentice gaffer whose child is still nursing, and is not what anyone would call an appropriate color or design, and appears unbilled. There's also some eleventh hour complication involving the ground level camera and the problem of keeping the commode's special monitor out of its upward shot, since video capture of a camera's own monitor causes what is known in the industry as feedback glare — the artist in such a case would see, not his own emergent *Victory*, but a searing and amorphous light.

THE PALE KING

§1

PAST THE FLANNEL plains and blacktop graphs and skylines of canted rust, and past the tobacco-brown river overhung with weeping trees and coins of sunlight through them on the water downriver, to the place beyond the windbreak, where untilled fields simmer shrilly in the A.M. heat: shatter-cane, lamb's-quarter, cutgrass, sawbrier, nutgrass, jimsonweed, wild mint, dandelion, foxtail, muscadine, spinecabbage, goldenrod, creeping charlie, butter-print, nightshade, ragweed, wild oat, vetch, butcher grass, invaginate volunteer beans, all heads gently nodding in a morning breeze like a mother's soft hand on your cheek. An arrow of starlings fired from the windbreak's thatch. The glitter of dew that stays where it is and steams all day. A sunflower, four more, one bowed, and horses in the distance standing rigid and still as toys. All nodding. Electric sounds of insects at their business. Ale-colored sunshine and pale sky and whorls of cirrus so high they cast no shadow. Insects all business all the time. Quartz and chert and schist and chondrite iron scabs in granite. Very old land. Look around you. The horizon trembling, shapeless. We are all of us brothers.

Some crows come overhead then, three or four, not a murder, on the wing, silent with intent, corn-bound for the pasture's wire beyond which one horse smells at the other's behind, the lead horse's tail obligingly lifted. Your shoes' brand incised in the dew. An alfalfa breeze. Socks' burrs. Dry scratching inside a culvert. Rusted wire and tilted posts more a symbol of restraint than a fence per se. NO HUNTING. The shush of the interstate off past the windbreak. The pasture's crows standing at angles, turning up patties to get at the worms underneath, the shapes of the worms incised in the overturned dung and baked by the sun all day until hardened, there to stay, tiny vacant lines in rows and inset curls that do not close because head never quite touches tail. Read these.

§5

It is this boy who dons the bright-orange bandolier and shepherds the lower grades' kids through the crosswalk outside school. This is after finishing his Meals on Wheels breakfast tour of the charity home for the aged downtown, whose administrator lunges to bolt her office door when she hears his cart's wheels in the hall. He has paid out of pocket for the steel whistle and the white gloves held palm-out at cars while children who did not dress themselves cross behind him, some trying to run despite walk, don't run!!, the happy-face sandwich board he also made himself. The autos whose drivers he knows he waves at and gives an extra-big smile and tosses some words of good cheer as the crosswalk clears and the cars peel out and barrel through, some joshing around a little by swerving to miss him only by inches as he laughs and dances aside and makes faces of pretended terror at the flanks and rear bumpers. (The time that one station wagon didn't miss him really *was* an accident, and he sent the lady several notes to make absolutely sure she knew he understood that, and asked a whole lot of people he hadn't yet gotten the opportunity to make friends with to sign his cast, and decorated the crutches very carefully with bits of colored ribbon and tinsel and adhesive sparkles, and even before the minimum six weeks the doctor sternly prescribed he'd donated the crutches to Calvin Memorial's pediatrics wing in order to brighten up some other less lucky and happy kid's convalescence, and by the end of the whole thing he'd been inspired to write a very long theme to enter in the annual Social Studies Theme Competition about how even a painful and debilitating accidental injury can yield new opportunities for making friends and reaching out to others, and while the theme didn't win or even get honorable mention he honestly didn't care, because he felt like writing the theme had been its own reward and that he'd gotten a lot out of the whole nine-draft process, and was honestly happy for the kids whose themes did win prizes, and told them he was 100-plus percent sure they deserved it and that if they wanted to preserve their prize themes and maybe even make display items out of them for their parents he'd be happy to type them up and laminate them and even fix any spelling errors he found if they'd like him to, and at home his father puts his hand on little Leonard's shoulder and says he's proud that his son's such a good sport, and offers to take him to Dairy Queen as a kind of reward, and Leonard tells his father he's grateful and that the gesture means a lot to him but that in all honesty he'd like it even more if they took the money his father would have spent on the ice cream and instead donated it either to Easter Seals or, better yet, to UNICEF, to go toward the needs of famine-ravaged Biafran kids who he knows for a fact have probably never even *heard* of ice cream, and says that he bets it'll end up giving both of them a better feeling even than the DQ would, and as the father slips the coins in the coin slot of the special bright-orange UNICEF volunteer cardboard pumpkin-bank, Leonard takes a moment to express concern about the father's facial tic again and to gently rib him about his reluctance to go in and have the family's MD look at it, noting again that according to the chart on the back of his bedroom door the father is three months overdue for his annual physical and that it's almost eight months past the date of his recommended tetanus booster.)

He serves as hall monitor for Periods 1 and 2 (he's half a grade ahead on credits) but gives far more official warnings than actual citations—he's there to serve, he feels, not run people down. Usually with the warnings he dispenses a smile and tells them you're young exactly once so enjoy it, and to go get out of here and make this day count why don't they. He does UNICEF and Easter Seals and starts a recycling program in three straight grades. He is healthy and scrubbed and always groomed just well enough to project basic courtesy and respect for the community of which he is a part, and he politely raises his hand in class for every question, but only if he's sure he knows not only the correct answer but the formulation of that answer that the teacher's looking for that will help advance the discussion of the overall topic they're covering that day, often staying after class to double-check with the teacher that his take on her general objectives is sound and to ask whether there was any way his in-class answers could have been better or more helpful.

The boy's mom has a terrible accident while cleaning the oven and is rushed to the hospital, and even though he's beside himself with concern and says constant prayers for her stabilization and recovery he volunteers to stay home and field calls and relay information to an alphabetized list of relatives and concerned family friends, and to make sure the mail and newspaper are brought in, and to keep the home's lights turned on and off in a random sequence at night as Officer Chuck of the Michigan State Police's Crime Stoppers public-school outreach program sensibly advises when grown-ups are suddenly called away from home, and also to call the gas company's emergency number (which he has memorized) to have them come check on what may well be a defective valve or circuit in the oven before anyone else in the family is exposed to risk of accidental harm, and also (secretly) to work on an immense display of bunting and pennants and WELCOME HOME and WORLD'S GREATEST MOM signs which he plans to use the garage's extendable ladder (with a responsible neighborhood adult holding it and supervising) to very carefully affix to the front of the home with water-soluble glue so that it'll be there to greet and cheer the mom when she's released from Critical Care with a totally clean bill of health, which Leonard calls his father repeatedly at the Critical Care ward pay phone to assure him that he has absolutely no doubt of, the totally clean bill of health, calling hourly right on the dot until there's some kind of mechanical problem with the pay phone and when he dials it he just gets a high tone, which he duly reports to the telephone company's special 1-616-TROUBLE line, remembering to include the specific pay phone's eight-digit Field Product Code (which he'd written down all of just in case) as the small-print technical material on the 1-616-TROUBLE line at the very back of the phone book recommends for most rapid and efficient service.

He can produce several different kinds of calligraphy and has been to origami camp (twice) and can do extraordinary freehand sketches of local flora and can whistle all six of Telemann's *Nouveaux Quatuors* as well as imitate just about any birdcall that Audubon could ever have thought of. He sometimes writes academic publishers about possible errors of category and/or syntax in their textbooks. Let's not even mention spelling bees. He can make over twenty different kinds of admiral, cowboy, clerical, and multiethnic hats out of ordinary newspaper, and he volunteers to visit the school's K–2 classrooms teaching the little kids how, an offer the Carl P. Robinson Elementary principal says he appreciates and has considered very carefully before declining. The principal loathes the mere sight of the boy but does not quite know why. He sees the boy in his sleep, at nightmares' ragged edges—the pressed checked shirt and hair's hard little part, the freckles and ready generous smile: anything he can do. The principal fantasizes about sinking a meat hook into Leonard Stecyk's bright-eyed little face and dragging the boy facedown behind his Volkswagen Beetle over the rough new streets of suburban Grand Rapids. The fantasies come out of nowhere and horrify the principal, who is a devout Mennonite.

Everyone hates the boy. It is a complex hatred, one that often causes the haters to feel mean and guilty and to hate themselves for feeling this way about such an accomplished and well-meaning boy, which then tends to make them involuntarily hate the boy even more for arousing such self-hatred. The whole thing is totally confusing and upsetting. People take a lot of aspirin when he's around. The boy's only real friends among kids are the damaged, the handicapped, the fat, the last-picked, the *non grata*—he seeks them out. All 316 invitations to his eleventh-birthday *BLOWOUT BASH*—322 invitations if you count the ones made on audiotape for the blind—are offset-printed on quality vellum with matching high-rag envelopes addressed in ornate Phillippian II calligraphy he's spent three weekends on, and each invitation details in Roman-numeraled outline form the itinerary's half-day at Six Flags, private PhD-guided tour of the Blanford Nature Center, and Reserved Banquet Area w/ Free Play at Shakee's Pizza and Indoor Arcade on Remembrance Drive (the whole day gratis and paid for out of the Paper and Aluminum Drives the boy got up at 4:00 A.M. all summer to organize and spearhead, the balance of the Drives' receipts going to the Red Cross and the parents of a Kentwood third-grader with terminal spina bifida who dreams above all else of seeing the Lions' Night Train Lane play live from his motorized wheelchair), and the invitations explicitly call the party this—a *BLOWOUT BASH*—in balloon-shaped font as the caption to an illustrated explosion of good cheer and -will and no-holds-barred-let-out-all-the-stops *FUN*, with the bold-faced proviso **PLEASE—NO PRESENTS REQUIRED** in each of each card's four corners; and the 316 invitations, sent via First-Class Mail to every student, instructor, substitute instructor, aide, administrator, and custodian at C. P. Robinson Elementary, yield a total attendance of nine celebrants (not counting parents or LPNs of the incapacitated), and yet an undauntedly fine time is had by all, and such is the consensus on the Honest Appraisal and Suggestion Cards (also vellum) circulated at party's end, the massive remainders of chocolate cake, Neapolitan ice cream, pizza, chips, caramel corn, Hershey's Kisses, Red Cross and Officer Chuck pamphlets on organ/tissue donation and the correct procedures to follow if approached by a stranger respectively, kosher pizza for the Orthodox, designer napkins, and dietetic soda in souvenir *I Survived Leonard Stecyk's 11th Birthday Blowout Bash 1964* plastic glasses w/ built-in lemniscate Krazy Straws the guests were to keep as mementos all donated to the Kent County Children's Home via procedures and transport that the birthday boy has initiated even while the big Twister free-for-all is under way, out of concerns about melted ice cream and staleness and flatness and the waste of a chance to help the less fortunate; and his father, driving the wood-panel station wagon and steadying his cheek with one hand, avows again that the boy beside him has a large, good heart, and that he is proud, and that if the boy's mother ever regains consciousness as they so very much hope, he knows she'll be just awful proud as well.

The boy makes As and enough occasional Bs to keep himself from getting a swelled head about marks, and his teachers shudder at the sound of even just his name. In the fifth grade he undertakes a district collection to provide a Special Fund of nickels for anyone at lunch who's already spent their milk money but still might for whatever reason want or feel they need more milk. The Jolly Holly Milk Company gets wind of it and puts a squib about the Fund and an automated line drawing of the boy on the side of some of their half-pint cartons. Two-thirds of the school ceases to drink milk, while the Special Fund itself grows so large that the principal has to requisition a small safe for his office. The principal is now taking Seconal to sleep and experiencing fine tremors, and on two separate occasions is cited for Failure to Yield at marked crosswalks.

A teacher in whose homeroom the boy suggests a charted reorganization of the coat hooks and boot boxes lining one wall so that the coat and galoshes of the student whose desk is nearest the door would themselves be nearest the door, and the second-nearest's second-nearest, and so on, speeding the pupils' egress to recess and reducing delays and possible quarrels and clots of half-bundled kids at the classroom door (which delays and clots the boy had taken the trouble this quarter to chart by statistical incidence, with relevant graphics and arrows but all names withheld), this tenured and highly respected veteran teacher ends up brandishing blunt scissors and threatening to kill first the boy and then herself, and is put on Medical Leave, during which she receives thrice-weekly Get Well cards, with neatly typed summaries of the class's activities and progress in her absence sprinkled with glitter and folded in perfect diamond shapes that open with just a squeeze of the two long facets inside (i.e., inside the cards), until the teacher's doctors order her mail to be withheld until improvement or at least stabilization in her condition warrants.

Right before 1965's big Halloween UNICEF collection three sixth-graders accost the boy in the southeast restroom after fourth period and do unspeakable things to him, leaving him hanging from a stall's hook by his underpants' elastic; and after being treated and released from the hospital (a different one than his mother is a patient in the long-term convalescent ward of), the boy refuses to identify his assailants and later circumspectly delivers to them individualized notes detailing his renunciation of any and all hard feelings about the incident, apologizing for whatever unwitting offense he might have given to provoke it, exhorting his attackers to please put the whole thing behind them and not in any way self-recriminate over it—especially down the line, because the boy's understanding was that these were the sorts of things that could sometimes really haunt you later on down the line in adulthood, citing one or two journal articles the attackers might have a look at if they wanted documentation on the long-term psychological effects of self-recrimination—and, in the notes, professing his personal hope that an actual friendship might conceivably result from the whole regrettable incident, along which lines he was also enclosing an invitation to attend a short no-questions-asked Conflict Resolution Roundtable the boy has persuaded a local community services outreach organization to sponsor after school the following Tuesday *'(Light Refreshments Served!),'* after which the boy's PE locker along with the four on either side are destroyed in an act of pyrotechnic vandalism that everyone on both sides in the subsequent court trial agrees got totally out of hand and was not a premeditated attempt to injure the night custodian or to do anything like the amount of structural damage to the Boys' locker room it ended up doing, and at which trial Leonard Stecyk appeals repeatedly to both sides' counsel for the opportunity to testify for the defense, if only as a character witness. A large percentage of the boy's classmates hide—take actual evasive action—when they see him coming. Eventually even the marginal and infirm stop returning his calls. His mother has to be turned and her limbs manipulated twice a day.

§6

THEY WERE UP on a picnic table at that one park by the lake, by the edge of the lake with part of a downed tree in the shallows half hidden by the bank. Lane A. Dean Jr. and his girlfriend, both in blue jeans and button-up shirts. They sat up on the table's top portion and had their shoes on the bench part that people sat on and picnicked in carefree times. They had gone to different high schools but the same junior college, where they had met in campus ministries. It was springtime, the park's grass was very green and the air suffused with honeysuckle and lilacs both, which was almost too much. There were bees, and the angle of the sun made the water of the shallows look dark. There had been more storms that week, with some downed trees and the sound of chainsaws all up and down his parents' street. Their postures on the picnic table were both the same forward kind with their shoulders rounded and elbows on their knees. In this position the girl rocked slightly and once put her face in her hands but she was not crying. Lane was very still and immobile and looking past the bank at the downed tree in the shallows and its ball of exposed roots going all directions and the tree's cloud of branches all half in the water. The only other individual nearby was a dozen spaced tables away by himself, standing upright. Looking at the torn-up hole in the ground there where the tree had gone over. It was still early yet and all the shadows wheeling right and shortening. The girl wore a thin old checked cotton shirt with pearl-colored snaps with the long sleeves down and she always smelled very good and clean, like someone you could trust and deeply care about even if you weren't in love. Lane Dean had liked the smell of her right away. His mother called her *down to earth* and liked her, thought she was good people, you could tell — she made this evident in little ways. The shallows lapped from different directions at the tree as if almost teething on it. Sometimes when alone and thinking or struggling to turn a matter over to Jesus Christ in prayer, he would find himself putting his fist in his palm and turning it slightly as if still playing and pounding his glove to stay sharp and alert in center. He did not do this now, it would be cruel and indecent to do this now. The older individual stood beside his picnic table, he was at it but not sitting, and looked also out of place in a suit coat or jacket and the kind of older men's hat Lane's grandfather wore in photos as a young insurance man. He appeared to be looking across the lake. If he moved, Lane didn't see it. He looked more like a picture than a man. There were not any ducks in view.

One thing Lane Dean did was reassure her again that he'd go with her and be there with her. It was one of the few safe or decent things he could really say. The second time he said it again now she shook her head and laughed in an unhappy way that was more just air out her nose. Her real laugh was different. Where he'd be was the waiting room, she said. That he'd be thinking about her and feeling bad for her, she knew, but he couldn't be in there with her. This was so obviously true that he felt like a ninny that he'd kept on about it and now knew what she had thought every time he went and said it; it hadn't brought her comfort or eased the burden at all. The worse he felt, the stiller he sat. The whole thing felt balanced on a knife or wire; if he moved to put his arm up or touch her the whole thing could tip over. He hated himself for sitting so frozen. He could almost visualize himself tiptoeing through something explosive. A big stupid-looking tiptoe like in a cartoon. The whole last black week had been this way and it was wrong. He knew it was wrong, he knew something was required of him and knew it was not this terrible frozen care and caution, but he pretended to himself he did not know what it was that was required. He pretended it had no name. He pretended that not saying aloud what he knew to be right and true was for her sake, was for the sake of her needs and feelings. He also worked dock and routing at UPS, besides school, but traded to get the day off after they'd decided together. Two days before, he had awakened very early and tried to pray but could not. He was freezing more and more solid, he felt like, but he hadn't thought of his father or the blank frozenness of his father, even in church, that once had filled him with such pity. This was the truth. Lane Dean Jr. felt sun on one arm as he pictured in his mind an image of himself on a train, waving mechanically to something that got smaller and smaller as the train pulled away. His father and his mother's father had the same birthday, a Cancer. Sheri's hair was colored an almost corn blond, very clean, the skin through the central part pink in the light. They'd sat up here long enough that only their right side was shaded now. He could look at her head, but not at her. Different parts of him felt unconnected to each other. She was smarter than him and they both knew it. It wasn't just school—Lane Dean was in accounting and business and did all right, he was hanging in there. She was a year older, she was twenty, but it was also more—she had always seemed to Lane to be on good terms with her life in a way age could not account for. His mother had put it that she *knew what it was she wanted,* which was nursing and not an easy program at Peoria Junior College, and plus she worked hostessing at the Embers and had bought her own car. She was serious in a way Lane liked. She had a cousin that died when she was thirteen, fourteen, that she'd loved and been close with. She only talked about it that once. He liked her smell and the downy hair on her arms and the way she exclaimed when something made her laugh. He had liked just being with her and talking to her. She was serious in her faith and values in a way that Lane had liked and now, sitting here with her on the table, found himself afraid of. This was an awful thing. He was starting to believe he might not be serious in his faith. He might be somewhat of a hypocrite, like the Assyrians in Isaiah, which would be a far graver sin than the appointment—he had decided he believed this. He was desperate to be good people, to still be able to feel he was good. He rarely before had thought of damnation and hell, that part of it didn't speak to his spirit, and in worship services he more just tuned himself out and tolerated hell when it came up, the same way you tolerate the job you have got to have to save up for what it is you want. Her tennis shoes had little things and items doodled on them from sitting in her class lectures. She stayed looking down like that. Little notes or reading assignments in Bic in her neat round hand on the rubber elements around the sneaker's rim. Lane A. Dean looking at her inclined head's side's barrettes in the shape of blue ladybugs. The appointment was for afternoon, but when the doorbell rang so early and his mother'd called to him up the stairs, he had known, and a terrible kind of blankness had commenced falling through him.

He told her that he did not know what to do. That he knew if he was the salesman of it and forced it upon her that was awful and wrong. But he was trying to understand, they'd prayed on it and talked it through from every different angle. Lane said how sorry she knew he was, and that if he was wrong in believing they'd truly decided together when they decided to make the appointment she should please tell him, because he thought he knew how she must have felt as it got closer and closer and how she must be so scared, but that what he couldn't tell was if it was more than that. He was totally still except for moving his mouth, it felt like. She did not reply. That if they needed to pray on it more and talk it through, why then he was here, he was ready, he said. He said the appointment could get moved back; if she just said the word they could call and push it back to take more time to be sure in the decision. It was still so early in it, they both knew that, he said. This was true, he felt this way, and yet he also knew he was also trying to say things that would get her to open up and say enough back that he could see her and read her heart and know what to say to get her to go through with it. He knew this without admitting to himself that this is what he wanted, for it would make him a hypocrite and a liar. He knew, in some locked-up little part of him, why it was that he'd gone to no one to open up and seek their life counsel, not Pastor Steve or the prayer partners at campus ministries, not his UPS friends or the spiritual counseling available through his parents' old church. But he did not know why Sheri herself had not gone to Pastor Steve—he could not read her heart. She was blank and hidden. He so fervently wished it never happened. He felt like he knew now why it was a true sin and not just a leftover rule from past society. He felt like he had been brought low by it and humbled and now did understand and believe that the rules were there for a reason. That the rules were concerned with him personally, as an individual. He'd promised God he had learned his lesson. But what if that, too, was a hollow promise, from a hypocrite who repented only after, who promised submission but really only wanted a reprieve? He might not even know his own heart or be able to read and know himself. He kept thinking also of 1 Timothy 6 and the hypocrite therein who *disputeth over words*. He felt a terrible inner resistance but could not feel what it was it so resisted. This was the truth. All the different angles and ways they had come at the decision together did not ever include it, the word—for had he once said it, avowed that he did love her, loved Sheri Fisher, then it would have all been transformed, it would be a different stance or angle but a difference in the very thing they were praying and deciding on together. Sometimes they had prayed together over the phone in a kind of half code in case anybody accidentally picked up another extension. She continued to sit as if thinking, in the pose of thinking like almost that one statue. They were on that one table. He was the one looking past her at the tree in the water. But he could not say he did, it was not true.

But nor did he ever open up and tell her straight out he did not love her. This may be his *lie by omission*. This may be the frozen resistance—were he to look straight at her and tell her he didn't, she would keep the appointment and go. He knew this. Something in him, though, some terrible weakness or lack of values, would not tell her. It felt like a muscle he just did not have. He didn't know why, he could not do it or even pray to do it. She believed he was good, serious in his values. Part of him seemed willing to more or less just about lie to someone with that kind of faith and trust and what did that make him? How could such a type of individual even pray? What it really felt like was a taste of the reality of what might be meant by hell. Lane Dean had never believed in hell as a lake of fire or a loving God consigning folks to a burning lake of fire—he knew in his heart this was not true. What he believed in was a living God of compassion and love and the possibility of a personal relationship with Jesus Christ through whom this love was enacted in human time. But sitting here beside this girl as unknown to him now as outer space, waiting for whatever she might say to unfreeze him, now he felt like he could see the edge or outline of what a real vision of hell might be. It was of two great and terrible armies within himself, opposed and facing each other, silent. There would be battle but no victor. Or never a battle—the armies would stay like that, motionless, looking across at each other and seeing therein something so different and alien from themselves that they could not understand, they could not hear each other's speech as even words or read anything from what their faces looked like, frozen like that, opposed and uncomprehending, for all human time. Two hearted, a hypocrite to yourself either way.

When he moved his head, the part of the lake farther out flashed with sun; the water up close wasn't black now and you could see into the shallows and see that all the water was moving but gently, this way and that, and in this same way he besought to return to himself as Sheri moved her leg and started to turn beside him. He could see the man in the suit and gray hat standing motionless now at the lake's rim, holding something under one arm and looking across at the opposite side where little forms on camp chairs sat there in a row in a way that meant they had lines in the water for crappie, which mostly only your blacks from the East Side ever did, and the little white shape at the row's end a Styrofoam creel. In his moment or time at the lake now just to come, Lane Dean first felt he could take this all in whole; everything seemed distinctly lit, for the circle of the pin oak's shade had rotated off all the way and they sat now in sun with their shadow a two-headed thing in the grass to the left before them. He was looking or gazing again at where the downed tree's branches seemed to bend so sharply just under the shallows' surface when he was given then to know that through all this frozen silence he'd despised he had, in truth, been praying all the while, or some little part of his heart he could not know or hear had, for he was answered now with a type of vision, what he later would call within his own mind a vision or *moment of grace*. He was not a hypocrite, just broken and split off like all men. Later on, he believed that what happened was he had a moment of almost seeing them both as Jesus might see them—as blind but groping, wanting to please God despite their inborn fallen nature. For in that same given moment he saw, quick as light, into Sheri's heart, and was made therein to know what would occur here as she finished turning to him and the man in the hat watched the fishing and the downed elm shed cells in the water. This down-to-earth girl who smelled good and wanted to be a nurse would take and hold one of his hands in both of hers to unfreeze him and make him look at her, and she would say that she cannot do it. That she is sorry she did not know this sooner, she hadn't meant to lie, she'd agreed because she wanted to believe she could, but she cannot. That she will carry this and have it, she has to. With her gaze clear and steady. That all night last night she prayed and searched herself and decided this is what love commands of her. That Lane should please please sweetie let her finish. That listen—this is her own decision and obliges him to nothing. That she knows he does not love her, not that way, has known it all this time, and that it's all right. That it is as it is and it's all right. She will carry this, and have it, and love it and make no claim on Lane except his good wishes and respecting what she has to do. That she releases him, all claim, and hopes he finishes up PJC and does so good in his life and has all joy and good things. Her voice will be clear and steady, and she will be lying, for Lane has been given to read her heart. To see her. One of the opposite side's blacks raises his arm in what might be greeting, or waving off a bee. There is a mower cutting grass someplace off behind them. It will be a terrible, make-or-break gamble born out of the desperation in Sheri Fisher's soul, the knowledge that she can neither do this thing today nor carry a child alone and shame her family. Her values block the way either way, Lane can see, and she has no other options or choice, this lie is not a sin. Galatians 4:16, *Have I then become your enemy?* She is gambling that he is good. There on the table, neither frozen nor yet moving, Lane Dean Jr. sees all this, and is moved with pity and with also something more, something without any name he knows, that is given to him to feel in the form of a question that never once in all the long week's thinking and division had even so much as occurred—why is he so sure he doesn't love her?

Why is one kind of love any different? What if he has no earthly idea what love is? What would even Jesus do? For it was just now he felt her two small strong soft hands on his, to turn him. What if he is just afraid, if the truth is no more than this, and if what to pray for is not even love but simple courage, to meet both her eyes as she says it and trust his heart?

§8

UNDER THE SIGN erected every May above the outer highway reading IT'S SPRING, THINK FARM SAFETY and through the north ingress with its own defaced name and signs addressed to soliciting and speed and universal glyph for children at play and down the blacktop's gauntlet of double-wide showpieces past the rottweiler humping nothing in crazed spasms at chain's end and the sound of frying through the kitchenette window of the trailer at the hairpin right and then hard left along the length of a speed bump into the dense copse as yet uncleared for new single-wides and the sound of dry things snapping and stridulation of bugs in the duff of the copse and the two bottles and bright plastic packet impaled on the mulberry twig, seeing through shifting parallax of saplings' branches sections then of trailers along the north park's anfractuous roads and lanes skirting the corrugate trailer where it was said the man left his family and returned sometime later with a gun and killed them all as they watched *Dragnet* and the torn abandoned sixteen-wide half overgrown by the edge of the copse where boys and their girls made strange agnate forms on pallets and left bright torn packs until a mishap with a stove blew the gas lead and ruptured the trailer's south wall in a great labial tear that exposes the trailer's gutted insides to view from the edge of the copse and the plurality of eyes as the needles and stems of a long winter noisomely crunch beneath a plurality of shoes where the copse leaves off at a tangent past the end of the undeveloped cul-de-sac where they come now at dusk to watch the parked car heave on its springs. The windows steamed nearly opaque and so alive in the chassis that it seems to move without running, the boat-sized car, squeak of struts and absorbers and a jiggle just short of true rhythm. The birds at dusk and the smell of snapped pine and a younger one's cinnamon gum. The shimmying motions resemble those of a car traveling at high speeds along a bad road, making the Buick's static aspect dreamy and freighted with something like romance or death in the gaze of the girls who squat at the copse's risen edge, appearing dyadic and eyes half again as wide and solemn, watching for the sometime passage of a limb's pale shape past a window (once a bare foot flat against it and itself atremble), moving incrementally forward and down each night in the week before true spring, soundlessly daring one another to go get up close to the heaving car and see in, which the only one who finally does so then sees naught but her own wide eyes reflected as from inside the glass comes a cry she knows too well, which wakes her again each time across the trailer's cardboard wall.

There were fires in the gypsum hills to the north, the smoke of which hung and stank of salt; then the pewter earrings vanished without complaint or even mention. Then a whole night's absence, two. The child as mother to the woman. These were auguries and signs: Toni Ware and her mother abroad again in endless night. Routes on maps that yield no sensible shape or figure when traced.

At night from the trailer's park the hills possessed of a dirty orange glow and the sounds of living trees exploding in the fires' heat did carry, and the noise of planes plowing the undulant air above and dropping thick tongues of talc. Some nights it rained fine ash which upon contacting turned to soot and kept all souls indoors such that throughout the park every trailer's window possessed of the underwater glow of televisions and when many were identically tuned the sounds of the programs came clear to the girl through the ash as if their own television were still with them. It had vanished without comment prior to their last move. That last time's sign.

The park's boys wore wide rumpled hats and cravats of thong and some displayed turquoise about their person, and of these one helped her empty the trailer's sanitary tank and then pressed her to fellate him in recompense, whereupon she promised that anything emerging from his trousers would not return there. No boy near her size had successfully pressed her since Houston and the two who put something in her pop that made them turn sideways in the air and she could not then fight and lay watching the sky while they did their distant business.

At sunset then the north and west were the same color. On clear nights she could read by the night sky's emberlight seated on the plastic box that served as stoop. The screen door had no screen but was still a screen door, which fact she thought upon. She could fingerpaint in the soot on the kitchenette's rangetop. In incendiary orange to the deepening twilight in the smell of creosote burning in the sharp hills upwind.

Her inner life rich and multivalent. In fantasies of romance it was she who fought and overcame thereon to rescue some object or figure that never in the reverie resolved or took to itself any shape or name.

After Houston her favorite doll had been the mere head of a doll, its hair prolixly done and the head's hole threaded to meet a neck's own thread; she had been eight when the body was lost and it lay now forever supine and unknowing in weeds while its head lived on.

The mother's relational skills were indifferent and did not include truthful or consistent speech. The daughter had learned to trust actions and to read sign in details of which the run of children are innocent. The battered road atlas had then appeared and lay athwart the counter's medial crack opened to the mother's home state over whose representation of her place of origin lay a spore of dried mucus spindled through with a red thread of blood. The atlas stayed open that way nigh on one week unreferred to; they ate around it. It gathered wind-drift ash through the torn screen. Ants vexed all the park's trailers, there being something in the fire's ash they craved. Their point of formication the high place where the kitchenette's woodgrain paneling had detached in prior heat and bowed outward and from which two vascular parallel columns of black ants descended. Standing eating out of cans at the anodized sink. Two flashlights and a drawer with different bits of candles which the mother eschewed for her cigarettes were her light unto the world. A little box of borax in each of the kitchenette's corners. The water in buckets from the coinwash tap, the trailer a standalone with sides' wires hanging and its owner's whereabouts unreckoned by the park's elders, whose lawn chairs sat unmolested by ash in the smoke tree's central shade. One of these, Mother Tia, told fortunes, leathery and tremorous and her face like a shucked pecan fully cowled in black and two isolate teeth like a spare at the Show Me Lanes, and owned her own cards and tray on which what ash collected showed white, calling her *chulla* and charging her no tariff on terms of the Evil Eye she claimed to fear when the girl looked at her through the screen's hole with the telescope of a rolled magazine. Two ribby and yellow-eyed dogs lay throbbing in the smoke tree's shade and rose only sometimes to bay at the planes as they harried the fires.

The sun overhead like a peephole into hell's own self-consuming heart.

Yet one more sign being when Mother Tia refused then to augur and doing so in terms of pleading for clemency instead of bare refusal to the reedy laughter of the shade's other elders and widows; no one understood why she feared the girl and she would not say, lower lip caught behind one tooth as she traced the special letter over and over on nothing in the air before her. Whom she would miss, and whose memory in trust therefore the doll's head also would carry.

The mother's relational skills being indifferent to this degree since the period of clinical confinement in University City MO wherein the mother had been denied visits for eighteen business days and the girl had evaded Family Services during this period and slept in an abandoned Dodge vehicle whose doors could be secured with coat hangers twisted just so.

The girl looked often at the open atlas and the city thereon marked with a sneeze. She had herself been born there, just outside, in the town that bore her own name. Her second experience of the kind her books made seem sweet through indifferent speech had occurred in the abandoned car in University City MO at the hands of a man who knew how to dislodge one coat hanger with the straightened hook of another and told her face beneath his fingerless mitten there were two different ways this right here could go.

The longest time she had ever subsisted wholly on shoplifted food was eight days. Not more than a competent shoplifter. Their time at Moab UT an associate once said that her pockets had no imagination and was soon thereafter pinched and made to spear litter by the highway as she and the mother had passed in the converted camper driven by 'Kick,' the seller of pyrite and self-made arrowheads around whom the mother said not ever one word but sat before the radio painting each nail a different color and who had once punched her stomach so hard she saw colors and smelled up close the carpet's grit base and could hear what her mother then did to distract 'Kick' from further attentions to this girl with the mouth on her. This being also how she learned to cut a brake line so the failure would be delayed until such time as the depth of the cut determined.

At night on the pallet in the ruddled glow she dreamt also of a bench by a pond and the somnolent mutter of ducks while the girl held the string of something that floated above with a painted face, a kite or balloon. Of another girl she would never see or know of.

Once on the nation's interstate highway system the mother had spoken of a headless doll she herself had kept and clung to through the hell on earth years of her Peoria girlhood and her own mother's *nervous illness* (her profile bunched up as she pronounced it) during which the mother's mother had refused to let her outside the house over which she had engaged itinerant men to nail found and abandoned hubcaps to every inch of the exterior in order to deflect the transmissions of one Jack Benny, a rich man whom the grandmother had come to believe was insane and sought *global thought control* by radio wave of a special pitch and hue. ("'Nobody that mean's going to let the world go" ' was an indirect quotation or hearsay when driving, which the mother could do while simultaneously smoking and using an emery board.) The girl made it her business to read signs and know the facts of her own history past and present. To beat broken glass into powder requires an hour with a portion of brick on a durable surface. She had shoplifted ground chuck and buns and kneaded powdered glass into the meat and cooked it on a windowscreen brazier at the rear of the abandoned Dodge and had left such painstaking meals of sandwich on the front seat for days running before the man who had pressed her used his coat hanger tool to jimmy the vehicle and steal them whereupon he returned no more; the mother then released into the girl's care soon. Imbrication by disk is impossible, but the grandmother's specifications were that each hubcap touch those on every possible side. Thus the electrification of one became the charge of all, to counter the waves' bombardment. The creation of a lethal field which jammed radios all down the block. Twice cited for diverting the home's amperage, the old woman had found a generator someplace that would run if noisily on kerosene and bounced and shook beside the bomb-shaped propane tank outside the kitchen. The young mother was sometimes permitted outside to bury the sparrows that alit on the home and sent up their souls in a single flash and bird-shaped ball of smoke.

The girl read stories about horses, bios, science, psychiatry, and *Popular Mechanics* when obtainable. She read history in a determined way. She read *My Struggle* and could not understand all the fuss. She read Wells, Steinbeck, Keene, Laura Wilder (twice), and Lovecraft. She read halves of many torn and castoff things. She read a coverless *Red Badge* and knew by sheer feel that its author had never seen war nor knew that past some extremity one floated just above the fear and could blinklessly watch it while doing what had to be done or allowed to stay alive.

The trailer park's boy who had pressed her there in the hanging smell of their own sewage now assembled his friends outside the trailer at night there to lurk and make inhuman sounds in the ashfall as the daughter's daughter drew circles within circles about her own given name on the map and the arteries leading thereto. The gypsum fires and the park's lit sign were the poles of the desert night. The boys burped and howled at the moon and the howls were nothing like the real thing and their laughter was strained and words indifferent to the love they said swelled them and would visit upon her past counting.

In these the mother's absences with men the girl sent for catalogues and Free Offers which daily did arrive by mail with samples of products that people with homes would buy to enjoy at their leisure like the girl, who considered herself home tutored and did not ride the bus with the park's children. These all possessed the stunned smeared look of those who are poor in one place; the trailers, sign, and passing trucks were the furniture of their world, which orbited but did not turn. The girl often imagined them in a rearview, receding, both arms raised in farewell.

Asbestos cloth cut carefully into strips one of which placed in the pay dryer when the mother of the would-be assailant had deposited her load and returned to the Circle K for more beer caused neither the boy nor mother to be seen anymore outside their double-wide, which rested on blocks. The boys' serenades ceased as well.

A soup can of sewage or roadkill carcass when placed beneath the blocks or plasticized lattice of a store-bought porch attachment would fill and afflict that trailer with a plague's worth of soft-bodied flies. A shade tree could be killed by driving a short length of copper tubing into its base a handsbreadth from ground; the leaves would commence to embrown straightaway. The trick with a brake or fuel line was to use strippers to whet it to almost nothing instead of cutting it clean through. It took a certain feel. Half an ounce of packets' aggregate sugar in the gas tank disabled all vehicles but required no art. Likewise a penny in the fuse box or red dye in a trailer's water tank accessible through the sanitation panel on all but late-year models of which the Vista Verde park had none.

Begat in one car and born in another. Creeping up in dreams to see her own conceiving.

The desert possessed of no echo and in this was like the sea from which it came. Sometimes at night the sounds of the fire carried, or the circling planes, or those of long-haul trucks on 54 for Santa Fe whose tires' plaint had the quality of distant surf's lalation; she lay listening on the pallet and imagined not the sea or the moving trucks themselves but whatever she right then chose. Unlike the mother or bodiless doll, she was free inside her head. An unbound genius, larger than any sun.

The girl read a biography of Hetty Green, the matricide and accused forger who had dominated the Stock Market while saving scraps of soap in a dented tin box she carried on her person, and who feared no living soul. She read *Macbeth* as a color comic with dialogue in boxes.

The performer Jack Benny had cupped his own face with a hand in a manner the mother, when lucid, had told her she'd seen as tender and pined for, dreamt of, inside the home and its carapace of electric shields while her own mother wrote letters to the FBI in code.

Near sunrise the red plains to the east undimmed and the terrible imperious heat of the day bestirred in its underground den; the girl placed the doll's head on the sill to watch the red eye open and small rocks and bits of litter cast shadows as long as a man.

Never once in five states worn a dress or leather shoes.

At dawn of the fires' eighth day her mother appeared in a vehicle made large by its corrugated shell behind whose wheel sat an unknown male. The side of the shell said LEER.

Thought blocking, overinclusion. Vagueness, overspeculation, woolly thinking, confabulation, word salad, stonewalling, aphasia. Delusions of persecution. Catatonic immobility, automatic obedience, affective flattening, dilute I/Thou, disordered cognition, loosened or obscure associations. Depersonalization. Delusions of centrality or grandeur. Compulsivity, ritualism. Hysterical blindness. Promiscuity. Solipsismus or ecstatic states (rare).

> This Girl's D./P.O.B.: 11-4-60, Anthony IL.
>
> Girl's Mother's D./P.O.B.: 4-8-43, Peoria IL.
>
> Most Recent Address: 17 Dosewallips Unit E, Vista Verde Estates Mobile Home Park, Organ NM 88052.
>
> Girl's H.W.E./H.: 5' 3", 95 lbs., Brown/Brown.
>
> Mother's Stated Occupations, 1966–1972 (from IRS Form 669-D [Certificate of Subordination of Federal Tax Lien, District 063(a)], 1972): Cafeteria Dish and Food Area Cleaning Assistant, Rayburn-Thrapp Agronomics, Anthony IL; Skilled Operator of Silkscreen Press Until Injury to Wrist, All City Uniform Company, Alton IL; Cashier, Convenient Food Mart Corporation, Norman OK and Jacinto City TX; Server, Stuckey's Restaurants Corp., Limon CO; Assistant Adhesive Product Mixing Scheduling Clerk, National Starch and Chemical Company, University City MO; Hostess and Beverage Server, Double Deuce Live Stage Night Club, Lordsburg NM; Contract Vendor, Cavalry Temporary Services, Moab UT; Canine Confinement Area Organization and Cleaning, Best Friends Kennel and Groom, Green Valley AZ; Ticket Agent and Substitute Night Manager, Riské's Live XX Adult Entertainment, Las Cruces NM.

They drove then once more at night. Below a moon that rose round before them. What was termed the truck's backseat was a narrow shelf on which the girl could sleep if she arranged her legs in the gap behind the real seats whose headrests possessed the dull shine of unwashed hair. The clutter and yeast smell bespoke a truck that was or had been lived in; the truck and its man smelled the same. The girl in cotton bodice and her jeans gone fugitive at the knees. The mother's conception of men was that she used them as a sorceress will dumb animals, as sign and object of her unnatural powers. Her spoken word aloud for these at which the girl gave no reproof, *familiar.* Swart and sideburned men who sucked wooden matches and crushed cans with their hands. Whose hats' brims had sweatlines like the rings of trees. Whose eyes crawled over you in the rearview. Men inconceivable as ever themselves being children or looking up naked at someone they trust, with a toy. To whom the mother talked like babies and let them treat her like a headless doll, *manhandle.*

At an Amarillo motel the girl had her own locked room out of earshot. The hangers were affixed to the closet's rod. The doll's head wore lipstick of pink crayon and looked at TV. The girl often wished she had a cat or some small pet to feed and reassure as she stroked its head. The mother feared winged insects and carried cans of spray. Mace on a chain and melted cosmetics and her faux-leather snap case for cigarettes and lighter at once in a handbag of imbricate red sequins the girl had produced for Christmas in Green Valley with only a very small tear near the base where the electronic tag had been forced with a file and then used to carry out the same bodice the girl now wore, on which stitched pink hearts formed a fenceline at breast level.

The truck smelled also of spoilt provision and had a window with vanished crank he rolled up and down with pliers. A card taped to one visor proclaimed that hairdressers teased it till it did stand up. His teeth were missing at one side; the glovebox was locked. The mother at thirty with face commencing to display the faint seams of the plan for the second face life had in store for her and which she feared would be her own mother's and in University City's confined time sat with knees bunched up rocking and scratched at herself essaying to ruin the face's plan. The sepia photo of the mother's mother at the girl's own age in a pinafore on horsehair seat rolled into the doll's head and carried with soapscraps and three library cards in her given name. Her diary in the round case's second lining. And the lone photo of her mother as a child outdoors in winter dazzle in so many coats and hats that she and the propane tank might be kin. The electrified house out of view and the circle of snowmelt around its base and the mother behind the little mother holding her upright; the child had had croup and such a fever she was feared not to live and her mother had realized she had no pictures of her baby to keep if she died and had bundled her up and sent her out into the snow to wait while she begged a snapshot with a neighbor's Land Camera so her baby might not be forgotten when she died. The photo distorted from long folding and no footprints in view anywhere in the picture's snow that the girl could see, the child's mouth wide open and eyes looking up at the man with the camera in trust that this made sense, this was how right life occurred. The girl's plans for the grandmother, much refined with age and accrued art, occupied much of the latest diary's first third.

Her mother and not the male was at the wheel when she woke to the clatter of gravel in Kansas. A truck stop receded as something upright ran in the road behind them and waved its hat. She asked where they were but did not ask after the man who through three states had driven with the same offending hand on the mother's thigh that had touched her, a hand studied through the seats' gap by the doll's head held just so and its detachment and airborne flight seen in the same dream the lurch and sounds first seemed part of. The daughter thirteen now and starting to look it. Her mother's eyes were distant and low-lidded in the company of men; now in Kansas she made faces at the rearview and chewed gum. 'Ride up front up out of there up here why don't you.' The gum smelt cinnamon and its folded foil could make a glovebox pick by wrapping round to smooth a file's emery at the point.

Outside a Portales rest stop, under a sun of beaten gold, the girl supine and half asleep in a porous nap on the little back shelf had suffered the man to hoist himself about behind the truck's wheel and form his hand into an unsensual claw and send it out over the seatback to squeeze her personal titty, to throttle the titty, eyes pale and unprurient, she playing dead and staring unblinking past him, the man's breathing audible and khaki cap pungent, manhandling the titty with what seemed an absent dispassion, leaving off only at the high heels' sound in the lot outside. Still a stark advance over the previous year's Cesar, who worked at painting highway signs and had green grains forever in the pores of his face and hands and required both mother and girl to keep the washroom door open no matter what their business inside, himself then in turn improved over Houston's district of warehouses and gutted lofts whereat had fallen in with them for two months 'Murray Blade,' the semiprofessional welder whose knife in its forearm's spring clip covered a tattoo of just that knife between two ownerless blue breasts the squeeze of a fist made swell at the sides which amused him. Men with leather vests and tempers who were tender when drunk in ways that made your back's skin pebble up.

The 54 highway east was not federal and the winds of oncoming rigs struck the truck and its shell and caused yaw the mother steered against. All windows down against the man's stored smell. An unmentionable thing in the glovebox the mother said to shut she couldn't look. The card with its entendre made French curls in their backwash and disappeared against the past road's shimmer.

West of Pratt KS they purchased and ate Convenient Mart burritos heated in the device provided for that purpose. A great huge unfinishable Slushee.

Behind her carapace of disks and foil the mother's mother held when madman Jack Benny or his spiral-eyed slaves came for them the best defense at hand was to play dead, to lie with blank eyes open and not blink or breathe while the men holstered their ray guns and walked about the house and looked at them, shrugging and telling one another they were too late because look here the woman and her nubile daughter were already deceased and best left be. Forced to practice together in the twin beds with open bottles of pills on the table betwixt and hands composed on their chests and eyes wide and breathing in such a slight way that the chest never rose. The older woman could hold her open eyes unblinking a very long time; the mother as child could not and they soon enough closed of their own, for a living child is no doll and does need to blink and breathe. The older woman said one could self-lubricate at will with the proper application of discipline and time. She said her decade on a carnival necklace and had a small nickel lock on the mailbox. Windows covered with foil in the crescents between the caps' black circles. The mother carried drops and always claimed her eyes were dry.

Riding up front was good. She did not ask about the truck's man. It was his truck they were in but he was not in the truck; it was hard to locate something to complain about in this. The mother's relatings were least indifferent when the two faced the same; she made small jokes and sang and sent small looks the daughter's way. All the world beyond the reach of the headlamps' beams was much obscured. Hers was her grandmother's maiden name, Ware. She could put her soles against the truck's black dash and look out between her knees, the whole of the headlights' tongue of road between them. The broken centerline shot Morse at them and the bone-white moon was round and clouds moved across it and took shape as they did so. First fingers then whole hands and trees of lightning fluttered on the west horizon; nothing came behind them. She kept looking for following lights or signs. The mother's lipstick was too bright for the shape of her mouth. The girl did not ask. The odds were high. The man was either the species of man who would file a report or else would essay to follow like a second 'Kick' and find them for leaving him waving his hat in the road. If she asked, the mother's face would go saggy as she thought of what to say when the truth was she hadn't thought at all. The girl's blessing and lot to know their two minds both as one, to hold the wheel as Murine was again applied.

They had a sit-down breakfast in Plepler MO in a rain that foamed the gutters and beat against the café's glass. The waitress in nurse-white had a craggy face and called them both honey and wore a button which said I have got but one nerve left and you are upon that nerve and flirted with the workingmen whose names she knew while steam came out of the kitchen over the counter above which she clipped sheets from her pad, and the girl used their toothbrush in a restroom whose lock had no hasp. The front door's hung bell sounded on use to signal custom. The mother wanted biscuits and hashbrowns and mush with syrup and they ordered and the mother sought a dry match and soon the girl heard her laughing at something the men at the counter said. Rain rolled through the street and cars passed slowly and their truck with its shell faced the table and still had its parking lights on, which she saw, and saw also within her mind the truck's legal owner still there in the road outside Kismet holding his hands extended into claws at the space where the truck had receded from view while the mother beat the wheel and blew hair from her eyes. The girl dragged toast through her yolk. Of the two men who entered and filled the next booth one had similar whiskers and eyes beneath a red cap gone black with rain. The waitress with her little stub pencil and pad said unto these:

'What are you settin' in a dirty booth for?'

'So as I can be closer to you, darling.'

'Why you could have set over right there and been closer yet.'

'Shoot.'

§9

Author's Foreword

AUTHOR HERE. Meaning the real author, the living human holding the pencil, not some abstract narrative persona. Granted, there sometimes is such a persona in *The Pale King,* but that's mainly a pro forma statutory construct, an entity that exists just for legal and commercial purposes, rather like a corporation; it has no direct, provable connection to me as a person. But this right here is me as a real person, David Wallace, age forty, SS no. 975-04-2012,[1] addressing you from my Form 8829–deductible home office at 725 Indian Hill Blvd., Claremont 91711 CA, on this fifth day of spring, 2005, to inform you of the following:

All of this is true. This book is really true.

I obviously need to explain. First, please flip back and look at the book's legal disclaimer, which is on the copyright page, verso side, four leaves in from the rather unfortunate and misleading front cover. The disclaimer is the unindented chunk that starts: 'The characters and events in this book are fictitious.' I'm aware that ordinary citizens almost never read disclaimers like this, the same way we don't bother to look at copyright claims or

---

1 Little-known fact: The only US citizens anywhere whose Social Security numbers start with the numeral 9 are those who are, or at some time were, contract employees of the Internal Revenue Service. Through its special relationship with the Social Security Administration, the IRS issues you a new SS number on the day your contract starts. It's like you're born again, ID-wise, when you enter the Service. Very few ordinary citizens know about this. There's no reason they should. But consider your own Social Security number, or those of the people close enough to you that you're entrusted with their SS. There's only one digit that these SS numbers never start with. That number is 9. 9's reserved for the Service. And if you're issued one, it stays with you for the rest of your life, even if you happen to have left the IRS long ago. It sort of marks you, numerically. Every April—and quarterly, of course, for those who are self-employed and pay quarterly ESTs—those tax returns and ESTs whose filers' SS numbers start with 9 are automatically pulled and routed through a special processing and exam program in the Martinsburg Computer Center. Your status in the system is forever altered. The Service knows its own, always.

Library of Congress specs or any of the dull pro forma boilerplate on sales contracts and ads that everyone knows is there just for legal reasons. But now I need you to read it, the disclaimer, and to understand that its initial 'The characters and events in this book…' includes this very Author's Foreword. In other words, this Foreword is defined by the disclaimer as itself fictional, meaning that it lies within the area of special legal protection established by that disclaimer. I need this legal protection in order to inform you that what follows[2] is, in reality, not fiction at all, but substantially true and accurate. That *The Pale King* is, in point of fact, more like a memoir than any kind of made-up story.

This might appear to set up an irksome paradox. The book's legal disclaimer defines everything that follows it as fiction, including this Foreword, but now here in this Foreword I'm saying that the whole thing is really nonfiction; so if you believe one you can't believe the other, & c., & c. Please know that I find these sorts of cute, self-referential paradoxes irksome, too—at least now that I'm over thirty I do—and that the very last thing this book is is some kind of clever metafictional titty-pincher. That's why I'm making it a point to violate protocol and address you here directly, as my real self; that's why all the specific identifying data about me as a real person got laid out at the start of this Foreword. So that I could inform you of the truth: The only bona fide 'fiction' here is the copyright page's disclaimer—which, again, is a legal device: The disclaimer's whole and only purpose is to protect me, the book's publisher, and the publisher's assigned distributors from legal liability. The reason why such protections are especially required here—why, in fact, the publisher[3] has

2 This is a term of art; what I really mean is that everything that surrounds this Foreword is essentially true. The Foreword's having now been moved seventy-nine pages into the text is due to yet another spasm of last-minute caution on the part of the publisher, re which please see just below.

3 At the advice of its corporate counsel, the publishing company has declined to be identified by name in this Author's Foreword, despite the fact that anyone who looks at the book's spine or title page will know immediately who the company is. Meaning it's an irrational constraint; but so be it. As my own counsel has observed, corporate attorneys are not paid to be totally rational, but they are paid to be totally cautious. And it is not hard to see why a registered US corporation like this book's publisher is going to be cautious about even the possibility of appearing to thumb its nose at the Internal Revenue Service or (this from some of the corporate counsel's hysterical early memos) to be 'abetting' an author's violation of the Nondisclosure Covenant that all Treasury employees are required to sign. Nevertheless—as my lawyer and I had to point out to them about 105 times before the company's counsel seemed to get it—the version of the Nondisclosure Covenant that's binding on *all* Treasury employees, not just on agents of the Bureau of Alcohol, Tobacco and Firearms and of the Secret Service, as formerly, was instituted in 1987, which happens to be the year that computers and a high-powered statistical for-

mula known as the ANADA (for 'Audit–No Audit Discriminant Algorithm') were first used in the examination of nearly all individual US tax returns. I know that's a pretty involved and confusing data-dump to inflict on you in a mere Foreword, but the crux here is that it is the ANADA,[a] and the constituents of its formula for determining which tax returns are most apt to yield additional revenue under audit, that the Service is concerned to protect, and that that was why the Nondisclosure Covenant was suddenly extended to IRS employees in 1987. But I had already left the Service in 1987. The worst of a certain personal unpleasantness had blown over, and I'd been accepted for transfer at another college, and by autumn of 1986 I was back on the East Coast and again up and running in the private sector, albeit of course still with my new SS number. My entire IRS career lasted from May 1985 through June 1986. Hence my exemption from the Covenant. Not to mention that I was hardly in a position to know anything compromising or specific about the ANADA. My Service post was totally low-level and regional. For the bulk of my time, I was a rote examiner, a.k.a. a 'wiggler' in the Service nomenclature. My contracted civil service rank was a GS-9, which at that time was the lowest full-time grade; there were secretaries and custodians who outranked me. And I was posted to Peoria IL, which is about as far from Triple-Six and the Martinsburg Center as anyone could imagine. Admittedly, at the same time—and this is what especially concerned the publishing company's counsel—Peoria was a REC, one of seven hubs of the IRS's Examination Division, which was precisely the division that got eliminated or, more accurately (though this is arguable), transferred from the Compliance Branch to the newly expanded Technical Branch, by the advent of the ANADA and a digital Fornix network. This is

> (a) By the way, no kidding about the formula's name. Were the Technical Branch statisticians aware that they were giving the algorithm such a heavy, almost thanatoid-sounding acronym? It's actually doubtful. As all too many Americans now know, computerized programs are totally, maddeningly literal and nonconnotative; and so were the people in Technical Branch.

rather more esoteric, contextless Service information than I'd anticipated having to ask you to swallow right at the beginning, and I can assure you that all this gets explained and/ or unfolded in much more graceful, dramatically apposite terms in the memoir itself, once it gets under way. For now, just so you're not totally flummoxed and bored, suffice it to say that Examinations is the IRS division tasked with combing and culling various kinds of tax returns and classifying some as '20s,' which is Service shorthand for tax returns that are to be forwarded to the relevant District office for audit. Audits themselves are conducted by revenue agents, who are usually GS-9s or -11s, and employed by the Audit Division. It's hard to put all this very smoothly or gracefully—and please know that none of this abstract information is all that vital to the mission of this Foreword. So feel free to skip or skim the following if you wish. And don't think the whole book will be like this, because it won't be. If you're burningly interested, though, each tax return pulled, for whatever reason(s) (some of which were smart and discerning and others, frankly, wacko and occult, depending on the wiggler), by a line examiner and forwarded for audit is supposed to be accompanied by an IRS Series 20 Internal Memo, which is where the term '20' comes from. Like most insular and (let's be frank) despised government agencies, the Service is rife with special jargon and code that seems overwhelming at first but then gets internalized so quickly and used so often that it becomes almost habitual. I still, sometimes, dream in Servicespeak. To return to the point, though, Examinations and Audits were two of the main divisions of the IRS's Compliance Branch, and the publishing company's house counsel's concern was that the IRS's own counsel could, if they were sufficiently aggrieved and wanted to make trouble over the Nondisclosure Covenant thing, argue that I and

insisted upon them as a precondition for acceptance of the manuscript and payment of the advance—is the same reason the disclaimer is, when you come right down to it, a lie.[4]

Here is the real truth: What follows is substantially true and accurate. At least, it's a mainly true and accurate partial record of what I saw and heard and did, of whom I knew and worked alongside and under, and of what-all eventuated at IRS Post 047, the Midwest Regional Examination Center, Peoria IL, in 1985–86. Much of the book is actually based on several different notebooks and journals I kept during my thirteen months as a rote examiner at the Midwest REC. ('Based' means more or less lifted right out of, for reasons that will doubtless become clear.) *The Pale King* is, in other words, a kind of vocational memoir. It is also supposed to function as a portrait of a bureaucracy—arguably the most important federal bureaucracy in American life—at a time of enormous internal struggle and soul-searching, the birth pains of what's come to be known among tax professionals as the New IRS.

In the interests of full disclosure, though, I should be explicit and say that the modifier in 'substantially true and accurate' refers not just to the inevitable subjectivity and bias of any memoir. The truth is that there are, in this nonfiction account, some slight changes and strategic rearrangements, most of these evolving through successive drafts in response to feedback from the book's editor, who was sometimes put in a very delicate position with respect to balancing literary and journalistic priorities, on the one hand, against legal and corporate concerns on the other. That's probably all I should say on that score. There is, of course, a whole tortuous backstory here involving the legal vetting of the manuscript's final three drafts. But you will be spared having to hear much about all this, if for no other reason than that relating that inside story would defeat the very pur-

---

several of the Post 047 REC coworkers and administrators who feature in this story should be grandfathered in under the constraints of the Nondisclosure Covenant, because we were not only employed by the Compliance Branch but posted at the REC that ended up figuring so prominently in the run-up to what came to be known variously as 'the New IRS,' 'the Spackman Initiative,' or just 'the Initiative,' which was ostensibly created by the Tax Reform Act of 1986 but was actually the result of a long, very complicated bureaucratic catfight between the Compliance Branch and the Technical Branch over Examinations and the Exam function in IRS operations. End of data-dump. If you're still reading, I hope enough of all that made sense for you to at least understand why the issue of whether or not I explicitly say the name of the publishing company was not one that I chose to spend a lot of time and editorial goodwill arguing about. You sort of have to pick your battles, as far as nonfiction goes.

4 (excepting the 'All rights reserved' part, of course)

pose of the repetitive, microscopically cautious vetting process and of all the myriad little changes and rearrangements to accommodate those changes that became necessary when, e.g., certain people declined to sign legal releases, or when one mid-sized company threatened legal action if its real name or identifying details of its actual past tax situation were used, disclaimer or no.[5]

In the final analysis, though, there are a lot fewer of these small, identity-obscuring changes and temporal rearrangements than one might have expected. For there are advantages to limiting a memoir's range to one single interval (plus relevant backstories) in what seems to us all now like the distant past. People don't much care anymore, for one thing. By which I mean people in this book. The publishing company's paralegals had far less trouble getting signed legal releases than counsel had predicted. The reasons for this are varied but (as my own lawyer and I had argued ahead of time) obvious. Of the persons named, described, and even sometimes projected into the consciousness of as so-called 'characters' in The Pale King, a majority have now left the Service. Of those remaining, several have reached levels of GS rank where they are more or less invulnerable.[6] Also, because of the time of year when drafts of the book were presented for their perusal, I am confident that certain other Service personnel were so busy and distracted that they did not really even read the

---

5 This latter is a good example of the sort of thing that threw the publisher's legal people into a swivet of anality and caution. People often don't understand how seriously large US corporations take even a threat of litigation. As I eventually realized, it's not even so much a question of whether or not the publisher would lose a lawsuit; what really concerns them is the cost of defending against it, and the effect of those costs on the company's liability insurance premiums, which are already a major operating expense. Legal trouble is, in other words, a bottom-line issue; and the editor or in-house counsel who exposes a publishing company to possible legal liability had better be able to demonstrate to his CFO that every last reasonable bit of caution and due diligence was exercised on the manuscript, lest he wear what we in Exams used to call 'the brown helmet.' At the same time, it isn't fair to attribute every last tactical change and deviation here to the publisher. I (meaning, again, the actual human David Wallace) also fear litigation. Like many Americans, I've been sued—twice, in fact, though both suits were meritless, and one was dismissed as frivolous before I was even deposed—and I know what so many of us know: Litigation is no fun, and it's worth one's time and trouble to try to head it off in advance whenever possible. Plus, of course, looming over the whole vetting-and-due-diligence process on The Pale King was the shadow of the Service, which no one in his right mind would ever even dream of wanting to piss off unnecessarily, or actually even to come to the full institutional attention of, since the Service, like civil litigation, can make your life miserable without ever getting one extra dime from you.

6 E.g., one is now an Assistant Regional Commissioner for Taxpayer Assistance in the Western Regional Commissioner's Office at Oxnard CA.

manuscript and, after waiting a decent interval to give the impression of close study and deliberation, signed the legal release so that they could feel they had one less thing they were supposed to do. A few also seemed flattered at the prospect of someone's having paid them enough notice to be able, years later, to remember their contributions. A handful signed because they have remained, through the years, my personal friends; one of these is probably the most valuable, profound friend I've ever made. Some are dead. Two turned out to be incarcerated, of which one of these was someone you never would have thought or suspected.

Not everyone signed legal releases; I don't mean to suggest that. Only that most did. Several also consented to be interviewed on-record. Where appropriate, parts of their tape-recorded responses have been transcribed directly into the text. Others have graciously signed additional releases authorizing the use of certain audio-visual recordings of them that were made in 1984 as part of an abortive IRS Personnel Division motivational and recruitment effort.[7] As an aggregate, they have provided reminiscences and concrete details that, when combined with the techniques of reconstructive journalism,[8] have yielded scenes of immense authority and realism, regardless of whether this author was actually corporeally right there on the scene at the time or not.

The point I'm trying to drive home here is that it's still all substantially true—i.e., the book this Foreword is part of—regardless of the various ways some of the forthcoming §s have had to be distorted, depersonalized, polyphonized, or otherwise jazzed up in order to conform to the specs of the legal disclaimer. This is not to say that this jazzing up is all just gratuitous titty-pinching; given the aforementioned legal-slash-commercial constraints, it's ended up being integral to the book's whole project. The idea, as both sides' counsel worked it out, is that you will regard features

---

7 A signed, notarized 2002 FOIA request for copies of these videotapes is on file at the Internal Revenue Service's Office of Public Information, 666 Independence Avenue, Washington DC....And yes: The Service's national HQ's street number really is '666.' So far as I know, it's nothing more than an unfortunate accident in the Treasury Department's assignment of office space after the Sixteenth Amendment was ratified in 1913. On the Regional levels, Service personnel tend to refer to the national office as 'Triple-Six'—the meaning of the term is obvious, though no one I was able to talk to seemed to know just when it came into use.

8 This loose term is meant to connote the dramatized reconstruction of an empirically real occurrence. It is a common and wholly respectable modern device used in both film (q.v. *The Thin Blue Line, Forrest Gump, JFK*) and literature (q.v. Capote's *In Cold Blood*, Wouk's *The Caine Mutiny*, Oates's *Zombie*, Crane's *The Red Badge of Courage*, Wolfe's *The Right Stuff*, & c., & c.).

like shifting p.o.v.s, structural fragmentation, willed incongruities, & c. as simply the modern literary analogs of 'Once upon a time...' or 'Far, far away, there once dwelt...' or any of the other traditional devices that signaled the reader that what was under way was fiction and should be processed accordingly. For as everyone knows, whether consciously or not, there's always a kind of unspoken contract between a book's author and its reader; and the terms of this contract always depend on certain codes and gestures that the author deploys in order to signal the reader what kind of book it is, i.e., whether it's made up vs. true. And these codes are important, because the subliminal contract for nonfiction is very different from the one for fiction.[9] What I'm trying to do right here, within the protective range of the copyright page's disclaimer, is to override the unspoken codes and to be 100 percent overt and forthright about the present contract's terms. *The Pale King* is basically a nonfiction memoir, with additional elements of reconstructive journalism, organizational psychology, elementary civics and tax theory, & c. Our mutual contract here is based on the presumptions of (a) my veracity, and (b) your understanding that any features or semions that might appear to undercut that veracity are in fact protective legal devices, not unlike the boilerplate that accompanies sweepstakes and civil contracts, and thus are not meant to be decoded or 'read' so much as merely acquiesced to as part of the cost of our doing business together, so to speak, in today's commercial climate.[10]

Plus there's the autobiographical fact that, like so many other nerdy, disaffected young people of that time, I dreamed of becoming an 'artist,' i.e., somebody whose adult job was original and creative instead of tedious and dronelike. My specific dream was of becoming an immortally great fiction writer à la Gaddis or Anderson, Balzac or Perec, & c.; and many of the notebook entries on which parts of this memoir are based were themselves literarily jazzed up and fractured; it's just the way I saw myself at the

---

9 The main way you can tell that the contracts are different is from our reactions to their breach. The feeling of betrayal or infidelity that the reader suffers if it turns out that a piece of ostensible nonfiction has made-up stuff in it (as has been revealed in some recent literary scandals, e.g. Kosinski's *Painted Bird* or that infamous Carcaterra book) is because the terms of the nonfiction contract have been violated. There are, of course, ways to quote-unquote cheat the reader in fiction, too, but these tend to be more technical, meaning internal to the story's own formal rules (see, e.g., the mystery novel's first-person narrator who doesn't reveal that he's actually the murderer until the last page, even though he obviously knew it all along and suppressed it just to jerk us around), and the reader tends to feel more aesthetically disappointed than personally dicked over.

10 Apologies for the preceding sentence, which is the product of much haggling and compromise with the publisher's legal team.

time. In some ways, you could say that my literary ambitions were the chief reason I was on hiatus from college and working at the Midwest REC at all, though most of that whole backstory is tangential and will be addressed only here in the Foreword, and very briefly, to wit:

In a nutshell, the truth is that the first pieces of fiction I was ever actually paid for involved certain other students at the initial college I went to, which was extremely expensive and highbrow and attended mainly by graduates of elite private schools in New York and New England. Without going into a whole lot of detail, let's just say that there were certain pieces of prose I produced for certain students on certain academic subjects, and that these pieces were fictional in the sense of having styles, theses, scholarly personas, and authorial names that were not my own. I think you get the idea. The chief motivation behind this little enterprise was, as it so often is in the real world, financial. It's not like I was desperately poor in college, but my family was far from wealthy, and part of my financial aid package involved taking out large student loans; and I was aware that student-loan debt tended to be very bad news for someone who wanted to pursue any sort of artistic career after college, since it's well known that most artists toil in ascetic obscurity for years before making any real money at their profession.

On the other hand, there were many students at that college whose families were in a position not only to pay their whole tuition but apparently also to give their kids money for whatever personal expenses came up, with no questions asked. 'Personal expenses' here refers to things like weekend ski trips, ridiculously expensive stereo systems, fraternity parties with fully stocked wet bars, & c. Not to mention that the entire campus was less than two acres, and yet most of the students had their own cars, which it also cost $400 per semester to park in one of the college lots. It was all pretty incredible. In many respects, this college was my introduction to the stark realities of class, economic stratification, and the very different financial realities that different sorts of Americans inhabited.

Some of these upper-class students were indeed spoiled, cretinous, and/ or untroubled by questions of ethics. Others were under great family pressure and failing, for whatever reasons, to work up to what their parents considered their true grade potential. Some just didn't manage their time and responsibilities well, and found themselves up against the wall on an assignment. I'm sure you get the basic picture. Let's just say that, as a way of positioning myself to pay off some of my loans at an accelerated rate, I provided a certain service. This service was not cheap, but I was quite good at it, and careful. E.g., I always demanded a large enough sample of a client's prior writing to determine how he tended to think and sound, and I never made the mistake of delivering something that was unrealistically superior to someone's own previous work. You can probably also see why these sorts of exercises would be good apprentice training for someone interested in so-called 'creative writing.'[11] The enterprise's proceeds were invested in a high-yield money market account; and interest rates at that time were high, whereas student loans don't even start accruing interest until one leaves school. The overall strategy was conservative, both financially and academically. It's not as if I was doing several of these commissioned fictional pieces a week or anything. I had plenty of my own work to do too, after all.

To anticipate a likely question, let me concede that the ethics here were gray at best. This is why I chose to be honest, just above, about not being impoverished or needing the extra income in order to eat or anything. I was not desperate. I was, though, trying to accumulate some savings against what I anticipated[12] to be debilitating post-grad debt. I am aware that this is not an excuse in the strict sense, but I do believe it serves as at least an explanation; and there were also other, more general factors and contexts that might be seen as mitigating. For one, the college itself turned out to have a lot of moral hypocrisy about it, e.g., congratulating itself on its diversity and the leftist piety of its politics while in reality going about the business of preparing elite kids to enter elite professions and make a great deal of money, thus increasing the pool of prosperous alumni donors. Without anyone ever discussing it or even allowing themselves to be aware of it, the college was a veritable temple of Mammon. I'm not kidding. For instance, the most popular major was economics, and the best and brightest of my class all seemed obsessed with a career on Wall Street, whose own public ethos at the time was 'Greed is good.' Not to mention that there were retail cocaine dealers on campus who made a lot more than I ever did. Those were just a few of what I might, if I chose, offer as extenuating factors. My own attitude about it was detached and professional, not unlike a lawyer's. The basic view I held was that, whereas there may have been elements of my enterprise that might technically qualify as aiding or abetting a client's decision to violate the college's Code of Academic Honesty, that decision, as well as the practical and moral responsibility for it, rested with the client. I was undertaking certain freelance writing assignments for pay; why certain students wanted certain papers of a certain

---

11 (which, FYI, there were few or no formal classes in at that time)
12 (correctly, it turned out)

length on certain topics, and what they chose to do with them after delivery, were not my business.

Suffice it to say that this view was not shared by the college's Judicial Board in late 1984. Here the story gets complex and a bit lurid, and an SOP memoir would probably linger on the details and the rank unfairnesses and hypocrisies involved. I'm not going to do that. I am, after all, mentioning all this only to provide some context for the ostensibly 'fictional'-looking formal elements of the non-SOP memoir that you have (I hope) bought and are now enjoying. Plus, of course, also to help explain what I was even doing in one of the most tedious and dronelike white-collar jobs in America during what should have been my junior year at an elite college,[13] so that this obvious question isn't left to hang distractingly all through the book (a type of distraction I personally despise, as a reader). Given these limited objectives, then, the whole Code-of-AH debacle is probably best sketched in broad schematic strokes, to wit:

(1a) Naive people are, more or less by definition, unaware that they're naive. (1b) I was, in retrospect, naive. (2) For various personal reasons, I was not a member of any campus fraternity, and so was ignorant of many of the bizarre tribal customs and practices in the college's so-called 'Greek' community. (3a) One of the college's fraternities had instituted the phenomenally stupid and shortsighted practice of placing behind their billiard room's wet bar a two-drawer file cabinet containing copies of certain recent exams, problem sets, lab reports, and term papers that had earned high grades, which were available for plagiarism. (3b) Speaking of phenomenally stupid, it turned out that not just one but *three* different members of this fraternity had, without bothering to consult the party from whom they'd commissioned and received them, tossed papers that were not technically their own into this communal file cabinet. (4) The paradox of plagiarism is that it actually requires a lot of care and hard work to pull off successfully, since the original text's style, substance, and logical sequences have to be modified enough so that the plagiarism isn't totally, insultingly obvious to the professor who's grading it. (5a) The type of spoiled, cretinous frat boy who goes into a communal file cabinet for a term paper on the use of implicit GNP price deflators in macroeconomic

---

13 Junior year, by the way, was when many of the college's other, more privileged students, including several who'd been my freelance clients, were enjoying their traditional 'semester abroad' at places like Cambridge and the Sorbonne. I'm just mentioning this. There's no expectation that you're going to wring your hands over whatever hypocrisy and unfairness you may discern in this state of affairs. In no sense is this Foreword a bid for sympathy. Plus it's all water long under the bridge now, obviously.

theory is also the type who will not know or care about the paradoxical extra work that good plagiarism requires. He will, however incredible it sounds, just plunk down and retype the thing, word for word. (5b) Nor, even more incredibly, will he take the trouble to verify that none of his fraternity brothers is planning to plagiarize the same term paper for the same course. (6) The moral system of a college fraternity turns out to be classically tribal, i.e., characterized by a deeply felt sense of honor, discretion, and loyalty to one's so-called 'brothers,' coupled with a complete, sociopathic lack of regard for the interests or even humanity of anyone outside that fraternal set.

Let's just end the sketch there. I doubt you need a whole diagram to anticipate what came down, nor much of a primer in US class dynamics to understand, of the eventual five students placed on academic probation or forced to retake certain courses vs. the one student formally suspended pending consideration of expulsion and possible[14] referral of the case to the Hampshire County District Attorney, which one of these was yours truly, the living author, Mr. David Wallace of Philo IL, to which tiny lifeless nothing town neither I nor my family were at all psyched about the prospect of having me return and sit around watching TV for the at least one and possibly two semesters that the college's administration was going to take its sweet time considering my fate.[15] Meanwhile, by the terms of the 1966 Federal Claims Collection Act's §106(c–d), the repayment clock on my Guaranteed Student Loans started running, as of 1 January 1985, at 6¼ percent interest.

Again, if any of that seems vague or ablated, it's because I am giving you a very stripped down, mission-specific version of just who and where I was, life-situation-wise, for the thirteen months I spent as an IRS examiner. Moreover, I'm afraid that just how I landed in this government post at all is a background item that I can explain only obliquely, i.e., by ostensibly explaining why I can't discuss it.[16] First, I'd ask you to bear in mind

---

14 (but highly unlikely, given the college's concern with its reputation and PR)

15 Sorry about that text sentence. The truth is that the whole frat-cabinet-and-cascading-scandal's-need-for-a-scapegoat situation still sometimes gets me jacked up, emotionally speaking. Two facts might make the durability of these emotions easier to understand: (a) of the five other students found by the J-Board to have either bought term papers or plagiarized from those who had, two ended up graduating *magna cum laude*, and (b) a third now serves on the college's Board of Trustees. I'll just leave those as stark facts and let you draw your own conclusions about the whole shabby affair. *Mendacem memorem esse oportet.*

16 And please forgive the contrivance here. Given the familio-legal strictures detailed just below, this kind of anti-explanation is the only permissible way for me to avoid having

the above-cited disinclination to have me return and serve out my limbo at home in Philo, which mutual reluctance in turn involves a whole lot of issues and history between my family and me that I couldn't get into even if I wanted to (see below). Second, I would inform you that the city of Peoria IL is roughly ninety miles from Philo, which is a distance that permits general familial monitoring without any of the sort of detailed, close-quarters knowledge that might confer feelings of concern or responsibility. Third, I could direct your attention to Congress's 1977 Fair Debt Collection Practices Act §1101, which turns out to override the Federal Claims Collection Act's §106(c–d) and to authorize deferment of Guaranteed Student Loan repayments for documented employees of certain government agencies, including guess which one. Fourth, I am allowed, after exhaustive negotiations with the publisher's counsel, to say that my thirteen-month contract, posting, and GS-9 civil service paygrade were the result of certain *sub-rosa* actions on the part of a certain unnamed relative[17] with unspecified connections to the Midwest Regional Commissioner's Office of a certain unnamed government agency. Last and most important, I am also permitted to say, albeit in language not wholly my own, that members of my family were almost unanimous in declining to sign the legal releases required for any further or more specific use, mention, or representation of the aforesaid relatives or any likeness thereof in any capacity, setting, form, or guise, inclusive of references *sine damno*, within the written work heretofore entitled *The Pale King*, and that this is why I can't get into anything more specific about the overall hows and whys. End of explanation of absence of real explanation, which, however irksome or opaque it may come off, is (again) still preferable to having the question of why/how I was working at the Midwest Regional Examination Center just hang there huge and unaddressed through the whole text to follow,[18] like the proverbial elephant in the room.

Here I should also probably address one other core-motivation-type question that bears on the matter of veracity and trust raised several ¶s above, viz., why a nonfiction memoir at all, since I'm primarily a fiction writer? Not to mention the question of why a memoir restricted to a single, long-past year I spent in exile from anything I even remotely cared about or was interested in, serving out time as little more than one tiny

---

my whole presence at IRS Post 047 be some enormous, unexplained, and unmotivated blank, which in certain types of fiction might be (technically) OK, but in a memoir would constitute a deep and essential breach of contract.

17 (*not* a parent)

18 Q.v. FN 2, *supra*.

ephemeral dronelike cog in an immense federal bureaucracy?[19] There are two different kinds of valid answer here, one being personal and the other more literary/humanistic. The personal stuff it's initially tempting to say is just none of your business... except that one disadvantage of addressing you here directly and in person in the cultural present of 2005 is the fact that, as both you and I know, there is no longer any kind of clear line between personal and public, or rather between private vs. performative. Among obvious examples are web logs, reality television, cell-phone cameras, chat rooms... not to mention the dramatically increased popularity of the memoir as a literary genre. Of course *popularity* is, in this context, a synonym for profitability; and actually that fact alone should suffice, personal-motivation-wise. Consider that in 2003, the average author's

---

19 The word *bureaucracy* is notwithstanding that part of the run-up to the whole 'New IRS' thing was an increasing anti- or post-bureaucratic mentality on the part of both Triple-Six and Region. See, for one quick example, this snippet from an interview with Mr. Donald Jones, a GS-13 Team Leader in the Midwest REC's Fats group from 1984 through 1990:

Perhaps it would help to define *bureaucracy*. The term. What we're talking about. All they said you had to do was refer to the dictionary. Administration characterized by diffusion of authority and adherence to inflexible rules of operation, unquote. Inflexible rules of operation. An administrative system in which the need or desire to follow complex procedures impedes effective action, unquote. They had transparencies of the definition projected up on the wall during meetings. They said he had them all recite them as nearly some type of catechism.

Meaning, in discursive terms, that the couple of years in question here saw one of the largest bureaucracies anywhere undergo a convulsion in which it tried to reconceive itself as a non- or even anti-bureaucracy, which at first might sound like nothing more than an amusing bit of bureaucratic folly. In fact, it was frightening; it was a little like watching an enormous machine come to consciousness and start trying to think and feel like a real human. The terror of concurrent films like *Terminator* and *Blade Runner* was based around just this premise... but of course in the case of the Service the convulsions, and fallout, although more diffuse and undramatic, had an actual impact on Americans' lives.

N.B. Mr. Jones's 'they' is referring to certain high-level figures who were exponents of the so-called 'Initiative,' which it is totally impractical here to try to explain abstractly (although q.v. Item 951458221 of §14, Interview Documentary, which consists of a long and probably not ideally focused version of such an explanation from Mr. Kenneth ['Type of Thing Ken'] Hindle, one of the oldest wigglers in the Rotes group to which I ended up [after a great deal of initial confusion and misassignment] being tasked), except to say that the only such figure anyone at our low level ever even laid eyes on was the Technical Branch's M. E. Lehrl and his strange team of intuitives and occult ephebes, who were (it emerged) tasked to help implement the Initiative as it pertained to Examinations. If that doesn't make any sense at this point, please don't worry about it. I went back and forth on the issue of what to explain here vs. what to let unfold in a more natural, dramatic way in the memoir itself. I finally decided to offer certain quick, potentially confusing explanations, betting that if they're too obscure or baroque right now you just won't pay much attention to them, which, again, I hasten to assure you is totally OK.

advance[20] for a memoir was almost 2.5 times that paid for a work of fiction. The simple truth is that I, like so many other Americans, have suffered reverses in the volatile economy of the last few years, and these reverses have occurred at the same time that my financial obligations have increased along with my age and responsibilities[21]; and meanwhile all sorts of US writers—some of whom I know personally, including one I actually had to lend money to for basic living expenses as late as spring 2001—have recently hit it big with memoirs,[22] and I would be a rank hypocrite if I pretended that I was less attuned and receptive to market forces than anyone else.

As all mature people know, though, it's possible for very different kinds of motives and emotions to coexist in the human soul. There is no way that a memoir like *The Pale King* could be written solely for financial gain. One paradox of professional writing is that books written solely for money and/ or acclaim will almost never be good enough to garner either. The truth is that the larger narrative encompassing this Foreword has significant social and artistic value. That might sound conceited, but rest assured that I wouldn't and couldn't have put three years' hard labor (plus an additional fifteen months of legal and editorial futzing) into *The Pale King* if I were

---

20 If you're interested, this term is shorthand for an unrefundable advance payment against the author's projected royalties (through a 7½%–15% set of progressive margins) on sales of a book. Since actual sales are difficult to predict, it is in the writer's financial interest to receive the largest possible advance, even though the lump-sum payment can create tax problems for the year of receipt (thanks largely to the 1986 Tax Reform Act's elimination of income averaging). And given, again, that predicting actual sales is an inexact science, the size of the up-front author advance that a publishing company is willing to pay for the rights to a book is the best tangible indication of the publisher's willingness to 'support' that book, w/ the latter term meaning everything from the number of copies printed to the size of the marketing budget. And this support is practically the only way for a book to gain the attention of a mass audience and to garner significant sales—like it or not, that's just the commercial reality today.

21 By age forty, artist or no, the reality is that only an imprudent chump would neglect to start saving and investing for eventual retirement, especially in this era of tax-deferred IRA and SEP-IRA plans with such generous annual tax-exempt caps—and extra-especially if you can S-corp yourself and let the corporation make an additional annual pension contribution, over and above your IRA, as a contractual 'employee benefit,' thereby exempting that extra amount from your taxable income, too. The tax laws right now are practically down on one knee, begging upper-income Americans to take advantage of this provision. The trick, of course, is earning enough to qualify as an upper-income American—*Deos fortioribus adesse*.

22 (Despite his sudden celebrity and windfall I am still, almost four years later, awaiting repayment of the loan's principal from this unnamed writer, which I mention not to whinge or be vindictive, but merely as one more small part of my financial condition *qua* motivation.)

not convinced it was true. Have, e.g., a look at the following, which was transcribed verbatim from remarks by Mr. DeWitt Glendenning Jr., the Director of the Midwest Regional Examination Center during most of my tenure there:

> If you know the position a person takes on taxes, you can determine [his] whole philosophy. The tax code, once you get to know it, embodies all the essence of [human] life: greed, politics, power, goodness, charity.

To these qualities that Mr. Glendenning ascribed to the code I would respectfully add one more: boredom. Opacity. User-unfriendliness.

This all can be put another way. It might sound a bit dry and wonkish, but that's because I'm boiling it down to the abstract skeleton:

1985 was a critical year for American taxation and for the Internal Revenue Service's enforcement of the US tax code. In brief, that year saw not only fundamental changes in the Service's operational mandate, but also the climax of an involved intra-Service battle between advocates and opponents of an increasingly automated, computerized tax system. For complex administrative reasons, the Midwest Regional Examination Center became one of the venues in which this battle's crucial phase played out.

But that's only part of it. As alluded to in an FN way above, subtending this operational battle over human vs. digital enforcement of the tax code was a deeper conflict over the very mission and *raison* of the Service, a conflict whose fallout extended from the corridors of power at Treasury and Triple-Six all the way down to the most staid and backwater District office. At the highest levels, the struggle here was between traditional or 'conservative'[23] officials who saw tax and its administration as an arena of social justice and civic virtue, on the one hand, and those more progressive, 'pragmatic' policymakers who prized the market model, efficiency, and a maximum return on the investment of the Service's annual budget. Distilled to its essence, the question was whether and to what extent the IRS should be operated like a for-profit business.

Probably that's all I should say right here in terms of summary. If you know how to search and parse government archives, you can find voluminous history and theory on just about every side of the debate. It's all in the public record.

But here's the thing. Both then and now, very few ordinary Americans

---

23 (meaning, somewhat confusingly, classically liberal)

know anything about all this. Nor much about the deep changes the Service underwent in the mid-1980s, changes that today directly affect the way citizens' tax obligations are determined and enforced. And the reason for this public ignorance is not secrecy. Despite the IRS's well-documented paranoia and aversion to publicity,[24] secrecy here had nothing to do with it. The real reason why US citizens were/are not aware of these conflicts, changes, and stakes is that the whole subject of tax policy and administration is dull. Massively, spectacularly dull.

It is impossible to overstate the importance of this feature. Consider, from the Service's perspective, the advantages of the dull, the arcane, the mind-numbingly complex. The IRS was one of the very first government agencies to learn that such qualities help insulate them against public protest and political opposition, and that abstruse dullness is actually a much more effective shield than is secrecy. For the great disadvantage of secrecy is that it's interesting. People are drawn to secrets; they can't help it. Keep in mind that the period we're talking was only a decade after Watergate. Had the Service tried to hide or cover up its conflicts and convulsions, some enterprising journalist(s) could have done an exposé that drew a lot of attention and interest and scandalous fuss. But this is not at all what happened. What happened was that much of the high-level policy debate played out for two years in full public view, e.g., in open hearings of the Joint Committee on Taxation, the Senate Treasury Procedures and Statutes Subcommittee, and the IRS's Deputy and Assistant Commissioners' Council. These hearings were collections of anaerobic men in drab suits who spoke a verbless bureaucratese—terms like 'strategic utilization template' and 'revenue vector' in place of 'plan' and 'tax'—and took days just to reach consensus on the order of items for discussion. Even in the financial press, there was hardly any coverage; can you guess why? If not, consider the fact that just about every last transcript, record, study, white paper, code amendment, revenue-ruling, and procedural memo has been available for public perusal since date of issue. No FOIA filing even required. But not one journalist seems ever to have checked them out, and with good reason: This stuff is solid rock. The eyes roll up white by the third or fourth ¶. You just have no idea.[25]

---

24 (attitudes that are not wholly unjustified, given TPs' hostility to the Service, politicians' habit of bashing the agency to score populist points, &c.)

25 I'm reasonably sure that I am the only living American who's actually read all these archives all the way through. I'm not sure I can explain how I did it. Mr. Chris Acquistipace, one of the GS-11 Chalk Leaders in our Rote Exams group, and a man of no small intuition and sensitivity, proposed an analogy between the public records sur-

Fact: The birth agonies of the New IRS led to one of the great and terrible PR discoveries in modern democracy, which is that if sensitive issues of governance can be made sufficiently dull and arcane, there will be no need for officials to hide or dissemble, because no one not directly involved will pay enough attention to cause trouble. No one will pay attention because no one will be interested, because, more or less *a priori*, of these issues' monumental dullness. Whether this PR discovery is to be regretted for its corrosive effect on the democratic ideal or celebrated for its enhancement of government efficiency depends, it seems, on which side one takes in the deeper debate over ideals vs. efficacy referenced on p. 82, resulting in yet another involuted loop that I won't tax your patience by trying to trace out or make hay of.

To me, at least in retrospect,[26] the really interesting question is why dullness proves to be such a powerful impediment to attention. Why we recoil from the dull. Maybe it's because dullness is intrinsically painful; maybe that's where phrases like 'deadly dull' or 'excruciatingly dull' come from. But there might be more to it. Maybe dullness is associated with psychic pain because something that's dull or opaque fails to provide enough stimulation to distract people from some other, deeper type of pain that is always there, if only in an ambient low-level way, and which most of us[27] spend nearly all our time and energy trying to distract ourselves from feeling, or at least from feeling directly or with our full attention. Admittedly, the whole thing's pretty confusing, and hard to talk about abstractly...but surely something must lie behind not just Muzak in dull or tedious places anymore but now also actual TV in waiting rooms, supermarkets' checkouts, airports' gates, SUVs' backseats. Walkmen, iPods, BlackBerries, cell phones that attach to your head. This terror of silence with nothing diverting to do. I can't think anyone really believes that today's so-called 'information society' is just about information. Everyone knows[28] it's about something else, way down.

The memoir-relevant point here is that I learned, in my time with the Service, something about dullness, information, and irrelevant complexity. About negotiating boredom as one would a terrain, its levels and

---

rounding the Initiative and the giant solid-gold Buddhas that flanked certain temples in ancient Khmer. These priceless statues, never guarded or secured, were safe from theft not despite but because of their value—they were too huge and heavy to move. Something about this sustained me.

26 (which is, after all, memoirs' specialty)

27 (whether or not we're consciously aware of it)

28 (again, whether consciously or not)

forests and endless wastes. Learned about it extensively, exquisitely, in my interrupted year. And now ever since that time have noticed, at work and in recreation and time with friends and even the intimacies of family life, that living people do not speak much of the dull. Of those parts of life that are and must be dull. Why this silence? Maybe it's because the subject is, in and of itself, dull... only then we're again right back where we started, which is tedious and irksome. There may, though, I opine, be more to it... as in vastly more, right here before us all, hidden by virtue of its size.

§33

Lane Dean Jr. with his green rubber pinkie finger sat at his Tingle table in his Chalk's row in the Rotes Group's wiggle room and did two more returns, then another one, then flexed his buttocks and held to a count of ten and imagined a warm pretty beach with mellow surf as instructed in orientation the previous month. Then he did two more returns, checked the clock real quick, then two more, then bore down and did three in a row, then flexed and visualized and bore way down and did four without looking up once except to put the completed files and memos in the two Out trays side by side up in the top tier of trays where the cart boys could get them when they came by. After just an hour the beach was a winter beach, cold and gray and the dead kelp like the hair of the drowned, and it stayed that way despite all attempts. Then three more, including one 1040A where the deductions for AGI were added wrong and the Martinsburg printout hadn't caught it and had to be amended on one of the Form 020-Cs in the lower left tray and then a lot of the same information filled out on the regular 20 you still had to do even if it was just a correspondence audit and the file going to Joliet instead of the District, each code for which had to be looked up on the pull-out thing he had to scoot the chair awkwardly over to pull out all the way. Then another one, then a plummeting inside of him as the wall clock showed that what he'd thought was another hour had not been. Not even close. 17 May 1985. Lord Jesus Christ have mercy on me a poor sinner. Crosschecking W-2s for the return's Line 7 off the place in the Martinsburg printout where the perforation if you wanted to separate the thing's sheets went right through the data and you had to hold it up against the light and almost sometimes guess, which his Chalk Leader said was a chronic bug with Systems but the wiggler was still accountable. The joke this week was how was an IRS rote examiner like a mushroom? Both kept in the dark and fed horseshit. He didn't know how mushrooms even worked, if it was true that you scooped waste on them. Sheri's cooking wasn't what you would call at the level of adding mushrooms. Then another return. The rule was, the more you looked at the clock the slower the time went. None of the wigglers wore a watch, except he saw that some kept them in their pockets for breaks. Clocks on Tingles were not allowed, nor coffee or pop. Try as he might he could not this last week help envisioning the inward lives of the older men to either side of him, doing this day after day. Getting up on a Monday and chewing their toast and putting their hats and coats on knowing what they were going out the door to come back to for eight hours. This was boredom beyond any boredom he'd ever felt. This made the routing desk at UPS look like a day at Six Flags. It was May 17, early morning, or early mid-morning you could maybe almost call it now. He could hear the squeak of the cart boys' carts someplace off at a distance where the vinyl panels between his Chalk's Tingles and the blond oriental fellow's Chalk one row up blocked the sight of them, the kids with the carts. One of the carts had a crazy wheel that chattered when the boy pushed it. Lane Dean always knew when that cart was coming down the rows. Chalk, Team, Group, Pod, Post, Division. He did another return, again the math squared and there were no itemizations on 34A and the printout's numbers for W-2 and 1099 and Forms 2440 and 2441 appeared to square and he filled out his codes for the middle tray's 402 and signed his name and ID number that some part of him still refused to quite get memorized so he had to unclip his badge and check it each time and then stapled the 402 to the return and put the file in the top tier's rightmost tray for 402s Out and refused to let himself count the number in the trays yet, and then unbidden came the thought that *boring* also meant something that drilled in and made a hole. His buttocks already ached from flexing, and the mere thought of envisioning the desolate beach unmanned him. He shut his eyes but instead of praying for inward strength now he found he was just looking at the strange reddish dark and the little flashes and floaters in there, that got almost hypnotic when you really looked at them. Then when he opened his eyes the In tray's stack of files looked to be still mainly the height it had been at 7:14 when he'd logged in in the Chalk Leader's notebook and started and there weren't enough files in his Out trays for Form 20s and 402s that he could see any over the side of the trays and he refused once more to stand up to check how many of them there were for he knew that would make it worse. He had the sensation of a great type of hole or emptiness falling through him and continuing to fall and never hitting the floor. Never before in his life up to now had he once thought of suicide. He was doing a return at the same time he fought with his mind, with the sin and affront of even the passing thought. The room was silent except for the adding machines and the chattering sound of that one kid's cart that had a crazy wheel as the cart boy brought it down a certain row with more files, but also he kept hearing in his head the sound a piece of paper makes when you tear it in half over and over. His six-man Chalk was a quarter of a row, separated off by the gray vinyl screens. A Team is four Chalks plus the Team Leader and a cart boy, some of these from Peoria College of Business. The screens could be moved around to reconfigure the room's layout. Similar rotes groups were in the rooms to either side. Far to the left past three other Chalks' rows was the Group Manager's office with the AGM's little cubicle of screens to the side of it. The pinkie rubbers were for traction on the forms for all deliberate speed. You were supposed to save the rubber at the end of the day. The overhead lights cast no shadow, even of your hand if you held it out like you were reaching at a tray. Doug and Amber Bellman of 402 Elk Court, Edina MN, who itemized and then some, elected to have $1 go to the Presidential Election Campaign Fund. It took several minutes to crosscheck everything on Schedule A but nothing qualified for the specs of a promising audit, even though Mr. Bellman had the jaggedy handwriting of a crazy man. Lane Dean had filed far fewer 20s than protocol called for. On Friday he had the fewest 20s of anyone else in the Chalk. Nobody'd said anything. All the wastebaskets were full of the curled strips of paper from the adding machines. Everyone's faces were the color of wet lead in the fluorescent light. You could make a semiprivate cubicle out of the screens like the Team Leader had. Then he looked up despite all best prior intentions. In four minutes it would be another hour, a half hour after that was the fifteen-minute break. Lane Dean imagined himself running around on the break waving his arms and shouting gibberish and holding ten cigarettes at once in his mouth like a panpipe. Year after year, a face the same color as your desk. Lord Jesus. Coffee wasn't allowed because of spills on the files, but on the break he'd have a big cup of coffee in each hand while he imagined himself running around the outside grounds shouting. He knew what he'd really do on the break was sit facing the wall clock in the lounge and despite prayers and effort sit counting the seconds tick off until he had to come back and do this again. And again and again and again. The imagined sound made him remember different times he'd seen people rip paper in half. He thought of a circus strongman tearing a phone book; he was bald and had a handlebar mustache and wore a stripy all-body swimsuit like people wore in the distant past. Lane Dean summoned all his will and bore down and did three returns in a row, and began imagining different high places to jump off of. He felt in a position to say he knew now that hell had nothing to do with fires or frozen troops. Lock a fellow in a windowless room to perform rote tasks just tricky enough to make him have to think, but still rote, tasks involving numbers that connected to nothing he'd ever see or care about, a stack of tasks that never went down, and nail a clock to the wall where he can see it, and just leave the man there to his mind's own devices. Tell him to pucker his butt and think beach when he starts to get antsy, and that would be just the word they'd use, *antsy*, like his mother. Let him find out in time's fullness what a joke the word was, that it didn't come anyplace close. He'd already dusted the desk with his cuff, moved his infant son's photo in its rattly little frame where the front glass slid a bit if you shook it. He'd already tried switching the green rubber over and doing the adding machine with his left hand, pretending he'd had a stroke and was bravely soldiering on. The rubber made the pinkie's tip all damp and pale beneath it. Unable to sit still at home, unable to look at anything for more than a second or two. The beach now had solid cement instead of sand and the water was gray and barely moved, just quivered a little, like Jell-O that's almost set. Unbidden came ways to kill himself with Jell-O. Lane Dean tried to control the rate of his heartbeat. He wondered if with enough practice and concentration you could stop your heart at will the same way you hold your breath — like this right here. His heart rate felt dangerously slow and he became scared and tried to keep his head inclined by rolling his eyes way up and compared the rate to the clock's second hand but the second hand seemed impossibly slow. The sound of ripping paper again and again. Some cart boys brought you files with everything you needed, some did not. The buzzer to bring a cart boy was just under the iron desk's edge, with a wire trailing down one of the desk's sides and little welded-on leg, but it didn't work. Atkins said the wiggler who'd been at the station before him, who'd got transferred someplace, had pressed on it so much it burnt the circuit. Small strange indentations in rows on the blotter's front edge were, Lane Dean had realized, the prints of teeth that somebody'd bent down and pressed real carefully into the blotter's edge so that the indentations went way down and stayed there. He felt he could understand. It was hard to keep from smelling his finger; at home he'd find himself doing it, staring into space at the table. His little baby boy's face worked better than the beach; he imagined him doing all sorts of things that he and his wife could talk about later, like curling his fist around one of their fingers or smiling when Sheri made that amazed face at him. He liked to watch her with the baby; for half a file it helped to have them in mind because they were why, they were what made this worthwhile and the right thing and he had to remember it but it kept slipping away down the hole that fell through him. Neither man on either side of him seemed to ever fidget or move except to reach up and lift things onto the desk from their Tingles' trays, like machines, and they were never in the lounge at break. Atkins claimed that after a year he could examine and crosscheck two files at once, but you never saw him try and do it, though he could whistle one song and hum a different one. Nugent's sister did the exorcist on the phone. Lane Dean watched out of the corner of his eye as a parrot-faced man by the central aisle dividing Teams pulled a file out of his tray and removed the return and detached the printout and centered both documents on his blotter. With his little homemade seat cushion and gray hat on its hook screwed into the 402s tray. Lane Dean stared down without seeing his own open file and imagined being that guy with his sad little cushion and customized banker's lamp and wondered what he possibly had or did in his spare time to make up for these soul-murdering eight daily hours that weren't even a quarter through until he just couldn't stand it and did three returns in a row in a kind of frenzy where he might have missed things and so on the next file went very slowly and painstakingly and found a discrepancy between the 1040's Schedule E and the RRA annuity tables for poor old Clive R. Terry of Alton's pissant railroad pension, but a discrepancy so small that you couldn't tell if the Martinsburg printout had even made an error or had just accepted a wide roundoff for time's sake given the amount at stake, and he had to fill out both an 020-C and a Memo 402-C(1) kicking the return over to the Group Manager's office to decide how to classify the error. Both had to be filled out with duplicated data on both sides, and signed. The whole issue was almost unbelievably meaningless and small. He thought about the word *meaning* and tried to summon up his baby's face without looking at the photo but all he could get was the heft of a full diaper and the plastic mobile over his crib turning in the breeze the box fan in the doorway made. No one in either congregation ever saw *The Exorcist;* it was against Catholic dogma and an obscenity. It was not entertainment. He imagined that the clock's second hand possessed awareness and knew that it was a second hand and that its job was to go around and around inside a circle of numbers forever at the same slow unvarying machinelike rate, going no place it hadn't already been a million times before, and imagining the second hand was so awful it made his breath catch in his throat and he looked quickly around to see if any of the examiners around him had heard it or were looking at him. When he started to see the baby's photo's face melting and lengthening and growing a long cleft jaw and the face aging years in just seconds and finally caving in from old age and falling away from the grinning yellow skull underneath, he knew he was half asleep and dreaming but did not know his own face was in his hands until he heard a human voice and opened his eyes but couldn't see who it went with and then smelled the pinkie's rubber right under his nose. He might have drooled on the open file.

Getting a little taste, I see.

It was a big older fellow with a seamed face and picket teeth. He wasn't from any Tingle that Lane Dean had ever observed from his own. The man had on a headlamp with a tan cotton band like some dentists wore and a type of thick black marker in his breast pocket. He smelled of hair oil and some kind of food. He had part of his bottom on the edge of Lane's desk and was cleaning under his thumbnail with a straightened-out paperclip and speaking softly. You could see an undershirt under his shirt; he wore no tie. He kept moving his upper body around in a slight kind of shape or circle, and the movements left a little bit of a visual trail. None of the wigglers in either adjoining row was paying attention to him. Dean checked the face in the photo to make sure he wasn't still dreaming.

They don't ever say it, though. Have you noticed? They talk around it. It's too manifest. As if talking about the air you're breathing, yes? It would be as if saying, I see so-and-so *with my eye*. What would be the point?

There was something wrong with one of his eyes; the pupil of the eye was bigger and stayed that way, making the eye look fixed. His headlamp wasn't on. The slow upper-body motions brought him in closer and then back and away and around again. It was very slight and slow.

Yes but now that you're getting a taste, consider it, the word. You know the one. Dean had the uneasy sense that the fellow wasn't strictly speaking *to* him, which would mean that he was more like ranting. The one eye looked fixedly past him. Although hadn't he just been thinking about a word? Was that word *dilated?* Had he said the word out loud? Lane Dean looked circumspectly to either side. The Group Manager's frosted door was shut.

Word appears suddenly in 1766. No known etymology. The Earl of March uses it in a letter describing a French peer of the realm. He didn't cast a shadow, but that didn't mean anything. For no reason, Lane Dean flexed his buttocks. In fact the first three appearances of *bore* in English conjoin it with the adjective *French*, that French bore, that boring Frenchman, yes? The French of course had *malaise, ennui*. See Pascal's fourth *Pensée*, which Lane Dean heard as *pantsy*. He was checking for errant spit on the file before him. One ham in dark-blue work pants was inches from his elbow. The man moved slightly back and forth like his waist was hinged. He appeared to be inspecting Lane Dean's upper body and face in a systematic gridlike fashion. His eyebrows were all over the place. The tan band was either soaked or stained. See La Rochefoucauld's or the Marquise du Deffand's well-known letters to Horace Walpole, specifically I believe Letter 96. But nothing in English prior to March, Earl of. This means a good five hundred years of no word for it you see, yes? He rotated slightly away. In no way was this a vision or moment. Lane Dean had heard of the phantom but never seen it. The phantom of the hallucination of repetitive concentration held for too long a time, like saying a word over and over until it kind of melted and got foreign. Mr. Wax's high hard gray hair was just visible four Tingles down. No word for the Latin *accidia* made so much of by monks under Benedict. For the Greek ακηδία. Also the hermits of third-century Egypt, the so-called *daemon meridianus*, when their prayers were stultified by pointlessness and tedium and a longing for violent death. Now Lane Dean was looking openly around as in like who is this fellow? The one eye was fixed at a point over past the row of vinyl screens. The tearing sound had gone, as had that one cart's squeaky wheel.

The fellow cleared his throat. Donne of course called it *lethargie*, and for a time it seems conjoined somewhat with melancholy, saturninia, *otiositas, tristitia* — that is, to be confused with sloth and torpor and lassitude and eremia and vexation and distemper and attributed to spleen, for example see Winchilsea's *black jaundice*, or of course Burton. The man was still on the same thumbnail. Quaker Green in I believe 1750 called it *spleenfog*. Hair oil made Lane Dean think of the barber's, of the stripy pole that seemed to spiral eternally upward but you could see when the shop closed and it stopped really didn't. The hair oil had a name. No one under sixty used it. Mr. Wax used a men's spray. The fellow appeared unconscious of his upper body's underwater X-shaped rotations. Two of the wigglers in a Team near the door had long beards and black derbies and bobbed at their Tingles as they examined returns but their bobbing was rapid and back and forth only; this was different. The examiners on either side didn't look up or pay attention; their fingers on the adders never slowed. Lane Dean couldn't tell if this was a sign of their professional concentration or something else. Some wore the rubber on the left pinkie, most on the right. Robert Atkins was ambidextrous; he could fill out different forms with each hand. The fellow on his left hadn't blinked once all morning that Dean had been able to see. And then suddenly up it pops. *Bore.* As if from Athena's forehead. Noun and verb, participle as adjective, whole nine yards. Origin unknown, really. We do not know. Nothing on it in Johnson.

Partridge's only entry is on *bored* as a subject complement and what preposition it takes, since *bored of* as opposed to *with* is a class marker which is all that ever really concerns Partridge. Class class class. The only Partridge Lane Dean knew was the same TV Partridge everybody else knew. He had no earthly idea what this guy was talking about but at the same time it unnerved him that he'd been thinking about *bore* as a word as well, the word, many returns ago. Philologists say it was a neologism—and just at the time of industry's rise, too, yes? of the mass man, the automated turbine and drill bit and bore, yes? Hollowed out? Forget Friedkin, have you seen *Metropolis*? All right, this really creeped Lane out. His inability to say anything to this guy or ask him what he even wanted felt a little like a bad dream as well. The night after his first day he'd dreamed of a stick that kept breaking over and over but never got smaller. The Frenchman pushing that uphill stone throughout eternity. Look for instance at L. P. Smith's *English Language*, '56 I believe, yes? It was the bad eye, the frozen eye, that seemed to inspect what he leaned toward. Posits certain neologisms as *arising from their own cultural necessity*—his words, I believe. Yes, he said. When the kind of experience that you're getting a man-sized taste of becomes possible, the word invents itself. The term. Now he switched nails. It was Vitalis that had soaked the headlamp's band, which looked more and more like a bandage. The Group Manager's door had his name on it painted on the same pebbled-glass window thing that older high schools have. Personnel's doors were the same. The wiggle rooms had windowless metal fire doors on struts up top, a newer model. Consider that the Oglok of Labrador have more than a hundred separate and distinct words for snow. Smith puts it as that when anything assumes sufficient relevance it finds its name. The name springs up under cultural pressure. Really quite interesting when you consider it. Now for the first time the fellow at the Tingle to the right turned briefly to give the man a look and turned just as fast back around when the man made his hands into claws and held them out at the other wiggler like a demon or someone possessed. The whole thing happened too fast to almost be real to Lane Dean. The wiggler turned a page in the file before him. Someone else had also called it that, *soul murdering*. Which now you will, too, yes? In the nineteenth century then suddenly the word's everywhere; see for example Kierkegaard's *Strange that boredom, in itself so staid and solid, should have such power to set in motion*. When he slid his big ham off the desktop the movement made the smell stronger; it was Vitalis and Chinese food, the food in the little white bucket with the wire handle, moo goo something. The room's light on the frosted glass was different because the door was slightly open, though Lane Dean hadn't seen the door open. It occurred to Lane Dean that he might pray.

It was the same gridlike swaying motion standing. The one eye was on the Group Manager's door, open a crack. Note too that *interesting* first appears just two years after *bore*. 1768. Mark this, two years *after*. Can this be so? He was halfway down the row; now the fellow with the cushion looked up and then back down right away. Invents itself, yes? Not all it invents. Then something Lane Dean heard as *bone after tea*. The man was gone when he reached the row's end. The file and its Schedules A/B and printout were right where they'd been, but Lane's son's picture was face-down. He let himself look up and saw that no time had passed at all, again.

§36

EVERY WHOLE PERSON has ambitions, objectives, initiatives, goals. This one particular boy's goal was to be able to press his lips to every square inch of his own body.

His arms to the shoulders and most of the legs beneath the knee were child's play. After these areas of his body, however, the difficulty increased with the abruptness of a coastal shelf. The boy came to understand that unimaginable challenges lay ahead of him. He was six.

There is little to say about the original animus or 'motive cause' of the boy's desire to press his lips to every square inch of his own body. He had been homebound one day with asthma, a rainy and distended morning, apparently looking through some of his father's promotional materials. Some of these survived the eventual fire. The boy's asthma was thought to be congenital.

The outside area of his foot beneath and around the lateral malleolus was the first to require any real contortion. (The young boy thought, at that point, of the lateral malleolus as the funny knob thing on his ankle.) The strategy, as he understood it, was to arrange himself on his bedroom's carpeted floor with the inside of his knee on the floor and his calf and foot at as close to a perfect 90-degree angle to his thigh as he could at that point manage. Then he had to lean as far over to the side as he could, bending out over the splayed ankle and the foot's outside, rotating his neck over and down and straining with his fully extended lips (the boy's idea of fully extended lips consisted at this point of the exaggerated pucker that signified kissing in children's cartoons) at a section of the foot's outside he had marked with a bull's-eye of soluble ink, struggling to breathe against the dextrorotated pressure of his ribs, stretching farther and farther to the side very early one morning until he felt a flat pop in the upper part of his back and then pain beyond naming somewhere between his shoulder blade and spine. The boy did not cry out or weep but merely sat silent in this tortured posture until his failure to appear for breakfast brought his father upstairs to the bedroom's door. The pain and resultant dyspnea kept the boy out of school for over a month. One can only wonder what a father might make of an injury like this in a six-year-old child.

The father's chiropractor, Doctor Kathy, was able to relieve the worst of the immediate symptoms. More important, it was Doctor Kathy who introduced the boy to the concepts of spine as microcosm and of spinal hygiene and postural echo and incrementalism in flexion. Doctor Kathy smelled faintly of fennel and seemed totally open and available and kind. The child lay prone on a tall padded table and placed his chin in a little cup. She manipulated his head, very gently but in a way that seemed to make things happen all the way down his back. Her hands were strong and soft and when she felt the boy's back he felt as if she were asking it questions and answering them all at the same time. She had charts on her wall with exploded views of the human spine and the muscles and fasciae and nerve bundles that surrounded the spine and were connected to it. No lollipops were anywhere in view. The specific stretching exercises Doctor Kathy gave the boy were for the splenius capitis and longissimus cervicis and the deep sheaths of nerve and muscle surrounding the boy's T2 and T3 vertebrae, which were what he had just injured. Doctor Kathy had reading glasses on a necklace and a green button-up sweater that looked as if it were made entirely of pollen. You could tell she talked to everybody the same way. She instructed the boy to perform the stretching exercises every single day and not to let boredom or a reduction in symptomology keep him from performing the rehabilitative exercises in a disciplined way. She said the long-term goal was not relief of present discomfort but neurological hygiene and health and a wholeness of body and mind he would someday appreciate very, very much. For the boy's father, Doctor Kathy prescribed an herbal relaxant.

Thus was Doctor Kathy the child's formal introduction both to incremental stretching and to the adult idea of quiet daily discipline and progress toward a long-term goal. This proved fortuitous. During his five weeks disabled with a subluxated T3 vertebra—often in such discomfort that not even his inhaler could help the asthma that struck whenever he experienced pain or distress—the heady enthusiasm of childhood had given way in the boy to a realization that the objective of pressing his lips to every square inch of himself was going to require maximum effort, discipline, and a commitment sustainable over periods of time he could not then (because of his age) imagine.

One thing Doctor Kathy had taken time out to show the boy was a freestanding 3-D model of a human spine that had not been taken proper care of in any real or significant way. It looked dark, stunted, necrotic, and sad. Its tubercles and soft tissues were inflamed, and the annulus fibrosus of its disks was the color of bad teeth. Up against the wall behind this model was a hand-lettered plaque or sign explaining about what Doctor Kathy liked to say were the two different types of payments for the spine and associated nervosa, which were *Now* and *Later.*

Most professional contortionists are, in fact, simply persons born with congenital atrophic/dystrophic conditions of major recti, or with acute lordotic flexion of the lumbar spine, or both. A majority display Chvostek's sign or other forms of ipsilateral spasticity. Very little effort or application is involved in their 'art,' therefore. In 1932, a preadolescent Ceylonese female was documented by British scholars of Tamil mysticism as capable of inserting into her mouth and down her esophagus both arms to the shoulder, one leg to the groin, and the other leg to just above the patella, and as thereupon able to spin unaided on the orally protrusive knee at rates in excess of 300 rpm. The phenomenon of suiphagia (i.e., 'self-swallowing') has subsequently been identified as a rare form of inanitive pica, in most cases caused by deficiencies in cadmium and/or zinc.

The insides of the small boy's thighs up to the medial fork of his groin took months even to prepare for, daily hours spent cross-legged and bowed, slowly and incrementally stretching the long vertical fasciae of his back and neck, the spinalis thoracis and levator scapulae, the iliocostalis lumborum all the way to the sacrum, and the interior thigh's dense and intransigent gracilis, pectineus, and adductor longus, which fuse below Scarpa's triangle and transmit sickening pain through the pubis whenever their range of flexibility is exceeded. Had anyone seen him during these two- and three-hour sessions, bringing his soles together and in to train the pectineus, bobbing slightly and then holding a deep cross-legged lean to work the great tight sheet of thoracolumbar fascia that connected his pelvis to his dorsal costae, the child would have appeared to that person either prayerful or catatonic, or both.

Once the thighs' anterior targets were achieved and touched with one or both lips, the upper portions of his genitals were simple, and were protrusively kissed and passed over even as plans for the ilium and outer buttocks were in conception. After these achievements would come the more difficult and neck-intensive contortions required to access the inner buttocks, perineum, and extreme upper groin.

The boy had turned seven.

The special place where he pursued his strange but newly mature objective was his room, which had wallpaper with a repeating jungle motif. The room's second-floor window yielded a view of the backyard's tree. Light from the sun came through the tree at different angles and intensities at different times of day and illuminated different parts of the boy as he stood, sat, inclined, or lay on the room's carpet, stretching and holding positions. His bedroom's carpet was white shag with a furry, polar aspect that the boy's father did not think went well with the walls' repeating scheme of tiger, zebra, lion, palm; but the father kept his feelings to himself.

Radical increase of the lips' protrusive range requires systematic exercise of maxillary fasciae such as the depressor septi, orbicularis oris, depressor anguli oris, depressor labii inferioris, and the buccinator, circumoral, and risorius groups. Zygomatic muscles are superficially involved. Praxis: Affix string to Wetherly button of at least 1.5" diameter borrowed from father's second-best raincoat; place button over upper and lower front teeth and enclose with lips; hold string fully extended at 90 degrees to face's plane and pull with gradually increasing tension on end, using lips to resist pull; hold for twenty seconds; repeat; repeat.

Sometimes his father sat on the floor outside the boy's bedroom with his back to the door. It's not clear whether the boy ever heard him listening for movement in the room, although the wood of the door sometimes made a creaky sound when the father sat against it or stood back up in the hallway or shifted his seated position against the door. The boy was in there stretching and holding contorted positions for extraordinary periods of time. The father was a somewhat nervous man, with a rushed, fidgety manner that always lent him an air of imminent departure. He had extensive entrepreneurial activities and was in motion much of the time. His place in most people's mental album was provisional, with something like a dotted line around it—the image of someone saying something friendly over his shoulder as he made for an exit. Most clients found the father made them uneasy. He was at his most effective on the phone.

By age eight, the child's long-term goal was beginning to affect his physical development. His teachers remarked changes in posture and gait. The boy's smile, which appeared by now constant because of the circumlabial hypertrophy's effects on the circumoral musculature, looked unusual also, rigid and overbroad and seeming, in one custodian's evaluative phrase, 'like nothing in this round world.'

*   *   *

Facts: Italian stigmatist Padre Pio carried wounds which penetrated the left hand and both feet medially throughout his lifetime. The Umbrian St. Veronica Giuliani presented with wounds in one hand as well as in her side, which wounds were observed to open and close on command. The eighteenth-century holy woman Giovanna Solimani permitted pilgrims to insert special keys in her hands' wounds and to turn them, reportedly facilitating those clients' own recovery from rationalist despair.

According to both St. Bonaventura and Tomas de Celano, St. Francis of Assisi's manual stigmata included baculiform masses of what presented as hardened black flesh extrudent from both volar planes. If and when pressure was applied to a palm's so-called 'nail,' a hardened black rod of flesh would immediately protrude from the back of the hand, just exactly as if a real so-called 'nail' were passing through the hand.

And yet (fact): Hands lack the anatomical mass required to support the weight of an adult human. Both Roman legal texts and modern examinations of first-century skeletons confirm that classical crucifixion required nails to be driven through the subject's wrists, not his hands. Hence the, quote, 'necessarily simultaneous *truth* and *falsity* of the stigmata' that existential theologist E. M. Cioran explicates in his 1937 *Lacrimi si sfinti*, the same monograph in which he refers to the human heart as 'God's open wound.'

Areas of the boy's midsection from navel to xiphoid process at the cleft of his ribs alone comprised nineteen months of stretching and postural exercises, the more extreme of which must have been very painful indeed. At this stage, further advances in flexibility were now subtle to the point of being undetectable without extremely precise daily record-keeping. Certain tensile limits in the flava, capsule, and process ligaments of the neck and upper back were gently but persistently stretched, the boy's chin placed to his (solubly arrowed and dotted) chest at mid-sternum and then slid incrementally down—1, sometimes 1.5 millimeters a day—and this catatonic and/or meditative posture held for an hour or more.

In the summer, during his early-morning routines, the tree outside the boy's window filled with grackles and became busy with grackles coming and going; and then, as the sun rose, the tree filled with the birds' harsh sounds, tearing sounds, which as the boy sat cross-legged with his chin to his chest sounded through the pane like rusty screws turning, some complexly stuck thing coming loose with a shriek. Past the southern exposure's tree were the foreshortened roofs of neighborhood homes and the fire hydrant and street sign of the cross-street and the forty-eight identical roofs of a low-income housing development beyond the cross-street, and, past the development, just at the horizon, the edges of the verdant cornfields that began at the city limits. In late summer the fields' green was more sallow, and later in the fall there was merely sad stubble, and in the winter the fields' bare earth looked like nothing so much as just what it was.

At his elementary school, where the boy's behavior was exemplary and his assignments completed and his progress charted at the medial apex of all relevant curves, he was, among his classmates, the sort of marginal social figure so marginal he was not even teased. As early as Grade 3, the boy had begun to develop along unusual physical lines as a result of his commitment to the objective; even so, something in his aspect or bearing served to place him outside the bounds of schoolyard cruelty. The boy followed classroom regulations and performed satisfactorily in group work. The written evaluations of his socialization described the boy not even as withdrawn or aloof but as 'calm,' 'unusually poised,' and 'self-containing [sic].' The boy gave neither trouble nor delight and was not much noticed. It is not known whether this bothered him. The vast majority of his time, energy, and attention belonged to the long-range objective and the daily disciplines thereby entailed.

Nor was it ever established precisely why this boy devoted himself to the goal of being able to press his lips to every square inch of his own body. It is not clear even that he conceived of the goal as an 'achievement' in any conventional sense. Unlike his father, he did not read Ripley and had never heard of the McWhirters — certainly it was no kind of stunt. Nor any sort of self-evection; this is verified; the boy had no conscious wish to 'transcend' anything. If someone had asked him, the boy would have said only that he'd decided he wanted to press his lips to every last micrometer of his own individual body. He would not have been able to say more than this. Insights or conceptions of his own physical 'inaccessibility' to himself (as we are all of us self-inaccessible and can, for example, touch parts of one another in ways that we could not even dream of with our own bodies) or of his complete determination, apparently, to pierce that veil of inaccessibility — to be, in some childish way, self-contained and -sufficient — these were beyond his conscious awareness. He was, after all, just a little boy.

His lips touched the upper aureoles of his left and right nipples in the autumn of his ninth year. The lips by this time were markedly large and protrusive; part of his daily disciplines were tedious button-and-string exercises designed to promote hypertrophy of the orbicularis muscles. The ability to extend his pursed lips as much as 10.4 centimeters had often been the difference between achieving part of his thorax and not. It had also been the orbicularis muscles, more than any outstanding advance in vertebral flexion, that had permitted him to access the rear areas of his scrotum and substantial portions of the papery skin around his anus before he turned nine. These areas had been touched, tagged on the four-sided chart inside his personal ledger, then washed clean of ink and forgotten. The boy's tendency was to forget each site once he had pressed his lips to it, as if the establishment of its accessibility made the site henceforth unreal for him and the site now in some sense 'existed' only on the four-faced chart.

Fully and exquisitely real for the boy in his eleventh year, however, remained those portions of his trunk he had not yet attempted: areas of his chest above the pectoralis minor and of his lower throat between clavicle and upper platysma, as well as the smooth and endless planes and tracts of his back (excluding lateral portions of the trapezius and rear deltoid, which he had achieved at eight and a half) extending upward from the buttocks.

Four separate licensed, bonded physicians apparently testified that the Bavarian mystic Therese Neumann's stigmata comprised corticate dermal structures that passed medially through both her hands. Therese Neumann's additional capacity for inedia was attested in writing by four Franciscan nuns who attended her in rotating shifts from 1927 to 1962 and confirmed that Therese lived for almost thirty-five years without food or liquid of any kind; her one recorded bowel movement (12 March 1928) was determined by laboratory analysis to comprise only mucus and empyreumatic bile.

A Bengali holy man known to followers as 'Prahansatha the Second' underwent periods of meditative chanting during which his eyes exited their sockets and ascended to float above his head, connected only by their dura mater cords, and thereupon underwent (i.e., the floating eyes did) rhythmically stylized rotary movements described by Western witnesses as evocative of dancing four-faced Shivas, of charmed snakes, of interwoven genetic helices, of the counterpointed figure-eight orbits of the Milky Way and Andromeda galaxies around each other at the perimeter of the Local Group, or of all four (supposedly) at once.

Studies of human algesia have established that the musculoskeletal structures most sensitive to painful stimulation are: the periosteum and joint capsules. Tendons, ligaments, and subchondral bone are classified as *significantly* pain-sensitive, while muscle and cortical bone's sensitivity has been established as *moderate*, and articular cartilage and fibrocartilage's as *mild*.

Pain is a wholly subjective experience and thus 'inaccessible' as a diagnostic object. Considerations of personality type also complicate the evaluation. As a general rule, however, the observed behavior of a patient in pain can provide a measure of (a) the pain's intensity and (b) the patient's ability to cope with it.

Common fallacies about pain include:

- People who are critically ill or gravely injured always experience intense pain.
- The greater the pain, the greater the extent and severity of damage.
- Severe chronic pain is symptomatic of incurable illness.

In fact, patients who are critically ill or gravely injured do not necessarily experience intense pain. Nor is the observed intensity of pain directly proportional to the extent or severity of damage; the correlation depends also on whether the 'pain pathways' of the anterolateral spinothalamic system are intact and functioning within established norms. In addition, the personality of a neurotic patient may accentuate felt pain, and a stoic or resilient personality may diminish its perceived intensity.

No one ever did ask him. His father believed only that he had an eccentric but very limber and flexible child, a child who'd taken Kathy Kessinger's homilies about spinal hygiene to heart the way some children will take things to heart and now spent a lot of time flexing and limbering his body, which as the queer heartcraft of children went was preferable to many other slack or damaging fixations the father could think of. The father, an entrepreneur who sold motivational tapes through the mail, worked out of a home office but was frequently away for seminars and mysterious evening sales calls. The family's home, which faced west, was tall and slender and contemporary; it resembled one half of a duplex town house from which the other half had been suddenly removed. It had olive-colored aluminum siding and was on a cul-de-sac at the northern end of which stood a side entrance to the county's third-largest cemetery, whose name was woven in iron above the main gate but not above that side entrance. The word that the father thought of when he thought of the boy was: *dutiful*, which surprised the man, for it was a rather old-fashioned word and he had no idea where it came from when he thought of him in there, from outside the door.

Doctor Kathy, who sometimes saw the boy for continuing prophylactic adjustments to his thoracic vertebrae, facets, and anterior rami, and was not a loon or a huckster in a shopping-center office but simply a DC who believed in the interpenetrating dance of spine, nervous system, spirit, and cosmos as totality—in the universe as an infinite system of neural connections that had evolved, at its highest point, an organism which could sustain consciousness of both itself and the universe at the same time, such that the human nervous system became the universe's way of being aware of and thus 'accessible [to]' itself—Doctor Kathy believed the patient to be a very quiet, inner-directed boy who had responded to a traumatic T3 subluxation with a commitment to spinal hygiene and neurospiritual integrity that might well signal a calling to chiropractic as an eventual career. It was she who had given the boy his first, comparatively simple stretching manuals, as well as the copies of B. R. Faucet's famous neuromuscular diagrams (©1961, Los Angeles College of Chiropractic) out of which the boy fashioned the freestanding four-sided cardboard chart that stood as if guarding his pillowless bed while he slept.

The father's belief in ATTITUDE as the overarching determinant of ALTITUDE had been unwavering since his own adolescence, during which awkward time he had discovered the works of Dale Carnegie and of the Willard and Marguerite Beecher Foundation, and had utilized these practical philosophies to bolster his own self-confidence and to improve his social standing—this standing, as well as all interpersonal exchanges and incidents which served as evidence thereof, was charted weekly and the charts and graphs displayed for ease of reference on the inside of his bedroom's closet door. Even as a provisional and secretly tortured adult, the father still worked tirelessly to maintain and improve his attitude and so influence his own altitude in personal achievement. To the medicine cabinet's mirror in the home's bathroom, for instance, where he could not help but reread and internalize them as he tended to personal grooming, were taped inspirational maxims such as:

'NO BIRD SOARS TOO HIGH, IF HE SOARS WITH HIS OWN
  WINGS — *BLAKE*'
'IF WE ABDICATE OUR INITIATIVE, WE BECOME PASSIVE —
  RECEPTIVE VICTIMS OF ON-COMING CIRCUMSTANCES — *BEECHER
  FOUNDATION*'

'DARE TO ACHIEVE!—*NAPOLEON HILL*'
'THE COWARD FLEES EVEN WHEN NO MAN PURSUETH—*BIBLE*'
'WHATEVER YOU CAN DO OR DREAM, YOU CAN BEGIN IT.
 BOLDNESS HAS GENIUS, POWER AND MAGIC IN IT. BEGIN IT
 NOW!—*GOETHE*'

and so forth, dozens or at times even scores of inspirational quotes and reminders, carefully printed in block capitals on small, fortune cookie–sized slips of paper and taped to the mirror as written reminders of the father's personal responsibility for whether he soared boldly, sometimes so many slips and pieces of tape that only a few slots of actual mirror were left above the bathroom's sink, and the father had to almost contort himself even to see to shave.

When the boy's father thought of himself, on the other hand, the word that came unbidden first to mind was always: *tortured*. Much of this secret torture—whose causes he perceived as impossibly complex and protean and involving both normal male sexual drives and highly abnormal personal weakness and lack of backbone—was actually quite simple to diagnose. Wedded at twenty to a woman about whom he'd known just one salient thing, this father-to-be had almost immediately found marriage's conjugal routines tedious and stifling; and the sense of monotony and sexual obligation (as opposed to sexual achievement) had caused in him a feeling that he felt must be almost like death. Even as a newlywed, he had begun to suffer from night terrors and to wake from nightmares of some terrible confinement feeling unable to move or breathe. These dreams did not exactly take any kind of psychiatric Einstein to interpret, the father knew, and after almost a year of inner struggle and complex self-analysis he had given in and begun seeing another woman, sexually. This woman, whom the father had met at a motivational seminar, was also married, and had a small child of her own, and they had agreed that this put some sensible limits and restrictions on the affair.

Within a short time, however, the father had begun to find this other woman kind of tedious and oppressive, as well. The fact that they lived separate lives and had little to talk about made the sex start to seem obligatory. It put too much weight on the physical sex, it seemed, and spoiled it. The father attempted to cool things off and to see the woman less, whereupon she in return also began to seem less interested and accessible than she had been. This was when the torture started. The father began to fear that the woman would break off the affair with him, either to resume monogamous sex with her husband or to take up with some other man.

This fear, which was a completely secret and interior torture, caused him to pursue the woman all over again even as he came more and more to despise her. The father, in short, longed to detach from the woman, but he didn't want the woman to be able to detach. He began to feel numb and even nauseous when he was with the other woman, but when he was away from her he felt tortured by thoughts of her with someone else. It seemed like an impossible situation, and the dreams of contorted suffocation came back more and more often. The only possible remedy that the father (whose son had just turned four) could see was not to detach from the woman he was having an affair with but to hang dutifully in there with the affair, but also to find and begin seeing a third woman, in secret and as it were 'on the side,' in order to feel—if only for a short time—the relief and excitement of an attachment freely chosen.

Thus began the father's true cycle of torture, in which the number of women with whom he was secretly involved and to whom he had sexual obligations steadily expanded, and in which not one of the women could be let go or given cause to detach and break it off, even as each became less and less a source of anything more than a sort of dutiful tedium of energy and time and the will to forge on in the face of despair.

The boy's mid- and upper back were the first areas of radical, perhaps even impossible unavailability to his own lips, presenting challenges to flexibility and discipline that occupied a vast percentage of his inner life in Grades 4 and 5. And beyond, of course, like the falls at a long river's end, lay the unimaginable prospects of achieving the back of his neck, the eight centimeters just below the chin's point, the galeae of his scalp's back and crown, the forehead and zygomatic ridge, the ears, nose, eyes—as well as the paradoxical *ding an sich* of his lips themselves, accessing which appeared to be like asking a blade to cut itself. These sites occupied a near-mythic place in the overall project: The boy revered them in such a way as to place them almost beyond the range of conscious intent. This boy was not by nature a 'worrier' (unlike himself, his father thought), but the inaccessibility of these last sites seemed so immense that it was as if their cast shadow fell across all the slow progress up toward his clavicle in the front and lumbar curvature in the rear that occupied his eleventh year, darkening the whole endeavor, a tenebrous shadow the boy chose to see as lending the enterprise a somber dignity rather than futility or pathos.

He did not yet know how, but he believed, as he approached pubescence, that his head would be his. He would find a way to access all of himself. He possessed nothing that anyone could ever call doubt, inside.

Afterword

This passage—which appeared posthumously in *The New Yorker* in 2011, with the title "Backbone," and became Chapter 36 of *The Pale King*—was one that David Foster Wallace had been working on for some time. He'd read a version of it at the Lannan Foundation in December 2000, and before that, in April 1999, he'd sent me an earlier draft, for possible inclusion in the magazine's first "20 Under 40" fiction issue. (Below the return address on the accompanying letter—"Fragmentco Unltd."—he wrote, "Dear D.T., Pursuant to our phone conversation of last Fri., here is as much of the Fragment as I can render readable in time to have this to you by week's end. In the wildly unlikely event that this Fragment does not meet your publication needs at this time, I would ask that you dispose of it thoroughly and irremediably—some combination of shredder and flame* is usually sufficient.... *[in that order...].” My apology, David, for whatever it's worth, for not having followed your instructions.) In the end, we ran a more polished piece in the issue—a story from Wallace's forthcoming "Brief Interviews with Hideous Men."

When I read the story again in 2011—significantly changed and expanded since its 1999 iteration—I was both awed and sorrow-struck. With the unearned privilege of hindsight, I could see how intricately, consciously or not, Wallace had reshaped his own process as a writer into his six-year-old hero's obsessive, torturous pursuit of perfection. The way that Wallace returned to this narrative, and others, again and again, removing, adding, adjusting, stretching, improving, had much in common with the way that the boy pursues his own dream, one that he knows, from the beginning, is quixotic and may even destroy him. The project begins as "child's play" and develops into a life's work, something that will require "maximum effort, discipline, and a commitment sustainable over periods of time that [the boy] could not then...imagine." Wallace is, of course, aware of the narcissism of this ambition: what could be more narcissistic than kissing "every square inch" of one's own body except perhaps exposing every square inch of oneself in writing? At the same time, the boy is a kind of saintly figure, his story repeatedly juxtaposed with those of holy men and women who have accomplished supernatural feats of physical endurance.

There's a certain defensiveness in that first line: "Every whole person has ambitions, objectives, initiatives, goals"— the insistence on "wholeness," the emphatic string of synonyms. The boy—an asthmatic who has trouble breathing, who seems to have lost his mother (she doesn't appear here; in the 1999 version, she died of "septic shock" after giving birth), who breaks his own back—is, arguably, not whole; marginalized, unloved, unkissed, he sets out to provide the missing kisses to himself. To do so, he must become someone else, or become two people: the kissed and the kisser, the child and his mother. "The difficulty increased with the abruptness of a coastal shelf," Wallace writes, in an echo, perhaps, of Philip Larkin's searing excoriation of parenthood "This Be the Verse": "Man hands on misery to man. / It deepens like a coastal shelf. / Get out as early as you can, / And don't have any kids yourself."

It's possible that the father in the story—the apparent opposite of his son, a man with a "lack of backbone" who feels trapped with one woman, adds another to his life, feels trapped, adds another, and so on, in his own "true cycle of torture"—also has something to tell us about Wallace's experience of writing *The Pale King*, an ever-expanding narrative with a multitude of beginnings and a multitude of characters, none of whom are ever entirely released from their service to the plot, though the nature of that service remains at times, perhaps purposefully, obscure.

And yet what I remember most about this story is the sudden joyous upward flight of its ending: a ringing declaration of ambition, of confidence, of optimism. Coming as it does after the bleakness of the child's fanatical isolation and of the father's emotional despair, its note of triumph feels even more ascendant: "He would find a way to access all of himself. He possessed nothing that anyone could ever call doubt, inside."

—Deborah Treisman

TEACHING
MATERIALS

Introduction

Good teachers are those who so love their subjects that they try with all their might and main to help students love them, too, forever. David seldom met a word he didn't enjoy playing with, making it jump through flaming hoops and perform feats of derring-do. (Or, as he might have said, daring-don't). When he was about four years old, he loved the sounds of *precocious, atrocious,* and *ferocious*, and he used them often (although he hadn't yet differentiated their definitions). When he was in high school, he would always ask, "Any thin, natal coverings?" when he came home. (He had discovered the word *caul*.) He was always eager to learn all he could about the language and how it works, and he was eager to share with his students, in a maximally palatable way, what he learned, knew, lived, and loved.

David was always interested in how other teachers plied their craft, and, like an engaging, appreciative, bandanna-wearing magpie, he would pick up shiny ideas from all over. Because both David and I assigned lots of writing, we were fond of groaning about composition and decomposition, grading and degrading. My constant mantra in the classroom was that good writers strive for clarity, courtesy, and conciseness, with an emphasis on courtesy because it's downright rude to expect a reader to wade through woolly constructions multiple times, trying to figure out what the writer is saying. I always read each student essay three times before I made a mark on the actual paper because first of all, I was eager to see how students responded to the assignment, then to identify the strengths and weaknesses of the effort, then to applaud the good stuff and make suggestions for revision of the less-good stuff. David adopted this practice and read each student piece three times, too, but he made marginal comments each time through, using different colored pens to differentiate. This Herculean time-and-labor-intensive practice blew his students' socks off and bolstered their efforts. He often called me with questions, sometimes during his office hours, when he had dinged a student for some grammatical breach but couldn't quite explain to the student exactly what made it a breach. His dad and I could hear the student chuckling in the background.

Even a person who had never heard of David could infer his character and personality from the materials he wrote for his students. His syllabi and teaching materials offer insight into a thoughtful, caring, funny, generous teacher who never stopped being a student. He was the kind of teacher who probably felt a bit guilty about accepting a salary for doing something he so enjoyed. Perhaps some of the pedagogical practices found in David's syllabi and handouts will be useful to teachers using *The David Foster Wallace Reader* in their classrooms.

— Sally Foster Wallace

DFW/SFW teaching-related correspondence:

Excerpt from a letter from David in 1987, when he was a TA at the University of Arizona:

> "I handed my papers back yesterday, and saw a burning effigy outside a frat party last night that looked a bit suspicious. It's lonely at the bottom (a quote from Auden.)"

Excerpt from a January 25, 1991, letter when he was an adjunct professor at Emerson College:

> "My students are nice, and though I was terribly anxious before the semester started, things are going better first-week-wise than they did last term. Mom, your object-and-subject exercise was a big hit, and it gave me a chance to see that these kids are really very acute readers; their trouble is that they know all this stuff in a vague intuitive way and haven't been given any sort of schema for organizing and using their instincts. Or so I hope. On the East Coast, stilted and phonily formal prose is more a problem than aint's and where-at's, it seems, so I am adopting the persona of the minimalist, which is a hoot."

DFW/SFW teaching/grammar-related e-mails:

DFW to SFW February 25, 2007

Yo. Question. Re the following sentence—"I have trouble being clear, concise, lucid, and brief."—are the four adjectives here adjectives, or are they subject complements. In "I am tall," I know that "tall" is a subj. coml.

I was taught that predicates following the verb "to be" are always subj. compl.'s, not adjectives/But is that still true when the form of "to be" is part of a participial phrase that is itself modifying something?

Help, oh Queen of R?!
/dw/

SFW to DFW February 26, 2007

A: Short answer: no.

Long answer: When I first clapped my beady, bloodshot blues on the beginning of your query quite early this morning, my reaction was "Yikes — clear and lucid are synonyms, as are concise and brief — why the wordiness"? Then, after reading your entire question, I was flummoxed, so I googled "subject complements in grammar" to help me think about this. There are a lot of links, some of them helpful.

My training in grammar (and it was Latin grammar) took place long before subject, object, and verb complements were designations. so my grammatical expertise is probably antiquated to the point of being of little use. However, your question triggered these synapses: clear, concise, lucid, and brief are inarguably adjectives that appear in the sentence's predicate, and I can't see any problem springing from calling them adjectives. "Being" here isn't behaving like a verb — it's behaving like a noun, and I think the rule you were taught pertains only to forms of "to be" that are functioning as verbs.

Meanwhile, back to that pesky wordiness. . . .

Love,
Scullery Maid of R

DFW to SFW February 27, 2007

Mom — Thanks. Note, though, the sexy po-mo way that the wordiness of the sentence helps undergird its claim (in a sort of Gillliganish way).

The sentence'll get cut, anyway — I'm doing this intro for the BAE 06, and so far it sounds like someone with a terrible fever. /dw/

SFW to DFW February 27, 2007

In the middle of yoga class yesterday, the realization smote me that the wordiness was intentional and clever and yours. (I originally thought that the sentence was a snippet from one of your students, and you were seeking a way to discuss it.) DUH!

LYL, Ma

DFW to SFW February 28, 2007

Yeah, but it'll get cut anyway. It's like the old joke: "My wife says I'm indecisive. but I'm not so sure..." har d har

DFW to SFW March 29, 2007

Mom: We were doing lie/lay last night, and someone asked me what the following tense is: "The tractor was lying in the yard." Is that the perpetual past? Why is it not laying, since "lay" is the past participle of "lie"? I sweated and ahem'd; I fingered my tie-knot. I didn't know what to say. /dw/

SFW to DFW March 29, 2007

Was lying is the past progressive (old-fashioned label)/continuous past (new one)—formed with the past form of *to be* (*was*) plus the present participle of the verb (*lying*). The past participle of *to lie* is *lain*. *Lay* is the past tense of *to lie*. Hope this helps. Unhand that tie-knot!

Love, Mom

DFW to SFW November 29, 2007

Q: Consider the sentence "I believe that John killed Fred." I was hectoring students last night about dropping "that's" in constructions, and I was arguing that "to believe" can function both transitively (I believe you) and intransitively (see supra), and then I wondered: Is "to believe" intransitive in "I believe that John killed Fred"? If so, then is the clause "John killed Fred" a subject complement, or an indirect object, or what? And what part of speech is "that" in the sentence? Can you help? :-) /dw/

SFW to DFW November 29, 2007

Yowser of a grammar question! My initial gut feeling was that THAT JOHN KILLED FRED is the direct object of BELIEVE, obviously transitive here. As you know, the test for transitiveness is to repeat the verb softly to yourself and then ask WHOM OR WHAT: The answer is THAT JOHN KILLED FRED. That's a direct object, to me. Just for cackles, I thought I'd check Bryan Garner, and ADMAU is pretty darn woolly here. On page 649, in section B, Wrongly Suppressed THAT, he says, "in formal writing, THAT is often ill-advisedly omitted" and then goes on to give good examples, but he never says what part of speech THAT is.

Then I used my Imac's dictionary twanger, which states that THAT functions as a conjunction when it introduces a subordinate clause expressing a statement or hypothesis. "She said that she was satisfied." "It is possible that we have misunderstood."
Bingo! I like this a lot.

Italics don't often make it through cyberspace successfully, so I've capitalized instead.

DFW to SFW November 29, 2007

A conjunction? What kind of conjunction? It sure isn't coordinating... /dw/

SFW to DFW November 30, 2007

According to my very recent research, THAT is one of a special group of SUBORDINATING conjunctions that introduce a complement clause: I wonder *WHETHER* he'll be late. I hope THAT he'll be on time.

English 64A   **First-Day Pop Quiz**   Name:

Please define or explain the following terms that people often use when talking technically about fiction-writing. If you don't know a term, skip it.

Developed versus Undeveloped Character

Point of View

Narrative Omniscience

Summary versus Scene

Plot

Freitag's Triangle

Unreliable Narrator

Genre Fiction versus Literary Fiction

Sentimentality

Voice

English 64A   Student Data Sheet

(Feel Free To Use Back)

Name:

Class & Major:

Campus Phone:

Email Address:

OK to include your phone/email in a Class Roster that we'll all have a copy of? Yes / No

Total # of finished pages of fiction you've written so far, lifetime:

Name two or three pieces of published fiction you've read that actually mean something to you. Explain what about each story gets to you so much, if you can.

Taken any kind of creative writing course before, ever? If so, when & where? What was the best thing about the class? What were some not-so-good things about it?

Explain what you'd like to get out of this course—like, what your con-sumer-expectations are. (It would help to be specific... and to be honest rather than just saying whatever it is you think the instructor wants to hear.)

How concerned are you about grades in this course? What do you expect your final grade to be based on? If you were the instructor for an Intro Fiction class, what criteria would you use for grading?

THINGS TO COPY

Syllabus
Student Data Sheet
Aug 31 Pop Quiz
Learning to Lie Exercise – 207-208 in brown *What If?*
Class Roster and Contact Info
Short-short Stories from What If (Get clean copy of "No One's a Mystery"
"Sudden Fiction or the Short-Short Story," Blue *What If*, pp. 220-221.
Dybek's "Pet Milk" in *Scribner Anthology*
Lydia Davis "Break It Down" from her book.
Saunders's "Isabel"
Linda Lloyd's "Poor Boy"
Elizabeth Graver's "Between" (1996 O Henrys, p. 285) – I own. COPIED 8/13
Homes's "A Real Doll"
Moody's "Twister."
King, "Man in Black Suit" (1996 O. Henry's, p. 3 – I own.] COPIED 8/13
Tom Paine, "Say Something Monsieur Eliot" – O. Henry's 96 p. 237 COPIED 8/13
Salinger's "The Laughing Man."
Walter Mosley's "The Thief" 1996 O. Henrys COPIED 8/13
Hemingway's "Clean, Well-Lighted."
Jerome Stern, "Don't Do This," *Crafting Fiction* p. 230 ff.

COURSE SYLLABUS
ENGLISH 170R, SPRING '03
SELECTED OBSCURE/ECLECTIC FICTIONS...

CLASS LOGISTICS Mondays and Wednesdays, 1:15–2:30, Crookshank 10

INSTRUCTOR David Wallace, 206 Crookshank, 607-8357

INSTRUCTOR'S OFFICE HOURS Mon. 8:00–9:00 AM, Tues. 4:30–5:30 PM, & by appt.

COURSE DESCRIPTION It's a 170-grade Advanced Seminar, meaning it's "speaking-intensive" and presupposes the basic set of lit-crit tools taught in English 67. Structurally, the course is meant to be more a colloquium than a prof.-led seminar. We are going to read and converse about nine novels (some of which are kind of long) dating from the 1930s–1970s. They're books that are arguably good and/or important but are not, in the main, read or talked about that much as of 2003. At the least, then, English 170R affords a chance to read some stuff you're not apt to get in other Lit classes. It would also be good to talk this term about the dynamics of the Lit canon and about why some important books get taught a lot in English classes and others do not—which will, of course, entail our considering what modifiers like "important," "good," and "influential" mean w/r/t modern fiction. We can approach the books from a variety of different critical, theoretical, and ideological perspectives, too, depending on students' backgrounds and interests. In essence, we can talk about whatever you wish to—provided that we do it cogently and well.

REQUIRED TEXTS All but a couple of the following are available in paperback at the Huntley Bookstore:
   (1) Renata Adler, *Speedboat* (*)
   (2) James Baldwin, *Giovanni's Room*
   (3) Djuna Barnes, *Nightwood*
   (4) Richard Brautigan, *Trout Fishing in America...In Watermelon Sugar*
   (5) Joan Didion, *Play It As It Lays*
   (6) Paula Fox, *Desperate Characters* (*)
   (7) Doris Lessing, *The Golden Notebook*
   (8) Walker Percy, *The Moviegoer*
   (9) Christina Stead, *The Man Who Loved Children*

N.B. (1) The two books marked with asterisks are not at the Huntley; you are responsible for tracking these down and getting a copy. They're not hard to find at used-type bookstores or through the Internet (abe.com, amazon.com, etc.). Paula Fox's *Desperate Characters* (© 1970) is in print in a new paperback edition from W.W. Norton & Co; its ISBN is 0-393-31894-X (please get that particular copy if you can). Renata Adler's *Speedboat* (© 1976) is apparently out of print right now, but there are lots of copies floating around the marketplace, especially of the Perennial Library trade paperback; that edition's ISBN is 0-06-097143-6.

N.B. (2) Please do not buy William Gaddis's *The Recognitions* even though Huntley's got it on 170R's Required Texts list. (Meaning feel free to buy it if you like, but it's not really on our list.)

COURSE REQUIREMENTS AND GRADING

ATTENDANCE AND PARTICIPATION Because the whole breath and bread of this course is discussion, your presence and involvement are required. You are allowed one unexcused absence without penalty; each additional unexcused absence will lower your final grade by one numeral.[1] For an absence to be excused, there must be an excellent reason and I must be notified in advance. Gross or chronic tardiness will quickly start counting as unexcused absences.

HOMEWORK, PREPARATION, AND RESPONSES TO READING As you can see from the SCHEDULE below, there's sometimes a lot of reading; and for the course to function, everybody's got to keep up all the time. A blunter way to say this is that you are required to do every iota of the assigned reading, on time and with care. Schedules and energies vary: please drop this course if you anticipate having difficulty keeping up when things get heavy. You will be required, moreover, to submit a one-page[2] response to each of the books we read this term. These minipapers should deal with some critical question about the book's meaning, technique, quality, etc., and should use a close reading of the text to support its points. They will usually be due on the last class-day we discuss each book, but the minipapers must not be mere rehashes of the class discussion—they need to represent your own thoughts/theses about some feature of the

---

1 That's one numeral of your overall term grade, not just of the A. & P. component. See p. 3 for the relevant percentages and my numerical grade-scale.

2 meaning one typed, single- or 1.5-spaced, 12-point-font page on 8.5 X 11 paper.

book. The minipapers also need to be clear, typo- and basic-error-free pieces of college-level writing.[3] They'll be graded. You're allowed to skip one of the nine minipapers without penalty; if you turn in all nine, I'll count only the eight highest grades. Note: No late minipapers will ever be accepted—if you have to miss class on the day one is due, you need to turn it in early.

LEADING CLASS DISCUSSIONS Once it's settled who's really enrolled, I will divide the class into two-member teams. Each team will be responsible for taking the lead in class discussion, at least twice, on a rotating basis. "Taking the lead" means giving a brief presentation and preparing topics and questions that will facilitate discussion of the day's material. Handouts and (brief) excerpts from outside sources are OK. I will be available for voluntary consultation with squads about their presentations either during office hours or at breakfast sometime early on Monday morning.

MAJOR ASSIGNMENTS[4] There's a 4-7-page midterm paper in which you'll do a close reading of some technical or thematic element in one of the books we've read so far. The final paper, due at the start of the last week of classes, will be 10-20 pages, will involve at least some outside research, and will need to make a complex, well-defined argument. You'll have to submit a proposal and annotated bibliography for the final paper several weeks ahead of time; and shortly before the paper is due, you'll submit a finished draft to a peer reviewer. By department rules for Advanced Seminars, the final paper must be in 100% MLA format, and late papers can be accepted only by prior arrangement with the instructor.

---

3 Written work with excessive typos, misspellings, or basic errors in usage/grammar will not be accepted for credit. At the very least, you'll have to redo the work and incur a penalty. If you believe this is just the usual start-of-term saber-rattling, be advised that some of the students in this course have had me as an instructor before—ask them whether I'm serious.

4 There are currently no quizzes or exams for this course; but I hereby reserve the right to begin quizzing and/or testing you in class if either (a) a sufficient number of students are not doing the assigned reading completely and carefully or (b) a sufficient number of students are not participating actively in discussions. If you remain enrolled in this course, do everyone a favor: come prepared, participate vigorously, and avert the possibility of a very nasty couple of in-class exams.

FINAL COURSE GRADES Here's a percentage-type breakdown:
- Attendance and Participation = 15%
- Eight minipapers = 15% total
- Leading class discussions = 10% total
- Midterm Paper = 20%
- Final Paper = 40%

FYI (1) I use numerals in computing grades, according to the following scale:

13 = A+ = Mind-blowingly good
12 = A = Extremely good
11 = A- = Very, very good
10 = B+ = Very good
9 = B = Good
8 = B- = High-average
7 = C+ = Average to low-average
6 = C = Mildly subpar
5 = C- = Severely subpar
4, 3, 2 = D Markedly poor; we need to talk
0 = F = Obvious.

FYI (2) As far as I can determine, my own grading standards are somewhat less inflated than the Pomona College norm. Of the 306 final grades I've given since 1987, the average (mean) is currently 7.375.

COURSE SCHEDULE (Subject to possible change as we proceed)

Day 1. Wed., 1/22: Intro, syllabus, student info sheets, etc.

Day 2. Mon, 1/27 Stead, *TMWLC*. Read Jarrell's "An Unread Book" (pp. v-xli), and Chs. One through Five (pp. 3-198). [Leading class: Instr.]

Day 3. Wed., 1/29 Stead. Read Chapters Six through Eight (pp. 199-365). [Leading class: Instr.]

Day 4. Mon., 2/3 Stead. Finish book. [Leading class: _____]

Day 5. Wed., 2/5   Stead. [Leading class: _____]

Day 6. Mon., 2/10   Barnes, *Nightwood*. Read Eliot's Intro and Weird Note to 2ⁿᵈ Ed. (pp. xi-xvii), and up to "WATCH-MAN, WHAT OF THE NIGHT?" (pp. 1-78). [Leading class: _____]

Day 7. Wed., 2/12   Barnes. Finish book. [Leading class: _____]

Mon., 2/17   NO CLASS — PRESIDENTS' DAY

Day 8. Wed., 2/19   Didion, *PIAIL*. Read first 47 chapters (pp. 3-125). [Leading class: _____]

Day 9. Mon., 2/24   Didion. Finish book. [Leading class: _____]

Day 10. Wed., 2/26   Baldwin, *GR*. Read Part One (pp. 3-72). [Leading class: _____]

Day 11. Mon, 3/3   Baldwin. Finish book. [Leading class: _____]

Wed., 3/5   NO CLASS — OPTIONAL CONFERENCES RE MIDTERM PAPER

Day 12. Mon, 3/10   Brautigan, *In WS*. Read up to "Something is Going to Happen" (pp. 1-75 in Huntley B.S. edition). [Leading class: _____]

Day 13. Wed., 3/12   Brautigan. Finish book. [Leading class: _____] Midterm papers due.

Mon., 3/17   SPRING RECESS

Wed., 3/19   DITTO

Day 14. Mon., 3/24   Percy, *Moviegoer*. Read Part One (pp. 3-63).
[Leading class: _____]

Day 15. Wed., 3/26   Percy. Read Parts Two and Three (pp. 64-166).
[Leading class: _____]

Day 16. Mon., 3/31   Percy. Finish book. [Leading class: _____]

Day 17. Wed., 4/2   Adler, *Speedboat*. Read up to "SPEEDBOAT"
(pp. 3-68 in Perennial Library edition).
[Leading class: _____]

Day 18. Mon., 4/7   Adler. Finish book. [Leading class: _____]

Wed., 4/9   NO CLASS — FINAL-PAPER PROPOSALS &
BIBLIOGRAPHIES DUE

Day 19. Mon, 4/14   Lessing, *TGN*. Read '93 and '71 Intros (p. vii-xvii),
and "FREE WOMEN: 1" (pp. 3-243).
[Leading class: _____]

Day 20. Wed., 4/16   Lessing. Read "FREE WOMEN: 2" (pp. 245-353).
[Leading class: _____]

Mon., 4/21   NO CLASS — OPTIONAL CONFERENCES RE FINAL PAPER

Day 21. Wed., 4/23   Lessing. Read "FREE WOMEN: 3" & "F.W.: 4" (pp.
355-580).
[Leading class: _____]

Day 22. Mon., 4/28   Lessing. Finish book.
[Leading class: _____]
Final-paper drafts due for peer review.

Day 23. Wed., 4/30   Fox, *DC*. Read Franzen's "No End to It"
(pp. vii-xiv), and Chs. One through Four (pp. 3-48
of Norton edition). [Leading class: _____]

Day 24. Mon., 5/5   Fox. Finish book. [Leading class: Instr.]
                     Final papers due; copy of peer-review document
                     due.

Day 25. Wed., 5/7   Final musings if any.

ENGLISH 170R
STUDENT INFO SHEET

NAME

HOMETOWN

CAMPUS PHONE

CAMPUS P.O. BOX

PLEASE NAME TWO NOVELS THAT REALLY MEAN SOMETHING TO YOU AND EXPLAIN WHY.

READ ANY OF THE BOOKS ON OUR LIST BEFORE, EVER? WHEN? WHAT DID YOU THINK?

If I remain enrolled in this course, I hereby promise to attend class faithfully, to complete all assignments in a timely and conscientious way, to participate fully in class discussions, and to contact Dave W. promptly about any problems or concerns.

SIGNATURE & DATE _____

ENGLISH 170R TEAMS

TEAM 1

TEAM 2

TEAM 3

TEAM 4

TEAM 5

TEAM 6

TEAM 7

TEAM 8

TEAM 9

TEAM 10

ENGLISH 170R   26 APRIL
SPECS AND GUIDELINES FOR PEER-REVIEW MISSIVE

Besides commenting by hand in the margins of the working draft itself, you need to type out a coherent general response—let's call it a letter. The letter and marked-up draft are due back to your partner at the start of class on 30 April. Make sure either to Xerox or print out a second copy of your letter, which you must hand in with your own final paper on 5 May. I will not grade these letters per se, but if it's obvious that you did a slight or shoddy job of reviewing your partner's draft, I will penalize your own paper.

A helpful letter on your partner's draft will probably include comments on all or most of the following issues, which I'm listing here for your convenience. You needn't address each item one after the other in the order they're listed here, though you may do so if it makes things easier.

1. Identify what appears to be the present draft's thesis or overall point. If you aren't sure just what it is, list the most likely possibilities.
2. Tell the author whether her thesis is interesting to you or not. Like, whether it adds anything substantive to your own reading(s) of the novel(s) in question. If it doesn't, you might suggest ways to make the thesis more interesting.
3. If, on the other hand, the overall thesis seems to you implausible, or unconvincing, or if you can see serious objections to it that the author hasn't addressed, tell her about them.
4. Describe, in no more than one short paragraph, the overall argument that's advanced in support of the thesis. If this seems impossible, explain why—try to identify areas you find confusing or unclear.
5. Identify two parts of the overall argument that seem comparatively strong/persuasive/effective.
6. Identify two parts of the overall argument that seem comparatively weak/unpersuasive/ineffective.
7. Does the author use any abstract terms or phrases (e.g., "despair," "gender," "happiness," "discover who she is") whose precise meanings in the paper aren't clear to you?
8. Tell the author how well the draft's parts fit together. Is she doing a good job of moving the reader coherently from one part of her argument to another? If not, try to identify some places where you got disoriented or couldn't figure out quite where in the discussion you were.
9. Tell the author whether her use of quotations from the novel(s) and/

or secondary sources seems effective. Do some of the quotations seem stuck in merely to satisfy the "Research" requirement? Are any quotations unnecessarily long? Are quotations introduced well, woven smoothly into the author's own prose, or do they just seem to hang there awkwardly? If you're already conversant with MLA format, are the quotations cited correctly?

10. Identify (in the margins of the draft if not in the letter) any basic syntactic errors you spotted that violate the Dept. Format and Style Sheet, or that have been covered in class during the semester. (Since final drafts that contain these sorts of errors will be severely penalized, you have a chance to do your partner a real service here.)

11. Keeping in mind that the author will have five days to revise this working draft, give at least two general suggestions for making the paper better.

E183A Fall '04

Guidelines for Writing Helpful Letters of Response to Colleagues' Stories

Reading other people's stories for discussion in a workshop, you will need to decide whether or not the piece succeeds as literary fiction, which elements of the present version do and do not work well, and what revisions might result in a more successful story. Then you will need to articulate these responses fully and clearly, giving specific examples wherever you can. Here are some questions you would do well to ask yourself as you read and re-read other people's work.*

1. **What has the writer set out to do? What is the story's meaning or purpose or point? Or agenda, or goal? What basic reaction do you think the writer is trying to get from the reader?**
2. **Has the writer actually done what she set out to do? Can you see gaps between what she thought she was doing and the way the story actually comes off?**
3. Does the story really begin where the writer starts it, or should it begin earlier or later?
4. Is the story too long for what it's trying to accomplish? Where might it profitably be cut?
5. Is the story too short? Does the writer only sketch or hint at things that need to be developed more fully? If so, which elements need more fleshing out?
6. Is the story's point of view appropriate, and is it consistent? Does the writer remain faithful to the vantage point she took when beginning the story: e.g., totally omniscient, or omniscient with respect to only one character, or objective?
7. Is the story's dialogue convincing? Does it sound like real human beings? Does their dialogue help to develop the story's central characters? Why or why not?
8. Are the characters 3-D, human, complex and developed? Or are

---

* In order to be genuinely helpful to the writer, your letter's answers to these questions must be concrete and specific, citing actual examples in the story wherever possible. The questions that tend to be most important in helpful criticism are numbered in bold font.

some of them only stereotypes, sketches? Which of the characters do you really feel you know?

9. Are the characters behaving consistently? Do their actions match the way the writer wants us to see them as people? Does the story give them sufficient motivation for doing what they do?

11. Is the writing natural and interesting? Does the story's narrator sound human, or is the writing puffed up and overly formal, such that the prose seems too 'written'?

12. Does the story's plot seem to move toward some climax, epiphany, or other unfolding of meaning? Or does it seem slow and static (or maybe rather random or chaotic)?

13. Is the story's overall sense of proportion appropriate? Is too much time devoted to characters or events that don't seem to contribute to the story's purpose? Is too little time devoted to characters or events that seem crucial to the real story?

14. If the story has left you with confusions or unanswered questions, what are they?

15. What are the strongest points of the story as it stands, the elements that have the strongest effect?

16. When revising, what two or three things seem most important for the writer to work on in order to make the story more successful?

Pomona College
English 183D Spring, 2008

Logistics

Wednesdays, 7:00–10:00, Crookshank 207

Inst: David Wallace

Inst. Office, Phone, and Email: Crookshank 101, 607-8357, ocapmycap@ca.rr.com

Inst. Office Hours: Wed., 6:00–7:00, Th., 3:00–4:00, and by appointment.

Description of Class

English 183D is a workshop course in *creative nonfiction*, which term denotes a broad category of prose works such as personal essays and memoirs, profiles, nature and travel writing, narrative essays, observational or descriptive essays, general-interest technical writing, argumentative or idea-based essays, general-interest criticism, literary journalism, and so on. The term's constituent words suggest a conceptual axis on which these sorts of prose works lie. As nonfiction, the works are connected to actual states of affairs in the world, are "true" to some reliable extent. If, for example, a certain event is alleged to have occurred, it must really have occurred; if a proposition is asserted, the reader expects some proof of (or argument for) its accuracy. At the same time, the adjective *creative* signifies that some goal(s) other than sheer truthfulness motivates the writer and informs her work. This creative goal, broadly stated, may be to interest readers, or to instruct them, or to entertain them, to move or persuade, to edify, to redeem, to amuse, to get readers to look more closely at or think more deeply about something that's worth their attention... or some combination(s) of these. *Creative* also suggests that this kind of nonfiction tends to bear traces of its own artificing; the essay's author usually wants us to see and understand her as the text's maker. This does not, however, mean that an essayist's main goal is simply to "share" or "express herself" or whatever feel-good term you might have got taught in high school. In the grown-up world, creative nonfiction is not *expressive* writing but rather *communicative* writing. And an axiom of communicative writing is that the reader does not automatically care about you (the writer), nor does she find you fascinating as a person, nor does she feel a deep natural interest in the same things that interest you. The reader, in fact, will feel about you, your subject, and your essay only what your written words themselves induce her to feel. An advantage of the workshop format is that it will allow you to hear what twelve reasonably intelligent adults have been induced to think and feel about each essay you write for the course.

Expenses

There are no required textbooks,* and I will provide free Xeroxes of all outside readings. You will, however, be responsible for making [12] high-quality, single-sided copies of each essay you distribute for workshop discussion. I may also ask some students to produce [12] copies of some other document or exercise.

Total Writing Workload for Class

(1) Let's say 24-39 pages of finished, high-quality nonfiction.

(2) A one-to-three-page letter of response to each one of your colleagues' essays—figure 30-35 letters total.

(3) A couple letters of response, for practice, on selected published essays.

(4) Additional individual exercises, rewrites, or other work assigned at your instructor's discretion.

Class Rules & Procedures

(1) For obvious reasons, you're required to attend every class. An absence will be excused only under extraordinary circumstances. Having more than one excused absence, and any unexcused ones at all, will result in a lowered final grade. After the first two weeks, chronic or flagrant tardiness will count as an unexcused absence.

(2) All assigned work needs to be totally completed by the time class starts.

(3) All the essays that you turn in must be written specifically for this course. You may not submit any work that was substantively begun before 15 January 2008.

(4) You need to have a special pocket-folder that's just for English 183D. This folder will function as your class portfolio, which must contain copies of all assigned work for the course (see (9) and (10) below). Please bring

---

* (A good dictionary and usage dictionary are strongly recommended. You're insane if you don't own these already.)

your portfolio to each class; and please put your name, the date, and some kind of rudimentary header on each piece of work therein.

(5) English 183D is to be a safe and serious critical venue. You should treat each peer's essay-drafts as confidential documents. No one outside this class gets to read them or know anything about them—not roommates, not mutual friends, not distant email buddies. If you discuss peers' essays with each other outside class, you must do so in a maximally private and respectful way.

(6) With a cap of twelve enrolled students, there is room in our workshop schedule for everyone to have three separate slots, and for each class meeting to comprise discussions of three different essays. This is a good number. Occasionally, though, a student will want to submit more than three pieces, or maybe two longer essays rather than three medium ones, etc. This is not impossible, but it makes for tricky scheduling—you need to confer with me individually (and soon) if you wish to submit something other than the normal three pieces.

(7) Once you sign up for a certain slot in the workshop rotation, that slot is *yours*. You can change or trade only with the whole class's permission. So please choose with care. We will fill out the first portion of the workshop schedule tonight and the remainder on 2 February.

(8) All workshop essays are to be distributed the week before the class in which they're to be discussed. There are two options here. Let's say you sign up to have an essay workshopped on Wed., 12 March. Either you can bring [12] copies to class for distribution on Wed., 5 March, or you can place the copies in the special E183D box outside my office door by 4:00 p.m. on Thurs., 6 March. But 4:00 p.m. on the Thursday before your assigned slot is the deadline. Don't be late. There are no "extensions" in workshop-type classes; your deadlines are obligations to [12] other adults. Finish editing and revising far enough ahead of time that you can accommodate computer or printer snafus.

(9) This class operates on the belief that you'll improve as a writer not just by writing a lot and receiving detailed criticism but also by becoming a more sophisticated and articulate critic of other writers' work. You are thus required to read each of your colleagues' essays at least twice, making helpful and specific comments on the manuscript copy wherever appropriate.* You will then compose a one-to-three-page letter to the

---

* For writers: One reason to double-space your essays and to give them generous margins is to give us space to write marginalia. For readers: Make sure that your margin comments are legible and lucid, and that they're directed to the author; the manuscript copy is not the place to jot notes to yourself. Example: "It's not clear how this sentence

essay's author, communicating your sense of the draft's strengths and weaknesses and making clear, specific suggestions for revision. At the top of each letter, please put your name, the author's name, the essay's title, and the date. Make a hard copy of each and every letter of response you write. Staple the original letter to your marked-up copy of the essay, so that at discussion's end they can all be returned to the author for private perusal. Place the copy of your letter in your class portfolio.

(10) Besides letter-copies and maybe a couple exercises, the only other things you're required to save in your portfolio are the instructor's copy of each essay you submit to class (i.e., the manuscript copy that I read and marked on, with my letter of response attached). I'll be collecting portfolios at the end of the term, but I also reserve the right to look through anyone's portfolio at any time—that's why you need to bring your portfolio to each class meeting.

(11) All written work for E183D must be high-quality printed in regular font and reasonable point-size. Everything must be double-spaced, with one-inch margins all around, and stapled. Your workshop essays must have a title page on which appear the piece's title, your name, and the date. Your last name and the page number should appear in the upper-right corner of p. 2 and of every page thereafter.* All copies must be complete, unsmudged, unfaint, and easily readable.

(12) For a variety of reasons, I probably will not put specific grades on your work when I hand it back to you. Anyone who has a problem with this should come speak to me personally; I may make an exception for someone with a professionally diagnosed anxiety disorder or something. And I will provide, at any point during the term, an estimate of her overall grade so far to any student who comes and asks me for it. (And anyone who appears to be heading for a final grade of 7 or below needn't worry about asking—I'll make it a point to let you know.

(13) Part of the grades you receive on written work in this course will depend on each document's presentation. *Presentation* here means evidence of care, of facility in written English, and of empathy for your readers. The essays you submit for group discussion need to be carefully proofread and

---

supports the conclusion you draw in the next paragraph" would be OK to write in the margin, whereas "Sentence sucks—make sure to ridicule author for this in class" would not.

* (FYI, *p. 2* means the second page of the actual essay; the title page doesn't count. And it's classier to omit the number on the first page of a document's text...so the first page you number should be the second page of the actual essay.)

edited for typos, misspellings, garbled constructions, and basic errors in usage and/or punctuation. "Creative" or not, E183D is an upper-division writing class, and work that appears sloppy or semiliterate will not be accepted for credit: you'll have to redo the piece and turn it back in, and there will be a grade penalty—a really severe one if it happens more than once.

Rough Components of Final Grade
  Essays = 60%
  Letters of Response = 20%
  Attendance, Quality & Quantity of Participation, Effort, Improvement, Alacrity of Carriage, Etc. = 20%.
  (N.B. The instructor's grade scale is numerical and goes like this: 13 = A+ = Mind-blowingly good; 12 = A = Extremely good; 11 = A- = Very, very good; 10 = B+ = Very good; 9 = B = Pretty good; 8 = B- = OK; 7 = C+ = Mildly subpar; 6 = C = Seriously subpar; 4, 3, 2 = D = Downright bad; 0 = F = Obvious.)

SEMESTER & WORKSHOP SCHEDULE

For Wed., 30 January: Read the following published essays: (1) Jo Ann Beard's "Werner," (2) Stephen Elliott's "Where I Slept," (3) George Orwell's "Politics and the English Language," (4) Donna Steiner's "Cold." Pick one of these essays, pretend that it's been written and distributed by an E183D colleague, and write a practice letter of response to it, being as specific and helpful as possible in detailing your impressions and reactions and suggestions for how the essay might be improved.

For Wed., 6 February: Read the following published essays: (1) David Gessner's "Learning to Surf," (2) Kathryn Harrison's "The Forest of Memory," (3) Hester Kaplan's "The Private Life of Skin," (4) George Saunders's "The Braindead Megaphone." Pick one of these essays, pretend that it's been written and distributed by an E183D colleague, and write a practice letter of response to it, being as specific and helpful as possible in detailing your impressions and reactions and suggestions for how the essay might be improved.

For Wed., 13 Feb. : Discussion of essays by:

——————————— , ——————————— , ———————————

For Wed., 20 Feb. : Discussion of essays by:

——————————— , ——————————— , ———————————

For Wed., 27 Feb. : Discussion of essays by:

——————————— , ——————————— , ———————————

For Wed., 5 March : Discussion of essays by:

——————————— , ——————————— , ———————————

For Wed., 12 March:

——————————— , ——————————— , ———————————

(**Essays for 26 March are to be distributed on 12 or 13 March**)

For Wed., 19 March: SPRING BREAK

For Wed., 26 March : Discussion of essays by:

——————————— , ——————————— , ———————————

For Wed., 2 April : Discussion of essays by:

——————————— , ——————————— , ———————————

For Wed., 9 April: Discussion of essays by:

——————————— , ——————————— , ———————————

For Wed., 16 April: Discussion of essays by:

——————————— , ——————————— , ———————————

For Wed., 23 April: Discussion of essays by:

—————————————, —————————————, —————————————

For Wed., 30 April: Discussion of essays by:

—————————————, —————————————, —————————————

For Wed., 7 May: Discussion of essays by:

—————————————, —————————————, —————————————

(** Portfolios Collected; Any/All Revisions Due**)

English 183D   Student Data Sheet

Name:

Class & Major:

Best Phone Number:

Best Email:

OK to include your phone/email info in a Class Roster for everyone to have? Yes / No

Approximate # of finished pages of creative nonfiction you've written so far, lifetime:

Name a couple pieces of literary nonfiction you've read that actually mean something to you. Explain why they're important to you, if you can.

Taken any kind of creative writing course before, ever? If so, when & where? What was the best thing about the class? What were some not-so-good things about it?

How do you expect the writing you'll be doing for this course to differ from the nonfiction writing you do in regular humanities classes?

How concerned are you about grades in this course? What do you expect your final grade to be based on? If you were the instructor for the class, what criteria would you use for determining students' grades?

ENGLISH 183A, 16 OCTOBER 2002—YOUR LIBERAL-ARTS $ AT WORK

(It would be really nice if people actually read these handouts and applied the prescriptions to their stories.)

1. *Can not* is not a synonym for *cannot*. "I cannot go to the store" means I can't go to the store. "I can not go to the store" means I have the power to refrain from going to the store. 99.999% of the time, what you mean to say is *cannot*.

2. "Joe is five years old" needs no hyphens. But when you turn the predicate into a compound adjective or compound noun, you do need hyphens: "Joe is a five-year-old chess prodigy"; "Joe, a five-year-old, mated the Grand Master in sixteen moves."

3. In dialogue, the "he said/she said" stuff is called attribution. Other attributions are various synonyms for or embellishments on *said*. As a general rule, you end a sentence of dialogue with a comma only when what follows is an attribution:
   "I hate you," she said.
   "I hate you, too," he replied, grinning fiendishly.
   If what follows a sentence(s) of dialogue is not an attribution, you normally end it with a period:
   "I hate you." She brandished the skillet menacingly.
   "Not nearly as much as I hate you." He prepared to duck.
   N.B. *Smiled, grinned, scowled,* etc. are not attributions, so:
   "I also hate your cat, your cooking, and that mud mask you wear to bed." He smiled bitterly.

4. Family names like *mother, father, mom, dad, uncle,* etc. need to be capitalized when they're proper nouns—"Why are you hitting me, Father?" "I'm scared of Aunt Regina, Mom"—but are lower-cased when they're common nouns: "My dad is abusive"; "Our aunt held seances whenever we visited, and I finally told my mom about it."

5. In literate usage, the correct relative pronoun to use for people is *who/whom*. "He is the man who loves me"; "The man whom I love is a podiatrist." Using *that* for people is, as of 2002, a perceived sign of ignorance or poor education (e.g., *PTL* in "The PTL Club" stands for "People That Love," which William Safire spent several *Times* columns sneering at). The point: In fiction, do not use the relative

pronoun *that* for people unless you specifically want literate readers to see the speaker/narrator as ignorant/uneducated/low-caste.

6. Please be alert to the difference between a hyphen and a dash, and do not use a hyphen when you need a dash. Most Word® programs have a nice dash that you can insert via the Insert/Symbols function (sometimes it's referred to as an *em-dash*, which is a long story that I'll spare you unless you ask). Or you can use two hyphens to signify a dash, as in "Wait -- didn't the podiatrist say not to use heat on that corn?" What's tricky is that a double-hyphen dash takes a space before and after (see *supra*), whereas a more professional-looking inserted em-dash does not take extra space:

"Wait—didn't the podiatrist say not to...?"

ENGLISH 183A, 30 OCTOBER 2002—YOUR LIBERAL-ARTS $ AT WORK

1. Though the words are logically converse, the distinction between *comprise* and *compose* is tricky, and 85% of writers misuse *comprise*, usually in sentences like "The USA is comprised of 50 states." Here's the easiest way to remember the relevant rule: when you have a large thing that's made up of several small things, the large thing *comprises* the small things, and the small things *compose* the large thing. Literate rewrites of the above sentence include "The USA comprises 50 states" and "The USA is composed of 50 states."

    (Perhaps an even easier mnemonic is this: the phrase *comprised of* is never right; whenever you need an *of*, you know the verb you want is *composed*.)

2. People are persistently confusing the comparative adverbs *like* and *as*. Here's the rule: when you're doing a simple comparison involving two constructions, you use *like* when what follows is just a noun; you use *as* when what follows is a clause (meaning noun + verb). So "Bob went crazy just like his father did" is wrong—"his father did" has both a noun and a verb—and should be revised to "Bob went crazy just as his father did." "Bob went crazy just like his father," though, is right. See the difference? (FYI, in the '70s there was a whole huge ad campaign for Winston cigarettes based around this distinction. The initial slogan was "Winston tastes good like a cigarette should," which some pedantic figure would correct by x-ing out the *like* and substituting *as* [and the *as* is, of course, correct, since "a cigarette should" contains both a noun and a verb], at which point the original speaker/writer would respond, "WHAT DO YOU WANT, GOOD GRAMMAR OR GOOD TASTE?" which was the mnemonic slogan that the advertisers wanted you to associate with Winstons.)

3. *Farther* and *further* are not interchangeable. *Farther* refers to additional distance—"How much farther is it to the rest stop?" "He hurled the dwarf much farther than Seamus had"—while *further* refers to additional extent or time—"I refuse to discuss this any further"; "There were further infractions, which the D.A. proceeded to list." The most common error is using *further* in reference to distance: "Canada is further away than Mexico" is wrong; "She was getting further into the deep woods" is wrong. Learn it; know it; live it.

ENGLISH 183A, 13 NOVEMBER 2002—YOUR LIBERAL-ARTS $ AT WORK

1. There is no such English construction as *a myriad of*. *Myriad* is just a plain old adjective. "There were myriad problems with the proposal" is fine; "There were a myriad of problems with the proposal" is wrong. It may be mnemonically helpful to keep in mind that *myriad* functions just like *numerous*. Sentences like "There were a numerous of problems with the proposal" are obviously f***ed up, but in fact the previous sentence is no wronger than "There were a myriad of problems...."

2. *Loan* is a noun; the associated verb is *to lend*. Constructions like "He loaned me his car" are OK only in extremely casual writing or from an uneducated narrator/character. Learn it; know it; live it.

3. It would be in your interests to learn and memorize the difference between the verbs *to compliment* and *to complement*, and between their respective nominalizations *compliment* and *complement*. The SpellChecker will not help you with this.

4. It is not necessarily wrong to start an SWE sentence with *And, But,* or *So;* but as a general rule, you should not follow them with a comma. A sentence like, for instance, "Or, maybe you've been in love with Veronica all along!" would be a lot better without the comma.

5. Let us continue to be on the watch for dangling participles. "Tapping first one key, then another and another, the sound of his typing became almost unnoticeable" is, of course, a dangling participle: the literal meaning here is that the sound was tapping first one key then another.... But not all participles end in *-ing*. Can you see that "Dressed in tight jeans and a T-shirt, his walk hinted at soft muscles hidden beneath his clothes" is also a dangling participle? If not, ask me: it's well worth your taking the trouble to learn.

6. *To peruse* actually means to read closely and with great care. It is therefore a total boner to employ it as a synonym for *to skim*.

7. The adjective *nauseous* actually means productive of nausea. If you say "I'm nauseous," you're really saying that you are sickening to others. The adjective that means nauseated is *nauseated*. Learn it; know it....

E 183A 6 October 2004

VALUE FOR YOUR LIBERAL-ARTS $

1a) We ate apples, hot dogs, cotton candy, and got home from the fair quite late.

1b) We have cool-sounding names, personalized capes, a whole myriad of weapons, and we take out the trash.

2) On the bus, I sat to myself as usual.

3a) A clean, white sign marks the end of the quarantine zone.

3b) We sat on an old, wooden bench in the garden.

4) Thick, gray, poison slowly fills the air.

5) There were hushed tones and muffled words—I couldn't understand what Lois' friends were saying.

6) I was unable to even remain in the same room with her.

7a) He plays the sax just like Charlie Parker does.

7b) As a doctor, the results of your EKG are of great concern to me.

7c) The clouds outside the window were dull and ashen. Lying low like they were, I knew that it was only a matter of time before the rain started.

8) We drive fast, so the poison cannot seep through our skin.

9) The gray clouds continued to drop rain off and on for the next few days.

10) In the mean time, I decided to retrieve the poster.

11) It was a difficult problem, and I had to mull for a long time.

E 183A   12-1-04

$ AT WORK

(a) She's the mother of a two-year-old who works sixteen hours a day.

(b) I was riding the pony I had had when I was a child along a river bank.

(c) She looks down and notices the dark Chinese dirt caking her boots that somehow made it through Customs unnoticed.

(d) I dozed afterwards as usual, but, unlike most days, I had a dream.

(e) "The first thing that needs to be done is we've got to unequivocally deny these accusations—Dick is not going to have this free air time unchallenged."

(f) He was a burden on not only himself but on those around him.

(g) She holds up a finger and he waits patiently until she finishes her gulp.

(h) They embrace, and she lies her head on his shoulder.

(i) "Alright, well have a good day. . ." he said.

(j) I soon approached a bridge, with steps down to the river bed.

(k) My wife heard my heavy steps, bounding precariously against the rocks and shrubbery of my subconscious.

(l) I would have hiked the six miles to the scene I sought right then, but I knew that I had to have everything, including the time of day, be the same if I were to find a resolution to the thump, thump, thump of her awful pulse.

(m) She sees a note left for her on the table next to the water glass with his new cell number and a suggestion that they get together for lunch.

NONFICTION

Derivative Sport in
Tornado Alley

When I left my boxed township of Illinois farmland to attend my dad's alma mater in the lurid jutting Berkshires of western Massachusetts, I all of a sudden developed a jones for mathematics. I'm starting to see why this was so. College math evokes and catharts a Midwesterner's sickness for home. I'd grown up inside vectors, lines and lines athwart lines, grids—and, on the scale of horizons, broad curving lines of geographic force, the weird topographical drain-swirl of a whole lot of ice-ironed land that sits and spins atop plates. The area behind and below these broad curves at the seam of land and sky I could plot by eye way before I came to know infinitesimals as easements, an integral as schema. Math at a hilly Eastern school was like waking up; it dismantled memory and put it in light. Calculus was, quite literally, child's play.

In late childhood I learned how to play tennis on the blacktop courts of a small public park carved from farmland that had been nitrogenized too often to farm anymore. This was in my home of Philo, Illinois, a tiny collection of corn silos and war-era Levittown homes whose native residents did little but sell crop insurance and nitrogen fertilizer and herbicide and collect property taxes from the young academics at nearby Champaign-Urbana's university, whose ranks swelled enough in the flush 1960s to make outlying non sequiturs like "farm and bedroom community" lucid.

Between the ages of twelve and fifteen I was a near-great junior tennis player. I made my competitive bones beating up on lawyers' and dentists' kids at little Champaign and Urbana Country Club events and was soon killing whole summers being driven through dawns to tournaments all over Illinois, Indiana, Iowa. At fourteen I was ranked seventeenth in the United States Tennis Association's Western Section ("Western" being the creakily ancient USTA's designation for the Midwest; farther west were the Southwest, Northwest, and Pacific Northwest sections). My flirtation with tennis excellence had way more to do with the township where I learned and trained and with a weird proclivity for intuitive math than it did with athletic talent. I was, even by the standards of junior competition in which everyone's a bud of pure potential, a pretty untalented tennis player. My hand-eye was OK, but I was neither large nor quick, had a near-concave chest and wrists so thin I could bracelet them with a thumb and pinkie, and could hit a tennis ball no harder or truer than most girls in my age bracket. What I could do was "Play the Whole Court." This was a piece of tennis truistics that could mean any number of things. In my case, it meant I knew my limitations and the limitations of what I stood inside, and adjusted thusly. I was at my very best in bad conditions.

Now, conditions in Central Illinois are from a mathematical perspective interesting and from a tennis perspective bad. The summer heat and wet-mitten humidity, the grotesquely fertile soil that sends grasses and broadleaves up through the courts' surface by main force, the midges that feed on sweat and the mosquitoes that spawn in the fields' furrows and in the conferva-choked ditches that box each field, night tennis next to impossible because the moths and crap-gnats drawn by the sodium lights form a little planet around each tall lamp and the whole lit court surface is aflutter with spastic little shadows.

But mostly wind. The biggest single factor in Central Illinois' quality of outdoor life is wind. There are more local jokes than I can summon about bent weather vanes and leaning barns, more downstate sobriquets for kinds of wind than there are in Malamut for snow. The wind had a personality, a (poor) temper, and, apparently, agendas. The wind blew autumn leaves into intercalated lines and arcs of force so regular you could photograph them for a textbook on Cramer's Rule and the cross-products of curves in 3-space. It molded winter snow into blinding truncheons that buried stalled cars and required citizens to shovel out not only driveways but the sides of homes; a Central Illinois "blizzard" starts only when the snowfall stops and the wind begins. Most people in Philo didn't comb their hair because why bother. Ladies wore those plastic flags tied down over their parlor-jobs so regularly I thought they were required for a real classy coiffure; girls on the East Coast outside with their hair hanging and tossing around looked wanton and nude to me. Wind wind etc. etc.

The people I know from outside it distill the Midwest into blank flatness, black land and fields of green fronds or five-o'clock stubble, gentle swells and declivities that make the topology a sadistic exercise in plotting quadrics, highway vistas so same and dead they drive motorists mad. Those from IN/WI/Northern IL think of their own Midwest as agronomics and commodity futures and corn-detasseling and bean-walking and seed-company caps, apple-cheeked Nordic types, cider and slaughter and football games with white fogbanks of breath exiting helmets. But in the odd central pocket that is Champaign-Urbana, Rantoul, Philo, Mahomet-Seymour, Mattoon, Farmer City, and Tolono, Midwestern life is informed and deformed by wind. Weatherwise, our township is on the eastern upcurrent of what I once heard an atmospherist in brown tweed call a Thermal Anomaly. Something about southward rotations of crisp air off the Great Lakes and muggy southern stuff from Arkansas and Kentucky miscegenating, plus an odd dose of weird zephyrs from the Mississippi valley three hours west. Chicago calls itself the Windy City, but Chicago, one big windbreak, does not know from a true religious-type wind. And meteorologists have nothing to tell people in Philo, who know perfectly well that the real story is that to the west, between us and the Rockies, there is basically nothing tall, and that weird zephyrs and stirs joined breezes and gusts and thermals and downdrafts and whatever out over Nebraska and Kansas and moved east like streams into rivers and jets and military fronts that gathered like avalanches and roared in reverse down pioneer oxtrails, toward our own personal unsheltered asses. The worst was spring, boys' high school tennis season, when the nets would stand out stiff as proud flags and an errant ball would blow clear to the easternmost fence, interrupting play on the next several courts. During a bad blow some of us would get rope out and tell Rob Lord, who was our fifth man in singles and spectrally thin, that we were going to have to tie him down to keep him from becoming a projectile. Autumn, usually about half as bad as spring, was a low constant roar and the massive clicking sound of continents of dry leaves being arranged into force-curves—I'd heard no sound remotely like this mega-clicking until I heard, at nineteen, on New Brunswick's Bay of Fundy, my first high-tide wave break and get sucked back out over a shore of polished pebbles. Summers were manic and gusty, then often around August deadly calm. The wind would just die some August days, and it was no relief at all; the cessation drove us nuts. Each August, we realized afresh how much the sound of wind had become part of the soundtrack to life in Philo. The sound of wind had become, for me, silence. When it went away, I was left with the squeak of the blood in my head and the aural glitter of all those little eardrum hairs quivering like a drunk in withdrawal. It was months after I moved to western MA before I could really sleep in the pussified whisper of New England's wind-sound.

To your average outsider, Central Illinois looks ideal for sports. The ground, seen from the air, strongly suggests a board game: anally precise squares of dun or khaki cropland all cut and divided by plumb-straight tar roads (in all farmland, roads still seem more like impediments than avenues). In winter, the terrain always looks like Mannington bathroom tile, white quadrangles where bare (snow), black where trees and scrub have shaken free in the wind. From planes, it always looks to me like Monopoly or Life, or a lab maze for rats; then, from ground level, the arrayed fields of feed corn or soybeans, fields furrowed into lines as straight as only an Allis-Chalmers and sextant can cut them, look laned like sprint tracks or Olympic pools, hashmarked for serious ball, replete with the angles and alleys of serious tennis. My part of the Midwest always looks laid down special, as if planned.

The terrain's strengths are also its weaknesses. Because the land seems so even, designers of clubs and parks rarely bother to roll it flat before laying the asphalt for tennis courts. The result is usually a slight list that only a player who spends a lot of time on the courts will notice. Because tennis courts are for sun- and eye-reasons always laid lengthwise north-south, and because the land in Central Illinois rises very gently as one moves east toward Indiana and the subtle geologic summit that sends rivers doubled back against their own feeders somewhere in the east of that state, the court's forehand half, for a rightie facing north, always seems physically uphill from the backhand—at a tournament in Richmond IN, just over the Ohio line, I noticed the tilt was reversed. The same soil that's so full of humus farmers have to be bought off to keep markets unflooded keeps clay courts chocked with jimson and thistle and volunteer corn, and it splits asphalt courts open with the upward pressure of broadleaf weeds whose pioneer-stock seeds are unthwarted by a half-inch cover of sealant and stone. So that all but the very best maintained courts in the most affluent Illinois districts are their own little rural landscapes, with tufts and cracks and underground-seepage puddles being part of the lay that one plays. A court's cracks always seem to start off to the side of the service box and meander in and back toward the service line. Foliated in pockets, the black cracks, especially against the forest green that contrasts with the barn red of the space outside the lines to signify fair territory, give the courts the eerie look of well-rivered sections of Illinois, seen from back aloft.

A tennis court, 78' × 27', looks, from above, with its slender rectangles of doubles alleys flanking its whole length, like a cardboard carton with flaps folded back. The net, 3.5 feet high at the posts, divides the court widthwise in half; the service lines divide each half again into backcourt and fore-. In the two forecourts, lines that run from the base of the net's center to the service lines divide them into 21' × 13.5' service boxes. The sharply precise divisions and boundaries, together with the fact that—wind and your more exotic-type spins aside—balls can be made to travel in straight lines only, make textbook tennis plane geometry. It is billiards with balls that won't hold still. It is chess on the run. It is to artillery and airstrikes what football is to infantry and attrition.

Tennis-wise, I had two preternatural gifts to compensate for not much physical talent. Make that three. The first was that I always sweated so much that I stayed fairly ventilated in all weathers. Oversweating seems an ambivalent blessing, and it didn't exactly do wonders for my social life in high school, but it meant I could play for hours on a Turkish-bath July day and not flag a bit so long as I drank water and ate salty stuff between matches. I always looked like a drowned man by about game four, but I didn't cramp, vomit, or pass out, unlike the gleaming Peoria kids whose hair never even lost its part right up until their eyes rolled up in their heads and they pitched forward onto the shimmering concrete. A bigger asset still was that I was extremely comfortable inside straight lines. None of the odd geometric claustrophobia that turns some gifted juniors into skittish zoo animals after a while. I found I felt best physically enwebbed in sharp angles, acute bisections, shaved corners. This was environmental. Philo, Illinois, is a cockeyed grid: nine north-south streets against six northeast-southwest, fifty-one gorgeous slanted-cruciform corners (the east and west intersection-angles' tangents could be evaluated integrally in terms of their secants!) around a three-intersection central town common with a tank whose nozzle pointed northwest at Urbana, plus a frozen native son, felled on the Salerno beachhead, whose bronze hand pointed true north. In the late morning, the Salerno guy's statue had a squat black shadow-arm against grass dense enough to putt on; in the evening the sun galvanized his left profile and cast his arm's accusing shadow out to the right, bent at the angle of a stick in a pond. At college it suddenly occurred to me during a quiz that the differential between the direction the statue's hand pointed and the arc of its shadow's rotation was first-order. Anyway, most of my memories of childhood—whether of furrowed acreage, or of a harvester's sentry duty along RR104W, or of the play of sharp shadows against the Legion Hall softball field's dusk—I could now reconstruct on demand with an edge and protractor.

I liked the sharp intercourse of straight lines more than the other kids I grew up with. I think this is because they were natives, whereas I was an infantile transplant from Ithaca, where my dad had Ph.D.'d. So I'd known, even horizontally and semiconsciously as a baby, something different, the tall hills and serpentine one-ways of upstate NY. I'm pretty sure I kept the amorphous mush of curves and swells as a contrasting backlight somewhere down in the lizardy part of my brain, because the Philo children I fought and played with, kids who knew and had known nothing else, saw nothing stark or new-worldish in the township's planar layout, prized nothing crisp. (Except why do I think it significant that so many of them wound up in the military, performing smart right-faces in razor-creased dress blues?)

Unless you're one of those rare mutant virtuosos of raw force, you'll find that competitive tennis, like money pool, requires geometric thinking, the ability to calculate not merely your own angles but the angles of response to your angles. Because the expansion of response-possibilities is quadratic, you are required to think n shots ahead, where n is a hyperbolic function limited by the sinh of opponent's talent and the cosh of the number of shots in the rally so far (roughly). I was good at this. What made me for a while near-great was that I could also admit the differential complication of wind into my calculations; I could think and play octally. For the wind put curves in the lines and transformed the game into 3-space. Wind did massive damage to many Central Illinois junior players, particularly in the period from April to July when it needed lithium badly, tending to gust without pattern, swirl and backtrack and die and rise, sometimes blowing in one direction at court level and in another altogether ten feet overhead. The precision in thinking required one to induct trends in percentage, thrust, and retaliatory angle—precision our guy and the other townships' volunteer coaches were good at abstracting about with chalk and board, attaching a pupil's leg to the fence with clothesline to restrict his arc of movement in practice, placing laundry baskets in different corners and making us sink ball after ball, taking masking tape and laying down Chinese boxes within the court's own boxes for drills and wind sprints—all this theoretical prep went out the window when sneakers hit actual court in a tournament. The best-planned, best-hit ball often just blew out of bounds, was the basic unlyrical problem. It drove some kids near-mad with the caprice and unfairness of it all, and on real windy days these kids, usually with talent out the bazoo, would have their first apoplectic racket-throwing tantrum in about the match's third game and lapse into a kind of sullen coma by the end of the first set, now bitterly *expecting* to get screwed over by wind, net, tape, sun. I, who was affectionately known as Slug because I was such a lazy turd in practice, located my biggest tennis asset in a weird robotic detachment from whatever unfairnesses of wind and weather I couldn't plan for. I couldn't begin to tell you how many tournament matches I won between the ages of twelve and fifteen against bigger, faster, more coordinated, and better-coached opponents simply by hitting balls unimaginatively back down the middle of the court in schizophrenic gales, letting the other kid play with more verve and panache, waiting for enough of his ambitious balls aimed near the lines to curve or slide via wind outside the green court and white stripe into the raw red territory that won me yet another ugly point. It wasn't pretty or fun to watch, and even with the Illinois wind I never could have won whole matches this way had the opponent not eventually had his small nervous breakdown, buckling under the obvious injustice of losing to a shallow-chested "pusher" because of the shitty rural courts and rotten wind that rewarded cautious automatism instead of verve and panache. I was an unpopular player, with good reason. But to say that I did not use verve or imagination was untrue. Acceptance is its own verve, and it takes imagination for a player to like wind, and I liked wind; or rather I at least felt the wind had some basic right to be there, and found it sort of interesting, and was willing to expand my logistical territory to countenace the devastating effect a 15- to 30-mph stutter-breeze swirling southwest to east would have on my best calculations as to how ambitiously to respond to Joe Perfecthair's topspin drive into my backhand corner.

The Illinois combination of pocked courts, sickening damp, and wind required and rewarded an almost Zen-like acceptance of things as they actually were, on-court. I won a lot. At twelve, I began getting entry to tournaments beyond Philo and Champaign and Danville. I was driven by my parents or by the folks of Gil Antitoi, son of a Canadian-history professor from Urbana, to events like the Central Illinois Open in Decatur, a town built and owned by the A. E. Staley processing concern and so awash in the stink of roasting corn that kids would play with bandannas tied over their mouths and noses; like the Western Closed Qualifier on the ISU campus in Normal; like the McDonald's Junior Open in the serious corn town of Galesburg, way out west by the River; like the Prairie State Open in Pekin, insurance hub and home of Caterpillar Tractor; like the Midwest Junior Clay Courts at a chichi private club in Peoria's pale version of Scarsdale.

Over the next four summers I got to see way more of the state than is normal or healthy, albeit most of this seeing was a blur of travel and crops, looking between nod-outs at sunrises abrupt and terribly candent over the crease between fields and sky (plus you could see any town you were aimed at the very moment it came around the earth's curve, and the only part of Proust that really moved me in college was the early description of the kid's geometric relation to the distant church spire at Combray), riding in station wagons' backseats through Saturday dawns and Sunday sunsets. I got steadily better; Antitoi, unfairly assisted by an early puberty, got radically better.

By the time we were fourteen, Gil Antitoi and I were the Central Illinois cream of our age bracket, usually seeded one and two at area tournaments, able to beat all but a couple of even the kids from the Chicago suburbs who, together with a contingent from Grosse Pointe MI, usually dominated the Western regional rankings. That summer the best fourteen-year-old in the nation was a Chicago kid, Bruce Brescia (whose penchant for floppy white tennis hats, low socks with bunnytails at the heel, and lurid pastel sweater vests testified to proclivities that wouldn't dawn on me for several more years), but Brescia and his henchman, Mark Mees of Zanesville OH, never bothered to play anything but the Midwestern Clays and some indoor events in Cook County, being too busy jetting off to like the Pacific Hard-courts in Ventura and Junior Wimbledon and all that. I played Brescia just once, in the quarters of an indoor thing at the Rosemont Horizon in 1977, and the results were not pretty. Antitoi actually got a set off Mees in the national Qualifiers one year. Neither Brescia nor Mees ever turned pro; I don't know what happened to either of them after eighteen.

Antitoi and I ranged over the exact same competitive territory; he was my friend and foe and bane. Though I'd started playing two years before he, he was bigger, quicker, and basically better than I by about age thir-teen, and I was soon losing to him in the finals of just about every tourna-ment I played. So different were our appearances and approaches and general gestalts that we had something of an epic rivalry from '74 through '77. I had gotten so prescient at using stats, surface, sun, gusts, and a kind of stoic cheer that I was regarded as a physical savant, a medicine boy of wind and heat, and could play just forever, sending back moonballs baroque with spin. Antitoi, uncomplicated from the get-go, hit the ever-living shit out of every round object that came within his ambit, aiming always for one of two backcourt corners. He was a Slugger; I was a Slug. When he was "on," i.e. having a good day, he varnished the court with me. When he wasn't at his best (and the countless hours I and David Saboe from Bloomington and Kirk Riehagen and Steve Cassil of Danville spent in meditation and seminar on just what variables of diet, sleep, romance, car ride, and even sock-color factored into the equation of Antitoi's mood and level day to day), he and I had great matches, real marathon wind-suckers. Of eleven finals we played in 1974, I won two.

Midwest junior tennis was also my initiation into true adult sadness. I had developed a sort of hubris about my Taoistic ability to control via non-control. I'd established a private religion of wind. I even liked to bike. Awfully few people in Philo bike, for obvious wind reasons, but I'd found a way to sort of tack back and forth against a stiff current, holding some wide book out at my side at about 120° to my angle of thrust—Bayne and Pugh's *The Art of the Engineer* and Cheiro's *Language of the Hand* proved to be the best airfoils—so that through imagination and verve and stoic cheer I could not just neutralize but use an in-your-face gale for biking. Similarly, by thirteen I'd found a way not just to accommodate but to *employ* the heavy summer winds in matches. No longer just mooning the ball down the center to allow plenty of margin for error and swerve, I was now able to use the currents kind of the way a pitcher uses spit. I could hit curves way out into cross-breezes that'd drop the ball just fair; I had a special wind-serve that had so much spin the ball turned oval in the air and curved left to right like a smart slider and then reversed its arc on the bounce. I'd developed the same sort of autonomic feel for what the wind would do to the ball that a standard-trans driver has for how to shift. As a junior tennis player, I was for a time a citizen of the concrete physical world in a way the other boys weren't, I felt. And I felt betrayed at around fourteen when so many of these single-minded flailing boys became abruptly mannish and tall, with sudden sprays of hair on their thighs and wisps on their lips and ropy arteries on their forearms. My fifteenth summer, kids I'd been beating easily the year before all of a sudden seemed overpowering. I lost in two semifinals, at Pekin and Springfield in '77, of events I'd beaten Antitoi in the finals of in '76. My dad just about brought me to my knees after the Springfield loss to some kid from the Quad Cities when he said, trying to console me, that it had looked like a boy playing a man out there. And the other boys sensed something up with me, too, smelled some breakdown in the odd détente I'd had with the elements: my ability to accommodate and fashion the exterior was being undercut by the malfunction of some internal alarm clock I didn't understand.

I mention this mostly because so much of my Midwest's communal psychic energy was informed by growth and fertility. The agronomic angle was obvious, what with my whole township dependent for tax base on seed, dispersion, height, and yield. Something about the adults' obsessive weighing and measuring and projecting, this special calculus of thrust and growth, leaked inside us children's capped and bandanna'd little heads out on the fields, diamonds, and courts of our special interests. By 1977 I was the only one of my group of jock friends with virginity intact. (I know this for a fact, and only because these guys are now schoolteachers and commoditists and insurers with families and standings to protect will I not share with you just how I know it.) I felt, as I became a later and later bloomer, alienated not just from my own recalcitrant glabrous little body, but in a way from the whole elemental exterior I'd come to see as my coconspirator. I knew, somehow, that the call to height and hair came from outside, from whatever apart from Monsanto and Dow made the corn grow, the hogs rut, the wind soften every spring and hang with the scent of manure from the plain of beanfields north between us and Champaign. My vocation ebbed. I felt uncalled. I began to experience the same resentment toward whatever children abstract as nature that I knew Steve Cassil felt when a soundly considered approach shot down the forehand line was blown out by a gust, that I knew Gil Antitoi suffered when his pretty kick-serve (he was the only top-flight kid from the slow weedy township courts to play serve-and-volley from the start, which is why he had such success on the slick cement of the West Coast when he went on to play for Cal-Fullerton) was compromised by the sun: he was so tall, and so stubborn about adjusting his high textbook service toss for solar conditions, that serving from the court's north end in early afternoon matches always filled his eyes with violet blobs, and he'd lumber around for the rest of the point, flailing and pissed. This was back when sunglasses were unheard of, on-court.

But so the point is I began to feel what they'd felt. I began, very quietly, to resent my physical place in the great schema, and this resentment and bitterness, a kind of slow root-rot, is a big reason why I never qualified for the sectional championships again after 1977, and why I ended up in 1980 barely making the team at a college smaller than Urbana High while kids I had beaten and then envied played scholarship tennis for Purdue, Fullerton, Michigan, Pepperdine, and even—in the case of Pete Bouton, who grew half a foot and forty IQ points in 1977—for the hallowed U of I at Urbana-Champaign.

Alienation-from-Midwest-as-fertility-grid might be a little on the overmetaphysical side, not to mention self-pitying. This was the time, after all, when I discovered definite integrals and antiderivatives and found my identity shifting from jock to math-wienie anyway. But it's also true that my whole Midwest tennis career matured and then degenerated under the aegis of the Peter Principle. In and around my township—where the courts were rural and budgets low and conditions so extreme that the mosquitoes sounded like trumpets and the bees like tubas and the wind like a five-alarm fire, that we had to change shirts between games and use our water jugs to wash blown field-chaff off our arms and necks and carry salt tablets in Pez containers—I was truly near-great: I could Play the Whole Court; I was In My Element. But all the more important tournaments, the events into which my rural excellence was an easement, were played in a different real world: the courts' surface was redone every spring at the Arlington Tennis Center, where the National Junior Qualifier for our region was held; the green of these courts' fair territory was so vivid as to distract, its surface so new and rough it wrecked your feet right through your shoes, and so bare of flaw, tilt, crack, or seam that it was totally disorienting. Playing on a perfect court was for me like treading water out of sight of land: I never knew where I was out there. The 1976 Chicago Junior Invitational was held at Lincolnshire's Bath and Tennis Club, whose huge warren of thirty-six courts was enclosed by all these troubling green plastic tarps attached to all the fences, with little archer-slits in them at eye level to afford some parody of spectation. These tarps were Wind-B-Gone windscreens, patented by the folks over at Cyclone Fence in 1971. They did cut down on the worst of the unfair gusts, but they also seemed to rob the court space of new air: competing at Lincolnshire was like playing in the bottom of a well. And blue bug-zapper lights festooned the lightposts when really major Midwest tournaments played into the night: no clouds of midges around the head or jagged shadows of moths to distinguish from balls' flights, but a real unpleasant zotting and frying sound of bugs being decommissioned just overhead; I won't pause to mention the smell. The point is I just wasn't the same, somehow, without deformities to play around. I'm thinking now that the wind and bugs and chuckholes formed for me a kind of inner boundary, my own personal set of lines. Once I hit a certain level of tournament facilities, I was disabled because I was unable to accommodate the absence of disabilities to accommodate. If that makes sense. Puberty-angst and material alienation notwithstanding, my Midwest tennis career plateaued the moment I saw my first windscreen.

Still strangely eager to speak of weather, let me say that my township, in fact all of East-Central Illinois, is a proud part of what meteorologists call Tornado Alley. Incidence of tornadoes all out of statistical proportion. I personally have seen two on the ground and five aloft, trying to assemble. Aloft tornadoes are gray-white, more like convulsions in the thunderclouds themselves than separate or protruding from them. Ground tornadoes are black only because of the tons of soil they suck in and spin around. The grotesque frequency of tornadoes around my township is, I'm told, a function of the same variables that cause our civilian winds: we are a coordinate where fronts and air masses converge. Most days from late March to June there are Tornado Watches somewhere in our TV stations' viewing area (the stations put a little graphic at the screen's upper right, like a pair of binoculars for a Watch and the Tarot deck's Tower card for a Warning, or something). Watches mean conditions are right and so on and so forth, which, big deal. It's only the rarer Tornado Warnings, which require a confirmed sighting by somebody with reliable sobriety, that make the Civil Defense sirens go. The siren on top of the Philo Middle School was a different pitch and cycle from the one off in the south part of Urbana, and the two used to weave in and out of each other in a godawful threnody. When the sirens blew, the native families went to their canning cellars or fallout shelters (no kidding); the academic families in their bright prefab houses with new lawns and foundations of flat slab went with whatever good-luck tokens they could lay hands on to the very most central point on the ground floor after opening every single window to thwart implosion from precipitous pressure drops. For my family, the very most central point was a hallway between my dad's study and a linen closet, with a reproduction of a Flemish annunciation scene on one wall and a bronze Aztec sunburst hanging with guillotinic mass on the other; I always tried to maneuver my sister under the sunburst.

If there was an actual Warning when you were outside and away from home—say at a tennis tournament in some godforsaken public park at some city fringe zoned for sprawl—you were supposed to lie prone in the deepest depression you could locate. Since the only real depressions around most tournament sites were the irrigation and runoff ditches that bordered cultivated fields, ditches icky with conferva and mosquito spray and always heaving with what looked like conventions of copperheads and just basically places your thinking man doesn't lie prone in under any circumstances, in practice at a Warned tournament you zipped your rackets into their covers and ran to find your loved ones or even your liked ones and just all milled around trying to look like you weren't about to lose sphincter-control. Mothers tended sometimes to wail and clutch childish heads to their bosoms (Mrs. Swearingen of Pekin was particularly popular for clutching even strange kids' heads to her formidable bosom).

I mention tornadoes for reasons directly related to the purpose of this essay. For one thing, they were a real part of Midwest childhood, because as a little kid I was obsessed with dread over them. My earliest nightmares, the ones that didn't feature mile-high robots from *Lost in Space* wielding huge croquet mallets (don't ask), were about shrieking sirens and dead white skies, a slender monster on the Iowa horizon, jutting less phallic than saurian from the lowering sky, whipping back and forth with such frenzy that it almost doubled on itself, trying to eat its own tail, throwing off chaff and dust and chairs; it never came any closer than the horizon; it didn't have to.

In practice, Watches and Warnings both seemed to have a kind of boy-and-wolf quality for the natives of Philo. They just happened too often.

Watches seemed especially irrelevant, because we could always see storms coming from the west way in advance, and by the time they were over, say, Decatur you could diagnose the basic condition by the color and height of the clouds: the taller the anvil-shaped thunderheads, the better the chance for hail and Warnings; pitch-black clouds were a happier sight than gray shot with an odd nacreous white; the shorter the interval between the sight of lightning and the sound of thunder, the faster the system was moving, and the faster the system, the worse: like most things that mean you harm, severe thunderstorms are brisk and no-nonsense.

I know why I stayed obsessed as I aged. Tornadoes, for me, were a transfiguration. Like all serious winds, they were our little stretch of plain's z coordinate, a move up from the Euclidian monotone of furrow, road, axis, and grid. We studied tornadoes in junior high: a Canadian high straight-lines it southeast from the Dakotas; a moist warm mass drawls on up north from like Arkansas: the result was not a Greek χ or even a Cartesian Γ but a circling of the square, a curling of vectors, concavation of curves. It was alchemical, Leibnizian. Tornadoes were, in our part of Central Illinois, the dimensionless point at which parallel lines met and whirled and blew up. They made no sense. Houses blew not out but in. Brothels were spared while orphanages next door bought it. Dead cattle were found three miles from their silage without a scratch on them. Tornadoes are omnipotent and obey no law. Force without law has no shape, only tendency and duration. I believe now that I knew all this without knowing it, as a kid.

The only time I ever got caught in what might have been an actual one was in June '78 on a tennis court at Hessel Park in Champaign, where I was drilling one afternoon with Gil Antitoi. Though a contemptible and despised tournament opponent, I was a coveted practice partner because I could transfer balls to wherever you wanted them with the mindless constancy of a machine. This particular day it was supposed to rain around suppertime, and a couple times we thought we'd heard the tattered edges of a couple sirens out west toward Monticello, but Antitoi and I drilled religiously every afternoon that week on the slow clayish Har-Tru of Hessel, trying to prepare for a beastly clay invitational in Chicago where it was rumored both Brescia and Mees would appear. We were doing butterfly drills—my crosscourt forehand is transferred back down the line to Antitoi's backhand, he crosscourts it to my backhand, I send it down the line to his forehand, four 45° angles, though the intersection of just his crosscourts makes an X, which is four 90's and also a crucifix rotated the same quarter-turn that a swastika (which involves eight 90° angles) is rotated on Hitlerian bunting. This was the sort of stuff that went through my head when I drilled. Hessel Park was scented heavily with cheese from the massive Kraft factory at Champaign's western limit, and it had wonderful expensive soft Har-Tru courts of such a deep piney color that the flights of the fluorescent balls stayed on one's visual screen for a few extra seconds, leaving trails, which is also why the angles and hieroglyphs involved in butterfly drill seem important. But the crux here is that butterflies are primarily a conditioning drill: both players have to get from one side of the court to the other between each stroke, and once the initial pain and wind-sucking are over—assuming you're a kid who's in absurd shape because he spends countless mindless hours jumping rope or running laps backward or doing star-drills between the court's corners or straight sprints back and forth along the perfect furrows of early beanfields each morning—once the first pain and fatigue of butterflies are got through, if both guys are good enough so that there are few unforced errors to break up the rally, a kind of fugue-state opens up inside you where your concentration telescopes toward a still point and you lose awareness of your limbs and the soft shush of your shoe's slide (you have to slide out of a run on Har-Tru) and whatever's outside the lines of the court, and pretty much all you know then is the bright ball and the octangled butterfly outline of its trail across the billiard green of the court. We had one just endless rally and I'd left the planet in a silent swoop inside when the court and ball and butterfly trail all seemed to surge brightly and glow as the daylight just plain went out in the sky overhead. Neither of us had noticed that there'd been no wind blowing the familiar grit into our eyes for several minutes—a bad sign. There was no siren. Later they said the C.D. alert network had been out of order. This was June 6, 1978. The air temperature dropped so fast you could feel your hairs rise. There was no thunder and no air stirred. I could not tell you why we kept hitting. Neither of us said anything. There was no siren. It was high noon; there was nobody else on the courts. The riding mower out over east at the softball field was still going back and forth. There were no depressions except a saprogenic ditch along the field of new corn just west. What could we have done? The air always smells of mowed grass before a bad storm. I think we thought it would rain at worst and that we'd play till it rained and then go sit in Antitoi's parents' station wagon. I do remember a mental obscenity—I had gut strings in my rackets, strings everybody with a high sectional ranking got free for letting the Wilson sales rep spray-paint a *W* across the racket face, so they were free, but I liked this particular string job on this racket, I liked them tight but not real tight, 62–63 p.s.i. on a Proflite stringer, and gut becomes pasta if it gets wet, but we were both in the fugue-state that exhaustion through repetition brings on, a fugue-state I've decided that my whole time playing tennis was spent chasing, a fugue-state I associated too with plowing and seeding and detasseling and spreading herbicides back and forth in sentry duty along perfect lines, up and back, or military marching on flat blacktop, hypnotic, a mental state at once flat and lush, numbing and yet exquisitely felt. We were young, we didn't know when to stop. Maybe I was mad at my body and wanted to hurt it, wear it down. Then the whole knee-high field to the west along Kirby Avenue all of a sudden flattened out in a wave coming toward us as if the field was getting steamrolled. Antitoi went wide west for a forehand cross and I saw the corn get laid down in waves and the sycamores in a copse lining the ditch point our way. There was no funnel. Either it had just materialized and come down or it wasn't a real one. The big heavy swings on the industrial swingsets took off, wrapping themselves in their chains around and around the top crossbar; the park's grass got laid down the same way the field had; the whole thing happened so fast I'd seen nothing like it; recall that Bimini H-Bomb film of the shock wave visible in the sea as it comes toward the ship's film crew. This all happened very fast but in serial progression: field, trees, swings, grass, then the feel like the lift of the world's biggest mitt, the nets suddenly and sexually up and out straight, and I seem to remember whacking a ball out of my hand at Antitoi to watch its radical west-east curve, and for some reason trying to run after this ball I'd just hit, but I couldn't have tried to run after a ball I had hit, but I remember the heavy gentle lift at my thighs and the ball curving back closer and my passing the ball and beating the ball in flight over the horizontal net, my feet not once touching the ground over fifty-odd feet, a cartoon, and then there was chaff and crud in the air all over and both Antitoi and I either flew or were blown pinwheeling for I swear it must have been fifty feet to the fence one court over, the easternmost fence, we hit the fence so hard we knocked it halfway down, and it stuck at 45°, Antitoi detached a retina and had to wear those funky Jabbar retina-goggles for the rest of the summer, and the fence had two body-shaped indentations like in cartoons where the guy's face makes a cast in the skillet that hit him, two catcher's masks of fence, we both got deep quadrangular lines impressed on our faces, torsos, legs' fronts, from the fence, my sister said we looked like waffles, but neither of us got badly hurt, and no homes got whacked—either the thing just ascended again for no reason right after, they do that, obey no rule, follow no line, hop up and down at something that might as well be will, or else it wasn't a real one. Antitoi's tennis continued to improve after that, but mine didn't.

1990

Afterword

When David Foster Wallace sat down to write this essay for *Harper's Magazine* in 1991, he was nearly thirty, very poor, and unable to write good fiction anymore, or so he said. Losing access to his fiction brain terrified him at an existential level. Through a few sustained explosions of creative work, his life had been defined, his gifts and sense of purpose discovered and confirmed. He was a bit like a star athlete famous for the feat, perhaps not repeatable, of making fastballs disappear into the upper deck. Other writers, male and American mostly (Malamud, Updike, DeLillo, more recently Chad Harbach), have linked creation's leap to that other secular ecstasy: the brief athletic peak. And indeed, DFW had a jock's connection to the theme. He had been, the essay tells us, a top competitive tennis player on the Midwestern junior circuit, an excellence marked above all else by the joy of living briefly in the body and the moment. Then this tennis zen went away, and he became an ordinary player, a worker and a grinder. When at twenty-one, he discovered his great gift for fiction—it poured out of him Mozartishly, a story in a morning, a novella in three weeks—he touched again the high sublime of racket-crashes-ball. This overflowing period of creativity ended four years later, just as he became perhaps the first famous writer of his generation. He was dubbed a genius in some circles, fiction's Natural, just as the work became like *work*—sluggish, slugged-out, fake (his word), and dogged by second thoughts.

This essay on the loss of grace in tennis speaks then to the passing of a writer's first ecstatic access to creation. Wallace mourns the loss and maps a paradox that would become the seed idea of later work. The paradox is that although we need to live in peaks, these hypostatic highs of sex, success, religion, love, creation, conception, childbirth, or yes sports, we can only fully *appreciate* the peaks when they are passed and passing. Why? Because ecstasy's power lies in its wordlessness, its ability to make of us a happy holy blank. Because appreciation is a *branch of thought*, it is only in falling, in coming down from ecstasy, that we can know that we have briefly touched the ultimate. It is only in the falling too that we try to find words for the sublime, seeking others who have known a God-truth-moment of their own, and so form the furtive, bruised communities that crop up in the world of D. F. Wallace. Ecstasy is best; thoughtlessness is God. In "appreciating" the absence of thought, describing it, forming our post-hoc support groups like the addicts in the AA meetings of *Infinite Jest* bereftly describing their own former highs, we paradoxically return to the realm of obsessive solipsistic self-analysis, the endless yammer of the head, which is downward and entropic and corrupt.

Is there any way out of the cycle? This essay suggests maybe. For while we live for the ecstatic, which is brief and inexplicable and carries a hard hangover, years can pass and a man can be in Boston at a desk and create in prose a second tennis ecstasy that is about *the loss of ecstasy* (note the Wallacean joke). This second artificial tennis ecstasy, this prosodic counterfeit, can—unlike the first real raw experience—forge a bond between the writer at his desk in 1991 and the readers in the future, and, unlike tornadoes, it can stay around awhile.

—Mark Costello

E Unibus Pluram

Television and U.S. Fiction

act natural

FICTION WRITERS AS a species tend to be oglers. They tend to lurk and to stare. They are born watchers. They are viewers. They are the ones on the subway about whose nonchalant stare there is something creepy, somehow. Almost predatory. This is because human situations are writers' food. Fiction writers watch other humans sort of the way gapers slow down for car wrecks: they covet a vision of themselves as *witnesses*.

But fiction writers tend at the same time to be terribly self-conscious. Devoting lots of productive time to studying closely how people come across to them, fiction writers also spend lots of less productive time wondering nervously how they come across to other people. How they appear, how they seem, whether their shirttail might be hanging out of their fly, whether there's maybe lipstick on their teeth, whether the people they're ogling can maybe size them up as somehow creepy, as lurkers and starers.

The result is that a majority of fiction writers, born watchers, tend to dislike being objects of people's attention. Dislike being watched. The exceptions to this rule—Mailer, McInerney—sometimes create the impression that most belletristic types covet people's attention. Most don't. The few who like attention just naturally get more attention. The rest of us watch.

Most of the fiction writers I know are Americans under 40. I don't know whether fiction writers under 40 watch more television than other American species. Statisticians report that television is watched over six hours a day in the average American household. I don't know any fiction writers who live in average American households. I suspect Louise Erdrich might. Actually I have never seen an average American household. Except on TV.

Right away you can see a couple of things that look potentially great, for U.S. fiction writers, about U.S. television. First, television does a lot of our predatory human research for us. American human beings are a slippery and protean bunch in real life, hard as hell to get any kind of universal handle on. But television comes equipped with just such a handle. It's an incredible gauge of the generic. If we want to know what American normality is—i.e. what Americans want to regard as normal—we can trust television. For television's whole raison is reflecting what people want to see. It's a mirror. Not the Stendhalian mirror that reflects the blue sky and mudpuddle. More like the overlit bathroom mirror before which the teenager monitors his biceps and determines his better profile. This kind of window on nervous American self-perception is simply invaluable in terms of writing fiction. And writers can have faith in television. There is a lot of money at stake, after all; and television owns the best demographers applied social science has to offer, and these researchers can determine precisely what Americans in the 1990s are, want, see—what we as Audience want to see ourselves as. Television, from the surface on down, is about desire. And, fiction-wise, desire is the sugar in human food.

The second great-seeming thing is that television looks to be an absolute godsend for a human subspecies that loves to watch people but hates to be watched itself. For the television screen affords access only one-way. A psychic ball-check valve. We can see Them; They can't see Us. We can relax, unobserved, as we ogle. I happen to believe this is why television also appeals so much to lonely people. To voluntary shut-ins. Every lonely human I know watches way more than the average U.S. six hours a day. The lonely, like the fictive, love one-way watching. For lonely people are usually lonely not because of hideous deformity or odor or obnoxiousness—in fact there exist today support- and social groups for persons with precisely these attributes. Lonely people tend, rather, to be lonely because they decline to bear the psychic costs of being around other humans. They are allergic to people. People affect them too strongly. Let's call the average U.S. lonely person Joe Briefcase. Joe Briefcase fears and loathes the strain of the special self-consciousness which seems to afflict him only when other real human beings are around, staring, their human sense-antennae abristle. Joe B. fears how he might appear, come across, to watchers. He chooses to sit out the enormously stressful U.S. game of appearance poker.

But lonely people, at home, alone, still crave sights and scenes, company. Hence television. Joe can stare at Them on the screen; They remain blind to Joe. It's almost like voyeurism. I happen to know lonely people who regard television as a veritable deus ex machina for voyeurs. And a lot of the criticism, the really rabid criticism less leveled than sprayed at networks, advertisers, and audiences alike, has to do with the charge that television has turned us into a nation of sweaty, slack-jawed voyeurs. This charge turns out to be untrue, but it's untrue for interesting reasons.

What classic voyeurism is is espial, i.e. watching people who don't know you're there as those people go about the mundane but erotically charged little businesses of private life. It's interesting that so much classic voyeurism involves media of framed glass—windows, telescopes, etc. Maybe the framed glass is why the analogy to television is so tempting. But TV-watching is different from genuine Peeping-Tomism. Because the people we're watching through TV's framed-glass screen are not really ignorant of the fact that somebody is watching them. In fact a whole *lot* of somebodies. In fact the people on television know that it is by virtue of this truly huge crowd of ogling somebodies that they are on the screen engaging in broad non-mundane gestures at all. Television does not afford true espial because television is performance, spectacle, which by definition requires watchers. We're not voyeurs here at all. We're just viewers. We are the Audience, megametrically many, though most often we watch alone: E Unibus Pluram.[1]

One reason fiction writers seem creepy in person is that by vocation they really *are* voyeurs. They need that straightforward visual theft of watching somebody who hasn't prepared a special watchable self. The only illusion in true espial is suffered by the voyee, who doesn't know he's giving off images and impressions. A problem with so many of us fiction writers under 40 using television as a substitute for true espial, however, is that TV "voyeurism" involves a whole gorgeous orgy of illusions for the pseudo-spy, when we watch. Illusion (1) is that we're voyeurs here at all: the "voyees" behind the screen's glass are only pretending ignorance. They know perfectly well we're out there. And that we're there is also very much on the minds of those behind the second layer of glass, viz. the lenses and monitors via which technicians and arrangers apply enormous ingenuity to hurl the visible images at us. What we see is far from stolen; it's proffered—illusion (2). And, illusion (3), what we're seeing through the framed panes isn't people in real situations that do or even could go on

---

1 This, and thus part of this essay's title, is from a marvelous toss-off in Michael Sorkin's "Faking It," published in Todd Gitlin, ed., *Watching Television*, Random House/Pantheon, 1987.

without consciousness of Audience. I.e., what young writers are scanning for data on some reality to fictionalize is *already* composed of fictional characters in highly formalized narratives. And, (4), we're not really even seeing "characters" at all: it's not Major Frank Burns, pathetic self-important putz from Fort Wayne, Indiana; it's Larry Linville of Ojai, California, actor stoic enough to endure thousands of letters (still coming in, even in syndication) from pseudo-voyeurs berating him for being a putz from Indiana. And then (5) it's ultimately of course not even actors we're espying, not even people: it's EM-propelled analog waves and ion streams and rear-screen chemical reactions throwing off phosphenes in grids of dots not much more lifelike than Seurat's own Impressionist commentaries on perceptual illusion. Good Lord and (6) the dots are coming out of our *furniture*, all we're really spying on is our own *furniture*, and our very own chairs and lamps and bookspines sit visible but unseen at our gaze's frame as we contemplate "Korea" or are taken "live to Jerusalem" or regard the plusher chairs and classier spines of the Huxtable "home" as illusory cues that this is some domestic interior whose membrane we have (slyly, unnoticed) violated — (7) and (8) and illusions ad inf.

Not that these realities about actors and phosphenes and furniture are unknown to us. We choose to ignore them. They are part of the disbelief we suspend. But it's an awfully heavy load to hoist aloft for six hours a day; illusions of voyeurism and privileged access require serious complicity from the viewer. How can we be made so willingly to acquiesce to the delusion that the people on the TV don't know they're being watched, to the fantasy that we're somehow transcending privacy and feeding on unself-conscious human activity? There might be lots of reasons why these unrealities are so swallowable, but a big one is that the performers behind the glass are — varying degrees of thespian talent notwithstanding — absolute *geniuses* at seeming unwatched. Make no mistake — seeming unwatched in front of a TV camera is an art. Take a look at how non-professionals act when a TV camera is pointed at them: they often spaz out, or else they go all stiff, frozen with self-consciousness. Even PR people and politicians are, in terms of being on camera, rank amateurs. And we love to laugh at how stiff and fake non-pros appear on television. How unnatural.

But if you've ever once been the object of that terrible blank round glass stare, you know all too well how paralyzingly self-conscious it makes you feel. A harried guy with earphones and a clipboard tells you to "act natural" as your face begins to leap around on your skull, struggling for a seeming-unwatched expression that feels so impossible because "seeming unwatched" is, like "acting natural," oxymoronic. Try hitting a golf ball right after someone asks you whether you in- or exhale on your backswing, or getting promised lavish rewards if you can avoid thinking of a green rhinoceros for ten seconds, and you'll get some idea of the truly heroic contortions of body and mind that must be required for a David Duchovny or Don Johnson to act unwatched as he's watched by a lens that's an overwhelming emblem of what Emerson, years before TV, called "the gaze of millions."[2]

For Emerson, only a certain very rare species of person is fit to stand this gaze of millions. It is not your normal, hardworking, quietly desperate species of American. The man who can stand the megagaze is a walking imago, a certain type of transcendent semihuman who, in Emerson's phrase, "carries the holiday in his eye." The Emersonian holiday that television actors' eyes carry is the promise of a vacation from human self-consciousness. Not worrying about how you come across. A total unallergy to gazes. It is contemporarily heroic. It is frightening and strong. It is also, of course, an act, for you have to be just abnormally self-conscious and self-controlled to appear unwatched before cameras and lenses and men with clipboards. This self-conscious appearance of unself-consciousness is the real door to TV's whole mirror-hall of illusions, and for us, the Audience, it is both medicine and poison.

For we gaze at these rare, highly-trained, unwatched-seeming people for six hours daily. And we love these people. In terms of attributing to them true supernatural assets and desiring to emulate them, it's fair to say we sort of worship them. In a real Joe Briefcase–world that shifts ever more starkly from some community of relationships to networks of strangers connected by self-interest and technology, the people we espy on TV offer us familiarity, community. Intimate friendship. But we split what we see. The characters may be our "close friends," but the *performers* are beyond strangers: they're imagos, demigods, and they move in a different sphere, hang out with and marry only each other, seem even as actors accessible to Audience only via the mediation of tabloid, talk show, EM signal. And yet both actors and characters, so terribly removed and filtered, seem so terribly, gloriously *natural* when we watch.

Given how much we watch and what watching means, it's inevitable, for those of us fictionists or Joe Briefcases who fancy ourselves voyeurs, to get the idea that these persons behind the glass — persons who are often

---

2 Quoted by Stanley Cavell in *Pursuits of Happiness,* Harvard U. Press, 1981; subsequent Emerson quotes ibid.

the most colorful, attractive, animated, *alive* people in our daily experience—are also people who are oblivious to the fact that they are watched. This illusion is toxic. It's toxic for lonely people because it sets up an alienating cycle (viz. "Why can't *I* be like that?" etc.), and it's toxic for writers because it leads us to confuse actual fiction-research with a weird kind of fiction-*consumption*. Self-conscious people's oversensitivity to real humans tends to put us before the television and its one-way window in an attitude of relaxed and total reception, rapt. We watch various actors play various characters, etc. For 360 minutes per diem, we receive unconscious reinforcement of the deep thesis that the most significant quality of truly alive persons is watchableness, and that genuine human worth is not just identical with but *rooted in* the phenomenon of watching. Plus the idea that the single biggest part of real watchableness is seeming to be unaware that there's any watching going on. Acting natural. The persons we young fiction writers and assorted shut-ins study, feel for, feel through most intently are, by virtue of a genius for feigned unself-consciousness, fit to stand people's gazes. And we, trying desperately to be nonchalant, perspire creepily on the subway.

the finger

Existentiovoyeuristic conundra notwithstanding, there's no denying the simple fact that people in the U.S.A. watch so much television basically because it's fun. I know I watch for fun, most of the time, and that at least 51% of the time I do have fun when I watch. This doesn't mean I do not take television seriously. One big claim of this essay is going to be that the most dangerous thing about television for U.S. fiction writers is that we don't take it seriously enough as both a disseminator and a definer of the cultural atmosphere we breathe and process, that many of us are so blinded by constant exposure that we regard TV the way Reagan's lame F.C.C. chairman Mark Fowler professed to see it in 1981, as "just another appliance, a toaster with pictures."[3]

It's undeniable, nevertheless, that watching television is pleasurable, and it may seem odd that so much of the pleasure my generation takes from television lies in making fun of it. But you have to remember that younger Americans grew up as much with people's disdain for TV as we did with TV itself. I knew it was a "vast wasteland" way before I knew

---

3 Bernard Nossiter, "The F.C.C.'s Big Giveaway Show," *Nation*, 10/26/85, p. 402.

who Newton Minow and Mark Fowler were. And it really is fun to laugh cynically at television—at the way the laughter from sitcoms' "live studio audiences" is always suspiciously constant in pitch and duration, or at the way travel is depicted on *The Flintstones* by having the exact same cut-rate cartoon tree, rock, and house go by four times. It's fun, when a withered June Allyson comes on-screen for Depend Adult Undergarments and says "If you have a bladder-control problem, you're not alone," to hoot and shout back "Well chances are you're alone *quite a bit,* June!"

Most scholars and critics who write about U.S. popular culture, though, seem both to take TV very seriously and to suffer terrible pain over what they see. There's this well-known critical litany about television's vapidity and irrealism. The litany is often even cruder and triter than the shows the critics complain about, which I think is why most younger Americans find professional criticism of television less interesting than professional television itself. I found solid examples of what I'm talking about on the first day I even looked. The *New York Times* Arts & Leisure Section for Sunday, 8/05/90, simply bulged with bitter critical derision for TV, and some of the most unhappy articles weren't about low-quality programming so much as about how TV's become this despicable instrument of cultural decay. In a summary review of all 1990's "crash and burn" summer box-office hits in which "realism...seems to have gone almost entirely out of fashion," it takes Janet Maslin only a paragraph to locate her true anti-reality culprit: "We may be hearing about 'real life' only on television shows made up of fifteen-second sound bites (in which 'real people' not only speak in brief, neat truisms but actually seem to think that way, perhaps as a result of having watched too much reality-molding television themselves)."[4] And one Stephen Holden, in what starts out as a scathing assessment of the pass pop music's come to, feels he knows perfectly well what's behind what he hates: "Pop music is no longer a world unto itself but an adjunct of television, whose stream of commercial images projects a culture in which everything is for sale and the only things that count are fame, power, and the body beautiful."[5] This stuff just goes on and on, article after article, in the *Times.* The only Arts & Leisure piece I could find with anything upbeat to say about TV that morning was a breathless article on how lots of Ivy League graduates are now flying straight from school to New York and Los Angeles to become television writers and are

---

4 Janet Maslin, "It's Tough for Movies to Get Real," *New York Times* Arts & Leisure Section, 8/05/90, p. 9.

5 Stephen Holden, "Strike The Pose: When Music Is Skin-Deep," ibid., p. 1.

clearing well over $200,000 to start and enjoying rapid advancement to harried clipboarded production status. In this regard, 8/05's *Times* is a good example of a strange mix that's been around for a few years now: weary contempt for television as a creative product and cultural force, combined with beady-eyed fascination about the actual behind-the-glass mechanics of making that product and projecting that force.

Surely I'm not alone in having acquaintances I hate to watch TV with because they so clearly loathe it—they complain relentlessly about the hackneyed plots, the unlikely dialogue, the Cheez-Whiz resolutions, the bland condescension of the news anchors, the shrill wheedling of the commercials—and yet are just as clearly obsessed with it, somehow *need* to loathe their six hours a day, day in and out. Junior advertising executives, aspiring filmmakers, and grad-school poets are in my experience especially prone to this condition where they simultaneously hate, fear, and need television, and try to disinfect themselves of whatever so much viewing might do to them by watching TV with weary contempt instead of the rapt credulity most of us grew up with. (Note that most fiction writers still tend to go for the rapt credulity.)

But, since the wearily contemptuous *Times* has its own demographic thumb to the pulse of readerly taste, it's probably safe to assume that most educated, *Times*-buying Americans are wearily disgusted by television, have this weird hate-/need-/fear-6-hrs.-daily gestalt about it. Published TV-scholarship sure reflects this mood. And the numbingly dull quality to most "literary" television analyses is due less to the turgid abstraction scholars employ to make television seem an OK object of aesthetic inquiry—q.v. part of an '86 treatise: "The form of my Tuesday evening's prime-time pleasure is structured by a dialectic of elision and rift among various windows through which...'flow' is more a circumstance than a product. The real output is the quantum, the smallest maneuverable broadcast bit."[6]—than to the jaded cynicism of TV-scholars who mock and revile the very phenomenon they've chosen as vocation. These scholars are like people who despise—I mean big-time, long-term despise—their spouses or jobs, but won't split up or quit. Critical complaint seems long ago to have degenerated into plain old whining. The important question about U.S. television is no longer whether there are some truly nasty problems involved in Americans' relation to television but rather what might possibly be done about them. On this question pop critics and scholars are resoundingly mute.

---

6 Sorkin in Gitlin, p. 163.

The fact is that it's only in the U.S. arts, particularly in certain strands of contemporary American fiction, that the really interesting questions about fin-de-siècle TV—What exactly is it about televisual culture that we hate so much? Why are we so immersed in it if we hate it so? What implications are there in our sustained, voluntary immersion in something we hate?—are being addressed. But they are also, weirdly, being asked and answered by television itself. This is another reason why most TV criticism seems so empty. Television's managed to become its own most profitable analyst.

Midmorning, 8/05/90, as I was scanning and sneering at the sneering tone of the aforementioned *Times* articles, a syndicated episode of *St. Elsewhere* was on TV, cleaning up in a Sunday-morning Boston market otherwise occupied by televangelists, infomercials, and the steroid- and polyurethane-ridden *American Gladiators,* itself not charmless but definitely a low-dose show. Syndication is another new area of public fascination, not only because huge cable stations like Chicago's WGN and Atlanta's TBS have upped the stakes from local to national, but because syndication is changing the whole creative philosophy of network television. Since it is in syndication deals (where the distributor gets both an up-front fee for a program and a percentage of the ad slots for his own commercials) that the creators of successful television series realize truly gross profits, many new programs are designed and pitched with both immediate prime-time and down-the-road syndication audiences in mind, and are now informed less by dreams of the ten-year-beloved-TV-institution-type run—*M*A*S*H, Cheers!*—than of a modest three-year run that will yield the 78 in-can episodes required for an attractive syndication package. By the way, I, like millions of other Americans, know this technical insider-type stuff because I saw a special three-part report about syndication on *Entertainment Tonight,* itself the first nationally syndicated "news" program and the first infomercial so popular that TV stations were willing to pay for it.

Sunday-morning syndication is also intriguing because it makes for juxtapositions as eerily apposite as anything French surrealists could come up with. Lovable warlocks on *Bewitched* and commercially Satanic heavy-metal videos on *Top Ten Countdown* run opposite air-brushed preachers decrying demonism in U.S. culture. You can surf back and forth between a televised mass's "This is my blood" and *Gladiators'* Zap breaking a civilian's nose with a polyurethane Bataka. Or, even better, have a look at 8/05/90's *St. Elsewhere* episode 94, originally broadcast in 1988, which airs in syndication on Boston's Channel 38 immediately following two back-to-back episodes of *The Mary Tyler Moore Show*, that icon of '70s pathos. The plots of the two *Mary Tyler Moore Shows* are unimportant here. But the *St. Elsewhere* episode that followed them was partly concerned with a cameo-role mental patient who presented with the delusional belief that he was Mary Richards from *The Mary Tyler Moore Show*. He further believed that a fellow cameo-role mental patient was Rhoda, that Dr. Westphal was Mr. Grant, and that Dr. Auschlander was Murray. This psychiatric subplot was a one-shot; it was resolved by episode's end. The pseudo-Mary (a sad lumpy-looking guy, portrayed by an actor whose name I didn't catch but who I remember used to play one of Dr. Hartley's neurotic clients on the old *Bob Newhart Show*) rescues the other cameo-role mental patient, whom he believes to be Rhoda and who has been furious in his denials that he is female, much less fictional (and who is himself played by the guy who used to play Mr. Carlin, Dr. Hartley's most intractable client), from assault by a bit-part hebephrene. In gratitude, Rhoda/Mr. Carlin/mental patient declares that he'll consent to be Rhoda if that's what Mary/neurotic client/mental patient wants. At this too-real generosity, the pseudo-Mary's psychotic break breaks. The sad lumpy guy admits to Dr. Auschlander that he's not Mary Richards. He's actually just a plain old amnesiac, a guy without a meaningful identity, existentially adrift. He has no idea who he is. He's lonely. He watches a lot of TV. He says he "figured it was better to believe I was a TV character than not to believe I was anybody." Dr. Auschlander takes the penitent patient for a walk in the wintery Boston air and promises that he, the identityless guy, can someday very probably find out who he really is, provided he can dispense with "the distraction of television." Extremely grateful and happy at this prognosis, the patient removes his own fuzzy winter beret and throws it into the air. The episode ends with a freeze of the airborne hat, leaving at least one viewer credulously rapt.

This would have been just another clever low-concept '80s TV story, where the final cap-tossing coyly undercuts Dr. Auschlander's putdown of television, were it not for the countless layers of ironic, involuted TV imagery and data that whirled around this incredibly high-concept installment. Because another of this episode's cameo stars, drifting through a different subplot, is one Betty White, Sue-Ann Nivens of the old *Mary Tyler Moore Show*, here playing a tortured NASA surgeon (don't ask). It is with almost tragic inevitability, then, that Ms. White, at 32 minutes into the episode, meets up with the TV-deluded pseudo-Mary in their respective tortured wanderings through the hospital's corridors, and that she greets the mental patient's inevitable joyful cries of "Sue-Ann!" with a too-straight face as she says that he must have her confused with someone else. Of the convoled levels of fantasy and reality and identity here—e.g. the patient simultaneously does, does not, and does have Betty White "confused" with Sue-Ann Nivens—we needn't speak in detail; doubtless a Yale Contemporary Culture dissertation is under way on Deleuze & Guattari and just this episode. But the most interesting levels of meaning here lie, and point, behind the lens. For NBC's *St. Elsewhere*, like *The Mary Tyler Moore Show* and *The Bob Newhart Show* before it, was created, produced, and guided into syndication by MTM Studios, owned by Mary Tyler Moore and overseen by her erstwhile husband, eventual NBC CEO Grant Tinker; and *St. Elsewhere*'s scripts and subplots are story-edited by Mark Tinker, Mary's stepson, Grant's heir. The deluded mental patient, an exiled, drifting veteran of one MTM program, reaches piteously out to the exiled, drifting (literally—*NASA*, for God's sake!) veteran of another MTM production, and her deadpan rebuff is scripted by MTM personnel, who accomplish the parodic undercut of MTM's Dr. Auschlander with the copyrighted MTM hat-gesture of one MTM veteran who's "deluded" he's another. Dr. A.'s Fowleresque dismissal of TV as just a "distraction" is less naïve than insane: there is nothing *but* television on this episode. Every character and conflict and joke and dramatic surge depends on involution, self-reference, metatelevision. It is in-joke within in-joke.

So then why do I get the in-joke? Because I, the viewer, outside the glass with the rest of the Audience, am *in* on the in-joke. I've seen Mary Tyler Moore's "real" toss of that fuzzy beret so often it's moved past cliché into warm nostalgia. I know the mental patient from *Bob Newhart*, Betty White from everywhere, *and* I know all sorts of intriguing irrelevant stuff about MTM Studios and syndication from *Entertainment Tonight*. I, the pseudo-voyeur, am indeed "behind the scenes," primed to get the in-joke. But it is not I the spy who have crept inside television's boundaries. It is vice versa. Television, even the mundane little businesses of its production, has become my—our—own interior. And we seem a jaded, weary, but willing and above all *knowledgeable* Audience. And this knowledgeability utterly transforms the possibilities and hazards of "creativity" in television. *St. Elsewhere*'s episode was nominated for a 1988 Emmy. For best original teleplay.

The best TV of the last five years has been about ironic self-reference like no previous species of postmodern art could ever have dreamed of. The colors of MTV videos, blue-black and lambently flickered, are the colors of television. *Moonlighting*'s David and *Bueller*'s Ferris throw asides to the viewer every bit as bald as an old melodrama villain's monologued gloat. Segments of the new late-night glitz-news *After Hours* end with a tease that features harried earphoned guys in the production booth ordering the tease. MTV's television-trivia game show, the dry-titled *Remote Control*, got so popular it burst out of its MTV-membrane and is now syndicated band-wide. The hippest commercials, with stark computerized settings and blank-faced models in mirrored shades and plastic slacks genuflecting before various forms of velocity, excitement, and prestige, seem like little more than TV's vision of how TV offers rescue to those lonely Joe Briefcases passively trapped into watching too much TV.

What explains the pointlessness of most published TV criticism is that television has become immune to charges that it lacks any meaningful connection to the world outside it. It's not that charges of nonconnection have become untrue but that they've become deeply irrelevant. It's that any such connection has become otiose. Television used to point beyond itself. Those of us born in, say, the '60s were trained by television to look where it pointed, usually at versions of "real life" made prettier, sweeter, livelier by succumbing to a product or temptation. Today's mega-Audience is way better trained, and TV has discarded what's not needed. A dog, if you point at something, will look only at your finger.

metawatching

It's not like self-reference is new to U.S. entertainment. How many old radio shows—Jack Benny, Burns and Allen, Abbott and Costello—were mostly about themselves as shows? "So, Lou, and you said I couldn't get a big star like Miss Lucille Ball to be a guest on our show, you little twerp." Etc. But once television introduces the element of watching, and once it informs an economy and culture like radio never could have, the referential stakes go way up. Six hours a day is more time than most people (consciously) do any other one thing. How human beings who absorb such high doses understand themselves will naturally change, become vastly more spectatorial, self-conscious. Because the practice of "watching" is expansive. Exponential. We spend enough time watching, pretty soon we start watching ourselves watching. Pretty soon we start to "feel" ourselves feeling, yearn to experience "experiences." And that American subspecies into fiction writing starts writing more and more about...

The emergence of something called Metafiction in the American '60s was hailed by academic critics as a radical aesthetic, a whole new literary form, literature unshackled from the cultural cinctures of mimetic narrative and free to plunge into reflexivity and self-conscious meditations on aboutness. Radical it may have been, but thinking that postmodern Metafiction evolved unconscious of prior changes in readerly taste is about as innocent as thinking that all those college students we saw on television protesting the Vietnam war were protesting only because they hated the Vietnam war. (They may have hated the war, but they also wanted to be seen protesting on television. TV was where they'd *seen* this war, after all. Why wouldn't they go about hating it on the very medium that made their hate possible?) Metafictionists may have had aesthetic theories out the bazoo, but they were also sentient citizens of a community that was exchanging an old idea of itself as a nation of doers and be-ers for a new vision of the U.S.A. as an atomized mass of self-conscious watchers and appearers. For Metafiction, in its ascendant and most important phases, was really nothing more than a single-order expansion of its own great theoretical nemesis, Realism: if Realism called it like it saw it, Metafiction simply called it as it saw itself seeing itself see it. This high-cultural postmodern genre, in other words, was deeply informed by the emergence of television and the metastasis of self-conscious watching. And (I claim) American fiction remains deeply informed by television . . . especially those strains of fiction with roots in postmodernism, which even at its rebellious Metafictional zenith was less a "response to" televisual culture than a kind of abiding-in-TV. Even back then, the borders were starting to come down.

It's strange that it took television itself so long to wake up to watching's potent reflexivity. Television shows about the business of television shows were rare for a long time. *The Dick van Dyke Show* was prescient, and Mary Moore carried its insight into her own decade-long exploration of local-market angst. Now, of course, there's been everything from *Murphy Brown* to *Max Headroom* to *Entertainment Tonight*. And with Letterman, Miller, Shandling, and Leno's battery of hip, sardonic, this-is-just-TV schticks, the circle back to the days of "We've just got to get Miss Ball on our show, Bud" has closed and come spiral, television's power to jettison connection and castrate protest fueled by the very ironic postmodern self-consciousness it had first helped fashion.

It will take a while, but I'm going to prove to you that the nexus where television and fiction converse and consort is self-conscious irony. Irony is, of course, a turf fictionists have long worked with zeal. And irony is important for understanding TV because "TV," now that it's gotten powerful enough to move from acronym to way of life, revolves off just the sorts of absurd contradictions irony's all about exposing. It is ironic that television is a syncretic, homogenizing force that derives much of its power from diversity and various affirmations thereof. It is ironic that an extremely canny and unattractive self-consciousness is necessary to create TV performers' illusion of unconscious appeal. That products presented as helping you express individuality can afford to be advertised on television only because they sell to enormous numbers of people. And so on.

Television regards irony sort of the way educated lonely people regard television. Television both fears irony's capacity to expose, and needs it. It needs irony because television was practically *made* for irony. For TV is a bisensuous medium. Its displacement of radio wasn't picture displacing sound; it was picture added. Since the tension between what's said and what's seen is irony's whole sales territory, classic televisual irony works via the conflicting juxtaposition of pictures and sounds. What's seen undercuts what's said. A scholarly article on network news describes a famous interview with a corporate guy from United Fruit on a CBS special about Guatemala: "I sure don't know of anybody being so-called 'oppressed,'" this guy, in a '70s leisure suit and bad comb-over, tells Ed Rabel. "I think this is just something that some reporters have thought up."[7] The whole interview is intercut with commentless footage of big-bellied kids in Guatemalan slums and union organizers lying in the mud with cut throats.

Television's classic irony function came into its own in the summer of 1974, as remorseless lenses opened to view the fertile "credibility gap" between the image of official disclaimer and the reality of high-level shenanigans. A nation was changed, as Audience. If even the president lies to you, whom are you supposed to trust to deliver the real? Television, that summer, got to present itself as the earnest, worried eye on the reality behind all images. The irony that television is itself a river of image, however, was apparent even to a twelve-year-old, sitting there, rapt. After '74 there seemed to be no way out. Images and ironies all over the place. It's not a coincidence that *Saturday Night Live,* that Athens of irreverent cynicism, specializing in parodies of (1) politics and (2) television, premiered the next fall (on television).

I'm worried when I say things like "television fears..." and "television presents itself..." because, even though it's kind of a necessary abstraction, talking about television as if it were an entity can easily slip into the worst sort of anti-TV paranoia, treating of TV as some autonomous diabolical

---

7 Daniel Hallin, "We Keep America On Top of the World," in Gitlin's anthology, p. 16.

corrupter of personal agency and community gumption. I am concerned to avoid anti-TV paranoia here. Though I'm convinced that television today lies, with a potency somewhere between symptom and synecdoche, behind a genuine crisis for U.S. culture and literature, I do not agree with reactionaries who regard TV as some malignancy visited on an innocent populace, sapping IQs and compromising SAT scores while we all sit there on ever fatter bottoms with little mesmerized spirals revolving in our eyes. Critics like Samuel Huntington and Barbara Tuchman who try to claim that TV's lowering of our aesthetic standards is responsible for a "contemporary culture taken over by commercialism directed to the mass market and necessarily to mass taste"[8] can be refuted by observing that their Propter Hoc isn't even Post Hoc: by 1830, de Tocqueville had already diagnosed American culture as peculiarly devoted to easy sensation and mass-marketed entertainment, "spectacles vehement and untutored and rude" that aimed "to stir the passions more than to gratify the taste."[9] Treating television as evil is just as reductive and silly as treating it like a toaster w/pictures.

It is of course undeniable that television is an example of Low Art, the sort of art that has to please people in order to get their money. Because of the economics of nationally broadcast, advertiser-subsidized entertainment, television's one goal—never denied by anybody in or around TV since RCA first authorized field tests in 1936—is to ensure as much watching as possible. TV is the epitome of Low Art in its desire to appeal to and enjoy the attention of unprecedented numbers of people. But it is not Low because it is vulgar or prurient or dumb. Television is often all these things, but this is a logical function of its need to attract and please Audience. And I'm not saying that television is vulgar and dumb because the people who compose Audience are vulgar and dumb. Television is the way it is simply because people tend to be extremely similar in their vulgar and prurient and dumb interests and wildly different in their refined and aesthetic and noble interests. It's all about syncretic diversity: neither medium nor Audience is faultable for quality.

Still, for the fact that individual American human beings are consuming vulgar, prurient, dumb stuff at the astounding average per-household dose of six hours a day—for this both TV and we need to answer. We are responsible basically because nobody is holding any weapons on us forcing us to spend amounts of time second only to sleep doing something that is,

---

8 Barbara Tuchman, "The Decline of Quality," *New York Times Magazine*, 11/02/80.

9 M. Alexis de Tocqueville, *Democracy in America*, Vintage, 1945 edition, pp. 57 and 73.

when you come right down to it, not good for us. Sorry to be a killjoy, but there it is: six hours a day is not good.

Television's greatest minute-by-minute appeal is that it engages without demanding. One can rest while undergoing stimulation. Receive without giving. In this respect, television resembles certain other things one might call Special Treats (e.g. candy, liquor), i.e. treats that are basically fine and fun in small amounts but bad for us in large amounts and *really* bad for us if consumed in the massive regular amounts reserved for nutritive staples. One can only guess at what volume of gin or poundage of Toblerone six hours of Special Treat a day would convert to.

On the surface of the problem, television is responsible for our rate of its consumption only in that it's become so terribly successful at its acknowledged job of ensuring prodigious amounts of watching. Its social accountability seems sort of like that of designers of military weapons: unculpable right up until they get a little too good at their job.

But the analogy between television and liquor is best, I think. Because (bear with me a second) I'm afraid good old average Joe Briefcase might be a teleholic. I.e., watching TV can become malignantly addictive. It may become malignantly addictive only once a certain threshold of quantity is habitually passed, but then the same is true of Wild Turkey. And by "malignant" and "addictive" I again do not mean evil or hypnotizing. An activity is addictive if one's relationship to it lies on that downward-sloping continuum between liking it a little too much and really needing it. Many addictions, from exercise to letter-writing, are pretty benign. But something is *malignantly* addictive if (1) it causes real problems for the addict, and (2) it offers itself as a relief from the very problems it causes.[10] A malignant addiction is also distinguished for spreading the problems of the addiction out and in in interference patterns, creating difficulties for relationships, communities, and the addict's very sense of self and spirit. In the abstract, some of this hyperbole might strain the analogy for you, but concrete illustrations of malignantly addictive TV-watching cycles aren't hard to come by. If it's true that many Americans are lonely, and if it's true that many lonely people are prodigious TV-watchers, and it's true that lonely people find in television's 2-D images relief from their stressful reluctance to be around real human beings, then it's also obvious that the more time spent at home alone watching TV, the less time spent in the world of real human beings, and that the less time spent in the real human

---

10 I didn't get this definition from any sort of authoritative source, but it seems pretty modest and commonsensical.

world, the harder it becomes not to feel inadequate to the tasks involved in being a part of the world, thus fundamentally apart from it, alienated from it, solipsistic, lonely. It's also true that to the extent one begins to view pseudo-relationships with Bud Bundy or Jane Pauley as acceptable alternatives to relationships with real people, one will have commensurately less conscious incentive even to try to connect with real 3-D persons, connections that seem pretty important to basic mental health. For Joe Briefcase, as for many addicts, the Special Treat begins to substitute for something nourishing and needed, and the original genuine hunger—less satisfied than bludgeoned—subsides to a strange objectless unease.

TV-watching as a malignant cycle doesn't even require special preconditions like writerly self-consciousness or neuroallergic loneliness. Let's for a second imagine Joe Briefcase as now just an average U.S. male, relatively unlonely, adjusted, married, blessed with 2.3 apple-cheeked issue, utterly normal, home from hard work at 5:30, starting his average six-hour stint in front of the television. Since Joe B. is average, he'll shrug at pollsters' questions and answer averagely that he most often watches television to "unwind" from those elements of his day and life he finds unpleasant. It's tempting to suppose that TV enables this unwinding simply because it offers an Auschlanderian "distraction," something to divert the mind from quotidian troubles. But would mere distraction ensure continual massive watching? Television offers way more than distraction. In lots of ways, television purveys and enables *dreams,* and most of these dreams involve some sort of transcendence of average daily life. The modes of presentation that work best for TV—stuff like "action," with shoot-outs and car wrecks, or the rapid-fire "collage" of commercials, news, and music videos, or the "hysteria" of prime-time soap and sitcom with broad gestures, high voices, too much laughter—are unsubtle in their whispers that, somewhere, life is quicker, denser, more interesting, more...well, *lively* than contemporary life as Joe Briefcase knows it. This might seem benign until we consider that what good old average Joe Briefcase does more than almost anything else in contemporary life is watch television, an activity which anyone with an average brain can see does not make for a very dense and lively life. Since television must seek to attract viewers by offering a dreamy promise of escape from daily life, and since stats confirm that so grossly much of ordinary U.S. life is watching TV, TV's whispered promises must somehow undercut television-watching in theory ("Joe, Joe, there's a world where life is lively, where nobody spends six hours a day unwinding before a piece of furniture") while reinforcing television-watching in practice ("Joe, Joe, your best and only access to this world is TV").

Well, average Joe Briefcase has an OK brain, and deep down inside he knows, as we do, that there's some kind of psychic shell-game going on in this system of conflicting whispers. But if it's so bald a delusion, why do he and we keep watching in such high doses? Part of the answer—a part which requires discretion lest it slip into anti-TV paranoia—is that the phenomenon of television somehow trains or conditions our viewership. Television has become able not only to ensure that we watch but somehow to inform our deepest responses to what's watched. Take jaded TV-critics, or our acquaintances who sneer at the numbing sameness of all the television they sit still for. I always want to grab these unhappy guys by the lapels and shake them until their teeth rattle and point to the absence of guns to their heads and ask why the hell they keep watching, then. But the truth is that there's some complex high-dose psychic transaction between TV and Audience whereby Audience gets trained to respond to and then like and then *expect* trite, hackneyed, numbing television shows, and to expect them to such an extent that when networks do occasionally abandon time-tested formulas Audience usually punishes them for it by not watching novel shows in sufficient numbers to let them get off the ground. Hence the networks' bland response to its critics that in the majority of cases—and until the rise of hip metatelevision you could count the exceptions on one hand—"different" or "high-concept" programming simply doesn't get ratings. High-quality television cannot stand up to the gaze of millions, somehow.

Now, it is true that certain PR techniques—e.g. shock, grotesquerie, or irreverence—can ease novel sorts of shows' rise to national demographic viability. Examples here might be the "shocking" *A Current Affair,* the "grotesque" *Real People,* the "irreverent" *Married...with Children.* But these programs, like most of those touted by the industry as "fresh" or "outrageous," turn out to be just tiny transparent variations on old formulas.

It's not fair to blame television's shortage of originality on any lack of creativity among network talent. The truth is that we seldom get a chance to know whether anybody behind any TV show is creative, or more accurately that they seldom get a chance to show us. Despite the unquestioned assumption on the part of pop-culture critics that television's poor old Audience, deep down, "craves novelty," all available evidence suggests, rather, that the Audience *really* craves sameness but thinks, deep down, that it *ought* to crave novelty. Hence the mixture of devotion and sneer on so many viewerly faces. Hence also the weird viewer complicity behind TV's sham "breakthrough programs": Joe Briefcase needs that PR-patina of "freshness" and "outrageousness" to quiet his conscience while he goes about getting from television what we've all been trained to want from it: some strangely American, profoundly shallow, and eternally temporary *reassurance*.

Particularly in the last decade, this tension in the Audience between what we do want and what we think we ought to want has been television's breath and bread. TV's self-mocking invitation to itself as indulgence, transgression, a glorious "giving in" (again, not exactly foreign to addictive cycles) is one of two ingenious ways it's consolidated its six-hour hold on my generation's cojones. The other is postmodern irony. The commercials for *Alf*'s Boston debut in a syndicated package feature the fat, cynical, gloriously decadent puppet (so much like Snoopy, like Garfield, like Bart, like Butt-Head) advising me to "Eat a whole lot of food and stare at the TV." His pitch is an ironic permission-slip to do what I do best whenever I feel confused and guilty: assume, inside, a sort of fetal position, a pose of passive reception to comfort, escape, reassurance. The cycle is self-nourishing.

guilty fictions

Not, again, that the cycle's root conflict is new. You can trace the opposition between what persons do and ought to desire at least as far back as Plato's chariot or the Prodigal's return. But the way entertainments appeal to and work within this conflict has been transformed in televisual culture. This culture-of-watching's relation to the cycle of indulgence, guilt, and reassurance has important consequences for U.S. art, and though the parallels are easiest to see w/r/t Warhol's Pop or Elvis's Rock, the most interesting intercourse is between television and American literature.

One of the most recognizable things about this century's postmodern fiction has always been the movement's strategic deployment of pop-cultural references—brand names, celebrities, television programs—in even its loftiest High Art projects. Think of just about any example of avant-garde U.S. fiction in the last twenty-five years, from Slothrop's passion for Slippery Elm throat lozenges and his weird encounter with Mickey Rooney in *Gravity's Rainbow*, to "You"'s fetish for the *New York Post*'s COMA BABY feature in *Bright Lights, Big City*, to Don DeLillo's pop-hip characters saying stuff to each other like "Elvis fulfilled the terms of the contract. Excess, deterioration, self-destructiveness, grotesque behavior, a physical bloating and a series of insults to the brain, self-delivered."[11]

The apotheosis of the pop in postwar art marked a whole new marriage between High and Low culture. For the artistic viability of postmodernism was a direct consequence, again, not of any new facts about art, but of facts about the new importance of mass commercial culture. Americans seemed no longer united so much by common beliefs as by common images: what binds us became what we stand witness to. Nobody sees this as a good change. In fact, pop-cultural references have become such potent metaphors in U.S. fiction not only because of how united Americans are in our exposure to mass images but also because of our guilty indulgent psychology with respect to that exposure. Put simply, the pop reference works so well in contemporary fiction because (1) we all recognize such a reference, and (2) we're all a little uneasy about how we all recognize such a reference.

The status of Low-cultural images in postmodern and contemporary fiction is very different from those images' place in postmodernism's artistic ancestors, e.g. the "dirty realism" of a Joyce or the ur-Dadaism of something like Duchamp's toilet sculpture. Duchamp's aesthetic display of that vulgarest of appliances served an exclusively theoretical end: it was making statements like "The Museum is the Mausoleum is the Men's Room," etc. It was an example of what Octavio Paz calls "Meta-irony,"[12] an attempt to reveal that categories we divide into superior/arty and inferior/vulgar are in fact so interdependent as to be coextensive. The use of Low references in a lot of today's High literary fiction, on the other hand, serves a less abstract agenda. It is meant (1) to help create a mood of irony and irreverence, (2) to make us uneasy and so "comment" on the vapidity of U.S. culture, and (3) most important, these days, to be just plain realistic.

Pynchon and DeLillo were ahead of their time. Today, the belief that pop images are basically just mimetic devices is one of the attitudes that separates most U.S. fiction writers under c. 40 from the writerly generation that precedes us, reviews us, and designs our grad-school curricula. This generation gap in conceptions of realism is, again, TV-dependent. The U.S. generation born after 1950 is the first for whom television was something to be lived with instead of just looked at. Our elders tend to regard the set rather as the flapper did the automobile: a curiosity turned

---

11 Don DeLillo, *White Noise*, Viking, 1985, p. 72.
12 Octavio Paz, *Children of the Mire*, Harvard U. Press, 1974, pp. 103–118.

treat turned seduction. For younger writers, TV's as much a part of reality as Toyotas and gridlock. We literally cannot imagine life without it. We're not different from our fathers in that television presents and defines our contemporary world. Where we are different is that we have no memory of a world without such electric definition. This is why the derision so many older fictionists heap on a "Brat Pack" generation they see as insufficiently critical of mass culture is at once understandable and misguided. It's true that there's something sad about the fact that David Leavitt's short stories' sole description of some characters is that their T-shirts have certain brand names on them. But the fact is that, for most of Leavitt's educated young readership, members of a generation raised and nourished on messages equating what one consumes with who one is, Leavitt's descriptions really do do the job. In our post-1950s, inseparable-from-TV association pool, brand loyalty really is synecdochic of character; this is simply a fact.

For those U.S. writers whose ganglia were formed pre-TV, those who are big on neither Duchamp nor Paz and who lack the oracular foresight of a DeLillo, the mimetic deployment of pop-culture icons seems at best an annoying tic and at worst a dangerous vapidity that compromises fiction's seriousness by dating it out of the Platonic Always where it ought to reside. In one of the graduate workshops I went through, a certain gray eminence kept trying to convince us that a literary story or novel should always eschew "any feature which serves to date it"[13] because "serious fiction must be Timeless." When we protested that, in his own well-known work, characters moved about electrically lit rooms, drove cars, spoke not Anglo-Saxon but postwar English, and inhabited a North America already separated from Africa by continental drift, he impatiently amended his proscription to those explicit references that would date a story in the "frivolous Now." When pressed for just what stuff evoked this F.N., he said of course he meant the "trendy mass-popular-media" reference. And here, at just this point, transgenerational discourse broke down. We looked at him blankly. We scratched our little heads. We didn't get it. This guy and his students simply did not conceive the "serious" world the same way. His automobiled Timeless and our MTV'd own were different.

If you read the big literary supplements, you've doubtless seen the intergenerational squabble this sort of scene typifies.[14] The plain fact is that certain things having to do with fiction production are different for young

---

13 This professor was the sort of guy who used "which" when the appropriate relative pronoun was the less fancy "that," to give you an idea.

14 If you want to see a typical salvo in this generation war, look at William Gass's "A Failing Grade for the Present Tense" in the 10/11/87 *New York Times Book Review*.

U.S. writers now. And television is at the vortex of most of the flux. Because younger writers are not only Artists probing for the nobler interstices in what Stanley Cavell calls the reader's "willingness to be pleased"; we are also, now, self-defined parts of the great U.S. Audience, and have our own aesthetic pleasure-centers; and television has formed and trained us. It won't do, then, for the literary establishment simply to complain that, for instance, young-written characters don't have very interesting dialogues with each other, that young writers' ears seem "tinny." Tinny they may be, but the truth is that, in younger Americans' experience, people in the same room don't do all that much direct conversing with each other. What most of the people I know do is they all sit and face the same direction and stare at the same thing and then structure commercial-length conversations around the sorts of questions that myopic car-crash witnesses might ask each other — "Did you just see what I just saw?" Plus, if we're going to talk about the virtues of "realism," the paucity of profound conversation in younger fiction seems accurately to reflect more than just our own generation — I mean six hours a day, in average households young and old, just how much conversation can really be going on? So now whose literary aesthetic seems "dated"?

In terms of literary history, it's important to recognize the distinction between pop and televisual references, on the one hand, and the mere use of TV-like techniques, on the other. The latter have been around in fiction forever. The Voltaire of *Candide,* for instance, uses a bisensuous irony that would do Ed Rabel proud, having Candide and Pangloss run around smiling and saying "All for the best, the best of all worlds" amid war-dead, pogroms, rampant nastiness, etc. Even the stream-of-consciousness guys who fathered Modernism were, on a very high level, constructing the same sorts of illusions about privacy-puncturing and espial on the forbidden that television has found so effective. And let's not even talk about Balzac.

It was in post-atomic America that pop influences on literature became something more than technical. About the time television first gasped and sucked air, mass popular U.S. culture seemed to become High-Art-viable as a collection of symbols and myth. The episcopate of this pop-reference movement were the post-Nabokovian Black Humorists, the Metafictionists and assorted franc-and latinophiles only later comprised by "postmodern." The erudite, sardonic fictions of the Black Humorists introduced a generation of new fiction writers who saw themselves as sort of avant-avant-garde, not only cosmopolitan and polyglot but also technologically literate, products of more than just one region, heritage, and theory, and citizens of a culture that said its most important stuff about itself via mass media. In this regard one thinks particularly of the Gaddis of *The Recognitions* and *JR*, the Barth of *The End of the Road* and *The Sot-Weed Factor*, and the Pynchon of *The Crying of Lot 49*. But the movement toward treating of the pop as its own reservoir of mythopoeia gathered momentum and quickly transcended both school and genre. Plucking from my shelves almost at random, I find poet James Cummins's 1986 *The Whole Truth*, a cycle of sestinas deconstructing Perry Mason. Here's Robert Coover's 1977 *A Public Burning*, in which Eisenhower buggers Nixon on-air, and his 1968 *A Political Fable*, in which the Cat in the Hat runs for president. I find Max Apple's 1986 *The Propheteers*, a novel-length imagining of Walt Disney's travails. Or here's part of poet Bill Knott's 1974 "And Other Travels":

> ...in my hand a cat o nine tails on every tip of which was Clearasil
> I was worried because Dick Clark had told the cameraman
> not to put the camera on me during the dance parts of the show
> because my skirts were too tight[15]

which serves as a great example because, even though this stanza appears in the poem without anything you'd normally call context or support, it is in fact *self*-supported by a reference we all, each of us, immediately get, conjuring as it does with *Bandstand* ritualized vanity, teenage insecurity, the management of spontaneous moments. It is the perfect pop image, at once slight and universal, soothing and discomfiting.

Recall that the phenomena of watching and consciousness of watching are by nature expansive. What distinguishes another, later wave of postmodern literature is a further shift from television-images as valid objects of literary allusion to television and metawatching as themselves valid *subjects*. By this I mean certain literature beginning to locate its raison in its commentary on/ response to a U.S. culture more and more of and for watching, illusion, and the video image. This involution of attention was first observable in academic poetry. See for instance Stephen Dobyns's 1980 "Arrested Saturday Night":

> This is how it happened: Peg and Bob had invited
> Jack and Roxanne over to their house to watch
> the TV, and on the big screen they saw Peg and Bob,
> Jack and Roxanne watching themselves watch
> themselves on progressively smaller TVs...[16]

---

15 In Bill Knott's *Love Poems to Myself, Book One*, Barn Dream Press, 1974.
16 In Stephen Dobyns's *Heat Death*, McLelland and Stewart, 1980.

or Knott's 1983 "Crash Course":

> I strap a TV monitor on my chest
> so that all who approach can see themselves
> and respond appropriately.[17]

The true prophet of this shift in U.S. fiction, though, was the aforementioned Don DeLillo, a long-underrated conceptual novelist who has made signal and image his unifying topoi the same way Barth and Pynchon had sculpted in paralysis and paranoia a decade earlier. DeLillo's 1985 *White Noise* sounded, to fledgling fictionists, a kind of televisual clarion-call. Scenelets like the following seemed especially important:

> Several days later Murray asked me about a tourist attraction known as the most photographed barn in America. We drove twenty-two miles into the country around Farmington. There were meadows and apple orchards. White fences trailed through the rolling fields. Soon the signs started appearing. THE MOST PHOTOGRAPHED BARN IN AMERICA. We counted five signs before we reached the site.... We walked along a cowpath to the slightly elevated spot set aside for viewing and photographing. All the people had cameras; some had tripods, telephoto lenses, filter kits. A man in a booth sold postcards and slides— pictures of the barn taken from the elevated spot. We stood near a grove of trees and watched the photographers. Murray maintained a prolonged silence, occasionally scrawling some notes in a little book.
>
> "No one sees the barn," he said finally.
>
> A long silence followed.
>
> "Once you've seen the signs about the barn, it becomes impossible to see the barn."
>
> He fell silent once more. People with cameras left the elevated site, replaced at once by others.
>
> "We're not here to capture an image. We're here to maintain one. Can you feel it, Jack? An accumulation of nameless energies."
>
> There was an extended silence. The man in the booth sold postcards and slides.
>
> "Being here is a kind of spiritual surrender. We see only what the others see. The thousands who were here in the past, those who will come in the future. We've agreed to be part of a collective perception.

---

17 In Bill Knott's *Becos*, Vintage, 1983.

This literally colors our vision. A religious experience in a way, like all tourism."

Another silence ensued.

"They are taking pictures of taking pictures," he said.[18]

I quote this at such length not only because it's too good to edit but also to draw your attention to two relevant features. One is the Dobyns-esque message here about the metastasis of watching. For not only are people watching a barn whose only claim to fame is being an object of watching, but the pop-culture scholar Murray is watching people watch a barn, and his friend Jack is watching Murray watch the watching, and we readers are pretty obviously watching Jack the narrator watch Murray watching, etc. If you leave out the reader, there's a similar regress of recordings of barn and barn-watching.

But more important are the complicated ironies at work in the scene. The scene itself is obviously absurd and absurdist. But most of the writing's parodic force is directed at Murray, the would-be transcender of spectation. Murray, by watching and analyzing, would try to figure out the how and whys of giving in to collective visions of mass images that have themselves become mass images only because they've been made the objects of collective vision. The narrator's "extended silence" in response to Murray's blather speaks volumes. But it's not to be taken as implying sympathy with the sheeplike photograph-hungry crowd. These poor Joe Briefcases are no less objects of ridicule for the fact that their "scientific" critic is himself being ridiculed. The narrative tone throughout is a kind of deadpan sneer, irony's special straight face, w/ Jack himself mute during Murray's dialogue — since to speak out loud in the scene would render the narrator a part of the farce (instead of a detached, transcendent "observer and recorder") and so himself vulnerable to ridicule. With his silence, DeLillo's alter ego Jack eloquently diagnoses the very disease from which he, Murray, barn-watchers, and readers all suffer.

i do have a thesis

I want to persuade you that irony, poker-faced silence, and fear of ridicule are distinctive of those features of contemporary U.S. culture (of which cutting-edge fiction is a part) that enjoy any significant relation to the

---

18 *White Noise*, pp. 12–13.

television whose weird pretty hand has my generation by the throat. I'm going to argue that irony and ridicule are entertaining and effective, and that at the same time they are agents of a great despair and stasis in U.S. culture, and that for aspiring fiction writers they pose especially terrible problems.

My two big premises are that, on the one hand, a certain subgenre of pop-conscious postmodern fiction, written mostly by young Americans, has lately arisen and made a real attempt to transfigure a world of and for appearance, mass appeal, and television; and that, on the other hand, tele-visual culture has somehow evolved to a point where it seems invulnerable to any such transfiguring assault. Television, in other words, has become able to capture and neutralize any attempt to change or even protest the attitudes of passive unease and cynicism that television requires of Audi-ence in order to be commercially and psychologically viable at doses of several hours per day.

image-fiction

The particular fictional subgenre I have in mind has been called by some editors post-postmodernism and by some critics Hyperrealism. Some of the younger readers and writers I know call it Image-Fiction. Image-Fiction is basically a further involution of the relations between lit and pop that blossomed with the '60s' postmodernists. If the postmodern church fathers found pop images valid *referents* and *symbols* in fiction, and if in the '70s and early '80s this appeal to the features of mass culture shifted from use to mention—i.e. certain avant-gardists starting to treat of pop and TV-watching as themselves fertile *subjects*—the new Fiction of Image uses the transient received myths of popular culture as a *world* in which to imagine fictions about "real," albeit pop-mediated, characters. Early uses of Imagist tactics can be seen in the DeLillo of *Great Jones Street,* the Coover of *Burning,* and in Max Apple, whose '70s short story "The Oranging of America" projects an interior life onto the figure of Howard Johnson.

But in the late '80s, despite publisher unease over the legalities of imag-ining private lives for public figures, a real bumper crop of this behind-the-glass stuff started appearing, authored largely by writers who didn't know or cross-fertilize one another. Apple's *Propheteers,* Jay Cantor's *Krazy Kat,* Coover's *A Night at the Movies, or You Must Remember This,* William T. Vollmann's *You Bright and Risen Angels,* Stephen Dixon's *Movies:*

Seventeen Stories, and DeLillo's own fictional hologram of Oswald in *Libra* are all notable post-'85 instances. (Observe too that, in another '80s medium, the arty *Zelig, Purple Rose of Cairo,* and *sex, lies, and videotape,* plus the low-budget *Scanners* and *Videodrome* and *Shockers,* all began to treat of mass-entertainment screens as permeable.)

It's in the last year that the Image-Fiction scene has really taken off. A. M. Homes's 1990 *The Safety of Objects* features a stormy love affair between a boy and a Barbie doll. Vollmann's 1989 *The Rainbow Stories* has Sonys as characters in Heideggerian parables. Michael Martone's 1990 *Fort Wayne Is Seventh on Hitler's List* is a tight cycle of stories about the Midwest's pop-culture giants—James Dean, Colonel Sanders, Dillinger—the whole project of which, spelled out in a preface about Image-Fiction's legal woes, involves "questioning the border between fact and fiction when in the presence of fame."[19] And Mark Leyner's 1990 campus smash *My Cousin, My Gastroenterologist,* less a novel than what the book's jacket copy describes as "a fiction analogue of the best drug you ever took," features everything from meditations on the color of Carefree Panty Shield wrappers to "Big Squirrel, the TV kiddie-show host and kung fu mercenary" to NFL instant replays in an "X-ray vision which shows leaping skeletons in a bluish void surrounded by 75,000 roaring skulls."[20]

One thing I have to insist you realize about this new subgenre is that it's distinguishable not just by a certain neo-postmodern technique but by a genuine socio-artistic agenda. The Fiction of Image is not just a use or mention of televisual culture but an actual *response* to it, an effort to impose some sort of accountability on a state of affairs in which more Americans get their news from television than from newspapers and in which more Americans every evening watch *Wheel of Fortune* than all three network news programs combined.

And please see that Image-Fiction, far from being a trendy avant-garde novelty, is almost atavistic. It is a natural adaptation of the hoary techniques of literary Realism to a '90s world whose defining boundaries have been deformed by electric signal. For one of realistic fiction's big jobs used to be to afford easements across borders, to help readers leap over the walls of self and locale and show us unseen or -dreamed-of people and cultures and ways to be. Realism made the strange familiar. Today, when we can eat Tex-Mex with chopsticks while listening to reggae and watching a Soviet-satellite newscast of the Berlin Wall's fall—i.e., when damn near

---

19 Martone, *Fort Wayne Is Seventh on Hitler's List,* Indiana U. Press, 1990, p. ix.
20 Leyner, *My Cousin, My Gastroenterologist,* Harmony/Crown, 1990, p. 82.

everything presents itself as familiar—it's not a surprise that some of today's most ambitious Realist fiction is going about trying to *make the familiar strange*. In so doing, in demanding fictional access behind lenses and screens and headlines and reimagining what human life might truly be like over there across the chasms of illusion, mediation, demographics, marketing, imago, and appearance, Image-Fiction is paradoxically trying to restore what's taken for "real" to three whole dimensions, to reconstruct a univocally round world out of disparate streams of flat sights.

That's the good news.

The bad news is that, almost without exception, Image-Fiction doesn't satisfy its own agenda. Instead, it most often degenerates into a kind of jeering, surfacey look "behind the scenes" of the very televisual front people already jeer at, a front they can already get behind the scenes of via *Entertainment Tonight* and *Remote Control*.

The reason why today's Image-Fiction isn't the rescue from a passive, addictive TV-psychology that it tries so hard to be is that most Image-Fiction writers render their material with the same tone of irony and self-consciousness that their ancestors, the literary insurgents of Beat and postmodernism, used so effectively to rebel against their own world and context. And the reason why this irreverent postmodern approach fails to help the new Imagists transfigure TV is simply that TV has beaten the new Imagists to the punch. The fact is that for at least ten years now, television has been ingeniously absorbing, homogenizing, and re-presenting the very same cynical postmodern aesthetic that was once the best alternative to the appeal of Low, over-easy, mass-marketed narrative. How TV's done this is blackly fascinating to see.

A quick intermission contra paranoia. By saying that Image-Fiction aims to "rescue" us from TV, I again am not suggesting that television has diabolic designs, or wants souls, or brainwashes people. I'm just referring again to the kind of natural Audience-conditioning consequent to high daily doses, a conditioning so subtle it can be observed best obliquely, through examples. And so if a term like "conditioning" still seems hyperbolic or hysterical to you, I'll ask you to consider for a moment the exemplary issue of prettiness. One of the things that make the people on television fit to stand the Megagaze is that they are, by ordinary human standards, extremely pretty. I suspect that this, like most television conventions, is set up with no motive more sinister than to appeal to the largest possible Audience—pretty people tend to be more appealing to look at than non-pretty people. But when we're talking about television, the combination of sheer Audience size and quiet psychic intercourse between images and oglers starts a cycle that both enhances pretty people's appeal and erodes us viewers' own security in the face of gazes. Because of the way human beings relate to narrative, we tend to identify with those characters we find appealing. We try to see ourselves in them. The same I.D.-relation, however, also means that we try to see them in ourselves. When everybody we seek to identify with for six hours a day is pretty, it naturally becomes more important to us to be pretty, to be viewed as pretty. Because prettiness becomes a priority for us, the pretty people on TV become all the more attractive, a cycle which is obviously great for TV. But it's less great for us civilians, who tend to own mirrors, and who also tend not to be anywhere near as pretty as the TV-images we want to identify with. Not only does this cause some angst personally, but the angst increases because, nationally, everybody else is absorbing six-hour doses and identifying with pretty people and valuing prettiness more, too. This very personal anxiety about our prettiness has become a national phenomenon with national consequences. The whole U.S.A. gets different about things it values and fears. The boom in diet aids, health and fitness clubs, neighborhood tanning parlors, cosmetic surgery, anorexia, bulimia, steroid-use among boys, girls throwing acid at each other because one girl's hair looks more like Farrah Fawcett's than another...are these supposed to be unrelated to each other? to the apotheosis of prettiness in a televisual culture?

It's not paranoid or hysterical to acknowledge that television in enormous doses affects people's values and self-perception in deep ways. Nor that televisual conditioning influences the whole psychology of one's relation to himself, his mirror, his loved ones, and a world of real people and real gazes. No one's going to claim that a culture all about watching and appearing is fatally compromised by unreal standards of beauty and fitness. But other facets of TV-training reveal themselves as more rapacious, more serious, than any irreverent fiction writer would want to take seriously.

irony's aura

It's widely recognized that television, with its horn-rimmed battery of statisticians and pollsters, is awfully good at discerning patterns in the flux of popular ideologies, absorbing those patterns, processing them, and then re-presenting them as persuasions to watch and to buy. Commercials targeted at the '80s' upscale Boomers, for example, are notorious for using processed versions of tunes from the rock culture of the '60s and '70s both to elicit the yearning that accompanies nostalgia and to yoke purchase of products with what for yuppies is a lost era of genuine conviction. Ford sport-vans are advertised with "This is the dawning of the age of the Aerostar"; Ford recently litigates with Bette Midler over the theft of her old vocals on "Do You Wanna Dance"; the CA Raisin Board's claymation raisins dance to "Heard It Through the Grapevine"; etc. If the cynical re-use of songs and the ideals they used to symbolize seems distasteful, it's not like pop musicians are paragons of noncommercialism themselves, and anyway nobody ever said selling was pretty. The effects of any one instance of TV absorbing and pablumizing cultural tokens seem innocuous enough. The recycling of whole cultural trends, and the ideologies that inform them, is a different story.

U.S. pop culture is just like U.S. serious culture in that its central tension has always set the nobility of individualism against the warmth of communal belonging. For its first twenty or so years, it seemed as though television sought to appeal mostly to the Group-Belonging side of the equation. Communities and bonding were extolled on early TV, even though TV itself, and especially its advertising, has from the outset projected itself at the lone viewer, Joe Briefcase, alone. (Television commercials always make their appeals to individuals, not groups, a fact that seems curious in light of the unprecedented size of TV's Audience, until one hears gifted salesmen explain how people are always most vulnerable, hence frightened, hence persuadable, when they are approached solo.)

Classic television commercials were all about the Group. They took the vulnerability of Joe Briefcase—sitting there, watching his furniture, lonely—and capitalized on it by linking purchase of a given product with Joe B.'s inclusion in some attractive community. This is why those of us over 21 can remember all those interchangeable old commercials featuring groups of pretty people in some ecstatic context, all having just way more fun than anybody has a license to have, and all united as Happy Group by the conspicuous fact that they're holding a certain bottle of pop or brand of snack—the blatant appeal here is that the relevant product can help Joe Briefcase belong:..."We're the Pepsi Generation...."

But since at least the '80s, the Individualist side of the great U.S. conversation has held sway in TV advertising. I'm not sure just why or how this happened. There are probably great connections to be traced—with Vietnam, youth culture, Watergate and recession and the New Right's rise—but the point is that a lot of the most effective TV commercials now make their appeal to the lone viewer in a terribly different way. Products are now most often pitched as helping the viewer "express himself," assert his individuality, "stand out from the crowd." The first instance I ever saw was a perfume vividly billed in the early '80s as reacting specially with each woman's "unique body chemistry" and creating "her own individual scent," the ad depicting a cattle-line of languid models waiting cramped and expressionless to get their wrists squirted one at a time, each smelling her moist individual wrist with a kind of biochemical revelation, then moving off in what a back-pan reveals to be different directions from the squirter. (We can ignore the obvious sexual connotations, squirting and all that; some tactics are changeless.) Or think of that recent series of over-dreary black-and-white Cherry 7-Up ads where the only characters who get to have color and stand out from their surroundings are the pink people who become pink at the exact moment they imbibe good old Cherry 7-Up. Examples of stand-apart ads are pretty much ubiquitous now.

Except for being sillier (e.g. products billed as distinguishing individuals from crowds sell to huge crowds of individuals), these ads aren't really any more complicated or subtle than the old Join-the-Fulfilling-Group ads that now seem so quaint. But the new Stand-Out-From-the-Pack ads' relation to their mass of lone viewers is both complex and ingenious. Today's best ads are still about the Group, but they now present the Group as something fearsome, something that can swallow you up, erase you, keep you from "being noticed." But noticed by whom? Crowds are still vitally important in the stand-apart ads' thesis on identity, but now a given ad's crowd, far from being more appealing, secure, and alive than the individual, functions as a mass of identical featureless eyes. The crowd is now, paradoxically, both (1) the "herd" in contrast to which the viewer's distinctive identity is to be defined and (2) the witnesses whose sight alone can confer distinctive identity. The lone viewer's isolation in front of his furniture is implicitly applauded—it's better, realer, these solipsistic ads imply, to fly solo—and yet it's also implicated as threatening, confusing, since after all Joe Briefcase is not an idiot, sitting here, and knows himself as a viewer to be guilty of the two big sins the ads decry: being a passive watcher (of TV) and being part of a great herd (of TV-watchers and Stand-Apart-product-buyers). How odd.

The surface of Stand-Out ads still presents a relatively unalloyed Buy This Thing, but the deep message of television w/r/t these ads looks to be that Joe Briefcase's ontological status as just one in a reactive watching mass is at some basic level shaky, contingent, and that true actualization of self would ultimately consist in Joe's becoming one of the images that are the *objects* of this great herd-like watching. That is, television's real pitch in these commercials is that it's better to be inside the TV than to be outside, watching.

The lonely grandeur of Stand-Apart advertising not only sells companies' products, then. It manages brilliantly to ensure—even in commercials that television gets paid to run—that ultimately it's TV, and not any specific product or service, that will be regarded by Joe B. as the ultimate arbiter of human worth. An oracle, to be consulted *a lot*. Advertising scholar Mark C. Miller puts it succinctly: "TV has gone beyond the explicit celebration of commodities to the implicit reinforcement of that spectatorial posture which TV requires of us."[21] Solipsistic ads are another way television ends up pointing at itself, keeping the viewer's relation to his furniture at once alienated and anaclitic.

Maybe, though, the relation of contemporary viewer to contemporary television is less a paradigm of infantilism and addiction than it is of the U.S.A.'s familiar relation to all the technology we equate at once with freedom and power and slavery and chaos. For, as with television, whether we happen personally to love technology, hate it, fear it, or all three, we still look relentlessly to technology for solutions to the very problems technology seems to cause—see e.g. catalysis for smog, S.D.I. for nuclear missiles, transplants for assorted rot.

And as with tech, so the gestalt of television expands to absorb all problems associated with it. The pseudo-communities of prime-time soaps like *Knots Landing* and *thirtysomething* are viewer-soothing products of the very medium whose ambivalence about the Group helps erode people's sense of connection. The staccato editing, sound bites, and summary treatment of knotty issues is network news' accommodation of an Audience whose attention span and appetite for complexity have naturally withered a bit after years of high-dose spectation. Etc.

But TV has technology-bred problems of its own. The advent of consumer cable, often with packages of over 40 channels, threatens networks and local affiliates alike. This is particularly true when the viewer is armed with a remote-control gizmo: Joe B. is still getting his six total hours of daily TV, but the amount of his retinal time devoted to any one option shrinks as he remote-scans a much wider band. Worse, the VCR, with its dreaded fast-forward and zap functions, threatens the very viability of commercials. Television advertisers' entirely sensible solution? Make the ads as appealing as the programs. Or at any rate try to keep Joe B. from disliking the commercials enough that he's willing to move his thumb to

---

21 Mark Crispin Miller, "Deride and Conquer," in Gitlin's anthology, p. 193.

check out 2½ minutes of *Hazel* on the Superstation while NBC sells lip balm. Make the ads prettier, livelier, full of enough rapidly juxtaposed visual quanta so that Joe's attention just doesn't get to wander, even if he remote-kills the volume. As one ad executive underputs it, "Commercials are becoming more like entertaining films."[22]

There's an obverse way, of course, to make commercials resemble programs. Have programs start to resemble commercials. That way the ads seem less like interruptions than like pace-setters, metronomes, commentaries on the shows' theory. Invent a *Miami Vice,* where there's little annoying plot to interrupt but an unprecedented emphasis on appearances, visuals, attitude, a certain "look."[23] Make music videos with the same amphetaminic pace and dreamy archetypal associations as ads — it doesn't hurt that videos are basically long music-commercials anyway. Or introduce the sponsor-supplied Infomercial that poses, in a lighthearted way, as a soft-news show, like *Amazing Discoveries* or those Robert Vaughn–hosted Hair-Loss Reports that haunt TV's wee cheap hours. Blur — just as postmodern lit did — the lines between genres, agendas, commercial art and arty commercials.

Still, television and its sponsors had a bigger long-term worry, and that was their shaky détente with the individual viewer's psyche. Given that television must revolve off basic antinomies about being and watching, about escape from daily life, the averagely intelligent viewer can't be all that happy about his daily life of high-dose watching. Joe Briefcase might have been happy enough *when* watching, but it was hard to think he could be too terribly happy *about* watching so much. Surely, deep down, Joe was uncomfortable with being one part of the biggest crowd in human history watching images that suggest that life's meaning consists in standing visibly apart from the crowd. TV's guilt/indulgence/reassurance cycle addresses these concerns on one level. But might there not be some deeper way to keep Joe Briefcase firmly in the crowd of watchers, by somehow associating his very viewership with transcendence of watching crowds? But that would be absurd. Enter irony.

I've claimed — so far sort of vaguely — that what makes television's hegemony so resistant to critique by the new Fiction of Image is that TV has coopted the distinctive forms of the same cynical, irreverent, ironic, absurdist post-WWII literature that the new Imagists use as touchstones.

---

22 At Foote, Cone and Belding, quoted by Miller — so the guy said it in the mid-'80s.

23 A similar point is made about *Miami Vice* in "We Build Excitement," Todd Gitlin's own essay in his anthology.

The fact is that TV's re-use of postmodern cool has actually evolved as an inspired solution to the keep-Joe-at-once-alienated-from-and-part-of-the-million-eyed-crowd problem. The solution entailed a gradual shift from oversincerity to a kind of bad-boy irreverence in the Big Face that TV shows us. This in turn reflected a wider shift in U.S. perceptions of how art was supposed to work, a transition from art's being a creative instantiation of real values to art's being a creative rejection of bogus values. And this wider shift, in its turn, paralleled both the development of the postmodern aesthetic and some deep and serious changes in how Americans chose to view concepts like authority, sincerity, and passion in terms of our willingness to be pleased. Not only are sincerity and passion now "out," TV-wise, but the very idea of pleasure has been undercut. As Mark C. Miller puts it, contemporary television "no longer solicits our rapt absorption or hearty agreement, but—like the ads that subsidize it—actually flatters us for the very boredom and distrust it inspires in us."[24]

Miller's 1986 "Deride and Conquer," far and away the best essay ever published about network advertising, details vividly an example of how TV's contemporary kind of appeal to the lone viewer works. It concerns a 1985–86 ad that won Clio Awards and still occasionally runs. It's that Pepsi commercial where a special Pepsi sound-van pulls up to a packed sweltering beach and the impish young guy in the van activates a lavish PA system and opens up a Pepsi and pours it into a cup up next to the microphone. And the dense glittered sound of much carbonation goes out over the beach's heat-wrinkled air, and heads turn vanward as if pulled with strings as his gulp and refreshed-sounding spirants and gasps are broadcast. And the final shot reveals that the sound-van is also a concession truck, and the whole beach's pretty population has now collapsed to a clamoring mass around the truck, everybody hopping up and down and pleading to be served first, as the camera's view retreats to an overhead crowd-shot and the slogan is flatly intoned: "Pepsi: the Choice of a New Generation." Truly a stunning commercial. But need one point out—as Miller's essay does in some detail—that the final slogan is here tongue-in-cheek? There's about as much "choice" at work in this commercial as there was in Pavlov's bell-kennel. The use of the word "choice" here is a dark joke. In fact the whole 30-second spot is tongue-in-cheek, ironic, self-mocking. As Miller argues, it's not really *choice* that the commercial is selling Joe Briefcase on, "but the total negation of choices. Indeed, the product itself is finally incidental to the pitch. The ad does not so much

---

24 Miller in Gitlin, p. 194.

extol Pepsi per se as recommend it by implying that a lot of people have been fooled into buying it. In other words, the point of this successful bit of advertising is that Pepsi has been advertised successfully."[25]

There are important things to realize here. First, this Pepsi ad is deeply informed by a fear of remote gizmos, zapping, and viewer disdain. An ad about ads, it uses self-reference to seem too hip to hate. It protects itself from the scorn today's TV-cognoscente feels for both the fast-talking hard-sell ads Dan Aykroyd parodied into oblivion on *Saturday Night Live* and the quixotic associative ads that linked soda-drinking with romance, prettiness, and Group-inclusion, ads that today's hip viewer finds old-fashioned and "manipulative." In contrast to a blatant Buy This Thing, the Pepsi commercial pitches parody. The ad is utterly up-front about what TV ads are popularly despised for doing, viz. using primal, flim-flam appeals to sell sugary crud to people whose identity is nothing but mass consumption. This ad manages simultaneously to make fun of itself, Pepsi, advertising, advertisers, and the great U.S. watching consuming crowd. In fact the ad is unctuous in its flattery of only one person: the lone viewer, Joe B., who even with an average brain can't help but discern the ironic contradiction between the "Choice" slogan (sound) and the Pavlovian orgy around the van (sight). The commercial invites Joe to "see through" the manipulation the beach's horde is rabidly buying. The commercial invites a complicity between its own witty irony and veteran viewer Joe's cynical, nobody's-fool appreciation of that irony. It invites Joe into an in-joke the Audience is the butt of. It congratulates Joe Briefcase, in other words, on transcending the very crowd that defines him. And entire crowds of Joe B.'s responded: the ad boosted Pepsi's market share through three sales quarters.

Pepsi's campaign is not unique. Isuzu Inc. hit pay dirt in the late '80s with its series of "Joe Isuzu" spots, featuring an oily, Satanic-looking salesman who told whoppers about Isuzu's genuine llama-skin upholstery and ability to run on tapwater. Though the ads never said much of anything about why Isuzus are in fact good cars, sales and awards accrued. The ads succeeded as parodies of how oily and Satanic car commercials are. They invited viewers to congratulate Isuzu's ads for being ironic, to congratulate themselves for getting the joke, and to congratulate Isuzu Inc. for being "fearless" and "irreverent" enough to acknowledge that car ads are ridiculous and that Audience is dumb to believe them. The ads invite the lone viewer to drive an Isuzu as some sort of anti-advertising statement. The ads

---

25 Ibid., p. 187.

successfully associate Isuzu-purchase with fearlessness and irreverence and the capacity to see through deception. You can now find successful television ads that mock TV-ad conventions almost anywhere you look, from Settlemeyer's Federal Express and Wendy's spots with their wizened, sped-up burlesques of commercial characters, to those hip Doritos splices of commercial spokesmen and campy old clips of *Beaver* and *Mr. Ed.*

Plus you can see this tactic of heaping scorn on pretentions to those old commercial virtues of authority and sincerity—thus (1) shielding the heaper of scorn from scorn and (2) congratulating the patron of scorn for rising above the mass of people who still fall for outmoded pretensions—employed to serious advantage on many of the television programs the commercials support. Show after show, for years now, has been either a self-acknowledged blank, visual, postmodern allusion- and attitude-fest, or, even more common, an uneven battle of wits between some ineffectual spokesman for hollow authority and his precocious children, mordant spouse, or sardonic colleagues. Compare television's treatment of earnest authority figures on pre-ironic shows—*The FBI*'s Erskine, *Star Trek*'s Kirk, *Beaver*'s Ward, *The Partridge Family*'s Shirley, *Hawaii Five-0*'s McGarrett—to TV's depiction of Al Bundy on *Married...with Children*, Mr. Owens on *Mr. Belvedere*, Homer on *The Simpsons*, Daniels and Hunter on *Hill Street Blues*, Jason Seaver on *Growing Pains*, Dr. Craig on *St. Elsewhere.*

The modern sitcom,[26] in particular, is almost wholly dependent for laughs and tone on the *M*A*S*H*-inspired savaging of some buffoonish spokesman for hypocritical, pre-hip values at the hands of bitingly witty insurgents. As Hawkeye savaged Frank and later Charles, so Herb is savaged by Jennifer and Carlson by J. Fever on *WKRP*, Mr. Keaton by Alex on *Family Ties*, boss by typing pool on *Nine to Five*, Seaver by whole family on *Pains*, Bundy by entire planet on *Married...w/* (the ultimate sitcom-parody of sitcoms). In fact, just about the only authority figures who retain any credibility on post-'80 shows (besides those like *Hill Street*'s Furillo and *Elsewhere*'s Westphal, who are beset by such relentless squalor and stress that simply hanging in there week after week renders them heroic) are those upholders of values who can communicate some irony about themselves, make fun of themselves before any merciless Group around them can move in for the kill—see Huxtable on *Cosby*, Belvedere

---

26 Miller's "Deride..." has a similar analysis of sitcoms, but Miller ends up arguing that the crux is some weird Freudio-patricidal element in how TV comedy views The Father.

on *Belvedere, Twin Peaks*'s Special Agent Cooper, Fox TV's Gary Shandling (the theme to whose show goes "This is the theme to Ga-ry's show"), and the ironic '80s' true Angel of Death, Mr. D. Letterman.

Its promulgation of cynicism about authority works to the general advantage of television on a number of levels. First, to the extent that TV can ridicule old-fashioned conventions right off the map, it can create an authority vacuum. And then guess what fills it. The real authority on a world we now view as constructed and not depicted becomes the medium that constructs our world-view. Second, to the extent that TV can refer exclusively to itself and debunk conventional standards as hollow, it is invulnerable to critics' charges that what's on is shallow or crass or bad, since any such judgments appeal to conventional, extra-televisual standards about depth, taste, quality. Too, the ironic tone of TV's self-reference means that no one can accuse TV of trying to put anything over on anybody. As essayist Lewis Hyde points out, self-mocking irony is always "Sincerity, with a motive."[27]

And, more to the original point, if television can invite Joe Briefcase into itself via in-gags and irony, it can ease that painful tension between Joe's need to transcend the crowd and his inescapable status as Audience-member. For to the extent that TV can flatter Joe about "seeing through" the pretentiousness and hypocrisy of outdated values, it can induce in him precisely the feeling of canny superiority it's taught him to crave, and can keep him dependent on the cynical TV-watching that alone affords this feeling.

And to the extent that it can train viewers to laugh at characters' unending put-downs of one another, to view ridicule as both the mode of social intercourse and the ultimate art-form, television can reinforce its own queer ontology of appearance: the most frightening prospect, for the well-conditioned viewer, becomes leaving oneself open to others' ridicule by betraying passé expressions of value, emotion, or vulnerability. Other people become judges; the crime is naïveté. The well-trained viewer becomes even more allergic to people. Lonelier. Joe B.'s exhaustive TV-training in how to worry about how he might come across, seem to watching eyes, makes genuine human encounters even scarier. But televisual irony has the solution: further viewing begins to seem almost like required research, lessons in the blank, bored, too-wise expression that Joe must learn how to wear for tomorrow's excruciating ride on the brightly lit

---

27 Lewis Hyde, "Alcohol and Poetry: John Berryman and the Booze Talking," *American Poetry Review*, reprinted in the *Pushcart Prize* anthology for 1987.

subway, where crowds of blank, bored-looking people have little to look at but each other.

What does TV's institutionalization of hip irony have to do with U.S. fiction? Well, for one thing, American literary fiction tends to be about U.S. culture and the people who inhabit it. Culture-wise, shall I spend much of your time pointing out the degree to which televisual values influence the contemporary mood of jaded weltschmerz, self-mocking materialism, blank indifference, and the delusion that cynicism and naïveté are mutually exclusive? Can we deny connections between an unprecedentedly powerful consensual medium that suggests no real difference between image and substance, on one hand, and stuff like the rise of Teflon presidencies, the establishment of nationwide tanning and liposuction industries, the popularity of "Vogueing" to a cynical synthesized command to "Strike a Pose"? Or, in contemporary art, that televisual disdain for "hypocritical" retrovalues like originality, depth, and integrity has no truck with those recombinant "appropriation" styles of art and architecture in which "past becomes pastiche," or with the repetitive solmizations of a Glass or a Reich, or with the self-conscious catatonia of a platoon of Raymond Carver wannabes?

In fact, the numb blank bored demeanor—what one friend calls the "girl-who's-dancing-with-you-but-would-obviously-rather-be-dancing-with-somebody-else" expression—that has become my generation's version of cool is all about TV. "Television," after all, literally means "seeing far"; and our six hours daily not only helps us feel up-close and personal at like the Pan-Am Games or Operation Desert Shield but also, inversely, trains us to relate to real live personal up-close stuff the same way we relate to the distant and exotic, as if separated from us by physics and glass, extant only as performance, awaiting our cool review. Indifference is actually just the '90s' version of frugality for U.S. young people: wooed several gorgeous hours a day for nothing but our attention, we regard that attention as our chief commodity, our social capital, and we are loath to fritter it. In the same regard, see that in 1990, flatness, numbness, and cynicism in one's demeanor are clear ways to transmit the televisual attitude of stand-out-transcendence—flatness and numbness transcend sentimentality, and cynicism announces that one knows the score, was last naïve about something at maybe like age four.

Whether or not 1990's youth culture seems as grim to you as it does to me, surely we can agree that the culture's TV-defined pop ethic has pulled a marvelous touché on the postmodern aesthetic that originally sought to co-opt and redeem the pop. Television has pulled the old dynamic of reference and redemption inside-out: it is now *television* that takes elements of the *postmodern*—the involution, the absurdity, the sardonic fatigue, the iconoclasm and rebellion—and bends them to the ends of spectation and consumption. This has been going on for a while. As early as '84, critics of capitalism were warning that "What began as a mood of the avant-garde has surged into mass culture."[28]

But postmodernism didn't just all of a sudden "surge" into television in 1984. Nor have the vectors of influence between the postmodern and the televisual been one-way. The chief connection between today's television and today's fiction is historical. The two share roots. For postmodern fiction—authored almost exclusively by young white overeducated males—clearly evolved as an intellectual expression of the "rebellious youth culture" of the '60s and '70s. And since the whole gestalt of youthful U.S. rebellion was made possible by a national medium that erased communicative boundaries between regions and replaced a society segmented by location and ethnicity with what rock music critics have called "a national self-consciousness stratified by generation,"[29] the phenomenon of TV had as much to do with postmodernism's rebellious irony as it did with Peaceniks' protest rallies.

In fact, by offering young, overeducated fiction writers a comprehensive view of how hypocritically the U.S.A. saw itself circa 1960, early television helped legitimize absurdism and irony as not just literary devices but sensible responses to a ridiculous world. For irony—exploiting gaps between what's said and what's meant, between how things try to appear and how they really are—is the time-honored way artists seek to illuminate and explode hypocrisy. And the television of lone-gunman westerns, paternalistic sitcoms, and jut-jawed law enforcement circa 1960 celebrated what by then was a deeply hypocritical American self-image. Miller describes nicely how the 1960s sitcom, like the westerns that preceded them,

> negated the increasing powerlessness of white-collar males with images of paternal strength and manly individualism. Yet by the time these sit-coms were produced, the world of small business [whose virtues were the Hugh Beaumontish ones of "self-possession, probity, and sound judgment"] had been...superseded by what

---

28 Fredric Jameson, "Postmodernism, or the Cultural Logic of Late Capitalism," *New Left Review* #146, Summer 1984, pp. 60–66.

29 Pat Auferhode, "The Look of the Sound," in good old Gitlin's anthology, p. 113.

C. Wright Mills called "the managerial demi-urge," and the virtues personified by... Dad were in fact passé.[30]

In other words, early U.S. TV was a hypocritical apologist for values whose reality had become attenuated in a period of corporate ascendancy, bureaucratic entrenchment, foreign adventurism, racial conflict, secret bombing, assassination, wiretaps, etc. It's not one bit accidental that post-modern fiction aimed its ironic crosshairs at the banal, the naïve, the sentimental and simplistic and conservative, for these qualities were just what '60s TV seemed to celebrate as distinctively American.

And the rebellious irony in the best postmodern fiction wasn't just credible as art; it seemed downright socially useful in its capacity for what counterculture critics called "a *critical negation* that would make it self-evident to everyone that the world is not as it seems."[31] Kesey's black parody of asylums suggested that our arbiters of sanity were often crazier than their patients; Pynchon reoriented our view of paranoia from deviant psychic fringe to central thread in the corporo-bureaucratic weave; DeLillo exposed image, signal, data and tech as agents of spiritual chaos and not social order. Burroughs's icky explorations of American narcosis exploded hypocrisy; Gaddis's exposure of abstract capital as deforming exploded hypocrisy; Coover's repulsive political farces exploded hypocrisy.

Irony in postwar art and culture started out the same way youthful rebellion did. It was difficult and painful, and productive—a grim diagnosis of a long-denied disease. The assumptions *behind* early postmodern irony, on the other hand, were still frankly idealistic: it was assumed that etiology and diagnosis pointed toward cure, that a revelation of imprisonment led to freedom.

So then how have irony, irreverence, and rebellion come to be not liberating but enfeebling in the culture today's avant-garde tries to write about? One clue's to be found in the fact that irony is *still around,* bigger than ever after 30 long years as the dominant mode of hip expression. It's not a rhetorical mode that wears well. As Hyde (whom I pretty obviously like) puts it, "Irony has only emergency use. Carried over time, it is the voice of the trapped who have come to enjoy their cage."[32] This is because irony, entertaining as it is, serves an almost exclusively negative function. It's critical and destructive, a ground-clearing. Surely this is the way our postmodern

---

30 Miller in Gitlin, p. 199.
31 Greil Marcus, *Mystery Train*, Dutton, 1976.
32 Hyde, op. cit.

fathers saw it. But irony's singularly unuseful when it comes to constructing anything to replace the hypocrisies it debunks. This is why Hyde seems right about persistent irony being tiresome. It is unmeaty. Even gifted ironists work best in sound bites. I find gifted ironists sort of wickedly fun to listen to at parties, but I always walk away feeling like I've had several radical surgical procedures. And as for actually driving cross-country with a gifted ironist, or sitting through a 300-page novel full of nothing but trendy sardonic exhaustion, one ends up feeling not only empty but somehow... oppressed.

Think, for a moment, of Third World rebels and coups. Third World rebels are great at exposing and overthrowing corrupt hypocritical regimes, but they seem noticeably less great at the mundane, non-negative task of then establishing a superior governing alternative. Victorious rebels, in fact, seem best at using their tough, cynical rebel-skills to avoid being rebelled against themselves—in other words, they just become better tyrants.

And make no mistake: irony tyrannizes us. The reason why our pervasive cultural irony is at once so powerful and so unsatisfying is that an ironist is *impossible to pin down*. All U.S. irony is based on an implicit "I don't really mean what I'm saying." So what *does* irony as a cultural norm mean to say? That it's impossible to mean what you say? That maybe it's too bad it's impossible, but wake up and smell the coffee already? Most likely, I think, today's irony ends up saying: "How totally *banal* of you to ask what I really mean." Anyone with the heretical gall to ask an ironist what he actually stands for ends up looking like an hysteric or a prig. And herein lies the oppressiveness of institutionalized irony, the too-successful rebel: the ability to interdict the *question* without attending to its *subject* is, when exercised, tyranny. It is the new junta, using the very tool that exposed its enemy to insulate itself.

This is why our educated teleholic friends' use of weary cynicism to try to seem superior to TV is so pathetic. And this is why the fiction-writing citizen of our televisual culture is in such very deep shit. What do you do when postmodern rebellion becomes a pop-cultural institution? For this of course is the second answer to why avant-garde irony and rebellion have become dilute and malign. They have been absorbed, emptied, and redeployed by the very televisual establishment they had originally set themselves athwart.

Not that television is culpable for any evil here. Just for immoderate success. This is, after all, what TV *does:* it discerns, decocts, and re-presents what it thinks U.S. culture wants to see and hear about itself. No one and everyone is at fault for the fact that television started gleaning rebellion and cynicism as the hip upscale Baby-Boomer *imago populi*. But the harvest has been dark: the forms of our best rebellious art have become mere gestures, schticks, not only sterile but perversely enslaving. How can even the idea of rebellion against corporate culture stay meaningful when Chrysler Inc. advertises trucks by invoking "The Dodge Rebellion"? How is one to be a bona fide iconoclast when Burger King sells onion rings with "Sometimes You Gotta Break the Rules"? How can an Image-Fiction writer hope to make people more critical of televisual culture by parodying television as a self-serving commercial enterprise when Pepsi and Subaru and FedEx parodies of self-serving commercials are already doing big business? It's almost a history lesson: I'm starting to see just why turn-of-the-last-century Americans' biggest fear was of anarchists and anarchy. For if anarchy actually *wins*, if rulelessness become the *rule*, then protest and change become not just impossible but incoherent. It'd be like casting a ballot for Stalin: you are voting for an end to all voting.

So here's the stumper for the U.S. writer who both breathes our cultural atmosphere and sees himself heir to whatever was neat and valuable in avant-garde literature: how to rebel against TV's aesthetic of rebellion, how to snap readers awake to the fact that our televisual culture has become a cynical, narcissistic, essentially empty phenomenon, when television regularly *celebrates* just these features in itself and its viewers? These are the very questions DeLillo's poor schmuck of a popologist was asking back in '85 about America, that most photographed of barns:

> "What was the barn like before it was photographed?" he said. "What did it look like, how was it different from other barns, how was it similar to other barns? We can't answer these questions because we've read the signs, seen the people snapping the pictures. We can't get outside the aura. We're part of the aura. We're here, we're now."
>
> He seemed immensely pleased by this.[33]

end of the end of the line

What responses to television's commercialization of the modes of literary protest seem possible, then, today? One obvious option is for the fiction writer to become reactionary, fundamentalist. Declare contemporary television evil and contemporary culture evil and turn one's back on the whole

---

33 *White Noise,* p. 13.

spandexed mess and invoke instead good old pre-1960s Hugh Beaumontish virtues and literal readings of the Testaments and be pro-Life, anti-Fluoride, antediluvian. The problem with this is that Americans who've opted for this tack seem to have one eyebrow straight across their forehead and knuckles that drag on the ground and really tall hair and in general just seem like an *excellent* crowd to want to transcend. Besides, the rise of Reagan/Bush/Gingrich showed that hypocritical nostalgia for a kinder, gentler, more Christian pseudo-past is no less susceptible to manipulation in the interests of corporate commercialism and PR image. Most of us will still take nihilism over neanderthalism.

Another option would be to adopt a somewhat more enlightened political conservatism that exempts viewer and networks alike from any complicity in the bitter stasis of televisual culture and which instead blames all TV-related problems on certain correctable defects in technology. Enter media futurologist George Gilder, a Hudson Institute senior fellow and author of *Life After Television: The Coming Transformation of Media and American Life*. The single most fascinating thing about *Life After Television* is that it's a book with *commercials*. Published in something called The Larger Agenda Series by one "Whittle Direct Books" in Federal Express Inc.'s Knoxville headquarters, the book sells for only $11.00 hard including postage, is big and thin enough to look great on executive coffee tables, and has very pretty full-page ads for Federal Express on every fifth page. The book's also largely a work of fiction, plus it's a heartrending dramatization of why anti-TV conservatives, motivated by simple convictions like "Television is at heart a totalitarian medium" whose "system is an alien and corrosive force in democratic capitalism," are going to be of little help with our ultraradical-TV problems, attached as conservative intellectuals are to their twin tired remedies for all U.S. ills, viz. the beliefs that (1) the discerning consumer-instincts of the Little Guy will correct all imbalances if only Big Systems will quit stifling his Freedom to Choose, and that (2) technology-bred problems can be resolved technologically.

Gilder's basic diagnosis runs thus. Television as we know and suffer it is "a technology with supreme powers but deadly flaws." The really fatal flaw is that the whole structure of television programming, broadcasting, and reception is still informed by the technological limitations of the old vacuum tubes that first enabled TV. The

> expense and complexity of these tubes used in television sets meant that most of the processing of signals would have to be done at the [networks],

a state of affairs which

> dictated that television would be a top-down system—in electronic terms, a "master-slave" architecture. A few broadcasting centers would originate programs for millions of passive receivers, or "dumb terminals."

By the time the transistor (which does essentially what vacuum tubes do but in less space at lower cost) found commercial applications, the top-down TV system was already entrenched and petrified, dooming viewers to docile reception of programs they were dependent on a very few networks to provide, and creating a "psychology of the masses" in which a trio of programming alternatives aimed to appeal to millions and millions of Joe B.'s. The TV signals are analog waves. Analogs are the required medium, since "With little storage or processing available at the set, the signals...would have to be directly displayable waves," and "analog waves directly simulate sound, brightness, and color." But analog waves can't be saved or edited by their recipient. They're too much like life: there in gorgeous toto one instant and then gone. What the poor TV viewer gets is only what he sees. This state of affairs has cultural consequences Gilder describes in apocalyptic detail. Even "High Definition Television" (HDTV), touted by the industry as the next big advance in entertainment, will, according to Gilder, be just the same vacuous emperor in a snazzier suit.

But for Gilder, TV, still clinging to the crowd-binding and hierarchical technologies of yesterdecade, is now doomed by the advances in microchip and fiber-optic technology of the last few years. The user-friendly microchip, which consolidates the activities of millions of transistors on one 49¢ wafer, and whose capacities will get even more attractive as controlled electron-conduction approaches the geodesic paradigm of efficiency, will allow receivers—TV sets—to do much of the image-processing that has hitherto been done "for" the viewer by the broadcaster. In another happy development, transporting images through glass fibers rather than via the EM spectrum will allow people's TV sets to be hooked up with each other in a kind of interactive net instead of all feeding passively at the transmitting teat of a single broadcaster. And fiber-optic transmissions have the further advantage that they conduct characters of information digitally. Since, as Gilder explains, "digital signals have an advantage over analog signals in that they can be stored and manipulated without deterioration" as well as being crisp and interferenceless as quality CDs, they'll allow the microchipped television receiver (and thus the viewer) to enjoy much of the discretion over selection, manipulation, and recombination of video images that is today restricted to the director's booth.

For Gilder, the new piece of furniture that will free Joe Briefcase from passive dependence on his furniture will be "the telecomputer, a personal computer adapted for video processing and connected by fiber-optic threads to other telecomputers around the world." The fibrous TC "will forever break the broadcast bottleneck" of television's One Over Many structure of image-dissemination. Now everybody'll get to be his own harried guy with earphones and clipboard. In the new millennium, U.S. television will finally become ideally, GOPishly democratic: egalitarian, interactive, and "profitable" without being "exploitative."

Boy does Gilder know his "Larger Agenda" audience. You can just see saliva overflowing lower lips in boardrooms as Gilder forecasts that the consumer's whole complicated fuzzy inconveniently transient world will become storable, manipulable, broadcastable, and viewable in the comfort of his own condo. "With artful programming of telecomputers, you could spend a day interacting on the screen with Henry Kissinger, Kim Basinger, or Billy Graham." Rather ghastly interactions to contemplate, perhaps, but then in Gilderland *each to his own:*

> Celebrities could produce and sell their own software. You could view the Super Bowl from any point in the stadium you choose, or soar above the basket with Michael Jordan. Visit your family on the other side of the world with moving pictures hardly distinguishable from real-life images. Give a birthday party for Grandma in her nursing home in Florida, bringing her descendents from all over the country to the foot of her bed in living color.

And not just warm 2-D images of family: *any* experience will be transferrable to image and marketable, manipulable, consumable. People will be able to

> go comfortably sight-seeing from their living room through high-resolution screens, visiting Third-World countries without having to worry about air fares or exchange rates…, you could fly an airplane over the Alps or climb Mount Everest—all on a powerful high-resolution display.

We will, in short, be able to engineer our own dreams.

So, in sum, a conservative tech writer offers a really attractive way of looking at viewer passivity, at TV's institutionalization of irony, narcissism, nihilism, stasis, loneliness. It's not our fault! It's outmoded technology's fault! If TV-dissemination were up to date, it would be impossible for it to "institutionalize" anything through its demonic "mass-psychology." Let's let Joe B., the little lonely average guy, be his own manipulator of video-bits. Once all experience is finally reduced to marketable image, once the receiving user of user-friendly receivers can break from the coffle and choose freely, Americanly, from an Americanly infinite variety of moving images *hardly distinguishable from real-life images,* and can then choose further just how he wishes to store, enhance, edit, recombine, and present those images to himself in the privacy of his very own home and skull, then TV's ironic, totalitarian grip on the American psychic cojones will be broken. !!!

Note that Gilder's semiconducted vision of a free, orderly video future is way more upbeat than postmodernism's old view of image and data. The novels of Pynchon and DeLillo revolve metaphorically off the concept of interference: the more connections, the more chaos, and the harder it is to cull any meaning from the seas of signal. Gilder would call their gloom outmoded, their metaphor infected with the deficiencies of the transistor:

> In all networks of wires and switches, except for those on the micro-chip, complexity tends to grow exponentially as the number of interconnections rises, [but] in the silicon maze of microchip technology...efficiency, not complexity, grows as the square of the number of interconnections to be organized.

Rather than a vacuous TV-culture drowning in cruddy images, Gilder foresees a TC-culture redeemed by a whole lot more to choose from and a whole lot more control over what you choose to...umm...see? pseudo-experience? dream?

It's wildly unrealistic to think that expanded choices alone will resolve our televisual bind. The advent of cable upped choices from 4 or 5 to 40+ synchronic alternatives, with little apparent loosening of television's grip on mass attitudes. It seems, rather, that Gilder sees the '90s' impending breakthrough as U.S. viewers' graduation from passive reception of fac-similes of experience to active manipulation of facsimiles of experience. It's worth questioning Gilder's definition of televisual "passivity." His new tech would indeed end "the passivity of mere reception." But the passivity of Audience, the acquiescence inherent in a whole culture of and about watching, looks unaffected by TCs.

The appeal of watching television has always involved fantasy. And contemporary TV has gotten vastly better at enabling the viewer's fantasy that he can transcend the limitations of individual human experience, that he can be inside the set, imago'd, "anyone, anywhere."[34] Since the limitations of being one human being involve certain restrictions on the number of different experiences possible to us in a given period of time, it's arguable that the biggest TV-tech "advances" of recent years have done little but abet this fantasy of escape from the defining limits of being human. Cable expanded our choices of evening realities; handheld gizmos let us leap instantly from one reality to another; VCRs let us commit experiences to an eidetic memory that permits re-experience at any time without loss or alteration. These advances sold briskly and upped average viewing-doses, but they sure haven't made U.S. televisual culture any less passive or cynical.

Of course, the downside of TV's big fantasy is that it's just a fantasy. As a Treat, my escape from the limits of genuine experience is neato. As a steady diet, though, it can't help but render my own reality less attractive (because in it I'm just one Dave, with limits and restrictions all over the place), render me less fit to make the most of it (because I spend all my time pretending I'm not in it), and render me ever more dependent on the device that affords escape from just what my escapism makes unpleasant.

It's tough to see how Gilder's soteriol vision of having more "control" over the arrangement of high-quality fantasy-bits is going to ease either the dependency that is part of my relation to TV or the impotent irony I must use to pretend I'm not dependent. Whether I'm "passive" or "active" as a viewer, I still must cynically pretend, because I'm still dependent, because my real dependency here is not on a single show or a few networks any more than the hophead's is on the Turkish florist or the Marseilles refiner. My real dependence is on the fantasies and the images that enable them, and thus on any technology that can make images both available and fantastic. Make no mistake: we *are* dependent on image-technology; and the better the tech, the harder we're hooked.

The paradox in Gilder's rosy forecast is the same as in all forms of artificial enhancement. The more enhancing the mediation—see for instance binoculars, amplifiers, graphic equalizers, or "moving pictures hardly distinguishable from real-life images"—the more direct, vivid, and real the experience *seems,* which is to say the more direct, vivid, and real the fantasy and dependence *are.* An exponential surge in the mass of televisual images, and a commensurate increase in my ability to cut, paste, magnify,

34 A term Gitlin uses in "We Build Excitement."

and combine them to suit my own fancy, can do nothing but render my interactive TC a more powerful enhancer and enabler of fantasy, my attraction to that fantasy stronger, the real experiences of which my TC offers more engaging and controllable simulacra paler and more frustrating to deal with, and me just a *whole* lot more dependent on my furniture. Jacking the number of choices and options up with better tech will remedy exactly nothing so long as no sources of insight on comparative worth, no guides to *why* and *how* to choose among experiences, fantasies, beliefs, and predilections, are permitted serious consideration in U.S. culture. Umm, insights and guides to value used to be among literature's jobs, didn't they? But then who's going to want to take such stuff seriously in ecstatic post-TV life, with Kim Basinger waiting to be interacted with?

Oh God, I've just reread my criticisms of Gilder. That he is naïve. That he is an ill-disguised apologist for corporate self-interest. That his book has commercials. That beneath its futuristic novelty it's just the same old American same-old that got us into this televisual mess. That Gilder vastly underestimates the intractability of the mess. Its hopelessness. Our gullibility, fatigue, disgust. My attitude, reading Gilder, has been sardonic, aloof, depressed. I have tried to make his book look ridiculous (which it is, but still). My reading of Gilder is televisual. I am in the aura.

Well, but at least good old Gilder is unironic. In this respect he's like a cool summer breeze compared to Mark Leyner, the young New Jersey medical-ad copywriter whose *My Cousin, My Gastroenterologist* is the biggest thing for campus hipsters since *The Fountainhead*. Leyner's novel exemplifies a third kind of literary response to our problem. For of course young U.S. writers can "resolve" the problem of being trapped in the televisual aura the same way French poststructuralists "resolve" their hopeless enmeshment in the logos. We can resolve the problem by celebrating it. Transcend feelings of mass-defined angst by genuflecting to them. We can be *reverently ironic.*

My Cousin, My Gastroenterologist is new not so much in kind as in degree. It is a methedrine compound of pop pastiche, offhand high tech, and dazzling televisual parody, formed with surreal juxtapositions and grammarless monologues and flash-cut editing, and framed with a relentless irony designed to make its frantic tone seem irreverent instead of repellent. You want sendups of commercial culture?

I had just been fired from McDonald's for refusing to wear a kilt during production launch week for their new McHaggis sandwich.

　　he picks up a copy of *das plumpe denken* new england's most disreputable german-language newsmagazine blast in egg cream factory kills philatelist he turns the page radioactive glow-in-the-dark semen found in canada he turns the page modern-day hottentots carry young in resealable sandwich bags he turns the page wayne newton calls mother's womb single-occupancy garden of eden morgan fairchild calls sally struthers loni anderson

what color is your mozzarella? i asked the waitress it's pink—it's the same color as the top of a mennen lady speed stick dispenser, y'know that color? no, maam I said it's the same color they use for the gillette daisy disposable razors for women...y'know that color? nope well, it's the same pink as pepto-bismol, y'know that color? oh yeah, I said, well do you have spaghetti?

You want mordant sendups of television?

Muriel got the *TV Guide,* flipped to Tuesday 8 P.M., and read aloud:...There's a show called "A Tumult of Pubic Hair and Bobbing Flaccid Penises as Sweaty Naked Chubby Men Run From the Sauna Screaming Snake! Snake!"...It also stars Brian Keith, Buddy Ebsen, Nipsey Russell, and Lesley Ann Warren

You like mocking self-reference? The novel's whole last chapter is a parody of its own "About the Author" page. Or maybe you're into hip identitylessness?

Grandma rolled up a magazine and hit Buzz on the side of the head....Buzz's mask was knocked loose. There was no skin beneath that mask. There were two white eyeballs protruding on stems from a mass of oozing blood-red musculature.

I can't tell if she's human or a fifth-generation gynemorphic android and I don't care

Parodic meditations on the boundaryless flux of televisual monoculture?

I'm stirring a pitcher of Tanqueray martinis with one hand and sliding a tray of frozen clams *oreganata* into the oven with my foot. God, these methedrine suppositories that Yogi Vithaldas gave me are good! As I iron a pair of tennis shorts I dictate a haiku into the tape recorder and then...do three minutes on the speedbag before making an origami praying mantis and then reading an article in *High Fidelity* magazine as I stir the coq au vin.

The decay of both the limits and the integrity of the single human self?

> There was a woman with the shrunken, wrinkled face of an eighty- or ninety-year-old. And this withered hag, this apparent octogenarian, had the body of a male Olympic swimmer. The long lean sinewy arms, the powerful V-shaped upper torso, without a single ounce of fat....
>
> to install your replacement head place the head assembly on neck housing and insert guide pins through mounting holes...if, after installing new head, you are unable to discern the contradictions in capitalist modes of production, you have either installed your head improperly or head is defective

In fact, one *of My Cousin, My Gastroenterologist*'s unifying obsessions is this latter juxtaposition of parts of selves, people and machines, human subjects and discrete objects. Leyner's fiction is, in this regard, an eloquent reply to Gilder's prediction that our TV-culture problems can be resolved by the dismantling of images into discrete chunks we can recombine however we wish. Leyner's world is a Gilderesque dystopia. The passivity and schizoid decay still endure for Leyner in his characters' reception of images and waves of data. The ability to *combine* them only adds a layer of disorientation: when all experience can be deconstructed and reconfigured, there become simply too many choices. And in the absence of any credible, noncommercial guides for living, the freedom to choose is about as "liberating" as a bad acid trip: each quantum is as good as the next, and the only standard of a particular construct's quality is its weirdness, incongruity, its ability to stand out from a crowd of other image-constructs and wow some Audience.

Leyner's own novel, in its amphetaminic eagerness to wow the reader, marks the far dark frontier of the Fiction of Image—literature's absorption of not just the icons, techniques, and phenomena of television, but of television's whole objective. *My Cousin, My Gastroenterologist*'s sole aim is, finally, to *wow*, to ensure that the reader is pleased and continues to read. The book does this by (1) flattering the reader with appeals to his erudite postmodern weltschmerz and (2) relentlessly reminding the reader that the author is smart and funny. The book itself is extremely funny, but it's not funny the way funny stories are funny. It's not that funny things happen here; it's that funny things are self-consciously imagined and pointed out, like a comedian's stock "You ever notice how...?" and "You ever wonder what would happen if...?"

Actually, Leyner's whole high-Imagist style most often resembles a kind of lapidary stand-up comedy:

> Suddenly Bob couldn't speak properly. He had suffered some form of spontaneous aphasia. But it wasn't total aphasia. He could speak, but only in a staccato telegraphic style. Here's how he described driving through the Midwest on Interstate 80: "Corn corn corn corn Stuckeys. Corn corn corn corn Stuckeys."
>
> there's a bar on the highway which caters almost exclusively to authority figures and the only drink it serves is lite beer and the only food it serves is surf and turf and the place is filled with cops and state troopers and gym teachers and green berets and toll attendants and game wardens and crossing guards and umpires

Leyner's fictional response to television is less a novel than a piece of witty, erudite, extremely high-quality prose television. Velocity and vividness replace development. People flicker in and out; events are garishly there and then gone and never referred to. There's a brashly irreverent rejection of "outmoded" concepts like integrated plot or enduring character. Instead there's a series of dazzlingly creative parodic vignettes, designed to appeal to the 45 seconds of near-Zen concentration we call the TV attention span. In the absence of a plot, unifying the vignettes are moods—antic anxiety, the overstimulated stasis of too many choices and no chooser's manual, irreverent brashness toward televisual reality. And, after the manner of films, music videos, dreams, and television programs, there are recurring "Key Images," here exotic drugs, exotic technologies, exotic foods, exotic bowel dysfunctions. And it is no accident that *My Cousin, My Gastroenterologist*'s central preoccupation is with digestion and elimination. Its mocking challenge to the reader is the same one presented by television's flood of realities and choices: ABSORB ME—PROVE YOU'RE CONSUMER ENOUGH.

Leyner's work, the best Image-Fiction yet, is both amazing and forgettable, wonderful and oddly hollow. I'm concluding by talking about it at length because, in its masterful reabsorption of the very features TV has itself absorbed from postmodern art, Leyner's book seems like the ultimate union of U.S. television and fiction. It seems also to cast the predicament of Image-Fiction itself into stark relief: the best stuff the subgenre's produced to date is hilarious, upsetting, sophisticated, and extremely shallow—doomed to shallowness by its desire to ridicule a TV-culture whose mockery of itself and all value already absorbs all ridicule. Leyner's attempt to "respond" to television via ironic genuflection is all too easily subsumed into the tired televisual ritual of mock-worship. It is dead on the page.

It's entirely possible that my plangent noises about the impossibility of rebelling against an aura that promotes and vitiates all rebellion say more about my residency inside that aura, my own lack of vision, than they do about any exhaustion of U.S. fiction's possibilities. The next real literary "rebels" in this country might well emerge as some weird bunch of anti-rebels, born oglers who dare somehow to back away from ironic watching, who have the childish gall actually to endorse and instantiate single-entendre principles. Who treat of plain old untrendy human troubles and emotions in U.S. life with reverence and conviction. Who eschew self-consciousness and hip fatigue. These anti-rebels would be outdated, of course, before they even started. Dead on the page. Too sincere. Clearly repressed. Backward, quaint, naïve, anachronistic. Maybe that'll be the point. Maybe that's why they'll be the next real rebels. Real rebels, as far as I can see, risk disapproval. The old postmodern insurgents risked the gasp and squeal: shock, disgust, outrage, censorship, accusations of socialism, anarchism, nihilism. Today's risks are different. The new rebels might be artists willing to risk the yawn, the rolled eyes, the cool smile, the nudged ribs, the parody of gifted ironists, the "Oh how *banal*." To risk accusations of sentimentality, melodrama. Of overcredulity. Of softness. Of willingness to be suckered by a world of lurkers and starers who fear gaze and ridicule above imprisonment without law. Who knows. Today's most engaged young fiction does seem like some kind of line's end's end. I guess that means we all get to draw our own conclusions. Have to. Are you immensely pleased.

1990

Afterword

It's tempting to read "E Unibus Pluram: Television and U.S. Fiction" through the filter of its moment; after all, the television culture Wallace critiques here no longer exists. Commercials, broadcast schedules, the primacy of the big screen...all have been transformed by the advent of the DVR, the computer, the tablet, the so-called smartphone. And yet, that's not really true, for the core of the essay remains—as it has since I first read it in 1993, in the *Review of Contemporary Fiction*—in the closing pages, which dissect George Gilder's digital glad-handing for the come-on that it is.

Gilder foresees a world in which networked televisions and computers "will forever break the broadcast bottleneck." For Wallace, this is sophistry at best, and at worst a kind of co-optation, in which the imagination itself is jeopardized. "Whether I'm 'passive' or 'active' as a viewer," he tells us, "I still must cynically pretend, because I'm still dependent....My real dependence is on the fantasies and the images that enable them, and thus on any technology that can make images both available and fantastic. Make no mistake: we *are* dependent on image-technology; and the better the tech, the harder we're hooked."

Make no mistake, indeed, for we now live in the world that Wallace, and not Gilder, envisioned, in which "image-technology," better and more ubiquitous screens, has transformed how we interact. It has become our water (to borrow a metaphor from Wallace's 2005 Kenyon College commencement address), interchangeably medium and message. Even our language is degraded: What do *friend* and *like* mean anymore?

I say this not as a Luddite; I'm as wrapped up in the image culture as anyone. But that only makes "E Unibus Pluram" all the more resonant. Wallace's long (and delightfully digressive) essay leads us to consider real emotion, real expression, not as some kind of game for saps but rather as the only thing that might redeem us, that might allow us to (re-)connect. "Irony," he writes, quoting Lewis Hyde, "has only emergency use. Carried over time, it is the voice of the trapped who have come to enjoy their cage."

This is an almost perfect evocation of the culture we've created, a culture "E Unibus Pluram" stands against. It is a cry in the dark, one that recognizes its futility and yet makes the effort all the same. ("It is entirely possible," Wallace writes, "that my plangent noises about the impossibility of rebelling against an aura that promotes and vitiates all rebellion say more about...my own lack of vision, than they do about any exhaustion of U.S. fiction's possibilities.") Where is the place for writers in this culture? Where is the place for the human heart? These are the questions Wallace is asking, and his earnest plea for, yes, a return to earnestness is both quixotic and the most essential sort of radical aesthetic stance.

—*David L. Ulin*

Getting Away from
Already Pretty Much Being
Away from It All

08/05/93/0800h. PRESS DAY IS a week or so before the Fair opens. I'm supposed to be at the grounds' Illinois Building by like 0900 to get Press Credentials. I imagine Credentials to be a small white card in the band of a fedora. I've never been considered Press before. My main interest in Credentials is getting into rides and stuff for free.

I'm fresh in from the East Coast to go to the Illinois State Fair for a swanky East-Coast magazine. Why exactly a swanky East-Coast magazine is interested in the Illinois State Fair remains unclear to me. I suspect that every so often editors at these magazines slap their foreheads and remember that about 90% of the United States lies between the Coasts and figure they'll engage somebody to do pith-helmeted anthropological reporting on something rural and heartlandish. I think they decided to engage me for this one because I actually grew up around here, just a couple hours' drive from downstate Springfield. I never did go to the State Fair, though, growing up—I pretty much topped out at the County Fair level.

In August it takes hours for the dawn fog to burn off. The air's like wet wool. 0800h. is too early to justify the car's AC. I'm on I-55 going S/SW. The sun's a blotch in a sky that isn't so much cloudy as opaque. The corn starts just past the breakdown lanes and goes right to the sky's hem. The August corn's as tall as a tall man. Illinois corn is now knee-high by about the 4th of May, what with all the advances in fertilizers and herbicides. Locusts chirr in every field, a brassy electric sound that Dopplers oddly in the speeding car. Corn, corn, soybeans, corn, exit ramp, corn, and every few miles an outpost way off on a reach in the distance—house, tree w/ tire-swing, barn, satellite dish. Grain silos are the only real skyline. The Interstate is dull and pale. The occasional other cars all look ghostly, their drivers' faces humidity-stunned. A fog hangs just over the fields like the land's mind or something. The temperature's over 80 and already climbing with the sun. It'll be 90+ by 1000h., you can tell: there's already that tightening quality to the air, like it's drawing itself in for a long siege.

Credentials 0900h., Welcome & Briefing 0915h., Press Tour on Special Tram 0945h.

I grew up in rural Illinois but haven't been back for a long time and can't say I've missed it—the yeasty heat, the lush desolation of limitless corn, the flatness.

But it's like bike-riding, in a way. The native body readjusts automatically to the flatness, and as your calibration gets finer, driving, you can start to notice that the dead-level flatness is only apparent. There are unevennesses, ups and downs, slight but rhythmic. Straight-shot I-55 will start, ever so slightly, to rise, maybe 5° over a mile, then go just as gentle back down, and then you see an overpass bridge ahead, over a river—the Salt Fork, the Sangamon. The rivers are swollen, but nothing like out around St. Louis. These gentle rises and then dips down to rivers are glacial moraines, edges of the old ice that shaved the Midwest level. The middling rivers have their origin in glacial runoff. The whole drive is a gentle sine wave like this, but it's like sea-legs: if you haven't spent years here you'll never feel it. To people from the Coasts, rural IL's topography's a nightmare, something to hunker down and speed through—the sky opaque, the dull crop-green constant, the land flat and dull and endless, a monotone for the eyes. For natives it's different. For me, at least, it got creepy. By the time I left for college the area no longer seemed dull so much as empty, lonely. Middle-of-the-ocean lonely. You can go weeks without seeing a neighbor. It gets to you.

08/05/0900h. But so it's still a week before the Fair, and there's something surreal about the emptiness of parking facilities so huge and complex that they have their own map. The parts of the Fairgrounds that I can see, pulling in, are half permanent structures and half tents and displays in various stages of erection, giving the whole thing the look of somebody half-dressed for a really important date.

08/05/0905h. The man processing Press Credentials is bland and pale and has a mustache and a short-sleeve knit shirt. In line before me are newshounds from *Today's Agriculture,* the *Decatur Herald & Review, Illinois Crafts Newsletter, 4-H News,* and *Livestock Weekly.* Press Credentials turn out to be just a laminated mugshot with a gator-clip for your pocket; not a fedora in the house. Two older ladies from a local horticulture organ behind me engage me in shoptalk. One of these ladies describes herself as the Unofficial Historian of the Illinois State Fair: she goes around giving slide shows on the Fair at nursing homes and Rotary lunches. She begins to emit historical data at a great rate — the Fair started in 1853; there was a Fair every year during the Civil War but not during WWII, plus no Fair in 1893 for some reason; the Governor has failed to cut the ribbon personally on Opening Day only twice; etc. It occurs to me I probably ought to have brought a notebook. I also notice I'm the only person in the room in a T-shirt. It's a fluorescent-lit cafeteria in something called the Illinois Building Senior Center, uncooled. All the local TV crews have their equipment spread out on tables and are lounging against walls talking about the apocalyptic 1993 floods to the immediate west, which floods are ongoing. They all have mustaches and short-sleeve knit shirts. In fact the only other males in the room without mustaches and golf-shirts are the local TV reporters, four of them, all in Eurocut suits. They are sleek, sweatless, deeply blue-eyed. They stand together up by the dais. The dais has a podium and a flag and a banner with GIVE US A WHIRL! on it, which I deduce is probably this year's Fair's Theme, sort of the way senior proms have a Theme. There's a compelling frictionlessness about the local TV reporters, all of whom have short blond hair and vaguely orange makeup. A vividness. I keep feeling a queer urge to vote for them for something.

The older ladies behind me tell me they've bet I'm here to cover either the auto racing or the pop music. They don't mean it unkindly. I tell them why I'm here, mentioning the magazine's name. They turn toward each other, faces alight. One (not the Historian) actually claps her hands to her cheeks.

"*Love* the recipes," she says.

"*Adore* the recipes," the Unofficial Historian says.

And I'm sort of impelled over to a table of all post-45 females, am introduced as on assignment from *Harper's* magazine, and everyone looks at one another with star-struck awe and concurs that the recipes really are first-rate, top-hole, the living end. One seminal recipe involving Amaretto and something called "Baker's chocolate" is being recalled and discussed when a loudspeaker's feedback brings the Fair's official Press Welcome & Briefing to order.

The Briefing is dull. We are less addressed than rhetorically bludgeoned by Fair personnel, product spokespeople, and middle-management State politicos. The words *excited, proud,* and *opportunity* are used a total of 76 times before I get distracted off the count. I've suddenly figured out that all the older ladies I'm at the table with have confused *Harper's* with *Harper's Bazaar*. They think I'm some sort of food writer or recipe scout, here to maybe vault some of the Midwestern food competition winners into the homemaker's big time. Ms. Illinois State Fair, tiara bolted to the tallest coiffure I've ever seen (bun atop bun, multiple layers, a veritable wedding cake of hair), is proudly excited to have the opportunity to present two corporate guys, dead-eyed and sweating freely in suits, who in turn report the excited pride of McDonald's and Wal-Mart at having the opportunity to be this year's Fair's major corporate sponsors. It occurs to me that if I allow the *Harper's-Bazaar*-food-scout misunderstanding to persist and circulate I can eventually show up at the Dessert Competition tents with my Press Credentials and they'll feed me free prize-winning desserts until I have to be carried off on a gurney. Older ladies in the Midwest can *bake*.

08/05/0950h. Under way at 4 mph on the Press Tour, on a kind of flatboat with wheels and a lengthwise bench so ridiculously high that everybody's feet dangle. The tractor pulling us has signs that say ETHANOL and AGRIPOWERED. I'm particularly keen to see the carnies setting up rides in the Fairgrounds' "Happy Hollow," but we head first to the corporate and political tents. Most every tent is still setting up. Workmen crawl over structural frames. We wave at them; they wave back; it's absurd: we're only going 4 mph. One tent says CORN: TOUCHING OUR LIVES EVERY DAY. There are massive many-hued tents courtesy of McDonald's, Miller Genuine Draft, Osco, Morton Commercial Structures Corp., the Land of Lincoln Soybean Association (LOOK WHERE SOYBEANS GO! on a half-up display), Pekin Energy Corp. (PROUD OF OUR SOPHISTICATED COMPUTER-CONTROLLED PROCESSING TECHNOLOGY), Illinois Pork Producers, and the John Birch Society (we'll be checking out that tent for sure). Two tents that say REPUBLICAN and DEMOCRAT. Other smaller tents for various Illinois officeholders. It's well up in the 90s and the sky is the color of old jeans. Over a system of crests to Farm Expo—twelve acres of wicked-looking needle-teethed harrows, tractors, harvesters and seeders—and then Conservation World, 22 acres I never do get straight on the conserving purpose of.

Then back around the rear of the big permanent structures—Artisans Bldg., Illinois Bldg. Senior Center, Expo Center (it says POULTRY on the tympanum, but it's the Expo Center)—passing tantalizingly close to Happy Hollow, where half-assembled rides stand in giant arcs and rays and shirtless guys with tattoos and wrenches slouch around them, fairly oozing menace and human interest—and I want a chance to chat with them before the Hollow opens and there's pressure to actually ride the carnival rides, since I am one of those people who gets sick on Near-Death-Experience carnival rides—but on at a crawl up a blacktop path to the Livestock Buildings on the Fairgrounds' west (upwind!) side. By this time, most of the Press is off the tram and walking in order to escape the tour's PA speaker, which is tinny and brutal. Horse Complex. Cattle Complex. Swine Barn. Sheep Barn. Poultry and Goat Barns. These are all long brick barracks open down both sides of their length. Inside some are stalls; others have pens divided into squares with aluminum rails. Inside, they're gray cement, dim and pungent, huge fans overhead, workers in overalls and waders hosing everything down. No animals yet, but the smells still hang from last year—horses' odors sharp, cows' rich, sheep's oily, swine's unspeakable. No idea what the Poultry Barn smelled like because I couldn't bring myself to go in. Traumatically pecked once, as a child, at the Champaign County Fair, I have a longstanding phobic thing about poultry.

The ethanol tractor's exhaust is literally flatulent-smelling as we crawl out past the Grandstand, where there will apparently be evening concerts and harness- and auto-racing—"WORLD'S FASTEST MILE DIRT TRACK"—and head for something called the Help Me Grow tent to interface with the state's First Lady, Brenda Edgar. It occurs to me that the 366-acre terrain of the Fairgrounds is awfully hilly for downstate IL; it's either a geologic anomaly or it's been man-enhanced. The Help Me Grow tent is on a grassy ridge that overlooks Happy Hollow. I think it's near where I parked. The dismantled-looking rides out below make the view complex. The Expo Center and Coliseum across the Hollow on an opposite ridge have odd neo-Georgian facades, a lot like the older buildings at the State U. over in Champaign. Nature-wise the view is lovely. The serious flooding's well to the west of Springfield, but we've had the same rains, and the grass here is lush and deep green, the trees' leaves balloon explosively like trees in Fragonard, and everything smells juicy and highly edible and still growing here in a month when I remember everything as tired and dry. The first sign of the Help Me Grow area is the nauseous bright red of Ronald McDonald's hair. He's capering around a small plasticky playground area under candy-stripe tenting. Though the Fair's ostensibly unopen, troupes of kids mysteriously appear and engage in rather rehearsed-looking play as we approach. Two of the kids are black, the first black people I've seen anywhere on the Fairgrounds. No parents in view. Just outside the tent, the Governor's wife stands surrounded by flinty-eyed aides. Ronald pretends to fall down. The Press forms itself into a kind of ring. There are several state troopers in khaki and tan, streaming sweat under their Nelson Eddy hats. My view isn't very good. Mrs. Edgar is cool and groomed and pretty in a lacquered way, of the sort of female age that's always suffixed with "-ish." Her tragic flaw is her voice, which sounds almost heliated. The Mrs. Edgar/McDonald's Help Me Grow Program, when you decoct the rhetoric, is basically a statewide crisis line for over-the-edge parents to call and get talked out of beating up their kids. The number of calls Mrs. Edgar says the line's fielded just this year is both de- and impressive. Shiny pamphlets are distributed. Ronald McDonald, speech slurry and makeup cottage-cheeseish in the heat, cues the kids to come over for some low-rent sleight of hand and Socratic banter. Lacking a real journalist's killer instinct, I've been jostled way to the back of the ring, and my view is obscured by the towering hair of Ms. Illinois State Fair, whose function on the Press Tour remains unclear. I don't want to asperse, but Ronald McDonald sounds like he's under the influence of something more than fresh country air. I drift away under the tent, where there's a metal watercooler. But no cups. It's hotter under the tent, and there's a reek of fresh plastic. All the toys and plastic playground equipment have signs that say COURTESY OF and then a corporate name. A lot of the photographers in the ring have on dusty-green safari vests, and they sit cross-legged in the sun, getting low-angle shots of Mrs. Edgar. There are no tough questions from the media. The tram's tractor is putting out a steady sweatsock-shape of blue-green exhaust. Right at the edge of the tent is where I notice that the grass is different: the grass under the tenting is a different grass, pine-green and prickly-looking, more like the St. Augustine grass of the deep U.S. South. Solid bent-over investigative journalism reveals that in fact it's artificial grass. A huge mat of plastic artificial grass has been spread over the knoll's real grass, under the candy-stripe tent. This may have been my only moment of complete East-Coast cynicism the whole day. A quick look under the edge of the fake grass mat reveals the real grass underneath, flattened and already yellowing.

One of the few things I still miss from my Midwest childhood was this weird, deluded but unshakable conviction that everything around me existed all and only *For Me*. Am I the only one who had this queer deep sense as a kid?—that everything exterior to me existed only insofar as it affected me somehow?—that all things were somehow, via some occult adult activity, specially arranged for my benefit? Does anybody else identify with this memory? The child leaves a room, and now everything in that room, once he's no longer there to see it, melts away into some void of potential or else (my personal childhood theory) is trundled away by occult adults and stored until the child's reentry into the room recalls it all back into animate service. Was this nuts? It was radically self-centered, of course, this conviction, and more than a little paranoid. Plus the *responsibility* it conferred: if the whole of the world dissolved and resolved each time I blinked, what if my eyes didn't open?

Maybe what I really miss now is the fact that a child's radical delusive self-centeredness doesn't cause him conflict or pain. His is the sort of regally innocent solipsism of like Bishop Berkeley's God: all things are nothing until his sight calls them forth from the void: his stimulation is the world's very being. And this is maybe why a little kid so fears the dark: it's not the possible presence of unseen fanged things in the dark, but rather the actual absence of everything his blindness has now erased. For me, at least, pace my folks' indulgent smiles, this was my true reason for needing a nightlight: it kept the world turning.

Plus maybe this sense of the world as all and only For-Him is why special ritual public occasions drive a kid right out of his mind with excitement. Holidays, parades, summer trips, sporting events. Fairs. Here the child's manic excitement is really exultation at his own power: the world will now not only exist For-Him but will present itself as *Special*-For-Him. Every hanging banner, balloon, gilded booth, clown-wig, turn of the wrench on a tent's erection—every bright bit signifies, refers. Counting down to the Special Event, time itself will alter, from a child's annular system of flashes and sweeps to a more adultish linear chronology—the concept of *looking forward to*—with successive moments ticking off toward a calendar-X'd telos, a new kind of fulfilling and apocalyptic End, the 0-hour of the Special Occasion, *Special,* of the garish and in all ways exceptional *Spectacle* which the child has made be and which is, he intuits at the same inarticulate depth as his need for a nightlight, For-Him alone, unique at the absolute center.

08/13/0925h. Official Opening. Ceremony, introductions, verbiage, bromides, really big brass shears for the ribbon across the Main Gate. It's cloudless and dry, but forehead-tighteningly hot. Noon will be a kiln. Knit-shirt Press and rabid early Fairgoers are massed from the Gate all the way out to Sangamon Avenue, where homeowners with plastic flags invite you to park on their lawn for $5.00. I gather "Little Jim" Edgar, the Governor, isn't much respected by the Press, most of whom are whispering about Michael Jordan's father's car being found but the father being missing, still. No anthropologist worth his helmet would be without the shrewd counsel of a colorful local, and I've brought a Native Companion here for the day (I can get people in free with my Press Credentials), and we're standing near the back. Governor E. is maybe fifty and greyhound-thin and has steel glasses and hair that looks carved out of feldspar. He radiates sincerity, though, after the hacks who introduced him, and speaks plainly and sanely and I think well — of both the terrible pain of the '93 Flood and the redemptive joy of seeing the whole state pull together to help one another, and of the special importance of this year's State Fair as a conscious affirmation of real community, of state solidarity and fellow-feeling and pride. Governor Edgar acknowledges that the state's really taken it on the chin in the last couple months, but that it's a state that's resilient and alive and most of all, he's reminded looking around himself here today, united, *together,* both in tough times and in happy times, happy times like for instance this very Fair. Edgar invites everybody to get in there and to have a really good time, and to revel in watching everybody else also having a good time, all as a kind of reflective exercise in civics, basically. The Press seem unmoved. I thought his remarks were kind of powerful, though.

And this Fair — the idea and now the reality of it — does seem to have something uniquely to do with state-as-community, a grand-scale togetherness. And it's not just the claustrophobic mash of people waiting to get inside. I can't get my finger onto just what's especially communitarian about an Illinois State Fair as opposed to like a New Jersey State Fair. I'd bought a notebook, but I left the car windows down last night and it got ruined by rain, and Native Companion kept me waiting getting ready to go and there wasn't time to buy a new notebook. I don't even have a pen, I realize. Whereas good old Governor Edgar has three different-colored pens in his knit shirt's breast pocket. This clinches it: you can always trust a man with multiple pens.

The Fair occupies space, and there's no shortage of space in downstate IL. The Fairgrounds take up 300+ acres on the east side of Springfield, a depressed capital of 109,000 where you can't spit without hitting some sort of Lincoln-site plaque. The Fair spreads itself out, and visually so. The Main Gate's on a rise, and through the two sagged halves of cut ribbon you get a great specular vantage on the whole thing — virgin and sun-glittered, even the tents looking fresh-painted. It seems garish and innocent and endless and aggressively Special. Kids are having like little like epileptic fits all around us, frenzied with a need to somehow take in everything at once.

I suspect that part of the self-conscious-community thing here has to do with space. Rural Midwesterners live surrounded by unpopulated land, marooned in a space whose emptiness starts to become both physical and spiritual. It is not just people you get lonely for. You're alienated from the very space around you, in a way, because out here the land's less an environment than a commodity. The land's basically a factory. You live in the same factory you work in. You spend an enormous amount of time with the land, but you're still alienated from it in some way. It's probably hard to feel any sort of Romantic spiritual connection to nature when you have to make your living from it. (Is this line of thinking somehow Marxist? Not when so many IL farmers still own their own land, I guess. This is a whole different kind of alienation.)

But so I theorize to Native Companion (who worked detassling summer corn with me in high school) that the Illinois State Fair's animating thesis involves some kind of structured interval of communion with both neighbor and space—the sheer *fact* of the land is to be celebrated here, its yields ogled and stock groomed and paraded, everything on decorative display. That what's Special here is the offer of a vacation from alienation, a chance for a moment to love what real life out here can't let you love. Native Companion, rummaging for her lighter, is about as interested in this stuff as she was about the child-as-empiricist-God-delusion horseshit back in the car, she apprises me.

08/13/1040h. The livestock venues are at full occupancy animal-wise, but we seem to be the only Fairgoers who've come right over from the Opening Ceremony to tour them. You can now tell which barns are for which animals with your eyes closed. The horses are in their own individual stalls, with half-height doors and owners and grooms on stools by the doors, a lot of them dozing. The horses stand in hay. Billy Ray Cyrus plays loudly on some stableboy's boom box. The horses have tight hides and apple-sized eyes that are set on the sides of their heads, like fish. I've rarely been this close to fine livestock. The horses' faces are long and somehow suggestive of coffins. The racers are lanky, velvet over bone. The draft and show horses are mammoth and spotlessly groomed and more or less odorless—the acrid smell in here is just the horses' pee. All their muscles are beautiful; the hides enhance them. Their tails whip around in sophisticated double-jointed ways, keeping the flies from mounting any kind of coordinated attack. (There really is such a thing as a horsefly.) The horses all make farty noises when they sigh, heads hanging over the short doors. They're not for petting, though. When you come close they flatten their ears and show big teeth. The grooms laugh to themselves as we jump back. These are special competitive horses, intricately bred, w/ high-strung artistic temperaments. I wish I'd brought carrots: animals can be bought, emotionally. Stall after stall of horses. Standard horse-type colors. They eat the same hay they stand in. Occasional feedbags look like gas masks. A sudden clattering spray-sound like somebody hosing down siding turns out to be a glossy chocolate stallion, peeing. He's at the back of his stall getting combed, and the door's wide open, and we watch him pee. The stream's an inch in diameter and throws up dust and hay and little chips of wood from the floor. We hunker down and have a look upward, and I sud-denly for the first time understand a certain expression describing certain human males, an expression I'd heard but never truly understood till just now, prone and gazing upward in some blend of horror and awe.

You can hear the cows all the way from the Horse Complex. The cow stalls are all doorless and open to view. I don't guess a cow presents much of an escape risk. The cows in here are white-spotted dun or black, or else white with big continents of dun or black. They have no lips and their tongues are wide. Their eyes roll and they have huge nostrils. I'd always thought of swine as the really nostrily barnyard animal, but cows have some serious nostrils going on, gaping and wet and pink or black. One cow has a sort of mohawk. Cow manure smells wonderful—warm and herbal and blameless—but cows themselves stink in a special sort of rich biotic way, rather like a wet boot. Some of the owners are scrubbing down their entries for the upcoming Beef Show over at the Coliseum (I have a detailed Media Guide, courtesy of Wal-Mart). These cows stand immobi-lized in webs of canvas straps inside a steel frame while ag-professionals scrub them down with a hose-and-brush thing that also oozes soap. The cows do not like this one bit. One cow we watch getting scrubbed for a while—whose face seems eerily reminiscent of former British P.M. Win-ston Churchill's face—trembles and shudders in its straps and makes the whole frame rock and clank, lowing, its eyes rolled almost to the whites. Native Companion and I cringe and make soft appalled noises. This cow's lowing starts all the other cows lowing, or maybe they just see what they're in for. The cow's legs keep half-buckling, and the owner kicks at them (the legs). The owner's face is intent but expressionless. White mucus hangs from the cow's snout. Other ominous dripping and gushings from else-where. It almost tips the steel frame over at one point, and the owner punches the cow in the ribs.

Swine have *fur!* I never thought of pigs as having fur. I've actually never been very close to a pig before, for olfactory reasons. Growing up over near

Urbana, the hot days when the wind blew from the U. of I. Swine Barns just southwest of our neighborhood were very grim days indeed. The U. of I. Swine Barns were actually what made my father finally knuckle under and let us get central AC. Swine smell, Native Companion reports her own father saying, "like Death his very own self is takin' a shit." The swine in here at the State Fair Swine Barn are show hogs, a breed called Poland China, their thin fur a kind of white crewcut over pink skin. A lot of the swine are down on their sides, stuporous and throbbing in the Barn's heat. The awake ones grunt. They stand and lie on very clean large-curd sawdust in low-fenced pens. A couple of barrows are eating both the sawdust and their own excrement. Again, we're the only tourists here. It also occurs to me that I didn't see a single farmer or ag-professional at the Opening Ceremony. It's like there are two different Fairs, different populations. A bullhorn on a wall announces that the Junior Pygmy Goat judging is under way over at the Goat Barn.

Pigs are in fact fat, and a lot of these swine are frankly huge — say ⅓ the size of a Volkswagen. Every once in a while you hear about farmers getting mauled or killed by swine. No teeth in view here, though the swine's hoofs look maul-capable — they're cloven and pink and kind of obscene. I'm not sure whether they're called hoofs or feet on swine. Rural Midwesterners learn by like second grade that there's no such word as "hooves." Some of the swine have large standing fans going in front of their pens, and twelve big ceiling-fans roar, but it's still stifling in here. The smell is both vomity and excremental, like some hideous digestive disorder on a grand scale. Maybe a cholera ward would come close. The owners and swineherds all have on rubber boots nothing like L. L. Bean East-Coast boots. Some of the standing swine commune through the bars of their pens, snouts almost touching. The sleeping swine thrash in dreams, their hind legs working. Unless they're in distress, swine grunt at a low constant pitch. It's a pleasant sound.

But now one butterscotch-colored swine is screaming. Distressed swine scream. The sound is both human and inhuman enough to make your hair stand. You can hear this one distressed swine all the way across the Barn. The professional swinemen ignore the pig, but we fuss on over, Native Companion making concerned baby-talk sounds until I shush her. The pig's sides are heaving; it's sitting up like a dog with its front legs quivering, screaming horribly. This pig's keeper is nowhere in sight. A small sign on its pen says it's a Hampshire Swine. It's having respiratory trouble, clearly: I'm guessing it inhaled either sawdust or excrement. Or else maybe it's just had it with the smell in here. Its front legs now buckle so it's on its side spasming. Whenever it can get enough breath together it screams. It's unendurable, but none of the ag-professionals comes vaulting over the pens to administer aid or anything. Native Companion and I are literally wringing our hands in sympathy. We both make plangent little noises at the pig. Native Companion tells me to go get somebody instead of standing there with my thumb up my butt. I feel enormous stress—nauseous smells, impotent sympathy, plus we're behind schedule: we are currently missing the Jr. Pygmy Goats, Philatelic Judging at the Expo Building, a 4-H Dog Show at something called Club Mickey D's, the Semifinals of the Midwest Arm-Wrestling Championships at the Lincoln Stage, a Ladies Camping Seminar, and the opening rounds of the Speed Casting Tournament over at the mysterious Conservation World. A swineherd kicks her Poland China sow awake so she can add more sawdust to its pen; Native Companion utters a pained sound. There are clearly exactly two Animal Rights advocates in this Swine Barn. We both can observe a kind of sullen, callous expertise in the demeanor of the ag-pros in here. A prime example of spiritual-alienation-from-land-as-factory, I posit. Except why take all the trouble to breed and train and care for a special animal and bring it all the way to the IL State Fair if you don't care anything about it?

Then it occurs to me that I had bacon yesterday and am even now looking forward to my first corn dog of the Fair. I'm standing here wringing my hands over a distressed swine and then I'm going to go pound down a corn dog. This is connected to my reluctance to charge over to a swine-pro and demand emergency resuscitative care for this agonized Hampshire. I can sort of picture the look the farmer would give me.

Not that it's profound, but I'm struck, amid the pig's screams and wheezes, by the fact that these agricultural pros do not see their stock as pets or friends. They are just in the agribusiness of weight and meat. They are unconnected even at the Fair, this self-consciously Special occasion of connection. And why not, maybe?—even at the Fair, their products continue to drool and smell and ingest their own excrement and scream, and the work just goes on and on. I can imagine what the ag-pros must think of us, cooing at the swine: we Fairgoers don't have to deal with the business of breeding and feeding our meat; our meat simply materializes at the corn-dog stand, allowing us to separate our healthy appetites from fur and screams and rolling eyes. We tourists get to indulge our tender Animal Rights feelings with our tummies full of bacon. I don't know how keen these sullen farmers' sense of irony is, but mine's been honed East-Coast keen, and I feel like a bit of a schmuck in the Swine Barn.

*   *   *

08/13/1150h. Since Native Companion was lured here for the day by the promise of free access to sphincter-loosening high-velocity rides, we make a quick descent into Happy Hollow. Most of the rides aren't even twirling hellishly yet. Guys with ratchet wrenches are still cranking away at the Ring of Fire. The giant Gondola Ferris Wheel is only half-assembled, and its seat-draped lower half resembles a hideous molary grin. It's over 100° in the sun, easy.

The Happy Hollow Carnival area's a kind of rectangular basin that extends east-west from near the Main Gate out to the steep pathless hillside just below Livestock. The Midway is made of dirt and flanked by carnival-game booths and ticket booths and rides. There's a merry-go-round and a couple of sane-paced kids' rides, but most of the rides down here look like genuine Near-Death Experiences. On this first morning the Hollow seems to be open only technically, and the ticket booths are unmanned, though heartbreaking little streams of AC'd air are blowing out through money-slots in the booths' glass. Attendance is sparse, and I notice none of the ag-pros or farm people are anywhere in sight down here. What there are are carnies. A lot of them slouch and slump in awnings' shade. Every one of them seems to chain-smoke. The Tilt-a-Whirl operator's got his boots up on his control panel reading a motorcycle-and-naked-lady magazine while two guys attach enormous rubber hoses to the ride's guts. We sidle over for a chat. The operator's 24 and from Bee Branch Arkansas, and has an earring and a huge tattoo of a motorcycle w/ naked lady on his triceps. He's way more interested in chatting with Native Companion than with me. He's been at this gig five years, touring with this one here same company here. Couldn't rightly say if he liked it or not, the gig: like as compared to what? Broke in the trade on the Toss-a-Quarter-Onto-the-Plates game and got, like, transferred over to the Tilt-a-Whirl in '91. He smokes Marlboro 100's but wears a cap that says WINSTON. He wants to know if Native Companion'd like to take a quick walk back across the Hollow and see something way out of the usual range of what she's used to. All around us are booths for various carny-type games. All the carny-game barkers have headset microphones; some are saying "Testing" and reciting their pitches' lines in tentative warm-up ways. A lot of the pitches seem frankly sexual: "You got to get it up to get it in"; "Take it out and lay'er down, only a dollar"; "Make it stand up. Two dollars five chances. Make it stand up." In the booths, rows of stuffed animals hang by their feet like game put out to cure. One barker's testing his mike by saying "Testes" instead of "Testing." It smells like machine grease and hair tonic down here, and there's already a spoiled, garbagey smell. My Media Guide says 1993's Happy Hollow is contracted to "...one of the largest owners of amusement attractions in the country," one Blomsness and Thebault All-Star Amusement Enterprises of Crystal Lake IL, up near Chicago. But the carnies themselves all seem to be from the middle South—Tennessee, Arkansas, Oklahoma. They are visibly unimpressed by the Press Credentials clipped to my shirt. They tend to look at Native Companion like she's food, which she ignores. There's very little of that childhood sense of all the games and rides being Special and For-Me, I have to say. I promptly lose $4.00 trying to "get it up and in" by tossing miniature basketballs into angled straw baskets in such a way that they don't bounce back out. The game's barker can toss the balls behind his back and get them to stay in, but he's right up next to the baskets. My shots carom out from eight feet away—the straw baskets look soft, but their bottoms make a suspicious steely sound when the balls hit.

It's so hot that we move in quick staggered vectors between areas of shade. I decline to take my shirt off because there'd be no way to display my Credentials. We zigzag gradually westward across the Hollow. I am keen to hit the Junior Beef Show which starts at 1300h. Then there are, of course, the Dessert Competition tents.

One of the fully assembled rides near the Hollow's west end is something called The Zipper. It's riderless but in furious motion, a kind of Ferris Wheel on amphetamines. Individual caged cars are hinged to spin on their own axes as they go around in a tight vertical ellipse. The machine looks less like a zipper than the head of a chain saw. Its off-white paint is chipped, and it sounds like a shimmying V-12, and in general it's something I'd run a mile in tight shoes to avoid riding. But Native Companion starts clapping and hopping around excitedly as we approach The Zipper. (This is a person who bungee jumps, to give you an idea.) And the operator at the controls sees her, waves back, and shouts down to Git on over and git some if she's a mind to. He claims they want to test The Zipper somehow. He's up on a kind of steel platform, elbowing a colleague next to him in a way I don't much like. We have no tickets, I point out, and none of the cash-for-ticket booths are manned. By now we're somehow at the base of the stairway up to the platform and control panel. The operator says without looking at me that the matter of tickets this early on Opening Day "Ain't no sweat off my balls." The operator's colleague conducts Native Companion up the waffled-steel steps and straps her into a cage, upping a thumb at the operator, who gives a sort of Rebel Yell and pulls a lever. Native C.'s cage begins to ascend. Pathetic little fingers appear in the cage's mesh. The Zipper operator is ageless and burnt-brown and has a

mustache waxed to wicked points like steers' horns, rolling a Drum cigarette with one hand as he nudges levers upward and the ellipse speeds up
and the individual cages start to spin independently on their hinges.
Native Companion is a blur of color inside her cage, but the operator and
colleague (whose jeans have worked down his hips to the point where the
top of his butt-crack is clearly visible) watch studiously as her spinning
cage and the clanking empty cages circle the ellipse approx. once a second.
I have a particular longstanding fear of things that spin independently
inside a larger spin. I can barely even watch this. The Zipper is the color of
unbrushed teeth, with big scabs of rust. The operator and colleague sit on a
little steel bench before a panel full of black-knobbed levers. Do testicles
themselves sweat? They're supposed to be very temperature-sensitive. The
colleague spits Skoal into a can he holds and tells the operator to "Well
then take her to Eight then you pussy." The Zipper begins to whine and
the thing to spin so fast that a detached car would surely be hurled into
orbit. The colleague has a small American flag folded into a bandanna
around his head. The empty cages shudder and clank as they whirl, spinning independently. One long scream, wobbled by Doppler, is coming
from Native C.'s cage, which is going around and around on its hinges
while a shape inside tumbles like stuff in a dryer. My particular neurological makeup (extremely sensitive: carsick, airsick, heightsick; my sister
likes to say I'm "lifesick") makes even just watching this an act of enormous personal courage. The scream goes on and on; it's nothing like a
swine's. Then the operator stops the ride abruptly with Native C.'s car at
the top, so she's hanging upside down inside the cage. I call up Is she OK,
but the response is just high-pitched noises. I see the two carnies gazing
upward very intently, shading their eyes. The operator's stroking his mustache contemplatively. The cage's inversion has made Native Companion's
dress fall up. They're ogling her nethers, obviously. As they laugh, the
sound literally sounds like "Tee hee hee hee." A less sensitive neurological
specimen probably would have stepped in at this point and stopped the
whole grotesque exercise. My own makeup leans more toward disassociation when under stress. A mother in shorts is trying to get a stroller up the
steps of the Funhouse. A kid in a *Jurassic Park* T-shirt is licking an enormous flat lollipop with a hypnotic spiral on it. A sign at a gas station we
passed on Sangamon Avenue was hand-lettered and said "BLU-BLOCK
SUNGLASSES — *Like Seen On TV.*" A Shell station off I-55 near Elkhart
sold cans of snuff out of a vending machine. 15% of the female Fairgoers
here have their hair in curlers. 25% are clinically fat. Midwestern fat people have no compunction about wearing shorts or halter-tops. A radio

reporter had held his recorder's mike up too close to a speaker during Governor E.'s opening remarks, causing hellacious feedback. Now the operator's joggling the choke-lever so The Zipper stutters back and forth, forward and backward, making N.C.'s top car spin around and around on its hinges. His colleague's T-shirt has a stoned Ninja Turtle on it, toking on a joint. There's a distended A# scream from the whirling cage, as if Native C.'s getting slow-roasted. I summon saliva to step in and really say something stern, but at this point they start bringing her down. The operator is deft at his panel; the car's descent is almost fluffy. His hands on the levers are a kind of parody of tender care. The descent takes forever — ominous silence from Native Companion's car. The two carnies are laughing and slapping their knee. I clear my throat twice. There's a trundly sound as Native Companion's car gets locked down at the platform. Jiggles of movement in the cage, and the door's latch slowly turns. I expect whatever husk of a human being emerges from the car to be hunched and sheet-white, dribbling fluids. Instead she sort of bounds out:

"That was fucking *great*. Joo see that? Son bitch spun that car *sixteen times,* joo see it?" This woman is native Midwestern, from my hometown. My prom date a dozen years ago. Now married, with three children, teaches water-aerobics to the obese and infirm. Her color is high. Her dress looks like the world's worst case of static cling. She's still got her *chewing gum* in, for God's sake. She turns to the carnies: "You sons bitches that was fucking *great. Ass*holes." The colleague is half-draped over the operator; they're roaring with laughter. Native Companion has her hands on her hips sternly, but she's grinning. Am I the only one who was in touch with the manifestly overt sexual-harassment element in this whole episode? She takes the steel stairs down three at a time and starts up the hillside toward the food booths. There is no sanctioned path up the incredibly steep hill on the Hollow's western side. Behind us the operator calls out: "They don't call me King of The Zipper for nuthin', sweet thang." She snorts and calls back over her shoulder "Oh you and whose fucking *platoon?*" and there's more laughter behind us.

I'm having a hard time keeping up on the slope. "Did you hear that?" I ask her.

"Jesus I thought I bought it for sure at the end that was so great. Fucking cornholers. But'd you *see* that one spin up top at the end, though?"

"Did you hear that Zipper King comment?" I say. She has her hand around my elbow and is helping me up the hillside's slick grass. "Did you sense something kind of sexual-harassmentish going on through that whole little sick exercise?"

"Oh for fuck's sake Slug it was *fun*." (Ignore the nickname.) "Son of a bitch spun that car *eighteen times*."

"They were looking up your *dress*. You couldn't see them, maybe. They hung you upside down at a great height and made your dress fall up and *ogled* you. They shaded their eyes and made comments to each other. I saw the whole thing."

"Oh for fuck's sake."

I slip a little bit and she catches my arm. "So this doesn't bother you? As a Midwesterner, you're unbothered? Or did you just not have an accurate sense of what was going on back there?"

"So if I noticed or I didn't, why does it have to be *my* deal? What, because there's assholes in the world I don't get to ride on The Zipper? I don't get to ever spin? Maybe I shouldn't ever go to the pool or ever get all girled up, just out of fear of assholes?" Her color is still high.

"So I'm curious, then, about what it would have taken back there, say, to have gotten you to lodge some sort of complaint with the Fair's management."

"You're so fucking *innocent*, Slug," she says. (The nickname's a long story; ignore it.) "Assholes are just assholes. What's getting hot and bothered going to do about it except keep me from getting to have fun?" She has her hand on my elbow this whole time—the hillside's a bitch.

"This is potentially key," I'm saying. "This may be just the sort of regional politico-sexual contrast the swanky East-Coast magazine is keen for. The core value informing a kind of willed politico-sexual stoicism on your part is your prototypically Midwestern appreciation of fun—"

"Buy me some pork skins, you dipshit."

"—whereas on the East Coast, politico-sexual indignation *is* the fun. In New York, a woman who'd been hung upside down and ogled would go get a whole lot of other women together and there'd be this frenzy of politico-sexual indignation. They'd confront the ogler. File an injunction. Management'd find itself litigating expensively—violation of a woman's right to nonharassed fun. I'm telling you. Personal and political fun merge somewhere just east of Cleveland, for women."

Native Companion kills a mosquito without looking at it. "And they all take Prozac and stick their finger down their throat too out there. They might ought to try just climbing on and spinning and ignoring assholes and saying Fuck 'em. That's pretty much all you can do with assholes."

"This could be integral."

* * *

08/13/1235h. Lunchtime. The Fairgrounds are a St. Vitus's dance of black-top footpaths, the axons and dendrites of mass spectation, connecting buildings and barns and corporate tents. Each path is flanked, pretty much along its whole length, by booths hawking food. There are tall Kaopectate-colored shacks that sell Illinois Dairy Council milkshakes for an off-the-scale $2.50—though they're mindbendingly good milkshakes, silky and so thick they don't even insult your intelligence with a straw or spoon, giving you instead a kind of small plastic trowel. There are uncountable pork options: Paulie's Pork Out, the Pork Patio, Freshfried Pork Skins, the Pork Street Cafe. The Pork Street Cafe is a "One Hundred Percent All-Pork Establishment," says its loudspeaker. "Ever last thing." I'm praying this doesn't include the beverages. No way I'm eating any pork after this morning's swine stress, anyway. And it's too hot even to think about the Dessert Competitions. It's at least 95° in the shade here due east of Livestock, and the breeze is shall we say fragrant. But food is getting bought and ingested at an incredible clip all up and down the path. The booths are ubiquitous, and each one has a line in front of it. Everybody's packed in together, eating as they walk. A peripatetic feeding frenzy. Native Companion is agitating for pork skins. Zipper or no, she's "*storvin'*," she says, "to *daith.*" She likes to put on a parodic hick accent whenever I utter a term like "peripatetic."

(You do not want details on what pork skins are.)

So along the path there are I.D.C. milkshakes (my lunch), Lemon Shake-Ups, Ice Cold Melon Man booths, Citrus Push-Ups, and Hawaiian Shaved Ice you can suck the syrup out of and then crunch the ice (my dessert). But a lot of what's getting bought and gobbled is to my mind not hot-weather food at all: bright-yellow popcorn that stinks of salt; onion rings big as leis; Poco Penos Stuffed Jalapeño Peppers; Zorba's Gyros; shiny fried chicken; Bert's Burritos—"BIG AS YOU'RE HEAD" (sic); hot Italian beef; hot New York City Beef (?); Jojo's Quick Fried Donuts (the only booth selling coffee, by the way); pizza by the shingle-sized slice and chitlins and Crab Rangoon and Polish sausage. (Rural Illinois' complete lack of ethnic identity creates a kind of postmodern embarrassment of riches—foods of every culture and creed become our own, quick-fried and served on cardboard and consumed on foot.) There are towering plates of "Curl Fries," which are pubic-hair-shaped and make people's fingers shine in the sun. Cheez-Dip Hot Dogs. Pony Pups. Hot Fritters. Philly Steak. Ribeye BBQ Corral. Joanie's Original ½-lb Burgers' booth's sign says 2 CHOICES—RARE OR MOOIN'. I can't believe people eat this kind of stuff in this kind of heat. The sky is cloudless and galvanized; the sun fairly pulses. There's the green reek of fried tomatoes. (Midwesterners say "tomāto.") The sound of myriad deep fryers forms a grisly sound-carpet all up and down the gauntlet of booths. The Original 1-lb Butterfly Pork Chop booth's sign says PORK: THE OTHER WHITE MEAT, the only discernible armwave to the health-conscious so far. Non-natives note, it's the Midwest: no nachos, no chili, no Evian, nothing Cajun.

But holy mackerel are there sweets: Fried Dough; Black Walnut Taffy; Fiddlesticks; Hot Crackerjack. Caramel apples for a felonious $1.50. Angel's Breath, known also as Dentist's Delight. Vanilla fudge that breaks a kind of weird sweat the minute it leaves its booth's freezer. The crowd moves at one slow pace, eating, dense-packed between the rows of booths. No ag-pros in sight. The crowd's adults are either pale or with the pink tinge of new burn, thin-haired and big-bellied in tight jeans, some downright fat and moving by sort of shifting their weight from side to side; boys minus shirts and girls in primary-colored halters; littler boys and girls in squads; parents with strollers; terribly pale academics in Bermudas and sandals; big women in curlers; lots of people carrying shopping bags; absurd floppy hats; almost all with '80s-fashion sunglasses — all seemingly eating, crowded together, twenty abreast, moving slowly, packed in, sweating, shoulders rubbing, the air deep-fried and spicy with antiperspirant and Coppertone, jowl to jowl. Picture Tokyo's rush-hour subway on an epic scale. It's a rare grand mass of Midwest humanity, eating and shuffling and rubbing, moving toward the Coliseum and Grandstand and Expo Building and the Livestock shows beyond. It's maybe significant that nobody looks like they're feeling oppressed or claustrophobic or bug-eyed at being airlessly hemmed in by the endless crowd we're all part of. Native Companion cusses and laughs when people step on her feet. Something East-Coast in me prickles at the bovine and herdlike quality of the crowd, though, i.e. us, hundreds of hands rising from paper tray to mouth as we jostle and press toward our respective attractions. From the air we'd look like some kind of Bataan March of docile consumption. (Native Companion laughs and says the batons aren't ever till the second day.) We're Jr.-Beef-Show-bound. You do not want to know what appalling combination of high-lipid foods N. Companion lunches on as we're borne by a living river toward prizewinning beef. The booths keep rolling past. There's Ace-High All-Butter Fudge. There are Rice-Krispie-squarish things called Krakkles. Angel Hair Cotton Candy. There are Funnel Cakes, viz. cake batter quick-fried to a tornadic spiral and rolled in sugared butter. Eric's Salt Water Taffy. Something called Zak's Fried Ice Cream. Another artery-clogger: Elephant Ears. An Elephant Ear is an album-sized expanse of oil-fried dough slathered with butter and cinnamon-sugar, sort of cinna-mon toast from hell, really and truly shaped like an ear, surprisingly yummy, it turns out, but sickly soft, the texture of adipose flesh, and unde-niably elephant-sized—no one's in line for Ears except the morbidly obese.

One food venue we fight across the current to check out special is a huge high-tech neonated stand: DIPPIN DOTS—*"Ice Cream Of The Future."* The countergirl sits on a tall stool shrouded in dry-ice steam and is at most thirteen years old, and my Press Credentials for the first time make someone's eyes widen, and we get free samples, little cups of what seem to be tiny little ice-cream pellets, fluorescent BB's that are kept, the countergirl swears to *God*, at 55° below 0—Oh *God* she doesn't *know* whether it's 0°C or 0°F; that wasn't in the DIPPIN DOTS training video. The pellets melt in your mouth, after a fashion. More like evaporate in your mouth. The taste is vivid, but the Dots' texture's weird, abstract. Futuristic. The stuff's intriguing but just too Jetsonian to really catch on. The countergirl spells her last name for us and wants to say Hey to some-one named Jody in return for the samples.

08/13/1310h. "Here we've got as balanced in dimension as any heifer you'll see today. A high-volume heifer but also solid on mass. Good to look at in terms of rib-length to -depth. Depth of forerib. Notice the depth of flank on the front quarter. We'd like to see maybe perhaps a little more muscle mass on the rear flank. Still, an outstanding heifer."

We're in the Jr. Livestock Center. A lot of cows move in a ring around the perimeter of the dirt circle, each cow led by an ag-family kid. The "Jr." pretty clearly refers to the owners, not the animals. Each cow's kid holds a long poker with a right-angled tooth at its end. They take turns prodding their cow into the center of the ring to move in a tighter circle while its vir-tues and liabilities are assessed. We're up in the stands. Native Companion is smitten. The Beef Show Official at the microphone looks uncannily like the actor Ed Harris, blue-eyed and somehow sexily bald. He's dressed just like the kids in the ring—dark new stiff jeans, check shirt, bandanna around neck. On him it doesn't look goofy. Plus he's got a stunning white cowboy hat. While Ms. Illinois Beef Queen presides from a dais decked with flowers sent over from the Horticulture Show, the Beef Official stands in the arena itself, his legs apart and his thumbs in his belt, 100% man, radiating livestock savvy. N.C. seems less smitten than decapitated, frankly.

"Okay this next heifer, a lot of depth of rib but a little tighter in the foreflank. A bit tighter-flanked, if you will, from the standpoint of capacity."

The cows' owners are farm kids, deep-rural kids from back-of-beyond counties like Piatt, Moultrie, Vermilion, all County Fair winners. They are earnest, nervous, pride-puffed. Dressed rurally up. Straw-colored crewcuts. High number of freckles per capita. They're kids remarkable for a kind of classic Rockwellian U.S. averageness, the products of balanced diets, vigorous labor, and solid GOP upbringings. The Jr. Livestock Center bleachers are over half-full, and it's all ag-people, farmers, parents mostly, many with video cameras. Cowhide vests and ornate dress-boots and simply amazing hats. Illinois farmers are rural and kind of inarticulate, but they are not poor. Just the amount of revolving credit you need to capitalize a fair-sized operation — seed and herbicide, heavy equipment, crop insurance — makes a lot of them millionaires on paper. Media dirges notwithstanding, banks are no more keen to foreclose on Midwestern farmers than they are on Third World nations; they're in that deeply. Nobody's in sunglasses or shorts; everyone's tanned in an earthtone, all-business way. And if the Fair's ag-pros are also stout, it's in a harder, squarer, somehow more *earned* way than the tourists on the paths outside. The bleachers' fathers have bushy eyebrows and simply enormous thumbs, I notice. Native C. keeps making growly throat noises about the Beef Official. The J.L.C. is cool and dim and spicy with livestock. The atmosphere's good-natured but serious. Nobody's eating any booth-food, and nobody's carrying the Fair's complimentary GOVERNOR EDGAR shopping bags.

"An excellent heifer from a profile standpoint."

"Here we have a low-volume heifer but with exceptional mass in the rear quarter."

I can't tell whose cow is winning.

"Certainly the most extreme heifer out here in terms of frame to depth."

Some of the cows looked drugged. Maybe they're just superbly trained. You can imagine these farm kids getting up every day so early they can see their breath and leading their cows in practice circles under the cold stars, then having to do all their chores. I feel good in here. The cows in the ring all have colored ribbons on their tails. The lows and snorts of other cows on deck echo under the stands' bleachers. Sometimes the bleachers shake like something's butting the struts down there.

There are baroque classifications I can't start to follow — Breed, Class, Age. A friendly ag-lady with a long tired face beside us explains the kids' pokers, though. They're called Show Sticks, used to arrange the cows' feet when they're standing, and to prod, scratch, swat, or stroke, depending. The lady's own boy took second in the "Polled Hereford" — that's him getting congratulated by Ms. IL Beef Queen for a *Livestock Weekly* photographer. Native Companion isn't crazy about the smells and bellows in here, but she says if her husband calls me up next week looking for her it'll mean she's decided to "up and follow that Ed Harris fellow home." This is even after I remark that he could use a little more depth in the forerib.

The cows are shampooed and mild-eyed and lovely, incontinence notwithstanding. They are also assets. The ag-lady beside us says her family's operation will realize maybe like $2,500 for the Hereford in the Winners Auction coming up. Illinois farmers call their farms "operations," rarely "farms" and never "spreads." The lady says $2,500 is "maybe about around half" what the family's spent on the heifer's breeding and upkeep and care. "We do this for pride," she says. This is more like it. Pride, care, selfless expense. The little boy's chest puffs out as the Official tips his blinding hat. Farm spirit. Oneness w/ crop and stock. I'm making mental notes till my temples throb. N.C. asks about the Official fellow. The ag-lady explains he's a beef buyer for a major Peoria packing plant and that the bidders in the upcoming Winners Auction (five brown suits and three string ties on the dais) are from McDonald's, Burger King, White Castle, etc. Meaning the mild-eyed winners have been sedulously judged as meat. The ag-lady has a particular bone to pick with McDonald's, "that always come in and overbid high on the champions and don't care about anything else. Mess up the pricing." Her husband confirms that they got "screwed back to front" on last year's bidding.

We skip the Junior Swine Show.

08/13/1400–1600h. We hurtle here and there, sort of surfing on the paths' crowds. Paid attendance today is 100,000+. A scum of clouds has cut the heat, but I'm on my third shirt. Society Horse Show at Coliseum. Wheat-Weaving Demonstration in Hobby, Arts & Crafts Bldg. Peonies like supernovas in the Horticulture Tent, where some of the older ladies from the Press Tour want to talk corn chowder recipes with me. We have no time. I'm getting the sort of overload-headache I always get in museums. Native C. is also stressed. And we're not the only tourists with that pinched glazed hurry-up look. There are just too many things to experience. Arm-Wrestling Finals where bald men fart audibly with effort. Assyrian National Council in the Fairgrounds' Ethnic Village — a riot of gesturing people in sheets. Everyone's very excited, at everything. Drum and Bugle Competition in Miller Lite Tent. On the crowded path outside Farm Expo a man engages in blatant frottage. Corn-fed young ladies in overalls cut off at the pockets. Hideous tottery Ronald McD. working the crowd at Club Mickey D's' 3-on-3 Hoops Competition—three of the six basketball players are black, the first black people I've seen here since Mrs. Edgar's hired kids. Pygmy Goat Show at Goat Barn. In the Media Guide: WALK ILLINOIS!(?), then Slide Show on Prairie Reclamation back over at Conservation World, then Open Poultry Judging, which I've decided to steel myself to see.

The afternoon becomes one long frisson of stress. I'm sure we'll miss something crucial. Native C. has zinc oxide on her nose and needs to get back home to pick up her kids. Plodding, elbowing. Seas of Fairgoing flesh, all looking, still eating. These Fairgoers seem to gravitate only to the crowded spots, the ones with long lines already. No one's playing any East-Coast games of Beat the Crowd. Midwesterners lack a certain cunning. Under stress they look like lost children. But no one gets impatient. Something adult and potentially integral strikes me. Why the Fairgoing tourists don't mind the crowds, lines, noise—and why I'm getting none of that old special sense of the Fair as uniquely For-Me. The State Fair here is For-*Us*. Self-consciously so. Not For-Me or -You. The Fair's deliberately *about* the crowds and jostle, the noise and overload of sight and smell and choice and event. It's Us showing off for Us.

A theory: Megalopolitan East-Coasters' summer vacations are literally getaways, flights-from—from crowds, noise, heat, dirt, the neural wear of too many stimuli. Thus ecstatic escapes to mountains, glassy lakes, cabins, hikes in silent woods. Getting Away From It All. Most East-Coasters see more than enough stimulating people and sights M-F, thank you; they stand in enough lines, buy enough stuff, elbow enough crowds, see enough spectacles. Neon skylines. Convertibles with 110-watt sound systems. Grotesques on public transport. Spectacles at every urban corner practically grabbing you by the lapels, commanding attention. The East-Coast existential treat is thus some escape from confines and stimuli—silence, rustic vistas that hold still, a turning inward: Away. Not so in the rural Midwest. Here you're pretty much Away all the time. The land here is big. Pool-table flat. Horizons in every direction. Even in comparatively citified Springfield, see how much farther apart the homes are, how broad the yards—compare with Boston or Philly. Here a seat to yourself on all public transport; parks the size of airports; rush hour a three-beat pause at a stop sign. And the farms themselves are huge, silent, mostly vacant space: you can't see your neighbor. Thus the vacation-impulse in rural IL is manifested as a flight-*toward*. Thus the urge physically to commune, melt, become part of a crowd. To see something besides land and corn and satellite TV and your wife's face. Crowds out here are a kind of adult nightlight. Hence the sacredness out here of Spectacle, Public Event. High school football, church social, Little League, parades, Bingo, market day, State Fair. All very big, very deep deals. Something in a Midwesterner sort of *actuates* at a Public Event. You can see it here. The faces in this sea of faces are like the faces of children released from their rooms. Governor Edgar's state spirit rhetoric at the Main Gate's ribbon rings true. The real Spectacle that draws us here is Us. The proud displays and the paths between them and the special-treat booths along the paths are less important than the greater-than-sum We that trudge elbow to elbow, pushing strollers and engaging in sensuous trade, expending months of stored-up attention. A neat inversion of the East-Coast's summer withdrawal. God only knows what the West Coast's like.

We're about 100 yards shy of the Poultry Building when I break down. I've been a rock about the prospect of Open Poultry Judging all day, but now my nerve totally goes. I can't go in there. Listen to the untold thousands of sharp squawking beaks in there, I say. Native Companion not unkindly offers to hold my hand, talk me through it. It's 93° and I have pygmy-goat shit on my shoe and am almost weeping with fear and embarrassment. I sit down on one of the green pathside benches to collect myself while N.C. goes to call home about her kids. I've never before realized that "cacophony" was onomatopoeic: the noise of the Poultry Bldg. is cacophonous and scrotum-tightening and totally horrible. I think it's what insanity must sound like. No wonder madmen clutch their heads and scream. There's also a thin stink, and lots of bits of feather are floating all over. And this is *outside* the Poultry Bldg. I hunch on the bench. When I was eight, at the Champaign County Fair, I was pecked without provocation, flown at and pecked by a renegade fowl, savagely, just under the right eye, the scar of which looks like a permanent zit.

Except of course one problem with the prenominate theory is that there's more than one Us, hence more than one State Fair. Ag-people at the Livestock barns and Farm Expo, non-farm civilians at the food-booths and touristy exhibits and Happy Hollow. The two groups do not much mix. Neither is the neighbor the other pines for.

Then there are the carnies. The carnies mix with no one, never seem to leave Happy Hollow. Late tonight, I'll watch them drop flaps to turn their carnival booths into tents. They'll smoke cheap dope and drink peppermint schnapps and pee out onto the Midway's dirt. I think carnies must be the rural U.S.'s gypsies — itinerant, insular, swarthy, unclean, not to be trusted. You are in no way drawn to them. They all have the same hard blank eyes as people in bus terminal bathrooms. They want your money and to look up your skirt; beyond that you're just blocking the view. Next week they'll dismantle and pack and haul up to the Wisconsin State Fair, where they'll again never set foot off the Midway they pee on.

The State Fair is rural IL's moment of maximum community, but even at a Fair whose whole raison is For-Us, Us's entail Thems, apparently. The carnies make an excellent Them. And the ag-people really hate them, the carnies. While I'm sitting there on the bench disassociating and waiting for N. Companion to come back, all of a sudden an old withered guy in an Illinois Poultry Association cap careers past on one of those weird three-wheeled carts, like a turbo-charged wheelchair, and runs neatly over my sneaker. This ends up being my one unassisted interview of the day, and it's brief. The old guy keeps revving his cart's engine like a biker. "*Traish*" he calls the carnies. "Lowlifes. Wouldn't let my own kids go off down there on a goddamn bet," gesturing down the hill at the twirling rides. He raises pullets down near Olney. He has something in his cheek. "Steal you blind. Drug-addicted and such. Swindle you nekked, them games. Traish. Me I ever year we drive up, why, I carry my wallet like this here," pointing to his hip. His wallet is on a big steel clip attached to a wire on his belt; the whole thing looks vaguely electrified.

Q: "But would they want to? Your kids I mean. Would they want to hit the Hollow, ride the rides, eat all-butter fudge, test various skills, mingle a little?"

He spits brownly. "*Hail* no. We all come for the shows." He means the Livestock Competitions. "See some folks, talk stock. Drink a beer. Work all year round raising 'em for showbirds. It's for pride. And to see folks. Shows're over Tuesday, why, we go on home." He looks like a bird himself. His face is mostly nose, his skin loose and pebbly like poultry's. His eyes are the color of denim. "Rest of all this here's for city people." Spits. He means Springfield, Decatur, Champaign. "Walk around, stand in line, eat junk, buy soovners. Give their wallet to the traish. Don't even know there's folks come here to work up here," gesturing at the barns. He spits again, leaning way out to the side of the cart to do it. "We come up to work, see some folks. Drink a beer. Bring our own goddamn food. Mother packs a hamper. Hail, what they'd want to go on down there?" I think meaning his kids. "Ain't no folks they know down there." He laughs. Asks my name. "It's good to see folks," he says. "We all stayin' up to the *mo*tel. Watch your wallet, boy." And he asks after my tire-treaded foot, very politely, before peeling out toward the chicken din.

08/14/1015h. Rested, rehydrated. No Native Companion along to ask embarrassing questions about why the reverential treatment; plenty of time for the *Harper's Bazaar* rumor to metastasize: I am primed to hit the Dessert Competitions.

08/14/1025h. Dessert Competitions.

08/14/1315h. Illinois State Fair Infirmary; then motel; then Springfield Memorial Medical Center Emergency Room for distention and possible rupture of transverse colon (false alarm); then motel; incapacitated till well after sunset; whole day a washout; incredibly embarrassing, unprofessional; indescribable. Delete entire day.

08/15/0600h. Upright and moving just outside the Hollow. Still transversely distressed, unrested; shaky but resolute. Sneakers already soaked. It rained in brutal sheets last night, damaged tents, tore up corn near the motel. Midwestern thunderstorms are real Old Testament skull-clutchers: Richter-Scale thunder, sideways rain, big zigzags of cartoon lightning. By the time I tottered back over last night Tammy Wynette had closed early at the Grandstand, but Happy Hollow went till midnight, a whole lot of neon in the rain.

The dawn is foggy. The sky looks like soap. An enfilade of snores from the booths-turned-tents along the Midway. Happy Hollow is a bog. Someone behind the lowered flaps of the shoot-2D-ducks-with-an-air-rifle booth is having a wicked coughing fit, obscenely punctuated. Distant sounds of dumpsters getting emptied. Twitters of various birds. The Blomsness-Thebault management trailer has a blinky electric burglar alarm on it. The goddamn cocks are at it already up in the Poultry Bldg. Thunder-mutters sound way off east over Indiana. Trees shudder and shed drops in the breeze. The blacktop paths are empty, eerie, shiny with rain.

08/15/0620h. Looking at legions of sleeping sheep. Sheep Building. I am the only waking human in here. It's cool and quiet. Sheep excrement has an evil vomity edge to it, but olfactorily it's not too bad in here. One or two sheep are upright but silent. No fewer than four ag-pros are in the pens sleeping right up next to their sheep, about which the less speculation the better as far as I'm concerned. The roof in here is leaky and most of the straw is sopped. There are little printed signs on every pen. In here are Yearling Ewes, Brood Ewes, Ewe Lambs, Fall Lambs. Breedwise we've got Corriedales, Hampshires, Dorset Horns, Columbias. You could get a Ph.D. just in sheep, from the looks of it. Rambouillets, Oxfords, Suffolks, Shropshires, Cheviots, Southdowns. And these are just like the major classes. I've forgotten to say you can't see the actual sheep. The actual corporeal sheep themselves are all in tight white bodysuits, cotton maybe, with eye- and mouth-holes. Like Superhero suits. Sleeping in them. Presumably to keep their wool clean until it's judged. No fun later when the temperature starts climbing, though, I bet.

Back outside. Floating protean ghosts of fog and evap on the paths. The Fairgrounds are creepy with everything set up but no one about. A creepy air of hasty abandonment, a feeling like you run home from kindergarten and the whole family's up and moved, left you. Plus nowhere dry to sit down and test out the notebook. (More like a tablet, purchased along w/ Bic ballpoint last night at the S.M.M.C. Card, Gift & Greeting shop. All they had was a little kid's tablet with that weird soft gray paper and some kind of purple brontosaurus-type character named Barney on the cover.)

08/15/0730h. Pentecostal Sunday Services in Twilight Ballroom. Services joyless, humorless, worshippers lean and starchy and dour like characters from Hals portraits. Not one person smiles the whole time, and there's no little interval where you get to go around shaking people's hands and wishing them Peace. It's already 80° but so damp that people's breath hangs in front of their face.

08/15/0820h. Press Room, 4th Floor, Illinois Bldg. I'm pretty much the only credentialed Press without a little plywood cubbyhole for mail and Press Releases. Two guys from an ag-newspaper are trying to hook a fax machine up to a rotary-phone jack. Michael Jordan's father's body has been found, and the wire services are going nuts in one corner. Wire service teletypes really do sound exactly like the background on old TV newscasts from childhood. Also, the East St. Louis levee's given way; National Guardsmen are being mobilized. (East St. Louis needs Guardsmen even when it's dry, from my experience.) A State Fair PR guy arrives for the daily Press Briefing. Coffee and unidentifiable muffinish things courtesy of Wal-Mart. I am hunched and pale. This P.M.'s highlights: Midwest Truck and Tractor Pull, the "Bill Oldani 100" U.S.A.C. auto race. Tonight's Grandstand Show's to be the poor old doddering Beach Boys, who I suspect now must make their entire living from State Fairs. The Beach Boys' "Special Guest" warm-up is to be America, another poor old doddering band. The PR guy cannot give away all his free Press Passes to the concert. Plus I learn I missed some law-and-order dramatics yesterday, apparently: two minors from Carbondale arrested riding The Zipper last night when a vial of cocaine fell out of one of their pockets and direct-hit a state trooper alertly eating a Lemon Push-Up on the Midway below; a reported rape or date-rape in Parking Lot 6; assorted bunkos and D&D's. Plus two separate reporters vomited on from a great height in two separate incidents under two separate Near-Death-Experience rides, trying to cover the Hollow.

08/15/0840h. A Macy's-float-sized inflatable Ronald, seated and eerily Buddha-like, presides over the north side of the Club Mickey D's tent. A family is having their picture taken in front of the inflatable Ronald, arranging their little kids in a careful pose. Notebook entry: *Why?*

08/15/0842h. Fourth trip to the bathroom in three hours. Elimination can be a dicey undertaking here. The Fair has scores of Midwest Potty-houses brand portable toilets at various strategic sites. Midwest Potty-houses are man-sized plastic huts, reminiscent of Parisian *pissoirs* but also utilized for *numero deux,* clearly. Each Midwest Pottyhouse has its own undulating shroud of flies, plus your standard heavy-use no-flush out-house smell, and I for one would rather succumb to a rupture than use a Pottyhouse, though the lines for them are long and sanguine. The only real restrooms are in the big exhibit buildings. The Coliseum's is like a grade school boys' room, especially the long communal urinal, a kind of huge porcelain trough. Performance- and other anxieties abound here, with upwards of twenty guys all flanking and facing each other, each with his unit out. All the men's rooms have hot-air blowers instead of paper towels, meaning you can't wash your face, and all have annoying faucet controls you have to keep a grip on to operate, meaning toothbrushing is a contorted affair. The highlight is watching Midwestern ag-guys struggle with suspenders and overall straps as they exit the stalls.

08/15/0847h. A quick scan of the Draft Horse Show. The Coliseum's interior is the size of a blimp hangar, with an elliptical dirt arena. The stands are permanent and set in cement and go on and up forever. The stands are maybe 5% full. Echoes are creepy, but the smell of the arena's moist earth is lush and nice. The draft horses themselves are enormous, eight feet high and steroidically muscled. I think they were originally bred to pull things; God only knows their function now. There are two- and three-year-old Belgian Stallions, Percherons, and the Bud-famous Clydesdales with their bellbottoms of hair. The Belgians are particularly thick through the chest and rear quarter (I'm starting to develop an eye for livestock). Again, the Official wears a simply bitching white cowboy hat and stands at ease, legs well apart. This one has a weak chin and something wrong with one of his eyelids, though, at least. All the competitors are again shampooed and combed, black and gunpowder-gray and the dull white of sea-foam, their tails cropped and the stumps decorated with girlish bows that look obscene against all this muscle. The horses' heads bob when they walk, rather like pigeons' heads. They're led in the now familiar concentric circles by their owners, big-bellied men in brown suits and string ties. At obscure PA commands, the owners break their animals into thundering canter, holding their bridles and running just under the head, stomachs bouncing around (the men's). The horses' hoofs throw up big clods of earth as they run, so that it sort of rains dirt for several yards behind them. They look mythic when they run. Their giant hoofs are black and have shiny age-striations like a tree-stump's rings.

It's something of a relief to see no fast-food buyers on the dais awaiting Auction. As with Beef, though, a young beauty queen in a tiara presides from a flower-decked throne. It's unclear just who she is: "Ms. Illinois Horseflesh" sounds unlikely, as does "Ms. Illinois Draft Horse." (Though there is a 1993 Illinois Pork Queen, over in Swine.)

08/15/0930h. Sun erumpent, mid-90s, puddles and mud trying to evaporate into air that's already waterlogged. Every smell just hangs there. The general sensation is that of being in the middle of an armpit. I'm once again at the capacious McDonald's tent, at the edge, the titanic inflatable clown presiding. (Why is there no Wal-Mart tent?) There's a fair-sized crowd in the basketball bleachers at one side and rows of folding chairs at the other. It's the Illinois State Jr. Baton-Twirling Finals. A metal loudspeaker begins to emit disco, and little girls pour into the tent from all directions, twirling and gamboling in vivid costume. There's a symphony of zippers from the seats and stands as video cameras come out by the score, and I can tell it's pretty much just me and a thousand parents.

The baroque classes and divisions, both team and solo, go from age three (!) to sixteen, with epithetic signifiers — e.g. the four-year-olds compose the Sugar 'N' Spice division, and so on. I'm in a chair right up front (but in the sun) behind the competition's judges, introduced as "Varsity Twirlers from the [why?] University of Kansas." They are four frosted blondes who smile a lot and blow huge grape bubbles.

The twirler squads are all from different towns. Mount Vernon and Kankakee seem especially rich in twirlers. The twirlers' spandex costumes, differently colored for each team, are paint-tight and really brief in the legs. The coaches are grim, tan, lithe-looking women, clearly twirlers once, on the far side of their glory now and very serious-looking, each with a clipboard and whistle. It's all a little like figure skating. The teams go into choreographed routines, each routine with a title and a designated disco or show tune, full of compulsory baton-twirling maneuvers with highly technical names. A mom next to me is tracking scores on what looks almost like an astrology chart, and is in no mood to explain anything to a novice baton-watcher. The routines are wildly complex, and the loudspeaker's play-by-play is mostly in code. All I can determine for sure is that I've bumbled into what has to be the single most spectator-hazardous event at the Fair. Missed batons go all over, whistling wickedly. The three-, four-, and five-year-olds aren't that dangerous, though they do spend most of their time picking up dropped batons and trying to hustle back into place—the parents of especially fumble-prone twirlers howl in fury from the stands while the coaches chew gum grimly—but the littler girls don't have the arm-strength to really endanger anybody, although one of the judges does take a Sugar 'N' Spice's baton across the bridge of the nose and has to be helped from the tent.

But when the seven- and eight-year-olds hit the floor for a series of "Armed Service Medleys" (spandex with epaulets and officers' caps and batons over shoulders like M-16s), errant batons start pinwheeling into the tent's ceiling, sides, and crowd with real force. I myself duck several times. A man just down the row takes one in the plexus and falls over in his metal chair with a horrid crash. The batons (one stray I picked up had REGULATION LENGTH embossed down the shaft) have white rubber stoppers on each end, but it's that dry hard kind of rubber, and the batons themselves are not light. I don't think it's an accident that police nightsticks are also called service batons.

Physically, even within same-age teams, there are marked incongruities in size and development. One nine-year-old is several heads taller than another, and they're trying to do an involved back-and-forth duet thing with just one baton, which ends up taking out a bulb in one of the tent's steel hanging lamps and showering part of the stands with glass. A lot of the younger twirlers look either anorexic or gravely ill. There are no fat baton-twirlers. The enforcement of this no-endomorph rule is probably internal: a fat person'd have to get exactly one look at herself in tight sequinned spandex to abandon all twirling ambitions for all time.

Ironically, it's the botched maneuvers that allow one to see how baton-twirling (which to me had always seemed sleight-of-handish and occult) works in terms of mechanics. It seems to consist not in twirling so much as sort of spinning the baton on your knuckle while the fingers underneath work and writhe furiously for some reason, maybe supplying torque. Some serious kinetic force is coming from somewhere, clearly. A sort of attempted sidearm-twirl sends a baton Xing out and hitting a big woman's kneecap with a ringing clang, and her husband puts his hand on her shoulder as she sits up very rigid and white, pop-eyed, her mouth a little bloodless hyphen. I miss good old Native Companion, who's the sort of person who can elicit conversation even from the recently baton-struck.

A team of ten-year-olds from the Gingersnap class have little cotton bunnytails on their costumes' bottoms and rigid papier-mâché ears, and they can do some serious twirling. A squad of eleven-year-olds from Towanda does an involved routine in tribute to Operation Desert Storm. To most of the acts there's either a cutesy ultrafeminine aspect or a stern butch military one; there's little in between. Starting with the twelve-year-olds — one team in black spandex that looks like cheesecake leotards — there is, I'm afraid, a frank sexuality that begins to get uncomfortable. You can already see some of the sixteen-year-olds out under the basketball hoop doing little warm-up twirls and splits, and they're disturbing enough to make me wish there was a copy of the state's criminal statutes handy and prominent. Also disturbing is that in an empty seat next to me is a gun, a rifle, real-looking, with a white wood stock, which who knows whether it's really real or part of an upcoming martial routine or what, that's been sitting here ownerless ever since the competition started.

Oddly, it's the cutesy feminine routines that result in the really serious casualties. A dad standing up near the stands' top with a Toshiba viewfinder to his eye takes a tomahawking baton directly in the groin and falls forward onto somebody eating a Funnel Cake, and they take out good bits of several rows below them, and there's an extended halt to the action, during which I decamp — steering way clear of the sixteen-year-olds on the basketball court — and as I clear the last row yet another baton comes *wharp-wharp*ing cruelly right over my shoulder, caroming viciously off big R.'s inflated thigh.

08/15/1105h. A certain swanky East-Coast organ is unfortunately denied journalistic impressions of the Illinois Snakes Seminar, the Midwestern Birds of Prey Demonstration, the Husband-Calling Contest, and something the Media Guide calls "The Celebrity 'Moo-Moo' Classic" — all of these clearly must-sees — because they're all also in venues right near the Food and Dessert Tent Grotto, which even the abstract thought of another proffered wedge of Chocolate Silk Triple-Layer Cake in the shape of Lincoln's profile produces a pulsing ache in the bulge I've still got on the left side of my abdomen. So right now I'm five acres and six hundred food-booths away from midday's must-see events, in the slow stream of people entering the Expo Bldg.

I'd planned on skipping the Expo Bldg., figuring it was full of like home-furniture-refinishing demos and futuristic mockups of Peoria's skyline. I'd had no idea it was... *air-conditioned*. Nor that it comprises a whole additional different IL State Fair with its own separate pros and patrons. It's not just that there are no carnies or ag-people in here. The place is jammed with people I've seen literally nowhere else on the Fairgrounds. It's a world and gala unto itself, self-sufficient: the fourth Us of the Fair.

The Expo Bldg.'s a huge enclosed mallish thing, AC'd down to 80°, with a cement floor and a hardwood mezzanine overhead. Every interior inch here is given over to adversion and commerce of a very special and lurid sort. Just inside the big east entrance a man with a headset mike is slicing up a block of wood and then a tomato, standing on a box in a booth that says *SharpKut*, hawking these spinoffs of Ginsu knives, "AS SEEN ON TV." Next door is a booth offering personalized pet-I.D. tags. Another's got the infamous mail-order-advertised Clapper, which turns on appliances automatically at the sound of two hands clapping (but also at the sound of a cough, sneeze, or sniff, I discover—caveat emp.). There's booth after booth, each with an audience whose credulity is heartrending. The noise in the Expo Bldg. is apocalyptic and complexly echoed, sound-carpeted by crying children and ceiling-fans' roar. A large percentage of the booths show signs of hasty assembly and say AS SEEN ON TV in bright brave colors. The booths' salesmen all stand raised to a slight height; all have headset microphones and speakers with built-in amps and rich neutral media voices.

It turns out these franchised Expo vendors, not unlike the Blomsness carnies (any comparison to whom makes the vendors show canine teeth, though), go from State Fair to State Fair all summer. One young man demonstrating QUICK 'N' BRITE—"A WHOLE NEW CONCEPT IN CLEANING"—was under the persistent impression that he was in Iowa.

There's a neon-bordered booth for something called a RAINBOW-VAC, a vacuum cleaner whose angle is that it uses water in its canister instead of a bag, and the canister is clear Lucite, so you get a graphic look at just how much dirt it's getting out of a carpet sample. People in polyester slacks and/or orthopedic shoes are clustered three-deep around this booth, greatly moved, but all I can think of is that the thing looks like the world's biggest heavy-use bong, right down to the water's color. There's a predictably strong odor surrounding the Southwestern Leatherworx booth. Likewise at Distressed Leather Luggage (missing hyphen? misplaced mod?). I'm not even halfway down one side of the Expo's main floor, list-wise. The mezzanine has still more booths. There's a booth that offers clock-faces superimposed on varnished photorealist paintings of Christ, John Wayne, Marilyn Monroe. There's a Computerized Posture Evaluation booth. A lot of the headsetted vendors are about my age or younger. Something ever so slightly over-groomed about them suggests a Bible-college background. It's just cool enough in here for a sweat-soaked shirt to get clammy. One vendor recites a pitch for Ms. Suzanne Somers's THIGHMASTER while a lady in a leotard lies on her side on the fiberboard counter and demonstrates the product. I'm in the Expo Bldg. almost two hours, and every time I look up the poor lady's still at it with the THIGHMASTER. Most of the Expo vendors won't answer questions and give me beady looks when I stand there making notes in the Barney tablet. But the THIGHMASTER lady—friendly, garrulous, violently cross-eyed, in (understandably) phenomenal physical condition—informs me she gets an hour off for lunch at 1400 but is back on her side all the way to closing at 2300. I remark that her thighs must be pretty well Mastered by now, and her leg sounds like a bannister when she raps her knuckle against it, and we have a good laugh together until her vendor finally makes her ask me to scram.

The Copper Kettle All-Butter Fudge booth does brisk air-conditioned business. There's something called a Full Immersion Body Fat Analysis for $8.50. A certain CompuVac Inc. offers a $1.50 Computerized Personality Analysis. Its booth's computer panel's tall and full of blinking lights and reel-to-reel tapes, like an old bad sci-fi-film computer. My own Personality Analysis, a slip of paper that protrudes like a tongue from a red-lit slot, says "Your Boldness of Nature is Ofset With The Fear Of Taking Risk" (sic^2). My suspicion that there's a guy hunched behind the blinking panel feeding its slot recycled fortune-cookie slips is overwhelming but unverifiable.

Booth after booth. A Xanadu of chintzola. Obscure non-stick cookware. "EYE GLASSES CLEANED FREE." A booth with anti-cellulite sponges. More DIPPIN DOTS futuristic ice cream. A woman with Velcro straps on her shoes gets fountain-pen ink out of a linen tablecloth with a Chapsticky-looking spot remover whose banner says "AS SEEN ON 'AMAZING DISCOVERIES,'" a wee-hour infomercial I'm kind of a fan of. A plywood booth that for $9.95 will take a photo and superimpose your face on either an FBI Wanted poster or a *Penthouse* cover. An MIA—BRING THEM HOME! booth staffed by women playing Go Fish. An anti-abortion booth called LIFESAVERS that lures you over with free candy. Sand Art. Shredded-Ribbon Art. Therm-L-Seal Double Pane Windows. An indescribable booth for "LATEST ADVANCE ROTARY NOSE HAIR CLIPPERS" whose other sign reads (I kid you not) *"Do Not Pull Hair From Nose, May Cause Fatal Infection."* Two different booths for collectible sports cards, "Top Ranked Investment Of The Nineties." And tucked way back on one curve of the mezzanine's ellipse: *yes:* black velvet paintings, including several of Elvis in pensive poses.

And people are buying this stuff. The Expo's unique products are targeted at a certain type of Midwestern person I'd all but forgotten. I'd somehow not noticed these persons' absence from the paths and exhibits. This is going to sound not just East-Coastish but elitist and snotty. But facts are facts. The special community of shoppers in the Expo Bldg. are a Midwestern subphylum commonly if unkindly known as Kmart People. Farther south they'd be a certain fringe-type of White Trash. Kmart People tend to be overweight, polyestered, grim-faced, toting glazed unhappy children. Toupees are the movingly obvious shiny square-cut kind, and the women's makeup is garish and often asymmetrically applied, giving many of the female faces a kind of demented look. They are sharp-voiced and snap at their families. They're the type you see slapping their kids in supermarket checkouts. They are people who work at like Champaign's Kraft and Decatur's A. E. Staley and think pro wrestling is real. I'm sorry, but this is all true. I went to high school with Kmart People. I know them. They own firearms and do not hunt. They aspire to own mobile homes. They read the *Star* without even a pretense of contempt and have toilet paper with little off-color jokes printed on it. A few of these folks might check out the Tractor Pull or U.S.A.C. race, but most are in the Expo to stay. This is what they've come for. They couldn't give one fat damn about ethanol exhibits or carnival rides whose seats are hard to squeeze into. Agriculture shmagriculture. And Gov. Edgar's a closet pinko: they heard it on Rush. They plod up and down, looking put out and intensely puzzled, as if they're sure what they've come for's got to be here someplace. I wish Native C. were here; she's highly quotable on the subject of Kmart People. One big girl with tattoos and a heavy-diapered infant wears a T-shirt that says "WARNING: I GO FROM 0 TO HORNEY IN 2.5 BEERS."

Have you ever wondered where these particular types of unfunny T-shirts come from? the ones that say things like "HORNEY IN 2.5" or

"Impeach President Clinton…AND HER HUSBAND TOO!!"? Mystery solved. They come from State Fair Expos. Right here on the main floor's a monster-sized booth, more like an open bodega, with shirts and laminated buttons and license-plate borders, all of which, for this subphylum, Testify. This booth seems integral, somehow. The seamiest fold of the Midwestern underbelly. The Lascaux Caves of a certain rural mentality. "40 Isn't Old…IF YOU'RE A TREE" and "The More Hair I Lose, The More Head I Get" and "Retired: No Worries, No Paycheck" and "I Fight Poverty…I WORK!!" As with *New Yorker* cartoons, there's an elusive sameness about the shirts' messages. A lot serve to I.D. the wearer as part of a certain group and then congratulate that group for its sexual dynamism—"Coon Hunters Do It All Night" and "Hairdressers Tease It Till It Stands Up" and "Save A Horse: Ride A Cowboy." Some presume a weird kind of aggressive relation between the shirt's wearer and its reader—"We'd Get Along Better…If You Were A BEER" and "Lead Me Not Into Temptation, I Know The Way MYSELF" and "What Part Of NO Don't You Understand?" There's something complex and compelling about the fact that these messages are not just uttered but *worn*, like they're a badge or credential. The message compliments the wearer somehow, and the wearer in turn endorses the message by spreading it across his chest, which fact is then in further turn supposed to endorse the wearer as a person of plucky or risqué wit. It's also meant to cast the wearer as an Individual, the sort of person who not only makes but wears a Personal Statement. What's depressing is that the T-shirts' statements are not only preprinted and mass-produced, but so dumbly unfunny that they serve to place the wearer squarely in that large and unfortunate group of people who think such messages not only Individual but funny. It all gets tremendously complex and depressing. The lady running the booth's register is dressed like a '68 Yippie but has a hard carny face and wants to know why I'm standing here memorizing T-shirts. All I can manage to tell her is that the "HORNEY" on these "2.5 BEERS"-shirts is misspelled; and now I really feel like an East-Coast snob, laying judgments and semiotic theories on these people who ask of life only a Republican in the White House and a black velvet Elvis on the wood-grain mantel of their mobile home. They're not hurting anybody. A good third of the people I went to high school with now probably wear these T-shirts, and proudly.

And I'm forgetting to mention the Expo Bldg.'s other nexus of commerce—church booths. The populist evangelism of the rural Midwest. An economy of spirit. It's not your cash they want. A Church of God booth offers a Computerized Bible Quiz. Its computer is CompuVacish in appearance. I go eighteen for twenty on the Quiz and am invited behind a chamois curtain for a "person-to-person faith exploration," which thanks anyway. The conventional vendors get along fine with the Baptists and Jews for Jesus who operate booths right near them. They all laugh and banter back and forth. The SharpKut guy sends all the vegetables he's microsliced over to the LIFESAVERS booth, where they put them out with the candy. The scariest spiritual booth is right up near the west exit, where something called Covenant Faith Triumphant Church has a big hanging banner that asks "WHAT IS THE *ONE* MAN MADE THING IN HEAVEN?" and I stop to ponder, which with charismatics is instant death, because a breastless bushy-browed woman is out around the booth's counter like a shot and in my personal space. She says "Give up? Give up do you?" I tell her I'll go ahead and bite. She's looking at me very intensely, but there's something off about her gaze: it's like she's looking *at* my eyes rather than *into* them. What one man-made thing, I ask. She puts her finger to her palm and makes screwing motions. Signifying coitus? (I don't say "coitus" out loud, though.) "Not but one thing," she says. "The holes in Christ's palms," screwing her finger in. It's scary. Except isn't it pretty well known that Roman crucifees were nailed at the wrists, since palm-flesh won't support weight? So but now I've been drawn into an actual dialogue, going so far as to let the lady take my arm and pull me toward the booth's counter. "Lookee here for a second now," she says. She has both hands around my arm. I feel a sinking in my gut; I'm programmed from childhood to know that I've made a serious error. A Midwestern child of academics gets trained early on to avoid these weird-eyed eager rural Christians who accost your space, to say Not Interested at the front door and No Thanks to mimeoed leaflets, to look right through streetcorner missionaries as if they were NYC panhandlers. I have erred. The woman more or less throws me up against the Covenant Faith counter, on which counter is a fine oak box, yay big, with a propped sign: "Where Will YOU Be When YOU Look Like THIS?" "Take you a look-see in here." The box has a hole in the top. Inside the box is a human skull. I'm pretty sure it's plastic. The interior lighting's tricky. But I'm pretty sure the skull isn't genuine. I haven't inhaled for over a minute now. The woman is looking at the side of my face. "Are you *sure* is the question," she says. I manage to make my straightening-up motion lead right into a backing-away motion. "Are you a hundred percent *sure*." Overhead, on the mezzanine, the THIGHMASTER lady's still at it, on her side, head on her arm, smiling cross-eyed into space.

*   *   *

08/15/1336h. I'm on a teetery stool watching the Prairie State Cloggers Competition in a Twilight Ballroom that's packed with ag-folks and well over 100°. An hour ago I'd nipped in here to get a bottle of soda-pop on my way to the Truck and Tractor Pull. By now the Pull's got to be nearly over, and in half an hour the big U.S.A.C. dirt-track auto race starts, which I've already reserved a ticket for. But I can't tear myself away from the scene in here. This is far and away the funnest, most emotionally intense thing at the Fair. Run, don't walk, to your nearest clogging venue.

I'd imagined goony Jed Clampett types in tattered hats and hobnail boots, a-stompin' and a-whoopin', etc. Clogging, Scotch-Irish in origin and the dance of choice in Appalachia, I guess did used to involve actual clogs and boots and slow stomps. But clogging has now miscegenated with square dancing and honky-tonk boogie to become a kind of intricately synchronized, absolutely kick-ass country tap dance.

There's teams from Pekin, Leroy, Rantoul, Cairo, Morton. They each do three numbers. The music is up-tempo country or 4/4 dance-pop. Each team has anywhere from four to ten dancers. They're 75% women. Few of the women are under 35, fewer still under 175 lbs. They're country mothers, red-cheeked gals with bad dye jobs and big pretty legs. They wear Westernwear tops and midiskirts with multiple ruffled slips underneath; and every once in a while they'll grab handfuls of cloth and flip the skirts up like cancan dancers. When they do this they either yip or whoop, as the spirit moves them. The men all have thinning hair and cheesy rural faces, and their skinny legs are rubberized blurs. The men's Western shirts have piping on the chest and shoulders. The teams are all color-coordinated — blue and white, black and red. The white shoes all the dancers wear look like golf shoes with metal taps clamped on.

Their numbers are to everything from shitkicker Waylon and Tammy to Aretha, Miami Sound Machine, Neil Diamond's "America." The routines have some standard tap-dance moves—sweep, flare, chorus-line kicking. But it's fast and sustained and choreographed down to the last wrist-flick. And square dancing's genes can be seen in the upright, square-shouldered postures on the floor, a kind of florally enfolding tendency to the choreography, some of which features high-speed promenades. But it's adrenaline-dancing, meth-paced and exhausting to watch because your own feet move; and it's erotic in a way that makes MTV look lame. The cloggers' feet are too fast to be seen, really, but they all tap out the exact same rhythm. A typical routine's is something like: *ta*tatata*ta*tatata*ta*tata. The variations around the basic rhythm are baroque. When they kick or spin, the two-beat absence of tap complexifies the pattern.

The audience is packed in right to the edge of the portable hardwood flooring. The teams are mostly married couples. The men are either rail-thin or have big hanging guts. A couple of the men are great fluid Astaire-like dancers, but mostly it's the women who compel. The males have constant sunny smiles, but the women look orgasmic; they're the really serious ones, transported. Their yips and whoops are involuntary, pure exclamation. They are arousing. The audience claps savvily on the back-beat and whoops when the women do. It's almost all folks from the ag and livestock shows—the flannel shirts, khaki pants, seed caps, and freckles. The spectators are soaked in sweat and extremely happy. I think this is the ag-community's Special Treat, a chance here to cut loose a little while their animals sleep in the heat. The psychic transactions between cloggers and crowd seem representative of the Fair as a whole: a culture talking to itself, presenting credentials for its own inspection. This is just a smaller and specialized rural Us—bean farmers and herbicide brokers and 4-H sponsors and people who drive pickup trucks because they really need them. They eat non-Fair food from insulated hampers and drink beer and pop and stomp in perfect time and put their hands on neighbors' shoulders to shout in their ear while the cloggers twirl and fling sweat on the crowd.

There are no black people in the Twilight Ballroom. The looks on the younger ag-kids' faces have this awakened astonished aspect, like they didn't realize their own race could dance like this. Three married couples from Rantoul, wearing full Western bodysuits the color of raw coal, weave an incredible filigree of high-speed tap around Aretha's "R-E-S-P-E-C-T," and there's no hint of racial irony in the room; the song has been made these people's own, emphatically. This '90s version of clogging does have something sort of pugnaciously white about it, a kind of performative nose-thumbing at Jackson and Hammer. There's an atmosphere in the room—not racist, but aggressively white. It's hard to describe. The atmosphere's the same at a lot of rural Midwest public events. It's not like if a black person came in he'd be ill-treated; it's more like it would just never occur to a black person to come in here.

I can barely hold the tablet to scribble journalistic impressions, the floor's rumbling under so many boots and sneakers. The record player's old-fashioned and the loudspeakers are shitty and it all sounds fantastic. Two little girls are playing jacks under the table I'm next to. Two of the dancing Rantoul wives are fat, but with great legs. Who could practice this kind of dancing as much as they must and stay fat? I think maybe rural Midwestern women are just congenitally big. But these people clog-ging get *down*. And they do it as a troupe, a collective, with none of the narcissistic look-at-me grandstanding of great dancers in rock clubs. They hold hands and whirl each other around and in and out, tapping like mad, their torsos upright and almost formal, as if only incidentally attached to the blur of legs below. It goes on and on. I'm rooted to my stool. Each team seems the best yet. On the crowd's other side across the floor I can see the old poultry farmer, he of the carny-hatred and electrified wallet. He's still got his billed poultry cap on, making a megaphone of his hands to whoop with the women, leaning way forward in his geriatric scooter, body bobbing like he's stomping in time while his little black boots stay clamped in their stays.

08/15/1636h. Trying to hurry to Grandstand; trapped in masses on central path out past FoodaRama. I'm eating a corn dog cooked in 100% soybean oil. I can hear the hornety engines of the U.S.A.C. 100 race, which must have started quite a while ago. Huge plume of track-dust hanging over Grandstand. Distant tinny burble of excited PA announcer. The corn dog tastes strongly of soybean oil, which itself tastes like corn oil that's been strained through an old gym towel. Tickets for the race are an obscene $13.50. Baton-twirling is *still* under way in the McD.'s tent. A band called Captain Rat and the Blind Rivets is playing at the Lincoln Stage, and as the path's mass goes by I can see dancers in there. They look jagged and arrhythmic and blank, bored in that hip young East-Coast-taught way, facing in instead of out, not touching their partners. The people not dancing don't even look at them, and after the clogging the whole thing looks unspeakably lonely and numb.

08/15/1645h. The official name of the race is the William "Wild Bill" Oldani Memorial 100 Sprint Car Race of the Valvoline-U.S.A.C. Silver Crown Series' True Value Championship Circuit. The Grandstand seats 9800 and is packed. The noise is beyond belief. The race is nearly over: the electric sign on the infield says LAP 92. The board says the leader is #26, except his black-and-green SKOAL car's in the middle of the pack. Apparently he's lapped people. The crowd's mostly men, very tan, smoking, mustaches, billed caps with automotive associations. Most of the spectators wear earplugs; the ones in the real know wear those thick airline-worker noise-filter earmuffs. The seventeen-page program is mostly impenetrable. There are either 49 or 50 cars, called either Pro Dirt or Silver Crown cars, and they're basically go-carts from hell, with a soapbox-derby chassis and huge dragster tires, gleaming tangles of pipes and spoilers jutting out all over, and unabashedly phallic bulges up front, where I suspect the engines are. What I know about auto racing could be inscribed with a dry Magic Marker on the lip of a Coke bottle. The program says these models are what they used to race at Indy in the 1950s. It's unclear whether that means these specific cars or this genre of car or what. I'm pretty sure "Indy" refers to the Indianapolis 500. The cars' cockpits are open and webbed in straps and roll bars; the drivers wear helmets the same color as their cars, with white ski-masky things over their faces to keep out the choking dust. The cars come in all hues. Most look to be sponsored by either Skoal or Marlboro. Pit crews in surgical white lean out into the track and flash obscure commands written on little chalkboards. The infield is clotted with trailers and tow trucks and Officials' stands and electric signs. Women in skimpy tops stand on different trailers, seeming very partisan indeed. It's all very confusing. Certain facts in the program just don't add up—like the Winner's Purse is only $9200, yet each car supposedly represents a six-figure annual investment for various sponsors. Whatever they invest in, it isn't mufflers. I can barely take my hands off my ears long enough to turn the program's pages. The cars sound almost like jets—that insectile whine—but with a diesely, lawn-mowerish component you can feel in your skull. Part of the problem is the raw concrete of the Grandstand's seating; another's the fact that the seating's on just one side of the Grandstand, on the straightaway. When the main mass of cars passes it's unendurable; your very skeleton hurts from the noise, and your ears are still belling when they come around again. The cars go like mad bats on the straightaways and then shift down for the tight turns, their rear tires wobbling in the dirt. Certain cars pass other cars, and some people cheer when they do. Down at the bottom of my section of seats a little boy held up on a cement fence-support by his father is rigid, facing away from the track, his hands clamped over his ears so hard his elbows stick way out, and his face is a rictus of pain as the cars go by. The little boy and I sort of rictus at each other. A fine dirty dust hangs in the air and coats everything, tongues included. Then all of a sudden binoculars come out and everyone stands as there's some sort of screeching slide and crash on a far turn, all the way across the infield; and firemen in full-length slickers and hats go racing out there in fire trucks, and the PA voice's pitch goes way up but is still incomprehensible, and a man with those airline earmuffs in the Officials' stands leans out and flails at the air with a bright-yellow flag, and the go-carts throttle down to autobahn speed, and the Official Pace Car (a Trans Am) comes out and leads them around, and everybody stands up, and I stand too. It's impossible to see anything but a swizzle stick of smoke above the far turn, and the engine noise is endurable and the PA silent, and the relative quiet hangs there while we all wait for news, and I look around hard at all the faces below the raised binoculars, but it's not at all clear what sort of news we're all hoping for.

08/15/1730h. Ten-minute line for an I.D.C. milkshake. Oily blacktop stink on heated paths. I ask a little kid to describe the taste of his Funnel Cake and he runs away. Ears still mossily ringing—everything sounds kind of car-phonish. Display of a 17.6-lb zucchini squash outside the Agri-Industries Pavilion. One big zucchini, all right. Several of the Dessert Tent ladies are at the Tupperware Retrospective (no kidding) right nearby, though, and I make myself scarce in a hurry. In the Coliseum, the only historical evidence of the Tractor Pull is huge ideograms of tire tracks, mounds of scored dirt, dark patches of tobacco juice, smells of burnt rubber and oil. Two buildings over is a curiously non-State-Pride-related exhibit, by the Harley Davidson Corporation, of "Motorcycles Of Distinction." Also a deltiology exhibit—card after card, some back from the 1940s, mostly of crops, thunderclouds massing at horizons, flat sweeps of very black land. In a broad tent next door's the "Motorsport Spectacular Exhibition," which is kind of surreal: a whole lot of really shiny and fast-looking sports cars in utter stasis, just sitting there, hoods up, innards exposed, clusters of older men in berets studying the cars with great intensity, some with white gloves and jeweler's loupes. Between two minor corporate tents is the serendipitous snout of the "Sertoma Mobile Hearing Test Trailer," inside which a woman with a receding hairline scores me overdecibeled but aurally hale. Fifteen whole minutes both in- and outside the huge STATE COMPTROLLER ROLAND BURRIS tent foils to uncover the tent's function. Next door, though, is a bus on display from the city of Peoria's All-Ethanol Bus System; it is painted to resemble a huge ear of corn. I don't know whether actual fleets of green-and-yellow corn-buses are deployed in Peoría or whether this is just a stunt.

08/15/1800h. Back again at the seemingly inescapable Club Mickey D's. All signs of baton-twirlers and fallen spectators have been erased. The tent's now set up for Illinois Golden Gloves Boxing. Out on the floor is a kind of square made up of four boxing rings. The rings are made out of clothesline and poles anchored by cement-filled tires, one ring per age division—Sixteens, Fourteens, Twelves, Tens(!). Here's another unhyped but riveting spectacle. If you want to see genuine interhuman violence, go check out a Golden Gloves tourney. None of your adult pros' silky footwork or Rope-a-Dope defenses here. Here asses are thoroughly kicked in what are essentially playground brawls with white-tipped gloves and brain-shaped headguards. The combatants' tank tops say things like "Rockford Jr. Boxing" and "Elgin Fight Club." The rings' corners have stools for the kids to sit on and get worked over by their teams' coaches. The coaches look like various childhood friends of mine's abusive fathers—florid, blue-jawed, bull-necked, flinty-eyed, the kind of men who bowl, watch TV in their underwear, and oversee sanctioned brawls. Now a fighter's mouthguard goes flying out of the Fourteens' ring, end over end, trailing strings of spit, and the crowd around that ring howls. In the Sixteens' ring is a Springfield kid, a local hero, one Darrell Hall, against a slim fluid Latino named Sullivano from Joliet. Hall outweighs Sullivano by a good twenty pounds. Hall also looks like just about every kid who ever beat me up in high school, right down to the wispy mustache and upper lip's cruel twist. The crowd around the Sixteens' ring is all his friends—guys with muscle shirts and varsity gym shorts and gelled hair, girls in cutoff overalls and complex systems of barrettes and scrunchies. There are repeated shouts of "Kick his *ass* Darrell!" The Latino sticks and moves. Somebody in this tent is smoking a joint, I can smell. The Sixteens can actually box. The ceiling's lights are bare bulbs in steel cones, hanging cockeyed from a day of batons. Everybody here pours sweat. A few people look askance at the little clicker I carry. The reincarnation of every high school cheerleader I ever pined for is in the Sixteens' crowd. The girls cry out and sort of frame their face in their hands whenever Darrell Hall gets hit. I do not know why cutoff overall shorts have evaded the East Coast's fashion ken; they are devastating. The fight in Fourteens is stopped for a moment to let the ref wipe a gout of blood from one kid's glove. Sullivano glides and jabs, sort of orbiting Hall. Hall is implacable, a hunched and feral fighter, boring in. Air explodes through his nose when he lands a blow. He keeps trying to back the Latino against the clothesline. People fan themselves with wood-handled fans from the Democratic Party. Mosquitoes work the crowd. The refs keep slapping at their necks. The rains have been bad, and the mosquitoes this August are the bad kind, big and vaguely hairy, field-bred, rapacious, the kind that can swarm on a calf overnight and the farmer finds his calf in the morning splay-legged and bled kosher. This actually happens. Mosquitoes are not to be fucked with out here. (East-Coast friends laugh at my dread of mosquitoes, and they make fun of the little battery-powered box I carry whenever I'm outside at night. Even in like NYC or Boston I carry it. It's from an obscure catalogue and produces a sound like a dragonfly—a.k.a. *odonata anisoptera*, sworn eternal foe to all mosquitoes everywhere—a faint high-speed clicking that sends any right-thinking mosquito out of its mind with fear. On East 55th, carrying the little box is maybe a bit neurotic; here, with me ripe and sweaty and tall in this crowd, the good old trusty clicker saves more than just my ass.) I can also see the Tens from this vantage, a vicious free-for-all between two tiny kids whose headguards make their heads look too big for their bodies. Neither ten-year-old has any interest in defense. Their shoes' toes touch as they windmill at each other, scoring at will. Scary dads chew gum in their corners. One kid's mouthguard keeps falling out. Now the Sixteens' crowd explodes as their loutish Darrell catches Sullivano with an uppercut that puts him on his bottom. Sullivano gamely rises, but his knees wobble and he won't face the ref. Hall raises both arms and faces the crowd, disclosing a missing incisor. The girls betray their cheerleading backgrounds by clapping and jumping up and down at the same time. Hall shakes his gloves at the ceiling as several girls call his name, and you can feel it in the air's very ions: Darrell Hall is going to get laid before the night's over.

The digital thermometer in the Ronald-god's big left hand reads 93° at 1815h. Behind him, big ominous scoop-of-coffee-ice-cream clouds are piling up at the sky's western reef, but the sun's still above them and very much a force. People's shadows on the paths are getting pointy. It's the part of the day when little kids go into jagged crying fits from what their parents naïvely call exhaustion. Cicadas chirr in the grass by the tent. The ten-year-olds stand literally toe to toe and whale the living shit out of each other. It's the sort of implausibly savage mutual beating you see in fight-movies. Their ring now has the largest crowd. The fight'll be all but impossible to score. But then it's over in an instant at the second intermission when one of the little boys, sitting on his stool, being whispered to by a coach with tattooed forearms, suddenly throws up. Prodigiously. For no apparent reason. It's kind of surreal. Vomit flies all over. Kids in the crowd go "Eeeyuuu." Several partially digested food-booth items are identifiable — maybe that's the apparent reason. The sick fighter starts to cry. His scary coach and the ref wipe him down and help him from the ring, not ungently. His opponent tentatively puts up his arms.

08/15/1930h. And there is, in this state with its origin and reason in food, a strong digestive subtheme running all through the '93 Fair. In a way, we're all here to be swallowed up. The Main Gate's maw admits us, slow tight-packed masses move peristaltically along complex systems of branching paths, engage in complex cash-and-energy transfers at the villi alongside the paths, and are finally — both filled and depleted — expelled out of exits designed for heavy flow. And there are the exhibits of food and of the production of food, the unending food-booths and the peripatetic consumption of food. The public Potties and communal urinals. The moist body-temp heat of the Fairgrounds. The livestock judged and applauded as future food while the animals stand in their own manure, chewing cuds.

Plus there are those great literalizers of all metaphor, little kids—boxers and fudge-gluttons, sunstroke-casualties, those who overflow just from the adrenaline of the Specialness of it all—the rural Midwesterners of tomorrow, all throwing up.

And so the old heavo-ho is the last thing I see at Golden Gloves Boxing and then the first thing I see at Happy Hollow, right at sunset. Standing with stupid Barney tablet on the Midway, looking up at the Ring of Fire—a set of flame-colored train cars sent around and around the inside of a 100-foot neon hoop, the operator stalling the train at the top and hanging the patrons upside down, jackknifed over their seatbelts, with loose change and eyeglasses raining down—looking up, I witness a single thick coil of vomit arc from a car; it describes a 100-foot spiral and lands with a meaty splat between two young girls whose T-shirts say something about volleyball and who look from the ground to each other with expressions of slapstick horror. And when the flame-train finally brakes at the ramp, a mortified-looking little kid totters off, damp and green, staggering over toward a Lemon Shake-Up stand.

I am basically scribbling impressions as I jog. I've put off a real survey of the Near-Death Experiences until my last hour, and I want to get everything catalogued before the sun sets. I've had some distant looks at the nighttime Hollow from up on the Press Lot's ridge and have an idea that being down here in the dark, amid all this rotating neon and the mechanical clowns and plunging machinery's roar and piercing screams and barkers' amplified pitches and high-volume rock, would be like every bad Sixties movie's depiction of a bum acid trip. It strikes me hardest in the Hollow that I am not spiritually Midwestern anymore, and no longer young—I do not like crowds, screams, loud noise, or heat. I'll endure these things if I have to, but they're no longer my idea of a Special Treat or sacred Community-interval. The crowds in the Hollow—mostly high school couples, local toughs, and kids in single-sex packs, as the demographics of the Fair shift to prime time—seem radically gratified, vivid, actuated, sponges for sensuous data, feeding on it all somehow. It's the first time I've felt truly lonely at the Fair.

Nor, I have to say, do I understand why some people will pay money to be careened and suspended and dropped and whipped back and forth at high speeds and hung upside down until they vomit. It seems to me like paying to be in a traffic accident. I do not get it; never have. It's not a regional or cultural thing. I think it's a matter of basic neurological makeup. I think the world divides neatly into those who are excited by the managed induction of terror and those who are not. I do not find terror exciting. I find it terrifying. One of my basic life goals is to subject my nervous system to as little total terror as possible. The cruel paradox of course is that this kind of makeup usually goes hand in hand with a delicate nervous system that's extremely easy to terrify. I'm pretty sure I'm more frightened looking up at the Ring of Fire than the patrons are riding it.

Happy Hollow has not one but two Tilt-a-Whirls. An experience called Wipe Out straps customers into fixed seats on a big lit disc that spins with a wobble like a coin that won't quite lie down. The infamous Pirate Ship puts forty folks in a plastic galley and swings it in a pendulous arc until they're facing straight up and then down. There's vomit on the sides of the Pirate Ship, too. The carny operating the P. Ship is made to wear an eyepatch and parrot and hook, on the tip of which hook burns an impaled Marlboro.

The operator of the Funhouse is slumped in a plastic control booth that reeks of sinsemilla.

The 104-foot Giant Gondola Wheel is a staid old Ferris wheel that puts you facing your seatmate in a kind of steel teacup. Its rotation is stately, but the cars at the top look like little lit thimbles, and you can hear thin female screams from up there as their dates grab the teacups' sides and joggle.

The lines are the longest for the really serious Near-Death Experiences: Ring of Fire, The Zipper, Hi Roller—which latter runs a high-speed train around the inside of an ellipse that is itself spinning at right angles to the train's motion. The crowds are dense and reek of repellent. Boys in fishnet shirts clutch their dates as they walk. There's something intensely *public* about young Midwestern couples. The girls have tall teased hair and bee-stung lips, and their eye makeup runs in the heat and gives them a vampirish aspect. The overt sexuality of modern high school girls is not just a Coastal thing. There's a Midwestern term, "drape," for the kind of girl who hangs onto her boyfriend in public like he's a tree in a hurricane. A lot of the girls on the Midway are drapes. I swing my trusty dragonfly-clicker before me in broad censerish arcs as I jog. I'm on a strict and compressed timetable. The Amour Express sends another little train at 60+ mph around a topologically deformed ring, half of which is enclosed in a fiberglass tunnel with neon hearts and arrows. Bug zappers up on the lightpoles are doing a brisk business. A fallen packet of Trojans lies near the row of Lucite cubes in which slack-jawed cranes try to pick up jewelry. The Hollow's basically an east-west vector, but I jog in rough figure-eights, passing certain venues several times. The Funhouse operator's sneakers are sticking out of his booth; the rest of him is out of view. Kids are running into the Funhouse for free. For a moment I'm convinced I've spotted Alan Thicke, of all celebrities, shooting an air rifle at a row of 2-D cardboard Iraqis for a *Jurassic Park* stuffed animal.

It seems journalistically irresponsible to describe the Hollow's rides without experiencing at least one of them firsthand. The Kiddie Kopter is a carousel of miniature Sikorsky prototypes rotating at a sane and dignified clip. The propellers on each helicopter rotate as well. My copter is admittedly a bit snug, even with my knees drawn up to my chest. I get kicked off the ride when the whole machine's radical tilt reveals that I weigh quite a bit more than the maximum 100 pounds, and I have to say that both the carny in charge and the other kids on the ride were unnecessarily snide about the whole thing. Each ride has its own PA speaker with its own charge of adrenalizing rock; the Kiddie Kopter's speaker is playing George Michael's "I Want Your Sex" as the little bastards go around. The late-day Hollow itself is an enormous sonic mash from which different sounds take turns protruding—mostly whistles, sirens, calliopes, mechanized clown-cackles, heavy-metal tunes, human screams hard to distinguish from recorded screams.

It isn't Alan Thicke, on closer inspection.

Both the Thunderboltz and the Octopus hurl free-spinning modular cars around a topologically complex plane. The Thunderboltz's north side and entrance ramp show still more evidence of gastric distress. Then there's the Gravitron, an enclosed, top-shaped structure inside which is a rubberized chamber that spins so fast you're mashed against the wall like a fly on a windshield. It's basically a centrifuge for the centrifugal separation of people's brains from those brains' blood supply. Watching people come out of the Gravitron is not a pleasant experience at all, and you do not want to know what the ground around the exit looks like. A small boy stands on one foot tugging the operator's khaki sleeve, crying that he lost a shoe in there. The best description of the carnies' tan is that they're somehow *sinisterly* tan. I notice that many of them have the low brow and prognathous jaw typically associated with Fetal Alcohol Syndrome. The carny operating the Scooter—bumper cars, fast, savage, underinsulated, a sure trip to the chiropractor—has been slumped in the same position in the same chair every time I've seen him, staring past the frantic cars and tearing up used ride-tickets with the vacant intensity of someone on a

Locked Ward. I lean casually against his platform's railing so that my Credentials dangle prominently and ask him in a neighborly way how he keeps from going out of his freaking mind with the boredom of his job. He turns his head very slowly, revealing a severe facial tic: "The fuck you talking bout."

The same two carnies as before are at The Zipper's controls, in the exact same clothes, looking up into the full cars and elbowing each other. The Midway smells of machine oil and fried food, smoke and Cutter repellent and mall-bought adolescent perfume and ripe trash in the bee-swarmed cans. The very Nearest-to-Death ride looks to be the Kamikaze, way down at the western end near the Zyklon roller coaster. Its neon sign has a grinning skull with a headband and says simply KAMIKAZE. It's a 70-foot pillar of white-painted iron with two 50-foot hammer-shaped arms hanging down, one on either side. The cars are at the end of these arms, twelve-seaters enclosed in clear plastic. The two arms swing ferociously around, as in 360°, vertically, and in opposite directions, so that at the top and bottom of every rotation it looks like your car is going to get smashed up against the other car and you can see faces in the other car hurtling toward you, gray with fright and squishy with G's. An eight-ticket, four-dollar waking nightmare.

No. Now I've found the worst one. It wasn't even here yesterday. It must have been brought in special. It may not even be part of the carnival proper. It's the SKY COASTER. The SKY COASTER stands regally aloof at the Hollow's far western edge, just past the Uphill-Bowling-for-Dinnerware game, in a kind of grotto formed by Blomsness-Thebault trailers and dismantled machinery. At first all you can see is the very-yellow of some piece of heavy construction equipment, then after a second there's some other, high-overhead stuff that from the east is just a tangle of Expressionist shadows against the setting sun. A small but steady stream of Fairgoers leads into the SKY COASTER grotto.

It's a 175-foot construction crane, a BRH-200, one of the really big mothers, with a tank's traction belts instead of wheels, a canary-yellow cab, and a long proboscis of black steel, 200 feet long, canted upward at maybe 70°. This is half of the SKY COASTER. The other half is a 100-foot+ tower assembly of cross-hatched iron that's been erected a couple hundred yards north of the crane. There's a folding table in front of the clothesline cordoning off the crane, and there's a line of people at the table. The woman taking their money is fiftyish and a compelling advertisement for sunscreen. Behind her on a vivid blue tarp are two meaty blond guys in SKY COASTER T-shirts helping the next customer strap himself into what looks like a combination straitjacket and utility belt, bristling with hooks and clips. It's not yet entirely clear what's going on. From here the noise of the Hollow behind is both deafening and muffled, like high tide behind a dike. My Media Guide, sweated into the shape of a buttock from my pocket, says: "If you thought bungee jumping was a thrill, wait until you soar high above the Fairgrounds on SKY COASTER. The rider is fastened securely into a full-body harness that hoists them [sic, hopefully] onto a tower and releases them to swing in a pendulum-like motion while taking in a spectacular view of the Fairgrounds below." The hand-printed signs at the folding table are more telling: "$40.00. AMEX Visa MC. NO REFUNDS. NO STOPPING HALF WAY UP." The two guys are leading the customer up the stairs of a construction platform maybe ten feet high. One guy's at each elbow, and I realize they're helping hold the customer up. Who would pay $40.00 for an experience you have to be held up even to walk toward? Why pay money to cause something to occur you will be grateful to survive? I simply do not get it. Plus there's also something slightly off about this customer, odd. For one thing, he's wearing tinted aviator glasses. No one in the rural Midwest wears aviator glasses, tinted or otherwise. Then I see what it really is. He's wearing $400 Banfi loafers. Without socks. This guy, now lying prone on the platform below the crane, is *from the East Coast*. He's a *ringer*. I almost want to shout it. A woman's on the blue tarp, already in harness, rubber-kneed, waiting her turn. A steel cable descends from the tip of the crane's proboscis, on its end a fist-sized clip. Another cable leads from the crane's cab along the ground to the tower, up through ring-tipped pitons all up the tower's side, and over a pulley right at the top, another big clip on the end. One of the blond guys waves the tower's cable down and brings it over to the platform. Both the crane's and tower's cables' clips are attached to the back of the East-Coast man's harness, fastened and locked. The man's trying to look around behind him to see what-all's attached to him as the two big blonds leave the platform. Yet another blond man in the crane's cab throws a lever, and the tower's cable pulls tight in the grass and up the tower's side and down. The crane's cable stays slack as the man is lifted into the air by the tower's cable. The harness covers his shorts and shirt, so he looks babe-naked as he rises. The one cable sings with tension as the East-Coaster is pulled slowly to the top of the tower. He's still stomach-down, limbs wriggling. At a certain height he starts to look like livestock in a sling. You can tell he's trying to swallow until his face gets too small to see. Finally he's all the way up at the top of the tower, his ass against the cable's pulley, trying not to writhe. I can barely take notes. They cruelly leave him up there awhile, slung, a smile of slack cable between him and the crane's tip. The grotto's crowd mutters and points, shading eyes against the red sun. One teenage boy describes the sight to another teenage boy as "Harsh." I myself am constructing a mental list of the violations I would undergo before I'd let anyone haul me ass-first to a great height and swing me like high-altitude beef. One of the blond guys has a bullhorn and is playing to the crowd's suspense, calling up to the slung East-Coaster: "Are. You. Ready." The East-Coaster's response-noises are more bovine than human. His tinted aviator glasses hang askew from just one ear; he doesn't bother to fix them. I can see what's going to happen. They're going to throw a lever and detach the tower-cable's clip, and the man in sockless Banfis will free-fall for what'll seem forever, until the crane's cable's slack is taken up and the line takes his weight and goes tight behind him and swings him way out over the grounds to the south, his arc's upward half almost as high as the tower was, and then he'll fall all over again, back, and get caught and swung the other way, back and forth, the man prone at the arc's trough and seeming to stand at either apex, swinging back and forth and erect and prone against a rare-meat sunset. And just as the crane's cab's blond reaches for his lever and the crowd mightily inhales, just then, I lose my nerve, in my very last moment at the Fair — I recall my childhood's serial nightmare of being swung or whipped in an arc that threatens to come full circle — and I decline to be part of this, even as witness — and I find, again, in extremis, access to childhood's other worst nightmare, the only sure way to obliterate all; and the sun and sky and plummeting Yuppie go out like a light.

1993

Afterword

For the past ten years, I have asked my undergraduate nonfiction class at Yale to read three pages from "Getting Away from Already Pretty Much Being Away from It All," David Foster Wallace's 1994 piece on the Illinois State Fair. Other readings for English 469 have changed, but not that one. I always assign those three pages — "08/13/1235h. Lunchtime" — at the beginning of the semester because they contain a mind-bending payload of writing lessons (*truly* mind-bending, as in "How could that tiny VW hold all those clowns?"). The very next week, the students write better. It sounds impossible, but it's true.

I ask my students to consider five things in the pages they've read.

The first is structure. This section of the piece surveys the fairground's lunch offerings. I read aloud a little outline I've made:

> I. Milkshakes
> II. Pork
> III. Sweet Stuff
> IV. Nonsweet Stuff
> V. More Sweet Stuff
> VI. Crowds & Fat People
> VII. More Sweet Stuff, climaxing with DIPPIN DOTS

I point out that Wallace has put sweet stuff in four different places and ask the students, who in other classes have been trained to group topics thematically, why he was so disorganized. One year out of two, someone says, *Because fairs are disorganized!* And then we talk about how creative nonfiction has no one-size-fits-all template: the structure can fit the subject.

The second is grammar. Wallace was a language snob, or, as he termed it in "Authority and American Usage," a SNOOT. He compiled handouts for his writing students at Amherst and Pomona with what-not-to-do examples from their own work: dangling modifiers, split infinitives, non-parallel phrases. Some of my students have never read Wallace before, and they have a vague idea that he was a wild and crazy guy who flouted the conventions of grammar and punctuation and would, by happy example, give them license to do the same. I ask someone to read aloud a 103-word sentence—the one that begins "The crowd's adults are either pale or with the pink tinge of a new burn"—whose thicket of predicate adjectives and appositives is meticulously subdivided by commas, semicolons, and dashes. *Oh*. It is instantly clear that although minimalists can afford to be a little hazy on mechanics (not that I recommend it), maximalists can't.

The third is wordplay. Wallace doesn't bend grammar, but he bends English. He loves Germanic compounds like "shingle-sized" (describing pizza slices), "Rice-Krispie-squarish" (describing Krakkles), and "pubic-hair-shaped" (describing Curl Fries). If no existing adjective can do exactly what he wants, he invents one—for instance, "Jetsonian" (describing DIPPIN DOTS). The students, ecumenical scholars of pop culture, all get the reference.

The fourth is lists. I ask someone to read this one aloud: "But holy mackerel are there sweets: Fried Dough; Black Walnut Taffy; Fiddlesticks; Hot Crackerjack. Caramel apples for a felonious $1.50. Angel's Breath, known also as Dentist's Delight. Vanilla fudge that breaks a kind of weird sweat the minute it leaves its booth's freezer." Notice anything about the sequence? Everyone does. *The items get longer and longer. Also funnier and funnier.* When you write a list, I suggest, put the least surprising items at the beginning and the longest/funniest/most ridiculous ones at the end.

The fifth is multisensory description. We all have noses, ears, tongues, and skin, but most people write as if they had only eyes. Not Wallace. That's how he makes us feel we're *at* the fair, not just reading about it. I ask for examples of each sense. Everyone speaks at once. *Sound-carpet of deep fryers! Air spicy with antiperspirant and Coppertone! Yummy Elephant Ears! The weird, abstract texture of DIPPIN DOTS!* I ask how they'd characterize "the green reek of fried tomatoes" and "bright-yellow popcorn that stinks of salt." It's Yale. At least four students cry out, *Synesthesia!*

One of the traditions of English 469 is that most of the authors on the syllabus have generously agreed to answer a single e-mailed question. We take the exercise seriously. Each student brings in a question. There is an election. It is an honor to win.

In 2006 and 2007, we sent questions to David Foster Wallace. The first year, the question was written by a sophomore named Dan Fromson: *In writing about the Illinois State Fair, you critique the animal-like fairgoers, and yet you also subtly mock your own voice as narrator. As a writer, how does one find a balance between mocking one's target and mocking oneself?*

You can imagine what it was like for a nineteen-year-old DFW fan to get a response—and not just a line or two but a 645-word mini-essay that opened with "Dear Mr. Fromson et al." and closed with "Tally Ho, David Wallace."

It began:

Well, hmm. You're about to get a more or less freewritten reply, which will be my attempt at simulating a live, sweaty, physically-present-type answer. Said answer being mainly: I don't know. At least I'm not sure whether (a) there is such a balance, and (b) if there is, whether finding it can be prescribed in any kind of formula. This isn't to say that I don't see your question's point—at least I think I do, although I did that piece a long time ago, and I don't have any copies of it here to look at. Part of me wants to object to "you critique the animal-like fairgoers," although I seem to recall stuff about clinically fat people engaged in peripatetic eating that made them look bovine. But I also recall a certain tenderness for the Midwesterners there (of whom I was, by origin and upbringing, one), and an attempt to explain, for the mainly cosmopolitan readers of *Harper's*, some of the effects rurality, physical distance, lack of stimulation, etc. have on people. Still, I must also admit that I got some pissed-off letters indeed from Midwesterners, along with some aggrieved press mentions in the Midwest—"Local boy goes off east and writes smart-ass article for hip New York mag," etc. Some people sure felt mocked, it would appear.

From the next paragraph:

I'd say that this is a dangerous kind of piece to do, because it sets up Narrator Persona challenges, more specifically the Asshole Problem. I'm sure you guys have seen it—it's death if the biggest sense the reader gets from a critical essay is that the narrator's a very critical person, or from a comic essay that the narrator's cruel or snooty. Hence the importance of being just as critical about oneself as one is about the stuff/people one's being critical of.

The Asshole Problem! What a magnificent concept! If you make fun of other people, you'll sound like an asshole unless you also make fun of yourself. When Dan read this paragraph aloud, his classmates immediately understood why Wallace had presented himself as a clueless reporter who forgot his pen, a wuss who was scared to ride the Zipper, an obnoxious poseur who used phrases like "regional politico-sexual contrast" and "postmodern embarrassment of riches."

The next year, a senior named Alex Borinsky asked: *Have you ever not written something for fear the subject might read it?*

Wallace sent Alex a response nearly as long as the last one. Yes, he said. He had backed out of book reviews because he didn't want to skewer the books. He had omitted personal details from a profile because they had been revealed in moments of indiscretion. He explained:

> On the one hand, a writer has to understand that his primary allegiance is to the reader, not to the article's subject. Excessive concern about subjects' feelings can lead to all sorts of dishonesty that the reader will be able to detect (whether this detection is conscious or not). On the other hand, life is short, and hard, and it seems like good policy to inflict the absolute minimum pain/humiliation on other people as we schlep through the day.

Alex and his classmates were glad to hear this. Wallace's descriptions of the fat fairgoers had troubled them. He *was* snide. But he was also kind. It was instructive to realize that one could be both.

David Foster Wallace died six days before my 2008 class. We talked about "Getting Away from Already Pretty Much Being Away from It All" and also about what Wallace had meant to the students who knew his work. It was a very quiet class.

We have continued to read those three pages every year, along with Wallace's responses to Dan and Alex. As a result, my students choose structures that fit their subjects. The maximalists among them see long sentences as an occasion for careful grammar rather than an excuse to avoid it. They play with language. They write good lists. They write multisensory descriptions. They use self-deprecation to avoid the Asshole Problem—a term they employ so frequently one might assume it was a staple of literary criticism. They try to inflict less pain/humiliation as they schlep through the day. Some of them close their e-mails to each other with "Tally Ho." They wish David Foster Wallace were alive, not only so he could continue to write but so they could ask him a question.

—Anne Fadiman

A Supposedly Fun Thing I'll Never Do Again

1

RIGHT NOW IT's Saturday 18 March, and I'm sitting in the extremely full coffee shop of the Fort Lauderdale Airport, killing the four hours between when I had to be off the cruise ship and when my flight to Chicago leaves by trying to summon up a kind of hypnotic sensuous collage of all the stuff I've seen and heard and done as a result of the journalistic assignment just ended.

I have seen sucrose beaches and water a very bright blue. I have seen an all-red leisure suit with flared lapels. I have smelled what suntan lotion smells like spread over 21000 pounds of hot flesh. I have been addressed as "Mon" in three different nations. I have watched 500 upscale Americans dance the Electric Slide. I have seen sunsets that looked computer-enhanced and a tropical moon that looked more like a sort of obscenely large and dangling lemon than like the good old stony U.S. moon I'm used to.

I have (very briefly) joined a Conga Line.

I've got to say I feel like there's been a kind of Peter Principle in effect on this assignment. A certain swanky East-Coast magazine approved of the results of sending me to a plain old simple State Fair last year to do a directionless essayish thing. So now I get offered this tropical plum assignment w/ the exact same paucity of direction or angle. But this time there's this new feeling of pressure: total expenses for the State Fair were $27.00 excluding games of chance. This time *Harper's* has shelled out over $3000 U.S. before seeing pithy sensuous description one. They keep saying—on the phone, Ship-to-Shore, very patiently—not to fret about it. They are sort of disingenuous, I believe, these magazine people. They say all they want is a sort of really big experiential postcard—go, plow the Caribbean in style, come back, say what you've seen.

I have seen a lot of really big white ships. I have seen schools of little fish with fins that glow. I have seen a toupee on a thirteen-year-old boy. (The glowing fish liked to swarm between our hull and the cement of the pier whenever we docked.) I have seen the north coast of Jamaica. I have seen and smelled all 145 cats inside the Ernest Hemingway Residence in Key West FL. I now know the difference between straight Bingo and Prize-O, and what it is when a Bingo jackpot "snowballs." I have seen camcorders that practically required a dolly; I've seen fluorescent luggage and fluorescent sunglasses and fluorescent pince-nez and over twenty different makes of rubber thong. I have heard steel drums and eaten conch fritters and watched a woman in silver lamé projectile-vomit inside a glass elevator. I have pointed rhythmically at the ceiling to the 2:4 beat of the exact same disco music I hated pointing at the ceiling to in 1977.

I have learned that there are actually intensities of blue beyond *very, very bright* blue. I have eaten more and classier food than I've ever eaten, and eaten this food during a week when I've also learned the difference between "rolling" in heavy seas and "pitching" in heavy seas. I have heard a professional comedian tell folks, without irony, "But seriously." I have seen fuchsia pantsuits and menstrual-pink sportcoats and maroon-and-purple warmups and white loafers worn without socks. I have seen professional blackjack dealers so lovely they make you want to run over to their table and spend every last nickel you've got playing blackjack. I have heard upscale adult U.S. citizens ask the Guest Relations Desk whether snorkeling necessitates getting wet, whether the skeetshooting will be held outside, whether the crew sleeps on board, and what time the Midnight Buffet is. I now know the precise mixological difference between a Slippery Nipple and a Fuzzy Navel. I know what a Coco Loco is. I have in one week been the object of over 1500 professional smiles. I have burned and peeled twice. I have shot skeet at sea. Is this enough? At the time it didn't seem like enough. I have felt the full clothy weight of a subtropical sky. I have jumped a dozen times at the shattering, flatulence-of-the-gods sound of a cruise ship's horn. I have absorbed the basics of mah-jongg, seen part of a two-day rubber of contract bridge, learned how to secure a life jacket over a tuxedo, and lost at chess to a nine-year-old girl.

(Actually it was more like I shot *at* skeet at sea.)

I have dickered over trinkets with malnourished children. I now know every conceivable rationale and excuse for somebody spending over $3000 to go on a Caribbean cruise. I have bitten my lip and declined Jamaican pot from an actual Jamaican.

I have seen, one time, from an upper deck's rail, way below and off the right rear hull, what I believe to have been a hammerhead shark's distinctive fin, addled by the starboard turbine's Niagaracal wake.

I have now heard—and am powerless to describe—reggae elevator music. I have learned what it is to become afraid of one's own toilet. I have acquired "sea legs" and would like now to lose them. I have tasted caviar and concurred with the little kid sitting next to me that it is: *blucky*.

I now understand the term "Duty Free."

I now know the maximum cruising speed of a cruise ship in knots.[1] I have had escargot, duck, Baked Alaska, salmon w/ fennel, a marzipan pelican, and an omelette made with what were alleged to be trace amounts of Etruscan truffle. I have heard people in deck chairs say in all earnestness that it's the humidity rather than the heat. I have been—thoroughly, professionally, and as promised beforehand—pampered. I have, in dark moods, viewed and logged every type of erythema, keratinosis, premelanomic lesion, liver spot, eczema, wart, papular cyst, potbelly, femoral cellulite, varicosity, collagen and silicone enhancement, bad tint, hair transplants that have not taken—i.e. I have seen nearly naked a lot of people I would prefer not to have seen nearly naked. I have felt as bleak as I've felt since puberty, and have filled almost three Mead notebooks trying to figure out whether it was Them or Just Me. I have acquired and nurtured a potentially lifelong grudge against the ship's Hotel Manager—whose name was Mr. Dermatis and whom I now and henceforth christen Mr. Dermatitis[2]—an almost reverent respect for my waiter, and a searing crush on the cabin steward for my part of Deck 10's port hallway, Petra, she of the dimples and broad candid brow, who always wore a nurse's starched and rustling whites and smelled of the cedary Norwegian disinfectant she swabbed bathrooms down with, and who cleaned my cabin within a cm of its life at least ten times a day but could never be caught in the actual *act* of cleaning—a figure of magical and abiding charm, and well worth a postcard all her own.

---

1 (though I never did get clear on just what a knot is)

2 Somewhere he'd gotten the impression I was an investigative journalist and wouldn't let me see the galley, Bridge, staff decks, *anything*, or interview any of the crew or staff in an on-the-record way, and he wore sunglasses inside, and epaulets, and kept talking on the phone for long stretches of time in Greek when I was in his office after I'd skipped the karaoke semifinals in the Rendez-Vous Lounge to make a special appointment to see him; I wish him ill.

2

More specifically: From 11 to 18 March 1995 I, voluntarily and for pay, underwent a 7-Night Caribbean (7NC) Cruise on board the m.v. *Zenith*,[3] a 47,255-ton ship owned by Celebrity Cruises Inc., one of the over twenty cruise lines that currently operate out of south Florida.[4] The vessel and facilities were, from what I now understand of the industry's standards, absolutely top-hole. The food was superb, the service impeccable, the shore excursions and shipboard activities organized for maximal stimulation down to the tiniest detail. The ship was so clean and so white it looked boiled. The Western Caribbean's blue varied between baby-blanket and fluorescent; likewise the sky. Temperatures were uterine. The very sun itself seemed preset for our comfort. The crew-to-passenger ratio was 1.2 to 2. It was a Luxury Cruise.

---

3 No wag could possibly resist mentally rechristening the ship the m.v. *Nadir* the instant he saw the *Zenith*'s silly name in the Celebrity brochure, so indulge me on this, but the rechristening's nothing particular against the ship itself.

4 There's also Windstar and Silversea, Tall Ship Adventures and Windjammer Barefoot Cruises, but these Caribbean Cruises are wildly upscale and smaller. The 20+ cruise lines I'm talking run the "Megaships," the floating wedding cakes with occupancies in four figures and engine-propellers the size of branch banks. Of the Megalines out of south FL there's Commodore, Costa, Majesty, Regal, Dolphin, Princess, Royal Caribbean, good old Celebrity. There's Renaissance, Royal Cruise Line, Holland, Holland America, Cunard, Cunard Crown, Cunard Royal Viking. There's Norwegian Cruise Line, there's Crystal, there's Regency Cruises. There's the Wal-Mart of the cruise industry, Carnival, which the other lines refer to sometimes as "Carnivore." I don't recall which line *The Love Boat*'s *Pacific Princess* was supposed to be with (I guess they were probably more like a CA-to-Hawaii-circuit ship, though I seem to recall them going all over the place), but now Princess Cruises has bought the name and uses poor old Gavin MacLeod in full regalia in their TV ads.

The 7NC Megaship cruiser is a type, a genre of ship all its own, like the destroyer. All the Megalines have more than one ship. The industry descends from those old patrician trans-Atlantic deals where the opulence combined with actually getting someplace—e.g. the *Titanic, Normandie,* etc. The present Caribbean Cruise market's various niches—Singles, Old People, Theme, Special Interest, Corporate, Party, Family, Mass-Market, Luxury, Absurd Luxury, Grotesque Luxury—have now all pretty much been carved and staked out and are competed for viciously (I heard off-the-record stuff about Carnival v. Princess that'd singe your brows). Megaships tend to be designed in America, built in Germany, registered out of Liberia or Monrovia; and they are both captained and owned, for the most part, by Scandinavians and Greeks, which is kind of interesting, since these are the same peoples who've dominated sea travel pretty much forever. Celebrity Cruises is owned by the Chandris Group; the X on their three ships' smokestacks turns out not to be an X but a Greek chi, for Chandris, a Greek shipping family so ancient and powerful they apparently regarded Onassis as a punk.

With a few minor niche-adaptive variations, the 7NC Luxury Cruise is essentially generic. All of the Megalines offer the same basic product. This product is not a service or a set of services. It's not even so much a good time (though it quickly becomes clear that one of the big jobs of the Cruise Director and his staff is to keep reassuring everybody that everybody's having a good time). It's more like a feeling. But it's also still a bona fide product—it's supposed to be *produced* in you, this feeling: a blend of relaxation and stimulation, stressless indulgence and frantic tourism, that special mix of servility and condescension that's marketed under configurations of the verb "to pamper." This verb positively studs the Megalines' various brochures: "...as you've never been pampered before," "...to pamper yourself in our Jacuzzis and saunas," "Let us pamper you," "Pamper yourself in the warm zephyrs of the Bahamas."

The fact that contemporary adult Americans also tend to associate the word "pamper" with a certain *other* consumer product is not an accident, I don't think, and the connotation is not lost on the mass-market Megalines and their advertisers. And there's good reason for them to iterate the word, and stress it.

3

This one incident made the Chicago news. Some weeks before I underwent my own Luxury Cruise, a sixteen-year-old male did a Brody off the upper deck of a Megaship—I think a Carnival or Crystal ship—a suicide. The news version was that it had been an unhappy adolescent love thing, a shipboard romance gone bad, etc. I think part of it was something else, something there's no way a real news story could cover.

There is something about a mass-market Luxury Cruise that's unbearably sad. Like most unbearably sad things, it seems incredibly elusive and complex in its causes and simple in its effect: on board the *Nadir*—especially at night, when all the ship's structured fun and reassurances and gaiety-noise ceased—I felt despair. The word's overused and banalified now, *despair,* but it's a serious word, and I'm using it seriously. For me it denotes a simple admixture—a weird yearning for death combined with a crushing sense of my own smallness and futility that presents as a fear of death. It's maybe close to what people call dread or angst. But it's not these things, quite. It's more like wanting to die in order to escape the unbearable feeling of becoming aware that I'm small and weak and selfish and going without any doubt at all to die. It's wanting to jump overboard.

I predict this'll get cut by the editor, but I need to cover some background. I, who had never before this cruise actually been on the ocean, have always associated the ocean with dread and death. As a little kid I used to memorize shark-fatality data. Not just attacks. Fatalities. The Albert Kogler fatality off Baker's Beach CA in 1959 (Great White). The U.S.S. *Indianapolis* smorgasbord off the Philippines in 1945 (many varieties, authorities think mostly Tigers and Blues)[5]; the most-fatalities-attributed-to-a-single-shark series of incidents around Matawan/Spring Lake NJ in 1916 (Great White again; this time they caught a *carcharias* in Raritan Bay NJ and found human parts *in gastro* (I know which parts, and whose)). In school I ended up writing three different papers on "The Castaway" section of *Moby-Dick,* the chapter where the cabin boy Pip falls overboard and is driven mad by the empty immensity of what he finds himself floating in. And when I teach school now I always teach Crane's horrific "The Open Boat," and I get bent out of shape when the kids find the story dull or jaunty-adventurish: I want them to feel the same marrow-level dread of the oceanic I've always felt, the intuition of the sea as primordial *nada,* bottomless, depths inhabited by cackling tooth-studded things rising toward you at the rate a feather falls. Anyway, hence the atavistic shark fetish, which I need to admit came back with a long-repressed vengeance on this Luxury Cruise,[6] and that I made such a fuss about the one (possible) dorsal fin I saw off starboard that my companions at supper's Table 64 finally had to tell me, with all possible tact, to shut up about the fin already.

I don't think it's an accident that 7NC Luxury Cruises appeal mostly to older people. I don't mean decrepitly old, but I mean like age-50+ people,

---

5 I'm doing this from memory. I don't need a book. I can still name every documented *Indianapolis* fatality, including some serial numbers and hometowns. (Hundreds of men lost, 80 classed as Shark, 7–10 August '45; the *Indianapolis* had just delivered Little Boy to the island of Tinian for delivery to Hiroshima, so ironists take note. Robert Shaw as Quint reprised the whole incident in 1975's *Jaws,* a film that, as you can imagine, was like fetish-porn to me at age thirteen.)

6 And I'll admit that on the very first night of the 7NC I asked the staff of the *Nadir's* Five-Star Caravelle Restaurant whether I could maybe have a spare bucket of *au jus* drippings from supper so I could try chumming for sharks off the back rail of the top deck, and that this request struck everybody from the maître d' on down as disturbing and maybe even disturbed, and that it turned out to be a serious journalistic faux pas, because I'm almost positive the maître d' passed this disturbing tidbit on to Mr. Dermatitis and that it was a big reason why I was denied access to stuff like the ship's galley, thereby impoverishing the sensuous scope of this article. (Plus it also revealed how little I understood the *Nadir's* sheer size: twelve decks and 150 feet up, the *au jus* drippings would have dispersed into a vague red cologne by the time they hit the water, with concentrations of blood inadequate to attract or excite a serious shark, whose fin would have probably looked like a pushpin from that height, anyway.)

for whom their own mortality is something more than an abstraction. Most of the exposed bodies to be seen all over the daytime *Nadir* were in various stages of disintegration. And the ocean itself (which I found to be salty as *hell*, like sore-throat-soothing-gargle-grade salty, its spray so corrosive that one temple-hinge of my glasses is probably going to have to be replaced) turns out to be basically one enormous engine of decay. Seawater corrodes vessels with amazing speed—rusts them, exfoliates paint, strips varnish, dulls shine, coats ships' hulls with barnacles and kelp-clumps and a vague ubiquitous nautical snot that seems like death incarnate. We saw some real horrors in port, local boats that looked dipped in a mixture of acid and shit, scabbed with rust and goo, ravaged by what they float in.

Not so the Megalines' ships. It's not an accident they're all so white and clean, for they're clearly meant to represent the Calvinist triumph of capital and industry over the primal decay-action of the sea. The *Nadir* seemed to have a whole battalion of wiry little Third World guys who went around the ship in navy-blue jumpsuits scanning for decay to overcome. Writer Frank Conroy, who has an odd little essaymercial in the front of Celebrity Cruises' 7NC brochure, talks about how "It became a private challenge for me to try to find a piece of dull bright-work, a chipped rail, a stain in the deck, a slack cable or anything that wasn't perfectly shipshape. Eventually, toward the end of the trip, I found a capstan[7] with a half-dollar-sized patch of rust on the side facing the sea. My delight in this tiny flaw was interrupted by the arrival, even as I stood there, of a crewman with a roller and a bucket of white paint. I watched as he gave the entire capstan a fresh coat of paint and walked away with a nod."

Here's the thing. A vacation is a respite from unpleasantness, and since consciousness of death and decay are unpleasant, it may seem weird that Americans' ultimate fantasy vacation involves being plunked down in an enormous primordial engine of death and decay. But on a 7NC Luxury Cruise, we are skillfully enabled in the construction of various fantasies of triumph over just this death and decay. One way to "triumph" is via the rigors of self-improvement; and the crew's amphetaminic upkeep of the *Nadir* is an unsubtle analogue to personal titivation: diet, exercise, megavitamin supplements, cosmetic surgery, Franklin Quest time-management seminars, etc.

There's another way out, too, w/r/t death. Not titivation but titillation. Not hard work but hard play. The 7NC's constant activities, parties, festivities, gaiety and song; the adrenaline, the excitement, the stimulation.

---

7 (apparently a type of nautical hoist, like a pulley on steroids)

It makes you feel vibrant, alive. It makes your existence seem noncontingent.[8] The hard-play option promises not a transcendence of death-dread so much as just drowning it out: "Sharing a laugh with your friends[9] in the lounge after dinner, you glance at your watch and mention that it's almost showtime.... When the curtain comes down after a standing ovation, the talk among your companions[10] turns to, 'What next?' Perhaps a visit to the casino or a little dancing in the disco? Maybe a quiet drink in the piano bar or a starlit stroll around the deck? After discussing all your options, everyone agrees: *'Let's do it all!'*"

Dante this isn't, but Celebrity Cruises' 7NC brochure is nevertheless an extremely powerful and ingenious piece of advertising. The brochure is magazine-size, heavy and glossy, beautifully laid out, its text offset by art-quality photos of upscale couples'[11] tanned faces locked in a kind of rictus of pleasure. All the Megalines put out brochures, and they're essentially interchangeable. The middle part of the brochures detail the different packages and routes. Basic 7NC's go to the Western Caribbean (Jamaica, Grand Cayman, Cozumel) or the Eastern Caribbean (Puerto Rico, Virgins), or something called the Deep Carribean (Martinique, Barbados, Mayreau). There are also 10- and 11-Night Ultimate Caribbean packages that hit pretty much every exotic coastline between Miami and the Panama Canal. The brochures' final sections' boilerplate always details costs,[12] passport stuff, Customs regulations, caveats.

But it's the first section of these brochures that really grabs you, the photos and italicized blurbs from *Fodor's Cruises* and *Berlitz,* the dreamy

---

8 The *Nadir's* got literally hundreds of cross-sectional maps of the ship on every deck, at every elevator and junction, each with a red dot and a YOU ARE HERE — and it doesn't take long to figure out that these are less for orientation than for some weird kind of reassurance.

9 Always constant references to "friends" in the brochures' text; part of this promise of escape from death-dread is that no cruiser is ever alone.

10 See?

11 Always couples in this brochure, and even in group shots it's always groups of couples. I never did get hold of a brochure for an actual Singles Cruise, but the mind reels. There was a "Singles Get Together" (sic) on the *Nadir* that first Saturday night, held in Deck 8's Scorpio Disco, which after an hour of self-hypnosis and controlled breathing I steeled myself to go to, but even the Get Together was 75% established couples, and the few of us Singles under like 70 all looked grim and self-hypnotized, and the whole affair seemed like a true wrist-slitter, and I beat a retreat after half an hour because *Jurassic Park* was scheduled to run on the TV that night, and I hadn't yet looked at the whole schedule and seen that *Jurassic Park* would play several dozen times over the coming week.

12 From $2500 to about $4000 for mass-market Megaships like the *Nadir,* unless you want a Presidential Suite with a skylight, wet bar, automatic palm-fronds, etc., in which case double that.

mise en scènes and breathless prose. Celebrity's brochure, in particular, is a real two-napkin drooler. It has little hypertextish offsets, boxed in gold, that say stuff like INDULGENCE BECOMES EASY and RELAX-ATION BECOMES SECOND NATURE and STRESS BECOMES A FAINT MEMORY. And these promises point to the third kind of death-and-dread-transcendence the *Nadir* offers, one that requires neither work nor play, the enticement that is a 7NC's real carrot and stick.

4

"Just standing at the ship's rail looking out to sea has a profoundly sooth-ing effect. As you drift along like a cloud on water, the weight of everyday life is magically lifted away, and you seem to be floating on a sea of smiles. Not just among your fellow guests but on the faces of the ship's staff as well. As a steward cheerfully delivers your drinks, you mention all of the smiles among the crew. He explains that every Celebrity staff member takes pleasure in making your cruise a completely carefree experience and treating you as an honored guest.[13] Besides, he adds, there's no place they'd rather be. Looking back out to sea, you couldn't agree more."

Celebrity's 7NC brochure uses the 2nd-person pronoun throughout. This is extremely appropriate. Because in the brochure's scenarios the

---

13 In response to some dogged journalistic querying, Celebrity's PR firm's Press Liaison (the charming and Debra Winger–voiced Ms. Wiessen) had this explanation for the cheery service: "The people on board—the staff—are really part of one big family—you probably noticed this when you were on the ship. They really love what they're doing and love serving people, and they pay attention to what everybody wants and needs."

This was not what I myself observed. What I myself observed was that the *Nadir* was one very tight ship, run by an elite cadre of very hard-ass Greek officers and supervisors, and that the preterite staff lived in mortal terror of these Greek bosses who watched them with enormous beadiness at all times, and that the crew worked almost Dickensianly hard, too hard to feel truly cheery about it. My sense was that Cheeriness was up there with Celerity and Servility on the clipboarded evaluation sheets the Greek bosses were constantly filling out on them: when they didn't know any guests were looking, a lot of the workers had the kind of pinched weariness about them that one associates with low-paid service employees in general, plus fear. My sense was that a crewman could get fired for a pretty small lapse, and that getting fired by these Greek officers might well involve a spotlessly shined shoe in the ass and then a really long swim.

What I observed was that the preterite workers did have a sort of affection for the passengers, but that it was a *comparative* affection—even the most absurdly demanding passenger seemed kind and understanding compared to the martinetism of the Greeks, and the crew seemed genuinely grateful for this, sort of the way we find even very basic human decency moving if we encounter it in NYC or Boston.

7NC experience is being not described but *evoked*. The brochure's real seduction is not an invitation to fantasize but rather a construction of the fantasy itself. This is advertising, but with a queerly authoritarian twist. In regular adult-market ads, attractive people are shown having a near-illegally good time in some scenario surrounding a product, and you are meant to fantasize that you can project yourself into the ad's perfect world via purchase of that product. In regular advertising, where your adult agency and freedom of choice have to be flattered, the purchase is prerequisite to the fantasy; it's the fantasy that's being sold, not any literal projection into the ad's world. There's no sense of any real kind of actual promise being made. This is what makes conventional adult advertisements fundamentally coy.

Contrast this coyness with the force of the 7NC brochure's ads: the near-imperative use of the second person, the specificity of detail that extends even to what you will say (*you will say* "I couldn't agree more" and "Let's do it all!"). In the cruise brochure's ads, you are excused from doing the work of constructing the fantasy. The ads do it for you. The ads, therefore, don't flatter your adult agency, or even ignore it—they supplant it.

And this authoritarian—near-parental—type of advertising makes a very special sort of promise, a diabolically seductive promise that's actually kind of honest, because it's a promise that the Luxury Cruise itself is all about honoring. The promise is not that you can experience great pleasure, but that you *will*. That they'll make certain of it. That they'll micromanage every iota of every pleasure-option so that not even the dreadful corrosive action of your adult consciousness and agency and dread can fuck up your fun. Your troublesome capacities for choice, error, regret, dissatisfaction, and despair will be removed from the equation. The ads promise that you will be able—finally, for once—truly to relax and have a good time, because you will *have no choice* but to have a good time.[14]

I am now 33 years old, and it feels like much time has passed and is passing faster and faster every day. Day to day I have to make all sorts of choices about what is good and important and fun, and then I have to live with the forfeiture of all the other options those choices foreclose. And I'm starting to see how as time gains momentum my choices will narrow and their foreclosures multiply exponentially until I arrive at some point

---

14 "YOUR PLEASURE," several Megalines' slogans go, "IS OUR BUSINESS." What in a regular ad would be a double entendre is here a triple entendre, and the tertiary connotation—viz. "MIND YOUR OWN BLOODY BUSINESS AND LET US PROFESSIONALS WORRY ABOUT YOUR PLEASURE, FOR CHRIST'S SAKE"—is far from incidental.

on some branch of all life's sumptuous branching complexity at which I am finally locked in and stuck on one path and time speeds me through stages of stasis and atrophy and decay until I go down for the third time, all struggle for naught, drowned by time. It is dreadful. But since it's my own choices that'll lock me in, it seems unavoidable—if I want to be any kind of grownup, I have to make choices and regret foreclosures and try to live with them.

Not so on the lush and spotless m.v. *Nadir*. On a 7NC Luxury Cruise, I pay for the privilege of handing over to trained professionals responsibility not just for my experience but for my *interpretation* of that experience—i.e. my pleasure. My pleasure is for 7 nights and 6.5 days wisely and efficiently managed...just as promised in the cruise line's advertising—nay, just as somehow already *accomplished* in the ads, with their 2nd-person imperatives, which make them not promises but predictions. Aboard the *Nadir*, just as ringingly foretold in the brochure's climactic p. 23, I get to do (in gold): "...something you haven't done in a long, long time: *Absolutely Nothing*."

How long has it been since you did Absolutely Nothing? I know exactly how long it's been for me. I know how long it's been since I had every need met choicelessly from someplace outside me, without my having to ask or even acknowledge that I needed. And that time I was floating, too, and the fluid was salty, and warm but not too-, and if I was conscious at all I'm sure I felt dreadless, and was having a really good time, and would have sent postcards to everyone wishing they were here.

5

A 7NC's pampering is a little uneven at first, but it starts at the airport, where you don't have to go to Baggage Claim because people from the Megaline get your suitcases for you and take them right to the ship.

A bunch of other Megalines besides Celebrity Cruises operate out of Fort Lauderdale,[15] and the flight down from O'Hare is full of festive-looking people dressed for cruising. It turns out the folks sitting next to me on the plane are booked on the *Nadir*. They're a retired couple from Chicago and this is their fourth Luxury Cruise in as many years. It is they who tell me about the news reports of the kid jumping overboard, and also

---

15 Celebrity, Cunard, Princess, and Holland America all use it as a hub. Carnival and Dolphin use Miami; others use Port Canaveral, Puerto Rico, the Bahamas, all over.

about a legendarily nasty outbreak of salmonella or *E. coli* or something on a Megaship in the late '70s that gave rise to the C.D.C.'s Vessel Sanitation program of inspections, plus about a supposed outbreak of Legionnaire's disease vectored by the jacuzzi on a 7NC Megaship two years ago—it was possibly one of Celebrity's three cruise ships, the lady (kind of the spokesman for the couple) isn't sure; it turns out she sort of likes to toss off a horrific detail and then get all vague and blasé when a horrified listener tries to pump her for details. The husband wears a fishing cap with a long bill and a T-shirt that says BIG DADDY.

7NC Luxury Cruises always start and finish on Saturday. Right now it's Saturday 11 March, 1020h., and we are deplaning. Imagine the day after the Berlin Wall came down if everybody in East Germany was plump and comfortable-looking and dressed in Caribbean pastels, and you'll have a pretty good idea what the Fort Lauderdale Airport terminal looks like today. Over near the back wall, a number of brisk-looking older ladies in vaguely naval outfits hold up printed signs—HLND, CELEB, CUND CRN. What you're supposed to do (the Chicago lady from the plane is kind of talking me through it as BIG DADDY shoulders us a path through the fray) what you're supposed to do is find your particular Megaline's brisk lady and sort of all coalesce around her as she walks with printed sign held high to attract still more cruisers and leads the growing ectoplasm of *Nadir*ites all out to buses that ferry us to the Piers and what we quixotically believe will be immediate and hassle-free boarding.

Apparently Ft. Laud. Airport is always just your average sleepy midsize airport six days a week and then every Saturday resembles the fall of Saigon. Half the terminal's mob consists of luggage-bearing people now flying home from 7NCs. They are Syrianly tan, and a lot of them have eccentric and vaguely hairy-looking souvenirs of various sizes and functions, and they all have a glazed spacey look about them that the Chicago lady avers is the telltale look of post-7NC Inner Peace. We pre-7NCs, on the other hand, all look pasty and stressed and somehow combat-unready.

Outside, we of the *Nadir* are directed to deectoplasmize ourselves and all line up along some sort of tall curb to await the *Nadir*'s special chartered buses. We are exchanging awkward don't-know-whether-to-smile-and-wave-or-not glances with a Holland America herd that's lining up on a grassy median parallel to us, and both groups are looking a little narrow-eyed at a Princess-bound herd whose buses are already pulling up. The Ft. Laud. Airport's porters and cabbies and white-bandoliered traffic cops and bus drivers are all Cuban. The retired Chicago couple, clearly wily veterans about lines by their fourth Luxury Cruise, has butted into place way up. A second Celebrity crowd-control lady has a megaphone and repeats over and over not to worry about our luggage, that it will follow us later, which I am apparently alone in finding chilling in its unwitting echo of the Auschwitz-embarkation scene in *Schindler's List*.

Where I am in the line: I'm between a squat and chain-smoking black man in an NBC Sports cap and several corporately dressed people wearing badges identifying them as with something called the Engler Corporation.[16] Way up ahead, the retired Chicago couple has spread a sort of parasol. There's a bumpy false ceiling of mackerel clouds moving in from the southwest, but overhead it's just wispy cirrus, and it's seriously hot standing and waiting in the sun, even without luggage or luggage-angst, and through a lack of foresight I'm wearing my undertakerish black wool suitcoat and an inadequate hat. But it feels good to perspire. Chicago at dawn was 18° and its sun the sort of wan and impotent March sun you can look right at. It is good to feel serious sun and see trees all frothy with green. We wait rather a long time, and the *Nadir* line starts to recoalesce into clumps as people's conversations have time to progress past the waiting-in-line small-talk stage. Either there was a mixup getting enough buses for people in on A.M. flights, or (my theory) the same Celebrity Cruises brain trust responsible for the wildly seductive brochure has decided to make certain elements of pre-embarkation as difficult and unpleasant as possible in order to sharpen the favorable contrast between real life and the 7NC experience.

Now we're riding to the Piers in a column of eight chartered Greyhounds. Our convoy's rate of speed and the odd deference other traffic shows gives the whole procession a kind of funereal quality. Ft. Laud. proper looks like one extremely large golf course, but the cruise lines' Piers are in something called Port Everglades, an industrial area, pretty clearly, zoned for Blight, with warehouses and transformer parks and stacked boxcars and vacant lots full of muscular and evil-looking Florida-type weeds. We pass a huge field of those hammer-shaped automatic oil derricks all bobbing fellatially, and on the horizon past them is a little fingernail clipping of shiny gray that I'm thinking must be the sea. Several different languages are in use on my bus. Whenever we go over bumps or

---

16 I was never in countless tries able to determine just what the Engler Corporation did or made or was about, but they'd apparently sent a quorum of their execs on this 7NC junket together as a weird kind of working vacation or intracompany convention or something.

train tracks, there's a tremendous mass clicking sound in here from all the cameras around everybody's neck. I haven't brought any sort of camera and feel a perverse pride about this.

The *Nadir*'s traditional berth is Pier 21. "Pier," though it had conjured for me images of wharfs and cleats and lapping water, turns out to denote something like what *airport* denotes, viz. a zone and not a thing. There is no real water in sight, no docks, no fishy smell or sodium tang to the air; but there are, as we enter the Pier zone, a lot of really big white ships that blot out most of the sky.

Now I'm writing this sitting in an orange plastic chair at the end of one of Pier 21's countless bolted rows of orange plastic chairs. We have debused and been herded via megaphone through 21's big glass doors, whereupon two more completely humorless naval ladies handed us each a little plastic card with a number on it. My card's number is 7. A few people sitting nearby ask me "what I am," and I figure out I'm to respond "a 7." The cards are by no means brand new, and mine has the vestigial whorls of a chocolate thumbprint in one corner.

From inside, Pier 21 seems kind of like a blimpless blimp hangar, high-ceilinged and very echoey. It has walls of unclean windows on three sides, at least 2500 orange chairs in rows of 25, a kind of desultory Snack Bar, and restrooms with very long lines. The acoustics are brutal and it's tremendously loud. Outside, rain starts coming down even though the sun's still shining. Some of the people in the rows of chairs appear to have been here for days: they have that glazed encamped look of people at airports in blizzards.

It's now 1132h., and boarding will not commence one second before 1400 sharp; a PA announcement politely but firmly declares Celebrity's seriousness about this.[17] The PA lady's voice is what you imagine a British supermodel would sound like. Everyone's clutching his numbered card like the cards are identity papers at Checkpoint Charley. There's an Ellis Island/pre-Auschwitz aspect to the massed and anxious waiting, but I'm uncomfortable trying to extend the analogy. A lot of the people waiting—Caribbeanish clothing notwithstanding—look Jewish to me, and I'm ashamed to catch myself thinking that I can determine Jewishness

---

17 The reason for the delay won't become apparent until next Saturday, when it takes until 1000h. to get everybody off the m.v. *Nadir* and vectored to appropriate transportation, and then from 1000 to 1400h. several battalions of jumpsuited Third World custodial guys will join the stewards in obliterating all evidence of us before the next 1374 passengers come on.

from people's appearance.[18] Maybe two-thirds of the total people in here are actually sitting in orange chairs. Pier 21's pre-boarding blimp hangar's not as bad as, say, Grand Central at 1715h. on Friday, but it bears little resemblance to any of the stressless pamper-venues detailed in the Celebrity brochure, which brochure I am not the only person in here thumbing through and looking at wistfully. A lot of people are also reading the *Fort Lauderdale Sentinel* and staring with subwayish blankness at other people. A kid whose T-shirt says SANDY DUNCAN'S EYE is carving something in the plastic of his chair. There are quite a few old people all travelling with really *desperately* old people who are pretty clearly the old people's parents. A couple different guys in different rows are field-stripping their camcorders with military-looking expertise. There's a fair share of WASP-looking passengers, as well. A lot of the WASPs are couples in their twenties and thirties, with a honeymoonish aspect to the way their heads rest on each other's shoulders. Men after a certain age simply should not wear shorts, I've decided; their legs are hairless in a way that's creepy; the skin seems denuded and practically crying out for hair, particularly on the calves. It's just about the only body-area where you actually want *more* hair on older men. Is this fibular hairlessness a result of years of chafing in pants and socks? The significance of the numbered cards turns out to be that you're supposed to wait here in Pier 21's blimp hangar until your number is called, then you board in "Lots."[19] So your number doesn't stand for you, but rather for the subherd of cruisers you're part of. Some 7NC-veterans nearby tell me that 7 is not a great Lot-number and advise me to get comfortable. Somewhere past the big gray doors behind the restrooms' roiling lines is an umbilical passage leading to what I assume is the actual *Nadir*, which outside the south wall's windows presents as a tall wall of total white. In the approximate center of the hangar is a long table where creamy-complected women in nursish white from Steiner of London Inc. are doing free little makeup and complexion consultations with women waiting to board, priming the economic pump.[20] The Chicago

---

18 For me, public places on the U.S. East Coast are full of these nasty little moments of racist observation and then internal P.C. backlash.

19 This term belongs to an eight-cruise veteran, a 50ish guy with blond bangs and a big ginger beard and what looks weirdly like a T-square sticking out of his carry-on, who's also the first person who offers me an unsolicited narrative on why he had basically no emotional choice right now but to come on a 7NC Luxury Cruise.

20 Steiner of London'll be on the *Nadir*, it turns out, selling herbal wraps and cellulite-intensive delipidizing massages and facials and assorted aesthetic pampering—they have a whole little wing in the top deck's Olympic Health Club, and it seems like they all but own the Beauty Salon on Deck 5.

lady and BIG DADDY are in the hangar's southeasternmost row of chairs playing Uno with another couple, who turn out to be friends they'd made on a Princess Alaska Cruise in '93.

Now I'm writing this sort of squatting with my bottom braced up against the hangar's west wall, which wall is white-painted cinderblocks, like a budget motel's wall, and also oddly clammy. By this time I'm down to slacks and T-shirt and tie, and the tie looks like it's been washed and hand-wrung. Perspiring has already lost its novelty. Part of what Celebrity Cruises is reminding us we're leaving behind is massed public waiting areas with no AC and indifferent ventilation. Now it's 1255h. Though the brochure says the *Nadir* sails at 1630h. EST and that you can board anytime from 1400 to then, all 1374 *Nadir* passengers look already to be massed here, plus what must be a fair number of relatives and well-wishers, etc.[21]

A major advantage to writing some sort of article about an experience is that at grim junctures like this pre-embarkation blimp hangar you can distract yourself from what the experience feels like by focusing on what look like items of possible interest for the article. This is the occasion I first see the thirteen-year-old kid with the toupee. He's slumped pre-adolescently in his chair with his feet up on some kind of rattan hamper while what I'll bet is his mom talks at him nonstop; he is staring into whatever special distance people in areas of mass public stasis stare into. His toupee isn't one of those horrible black shiny incongruous Howard Cosell toupees, but it's not great either; it's an unlikely orange-brown, and its texture is like one of those local-TV-anchorman toupees where if you tousled the hair it would get broken instead of mussed. A lot of the people from the Engler Corporation are massed in some kind of round informal conference or meeting over near the Pier's glass doors, looking from the distance rather like a rugby scrum. I've decided the perfect description of the orange of the hangar's chairs is *waiting-room* orange. Several driven-looking corporate guys are talking into cellular phones while their wives look stoic. Close to a dozen confirmed sightings of J. Redfield's *The Celestine Prophecy*. The acoustics in here have the nightmarishly echoey quality of some of the Beatles' more conceptual stuff. At the Snack Bar, a plain old candy bar is $1.50, and soda-pop's even more. The line for the men's room extends NW almost to the Steiner of London table. Several Pier

---

21 Going on a 7NC Luxury Cruise is like going to the hospital or college in this respect: it seems to be SOP for a mass of relatives and well-wishers to accompany you right up to the jumping-off point and then have to finally leave, w/ lots of requisite hugs and tears.

personnel with clipboards are running around w/o any discernible agenda. The crowd has a smattering of college-age kids, all with complex haircuts and already wearing poolside thongs. A little kid right near me is wearing the exact same kind of hat I am, which I might as well admit right now is a full-color Spiderman cap.[22]

I count over a dozen makes of camera just in the little block of orange chairs within camera-make-discernment range. That's not counting camcorders.

The dress code in here ranges from corporate-informal to tourist-tropical. I am the sweatiest and most disheveled person in view, I'm afraid.[23] There is nothing even remotely nautical about the smell of Pier 21. Two male Engler executives excluded from the corporate scrum are sitting together at the end of the nearest row, right leg over left knee and joggling their loafers in perfect unconscious sync. Every infant within earshot has a promising future in professional opera, it sounds like. Also, every infant being carried or held is being carried or held by its female parent. Over 50% of the purses and handbags are wicker/rattan. The women all somehow give the impression of being on magazine diets. The median age here is at least 45.

A Pier person runs by with an enormous roll of crepe. Some sort of fire alarm's been going for the last fifteen minutes, nerve-janglingly, ignored by everyone because the British bombshell at the PA and the Celebrity people with clipboards also appear to be ignoring it. Also now comes what sounds at first like a sort of tuba from hell, two five-second blasts that ripple shirt-fronts and contort everyone's faces. It turns out it's Holland America's S.S. *Westerdam*'s ship's horn outside, announcing All-Ashore-That's-Going because departure is imminent.

Every so often I remove the hat, towel off, and sort of orbit the blimp hangar, eavesdropping, making small-talk. Over half the passengers I chat up turn out to be from right around here in south Florida. Nonchalant eavesdropping provides the most fun and profit, though: an enormous number of small-talk-type conversations are going on all over the hangar. And a major percentage of this overheard chitchat consists of passengers explaining to other passengers why they signed up for this 7NC Cruise. It's like the universal subject of discussion in here, like chitchatting in the dayroom of a mental ward: "So, why are *you* here?" And the striking

---

22 Long story, not worth it.

23 Another odd demographic truth is that whatever sorts of people are neurologically disposed to go on 7NC Luxury Cruises are also neurologically disposed not to sweat—the one venue of exception on board the *Nadir* was the Mayfair Casino.

constant in all the answers is that not once does somebody say they're going on this 7NC Luxury Cruise just to go on a 7NC Luxury Cruise. Nor does anybody refer to stuff about travel being broadening or a mad desire to parasail. Nobody even mentions being mesmerized by Celebrity's fantasy-slash-promise of pampering in uterine stasis—in fact the word "pamper," so ubiquitous in the Celebrity 7NC brochure, is not once in my hearing uttered. The word that gets used over and over in the explanatory small-talk is: *relax*. Everybody characterizes the upcoming week as either a long-put-off reward or as a last-ditch effort to salvage sanity and self from some inconceivable crockpot of pressure, or both.[24] A lot of the explanatory narratives are long and involved, and some are sort of lurid. Two different conversations involve people who've just finally buried a relative they'd been nursing at home for months as the relative lingered hideously. A floral wholesaler in an aqua MARLINS shirt talks about how he's managed to drag the battered remnants of his soul through the Xmas-to-Valentine rush only by dangling in front of himself the carrot of this week of total relaxation and renewal. A trio of Newark cops all just retired and had promised themselves a Luxury Cruise if they survived their 20. A couple from Fort Lauderdale sketch a scenario in which they've sort of been shamed by friends into 7NC Luxury Cruising, as if they were native New Yorkers and the *Nadir* the Statue of Liberty.

By the way, I have now empirically verified that I am the only ticketed adult here without some kind of camera equipment.

At some point, unnoticed, Holland's *Westerdam*'s snout has withdrawn from the west window: the window is clear, and a brutal sun is shining through a patchy steam of evaporated rain. The blimp hangar's emptier by half now, and quiet. BIG DADDY and spouse are long gone. They have called Lots 5 through 7 all in a sort of bunch, and I and pretty much the whole massed Engler Corporation contingent are now moving in a kind of columnar herd toward Passport Checks and the Deck 3[25] gangway

---

24 I'm pretty sure I know what this syndrome is and how it's related to the brochure's seductive promise of total self-indulgence. What's in play here, I think, is the subtle universal shame that accompanies self-indulgence, the need to explain to just about anybody why the self-indulgence isn't in fact really self-indulgence. Like: I never go get a massage just to get a massage, I go because this old sports-related back injury's killing me and more or less *forcing* me to get a massage; or like: I never just "want" a cigarette, I always "*need*" a cigarette.

25 Like all Megaships, the *Nadir* designates each deck with some 7NC-related name, and on the Cruise it got confusing because they never referred to decks by numbers and you could never remember whether e.g. the Fantasy Deck was Deck 7 or 8. Deck 12 is called the Sun Deck, 11 is the Marina Deck, 10 I forget, 9's the Bahamas Deck, 8 Fantasy

beyond. And now we are getting greeted (each of us) by not one but two Aryan-looking hostesses from the Hospitality staff, and now moving over plush plum carpet to the interior of what one presumes is the actual *Nadir*, washed now in high-oxygen AC that seems subtly balsam-scented, pausing for a second, if we wish, to have our pre-Cruise photo taken by the ship's photographer,[26] apparently for some kind of Before/After souvenir ensemble they'll try to sell us at week's end; and I start seeing the first of more WATCH YOUR STEP signs this coming week than anyone could count, because a Megaship's architecture's flooring is totally jerry-rigged-looking and uneven and everywhere there are sudden little six-inch steplets up and down; and there's the delicious feel of sweat drying and the first nip of AC chill, and I suddenly can't even remember what the squall of a prickly-heated infant sounds like anymore, not in the plushly cushioned little corridors I'm walked through. One of the two Hospitality hostesses seems to have an orthopedic right shoe, and she walks with a very slight limp, and somehow this detail seems terribly moving.

And as Inga and Geli of Hospitality walk me on and in (and it's an endless walk—up, fore, aft, serpentine through bulkheads and steel-railed corridors with mollified jazz out of little round speakers in a beige enamel ceiling I could reach an elbow up and touch), the whole three-hour pre-cruise gestalt of shame and explanation and Why Are You Here is transposed utterly, because at intervals on every wall are elaborate cross-sectioned maps and diagrams, each with a big and reassuringly jolly red dot with YOU ARE HERE, which assertion preempts all inquiry and signals that explanations and doubt and guilt are now left back there with all else we're leaving behind, handing over to pros.

And the elevator's made of glass and is noiseless, and the hostesses

---

and 7 Galaxy (or vice versa), 6 I never did get straight. 5 is the Europa Deck and comprises kind of the *Nadir*'s corporate nerve center and is one huge high-ceilinged bank-looking lobby with everything done in lemon and salmon with brass plating around the Guest Relations Desk and Purser's Desk and Hotel Manager's Desk, and plants, and massive pillars with water running down them with a sound that all but drives you to the nearest urinal. 4 is all cabins and is called I think the Florida Deck. Everything below 4 is all business and unnamed and off-limits w/ the exception of the smidgeon of 3 that has the gangway. I'm henceforth going to refer to the Decks by number, since that's what I had to know in order to take the elevator anywhere. Decks 7 and 8 are where the serious eating and casinoing and discos and entertainment are; 11 has the pools and café; 12 is on top and laid out for serious heliophilia.

26 (a thoroughly silly and superfluous job if ever there was one, on this 7N photocopia)

smile slightly and gaze at nothing as all together we ascend, and it's a very close race which of these two hostesses smells better in the enclosed chill.

And now we're passing little teak-lined shipboard shops with Gucci, Waterford and Wedgwood, Rolex and Raymond Weil, and there's a crackle in the jazz and an announcement in three languages about Welcome and *Willkommen* and how there'll be a Compulsory Lifeboat Drill an hour after sailing.

At 1515h. I am installed in *Nadir* Cabin 1009 and immediately eat almost a whole basket of free fruit and lie on a really nice bed and drum my fingers on my swollen tummy.

6

Departure at 1630h. turns out to be a not untasteful affair of crepe and horns. Each deck's got walkways outside, with railings made of some kind of really good wood. It's now overcast, and the ocean way below is dull-colored and frothy, etc. It smells less fishy or oceany than just salty. Our horn is even more planet-shattering than the *Westerdam*'s horn. Most of the people exchanging waves with us are cruisers along the rails of the decks of other 7NC Megaships, also just leaving, so it's a surreal little scene—it's hard not to imagine all of us cruising the whole Western Caribbean in a parallel pack, all waving at one another the entire time. Docking and leaving are the two times a Megacruiser's Captain is actually steering the ship; and m.v. *Nadir* Captain G. Panagiotakis has wheeled us around and pointed our snout at the open sea, and we, large and white and clean, are under sail.

7

The whole first two days and nights are bad weather, with high-pitched winds and heaving seas, spume[27] lashing the porthole's glass, etc. For 40+ hours it's more like a Luxury North Sea Cruise, and the Celebrity staff

---

27 The single best new vocab word from this week: *spume* (second-best was *scheisser*, which one German retiree called another German retiree who kept beating him at darts).

goes around looking regretful but not apologetic,[28] and in all fairness it's hard to find a way to blame Celebrity Cruises Inc. for the weather.[29]

On gale-force days like the first two, passengers are advised to enjoy the view from the railings on the lee side of the *Nadir*. The one other guy who ever joins me in trying out the non-lee side has his glasses blown off by the wind, and he does not appreciate my remarking to him that round-the-ear cable arms are better for high-wind view-enjoying. I keep waiting to see somebody from the crew wearing the traditional yellow slicker, but no luck. The railing I do most of my contemplative gazing from is on Deck 10, so the sea is way below, and the sounds of it slopping and heaving around are far-away and surflike, and visually it's a little like looking down into a flushing toilet. No fins in view.

In heavy seas, hypochondriacs are kept busy taking their gastric pulse every couple seconds and wondering whether what they're feeling is maybe the onset of seasickness and/or gauging the exact level of seasickness they're feeling. Seasickness-wise, though, it turns out that heavy seas are sort of like battle: there's no way to know ahead of time how you'll react. A test of the deep and involuntary stuff of a man. I myself turn out not to get seasick. An apparent immunity, deep and unchosen, and slightly miraculous, given that I have every other kind of motion sickness listed in the *PDR* and cannot take anything for it.[30] For the whole first rough-sea day I puzzle about the fact that every other passenger on the m.v. *Nadir* looks to have received identical little weird shaving cuts below their left ear—which in the case of female passengers seems especially strange—until I learn that the little round Band-Aidish things on everybody's neck are these special new nuclear-powered transdermal motion sickness *patches*, which apparently now nobody with any kind of clue about 7NC Luxury Cruising leaves home without.

Patches notwithstanding, a lot of the passengers get seasick anyway, these first two howling days. It turns out that a seasick person really does look green, though it's an odd, ghostly green, pasty and toadish, and more than a little corpselike when the seasick person is dressed in formal dinnerwear.

For the first two nights, who's feeling seasick and who's not and who's

---

28 (this expression resembling a kind of facial shoulder-shrug, as at fate)

29 (Though I can't help noting that the weather in the Celebrity 7NC brochure was substantially nicer.)

30 I have a deep and involuntary reaction to Dramamine whereby it sends me pitching forward to lie prone and twitching wherever I am when the drug kicks in, so I'm sailing the *Nadir* cold turkey.

not now but was a little while ago or isn't feeling it yet but thinks it's maybe coming on, etc., is a big topic of conversation at good old Table 64 in the Five-Star Caravelle Restaurant.[31] Common suffering and fear of suffering turn out to be a terrific icebreaker, and ice-breaking is important, because on a 7NC you eat at the same designated table with the same companions all seven nights.[32] Discussing nausea and vomiting while eat-

---

[31] This is on Deck 7, the serious dining room, and it's never called just the "Caravelle Restaurant" (and *never* just "the Restaurant")—it's always "The Five-Star Caravelle Restaurant."

[32] There were seven other people with me at good old Table 64, all from south Florida—Miami, Tamarac, Fort Lauderdale itself. Four of the people knew each other in private landlocked life and had requested to be at the same table. The other three people were an old couple and their granddaughter, whose name was Mona.

I was the only first-time Luxury Cruiser at Table 64, and also the only person who referred to the evening meal as "supper," a childhood habit I could not seem to be teased out of.

With the conspicuous exception of Mona, I liked all my tablemates a lot, and I want to get a description of supper out of the way in a fast footnote and avoid saying much about them for fear of hurting their feelings by noting any weirdnesses or features that might seem potentially mean. There were some pretty weird aspects to the Table 64 ensemble, though. For one thing, they all had thick and unmistakable NYC accents, and yet they swore up and down that they'd all been born and raised in south Florida (although it did turn out that all the T64 adults' own parents had been New Yorkers, which when you think about it is compelling evidence of the durability of a good thick NYC accent). Besides me there were five women and two men, and both men were completely silent except on the subjects of golf, business, transdermal motion sickness prophylaxis, and the legalities of getting stuff through Customs. The women carried Table 64's conversational ball. One of the reasons I liked all these women (except Mona) so much was because they laughed really hard at my jokes, even lame or very obscure jokes; although they all had this curious way of laughing where they sort of *screamed* before they laughed, I mean really and discernibly screamed, so that for one excruciating second you could never tell whether they were getting ready to laugh or whether they were seeing something hideous and screamworthy over your shoulder across the 5☆C.R., and this was disconcerting all week. Also, like many other 7NC Luxury Cruise passengers I observed, they all seemed to be uniformly stellar at anecdotes and stories and extended-set-up jokes, employing both hands and faces to maximum dramatic effect, knowing when to pause and when to go run-on, how to double-take and how to set up a straight man.

My favorite tablemate was Trudy, whose husband was back home in Tamarac managing some sudden crisis at the couple's cellular phone business and had given his ticket to Alice, their heavy and very well-dressed daughter, who was on spring break from Miami U, and who was for some reason extremely anxious to communicate to me that she had a Serious Boyfriend, the name of which boyfriend was Patrick. Alice's part of most of our interfaces consisted of remarks like: "You hate fennel? What a coincidence: my boyfriend Patrick absolutely *detests* fennel"; "You're from Illinois? What a coincidence: my boyfriend Patrick has an aunt whose first husband was from Indiana, which is right near Illinois"; "You have four limbs? What a coincidence:...," and so on. Alice's continual assertion of her relationship-status may have been a defensive tactic against Trudy, who kept pulling professionally retouched 4 × 5 glossies of Alice out of her purse and showing them to me with Alice sitting right there, and who, every time Alice mentioned Patrick, suffered some sort of weird facial tic or grimace where one side's canine tooth showed and the other side's didn't. Trudy was 56, the same age as my own dear personal Mom, and looked—Trudy did, and I mean this in the nicest possible way—like Jackie Gleason in drag, and had a particularly loud pre-laugh scream that was a real arrhythmia-producer, and was the one who coerced me into Wednesday night's Conga Line, and got me strung out on Snowball Jackpot Bingo, and also was an incredible lay authority on 7NC Luxury Cruises, this being her sixth in a decade—she and her friend Esther (thin-faced, subtly ravaged-looking, the distaff part of the couple from Miami) had tales to tell about Carnival, Princess, Crystal, and Cunard too fraught with libel-potential to reproduce here, and one long review of what was apparently the worst cruise line in 7NC history—one "American Family Cruises," which folded after just sixteen months—involving outrages too literally incredible to be believed from any duo less knowledgeable and discerning than Trudy and Esther.

Plus it started to strike me that I had never before been party to such a minute and exacting analysis of the food and service of a meal I was just at that moment eating. Nothing escaped the attention of T and E—the symmetry of the parsley sprigs atop the boiled baby carrots, the consistency of the bread, the flavor and mastication-friendliness of various cuts of meat, the celerity and flambé technique of the various pastry guys in tall white hats who appeared tableside when items had to be set on fire (a major percentage of the desserts in the 5☆C.R. had to be set on fire), and so on. The waiter and busboy kept circling the table, going "Finish? Finish?" while Esther and Trudy had exchanges like:

"Honey you don't look happy with the conch, what's the problem."

"I'm fine. It's fine. Everything's fine."

"Don't lie. Honey with that face who could lie. Frank am I right? This is a person with a face incapable of lying. Is it the potatoes or the conch? Is it the conch?"

"There's nothing wrong Esther darling I swear it."

"You're not happy with the conch."

"All right. I've got a problem with the conch."

"Did I tell you? Frank did I tell her?"

[Frank silently probes own ear with pinkie.]

"Was I right? I could tell just by looking you weren't happy."

"I'm fine with the potatoes. It's the conch."

"Did I tell you about seasonal fish on ships? What did I tell you?"

"The potatoes are good."

Mona is eighteen. Her grandparents have been taking her on a Luxury Cruise every spring since she was five. Mona always sleeps through both breakfast and lunch and spends all night at the Scorpio Disco and in the Mayfair Casino playing the slots. She's 6' 2" if she's an inch. She's going to attend Penn State next fall because the agreement was that she'd receive a 4-Wheel-Drive vehicle if she went someplace where there might be snow. She was unabashed in recounting this college-selection criterion. She was an incredibly demanding passenger and diner, but her complaints about slight aesthetic and gustatory imperfections at table lacked Trudy and Esther's discernment and integrity and came off as simply churlish. Mona was also kind of strange-looking: a body like Brigitte Nielsen or some centerfold on steroids, and above it, framed in resplendent and frizzless blond hair, the tiny delicate pale unhappy face of a kind of corrupt doll. Her grandparents, who retired every night right after supper, always made a small ceremony after dessert of handing Mona $100 to "go have some fun" with. This $100 bill was always in one

ing intricately prepared and heavy gourmet foods doesn't seem to bother anybody.

Even in heavy seas, 7NC Megaships don't yaw or throw you around or send bowls of soup sliding across tables. Only a certain subtle unreality to your footing lets you know you're not on land. At sea, a room's floor feels somehow 3-D, and your footing demands a slight attention good old planar static land never needs. You don't ever quite hear the ship's big engines, but when your feet are planted you can feel them, a kind of spinal throb — it's oddly soothing.

Walking is a little dreamy also. There are constant slight shifts in torque from the waves' action. When heavy waves come straight at a Megaship's snout, the ship goes up and down along its long axis — this is called *pitching*. It produces a disorienting deal where you feel like you're walking on a very slight downhill grade and then level and then on a very slight uphill grade. Some evolutionary retrograde reptile-brain part of the CNS is apparently reawakened, though, and manages all this so automatically that it requires a good deal of attention to notice anything more than that walking feels a little dreamy.

Rolling, on the other hand, is when waves hit the ship from the side and

---

of those little ceremonial bank envelopes that has B. Franklin's face staring out of a porthole-like window in the front, and written on the envelope in red Magic Marker was always "We Love You, Honey." Mona never once said thank you for the money. She also rolled her eyes at just about everything her grandparents said, a habit that quickly drove me up the wall.

I find I'm not as worried about saying potentially mean stuff about Mona as I am about Trudy and Alice and Esther and Esther's mute smiling husband Frank.

Apparently Mona's special customary little gig on 7NC Luxury Cruises is to lie to the waiter and maître d' and say that Thursday is her birthday, so that at the Formal supper on Thursday she gets bunting and a heart-shaped helium balloon tied to her chair and her own cake and pretty much the whole restaurant staff comes out and forms a circle around her and sings to her. Her real birthday, she informs me on Monday, is 29 July, and when I observe that 29 July is also the birthday of Benito Mussolini, Mona's grandmother shoots me kind of a death-look, though Mona herself is excited at the coincidence, apparently confusing the names *Mussolini* and *Maserati*. Because it just so happens that Thursday 16 March really *is* the birthday of Trudy's daughter Alice, and because Mona declines to forfeit her fake birthday claim and instead counterclaims that her and Alice's sharing bunting and natal attentions at 3/16's Formal supper promises to be "radical," Alice has decided that she wishes Mona all kinds of ill, and by Tuesday 14 March Alice and I have established a kind of anti-Mona alliance, and we amuse each other across Table 64 by making subtly disguised little strangling and stabbing motions whenever Mona says anything, a set of disguised motions Alice told me she learned at various excruciating public suppers in Miami with her Serious Boyfriend Patrick, who apparently hates almost everyone he eats with.

make it go up and down along its crosswise axis.[33] When the m.v. *Nadir* rolls, what you feel is a very slight increase in the demands placed on the muscles of your left leg, then a strange absence of all demand, then demands on the right leg. The demands shift at the rate of a very long thing swinging, and again the action is usually so subtle that it's almost a meditative exercise to stay conscious of what's going on.

We never pitch badly, but every once in a while some really big *Poseidon Adventure*–grade single wave must come and hit the *Nadir*'s side, because every once in a while the asymmetric leg-demands won't stop or reverse and you keep having to put more and more weight on one leg until you're exquisitely close to tipping over and have to grab something.[34] It happens very quickly and never twice in a row. The cruise's first night features some really big waves from starboard, and in the casino after supper it's hard to tell who's had too much of the '71 Richebourg and who's just doing a roll-related stagger. Add in the fact that most of the women are wearing high heels, and you can imagine some of the vertiginous staggering/flailing/clutching that goes on. Almost everyone on the *Nadir* has come on in couples, and when they walk during heavy seas they tend to hang on each other like freshman steadies. You can tell they like it—the women have this trick of sort of folding themselves into the men and snuggling as they walk, and the men's postures improve and their faces firm up and you can tell they feel unusually solid and protective. A 7NC Luxury Cruise is full of these odd little unexpected romantic nuggets like trying to help each other walk when the ship rolls—you can sort of tell why older couples like to cruise.

Heavy seas are also great for sleep, it turns out. The first two mornings, there's hardly anybody at Early Seating Breakfast. Everybody sleeps in. People with insomnia of years' standing report uninterrupted sleep of nine hours, ten hours. Their eyes are wide and childlike with wonder as they report this. Everybody looks younger when they've had a lot of sleep. There's rampant daytime napping, too. By week's end, when we'd had all manner of weather, I finally saw what it was about heavy seas and

---

33 (Which, again, w/ a Megaship like this is subtle—even at its worst, the rolling never made chandeliers tinkle or anything fall off surfaces, though it did keep a slightly unplumb drawer in Cabin 1009's complex Wondercloset rattling madly in its track even after several insertions of Kleenex at strategic points.)

34 This on-the-edge moment's exquisiteness is something like the couple seconds between knowing you're going to sneeze and actually sneezing, some kind of marvelous distended moment of transferring control to large automatic forces. (The sneeze-analogy thing might sound freaky, but it's true, and Trudy's said she'll back me up.)

marvelous rest: in heavy seas you feel rocked to sleep, with the windows' spume a gentle shushing, the engines' throb a mother's pulse.

8

Did I mention that famous writer and Iowa Writers' Workshop Chairperson Frank Conroy has his own experiential essay about cruising right there in Celebrity's 7NC brochure? Well he does, and the thing starts out on the Pier 21 gangway that first Saturday with his family:[35]

> With that single, easy step, we entered a new world, a sort of alternate reality to the one on shore. Smiles, handshakes, and we were whisked away to our cabin by a friendly young woman from Guest Relations.

Then they're outside along the rail for the *Nadir*'s sailing:

> ... We became aware that the ship was pulling away. We had felt no warning, no trembling of the deck, throbbing of the engines or the like. It was as if the land were magically receding, like some ever-so-slow reverse zoom in the movies.

This is pretty much what Conroy's whole "My Celebrity Cruise, or *'All This and a Tan, Too'*" is like. Its full implications didn't hit me until I reread it supine on Deck 12 the first sunny day. Conroy's essay is graceful and lapidary and attractive and assuasive. I submit that it is also completely sinister and despair-producing and bad. Its badness does not consist so much in its constant and mesmeric references to fantasy and alternate realities and the palliative powers of pro pampering—

> I'd come on board after two months of intense and moderately stressful work, but now it seemed a distant memory.
> I realized it had been a week since I'd washed a dish, cooked a meal, gone to the market, done an errand or, in fact, anything at all

---

35 Conroy took the same Luxury Cruise as I, the Seven-Night Western Caribbean on the good old *Nadir*, in May '94. He and his family cruised for free. I know details like this because Conroy talked to me on the phone, and answered nosy questions, and was frank and forthcoming and in general just totally decent-seeming about the whole thing.

requiring a minimum of thought and effort. My toughest decisions had been whether to catch the afternoon showing of *Mrs. Doubtfire* or play bingo.

—nor in the surfeit of happy adjectives, nor so much in the tone of breathless approval throughout—

For all of us, our fantasies and expectations were to be exceeded, to say the least.

When it comes to service, Celebrity Cruises seems ready and able to deal with anything.

Bright sun, warm still air, the brilliant blue-green of the Caribbean under the vast lapis lazuli dome of the sky....

The training must be rigorous, indeed, because the truth is, the service was impeccable, and impeccable in every aspect from the cabin steward to the sommelier, from the on-deck waiter to the Guest Relations manager, from the ordinary seaman who goes out of his way to get your deck chair to the third mate who shows you the way to the library. It is hard to imagine a more professional, polished operation, and I doubt that many in the world can equal it.

Rather, part of the essay's real badness can be found in the way it reveals once again the Megaline's sale-to-sail agenda of micromanaging not only one's perceptions of a 7NC Luxury Cruise but even one's own interpretation and articulation of those perceptions. In other words, Celebrity's PR people go and get one of the U.S.A.'s most respected writers to pre-articulate and -endorse the 7NC experience, and to do it with a professional eloquence and authority that few lay perceivers and articulators could hope to equal.[36]

But the really major badness is that the project and placement of "My Celebrity Cruise..." are sneaky and duplicitous and far beyond whatever eroded pales still exist in terms of literary ethics. Conroy's "essay" appears as an insert, on skinnier pages and with different margins from the rest of the brochure, creating the impression that it has been excerpted from some large and objective thing Conroy wrote. But it hasn't been. The truth is that Celebrity Cruises paid Frank Conroy upfront to write it,[37] even

---

36 E.g. after reading Conroy's essay on board, whenever I'd look up at the sky it wouldn't be the sky I was seeing, it was the *vast lapis lazuli dome of the sky*.

37 Pier 21 having seasoned me as a recipient of explanatory/justificatory narratives, I was able to make some serious journalistic phone inquiries about how Professor Conroy's essaymercial came to be, yielding two separate narratives:

though nowhere in or around the essay is there anything acknowledging that it's a paid endorsement, not even one of the little "So-and-so has been compensated for his services" that flashes at your TV screen's lower right during celebrity-hosted infomercials. Instead, inset on this weird essay-mercial's first page is an author-photoish shot of Conroy brooding in a black turtleneck, and below the photo is an author-bio with a list of Con-roy's books that includes the 1967 classic *Stop-Time*, which is arguably the best literary memoir of the twentieth century and is one of the books that first made poor old yours truly want to try to be a writer.

In other words, Celebrity Cruises is presenting Conroy's review of his 7NC Cruise as an essay and not a commercial. This is extremely bad. Here is the argument for why it's bad. Whether it honors them well or not, an essay's fundamental obligations are supposed to be to the reader. The reader, on however unconscious a level, understands this, and thus tends to approach an essay with a relatively high level of openness and credulity. But a commercial is a very different animal. Advertisements have certain formal, legal obligations to truthfulness, but these are broad enough to allow for a great deal of rhetorical maneuvering in the fulfillment of an advertisement's primary obligation, which is to serve the financial inter-ests of its sponsor. Whatever attempts an advertisement makes to interest and appeal to its readers are not, finally, for the reader's benefit. And the reader of an ad knows all this, too—that an ad's appeal is by its very nature *calculated*—and this is part of why our state of receptivity is differ-ent, more guarded, when we get ready to read an ad.[38]

In the case of Frank Conroy's "essay," Celebrity Cruises[39] is trying to position an ad in such a way that we come to it with the lowered guard and

---

(1) From Celebrity Cruises' PR liaison Ms. Wiessen (after a two-day silence that I've come to understand as the PR-equivalent of covering the microphone with your hand and leaning over to confer w/ counsel): "Celebrity saw an article he wrote in *Travel and Leisure* magazine, and they were really impressed with how he could create these mental post-cards, so they went to ask him to write about his Cruise experience for people who'd never been on a Cruise before, and they did pay him to write the article, and they really took a gamble, really, because he'd never been on a Cruise before, and they had to pay him whether he liked it or not, and whether they liked the article or not, but... [dry little chuckle] obviously they liked the article, and he did a good job, so that's the Mr. Conroy story, and those are his perspectives on his experience."

(2) From Frank Conroy (with the small sigh that precedes a certain kind of weary candor): "I prostituted myself."

38 This is the reason why even a really beautiful, ingenious, powerful ad (of which there are a lot) can never be any kind of real art: an ad has no status as gift, i.e. it's never really *for* the person it's directed at.

39 (with the active complicity of Professor Conroy, I'm afraid)

leading chin we properly reserve for coming to an essay, for something that is art (or that is at least trying to be art). An ad that pretends to be art is—at absolute best—like somebody who smiles warmly at you only because he wants something from you. This is dishonest, but what's sinister is the cumulative effect that such dishonesty has on us: since it offers a perfect facsimile or simulacrum of goodwill without goodwill's real spirit, it messes with our heads and eventually starts upping our defenses even in cases of genuine smiles and real art and true goodwill. It makes us feel confused and lonely and impotent and angry and scared. It causes despair.[40]

At any rate, for this particular 7NC consumer, Conroy's ad-as-essay ends up having a truthfulness about it that I'm quite sure is unintentional. As my week on the *Nadir* wore on, I began to see this essaymercial as a perfect ironic reflection of the mass-market-Cruise experience itself. The essay is polished, powerful, impressive, clearly the best that money can buy. It presents itself as for my benefit. It manages my experiences and my interpretation of those experiences and takes care of them in advance for me. It seems to care about me. But it doesn't, not really, because first and foremost it wants something from me. So does the Cruise itself. The pretty setting and glittering ship and dashing staff and sedulous servants and

---

40 This is related to the phenomenon of the Professional Smile, a national pandemic in the service industry; and noplace in my experience have I been on the receiving end of as many Professional Smiles as I am on the *Nadir,* maître d's, Chief Stewards, Hotel Managers' minions, Cruise Director—their P.S.'s all come on like switches at my approach. But also back on land at banks, restaurants, airline ticket counters, on and on. You know this smile—the strenuous contraction of circumoral fascia w/ incomplete zygomatic involvement—the smile that doesn't quite reach the smiler's eyes and that signifies nothing more than a calculated attempt to advance the smiler's own interests by pretending to like the smilee. Why do employers and supervisors force professional service people to broadcast the Professional Smile? Am I the only consumer in whom high doses of such a smile produce despair? Am I the only person who's sure that the growing number of cases in which totally average-looking people suddenly open up with automatic weapons in shopping malls and insurance offices and medical complexes and McDonald'ses is somehow causally related to the fact that these venues are well-known dissemination-loci of the Professional Smile?

Who do they think is fooled by the Professional Smile?

And yet the Professional Smile's absence now *also* causes despair. Anybody who's ever bought a pack of gum in a Manhattan cigar store or asked for something to be stamped FRAGILE at a Chicago post office or tried to obtain a glass of water from a South Boston waitress knows well the soul-crushing effect of a service worker's scowl, i.e. the humiliation and resentment of being denied the Professional Smile. And the Professional Smile has by now skewed even my resentment at the dreaded Professional Scowl: I walk away from the Manhattan tobacconist resenting not the counterman's character or absence of goodwill but his lack of *professionalism* in denying me the Smile. What a fucking mess.

solicitous fun-managers all want something from me, and it's not just the price of my ticket—they've already got that. Just what it is that they want is hard to pin down, but by early in the week I can feel it, and building: it circles the ship like a fin.

9

Celebrity's fiendish brochure does not lie or exaggerate, however, in the luxury department. I now confront the journalistic problem of not being sure how many examples I need to list in order to communicate the atmosphere of sybaritic and nearly insanity-producing pampering on board the m.v. *Nadir*.

How about for just one example Saturday 11 March, right after sailing but before the North Sea weather hits, when I want to go out to Deck 10's port rail for some introductory vista-gazing and thus decide I need some zinc oxide for my peel-prone nose. My zinc oxide's still in my big duffel bag, which at that point is piled with all Deck 10's other luggage in the little area between the 10-Fore elevator and the 10-Fore staircase while little men in cadet-blue Celebrity jumpsuits, porters—entirely Lebanese, this squad seemed to be—are cross-checking the luggage tags with the *Nadir*'s passenger list Lot #s and organizing the luggage and taking it all up the Port and Starboard halls to people's cabins.

And but so I come out and spot my duffel among the luggage, and I start to grab and haul it out of the towering pile of leather and nylon, with the idea that I can just whisk the bag back to 1009 myself and root through it and find my good old ZnO;[41] and one of the porters sees me starting to grab the bag, and he dumps all four of the massive pieces of luggage he's staggering with and leaps to intercept me. At first I'm afraid he thinks I'm some kind of baggage thief and wants to see my claim-check or something. But it turns out that what he wants is my duffel: he wants to carry it to 1009 for me. And I, who am about half again this poor herniated little guy's size (as is the duffel bag itself), protest politely, trying to be considerate, saying Don't Fret, Not a Big Deal, Just Need My Good Old ZnO. I indicate to the porter that I can see they have some sort of incredibly organized ordinal luggage-dispersal system under way here and that I don't mean to disrupt it or make him carry a Lot #7 bag before a Lot #2 bag or

---

41 (Which by the way trust me, I used to lifeguard part-time, and fuck this SPF hooha: good old ZnO will keep your nose looking like a newborn's.)

anything, and no I'll just get the big old heavy weather stained sucker out of here myself and give the little guy that much less work to do.

And then now a very strange argument indeed ensues, me v. the Lebanese porter, because it turns out I am putting this guy, who barely speaks English, in a terrible kind of sedulous-service double-bind, a paradox of pampering: viz. the The-Passenger's-Always-Right-versus-Never-Let-A-Passenger-Carry-His-Own-Bag paradox. Clueless at the time about what this poor little Lebanese man is going through, I wave off both his high-pitched protests and his agonized expression as mere servile courtesy, and I extract the duffel and lug it up the hall to 1009 and slather the old beak with ZnO and go outside to watch the coast of Florida recede cinematically à la F. Conroy.

Only later did I understand what I'd done. Only later did I learn that that little Lebanese Deck 10 porter had his head just about chewed off by the (also Lebanese) Deck 10 Head Porter, who'd had his own head chewed off by the Austrian Chief Steward, who'd received confirmed reports that a Deck 10 passenger had been seen carrying his own luggage up the Port hallway of Deck 10 and now demanded rolling Lebanese heads for this clear indication of porterly dereliction, and had reported (the Austrian Chief Steward did) the incident (as is apparently SOP) to an officer in the Guest Relations Dept., a Greek officer with Revo shades and a walkie-talkie and officerial epaulets so complex I never did figure out what his rank was; and this high-ranking Greek guy actually came around to 1009 after Saturday's supper to apologize on behalf of practically the entire Chandris shipping line and to assure me that ragged-necked Lebanese heads were even at that moment rolling down various corridors in piacular recompense for my having had to carry my own bag. And even though this Greek officer's English was in lots of ways better than mine, it took me no less than ten minutes to express my own horror and to claim responsibility and to detail the double-bind I'd put the porter in — brandishing at relevant moments the actual tube of ZnO that had caused the whole snafu — ten or more minutes before I could get enough of a promise from the Greek officer that various chewed-off heads would be reattached and employee records unbesmirched to feel comfortable enough to allow the officer to leave;[42] and the whole incident was incredibly frazzling and

---

42 In further retrospect, I think the only thing I really persuaded the Greek officer of was that I was very weird, and possibly unstable, which impression I'm sure was shared with Mr. Dermatitis and combined with that same first night's *au-jus*-as-shark-bait request to destroy my credibility with Dermatitis before I even got in to see him.

angst-fraught and filled almost a whole Mead notebook and is here recounted in only its barest psychoskeletal outline.

It is everywhere on the *Nadir* you look: evidence of a steely determination to indulge the passenger in ways that go far beyond any halfway-sane passenger's own expectations.[43] Some wholly random examples: My cabin bathroom has plenty of thick fluffy towels, but when I go up to lie in the sun[44] I don't have to take any of my cabin's towels, because the two upper decks' sun areas have big carts loaded with even thicker and fluffier towels. These carts are stationed at convenient intervals along endless rows of gymnastically adjustable deck chairs that are themselves phenomenally fine deck chairs, sturdy enough for even the portliest sunbather but also narcoleptically comfortable, with heavy-alloy skeletons over which is stretched some exotic material that combines canvas's quick-drying durability with cotton's absorbency and comfort—the material's precise composition is mysterious, but it's a welcome step up from public pools' deck chairs' surface of Kmartish plastic that sticks and produces farty suction-noises whenever you shift your sweaty weight on it—and the *Nadir*'s chairs' material is not striated or cross-hatched in some web but is a solid expanse stretched drum-tight over the frame, so that you don't get those weird pink chair-stripes on the side you're lying on. Oh, and each upper deck's carts are manned by a special squad of full-time Towel Guys, so that, when you're well-done on both sides and ready to quit and spring easily out of the deck chair, you don't have to pick up your towel and take it with you or even bus it into the cart's Used Towel slot, because a Towel Guy materializes the minute your fanny leaves the chair and removes your towel for you and deposits it in the slot. (Actually the Towel Guys are such overachievers about removing used towels that even if you just get up for a second to reapply ZnO or gaze contemplatively out over the railing, often when you turn back around your towel's gone, and your deck chair's refolded to the uniform 45° at-rest angle, and you have to readjust your chair all over again and go to the cart to get a fresh fluffy towel, of which there's admittedly not a short supply.)

Down in the Five-Star Caravelle Restaurant, the waiter[45] will not only

---

43 One of Celebrity Cruises' slogans asserts that they Look Forward To Exceeding Your Expectations—they say it a lot, and they are sincere, though they are either disingenuous about or innocent of this Excess's psychic consequences.

44 (to either Deck 11's pools or Deck 12's Temple of Ra)

45 Table 64's waiter is Tibor, a Hungarian and a truly exceptional person, about whom if there's any editorial justice you will learn a lot more someplace below.

bring you, e.g., lobster—as well as seconds and even thirds on lobster[46]—with methamphetaminic speed, but he'll also incline over you[47] with gleaming claw-cracker and surgical fork and dismantle the lobster for you, saving you the green goopy work that's the only remotely rigorous thing about lobster.

At the Windsurf Cafe, up on Deck 11 by the pools, where there's always an informal buffet lunch, there's never that bovine line that makes most cafeterias such a downer, and there are about 73 varieties of entrée alone, and incredibly good coffee; and if you're carrying a bunch of notebooks or even just have too many things on your tray, a waiter will materialize as you peel away from the buffet and will carry your tray—i.e. even though it's a cafeteria there're all these waiters standing around, all with Nehru-esque jackets and white towels draped over left arms that are always held in the position of broken or withered arms, watching you, the waiters, not quite making eye-contact but scanning for any little way to be of service, plus plum-jacketed sommeliers walking around to see if you need a non-buffet libation...plus a whole other crew of maître d's and supervisors watching the waiters and sommeliers and tall-hatted buffet-servers to make sure they're not even thinking of letting you do something for yourself that they could be doing for you.[48]

Every public surface on the m.v. *Nadir* that isn't stainless steel or glass or varnished parquet or dense and good-smelling sauna-type wood is plush blue carpet that never naps and never has a chance to accumulate even one flecklet of lint because jumpsuited Third World guys are always at it with Siemens A.G. high-suction vacuums. The elevators are Euroglass and yellow steel and stainless steel and a kind of wood-grain material that looks too shiny to be real wood but makes a sound when you thump it that's an awful lot like real wood.[49] The elevators and stairways between

---

46 Not until Tuesday's lobster night at the 5☆C.R. did I really emphatically understand the Roman phenomenon of the vomitorium.

47 (not invasively or obtrusively or condescendingly)

48 Again, you never have to bus your tray after eating at the Windsurf, because the waiters leap to take them, and again the zeal can be a hassle, because if you get up just to go get another peach or something and still have a cup of coffee and some yummy sandwich crusts you've been saving for last a lot of times you come back and the tray and the crusts are gone, and I personally start to attribute this oversedulous busing to the reign of Hellenic terror the waiters labor under.

49 The many things on the *Nadir* that were wood-grain but not real wood were such marvelous and painstaking imitations of wood that a lot of times it seemed like it would have been simpler and less expensive simply to have used real wood.

decks[50] seem to be the particular objects of the anal retention of a whole special Elevator-and-Staircase custodial crew.[51, 52]

And let's don't forget Room Service, which on a 7NC Luxury Cruise is called Cabin Service. Cabin Service is in addition to the eleven scheduled daily opportunities for public eating, and it's available 24/7, and it's free: all you have to do is hit x72 on the bedside phone, and ten or fifteen minutes later a guy who wouldn't even *dream* of hitting you up for a gratuity appears with this...this *tray:* "Thinly Sliced Ham and Swiss Cheese on White Bread with Dijon Mustard," "The Combo: Cajun Chicken with Pasta Salad, and Spicy Salsa," on and on, a whole page of sandwiches and platters in the Services Directory—and the stuff deserves to be capitalized, believe me. As a kind of semi-agoraphobe who spends massive amounts of time in my cabin, I come to have a really complex dependency/shame relationship with Cabin Service. Since finally getting around to reading the Services Directory and finding out about it Monday night, I've ended up availing myself of Cabin Service every night—more like twice a night, to be honest—even though I find it extremely embarrassing to be calling up x72 asking to have even *more* rich food brought to me

50 Two broad staircases, Fore and Aft, both of which reverse their zag-angle at each landing, and the landings themselves have mirrored walls, which is wickedly great because via the mirrors you can check out female bottoms in cocktail dresses ascending one flight above you without appearing to be one of those icky types who check out female bottoms on staircases.

51 During the first two days of rough seas, when people vomited a lot (especially after supper and apparently *extra*-especially on the elevators and stairways), these puddles of vomit inspired a veritable feeding frenzy of Wet/Dry Vacs and spot-remover and all-trace-of-odor-eradicator chemicals applied by this Elite Special Forces-type crew.

52 By the way, the ethnic makeup of the *Nadir*'s crew is a melting-pot mélange on the order of like a Benetton commercial, and it's a constant challenge to trace the racio-geographical makeup of the employees' various hierarchies. All the big-time officers are Greek, but then it's a Greek-owned ship so what do you expect. Them aside, it at first seems like there's some basic Eurocentric caste system in force: waiters, busboys, beverage waitresses, sommeliers, casino dealers, entertainers, and stewards seem mostly to be Aryans, while the porters and custodians and swabbies tend to be your swarthier types—Arabs and Filipinos, Cubans, West Indian blacks. But it turns out to be more complex than that, because the Chief Stewards and Chief Sommeliers and maître d's who so beadily oversee the Aryan servants are *themselves* swarthy and non-Aryan—e.g. our maître d' at the 5☆C.R. is Portuguese, with the bull neck and heavy-lidded grin of a Teamsters official, and gives the impression of needing only some very subtle prearranged signal to have a $10000-an-hour prostitute or unimaginable substances delivered to your cabin; and our whole T64 totally loathes him for no single pinpointable reason, and we've all agreed in advance to fuck him royally on the tip at week's end.

when there've already been eleven gourmet eating-ops that day.[53] Usually what I do is spread out my notebooks and *Fielding's Guide to Worldwide Cruising 1995* and pens and various materials all over the bed, so when the Cabin Service guy appears at the door he'll see all this belletristic material and figure I'm working really hard on something belletristic right here in the cabin and have doubtless been too busy to have hit all the public meals and am thus legitimately entitled to the indulgence of Cabin Service.[54]

But it's my experience with the cabin cleaning that's maybe the ultimate example of stress from a pampering so extravagant that it messes with your head. Searing crush or no, the fact of the matter is I rarely even see 1009's cabin steward, the diaphanous and epicanthically doe-eyed Petra. But I have good reason to believe she sees me. Because every time I leave 1009 for more than like half an hour, when I get back it's totally cleaned and dusted down again and the towels replaced and the bathroom agleam. Don't get me wrong: in a way it's great. I am kind of a slob, and I'm in Cabin 1009 a lot, and I also come and go a lot,[55] and when I'm in here in 1009 I sit in bed and write in bed while eating fruit and generally mess up the bed. But then whenever I dart out and then come back, the bed is freshly made up and hospital-cornered and there's another mint-centered chocolate on the pillow.[56]

I fully grant that mysterious invisible room-cleaning is in a way great, every true slob's fantasy, somebody materializing and deslobbing your room and then dematerializing—like having a mom without the guilt.

---

53 This is counting the Midnight Buffet, which tends to be a kind of lamely lavish Theme-slash-Costume-Partyish thing, w/ Theme-related foods—Oriental, Caribbean, Tex-Mex—and which I plan in this essay to mostly skip except to say that Tex-Mex Night out by the pools featured what must have been a seven-foot-high ice sculpture of Pancho Villa that spent the whole party dripping steadily onto the mammoth sombrero of Tibor, Table 64's beloved and extremely cool Hungarian waiter, whose contract forces him on Tex-Mex Night to wear a serape and a straw sombrero with a 17" radius[53a] and to dispense Four Alarm chili from a steam table placed right underneath an ice sculpture, and whose pink and birdlike face on occasions like this expressed a combination of mortification and dignity that seem somehow to sum up the whole plight of postwar Eastern Europe.

53a (He let me measure it when the reptilian maître d' wasn't looking.)

54 (I know, like I'm sure this guy even cares.)

55 This was primarily because of the semi-agoraphobia—I'd have to sort of psych myself up to leave the cabin and go accumulate experiences, and then pretty quickly out there in the general population my will would break and I'd find some sort of excuse to scuttle back to 1009. This happened quite a few times a day.

56 (This FN right here's being written almost a week after the Cruise ended, and I'm still living mainly on these hoarded mint-centered chocolates.)

But there is also, I think, a creeping guilt here, a deep accretive uneasiness, a discomfort that presents—at least in my own case—as a weird kind of pampering-paranoia.

Because after a couple days of this fabulous invisible room-cleaning, I start to wonder how exactly Petra knows when I'm in 1009 and when I'm not. It's now that it occurs to me how rarely I ever see her. For a while I try experiments like all of a sudden darting out into the 10-Port hallway to see if I can see Petra hunched somewhere keeping track of who is decabining, and I scour the whole hallway-and-ceiling area for evidence of some kind of camera or monitor tracking movements outside the cabin doors—zilch on both fronts. But then I realize that the mystery's even more complex and unsettling than I'd first thought, because my cabin gets cleaned always and only during intervals where I'm gone more than half an hour. When I go out, how can Petra or her supervisors possibly know how long I'm going to be gone? I try leaving 1009 a couple times and then dashing back after 10 or 15 minutes to see whether I can catch Petra *in delicto,* but she's never there. I try making a truly unholy mess in 1009 and then leaving and hiding somewhere on a lower deck and then dashing back after exactly 29 minutes—and again when I come bursting through the door there's no Petra and no cleaning. Then I leave the cabin with exactly the same expression and appurtenances as before and this time stay hidden for 31 minutes and then haul ass back—and this time again no sighting of Petra, but now 1009 is sterilized and gleaming and there's a mint on the pillow's fresh new case. Know that I carefully scrutinize every inch of every surface I pass as I circle the deck during these little experiments—no cameras or motion sensors or anything in evidence anywhere that would explain how They know.[57] So now for a while I theorize that somehow a special crewman is assigned to each passenger and follows that passenger at all times, using extremely sophisticated techniques of personal surveillance and reporting the passenger's movements and activities and projected time of cabin-return back to Steward HQ or something, and so for about a day I try taking extreme evasive actions—whirling sud-

---

57 The answer to why I don't just ask Petra how she does it is that Petra's English is extremely limited and primitive, and in sad fact I'm afraid my whole deep feeling of attraction and connection to Petra the Slavanian steward has been erected on the flimsy foundation of the only two English clauses she seems to know, one or the other of which clauses she uses in response to every statement, question, joke, or protestation of undying devotion: "Is no problem" and "You are a funny thing."

denly to check behind me, popping around corners, darting in and out of Gift Shops via different doors, etc. — never one sign of anybody engaged in surveillance. I never develop even a plausible theory about how They do it. By the time I quit trying, I'm feeling half-crazed, and my counter-surveillance measures are drawing frightened looks and even some temple-tapping from 10-Port's other guests.

I submit that there's something deeply mind-fucking about the Type-A-personality service and pampering on the *Nadir*, and that the manic invisible cabin-cleaning provides the clearest example of what's creepy about it. Because, deep down, it's not *really* like having a mom. *Pace* the guilt and nagging, etc., a mom cleans up after you largely because she loves you — you are the point, the object of the cleaning somehow. On the *Nadir*, though, once the novelty and convenience have worn off, I begin to see that the phenomenal cleaning really has nothing to do with me. (It's been particularly traumatic for me to realize that Petra is cleaning Cabin 1009 so phenomenally well simply because she's under orders to do so, and thus (obviously) that she's not doing it for me or because she likes me or thinks I'm No Problem or A Funny Thing — in fact she'd clean my cabin just as phenomenally well even if I were a dork — and maybe conceivably behind the smile does consider me a dork, in which case what if in fact I really am a dork? — I mean, if pampering and radical kindness don't seem motivated by strong affection and thus don't somehow affirm one or help assure one that one is not, finally, a dork, of what final and significant value is all this indulgence and cleaning?)

The feeling's not all that dissimilar to the experience of being a guest in the home of somebody who does things like sneak in in the A.M. and make your guest bed up for you while you're in the shower and fold your dirty clothes or even launder them without being asked to, or who empties your ashtray after each cigarette you smoke, etc. For a while, with a host like this, it seems great, and you feel cared about and prized and affirmed and worthwhile, etc. But then after a while you begin to intuit that the host isn't acting out of regard or affection for you so much as simply going around obeying the imperatives of some personal neurosis having to do with domestic cleanliness and order…which means that, since the ulti-mate point and object of the cleaning isn't you but rather cleanliness and order, it's going to be a relief for her when you leave. Meaning her hygienic pampering of you is actually evidence that she doesn't want you around. The *Nadir* doesn't have the Scotchguarded carpet or plastic-wrapped fur-niture of a true anal-type host like this, but the psychic aura's the same, and so's the projected relief of getting out.

10

I don't know how well a claustrophobe would do, but for the agoraphobe a 7NC Luxury Megacruiser presents a whole array of attractively enclosing options. The agoraphobe can choose not to leave the ship,[58] or can restrict herself only to certain decks, or can decline to leave the particular deck her cabin is on, or can eschew the view-conducive open-air railings on either side of that certain deck and keep exclusively to the deck's interior enclosed part. Or the agoraphobe can simply not leave her cabin at all.

I—who am not a true, can't-even-go-to-the-supermarket-type agoraphobe, but am what might be called a "borderline-" or "semi-agoraphobe"—come nevertheless to love very deeply Cabin 1009, Exterior Port.[59] It is made of a fawn-colored enamelish polymer and its walls are extremely thick and solid: I can drum annoyingly on the wall above my bed for up to five minutes before my aft neighbors pound (very faintly) back in annoyance. The cabin is thirteen size-11 Keds long by twelve Keds wide, with a little peninsular vestibule protruding out toward a cabin door that's got three separate locking technologies and trilingual lifeboat instructions bolted to its inside and a whole deck of DO NOT DISTURB cards hanging from the inside knob.[60] The vestibule is one-and-one-half times as wide as I. The cabin's bathroom is off one side of the vestibule, and off the other side is the Wondercloset, a complicated honeycomb of shelves and drawers and hangers and cubbyholes and Personal Fireproof Safe. The Wondercloset is so intricate in its utilization of every available cubic cm that all I can say is it must have been designed by a very organized person indeed.

All the way across the cabin, there's a deep enamel ledge running along the port wall under a window that I think is called my porthole.[61] As are

---

58 (At sea this is small agorapotatoes, but in port, once the doors open and the gangway extends, it represents a true choice and is thus agoraphobically valid.)

59 "1009" indicates that it's on Deck 10, and "Port" refers to the side of the ship it's on, and "Exterior" means that I have a window. There are also, of course, "Interior" cabins off the inner sides of the decks' halls, but I hereby advise any prospective 7NC passenger with claustrophobic tendencies to make sure and specify "Exterior" when making cabin-reservations.

60 The non-U.S. agoraphobe will be heartened to know that this deck includes "BITTE NICHT STÖREN," "PRIÈRE DE NE PAS DÉRANGER," "SI PREGA NON DISTURBARE," and (my personal favorite) "FAVOR DE NO MOLESTAR."

61 If you're either a little kid or an anorectic you can probably sit on this ledge to do your dreamy contemplative sea-gazing, but a raised and buttock-hostile lip at the ledge's outer border makes this impractical for a full-size adult.

the portholes in ships on TV, this porthole is indeed round, but it is not small, and in terms of its importance to the room's mood and *raison* it resembles a cathedral's rose window. It's made of that kind of very thick glass that Drive-Up bank tellers stand behind. In the corner of the port-hole's glass is this:

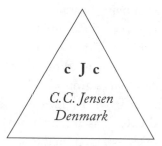

You can thump the glass with your fist w/o give or vibration. It's really good glass. Every morning at exactly 0834h. a Filipino guy in a blue jumpsuit stands on one of the lifeboats that hang in rows between Decks 9 and 10 and sprays my porthole with a hose, to get the salt off, which is fun to watch.

Cabin 1009's dimensions are just barely on the good side of the line between very very snug and cramped. Packed into its near-square are a big good bed and two bedside tables w/ lamps and an 18" TV with five At-Sea Cable® options, two of which show continuous loops of the Simpson trial.[62] There's also a white enamel desk that doubles as a vanity, and a round glass table on which is a basket that's alternately filled with fresh fruit and with husks and rinds of same. I don't know whether it's SOP or a subtle jour-nalistic perq, but every time I leave the cabin for more than the requisite half-hour I come back to find a new basket of fruit, covered in snug blue-tinted Saran, on the glass table. It's good fresh fruit and it's always there. I've never eaten so much fruit in my life.

Cabin 1009's bathroom deserves extravagant praise. I've seen more

---

62 There are also continual showings of about a dozen second-run movies, via what I get the sense is a VCR somewhere right here on board, because certain irregularities in tracking show up in certain films over and over. The movies run 24/7, and I end up watch-ing several of them so many times that I can now do their dialogue verbatim. These mov-ies include *It Could Happen to You* (the *It's a Wonderful Life*-w/-lottery-twist thing), *Jurassic Park* (which does not stand up well: its essential plotlessness doesn't emerge until the third viewing, but after that the semi-agoraphobe treats it like a porno flic, twiddling his thumbs until the T. Rex and Velociraptor parts (which do stand up well)), *Wolf* (stupid), *The Little Rascals* (nauseous), *Andre* (kind of *Old Yeller* with a seal), *The Client* (with another incredibly good child actor—where do they *get* all these Olivier-grade children?), and *Renaissance Man* (w/ Danny DeVito, a movie that tugs at your sentiments like a dog at a pantcuff, except it's hard not to like any movie that has an academic as the hero).

than my share of bathrooms, and this is one bitchingly nice bathroom. It is five-and-a-half Keds to the edge of the shower's step up and sign to Watch Your Step. The room's done in white enamel and gleaming brushed and stainless steel. Its overhead lighting is luxury lighting, some kind of blue-intensive Eurofluorescence that's run through a diffusion filter so it's diagnostically acute without being brutal.[63] Right by the light switch is an Alisco Sirocco-brand hairdryer that's brazed right onto the wall and comes on automatically when you take it out of the mount; the Sirocco's *High* setting just about takes your head off. Next to the hairdryer there's both 115v and 230v sockets, plus a grounded 110v for razors.

The sink is huge and its bowl deep without seeming precipitous or ungentle of grade. Good C.C. Jensen plate mirror covers the whole wall over the sink. The steel soap dish is striated to let sog-water out and minimize that annoying underside-of-the-bar slime. The ingenious consideration of the anti-slime soap dish is particularly affecting.

Keep in mind that 1009 is a mid-price single cabin. The mind positively reels at what a luxury-penthouse-type cabin's bathroom must be like.[64]

And so but simply enter 1009's bathroom and hit the overhead lights and on comes an automatic exhaust fan whose force and aerodynamism give steam or your more offensive-type odors just no quarter at all.[65] The fan's suction is such that if you stand right underneath its louvered vent it makes your hair stand straight up on your head, which together with the concussive and abundantly rippling action of the Sirocco hairdryer makes for hours of fun in the lavishly lit mirror.

The shower itself overachieves in a big way. The Hot setting's water is exfoliatingly hot, but it takes only one preset manipulation of the shower-knob to get perfect 98.6° water. My own personal home should have such

---

63 What it is is lighting for upscale and appearance-conscious adults who want a clear picture of whatever might be aesthetically problematic that day but also want to be reassured that the overall aesthetic situation is pretty darn good.

64 Attempts to get to see a luxury cabin's loo were consistently misconstrued and rebuffed by upscale penthouse-type *Nadir*ites—there are disadvantages to Luxury Cruising as a civilian and not identifiable Press.

65 1009's bathroom always smells of a strange but not unnice Norwegian disinfectant whose scent resembles what it would smell like if someone who knew the exact organochemical composition of a lemon but had never in fact smelled a lemon tried to synthesize the scent of a lemon. Kind of the same relation to a real lemon as a Bayer's Children's Aspirin to a real orange.

The cabin itself, on the other hand, after it's been cleaned, has no odor. None. Not in the carpets, the bedding, the insides of the desk's drawers, the wood of the Wondercloset's doors: nothing. One of the very few totally odorless places I've ever been in. This, too, eventually starts giving me the creeps.

water pressure: the showerhead's force pins you helplessly to the stall's opposite wall, and at 98.6° the head's MASSAGE setting makes your eyes roll up and your sphincter just about give.[66] The showerhead and its flexible steel line are also detachable, so you can hold the head and direct its punishing stream just at e.g. your particularly dirty right knee or something.[67]

Toiletry-wise, flanking the sink's mirror are broad shallow bolted steel minibaskets with all sorts of free stuff in them. There's Caswell-Massey Conditioning Shampoo in a convenient airplane-liquor-size bottle. There's Caswell-Massey Almond and Aloe Hand and Body Emulsion With Silk. There's a sturdy plastic shoehorn and a chamois mitt for either eyeglasses or light shoeshining—both these items are the navy-blue-on-searing-white that are Celebrity's colors.[68] There's not one but *two* fresh showercaps at all times. There's good old unpretentious unswishy Safeguard soap. There's washcloths w/o nubble or nap, and of course towels you want to propose to.

In the vestibule's Wondercloset are extra chamois blankets and hypoallergenic pillows and plastic CELEBRITY CRUISES–emblazoned bags of all different sizes and configurations for your laundry and optional dry cleaning, etc.[69]

But all this is still small potatoes compared to 1009's fascinating and potentially malevolent toilet. A harmonious concordance of elegant form and vigorous function, flanked by rolls of tissue so soft as to be without the usual perforates for tearing, my toilet has above it this sign:

THIS TOILET IS CONNECTED TO A **VACUUM SEWAGE SYSTEM.** PLEASE DO NOT THROW INTO THE TOILET ANYTHING THAN ORDINARY TOILET WASTE AND TOILET PAPER[70]

---

66 Perhaps designed with this in mind, the shower's floor has a 10° grade from all sides to the center's drain, which drain is the size of a lunch plate and has audibly aggressive suction.

67 This detachable and concussive showerhead can allegedly also be employed for non-hygienic and even prurient purposes, apparently. I overheard guys from a small U. of Texas spring-break contingent (the only college-age group on the whole *Nadir*) regale each other about their ingenuity with the showerhead. One guy in particular was fixated on the idea that somehow the shower's technology could be rigged to administer fellatio if he could just get access to a "metric ratchet set"—your guess here is as good as mine.

68 The *Nadir* itself is navy trim on a white field, and all the Megalines have their own trademark color schemes—lime-green on white, aqua on white, robin's-egg on white, barn-red on white (white apparently being a constant).

69 You can apparently get "Butler Service" and automatic-send-out dry cleaning and shoeshining, all at prices that I'm told are not out of line, but the forms you have to fill out and hang on your door for all this are wildly complex, and I'm scared of setting in motion mechanisms of service that seem potentially overwhelming.

70 The missing predicative preposition here is *sic*—ditto what looks to be an implied image of thrown excrement—but the mistakes seem somehow endearing, humanizing, and this toilet needed all the humanizing it could get.

Yes that's right a *vacuum toilet*. And, as with the exhaust fan above, not a lightweight or unambitious vacuum. The toilet's flush produces a brief but traumatizing sound, a kind of held high-B gargle, as of some gastric disturbance on a cosmic scale. Along with this sound comes a concussive suction so awesomely powerful that it's both scary and strangely comforting—your waste seems less removed than *hurled* from you, and hurled with a velocity that lets you feel as though the waste is going to end up someplace so far away from you that it will have become an abstraction...a kind of existential-level sewage treatment.[71, 72]

---

71 It's pretty hard not to see connections between the exhaust fan and the toilet's vacuums—an almost Final Solution–like eradication of animal wastes and odors (wastes and odors that are by all rights a natural consequence of Henry VIII–like meals and unlimited free Cabin Service and fruit baskets)—and the death-denial/-transcendence fantasies that the 7NC Luxury Megacruise is trying to enable.

72 The *Nadir*'s VACUUM SEWAGE SYSTEM begins after a while to hold such a fascination for me that I end up going hat in hand back to Hotel Manager Dermatitis to ask once again for access to the ship's nether parts, and once again I pull a boner with Dermatitis: I innocently mention my specific fascination with the ship's VACUUM SEWAGE SYSTEM—which boner is consequent to another and prior boner by which I'd failed to discover in my pre-boarding researches that there'd been, just a few months before this, a tremendous scandal in which the I think *QE2* Megaship had been discovered dumping waste over the side in mid-voyage, in violation of numerous national and maritime codes, and had been videotaped doing this by a couple of passengers who subsequently apparently sold the videotape to some network newsmagazine, and so the whole Megacruise industry was in a state of almost Nixonian paranoia about unscrupulous journalists trying to manufacture scandals about Megaships' handling of waste. Even behind his mirrored sunglasses I can tell that Mr. Dermatitis is severely upset about my interest in sewage, and he denies my request to eyeball the V.S.S. with a complex defensiveness that I couldn't even begin to chart out here. It is only later that night (Wednesday 3/15), at supper, at good old Table 64 in the 5☆C.R., that my cruise-savvy tablemates fill me in on the *QE2* waste-scandal, and they scream[72a] with mirth at the clay-footed naïveté with which I'd gone to Dermatitis with what was in fact an innocent if puerile fascination with hermetically-evacuated waste; and such is my own embarrassment and hatred of Mr. Dermatitis by this time that I begin to feel like if the Hotel Manager really *does* think I'm some kind of investigative journalist with a hard-on for shark dangers and sewage scandals then he might think it would be worth the risk to have me harmed in some way; and through a set of neurotic connections I won't even try to defend, I, for about a day and a half, begin to fear that the *Nadir*'s Greek episcopate will somehow contrive to use the incredibly potent and forceful 1009 toilet itself for the assassination—I don't know, that they'll like somehow lubricate the bowl and up the suction to where not just my waste but I myself will be sucked down through the seat's opening and hurled into some kind of abstract septic holding-tank.

72a (literally)

11

Traveling at sea for the first time is a chance to realize that the ocean is not one ocean. The water changes. The Atlantic that seethes off the eastern U.S. is glaucous and lightless and looks mean. Around Jamaica, though, it's more like a milky aquamarine, and translucent. Off the Cayman Islands it's an electric blue, and off Cozumel it's almost purple. Same sort of deal with the beaches. You can tell right away that south Florida's sand is descended from rocks: it hurts your bare feet and has that sort of minerally glitter to it. But Ocho Rios's beach is more like dirty sugar, and Cozumel's is like clean sugar, and at places along the coast of Grand Cayman the sand's texture is more like flour, silicate, its white as dreamy and vaporous as clouds' white. The only real constant to the nautical topography of the m.v. *Nadir*'s Caribbean is something about its unreal and almost retouched-looking prettiness[73] — it's impossible to describe quite right, but the closest I can come is to say that it all looks: *expensive.*

12

Mornings in port are a special time for the semi-agoraphobe, because just about everybody else gets off the ship and goes ashore for Organized Shore Excursions or for unstructured peripatetic tourist stuff, and the m.v. *Nadir*'s upper decks have the eerily delicious deserted quality of your folks' house when you're home sick as a kid and everybody else is off at work and school, etc. Right now it's 0930h. on 15 March (Ides Wednesday) and we're docked off Cozumel, Mexico. I'm on Deck 12. A couple guys in software-company T-shirts jog fragrantly by every couple minutes,[74] but other than that it's just me and the ZnO and hat and about a thousand empty and identically folded high-quality deck chairs. The 12-Aft Towel Guy has almost nobody to exercise his zeal on, and by 1000h. I'm on my fifth new towel.

Here the semi-agoraphobe can stand alone at the ship's highest port rail

---

73 It is not "beautiful"; it is "pretty." There's a difference.

74 Seven times around Deck 12 is a mile, and I'm one of very few *Nadir*ites under about 70 who doesn't jog like a fiend up here now that the weather's nice. Early A.M. is the annular rush-hour of Deck 12 jogging. I've already seen a couple of juicy and Keystone-quality jogging collisions.

and gaze pensively out to sea. The sea off Cozumel is a kind of watery indigo through which you can see the powder-white of the bottom. In the middle distance, underwater coral formations are big cloud-shapes of deep purple. You can see why people say of calm seas that they're "glassy": at 1000h. the sun assumes a kind of Brewster's Angle w/r/t the surface and the harbor lights up as far as the eye can see: the water moves a million little ways at once, and each move makes a sparkle. Out past the coral, the water gets progressively darker in orderly baconish stripes—I think this phenomenon has to do with perspective. It's all extremely pretty and peaceful. Besides me and the T.G. and the orbiting joggers, there's only a supine older lady reading *Codependent No More* and a man standing way up at the fore part of the starboard rail videotaping the sea. This sad and cadaverous guy, who by the second day I'd christened Captain Video, has tall hard gray hair and Birkenstocks and very thin hairless calves, and he is one of the cruise's more prominent eccentrics.[75] Pretty much everybody on the *Nadir* qualifies as camera-crazy, but Captain Video camcords absolutely *everything*, including meals, empty hallways, endless games of geriatric bridge—even leaping onto Deck 11's raised stage during Pool Party to get the crowd from the musicians' angle. You can tell that the magnetic record of Captain Video's Megacruise experience is going to be this Warholianly dull thing that is exactly as long as the Cruise itself. Captain Vid-

---

75 Other eccentrics on this 7NC include: the thirteen-year-old kid with the toupee, who wears his big orange life jacket all week and sits on the wood floor of the upper decks reading Jose Philip Farmer paperbacks with three different boxes of Kleenex around him at all times; the bloated and dead-eyed guy who sits in the same chair at the same 21 table in the Mayfair Casino every day from 1200h. to 0300h., drinking Long Island Iced Tea and playing 21 at a narcotized underwater pace. There's The Guy Who Sleeps By The Pool, who does just what his name suggests, except he does it all the time, even in the rain, a hairy-stomached guy of maybe 50, a copy of *Megatrends* open on his chest, sleeping w/o sunglasses or sunblock, w/o moving, for hours and hours, in full and high-watt sun, and never in my sight burns or wakes up (I suspect that at night they move him down to his room on a gurney). There's also the two unbelievably old and cloudy-eyed couples who sit in a quartet in upright chairs just inside the clear plastic walls that enclose the area of Deck 11 that has the pools and Windward Cafe, facing out, i.e. out through the plastic sheeting, watching the ocean and ports like they're something on TV, and also never once visibly moving.

It seems relevant that most of the *Nadir*'s eccentrics are eccentric in *stasis*: what distinguishes them is their doing the same thing hour after hour and day after day without moving. (Captain Video is an active exception. People are surprisingly tolerant of Captain Video until the second-to-last night's Midnight Caribbean Blow-Out by the pools, when he keeps breaking into the Conga Line and trying to shift its course so that it can be recorded at better advantage; then there is a kind of bloodless but unpleasant uprising against Captain Video, and he lays low for the rest of the Cruise, possibly organizing and editing his tapes.)

eo's the only passenger besides me who I know for a fact is cruising without a relative or companion, and certain additional similarities between C.V. and me (the semi-agoraphobic reluctance to leave the ship in port, for one thing) tend to make me uncomfortable, and I try to avoid him as much as possible.

The semi-agoraphobe can also stand at Deck 12's starboard rail and look way down at the army of *Nadir* passengers being disgorged by the Deck 3 egress. They keep pouring out the door and down the narrow gangway. As each person's sandal hits the pier, a sociolinguistic transformation from *cruiser* to *tourist* is effected. At this very moment, 1300+ upscale tourists with currency to unload and experiences to experience and record compose a serpentine line stretching all the way down the Cozumel pier, which pier is poured cement and a good quarter-mile long and leads to the TOURISM CENTER,[76] a kind of mega-Quonset structure where Organized Shore Excursions[77] and cabs or mopeds into San Miguel are available. The word around good old Table 64 last night was that in primitive and incredibly poor Cozumel the U.S. dollar is treated like a UFO: "They worship it when it lands."

Locals along the Cozumel pier are offering *Nadir*ites a chance to have their picture taken holding a very large iguana. Yesterday, on the Grand Cayman pier, locals had offered them the chance to have their picture taken with a guy wearing a peg-leg and hook, while off the *Nadir*'s port bow a fake pirate ship plowed back and forth across the bay all morning, firing blank broadsides and getting on everybody's nerves.

The *Nadir*'s crowds move in couples and quartets and groups and packs; the line undulates complexly. Everybody's shirt is some kind of pastel and is festooned with the cases of recording equipment, and 85% of the females have white visors and wicker purses. And everybody down below has on sunglasses with this year's fashionable accessory, a padded fluorescent cord that attaches to the glasses' arms so the glasses can hang around your neck and you can put them on and take them off a lot.[78]

---

76 (its sign's in English, significantly)

77 In Ocho Rios on Monday the big tourist-draw was apparently some sort of waterfall a whole group of *Nadir*ites could walk up inside with a guide and umbrellas to protect their cameras. In Grand Cayman yesterday the big thing was Duty-Free rum and something called Bernard Passman Black Coral Art. Here in Cozumel it's supposedly silver jewelry hawked by hard-dickering peddlers, and more Duty-Free liquor, and a fabled bar in San Miguel called Carlos and Charlie's where they allegedly give you shots of something that's mostly lighter fluid.

78 Apparently it's no longer in fashion to push the frames of the sunglasses up to where they ride just above the crown of your skull, which is what I used to see upscale

Off to my right (southeast), now, another Megacruiser is moving in for docking someplace that must be pretty close to us, judging by its approach-vector. It moves like a force of nature and resists the idea that so much mass is being steered by anything like a hand on a tiller. I can't imagine what trying to maneuver one of these puppies into the pier is like. Parallel parking a semi into a spot the same size as the semi with a blindfold on and four tabs of LSD in you might come close. There's no empirical way to know: they won't even let me near the ship's Bridge, not after the *au-jus* snafu. Our docking this morning at sunrise involved an antlike frenzy of crewmen and shore personnel and an anchor[79] that spilled from the ship's navel and upward of a dozen ropes complexly knotted onto what look like giant railroad ties studding the pier. The crew insist on calling the ropes "lines" even though each one is at least the same diameter as a tourist's head.

I cannot convey to you the sheer and surreal scale of everything: the towering ship, the ropes, the ties, the anchor, the pier, the vast lapis lazuli dome of the sky. The Caribbean is, as ever, odorless. The floor of Deck 12 is tight-fitted planks of the same kind of corky and good-smelling wood you see in saunas.

Looking down from a great height at your countrymen waddling in expensive sandals into poverty-stricken ports is not one of the funner moments of a 7NC Luxury Cruise, however. There is something inescapably *bovine* about an American tourist in motion as part of a group. A certain greedy placidity about them. Us, rather. In port we automatically become *Peregrinator americanus, Die Lumpenamerikaner.* The Ugly Ones. For me, boviscopophobia[80] is an even stronger motive than semi-agoraphobia for staying on the ship when we're in port. It's in port that I feel most implicated, guilty by perceived association. I've barely been out of the U.S.A. before, and never as part of a high-income herd, and in port—even up here above it all on Deck 12, just watching—I'm newly and unpleasantly conscious of being an American, the same way I'm always suddenly conscious of being white every time I'm around a lot of nonwhite people. I cannot help imagining us as we appear to them, the

---

sunglasses-wearers do a lot; the habit has now gone the way of tying your white Lacoste tennis sweater's arms across your chest and wearing it like a cape.

79 The anchor is gigantic and must weigh a hundred tons, and—delightfully—it really is anchor-shaped, i.e. the same shape as anchors in tattoos.

80 (= the morbid fear of being seen as bovine)

impassive Jamaicans and Mexicans,[81] or especially to the non-Aryan preterite crew of the *Nadir*. All week I've found myself doing everything I can
to distance myself in the crew's eyes from the bovine herd I'm part of, to
somehow unimplicate myself: I eschew cameras and sunglasses and pastel
Caribbeanwear; I make a big deal of carrying my own cafeteria tray and
am effusive in my thanks for the slightest service. Since so many of my
shipmates shout, I make it a point of special pride to speak extra-quietly to
crewmen whose English is poor.

At 1035h. there are just one or two small clouds in a sky so blue here it
hurts. Every dawn so far in port has been overcast. Then the ascending
sun gathers force and disperses the clouds somehow, and for an hour or so
the sky looks shredded. Then by 0800h. an endless blue opens up like an
eye and stays that way all A.M., one or two clouds always in the distance, as
if for scale.

There are massed formicatory maneuvers among pier workers with
ropes and walkie-talkies down there now as this other bright-white Megaship moves slowly in toward the pier from the right.

And then in the late A.M. the isolate clouds overhead start moving
toward one another, and in the early P.M. they begin very slowly interlock-
ing like jigsaw pieces, and by evening the puzzle will be solved and the sky
will be the color of old dimes.[82]

But of course all this ostensibly unimplicating behavior on my part is
itself motivated by a self-conscious and somewhat condescending concern
about how I appear to others that is (this concern) 100% upscale American. Part of the overall despair of this Luxury Cruise is that no matter
what I do I cannot escape my own essential and newly unpleasant Ameri-

---

81 And in my head I go around and around about whether my fellow *Nadir*ites suffer
the same steep self-disgust. From a height, watching them, I usually imagine that the
other passengers are oblivious to the impassively contemptuous gaze of the local mer-
chants, service people, photo-op-with-lizard vendors, etc. I usually imagine that my fellow tourists are too bovinely self-absorbed to even notice how we're looked at. At other
times, though, it occurs to me that the other Americans on board quite possibly feel the
same vague discomfort about their bovine-American role in port that I do, but that they
refuse to let their boviscopophobia rule them: they've paid good money to have fun and be
pampered and record some foreign experiences, and they'll be goddamned if they're
going to let some self-indulgent twinge of neurotic projection about how their American-
ness appears to malnourished locals detract from the 7NC Luxury Cruise they've worked
and saved for and decided they deserve.

82 This dawn-and-dusk cloudiness was a pattern. In all, three of the week's days
could be called substantially cloudy, and it rained a bunch of times, including all Friday in
port in Key West. Again, I can see no way to blame the *Nadir* or Celebrity Cruises Inc.
for this happenstance.

canness. This despair reaches its peak in port, at the rail, looking down at what I can't help being one of. Whether up here or down there, I am an American tourist, and am thus *ex officio* large, fleshy, red, loud, coarse, condescending, self-absorbed, spoiled, appearance-conscious, ashamed, despairing, and greedy: the world's only known species of bovine carnivore.

Here, as in the other ports, Jet Skis buzz the *Nadir* all morning. There's about half a dozen this time. Jet Skis are the mosquitoes of Caribbean ports, annoying and irrelevant and apparently always there. Their noise is a cross between a gargle and a chain saw. I am tired of Jet Skis already and have never even been on a Jet Ski. I remember reading somewhere that Jet Skis are incredibly dangerous and accident-prone, and I take a certain unkind comfort in this as I watch blond guys with washboard stomachs and sunglasses on fluorescent cords buzz around making hieroglyphs of foam.

Instead of fake pirate ships, in Cozumel there are glass-bottom boats working the waters around the coral shadows. They move sluggishly because they're terribly overloaded with cruisers on an Organized Shore Excursion. What's neat about the sight is that everybody on the boats is looking straight down, a good 100+ people per boat—it looks prayerful somehow, and sets off the boat's driver, a local who stares dully ahead at the same nothing all drivers of all kinds of mass transport stare at.[83]

A red and orange parasail hangs dead still on the port horizon, a stick-figure dangling.

The 12-Aft Towel Guy, a spectral Czech with eyes so inset they're black from brow-shadow, stands very straight and expressionless by his cart, playing what looks like Rock-Paper-Scissors with himself. I've learned that the 12-Aft Towel Guy is immune to chatty journalistic probing—he gives me a look of what I can only call *withering neutrality* whenever I go get another towel. I am reapplying ZnO. Captain Video isn't filming now but is looking at the harbor through a square he's made of his hands. He's the type where you can tell without even looking closely that he's talking to himself. This other Megacruise ship is now docking right next to us, a procedure which apparently demands a lot of coded blasts on its world-ending horn. But maybe the single best A.M. visual in the harbor is another big organized 7NC-tourist thing: A group of *Nadir*ites is learning

---

83 A further self-esteem-lowerer is how bored all the locals look when they're dealing with U.S. tourists. We bore them. Boring somebody seems way worse than offending or disgusting him.

to snorkel in the lagoonish waters just offshore; off the port bow I can see a good 150 solid citizens floating on their stomachs, motionless, the classic Dead Man's Float, looking like the massed and floating victims of some hideous mishap—from this height a macabre and riveting sight. I have given up looking for dorsal fins in port. It turns out that sharks, apparently being short on aesthetic sense, are never seen in pretty Caribbean ports, though a couple Jamaicans had lurid if dubious stories of barracudas that could take off a limb in one surgical drive-by. Nor in Caribbean ports is there ever any evident kelp, glasswort, algaeic scuz, or any of the sapropel the regular ocean's supposed to have. Probably sharks like murkier and scuzzier waters; potential victims could see them coming too easily down here.

Speaking of carnivores, Carnival Cruises Inc.'s good ships *Ecstasy* and *Tropicale* are both anchored all the way across the harbor. In port, Carnival Megaships tend to stay sort of at a distance from other cruise ships, and my sense is that the other ships think this is just as well. The Carnival ships have masses of 20ish-looking people hanging off the rails and seem at this distance to throb slightly, like a hi-fi's woofer. The rumors about Carnival 7NC's are legion, one such rumor being that their Cruises are kind of like floating meat-market bars and that their ships bob with a conspicuous carnal *squeakatasqueakata* at night. There's none of this kind of concupiscent behavior aboard the *Nadir*, I'm happy to say. By now I've become a kind of 7NC snob, and when Carnival or Princess is mentioned in my presence I feel my face automatically assume Trudy and Esther's expression of classy distaste.

But so there they are, the *Ecstasy* and *Tropicale;* and now right up alongside the *Nadir* on the other side of the pier is finally docked and secured the m.v. *Dreamward*, with the peach-on-white color scheme that I think means it's owned by Norwegian Cruise Line. Its Deck 3 gangway protrudes and almost touches our Deck 3 gangway—sort of obscenely—and the *Dreamward*'s passengers, identical in all important respects to the *Nadir*'s passengers, are now streaming down the gangway and massing and moving down the pier in a kind of canyon of shadow formed by the tall walls of our two ships' hulls. The hulls hem them in and force a near-defile that stretches endlessly. A lot of the *Dreamward*'s passengers turn and crane to marvel at the size of what's just disgorged them. Captain Video, now inclined way over the starboard rail so that only the toes of his sandals are still touching deck, is filming them as they look up at us, and more than a few of the *Dreamward*ites way below lift their own camcorders and point them up our way in a kind of almost defensive or retaliatory gesture, and for just a moment they and C.V. compose a tableau that looks almost classically postmodern.

Because the *Dreamward* is lined up right next to us, almost porthole to porthole, with its Deck 12's port rail right up flush[84] against our Deck 12's starboard rail, the *Dreamward*'s semi-agoraphobic shore-shunners and I can stand at the rails and sort of check each other out in the sideways way of two muscle cars lined up at a stoplight. We can sort of see how we stack up against each other. I can see the *Dreamward*'s rail-leaners looking the *Nadir* up and down. Their faces are shiny with high-SPF sunblock. The *Dreamward* is blindingly white, white to a degree that seems somehow aggressive and makes the *Nadir*'s own white look more like buff or cream. The *Dreamward*'s snout is a little more tapered and aerodynamic-looking than our snout, and its trim is a kind of fluorescent peach, and the beach umbrellas around its Deck 11 pools[85] are also peach—our beach umbrellas are light orange, which has always seemed odd given the white-and-navy motif of the *Nadir*, and now seems to me ad hoc and shabby. The *Dreamward* has more pools on Deck 11 than we do, plus what looks like a whole other additional pool behind glass on Deck 6; and their pools' blue is that distinctive chlorine-blue—the *Nadir*'s two small pools are both seawater and kind of icky, even though the pools in the Celebrity brochure had sneakily had that electric-blue look of good old chlorine.

On all its decks, all the way down, the *Dreamward*'s cabins have little white balconies for private open-air sea-gazing. Its Deck 12 has a full-court basketball setup with color-coordinated nets and backboards as white as communion wafers. I notice that each of the myriad towel carts on the *Dreamward*'s Deck 12 is manned by its very own Towel Guy, and that their Towel Guys are ruddily Nordic and nonspectral and have nothing resembling withering neutrality or boredom about their mien.

The point is that, standing here next to Captain Video, looking, I start to feel a covetous and almost prurient envy of the *Dreamward*. I imagine its interior to be cleaner than ours, larger, more lavishly appointed. I imagine the *Dreamward*'s food being even more varied and punctiliously prepared, the ship's Gift Shop less expensive and its casino less depressing and its stage entertainment less cheesy and its pillow mints bigger. The little private balconies outside the *Dreamward*'s cabins, in particular, seem

---

84 (which on scale of these ships means something around 100 m)

85 On all 7NC Megaships, Deck 12 forms a kind of mezzanineish ellipse over Deck 11, which is always about half open-air (11 is) and always has pools surrounded by plastic/Plexiglas walls.

just way superior to a porthole of bank-teller glass, and suddenly private balconies seem absolutely crucial to the whole 7NC Megaexperience I'm expected to try to convey.

I spend several minutes fantasizing about what the bathrooms might be like on the good old *Dreamward*. I imagine its crew quarters being open for anybody at all to come down and moss out and shoot the shit, and the *Dreamward*'s crew being open and genuinely friendly, with M.A.s in English and whole leatherbound and neatly printed diaries full of nautical lore and wry engaging 7NC observations. I imagine the *Dreamward*'s Hotel Manager to be an avuncular Norwegian with a rag sweater and a soothing odor of Borkum Rif about him, a guy w/o sunglasses or hauteur who throws open the pressurized doors to the *Dreamward*'s Bridge and galley and Vacuum Sewage System and personally takes me through, offering pithy and quotable answers to questions before I've even asked them. I experience a sudden rush of grievance against *Harper's* magazine for booking me on the m.v. *Nadir* instead of the *Dreamward*. I calculate by eye the breadth of the gap I'd have to jump or rappel to switch to the *Dreamward*, and I mentally sketch out the paragraphs that would detail such a bold and William T. Vollmannish bit of journalistic derring-do as literally jumping from one 7NC Megaship to another.

This saturnine line of thinking proceeds as the clouds overhead start to coalesce and the sky takes on its regular clothy P.M. weight. I am suffering here from a delusion, and I know it's a delusion, this envy of another ship, and still it's painful. It's also representative of a psychological syndrome that I notice has gotten steadily worse as the Cruise wears on, a mental list of dissatisfactions and grievances that started picayune but has quickly become nearly despair-grade. I know that the syndrome's cause is not simply the contempt bred of a week's familiarity with the poor old *Nadir,* and that the source of all the dissatisfactions isn't the *Nadir* at all but rather plain old humanly conscious me, or, more precisely, that ur-American part of me that craves and responds to pampering and passive pleasure: the Dissatisfied Infant part of me, the part that always and indiscriminately WANTS. Hence this syndrome by which, for example, just four days ago I experienced such embarrassment over the perceived self-indulgence of ordering even more gratis food from Cabin Service that I littered the bed with fake evidence of hard work and missed meals, whereas by last night I find myself looking at my watch in real annoyance after fifteen minutes and wondering where the fuck *is* that Cabin Service guy with the tray already. And by now I notice how the tray's sandwiches are kind of small, and how the wedge of dill pickle[86] always soaks into the starboard crust of the bread, and how the damn Port hallway is too narrow to really let me put the used Cabin Service tray outside 1009's door at night when I'm done eating, so that the tray sits in the cabin all night and in the A.M. adulterates the olfactory sterility of 1009 with a smell of rancid horse-radish, and how this seems, by the Luxury Cruise's fifth day, deeply dissatisfying.

Death and Conroy notwithstanding, we're maybe now in a position to appreciate the lie at the dark heart of Celebrity's brochure. For this—the promise to sate the part of me that always and only WANTS—is the central fantasy the brochure is selling. The thing to notice is that the real fantasy here isn't that this promise will be kept, but that such a promise is keepable at all. This is a big one, this lie.[87] And of course I want to believe it—fuck the Buddha—I want to believe that maybe this Ultimate Fantasy Vacation will be *enough* pampering, that this time the luxury and pleasure will be so completely and faultlessly administered that my Infantile part will be sated.[88]

But the Infantile part of me is insatiable—in fact its whole essence or *dasein* or whatever lies in its a priori insatiability. In response to any environment of extraordinary gratification and pampering, the Insatiable Infant part of me will simply adjust its desires upward until it once again levels out at its homeostasis of terrible dissatisfaction. And sure enough, on the *Nadir* itself, after a few days of delight and then adjustment, the Pamper-swaddled part of me that WANTS is now back, and with a vengeance. By Ides Wednesday I'm acutely conscious of the fact that the AC vent in my cabin hisses (*loudly*), and that though I can turn off the reggae Muzak coming out of the speaker in the cabin I cannot turn off the even louder ceiling-speaker out in the 10-Port hall. By now I notice that when Table 64's towering busboy uses his crumb-scoop to clear crumbs off the tablecloth between courses he never seems to get quite *all* the crumbs. By now the nighttime rattle of my Wondercloset's one off-plumb drawer

---

86 (I hate dill pickles, and C.S. churlishly refuses to substitute gherkins or butter chips)

87 It may well be *the* Big One, come to think of it.

88 The fantasy they're selling is the whole reason why all the subjects in all the brochures' photos have facial expressions that are at once orgasmic and oddly slack: these expressions are the facial equivalent of going "*Aaaahhhhh,*" and the sound is not just that of somebody's Infantile part exulting in finally getting the total pampering it's always wanted but also that of the relief all the other parts of that person feel when the Infantile part finally *shuts up*.

sounds like a jackhammer. Mavourneen of the high seas or no, when Petra makes my bed not all the hospital corners are at *exactly* the same angle. My desk/vanity has a small but uncannily labial-looking hairline crack in the bevel of its top's right side, which crack I've come to hate because I can't help looking right at it when I open my eyes in bed in the morning. Most of the nightly Celebrity Showtime live entertainment in the Celebrity Show Lounge is so bad it's embarrassing, and there's a repellent hotel-art-type seascape on the aft wall of 1009 that's bolted to the wall and can't be removed or turned around, and Caswell-Massey Conditioning Shampoo turns out to be harder to rinse all the way out than most other shampoos, and the ice sculptures at the Midnight Buffet sometimes look hurriedly carved, and the vegetable that comes with my entrée is continually over-cooked, and it's impossible to get really *numbingly* cold water out of 1009's bathroom tap.

I'm standing here on Deck 12 looking at a *Dreamward* that I bet has cold water that'd turn your knuckles blue, and, like Frank Conroy, part of me realizes that I haven't washed a dish or tapped my foot in line behind somebody with multiple coupons at a supermarket checkout in a week; and yet instead of feeling refreshed and renewed I'm anticipating just how totally stressful and demanding and unpleasurable regular landlocked adult life is going to be now that even just the premature removal of a towel by a sepulchral crewman seems like an assault on my basic rights, and plus now the sluggishness of the Aft elevator is an outrage, and the absence of 22.5-lb dumbbells in the Olympic Health Club's dumbbell rack is a personal affront. And now as I'm getting ready to go down to lunch I'm mentally drafting a really mordant footnote on my single biggest peeve about the *Nadir: soda-pop is not free,* not even at dinner: you have to order a Mr. Pibb from the 5☆C.R.'s maddeningly E.S.L.-hampered cocktail waitress just like it was a fucking Slippery Nipple, and then you have to sign for it right there at the table, and they *charge* you—and they don't even *have* Mr. Pibb; they foist Dr Pepper on you with a maddeningly unapologetic shrug when any *fool* knows Dr Pepper is *no substitute* for Mr. Pibb, and it's an absolute goddamned travesty, or at any rate extremely dissatisfying indeed.[89]

---

89 This right here is not the mordant footnote projected *supra*, but the soda-pop issue bears directly on what was for me one of the true mysteries of this Cruise, viz. how Celebrity makes a profit on Luxury 7NCs. If you accept *Fielding's Worldwide Cruises 1995*'s per diem on the *Nadir* of about $275.00 a head, then you consider that the m.v. *Nadir* itself cost Celebrity Cruises $250 million to build in 1992, and that it's got 600

employees of whom at least the upper echelons have got to be making serious money (the whole Greek contingent had the unmistakable set of mouth that goes with salaries in six figures), plus simply hellacious fuel costs — plus port taxes and insurance and safety equipment and space-age navigational and communications gear and a computerized tiller and state-of-the-art maritime sewage — and then start factoring in the luxury stuff, the top-shelf decor and brass ceiling-tile, chandeliers, a good three dozen people aboard as nothing more than twice-a-week stage entertainers, plus then the professional Head Chef and the lobster and Etruscan truffles and the cornucopic fresh fruit and the imported pillow mints ... then, even playing it very conservative, you cannot get the math to add up. There doesn't look to be any way Celebrity can be coming out ahead financially. And yet the sheer number of different Megalines offering 7NCs constitutes reliable evidence that Luxury Cruises must be very profitable indeed. Again, Celebrity's PR lady Ms. Wiessen was — notwithstanding a phone-voice that was a total pleasure to listen to — not particularly helpful with this mystery:

> The answer to their affordability, how they offer such a great product, is really based on their management. They really are in touch with all the details of what's important to the public, and they pay a lot of attention to those details.

Libation revenues provide part of the real answer, it turns out. It's a little bit like the microeconomics of movie theaters. When you hear how much of the gate they have to kick back to films' distributors, you can't figure out how theaters stay in business. But of course you can't go just by ticket revenues, because where movie theaters really make their money is at the concession stand.

The *Nadir* sells a shitload of drinks. Full-time beverage waitresses in khaki shorts and Celebrity visors are unobtrusively everywhere — poolside, on Deck 12, at meals, entertainments, Bingo. Soda-pop is $2.00 for a very skinny glass (you don't pay cash right there; you sign for it and then they sock you with a printed Statement of Charges on the final night), and exotic cocktails like Wallbangers and Fuzzy Navels go as high as $5.50. The *Nadir* doesn't do tacky stuff like oversalt the soup or put bowls of pretzels all over the place, but a 7NC Luxury Cruise's crafted atmosphere of indulgence and endless partying — "Go on, You Deserve It" — more than conduces to freeflowing wine. (Let's not forget the cost of a fine wine w/ supper, the ever-present sommeliers.) Of the different passengers I asked, more than half estimated their party's total beverage tab at over $500. And if you know even a little about the beverage markups in any restaurant/bar operation, you know a lot of that $500's going to end up as net profit. Other keys to profitability: a lot of the ship's service staff's income isn't figured into the price of the Cruise ticket: you have to tip them at week's end or they're screwed (another peeve is that the Celebrity brochure neglects to mention this). And it turns out that a lot of the paid entertainment on the *Nadir* is "vended out" — agencies contract with Celebrity Cruises to supply teams like the Matrix Dancers for all the stage shows, the Electric Slide lessons, etc.

Another contracted vendor is Deck 8's Mayfair Casino, whose corporate proprietor pays a flat weekly rate plus an unspecified percentage to the *Nadir* for the privilege of sending their gorgeous dealers and four-deck shoes against passengers who've learned the rules of 21 and Caribbean Stud Poker from an "Educational Video" that plays continuously on one of the At-Sea TV's channels. I didn't spend all that much time in the Mayfair Casino — the eyes of 74-year-old Cleveland grandmothers pumping quarters into the slots of twittering machines are not much fun to spend time looking at — but I was in there long enough to see that if the *Nadir* gets even a 10% vig on the Mayfair's weekly net, then Celebrity is making a killing.

13

Every night, the 10-Port cabin steward, Petra, when she turns down your bed, leaves on your pillow—along with the day's last mint and Celebrity's printed card wishing you sweet dreams in six languages—the next day's *Nadir Daily*, a phatic little four-page ersatz newspaper printed on white vellum in a navy-blue font. The *ND* has historical nuggets on upcoming ports, pitches for Organized Shore Excursions and specials in the Gift Shop, and stern stuff in boxes with malaprop-headlines like QUARANTINES ON TRANSIT OF FOOD and MISUSE OF DRUG ACTS 1972.[90]

Right now it's Thursday 16 March, 0710h., and I'm alone at the 5☆C.R.'s Early Seating Breakfast, Table 64's waiter and towering busboy hovering nearby.[91] We've rounded the final turn and are on our return trajectory toward Key West, and today is one of the week's two "At-Sea" days when shipboard activities are at their densest and most organized; and this is the day I've picked to use the *Nadir Daily* as a Baedeker as I leave Cabin 1009 for a period well in excess of half an hour and plunge headfirst into the recreational fray and keep a precise and detailed log of some really representative experiences as together now we go In Quest of Managed

---

90 Snippet of latter item: "All persons entering each island [?] are warned that it is a CRIMINAL OFFENSE to import or have possession of narcotics and other Controlled Drugs, including marijuana. Penalties for drug offenders are severe." Half of the Port Lecture before we hit Jamaica consisted of advice about stuff like two-timing street dealers who'll sell you a quarter-oz. of crummy pot and then trot down to a constable and collect a bounty for fingering you. Conditions in the local jails are described just enough to engage the grimmer parts of the imagination.

Celebrity Cruises' own onboard drug policy remains obscure. Although there are always a half-dozen humorless Security guys standing burlily around the *Nadir*'s gangway in port, you never get searched when you reboard. I never saw or smelled evidence of drug use on the *Nadir*—as with concupiscence, it just doesn't seem like that kind of crowd. But there must be colorful incidents in the *Nadir*'s past, because the Cruise staff became almost operatic in their cautions to us as we headed back to Fort Lauderdale on Friday, though every warning was preceded by an acknowledgment that the exhortation to flush/toss anything Controlled *surely* couldn't apply to anyone on this particular cruise. Apparently Fort Lauderdale's Customs guys regard homebound 7NC passengers sort of the way small-town cops regard out-of-state speeders in Saab Turbos. An old veteran of many 7NCLCs told one of the U. Texas kids ahead of me in the Customs line the last day "Kiddo, if one of those dogs stops at your bag, you better hope he lifts his leg."

91 It's a total mystery when these waiters sleep. They serve at the Midnight Buffet every night, and then help clean up after, and then they appear in the 5☆C.R. in clean tuxes all over again at 0630h. the next day, always so fresh and alert they look slapped.

Fun. So everything that follows from here on out is from this day's p.&d. experiential log:

0645h.: A triple ding from the speakers in cabin and halls and then a cool female voice says Good Morning, the date, the weather, etc. She says it in a gentle accented English, repeats it in an Alsatian-sounding French, then again in German. She can make even German sound lush and postcoital. Hers is not the same PA voice as at Pier 21, but it's got the exact same quality of sounding the way expensive perfume smells.

0650–0705h.: Shower, play with Alisco Sirocco hairdryer & exhaust fan & hair in bathroom mirror, read from *Daily Meditations for the Semiphobically Challenged*, go over *Nadir Daily* with yellow HiLiter pen.

0708–0730h.: E.S. Breakfast at Table 64 in 5☆C.R. Last night everybody announced intentions to sleep through breakfast and grab some scones or something at the Windsurf Cafe later. So I'm alone at Table 64, which is large and round and right up next to a starboard window.

Table 64's waiter's name is, as mentioned before, Tibor. Mentally I refer to him as "The Tibster," but never out loud. Tibor has dismantled my artichokes and my lobsters and taught me that extra-well-done is not the only way meat can be palatable. We have sort of bonded, I feel. He is 35 and about 5'4" and plump, and his movements have the birdlike economy characteristic of small plump graceful men. Menu-wise, Tibor advises and recommends, but without the hauteur that's always made me hate the gastropedantic waiters in classy restaurants. Tibor is omnipresent without being unctuous or oppressive; he is kind and warm and fun. I sort of love him. His hometown is Budapest and he has a postgraduate degree in Restaurant Management from an unpronounceable Hungarian college. His wife back home is expecting their first child. He is the Head Waiter for Tables 64–67 at all three meals. He can carry three trays w/o precarity and never looks harried or on-the-edge the way most multitable waiters look. He seems like he cares. His face is at once round and pointy, and rosy. His tux never wrinkles. His hands are soft and pink, and his thumb-joint's skin is unwrinkled, like the thumb-joint of a small child.

Tibor's cuteness has been compared by the women at Table 64 to that of a button. But I have learned not to let his cuteness fool me. Tibor is a pro. His commitment to personally instantiating the *Nadir*'s fanatical commitment to excellence is the one thing about which he shows no sense of humor. If you fuck with him in this area he will feel pain and will make no effort to conceal it. See for example the second night, Sunday, at supper: Tibor was circling the table and asking each of us how our entrée was, and we all regarded this as just one of those perfunctory waiter-questions and all perfunctorily smiled and cleared our mouths and said Fine, Fine — and Tibor finally stopped and looked down at us all with a pained expression and changed his timbre slightly so it was clear he was addressing the whole table: "Please. I ask each: is excellent? Please. If excellent, you say, and I am happy. If not excellent, please: do not say excellent. Let me fix. Please." There was no hauteur or pedantry as he addressed us. He just meant what he said. His expression was babe-naked, and we heard him, and nothing was perfunctory again.

Good old Wojtek, the towering bespectacled Pole, age 22 and at least 6'8", Table 64's busboy — in charge of water, bread supply, crumb-removal, and using a big tower of a mill to put pepper on pretty much anything you don't lean forward and cover with your upper body — good old Wojtek works exclusively with Tibor, and they have an involved minuet of service that's choreographed down to the last pivot, and they speak quietly to each other in a Slavicized German pidgin you can tell they've evolved through countless quiet professional exchanges; and you can tell Wojtek reveres Tibor as much as the rest of us do.

This morning The Tibster wears a red bow tie and smells faintly of sandalwood. Early Seating Breakfast is the best time to be around him, because he's not very busy and can be initiated into chitchat without looking pained at neglecting his duties. He doesn't know I'm on the *Nadir* as a pseudojournalist. I'm not sure why I haven't told him — somehow I think it might make things hard for him. During E.S.B. chitchat I never ask him anything about Celebrity Cruises or the *Nadir*,[92] not out of deference to Mr. Dermatitis's pissy injunctions but because I feel like I'd just about die if Tibor got into trouble on my account.

Tibor's ambition is someday to return to Budapest[93] for good and with his *Nadir*-savings open a sort of newspaper-and-beret-type sidewalk cafe that specializes in something called Cherry Soup. With this in mind, two days from now in Ft. Lauderdale I'm going to tip The Tibster way, way more than the suggested $3.00 U.S./diem,[94] balancing out total expenses by radically undertipping both the liplessly sinister maître d' and our

---

92 (except for precise descriptions of whatever dorsal fins he's seen)

93 (he pronounces the "-pest" part of this "-persht")

94 The last night's *ND* breaks the news about tipping and gives tactful "suggestions" on going rates.

sommelier, an unctuously creepy Ceylonese guy the whole table has christened The Velvet Vulture.

0815h.: Catholic Mass is celebrated with Father DeSandre, Location: Rainbow Room, Deck 8.[95]

There's no chapel per se on the *Nadir*. The Father sets up a kind of folding credence table in the Rainbow Room, the most aftward of the Fantasy Deck lounges, done in salmon and sere yellow with dados of polished bronze. Genuflecting at sea turns out to be a tricky business. There are about a dozen people here. The Father's backlit by a big port window, and his homily is mercifully free of nautical puns or references to life being a voyage. The communal beverage is a choice of either wine or Welch's-brand unsweetened grape juice. Even the *Nadir*'s daily mass's communion wafers are unusually yummy, biscuitier than your normal host and with a sweet tinge to the pulp it becomes in your teeth.[96] Cynical observations about how appropriate it is that a 7NC Luxury Cruise's daily worship is held in an overdecorated bar seem too easy to take up space on. Just how a diocesan priest gets a 7NC Megacruiser as a parish—whether Celebrity maybe has clerics on retainer, sort of like the army, and they get assigned to different ships in rotation, and whether the R.C. Church gets paid just like the other vendors who provide service and entertainment personnel, etc.—will I'm afraid be forever unclear: Father DeSandre explains he has no time after the recessional for professional queries, because of

0900h.: Wedding Vow Renewal with Father DeSandre. Same venue, same porta-altar setup. No married couples show up to renew their wedding vows, though. There's me and Captain Video and maybe a dozen other *Nadir*ites sitting around in salmon chairs, and a beverage waitress makes a couple circuits with her visor and pad, and Father DeS. stands patiently in his cassock and white cope till 0920, but no older-type couples appear or step forward to renew. A few of the people in the R.R. sit in proximities and attitudes that show they're couples, but they sort of apologetically tell the Father they're not even married; the surprisingly cool and laid back Father DeS.'s invitation to make use of the setup and twin candles and priest w/ sacramentary *Book of Rites* opened to just the right page produces some shy laughter from the couples, but no takers. I don't know

---

95 All boldface stuff is verbatim and *sic* from today's *Nadir Daily*.
96 If Pepperidge Farm made communion wafers, these would be them.

what to make of the W.V.R.'s no-shows in terms of death/despair/pampering/insatiability issues.

0930h.: The Library is open for check-out of games, cards, and books, Location: Library,[97] Deck 7.

The *Nadir*'s Library is a little glassed-in salon set obliquely off Deck 7's Rendez-Vous Lounge. The Library's all good wood and leather and three-way lamping, an extremely pleasant place, but it's open only at weird and inconvenient times. Only one wall is even shelved, and most of the books are the sorts of books you see on the coffeetables of older people who live in condominiums near unchallenging golf courses: folio-sized, color-plated, with titles like *Great Villas of Italy* and *Famous Tea Sets of the Modern World*, etc. But it's a great place to just hang around and moss out, the Library. Plus this is where the chess sets are. This week also features an unbelievably large and involved jigsaw puzzle that sits about half-done on an oak table in the corner, which all sorts of different old people come in and work on in shifts. There's also a seemingly endless game of contract bridge always going on in the Card Room right next door, and the bridge players' motionless silhouettes are always there through the frosted glass between Library and C.R. when I'm mossing out and playing with the chess sets.

The *Nadir*'s Library's got cheapo Parker Brothers chess sets with hollow plastic pieces, which any good chess player has got to like.[98] I'm not nearly as good at chess as I am at Ping-Pong, but I'm pretty good. Most of the time on the *Nadir* I play chess with myself (not as dull as it may sound), for I have determined that—no offense—the sorts of people who go on 7NC Megacruises tend not to be very good chess players.

Today, however, is the day I am mated in 23 moves by a nine-year-old girl. Let's not spend a lot of time on this. The girl's name is Deirdre. She's one of very few little kids on board not tucked out of sight in Deck 4's Daycare Grotto.[99] Deirdre's mom never leaves her in the Grotto but also

---

97 Duh.

98 Heavy expensive art-carved sets are for dorks.

99 This is something else Mr. Dermatitis declined to let me see, but by all reports the daycare on these Megaships is phenomenal, w/ squads of nurturing and hyperkinetic young daycare ladies keeping the kids manically stimulated for up to ten-hour stretches via an endless number of incredibly well-structured activities, so tuckering the kids out that they collapse mutely into bed at 2000h. and leave their parents free to plunge into the ship's nightlife and Do It All.

never leaves her side, and has the lipless and flinty-eyed look of a parent whose kid is preternaturally good at something.

I probably should have seen this and certain other signs of impending humiliation as the kid first comes over as I'm sitting there trying a scenario where both sides of the board deploy a Queen's Indian and tugs on my sleeve and asks if I'd maybe like to play. She really does tug on my sleeve, and calls me Mister, and her eyes are roughly the size of sandwich plates. In retrospect it occurs to me that this girl was a little *tall* for nine, and worn-looking, slump-shouldered, the way usually only much older girls get—a kind of poor psychic posture. However good she may be at chess, this is not a happy little girl. I don't suppose that's germane.

Deirdre pulls up a chair and says she usually likes to be black and informs me that in lots of cultures black isn't thanatotic or morbid but is the spiritual equivalent of what white is in the U.S. and that in these other cultures it's *white* that's morbid. I tell her I already know all that. We start. I push some pawns and Deirdre develops a knight. Deirdre's mom watches the whole game from a standing position behind the kid's seat,[100] motionless except for her eyes. I know within seconds that I despise this mom. She's like some kind of stage-mother of chess. Deirdre seems like an OK type, though—I've played precocious kids before, and at least Deirdre doesn't hoot or smirk. If anything, she seems a little sad that I don't turn out to be more of a stretch for her.

My first inkling of trouble is on the fourth move, when I fianchetto and Deirdre knows what I'm doing is fianchettoing and uses the term correctly, again calling me Mister. The second ominous clue is the way her little hand keeps flailing out to the side of the board after she moves, a sign that she's used to a speed clock. She swoops in with her developed QK and forks my queen on the twelfth move and after that it's only a matter of time. It doesn't really matter. I didn't even *start* playing chess until my late twenties. On move 17 three desperately old and related-looking people at the jigsaw puzzle table kind of totter over and watch as I hang my rook and the serious carnage starts. It doesn't really matter. Neither Deirdre nor the hideous mom smiles when it's over; I smile enough for everybody. None of us says anything about maybe playing again tomorrow.

---

100 The only chairs in the Library are leather wing chairs with low seats, so only Deirdre's eyes and nose clear the board's table as she sits across from me, adding a Kilroy-ishly surreal quality to the humiliation.

0945–1000h.: Back briefly for psychic recharging in good old 1009E.P., I eat four pieces of some type of fruit that's like a tiny oversweetened tangerine and watch, for the fifth time this week, the Velociraptors-stalk-precocious-children-in-gleaming-institutional-kitchen part of *Jurassic Park*, noting an unprecedented sympathy for the Velociraptors this time around.

1000–1100h.: Three simultaneous venues of Managed Fun, all aft on Deck 9: **Darts Tournament, take aim and hit the bull's-eye!; Shuffleboard Shuffle, join your fellow guests for a morning game; Ping Pong Tournament, meet the Cruise Staff at the tables, Prizes to the Winners!**

Organized shuffleboard has always filled me with dread. Everything about it suggests infirm senescence and death: it's like it's a game played on the skin of a void and the rasp of the sliding puck is the sound of that skin getting abraded away bit by bit. I also have a morbid but wholly justified fear of darts, stemming from a childhood trauma too involved and hair-raising to discuss here, and as an adult I avoid darts like cholera.

What I'm here for is the Ping-Pong. I am an exceptionally good Ping-Pong player. The *ND*'s use of "Tournament" is euphemistic, though, because there are never any draw sheets or trophies in sight, and no other *Nadir*ites are ever playing. The constant high winds on 9-Aft may account for Ping-Pong's light turnout. Today three tables are set up (well off to the side of the Darts Tournament, which given the level of darts-play over there seems judicious), and the m.v. *Nadir*'s very own Ping-Pong Pro (or "3P," as he calls himself) stands cockily by the center table, amusing himself by bouncing a ball off the paddle between his legs and behind his back. He turns when I crack my knuckles. I've come to Ping-Pong three different times already this week, and nobody's ever here except the good old 3P, whose real first name is Winston. He and I are now at the point where we greet each other with the curt nods of old and mutually respected foes.

Below the center table is an enormous box of fresh Ping-Pong balls, and apparently several more of these boxes are in the storage locker behind the Golf-Drive Net, which again seems judicious given the number of balls in each game that get smashed or blown out to sea.[101] They also have a big peg-studded board on the bulkhead's wall with over a dozen different paddles, both the plain-wooden-grip-and-head-with-thin-skin-of-cheap-

---

101 I imagine it would be pretty interesting to trail a Megaship through a 7NC Cruise and just catalogue the trail of stuff that bobs in its wake.

pebbly-rubber kind and the fancy-wrapped-grip-and-head-with-thick-mushy-skin-of-unpebbled-rubber kind, all in Celebrity's snazzy white/navy motif.[102]

I am, as I believe I may already have stated, an extraordinarily fine Ping-Pong player,[103] and it turns out that I am an even finer Ping-Pong player outdoors in tricky tropical winds; and, although Winston is certainly a good enough player to qualify as a 3P on a ship where interest in Ping-Pong is shall we say less than keen, my record against him thus far is eight wins and only one loss, with that one loss being not only a very close loss but also consequent to a number of freakish gusts and a net that Winston himself admitted later may not have been regulation I.T.T.F. height and tension. Winston is under the curious (and false) impression that we've got some kind of tacit wager going on whereby if the 3P ever beats me three games out of five he gets my full-color Spiderman hat, which hat he covets and which hat I wouldn't dream ever of playing serious Ping-Pong without.

Winston only moonlights as a 3P. His primary duty on the *Nadir* is serving as Official Cruise Deejay in Deck 8's Scorpio Disco, where every night he stands behind an incredible array of equipment wearing hornrim sunglasses and working both the CD player and the strobes frantically till well after 0200h., which may account for a sluggish and slightly dazed quality to his A.M. Ping-Pong. He is 26 years old and, like much of the *Nadir*'s Cruise and Guest Relations staff, is good-looking in the vaguely unreal way soap opera actors and models in Sears catalogues are good-looking. He has big brown Help-Me eyes and a black fade that's styled into the exact shape of a nineteenth-century blacksmith's anvil, and he plays Ping-Pong with his thick-skinned paddle's head down in the chopsticky way of people who've received professional instruction.

Outside and aft, the *Nadir*'s engines' throb is loud and always sounds weirdly lopsided. 3P Winston and I have both reached that level of almost Zen-like Ping-Pong mastery where the game kind of plays us — the lunges and pirouettes and smashes and recoveries are automatic outer instantiations of a kind of intuitive harmony between hand and eye and primal

---

102 Only the fear of an impromptu Fort Lauderdale Customs search and discovery keeps me from stealing one of these paddles. I confess that I did end up stealing the chamois eyeglass-cleaners from 1009's bathroom, though maybe you're meant to take those home anyway — I couldn't tell whether they fell into the Kleenex category or the towel category.

103 I've sure never lost to any prepubescent females in fucking *Ping-Pong*, I can tell you.

Urge To Kill—in a way that leaves our forebrains unoccupied and capable of idle chitchat as we play:

"Wicked hat. I want that hat. Boss hat."

"Can't have it."

"Wicked motherfucking hat. Spiderman be dope."[104]

"Sentimental value. Long story behind this hat."

Insipidness notwithstanding, I've probably exchanged more total words with 3P Winston on this 7NC Luxury Cruise than I have with anybody else.[105] As with good old Tibor, I don't probe Winston in any serious journalistic way, although in this case it's not so much because I fear getting the 3P in trouble as because (nothing against good old Winston personally) he's not exactly the brightest bulb in the ship's intellectual chandelier, if you get my drift. E.g. Winston's favorite witticism when deejaying in the Scorpio Disco is to muff or spoonerize some simple expression and then laugh and slap himself in the head and go "Easy for me to say!" According to Mona and Alice, he's also unpopular with the younger crowd at the Scorpio Disco because he always wants to play Top-40ish homogenized rap instead of real vintage disco.[106]

It's also not necessary to ask Winston much of anything at all, because he's an incredible chatterbox when he's losing. He's been a student at the U. of South Florida for a rather mysterious seven years, and has taken this year off to "get fucking *paid* for a change for a while" on the *Nadir*. He claims to have seen all manner of sharks in these waters, but his descriptions don't inspire much real confidence or dread. We're in the middle of our second game and on our fifth ball. Winston says he's had the chance to do some serious ocean-gazing and soul-searching during his off hours these last few months and has decided to return to U.S.F. in Fall '95 and start college more or less all over, this time majoring not in Business Administration but in something he claims is called "Multimediated Production."

"They have a department in that?"

---

104 Winston also sometimes seemed to suffer from the verbal delusion that he was an urban black male; I have no idea what the story is on this or what conclusions to draw from it.

105 This is not counting my interfaces with Petra, which though lengthy and verbose tended of course to be one-sided except for "You are a funny thing, you."

106 The single most confounding thing about the young and hip cruisers on the *Nadir* is that they seem truly to love the exact same cheesy disco music that we who were young and hip in the late '70s loathed and made fun of, boycotting Prom when Donna Summer's "MacArthur Park" was chosen Official Prom Theme, etc.

"It's this interdisciplinarian thing. It's going to be fucking *phat,* Homes. You know. CD-ROM and shit. Smart chips. Digital film and shit."

I'm up 18–12. "Sport of the future."

Winston agrees. "It's where it's all going to be at. The Highway. Interactive TV and shit. Virtual Reality. *Interactive* Virtual Reality."

"I can see it now," I say. The game's almost over. "The Cruise of the Future. The *Home Cruise.* The Caribbean Luxury Cruise you don't have to leave home for. Strap on the old goggles and electrodes and off you go."

"Word up."

"No passports. No seasickness. No wind or sunburn or insipid Cruise staff.[107] Total Virtual Motionless Stay-At-Home Simulated Pampering."

"Word."

1105h.: Navigation Lecture — Join Captain Nico and learn about the ship's Engine Room, the Bridge, and the basic "nuts 'n bolts" of the ship's operation!

The m.v. *Nadir* can carry 460,000 gallons of nautical-grade diesel fuel. It burns between 40 and 70 tons of this fuel a day, depending on how hard it's traveling. The ship has two turbine engines on each side, one big "Papa" and one (comparatively) little "Son."[108] Each engine has a propeller that's 17 feet in diameter and is adjustable through a lateral rotation of 23.5° for maximum torque. It takes the *Nadir* 0.9 nautical miles to come to a complete stop from its standard speed of 18 knots. The ship can go slightly faster in certain kinds of rough seas than it can go in calm seas — this is for technical reasons that won't fit on the napkin I'm taking notes on. The ship has a rudder, and the rudder has two complex alloy "flaps" that somehow interconfigure to allow a 90° turn. Captain Nico's[109] English is not going to win any elocution ribbons, but he is a veritable blowhole of hard data. He's about my age and height but is just ridiculously good-looking,[110] like an extremely fit and tan Paul Auster. The

---

107 Interfacing with Winston could be kind of depressing in that the urge to make cruel sport of him was always irresistible, and he never acted offended or even indicated he knew he was being made sport of, and you went away afterward feeling like you'd just stolen coins from a blind man's cup or something.

108 Choosing from among 2^4 options, they can run on all four, or one Papa and one Son, or two Sons, etc. My sense is that running on Sons instead of Papas is kind of like switching from warp drive to impulse power.

109 The *Nadir* has a Captain, a Staff Captain, and four Chief Officers. Captain Nico is actually one of these Chief Officers; I do not know why he's called Captain Nico.

110 Something else I've learned on this Luxury Cruise is that no man can ever look any better than he looks in the white full-dress uniform of a naval officer. Women of all

venue here is Deck 11's Fleet Bar,[111] all blue and white and trimmed in stainless steel, and so abundantly fenestrated that the sunlight makes Captain Nico's illustrative slides look ghostly and vague. Captain Nico wears Ray-Bans but w/o a fluorescent cord. Thursday 16 March is also the day my paranoia about Mr. Dermatitis's contriving somehow to jettison me from the *Nadir* via Cabin 1009's vacuum toilet is at its emotional zenith, and I've decided in advance to keep a real low journalistic profile at this event. I ask a total of just one little innocuous question, right at the start, and Captain Nico responds with a witticism—

"How do we start engines? Not with the key of ignition, I can tell you!"

—that gets a large and rather unkind laugh from the crowd.

It turns out that the long-mysterious "m.v." in "m.v. *Nadir*" stands for "motorized vessel." The m.v. *Nadir* cost $250,310,000 U.S. to build. It was christened in Papenburg FRG in 10/92 with a bottle of ouzo instead of champagne. The *Nadir*'s three onboard generators produce 9.9 megawatts of power. The ship's Bridge turns out to be what lies behind the very intriguing triple-locked bulkhead near the aft towel cart on Deck 11. The

---

ages and estrogen-levels swooned, sighed, wobbled, lash-batted, growled, and hubba'd when one of these navally resplendent Greek officers went by, a phenomenon that I don't imagine helped the Greeks' humility one bit.

111 The Fleet Bar was also the site of **Elegant Tea Time** later that same day, where elderly female passengers wore long white stripper-gloves and pinkies protruded from cups, and where among my breaches of **Elegant Tea Time** etiquette apparently were: (a) imagining people would be amused by the tuxedo-design T-shirt I wore because I hadn't taken seriously the Celebrity brochure's instruction to bring a real tux on the Cruise; (b) imagining the elderly ladies at my table would be charmed by the off-color Rorschach jokes I made about the rather obscene shapes the linen napkins at each place were origami-folded into; (c) imagining these same ladies might be interested to learn what sorts of things have to be done to a goose over its lifetime in order to produce pâté-grade liver; (d) putting a 3-ounce mass of what looked like glossy black buckshot on a big white cracker and then putting the whole cracker in my mouth; (e) assuming one second thereafter a facial expression I'm told was, under even the most charitable interpretation, inelegant; (f) trying to respond with a full mouth when an elderly lady across the table with a pince-nez and buff-colored gloves and lipstick on her right incisor told me this was Beluga caviar, resulting in (f(1)) the expulsion of several crumbs and what appeared to be a large black bubble and (f(2)) the distorted production of a word that I was told sounded to the entire table like a genital expletive; (g) trying to spit the whole indescribable nauseous glob into a flimsy *paper* napkin instead of one of the plentiful and sturdier *linen* napkins, with results I'd prefer not to describe in any more detail than as *unfortunate;* and (h) concurring, when the little kid (in a bow tie and [no kidding] *tuxedo-shorts*) seated next to me pronounced Beluga caviar "blucky," with a spontaneous and unconsidered expression that was, indeed and unmistakably, a genital expletive.

Let us draw the curtain of charity over the rest of that particular bit of Managed Fun. This will, at any rate, explain the 1600h.–1700h. lacuna in today's p.&d. log.

Bridge is "where the equipments are—radars, indication of weathers and all these things."

Two years of sedulous postgraduate study is required of officer-wannabes just to get a handle on the navigational math involved; "also there is much learning for the computers."

Of the 40 or so *Nadir*ites at this lecture, the total number of women is: 0. Captain Video is here, of course, Celebrating the Moment from a cam-corded crouch on the Fleet Bar's steel bartop; he's wearing a nylon warm-up suit of fluorescent maroon and purple that makes him look like a huge macaw, and his knees crackle whenever he shifts position and rehunches. By this time Captain Video's really getting on my nerves.

A deeply sunburned man next to me is taking notes with a Mont Blanc pen in a leatherbound notebook with ENGLER embossed on it.[112] Just one moment of foresight on the way from Ping-Pong to Fleet Bar would have prevented my sitting here trying to take notes on paper napkins with a big felt-tip HiLiter. The *Nadir*'s officers have their quarters, mess, and a private bar on Deck 3, it turns out. "In the Bridge also we have different compass to see where we are going." The ship's four patro-filial turbines cannot ever be turned off except in drydock. What they do to deactivate an engine is simply disengage its propeller. It turns out that parallel park-ing a semi on LSD doesn't even come close to what Captain G. Pana-giotakis experiences when he docks the m.v. *Nadir*. The Engler man next to me is drinking a $5.50 Slippery Nipple, which comes with not one but two umbrellas in it. The rest of the *Nadir*'s crew's quarters are on Deck 2, which also houses the ship's laundry and "the areas of processing of gar-bage and wastes." Like all Megacruisers, the *Nadir* needs no tugboat in port; this is because it's got "the sternal thrusters and bow thrusters."[113]

The lecture's audience consists of bald solid thick-wristed men over 50 who all look like the kind of guy who rises to CEO a company out of that company's engineering dept. instead of some fancy MBA program.[114] A number of them are clearly Navy veterans or yachtsmen or something.

---

112 All week the Englerites have been a fascinating subcultural study in their own right—moving only in herds and having their own special Organized Shore Excursions and constantly reserving big party-rooms with velveteen ropes and burly guys standing by them with their arms crossed checking credentials—but there hasn't been room in this essay to go into any serious Englerology.

113 (not—mercifully—"bowal thrusters")

114 In other words, the self-made brass-balled no-bullshit type of older U.S. male whom you least want the dad to turn out to be when you go over to a girl's house to take her to a movie or something with dishonorable intentions rattling around in the back of your mind—an ur-authority figure.

They all compose a very knowledgeable audience and ask involved questions about the bore and stroke of the engines, the management of multiradial torque, the precise distinctions between a C-Class Captain and a B-Class Captain. My attempts at technical notes are bleeding out into the paper napkins until the yellow letters are all ballooned and goofy like subway graffiti. The male 7NC cruisers all want to know stuff about the hydrodynamics of midship stabilizers. They're all the kind of men who look like they're smoking cigars even when they're not smoking cigars. Everybody's complexion is hectic from sun and salt spray and a surfeit of Slippery Nipples. 21.4 knots is a 7NC Megaship's maximum possible cruising speed. There's no way I'm going to raise my hand in this kind of crowd and ask what a knot is.

Several unreproducible questions concern the ship's system of satellite navigation. Captain Nico explains that the *Nadir* subscribes to something called GPS: "This Global Positioning System is using the satellites above to know the position at all times, which gives this data to the computer." It emerges that when we're not negotiating ports and piers, a kind of computerized Autocaptain pilots the ship.[115] There's no actual "tiller" or "con" anymore, is the sense I get; there's certainly no protrusive-spoked wooden captain's wheel like these that line the walls of the jaunty Fleet Bar, each captain's wheel centered with thole pins that hold up a small and verdant fern.

1150h.: There's never a chance to feel actual physical hunger on a Luxury Cruise, but when you've gotten accustomed to feeding seven or eight times a day, a certain foamy emptiness in the gut always lets you know when it's time to feed again.

Among the *Nadir*ites, only the radically old and formalphiliacal hit Luncheon at the 5☆C.R., where you can't wear swim trunks or a floppy hat. The really happening place for lunch is the buffet at the Windsurf Cafe off the pools and plasticene grotto on Deck 11. Just inside both sets of the Windsurf's automatic doors, in two big bins whose sides are deco-

---

115 This helps explain why Captain G. Panagiotakis usually seems so phenomenally unbusy, why his real job seems to be to stand in various parts of the *Nadir* and try to look vaguely presidential, which he would (look presidential) except for the business of wearing sunglasses inside,[151a] which makes him look more like a Third World strongman.

    115a All the ship's officers wore sunglasses inside, it turned out, and always stood off to the side of everything with their hands behind their backs, usually in groups of three, conferring hieratically in technical Greek.

rated to look like coconut skin, are cornucopiae of fresh fruit[116] presided over by ice sculptures of a madonna and a whale. The crowds' flow is skillfully directed along several different vectors so that delays are minimal, and the experience of waiting to feed in the Windsurf Cafe is not as bovine as lots of other 7NC experiences.

Eating in the Windsurf Cafe, where things are out in the open and not brought in from behind a mysterious swinging door, makes it even clearer that everything ingestible on the *Nadir* is designed to be absolutely top-of-the-line: the tea isn't Lipton but *Sir Thomas Lipton* in a classy individual vacuum packet of buff-colored foil; the lunch meat is the really good fat-and gristle-free kind that gentiles usually have to crash kosher delis to get; the mustard is something even fancier-tasting than Grey Poupon that I keep forgetting to write down the brand of. And the Windsurf Cafe's coffee — which burbles merrily from spigots in big brushed-steel dispensers — the coffee is, quite simply, the kind of coffee you marry somebody for being able to make. I normally have a firm and neurologically imperative one-cup limit on coffee, but the Windsurf's coffee is so good,[117] and the job of deciphering the big yellow Rorschachian blobs of my Navigation Lecture notes so taxing, that on this day I exceed my limit, by rather a lot, which may help explain why the next few hours of this log get kind of kaleidoscopic and unfocused.

1240h.: I seem to be out on 9-Aft hitting golf balls off an Astroturf square into a dense-mesh nylon net that balloons impressively out toward the sea when a golf ball hits it. Thanatotic shuffleboard continues over to starboard; no sign of 3P or any Ping-Pong players or any paddles left behind; ominous little holes in deck, bulkhead, railing, and even the Astroturf square testify to my wisdom in having steered way clear of the A.M. Darts Tourney.

1314h.: I am now seated back in Deck 8's Rainbow Room watching "Ernst," the *Nadir*'s mysterious and ubiquitous Art Auctioneer,[118] mediate spirited bidding for a signed Leroy Neiman print. Let me iterate this. Bid-

---

116 As God is my witness no more fruit ever again in my whole life.

117 And it's just coffee qua coffee — it's not Blue Mountain Hazlenut Half-Caf or Sudanese Vanilla With Special Chicory Enzymes or any of that bushwa. The *Nadir*'s is a level-headed approach to coffee that I hereby salute.

118 One of very few human beings I've ever seen who is both blond and murine-looking, Ernst today is wearing white loafers, green slacks, and a flared sportcoat whose pink I swear can be described only as menstrual.

ding is spirited and fast approaching four figures for a signed Leroy Neiman print—not a signed Leroy Neiman, a signed Leroy Neiman *print*.

1330h.: Poolside Shenanigans! Join Cruise Director Scott Peterson and Staff for some crazy antics and the Men's Best Legs Contest judged by all the ladies at poolside!

Starting to feel the first unpleasant symptoms of caffeine toxicity, hair tucked at staff suggestion into a complimentary Celebrity Cruises swimcap, I take full and active part in the prenominate Shenanigans, which consist mostly of a tourney-style contest where gals in the Gal division and then guys in the Guy division have to slide out on a plastic telephone pole slathered with Vaseline[119] and face off against another gal/guy and try to knock each other off the pole and into the pool's nauseous brine by hitting each other with pillowcases filled with balloons. I make it through two rounds and then am knocked off by a hulking and hairy-shouldered Milwaukee newlywed who actually *hits me with his fist*—which as people start to lose their balance and compensate by leaning far forward[120] can happen—knocking my swimcap almost clear off my head and toppling me over hard to starboard into a pool that's not only got a really high Na-content but is also now covered with a shiny and full-spectrum scum of Vaseline, and I emerge so icky and befouled and cross-eyed from the guy's right hook that I blow what should have been a very legitimate shot at the title in the Men's Best Legs Contest, in which I end up placing third but am told later I would have won the whole thing except for the scowl, swollen and strabismic left eye, and askew swimcap that formed a contextual backdrop too downright goofy to let the full force of my gams' shapeliness come through to the judges.

1410h.: I seem now to be at the daily Arts & Crafts seminar in some sort of back room of the Windsurf Cafe, and aside from noting that I seem to be the only male here under 70 and that the project under construction on the table before me involves Popsicle sticks and crepe and a type of glue too runny and instant-adhesive to get my trembling overcaffeinated hands anywhere near, I have absolutely no fucking idea what's going on. 1415h.: In the public loo off the elevators on Deck 11-Fore, which has four urinals and three commodes, all Vacuum-Suction, which if activated one after the other

---

119 (the pole)

120 This is what I did, leaned too far forward and into the guy's fist that was clutching the hem of his pillowcase, which is why I didn't cry Foul, even though the vision in my right eye still drifts in and out of focus even back here on land a week later.

in rapid succession produce a cumulative sound that is exactly like the climactic D^b-$G^{\#}$ melisma at the end of the 1983 Vienna Boys Choir's seminal recording of the medievally lugubrious *Tenebrae Factae Sunt*. 1420h.: And now I'm in Deck 12's Olympic Health Club, in the back area, the part that's owned by Steiner of London,[121] where the same creamy-faced French women who'd worked 3/11's crowd at Pier 21 now all hang out, and I'm asking to be allowed to watch one of the "Phytomer/Ionithermie Combination Treatment De-Toxifying Inch Loss Treatments"[122] that some of the heftier ladies on board have been raving about, and I am being told that it's not really a spectator-type thing, that there's nakedness involved, and that if I want to see a P./I.C.T.D.-T.I.L.T. it's going to have to be as the subject of one; and between the quoted price of the treatment and the sensuous recall of the smell of my own singed nostril-hair in Chem. 205 in 1983, I opt to forfeit this bit of managed pampering. If you back off from something really big, the creamy ladies then try to sell you on a facial, which they say "a great large number" of male *Nadir*ites have pampered themselves with this week, but I also decline the facial, figuring that at this point in the week the procedure for me would consist mostly in exfoliating half-peeled skin. 1425h.: Now I'm in the small public loo of the Olympic Health Club, a one-holer notable only because O. Newton-John's "Let's Get Physical" plays on an apparently unending loop out of the overhead speaker. I'll go ahead and admit that I have, this week, come in a couple times between UV bombardments and pumped a little iron here in the *Nadir*'s Olympic Health Club. Except in the O.H.C. it's more like pumping ultrarefined titanium alloy: all the weights are polished stainless steel, and the place is one of these clubs

---

121 (also in the *ND* known as Steiner Salons and Spas at Sea)

122 So you can see why nobody with a nervous system would want to miss watching one of these, some hard data from the Steiner brochure:

IONITHERMIE—HOW DOES IT WORK? Firstly you will be measured in selected areas. The skin is marked and the readings are recorded on your program. Different creams, gels and ampoules are applied. These contain extracts effective in breaking down and emulsifying fat. Electrodes using faradism and galvanism are placed in position and a warm blue clay covers the full area. We are now ready to start your treatment. The galvanism accelerates the products into your skin, and the faradism exercises your muscles.[122a] The cellulite or 'lumpy fat,' which is so common amongst women, is emulsified by the treatment, making it easier to drain the toxins from the body and disperse them, giving your skin a smoother appearance.

122a And, as somebody who once brushed up against a college chemistry lab's live induction coil and had subsequently to be pried off the thing with a wooden mop handle, I can personally vouch for the convulsive-exercise benefit of faradic current.

with mirrors on all four walls that force you into displays of public self-scrutiny that are as excruciating as they are irresistible, and there are huge and insectile-looking pieces of machinery that mimic the aerobic demands of staircases and rowboats and racing bikes and improperly waxed cross-country skis, etc., complete with heart-monitor electrodes and radio headphones; and on these machines there are people in spandex whom you really want to take aside and advise in the most tactful and loving way not to wear spandex.

1430h.: We're back down in the good old Rainbow Room for **Behind the Scenes — Meet your Cruise Director Scott Peterson and find out what it's really like to work on a Cruise Ship!**

Scott Peterson is a deeply tan 39-year-old male with tall rigid hair, a constant high-watt smile, an escargot mustache, and a gleaming Rolex — basically the sort of guy who looks entirely at home in sockless white loafers and a mint-green knit shirt from Lacoste. He is also one of my least favorite Celebrity Cruises employees, though with Scott Peterson it's a case of mildly enjoyable annoyance rather than the terrified loathing I feel for Mr. Dermatitis.

The very best way to describe Scott Peterson's demeanor is that it looks like he's constantly posing for a photograph nobody is taking.[123] He mounts the Rainbow Room's low brass dais and reverses his chair and sits like a cabaret singer and begins to hold forth. There are maybe 50 people attending, and I have to admit that some of them seem to like Scott Peterson a lot, and really do enjoy his talk, a talk that, not surprisingly, turns out to be more about what it's like to be Scott Peterson than what it's like to work on the good old *Nadir*. Topics covered include where and under what circumstances Scott Peterson grew up, how Scott Peterson got interested in cruise ships, how Scott Peterson and his college roommate got their first jobs together on a cruise ship, some hilarious booboos in Scott Peterson's first months on the job, every celebrity Scott Peterson has personally met and shaken the hand of, how much Scott Peterson loves the

---

123 He's also a bit like those small-town politicians and police chiefs who go to shameless lengths to get mentioned in the local newspaper. Scott Peterson's name appears in each day's *Nadir Daily* over a dozen times: **"Backgammon Tournament with your Cruise Director Scott Peterson"; " 'The World Goes Round' with Jane McDonald, Michael Mullane, and the Matrix Dancers, and your host, Cruise Director Scott Peterson"; "Ft. Lauderdale Disembarkation Talk — Your Cruise Director Scott Peterson explains everything you need to know about your transfer from the ship in Ft. Lauderdale";** etc., ad naus.

people he gets to meet working on a cruise ship, how much Scott Peterson loves just working on a cruise ship in general, how Scott Peterson met the future Mrs. Scott Peterson working on a cruise ship, and how Mrs. Scott Peterson now works on a different cruise ship and how challenging it is to sustain an intimate relation as warm and in all respects wonderful as that of Mr. and Mrs. Scott Peterson when you (i.e., Mr. and Mrs. Scott Peterson) work on different cruise ships and lay eyes on each other only about every sixth week, except how but now Scott Peterson's tickled to be able to announce that Mrs. Scott Peterson happens to be on a well-earned vacation and is as a rare treat here this week cruising on the m.v. *Nadir* with him, Scott Peterson, and is as a matter of fact right here with us in the audience today, and wouldn't Mrs. S.P. like to stand up and take a bow.

I swear I am not exaggerating: this occasion is a real two-handed head-clutcher, awesome in its ickiness. But now, just as I need to leave in order not to be late for 1500h.'s much-anticipated skeetshooting, Scott Peterson starts to relate an anecdote that engages my various onboard dreads and fascinations enough for me to stay and try to write down. Scott Peterson tells us how his wife, Mrs. Scott Peterson, was in the shower in the Mr. and Mrs. Scott Peterson Suite on Deck 3 of the *Nadir* the other night when — one hand goes up in the gesture of someone searching for just the right delicate term — when nature called. So Mrs. Scott Peterson apparently gets out of the shower still wet and sits down on Scott Peterson's stateroom's bathroom's commode. Scott Peterson, in a narrative aside, says how perhaps we've all noticed that the commodes on the m.v. *Nadir* are linked to a state-of-the-art Vacuum Sewage System that happens to generate not a weak or incidental flush-suction. Other *Nadir*ites besides just me must fear their toilet, because this gets a big jagged tension-related laugh. Mrs. Scott Peterson[124] is sinking lower and lower in her salmon-colored chair. Scott Peterson says but so Mrs. Scott Peterson sits down on the commode, still naked and wet from the shower, and attends to nature's summons, and when she's done she reaches over and hits the commode's Flush mechanism, and Scott Peterson says that, in Mrs. Scott Peterson's wet slick condition, the incredible suction of the *Nadir*'s state-of-the-art V.S.S. starts actually *pulling her down through the seat's central hole*,[125] and apparently Mrs. Scott Peterson is just a bit too broad abeam to

---

124 Mrs. S.P. is an ectomorphic and sort of leather-complected British lady in a big-brimmed sombrero, which sombrero I observe her now taking off and stowing under her brass table as she loses altitude in the chair.

125 At this point in the anecdote I'm absolutely rigid with interest and empathic terror, which will help explain why it's such a huge letdown when this whole anecdote turns

get sucked down all the way and hurled into some abstract excremental void but rather *sticks*, wedged, halfway down in the seat's hole, and can't get out, and is of course stark naked, and starts screeching for help (by now the live Mrs. Scott Peterson seems very interested in something going on down underneath her table, and mostly only her left shoulder—leather-brown and stippled with freckles—is visible from where I'm sitting); and Scott Peterson tells us that he, Scott Peterson, hears her and comes rushing into the bathroom from the stateroom where he'd been practicing his Professional Smile in the bedside table's enormous vanity mirror,[126] comes rushing in and sees what's happened to Mrs. Scott Peterson and tries to pull her out—her feet kicking pathetically and buttocks and pop-liteals purpling from the seat's adhesive pressure—but he can't pull her out, she's been wedged in too tight by the horrific V.S.S. suction, and so thanks to some quick thinking Scott Peterson gets on the phone and calls one of the *Nadir*'s Staff Plumbers, and the Staff Plumber says Yes Sir Mr. Scott Peterson Sir I'm on my way, and Scott Peterson runs back into the bathroom and reports to Mrs. Scott Peterson that professional help is on the way, at which point it only then occurs to Mrs. Scott Peterson that she's starkers, and that not only are her ectomorphic breasts exposed to full Eurofluorescent view but a portion of her own personal pudendum is clearly visible above the rim of the occlusive seat that holds her fast,[127] and she screeches Britishly at Scott Peterson to for the bloody love of Christ do something to cover her legally betrothed nethers against the swart blue-collar gaze of the impending Staff Plumber, and so Scott Peterson goes and gets Mrs. Scott Peterson's favorite sun hat, a huge sombrero, in fact the very same huge sombrero Scott Peterson's beloved wife is wearing right...umm, just a couple seconds ago was wearing right here in this very Rainbow Room; and but so via the quick and resourceful thinking of Scott Peterson the sombrero is brought from the stateroom into the bath-room and placed over Mrs. Scott Peterson's inbent concave naked thorax, to cover her private parts. And the *Nadir*'s Staff Plumber knocks and comes in all overlarge and machine-oil-redolent, w/ tool-belt ajingle, and

---

out to be nothing but a cheesy Catskills-type joke, one that Scott Peterson has clearly been telling once a week for eons (although maybe not with poor Mrs. Scott Peterson actually sitting right there in the audience, and I find myself hopefully imagining all sorts of nuptial vengeance being wreaked on Scott Peterson for embarrassing Mrs. Scott Peterson like that), the dweeb.

126 [authorial postulate]

127 [Again an authorial postulate, but it's the only way to make sense of the remedy she's about to resort to (at this point I still don't know this is all just a corny joke—I'm rigid and bug-eyed with empathic horror for both the intra- and extranarrative Mrs. S.P.).]

badly out of breath, and sure enough swart, and he comes into the bathroom and appraises the situation and takes certain complex measurements and performs some calculations and finally tells Mr. Scott Peterson that he thinks he (the Staff Plumber) can get indeed get Mrs. Scott Peterson out of the toilet seat, but that extracting that there Mexican fellow in there with Mrs. S.P. is going to be a whole nother story.

1305h.: I've darted just for a second into Deck 7's Celebrity Show Lounge to catch some of the rehearsals for tomorrow night's climactic Passenger Talent Show. Two crew-cut and badly burned U. Texas guys are doing a minimally choreographed dance number to a recording of "Shake Your Groove Thing." Asst. Cruise Director "Dave the Bingo Boy" is coordinating activities from a canvas director's chair at stage left. A septuagenarian from Halifax VA tells four ethnic jokes and sings "One Day at a Time (Sweet Jesus)." A retired Century 21 Realtor from Idaho does a long drum solo to "Caravan." The climactic Passenger Talent Show is apparently a 7NC tradition, as was Tuesday night's Special Costume Party.[128] Some of the *Nadir*ites are deeply into this stuff and have brought their own costumes, music, props. A lithe Canadian couple does a tango complete w/ pointy black shoes and an interdental rose. Then the finale of the P.T.S. is apparently going to be four consecutive stand-up comedy routines delivered by very old men. These men totter on one after the other. One has one of those three-footed canes, another a necktie that looks uncannily like a Denver omelette, another an excruciating stutter. What follow are four successive interchangeable routines where the manner and humor are like exhumed time capsules of the 1950s: jokes about how impossible it is to understand women, about how very much men want to play golf and how their wives try to keep them from playing golf, etc. The routines have the same kind of flamboyant unhipness that makes my own grandparents objects of my pity, awe, and embarrassment all at once. One of the senescent quartet refers to his appearance tomorrow night as a "gig." The one with the tridential cane stops suddenly in the middle of a long joke about skipping his wife's funeral to play golf and, pointing the cane's tips at Dave the Bingo Boy, demands an immediate and accurate estimate of what the attendance will be for tomorrow night's Passenger Talent Show.

---

128 It was this kind of stuff that combined with the micromanagement of activities to make the *Nadir* weirdly reminiscent of the summer camp I attended for three straight Julys in early childhood, another venue where the food was great and everyone was sunburned and I spent as much time as possible in my cabin avoiding micromanaged activities.

Dave the Bingo Boy sort of shrugs and looks at his emery board and says that it's hard to say, that it like varies week to week, whereupon the old guy kind of brandishes his cane and says well it better be substantial because he *goddamn* well hates playing to an empty house.

1320h.: The *ND* neglects to mention that the skeetshooting is a *competitive* Organized Activity. The charge is $1.00 a shot, but you have to purchase your shots in sets of 10, and there's a large and vaguely gun-shaped plaque for the best X/10 score. I arrive at 8-Aft late; a male *Nadir*ite is already shooting skeet, and several other men have formed a line and are waiting to shoot skeet. The *Nadir*'s wake is a big fizzy V way below the aft rail. Two sullen Greek NCOs run the show, and between their English and their earmuffs and the background noise of shotguns—plus the fact that I've never touched any kind of gun before and have only the vaguest idea of which end even to point—negotiations over my late entry and the forwarding of the skeetshooting bill to *Harper's* are lengthy and involved.

I am seventh and last in line. The other contestants in line refer to the skeet as "traps" or "pigeons," but what they really look like is tiny discuses painted the Day-Glo orange of high-cost huntingwear. The orange, I posit, is for ease of visual tracking, and the color must really help, because the trim bearded guy in aviator glasses currently shooting is perpetrating absolute skeetocide in the air over the ship.

I assume you already know the basic skeetshooting conventions from movies and TV: the lackey at the weird little catapultish device, the bracing and pointing and order to *Pull,* the combination thud and *kertwang* of the catapult, the brisk crack of the weapon, and the midair disintegration of the luckless skeet. Everybody in line with me is male, though there are a number of females in the crowd that's watching the competition from the 9-Aft balcony above and behind us.

From the line, watching, three things are striking: (a) what on TV is a brisk crack is here a whooming roar that apparently is what a shotgun really sounds like; (b) skeetshooting looks comparatively easy, because now the stocky older guy who's replaced the trim bearded guy at the rail is also blowing these fluorescent skeet away one after the other, so that a steady rain of lumpy orange crud is falling into the *Nadir*'s wake; (c) a flying skeet,[129] when shot, undergoes a frighteningly familiar-looking mid-flight peripeteia—erupting material, changing vector, and plummeting

---

129 (these skeet made, I posit, from some kind of extra-brittle clay for maximum frag)

seaward in a distinctive corkscrewy way that all eerily recalls footage of the 1986 *Challenger* disaster.

Striking thing (b) turns out to be an illusion, one not unlike the illusion I'd had about the comparative easiness of golf from watching golf on TV before I'd actually ever tried to play golf. The shooters who precede me do all seem to fire with a kind of casual scorn, and they all get 8/10 or above. But it turns out that, of these six guys, three have military-combat backgrounds, another two are insufferable East-Coast retro-Yuppie brothers who spend weeks every year hunting various fast-flying species with their "Papa" in southern Canada, and the last has not only his own earmuffs, plus his own shotgun in a special crushed-velvet-lined case, but also his own skeetshooting range in his backyard[130] in North Carolina. When it's finally my turn, the earmuffs they give me have somebody else's ear-oil on them and don't fit my head. The gun itself is shockingly heavy and stinks of what I'm told is cordite, small pubic spirals of which are still exiting the barrel from the Korea-vet who preceded me and is tied for first with 10/10. The two Yuppie brothers are the only entrants even near my age; both got scores of 9/10 and are now appraising me coolly from identical prep-school-slouch positions against the starboard rail. The Greek non-coms seem extremely bored. I am handed the heavy gun and told to "be bracing a hip" against the aft rail and then to place the stock of the weapon against no *not* the shoulder of my hold-the-gun arm but the shoulder of my pull-the-trigger arm — my initial error in this latter regard results in a severely distorted aim that makes the Greek by the catapult do a rather neat drop-and-roll.

OK, let's not spend a lot of time drawing this whole incident out. Let me simply say that, yes, my own skeetshooting score was noticeably lower than the other entrants' scores, then simply make a few disinterested observations for the benefit of any novice contemplating shooting skeet from the rolling stern of a 7NC Megaship, and then we'll move on: (1) A certain level of displayed ineptitude with a firearm will cause everyone in the vicinity who knows anything about firearms to converge on you all at the same time with cautions and advice and handy tips passed down from Papa. (2) A lot of the advice in (1) boils down to exhortations to "lead" the launched skeet, but nobody explains whether this means that the gun's barrel should move across the sky with the skeet or should instead lie in a sort of static ambush along some point in the skeet's projected path. (3) TV skeetshooting is not totally unrealistic in that you really are supposed

---

130 !

to say *"Pull"* and the weird little catapultish thing really does produce a kertwanging thud. (4) Whatever a "hair trigger" is, a shotgun does not have one. (5) If you've never fired a gun before, the urge to close your eyes at the precise moment of concussion is, for all practical purposes, irresistible. (6) The well-known "kick" of a fired shotgun is no misnomer: it does indeed feel like being kicked, and hurts, and sends you back several steps with your arms pinwheeling wildly for balance, which, when you're holding a gun, results in mass screaming and ducking and then on the next shot a conspicuous thinning of the crowd in the 9-Aft gallery above.

Finally, (7), know that an unshot skeet's movement against the vast lapis lazuli dome of the open ocean's sky is sun-like—i.e. orange and parabolic and right-to-left—and that its disappearance into the sea is edge-first and splashless and sad.

1600h.–1700h.: Lacuna.

1700h.–1815h.: Shower, personal grooming, third viewing of the heart-tweaking last act of *Andre,* attempted shower-steam-rehabilitation of wool slacks and funereal sportcoat for tonight's 5☆C.R. supper, which in the *ND* is designated sartorially "Formal."[131]

---

131 Look, I'm not going to spend a lot of your time or my emotional energy on this, but if you are male and you ever do decide to undertake a 7NC Luxury Cruise, be smart and take a piece of advice I did not take: *bring Formalwear.* And I do not mean just a coat and tie. A coat and tie are appropriate for the two 7NC suppers designated "Informal" (which term apparently comprises some purgatorial category between "Casual" and "Formal"), but for Formal supper you're supposed to wear either a tuxedo or something called a "dinner jacket" that as far as I can see is basically the same as a tuxedo. I, dickhead that I am, decided in advance that the idea of Formalwear on a tropical vacation was absurd, and I steadfastly refused to buy or rent a tux and go through the hassle of trying to figure out how even to pack it. I was both right and wrong: yes, the Formalwear thing is absurd, but since every *Nadir*ite except me went ahead and dressed up in absurd Formalwear on Formal nights, I—having, of course, ironically enough spurned a tux precisely because of absurdity-considerations—was the one who ends up looking absurd at Formal 5☆C.R. suppers—painfully absurd in the tuxedo-motif T-shirt I wore on the first Formal night, and then even more painfully absurd on Thursday in the funereal sportcoat and slacks I'd gotten all sweaty and rumpled on the plane and at Pier 21. No one at Table 64 said anything about the absurd informality of my Formal-supper dress, but it was the sort of deeply tense absence of comment which attends only the grossest and most absurd breaches of social convention, and which after the Elegant Tea Time debacle pushed me right to the very edge of ship-jumping.

Please, let my dickheadedness and humiliation have served some purpose: take my advice and *bring Formalwear,* no matter how absurd it seems, if you go.

1815h.: The cast and general atmospherics of the 5☆C.R.'s T64 have already been covered. Tonight's supper is exceptional only in its tension. The hideous Mona has, recall, opted to represent today as her birthday to Tibor and the maître d', resulting tonight in bunting and a tall cake and a chair-balloon, plus in Wojtek leading a squad of Slavic busboys in a ceremonial happy-birthday mazurka around Table 64, and in an overall smug glow of satisfaction from Mona (who when The Tibster sets her cake down before her claps her hands once before her face like a small depraved child) and in an expression of blank tolerance from Mona's grandparents that's impossible to read or figure.

Additionally, Trudy's daughter Alice—whose birthday, recall, really *is* today—has in silent protest against Mona's fraud said nothing all week to Tibor about it—i.e. her own birthday—and sits tonight across from Mona wearing just the sort of face you would expect from one privileged child watching another privileged child receive natal treats and attentions that are by all rights her own.

The result of all this is that stony-faced Alice and I[132] have tonight established a deep and high-voltage bond across the table, united in our total disapproval and hatred of Mona, and are engaging in a veritable ballet of coded little stab-, strangle-, and slap-Mona pantomimes for each other's amusement, Alice and I are, which I've got to say is for me a fun and therapeutic anger-outlet after the day's tribulations.

But the supper's tensest development is that Alice's mother and my own new friend Trudy—whose purslane-and-endive salad, rice pilaf, and Tender Medallions of Braised Veal are simply too perfect tonight to engage any of her critical attention, and who I should mention has, all week, made little secret of the fact that she's not exactly crazy about Alice's Serious Boyfriend Patrick, or about his and Alice's Serious Relationship[133]—that Trudy notices and misconstrues my and Alice's coded gestures and stifled giggles as signs of some kind of burgeoning romantic connection between us, and Trudy begins yet once again extracting and spreading out her purse's 4×5s of Alice, and relating little tales of Alice's childhood designed to make Alice appear adorable, and talking Patrick

---

132 (an I who, recall, am reeling from the triple whammy of first ballistic humiliation and then Elegant Tea Time disgrace and now being the only person anywhere in sight in a sweat-crusted wool sportcoat instead of a glossy tux, and am having to order and chug three Dr Peppers in a row to void my mouth of the intransigent aftertaste of Beluga caviar)

133 (which S.R. apparently includes living together on Alice's $$ and "co-owning" Alice's 1992 Saab)

down, and in general I have to say acting like a procuress...and this would be bad enough, tension-wise (especially when Esther gets into the act), but now poor Alice—who, even though deeply preoccupied with birthday-deprivation and Mona-hatred, is by no means dim or unperceptive—quickly sees what Trudy's doing, and, apparently terrified that I might possibly share her mother's misperception of my connection with her as anything more than an anti-Mona alliance, begins directing my way a kind of Ophelia-type mad monologue of unconnected Patrick-references and Patrick-anecdotes, all of which causes Trudy to start making her weird dentally asymmetric grimace at the same time she begins cutting at her Tender Medallions of Braised Veal so hard that the sound of her knife against the 5☆C.R.'s bone china gives everybody at the table tooth-shivers; and the mounting tension causes fresh sweatstains to appear in the underarms of my funereal sportcoat and spread nearly to the perimeter of the faded salty remains of Pier 21's original sweatstains; and when Tibor makes his customary post-entrée circuit of the table and asks How Is All Of Everything, I am for the first time since the educational second night unable to say anything other than: Fine.

2045h.

CELEBRITY SHOWTIME

Celebrity Cruises Proudly Presents

HYPNOTIST

NIGEL ELLERY

Hosted by your Cruise Director Scott Peterson

PLEASE NOTE: *Video and audio taping of all shows is strictly prohibited.*
Children, please remain seated with your parents during shows.
No children in the front row.

CELEBRITY SHOW LOUNGE

Other Celebrity Showtime headline entertainments this week have included a Vietnamese comedian who juggles chain saws, a husband-and-wife team that specializes in Broadway love medleys, and, most notably, a singing impressionist named Paul Tanner, who made simply an enormous impression on Table 64's Trudy and Esther, and whose impressions of Engelbert Humperdinck, Tom Jones, and particularly Perry Como were apparently so stirring that a second Popular Demand Encore Performance by Paul Tanner has been hastily scheduled to follow tomorrow night's climactic Passenger Talent Show.[134]

Stage-hypnotist Nigel Ellery is British[135] and looks uncannily like 1950s B-movie villain Kevin McCarthy. Introducing him, Cruise Director Scott Peterson informs us that Nigel Ellery "has had the honor of hypnotizing both Queen Elizabeth II and the Dalai Lama."[136] Nigel Ellery's act combines hypnotic highjinks with a lot of rather standard Borscht Belt patter and audience abuse. And it ends up being such a ridiculously apposite symbolic microcosm of the week's whole 7NC Luxury Cruise experience that it's almost like a setup, some weird form of journalistic pampering.

First off, we learn that not everyone is susceptible to serious hypnosis — Nigel Ellery puts the C.S.L.'s whole 300+ crowd through some simple in-your-seat tests[137] to determine who in the C.S.L.'s crowd is "suggestibly gifted" enough to participate in the "fun" to come.

Second, when the six most suitable subjects — all still locked in complex contortions from the in-your-seat tests — are assembled onstage, Nigel Ellery spends a long time reassuring them and us that absolutely nothing will happen that they do not wish to have happen and voluntarily submit to. He then persuades a young lady from Akron that a loud male Hispanic voice is issuing from the left cup of her brassiere. Another lady is

---

134 At least guaranteeing the old *Nadir*ite comedian w/ cane a full house, I guess.

135 His accent indicates origins in London's East End.

136 (Not, one would presume, at the same time.)

137 One is: Lace your fingers together and put them in front of your face and then unlace just your index fingers and have them sort of face each other and imagine an irresistible magnetic force drawing them together and see whether the two fingers do indeed as if by magic move slowly and inexorably together until they're pressed together whorl to whorl. From a really scary and unpleasant experience in seventh grade,[137a] I already know I'm excessively suggestible, and I skip all the little tests, since no force on earth could ever get me up on a hypnotist's stage in front of over 300 entertainment-hungry strangers.

137a (viz. when at a school assembly a local psychologist put us all under a supposedly light state of hypnosis for some "Creative Visualization," and ten minutes later everybody in the auditorium came out of the hypnosis except unfortunately yours truly, and I ended up spending four irreversibly entranced and pupil-dilated hours in the school nurse's office, with the increasingly panicked shrink trying more and more drastic devices for bringing me out of it, and my parents very nearly litigated over the whole episode, and I calmly and matter-of-factly decided to steer well clear of all hypnosis thereafter)

induced to smell a horrific odor coming off the man in the chair next to her, a man who himself believes that the seat of his chair periodically heats to 100°C. The other three subjects respectively flamenco, believe they are not just nude but woefully ill-endowed, and are made to shout "Mommy, I want a wee-wee!" whenever Nigel Ellery utters a certain word. The audience laughs very hard at all the right times. And there is something genuinely funny (not to mention symbolically microcosmic) about watching these well-dressed adult cruisers behave strangely for no reason they understand. It is as if the hypnosis enables them to construct fantasies so vivid that the subjects do not even know they are fantasies. As if their heads were no longer their own. Which is of course funny.

Maybe the single most strikingly comprehensive 7NC symbol, though, is Nigel Ellery himself. The hypnotist's boredom and hostility are not only undisguised, they are incorporated kind of ingeniously into the entertainment itself: Ellery's boredom gives him the same air of weary expertise that makes us trust doctors and policemen, and his hostility—via the same kind of phenomenon that makes Don Rickles a big star in Las Vegas, I guess—is what gets the biggest roars of laughter from the lounge's crowd. The guy's stage persona is extremely hostile and mean. He does unkind imitations of people's U.S. accents. He ridicules questions from both the subjects and the audience. He makes his eyes burn Rasputinishly and tells people they're going to wet the bed at exactly 3:00 A.M. or drop trou at the office in exactly two weeks. The spectators—mostly middle-aged, it looks like—rock back and forth with mirth and slap their knee and dab at their eyes with hankies. Each moment of naked ill will from Ellery is followed by an enormous circumoral constriction and a palms-out assurance that he's just kidding and that he loves us and that we are a simply marvelous bunch of human beings who are clearly having a very good time indeed.

For me, at the end of a full day of Managed Fun, Nigel Ellery's act is not particularly astounding or side-splitting or entertaining—but neither is it depressing or offensive or despair-fraught. What it is is weird. It's the same sort of weird feeling that having an elusive word on the tip of your tongue evokes. There's something crucially key about Luxury Cruises in evidence here: being entertained by someone who clearly dislikes you, and feeling that you deserve the dislike at the same time that you resent it. All six subjects are now lined up doing syncopated Rockette kicks, and the show is approaching its climax, Nigel Ellery at the microphone getting us ready for something that will apparently involve furiously flapping arms and the astounding mesmeric illusion of flight. Because my own dangerous susceptibility makes it important that I not follow Ellery's hypnotic suggestions too closely or get too deeply involved, I find myself, in my comfortable navy-blue seat, going farther and farther away inside my head, sort of Creatively Visualizing a kind of epiphanic Frank Conroy–type moment of my own, pulling mentally back, seeing the hypnotist and subjects and audience and Celebrity Show Lounge and deck and then whole motorized vessel itself with the eyes of someone not aboard, visualizing the m.v. *Nadir* at night, right at this moment, steaming north at 21.4 knots, with a strong warm west wind pulling the moon backwards through a skein of clouds, hearing muffled laughter and music and Papas' throb and the hiss of receding wake and seeing, from the perspective of this nighttime sea, the good old *Nadir* complexly aglow, angelically white, lit up from within, festive, imperial, palatial…yes, this: like a palace: it would look like a kind of floating palace, majestic and terrible, to any poor soul out here on the ocean at night, alone in a dinghy, or not even in a dinghy but simply and terribly floating, a man overboard, treading water, out of sight of all land. This deep and creative visual trance—N. Ellery's true and accidental gift to me—lasted all through the next day and night, which period I spent entirely in Cabin 1009, in bed, mostly looking out the spotless porthole, with trays and various rinds all around me, feeling maybe a little bit glassy-eyed but mostly good—good to be on the *Nadir* and good soon to be off, good that I had survived (in a way) being pampered to death (in a way)—and so I stayed in bed. And even though the tranced stasis caused me to miss the final night's climactic P.T.S. and the Farewell Midnight Buffet and then Saturday's docking and a chance to have my After photo taken with Captain G. Panagiotakis, subsequent reentry into the adult demands of landlocked real-world life wasn't nearly as bad as a week of Absolutely Nothing had led me to fear.

1995

The Nature of the Fun

THE BEST METAPHOR I know of for being a fiction writer is in Don DeLillo's *Mao II,* where he describes a book-in-progress as a kind of hideously damaged infant that follows the writer around, forever crawling after the writer (i.e., dragging itself across the floor of restaurants where the writer's trying to eat, appearing at the foot of the bed first thing in the morning, etc.), hideously defective, hydrocephalic and noseless and flipper-armed and incontinent and retarded and dribbling cerebrospinal fluid out of its mouth as it mewls and blurbles and cries out to the writer, wanting love, wanting the very thing its hideousness guarantees it'll get: the writer's complete attention.

The damaged-infant trope is perfect because it captures the mix of repulsion and love the fiction writer feels for something he's working on. The fiction always comes out so horrifically defective, so hideous a betrayal of all your hopes for it—a cruel and repellent caricature of the perfection of its conception—yes, understand: grotesque because *imperfect.* And yet it's yours, the infant is, it's *you,* and you love it and dandle it and wipe the cerebrospinal fluid off its slack chin with the cuff of the only clean shirt you have left because you haven't done laundry in like three weeks because finally this one chapter or character seems like it's finally trembling on the edge of coming together and working and you're terrified to spend any time on anything other than working on it because if you look away for a second you'll lose it, dooming the whole infant to continued hideousness. And but so you love the damaged infant and pity it and care for it; but also you hate it—*hate* it—because it's deformed, repellent, because something grotesque has happened to it in the parturition from head to page; hate it because its deformity is *your* deformity (since if you were a better fiction writer your infant would of course look like one of those babies in catalogue ads for infantwear, perfect and pink and cerebrospinally continent) and its every hideous incontinent breath is a devastating indictment of *you,* on all levels...and so you want it dead, even as you dote and love and wipe it and dandle it and sometimes even apply CPR when it seems like its own grotesqueness has blocked its breath and it might die altogether.

The whole thing's all very messed up and sad, but simultaneously it's also tender and moving and noble and cool—it's a genuine *relationship*, of a sort—and even at the height of its hideousness the damaged infant somehow touches and awakens what you suspect are some of the very best parts of you: maternal parts, dark ones. You love your infant very much. And you want others to love it, too, when the time finally comes for the damaged infant to go out and face the world.

So you're in a bit of a dicey position: you love the infant and want others to love it, but that means you hope others won't see it *correctly*. You want to sort of fool people: you want them to see as perfect what you in your heart know is a betrayal of all perfection.

Or else you don't want to fool these people; what you want is you want them to see and love a lovely, miraculous, perfect, ad-ready infant and to be *right, correct,* in what they see and feel. You want to be terribly wrong: you want the damaged infant's hideousness to turn out to have been nothing but your own weird delusion or hallucination. But that'd mean you were crazy: you have seen, been stalked by, and recoiled from hideous deformities that in fact (others persuade you) aren't there at all. Meaning you're at least a couple fries short of a Happy Meal, surely. But worse: it'd also mean you see and despise hideousness in a thing *you* made (and love), in your spawn, in in certain ways *you*. And this last, best hope—this'd represent something way worse than just very bad parenting; it'd be a terrible kind of self-assault, almost self-torture. But that's still what you most want: to be completely, insanely, suicidally wrong.

But it's still all a lot of fun. Don't get me wrong. As to the nature of that fun, I keep remembering this strange little story I heard in Sunday school when I was about the size of a fire hydrant. It takes place in China or Korea or someplace like that. It seems there was this old farmer outside a village in the hill country who worked his farm with only his son and his beloved horse. One day the horse, who was not only beloved but vital to the labor-intensive work on the farm, picked the lock on his corral or whatever and ran off into the hills. All the old farmer's friends came around to exclaim what bad luck this was. The farmer only shrugged and said, "Good luck, bad luck, who knows?" A couple days later the beloved horse returned from the hills in the company of a whole priceless herd of wild horses, and the farmer's friends all come around to congratulate him on what good luck the horse's escape turned out to be. "Good luck, bad luck, who knows?" is all the farmer says in reply, shrugging. The farmer now strikes me as a bit Yiddish-sounding for an old Chinese farmer, but this is how I remember it. But so the farmer and his son set about breaking the wild horses, and one of the horses bucks the son off his back with such wild force that the son breaks his leg. And here come the friends to commiserate with the farmer and curse the bad luck that had ever brought these accursed wild horses onto his farm. The old farmer just shrugs and says, "Good luck, bad luck, who knows?" A few days later the Imperial Sino-Korean Army or something like that comes marching through the village, conscripting every able-bodied male between like ten and sixty for cannon-fodder for some hideously bloody conflict that's apparently brewing, but when they see the son's broken leg, they let him off on some sort of feudal 4-F, and instead of getting shanghaied the son stays on the farm with the old farmer. Good luck? Bad luck?

This is the sort of parabolic straw you cling to as you struggle with the issue of fun, as a writer. In the beginning, when you first start out trying to write fiction, the whole endeavor's about fun. You don't expect anybody else to read it. You're writing almost wholly to get yourself off. To enable your own fantasies and deviant logics and to escape or transform parts of yourself you don't like. And it works—and it's terrific fun. Then, if you have good luck and people seem to like what you do, and you actually get to get paid for it, and get to see your stuff professionally typeset and bound and blurbed and reviewed and even (once) being read on the AM subway by a pretty girl you don't even know, it seems to make it even *more* fun. For a while. Then things start to get complicated and confusing, not to mention scary. Now you feel like you're writing for other people, or at least you hope so. You're no longer writing just to get yourself off, which—since any kind of masturbation is lonely and hollow—is probably good. But what replaces the onanistic motive? You've found you very much enjoy having your writing liked by people, and you find you're extremely keen to have people like the new stuff you're doing. The motive of pure personal fun starts to get supplanted by the motive of being liked, of having pretty people you don't know like you and admire you and think you're a good writer. Onanism gives way to attempted seduction, as a motive. Now, attempted seduction is hard work, and its fun is offset by a terrible fear of rejection. Whatever "ego" means, your ego has now gotten into the game. Or maybe "vanity" is a better word. Because you notice that a good deal of your writing has now become basically showing off, trying to get people to think you're good. This is understandable. You have a great deal of yourself on the line, now, writing—your vanity is at stake. You discover a tricky thing about fiction writing: a certain amount of vanity is necessary to be able to do it at all, but any vanity above that certain amount is lethal. At this point 90+ percent of the stuff you're writing is motivated and informed by an overwhelming need to be liked. This results in shitty fiction. And the shitty work must get fed to the wastebasket, less because of any sort of artistic integrity than simply because shitty work will make you disliked. At this point in the evolution of writerly fun, the very thing that's always motivated you to write is now also what's motivating you to feed your writing to the wastebasket. This is a paradox and a kind of double bind, and it can keep you stuck inside yourself for months or even years, during which you wail and gnash and rue your bad luck and wonder bitterly where all the *fun* of the thing could have gone.

The smart thing to say, I think, is that the way out of this bind is to work your way somehow back to your original motivation: fun. And, if you can find your way back to the fun, you will find that the hideously unfortunate double bind of the late vain period turns out really to have been good luck for you. Because the fun you work back to has been transfigured by the unpleasantness of vanity and fear, an unpleasantness you're now so anxious to avoid that the fun you rediscover is a way fuller and more large-hearted kind of fun. It has something to do with Work as Play. Or with the discovery that disciplined fun is more fun than impulsive or hedonistic fun. Or with figuring out that not all paradoxes have to be paralyzing. Under fun's new administration, writing fiction becomes a way to go deep inside yourself and illuminate precisely the stuff you don't want to see or let anyone else see, and this stuff usually turns out (paradoxically) to be precisely the stuff all writers and readers share and respond to, feel. Fiction becomes a weird way to countenance yourself and to tell the truth instead of being a way to escape yourself or present yourself in a way you figure you will be maximally likable. This process is complicated and confusing and scary, and also hard work, but it turns out to be the best fun there is.

The fact that you can now sustain the fun of writing only by confronting the very same unfun parts of yourself you'd first used writing to avoid or disguise is another paradox, but this one isn't any kind of bind at all. What it is is a gift, a kind of miracle, and compared to it the reward of strangers' affection is as dust, lint.

— 1998

Some Remarks on Kafka's Funniness from Which Probably Not Enough Has Been Removed

ONE REASON FOR my willingness to speak publicly on a subject for which I am direly underqualified is that it affords me a chance to declaim for you a short story of Kafka's that I have given up teaching in literature classes and miss getting to read aloud. Its English title is "A Little Fable":

> "Alas," said the mouse, "the world is growing smaller every day. At the beginning it was so big that I was afraid, I kept running and running, and I was glad when at last I saw walls far away to the right and left, but these long walls have narrowed so quickly that I am in the last chamber already, and there in the corner stands the trap that I must run into." "You only need to change your direction," said the cat, and ate it up.

For me, a signal frustration in trying to read Kafka with college students is that it is next to impossible to get them to see that Kafka is funny. Nor to appreciate the way funniness is bound up with the power of his stories. Because, of course, great short stories and great jokes have a lot in common. Both depend on what communications theorists sometimes call *exformation*, which is a certain quantity of vital information removed from but evoked by a communication in such a way as to cause a kind of explosion of associative connections within the recipient.[1] This is probably why the effect of both short stories and jokes often feels sudden and

---

1 Compare e.g. in this regard the whole "What was the old man in despair about?"–"Nothing" interchange in the opening pages of Hemingway's "A Clean, Well-Lighted Place" with water-cooler zingers like "The big difference between a White House intern and a Cadillac is that not everybody's been in a Cadillac." Or consider the single word "Goodbye" at the end of Vonnegut's "Report on the Barnhouse Effect" vs. the function of "The fish!" as a response to "How many surrealists does it take to screw in a lightbulb?"

percussive, like the venting of a long-stuck valve. It's not for nothing that Kafka spoke of literature as "a hatchet with which we chop at the frozen seas inside us." Nor is it an accident that the technical achievement of great short stories is often called *compression*—for both the pressure and the release are already inside the reader. What Kafka seems able to do better than just about anyone else is to orchestrate the pressure's increase in such a way that it becomes intolerable at the precise instant it is released.

The psychology of jokes helps account for part of the problem in teaching Kafka. We all know that there is no quicker way to empty a joke of its peculiar magic than to try to explain it—to point out, for example, that Lou Costello is mistaking the proper name *Who* for the interrogative pronoun *who,* and so on. And we all know the weird antipathy such explanations arouse in us, a feeling of not so much boredom as offense, as if something has been blasphemed. This is a lot like the teacher's feelings at running a Kafka story through the gears of your standard undergrad critical analysis—plot to chart, symbols to decode, themes to exfoliate, etc. Kafka, of course, would be in a unique position to appreciate the irony of submitting his short stories to this kind of high-efficiency critical machine, the literary equivalent of tearing the petals off and grinding them up and running the goo through a spectrometer to explain why a rose smells so pretty. Franz Kafka, after all, is the story writer whose "Poseidon" imagines a sea god so overwhelmed with administrative paperwork that he never gets to sail or swim, and whose "In the Penal Colony" conceives description as punishment and torture as edification and the ultimate critic as a needled harrow whose coup de grâce is a spike through the forehead.

Another handicap, even for gifted students, is that—unlike, say, those of Joyce or Pound—the exformative associations that Kafka's work creates are not intertextual or even historical. Kafka's evocations are, rather, unconscious and almost sort of sub-archetypal, the primordial little-kid stuff from which myths derive; this is why we tend to call even his weirdest stories *nightmarish* rather than *surreal.* The exformative associations in Kafka are also both simple and extremely rich, often just about impossible to be discursive about: imagine, for instance, asking a student to unpack and organize the various signification networks behind *mouse, world, running, walls, narrowed, chamber, trap, cat,* and *cat eats mouse.*

Not to mention that the particular kind of funniness Kafka deploys is deeply alien to students whose neural resonances are American.[2] The fact

---

2 I'm not referring to lost-in-translation stuff here. Tonight's whole occasion[*] notwithstanding, I have to confess that I have very little German, and the Kafka I know and

is that Kafka's humor has almost none of the particular forms and codes of contemporary US amusement. There's no recursive wordplay or verbal stunt-pilotry, little in the way of wisecracks or mordant lampoon. There is no body-function humor in Kafka, nor sexual entendre, nor stylized attempts to rebel by offending convention. No Pynchonian slapstick with banana peels or rogue adenoids. No Rothish priapism or Barthish meta-parody or Woody Allen–type kvetching. There are none of the ba-bing ba-bang reversals of modern sitcoms; nor are there precocious children or profane grandparents or cynically insurgent coworkers. Perhaps most alien of all, Kafka's authority figures are never just hollow buffoons to be ridiculed, but are always absurd and scary and sad all at once, like "In the Penal Colony"'s Lieutenant.

My point is not that his wit is too subtle for US students. In fact, the only halfway effective strategy I've come up with for exploring Kafka's funniness in class involves suggesting to students that much of his humor is actually sort of unsubtle—or rather anti-subtle. The claim is that Kafka's funniness depends on some kind of radical literalization of truths we tend to treat as metaphorical. I opine to them that some of our most profound collective intuitions seem to be expressible only as figures of speech, that that's why we call these figures of speech *expressions*. With respect to "The Metamorphosis," then, I might invite students to consider what is really being expressed when we refer to someone as *creepy* or *gross* or say that he is forced to *take shit* as part of his job. Or to reread "In the Penal Colony" in light of expressions like *tongue-lashing* or *tore him a new asshole* or the gnomic "By middle age, everyone's got the face they deserve." Or to approach "A Hunger Artist" in terms of tropes like *starved for attention* or *love-starved* or the double entendre in the term *self-denial,* or even as innocent a factoid as that the etymological root of *anorexia* happens to be the Greek word for longing.

The students usually end up engaged here, which is great; but the teacher still sort of writhes with guilt, because the comedy-as-literalization-of-metaphor tactic doesn't begin to countenance the deeper alchemy by which Kafka's comedy is always also tragedy, and this tragedy always also an immense and reverent joy. This usually leads to an excruciating hour during which I backpedal and hedge and warn students that, for all their

---

teach is Mr. and Mrs. Muir's Kafka, and though Lord only knows how much more I'm missing, the funniness I'm talking about is funniness that's right there in the good old Muirs' English version.

*[= a PEN American Center event concerning a big new translation of *The Castle* by a man from I think Princeton. In case it's not obvious, that's what this whole document is—the text of a very quick speech.]

wit and exformative voltage, Kafka's stories are *not* fundamentally jokes, and that the rather simple and lugubrious gallows humor that marks so many of Kafka's personal statements—stuff like "There is hope, but not for us"—is not what his stories have got going on.

What Kafka's stories have, rather, is a grotesque, gorgeous, and thoroughly modern complexity, an ambivalence that becomes the multivalent Both/And logic of the, quote, "unconscious," which I personally think is just a fancy word for soul. Kafka's humor—not only not neurotic but *anti*-neurotic, heroically sane—is, finally, a religious humor, but religious in the manner of Kierkegaard and Rilke and the Psalms, a harrowing spirituality against which even Ms. O'Connor's bloody grace seems a little bit easy, the souls at stake pre-made.

And it is this, I think, that makes Kafka's wit inaccessible to children whom our culture has trained to see jokes as entertainment and entertainment as reassurance.[3] It's not that students don't "get" Kafka's humor but that we've taught them to see humor as something you *get*—the same way we've taught them that a self is something you just *have*. No wonder they cannot appreciate the really central Kafka joke: that the horrific struggle to establish a human self results in a self whose humanity is inseparable from that horrific struggle. That our endless and impossible journey toward home is in fact our home. It's hard to put into words, up at the blackboard, believe me. You can tell them that maybe it's good they don't "get" Kafka. You can ask them to imagine his stories as all about a kind of

---

3 There are probably whole Johns Hopkins U. Press books to be written on the lallating function that humor serves in today's US psyche. A crude way to put the whole thing is that our present culture is, both developmentally and historically, adolescent. And since adolescence is acknowledged to be the single most stressful and frightening period of human development—the stage when the adulthood we claim to crave begins to present itself as a real and narrowing system of responsibilities and limitations (taxes, death) and when we yearn inside for a return to the same childish oblivion we pretend to scorn*—it's not difficult to see why we as a culture are so susceptible to art and entertainment whose primary function is *escape*, i.e. fantasy, adrenaline, spectacle, romance, etc. Jokes are a kind of art, and because most of us Americans come to art now essentially to escape ourselves—to pretend for a while that we're not mice and walls are parallel and the cat can be outrun—it's understandable that most of us are going to view "A Little Fable" as not all that funny, or maybe even see it as a repulsive instance of the exact sort of downer-type death-and-taxes reality for which "real" humor serves as a respite.

*(Do you think it's a coincidence that college is when many Americans do their most serious fucking and falling-down drinking and generally ecstatic Dionysian-type reveling? It's not. College students are adolescents, and they're terrified, and they're dealing with their terror in a distinctively US way. Those naked boys hanging upside-down out of their frat house's windows on Friday night are simply trying to buy a few hours' escape from the grim adult stuff that any decent school has forced them to think about all week.)

door. To envision us approaching and pounding on this door, increasingly hard, pounding and pounding, not just wanting admission but needing it; we don't know what it is but we can feel it, this total desperation to enter, pounding and ramming and kicking. That, finally, the door opens... and it opens *outward*—we've been inside what we wanted all along. Das ist komisch.

1999

"Save up to 50%, and More!" Between you and I. On accident. Somewhat of a. Kustom Kar Kare Autowash. "The cause was due to numerous factors." "Orange Crush — A Taste That's All It's Own." "Vigorex: Helping men conquer sexual issues." "Equal numbers of both men and women opposed the amendment." Feedback. "As drinking water becomes more and more in short supply." "IMATION — Borne of 3M Innovation." Point in time. Time frame. "At this point in time, the individual in question was observed, and subsequently apprehended by authorities." Here for you, there for you. *Fail to comply with* for *violate*. Comprised of. From whence. *Quote* for *quotation*. *Nauseous* for *nauseated*. Besides the point. To mentor, to parent. To partner. To critique. *Indicated* for *said*. *Parameters* for *limits* and *options* for *choices* and *viable options* for *options* and *workable solution* for *solution*. In point of fact. Prior to this time. As of this point in the time frame. Serves to. Tends to be. *Convince* for *persuade, portion* for *part*. Commence to, cease to. Expedite. *Request* for *ask. Eventuate* for *happen*. Subsequent to this time. Facilitate. "Author's Foreward." Aid in. Utilize. Detrimental. Equates with. In regards to. "It has now made its way into the mainstream of verbal discourse." Tragic, tragedy. *Grow* as non-ag. transitive. *Keep* for *stay*. "To demonstrate the power of Epson's New Stylus Color Inkjet Printer with 1440 d.p.i., just listen:" Could care less. Personal issues, core issues. Fellow colleagues. Goal-orientated. Resources. To share. Feelings. Nurture, empower, recover. *Valid* for *true*. Authentic. Productive, unproductive. "I choose to view my opponent's negative attacks as unproductive to the real issues facing the citizens of this campaign." Incumbent upon. Mandate. Plurality. *Per anum.* Conjunctive adverbs in general. Instantaneous. *Quality* as adj. Proactive. Proactive Mission Statement. Positive feedback. A positive role model. Compensation. Validation. As for example. True facts are often impactful. "Call now for your free gift!" I only wish. Not too good of a. *Potentiality* for *potential.* Pay the consequences of. Obligated. At this juncture. To reference. To process. Process. The process of. The healing process. The grieving process. "Processing of feelings is a major component of the grieving process." To transition. Commensurant. "Till the stars fall from the sky/For you and I." Working together. Efficacious, effectual. Lifestyle. This phenomena, these criterion. Irregardless. *If* for *whether. As* for *because.* "Both sides are working together to achieve a workable consensus." Dysfunctional family of origin. S.O. To nest. Support. Relate to. Merge together. KEEP IN OWN LANE. For whomever wants it. "My wife and myself wish to express our gratitude and thanks to you for being there to support us at this difficult time in our life." Diversity. Quality time. Values, family values. To conference. "French provincial twin bed with canape and box spring, $150." Take a wait-and-see attitude. Cum-N-Go Quik Mart. Travelodge. Self-confessed. Precise estimate. More correct. Very possible, very unique. "Travel times on the expressways are reflective of its still being bad out there." Budgetel. More and more inevitable. EZPAY. RENT2OWN. MENS' ROOM. LADY'S ROOM. *Individual* for *person. Whom* for *who, that* for *who.* "The accident equated to a lot of damage." *Ipse dixie.* Falderol. "'Waiting on' is a dialectical locution on the rise and splitting its meaning." Staunch the flow. AM in the morning. *Forte* as "*for*tay." Advisement. Most especially. Sum total. Final totals. Complete dearth. "You can donate your used car or truck in any condition." At present. At the present time. *Challenge* for *problem, challenging* for *hard.* Closure. Judgement. Nortorious. Miniscule. Mischievious. "Both died in an apartment Dr. Kevorkian was leasing after inhaling carbon monoxide." Bald-faced. "No obligation required!" ☺

*Authority and American Usage**

Acknowledgements. To give off the impression. Instrumentality. Suffice to say. "The third-leading cause of death of both American men and women." *Positive* for *good.* Alright. "This begs the question, why are our elected leaders silent on this issue?" To reference. To privilege, to gender. "DiBlasi's work shows how sex can bring people together and pull them apart." "Come in and take advantage of our knowledgeable staff!" "We get the job done, not make excuses." In so far as. "Chances of rain are prevalent." NO TRUCK'S. Beyond the pail. National Highway Traffic Safety Administration Rule and Regulation Amendment Task Force. *Further* for *farther.* "The Fred Pryor Seminar has opened my eyes to better time management techniques. Also it has given real life situations and how to deal with them effectively." Hands-on, can-do. "Each of the variants indicated in boldface type count as an entry." Visualize, visualization. "Insert and tighten metric calibrated hexscrews (K) into arc (C) comprised of intersecting vertical pieces (A) along transverse section of Structure." Creativity, creative. To message, to send a message, to bring our message to. To reach out to. Context. A factor, a major factor, a decisive factor. Myriads of decisive factors. "It is a federal requirement to comply with all safety regulations on this flight." In this context, of this context. On a frequent basis. From the standpoint of. Contextualization. Within the parameters of this context. Decontextualization. Defamiliarization. Disorientated. "The artist's employment of a radical visual idiom serves to decontextualize both conventional modes of representation and the patriarchal contexts on which such traditional hegemonic notions as representation, tradition, and even conventional contextualization have come to be seen as depending for their canonical privileging as aestheto-interpretive mechanisms." I don't feel well but expect to recoup. "As parents, the responsibility of talking to your kids about drugs is up to you." Who would of thought? Last and final call. Achieve. Achievement. Excellence. Pursuit of a standard of total excellence. Partial completion. An astute observance. *Misrepresent* for *lie.* A long-standing tradition of achievement in the arena of excellence. "All dry cleaners are not the same." Visible to the eye. *Which* for *that, I* for *me.* That which. With regards to this issue. *Data* as singular, *media* as singular, *graffiti* as singular. *Remain* for *stay.* On-task. *Escalate* as transitive. Community. "Iran must realize that it cannot flaunt with impunity the expressed will and law of the world community." Community support. Community-based. Broad appeal. Rally support. Outpourings of support. "Tried to lay the cause at the feet of Congress." Epidemic proportions. Proportionate response. Feasibility. "This anguishing national ordeal." Bipartisan, nonpartisan. Widespread outbreaks. Constructive dialogue. To appeal for. To impact. Hew and cry. From this aspect. Hayday. Appropriate, inappropriate. Contingency. Contingent upon. Every foreseeable contingency. Audible to the ear. *As* for *since.* Palpably quiet. "The enormity of this administration's accomplishments." Frigid temperatures. Loud volume. "Surrounded on all sides, my workable options at this time are few in number." Chaise lounge, nucular, deep-seeded, bedroom suit, reek havoc. "Her ten-year rein atop the competition? The reason why is because she still continues to hue to the basic fundamentals." Ouster. Lucrative salaries, expensive prices. *Forgo* for *forego* and vice versa. Breech of conduct. Award for meretricious service. Substantiate, unsubstantiated, substantial. Re-elected to another term. Fulsome praise. Service. Public service. "A tradition of servicing your needs." "A commitment to accountability in a lifetime of public service." I thought to myself. As best as we can. WAVE ALL INTEREST FOR 90 DAYS. "But I also want to have — be the president that protects the rights of, of people to, to have arms. And that — so you don't go so far that the legitimate rights on some legislation are, are, you know, impinged on." "Dr. Charles Frieses' theories." Conflict. Conflict-resolution. The mutual advantage of both sides in this widespread conflict. "We will make a determination in terms of an appropriate response." Impact, to impact. Future plans. Don't go there! PLEASE WAIT HERE UNTIL NEXT AVAILABLE CLERK. Fellow countrymen. *Misappropriate* for *steal.* Off of. I'll be there momentarily. At some later point in time. I'm not adverse to that. Have a good one. Luv ya. Alot.

*(or, "POLITICS AND THE ENGLISH LANGUAGE" IS REDUNDANT)

Dilige et quod vis fac.
– AUGUSTINE

DID YOU KNOW that probing the seamy underbelly of US lexicography reveals ideological strife and controversy and intrigue and nastiness and fervor on a near-Lewinskian scale?

For instance, did you know that some modern dictionaries are notoriously liberal and others notoriously conservative, and that certain conservative dictionaries were actually conceived and designed as corrective responses to the "corruption" and "permissiveness" of certain liberal dictionaries? That the oligarchic device of having a special "Distinguished Usage Panel...of outstanding professional speakers and writers" is some dictionaries' attempt at a compromise between the forces of egalitarianism and traditionalism in English, but that most linguistic liberals dismiss the Usage Panel device as mere sham-populism, as in e.g. "Calling upon the opinions of the elite, it claims to be a democratic guide"?

Did you know that US lexicography even *had* a seamy underbelly?

The occasion for this article is Oxford University Press's recent release of Mr. Bryan A. Garner's *A Dictionary of Modern American Usage*, a book that Oxford is marketing aggressively and that it is my assigned function to review. It turns out to be a complicated assignment. In today's US, a typical book review is driven by market logic and implicitly casts the reader in the role of consumer. Rhetorically, its whole project is informed by a question that's too crass ever to mention up front: "Should you buy this book?" And because Bryan A. Garner's usage dictionary belongs to a particular subgenre of a reference genre that is itself highly specialized and particular, and because at least a dozen major usage guides have been published in the last couple years and some of them have been quite good indeed,[1] the central unmentionable question

---

1 (the best and most substantial of these being *The American Heritage Book of English*

here appends the prepositional comparative "...rather than *that* book?" to the main clause and so entails a discussion of whether and how *ADMAU* is different from other recent specialty-products of its kind.

The fact of the matter is that Garner's dictionary is extremely good, certainly the most comprehensive usage guide since E. W. Gilman's *Webster's Dictionary of English Usage,* now a decade out of date.[2] But the really salient and ingenious features of *A Dictionary of Modern American Usage* involve issues of rhetoric and ideology and style, and it is impossible to describe why these issues are important and why Garner's management of them borders on genius without talking about the historical context[3] in which *ADMAU* appears, and this context turns out to be a veritable hurricane of controversies involving everything from technical linguistics and public education to political ideology,[4] and these controversies take a certain amount of time to unpack before their relation to what makes Garner's dictionary so eminently worth your hard-earned reference-book dollar can even be established; and in fact there's no way even to begin the whole harrowing polymeric discussion without first taking a moment to establish and define the highly colloquial term *SNOOT.*

From one perspective, a certain irony attends the publication of any good new book on American usage. It is that the people who are going to be

---

Usage, Jean Eggenschwiler's *Writing: Grammar, Usage, and Style,* and Oxford/Clarendon's own *The New Fowler's Modern English Usage*)

2 *The New Fowler's* is also extremely comprehensive and fine, but its emphasis is on British usage.

3 Sorry about this phrase; I hate this phrase, too. This happens to be one of those very rare times when "historical context" is the phrase to use and there is no equivalent phrase that isn't even worse (I actually tried "lexico-temporal backdrop" in one of the middle drafts, which I think you'll agree is not preferable).

INTERPOLATION

The above ¶ is motivated by the fact that this reviewer nearly always sneers and/or winces when he sees a phrase like "historical context" deployed in a piece of writing and thus hopes to head off any potential sneers/winces from the reader here, especially in an article about felicitous usage. One of the little personal lessons I've learned in working on this essay is that being chronically inclined to sneer/wince at other people's usage tends to make me chronically anxious about other people's sneering/wincing at my usage. It is, of course, possible that this bivalence is news to nobody but me; it may be just a straightforward instance of Matt. 7:1's thing about "Judge not lest ye be judged." In any case, the anxiety seems worth acknowledging up front.

4 One of the claim-clusters I'm going to spend a lot of both our time arguing for is that issues of English usage are fundamentally and inescapably political, and that putatively disinterested linguistic authorities like dictionaries are always the products of certain ideologies, and that as authorities they are accountable to the same basic standards of sanity and honesty and fairness as our political authorities.

interested in such a book are also the people who are least going to need it—i.e., that offering counsel on the finer points of US English is preaching to the choir. The relevant choir here comprises that small percentage of American citizens who actually care about the current status of double modals and ergative verbs. The same sorts of people who watched *The Story of English* on PBS (twice) and read Safire's column with their half-caff every Sunday. The sorts of people who feel that special blend of wincing despair and sneering superiority when they see EXPRESS LANE—10 ITEMS OR LESS or hear *dialogue* used as a verb or realize that the founders of the Super 8 Motel chain must surely have been ignorant of the meaning of *suppurate*. There are lots of epithets for people like this—Grammar Nazis, Usage Nerds, Syntax Snobs, the Grammar Battalion, the Language Police. The term I was raised with is *SNOOT*.[5] The word might be slightly self-mocking, but those other terms are outright dysphemisms. A SNOOT can be loosely defined as somebody who knows what *dysphemism* means and doesn't mind letting you know it.

I submit that we SNOOTs are just about the last remaining kind of truly elitist nerd. There are, granted, plenty of nerd-species in today's America, and some of these are elitist within their own nerdy purview (e.g., the skinny, carbuncular, semi-autistic Computer Nerd moves instantly up on the totem pole of status when your screen freezes and now you need his help, and the bland condescension with which he performs the two occult keystrokes that unfreeze your screen is both elitist and situationally valid). But the SNOOT's purview is interhuman life itself. You don't, after all (despite withering cultural pressure), have to use a computer, but you can't escape language: language is everything and everywhere; it's what lets us have anything to do with one another; it's what separates us from animals; Genesis 11:7–10 and so on. And we SNOOTs know when and how to hyphenate phrasal adjectives and to keep participles from dangling, and we know that we know, and we know how very few other Americans know this stuff or even care, and we judge them accordingly.

In ways that certain of us are uncomfortable with, SNOOTs' attitudes

---

5 SNOOT (*n*) (*highly colloq*) is this reviewer's nuclear family's nickname à clef for a really extreme usage fanatic, the sort of person whose idea of Sunday fun is to hunt for mistakes in the very prose of Safire's column. This reviewer's family is roughly 70 percent SNOOT, which term itself derives from an acronym, with the big historical family joke being that whether S.N.O.O.T. stood for "Sprachgefühl Necessitates Our Ongoing Tendance" or "Syntax Nudniks Of Our Time" depended on whether or not you were one.

about contemporary usage resemble religious/political conservatives' attitudes about contemporary culture.[6] We combine a missionary zeal and a near-neural faith in our beliefs' importance with a curmudgeonly hell-in-a-handbasket despair at the way English is routinely defiled by supposedly literate adults.[7] Plus a dash of the elitism of, say, Billy Zane in *Titanic*—a fellow SNOOT I know likes to say that listening to most people's public English feels like watching somebody use a Stradivarius to pound nails. We[8]

6 This is true in my own case, at any rate—plus also the "uncomfortable" part. I teach college English part-time. Mostly Lit, not Composition. But I am so pathologically obsessed with usage that every semester the same thing happens: once I've had to read my students' first set of papers, we immediately abandon the regular Lit syllabus and have a three-week Emergency Remedial Usage and Grammar Unit, during which my demeanor is basically that of somebody teaching HIV prevention to intravenous-drug users. When it emerges (as it does, every term) that 95 percent of these intelligent upscale college students have never been taught, e.g., what a clause is or why a misplaced *only* can make a sentence confusing or why you don't just automatically stick in a comma after a long noun phrase, I all but pound my head on the blackboard; I get angry and self-righteous; I tell them they should sue their hometown school boards, and mean it. The kids end up scared, both of me and for me. Every August I vow silently to *chill about usage* this year, and then by Labor Day there's foam on my chin. I can't seem to help it. The truth is that I'm not even an especially good or dedicated teacher; I don't have this kind of fervor in class about anything else, and I know it's not a very productive fervor, nor a healthy one—it's got elements of fanaticism and rage to it, plus a snobbishness that I know I'd be mortified to display about anything else.

7 N.B. that this article's own title page features blocks of the typical sorts of contemporary boners and clunkers and oxymorons and solecistic howlers and bursts of voguish linguistic methane that tend to make a SNOOT's cheek twitch and forehead darken. (N.B. further that it took only about a week of semi-attentive listening and note-taking to assemble these blocks—the Evil is all around us.)

8 Please note that the strategically repeated 1-P pronoun is meant to iterate and emphasize that this reviewer is very much one too, a SNOOT, plus to connote the nuclear family mentioned *supra*. SNOOTitude runs in families. In *ADMAU*'s preface, Bryan Garner mentions both his father and grandfather and actually uses the word *genetic*, and it's probably true: 90 percent of the SNOOTs I know have at least one parent who is, by profession or temperament or both, a SNOOT. In my own case, my mom is a Comp teacher and has written remedial usage books and is a SNOOT of the most rabid and intractable sort. At least part of the reason I am a SNOOT is that for years my mom brainwashed us in all sorts of subtle ways. Here's an example. Family suppers often involved a game: if one of us children made a usage error, Mom would pretend to have a coughing fit that would go on and on until the relevant child had identified the relevant error and corrected it. It was all very self-ironic and lighthearted; but still, looking back, it seems a bit excessive to pretend that your small child is actually *denying you oxygen* by speaking incorrectly. The really chilling thing, though, is that I now sometimes find myself playing this same "game" with my own students, complete with pretend pertussion.

INTERPOLATION

As something I'm all but sure *Harper's* will excise, I will also insert that we even had a fun but retrospectively chilling little family *song* that Mom and we little SNOOTlets would

are the Few, the Proud, the More or Less Constantly Appalled at Everyone Else.

THESIS STATEMENT FOR WHOLE ARTICLE

Issues of tradition vs. egalitarianism in US English are at root political issues and can be effectively addressed only in what this article hereby terms a "Democratic Spirit." A Democratic Spirit is one that combines rigor and humility, i.e., passionate conviction plus a sedulous respect for the convictions of others. As any American knows, this is a difficult spirit to cultivate and maintain, particularly when it comes to issues you feel strongly about. Equally tough is a DS's criterion of 100 percent intellectual integrity—you have to be willing to look honestly at yourself and at your motives for believing what you believe, and to do it more or less continually.

This kind of stuff is advanced US citizenship. A true Democratic Spirit is up there with religious faith and emotional maturity and all those other top-of-the-Maslow-Pyramid-type qualities that people spend their whole lives working on. A Democratic Spirit's constituent rigor and humility and self-honesty are, in fact, so hard to maintain on certain issues that it's almost irresistibly tempting to fall in with some established dogmatic camp and to follow that camp's line on the issue and to let your position

---

sing in the car on long trips while Dad silently rolled his eyes and drove (you have to remember the theme to *Underdog* in order to follow the song):

> *When idiots in this world appear*
> *And fail to be concise or clear*
> *And solecisms rend the ear*
> *The cry goes up both far and near*
> *for Blunderdog*
> *Blunderdog*
> *Blunderdog*
> *Blunderdog*
> *Pen of iron, tongue of fire*
> *Tightening the wid'ning gyre*
> *Blunderdo-O-O-O-O-O...*
> *[etc.]* *

* (Since this'll almost surely get cut, I'll admit that, yes, I, as a kid, was in fact the author of this song. But by this time I'd been thoroughly brainwashed. It was sort of our family's version of "100 Bottles...Wall." My mother was the one responsible for the "wid'ning gyre" line in the refrain, which after much debate was finally substituted for a supposedly "forced" rhyme for *fire* in my own original lyrics—and again, years later, when I actually understood the apocalyptic thrust of that Yeats line I was, retrospectively, a bit chilled.)

harden within the camp and become inflexible and to believe that the other camps[9] are either evil or insane and to spend all your time and energy trying to shout over them.

I submit, then, that it is indisputably easier to be Dogmatic than Democratic, especially about issues that are both vexed and highly charged. I submit further that the issues surrounding "correctness" in contemporary American usage are both vexed and highly charged, and that the fundamental questions they involve are ones whose answers have to be literally *worked out* instead of merely found.

A distinctive feature of *ADMAU* is that its author is willing to acknowledge that a usage dictionary is not a bible or even a textbook but rather just the record of one bright person's attempts to work out answers to certain very difficult questions. This willingness appears to me to be informed by a Democratic Spirit. The big question is whether such a spirit compromises Bryan Garner's ability to present himself as a genuine "authority" on issues of usage. Assessing Garner's book, then, requires us to trace out the very weird and complicated relationship between Authority and Democracy in what we as a culture have decided is English. That relationship is, as many educated Americans would say, still in process at this time.

A Dictionary of Modern American Usage has no Editorial Staff or Distinguished Panel. It's been conceived, researched, and written *ab ovo usque ad mala* by Mr. Bryan A. Garner. This Garner is an interesting guy. He's both a lawyer and a usage expert (which seems a bit like being both a narcotics wholesaler and a DEA agent). His 1987 *A Dictionary of Modern Legal Usage* is already a minor classic; and now, instead of practicing law anymore, he goes around conducting writing seminars for JDs and doing prose-consulting for various judicial bodies. Garner's also the founder of something called the H. W. Fowler Society,[10] a worldwide group of usage Trekkies who like to send one another linguistic boners clipped from dif-

---

9 (It seems to be a natural law that camps form only in opposition to other camps and that there are always at least two w/r/t any difficult issue.)

10 If Samuel Johnson is the Shakespeare of English usage, think of Henry Watson Fowler as the Eliot or Joyce. His 1926 *A Dictionary of Modern English Usage* is the granddaddy of modern usage guides, and its dust-dry wit and blushless imperiousness have been models for every subsequent classic in the field, from Eric Partridge's *Usage and Abusage* to Theodore Bernstein's *The Careful Writer* to Wilson Follett's *Modern American Usage* to Gilman's '89 *Webster's*.

ferent periodicals. You get the idea. This Garner is one serious and very hard-core SNOOT.

The lucid, engaging, and extremely sneaky preface to *ADMAU* serves to confirm Garner's SNOOTitude in fact while undercutting it in tone. For one thing, whereas the traditional usage pundit cultivates a remote and imperial persona—the kind who uses *one* or *we* to refer to himself—Garner gives us an almost Waltonishly endearing sketch of his own background:

> I realized early—at the age of 15[11]—that my primary intellectual interest was the use of the English language.... It became an all-consuming passion.... I read everything I could find on the subject. Then, on a wintry evening while visiting New Mexico at the age of 16, I discovered Eric Partridge's *Usage and Abusage*. I was enthralled. Never had I held a more exciting book.... Suffice it to say that by the time I was 18, I had committed to memory most of Fowler, Partridge, and their successors.

Although this reviewer regrets the bio-sketch's failure to mention the rather significant social costs of being an adolescent whose overriding passion is English usage,[12] the critical hat is off to yet another personable preface-section, one that Garner entitles "First Principles": "Before going any further, I should explain my approach. That's an unusual thing for the author of a usage dictionary to do—unprecedented, as far as I know. But a guide to good writing is only as good as the principles on which it's based. And users should be naturally interested in those principles. So, in the interests of full disclosure..."[13]

The "unprecedented" and "full disclosure" here are actually good-natured digs at Garner's Fowlerite predecessors, and a slight nod to one

---

11 (Garner prescribes spelling out only numbers under ten. I was taught that this rule applies just to Business Writing and that in all other modes you spell out one through nineteen and start using cardinals at 20. *De gustibus non est disputandum*.)

12 From personal experience, I can assure you that any kid like this is going to be at best marginalized and at worst savagely and repeatedly Wedgied—see *sub*.

13 What follow in the preface are "the ten critical points that, after years of working on usage problems, I've settled on." These points are too involved to treat separately, but a couple of them are slippery in the extreme—e.g., "10. **Actual Usage**. In the end, the actual usage of educated speakers and writers is the overarching criterion for correctness," of which both "educated" and "actual" would really require several pages of abstract clarification and qualification to shore up against Usage Wars–related attacks, but which Garner rather ingeniously elects to define and defend via their application in his dictionary itself. Garner's ability not only to stay out of certain arguments but to render them irrelevant ends up being very important—see much *sub*.

camp in the wars that have raged in both lexicography and education ever since the notoriously liberal *Webster's Third New International Dictionary* came out in 1961 and included terms like *heighth* and *irregardless* without any monitory labels on them. You can think of *Webster's Third* as sort of the Fort Sumter of the contemporary Usage Wars. These wars are both the context and the target of a very subtle rhetorical strategy in *A Dictionary of Modern American Usage,* and without talking about them it's impossible to explain why Garner's book is both so good and so sneaky.

We regular citizens tend to go to The Dictionary for authoritative guidance.[14] Rarely, however, do we ask ourselves who exactly decides what gets in The Dictionary or what words or spellings or pronunciations get deemed substandard or incorrect. Whence the authority of dictionary-makers to decide what's OK and what isn't? Nobody elected them, after all. And simply appealing to precedent or tradition won't work, because what's considered correct changes over time. In the 1600s, for instance, the second-singular took a singular conjugation—"You is." Earlier still, the standard 2-S pronoun wasn't *you* but *thou*. Huge numbers of now-acceptable words like *clever, fun, banter,* and *prestigious* entered English as what usage authorities considered errors or egregious slang. And not just usage conventions but English itself changes over time; if it didn't, we'd all still be talking like Chaucer. Who's to say which changes are natural and good and which are corruptions? And when Bryan Garner or E. Ward Gilman do in fact presume to say, why should we believe them?

These sorts of questions are not new, but they do now have a certain urgency. America is in the midst of a protracted Crisis of Authority in matters of language. In brief, the same sorts of political upheavals that produced everything from Kent State to Independent Counsels have produced an influential contra-SNOOT school for whom normative standards of English grammar and usage are functions of nothing but custom and the ovine docility of a populace that lets self-appointed language experts boss them around. See for example MIT's Steven Pinker in a famous *New Republic* article—"Once introduced, a prescriptive rule is very hard to eradicate, no matter how ridiculous. Inside the writing establishment, the rules survive by the same dynamic that perpetuates ritual genital mutilations"—or, at a somewhat lower emotional pitch, Bill Bryson in *Mother Tongue: English and How It Got That Way:*

---

14 There's no better indication of The Dictionary's authority than that we use it to settle wagers. My own father is still to this day living down the outcome of a high-stakes bet on the correct spelling of *meringue*, a bet made on 14 September 1978.

Who sets down all those rules that we know about from child-hood—the idea that we must never end a sentence with a preposition or begin one with a conjunction, that we must use *each other* for two things and *one another* for more than two...? The answer, surprisingly often, is that no one does, that when you look into the background of these "rules" there is often little basis for them.

In *ADMAU*'s preface, Garner himself addresses the Authority question with a Trumanesque simplicity and candor that simultaneously disguise the author's cunning and exemplify it:

As you might already suspect, I don't shy away from making judgments. I can't imagine that most readers would want me to. Linguists don't like it, of course, because judgment involves subjectivity.[15] It isn't scientific. But rhetoric and usage, in the view of most professional writers,[16] aren't scientific endeavors. You[17] don't want dispassionate descriptions; you want sound guidance. And that requires judgment.

---

15 This is a clever half-truth. Linguists compose only one part of the anti-judgment camp, and their objections to usage judgments involve way more than just "subjectivity."

16 Notice, please, the subtle appeal here to the same "writing establishment" that Steven Pinker scorns. This isn't accidental; it's rhetorical.* What's crafty is that this is one of several places where Garner uses professional writers and editors as support for his claims, but in the preface he also treats these language pros as the primary *audience* for *ADMAU*, as in e.g. "The problem for professional writers and editors is that they can't wait idly to see what direction the language takes. Writers and editors, in fact, influence that direction: they must make decisions.... That has traditionally been the job of the usage dictionary: to help writers and editors solve editorial predicaments."

This is the same basic rhetorical move that President R. W. Reagan perfected in his televised Going-Over-Congress's-Head-to-the-People addresses, one that smart politicians ever since have imitated. It consists in citing the very audience you're addressing as the source of support for your proposals: "I'm pleased to announce tonight that we are taking the first steps toward implementing the policies that you elected me to implement," etc. The tactic is crafty because it (1) flatters the audience, (2) disguises the fact that the rhetor's purpose here is actually to persuade and rally support, not to inform or celebrate, and (3) preempts charges from the loyal opposition that the actual policy proposed is in any way contrary to the interests of the audience. I'm not suggesting that Bryan Garner has any particular political agenda. I'm simply pointing out that *ADMAU*'s preface is fundamentally rhetorical in the same way that Reagan's little Chats With America were.

*(In case it's not totally obvious, be advised that this article is using the word *rhetoric* in its strict traditional sense, something like "the persuasive use of language to influence the thoughts and actions of an audience.")

17 See?

Whole monographs could be written just on the masterful rhetoric of this passage. Besides the FN 16 stuff, note for example the ingenious equivocation of *judgment,* which in "I don't shy away from making judgments" means actual rulings (and thus invites questions about Authority), but in "And that requires judgment" refers instead to perspicacity, discernment, reason. As the body of *ADMAU* makes clear, part of Garner's overall strategy is to collapse these two different senses of *judgment,* or rather to use the second sense as a justification for the first. The big things to recognize here are (1) that Garner wouldn't be doing any of this if he weren't *keenly* aware of the Authority Crisis in modern usage, and (2) that his response to this crisis is—in the best Democratic Spirit—rhetorical.

So...

COROLLARY TO THESIS STATEMENT FOR WHOLE ARTICLE

The most salient and timely feature of Bryan A. Garner's dictionary is that its project is both lexicographical and rhetorical. Its main strategy involves what is known in classical rhetoric as the Ethical Appeal. Here the adjective, derived from the Greek *ēthos,* doesn't mean quite what we usually mean by *ethical.* But there are affinities. What the Ethical Appeal amounts to is a complex and sophisticated "Trust me." It's the boldest, most ambitious, and also most democratic of rhetorical Appeals because it requires the rhetor to convince us not just of his intellectual acuity or technical competence but of his basic decency and fairness and sensitivity to the audience's own hopes and fears.[18]

These latter are not qualities one associates with the traditional SNOOT usage-authority, a figure who for many Americans exemplifies snobbishness and anality, and one whose modern image is not helped by stuff like *The American Heritage Dictionary*'s Distinguished Usage Panelist Morris Bishop's "The arrant solecisms of the ignoramus are here often omitted entirely, 'irregardless' of how he may feel about this neglect" or critic John Simon's "The English language is being treated nowadays exactly as slave traders once handled their merchandise." Compare those lines' authorial personas with Garner's in, e.g., "English usage is so challenging that even experienced writers need guidance now and then."

The thrust here is going to be that *A Dictionary of Modern American Usage* earns Garner pretty much all the trust his Ethical Appeal asks us for. What's interesting is that this trust derives not so much from the

---

18 In this last respect, recall for example W. J. Clinton's "I feel your pain," which was a blatant if not especially deft Ethical Appeal.

book's lexicographical quality as from the authorial persona and spirit it cultivates. *ADMAU* is a feel-good usage dictionary in the very best sense of *feel-good*. The book's spirit marries rigor and humility in such a way as to let Garner be extremely prescriptive without any appearance of evangelism or elitist put-down. This is an extraordinary accomplishment. Understanding why it's basically a *rhetorical* accomplishment, and why this is both historically significant and (in this reviewer's opinion) politically redemptive, requires a more detailed look at the Usage Wars.

You'd definitely know that lexicography had an underbelly if you read the different little introductory essays in modern dictionaries—pieces like *Webster's DEU*'s "A Brief History of English Usage" or *Webster's Third*'s "Linguistic Advances and Lexicography" or *AHD-2*'s "Good Usage, Bad Usage, and Usage" or *AHD-3*'s "Usage in the Dictionary: The Place of Criticism." But almost nobody ever bothers with these little intros, and it's not just their six-point type or the fact that dictionaries tend to be hard on the lap. It's that these intros aren't actually written for you or me or the average citizen who goes to The Dictionary just to see how to spell (for instance) *meringue*. They're written for other lexicographers and critics; and in fact they're not really introductory at all, but polemical. They're salvos in the Usage Wars that have been under way ever since editor Philip Gove first sought to apply the value-neutral principles of structural linguistics to lexicography in *Webster's Third*. Gove's now-famous response to conservatives who howled[19] when *W3* endorsed *OK* and described *ain't* as "used colloquially by educated speakers in many regions of the United States" was this: "A dictionary should have no truck with artificial notions of correctness or superiority. It should be descriptive and not prescriptive." Gove's terms stuck and turned epithetic, and linguistic conservatives are now formally known as Prescriptivists and linguistic liberals as Descriptivists.

The former are better known, though not because of dictionaries' prologues or scholarly Fowlerites. When you read the columns of William

---

19 Really, *howled:* Blistering reviews and outraged editorials from across the country—from the *Times* and *The New Yorker* and the *National Review* and good old *Life,* or see e.g. this from the January '62 *Atlantic Monthly:* "We have seen a novel dictionary formula improvised, in great part, out of snap judgments and the sort of theoretical improvement that in practice impairs; and we have seen the gates propped wide open in enthusiastic hospitality to miscellaneous confusions and corruptions. In fine, the anxiously awaited* work that was to have crowned cisatlantic linguistic scholarship with a particular glory turns out to be a scandal and a disaster."

*(*Sic*—should obviously be "eagerly awaited." *Nemo mortalium omnibus horis sapit.*)

Safire or Morton Freeman or books like Edwin Newman's *Strictly Speaking* or John Simon's *Paradigms Lost*, you're actually reading Popular Prescriptivism, a genre sideline of certain journalists (mostly older males, the majority of whom actually do wear bow ties[20]) whose bemused irony often masks a Colonel Blimp's rage at the way the beloved English of their youth is being trashed in the decadent present. Some Pop Prescriptivism is funny and smart, though much of it just sounds like old men grumbling about the vulgarity of modern mores.[21] And some PP is offensively small-minded and knuckle-dragging, such as *Paradigms Lost*'s simplistic dismissal of Standard Black English: "As for 'I be,' 'you be,' 'he be,' etc., which should give us all the heebie-jeebies, these may indeed be comprehensible, but they go against all accepted classical and modern grammars and are the product not of a language with its roots in history but of ignorance of how a language works." But what's really interesting is that the plutocratic tone and styptic wit of Newman and Safire and the best of the Pop Prescriptivists are modeled after the mandarin-Brit personas of Eric Partridge and H. W. Fowler, the same twin towers of scholarly Prescriptivism whom Garner talks about revering as a kid.[22]

Descriptivists, on the other hand, don't have weekly columns in the *Times*. These guys tend to be hard-core academics, mostly linguists or

---

20 It's true: Newman, Simon, Freeman, James J. Kilpatrick...can George F. Will's bestseller on usage be long in coming?

21 Even the late Edwin Newman, the most thoughtful and least hemorrhoidal of the pop SNOOTs, sometimes let his Colonel B. poke out, as in e.g. "I have no wish to dress as many younger people do nowadays....I have no wish to impair my hearing by listening to their music, and a communication gap between an electronic rock group and me is something I devotedly cherish and would hate to see disappear."

22 Note for instance the mordant pith (and royal *we*) of this random snippet from Partridge's *Usage and Abusage:*

> **anxious of.** 'I am not hopeless of our future. But I am profoundly anxious of it,' Beverley Nichols, *News of England,* 1938: which made us profoundly anxious *for* (or *about*)—not *of*—Mr. Nichols's literary future.

Or observe the near-Himalayan condescension of Fowler, here on some people's habit of using words like *viable* or *verbal* to mean things the words don't really mean:

> **slipshod extension**...is especially likely to occur when some accident gives currency among the uneducated to words of learned origin, & the more if they are isolated or have few relatives in the vernacular....The original meaning of *feasible* is simply doable (L. *facere* do); but to the unlearned it is a mere token, of which he has to infer the value from the contexts in which he hears it used, because such relatives as it has in English—*feat, feature, faction,* &c.—either fail to show the obvious family likeness to which he is accustomed among families of indigenous words, or are (like *malfeasance*) outside his range.

Comp theorists. Loosely organized under the banner of structural (or "descriptive") linguistics, they are doctrinaire positivists who have their intellectual roots in Comte and Saussure and L. Bloomfield[23] and their ideological roots firmly in the US Sixties. The brief explicit mention Garner's preface gives this crew—

> Somewhere along the line, though, usage dictionaries got hijacked by the descriptive linguists,[24] who observe language scientifically. For the pure descriptivist, it's impermissible to say that one form of language is any better than another: as long as a native speaker says it, it's OK—and anyone who takes a contrary stand is a dunderhead.... Essentially, descriptivists and prescriptivists are approaching different problems. Descriptivists want to record language as it's actually used, and they perform a useful function—although their audience is generally limited to those willing to pore through vast tomes of dry-as-dust research.[25]

—is disingenuous in the extreme, especially the "approaching different problems" part, because it vastly underplays the Descriptivists' influence on US culture. For one thing, Descriptivism so quickly and thoroughly took over English education in this country that just about everybody who started junior high after c. 1970 has been taught to write Descriptively—via "freewriting," "brainstorming," "journaling"—a view of writing as self-exploratory and -expressive rather than as communicative, an abandonment of systematic grammar, usage, semantics, rhetoric, etymol-

---

23 FYI, Leonard Bloomfield's 1933 *Language* pretty much founded descriptive linguistics by claiming that the proper object of study was not language but something called "language behavior."

24 Utter bushwa: As *ADMAU*'s body makes clear, Garner knows precisely where along the line the Descriptivists started influencing usage guides.

25 His SNOOTier sentiments about linguists' prose emerge in Garner's preface via his recollection of studying under certain eminent Descriptivists in college: "The most bothersome thing was that they didn't write well: their offerings were dreary gruel. If you doubt this, go pick up any journal of linguistics. Ask yourself whether the articles are well-written. If you haven't looked at one in a while, you'll be shocked."

INTERPOLATION

Garner's aside about linguists' writing has wider applications, though *ADMAU* mostly keeps them implicit. The truth is that most US academic prose is appalling—pompous, abstruse, claustral, inflated, euphuistic, pleonastic, solecistic, sesquipidelian, Heliogabaline, occluded, obscure, jargon-ridden, empty: resplendently dead. See textual INTERPOLATION much below.

ogy. For another thing, the very language in which today's socialist, feminist, minority, gay, and environmental movements frame their sides of
political debates is informed by the Descriptivist belief that traditional
English is conceived and perpetuated by Privileged WASP Males[26] and is
thus inherently capitalist, sexist, racist, xenophobic, homophobic, elitist:
unfair. Think Ebonics. Think Proposition 227. Think of the involved contortions people undergo to avoid using *he* as a generic pronoun, or of the
tense, deliberate way white males now adjust their vocabularies around
non-w.m.'s. Think of the modern ubiquity of spin or of today's endless
rows over just the *names* of things—"Affirmative Action" vs. "Reverse
Discrimination," "Pro-Life" vs. "Pro-Choice,"* "Undocumented Worker"
vs. "Illegal Alien," "Perjury" vs. "Peccadillo," and so on.

*INTERPOLATION
EXAMPLE OF THE APPLICATION OF WHAT THIS ARTICLE'S
THESIS STATEMENT CALLS A DEMOCRATIC SPIRIT TO A
HIGHLY CHARGED POLITICAL ISSUE, WHICH EXAMPLE
IS MORE RELEVANT TO GARNER'S *ADMAU* THAN IT
MAY INITIALLY APPEAR

In this reviewer's opinion, the only really coherent position on the
abortion issue is one that is both Pro-Life *and* Pro-Choice.

Argument: As of 4 March 1999, the question of defining human
life *in utero* is hopelessly vexed. That is, given our best present medical and philosophical understandings of what makes something not
just a living organism but a person, there is no way to establish at just
what point during gestation a fertilized ovum becomes a human
being. This conundrum, together with the basically inarguable
soundness of the principle "When in irresolvable doubt about
whether something is a human being or not, it is better not to kill it,"
appears to me to require any reasonable American to be Pro-Life. At
the same time, however, the principle "When in irresolvable doubt
about something, I have neither the legal nor the moral right to tell
another person what to do about it, especially if that person feels that
s/he is *not* in doubt" is an unassailable part of the Democratic
pact we Americans all make with one another, a pact in which
each adult citizen gets to be an autonomous moral agent; and this

---

26 (which is in fact true)

principle appears to me to require any reasonable American to be Pro-Choice.

This reviewer is thus, as a private citizen and an autonomous agent, both Pro-Life and Pro-Choice. It is not an easy or comfortable position to maintain. Every time someone I know decides to terminate a pregnancy, I am required to believe simultaneously that she is doing the wrong thing and that she has every right to do it. Plus, of course, I have both to believe that a Pro-Life + Pro-Choice stance is the only really coherent one *and* to restrain myself from trying to force that position on other people whose ideological or religious convictions seem (to me) to override reason and yield a (in my opinion) wacko dogmatic position. This restraint has to be maintained even when somebody's (to me) wacko dogmatic position appears (to me) to reject the very Democratic tolerance that is keeping me from trying to force my position on him/her; it requires me not to press or argue or retaliate even when somebody calls me Satan's Minion or Just Another Shithead Male, which forbearance represents the really outer and tooth-grinding limits of my own personal Democratic Spirit.

Wacko name-calling notwithstanding, I have encountered only one serious kind of objection to this Pro-Life + Pro-Choice position. But it's a powerful objection. It concerns not my position per se but certain facts about me, the person who's developed and maintained it. If this sounds to you both murky and extremely remote from anything having to do with American usage, I promise that it becomes almost excruciatingly clear and relevant below.

The Descriptivist revolution takes a little time to unpack, but it's worth it. The structural linguists' rejection of conventional usage rules in English depends on two main kinds of argument. The first is academic and methodological. In this age of technology, some Descriptivists contend, it's the scientific method—clinically objective, value-neutral, based on direct observation and demonstrable hypothesis—that should determine both the content of dictionaries and the standards of "correct" English. Because language is constantly evolving, such standards will always be fluid. Philip Gove's now-classic introduction to *Webster's Third* outlines this type of Descriptivism's five basic edicts: "1—Language changes constantly; 2—Change is normal; 3—Spoken language *is* the language; 4—Correctness rests upon usage; 5—All usage is relative."

These principles look prima facie OK—simple, commonsensical, and couched in the bland s.-v.-o. prose of dispassionate science—but in fact they're vague and muddled and it takes about three seconds to think of reasonable replies to each one of them, viz.:

1—All right, but how much and how fast?

2—Same thing. Is Hericlitean flux as normal or desirable as gradual change? Do some changes serve the language's overall pizzazz better than others? And how many people have to deviate from how many conventions before we say the language has actually changed? Fifty percent? Ten percent? Where do you draw the line? Who draws the line?

3—This is an old claim, at least as old as Plato's *Phaedrus*. And it's specious. If Derrida and the infamous Deconstructionists have done nothing else, they've successfully debunked the idea that speech is language's primary instantiation.[27] Plus consider the weird arrogance of Gove's (3) with respect to correctness. Only the most mullah-like Prescriptivists care all that much about spoken English; most Prescriptive usage guides concern Standard *Written* English.[28]

4—Fine, but whose usage? Gove's (4) begs the whole question. What he wants to suggest here, I think, is a reversal of the traditional entailment-relation between abstract rules and concrete usage: instead of usage's ideally corresponding to a rigid set of regulations, the regulations ought to correspond to the way real people are actually using the language. Again, fine, but which people? Urban Latinos? Boston Brahmins? Rural Midwesterners? Appalachian Neogaelics?

5—*Huh?* If this means what it seems to mean, then it ends up biting Gove's whole argument in the ass. Principle (5) appears to imply that the correct answer to the above "which people?" is: All of them. And it's easy to show why this will not stand up as a lexicographical principle. The most

---

27 (Q.v. the "Pharmakon" stuff in Derrida's *La dissémination*—but you'd probably be better off just trusting me.)

28 Standard Written English (SWE) is sometimes called Standard English (SE) or Educated English, but the basic inditement-emphasis is the same. See for example *The Little, Brown Handbook*'s definition of Standard English as "the English normally expected and used by educated readers and writers."

SEMI-INTERPOLATION

Plus let's note that Garner's preface explicitly characterizes his dictionary's intended audience as "writers and editors." And even the recent ads for *ADMAU* in organs like the *New York Review of Books* are built around the slogan "If you like to WRITE… **Refer to us.**"*

*(Your SNOOT reviewer cannot help observing, w/r/t this ad, that the opening *r* in its **Refer** shouldn't be capitalized after a dependent clause + ellipsis. *Quandoque bonus dormitat Homerus.*)

obvious problem with it is that not everything can go in The Dictionary. Why not? Well, because you can't actually observe and record every last bit of every last native speaker's "language behavior," and even if you could, the resultant dictionary would weigh four million pounds and need to be updated hourly.[29] The fact is that any real lexicographer is going to have to make choices about what gets in and what doesn't. And these choices are based on . . . what? And so we're right back where we started.

It is true that, as a SNOOT, I am naturally predisposed to look for flaws in Gove et al.'s methodological argument. But these flaws still seem awfully easy to find. Probably the biggest one is that the Descriptivists' "scientific lexicography"—under which, keep in mind, the ideal English dictionary is basically number-crunching: you somehow observe every linguistic act by every native/naturalized speaker of English and put the sum of all these acts between two covers and call it The Dictionary—involves an incredibly crude and outdated understanding of what *scientific* means. It requires a naive belief in scientific Objectivity, for one thing. Even in the physical sciences, everything from quantum mechanics to Information Theory has shown that an act of observation is itself part of the phenomenon observed and is analytically inseparable from it.

If you remember your old college English classes, there's an analogy here that points up the trouble scholars get into when they confuse observation with interpretation. It's the New Critics.[30] Recall their belief that literary criticism was best conceived as a "scientific" endeavor: the critic was a neutral, careful, unbiased, highly trained observer whose job was to find and objectively describe meanings that were right there, literally inside pieces of literature. Whether you know what happened to New Criticism's reputation depends on whether you took college English after c. 1975; suffice it to say that its star has dimmed. The New Critics had the same basic problem as Gove's Methodological Descriptivists: they believed that there was such a thing as unbiased observation. And that linguistic meanings could exist "Objectively," separate from any interpretive act.

The point of the analogy is that claims to Objectivity in language study are now the stuff of jokes and shudders. The positivist assumptions that

---

29 Granted, some sort of 100 percent compendious real-time Megadictionary might conceivably be possible online, though it would take a small army of lexical webmasters and a much larger army of *in situ* actual-use reporters and surveillance techs; plus it'd be GNP-level expensive (. . . plus what would be the point?).

30 *New Criticism* refers to T. S. Eliot and I. A. Richards and F. R. Leavis and Cleanth Brooks and Wimsatt & Beardsley and the whole autotelic Close Reading school that dominated literary criticism from the Thirties to well into the Seventies.

underlie Methodological Descriptivism have been thoroughly confuted and displaced—in Lit by the rise of post-structuralism, Reader-Response Criticism, and Jaussian Reception Theory, in linguistics by the rise of Pragmatics—and it's now pretty much universally accepted that (a) meaning is inseparable from some act of interpretation and (b) an act of interpretation is always somewhat biased, i.e., informed by the interpreter's particular ideology. And the consequence of (a)+(b) is that there's no way around it—decisions about what to put in The Dictionary and what to exclude are going to be based on a lexicographer's ideology. And every lexicographer's got one. To presume that dictionary-making can somehow avoid or transcend ideology is simply to subscribe to a particular ideology, one that might aptly be called Unbelievably Naive Positivism.

There's an even more important way Descriptivists are wrong in thinking that the scientific method developed for use in chemistry and physics is equally appropriate to the study of language. This one doesn't depend on stuff about quantum uncertainty or any kind of postmodern relativism. Even if, as a thought experiment, we assume a kind of 19th-century scientific realism—in which, even though some scientists' interpretations of natural phenomena might be biased,[31] the natural phenomena themselves can be supposed to exist wholly independent of either observation or interpretation—it's still true that no such realist supposition can be made about "language behavior," because such behavior is both *human* and fundamentally *normative*.

To understand why this is important, you have only to accept the proposition that language is by its very nature public—i.e., that there is no such thing as a private language[32]—and then to observe the way Descrip-

---

31 ("EVIDENCE OF CANCER LINK REFUTED BY TOBACCO INSTITUTE RESEARCHERS")

32 This proposition is in fact true, as is interpolatively demonstrated just below, and although the demonstration is persuasive it is also, as you can see from the size of this FN, lengthy and involved and rather, umm, dense, so that once again you'd maybe be better off simply granting the truth of the proposition and forging on with the main text.

INTERPOLATIVE DEMONSTRATION OF THE FACT THAT THERE
IS NO SUCH THING AS A PRIVATE LANGUAGE

It is sometimes tempting to imagine that there can be such a thing as a private language. Many of us are prone to lay-philosophizing about the weird privacy of our own mental states, for example; and from the fact that when my knee hurts only I can feel it, it's tempting to conclude that for me the word *pain* has a very subjective internal meaning that only I can truly understand. This line of thinking is sort of like the adolescent pot-smoker's terror that his own inner experience is both private and unverifiable, a syndrome that is technically known as Cannabic Solipsism. Eating Chips Ahoy! and staring very intently at the television's network PGA event, for instance, the adolescent pot-

tivists seem either ignorant of this fact or oblivious to its consequences, as in for example one Dr. Charles Fries's introduction to an epigone of *Webster's Third* called *The American College Dictionary:*

> A dictionary can be an "authority" only in the sense in which a book of chemistry or physics or of botany can be an "authority"—by the

---

smoker is struck by the ghastly possibility that, e.g., what he sees as the color green and what other people call "the color green" may in fact not be the same color-experiences at all: the fact that both he and someone else call Pebble Beach's fairways green and a stoplight's GO signal green appears to guarantee only that there is a similar consistency in their color-experiences of fairways and GO lights, not that the actual subjective quality of those color-experiences is the same; it could be that what the ad. pot-smoker experiences as green everyone else actually experiences as blue, and that what we "mean" by the word *blue* is what he "means" by *green*, etc. etc., until the whole line of thinking gets so vexed and exhausting that the a. p.-s. ends up slumped crumb-strewn and paralyzed in his chair.

The point here is that the idea of a private language, like private colors and most of the other solipsistic conceits with which this reviewer has at various times been afflicted, is both deluded and demonstrably false.

In the case of private language, the delusion is usually based on the belief that a word like *pain* or *tree* has the meaning it does because it is somehow "connected" to a feeling in my knee or to a picture of a tree in my head. But as Mr. L. Wittgenstein's *Philosophical Investigations* proved in the 1950s, words actually have the meanings they do because of certain rules and verification tests that are imposed on us from outside our own subjectivities, viz., by the community in which we have to get along and communicate with other people. Wittgenstein's argument centers on the fact that a word like *tree* means what it does for me because of the way the community I'm part of has tacitly agreed to use *tree*. What makes this observation so powerful is that Wittgenstein can prove that it holds true even if I am an angst-ridden adolescent pot-smoker who believes that there's no way I can verify that what I mean by *tree* is what anybody else means by *tree*. Wittgenstein's argument is very technical but goes something like:

(1) A word has no meaning apart from how it is actually used, and even if

(2) "The question of whether my use agrees with others has been given up as a bad job,"* still,

(3) The only way a word can be used meaningfully even to myself is if I use it "correctly," with

(4) *Correctly* here meaning "consistently with my own definition" (that is, if I use *tree* one time to mean a tree and then the next time turn around and use *tree* to mean a golf ball and then the next time willy-nilly use *tree* to mean a certain brand of high-cal corporate cookie, etc., then, even in my own little solipsistic universe, *tree* has ceased really to "mean" anything at all), but

(5) The criterion of consistency-with-my-own-definition is satisfiable only if there exist certain rules that are independent of any one individual language-user (viz., in this case, me). Without the existence of these external rules, there is no difference between the statement "I am in fact using *tree* consistently with my own definition" and the statement "I happen to be under the impression that I am using *tree* consistently with my own definition." Wittgenstein's basic way of putting it is:

accuracy and the completeness of its record of the observed facts of the field examined, in accord with the latest principles and techniques of the particular science.

Now how is it to be decided whether I have used the [privately defined] word consistently? What will be the difference between my having used it consistently and its *seeming* to me that I have? Or has this distinction vanished?...If the distinction between 'correct' and 'seems correct' has disappeared, then so has the concept *correct*. It follows that the 'rules' of my private language are only *impressions* of rules. My impression that I follow a rule does not confirm that I follow the rule, unless there can be something that will prove my impression correct. "And that something cannot be another impression—for this would be as if someone were to buy several copies of the morning paper to assure himself that what it said was true."

Step (5) is the real kicker; step (5) is what shows that even if the involuted adolescent decides that he has his own special private definition of *tree*, he himself cannot make up the "rules of consistency" via which he confirms that he's using *tree* the way he privately defined it—i.e., "The proof that I am following a rule must appeal to something *independent* of my impression that I am."

If you are thinking that all this seems not just hideously abstract but also irrelevant to the Usage Wars or to anything you have any interest in at all, I submit that you are mistaken. If words' and phrases' meanings depend on transpersonal rules and these rules on community consensus,[†] then language is not only non-private but also irreducibly *public, political,* and *ideological*. This means that questions about our national consensus on grammar and usage are actually bound up with every last social issue that millennial America's about—class, race, sex, morality, tolerance, pluralism, cohesion, equality, fairness, money: you name it.

And if you at least provisionally grant that meaning is use and language public and communication impossible without consensus and rules, you're going to see that the Descriptivist argument is open to the objection that its ultimate aim—the abandonment of "artificial" linguistic rules and conventions—would make language itself impossible. As in Genesis 11:1–10–grade impossible, a literal Babel. There have to be *some* rules and conventions, no? We have to agree that *tree* takes *e*'s and not *u*'s and denotes a large woody thing with branches and not a small plastic thing with dimples and TITLEIST on it, right? And won't this agreement automatically be "artificial," since it's human beings making it? Once you accept that at least some artificial conventions are necessary, then you can get to the really hard and interesting questions: which conventions are necessary? and when? and where? and who gets to decide? and whence their authority to do so? And because these are the very questions that Gove's crew believes Dispassionate Science can transcend, their argument appears guilty of both *petitio principii* and *ignoratio elenchi*, and can pretty much be dismissed out of hand.

*Because *The Investigations'* prose is extremely gnomic and opaque and consists largely of Wittgenstein having weird little imaginary dialogues with himself, the quotations here are actually from Norman Malcolm's definitive paraphrase of L.W.'s argument, in which paraphrase Dr. Malcolm uses single quotation marks for tone quotes and double quotation marks for when he's actually quoting Wittgenstein—which, when I myself am quoting Malcolm quoting Wittgenstein's tone quotes, makes for a rather irksome surfeit of quotation marks, admittedly; but using Malcolm's exegesis allows this interpolative demonstration to be about 60 percent shorter than it would be if we were to grapple with Wittgenstein directly.

This is so stupid it practically drools. An "authoritative" physics text presents the results of *physicists'* observations and *physicists'* theories about those observations. If a physics textbook operated on Descriptivist principles, the fact that some Americans believe electricity flows better downhill (based on the observed fact that power lines tend to run high above the homes they serve) would require the Electricity Flows Better Downhill Hypothesis to be included as a "valid" theory in the textbook—just as, for Dr. Fries, if some Americans use *infer* for *imply* or *aspect* for *perspective*, these usages become *ipso facto* "valid" parts of the language. The truth is that structural linguists like Gove and Fries are not scientists at all; they're pollsters who misconstrue the importance of the "facts" they are recording. It isn't scientific phenomena they're observing and tabulating, but rather a set of human behaviors, and a lot of human behaviors are—to be blunt—moronic. Try, for instance, to imagine an "authoritative" ethics textbook whose principles were based on what most people actually *do*.

Grammar and usage conventions are, as it happens, a lot more like ethical principles than like scientific theories. The reason the Descriptivists can't see this is the same reason they choose to regard the English language as the sum of all English utterances: they confuse mere regularities with *norms*.

Norms aren't quite the same as rules, but they're close. A norm can be defined here simply as something that people have agreed on as the optimal way to do things for certain purposes. Let's keep in mind that language didn't come into being because our hairy ancestors were sitting around the veldt with nothing better to do. Language was invented to serve certain very specific purposes—"That mushroom is poisonous"; "Knock these two rocks together and you can start a fire"; "This shelter is mine!" and so on. Clearly, as linguistic communities evolve over time, they discover that some ways of using language are better than others—not better *a priori,* but better with respect to the community's purposes. If we assume that one such purpose might be communicating which kinds of food are safe to eat, then we can see how, for example, a misplaced modifier could violate an important norm: "People who eat that kind of mushroom often get sick" confuses the message's recipient about whether he'll get sick only if he eats the mushroom frequently or whether he stands a

---

†There's a whole argument for this, but intuitively you can see that it makes sense: if the rules can't be subjective, and if they're not actually "out there" floating around in some kind of metaphysical hyperreality (a floating hyperreality that you can believe in if you wish, but you should know that people with beliefs like this usually get forced to take medication), then community consensus is really the only plausible option left.

good chance of getting sick the very first time he eats it. In other words, the fungiphagic community has a vested practical interest in excluding this kind of misplaced modifier from acceptable usage; and, given the purposes the community uses language for, the fact that a certain percentage of tribesmen screw up and use misplaced modifiers to talk about food safety does not *eo ipso* make m.m.'s a good idea.

Maybe now the analogy between usage and ethics is clearer. Just because people sometimes lie, cheat on their taxes, or scream at their kids, this doesn't mean that they think those things are "good."[33] The whole point of establishing norms is to help us evaluate our actions (including utterances) according to what we as a community have decided our real interests and purposes are. Granted, this analysis is oversimplified; in practice it's incredibly hard to arrive at norms and to keep them at least minimally fair or sometimes even to agree on what they are (see e.g. today's Culture Wars). But the Descriptivists' assumption that all usage norms are arbitrary and dispensable leads to—well, have a mushroom.

The different connotations of *arbitrary* here are tricky, though—and this sort of segues into the second main kind of Descriptivist argument. There is a sense in which specific linguistic conventions really *are* arbitrary. For instance, there's no particular metaphysical reason why our word for a four-legged mammal that gives milk and goes moo is *cow* and not, say, *prtlmpf.* The uptown term for this is "the arbitrariness of the linguistic sign,"[34] and it's used, along with certain principles of cognitive science and generative grammar, in a more philosophically sophisticated version of Descriptivism that holds the conventions of SWE to be more like the niceties of fashion than like actual norms. This "Philosophical Descriptivism" doesn't care much about dictionaries or method; its target is the stan-

---

33 In fact, the Methodological Descriptivists' reasoning is known in social philosophy as the "Well, Everybody Does It" fallacy—i.e., if a lot of people cheat on their taxes, that means it's somehow morally OK to cheat on your taxes. Ethics-wise, it takes only two or three deductive steps to get from there to the sort of State of Nature where everybody's hitting each other over the head and stealing their groceries.

34 This phrase is attributable to Ferdinand de Saussure, the Swiss philologist who more or less invented modern technical linguistics, separating the study of language as an abstract formal system from the historical and comparative emphases of 19th-century philology. Suffice it to say that the Descriptivists like Saussure a *lot*. Suffice it also to say that they tend to misread him and take him out of context and distort his theories in all kinds of embarrassing ways—e.g., Saussure's "arbitrariness of the linguistic sign" means something other and far more complicated than just "There's no ultimate necessity to English speakers' saying *cow*." (Similarly, the structural linguists' distinction between "language behavior" and "language" is based on a simplistic misreading of Saussure's distinction between *"parole"* and *"langue."*)

dard SNOOT claim that prescriptive rules have their ultimate justification in the community's need to make its language meaningful and clear.

Steven Pinker's 1994 *The Language Instinct* is a good and fairly literate example of this second kind of Descriptivist argument, which, like the Gove-et-al. version, tends to deploy a jr.-high-filmstrip SCIENCE: POINTING THE WAY TO A BRIGHTER TOMORROW—type tone:

> [T]he words "rule" and "grammar" have very different meanings to a scientist and a layperson. The rules people learn (or, more likely, fail to learn) in school are called "prescriptive" rules, prescribing how one *ought* to talk. Scientists studying language propose "descriptive" rules, describing how people *do* talk. Prescriptive and descriptive grammar are simply different things.[35]

The point of this version of Descriptivism is to show that the descriptive rules are more fundamental and way more important than the prescriptive rules. The argument goes like this. An English sentence's being *meaningful* is not the same as its being *grammatical*. That is, such clearly ill-formed constructions as "Did you seen the car keys of me?" or "The show was looked by many people" are nevertheless comprehensible; the sentences do, more or less, communicate the information they're trying to get across. Add to this the fact that nobody who isn't damaged in some profound Oliver Sacksish way actually ever makes these sorts of very deep syntactic errors[36] and you get the basic proposition of N. Chomsky's generative linguistics, which is that there exists a Universal Grammar beneath and common to all languages, plus that there is probably an actual part of the human brain that's imprinted with this Universal Grammar the same way birds' brains are imprinted with Fly South and dogs' with Sniff Genitals. There's all kinds of compelling evidence and support for these ideas, not least of which are the advances that linguists and cognitive scientists and AI researchers have been able to make with them, and the theories have a lot of credibility, and they are adduced by the Philosophical

---

35 (If that last line of Pinker's pourparler reminds you of Garner's "Essentially, descriptivists and prescriptivists are approaching different problems," be advised that the similarity is neither coincidence nor plagiarism. One of the many cunning things about *ADMAU*'s preface is that Garner likes to take bits of Descriptivist rhetoric and use them for very different ends.)

36 Pinker puts it this way: "No one, not even a valley girl, has to be told not to say *Apples the eat boy* or *The child seems sleeping* or *Who did you meet John and?* or the vast, vast majority of the millions of trillions of mathematically possible combinations of words."

Descriptivists to show that since the really *important* rules of language are at birth already hardwired into people's neocortex, SWE prescriptions against dangling participles or mixed metaphors are basically the linguistic equivalent of whalebone corsets and short forks for salad. As Steven Pinker puts it, "When a scientist considers all the hightech mental machinery needed to order words into everyday sentences, prescriptive rules are, at best, inconsequential decorations."

This argument is not the barrel of drugged trout that Methodological Descriptivism was, but it's still vulnerable to objections. The first one is easy. Even if it's true that we're all wired with a Universal Grammar, it doesn't follow that *all* prescriptive rules are superfluous. Some of these rules really do seem to serve clarity and precision. The injunction against two-way adverbs ("People who eat this often get sick") is an obvious example, as are rules about other kinds of misplaced modifiers ("There are many reasons why lawyers lie, some better than others") and about relative pronouns' proximity to the nouns they modify ("She's the mother of an infant daughter who works twelve hours a day").

Granted, the Philosophical Descriptivist can question just how absolutely necessary these rules are: it's quite likely that a recipient of clauses like the above could figure out what they mean from the sentences on either side or from the overall context or whatever.[37] A listener can usually figure out what I really mean when I misuse *infer* for *imply* or say *indicate* for *say,* too. But many of these solecisms—or even just clunky redundancies like "The door was rectangular in shape"—require at least a couple extra nanoseconds of cognitive effort, a kind of rapid sift-and-discard process, before the recipient gets it. Extra work. It's debatable just how much extra work, but it seems indisputable that we put *some* extra interpretive burden on the recipient when we fail to honor certain conventions. W/r/t confusing clauses like the above, it simply seems more "considerate" to follow the rules of correct English...just as it's more "considerate" to de-slob your home before entertaining guests or to brush your teeth before picking up a date. Not just more considerate but more *respectful* somehow—both of your listener/reader and of what you're trying to get across. As we sometimes also say about elements of fashion and etiquette, the way you use English "makes a statement" or "sends a message"—even though these statements/messages often have nothing to do with the actual information you're trying to communicate.

---

37 (FYI, there happens to be a whole subdiscipline of linguistics called Pragmatics that essentially studies the way statements' meanings are created by various contexts.)

We've now sort of bled into a more serious rejoinder to Philosophical Descriptivism: from the fact that linguistic communication is not strictly dependent on usage and grammar it does *not* necessarily follow that the traditional rules of usage and grammar are nothing but "inconsequential decorations." Another way to state this objection is that something's being "decorative" does not necessarily make it "inconsequential." Rhetoric-wise, Pinker's flip dismissal is very bad tactics, for it invites precisely the question it's begging: inconsequential *to whom?*

A key point here is that the resemblance between usage rules and certain conventions of etiquette or fashion is closer than the Philosophical Descriptivists know and far more important than they understand. Take, for example, the Descriptivist claim that so-called correct English usages like *brought* rather than *brung* and *felt* rather than *feeled* are arbitrary and restrictive and unfair and are supported only by custom and are (like irregular verbs in general) archaic and incommodious and an all-around pain in the ass. Let us concede for the moment that these claims are 100 percent reasonable. Then let's talk about pants. Trousers, slacks. I suggest to you that having the so-called correct subthoracic clothing for US males be pants instead of skirts is arbitrary (lots of other cultures let men wear skirts), restrictive and unfair (US females get to wear either skirts or pants), based solely on archaic custom (I think it's got to do with certain traditions about gender and leg-position, the same reasons women were supposed to ride sidesaddle and girls' bikes don't have a crossbar), and in certain ways not only incommodious but illogical (skirts are more comfortable than pants;[38] pants ride up; pants are hot; pants can squish the 'nads and reduce fertility; over time pants chafe and erode irregular sections of men's leg-hair and give older men hideous half-denuded legs; etc. etc.). Let us grant—as a thought experiment if nothing else—that these are all sensible and compelling objections to pants as an androsartorial norm. Let us, in fact, in our minds and hearts say yes—*shout* yes—to the skirt, the kilt, the toga, the sarong, the jupe. Let us dream of or even in our spare time work toward an America where nobody lays any arbitrary sumptuary prescriptions on anyone else and we can all go around as comfortable and aerated and unchafed and motile as we want.

And yet the fact remains that in the broad cultural mainstream of millennial America, men do not wear skirts. If you, the reader, are a US male, and even if you share my personal objections to pants and dream as I do of a cool and genitally unsquishy American Tomorrow, the odds are still 99.9

---

38 (presumably)

percent that in 100 percent of public situations you wear pants/slacks/ shorts/trunks. More to the point, if you are a US male and also have a US male child, and if that child might happen to come to you one evening and announce his desire/intention to wear a skirt rather than pants to school the next day, I am 100 percent confident that you are going to discourage him from doing so. *Strongly* discourage him. You could be a Molotov-tossing anti-pants radical or a kilt manufacturer or Dr. Steven Pinker himself—you're going to stand over your kid and be prescriptive about an arbitrary, archaic, uncomfortable, and inconsequentially decorative piece of clothing. Why? Well, because in modern America any little boy who comes to school in a skirt (even, say, a modest all-season midi) is going to get stared at and shunned and beaten up and called a total geekoid by a whole lot of people whose approval and acceptance are important to him.[39] In our present culture, in other words, a boy who wears a skirt is "making a statement" that is going to have all kinds of gruesome social and emotional consequences for him.

You can probably see where this is headed. I'm going to describe the intended point of the pants analogy in terms that I'm sure are simplistic—doubtless there are whole books in Pragmatics or psycholinguistics or something devoted to unpacking this point. The weird thing is that I've seen neither Descriptivists nor SNOOTs deploy it in the Wars.[40, 41]

When I say or write something, there are actually a whole lot of different things I am communicating. The propositional content (i.e., the verbal information I'm trying to convey) is only one part of it. Another part is stuff about me, the communicator. Everyone knows this. It's a function of the fact that there are so many different well-formed ways to say the same basic thing, from e.g. "I was attacked by a bear!" to "Goddamn bear tried

---

39 In the case of little Steve Pinker Jr., these people are the boy's peers and teachers and crossing guards. In the case of adult cross-dressers and drag queens who have jobs in the straight world and wear pants to those jobs, it's bosses and coworkers and customers and people on the subway. For the die-hard slob who nevertheless wears a coat and tie to work, it's mostly his boss, who doesn't want his employees' clothes to send clients "the wrong message." But it's all basically the same thing.

40 Even Garner scarcely mentions it, and just once in his dictionary's miniessay on CLASS DISTINCTIONS: "[M]any linguistic pratfalls can be seen as class indicators—even in a so-called classless society such as the United States." And when Bryan A. Garner uses a clunky passive like "can be seen" as to distance himself from an issue, you know something's in the air.·

41 In fact, pretty much the only time one ever hears the issue made wholly explicit is in radio ads for tapes that promise to improve people's vocabularies. These ads tend to be extremely ominous and intimidating and always start out with "DID YOU KNOW PEOPLE JUDGE YOU BY THE WORDS YOU USE?"

to kill me!" to "That ursine juggernaut did essay to sup upon my person!" and so on. Add the Saussurian/Chomskian consideration that many grammatically ill-formed sentences can also get the propositional content across—"Bear attack Tonto, Tonto heap scared!"—and the number of subliminal options we're scanning/sorting/interpreting as we communicate with one another goes transfinite very quickly. And different levels of diction and formality are only the simplest kinds of distinction; things get way more complicated in the sorts of interpersonal communication where social relations and feelings and moods come into play. Here's a familiar kind of example. Suppose that you and I are acquaintances and we're in my apartment having a conversation and that at some point I want to terminate the conversation and not have you be in my apartment anymore. Very delicate social moment. Think of all the different ways I can try to handle it: "Wow, look at the time"; "Could we finish this up later?"; "Could you please leave now?"; "Go"; "Get out"; "Get the hell out of here"; "Didn't you say you had to be someplace?"; "Time for you to hit the dusty trail, my friend"; "Off you go then, love"; or that sly old telephone-conversation-ender: "Well, I'm going to let you go now"; etc. etc." And then think of all the different factors and implications of each option.[42]

The point here is obvious. It concerns a phenomenon that SNOOTs blindly reinforce and that Descriptivists badly underestimate and that scary vocab-tape ads try to exploit. People really do judge one another according to their use of language. Constantly. Of course, people are constantly judging one another on the basis of all kinds of things—height, weight, scent, physiognomy, accent, occupation, make of vehicle[43]—and, again, doubtless it's all terribly complicated and occupies whole battalions of sociolinguists. But it's clear that at least one component of all this interpersonal semantic judging involves *acceptance,* meaning not some touchy-

---

42 To be honest, the example here has a special personal resonance for this reviewer because in real life I always seem to have a hard time winding up a conversation or asking somebody to leave, and sometimes the moment becomes so delicate and fraught with social complexity that I'll get overwhelmed trying to sort out all the different possible ways of saying it and all the different implications of each option and will just sort of blank out and do it totally straight—"I want to terminate the conversation and not have you be in my apartment anymore"—which evidently makes me look either as if I'm very rude and abrupt or as if I'm semi-autistic and have no sense of how to wind up a conversation gracefully. Somehow, in other words, my reducing the statement to its bare propositional content "sends a message" that is itself scanned, sifted, interpreted, and judged by my auditor, who then sometimes never comes back. I've actually lost friends this way.

43 (...not to mention color, gender, ethnicity—you can see how fraught and charged all this is going to get)

feely emotional affirmation but actual acceptance or rejection of someone's bid to be regarded as a peer, a member of somebody else's collective or community or Group. Another way to come at this is to acknowledge something that in the Usage Wars gets mentioned only in very abstract terms: "correct" English usage is, as a practical matter, a function of whom you're talking to and of how you want that person to respond—not just to your utterance but also to *you*. In other words, a large part of the project of any communication is rhetorical and depends on what some rhet-scholars call "Audience" or "Discourse Community."[44] It is the present existence in the United States of an enormous number of different Discourse Communities, plus the fact that both people's use of English and their interpretations of others' use are influenced by rhetorical assumptions, that are central to understanding why the Usage Wars are so politically charged and to appreciating why Bryan Garner's *ADMAU* is so totally sneaky and brilliant and modern.

Fact: There are all sorts of cultural/geographical dialects of American English—Black English, Latino English, Rural Southern, Urban Southern, Standard Upper-Midwest, Maine Yankee, East-Texas Bayou, Boston Blue-Collar, on and on. Everybody knows this. What not everyone knows—especially not certain Prescriptivists—is that many of these non-SWE-type dialects have their own highly developed and internally consistent grammars, and that some of these dialects' usage norms actually make more linguistic/aesthetic sense than do their Standard counterparts.* Plus, of course, there are also innumerable sub- and subsubdialects[45] based on all sorts of things that have nothing to do with locale or ethnicity—Medical-School English, Twelve-Year-Old-Males-Whose-Worldview-Is-Deeply-Informed-by-*South-Park* English—that are nearly

---

44 *Discourse Community* is a rare example of academic jargon that's actually a valuable addition to SWE because it captures something at once very complex and very specific that no other English term quite can.*

*(The above, while true, is an obvious attempt to preempt readerly sneers/winces at the term's continued deployment in this article.)

45 Just how tiny and restricted a subdialect can get and still be called a subdialect isn't clear; there might be very firm linguistic definitions of what's a dialect and what's a subdialect and what's a subsub-, etc. Because I don't know any better and am betting you don't either, I'm going to use *subdialect* in a loose inclusive way that covers idiolects as distinctive as Peorians-Who-Follow-Pro-Wrestling-Closely or Geneticists-Who-Specialize-in-Hardy-Weinberg-Equilibrium. *Dialect* should probably be reserved for major players like Standard Black English et al.

incomprehensible to anyone who isn't inside their very tight and specific Discourse Community (which of course is part of their function[46]).

*INTERPOLATION
POTENTIALLY DESCRIPTIVIST-LOOKING EXAMPLE
OF SOME GRAMMATICAL ADVANTAGES OF A
NON-STANDARD DIALECT THAT THIS REVIEWER
ACTUALLY KNOWS ABOUT FIRSTHAND

I happen to have two native English dialects—the SWE of my hyper-educated parents and the hard-earned Rural Midwestern of most of my peers. When I'm talking to RMs, I tend to use constructions like "Where's it at?" for "Where is it?" and sometimes "He don't" instead of "He doesn't." Part of this is a naked desire to fit in and not get rejected as an egghead or fag (see *sub*). But another part is that I, SNOOT or no, believe that these RMisms are in certain ways superior to their Standard equivalents.

For a dogmatic Prescriptivist, "Where's it at?" is double-damned as a sentence that not only ends with a preposition but whose final preposition forms a redundancy with *where* that's similar to the redundancy in "the reason is because" (which latter usage I'll admit makes me dig my nails into my palms). Rejoinder: First off, the avoid-terminal-prepositions rule is the invention of one Fr. R. Lowth, an 18th-century British preacher and indurate pedant who did things like spend scores of pages arguing for *hath* over the trendy and degenerate *has*. The a.-t.-p. rule is antiquated and stupid and only the most ayotolloid SNOOT takes it seriously. Garner himself calls the rule "stuffy" and lists all kinds of useful constructions like "a person I have great respect for" and "the man I was listening to" that we'd have to discard or distort if we really enforced it.

Plus, the apparent redundancy of "Where's it at?"[47] is offset by its metrical logic: what the *at* really does is license the contraction of *is*

---

46 (Plus it's true that whether something gets called a "subdialect" or "jargon" seems to depend on how much it annoys people outside its Discourse Community. Garner himself has miniessays on AIRPLANESE, COMPUTERESE, LEGALESE, and BUREAUCRATESE, and he more or less calls all of them jargon. There is no *ADMAU* miniessay on DIALECTS, but there is one on JARGON, in which such is Garner's self-restraint that you can almost hear his tendons straining, as in "[Jargon] arises from the urge to save time and space—and occasionally to conceal meaning from the uninitiated.")

47 (a redundancy that's a bit arbitrary, since "Where's it *from?*" isn't redundant [mainly because *whence* has receded into semi-archaism])

after the interrogative adverb. You can't say "Where's it?" So the choice is between "Where is it?" and "Where's it at?", and the latter, a strong anapest, is prettier and trips off the tongue better than "Where is it?", whose meter is either a clunky monosyllabic-foot + trochee or it's nothing at all.

Using "He don't" makes me a little more uncomfortable; I admit that its logic isn't quite as compelling. Nevertheless, a clear trend in the evolution of English from Middle to Modern has been the gradual regularizing of irregular present-tense verbs,[48] a trend justified by the fact that irregulars are hard to learn and to keep straight and have nothing but history going for them. By this reasoning, Standard Black English is way out on the cutting edge of English with its abandonment of the 3-S present in *to do* and *to go* and *to say* and its marvelously streamlined six identical present-tense inflections of *to be*. (Granted, the conjugation "he be" always sounds odd to me, but then SBE is not one of my dialects.)

This is probably the place for your SNOOT reviewer openly to concede that a certain number of traditional prescriptive rules really are stupid and that people who insist on them (like the legendary assistant to Margaret Thatcher who refused to read any memo with a split infinitive in it, or the jr.-high teacher I had who automatically graded you down if you started a sentence with *Hopefully*) are that very most contemptible and dangerous kind of SNOOT, the SNOOT Who Is Wrong. The injunction against split infinitives, for instance, is a consequence of the weird fact that English grammar is modeled on Latin even though Latin is a synthetic language and English is an analytic language.[49] Latin infinitives consist of one word and are impossible to as it were split, and the earliest English Prescriptivists — so enthralled with Latin that their English usage guides were actually *written* in Latin[50] — decided that English infinitives shouldn't be split either. Garner himself takes out after the s.i. rule in his miniessays on both SPLIT INFINITIVES and SUPERSTI-

---

48 E.g., for a long time English had a special 2-S present conjugation—"thou lovest," "thou sayest"—that now survives only in certain past tenses (and in the present of *to be*, where it consists simply in giving the 2-S a plural inflection).

49 A synthetic language uses grammatical inflections to dictate syntax, whereas an analytic languages uses word order. Latin, German, and Russian are synthetic; English and Chinese are analytic.

50 (Q.v. for example Sir Thomas Smith's cortex-withering *De Recta et Emendata Linguae Anglicae Scriptione Dialogus* of 1568.)

TIONS.[51]And *Hopefully* at the beginning of a sentence, as a certain cheeky eighth-grader once (to his everlasting social cost) pointed out in class, actually functions not as a misplaced modal auxiliary or as a manner adverb like *quickly* or *angrily* but as a sentence adverb (i.e., as a special kind of "veiled reflexive" that indicates the speaker's attitude about the state of affairs described by the rest of the sentence—examples of perfectly OK sentence adverbs are *clearly, basically, luckily*), and only SNOOTs educated in the high-pedantic years 1940–1960 blindly proscribe it or grade it down.

The cases of split infinitives and *Hopefully* are in fact often trotted out by dogmatic Descriptivists as evidence that all SWE usage rules are arbitrary and dumb (which is a bit like pointing to Pat Buchanan as evidence that all Republicans are maniacs). FYI, Garner rejects *Hopefully*'s knee-jerk proscription, too, albeit grudgingly, saying "the battle is lost" and including the adverb in his miniessay on SKUNKED TERMS, which is his phrase for a usage that is "hotly disputed...any use of it is likely to distract some readers." (Garner also points out something I'd never quite realized, which is that *hopefully*, if misplaced/mispunctuated in the body of a sentence, can create some of the same two-way ambiguities as other adverbs, as in e.g. "I will borrow your book and hopefully read it soon.")

Whether we're conscious of it or not, most of us are fluent in more than one major English dialect and in several subdialects and are probably at least passable in countless others. Which dialect you choose to use depends, of course, on whom you're addressing. More to the point, I submit that the dialect you use depends mostly on what sort of Group your listener is part of and on whether you wish to present yourself as a fellow member of that Group. An obvious example is that traditional upper-class English has certain dialectal differences from lower-class English and that schools used to have courses in elocution whose whole *raison* was to teach

---

51 N.B., though, that he's sane about it. Some split infinitives really are clunky and hard to parse, especially when there are a lot of words between *to* and the verb ("We will attempt to swiftly and to the best of our ability respond to these charges"), which Garner calls "wide splits" and sensibly discourages. His overall verdict on split infinitives—which is that some are "perfectly proper" and some iffy and some just totally bad news, and that no one wide tidy dogmatic ukase can handle all s.i. cases, and thus that "knowing when to split an infinitive requires a good ear and a keen eye"—is a fine example of the way Garner distinguishes sound and helpful Descriptivist objections from wacko or dogmatic objections and then incorporates the sound objections into a smarter and more flexible Prescriptivism.

people how to speak in an upper-class way. But usage-as-inclusion is about much more than class. Try another sort of thought experiment: A bunch of US teenagers in clothes that look several sizes too large for them are sitting together in the local mall's food court, and imagine that a 53-year-old man with jowls, a comb-over, and clothes that fit perfectly comes over to them and says he was scoping them and thinks they're totally rad and/or phat and asks is it cool if he just kicks it and chills with them here at their table. The kids' reaction is going to be either scorn or embarrassment for the guy—most likely a mix of both. Q: Why? Or imagine that two hard-core young urban black guys are standing there talking and I, who am resoundingly and in all ways white, come up and greet them with "Yo" and address one or both as "Brother" and ask "s'up, s'goin' on," pronouncing *on* with that NYCish ōō-ŏ diphthong that Young Urban Black English deploys for a standard o. Either these guys are going to think that I am mocking them and be offended or they are going to think I am simply out of my mind. No other reaction is remotely foreseeable. Q: Why?

Why: A dialect of English is learned and used either because it's your native vernacular or because it's the dialect of a Group by which you wish (with some degree of plausibility) to be accepted. And although it is a major and vitally important one, SWE is only one dialect. And it is never, or at least hardly ever,[52] anybody's only dialect. This is because there are—as you and I both know and yet no one in the Usage Wars ever seems to mention—situations in which faultlessly correct SWE is *not* the appropriate dialect.

Childhood is full of such situations. This is one reason why SNOOT-lets tend to have such a hard social time of it in school. A SNOOTlet is a little kid who's wildly, precociously fluent in SWE (he is often, recall, the offspring of SNOOTs). Just about every class has a SNOOTlet, so I know you've seen them—these are the sorts of six-to-twelve-year-olds who use *whom* correctly and whose response to striking out in T-ball is to shout "How incalculably dreadful!" The elementary-school SNOOTlet is one of the earliest identifiable species of academic geekoid and is duly despised by his peers and praised by his teachers. These teachers usually don't see the incredible amounts of punishment the SNOOTlet is receiving from his classmates, or if they do see it they blame the classmates and shake their heads sadly at the vicious and arbitrary cruelty of which children are capable.

---

52 (It is, admittedly, difficult to imagine William F. Buckley using or perhaps even being aware of anything besides SWE.)

Teachers who do this are dumb. The truth is that his peers' punishment of the SNOOTlet is not arbitrary at all. There are important things at stake. Little kids in school are learning about Group-inclusion and -exclusion and about the respective rewards and penalties of same and about the use of dialect and syntax and slang as signals of affinity and inclusion. They're learning about Discourse Communities. Little kids learn this stuff not in Language Arts or Social Studies but on the playground and the bus and at lunch. When his peers are ostracizing the SNOOTlet or giving him monstrous quadruple Wedgies or holding him down and taking turns spitting on him, there's serious learning going on. Everybody here is learning except the little SNOOT[53]—in fact, what the SNOOTlet is being punished for is precisely his *failure* to learn. And his Language Arts teacher—whose own Elementary Education training prizes "linguistic facility" as one of the "social skills" that ensure children's "developmen-

---

53   AMATEUR DEVELOPMENTAL-SOCIOLINGUISTIC INTERPOLATION #1

The SNOOTlet is, as it happens, an indispensable part of the other children's playground education. School and peers are kids' first socialization outside the family. In learning about Groups and Group tectonics, the kids are naturally learning that a Group's identity depends as much on exclusion as inclusion. They are, in other words, starting to learn about Us and Them, and about how an Us always needs a Them because being not-Them is essential to being Us. Because they're little children and it's school, the obvious Them is the teachers and all the values and appurtenances of the teacher-world.* This teacher-Them helps the kids see how to start to be an Us, but the SNOOTlet completes the puzzle by providing a kind of missing link: he is the traitor, the Us who is in fact not Us but *Them*. The SNOOTlet, who at first appears to be one of Us because like Us he's three feet tall and runny-nosed and eats paste, nevertheless speaks an erudite SWE that signals membership not in Us but in Them, which since Us is defined as not-Them is equivalent to a rejection of Us that is also a *betrayal* of Us precisely because the SNOOTlet is a kid, i.e., one of Us.

Point: The SNOOTlet is teaching his peers that the criteria for membership in Us are not just age, height, paste-ingestion, etc., that in fact Us is primarily a state of mind and a set of sensibilities. An ideology. The SNOOTlet is also teaching the kids that Us has to be *extremely vigilant* about persons who may at first appear to be Us but are in truth *not* Us and may need to be identified and excluded *at a moment's notice*. The SNOOTlet is not the only type of child who can serve as traitor: the Teacher's Pet, the Tattletale, the Brown-Noser, and the Mama's Boy can also do nicely...just as the Damaged and Deformed and Fat and Generally Troubled children all help the nascent mainstream Us-Groups refine the criteria for in- and exclusion.

In these crude and fluid formations of ideological Groupthink lies American kids' real socialization. We all learn early that community and Discourse Community are the same thing, and a fearsome thing indeed. It helps to know where We come from.

*(Plus, because the teacher-Them are tall humorless punishers/rewarders, they come to stand for all adults and—in a shadowy, inchoate way—for the Parents, whose gradual shift from composing Us to defining Them is probably the biggest ideological adjustment of childhood.)

tally appropriate peer rapport,"[54] but who does not or cannot consider the possibility that linguistic facility might involve more than lapidary SWE—is unable to see that her beloved SNOOTlet is actually *deficient* in Language Arts. He has only one dialect. He cannot alter his vocabulary, usage, or grammar, cannot use slang or vulgarity; and it's these abilities that are really required for "peer rapport," which is just a fancy academic term for being accepted by the second-most-important Group in the little kid's life.[55] If he is sufficiently in thrall to his teachers and those teachers are sufficiently clueless, it may take years and unbelievable amounts of punishment before the SNOOTlet learns that you need more than one dialect to get along in school.

This reviewer acknowledges that there seems to be some, umm, personal stuff getting dredged up and worked out here;[56] but the stuff is germane. The point is that the little A+ SNOOTlet is actually in the same dialectal position as the class's "slow" kid who can't learn to stop using *ain't* or *bringed*. Exactly the same position. One is punished in class, the other on the playground, but both are deficient in the same linguistic skill—viz., the ability to move between various dialects and levels of "correctness," the ability to communicate one way with peers and another way with teachers and another with family and another with T-ball coaches and so on. Most of these dialectal adjustments are made below the level of conscious awareness, and our ability to make them seems part psychological and part something else—perhaps something hardwired into the same motherboard as Universal Grammar—and in truth this ability is a much better indicator of a kid's raw "verbal IQ" than test scores or grades, since US English classes do far more to retard dialectal talent than to cultivate it.

---

54 (Elementary Ed professors really do talk this way.)

55   AMATEUR DEVELOPMENTAL-SOCIOLINGUISTIC INTERPOLATION #2

And by the time the SNOOTlet hits adolescence it'll have supplanted the family to become the *most* important Group. And it will be a Group that depends for its definition on a rejection of traditional Authority.* And because it is the recognized dialect of mainstream adult society, there is no better symbol of traditional Authority than SWE. It is not an accident that adolescence is the time when slang and code and subdialects of subdialects explode all over the place and parents begin to complain that they can hardly even understand their kids' language. Nor are lyrics like "I can't get no / Satisfaction" an accident or any kind of sad commentary on the British educational system. Jagger et al. aren't stupid; they're rhetoricians, and they know their audience.

*(That is, the teacher-/parent-Them becomes the Establishment, Society—Them becomes THEM.)

56 (The skirt-in-school scenario was not personal stuff, though, FYI.)

EXAMPLE OF HOW CONCEPTS OF RHETORIC AND DIALECT AND GROUP-INCLUSION CAN HELP MAKE SENSE OF SOME OF THE USAGE WARS' CONSTITUENT BATTLES

Well-known fact: In neither K–12 nor college English are systematic SWE grammar and usage much taught anymore. It's been this way for more than 20 years, and the phenomenon drives Prescriptivists nuts; it's one of the big things they cite as evidence of America's gradual murder of English. Descriptivists and English-Ed specialists counter that grammar and usage have been abandoned because scientific research has proved that studying SWE conventions doesn't help make kids better writers.[57] Each side in the debate tends to regard the other as mentally ill or/and blinded by ideology. Neither camp appears ever to have considered whether maybe the *way* prescriptive SWE was traditionally taught had something to do with its inutility.

By *"way"* here I'm referring not so much to actual method as to spirit or attitude. Most traditional teachers of English grammar have, of course, been dogmatic SNOOTs, and like most dogmatists they've been extremely stupid about the rhetoric they used and the audience they were addressing. I refer specifically to these teachers'[58] assumption that SWE is the sole appropriate English dialect and that the only reasons anyone could fail to see this are ignorance or amentia or grave deficiencies in character. As rhetoric, this sort of attitude works only in sermons to the choir, and as pedagogy it's disastrous, and in terms of teaching writing it's especially bad because it commits precisely the error that most Freshman Composition classes spend all semester trying to keep kids from making—the error of *presuming* the very audience-agreement that it is really their rhetorical job to *earn*.[59] The reality is that an average US student is going to

---

57 There is a respectable body of English-Ed research to back up this claim, the best known being the Harris, Bateman-Zidonis, and Mellon studies of the 1960s.

58 There are still some of them around, at least here in the Midwest. You know the type: lipless, tweedy, cancrine—old maids of both genders. If you ever had one (as I did, 1976–77), you surely remember him.

59   INTERPOLATIVE BUT RELEVANT, IF ONLY BECAUSE THE ERROR HERE
        IS ONE THAT GARNER'S *ADMAU* MANAGES NEVER ONCE TO MAKE
This kind of mistake results more from a habit of mind than from any particular false premise—it is a function not of fallacy or ignorance but of self-absorption. It also happens to be the most persistent and damaging error that most college writers make, and one so deeply rooted that it often takes several essays and conferences and revisions to get them to even see what the problem is. Helping them eliminate the error involves drumming into student writers two big injunctions: (1) Do not presume that the reader can

take the trouble to master the difficult conventions of SWE only if he sees SWE's relevant Group or Discourse Community as one he'd like to be part of. And in the absence of any sort of argument for why the correct-SWE Group is a good or desirable one (an argument that, recall, the traditional teacher hasn't given, because he's such a dogmatic SNOOT he sees no need to), the student is going to be reduced to evaluating the desirability of the SWE Group based on the one obvious member of that Group he's encountered, namely the SNOOTy teacher himself. And what right-thinking average kid would want to be part of a Group represented by so smug, narrow, self-righteous, condescending, utterly uncool a personage as the traditional Prescriptivist teacher?

I'm not trying to suggest here that an effective SWE pedagogy would require teachers to wear sunglasses and call students Dude. What I am suggesting is that the rhetorical situation of a US English class—a class composed wholly of young people whose Group identity is rooted in defiance of Adult Establishment values, plus also composed partly of minorities whose primary dialects are different from SWE—requires the teacher to come up with overt, honest, and compelling arguments for why SWE is a dialect worth learning.

These arguments are hard to make. Hard not intellectually but emotionally, politically. Because they are baldly elitist.[60] The real truth, of course, is that SWE is the dialect of the American elite. That it was invented, codified, and promulgated by Privileged WASP Males and is perpetuated as "Standard" by same. That it is the shibboleth of the Estab-

---

read your mind—anything that you want the reader to visualize or consider or conclude, you must provide; (2) Do not presume that the reader feels the same way that you do about a given experience or issue—your argument cannot just assume as true the very things you're trying to argue for.

Because (1) and (2) seem so simple and obvious, it may surprise you to know that they are actually *incredibly hard* to get students to understand in such a way that the principles inform their writing. The reason for the difficulty is that, in the abstract, (1) and (2) are intellectual, whereas in practice they are more things of the spirit. The injunctions require of the student both the imagination to conceive of the reader as a separate human being and the empathy to realize that this separate person has preferences and confusions and beliefs of her own, p/c/b's that are just as deserving of respectful consideration as the writer's. More, (1) and (2) require of students the humility to distinguish between a universal truth ("This is the way things are, and only an idiot would disagree") and something that the writer merely opines ("My reasons for recommending this are as follows:"). These sorts of requirements are, of course, also the elements of a Democratic Spirit. I therefore submit that the hoary cliché "Teaching the student to write is teaching the student to think" sells the enterprise way short. Thinking isn't even half of it.

60 (Or rather the arguments require us openly to acknowledge and talk about elitism, whereas a traditional dogmatic SNOOT's pedagogy is merely elitism in action.)

lishment, and that it is an instrument of political power and class division and racial discrimination and all manner of social inequity. These are shall we say rather *delicate* subjects to bring up in an English class, especially in the service of a pro-SWE argument, and *extra*-especially if you yourself are both a Privileged WASP Male and the teacher and thus pretty much a walking symbol of the Adult Establishment. This reviewer's opinion, though, is that both students and SWE are way better served if the teacher makes his premises explicit and his argument overt—plus it obviously helps his rhetorical credibility if the teacher presents himself as an advocate of SWE's utility rather than as some sort of prophet of its innate superiority.

Because the argument for SWE is both most delicate and (I believe) most important with respect to students of color, here is a condensed version of the spiel I've given in private conferences[61] with certain black students who were (a) bright and inquisitive as hell and (b) deficient in what US higher education considers written English facility:

> I don't know whether anybody's told you this or not, but when you're in a college English class you're basically studying a foreign dialect. This dialect is called Standard Written English. [Brief overview of major US dialects à la page 882.] From talking with you and reading your first couple essays, I've concluded that your own primary dialect is [one of three variants of SBE common to our region]. Now, let me spell something out in my official teacher-voice: the SBE you're fluent in is different from SWE in all kinds of important ways. Some of these differences are grammatical—for example, double negatives are OK in Standard Black English but not in SWE, and SBE and SWE conjugate certain verbs in totally different ways. Other differences have more to do with style—for instance, Standard Written English tends to use a lot more subordinate clauses in the early parts of sentences, and it sets off most of these early subordinates with commas, and under SWE rules, writing that doesn't do this tends to look "choppy." There are tons of differences like that. How much of this stuff do you already know? [STANDARD RESPONSE = some variation on "I know from the grades and comments on my papers that the English profs here don't think I'm a good writer."] Well, I've got good news and bad news. There are some otherwise smart English profs who aren't very aware that there are real dialects of English

---

61 (I'm not a total idiot.)

other than SWE, so when they're marking up your papers they'll put, like, "Incorrect conjugation" or "Comma needed" instead of "SWE conjugates this verb differently" or "SWE calls for a comma here." That's the good news—it's not that you're a bad writer, it's that you haven't learned the special rules of the dialect they want you to write in. Maybe that's not such good news, that they've been grading you down for mistakes in a foreign language you didn't even know was a foreign language. That they won't let you write in SBE. Maybe it seems unfair. If it does, you're probably not going to like this other news: I'm not going to let you write in SBE either. In my class, you have to learn and write in SWE. If you want to study your own primary dialect and its rules and history and how it's different from SWE, fine—there are some great books by scholars of Black English, and I'll help you find some and talk about them with you if you want. But that will be outside class. In class—in my English class—you will have to master and write in Standard Written English, which we might just as well call "Standard White English" because it was developed by white people and is used by white people, especially educated, powerful white people. [RESPONSES at this point vary too widely to standardize.] I'm respecting you enough here to give you what I believe is the straight truth. In this country, SWE is perceived as the dialect of education and intelligence and power and prestige, and anybody of any race, ethnicity, religion, or gender who wants to succeed in American culture has got to be able to use SWE. This is just How It Is. You can be glad about it or sad about it or deeply pissed off. You can believe it's racist and unfair and decide right here and now to spend every waking minute of your adult life arguing against it, and maybe you should, but I'll tell you something—if you ever want those arguments to get listened to and taken seriously, you're going to have to communicate them in SWE, because SWE is the dialect our nation uses to talk to itself. African-Americans who've become successful and important in US culture know this; that's why King's and X's and Jackson's speeches are in SWE, and why Morrison's and Angelou's and Baldwin's and Wideman's and Gates's and West's books are full of totally ass-kicking SWE, and why black judges and politicians and journalists and doctors and teachers communicate professionally in SWE. Some of these people grew up in homes and communities where SWE was the native dialect, and these black people had it much easier in school, but the ones who didn't grow up with SWE realized at some point that they had to learn it and become able to write fluently in it, and so they did. And [STUDENT'S NAME], you're going to learn to use it, too, because I am going to make you.

I should note here that a couple of the students I've said this stuff to were offended—one lodged an Official Complaint—and that I have had more than one colleague profess to find my spiel "racially insensitive." Perhaps you do, too. This reviewer's own humble opinion is that some of the cultural and political realities of American life are themselves racially insensitive and elitist and offensive and unfair, and that pussyfooting around these realities with euphemistic doublespeak is not only hypocritical but toxic to the project of ever really changing them.

ANOTHER KIND OF USAGE WARS–RELATED EXAMPLE, THIS ONE WITH A PARTICULAR EMPHASIS ON DIALECT AS A VECTOR OF SELF-PRESENTATION VIA POLITENESS[62]

Traditionally, Prescriptivists tend to be political conservatives and Descriptivists tend to be liberals. But today's most powerful influence on the norms of public English is actually a stern and exacting form of liberal Prescriptivism. I refer here to Politically Correct English (PCE), under whose conventions failing students become "high-potential" students and poor people "economically disadvantaged" and people in wheelchairs "differently abled" and a sentence like "White English and Black English are different, and you better learn White English or you're not going to get good grades" is not blunt but "insensitive." Although it's common to make jokes about PCE (referring to ugly people as "aesthetically challenged" and so on), be advised that Politically Correct English's various pre- and proscriptions are taken very seriously *indeed* by colleges and corporations

---

62   ESPECIALLY GOOD EPIGRAPHS FOR THIS SECTION
"Passive voice verbs, in particular, may deny female agency."

—DR. MARILYN SCHWARTZ AND THE TASK FORCE ON
BIAS-FREE LANGUAGE OF THE ASSOCIATION OF
AMERICAN UNIVERSITY PRESSES

"He raised his voice suddenly, and shouted for dinner. Servants shouted back that it was ready. They meant that they wished it was ready, and were so understood, for nobody moved."

—E. M. FORSTER

and government agencies, whose institutional dialects now evolve under the beady scrutiny of a whole new kind of Language Police.

From one perspective, the rise of PCE evinces a kind of Lenin-to-Stalinesque irony. That is, the same ideological principles that informed the original Descriptivist revolution—namely, the rejections of traditional authority (born of Vietnam) and of traditional inequality (born of the civil rights movement)—have now actually produced a far more inflexible Prescriptivism, one largely unencumbered by tradition or complexity and backed by the threat of real-world sanctions (termination, litigation) for those who fail to conform. This is funny in a dark way, maybe, and it's true that most criticisms of PCE seem to consist in making fun of its trendiness or vapidity. This reviewer's own opinion is that prescriptive PCE is not just silly but ideologically confused and harmful to its own cause.

Here is my argument for that opinion. Usage is always political, but it's complexly political. With respect, for instance, to political change, usage conventions can function in two ways: on the one hand they can be a *reflection* of political change, and on the other they can be an *instrument* of political change. What's important is that these two functions are different and have to be kept straight. Confusing them—in particular, mistaking for political efficacy what is really just a language's political symbolism—enables the bizarre conviction that America ceases to be elitist or unfair simply because Americans stop using certain vocabulary that is historically associated with elitism and unfairness. This is PCE's core fallacy—that a society's mode of expression is productive of its attitudes rather than a product of those attitudes[63]—and of course it's nothing but the obverse of the politically conservative SNOOT's delusion that social change can be retarded by restricting change in standard usage.[64]

Forget Stalinization or Logic 101–level equivocations, though. There's a grosser irony about Politically Correct English. This is that PCE purports to be the dialect of progressive reform but is in fact—in its Orwellian substitution of the euphemisms of social equality for social equality itself—of vastly more help to conservatives and the US status quo than traditional SNOOT prescriptions ever were. Were I, for instance, a political conservative who opposed using taxation as a means of redistributing national wealth, I would be delighted to watch PC progressives spend

---

63 (A pithier way to put this is that *politeness* is not the same as *fairness*.)

64 E.g., this is the reasoning behind Pop Prescriptivists' complaint that shoddy usage signifies the Decline of Western Civilization.

their time and energy arguing over whether a poor person should be described as "low-income" or "economically disadvantaged" or "pre-prosperous" rather than constructing effective public arguments for redistributive legislation or higher marginal tax rates. (Not to mention that strict codes of egalitarian euphemism serve to burke the sorts of painful, unpretty, and sometimes offensive discourse that in a pluralistic democracy lead to actual political change rather than symbolic political change. In other words, PCE acts as a form of censorship, and censorship always serves the status quo.)

As a practical matter, I strongly doubt whether a guy who has four small kids and makes $12,000 a year feels more empowered or less ill-used by a society that carefully refers to him as "economically disadvantaged" rather than "poor." Were I he, in fact, I'd probably find the PCE term insulting—not just because it's patronizing (which it is) but because it's hypocritical and self-serving in a way that oft-patronized people tend to have really good subliminal antennae for. The basic hypocrisy about usages like "economically disadvantaged" and "differently abled" is that PCE advocates believe the beneficiaries of these terms' compassion and generosity to be poor people and people in wheelchairs, which again omits something that everyone knows but nobody except the scary vocabulary-tape ads' announcer ever mentions—that part of any speaker's motive for using a certain vocabulary is always the desire to communicate stuff about himself. Like many forms of Vogue Usage,[65] PCE functions primarily to signal and congratulate certain virtues in the speaker—scrupulous egalitarianism, concern for the dignity of all people, sophistication about the political implications of language—and so serves the self-regarding

---

65 *A Dictionary of Modern American Usage* includes a miniessay on VOGUE WORDS, but it's a disappointing one in which Garner does little more than list VWs that bug him and say that "vogue words have such a grip on the popular mind that they come to be used in contexts in which they serve little purpose." This is one of the rare places in *ADMAU* where Garner is simply wrong. The real problem is that every sentence blends and balances at least two different communicative functions—one the transmission of raw info, the other the transmission of certain stuff about the speaker—and Vogue Usage throws this balance off. Garner's "serve little purpose" is exactly incorrect: vogue words serve *too much* the purpose of presenting the speaker in a certain light (even if this is merely as with-it or hip), and people's odd little subliminal BS-antennae pick this imbalance up, and that's why even nonSNOOTs often find Vogue Usages irritating and creepy. It's the same phenomenon as when somebody goes out of her way to be incredibly solicitous and complimentary and nice to you and after a while you begin to find her solicitude creepy: you are sensing that a disproportionately large part of this person's agenda consists in trying to present herself as Nice.

interests of the PC far more than it serves any of the persons or groups renamed.*†

*INTERPOLATION

The unpleasant truth is that the same self-serving hypocrisy that informs PCE tends to infect and undermine the US Left's rhetoric in almost every debate over social policy. Take the ideological battle over wealth-redistribution via taxes, quotas, Welfare, enterprise zones, AFDC/TANF, you name it. As long as redistribution is conceived as a form of charity or compassion (and the Bleeding Left appears to buy this conception every bit as much as the Heartless Right), then the whole debate centers on utility—"Does Welfare help poor people get on their feet or does it foster passive dependence?" "Is government's bloated social-services bureaucracy an effective way to dispense charity?" and so on—and both camps have their arguments and preferred statistics, and the whole thing goes around and around....

Opinion: The mistake here lies in both sides' assumption that the real motives for redistributing wealth are charitable or unselfish. The conservatives' mistake (if it is a mistake) is wholly conceptual, but for the Left the assumption is also a serious tactical error. Progressive liberals seem incapable of stating the obvious truth: that we who are well off should be willing to share more of what we have with poor people not for the poor people's sake but for our own; i.e., we should share what we have in order to become less narrow and frightened and lonely and self-centered people. No one ever seems willing to acknowledge aloud the thoroughgoing *self-interest* that underlies all impulses toward economic equality—especially not US progressives, who seem so invested in an image of themselves as Uniquely Generous and Compassionate and Not Like Those Selfish Conservatives Over There that they allow the conservatives to frame the debate in terms of charity and utility, terms under which redistribution seems far less obviously a good thing.

I'm talking about this example in such a general, simplistic way because it helps show why the type of leftist vanity that informs PCE is actually inimical to the Left's own causes. For in refusing to abandon the idea of themselves as Uniquely Generous and Compassionate (i.e., as morally superior), progressives lose the chance to frame their redistributive arguments in terms that are both realistic and realpolitikal. One such argument would involve a complex, sophisticated analysis of what we really mean by *self-interest*, particularly the distinctions between short-term financial self-interest and longer-term moral or social self-interest. As it is, though, liberals' vanity tends to grant conservatives a monopoly on appeals to self-interest, enabling the conservatives to depict progressives as pie-in-the-sky idealists and themselves as real-world back-pocket pragmatists. In short, leftists' big mistake here is not conceptual or ideological but spiritual and rhetorical—their narcissistic attachment to assumptions that maximize their own appearance of virtue tends to cost them both the theater and the war.

†INTERPOLATION
EXAMPLE OF A SNOOT-RELATED ISSUE IN THE
FACE OF WHOSE MALIGNANCY THIS REVIEWER'S
DEMOCRATIC SPIRIT GIVES OUT ALTOGETHER,
ADMITTEDLY

This issue is Academic English, a verbal cancer that has metastasized now to afflict both scholarly writing—

> If such a sublime cyborg would insinuate the future as post-Fordist subject, his palpably masochistic locations as ecstatic agent of the sublime superstate need to be decoded as the "now all-but-unreadable DNA" of the fast industrializing Detroit, just as his Robocop-like strategy of carceral negotiation and street control remains the tirelessly American one of inflicting regeneration through violence upon the racially heteroglassic wilds and others of the inner city.[66]

—and prose as mainstream as the *Village Voice*'s—

> At first encounter, the poems' distanced cerebral surfaces can be daunting, evading physical location or straightforward emotional arc. But this seeming remoteness quickly reveals a very real passion, centered in the speaker's struggle to define his evolving self-construction.

---

66 FYI, this snippet, which appears in *ADMAU*'s miniessay on OBSCURITY, is quoted from a 1997 *Sacramento Bee* article entitled "No Contest: English Professors Are Worst Writers on Campus."

Maybe it's a combination of my SNOOTitude and the fact that I end up having to read a lot of it for my job, but I'm afraid I regard Academic English not as a dialectal variation but as a grotesque debasement of SWE, and loathe it even more than the stilted incoherences of Presidential English ("This is the best and only way to uncover, destroy, and prevent Iraq from reengineering weapons of mass destruction") or the mangled pieties of BusinessSpeak ("Our Mission: to proactively search and provide the optimum networking skills and resources to service the needs of your growing business"); and in support of this total contempt and intolerance I cite no less an authority than Mr. G. Orwell, who 50 years ago had AE pegged as a "mixture of vagueness and sheer incompetence" in which "it is normal to come across long passages which are almost completely lacking in meaning."[67]

It probably isn't the whole explanation, but as with the voguish hypocrisy of PCE, the obscurity and pretension of Academic English can be attributed in part to a disruption in the delicate rhetorical balance between language as a vector of meaning and language as a vector of the writer's own résumé. In other words, it is when a scholar's vanity/insecurity leads him to write *primarily* to communicate and reinforce his own status as an Intellectual that his English is deformed by pleonasm and pretentious diction (whose function is to signal the writer's erudition) and by opaque abstraction (whose function is to keep anybody from pinning the writer down to a definite assertion that can maybe be refuted or shown to be silly). The latter characteristic, a level of obscurity that often makes it just about impossible to figure out what an AE sentence is really saying,[68] so closely resembles political and corporate doublespeak ("revenue

---

67 This was in his 1946 "Politics and the English Language," an essay that despite its date (and the basic redundancy of its title) remains the definitive SNOOT statement on Academese. Orwell's famous AE translation of the gorgeous "I saw under the sun that the race is not to the swift" part of Ecclesiastes as "Objective consideration of contemporary phenomena compels the conclusion that success or failure in competitive activities exhibits no tendency to be commensurate with innate capacity, but that a considerable element of the unpredictable must invariably be taken into account" should be tattooed on the left wrist of every grad student in the anglophone world.

68 If you still think assertions like that are just SNOOT hyperbole, see also e.g. Dr. Fredric Jameson, author of *The Geopolitical Aesthetic* and *The Prison-House of Language*, whom *The Johns Hopkins Guide to Literary Theory and Criticism* calls "one of the foremost contemporary Marxist literary critics writing in English." Specifically, have a look at the first sentence of Dr. Jameson's 1992 *Signatures of the Visible*—

enhancement," "downsizing," "proactive resource-allocation restructuring") that it's tempting to think AE's real purpose is concealment and its real motivation fear.[69]

The insecurities that drive PCE, AE, and vocab-tape ads are far from groundless, though. These are tense linguistic times. Blame it on Heisenbergian uncertainty or postmodern relativism or Image Over Substance or the ubiquity of advertising and PR or the rise of Identity Politics or whatever you will—we live in an era of terrible preoccupation with presentation and interpretation, one in which the relations between who someone is and what he believes and how he "expresses himself"[70] have been thrown into big-time flux. In rhetorical terms, certain long-held distinctions between the Ethical Appeal, Logical Appeal (= an argument's plausibility or soundness, from *logos*), and Pathetic Appeal (= an argument's emotional impact, from *pathos*) have now pretty much collapsed—or rather the different sorts of Appeals now affect and are affected by one another in ways that make it nearly impossible to advance an argument on "reason" alone.

A vividly concrete illustration here concerns the Official Complaint that a certain black undergraduate filed against me after one of my little *in camera* spiels described on pages 891–93. The complainant was (I opine)

> The visual is *essentially* pornographic, which is to say that it has its end in rapt, mindless fascination; thinking about its attributes becomes an adjunct to that, if it is unwilling to betray its object; while the most austere films necessarily draw their energy from the attempt to repress their own excess (rather than from the thankless effort to discipline the viewer).

—in which not only is each of its three main independent clauses totally obscure and full of predicates without evident subjects and pronouns without clear antecedents, but whatever connection between those clauses justifies stringing them together into one long semicolonic sentence is anyone's guess at all.

Please be advised (a) that the above sentence won 1997's First Prize in the World's Worst Writing Contest held annually at Canterbury University in New Zealand, a competition in which American academics regularly sweep the field, and (b) that F. Jameson was and is an extremely powerful and influential and oft-cited figure in US literary scholarship, which means (c) that if you have kids in college, there's a good chance that they are being taught how to write by high-paid adults for whom the above sentence is a model of erudite English prose.

69 Even in Freshman Comp, bad student essays are far, far more often the products of fear than of laziness or incompetence. In fact, it often takes so long to identify and help with students' fear that the Freshman Comp teacher never gets to find out whether they might have other problems, too.

70 (Notice the idiom's syntax—it's never "expresses his beliefs" or "expresses his ideas.")

wrong, but she was not crazy or stupid; and I was able later to see that I did bear some responsibility for the whole nasty administrative swivet. My culpability lay in gross rhetorical naïveté. I'd seen my speech's primary Appeal as Logical: the aim was to make a conspicuously blunt, honest argument for SWE's utility. It wasn't pretty, maybe, but it was true, plus so manifestly bullshit-free that I think I expected not just acquiescence but gratitude for my candor.[71] The problem I failed to see, of course, lay not with the argument per se but with the person making it — namely me, a Privileged WASP Male in a position of power, thus someone whose statements about the primacy and utility of the Privileged WASP Male dialect appeared not candid/hortatory/authoritative/true but elitist/high-handed/authoritarian/racist. Rhetoric-wise, what happened was that I allowed the substance and style of my Logical Appeal to completely torpedo my Ethical Appeal: what the student heard was just another PWM rationalizing why his Group and his English were top dog and ought "logically" to stay that way (plus, worse, trying to use his academic power over her to coerce her assent[72]).

If for any reason you happen to find yourself sharing this particular student's perceptions and reaction,[73] I would ask that you bracket your feelings just long enough to recognize that the PWM instructor's very modern rhetorical dilemma in that office was not much different from the dilemma faced by any male who makes a Pro-Life argument, or any atheist who argues against creation science, or any caucasian who opposes Affirmative Action, or any African-American who decries racial profiling, or anyone over eighteen who tries to make a case for raising the legal driving age to eighteen, etc. The dilemma has nothing to do with whether the arguments themselves are plausible or right or even sane, because the debate rarely gets that far — any opponent with sufficiently strong feelings or a dogmatic bent can discredit the argument and pretty much foreclose all further discussion with a rejoinder we Americans have come to know well: "Of course *you'd* say that"; "Easy for *you* to say"; "What right do *you* have to...?"

---

71 (Please just don't even say it.)

72 (The student professed to have been especially traumatized by the climactic "I am going to make you," which was indeed a rhetorical boner.)

73 FYI, the dept. chair and dean did not, at the Complaint hearing, share her reaction...though it would be disingenuous not to tell you that they happened also to be PWMs, which fact was also remarked on by the complainant, such that the whole proceeding got pretty darn tense indeed, before it was over.

Now (still bracketing) consider the situation of any reasonably intelligent and well-meaning SNOOT who sits down to prepare a prescriptive usage guide. It's the millennium, post-everything: whence the authority to make any sort of credible Appeal for SWE at all?

ARTICLE'S CRUX:
WHY BRYAN A. GARNER IS A GENIUS (I)

It isn't that *A Dictionary of Modern American Usage* is perfect. It doesn't seem to cover *conversant in* vs. *conversant with*, for example, or *abstruse* vs. *obtuse*, or to have anything on *hereby* and *herewith* (which I tend to use interchangeably but always have the uneasy feeling I'm screwing up). Garner's got a good discussion of *used to* but nothing on *supposed to*. Nor does he give any examples to help explain irregular participles and transitivity ("The light shone" vs. "I shined the light," etc.), and these would seem to be more important than, say, the correct spelling of *huzzah* or the plural of *animalculum*, both of which get discussed. In other words, a rock-ribbed SNOOT is going to be able to find stuff to kvetch about in any usage dictionary, and *ADMAU* is no exception.

But it's still really, really good. Except for the VOGUE WORDS snafu and the absence of a pronunciation entry on *trough*,[74] the above were pretty much the only quibbles this reviewer could find. *ADMAU* is thorough and timely and solid, as good as Follett's and Gilman's and the handful of other great American usage guides of the century. Their format—which was Fowler's—is *ADMAU*'s, too: concise entries on individual words and phrases and expository cap-titled MINIESSAYS on any issue broad enough to warrant more general discussion. Because of both his Fowler Society and the advent of online databases, though, Garner has access to many more examples of actual published SWE than did Gilman nine years ago, and he uses them to great, if lengthy, effect. But none of this is why Bryan Garner is a genius.

ADMAU is a collection of judgments and so is in no way Descriptivist,

---

74 To be honest, I noticed this omission only because midway through working on this article I happened to use the word *trough* in front of the same SNOOT friend who compares public English to violin-hammering, and he fell sideways out of his chair, and it emerged that I have somehow all my life misheard *trough* as ending with a *th* instead of an *f* and thus have publicly mispronounced it God only knows how many scores of times, and I all but burned rubber getting home to see whether perhaps the error was so common and human and understandable that *ADMAU* had a good-natured entry on it—but no such luck, which in fairness I don't suppose I can really blame Garner for.

but Garner structures his judgments very carefully to avoid the elitism and anality of traditional SNOOTitude. He does not deploy irony or scorn or caustic wit, nor tropes or colloquialisms or contractions…or really any sort of verbal style at all. In fact, even though Garner talks openly about himself and uses the 1-S pronoun throughout the whole dictionary, his personality is oddly effaced, neutralized. It's like he's so bland he's barely there. For instance, as this reviewer was finishing the book's final entry,[75] it struck me that I had no idea whether Bryan A. Garner was black or white, gay or straight, Democrat or Dittohead. What was even more striking was that I hadn't once wondered about any of this up to now; something about Garner's lexical persona kept me from ever asking where the guy was coming from or what particular agendas or ideologies were informing what he had admitted right up front were "value judgments." This seemed very odd indeed. Bland people can have axes to grind, too, so I decided that *bland* probably wasn't the right word to describe Garner's *ADMAU* persona. The right word was probably more like *objective,* but with a little *o,* as in "disinterested," "reasonable." Then something kind of obvious occurred to me, but in an unobvious way—this small-*o* kind of objectivity was very different from the metaphysical, capital *O*–type Objectivity whose postmodern loss had destroyed (I'd pretty much concluded) any possibility of genuine Authority in issues of usage.

Then it occurred to me that if *Objectivity* still had a lowercase sense unaffected by modern relativism, maybe *Authority* did as well. So, just as I'd done w/r/t Garner's use of *judgment,* I went to my trusty conservative *American Heritage Dictionary* and looked up *authority.*

Does any of this make sense? Because this was how I discovered that Bryan Garner is a genius.

WHY BRYAN A. GARNER IS
A GENIUS (II)

Bryan Garner is a genius because *A Dictionary of Modern American Usage* just about completely resolves the Usage Wars' problem of Authority. The book's solution is both semantic and rhetorical. Garner manages to collapse the definitions of certain key terms and to control the compresence of rhetorical Appeals so cleverly that he is able to transcend both Usage Wars camps and simply tell the truth, and to tell the truth in a way that does not torpedo his own credibility but actually enhances it. His argu-

---

75 (on *zwieback* vs. *zweiback*)

mentative strategy is totally brilliant and totally sneaky, and part of both qualities is that it usually doesn't seem like there's even an argument going on at all.

WHY BRYAN A. GARNER IS
A GENIUS (III)

Rhetorically, traditional Prescriptivists depend almost entirely on the Logical Appeal. One reason they are such inviting targets for liberal scorn is their arrogance, and their arrogance is based on their utter disdain for considerations of persona or persuasion. This is not an exaggeration. Doctrinaire Prescriptivists conceive of themselves not as advocates of correct English but as avatars of it. The truth of what they prescribe is itself their "authority" for prescribing it; and because they hold the truth of these prescriptions to be self-evident, they regard those Americans who reject or ignore the prescriptions as "ignoramuses" who are pretty much beneath notice except as evidence for the general deterioration of US culture.

Since the only true audience for it is the Prescriptivists themselves, it really doesn't matter that their argument is almost Euthyphrotically circular—"It's the truth because we say so, and we say so because it's the truth." This is dogmatism of a purity you don't often see in this country, and it's no accident that hard-core Prescriptivists are just a tiny fringe-type element of today's culture. The American Conversation is an argument, after all, and way worse than our fear of error or anarchy or Gomorrahl decadence is our fear of theocracy or autocracy or any ideology whose project is not to argue or persuade but to adjourn the whole debate *sine die*.[76]

The hard-line Descriptivists, for all their calm scientism and avowed preference for fact over value, rely mostly on rhetorical *pathos,* the visceral emotional Appeal. As mentioned, the relevant emotions here are Sixties-ish in origin and leftist in temperament—an antipathy for conventional Authority and elitist put-downs and uptight restrictions and casuistries and androcaucasian bias and snobbery and overt smugness of any sort...i.e., for the very attitudes embodied in the prim glare of the grammarian and the languid honk of Buckley-type elites, which happen to be the two most visible species of SNOOT still around. Whether Methodological or Philosophical or pseudo-progressive, Descriptivists are, all and

---

76 It's this logic (and perhaps this alone) that keeps protofascism or royalism or Maoism or any sort of really dire extremism from achieving mainstream legitimacy in US politics—how does one vote for No More Voting?

essentially, demagogues; and dogmatic Prescriptivists are actually their most valuable asset, since Americans' visceral distaste for dogmatism and elitist fatuity gives Descriptivism a ready audience for its Pathetic Appeal.

What the Descriptivists haven't got is logic. The Dictionary can't sanction everything, and the very possibility of language depends on rules and conventions, and Descriptivism offers no *logos* for determining which rules and conventions are useful and which are pointless/oppressive, nor any arguments for how and by whom such determinations are to be made. In short, the Descriptivists don't have any kind of Appeal that's going to persuade anyone who doesn't already have an EAT THE RICH–type hatred of Authority per se. Homiletically speaking, the only difference between the Prescriptivists and the Descriptivists is that the latter's got a bigger choir.

Mr. Bryan A. Garner recognizes something that neither of these camps appears to get: given 40 years of the Usage Wars, "authority" is no longer something a lexicographer can just presume *ex officio*. In fact, a large part of the project of any contemporary usage dictionary will consist in *establishing* this authority. If that seems rather obvious, be apprised that nobody before Garner seems to have figured it out — that the lexicographer's challenge now is to be not just accurate and comprehensive but *credible*. That in the absence of unquestioned, capital-*A* Authority in language, the reader must now be moved or persuaded to grant a dictionary its authority, freely and for what appear to be good reasons.

Garner's *A Dictionary of Modern American Usage* is thus both a collection of information and a piece of Democratic[77] rhetoric. Its primary Appeal is Ethical, and its goal is to recast the Prescriptivist's persona: the author presents himself not as a cop or a judge but as more like a doctor or lawyer. This is an ingenious tactic. In the same sort of move we can see him make w/r/t *judgment* and *objective*, Garner here alters the relevant *AHD* definitions of *authority* from (1) "The right and power to command, enforce laws, exact obedience, determine, or judge" / "A person or group invested with this power" to (2) "Power to influence or persuade resulting from knowledge or experience" / "An accepted source of expert information or advice." *ADMAU*'s Garner, in other words, casts himself as an authority not in an *autocratic* sense but in a *technocratic* sense. And the technocrat is not only a thoroughly modern and palatable image of authority but also immune to the charges of elitism/classism that have hobbled traditional Prescriptivism. After all, do we call a doctor or lawyer "elitist"

---

77 (meaning *literally* Democratic — it Wants Your Vote)

when he presumes to tell us what we should eat or how we should do our taxes?

Of course, Garner really *is* a technocrat. He's an attorney, recall, and in *ADMAU* he cultivates just the sort of persona good jurists project: knowledgeable, reasonable, dispassionate, fair. His judgments about usage tend to be rendered like legal opinions—exhaustive citation of precedent (other dictionaries' judgments, published examples of actual usage) combined with clear, logical reasoning that's always informed by the larger consensual purposes SWE is meant to serve.

Also technocratic is Garner's approach to the whole issue of whether anybody's even going to be interested in his 700 pages of fine-pointed counsel. Like any mature specialist, he simply assumes that there are good practical reasons why some people choose to concern themselves with his area of expertise; and his attitude about the fact that most Americans "could care less" about SWE usage isn't scorn or disapproval but the phlegmatic resignation of a professional who realizes that he can give good advice but can't make you take it:

> The reality I care about most is that some people still want to use the language well.[78] They want to write effectively; they want to speak effectively. They want their language to be graceful at times and powerful at times. They want to understand how to use words well, how to manipulate sentences, and how to move about in the language without seeming to flail. They want good grammar, but they want more: they want rhetoric[79] in the traditional sense. That is, they want to use the language deftly so that it's fit for their purposes.

It's now possible to see that all the autobiographical stuff in *ADMAU*'s preface does more than just humanize Mr. Bryan A. Garner. It also serves to detail the early and enduring passion that helps make someone a credible technocrat—we tend to like and trust experts whose expertise is born of a real love for their specialty instead of just a desire to be expert at something. In fact, it turns out that *ADMAU*'s preface quietly and steadily

---

78 The last two words of this sentence, of course, are what the Usage Wars are all about—whose "language" and whose "well"? The most remarkable thing about the sentence is that coming from Garner it doesn't sound naive or obnoxious but just...reasonable.

79 (Did you think I was kidding?)

invests Garner with every single qualification of modern technocratic authority: passionate devotion, reason and accountability (recall "in the interests of full disclosure, here are the ten critical points..."), experience ("...that, after years of working on usage problems, I've settled on"), exhaustive and tech-savvy research ("For contemporary usage, the files of our greatest dictionary makers pale in comparison with the full-text search capabilities now provided by NEXIS and WESTLAW"[80]), an even and judicious temperament (see e.g. this from his HYPERCORREC-TION: "Sometimes people strive to abide by the strictest etiquette, but in the process behave inappropriately"[81]), and the sort of humble integrity (for instance, including in one of the entries a past published usage-error of his own) that not only renders Garner likable but transmits the kind of reverence for English that good jurists have for the law, both of which are bigger and more important than any one person.

Probably the most ingenious and attractive thing about his dictionary's Ethical Appeal, though, is Garner's scrupulousness about considering the reader's own hopes and fears and reasons for caring enough about usage to bother with something like *ADMAU* at all. These reasons, as Garner makes clear, tend to derive from a reader's concern about his/her *own* linguistic authority and rhetorical persona and ability to convince an audience that he/she cares. Again and again, Garner frames his prescriptions in rhetorical terms: "To the writer or speaker for whom credibility is important, it's a good idea to avoid distracting *any* readers or listeners"; "Whatever you do, if you use *data* in a context in which its number becomes known, you'll bother some of your readers." *A Dictionary of Modern American Usage*'s real thesis, in other words, is that the purposes of the expert authority and the purposes of the lay reader are identical, and identically rhetorical—which I submit is about as Democratic these days as you're going to get.

---

80 Cunning—what is in effect Garner's blowing his own archival horn is cast as humble gratitude for the resources made available by modern technology. Plus notice also Garner's implication here that he's once again absorbed the sane parts of Descriptivism's cast-a-wide-net method: "Thus, the prescriptive approach here is leavened by a thorough canvassing of actual usage in modern edited prose."

81 (Here, this reviewer's indwelling and ever-vigilant SNOOT can't help but question Garner's deployment of a comma before the conjunction in this sentence, since what follows the conjunction is neither an independent clause nor any sort of plausible complement for "strive to." But respectful disagreement between people of goodwill is of course Democratically natural and healthy and, when you come right down to it, kind of fun.)

BONUS FULL-DISCLOSURE INFO ON THE SOURCES OF CERTAIN STUFF THAT DOES OR SHOULD APPEAR INSIDE QUOTATION MARKS IN THIS ARTICLE

p. 855 "Distinguished Usage Panel..." = Morris Bishop, "Good Usage, Bad Usage, and Usage," an intro to the 1976 New College Edition of *The American Heritage Dictionary of the English Language*, published by Houghton Mifflin Co.

p. 855 "Calling upon the opinions of the elite..." = John Ottenhoff, "The Perils of Prescriptivism: Usage Notes and *The American Heritage Dictionary*," *American Speech*, v. 31 #3, 1996, p. 274.

p. 861 "I realized early..." = *ADMAU*, preface, pp. xiv–xv.

p. 861 "Before going any..." = *Ibid.*, p. x.

p. 861 FN 13 "the ten critical points..." = *Ibid.*, pp. x–xi.

p. 862 "Once introduced, a prescriptive..." = Steven Pinker, "Grammar Puss" (excerpted from ch. 12 of Pinker's book *The Language Instinct*, Morrow, 1994), which appeared in the *New Republic* on 31 Jan. '94 (p. 20). Some of the subsequent Pinker quotations are from the *NR* excerpt because they tend to be more compact.

p. 863 "Who sets down...?" = p. 141 of Bryson's *Mother Tongue* (Avon, 1990).

p. 863 "As you might already..." = *ADMAU*, preface, p. xiii.

p. 863 FN 16 "The problem for professional..." = *Ibid.*, p. xi; plus the traditional-type definition of *rhetoric* is adapted from p. 1114 of the 1976 *AHD*.

p. 864 "The arrant solecisms..." = Bishop, 1976 *AHD* intro, p. xxiii.

p. 864 "The English language is being..." = John Simon, *Paradigms Lost: Reflections on Literacy and Its Decline* (Crown, 1980), p. 106.

p. 865 FN 19 "We have seen a novel..." = Wilson Follett, "Sabotage in Springfield," the *Atlantic Monthly*, January '62, p. 73.

p. 865 "A dictionary should have no..." = P. Gove in a letter to the *New York Times* replying to their howling editorial, said letter reprinted in Sledd and Ebbitt, eds., *Dictionaries and That Dictionary* (Scott, Foresman, 1962), p. 88.

p. 866 FN 21 Newman's "I have no wish..." = *Strictly Speaking: Will America Be the Death of English?* (Bobbs-Merrill, 1974), p. 10.

p. 866 Simon's "As for 'I be,'..." = *Paradigms Lost*, pp. 165–166.

p. 866 FN 22 The Partridge quotation is from p. 36 of *Usage and Abusage*

(Hamish Hamilton, 1947). The Fowler snippet is from *A Dictionary of Modern English Usage* (Oxford, 1927), pp. 540–541.

p. 867 "Somewhere along the line…" = *ADMAU*, preface, p. xi.

p. 867 FN 25 "The most bothersome…" = *Ibid.*, preface, p. xv.

p. 869 "1—Language changes…" = Philip Gove, "Linguistic Advances and Lexicography," Introduction to *Webster's Third*. Reprinted in Sledd and Ebbitt; Gove's axioms appear therein on p. 67.

p. 870 FN 28 "the English normally expected…" = p. 459 of *The Little, Brown Handbook*, Fourth Edition (Scott, Foresman, 1989).

pp. 873–74 FN 32 Norman Malcolm's exegesis of Wittgenstein's private-language argument (which argument occupies sections 258–265 of the *Philosophical Investigations*) appears in Malcolm's *Knowledge and Certainty* (Prentice-Hall, 1963), pp. 98–99.

p. 873 "A dictionary can be…" = "Usage Levels and Dialect Distribution," intro to the *American College Dictionary* (Random House, 1962), p. xxv; reprinted in Gove's letter to the *NYT*.

p. 877 "[T]he words 'rule'…" = S. Pinker, *The Language Instinct*, p. 371. The chunk also appears in Pinker's "Grammar Puss" *New Republic* article, p. 19.

p. 877 FN 36 "No one, not even…" = *The Language Instinct*, p. 372.

pp. 878 "When a scientist…" = "Grammar Puss," p. 19.

p. 880 FN 40 Garner's class distinctions miniessay is on *ADMAU*'s pp. 124–126.

p. 883 FN 46 "[Jargon] arises from…" = *ADMAU*, p. 390.

p. 885 FN 51 "knowing when to split…" = *Ibid.*, pp. 616–617.

p. 885 "hotly disputed…" = *ADMAU*'s skunked terms miniessay, which is on pp. 603–604.

p. 889 FN 57 A concise overview of these studies can be found in Janice Neuleib's "The Relation of Formal Grammar to Composition," *College Composition and Communication*, October '77.

p. 893 FN 62 Dr. Schwartz and the Task Force are listed as the authors of *Guidelines for Bias-Free Writing* (Indiana U. Press, 1995), in which the quoted sentence appears on p. 28. The Forster snippet is from the opening chapter of *A Passage to India*.

p. 895 FN 65 "vogue words have such a grip…" = *ADMAU*, p. 682.

p. 897 "At first encounter…" = Karen Volkman's review of Michael Palmer's *The Lion Bridge: Selected Poems* in the *Village Voice Literary Supplement*, October '98, p. 6.

p. 897 FN 66 The obscurity miniessay is on p. 462 of *ADMAU*.

p. 898 "This is the best and only way..." = President Clinton verbatim in mid-November '98.

p. 898 & p. 898 FN 67 Quoted bits of Orwell's "Politics and the English Language" are from the essay as it appears in, e.g., Hunt and Perry, eds., *The Dolphin Reader*, Fifth Edition (Houghton Mifflin, 1999), pp. 670–682.

p. 899 FN 68 The Jameson sentence also appears in *ADMAU*'s miniessay on OBSCURITY, p. 462; plus it appears in the same *Sacramento Bee* article mentioned in FN 66.

p. 904 The various quoted definitions of *authority* here come from *The American Heritage Dictionary*, Third Edition (Houghton Mifflin, 1992), p. 124.

p. 905 "The reality I care about..." = *ADMAU*, preface, pp. ix–x. The next five quotation-snippets—on pp. 123–124 and in FN 80—are also from the preface.

p. 906 "Sometimes people strive to..." = *ADMAU*, p. 345.

p. 906 "To the writer or speaker for whom..." = *Ibid.*, p. 604.

p. 906 "Whatever you do..." = *Ibid.*, p. 186.

1999

The View from Mrs. Thompson's

Location: Bloomington, Illinois
Dates: 11–13 September 2001
Subject: Obvious

SYNECDOCHE In true Midwest fashion, people in Bloomington aren't unfriendly but do tend to be reserved. A stranger will smile warmly at you, but there normally won't be any of that strangerly chitchat in waiting areas or checkout lines. But now, thanks to the Horror, there's something to talk about that overrides all inhibition, as if we were somehow all standing right there and just saw the same traffic accident. Example: Overheard in the checkout line at Burwell Oil (which is sort of the Neiman Marcus of gas station/ convenience store plazas — centrally located athwart both one-way main drags, and with the best tobacco prices in town, it's a municipal treasure) between a lady in an Osco cashier's smock and a man in a dungaree jacket cut off at the shoulders to make a sort of homemade vest: "With my boys they thought it was all some movie like that *Independence Day*, till then they started to notice how it was the same movie on all the channels." (The lady didn't say how old her boys were.)

WEDNESDAY Everyone has flags out. Homes, businesses. It's odd: you never see anybody putting out a flag, but by Wednesday morning there they all are. Big flags, small, regular flag-sized flags. A lot of homeowners here have those special angled flag-holders by their front door, the kind whose brace takes four Phillips screws. Plus thousands of the little handheld flags-on-a-stick you normally see at parades — some yards have dozens of these stuck in the ground all over, as if they'd somehow all just sprouted overnight. Rural-road people attach the little flags to their mailboxes out by the street. A good number of vehicles have them wedged in their grille or attached to the antenna. Some upscale people have actual poles; their flags are at half-mast. More than a few large homes around Franklin Park or out on the east side even have enormous multi-story flags hanging gonfalon-style down over their facades. It's a total mystery where people can buy flags this big or how they got them up there, or when.

My own next-door neighbor, a retired bookkeeper and USAF vet whose home- and lawn-care are nothing short of phenomenal, has a regulation-size anodized flagpole secured in eighteen inches of reinforced cement that none of the other neighbors like very much because they feel it draws lightning. He says there's a very particular etiquette to having your flag at half-mast: you're supposed to first run it all the way up to the finial at the top and *then* bring it halfway down. Otherwise it's some kind of insult. His flag is out straight and popping smartly in the wind. It's far and away the biggest flag on our street. You can also hear the wind in the cornfields just south; it sounds roughly the way light surf sounds when you're two dunes back from the shore. Mr. N——'s pole's halyard has metal elements that clank against the pole when it's windy, which is something else the neighbors don't much care for. His driveway and mine are almost right together, and he's out here on a stepladder polishing his pole with some kind of special ointment and a chamois cloth—I shit you not—although in the morning sun it's true that his metal pole does shine like God's own wrath.

"Hell of a nice flag and display apparatus, Mr. N——."

"Ought to be. Cost enough."

"Seen all the other flags out everywhere this morning?"

This gets him to look down and smile, if a bit grimly. "Something, isn't it." Mr. N—— is not what you'd call the friendliest next-door neighbor. I really only know him because his church and mine are in the same softball league, for which he serves with great seriousness and precision as his team's statistician. We are not close. Nevertheless he's the first one I ask:

"Say, Mr. N——, suppose somebody like a foreign person or a TV reporter or something were to come by and ask you what the purpose of all these flags after what happened yesterday was, exactly—what do you think you'd say?"

"Why" (after a little moment of him giving me the same sort of look he usually gives my lawn), "to show our support towards what's going on, as Americans."*

---

*Plus: Selected other responses from various times during the day's flag-hunt when circumstances permitted the question to be asked without one seeming like a smartass or loon:

"To show we're Americans and we're not going to bow down to nobody";

The overall point being that on Wednesday here there's a weird accretive pressure to have a flag out. If the purpose of displaying a flag is to make a statement, it seems like at a certain point of density of flags you're making more of a statement if you *don't* have a flag out. It's not totally clear what statement this would be, though. What if you just don't happen to have a flag? Where has everyone gotten these flags, especially the little ones you can fasten to your mailbox? Are they all from the Fourth of July and people just save them, like Christmas ornaments? How do they know to do this? There's nothing in the Yellow Pages under *Flag.* At some point there starts to be actual tension. Nobody walks by or stops their car and says, "Hey, how come your house doesn't have a flag?," but it gets easier and easier to imagine them thinking it. Even a sort of half-collapsed house down the street that everybody thought was abandoned has one of the little flags on a stick in the weeds by the driveway. None of Bloomington's grocery stores turn out to stock flags. The big novelty shop downtown has nothing but Halloween stuff. Only a few businesses are actually open, but even the closed ones are now displaying some sort of flag. It's almost surreal. The VFW hall is obviously a good bet, but it can't open until noon if at all (it has a bar). The counter lady at Burwell Oil references a certain hideous KWIK-N-EZ convenience store out by I-55 at which she's pretty sure she recalls seeing some little plastic flags back in the racks with all the bandannas and NASCAR caps, but by the time I get down there they all turn out to be gone, snapped up by parties unknown. The cold reality is that there is not a flag to be had in this town. Stealing one out of somebody's yard is clearly just out of the question. I'm standing in a fluorescent-lit KWIK-N-EZ afraid to go home. All those people dead, and I'm sent to the edge by a plastic flag. It doesn't get really bad until people come over and ask if I'm OK and I have to lie and say it's a Benadryl reaction (which in fact can happen).

...And so on until, in one more of the Horror's weird twists of fate and circumstance, it's the KWIK-N-EZ proprietor himself (a Pakistani, by the way) who offers solace and a shoulder and a strange kind of unspoken understanding, and who lets me go back and sit in the stockroom amid every conceivable petty vice and indulgence America has to offer and

---

"It's a classic pseudo-archetype, a reflexive semion designed to preempt and negate the critical function" (grad student);

"For pride."

"What they do is symbolize unity and that we're all together behind the victims in this war and they've fucked with the wrong people this time, amigo."

compose myself, and who only slightly later, over styrofoam cups of a strange kind of perfumey tea with a great deal of milk in it, suggests construction paper and "Magical Markers," which explains my now-beloved and proudly displayed homemade flag.

AERIAL & GROUND VIEWS Everyone here gets the local news organ, the *Pantagraph*, which is roundly loathed by most of the natives I know. Imagine, let's say, a well-funded college newspaper co-edited by Bill O'Reilly and Martha Stewart. Wednesday's headline is: **ATTACKED!** After two pages of AP stuff, you get to the real *Pantagraph*. Everything to follow is *sic*. Wednesday's big local headers are: STUNNED CITIZENS RUN THROUGH MANY EMOTIONS; CLERGY OPEN ARMS TO HELP PEOPLE DEAL WITH TRAGEDY; ISU PROFESSOR: B-N NOT A LIKELY TARGET; PRICES ROCKET AT GAS PUMPS; AMPUTEE GIVES INSPIRATIONAL SPEECH. There's a half-page photo of a student at Bloomington Central Catholic HS saying the rosary in response to the Horror, which means that some staff photographer came in and popped a flash in the face of a traumatized kid at prayer. The Op-Ed column for 9/12 starts out: "The carnage we have seen through the eyes of lenses in New York City and Washington, D.C., still seems like an R-rated movie out of Hollywood."

Bloomington is a city of 65,000 in the central part of a state that is extremely, emphatically flat, so that you can see the town's salients from way far away. Three major interstates converge here, and several rail lines. The town's almost exactly halfway between Chicago and St. Louis, and its origins involve being an important train depot. Bloomington is the birthplace of Adlai Stevenson and the putative hometown of Colonel Blake on *M*A*S*H*. It has a smaller twin city, Normal, that's built around a public university and is a whole different story. Both towns together are like 110,000 people.

As Midwest cities go, the only remarkable thing about Bloomington is its prosperity. It is all but recession-proof. Some of this is due to the county's farmland, which is world-class fertile and so expensive per acre that a civilian can't even find out how much it costs. But Bloomington is also the national HQ for State Farm, which is the great dark god of US consumer insurance and for all practical purposes owns the town, and because of which Bloomington's east side is now all smoked-glass complexes and Build to Suit developments and a six-lane beltway of malls and franchises that's killing off the old downtown, plus an ever-wider split between the town's two basic classes and cultures, so well and truly symbolized by the SUV and the pickup truck, respectively.*

Winter here is a pitiless bitch, but in the warm months Bloomington is a lot like a seaside community except here the ocean is corn, which grows steroidically and stretches to the earth's curve in all directions. The town itself in summer is intensely green—streets bathed in tree-shade and homes' explosive gardens and dozens of manicured parks and ballfields and golf courses you almost need eye protection to look at, and broad weedless fertilized lawns all made to line up exactly flush to the sidewalk with special edging tools.† To be honest, it's all a little creepy, especially in high summer, when nobody's out and all that green just sits in the heat and seethes.

Like most Midwest towns, B-N is crammed with churches: four full pages in the phone book. Everything from Unitarian to bugeyed Pentecostal. There's even a church for agnostics. But except for church—plus I guess your basic parades, fireworks, and a couple corn festivals—there isn't much public community. Everybody has his family and neighbors and tight little circle of friends. Folks keep to themselves (the native term for light conversation is *visit*). They basically all play softball or golf and grill out, and watch their kids play soccer, and sometimes go to mainstream movies...

...And they watch massive, staggering amounts of TV. I don't just mean the kids, either. Something that's obvious but important to keep in mind re Bloomington and the Horror is that reality—any felt sense of a larger world—is mainly televisual. New York's skyline, for instance, is as recognizable here as anyplace else, but what it's recognizable from is TV. TV's also a more social phenomenon than on the East Coast, where in my experience people are almost constantly leaving home to go meet other people face-to-face in public places. There don't really tend to be parties or mixers per se so much here—what you do in Bloomington is all get together at somebody's house and watch something.

In Bloomington, therefore, to have a home without a TV is to become a kind of constant and Kramer-like presence in others' homes, a perpetual guest of folks who can't quite understand why somebody wouldn't own a TV but are totally respectful of your need to watch TV, and who will offer

---

Pace some people's impression, the native accent around here isn't southern so much as just rural. The town's corporate transplants, on the other hand, have no accent at all—in Mrs. Bracero's phrase, State Farm people "sound like the folks on TV."

†People here are deeply, deeply into lawn-care; my own neighbors mow about as often as they shave.

you access to their TV in the same instinctive way they'd bend to offer a hand if you fell down in the street. This is especially true for some kind of must-see, crisis-type situation like the 2000 election or this week's Horror. All you have to do is call someone you know and say you don't have a TV: "Well shoot, boy, get over here."

TUESDAY There are maybe ten days a year when it's gorgeous in Bloomington, and 11 September is one of them. The air is clear and temperate and wonderfully dry after several weeks of what's felt very much like living in someone's armpit. It's just before serious harvesting starts, when the region's pollen is at its worst, and a good percentage of the city is stoned on Benadryl, which as you probably know tends to give the early morning a kind of dreamy, underwater quality. Time-wise, we're an hour behind the East Coast. By 8:00, everybody with a job is at it, and just about everybody else is home drinking coffee and blowing their nose and watching *Today* or one of the other network AM shows that all broadcast (it goes without saying) from New York. At 8:00 on Tuesday I personally was in the shower, trying to listen to a Bears postmortem on WSCR Sports Radio in Chicago.

The church I belong to is on the south side of Bloomington, near where my house is. Most of the people I know well enough to ask if I can come over and watch their TV are members of my church. It's not one of those churches where people throw Jesus' name around a lot or talk about the End Times, but it's fairly serious, and people in the congregation get to know each other well and to be pretty tight. As far as I know, all the congregants are natives of the area. Most are working-class or retired from same. There are some small-business owners. A fair number are veterans and/or have kids in the military or — especially — in the Reserves, because for many of these families that's what you do to pay for college.

The house I end up sitting with shampoo in my hair watching most of the actual unfolding Horror at belongs to Mrs. Thompson, who is one of the world's cooler seventy-four-year-olds and exactly the kind of person who in an emergency even if her phone is busy you know you can just come on over. She lives about a mile away from me on the other side of a mobile-home park. The streets are not crowded, but they're also not as empty as they're going to get. Mrs. Thompson's is a tiny immaculate one-story home that on the West Coast would be called a bungalow and on the south side of Bloomington is called a house. Mrs. Thompson is a long-time member and a leader in the congregation, and her living room tends to be kind of a gathering place. She's also the mom of one of my very best friends here, F——, who was in the Rangers in Vietnam and got shot in the knee and now works for a contractor installing various kinds of franchise stores in malls. He's in the middle of a divorce (long story) and living with Mrs. T. while the court decides on the disposition of his house. F—— is one of those veterans who doesn't talk about the war or belong to the VFW but is sometimes preoccupied in a dark way, and goes quietly off to camp by himself over Memorial Day weekend, and you can tell that he carries some serious shit in his head. Like most people who work construction, he wakes up very early and was long gone by the time I got to his mom's, which happened to be just after the second plane hit the South Tower, meaning probably around 8:10.

In retrospect, the first sign of possible shock was the fact that I didn't ring the bell but just came on in, which normally here one would never do. Thanks in part to her son's trade connections, Mrs. T. has a forty-inch flat-panel Philips TV on which Dan Rather appears for a second in shirtsleeves with his hair slightly mussed. (People in Bloomington seem overwhelmingly to prefer CBS News; it's unclear why.) Several other ladies from church are already over here, but I don't know if I exchanged greetings with anyone because I remember when I came in everybody was staring transfixed at one of the very few pieces of video CBS never reran, which was a distant wide-angle shot of the North Tower and its top floors' exposed steel lattice in flames, and of dots detaching from the building and moving through smoke down the screen, which then a sudden jerky tightening of the shot revealed to be actual people in coats and ties and skirts with their shoes falling off as they fell, some hanging onto ledges or girders and then letting go, upside-down or wriggling as they fell and one couple almost seeming (unverifiable) to be hugging each other as they fell those several stories and shrank back to dots as the camera then all of a sudden pulled back to the long view—I have no idea how long the clip took—after which Dan Rather's mouth seemed to move for a second before any sound emerged, and everyone in the room sat back and looked at one another with expressions that seemed somehow both childlike and terribly old. I think one or two people made some sort of sound. I'm not sure what else to say. It seems grotesque to talk about being traumatized by a piece of video when the people in the video were dying. Something about the shoes also falling made it worse. I think the older ladies took it better than I did. Then the hideous beauty of the rerun clip of the second plane hitting the tower, the blue and silver and black and spectacular orange of it, as more little moving dots fell. Mrs. Thompson was in her chair, which is a rocker with floral cushions. The living room has two other chairs, and a huge corduroy sofa that F—— and I had had to take the front door off its hinges to get in the house. All the seats were occupied, meaning I think five or six other people, most women, all these over fifty, and there were more voices in the kitchen, one of which was very upset-sounding and belonged to the psychologically delicate Mrs. R——, who I don't know very well but is said to have once been a beauty of great local repute. Many of the people are Mrs. T.'s neighbors, and some are still in robes, and at various times people leave to go home and use the phone and come back, or leave altogether (one younger lady went to go take her children out of school), and other people came. At one point, around the time the South Tower was falling so perfectly-seeming down into itself (I remember thinking that it was falling the way an elegant lady faints, but it was Mrs. Bracero's normally pretty much useless and irritating son, Duane, who pointed out that what it really looked like is if you took some film of a NASA liftoff and ran it backward, which now after several re-viewings does seem dead on), there were at least a dozen people in the house. The living room was dim because in summer here everyone always keeps their drapes pulled.*

Is it normal not to remember things very well after only a couple days, or at any rate the order of things? I know at some point for a while there was the sound outside of some neighbor mowing his lawn, which seemed totally bizarre, but I don't remember if anybody remarked on it. Sometimes it seemed like nobody said anything and sometimes like everybody was talking at once. There was also a lot of telephonic activity. None of these women carry cell phones (Duane has a pager whose function is unclear), so it's just Mrs. T.'s old wall-mount in the kitchen. Not all the calls made rational sense. One side effect of the Horror was an overwhelming desire to call everyone you loved. It was established early on that you couldn't get New York—dialing 212 yielded only a weird whooping sound. People keep asking Mrs. T.'s permission until she tells them to knock it off and for heaven's sake just use the phone. Some of the ladies reach their husbands, who are apparently all gathered around TVs and radios at their various workplaces; for a while bosses are too shocked to think to send people home. Mrs. T. has coffee on, but another sign of

---

*Mrs. Thompson's living room is prototypical working-class Bloomington, too: double-pane windows, white Sears curtains w/ valence, catalogue clock with a background of mallards, woodgrain magazine rack with *CSM* and *Reader's Digest*, inset bookshelves used to display little collectible figurines and framed photos of relatives and their families. There are two knit samplers w/ the Desiderata and Prayer of St. Francis, antimacassars on every good chair, and wall-to-wall carpet so thick that you can't see your feet (people take their shoes off at the door—it's basic common courtesy).

crisis is that if you want some you have to go get it yourself—usually it just sort of appears. From the door to the kitchen I remember seeing the second tower fall and being confused about whether it was a replay of the first tower falling. Another thing about the hay fever is that you can't ever be totally sure someone's crying, but over the two hours of first-run Horror, with bonus reports of the crash in PA and Bush being moved into a SAC bunker and a car bomb that's gone off in Chicago (the latter then retracted), pretty much everybody either cries or comes very close, according to his or her relative abilities. Mrs. Thompson says less than almost anyone. I don't think she cries, but she doesn't rock in her chair as usual, either. Her first husband's death was apparently sudden and grisly, and I know at times during the war F—— would be out in the field and she wouldn't hear from him for weeks at a time and didn't know whether he was even alive. Duane Bracero's main contribution is to keep iterating how much like a movie it all seems. Duane, who's at least twenty-five but still lives at home while supposedly studying to be a welder, is one of these people who always wears camouflage T-shirts and paratrooper boots but would never dream of actually enlisting (as, to be fair, neither would I). He has also kept his hat, the front of which promotes something called SLIPKNOT, on his head indoors in Mrs. Thompson's house. It always seems to be important to have at least one person in the vicinity to hate.

It turns out the cause of poor tendony Mrs. R——'s meltdown in the kitchen is that she has either a grandniece or removed cousin who's doing some type of internship at Time, Inc., in the Time-Life Building or whatever it's called, about which Mrs. R—— and whoever she's managed to call know only that it's a vertiginously tall skyscraper someplace in New York City, and she's out of her mind with worry, and two other ladies have been out here the whole time holding both her hands and trying to decide whether they should call her doctor (Mrs. R—— has kind of a history), and I end up doing pretty much the only good I do all day by explaining to Mrs. R—— where midtown Manhattan is. It thereupon emerges that none of the people here I'm watching the Horror with—not even the couple ladies who'd gone to see *Cats* as part of some group tour thing through the church in 1991—have even the vaguest notion of New York's layout and don't know, for example, how radically far south the Financial District and Statue of Liberty are; they have to be shown this via pointing out the ocean in the foreground of the skyline they all know so well (from TV).

The half-assed little geography lesson is the start of a feeling of alienation from these good people that builds in me all throughout the part of the Horror where people flee rubble and dust. These ladies are not stupid, or ignorant.

Mrs. Thompson can read both Latin and Spanish, and Ms. Voigtlander is a certified speech therapist who once explained to me that the strange gulping sound that makes NBC's Tom Brokaw so distracting to listen to is an actual speech impediment called a *glottal L*. It was one of the ladies out in the kitchen supporting Mrs. R—— who pointed out that 11 September is the anniversary of the Camp David Accords, which was certainly news to me.

What these Bloomington ladies are, or start to seem to me, is innocent. There is what would strike many Americans as a marked, startling lack of cynicism in the room. It does not, for instance, occur to anyone here to remark on how it's maybe a little odd that *all three* network anchors are in shirtsleeves, or to consider the possibility that Dan Rather's hair's being mussed might not be wholly accidental, or that the constant rerunning of horrific footage might not be just in case some viewers were only now tuning in and hadn't seen it yet. None of the ladies seem to notice the president's odd little lightless eyes appear to get closer and closer together throughout his taped address, nor that some of his lines sound almost plagiaristically identical to those uttered by Bruce Willis (as a right-wing wacko, recall) in *The Siege* a couple years back. Nor that at least some of the sheer weirdness of watching the Horror unfold has been how closely various shots and scenes have mirrored the plots of everything from *Die Hard I–III* to *Air Force One*. Nobody's near hip enough to lodge the sick and obvious po-mo complaint: We've Seen This Before. Instead, what they do is all sit together and feel really bad, and pray. No one in Mrs. Thompson's crew would ever be so nauseous as to try to get everybody to pray aloud or form a prayer circle, but you can still tell what they're all doing.

Make no mistake, this is mostly a good thing. It forces you to think and do things you most likely wouldn't alone, like for instance while watching the address and eyes to pray, silently and fervently, that you're wrong about the president, that your view of him is maybe distorted and he's actually far smarter and more substantial than you believe, not just some soulless golem or nexus of corporate interests dressed up in a suit but a statesman of courage and probity and... and it's good, this is good to pray this way. It's just a bit lonely to have to. Truly decent, innocent people can be taxing to be around. I'm not for a moment trying to suggest that everyone I know in Bloomington is like Mrs. Thompson (e.g., her son F—— isn't, though he's an outstanding person). I'm trying, rather, to explain how some part of the horror of the Horror was knowing, deep in my heart, that whatever America the men in those planes hated so much was far more my America, and F——'s, and poor old loathsome Duane's, than it was these ladies'.

2001

Consider the Lobster

THE ENORMOUS, PUNGENT, and extremely well-marketed Maine Lobster Festival is held every late July in the state's midcoast region, meaning the western side of Penobscot Bay, the nerve stem of Maine's lobster industry. What's called the midcoast runs from Owl's Head and Thomaston in the south to Belfast in the north. (Actually, it might extend all the way up to Bucksport, but we were never able to get farther north than Belfast on Route 1, whose summer traffic is, as you can imagine, unimaginable.) The region's two main communities are Camden, with its very old money and yachty harbor and five-star restaurants and phenomenal B&Bs, and Rockland, a serious old fishing town that hosts the festival every summer in historic Harbor Park, right along the water.[1]

Tourism and lobster are the midcoast region's two main industries, and they're both warm-weather enterprises, and the Maine Lobster Festival represents less an intersection of the industries than a deliberate collision, joyful and lucrative and loud. The assigned subject of this *Gourmet* article is the 56th Annual MLF, 30 July–3 August 2003, whose official theme this year was "Lighthouses, Laughter, and Lobster." Total paid attendance was over 100,000, due partly to a national CNN spot in June during which a senior editor of *Food & Wine* magazine hailed the MLF as one of the best food-themed galas in the world. 2003 festival highlights: concerts by Lee Ann Womack and Orleans, annual Maine Sea Goddess beauty pageant, Saturday's big parade, Sunday's William G. Atwood Memorial Crate Race, annual Amateur Cooking Competition, carnival rides and midway attractions and food booths, and the MLF's Main Eating Tent, where something over 25,000 pounds of fresh-caught Maine lobster is consumed after preparation in the World's Largest Lobster Cooker near the grounds' north entrance. Also available are lobster rolls, lobster turn-

---

1 There's a comprehensive native apothegm: "Camden by the sea, Rockland by the smell."

overs, lobster sauté, Down East lobster salad, lobster bisque, lobster ravioli, and deep-fried lobster dumplings. Lobster thermidor is obtainable at a sit-down restaurant called the Black Pearl on Harbor Park's northwest wharf. A large all-pine booth sponsored by the Maine Lobster Promotion Council has free pamphlets with recipes, eating tips, and Lobster Fun Facts. The winner of Friday's Amateur Cooking Competition prepares Saffron Lobster Ramekins, the recipe for which is now available for public downloading at www.mainelobsterfestival.com. There are lobster T-shirts and lobster bobblehead dolls and inflatable lobster pool toys and clamp-on lobster hats with big scarlet claws that wobble on springs. Your assigned correspondent saw it all, accompanied by one girlfriend and both his own parents—one of which parents was actually born and raised in Maine, albeit in the extreme northern inland part, which is potato country and a world away from the touristic midcoast.[2]

For practical purposes, everyone knows what a lobster is. As usual, though, there's much more to know than most of us care about—it's all a matter of what your interests are. Taxonomically speaking, a lobster is a marine crustacean of the family Homaridae, characterized by five pairs of jointed legs, the first pair terminating in large pincerish claws used for subduing prey. Like many other species of benthic carnivore, lobsters are both hunters and scavengers. They have stalked eyes, gills on their legs, and antennae. There are a dozen or so different kinds worldwide, of which the relevant species here is the Maine lobster, *Homarus americanus*. The name "lobster" comes from the Old English *loppestre*, which is thought to be a corrupt form of the Latin word for locust combined with the Old English *loppe*, which meant spider.

Moreover, a crustacean is an aquatic arthropod of the class Crustacea, which comprises crabs, shrimp, barnacles, lobsters, and freshwater crayfish. All this is right there in the encyclopedia. And arthropods are members of the phylum Arthropoda, which phylum covers insects, spiders, crustaceans, and centipedes/millipedes, all of whose main commonality, besides the absence of a centralized brain-spine assembly, is a chitinous exoskeleton composed of segments, to which appendages are articulated in pairs.

The point is that lobsters are basically giant sea insects.[3] Like most arthropods, they date from the Jurassic period, biologically so much older

---

2 N.B. All personally connected parties have made it clear from the start that they do not want to be talked about in this article.

3 Midcoasters' native term for a lobster is, in fact, "bug," as in "Come around on Sunday and we'll cook up some bugs."

than mammalia that they might as well be from another planet. And they are—particularly in their natural brown-green state, brandishing their claws like weapons and with thick antennae awhip—not nice to look at. And it's true that they are garbagemen of the sea, eaters of dead stuff,[4] although they'll also eat some live shellfish, certain kinds of injured fish, and sometimes one another.

But they are themselves good eating. Or so we think now. Up until sometime in the 1800s, though, lobster was literally low-class food, eaten only by the poor and institutionalized. Even in the harsh penal environment of early America, some colonies had laws against feeding lobsters to inmates more than once a week because it was thought to be cruel and unusual, like making people eat rats. One reason for their low status was how plentiful lobsters were in old New England. "Unbelievable abundance" is how one source describes the situation, including accounts of Plymouth Pilgrims wading out and capturing all they wanted by hand, and of early Boston's seashore being littered with lobsters after hard storms—these latter were treated as a smelly nuisance and ground up for fertilizer. There is also the fact that premodern lobster was cooked dead and then preserved, usually packed in salt or crude hermetic containers. Maine's earliest lobster industry was based around a dozen such seaside canneries in the 1840s, from which lobster was shipped as far away as California, in demand only because it was cheap and high in protein, basically chewable fuel.

Now, of course, lobster is posh, a delicacy, only a step or two down from caviar. The meat is richer and more substantial than most fish, its taste subtle compared to the marine-gaminess of mussels and clams. In the US pop-food imagination, lobster is now the seafood analog to steak, with which it's so often twinned as Surf 'n' Turf on the really expensive part of the chain steakhouse menu.

In fact, one obvious project of the MLF, and of its omnipresently sponsorial Maine Lobster Promotion Council, is to counter the idea that lobster is unusually luxe or unhealthy or expensive, suitable only for effete palates or the occasional blow-the-diet treat. It is emphasized over and over in presentations and pamphlets at the festival that lobster meat has fewer calories, less cholesterol, and less saturated fat than chicken.[5] And in the Main Eating Tent, you can get a "quarter" (industry shorthand for a 1¼-pound lobster), a four-ounce cup of melted butter, a bag of chips, and a

---

4 Factoid: Lobster traps are usually baited with dead herring.

5 Of course, the common practice of dipping the lobster meat in melted butter torpedoes all these happy fat-specs, which none of the council's promotional stuff ever mentions, any more than potato industry PR talks about sour cream and bacon bits.

soft roll w/ butter-pat for around $12.00, which is only slightly more expensive than supper at McDonald's.

Be apprised, though, that the Maine Lobster Festival's democratization of lobster comes with all the massed inconvenience and aesthetic compromise of real democracy. See, for example, the aforementioned Main Eating Tent, for which there is a constant Disneyland-grade queue, and which turns out to be a square quarter mile of awning-shaded cafeteria lines and rows of long institutional tables at which friend and stranger alike sit cheek by jowl, cracking and chewing and dribbling. It's hot, and the sagged roof traps the steam and the smells, which latter are strong and only partly food-related. It is also loud, and a good percentage of the total noise is masticatory. The suppers come in styrofoam trays, and the soft drinks are iceless and flat, and the coffee is convenience-store coffee in more styrofoam, and the utensils are plastic (there are none of the special long skinny forks for pushing out the tail meat, though a few savvy diners bring their own). Nor do they give you near enough napkins considering how messy lobster is to eat, especially when you're squeezed onto benches alongside children of various ages and vastly different levels of fine-motor development—not to mention the people who've somehow smuggled in their own beer in enormous aisle-blocking coolers, or who all of a sudden produce their own plastic tablecloths and spread them over large portions of tables to try to reserve them (the tables) for their own little groups. And so on. Any one example is no more than a petty inconvenience, of course, but the MLF turns out to be full of irksome little downers like this—see for instance the Main Stage's headliner shows, where it turns out that you have to pay $20 extra for a folding chair if you want to sit down; or the North Tent's mad scramble for the Nyquil-cup-sized samples of finalists' entries handed out after the Cooking Competition; or the much-touted Maine Sea Goddess pageant finals, which turn out to be excruciatingly long and to consist mainly of endless thanks and tributes to local sponsors. Let's not even talk about the grossly inadequate Port-A-San facilities or the fact that there's nowhere to wash your hands before or after eating. What the Maine Lobster Festival really is is a midlevel county fair with a culinary hook, and in this respect it's not unlike Tidewater crab festivals, Midwest corn festivals, Texas chili festivals, etc., and shares with these venues the core paradox of all teeming commercial demotic events: It's not for everyone.[6] Nothing against the euphoric senior editor of *Food &*

---

6 In truth, there's a great deal to be said about the differences between working-class Rockland and the heavily populist flavor of its festival versus comfortable and elitist

Wine, but I'd be surprised if she'd ever actually been here in Harbor Park, amid crowds of people slapping canal-zone mosquitoes as they eat deep-fried Twinkies and watch Professor Paddywhack, on six-foot stilts in a raincoat with plastic lobsters protruding from all directions on springs, terrify their children.

Lobster is essentially a summer food. This is because we now prefer our lobsters fresh, which means they have to be recently caught, which for both tactical and economic reasons takes place at depths less than 25 fathoms. Lobsters tend to be hungriest and most active (i.e., most trappable) at summer water temperatures of 45–50 degrees. In the autumn, most Maine lobsters migrate out into deeper water, either for warmth or to avoid the heavy waves that pound New England's coast all winter. Some burrow into the bottom. They might hibernate; nobody's sure. Summer is also lobsters' molting season—specifically early- to mid-July. Chitinous arthropods grow by molting, rather the way people have to buy bigger clothes as they age and gain weight. Since lobsters can live to be over 100, they can

---

Camden with its expensive view and shops given entirely over to $200 sweaters and great rows of Victorian homes converted to upscale B&Bs. And about these differences as two sides of the great coin that is US tourism. Very little of which will be said here, except to amplify the above-mentioned paradox and to reveal your assigned correspondent's own preferences. I confess that I have never understood why so many people's idea of a fun vacation is to don flip-flops and sunglasses and crawl through maddening traffic to loud, hot, crowded tourist venues in order to sample a "local flavor" that is by definition ruined by the presence of tourists. This may (as my festival companions keep pointing out) all be a matter of personality and hardwired taste: the fact that I do not like tourist venues means that I'll never understand their appeal and so am probably not the one to talk about it (the supposed appeal). But, since this FN will almost surely not survive magazine-editing anyway, here goes:

   As I see it, it probably really is good for the soul to be a tourist, even if it's only once in a while. Not good for the soul in a refreshing or enlivening way, though, but rather in a grim, steely-eyed, let's-look-honestly-at-the-facts-and-find-some-way-to-deal-with-them way. My personal experience has not been that traveling around the country is broadening or relaxing, or that radical changes in place and context have a salutary effect, but rather that intranational tourism is radically constricting, and humbling in the hardest way—hostile to my fantasy of being a true individual, of living somehow outside and above it all. (Coming up is the part that my companions find especially unhappy and repellent, a sure way to spoil the fun of vacation travel:) To be a mass tourist, for me, is to become a pure late-date American: alien, ignorant, greedy for something you cannot ever have, disappointed in a way you can never admit. It is to spoil, by way of sheer ontology, the very unspoiledness you are there to experience. It is to impose yourself on places that in all non-economic ways would be better, realer, without you. It is, in lines and gridlock and transaction after transaction, to confront a dimension of yourself that is as inescapable as it is painful: As a tourist, you become economically significant but existentially loathsome, an insect on a dead thing.

also get to be quite large, as in 30 pounds or more—though truly senior lobsters are rare now because New England's waters are so heavily trapped.[7] Anyway, hence the culinary distinction between hard- and soft-shell lobsters, the latter sometimes a.k.a. shedders. A soft-shell lobster is one that has recently molted. In midcoast restaurants, the summer menu often offers both kinds, with shedders being slightly cheaper even though they're easier to dismantle and the meat is allegedly sweeter. The reason for the discount is that a molting lobster uses a layer of seawater for insulation while its new shell is hardening, so there's slightly less actual meat when you crack open a shedder, plus a redolent gout of water that gets all over everything and can sometimes jet out lemonlike and catch a tablemate right in the eye. If it's winter or you're buying lobster someplace far from New England, on the other hand, you can almost bet that the lobster is a hard-shell, which for obvious reasons travel better.

As an à la carte entrée, lobster can be baked, broiled, steamed, grilled, sautéed, stir-fried, or microwaved. The most common method, though, is boiling. If you're someone who enjoys having lobster at home, this is probably the way you do it, since boiling is so easy. You need a large kettle w/ cover, which you fill about half full with water (the standard advice is that you want 2.5 quarts of water per lobster). Seawater is optimal, or you can add two tbsp salt per quart from the tap. It also helps to know how much your lobsters weigh. You get the water boiling, put in the lobsters one at a time, cover the kettle, and bring it back up to a boil. Then you bank the heat and let the kettle simmer—ten minutes for the first pound of lobster, then three minutes for each pound after that. (This is assuming you've got hard-shell lobsters, which, again, if you don't live between Boston and Halifax is probably what you've got. For shedders, you're supposed to subtract three minutes from the total.) The reason the kettle's lobsters turn scarlet is that boiling somehow suppresses every pigment in their chitin but one. If you want an easy test of whether the lobsters are done, you try pulling on one of their antennae—if it comes out of the head with minimal effort, you're ready to eat.

A detail so obvious that most recipes don't even bother to mention it is that each lobster is supposed to be alive when you put it in the kettle. This is part of lobster's modern appeal—it's the freshest food there is. There's no decomposition between harvesting and eating. And not only do lobsters require no cleaning or dressing or plucking, they're relatively easy for

---

7 Datum: In a good year, the US industry produces around 80,000,000 pounds of lobster, and Maine accounts for more than half that total.

vendors to keep alive. They come up alive in the traps, are placed in containers of seawater, and can—so long as the water's aerated and the animals' claws are pegged or banded to keep them from tearing one another up under the stresses of captivity[8]—survive right up until they're boiled. Most of us have been in supermarkets or restaurants that feature tanks of live lobsters, from which you can pick out your supper while it watches you point. And part of the overall spectacle of the Maine Lobster Festival is that you can see actual lobstermen's vessels docking at the wharves along the northeast grounds and unloading fresh-caught product, which is transferred by hand or cart 150 yards to the great clear tanks stacked up around the festival's cooker—which is, as mentioned, billed as the World's Largest Lobster Cooker and can process over 100 lobsters at a time for the Main Eating Tent.

So then here is a question that's all but unavoidable at the World's Largest Lobster Cooker, and may arise in kitchens across the US: Is it all right to boil a sentient creature alive just for our gustatory pleasure? A related set of concerns: Is the previous question irksomely PC or sentimental? What does "all right" even mean in this context? Is the whole thing just a matter of personal choice?

As you may or may not know, a certain well-known group called People for the Ethical Treatment of Animals thinks that the morality of lobster-boiling is not just a matter of individual conscience. In fact, one of the very first things we hear about the MLF... well, to set the scene: We're coming in by cab from the almost indescribably odd and rustic Knox County Airport[9] very late on the night before the festival opens, sharing the cab with a wealthy political consultant who lives on Vinalhaven Island in the bay half the year (he's headed for the island ferry in Rockland). The consultant and cabdriver are responding to informal journalistic probes about how

---

8 N.B. Similar reasoning underlies the practice of what's termed "debeaking" broiler chickens and brood hens in modern factory farms. Maximum commercial efficiency requires that enormous poultry populations be confined in unnaturally close quarters, under which conditions many birds go crazy and peck one another to death. As a purely observational side-note, be apprised that debeaking is usually an automated process and that the chickens receive no anesthetic. It's not clear to me whether most *Gourmet* readers know about debeaking, or about related practices like dehorning cattle in commercial feed lots, cropping swine's tails in factory hog farms to keep psychotically bored neighbors from chewing them off, and so forth. It so happens that your assigned correspondent knew almost nothing about standard meat-industry operations before starting work on this article.

9 The terminal used to be somebody's house, for example, and the lost-luggage-reporting room was clearly once a pantry.

people who live in the midcoast region actually view the MLF, as in is the festival just a big-dollar tourist thing or is it something local residents look forward to attending, take genuine civic pride in, etc. The cabdriver (who's in his seventies, one of apparently a whole platoon of retirees the cab company puts on to help with the summer rush, and wears a US-flag lapel pin, and drives in what can only be called a very *deliberate* way) assures us that locals do endorse and enjoy the MLF, although he himself hasn't gone in years, and now come to think of it no one he and his wife know has, either. However, the demilocal consultant's been to recent festivals a couple times (one gets the impression it was at his wife's behest), of which his most vivid impression was that "you have to line up for an ungodly long time to get your lobsters, and meanwhile there are all these ex–flower children coming up and down along the line handing out pamphlets that say the lobsters die in terrible pain and you shouldn't eat them."

And it turns out that the post-hippies of the consultant's recollection were activists from PETA. There were no PETA people in obvious view at the 2003 MLF,[10] but they've been conspicuous at many of the recent festivals. Since at least the mid-1990s, articles in everything from the *Camden Herald* to the *New York Times* have described PETA urging boycotts of the Maine Lobster Festival, often deploying celebrity spokesmen like Mary Tyler Moore for open letters and ads saying stuff like "Lobsters are extraordinarily sensitive" and "To me, eating a lobster is out of the question." More concrete is the oral testimony of Dick, our florid and extremely gregarious rental-car liaison,[11] to the effect that PETA's been around so much during recent years that a kind of brittlely tolerant homeostasis now

---

10 It turned out that one Mr. William R. Rivas-Rivas, a high-ranking PETA official out of the group's Virginia headquarters, was indeed there this year, albeit solo, working the festival's main and side entrances on Saturday, 2 August, handing out pamphlets and adhesive stickers emblazoned with "Being Boiled Hurts," which is the tagline in most of PETA's published material about lobsters. I learned that he'd been there only later, when speaking with Mr. Rivas-Rivas on the phone. I'm not sure how we missed seeing him *in situ* at the festival, and I can't see much to do except apologize for the oversight—although it's also true that Saturday was the day of the big MLF parade through Rockland, which basic journalistic responsibility seemed to require going to (and which, with all due respect, meant that Saturday was maybe not the best day for PETA to work the Harbor Park grounds, especially if it was going to be just one person for one day, since a lot of diehard MLF partisans were off-site watching the parade (which, again with no offense intended, was in truth kind of cheesy and boring, consisting mostly of slow homemade floats and various midcoast people waving at one another, and with an extremely annoying man dressed as Blackbeard ranging up and down the length of the crowd saying "Arrr" over and over and brandishing a plastic sword at people, etc.; plus it rained)).

11 By profession, Dick is actually a car salesman; the midcoast region's National Car Rental franchise operates out of a Chevy dealership in Thomaston.

obtains between the activists and the festival's locals, e.g.: "We had some incidents a couple years ago. One lady took most of her clothes off and painted herself like a lobster, almost got herself arrested. But for the most part they're let alone. [Rapid series of small ambiguous laughs, which with Dick happens a lot.] They do their thing and we do our thing."

This whole interchange takes place on Route 1, 30 July, during a four-mile, 50-minute ride from the airport[12] to the dealership to sign car-rental papers. Several irreproducible segues down the road from the PETA anecdotes, Dick—whose son-in-law happens to be a professional lobster-man and one of the Main Eating Tent's regular suppliers—explains what he and his family feel is the crucial mitigating factor in the whole morality-of-boiling-lobsters-alive issue: "There's a part of the brain in people and animals that lets us feel pain, and lobsters' brains don't have this part."

Besides the fact that it's incorrect in about nine different ways, the main reason Dick's statement is interesting is that its thesis is more or less echoed by the festival's own pronouncement on lobsters and pain, which is part of a Test Your Lobster IQ quiz that appears in the 2003 MLF program courtesy of the Maine Lobster Promotion Council:

> The nervous system of a lobster is very simple, and is in fact most similar to the nervous system of the grasshopper. It is decentralized with no brain. There is no cerebral cortex, which in humans is the area of the brain that gives the experience of pain.

Though it sounds more sophisticated, a lot of the neurology in this latter claim is still either false or fuzzy. The human cerebral cortex is the brain-part that deals with higher faculties like reason, metaphysical self-awareness, language, etc. Pain reception is known to be part of a much older and more primitive system of nociceptors and prostaglandins that are managed by the brain stem and thalamus.[13] On the other hand, it

---

12 The short version regarding why we were back at the airport after already arriving the previous night involves lost luggage and a miscommunication about where and what the midcoast's National franchise was—Dick came out personally to the airport and got us, out of no evident motive but kindness. (He also talked nonstop the entire way, with a very distinctive speaking style that can be described only as manically laconic; the truth is that I now know more about this man than I do about some members of my own family.)

13 To elaborate by way of example: The common experience of accidentally touching a hot stove and yanking your hand back before you're even aware that anything's going on is explained by the fact that many of the processes by which we detect and avoid painful stimuli do not involve the cortex. In the case of the hand and stove, the brain is bypassed altogether; all the important neurochemical action takes place in the spine.

is true that the cerebral cortex is involved in what's variously called suffering, distress, or the emotional experience of pain—i.e., experiencing painful stimuli as unpleasant, very unpleasant, unbearable, and so on.

Before we go any further, let's acknowledge that the questions of whether and how different kinds of animals feel pain, and of whether and why it might be justifiable to inflict pain on them in order to eat them, turn out to be extremely complex and difficult. And comparative neuroanatomy is only part of the problem. Since pain is a totally subjective mental experience, we do not have direct access to anyone or anything's pain but our own; and even just the principles by which we can infer that other human beings experience pain and have a legitimate interest in not feeling pain involve hard-core philosophy—metaphysics, epistemology, value theory, ethics. The fact that even the most highly evolved nonhuman mammals can't use language to communicate with us about their subjective mental experience is only the first layer of additional complication in trying to extend our reasoning about pain and morality to animals. And everything gets progressively more abstract and convoluted as we move farther and farther out from the higher-type mammals into cattle and swine and dogs and cats and rodents, and then birds and fish, and finally invertebrates like lobsters.

The more important point here, though, is that the whole animal-cruelty-and-eating issue is not just complex, it's also uncomfortable. It is, at any rate, uncomfortable for me, and for just about everyone I know who enjoys a variety of foods and yet does not want to see herself as cruel or unfeeling. As far as I can tell, my own main way of dealing with this conflict has been to avoid thinking about the whole unpleasant thing. I should add that it appears to me unlikely that many readers of *Gourmet* wish to think about it, either, or to be queried about the morality of their eating habits in the pages of a culinary monthly. Since, however, the assigned subject of this article is what it was like to attend the 2003 MLF, and thus to spend several days in the midst of a great mass of Americans all eating lobster, and thus to be more or less impelled to think hard about lobster and the experience of buying and eating lobster, it turns out that there is no honest way to avoid certain moral questions.

There are several reasons for this. For one thing, it's not just that lobsters get boiled alive, it's that you do it yourself—or at least it's done specifically for you, on-site.[14] As mentioned, the World's Largest Lobster

---

14 Morality-wise, let's concede that this cuts both ways. Lobster-eating is at least not abetted by the system of corporate factory farms that produces most beef, pork, and

Cooker, which is highlighted as an attraction in the festival's program, is right out there on the MLF's north grounds for everyone to see. Try to imagine a Nebraska Beef Festival[15] at which part of the festivities is watching trucks pull up and the live cattle get driven down the ramp and slaughtered right there on the World's Largest Killing Floor or something — there's no way.

The intimacy of the whole thing is maximized at home, which of course is where most lobster gets prepared and eaten (although note already the semiconscious euphemism "prepared," which in the case of lobsters really means killing them right there in our kitchens). The basic scenario is that we come in from the store and make our little preparations like getting the kettle filled and boiling, and then we lift the lobsters out of the bag or whatever retail container they came home in...whereupon some uncomfortable things start to happen. However stuporous a lobster is from the trip home, for instance, it tends to come alarmingly to life when placed in boiling water. If you're tilting it from a container into the steaming kettle, the lobster will sometimes try to cling to the container's sides or even to hook its claws over the kettle's rim like a person trying to keep from going over the edge of a roof. And worse is when the lobster's fully immersed. Even if you cover the kettle and turn away, you can usually hear the cover rattling and clanking as the lobster tries to push it off. Or the creature's claws scraping the sides of the kettle as it thrashes around. The lobster, in other words, behaves very much as you or I would behave if we were plunged into boiling water (with the obvious exception of screaming[16]). A

---

chicken. Because, if nothing else, of the way they're marketed and packaged for sale, we eat these latter meats without having to consider that they were once conscious, sentient creatures to whom horrible things were done. (N.B. "Horrible" here meaning really, really horrible. Write off to PETA or peta.org for their free "Meet Your Meat" video, narrated by Mr. Alec Baldwin, if you want to see just about everything meat-related you don't want to see or think about. (N.B.$_2$ Not that PETA's any sort of font of unspun truth. Like many partisans in complex moral disputes, the PETA people are fanatics, and a lot of their rhetoric seems simplistic and self-righteous. But this particular video, replete with actual factory-farm and corporate-slaughterhouse footage, is both credible and traumatizing.))

15 Is it significant that "lobster," "fish," and "chicken" are our culture's words for both the animal and the meat, whereas most mammals seem to require euphemisms like "beef" and "pork" that help us separate the meat we eat from the living creature the meat once was? Is this evidence that some kind of deep unease about eating higher animals is endemic enough to show up in English usage, but that the unease diminishes as we move out of the mammalian order? (And is "lamb"/"lamb" the counterexample that sinks the whole theory, or are there special, biblico-historical reasons for that equivalence?)

16 There's a relevant populist myth about the high-pitched whistling sound that sometimes issues from a pot of boiling lobster. The sound is really vented steam from the

blunter way to say this is that the lobster acts as if it's in terrible pain, causing some cooks to leave the kitchen altogether and to take one of those
little lightweight plastic oven-timers with them into another room and
wait until the whole process is over.

There happen to be two main criteria that most ethicists agree on for
determining whether a living creature has the capacity to suffer and so has
genuine interests that it may or may not be our moral duty to consider.[17]
One is how much of the neurological hardware required for pain-experience
the animal comes equipped with—nociceptors, prostaglandins, neuronal
opioid receptors, etc. The other criterion is whether the animal demonstrates behavior associated with pain. And it takes a lot of intellectual
gymnastics and behaviorist hairsplitting not to see struggling, thrashing,
and lid-clattering as just such pain-behavior. According to marine zoolo-
gists, it usually takes lobsters between 35 and 45 seconds to die in boiling
water. (No source I could find talks about how long it takes them to die in
superheated steam; one rather hopes it's faster.)

There are, of course, other ways to kill your lobster on-site and so
achieve maximum freshness. Some cooks' practice is to drive a sharp
heavy knife point-first into a spot just above the midpoint between the
lobster's eyestalks (more or less where the Third Eye is in human foreheads). This is alleged either to kill the lobster instantly or to render it
insensate, and is said at least to eliminate some of the cowardice involved
in throwing a creature into boiling water and then fleeing the room. As far
as I can tell from talking to proponents of the knife-in-head method, the
idea is that it's more violent but ultimately more merciful, plus that a
willingness to exert personal agency and accept responsibility for stabbing
the lobster's head honors the lobster somehow and entitles one to eat it

---

layer of seawater between the lobster's flesh and its carapace (this is why shedders whistle
more than hard-shells), but the pop version has it that the sound is the lobster's rabbit-like
death-scream. Lobsters communicate via pheromones in their urine and don't have anything close to the vocal equipment for screaming, but the myth's very persistent—which
might, once again, point to a low-level cultural unease about the boiling thing.

17 "Interests" basically means strong and legitimate preferences, which obviously
require some degree of consciousness, responsiveness to stimuli, etc. See, for instance, the
utilitarian philosopher Peter Singer, whose 1974 *Animal Liberation* is more or less the
bible of the modern animal-rights movement:

> It would be nonsense to say that it was not in the interests of a stone to be kicked
> along the road by a schoolboy. A stone does not have interests because it cannot
> suffer. Nothing that we can do to it could possibly make any difference to its wel-
> fare. A mouse, on the other hand, does have an interest in not being kicked along
> the road, because it will suffer if it is.

(there's often a vague sort of Native American spirituality-of-the-hunt flavor to pro-knife arguments). But the problem with the knife method is basic biology: Lobsters' nervous systems operate off not one but several ganglia, a.k.a. nerve bundles, which are sort of wired in series and distributed all along the lobster's underside, from stem to stern. And disabling only the frontal ganglion does not normally result in quick death or unconsciousness.

Another alternative is to put the lobster in cold saltwater and then very slowly bring it up to a full boil. Cooks who advocate this method are going on the analogy to a frog, which can supposedly be kept from jumping out of a boiling pot by heating the water incrementally. In order to save a lot of research-summarizing, I'll simply assure you that the analogy between frogs and lobsters turns out not to hold—plus, if the kettle's water isn't aerated seawater, the immersed lobster suffers from slow suffocation, although usually not decisive enough suffocation to keep it from still thrashing and clattering when the water gets hot enough to kill it. In fact, lobsters boiled incrementally often display a whole bonus set of gruesome, convulsionlike reactions that you don't see in regular boiling.

Ultimately, the only certain virtues of the home-lobotomy and slow-heating methods are comparative, because there are even worse/crueler ways people prepare lobster. Time-thrifty cooks sometimes microwave them alive (usually after poking several vent-holes in the carapace, which is a precaution most shellfish-microwavers learn about the hard way). Live dismemberment, on the other hand, is big in Europe—some chefs cut the lobster in half before cooking; others like to tear off the claws and tail and toss only these parts into the pot.

And there's more unhappy news respecting suffering-criterion number one. Lobsters don't have much in the way of eyesight or hearing, but they do have an exquisite tactile sense, one facilitated by hundreds of thousands of tiny hairs that protrude through their carapace. "Thus it is," in the words of T. M. Prudden's industry classic *About Lobster*, "that although encased in what seems a solid, impenetrable armor, the lobster can receive stimuli and impressions from without as readily as if it possessed a soft and delicate skin." And lobsters do have nociceptors,[18] as well as invertebrate ver-

---

18 This is the neurological term for special pain-receptors that are "sensitive to potentially damaging extremes of temperature, to mechanical forces, and to chemical substances which are released when body tissues are damaged."

sions of the prostaglandins and major neurotransmitters via which our own brains register pain.

Lobsters do not, on the other hand, appear to have the equipment for making or absorbing natural opioids like endorphins and enkephalins, which are what more advanced nervous systems use to try to handle intense pain. From this fact, though, one could conclude either that lobsters are maybe even *more* vulnerable to pain, since they lack mammalian nervous systems' built-in analgesia, or, instead, that the absence of natural opioids implies an absence of the really intense pain-sensations that natural opioids are designed to mitigate. I for one can detect a marked upswing in mood as I contemplate this latter possibility. It could be that their lack of endorphin/enkephalin hardware means that lobsters' raw subjective experience of pain is so radically different from mammals' that it may not even deserve the term "pain." Perhaps lobsters are more like those frontal-lobotomy patients one reads about who report experiencing pain in a totally different way than you and I. These patients evidently do feel physical pain, neurologically speaking, but don't dislike it—though neither do they like it; it's more that they feel it but don't feel anything *about* it—the point being that the pain is not distressing to them or something they want to get away from. Maybe lobsters, who are also without frontal lobes, are detached from the neurological-registration-of-injury-or-hazard we call pain in just the same way. There is, after all, a difference between (1) pain as a purely neurological event, and (2) actual suffering, which seems crucially to involve an emotional component, an awareness of pain as unpleasant, as something to fear/dislike/want to avoid.

Still, after all the abstract intellection, there remain the facts of the frantically clanking lid, the pathetic clinging to the edge of the pot. Standing at the stove, it is hard to deny in any meaningful way that this is a living creature experiencing pain and wishing to avoid/escape the painful experience. To my lay mind, the lobster's behavior in the kettle appears to be the expression of a *preference;* and it may well be that an ability to form preferences is the decisive criterion for real suffering.[19] The logic of this (preference → suffering) relation may be easiest to see in the negative case. If you cut certain kinds of worms in half, the halves will often keep crawling around and going about their vermiform business as if nothing

---

19 "Preference" is maybe roughly synonymous with "interests," but it is a better term for our purposes because it's less abstractly philosophical—"preference" seems more personal, and it's the whole idea of a living creature's personal experience that's at issue.

had happened. When we assert, based on their post-op behavior, that these worms appear not to be suffering, what we're really saying is that there's no sign the worms know anything bad has happened or would *prefer* not to have gotten cut in half.

Lobsters, though, are known to exhibit preferences. Experiments have shown that they can detect changes of only a degree or two in water temperature; one reason for their complex migratory cycles (which can often cover 100-plus miles a year) is to pursue the temperatures they like best.[20] And, as mentioned, they're bottom-dwellers and do not like bright light — if a tank of food-lobsters is out in the sunlight or a store's fluorescence, the lobsters will always congregate in whatever part is darkest. Fairly solitary in the ocean, they also clearly dislike the crowding that's part of their captivity in tanks, since (as also mentioned) one reason why lobsters' claws are banded on capture is to keep them from attacking one another under the stress of close-quarter storage.

In any event, at the MLF, standing by the bubbling tanks outside the World's Largest Lobster Cooker, watching the fresh-caught lobsters pile over one another, wave their hobbled claws impotently, huddle in the rear corners, or scrabble frantically back from the glass as you approach, it is difficult not to sense that they're unhappy, or frightened, even if it's some rudimentary version of these feelings... and, again, why does rudimentariness even enter into it? Why is a primitive, inarticulate form of suffering

---

20 Of course, the most common sort of counterargument here would begin by objecting that "like best" is really just a metaphor, and a misleadingly anthropomorphic one at that. The counterarguer would posit that the lobster seeks to maintain a certain optimal ambient temperature out of nothing but unconscious instinct (with a similar explanation for the low-light affinities upcoming in the main text). The thrust of such a counterargument will be that the lobster's thrashings and clankings in the kettle express not unpreferred pain but involuntary reflexes, like your leg shooting out when the doctor hits your knee. Be advised that there are professional scientists, including many researchers who use animals in experiments, who hold to the view that nonhuman creatures have no real feelings at all, merely "behaviors." Be further advised that this view has a long history that goes all the way back to Descartes, although its modern support comes mostly from behaviorist psychology.

To these what-looks-like-pain-is-really-just-reflexes counterarguments, however, there happen to be all sorts of scientific and pro–animal rights counter-counterarguments. And then further attempted rebuttals and redirects, and so on. Suffice it to say that both the scientific and the philosophical arguments on either side of the animal-suffering issue are involved, abstruse, technical, often informed by self-interest or ideology, and in the end so totally inconclusive that as a practical matter, in the kitchen or restaurant, it all still seems to come down to individual conscience, going with (no pun) your gut.

less urgent or uncomfortable for the person who's helping to inflict it by paying for the food it results in? I'm not trying to give you a PETA-like screed here—at least I don't think so. I'm trying, rather, to work out and articulate some of the troubling questions that arise amid all the laughter and saltation and community pride of the Maine Lobster Festival. The truth is that if you, the festival attendee, permit yourself to think that lobsters can suffer and would rather not, the MLF begins to take on the aspect of something like a Roman circus or medieval torture-fest.

Does that comparison seem a bit much? If so, exactly why? Or what about this one: Is it possible that future generations will regard our present agribusiness and eating practices in much the same way we now view Nero's entertainments or Mengele's experiments? My own initial reaction is that such a comparison is hysterical, extreme—and yet the reason it seems extreme to me appears to be that I believe animals are less morally important than human beings;[21] and when it comes to defending such a belief, even to myself, I have to acknowledge that (a) I have an obvious selfish interest in this belief, since I like to eat certain kinds of animals and want to be able to keep doing it, and (b) I haven't succeeded in working out any sort of personal ethical system in which the belief is truly defensible instead of just selfishly convenient.

Given this article's venue and my own lack of culinary sophistication, I'm curious about whether the reader can identify with any of these reactions and acknowledgments and discomforts. I'm also concerned not to come off as shrill or preachy when what I really am is more like confused. For those *Gourmet* readers who enjoy well-prepared and -presented meals involving beef, veal, lamb, pork, chicken, lobster, etc.: Do you think much about the (possible) moral status and (probable) suffering of the animals involved? If you do, what ethical convictions have you worked out that permit you not just to eat but to savor and enjoy flesh-based viands (since of course refined *enjoyment,* rather than mere ingestion, is the whole point of gastronomy)? If, on the other hand, you'll have no truck with confusions or convictions and regard stuff like the previous paragraph as just so much fatuous navel-gazing, what makes it feel truly okay, inside, to just dismiss the whole thing out of hand? That is, is your refusal to think about any of this the product of actual thought, or is it just that you don't want to

---

21 Meaning *a lot* less important, apparently, since the moral comparison here is not the value of one human's life vs. the value of one animal's life, but rather the value of one animal's life vs. the value of one human's taste for a particular kind of protein. Even the most diehard carniphile will acknowledge that it's possible to live and eat well without consuming animals.

think about it? And if the latter, then why not? Do you ever think, even idly, about the possible reasons for your reluctance to think about it? I am not trying to bait anyone here—I'm genuinely curious. After all, isn't being extra aware and attentive and thoughtful about one's food and its overall context part of what distinguishes a real gourmet? Or is all the gourmet's extra attention and sensibility just supposed to be sensuous? Is it really all just a matter of taste and presentation?

These last few queries, though, while sincere, obviously involve much larger and more abstract questions about the connections (if any) between aesthetics and morality—about what the adjective in a phrase like "The Magazine of Good Living" is really supposed to mean—and these questions lead straightaway into such deep and treacherous waters that it's probably best to stop the public discussion right here. There are limits to what even interested persons can ask of each other.

2004

Afterword

I am a lifelong vegetarian, so it was his lobster essay that sealed my David Foster Wallace deal forever. It's so slyly unconvincing and sidelong that you don't realize until the end what he has accomplished on behalf of the lobster (and all the other kitchen-tormented creatures of sea and land).

Notice that he doesn't really get into boiling them alive until page eight, and notice also that in the end his conclusion is so modest, and so mannerly—he is not trying to bait anyone here, he is genuinely curious—that the reader finds herself, somehow, in the position of taking a firmer and more strident stance on behalf of the lobster than our correspondent. All we can tell for sure, he concludes, is that the lobster is exhibiting an expression of a *preference* not to be boiled alive—but then he gently (almost) retracts that as well in a footnote, arguing with himself here and there in the essay, so that we don't have to.

I teach it nearly every semester, just so I can have the pleasure of asking students at the end how they feel about eating something that has been boiled alive. It's what determines their grade.

—*Jo Ann Beard*

Federer Both Flesh and Not

ALMOST ANYONE WHO loves tennis and follows the men's tour on television has, over the last few years, had what might be termed Federer Moments. These are times, watching the young Swiss at play, when the jaw drops and eyes protrude and sounds are made that bring spouses in from other rooms to see if you're OK. The Moments are more intense if you've played enough tennis to understand the impossibility of what you just saw him do. We've all got our examples. Here is one. It's the finals of the 2005 U.S. Open, Federer serving to Andre Agassi early in the fourth set. There's a medium-long exchange of groundstrokes, one with the distinctive butterfly shape of today's power-baseline game, Federer and Agassi yanking each other from side to side, each trying to set up the baseline winner...until suddenly Agassi hits a hard heavy cross-court backhand that pulls Federer way out wide to his ad (= his left) side, and Federer gets to it but slices the stretch backhand short, a couple feet past the service line, which of course is the sort of thing Agassi dines out on, and as Federer's scrambling to reverse and get back to center, Agassi's moving in to take the short ball on the rise, and he smacks it hard right back into the same ad corner, trying to wrong-foot Federer, which in fact he does—Federer's still near the corner but running toward the centerline, and the ball's heading to a point behind him now, where he just was, and there's no time to turn his body around, and Agassi's following the shot in to the net at an angle from the backhand side...and what Federer now does is somehow instantly reverse thrust and sort of skip backward three or four steps, impossibly fast, to hit a forehand out of his backhand corner, all his weight moving backward, and the forehand is a topspin screamer down the line past Agassi at net, who lunges for it but the ball's past him, and it flies straight down the sideline and lands exactly in the deuce corner of Agassi's side, a winner—Federer's still dancing backward as it lands. And there's that familiar little second of shocked silence from the New York crowd before it erupts, and John McEnroe with his color man's headset on TV says (mostly to himself, it sounds like), "How do you hit a winner from that position?" And he's right: given Agassi's position and world-class quickness, Federer had to send that ball down a two-inch pipe of space in order to pass him, which he did, moving backward, with no setup time and none of his weight behind the shot. It was impossible. It was like something out of *The Matrix*. I don't know what-all sounds were involved, but my spouse says she hurried in and there was popcorn all over the couch and I was down on one knee and my eyeballs looked like novelty-shop eyeballs.

Anyway, that's one example of a Federer Moment, and that was merely on TV—and the truth is that TV tennis is to live tennis pretty much as video porn is to the felt reality of human love.

Journalistically speaking, there is no hot news to offer you about Roger Federer. He is, at twenty-five, the best tennis player currently alive. Maybe the best ever. Bios and profiles abound. *60 Minutes* did a feature on him just last year. Anything you want to know about Mr. Roger N.M.I. Federer—his background, his hometown of Basel, his parents' sane and unexploitative support of his talent, his junior tennis career, his early problems with fragility and temper, his beloved junior coach, how that coach's accidental death in 2002 both shattered and annealed Federer and helped make him what he now is, Federer's thirty-nine career singles titles, his eight Grand Slams, his unusually steady and mature commitment to the girlfriend who travels with him (which on the men's tour is rare) and handles his affairs (which on the men's tour is unheard-of), his old-school stoicism and mental toughness and good sportsmanship and evident overall decency and thoughtfulness and charitable largesse—it's all just a Google search away. Knock yourself out.

This present article is more about a spectator's experience of Federer, and its context. The specific thesis here is that if you've never seen the young man play live, and then do, in person, on the sacred grass of Wimbledon, through the literally withering heat and then wind and rain of the '06 fortnight, then you are apt to have what one of the tournament's press bus drivers describes as a "bloody near-religious experience." It may be tempting, at first, to hear a phrase like this as just one more of the overheated tropes that people resort to as they try to describe the feeling of Federer Moments. But the driver's phrase turns out to be true—literally, for an instant ecstatically—though it takes some time and serious watching to see this truth emerge.

Beauty is not the goal of competitive sports, but high-level sports are a prime venue for the expression of human beauty. The relation is roughly that of courage to war.

The human beauty we're talking about here is beauty of a particular type; it might be called kinetic beauty. Its power and appeal are universal. It has nothing to do with sex or cultural norms. What it seems to have to do with, really, is human beings' reconciliation with the fact of having a body.[1]

Of course, in men's sports no one ever talks about beauty, or grace, or the body. Men may profess their "love" of sports, but that love must always be cast and enacted in the symbology of war: elimination vs. advance, hierarchy of rank and standing, obsessive stats and technical analysis, tribal and/or nationalist fervor, uniforms, mass noise, banners, chest-thumping, face-painting, etc. For reasons that are not well understood, war's codes are safer for most of us than love's. You too may find them so, in which case Spain's mesomorphic and totally martial Rafael Nadal is the man's man for you — he of the unsleeved biceps and Kabuki self-exhortations. Plus Nadal is also Federer's nemesis, and the big surprise of this year's Wimbledon, since he's a clay-court specialist and no one expected him to make it past the first few rounds here. Whereas Federer, through the semifinals, has provided no surprise or competitive drama at all. He's outplayed each opponent so completely that the TV and print press are worried his matches are dull and can't compete effectively with the nationalist fervor of the World Cup.[2]

July 9's men's final, though, is everyone's dream. Nadal vs. Federer is a replay of last month's French Open final, which Nadal won. Federer has so far lost only four matches all year, but they've all been to Nadal. Still, most of these matches have been on slow clay, Nadal's best surface. Grass is Federer's best. On the other hand, the first week's heat has baked out some of the Wimbledon courts' slickness and made them slower. There's also the fact that Nadal

---

1 There's a great deal that's bad about having a body. If this is not so obviously true that no one needs examples, we can just quickly mention pain, sores, odors, nausea, aging, gravity, sepsis, clumsiness, illness, limits — every last schism between our physical wills and our actual capacities. Can anyone doubt we need help being reconciled? Crave it? It's your body that dies, after all.

There are wonderful things about having a body, too, obviously — it's just that these things are much harder to feel and appreciate in real time. Rather like certain kinds of rare, peak-type sensuous epiphanies ("I'm so glad I have eyes to see this sunrise!," etc.), great athletes seem to catalyze our awareness of how glorious it is to touch and perceive, move through space, interact with matter. Granted, what great athletes can do with their bodies are things that the rest of us can only dream of. But these dreams are important — they make up for a lot.

2 The U.S. media here are especially worried because no Americans of either sex survived into even the quarterfinals this year. (If you're into obscure statistics, it's the first time this has happened at Wimbledon since 1911.)

has adjusted his clay-based game to grass—moving in closer to the baseline on his groundstrokes, amping up his serve, overcoming his allergy to the net. He beat the absolute shit out of Agassi in the third round. The networks are in ecstasies. Before the match, on Centre Court, behind the glass slits above the south backstop, as the linesmen are coming out on court in their new Ralph Lauren uniforms that look so much like children's navalwear, the broadcast commentators can be seen practically bouncing up and down in their chairs. This Wimbledon final's got the revenge narrative, the king-vs.-regicide dynamic, the stark character contrasts. It's the passionate machismo of southern Europe versus the intricate clinical artistry of the north. Dionysus and Apollo. Cleaver and scalpel. Southpaw and righty. Numbers 2 and 1 in the world. Nadal, the man who's taken the modern power-baseline game just as far as it goes...versus a man who's transfigured that modern game, whose precision and variety are as big a deal as his pace and foot-speed, but who may be peculiarly vulnerable to, or psyched out by, that first man. A British sportswriter, exulting with his mates in the press section, says, twice, "It's going to be a war."

Plus it's in the cathedral of Centre Court. And the men's final is always on the fortnight's second Sunday, the symbolism of which Wimbledon emphasizes by always omitting play on the first Sunday. And the spattery gale that has knocked over parking signs and everted umbrellas all morning suddenly quits an hour before match time, the sun emerging just as Centre Court's tarp is rolled back and the net posts are driven home.

Federer and Nadal come out to applause, make their ritual bows to the nobles' box. The Swiss is in the buttermilk-colored sport coat that Nike's gotten him to wear for Wimbledon this year. On Federer, and perhaps on him alone, it doesn't look absurd with shorts and sneakers. The Spaniard eschews all warm-up clothing, so you have to look at his muscles right away. He and the Swiss are both in all-Nike, up to the very same kind of tied white Nike hankie with the swoosh positioned right above the third eye. Nadal tucks his hair under his hankie, but Federer doesn't, and smoothing and fussing with the bits of hair that fall over the hankie is the main Federer tic TV viewers get to see; likewise Nadal's obsessive retreat to the ballboy's towel between points. There happen to be other tics and habits, though, tiny perks of live viewing. There's the great care Roger Federer takes to hang the sport coat over his spare courtside chair's back, just so, to keep it from wrinkling—he's done this before each match here, and something about it seems childlike and weirdly sweet. Or the way he inevitably changes out his racket sometime in the second set, the new one always in the same clear plastic bag closed with blue tape, which he takes off carefully and always hands to a ballboy to dispose of. There's Nadal's habit of constantly picking his long shorts out of his bottom as he bounces the ball before serving, his way of always cutting his eyes warily from side to side as he walks the baseline, like a convict expecting to be shanked. And something odd on the Swiss's serve, if you look very closely. Holding ball and racket out in front, just before starting the motion, Federer always places the ball precisely in the V-shaped gap of the racket's throat, just below the head, just for an instant. If the fit isn't perfect, he adjusts the ball until it is. It happens very fast, but also every time, on both first serves and second.

Nadal and Federer now warm each other up for precisely ten minutes; the umpire keeps time. There's a very definite order and etiquette to these pro warm-ups, which is something that television has decided you're not interested in seeing. Centre Court holds thirteen thousand and change. Another several thousand have done what people here do willingly every year, which is to pay a stiff General Admission at the gate and then gather, with hampers and mosquito spray, to watch the match on an enormous TV screen outside Court 1. Your guess here is probably as good as anyone's.

Right before play, up at the net, there's a ceremonial coin-toss to see who'll serve first. It's another Wimbledon ritual. The honorary coin-tosser this year is William Caines, assisted by the umpire and tournament referee. William Caines is a seven-year-old from Kent who contracted liver cancer at age two and somehow survived after surgery and horrific chemo. He's here representing Cancer Research UK. He's blond and pink-cheeked and comes up to about Federer's waist. The crowd roars its approval of the honorary toss. Federer smiles distantly the whole time. Nadal, just across the net, keeps dancing in place like a boxer, swinging his arms from side to side. I'm not sure whether the U.S. networks show the coin-toss or not, whether this ceremony's part of their contractual obligation or whether they get to cut to commercial. As William Caines is ushered off, there's more cheering, but it's scattered and disorganized; most of the crowd can't quite tell what to do. It's like once the ritual's over, the reality of why this child was part of it sinks in. There's a feeling of something important, something both uncomfortable and not, about a child with cancer tossing this dream-final's coin. The feeling, what-all it might mean, has a tip-of-the-tongue-type quality that remains elusive for at least the first two sets.[3]

---

3 Actually, this is not the only Federer-and-sick-child incident of Wimbledon's second week. Three days prior to the men's final, a Special One-on-One Interview with Mr. Roger Federer* takes place in a small, crowded International Tennis Federation office just off the third floor of the Press Center. Right afterward, as the ATP player-rep is ush-

*   *   *

A top athlete's beauty is next to impossible to describe directly. Or to evoke. Federer's forehand is a great liquid whip, his backhand a one-hander that he can drive flat, load with topspin, or slice—the slice with such snap that the ball turns shapes in the air and skids on the grass to maybe ankle height. His serve has world-class pace and a degree of placement and variety no one else comes close to; the service motion is lithe and uneccentric, distinctive (on TV) only in a certain eel-like all-body snap at the moment of impact. His anticipation and court sense are otherworldly, and his footwork is the best in the game—as a child, he was also a soccer prodigy. All this is true, and yet none of it really explains anything or evokes the experience of watching this man play. Of witnessing, firsthand, the beauty and genius of his game. You more have to come at the aesthetic stuff obliquely, to talk around it, or—as Aquinas did with his own ineffable subject—to try to define it in terms of what it is not.

One thing it is not is televisable. At least not entirely. TV tennis has its advantages, but these advantages have disadvantages, and chief among them is a certain illusion of intimacy. Television's slow-mo replays, its close-ups and graphics, all so privilege viewers that we're not even aware of how much is lost in broadcast. And a large part of what's lost is the sheer physicality of top tennis, a sense of the speeds at which the ball is

---

ering Federer out the back door for his next scheduled obligation, one of the ITF guys (who's been talking loudly on the telephone through the whole Special Interview) now comes up and asks for a moment of Roger's time. The man, who has the same slight, generically foreign accent as all ITF guys, says: "Listen, I hate doing this. I don't do this, normally. It's for my neighbor. His kid has a disease. They will do a fund-raiser, it's planned, and I'm asking can you sign a shirt or something, you know—something." He looks mortified. The ATP rep is glaring at him. Federer, though, just nods, shrugs: "No problem. I'll bring it tomorrow." Tomorrow's the men's semifinal. Evidently the ITF guy has meant one of Federer's own shirts, maybe from the match, with Federer's actual sweat on it. (Federer throws his used wristbands into the crowd after matches, and the people they land on seem pleased rather than grossed out.) The ITF guy, after thanking Federer three times very fast, shakes his head: "I hate doing this." Federer, still halfway out the door: "It's no problem." And it isn't. Like all pros, Federer changes his shirt a few times during matches, and he can just have somebody save one, and then he'll sign it. It's not like Federer's being Gandhi here—he doesn't stop and ask for details about the kid or his illness. He doesn't pretend to care more than he does. The request is just one more small, mildly distracting obligation he has to deal with. But he does say yes, and he will remember—you can tell. And it won't distract him; he won't permit it. He's good at this kind of stuff, too.

*(Only considerations of space and basic believability prevent a full description of the hassles involved in securing such a One-on-One. In brief, it's rather like the old story of someone climbing an enormous mountain to talk to the man seated lotus on top, except in this case the mountain is composed entirely of sports-bureaucrats.)

moving and the players are reacting. This loss is simple to explain. TV's priority, during a point, is coverage of the whole court, a comprehensive view, so that viewers can see both players and the overall geometry of the exchange. TV therefore chooses a specular vantage that is overhead and behind one baseline. You, the viewer, are above and looking down from behind the court. This perspective, as any art student will tell you, "foreshortens" that court. Real tennis, after all, is three-dimensional, but a TV screen's image is only 2-D. The dimension that's lost (or rather distorted) on the screen is the real court's length, the seventy-eight feet between baselines; and the speed with which the ball traverses this length is a shot's pace, which on TV is obscured, and in person is fearsome to behold. That may sound abstract or overblown, in which case by all means go in person to some professional tournament—especially to the outer courts in early rounds, where you can sit twenty feet from the sideline—and sample the difference for yourself. If you've watched tennis only on television, you simply have no idea how hard these pros are hitting the ball, how fast the ball is moving,[4] how little time the players have to get to it, and how quickly they're able to move and rotate and strike and recover. And none are faster, or more deceptively effortless about it, than Roger Federer.

Interestingly, what is less obscured in TV coverage is Federer's intelligence, since this intelligence often manifests as angle. Federer is able to see, or create, gaps and angles for winners that no one else can envision, and television's perspective is perfect for viewing and reviewing these Federer Moments. What's harder to appreciate on TV is that these spectacular-looking angles and winners are not coming from nowhere—they're often set up several shots ahead, and depend as much on Federer's manipulation of opponents' positions as they do on the pace or placement of the coup de grâce. And understanding how and why Federer is able to move other world-class athletes around this way requires, in turn, a better technical understanding of the modern power-baseline game than TV—again—is set up to provide.

---

4 Top men's serves often reach speeds of 125–135 m.p.h., true, but what all the radar signs and graphics neglect to tell you is that male power-baseliners' groundstrokes themselves are often traveling at over 90 m.p.h., which is the speed of a big-league fastball. If you get down close enough to a pro court, you can hear an actual *sound* coming off the ball in flight, a kind of liquid hiss, from the combination of pace and spin. Close up and live, you'll also understand better the "open stance" that's become such an emblem of the power-baseline game. The term, after all, just means not turning one's side all the way to the net before hitting a groundstroke, and one reason why so many power-baseliners hit from the open stance is that the ball now is coming too fast for them to get turned all the way.

*   *   *

Wimbledon is strange. Verily it is the game's Mecca, the cathedral of tennis; but it would be easier to sustain the appropriate level of on-site veneration if the tournament weren't so intent on reminding you over and over that it's the cathedral of tennis. There's a peculiar mix of stodgy self-satisfaction and relentless self-promotion and -branding. It's a bit like the sort of authority figure whose office wall has every last plaque, diploma, and award he's ever gotten, and every time you come into the office you're forced to look at the wall and say something to indicate that you're impressed. Wimbledon's own walls, along nearly every significant corridor and passage, are lined with posters and signs featuring shots of past champions, lists of Wimbledon facts and trivia, historic lore, and so on. Some of this stuff is interesting; some is just odd. The Wimbledon Lawn Tennis Museum, for instance, has a collection of all the various kinds of rackets used here through the decades, and one of the many signs along the Level 2 passage of the Millennium Building[5] promotes this exhibit with both photos and didactic text, a kind of History of the Racket. Here, *sic,* is the climactic end of this text:

> Today's lightweight frames made of space-age materials like graphite, boron, titanium and ceramics, with larger heads—mid-size (90–95 square inches) and over-size (110 square inches)—have totally transformed the character of the game. Nowadays it is the powerful hitters who dominate with heavy topspin. Serve-and-volley players and those who rely on subtlety and touch have virtually disappeared.

It seems odd, to say the least, that such a diagnosis continues to hang here so prominently in the fourth year of Federer's reign over Wimbledon, since the Swiss has brought to men's tennis degrees of touch and subtlety unseen since (at least) the days of McEnroe's prime. But the sign's really just a testament to the power of dogma. For almost two decades, the party line's been that certain advances in racket technology, conditioning, and weight training have transformed pro tennis from a game of quickness and finesse into one of athleticism and brute power. And, as an etiology of today's power-baseline game, this party line is broadly accurate. Today's pros truly are measurably bigger, stronger, and better conditioned,[6] and

---

5 This is the large (and presumably six-year-old) structure where Wimbledon's administration, players, and media all have their respective areas and HQs.

6 (Some, like Nadal or Serena Williams, look more like cartoon superheroes than people.)

high-tech composite rackets really have increased their capacities for pace and spin. How, then, someone of Roger Federer's consummate finesse has come to dominate the men's tour is a source of wide and dogmatic confusion.

There are three kinds of valid explanation for Federer's ascendancy. One kind involves mystery and metaphysics and is, I think, closest to the real truth. The others are more technical and make for better journalism.

The metaphysical explanation is that Roger Federer is one of those rare, preternatural athletes who appear to be exempt, at least in part, from certain physical laws. Good analogs here include Michael Jordan,[7] who could not only jump inhumanly high but actually hang there a beat or two longer than gravity allows, and Muhammad Ali, who really could "float" across the canvas and land two or three jabs in the clock-time required for one. There are

---

7 When asked, during the aforementioned Special One-on-One Interview, for examples of other athletes whose performances might seem beautiful to him, Federer mentions Jordan first, then Kobe Bryant, then "a soccer player like—guys who play very relaxed, like a Zinédine Zidane or something: he does great effort, but he seems like he doesn't need to try hard to get the results."

Federer's response to the subsequent question, which is what-all he makes of it when pundits and other players describe his own game as "beautiful," is interesting mainly because the response is pleasant, intelligent, and cooperative—as is Federer himself—without ever really saying anything (because, in fairness, what could one say about others' descriptions of him as beautiful? What would you say? It's ultimately a stupid question):

"It's always what people see first—for them, that's what you are 'best at.' When you used to watch John McEnroe, you know, the first time, what would you see? You would see a guy with incredible talent, because the way he played, nobody played like this. The way he played the ball, it was just all about *feel*. And then you go over to Boris Becker, and right away you saw a *powerful* player, you know?* When you see me play, you see a 'beautiful' player—and maybe after that you maybe see that he's fast, maybe you see that he's got a good forehand, maybe then you see that he has a good serve. First, you know, you have a base, and to me, I think it's great, you know, and I'm very lucky to be called basically 'beautiful,' you know, for style of play. Other ones have the 'grinder' [quality] first, [some] other ones are the 'power player,' [still] other ones are 'the quick guy.' With me it's, like, 'the beautiful player,' and that's really cool."

*(N.B. Federer's big conversational tics are "maybe" and "you know." Ultimately, these tics are helpful because they serve as reminders of how appallingly young he really is. If you're interested, the world's best tennis player is wearing white warm-up pants and a long-sleeved white microfiber shirt, possibly Nike. No sport coat, though. His handshake is only moderately firm, though the hand itself is like a carpentry rasp (for obvious reasons, tennis players tend to be very callusy). He's a bit bigger than TV makes him seem—broader-shouldered, deeper in the chest. He's next to a table that's covered with visors and headbands, which he's been autographing with a Sharpie. He sits with his legs crossed and smiles pleasantly and seems very relaxed; he never fidgets with the Sharpie. One's overall impression is that Roger Federer is either a very nice guy or a guy who's very good at dealing with the media—or [most likely] both.)

probably a half-dozen other examples since 1960. And Roger Federer is of this type—a type that one could call genius, or mutant, or avatar. He is never hurried or off-balance. The approaching ball hangs, for him, a split-second longer than it ought to. His movements are lithe rather than athletic. Like Ali, Jordan, Maradona, and Gretzky, he seems both less and more substantial than the men he faces. Particularly in the all-white that Wimbledon enjoys getting away with still requiring, he looks like what he may well (I think) be: a creature whose body is both flesh and, somehow, light.

This thing about the ball cooperatively hanging there, slowing down, as if susceptible to the Swiss's will—there's real metaphysical truth here. And in the following anecdote. After a July 7 semifinal in which Federer destroyed Jonas Bjorkman—not just beat him, *destroyed* him—and just before a requisite post-match news conference in which Bjorkman, who's friendly with Federer, says he was pleased to "have the best seat in the house" to watch the Swiss "play the nearest to perfection you can play tennis," Federer and Bjorkman are evidently chatting and joking around, and Bjorkman asks him just how unnaturally big the ball was looking to him out there, and Federer confirms that it was "like a bowling ball or basketball." He means it just as a bantery, modest way to make Bjorkman feel better, to confirm that he's surprised by how unusually well he played today; but he's also revealing something about what tennis is like for him. Imagine that you're a person with preternaturally good reflexes and coordination and speed, and that you're playing high-level tennis. Your experience, in play, will not be that you possess phenomenal reflexes and speed; rather, it will seem to you that the tennis ball is quite large and slow-moving, and that you always have plenty of time to hit it. That is, you won't experience anything like the (empirically real) quickness and skill that the live audience, watching tennis balls move so fast they hiss and blur, will attribute to you.[8]

Velocity's just one part of it. Now we're getting technical. Tennis is

---

8 Special One-on-One support from the man himself for this claim: "It's interesting, because this week, actually, Ancic [comma Mario, the towering Top-Ten Croatian whom Federer beat in Wednesday's quarterfinal] played on Centre Court against my friend, you know, the Swiss player Wawrinka [comma Stanislas, Federer's Davis Cup teammate], and I went to see it out where, you know, my girlfriend Mirka [Vavrinec, a former Top 100 female player, knocked out by injury, who now basically functions as Federer's Alice B. Toklas] usually sits, and I went to see—for the first time since I have come here to Wimbledon, I went to see a match on Centre Court, and I was also surprised, actually, how fast, you know, the serve is and how fast you have to react to be able to get the ball back, especially when a guy like Mario [Ancic, who's known for his vicious serve] serves, you know? But then once you're on the court yourself, it's totally different, you know, because all you see is the ball, really, and you don't see the speed of the ball...."

often called a game of inches, but the cliché is mostly referring to where a shot lands. In terms of a player's hitting an incoming ball, tennis is actually more a game of micrometers: vanishingly tiny changes around the moment of impact will have large effects on how and where the ball travels. The same principle explains why even the smallest imprecision in aiming a rifle will still cause a miss if the target's far enough away.

By way of illustration, let's slow things way down. Imagine that you, a tennis player, are standing just behind your deuce corner's baseline. A ball is served to your forehand—you pivot (or rotate) so that your side is to the ball's incoming path and start to take your racket back for the forehand return. Keep visualizing up to where you're about halfway into the stroke's forward motion; the incoming ball is now just off your front hip, maybe six inches from point of impact. Consider some of the variables involved here. On the vertical plane, angling your racket face just a couple degrees forward or back will create topspin or slice, respectively; keeping it perpendicular will produce a flat, spinless drive. Horizontally, adjusting the racket face ever so slightly to the left or right, and hitting the ball maybe a millisecond early or late, will result in a cross-court versus down-the-line return. Further slight changes in the curves of your groundstroke's motion and follow-through will help determine how high your return passes over the net, which, together with the speed at which you're swinging (along with certain characteristics of the spin you impart), will affect how deep or shallow in the opponent's court your return lands, how high it bounces, etc. These are just the broadest distinctions, of course—like, there's heavy topspin vs. light topspin, sharply cross-court vs. only slightly cross-court, etc. There are also the issues of how close you're allowing the ball to get to your body, what grip you're using, the extent to which your knees are bent and/or weight's moving forward, and whether you're able simultaneously to watch the ball and to see what your opponent's doing after he serves. These all matter, too. Plus there's the fact that you're not putting a static object into motion here but rather reversing the flight and (to a varying extent) spin of a projectile coming toward you—coming, in the case of pro tennis, at speeds that make conscious thought impossible. Mario Ancic's first serve, for instance, often comes in around 130 m.p.h. Since it's seventy-eight feet from Ancic's baseline to yours, that means it takes 0.41 seconds for his serve to reach you.[9] This is less than the time it takes to blink quickly, twice.

---

9 We're doing the math here with the ball traveling as the crow flies, for simplicity. Please do not write in with corrections. If you want to factor in the serve's bounce and so

The upshot is that pro tennis involves intervals of time too brief for deliberate action. Temporally, we're more in the operative range of reflexes, purely physical reactions that bypass conscious thought. And yet an effective return of serve depends on a large set of decisions and physical adjustments that are a whole lot more involved and intentional than blinking, jumping when startled, etc.

Successfully returning a hard-served tennis ball requires what's sometimes called "the kinesthetic sense," meaning the ability to control the body and its artificial extensions through complex and very quick systems of tasks. English has a whole cloud of terms for various parts of this ability: feel, touch, form, proprioception, coordination, hand-eye coordination, kinesthesia, grace, control, reflexes, and so on. For promising junior players, refining the kinesthetic sense is the main goal of the extreme daily practice regimens we often hear about.[10] The training here is both muscular and neurological. Hitting thousands of strokes, day after day, develops the ability to do by "feel" what cannot be done by regular conscious thought. Repetitive practice like this often looks tedious or even cruel to an outsider, but the outsider can't feel what's going on inside the player—tiny adjustments, over and over, and a sense of each change's effects that gets more and more acute even as it recedes from normal consciousness.[11]

The time and discipline required for serious kinesthetic training are one reason why top pros are usually people who've devoted most of their waking lives to tennis, starting (at the very latest) in their early teens. It was, for example, at age thirteen that Roger Federer finally gave up soccer, and a recognizable childhood, and entered Switzerland's national tennis training center in Ecublens. At sixteen, he dropped out of classroom studies and started serious international competition.

It was only weeks after quitting school that Federer won Junior Wimbledon. Obviously, this is something that not every junior who devotes

---

compute the total distance traveled by the ball as the sum of an oblique triangle's* two shorter legs, then by all means go ahead—you'll end up with between two and five additional hundredths of a second, which is not significant.

*(The slower a tennis court's surface, the closer to a right triangle you're going to have. On fast grass, the bounce's angle is always oblique.)

10 Conditioning is also important, but this is mainly because the first thing that physical fatigue attacks is the kinesthetic sense. (Other antagonists are fear, self-consciousness, and extreme upset—which is why fragile psyches are rare in pro tennis.)

11 The best lay analogy is probably to the way an experienced driver can make all of good driving's myriad little decisions and adjustments without having to pay real attention to them.

himself to tennis can do. Just as obviously, then, there is more than time and training involved—there is also sheer talent, and degrees of it. Extraordinary kinesthetic ability must be present (and measurable) in a kid just to make the years of practice and training worthwhile...but from there, over time, the cream starts to rise and separate. So one type of technical explanation for Federer's dominion is that he's just a bit more kinesthetically talented than the other male pros. Only a little bit, since everyone in the Top 100 is himself kinesthetically gifted—but, then, tennis is a game of inches.

This answer is plausible but incomplete. It would probably not have been incomplete in 1980. In 2006, though, it's fair to ask why this kind of talent still matters so much. Recall what is true about dogma and Wimbledon's sign. Kinesthetic virtuoso or no, Roger Federer is now dominating the largest, strongest, fittest, best-trained and -coached field of male pros who've ever existed, with everyone using a kind of nuclear racket that's said to have made the finer calibrations of kinesthetic sense irrelevant, like trying to whistle Mozart during a Metallica concert.

According to reliable sources, honorary coin-tosser William Caines's backstory is that one day, when he was two and a half, his mother found a lump in his tummy, and took him to the doctor, and the lump was diagnosed as a malignant liver tumor. At which point one cannot, of course, imagine...a tiny child undergoing chemo, serious chemo, his mother having to watch, carry him home, nurse him, then bring him back to that place for more chemo. How did she answer her child's question—the big one, the obvious one? And who could answer hers? What could any priest or pastor say that wouldn't be grotesque?

It's 2-1 Nadal in the final's second set, and he's serving. Federer won the first set at love but then flagged a bit, as he sometimes does, and is quickly down a break. Now, on Nadal's ad, there's a sixteen-stroke point. Nadal is serving twenty m.p.h. faster than he did in Paris, and this one's down the center. Federer floats a soft forehand high over the net, which he can get away with because Nadal never comes in behind his serve. The Spaniard now hits a characteristically heavy topspin forehand deep to Federer's backhand; Federer comes back with an even heavier topspin backhand, almost a clay-court shot. It's unexpected and backs Nadal up, slightly, and his response is a low hard short ball that lands just past the service line's T on Federer's forehand side. Against most other opponents, Federer could simply end the point on a ball like this, but one reason Nadal gives him trouble is that he's faster than the others, can get to stuff they can't; and so Federer here just hits a flat, medium-hard cross-court forehand, going not for a winner but for a low, shallowly angled ball that forces Nadal up and out to the deuce side, his backhand. Nadal, on the run, backhands it hard down the line to Federer's backhand; Federer slices it right back down the same line, slow and floaty with backspin, making Nadal return to the same spot. Nadal slices the ball right back—three shots now all down the same line—and Federer slices the ball to the same spot yet again, this one even slower and floatier, and Nadal gets planted and hits a big two-hander down the same line—it's like Nadal's camped out now on his deuce side; he's no longer moving all the way back to the baseline's center between shots; Federer's hypnotized him a little. Federer now hits a very hard, deep topspin backhand, the kind that hisses, to a point just slightly on the ad side of Nadal's baseline, which Nadal gets to and forehands cross-court; and Federer responds with an even harder, heavier cross-court backhand, baseline-deep and moving so fast that Nadal has to hit the forehand off his back foot and then scramble to get to center as the shot lands maybe two feet short on Federer's backhand side again. Roger Federer steps to this ball and now hits a totally different cross-court backhand, this one much shorter and sharper-angled, an angle no one would anticipate, and so heavy and blurred with topspin that it lands shallow and just inside the sideline and takes off hard after the bounce, and Nadal can't move in to cut it off and can't get to it laterally along the baseline, because of all the angle and topspin—end of point. It's a spectacular winner, a Federer Moment; but, watching it live, you can see that it's also a winner that Federer started setting up four or even five shots earlier. Everything after that first down-the-line slice was designed by the Swiss to maneuver Nadal and lull him and disrupt his rhythm and balance and open up that last, unimaginable angle—an angle that would have been impossible without extreme topspin.

Extreme topspin is the hallmark of today's power-baseline game. This is something that Wimbledon's sign gets right.[12] Why topspin is so key, though, is not commonly understood. What's commonly understood is that high-tech composite rackets impart much more pace to the ball, rather like aluminum baseball bats as opposed to good old lumber. But

---

12 (…assuming, that is, that the sign's "with heavy topspin" is modifying "dominate" rather than "powerful hitters," which actually it might or might not—British grammar is a bit dodgy)

that dogma is false. The truth is that, at the same tensile strength, carbon-based composites are lighter than wood, and this allows modern rackets to be a couple ounces lighter and at least an inch wider across the face than the vintage Kramer and Maxply. It's the width of the face that's vital. A wider face means there's more total string area, which means the sweet spot's bigger. With a composite racket, you don't have to meet the ball in the precise geometric center of the strings in order to generate good pace. Nor must you be spot-on to generate topspin, a spin that (recall) requires a tilted face and upwardly curved stroke, brushing over the ball rather than hitting flat through it—this was quite hard to do with wood rackets, because of their smaller face and niggardly sweet spot. Composites' lighter, wider heads and more generous centers let players swing faster and put way more topspin on the ball...and, in turn, the more topspin you put on the ball, the harder you can hit it, because there's more margin for error. Topspin causes the ball to pass high over the net, describe a sharp arc, and come down fast into the opponent's court (instead of maybe soaring out).

So the basic formula here is that composite rackets enable topspin, which in turn enables groundstrokes vastly faster and harder than twenty years ago—it's common now to see male pros pulled up off the ground and halfway around in the air by the force of their strokes, which in the old days was something one saw only in Jimmy Connors.

Connors was not, by the way, the father of the power-baseline game. He whaled mightily from the baseline, true, but his groundstrokes were flat and spinless and had to pass very low over the net. Nor was Björn Borg a true power-baseliner. Both Borg and Connors played specialized versions of the classic baseline game, which had evolved as a counterforce to the even more classic serve-and-volley game, which was itself the dominant form of men's power tennis for decades, and of which John McEnroe was the greatest modern exponent. You probably know all this, and may also know that McEnroe toppled Borg and then more or less ruled the men's game until the appearance, around the early mid-1980s, of (a) modern composite rackets[13] and (b) Ivan Lendl, who played with an early form of composite and was the true progenitor of power-baseline tennis.[14]

---

13 (which neither Connors nor McEnroe could switch to with much success—their games were fixed around pre-modern rackets)

14 Formwise, with his whippy forehand, lethal one-hander, and merciless treatment of short balls, Lendl somewhat anticipated Federer. But the Czech was also stiff, cold, and brutal; his game was awesome but not beautiful. (My college doubles partner used to describe watching Lendl as like getting to see *Triumph of the Will* in 3-D.)

Ivan Lendl was the first top pro whose strokes and tactics appeared to be designed around the special capacities of the composite racket. His goal was to win points from the baseline, via either passing shots or outright winners. His weapon was his groundstrokes, especially his forehand, which he could hit with overwhelming pace because of the amount of top-spin he put on the ball. The blend of pace and topspin also allowed Lendl to do something that proved crucial to the advent of the power-baseline game. He could pull off radical, extraordinary angles on hard-hit ground-strokes, mainly because of the speed with which heavy topspin makes the ball dip and land without going wide. In retrospect, this changed the whole physics of aggressive tennis. For decades, it had been angle that made the serve-and-volley game so lethal. The closer one is to the net, the more of the opponent's court is open—the classic advantage of volleying was that you could hit angles that would go way wide if attempted from the baseline or midcourt. But topspin on a groundstroke, if it's really extreme, can bring the ball down fast and shallow enough to exploit many of these same angles. Especially if the groundstroke you're hitting is off a somewhat short ball—the shorter the ball, the more angles are possible. Pace, topspin, and aggressive baseline angles: and lo, it's the power-base-line game.

It wasn't that Ivan Lendl was an immortally great tennis player. He was simply the first top pro to demonstrate what heavy topspin and raw power could achieve from the baseline. And, most important, the achievement was replicable, just like the composite racket. Past a certain threshold of physical talent and training, the main requirements were athleticism, aggression, and superior strength and conditioning. The result (omitting various complications and subspecialties[15]) has been men's pro tennis for the last twenty years: ever bigger, stronger, fitter players generating unprecedented pace and topspin off the ground, trying to force the short or weak ball that they can put away.

Illustrative stat: When Lleyton Hewitt defeated David Nalbandian in the 2002 Wimbledon men's final, there was not one single serve-and-volley point.[16]

The generic power-baseline game is not boring—certainly not com-pared with the two-second points of old-time serve-and-volley or the moon-ball tedium of classic baseline attrition. But it is somewhat static

---

15 See, for one example, the continued effectiveness of some serve-and-volley (mainly in the adapted, heavily ace- and quickness-dependent form of a Sampras or Rafter) on fast courts through the 1990s.

16 It's also illustrative that 2002 was Wimbledon's last pre-Federer final.

954 • THE DAVID FOSTER WALLACE READER

and limited; it is not, as pundits have publicly feared for years, the evolutionary endpoint of tennis. The player who's shown this to be true is Roger Federer. And he's shown it from *within* the modern game.

This *within* is what's important here; this is what a purely neural account leaves out. And it is why sexy attributions like touch and subtlety must not be misunderstood. With Federer, it's not either/or. The Swiss has every bit of Lendl's and Agassi's pace on his groundstrokes, and leaves the ground when he swings, and can out-hit even Nadal from the backcourt.[17] What's strange and wrong about Wimbledon's sign, really, is its overall dolorous tone. Subtlety, touch, and finesse are not dead in the power-baseline era. For it is, still, in 2006, very much the power-baseline era: Roger Federer is a first-rate, kick-ass power-baseliner. It's just that that's not all he is. There's also his intelligence, his occult anticipation, his court sense, his ability to read and manipulate opponents, to mix spins and speeds, to misdirect and disguise, to use tactical foresight and peripheral vision and kinesthetic range instead of just rote pace—all this has exposed the limits, and possibilities, of men's tennis as it's now played.

---

17 In the '06 final's third set, at three games all and 30-15, Nadal kicks his second serve high to Federer's backhand. Nadal's clearly been coached to go high and heavy to Federer's backhand, and that's what he does, point after point. Federer slices the return back to Nadal's center and two feet short—not short enough to let the Spaniard hit a winner, but short enough to draw him slightly into the court, whence Nadal winds up and puts all his forehand's strength into a hard heavy shot to (again) Federer's backhand. The pace he's put on the ball means that Nadal is still backpedaling to his baseline as Federer leaves his feet and cranks a very hard topspin backhand down the line to Nadal's deuce side, which Nadal—out of position but world-class fast—reaches and manages to one-hand back deep to (again) Federer's backhand side, but this ball's floaty and slow, and Federer has time to step around and hit an inside-out forehand, a forehand as hard as anyone's hit all tournament, with just enough topspin to bring it down in Nadal's ad corner, and the Spaniard gets there but can't return it. Big ovation. Again, what looks like an overwhelming baseline winner was actually set up by that first clever semi-short slice and Nadal's own predictability about where and how hard he'll hit every ball. Federer surely whaled that last forehand, though. People are looking at each other and applauding. The thing with Federer is that he's Mozart and Metallica at the same time, and the harmony's somehow exquisite.

By the way, it's right around here, or the next game, watching, that three separate inner-type things come together and mesh. One is a feeling of deep personal privilege at being alive to get to see this; another is the thought that William Caines is probably somewhere here in the Centre Court crowd, too, watching, maybe with his mum. The third thing is a sudden memory of the earnest way the press bus driver promised just this experience. Because there is one. It's hard to describe—it's like a thought that's also a feeling. One wouldn't want to make too much of it, or to pretend that it's any sort of equitable balance; that would be grotesque. But the truth is that whatever deity, entity, energy, or random genetic flux produces sick children also produced Roger Federer, and just look at him down there. Look at that.

...Which sounds very high-flown and nice, of course, but please understand that with this guy it's not high-flown or abstract. Or nice. In the same emphatic, empirical, dominating way that Lendl drove home his own lesson, Roger Federer is showing that the speed and strength of today's pro game are merely its skeleton, not its flesh. He has, figuratively and literally, re-embodied men's tennis, and for the first time in years the game's future is unpredictable. You should have seen, on the grounds' outside courts, the variegated ballet that was this year's Junior Wimbledon. Drop volleys and mixed spins, off-speed serves, gambits planned three shots ahead—all as well as the standard-issue grunts and booming balls. Whether anything like a nascent Federer was here among these juniors can't be known, of course. Genius is not replicable. Inspiration, though, is contagious, and multiform—and even just to see, close up, power and aggression made vulnerable to beauty is to feel inspired and (in a fleeting, mortal way) reconciled.

2006

Afterword

Part of my excitement in reading Wallace's Federer essay involves the special torque he puts on what we called the "mimetic fallacy" back in college. Briefly: You don't convey boredom by being boring, or confusion by being confusing. But there are exceptions. In this essay, Wallace presents the sui generis brilliance of Roger Federer's tennis-playing by not only deploying his own brilliantly sui generis writing chops, but doing so within a subtly apt structural frame. For starters, he draws on the more kinetic and athletic register of his prose (as opposed to, say, his more abstract, concept-parsing register), and in the process he incorporates—channels—the tactical intelligence he ascribes to Federer through the staggered progression of the essay. Finally, in the closing section, he makes a very bold move that asks to be seen as his own mirroring homage to the game he has been writing about: Federer vs. Nadal, Wimbledon 2006.

Wallace was a nationally top-seeded tennis player in his teens, and he has written about the game in essays as well as in sections of *Infinite Jest*. He had the double advantage of being both a participant-insider, a connoisseur of the game's tactile nuances, and being Wallace, which is to say possessing a mind of great refractive analytical power, one that could do justice to the strategic cat's cradle of any high-level face-off. I speak as a nonplayer, nonwatcher, and my own learn-as-you-go reading testifies to this writer's ability to simultaneously illuminate the game—its physical scope and demand—*and* allow me to see it as an art form on a par with any other. That is a kind of seeing that cannot be unseen. As the cliché goes: I will never think of tennis in the same way again.

In his best passages you can feel Wallace's prose strain for that extra bit of reach, the thrust of a still keener accuracy. He writes: "Federer's forehand is a great liquid whip, his backhand a one-hander that he can drive flat, load with topspin, or slice—the slice with such snap that the ball turns shapes in the air and skids on the grass to maybe ankle height." That "liquid whip," that sense of the ball turning "shapes in the air"—we feel the language mime Federer's own transcending of normal physical limits.

Just as any brilliant serve or return is but one moment in a greater unfolding contest, so are Wallace's various tours de force also moves in the essay's unfolding strategy. The logistics are canny. First, he introduces the Wimbledon match that will showcase Federer at the very top of his game. Then he draws back, digresses, fills in various perspectives and bits of background. There is the held breath of the coin toss. Then the switch to more background. Wallace uses the time-honored technique of building suspense, and at the same time he gives us the insider's vision of the game's complexity. He attunes us to its amazing subtleties and surprises, even as he moves toward one of his own devising. One that we get only on a double take, after it's over. All this time, you see, we have been reading, as trained, toward the climactic moments of the match. And then, then—where are they? Why, he dropped them just over the net, far from where he had us scrambling. *Into a footnote*. We've heard of journalists burying the lead, but this is something else: burying the climax. In the reduced-size print of a footnote, just where we would be most apt to read right by it. Point and game.

—Sven Birkerts

About the Contributors

Jo Ann Beard is the author of the novel *In Zanesville* and the essay collection *The Boys of My Youth*.

Sven Birkerts is the author of nine books, including *The Gutenberg Elegies: The Fate of Reading in an Electronic Age, My Sky Blue Trades,* and, most recently, *The Other Walk: Essays.* His next collection, *On or About: Writing the Digital Divide,* will be published by Graywolf Press. Editor of the journal *AGNI,* he also directs the Bennington Writing Seminars.

Mark Costello is the author of two novels, including the National Book Award finalist *Big If.* He lives in New York City.

Kevin J. H. Dettmar is W. M. Keck Professor and Chair of English at Pomona College. He is the author or editor of a number of scholarly books on modernist literature and popular music studies.

Anne Fadiman is the author of *At Large and At Small, Ex Libris,* and *The Spirit Catches You and You Fall Down,* and is at work on a short memoir about her father and wine. She is the Francis Writer-in-Residence at Yale.

Gerald Howard is an executive editor at Doubleday. He acquired and edited David Foster Wallace's first novel, *The Broom of the System,* when he was an editor at Penguin Books in the 1980s, and he subsequently published Wallace's story collection *Girl with Curious Hair* at W. W. Norton.

Born in London, **Hari Kunzru** is the author of the novels *The Impressionist* (2002), *Transmission* (2004), *My Revolutions* (2007), and *Gods Without Men* (2011), as well as a short- story collection, *Noise* (2006), and a novella, *Memory Palace* (2013). He was a 2008 Cullman Fellow at the New York Public Library and is a 2014 Guggenheim Fellow. He lives in New York City.

Nam Le is the author of *The Boat*.

Nick Maniatis is the owner of The Howling Fantods (http://www.the-howlingfantods.com/dfw), a website that has been dedicated to promoting the works of David Foster Wallace for eighteen years. He is also an English teacher at Campbell High School in Canberra, Australia.

Deborah Treisman is the Fiction Editor of *The New Yorker*.

David L. Ulin is the author, most recently, of the novella *Labyrinth*. His other books include *The Lost Art of Reading: Why Books Matter in a Distracted Time* and the Library of America's *Writing Los Angeles: A Literary Anthology*, which won a California Book Award. He is book critic of the *Los Angeles Times*.

A graduate of Mount Holyoke College, **Sally Foster Wallace** received her MA in English from the University of Illinois. From 1973 until her retirement in 2003, she was a professor of English at Parkland College in Champaign, Illinois. The Council for the Advancement and Support of Education named her the national Outstanding Community Colleges Professor of 1996. She is the author of *Practically Painless English*.

Copyright Acknowledgments

Chapter 33, published as "Wiggle Room" in *The New Yorker* in 2009; Chapter 36, published as "Backbone" in *The New Yorker* in 2011.

"Derivative Sport in Tornado Alley" originally published in *Harper's* in 1992 under the title "Tennis, Trigonometry, Tornadoes," and as "Derivative Sport in Tornado Alley" in the anthology *Townships*, ed. Michael Martone (University of Iowa Press, 1993), and in *A Supposedly Fun Thing I'll Never Do Again* (Little, Brown and Company, 1997).

"E Unibus Pluram: Television and U.S. Fiction" originally published in *The Review of Contemporary Fiction* in 1993, and in *A Supposedly Fun Thing I'll Never Do Again* (Little, Brown and Company, 1997).

"Getting Away from Already Pretty Much Being Away from It All" originally published in *Harper's* in 1994 under the title "Ticket to the Fair," and as "Getting Away from Already Pretty Much Being Away from It All" in *A Supposedly Fun Thing I'll Never Do Again* (Little, Brown and Company, 1997).

"A Supposedly Fun Thing I'll Never Do Again" originally published in *Harper's* in 1996 under the title "Shipping Out," and as "A Supposedly Fun Thing I'll Never Do Again" in *A Supposedly Fun Thing I'll Never Do Again* (Little, Brown and Company, 1997).

"The Nature of the Fun" originally published in *Fiction Writer* in 1998, and in *Both Flesh and Not* (Little, Brown and Company, 2012).

"Some Remarks on Kafka's Funniness from Which Probably Not Enough Has Been Removed" originally published in *Harper's* in 1998 under the title "Laughing with Kafka," and as "Some Remarks on Kafka's Funniness from Which Probably Not Enough Has Been Removed" in *Consider the Lobster* (Little, Brown and Company, 2005).

"Authority and American Usage" originally published in *Harper's* in 2001 under the title "Tense Present: Democracy, English, and Wars over Usage," and as "Authority and American Usage" in *Consider the Lobster* (Little, Brown and Company, 2005).

"The View from Mrs. Thompson's" originally published in *Rolling Stone* in 2001, and in *Consider the Lobster* (Little, Brown and Company, 2005).

About the Author

David Foster Wallace was born in Ithaca, New York, in 1962 and raised in Illinois, where he was a regionally ranked junior tennis player. He received bachelor of arts degrees in philosophy and English from Amherst College; his senior English thesis, the novel *The Broom of the System*, was published in 1987, and his senior philosophy thesis was published as *Fate, Time, and Language* in 2010. He earned a master of fine arts at the University of Arizona. His second novel, *Infinite Jest*, was published in 1996. He also published the story collections *Girl with Curious Hair*, *Brief Interviews with Hideous Men*, and *Oblivion*; the essay collections *A Supposedly Fun Thing I'll Never Do Again* and *Consider the Lobster*; a book about hip-hop, written with his friend Mark Costello, *Signifying Rappers*; and a book about infinity, *Everything and More*. Over the years Wallace taught at Emerson College, Illinois State University, and Pomona College. He was awarded the MacArthur Fellowship, a Lannan Literary Award, and the Whiting Writers' Award and served on the Usage Panel for *The American Heritage Dictionary of the English Language*. He died in 2008. His last novel, *The Pale King*, was published in 2011 and was a finalist for the Pulitzer Prize.